U0922430

2017
江苏统计年鉴
JIANGSU STATISTICAL YEARBOOK

（总第34期 №.34）

江　苏　省　统　计　局
国家统计局江苏调查总队　编

Compiled by
Jiangsu Provincial Statistics Bureau
Survey Office of the National Bureau of Statistics in Jiangsu

图书在版编目(CIP)数据

江苏统计年鉴. 2017 : 汉英对照 / 江苏省统计局，国家统计局江苏调查总队编. — 北京 : 中国统计出版社，2017.8

ISBN 978 - 7 - 5037 - 8208 - 4

Ⅰ. ①江… Ⅱ. ①江… ②国… Ⅲ. ①统计资料 - 江苏省 - 2017 - 年鉴 - 汉、英 Ⅳ. ①C832.53 - 54

中国版本图书馆 CIP 数据核字(2017)第 171446 号

江苏统计年鉴-2017

作　　者 / 江苏省统计局　国家统计局江苏调查总队
责任编辑 / 佘竞雄　李潇潇　王立群
执行编辑 / 宣　严
装帧设计 / 奚　磊
出版发行 / 中国统计出版社
地　　址 / 北京市丰台区西三环南路甲 6 号
邮政编码 / 100073
电　　话 / 邮购(010)63376909　书店(010)68783171
网　　址 / http://www.zgtjcbs.com
印　　刷 / 南京人民印刷厂
经　　销 / 新华书店
开　　本 / 880 mm × 1230 mm　1/16
字　　数 / 1948 千字
印　　张 / 47.5　1 彩页
版　　别 / 2017 年 8 月第 1 版
版　　次 / 2017 年 8 月第 1 次印刷
定　　价 / 460.00 元

本书附同版本 CD - ROM 一张，光盘内容以书面文字为准。
如有印装差错，由本社发行部调换。

《江苏统计年鉴－2017》

编委会和编辑人员

Jiangsu Statistical Yearbook – 2017

EDITORIAL BOARD AND EDITORIAL STAFF

编者说明

一、《江苏统计年鉴－2017》(以下简称《年鉴》)是一部全面、系统反映江苏省2016年及历史重要年份国民经济和社会发展情况的资料性年刊,收录了江苏省及各地区大量的经济社会发展统计信息。

二、《年鉴》分为二十一个部分:1. 综合,2. 国民经济核算,3. 人口、就业和工资,4. 价格指数,5. 人民生活,6. 固定资产投资,7. 财政、金融,8. 对外经济贸易,9. 能源、资源、环境,10. 农业,11. 工业,12. 建筑业,13. 运输、邮电和服务业,14. 批发零售、住宿餐饮和旅游,15. 科技、教育,16. 文化、体育、卫生,17. 公共管理、社会保障和社会组织, 18. 城市经济与建设,19. 区域经济,20. 市县社会经济,21. 县(市)社会经济发展序列。另附录全国分省主要指标。为方便读者使用,各篇章前设有《简要说明》,对本篇章的主要内容、资料来源、统计范围、统计方法以及历史变动情况予以简要概述,篇末附有《主要统计指标解释》。

三、《年鉴》资料大部分来自年度统计报表,一部分来自抽样调查等。全国分省资料来自国家统计局出版的有关统计资料。

四、《年鉴》中所使用的度量衡单位均采用国际统一标准计量单位。

五、《年鉴》中国民经济行业分类按2011年国家标准《国民经济行业分类》(GB/T4754－2011)执行。

六、《年鉴》总量指标计算所采用的价格均为现行价格。

七、《年鉴》部分数据合计数或相对数由于单位取舍不同产生的计算误差未作机械调整。

八、《年鉴》表中"..."表示数据不足本表最小单位数;"空格"表示该项统计指标数据不详或无该项数据;"#"表示其中的主要项。

感谢国内外广大读者多年来对《年鉴》编辑出版工作的支持和帮助,欢迎继续提出宝贵意见,使《年鉴》的形式和内容更趋完善。

EDITOR'S NOTES

Ⅰ. *Jiangsu Statistical Yearbook 2017* (abbreviated as Yearbook hereafter) is an annual publication which provides comprehenisive and systematic data series about the national economy and social development in Jiangsu Province in 2016 and some selected data series in historically important years. It includes much statistical information on social and economic development in the province and in various regions.

Ⅱ. The Yearbook contatins the following twenty-one parts: 1. General Survey, 2. National Accounts, 3. Population, Employment and Wages, 4. Price Indices, 5. People's Living Conditions, 6. Investment in Fixed Assets, 7. Government Finance, Financial Intermediation, 8. Foreign Trade and Economic Cooperation, 9. Energy, Resourceand Environment, 10. Agriculture, 11. Industry, 12. Construction, 13. Transport, Postal and Telecommunication Services, Service Industry, 14. Wholesale and Retail Trade, Hotels, Catering Services and Tourism, 15. Science and Technology, Education, 16. Culture, Sports and Public Health, 17. Public Management, Social Security and Social Organizations, 18. Urban Economy and Construction, 19. Regional Economy, 20. Social Economy of Cities and Counties, 21. Social Economy Development Alignment of Counties(Cities), Appendix, Major Indicators by Region. To facilitate readers, the Brief Introduction at the beginning of each chapter provides a summary of the main contents of the chapter, data sources, statistical scope, statistical methods and historical changes. At the end of each chapter, Explanatory Notes on Main Statistical Indicators are included.

Ⅲ. The major data sources of this publication are obtained from annual statistical reports, and some from sample surveys. National major indicators grouped by provinces are obtained from relative statistical data published by the National Bureau of Statistics of China.

Ⅳ. The units of measurement used in the Yearbook are all internationally standard measurement units.

Ⅴ. The classification of national economic industry used in the Yearbook is the national standard of 2011's "The Classification on National Economic Industry", i. e. (GB/T4754 - 2011).

Ⅵ. The price used for gross indicator's calculating are current prise.

Ⅶ. Statistical dicrepancies due to rouding are not adjusted.

Ⅷ. In the Yearbook, "…" indicates that the figure is not large enough to be measured with the samllest unit in the table; (blank) indicates that the figure is not available, "#" indicates the major component items.

We express thanks to the general readers of domestic and abroad for supporting and helping the work of compilcation and publication of the Yearbook. We sincerely welcome conitinued valuable suggestions from the general readers so that the form and content of the Yearbook can be further improved.

目 录

CONTENTS

1 综 合

General Survey

1 - 1 行政区划(2016 年) …………………………………………………… (7)
Administrative Divisions(2016)

1 - 2 国民经济和社会发展总量与速度指标 …………………………………… (8)
Principal Aggregate Indicators on National Economic and Social Development and Growth Rate

1 - 3 国民经济和社会发展结构指标 ……………………………………………… (16)
Composition Indicators on National Economic and Social Development

1 - 4 国民经济和社会发展比例和效益指标 …………………………………… (20)
Indicators on National Economic and Social Development

1 - 5 江苏国民经济占全国的比重 (2016 年) ……………………………………… (22)
Percentage of Jiangsu's National Economy in the Country (2016)

1 - 6 江苏的一天 ………………………………………………………………… (23)
One Day in Jiangsu

1 - 7 全省人均国民经济主要指标 ……………………………………………… (24)
Major Per Capita Indicators of Jiangsu National Economy

1 - 8 全省法人单位数及从业人员数 …………………………………………… (25)
Number of Corporations and Empolyment

1 - 9 个体工商业基本情况 (2016 年) …………………………………………… (27)
Basic Conditions of Self-employment Business (2016)

1 - 10 私营企业基本情况 (2016 年) …………………………………………… (28)
Basic Conditions of Private Enterprises (2016)

2 国民经济核算

National Accounts

2 - 1 主要年份总产出 …………………………………………………………… (37)
Total Output in Major Years

2－2　主要年份总产出指数 …… (38)
Indices of Total Output in Major Years
2－3　主要年份地区生产总值 …… (39)
Gross Domestic Product in Major Years
2－4　主要年份地区生产总值构成 …… (40)
Composition of Gross Domestic Product in Major Years
2－5　不变价地区生产总值 …… (41)
Gross Domestic Product at Constant Price
2－6　主要年份地区生产总值指数 …… (42)
Indices of Gross Domestic Product in Major Years
2－7　主要年份地区生产总值定基指数 …… (43)
Fixed-base Indices of Gross Domestic Product in Major Years
2－8　分行业地区生产总值 …… (44)
Gross Domestic Product by Sector
2－9　分行业地区生产总值构成 …… (45)
Composition of Gross Domestic Product by Sector
2－10　分市分行业地区生产总值(2016 年) …… (46)
Composition of Gross Domestic Product by Sector and Region(2016)
2－11　三次产业对地区生产总值的贡献率和拉动 …… (48)
Contribution Share and Contribution of the Three Strata of Industry to GDP Growth
2－12　分市地区生产总值 …… (50)
Gross Domestic Product by Region
2－13　分市地区生产总值构成 …… (56)
Composition of Gross Domestic Product by Region
2－14　分市地区生产总值指数 …… (60)
Indices of Gross Domestic Product by Region
2－15　按收入法计算的地区生产总值(2016 年) …… (65)
Income Approach Components of Gross Domestic Product (2016)
2－16　主要年份按收入法计算的地区生产总值 …… (67)
Income Approach Components of Gross Domestic Product in Major Years
2－17　按支出法计算的地区生产总值 …… (68)
Gross Domestic Product by Expenditure Approach
2－18　按支出法计算的地区生产总值构成 …… (69)
Composition of Gross Domestic Product by Expenditure Approach
2－19　按支出法计算的地区生产总值指数 …… (70)
Indices of Gross Domestic Product by Expenditure Approach

3　人口、就业和工资

Population, Employment and Wages

3－1　全省人口数、户数(常住) …… (77)
Population and Households(Permanent)

3－2 全省市、镇、乡村人口数及其构成 …… (78)
City, Town, Country Population and It's Composition
3－3 全省人口自然变动 …… (79)
Natural Change of Population
3－4 全省人口数、户数(户籍) …… (80)
Population and Households(Registered)
3－5 全省历次人口普查主要数据 …… (81)
Major Data of All Previous Provincial Population Census
3－6 按地区分常住人口 …… (82)
Permanent Population by Region
3－7 全省人口年龄构成情况(2016 年 11 月 1 日零时) …… (83)
Composition of Population Grouped by Age (0 o'clock on November 1,2016)
3－8 全省人口受教育程度情况 (2016 年 11 月 1 日零时) …… (84)
Educated Situation of Population (0 o'clock on November 1,2016)
3－9 全省 15 岁及以上人口的婚姻状况 (2016 年 11 月 1 日零时) …… (84)
Marriage Status of Population Aged 15 and Over (0 o'clock on November 1,2016)
3－10 全省 16 岁及以上人口经济活动情况 (2016 年 11 月 1 日零时) …… (85)
Condition of Economic Activities of Age 16 and Above Population(0 o'clock on November 1,2016)
3－11 就业基本情况 …… (86)
Employment
3－12 就业人数 …… (87)
Number of Employed Persons
3－13 分三次产业的就业人数 …… (88)
Number of Employed Persons by Three Types of Industries
3－14 分地区就业人数 …… (89)
Number of Employed Persons by Region
3－15 城镇非私营单位就业人员数 (2016 年) …… (90)
Number of Employed Persons in Urban Units (2016)
3－16 分细行业城镇非私营单位就业人员数 (2016 年) …… (91)
Number of Employed Persons in Urban Units by Sector in Detail(2016)
3－17 分地区城镇非私营单位就业人员数(2016 年) …… (94)
Number of Employed Persons in Urban Units by Region(2016)
3－18 分行业城镇非私营单位女性就业人员数(2016 年) …… (96)
Number of Employed Women in Urban Units by Sector (2016)
3－19 城镇失业人数及失业率 …… (97)
Number of Urban Unemployed Persons and Unemployed Rate
3－20 在岗职工工资总额及指数 …… (98)
Total Wage Bill of Staff and Workers and Related Index
3－21 城镇非私营单位就业人员工资总额(2016 年) …… (99)
Total Wages of Employed Persons in Urban Units (2016)
3－22 制造业城镇非私营单位就业人员工资总额(2016 年) …… (100)
Total Wages of Manufacturing Employees in Urban Units (2016)

3－23 在岗职工平均工资及指数 …… (101)
Average Wage of Staff and Workers and Related Indices
3－24 在岗职工平均工资指数 …… (102)
Average Wage Indices of Staff and Workers
3－25 城镇非私营单位就业人员平均工资(2016 年) …… (103)
Average Wage of Employed Persons in Urban Units (2016)
3－26 分地区城镇非私营单位就业人员平均工资 …… (104)
Average Wage of Employed Persons in Urban Units by Region
3－27 分细行业城镇非私营单位就业人员平均工资(2016 年) …… (105)
Average Wage of Employed Persons in Urban Units by Sector in Detail(2016)
3－28 制造业城镇非私营单位就业人员平均工资 (2016 年) …… (108)
Average Wage of Employed Persons in Manufacturing of Urban Units (2016)
3－29 城镇私营单位就业人员平均工资 …… (109)
Average Wage of Employed Persons in Urban Private Units

4 价格指数

Price Indices

4－1 各种价格指数 …… (120)
Price Indices
4－2 各种价格定基指数 …… (121)
Fixed-base Price Indices
4－3 居民消费价格分类指数 (2016 年) …… (122)
Consumer Price Indices by Category (2016)
4－4 商品零售价格分类指数(2016 年) …… (124)
Retail Price Indices by Categories (2016)
4－5 工业生产者出厂价格指数 …… (125)
Producer Price Indices for Industrial Products
4－6 分部门工业生产者出厂价格指数 …… (125)
Producer Price Indices for Industrial Products by Industry
4－7 分行业工业生产者出厂价格指数 …… (126)
Producer Price Indices for Industrial Products by Sector
4－8 工业生产者购进价格指数 …… (128)
Purchasing Price Indices for Industrial Products
4－9 固定资产投资价格指数 …… (128)
Price Indices for Investment in Fixed Assets
4－10 房地产价格指数 …… (128)
Real Estate Price Indices

5 人民生活

People's Living Conditions

5－1 人民生活水平情况 …… (134)
Basic Statistics on People's Living Standard

5－2 农村居民家庭人均收入及恩格尔系数 …… (137)
Per Capita Annual Income and Engle Coefficient of Rural Households

5－3 城镇居民家庭人均收入及恩格尔系数 …… (138)
Per Capita Annual Income and Engle Coefficient of Urban Households

5－4 居民家庭基本情况 …… (139)
Basic Conditions of Residents

5－5 不同收入组城镇常住居民家庭基本情况(2016 年) …… (140)
Basic Conditions of Urban Residents by Income(2016)

5－6 不同收入组农村常住居民家庭基本情况(2016 年) …… (141)
Basic Conditions of Rural Residents by Income(2016)

5－7 居民家庭平均每人主要消费品消费量 …… (143)
Per Capita Consumption on Major Consumer Goods of Residents

5－8 不同收入组城镇常住居民家庭平均每人主要消费品消费量(2016 年) …… (144)
Per Capita Consumption on Major Consumer Goods of Urban Residents by Income(2016)

5－9 不同收入组农村常住居民家庭平均每人主要消费品消费量(2016 年) …… (145)
Per Capita Consumption on Major Consumer Goods of
Rural Residents by Income(2016)

5－10 居民家庭平均购买商品数量 …… (146)
Annual Purchases of Commodities of Residents

5－11 不同收入组城镇常住居民家庭平均购买商品数量(2016 年) …… (147)
Annual Purchases of Commodities of Urban Residents by Income(2016)

5－12 不同收入组农村常住居民家庭平均购买商品数量(2016 年) …… (148)
Annual Purchases of Commodities of Rural Residents by Income(2016)

5－13 居民家庭平均每百户年末耐用品拥有量 …… (149)
Ownership of Major Durable Consumer Goods per 100 Residents at Year-end

5－14 不同收入组城镇常住居民家庭平均每百户年末耐用品拥有量(2016 年) …… (150)
Ownership of Major Durable Consumer Goods per 100 Urban Residents by Income at Year-end(2016)

5－15 不同收入组农村常住居民家庭平均每百户年末耐用品拥有量(2016 年) …… (151)
Ownership of Major Durable Consumer Goods per 100 Rural Residents by Income at Year-end(2016)

5－16 分地区城镇常住居民家庭基本情况(2016 年) …… (152)
Basic Conditions of Urban Residents by Region(2016)

5－17 分地区农村常住居民家庭基本情况(2016 年) …… (154)
Basic Conditions of Rural Residents by Region(2016)

5－18 农村常住居民家庭房屋情况 …… (156)
Housing Conditions of Rural Residents

6 固定资产投资

Investment in Fixed Assets

6－1 固定资产投资主要指标 …………………………………………………………………………………………（161）
Major Indicators of Investment in Fixed Assets
6－2 固定资产投资额 ………………………………………………………………………………………………（162）
Investment in Fixed Assets
6－3 按登记注册类型分固定资产投资 …………………………………………………………………………（163）
Investment in Fixed Assets by Registration Status
6－4 按资金来源和构成分固定资产投资 ………………………………………………………………………（164）
Investment in Fixed Assets by Sources of Finance and Use of Funds
6－5 按构成分固定资产投资(2016 年) ………………………………………………………………………（166）
Investment in Fixed Assets by Use of Funds(2016)
6－6 按建设性质分固定资产投资(2016 年) ……………………………………………………………………（169）
Investment in Fixed Assets by Type of Construction(2016)
6－7 按隶属关系和注册类型分固定资产投资(2016 年) ………………………………………………………（172）
Investment in Fixed Assets by Jurisdiction of Management and Registration Status(2016)
6－8 按行业分施工投产项目个数(2016 年) ……………………………………………………………………（178）
Number of Projects Under Construction and Put into Use by Sector(2016)
6－9 国有单位固定资产投资 ……………………………………………………………………………………（181）
Investment of State-owned Units in Capital Construction
6－10 分市固定资产投资(2016 年) ………………………………………………………………………………（182）
Investment by Region (2016)
6－11 房地产开发投资主要指标 …………………………………………………………………………………（184）
Major Indicaotrs of Real Estate Investment
6－12 房地产开发企业经营情况 …………………………………………………………………………………（185）
Operating Statistics on Enterprises for Real Estate Development
6－13 按登记注册类型分房地产开发投资(2016 年) ……………………………………………………………（186）
Investment in Real Estate Development by Registration Status(2016)
6－14 分市房地产开发投资(2016 年) ……………………………………………………………………………（190）
Real Estate Investment by Region (2016)

7 财政、金融

Government Finance, Financial Intermediation

7－1 历年财政收支 …………………………………………………………………………………………………（200）
Financial Revenue and Expenditure over the Years
7－2 公共财政收支 …………………………………………………………………………………………………（201）
Public Financial Budget Revenue and Expenditure

7－3　分市财政收支(2016 年) …………………………………………………………………………… (202)

Financial Revenue and Expenditure by Region (2016)

7－4　历年金融机构存贷款 ………………………………………………………………………………… (204)

The Balance of Deposits of Financial Institutions over the Years

7－5　金融机构存贷款年末余额(2016) ……………………………………………………………… (205)

Deposits and Loans of Financial Institutions at Year-end(2016)

7－6　分地区金融机构本外币存贷款年末余额(2016 年) ……………………………………………… (206)

Deposits and Loans of Financial Institutions at Year-end by Region(RMB and Foreign Currency)(2016)

7－7　分地区金融机构人民币存贷款年末余额(2016 年) ……………………………………………… (208)

Deposits and Loans of Financial Institutions at Year-end by Region(RMB)(2016)

7－8　分地区金融机构外汇存贷款年末余额(2016 年) ………………………………………………… (210)

Deposits and Loans of Financial Institutions at Year-end by Region(Foreign Currency)(2016)

7－9　分行业金融机构贷款年末余额 ………………………………………………………………… (212)

Loans of Financial Institutions at Year-end by Sector

7－10　分市分行业金融机构本外币贷款年末余额 (2016 年) ………………………………………… (214)

Deposits and Loans of Financial Institutions at Year-end by Region and Sector (2016)

7－11　金融机构人员情况表 ……………………………………………………………………………… (216)

Number of Institutions and Staff and Workers of Banking Organizations

7－12　保险业务主要指标 ………………………………………………………………………………… (217)

Major Indicators of Insurance Business

7－13　江苏辖区证券市场基本情况 …………………………………………………………………… (218)

Basic Information of Securities Markets within Jiangsu

8　对外经济贸易

Foreign Trade and Economic Cooperation

8－1　对外经济主要指标 ………………………………………………………………………………… (224)

Major Indicators of Foreign Trade and Economic Cooperation

8－2　人民币对主要外币年平均汇价(中间价) ………………………………………………………… (225)

Average Exchange Rate of RMB Yuan Against Main Convertible Currencies (Middle Price)

8－3　对外贸易进出口总额 ……………………………………………………………………………… (226)

Total Imports and Exports

8－4　按贸易方式和经济类型分的进口额 ……………………………………………………………… (227)

Total Imports by Type of Trade and Ownership

8－5　按贸易方式和经济类型分的出口额 ……………………………………………………………… (227)

Total Exports by Type of Trade and Ownership

8－6　进口商品分类总额 ………………………………………………………………………………… (228)

Total Value of Imports by Category of Commodities

8－7　出口商品分类总额 ………………………………………………………………………………… (228)

Total Value of Exports by Category of Commodities

8－8　进出口商品细分类总额（2016 年） ……………………………………………………………………… (229)

Value of Imports and Exports by Category of Commodities (2016)

8－9　进出口商品细分类总额(RMB)(2016 年) ……………………………………………………………… (231)

Value of Imports and Exports by Category of Commodities(RMB)(2016)

8－10　进出口商品主要国家和地区 ……………………………………………………………………… (233)

Imports and Exports Value by Country and Region

8－11　进出口商品主要国家和地区(RMB) …………………………………………………………… (235)

Imports and Exports Value by Country and Region(RMB)

8－12　主要商品进口数量和金额 ………………………………………………………………………… (237)

Major Import Commodities in Volume and Value

8－13　主要商品进口数量和金额(RMB) ……………………………………………………………… (241)

Major Import Commodities in Volume and Value(RMB)

8－14　主要商品出口数量和金额 ………………………………………………………………………… (245)

Major Export Commodities in Volume and Value

8－15　主要商品出口数量和金额(RMB) ……………………………………………………………… (249)

Major Export Commodities in Volume and Value(RMB)

8－16　协议注册外资项目 ………………………………………………………………………………… (253)

Agreement Registered Foreign Investment Project

8－17　协议注册外资 ……………………………………………………………………………………… (253)

Agreement Registered Foreign

8－18　实际使用外资 ……………………………………………………………………………………… (254)

Actual Use of Foreign Capital

8－19　按行业分外商直接投资(2016 年) ……………………………………………………………… (255)

Foreign Direct Investment Grouped by Sector(2016)

8－20　按国家或地区分外商直接投资 …………………………………………………………………… (257)

Foreign Direct Investment by Country or Region

8－21　年末登记外商投资企业行业分布情况(2016 年) ……………………………………………… (258)

Sector Distribution Registered of Foreign-funded Enterprises at Year-end(2016)

8－22　对外承包工程 ……………………………………………………………………………………… (259)

Contracted Projects with Foreign Countries

8－23　对外劳务合作 ……………………………………………………………………………………… (260)

Labor Services Cooperation with Foreign Countries

8－24　境外投资情况 ……………………………………………………………………………………… (261)

Information of Overseas Investment

8－25　境外投资主要国别地区情况 ……………………………………………………………………… (262)

Information of Overseas Investment to Main Countries or Regions

8－26　分行业境外投资情况 ……………………………………………………………………………… (265)

Information of Overseas Investment by Sector

8－27　分地区境外投资情况 ……………………………………………………………………………… (268)

Information of Overseas Investment by Region

9　能源、资源、环境

Energy, Resource and Environment

9－1　主要城市月平均气温(2016 年) ……………………………………………… (273)

Monthly Average Temperature of Major Cities (2016)

9－2　主要城市月降水量 (2016 年) ……………………………………………… (273)

Monthly Precipitation of Major Cities (2016)

9－3　水资源总量 (2016 年) ……………………………………………… (274)

Water Resources (2016)

9－4　农村自然灾害情况 ……………………………………………… (274)

Basic Siatistics on Rural Natural Disaster

9－5　规模以上工业企业主要能源消费量 ……………………………………………… (275)

Major Energy Consumption of above Designated Industrial Enterprises

9－6　规模以上工业企业平均每天主要能源消费量 ……………………………………………… (275)

Average Daily Energy Consumption of above Designated Industrial Enterprises

9－7　综合能源平衡表 ……………………………………………… (276)

Aggregate Balance Sheet of Energy

9－8　江苏电网生产经营综合情况 ……………………………………………… (278)

General Production and Business of Jiangsu Power Grid

9－9　全社会用电情况 ……………………………………………… (280)

Basic Situation of Total Electricity Consumption

9－10　分地区全社会用电量 ……………………………………………… (282)

Electricity Consumption by Region

9－11　分地区工业用电量 ……………………………………………… (284)

Industrial Electricity Consumption by Region

9－12　主要发电厂发电情况 ……………………………………………… (286)

Electricity Production of Major Power Plants

9－13　环境保护基本情况 ……………………………………………… (288)

Basic Statistics on Environmental Protection

10　农　业

Agriculture

10－1　农业基本情况 ……………………………………………… (296)

Basic Statistics of Agriculture

10－2　农业现代化情况 ……………………………………………… (297)

Statistics on Agricultural Modernization

10－3　主要年份农林牧渔业总产值 ……………………………………………… (298)

Gross Output Value of Agriculture, Forestry, Animal Husbandry and Fishery in Major Years

10-4 主要年份农林牧渔业总产值指数 …… (299)
Indices of Gross Output Value of Agriculture, Forestry, Animal Husbandry and Fishery in Major Years
10-5 主要年份农林牧渔业总产值定基指数 …… (300)
Fixed-base Indices of Gross Output Value of Agriculture, Forestry, Animal Husbandry and Fishery in Major Years
10-6 农林牧渔业分项产值 …… (301)
Gross Output Value of Agriculture, Forestry, Animal Husbandry and Fishery by Branch
10-7 农作物播种面积 …… (302)
Total Sown Areas of Farm Crops
10-8 主要农作物种植结构 …… (304)
Planting Structure of Major Farm Crops
10-9 主要农作物播种面积和产量(2016年) …… (305)
Total Sown Areas of Farm Crops and Output (2016)
10-10 主要农产品产量 …… (306)
Output of Major Farm Crops
10-11 人均占有主要农产品产量 …… (307)
Per Capita Output of Major Farm Products
10-12 蚕、茶、果生产情况 …… (308)
Statistics on Silkworm Cocoons, Tea and Fruits
10-13 林业生产情况 …… (309)
Statistics on Forestry
10-14 畜牧业生产情况 …… (310)
Statistics on Livestock
10-15 水产品产量 …… (311)
Output of Aquatic Products
10-16 主要农业机械和农产品加工机械年底拥有量 …… (312)
Agricultural Machinery and Machinery for Processing Farm Products at Year-end
10-17 农业主要经济效益指标 …… (314)
Main Indicators on Economic Benefit of Agriculture
10-18 国有农场基本情况 …… (315)
Basic Statistics on State Farms
10-19 分市农业基本情况(2016年) …… (316)
Basic Statistics of Agriculture by Region (2016)

11 工 业
Industry

11-1 1998—2016年规模以上工业企业主要经济指标 …… (323)
Main Indicators of Industrial Enterprises above Designated Size(1998—2016)

11－2　规模以上工业企业单位数和产销总值(2016 年) …… (325)
Number of Industrial Enterprises above Designated Size and Their Total Value of Gross Output and Sales (2016)
11－3　分市规模以上工业总产值(2016 年) …… (328)
Gross Industrial Output Value above Designated Size by Region (2016)
11－4　规模以上工业企业主要经济指标(2016 年) …… (334)
Main Economic Indicators of above Designated Size Industrial Enterprises(2016)
11－5　规模以上工业企业主要经济效益指标 (2016 年) …… (346)
Main Indicators on Economic Benefit of above Designated Size Industrial Enterprises(2016)
11－6　国有控股工业企业主要经济指标 (2016 年) …… (352)
Main Economic Indicators of State Shareholding Industrial Enterprises(2016)
11－7　国有控股工业企业主要经济效益指标 (2016 年) …… (360)
Main Indicators on Economic Benefit of State Shareholding Industrial Enterprises(2016)
11－8　私营工业企业主要经济指标 (2016 年) …… (364)
Main Economic Indicators of Private Industrial Enterprises(2016)
11－9　私营工业企业主要经济效益指标 (2016 年) …… (372)
Main Indicators on Economic Benefit of Private Industrial Enterprises(2016)
11－10　外商投资和港澳台商投资工业企业主要经济指标 (2016 年) …… (376)
Main Economic Indicators of Industrial Enterprises with Hong Kong, Macao, Taiwan and Foreign Funds (2016)
11－11　外商投资和港澳台商投资工业企业主要经济效益指标(2016 年) …… (384)
Main Indicators on Economic Benefit of Industrial Enterprises with Hong Kong, Macao, Taiwan and Foreign Funds (2016)
11－12　大中型工业企业主要经济指标(2016 年) …… (388)
Main Economic Indicators of Big and Medium Size Industrial Enterprises (2016)
11－13　大中型工业企业主要经济效益指标 (2016 年) …… (396)
Main Indicators on Economic Benefit of Big and Medium Size Industrial Enterprises (2016)
11－14　主要年份工业主要产品产量 …… (400)
Output of Main Industrial Products in Major Years
11－15　规模以上工业企业主要产品生产、销售、库存 (2016 年) …… (401)
Main Indicators on Economic Benefit of above Designated Size Industrial Enterprises(2016)

12　建筑业

Construction

12－1　建筑施工企业概况 …… (409)
Basic Statistics on Construction Enterprises
12－2　建筑业企业主要经济指标 …… (413)
Main Economic Indicators on Construction Enterprises
12－3　按登记注册类型分建筑业企业主要经济指标(2016 年) …… (414)
Main Economic Indicators on Construction Enterprises by Registration Status (2016)
12－4　按登记注册类型分建筑业企业财务状况(2016 年) …… (416)
Financial Indicators on Construction Enterprises by Registration Status (2016)

12－5　按行业分建筑业企业主要经济指标和财务状况(2016 年) ………… (418)
Main Economic Indicators on Construction Enterprises by Sector (2016)

12－6　按地区分建筑业企业主要指标 ………… (419)
Main Indicators on Construction Enterprises by Region

13　运输、邮电和服务业

Transport, Postal and Telecommunication Services, Service Industry

13－1　交通运输基本情况 ………… (429)
Basic Statistics of Transport

13－2　客运量 ………… (430)
Passenger Traffic

13－3　旅客周转量 ………… (431)
Turnover Volume of Passenger Traffic

13－4　货运量 ………… (432)
Freight Traffic

13－5　货物周转量 ………… (433)
Turnover Volume of Freight Traffic

13－6　全社会港口码头泊位和通过能力 ………… (434)
Number of Berths and Traffic Capacity in All Port

13－7　主要港口吞吐量 ………… (434)
Volume of Freight and Passenger Handled at Major Ports

13－8　全省民用车辆拥有量(2016 年) ………… (436)
Number of Civil Motor Vehicles(2016 年)

13－9　个人车辆拥有量 ………… (436)
Number of Private-owned Vehicles

13－10　全省公路运输汽车拥有量 ………… (437)
Number of Transport Motor Vehicles

13－11　全社会运输船舶拥有量 ………… (437)
Number of Transport Vessels

13－12　分市交通运输基本情况 (2016 年) ………… (438)
Basic Statistics of Transport by Region (2016)

13－13　邮电业务基本情况 ………… (440)
Basic Conditions of Post and Telecommunication Services

13－14　分市邮电业务基本情况(2016 年) ………… (442)
Basic Conditions of Post and Telecommunication Services by Region (2016)

13－15　规模以上服务业企业主要经济指标 ………… (444)
Main Indicators of Service Industrial Enterprises above Designated Size

14 批发零售、住宿餐饮和旅游

Wholesale and Retail Trade, Hotels, Catering Services and Tourism

14-1 国内贸易基本情况 …… (453)
Basic Conditions of Domestic Trade

14-2 按行业分社会消费品零售总额 …… (454)
Total Retail Sales of Consumer Goods by Sector

14-3 按地区分社会消费品零售总额(2016年) …… (455)
Total Retail Sales of Consumer Goods by Region (2016)

14-4 限额以上批发和零售业基本情况(2016年) …… (456)
Basic Conditions of Enterprises above Designated Size in Wholesale and Retail Trades(2016)

14-5 批发和零售业商品购销存总额(2016年) …… (460)
Total Value of Commodity Purchasing,Sales and Inventory of Enterprises above Designated Size in Wholesale and Retail Sale Trade(2015)

14-6 限额以上批发和零售业企业财务状况(2016年) …… (464)
Financial Indicators of Enterprises above Designated Size in Wholesale and Retail Trade(2016)

14-7 限额以上住宿和餐饮业基本情况(2016年) …… (472)
Basic Conditions of Enterprises above Designated Size in Hotel and Catering Trade(2016)

14-8 住宿和餐饮业经营情况(2016年) …… (476)
Business of Enterprises of Hotels and Catering Services(2016)

14-9 限额以上住宿和餐饮业企业财务状况(2016年) …… (480)
Financial Indicators of Enterprises above Designated Size in Hotel and Catering Industry (2016)

14-10 批发和零售业、住宿和餐饮业连锁总店经营情况(2016年) …… (486)
Management Conditions of General Chain Stores of Wholesale and Retail Sale Trade, Hotel and Catering Trade Service (2016)

14-11 亿元以上商品交易市场基本情况(2016年) …… (488)
Basic Condition of Transaction Markets with Transaction Value over 100 Million Yuan (2016)

14-12 省外批发和零售业、住宿和餐饮业连锁总店在江苏分店经营情况(2016) …… (494)
Management Conditions of Branch Stores of Wholesale and Retail Sale Trade Hotel and Catering Trade of General Chain Stores of Other Province in Jiangsu(2016)

14-13 旅游业主要指标 …… (495)
Main Indicators of Tourism

14-14 接待海外旅游者人数和收入 …… (497)
Number of Overseas Tourists Received and Earnings

15 科技、教育

Science and Technology, Education

15-1 科技活动基本情况 …… (503)
Basic Statistics on Scientific and Technical Activities

15－2　研究与发展课题情况 …………………………………………………………………………………………（503）
Research and Development Projects
15－3　县级以上政府部门所属研究与开发机构(2016 年) …………………………………………………………（504）
State-owned Research and Development Institutions above County Level(2016)
15－4　县级以上政府部门所属研究与开发机构课题情况(2016 年) ……………………………………………（506）
Projects of State-owned Research and Development Institutions above County Level(2016)
15－5　县级以上政府部门所属研究与开发机构基本情况 ……………………………………………………（508）
Basic Statistics on State-owned Research and Development Institutions above County Level
15－6　县级以上政府部门所属研究与开发机构成果 …………………………………………………………（508）
Achievements of State-owned Research and Development Institutions above County Level
15－7　规上工业企业研发情况 ………………………………………………………………………………（509）
Basic Statistics on Scientific and Technical Research Activities of above Designated Size Industrial Enterprises
15－8　大中型工业企业研发情况 ……………………………………………………………………………（510）
Basic Statistics on Scientific and Technical Research Activities of Large and Medium-sized Industrial Enterprises
15－9　规上工业企业研究与发展经费内部支出 ………………………………………………………………（511）
Basic Statistics on Intramural R&D Expenditure of above Designated Size Industrial Enterprises
15－10　大中型工业企业研究与发展经费内部支出 ……………………………………………………………（513）
Basic Statistics on Intramural R&D Expenditure of Large and Medium-sized Industrial Enterprises
15－11　高等学校科技活动情况 ……………………………………………………………………………（515）
Basic Statistics on Scientific and Technical Activities of Institutions of Higher Education
15－12　高新技术产业产值 …………………………………………………………………………………（516）
Output Value in High-tech Industry
15－13　各类专业技术人员数 ………………………………………………………………………………（517）
Number of Scientific and Technical Personnels
15－14　三种专利申请受理量 ………………………………………………………………………………（518）
Application for Three Kinds of Patents Accepted
15－15　三种专利授权量 ……………………………………………………………………………………（518）
Three Kinds of Patents Granted
15－16　全省产品质量监督检查情况 (2016 年) ……………………………………………………………（519）
Results of Sampling Check on the Quality of Products under Provincial Supervision (2016)
15－17　教育事业基本情况 …………………………………………………………………………………（520）
Basic Statistics on Education
15－18　各级各类教育事业(2016 年) ………………………………………………………………………（521）
Basic Statistics on Education by Level and Type (2016)
15－19　全省研究生数 ………………………………………………………………………………………（522）
Number of Postgraduates
15－20　各级各类学校女在校学生和女专任教师数 ……………………………………………………………（522）
Number of Female Students Enrollment and Teachers by Level and Type of Schools
15－21　普通高等教育分科学生数(2016 年) ………………………………………………………………（523）
Student Enrollment in Regular Higher Education by Field of Study (2016)

15－22　分市教育事业基本情况(2016 年) …………………………………………………………………… (524)
Basic Statistics on Education by Region (2016)
15－23　每万人口在校学生数和中小学升学情况 ……………………………………………………………… (526)
Number of Students Per 10000 Population and Enrollment Rate of Secondary and Primary Schools
15－24　各级学校教师负担学生数 ……………………………………………………………………………… (527)
Student-teacher Ratio by Level of School

16　文化、体育、卫生

Culture, Sports and Public Health

16－1　文化艺术和文物事业机构、人员情况 ……………………………………………………………… (535)
Number of Cultural Institution and Personnel
16－2　群众艺术馆、文化馆站业务活动及经费情况 (2016 年) ……………………………………………… (536)
Basic Statistics on Activities and Expenditures of Mass Art Centers and Cultural Centers (2016)
16－3　公共图书馆业务活动及经费情况 (2016 年) ………………………………………………………… (536)
Facilities, Services and Expenditures of Public Libraries (2016)
16－4　报纸、期刊出版情况 (2016 年) ……………………………………………………………………… (537)
Basic Statistics on Newspaper and Periodicals Published (2016)
16－5　图书出版情况(2016 年) ……………………………………………………………………………… (537)
Basic Statistics on Books Published (2016)
16－6　分地区公共图书馆基本情况 (2016 年) ……………………………………………………………… (538)
Statistics on Public Libraries by Region (2016)
16－7　广播、电视事业发展情况 …………………………………………………………………………… (540)
Basic Statistics on Broadcasting and Television Stations
16－8　广播、电视节目制作时间 …………………………………………………………………………… (540)
Time of Production of Broadcasting and TV Programs
16－9　分地区规模以上文化及相关产业法人单位数 (2016 年底) ………………………………………… (541)
Number of Legal Persons of Culture and Relavant Industry above Ddesignated Size by Region at Year-end (2016)
16－10　分地区规模以上文化制造业企业基本情况 (2016 年) ……………………………………………… (542)
Basic Conditions of Cultural Manufacturing Enterprises above Designated Size by Region (2016)
16－11　分地区限额以上文化批发和零售业企业基本情况 (2016 年) ……………………………………… (543)
Basic Conditions of Enterprises of Wholesale and Retail of Culture above Designated Size by Region (2016)
16－12　分地区重点文化服务业企业基本情况 (2016 年) …………………………………………………… (544)
Basic Conditions of Major Enterprises of Services of Culture by Region (2016)
16－13　体育系统职工人数 (2016 年) ……………………………………………………………………… (545)
Number of Staff and Workers in Sports Commissions (2016)
16－14　等级运动员、裁判员人数 ………………………………………………………………………… (545)
Number of Athletes and Referees in Grades
16－15　运动员在各级比赛中获奖牌情况(2016 年) ………………………………………………………… (545)
Awards for Athletes in Competitions of All Levels (2016)

16－16 卫生事业基本情况（2016 年） …… （546）
Basic Statistics on Health Care（2016）
16－17 卫 生 机 构 数 …… （547）
Number of Health Care Institutions
16－18 卫生机构人员数 …… （548）
Number of Persons Engaged in Health Care Institutions
16－19 卫生机构床位数 …… （549）
Number of Beds in Health Care Institutions
16－20 医疗机构门诊情况（2016 年） …… （550）
Service of Health Institutions（2016）
16－21 医疗机构住院服务、病床使用情况（2016 年） …… （551）
Situation of Hospitalization Service and Beds Utilization of Health Institutions（2016）
16－22 法定报告传染病发病及死亡情况（2016 年） …… （552）
Legal Report on Infection Disease Incidence and Death（2016）
16－23 孕产妇及婴儿死亡率 …… （552）
Death Rate of Pregnant Women and Babies

17 公共管理、社会保障和社会组织

Public Management, Social Security and Social Organizations

17－1 档案事业机构人员数（2016 年） …… （557）
Number of Persons and Institutions of Archives（2016）
17－2 档案馆档案资料馆藏和利用情况 …… （557）
Conditions of Files Stored and Used in Archives
17－3 律师、公证及调解工作基本情况 …… （558）
Basic Statistics on Lawyers, Notarization and Mediation
17－4 国内公证文书分类 …… （559）
Domestic Notarial Documents by Type
17－5 涉外公证文书分类 …… （559）
Foreign-related Notarial Documents by Type
17－6 民政行业单位基本情况 …… （560）
Basic Conditions of Affairs Agencies
17－7 民政事业费支出情况 …… （561）
Operating Expenses for Civil Administration
17－8 提供住宿的社会服务机构基本情况（2016 年） …… （562）
Basic Statistics of Provide Accommodation Social service Agencies(2016)
17－9 残疾人事业基本情况 …… （563）
Basic Statistics of People with Disabilities
17－10 婚姻登记和离婚情况 …… （565）
Number of Marriages and Divorces

17－11　社会保险基本情况 …………………………………………………………………………………… (566)
Basic Statistics of Social Insurance
17－12　社会保险基金收支及累计结余 ……………………………………………………………………… (567)
Revenue, Expenses and Balance of Social Insurance Fund
17－13　工会、妇联基本情况 ………………………………………………………………………………… (568)
Basic Statistics on Labour Union and Women's Federation
17－14　公安机关立案的刑事案件情况 ……………………………………………………………………… (569)
Criminal Cases Registered in Public Security Organs
17－15　公安机关受理、查处治安案件情况 ………………………………………………………………… (569)
Offense Cases Against Public Order Handled by Public Security Organs
17－16　交通事故情况(2016 年) …………………………………………………………………………… (570)
Basic Statistics on Traffic Accidents (2016)
17－17　火灾事故情况(2016 年) …………………………………………………………………………… (570)
Basic Statistics on Fire Accidents (2016)
17－18　人民检察院直接立案侦查案件情况 (2016 年) ……………………………………………………… (571)
Cases under Direct Investigation by People's Procuratorate(2016)
17－19　人民检察院审查批准、决定逮捕犯罪嫌疑人和提起公诉被告人情况 (2016 年) …………………… (571)
Arrests of Criminal Suspects and Defendants under Public Prosecution Approved by People's Procuratorate(2016)
17－20　人民检察院处理申诉案件情况 (2016 年) ………………………………………………………… (572)
Appeals Handled by People's Procuratorate(2016)
17－21　人民法院审理刑事一审案件收结案情况 …………………………………………………………… (572)
First Trial Criminal Cases Accepted and Settled by Courts
17－22　人民法院审理婚姻家庭、继承一审案件收结案情况 (2016 年) …………………………………… (573)
First Trial Civil Cases of Marriages, Family Affairs and Inheritance Accepted and Settled by Courts(2016)
17－23　人民法院审理合同纠纷一审案件收结案情况 (2016 年) …………………………………………… (573)
First Trial Cases of Contracts Disputes Accepted and Settled by Courts (2016)
17－24　人民法院审理权属、侵权纠纷及其他民事一审收结案情况 (2016 年) …………………………… (574)
First Trial Cases of Disputes of Right, Infringement of Right and Other Civil Affairs Accepted and Settled by Courts(2016)
17－25　人民法院行政一审案件收结案情况 (2016 年) …………………………………………………… (574)
First Trial Administrative Cases Accepted and Settled by Courts(2016)

18　城市经济与建设

Urban Economy and Construction

18－1　城市公用事业基本情况 ………………………………………………………………………… (579)
Basic Statisics on Urban Public Utilities
18－2　城市自来水情况 ……………………………………………………………………………………… (580)
Basic Statistics on Tap Water Supply in Cities
18－3　城市煤气、液化石油气情况 ………………………………………………………………………… (581)
Basic Statistics on Supply of Gas and Liquefied Petroleum Gas in Cities

18－4　城市市政工程情况 …………………………………………………………………… (582)

Basic Statistics on Municipal Engineering in Cities

18－5　城市园林绿化情况 …………………………………………………………………… (583)

Basic Statistics on Parks, Gardens and Green Areas in Cities

18－6　城市环境卫生情况 …………………………………………………………………… (584)

Basic Statistics on Urban Environmental Sanitation

18－7　城市公共汽(电)车、出租汽车情况 …………………………………………………… (585)

Basic Statistics on Buses (Trolley Buses) and Taxis in Cities

18－8　主要城市土地面积、人口情况 (2016 年) ……………………………………………… (586)

Land Area and Population of Major Cities(2016)

18－9　主要城市就业情况 (2016 年) ………………………………………………………… (586)

Employment of Major Cities(2016)

18－10　主要城市地区生产总值及指数 (2016 年) …………………………………………… (587)

Gross Domestic Product of Major Cities(2016)

18－11　主要城市固定资产投资 (2016 年) ………………………………………………… (587)

Investment in Fixed Assets of Major Cities(2016)

18－12　主要城市工业基本情况 (2016 年) ………………………………………………… (588)

Basic Statistics on Industry of Major Cities(2016)

18－13　主要城市工业总产值 (2016 年) …………………………………………………… (588)

Gross Output Value of Industry of Major Cities(2016)

18－14　主要城市财政、金融 (2016 年) …………………………………………………… (589)

Government Revenue and Expenditures of Major Cities(2016)

18－15　主要城市贸易、外经(2016 年) …………………………………………………… (589)

Domestic Trade and Foreign Economy of Major Cities(2016)

18－16　主要城市邮电、电力 (2016 年) …………………………………………………… (590)

Post and Telecommunication Service and Power Consumption of Major Cities(2016)

18－17　主要城市文教、科技、卫生(2016 年) ……………………………………………… (590)

Culture, Education, Science and Technology and Public Health of Major Cities(2016)

18－18　主要城市居民收支情况 (2016 年) ………………………………………………… (591)

Household Income and Expenditure of Major Cities(2016)

18－19　市辖区主要指标 (2016 年) ………………………………………………………… (592)

Major Indicators of Municipal Districts(2016)

18－20　市辖区法人单位数 (2016 年) ……………………………………………………… (596)

Number of Corporations of Municipal District(2016)

18－21　市辖区人口、面积(2016 年) ……………………………………………………… (598)

Population and Land Area of Municipal District(2016)

18－22　市辖区就业人员(2016 年) ………………………………………………………… (599)

Employment of Municipal District(2016)

18－23　市辖区地区生产总值(2016 年) …………………………………………………… (600)

Gross Domestic Product of Municipal District(2016)

18－24 市辖区投资、财政收支(2016 年) …… (601)
Investment, Government Revenue and Expenditure of Municipal District (2016)
18－25 市辖区规模以上工业产值(2016 年) …… (602)
Gross Output Value of above Designated Size Industry of Municipal District (2016)
18－26 市辖区规模以上工业效益(2016 年) …… (603)
Economic Benefit of above Designated Size Industry of Municipal District (2016)
18－27 市辖区贸易、外资(2016 年) …… (604)
Trade and Foreign Economy of Municipal District(2016)
18－28 市辖区教育、卫生、收入(2016 年) …… (605)
Education, Public Health and Income of Municipal District(2016)

19 区域经济

Regional Economy

19－1 三大区域主要经济指标(2016 年) …… (611)
Major Economic Indicators of Three Regions (2016)
19－2 三大区域经济社会基本情况(2016 年) …… (612)
Basic Statistics on Economy and Society of Three Regions (2016)
19－3 江苏主要指标占长江三角洲比重 (2016 年) …… (628)
Proportion of Main Indicators of Jiangsu in Yangtze River Delta (2016)
19－4 沿江开发区域主要指标占全省比重 (2016 年) …… (629)
Proportion of Main Indicators of Development Zones along the Yangtze River in Jiangsu Province (2016)
19－5 沿江地区主要指标 (2016 年) …… (630)
Main Indicators of the Region along the Yangtze River (2016)
19－6 沿海地区主要指标 (2016 年) …… (637)
Main Indicators of the Coastal Regions(2016)
19－7 沿东陇海线地区主要指标 (2016 年) …… (644)
Main Indicators of the East Region along the Long-hai Railway(2016)

20 市县社会经济

Social Economy of Cities and Counties

20－1 人口(2016 年) …… (649)
Population (2016)
20－2 户数及土地面积 (2016 年) …… (651)
Number of Households and Land Area (2016)
20－3 法人单位数(2016 年) …… (653)
Number of Corporations (2016)

20－4 年末就业人员（2016年）……………………………………………………………………………………（655）
Number of Employed Persons（Year-end）（2016）
20－5 乡村就业人员（2016年）……………………………………………………………………………………（657）
Rural Employment（2016）
20－6 地区生产总值（2016年）……………………………………………………………………………………（659）
Gross Domestic Product（2016）
20－7 地区生产总值构成（2015年）………………………………………………………………………………（661）
Composition and Indices of Gross Domestic Product（2015）
20－8 农林牧渔业总产值（2016年）………………………………………………………………………………（663）
Gross Output Value of Agriculture，Forestry，Animal Husbandry and Fishery（2016）
20－9 农业生产情况（2016年）……………………………………………………………………………………（665）
Basic Conditions of Agricultural Production（2016）
20－10 农产品产量（2016年）……………………………………………………………………………………（667）
Output of Agricultural Products（2016）
20－11 工业总产值（2016年）……………………………………………………………………………………（669）
Gross Output Value of Industry（2016）
20－12 工业企业主要经济指标（2016年）…………………………………………………………………………（671）
Major Economic Indicators on Industrial Enterprises（2016）
20－13 交通运输（2016年）………………………………………………………………………………………（673）
Transportation（2016）
20－14 邮电、电力（2016年）……………………………………………………………………………………（675）
Postal and Telecommunications，Power Services（2016）
20－15 固定资产投资完成额（2016年）…………………………………………………………………………（677）
Completed Investment in Fixed Assets（2016）
20－16 国内贸易、对外经济（2016年）…………………………………………………………………………（679）
Domestic and Foreign Trade，Foreign Economy（2016）
20－17 财政、金融（2016年）……………………………………………………………………………………（681）
Government Finance，Financial Intermediation（2016）
20－18 科技、教育（2016年）……………………………………………………………………………………（683）
Science，Technology and Education（2016）
20－19 文化、卫生（2016年）……………………………………………………………………………………（685）
Culture and Public Health（2016）
20－20 人民生活（2016年）………………………………………………………………………………………（688）

21 县（市）社会经济发展序列

Social Economy Development Alignment of Counties

21－1 年末户籍人口（2016年）……………………………………………………………………………………（695）
Total Registered Population at Year-end（2016）
21－2 地区生产总值（2016年）……………………………………………………………………………………（696）
Gross Domestic Product（2016）

21－3 第一产业增加值（2016 年）…………（697）
Value-added of the Primary Industry（2016）
21－4 第二产业增加值（2016 年）…………（698）
Value-added of the Secondary Industry（2016）
21－5 第三产业增加值（2016 年）…………（699）
Value-added of the Tertiary Industry（2016）
21－6 全部工业增加值(2016 年)…………（700）
Value-added of All Industries（2016）
21－7 人均地区生产总值（2016 年）…………（701）
Per Capita Gross Domestic Product（2016）
21－8 固定资产投资（2016 年）…………（702）
Completed Investment in Fixed Assetes（2016）
21－9 一般公共预算收入（2016 年）…………（703）
General Public Budget Revenue(2016)
21－10 人均一般公共预算收入(2016 年)…………（704）
Per Capita General Public Budget Revenue(2016)
21－11 粮食产量(2016 年)…………（705）
Output of Grain（2016）
21－12 油料产量(2016 年)…………（706）
Output of Oil-bearing Crops（2016）
21－13 规模以上工业企业利润总额（2016 年）…………（707）
Profits of above Designated Size Industrial Enterprises（2016）
21－14 社会消费品零售总额（2016 年）…………（708）
Total Retail Sale of Consumer Goods（2016）
21－15 出口总额(2016 年)…………（709）
Total Exports（2016）
21－16 实际使用外资(2016 年)…………（710）
Actual Use of Foreign Capital(2016)
21－17 金融机构各项存款余额(2016 年)…………（711）
The Balance of Deposits of Financial Institutions（2016）
21－18 金融机构各项贷款余额(2016 年)…………（712）
The Balance of Loans of Financial Institutions（2016）
21－19 居民人均可支配收入(2016 年)…………（713）
Per Capita Disposable Income of Residents(2016)
21－20 城镇常住居民人均可支配收入（2016 年）…………（714）
Per Capita Disposable Income of Urban Permanent Residents(2016)
21－21 农村常住居民人均可支配收入(2016 年)…………（715）
Per Capita Disposable Income of Rural Permanent Residents(2016)

附录　全国分省主要指标

Appendix. Major Indicators by Region

附录 1－1　人口及地区生产总值（2016 年）…… （719）

Population and Gross Domestic Product（2016）

附录 1－2　地区生产总值构成及增速（2016 年）…… （720）

Structure and Growth Rate of Gross Domestic Product（2016）

附录 1－3　固定资产投资完成额（2016 年）…… （721）

Completed Investment in Fixed Assets（2016）

附录 1－4　居民人均收入与支出(2016 年）…… （722）

Per Capita Disposable Income and Comsumption Expenditure of Residents(2016)

附录 1－5　居民消费价格指数(2016 年）…… （723）

Consumer Price Index(2016)

附录 1－6　农林牧渔业总产值和增速(2016 年）…… （724）

Gross Output Value and Growth Rate of Agriculture, Forestry, Animal Husbandry and Fishery（2016）

附录 1－7　主要农产品产量（2016 年）…… （725）

Output of Major Agricultural Products（2016）

附录 1－8　规模以上工业企业主要经济指标(2016 年）…… （726）

Main Economic Indicators of above Designated Size Industrial Enterprises（2016）

附录 1－9　主要工业产品产量(2016 年）…… （727）

Output of Major Industrial Products（2016）

附录 1－10　建筑业主要指标(2016 年）…… （728）

Main Indicators on Construction（2016）

附录 1－11　客运量和旅客周转量（2016 年）…… （729）

Passenger Traffic and Turnover Volume of Passenger Traffic（2016）

附录 1－12　货运量和货物周转量（2016 年）…… （730）

Freight Traffic and Turnover Volume of Freight Traffic（2016）

附录 1－13　国内外贸易（2016 年）…… （731）

Domestic and Foreign Trade（2016）

1

综　合

General Survey

简 要 说 明

本篇章主要内容和资料来源

一、综合资料主要包括行政区划、国民经济和社会发展综合资料、私营个体统计资料等。

二、行政区划资料，由民政部门根据截止到上一年末全省行政区划变更情况整理提供。

三、国民经济综合资料是抽取全书的精华，通过对各篇章主要统计指标及其速度、结构、比例和效益等的加工计算，反映国民经济和社会发展的总体情况。

四、基本单位统计资料根据基本单位统计年报汇总整理。

五、私营个体统计资料，由工商行政管理部门整理提供。

Brief Introduction

Main Contents and Sources of Data

Ⅰ. This chapter consists of four parts: divisions of administrative areas, summary data on the national economy and social development, basic unit of statistics, private and individual statistics.

Ⅱ. Date about divisions of administrative areas is provided by Civil Affairs bureau which given the change of the administrative divisions end of year.

Ⅲ. The summary data on the national economy reflect the overall situation of the economic and social development by presenting further processed statistics including growth, structure, ratio, and efficiency data derived from other chapters.

Ⅳ. Date of basic unit is come from basic unit of statistics annual report. .

Ⅴ. Date of private and individual economy provided by Department of Business Administration.

自然概况

位　置

江苏简称苏，位于我国大陆东部沿海中心，介于东经116°18′-121°57′，北纬30°45′-35°20′之间。东濒黄海，西连安徽，北接山东，东南与浙江和上海毗邻。

江苏地处美丽富饶的长江三角州，平原辽阔，主要有苏南平原，江淮平原、黄淮平原和东部滨海平原，自然条件优越，经济基础较好。

面　积

全省面积10.72万平方公里，占全国总面积的1.1%，海岸线长954公里。

河　流

全省境内河川交错，水网密布，长江横穿东西425多公里，大运河纵贯南北718公里，西南部有秦淮河，北部有苏北灌溉总渠、新沭河、通扬运河等。有大小湖泊290多个，全国五大淡水湖，江苏得其二，太湖和洪泽湖象两面大明镜，分别镶嵌在水乡江南和苏北平原。

资　源

江苏以地形地势低平，河湖众多为特点，平原、水面所占比例之大，在全国居首位，成为江苏一大地理优势。水产资源丰富，有广阔的海涂、浅海，东部沿海渔场面积达15.4万平方公里，其中包括著名的吕泗、海州湾等四大渔场，盛产黄鱼、带鱼、昌鱼、虾类、蟹类及贝藻类等。江苏也是全国河蟹、鳗鱼苗的主要产地。内陆水面4000多万亩，养殖面积1148万亩，有淡水鱼类140余种，已利用的有40多种。矿产资源分布广泛，品种较多，已发现的有133种。能源矿产主要有煤炭、石油和天然气；非金属矿产有硫、磷、钠盐、水晶、兰晶石、蓝宝石、金刚石、高岭土、石灰石、石英砂、大理石、陶瓷粘土；金属矿产有铁、铜、铅、锌、银、金、锶、锰等。粘土类矿产、建材类矿产、化工原料矿产、冶金辅助原料矿产、特种用途矿产和有色金属矿产，是江苏矿产资源的优势。

气　候

全省气候具有明显的季风特征，处于亚热带向暖温带过渡地带，大致以淮河—灌溉总渠一线为界，以南属亚热带湿润季风气候，以北属暖温带湿润季风气候。全省气候温和，雨量适中，四季分明。

Natural Resources

Location

Jiangsu (Short for Su) lies in the east of the country. It is situated in the center of the costal area, between 116°18′ - 121°57′E and 30°45′ - 35°20′N, with Yellowsea on the east, Anhui province on the west, Shandong on the north, and Zhejiang and Shanghai as its neighbours on the southeast.

Jiangsu seats on the beautiful and abundant Yangtze River Delta. Composed of vast plains, mainly South-Su, Jianghuai, Huanghuai and eastern plain by the sea, the province provides favorable natural conditions and good economic bases.

Area

The area of Jiangsu is 107.2 thousand square kilometres, occupied 1.1 % of the total national area,The coastline of the province is as long as 954 kilmetres.

Rivers and Lakes

In Jiangsu, there are rivers crisscrossing throughout the province, and distributes the network of waterways. The Yangtze River travels the whole area of Jiangsu, from west to east, for more than 400 kilometres. The Grand Canal flows south to north for 690 kilometres. There are Qinhuai River in the southeast of Jiangsu, Subei general irrigation canal, Xinshu River and Tongyang canal etc. in the north part. Among the 290 lakes of varying size in Jiangsu, the Taihu Lake and Hongzehu Lake are both listed among the national "Five Large Fresh Water Lakes", like two bright mirrors inlaid respectively into the southern region of the Changjiang River and Subei Plain.

Resources

The province is characteristic of topographical features in low and flat terrains, with numerous rivers and lakes. The proportion of plain and watersurface area is so large that it ranks the first in China and become a geographical superiority proportion. There are plentiful aquatic resources, vast shallow sea beaches and epeiric seas. There are 154 thousand square kilometres of fishing grounds on the eastern coastal area, composed of the four famous fishing grounds such as Lusi and Haizhouwan etc., abound in yellow croaker, hairtail, butterfish, shrimp and crab, and shellfish and algae. Jiangsu is also a main production area of crabs and young eels in the country. There are more than 40 million mu of interior water surface, with 11.48 million mu of aquatic farm. Among 140 kinds and more of flesh water fishes, over 40 are utilized. Numerous varieties of mineral resources are widely dispersed, 133 kinds of them have been discovered. The main sources of energy and minerals dispersed in Jiangsu are coal, petroleum and natural gas. Nonmetallic minerals contain sulphur, phosphorus, sodium, crystal, dyanite, sapphire, diamond, kaolin, limestone, quartzite, marble and pottery clay. Metallic minerals contain iron, copper, lead, zinc, silver, gold, strontium and manganese. The minerals as clay, construction materials, sand, chemical raw materials, metallurgical assistance raw materials, special purpose minerals and non-ferrous metal minerals become a mineral superiority of Jiangsu.

Climate

Located in a transition area from subtripical zone to temperature zone, Jiangsu shows a distinct characteristic of monsoon. Taking the Huaihe river to general irrigation canal as an approximate line of demarcation, the climate to the south of the line belongs to monsoon of tropical moist zone, while the climate to the north of the line belongs to monsoon of warm moist zone. Jiangsu has a warm climate, with moderate rainfall and distinct seasons.

综　合
GENERAL SURVEY

从数字看 2016 年的江苏
Jiangsu in Statistics　’2016

江 苏 的 地 位
Position of Jiangsu in the Country

地区生产总值	Gross Domestic Product	占全国	10.20%	10.2 percent of China
#第三产业	Tertiary Industry	占全国	10.0%	10.0 percent of China
人均地区生产总值	Per Capital GDP	高于全国	41277 元	Over 41277 yuan
固定资产投资	Investment in Fixed Assets	占全国	8.3%	8.3 percent of China
社会消费品零售总额	Total Retail Sales of Consumer Goods	占全国	8.6%	8.6 percent of China
进出口总额	Total Imports and Exports	占全国	13.8%	13.8 percent of China
#出口总额	Total Exports	占全国	15.2%	15.2 percent of China
粮食产量	Output of Grain	占全国	5.6%	5.6 percent of China
钢材产量	Output of Steel	占全国	13.7%	13.7 percent of China
发电量	Output of Electricity	占全国	7.6%	7.6 percent of China
居民人均可支配收入	Per Capita Disposable Income of Residents	高于全国	8249 元	Over 8249 yuan
城镇常住居民人均可支配收入	Per Capita Disposable Income of Urban Permanent Residents	高于全国	6536 元	Over 6536 yuan
农村常住居民人均可支配收入	Per Capita Disposable Income of Rural Permanent Residents	高于全国	5243 元	Over 5243 yuan

江 苏 的 人 口
Population of Jiangsu

年末常住人口	Permanent Population at Year-end	7998.60	万人	(10000 persons)
年末户籍人口	Registered Population at Year-end	7775.66	万人	(10000 persons)
就业人员	Employment	4756.22	万人	(10000 persons)
出生人口	Births	77.96	万人	(10000 persons)
死亡人口	Deaths	56.15	万人	(10000 persons)
结婚人数	Marriages	71.61	万对	(10000 couples)
离婚人数	Divorces	26.13	万对	(10000 couples)
人口密度	Density of Population	746	人/平方公里	(person/sq. km)
人口平均期望寿命(2015 年)	Life Expectancy(2015)	77.51	岁	(year)
男	Male	75.50	岁	(year)
女	Female	79.52	岁	(year)

江苏的经济发展
Economic Development of Jiangsu

		1979—2016年平均增长(%) 1979—2016 Average Annual Growth Rate(%)	2011—2016年平均增长(%) 2011—2016 Average Annual Growth Rate(%)
地区生产总值	Gross Domestic Product	12.1	9.3
第一产业	Primary Industry	4.4	3.1
第二产业	Secondary Industry	13.4	9.3
第三产业	Tertiary Industry	13.8	9.9
#工业	Industry	13.5	9.5
全社会固定资产投资	Total Investment in Fixed Assets	22.6	14.5
一般公共预算收入	General Public Budget Revenue	13.7	12.2
社会消费品零售总额	Total Retail Sales of Consumer Goods	16.6	13.3
出口总额	Total Exports	19.1	2.8

江苏的一天
One Day in Jiangsu

地区生产总值	Gross Domestic Product	208.46	亿元	(100 million yuan)
第一产业	Primary Industry	11.17	亿元	(100 million yuan)
第二产业	Secondary Industry	91.92	亿元	(100 million yuan)
第三产业	Tertiary Industry	105.37	亿元	(100 million yuan)
#工业	Industry	80.93	亿元	(100 million yuan)
财政收入	Government Revenue	53.33	亿元	(100 million yuan)
货物运输量	Freight Traffic	590.82	万吨	(10000 tons)
竣工房屋面积	Floor Space of Residential Housing Completed	205.45	万平方米	(10000 sq. m)
社会消费品零售总额	Total Retail Sales of Consumer Goods	78.65	亿元	(100 million yuan)
出口总额	Total Exports	8.75	亿美元	(USD 100 million)
出版报纸	Newspapers Published	638.55	万份	(10000 copies)
邮寄函件	Letters Delivered	91.23	万件	(10000 pieces)

1－1 行 政 区 划（2016年）
Administrative Divisions(2016)

单位:个 (unit)

市 名	City	各级市单位数 Number of Cities at All Levels	县级单位数 Number of Counties	县 County	县级市 Cities at County Level	市辖区 Districts Under the Jurisdiction of Cities
全 省	**Total**	**13**	**96**	**20**	**21**	**55**
南京市	Nanjing	1	11			11
无锡市	Wuxi	1	7		2	5
徐州市	Xuzhou	1	10	3	2	5
常州市	Changzhou	1	6		1	5
苏州市	Suzhou	1	9		4	5
南通市	Nantong	1	8	2	3	3
连云港市	Lianyungang	1	6	3		3
淮安市	Huaian	1	7	3		4
盐城市	Yancheng	1	9	5	1	3
扬州市	Yangzhou	1	6	1	2	3
镇江市	Zhenjiang	1	6		3	3
泰州市	Taizhou	1	6		3	3
宿迁市	Suqian	1	5	3		2

1－1 续表 Continued

单位:个 (unit)

市 名	City	镇 Town	乡 Township	街道办事处 Subdistrict Office	村民委员会 Village Committee	居民委员会 Neighbourhood Committee
全 省	**Total**	**763**	**69**	**455**	**14477**	**7079**
南京市	Nanjing	13		87	287	944
无锡市	Wuxi	30		51	639	590
徐州市	Xuzhou	97		66	2041	650
常州市	Changzhou	36		25	645	394
苏州市	Suzhou	55		41	1036	1128
南通市	Nantong	65		37	1304	606
连云港市	Lianyungang	50	10	29	1432	251
淮安市	Huaian	84	20	21	1451	246
盐城市	Yancheng	96		26	1826	617
扬州市	Yangzhou	62	5	14	1005	374
镇江市	Zhenjiang	31		25	490	271
泰州市	Taizhou	71	5	20	1425	437
宿迁市	Suqian	73	29	13	896	571

1－2 国民经济和社会发展总量与速度指标

指标	Item	总量指标 1978	1990	2000	2010
人口与就业	**Population and Employment**				
人口（万人）	**Population**（10000 persons）				
年末人口	Population at Year-end	5834.32	6766.90	7327.24	7869.34
城镇人口	Urban	800.77	1458.94	3040.81	4767.63
乡村人口	Rural	5033.55	5307.96	4286.43	3101.71
就业（万人）	**Employment**（10000 persons）				
就业人数	Employment	2777.72	4225.02	4418.14	4754.68
#职工人数	Staff and Workers	581.50	879.85	673.25	710.58
#国有单位	State-owned Units	366.37	536.88	411.40	263.95
年末城镇登记失业人数	Unemployment Registered in Urban Area		22.52	30.36	40.65
宏观经济	**Macroeconomy**				
国民经济核算（亿元）	**National Economic Accounting**（100 million yuan）				
地区生产总值	Gross Domestic Product	249.24	1416.50	8553.69	41425.48
第一产业	Primary Industry	68.71	355.17	1048.34	2540.10
第二产业	Secondary Industry	131.09	692.59	4435.89	21753.93
第三产业	Tertiary Industry	49.44	368.74	3069.46	17131.45
支出法地区生产总值	Gross Domestic Expenditures				
#最终消费	Final Consumption Expenditure	130.55	717.36	3710.72	17238.08
居民消费	Resident Consumption	115.15	608.29	2815.51	10942.82
政府消费	Government Consumption Expenditure	15.40	109.07	895.21	6295.26
资本形成总额	Gross Capital Formation	77.98	588.44	4044.78	21173.29
固定资本形成	Fixed Capital Formation	40.40	374.12	3225.42	20709.14
存货增加	Changes in Stock	37.58	214.32	819.36	464.15
固定资产投资（亿元）	**Investment in Fixed Assets**（100 million yuan）				
全社会固定资产投资	Total Investment in Fixed Assets	21.75	356.30	2995.43	22020.73
#国有单位	State-owned Units	20.70	134.86	1200.01	4438.46
集体单位	Collective-owned Units	1.05	74.87	455.86	902.96
#房地产开发	Real Estale Development		11.71	358.72	4299.38
财政（亿元）	**Finance**（100 million yuan）				
一般公共预算收入	General Public Budget Revenue	61.09	136.20	448.31	4079.86
一般公共预算支出	General Public Budget Expenditure	28.38	100.97	591.28	4914.06

Principal Aggregate Indicators on National Economic and Social Development and Growth Rate

Aggregate Data		速度指标 Indicies and Growth Rate							
		2016年比下列各年增长(%) Index (2016 as percentage of the following years)					年平均增长(%) Average Annual Growth Rate		
2015	2016	1978	1990	2000	2010	2015	1979 ~ 2016	2001 ~ 2016	2011 ~ 2016
7976.30	7998.60	37.1	18.2	9.2	1.6	0.3	0.8	0.5	0.3
5305.83	5416.65	576.4	271.3	78.1	13.6	2.1	5.2	3.7	2.1
2670.47	2581.95	-48.7	-51.4	-39.8	-16.8	-3.3	-1.7	-3.1	-3.0
4758.50	4756.22	71.2	12.6	7.7	0.0	0.0	1.4	0.5	0.01
1552.08	1497.30	157.5	70.2	122.4	110.7	-3.5	2.5	5.1	13.2
294.31	289.86	-20.9	-46.0	-29.5	9.8	-1.5	-0.6	-2.2	1.6
36.01	35.21		56.3	16.0	-13.4	-2.2		0.9	-2.4
70116.38	76086.17	7595.3	2091.6	489.4	70.2	7.8	12.1	11.7	9.3
3986.05	4077.18	422.4	179.1	70.6	20.0	0.7	4.4	3.4	3.1
32044.45	33550.54	11778.8	2843.3	561.0	70.5	6.6	13.4	12.5	9.3
34085.88	38458.45	13515.0	2633.4	531.2	76.6	9.7	13.8	12.2	9.9
35041.42									
25245.17									
9796.25									
30600.62									
29940.82									
659.80									
46246.87	49663.21	228236.6	13838.6	1558.0	125.5	7.4	22.6	19.2	14.5
8901.58	8236.65	39690.6	6007.6	586.4	85.6	-7.5	17.1	12.8	10.9
1872.50	806.51	76710.8	977.2	76.9	-10.7	-56.9	19.1	3.6	-1.9
8153.68	8956.37		76384.8	2396.8	108.3	9.8		22.3	13.0
8028.59	8121.23	13193.9	5862.7	1711.5	99.1	1.2	13.7	19.8	12.2
9687.58	9981.96	35072.5	9786.1	1588.2	103.1	3.0	16.7	19.3	12.5

1-2 续表 1

指标	Item	总量指标 1978	1990	2000	2010
物价 （上年=100）	**Price (preceding year=100)**				
居民消费价格指数	General Consumer Price Index	100.1	103.2	100.1	103.8
商品零售价格指数	General Retail Price Index	100.2	102.3	98.6	103.2
工业生产者出厂价格指数	Ex -factory Price Index of Industrial Producers			101.1	107.3
利用外资 （亿美元）	**Utilization of Foreign Capital (USD 100 million)**				
协议注册外资	Agreement Registered Foreign		2.44	106.11	568.33
实际使用投资	Actual Use of Foreign Capital		1.41	64.24	284.98
产 业	**Industry**				
农业	**Agriculture**				
农林牧渔业劳动力 （万人）	Number of Persons Engaged in Agriculture, Forestry, Animal Husbandry and Fishery (10000 persons)	2030.67	1714.49	1480.22	859.83
农林牧渔业总产值 （亿元）	Gross Output Value of Agriculture, Forestry, Animal Husbandry and Fishery (100 million yuan)	105.87	580.53	1869.73	4297.14
主要农产品产量 （万吨）	Output of Major Farm Products (10000 tons)				
粮食	Grain	2400.65	3264.15	3106.63	3235.10
棉花	Cotton	47.54	46.42	31.45	26.08
油料	Oil-bearing Crops	37.44	112.39	225.65	151.97
糖料	Sugar Crops	6.88	22.26	28.26	10.27
蚕茧	Silkworm Cocoons	2.63	12.00	9.01	7.91
猪牛羊肉	Pork, Beef and Mutton		158.38	227.41	223.91
水产品	Aquatic Products	39.76	118.25	308.79	460.44
工业	**Industry**				
全部工业增加值 （亿元）	Added Value of All Industties (100 million yuan)	117.10	634.13	3848.52	19277.65
主要工业产品产量 （万吨）	Output of Major Industrial Products (10000 tons)				
粗钢	Steel	54.51	190.18	617.16	6242.75
钢材	Rolled-steel	60.31	203.01	1401.83	9122.95
发电量 （亿千瓦小时）	Electricity (100 million kW·h)	126.42	404.47	909.69	3358.98
原煤	Coal	1707.02	2407.79	2479.02	2122.48
农用化肥(折100%)	Chemical Furtilizers	72.18	145.90	192.38	241.96
化学农药	Chemical Pesticide	4.92	4.51	17.23	61.76
水泥	Cement	444.10	1532.89	4599.52	15647.46
化学纤维	Chemical Fiber	2.11	40.76	190.99	1027.19
彩色电视机 （万台）	Color Television Sets (10000 units)	0.03	36.64	127.66	1766.89
家用电冰箱 （万台）	Household Refrigerators (10000 units)		83.18	285.17	812.49
建筑业	**Construction**				
建筑业从事主营业务活动的从业人员平均人数 （万人）	The average number of employees engaged in principal Business (10000 persons)		124.31	221.48	598.98
建筑业总产值 （亿元）	Gross Output Value (100 million yuan)		147.23	1546.17	12405.90
施工房屋面积 （万平方米）	Floor Space of Building Under Construction (10000 sq.m)		5241	21287	119036
竣工房屋面积 （万平方米）	Floor Space of Building Completed (10000 sq.m)		3308	12330	48560

1－2 Continued 1

Aggregate Data		速度指标 Indicies and Growth Rate							
		2016年比下列各年增长(%) Index (2016 as percentage of the following years)					年平均增长(%) Average Annual Growth Rate		
2015	2016	1978	1990	2000	2010	2015	1979～2016	2001～2016	2011～2016
101.7	102.3	538.7	199.7	45.6	17.5	2.2	5.0	2.4	2.7
100.6	100.8	366.2	121.3	23.3	11.5	0.8	4.1	1.3	1.8
95.3	98.1		77.7	11.7	－7.1	－1.9		0.7	－1.2
393.61	431.39		17568.5	306.6	－24.1	9.6		9.2	－4.5
242.75	245.43		17294.0	282.1	－13.9	1.1		8.7	－2.5
747.41	736.12	－63.7	－57.1	－50.3	－14.4	－1.5	－2.6	－4.3	－2.6
7030.76	7235.06	653.9	279.6	80.5	19.4	0.8	5.5	3.8	3.0
3561.34	3466.01	44.4	6.2	11.6	7.1	－2.7	1.0	0.7	1.2
11.69	7.38	－84.5	－84.1	－76.5	－71.7	－36.9	－4.8	－8.7	－19.0
143.11	131.93	252.4	17.4	－41.5	－13.2	－7.8	3.4	－3.3	－2.3
9.50	9.03	31.2	－59.5	－68.1	－12.1	－5.0	0.7	－6.9	－2.1
4.97	3.95	50.2	－67.1	－56.2	－50.1	－20.5	1.1	－5.0	－10.9
237.20	227.73		43.8	0.1	1.7	－4.0		0.0	0.3
522.11	523.15	1215.8	342.4	69.4	13.6	0.2	7.0	3.3	2.2
27996.43	29689.92	12309.2	2863.3	594.9	72.2	6.9	13.5	12.9	9.5
10995.17	11080.49	20227.4	5726.3	1695.4	77.5	0.8	15.0	19.8	10.0
13560.81	13469.72	22234.1	6535.0	860.9	47.6	－0.7	15.3	15.2	6.7
4351.78	4667.73	3592.2	1054.0	413.1	39.0	7.3	10.0	10.8	5.6
1918.90	1367.91	－19.9	－43.2	－44.8	－35.6	－28.7	－0.6	－3.6	－7.1
203.76	207.17	187.0	42.0	7.7	－14.4	1.7	2.8	0.5	－2.6
105.53	120.55	2350.2	2573.0	599.7	95.2	14.2	8.8	12.9	11.8
18013.66	17989.78	3950.8	1073.6	291.1	15.0	－0.1	10.2	8.9	2.4
1430.62	1458.19	69009	3477.5	663.5	42.0	1.9	18.8	13.5	6.0
1626.20	1839.38	6131170	4920.1	1340.8	4.1	13.1	33.7	18.1	0.7
907.65	945.75		1037.0	231.6	16.4	4.2		7.8	2.6
833.31	845.84		580.4	281.9	41.2	1.5		8.7	5.9
24785.81	25791.76		17418.0	1568.1	107.9	4.1		19.2	13.0
215592	221494		4126.2	940.5	86.1	2.7		15.8	10.9
76824	74990		2167.0	508.2	54.4	－2.4		11.9	7.5

指　标 Item		总量指标 1978	1990	2000	2010
交通运输	**Transportation**				
货运量 （万吨）	Freight Traffic (10000 tons)	14626	49399	90436	188565
#铁路	Railways	3224	4235	4077	6374
公路	Highways	4488	27904	59056	123500
水运	Waterways	6557	15908	25902	48702
客运量 （万人）	Passenger Traffic (10000 persons)	25621	48339	107244	226627
#铁路	Railways	2752	4788	4891	9711
公路	Highways	18694	41850	101713	215850
水运	Waterways	4175	1701	514	590
港口货物吞吐量 （万吨）	Volume of Freight Handled at Seaports (10000 tons)	10183	17002	39200	158977
邮电通信业	**Postal and Telecommunications Services**				
邮电业务总量 （亿元）	Total Business Revenue (100 million yuan)	1.83	9.98	323.45	2194.60
函件 （亿件）	Number of Letters Delivered (100 million pieces)	1.63	3.30	5.74	9.36
年末固定电话用户 （万户）	Number of Eited Telephone Subseribers at Year-end (10000 househalds)			1138.06	2498.80
城市	Urban			535.43	1527.80
农村	Rural			602.63	971.00
年末移动电话用户 （万户）	Number of Mobile Telephone Subseribers at Year-end (10000 households)			619.50	5923.10
国内商业	**Domestic Trade**				
社会消费品零售总额 （亿元）	Total Retail Sales of Consumer Goods (100 million yuan)	84.79	515.43	2908.46	13606.34
对外经济贸易和旅游	**Foreign Trade and Tourism**				
进出口总额 （亿美元）	Total Imports and Exports (USD 100 million)	4.27	41.39	456.38	4657.93
进口	Imports	0.09	11.95	198.69	1952.43
出口	Exports	4.18	29.44	257.70	2705.50
接待海外旅游人数 （万人）	Number of International Tourists Received (10000 persons)	11.33	72.48	160.94	653.55
金融保险 （亿元）	**Banking and Insurance (100 million yuan)**				
金融机构存款	Deposits of Banking System	60.72	860.33	8400.75	58984.14
金融机构贷款	Loans of Banking System	115.29	1013.45	5967.66	42121.04
国内保险保费收入	Domestic Premium		9.31	132.03	1162.67
教育、科技、文化	**Education, Science and Technology and Culture**				
教育	**Education**				
高等学校本专科在校学生 （万人）	Students Enrollment in Institutions of Higher Education (10000 persons)	6.05	14.69	45.19	164.94
中等专业学校在校学生 （万人）	Students Enrollment in Specialized Secondary Schools (10000 persons)	3.84	13.99	43.62	68.30
普通中学在校学生 （万人）	Students Enrollment in Regular Secondary Schools (10000 persons)	385.85	281.97	373.64	368.61
小学在校学生 （万人）	Students Enrollment in Primary Schools (10000 persons)	868.90	612.29	718.55	398.78
科技	**Science and Technology**				
县以上科研机构数 （个）	Number of Scientific & Technological Research Institutions of County Level and Above (unit)		326	313	135
各类专业技术人员 （万人）	Scientific and Technical Personnel (10000 persons)	22.18	158.86	194.24	140.53

1－2 Continued 2

Aggregate Data		速度指标 Indicies and Growth Rate							
2015	2016	2016年比下列各年增长(%) Index (2016 as percentage of the following years)					年平均增长(%) Average Annual Growth Rate		
		1978	1990	2000	2010	2015	1979～2016	2001～2016	2011～2016
211648	215651					1.9			
5066	5335					5.3			
113351	117166					3.4			
80343	79314					－1.3			
153943	134605					－12.6			
16116	17814					10.5			
134553	113493					－15.7			
2392	2272					－5.0			
233289	241487	2271.5	1320.3	516.0	51.9	3.5	8.7	12.0	7.2
2280.60	3431.23	187399	34281.1	960.8	56.3	50.5	21.9	15.9	7.7
4.88	3.33	104.3	0.9	－42.0	－64.4	－31.8	1.9	－3.3	－15.8
1972.99	1708.33			50.1	－31.6	－13.4		2.6	－6.1
1217.98	1096.96			104.9	－28.2	－9.9		4.6	－5.4
755.01	611.37			1.5	－37.0	－19.0		0.1	－7.4
8227.33	8198.75			1223.4	38.4	－0.3		17.5	5.6
25876.77	28707.12	33757	5469.5	887.0	111.0	10.9	16.6	15.4	13.3
5456.14	5096.12	119110	12212.2	1016.6	9.4	－6.6	20.5	16.3	1.5
2069.45	1902.68	2106968	15818.3	857.6	－2.5	－8.1	30.0	15.2	－0.4
3386.68	3193.44	76214	10748.0	1139.2	18.0	－5.7	19.1	17.0	2.8
305.01	329.77	2811	355.0	104.9	－49.5	8.1	9.3	4.6	－10.8
107873.0251	121106.58	199351	13976.8	1341.6	105.3	12.3	22.1	18.1	12.7
78866.34	91107.60	78925	8889.8	1426.7	116.3	15.5	19.2	18.6	13.7
1989.91	2690.25		28796.3	1937.6	131.4	35.2		20.7	15.0
171.57	174.58	2785.6	1088.4	286.3	5.8	1.8	9.3	8.8	1.0
51.89	51.13	1231.5	265.5	17.2	－25.1	－1.5	7.1	1.0	－4.7
284.52	290.10	－24.8	2.9	－22.4	－21.3	2.0	－0.7	－1.6	－3.9
499.64	522.20	－39.9	－14.7	－27.3	30.9	4.5	－1.3	－2.0	4.6
130	124		－62.0	－60.4	－8.1	－4.6		－5.6	－1.4
118.43	118.42	433.9	－25.5	－39.0	－15.7	0.0	4.5	－3.0	－2.8

指标	Item	总量指标 1978	1990	2000	2010
#工程技术人员	Engineering Personnel	7.83	31.84	44.84	19.00
文化	**Culture**				
图书出版量 (亿册)	Books Published (100 million copies)	1.94	3.44	3.47	5.17
杂志出版量 (万册)	Magazines Issued (10000 copies)	535	4107	11008	10475
报纸出版量 (亿份)	Newspapers Issued (100 million copies)	2.45	8.27	23.34	27.12
家庭、生活、环境	**Family, People's Livelihood and Environment**				
家庭	**Family**				
总户数 (万户)	Total Househalds (10000 households)	1423.11	1806.78	2220.38	2564.59
城镇居民平均每户家庭人口 (人)	Average Household Size in Urban Areas (person)		3.34	3.07	2.79
农村居民平均每户家庭人口 (人)	Average Household Size in Rural Areas (person)		4.10	3.74	3.68
居住	**Housing**				
城镇居民人均住房建筑面积 (平方米)	Per Capita Net Floor Space of Urban Residents (sq. m)	5.7	17.29	25.54	33.39
农村居民人均住房建筑面积 (平方米)	Per Capita Net Floor Space of Rural Residents (sq. m)	9.7	25.20	33.70	46.33
生活	**People's Livelihood**				
城镇常住居民人均可支配收入 (元)	Per Capita Annual Disposable Income of Urban Residents (yuan)	288	1464	6800	22944
农村常住居民人均可支配收入 (元)	Per Capita Annual Disposable Income of Rural Residents (yuan)	155	884	3595	9118
工资	**Wages and Welfare**				
工资总额 (亿元)	Total Wages of Staff and Workers (100 million yuan)	29.05	184.60	705.36	2841.33
职工平均工资 (元)	Average Wage of Staff and Workers (yuan)	513	2129	10299	40505
卫生	**Health Care**				
卫生机构数 (个)	Number of Health Care Organizations (unit)	9277	12366	12813	30961
#医院卫生院	Hospital and Commune Hospitals	2428	2491	2511	2433
床位数 (万张)	Number of Hospital Beds (10000 units)	12.29	16.45	17.31	26.97
#医院卫生院	Hospital and Commune Hospitals	11.07	14.54	16.18	24.74
卫生技术人员数 (万人)	Number of Medical Technical Personnels (10000 persons)	14.00	21.35	25.36	32.84
#医生	Doctors	5.70	9.94	11.44	12.90
市政建设	**Urban Civil Construction**				
自来水供水量 (亿吨)	Volume of Tap Water Supply (100 million tons)	3.51	25.67	35.34	48.28
排水管道长度 (公里)	Length of Sewer Pipelines (km)	1503	4099	11097	46867
年末实有道路长度 (公里)	Year-end Length of Paved Roads (km)	1893	5812	11011	31899
环境	**Environment**				
工业废水排放量 (亿吨)	Volume of Industrial Waste Water Discharged (100 million tons)		24.24	20.19	26.38
工业二氧化硫排放量 (万吨)	Volume of Industrial sulfur dioxide (10000 tons)			84.33	100.25
工业烟(粉)尘排放量 (万吨)	Volume of Industrial Dust Removed (10000 tons)			37.47	45.00

1－2 Continued 3

Aggregate Data		速度指标 Indicies and Growth Rate							
2015	2016	2016年比下列各年增长(%) Index (2016 as percentage of the following years)					年平均增长(%) Average Annual Growth Rate		
		1978	1990	2000	2010	2015	1979～2016	2001～2016	2011～2016
11.46	11.77	50.4	-63.0	-73.7	-38.0	2.8	1.1	-8.0	-7.7
6.23	6.24	221.7	81.4	79.9	20.7	0.2	3.1	3.7	3.2
11431	11954	2134.4	191.1	8.6	14.1	4.6	8.5	0.5	2.2
26.39	23.31	851.3	181.8	-0.1	-14.1	-11.7	6.1	0.0	-2.5
2617.80	2621.20	84.2	45.1	18.1	2.2	0.1	1.6	1.0	0.4
2.98	2.97		-11.1	-3.3	6.5	-0.2		-0.2	1.0
2.96	2.98		-27.3	-20.3	-19.0	0.6		-1.4	-3.5
39.62	40.30	607.0	133.1	57.8	20.7	1.7	5.3	2.9	3.2
54.95	56.90	486.6	125.8	68.8	22.8	3.5	4.8	3.3	3.5
37173	40152	13830.6	2640.4	490.0	74.9	8.0	13.9	11.7	9.8
16257	17606	11257.7	1891.5	389.7	93.1	8.3	13.3	10.4	11.6
9802.41	10583.16	36330.8	5633.0	1400.4	272.5	8.0	16.8	18.4	24.5
67200	72684	14068.4	3314.0	605.7	79.4	8.2	13.9	13.0	10.2
31925	32135	246.4	159.9	150.8	3.8	0.7	3.3	5.9	0.6
2616	2720	12.0	9.2	8.3	11.8	4.0	0.3	0.5	1.9
41.36	44.31	260.5	169.4	156.0	64.3	7.1	3.4	6.1	8.6
38.49	41.50	274.9	185.4	156.5	67.7	7.8	3.5	6.1	9.0
48.70	51.71	269.3	142.2	103.9	57.5	6.2	3.5	4.6	7.9
18.92	20.47	259.1	105.9	78.9	58.7	8.2	3.4	3.7	8.0
50.68	53.31	1418.8	107.7	50.8	10.4	5.2	7.4	2.6	1.7
70048	72823	4745.2	1676.6	556.2	55.4	4.0	10.8	12.5	7.6
40749	44999	2277.2	674.3	308.7	41.1	10.4	8.7	9.2	5.9
20.64									
83.51									
65.45									

1－3 国民经济和社会发展结构指标

Composition Indicators on National Economic and Social Development

单位:% (%)

指标	Item	1978	2000	2005	2010	2015	2016
人口与就业	**Population and Employment**						
人口	**Population**						
城乡结构	Urban and Rural Structure						
城镇	Urban	13.7	41.5	50.5	60.6	66.5	67.7
乡村	Rural	86.3	58.5	49.5	39.4	33.5	32.3
性别结构	Sexual Structure						
男	Male	50.6	50.6	50.0	50.4	50.3	50.6
女	Female	49.4	49.4	50.0	49.6	49.7	49.4
就业	**Employment**						
产业结构	Industrial Structure						
第一产业	Primary Industry	69.7	42.8	30.9	22.3	18.4	17.7
第二产业	Secondary Industry	19.6	30.2	37.2	42.0	43.0	43.0
第三产业	Tertiary Industry	10.7	27.0	31.9	35.7	38.6	39.3
经济类型结构	Structures by Ownership						
城镇非私营单位从业人员	Staff and Workers Employed in Urban Units	20.9	15.7	13.7	16.1	32.6	31.5
国有单位	State-owned	13.2	9.5	6.2	5.9	6.2	6.1
城镇集体单位	Collective-owned	7.7	2.7	0.8	0.6	0.7	0.7
其他单位	Others		3.5	6.7	9.5	25.7	24.7
城镇私营企业和个体就业人员	Urban Private Enterprises and Self-employed Workers	0.1	4.0	12.8	27.3	41.6	48.3
其他	Others	79.0	80.3	73.5	56.6	25.8	20.2
宏观经济	**Macro Economy**						
国民经济核算	**National Economic Accounting**						
地区生产总值产业结构	Industrial Structures						
第一产业	Primary Industry	27.6	12.2	7.9	6.1	5.7	5.4
第二产业	Secondary Industry	52.6	51.9	56.6	52.5	45.7	41.1
第三产业	Tertiary Industry	19.8	35.9	35.6	41.4	48.6	50.5
地区生产总值支出结构	Domestic Expenditures						
最终消费	Total Consumption	52.4	43.4	41.2	41.6	50.0	
居民消费	Resident Consumption	46.2	32.9	28.7	26.4	36.0	
政府消费	Government Consumption Expenditure	6.2	10.5	12.5	15.2	14.0	
资本形成总额	Gross Capital Formation	31.3	47.3	50.9	51.1	43.6	
固定资本	Fixed Capital Formation	16.2	37.7	47.8	50.0	42.7	
存货增加	Changes in Stock	15.1	9.6	3.1	1.1	0.9	
净出口	Net Exports	16.3	9.3	7.9	7.3	6.4	
投资	**Investment**						
经济类型结构	Structure by Ownership						
国有经济	State-owned	95.2	40.1	23.8	20.1	19.4	16.7

1－3 续表1 Continued 1

单位:% (%)

指标	Item	1978	2000	2005	2010	2015	2016
集体经济	Collective-owned	4.8	15.2	5.1	4.2	4.1	1.6
港澳台及外商投资经济	Hong Kong, Macao, Taiwan and Foreign Investment Economy		12.1	17.9	13.7	8.5	9.5
私营个体经济	Private and Individuals		10.9	30.0	35.9	46.3	47.4
其他经济	Others		21.7	23.2	26.1	21.7	24.7
资金来源结构	Structure of Funded Sources						
国家预算资金	State Budgetary Appropriation		2.5	0.7	1.1	1.6	1.8
国内贷款	Domestic Loans		16.3	13.8	12.6	9.6	10.6
利用外资	Foreign Investment		9.4	9.1	4.4	1.9	1.1
自筹资金	Fundraising		61.0	63.3	63.1	72.5	66.6
其他投资	Others		10.8	13.1	18.8	14.4	19.9
财 政	**Government Finance**						
一般公共预算支出结构	Structure of General Public Budgetary Expenditure						
#农林水事务	Operating Expenses of Agriculture, Forestry and Water	25.1	7.9	5.8	10.0	10.4	9.9
教育支出	Education	10.8	19.9	15.4	17.6	18.0	18.5
利用外资	**Utilization of Foreign Capital**						
实际外商直接投资结构	Structure of Foreign Direct Investment						
合资经营企业	Joint Venture Enterprises		35.4	18.9	16.6	19.0	22.2
合作经营企业	Cooperative Operation Enterprises		5.6	1.5	0.9	0.6	0.9
独资经营企业	Foreign Solely Funded Enterprises		59.0	79.0	80.1	76.5	74.4
外商投资股份制企业	Share Holding with Foreign Investment		0.04	0.7	2.3	4.0	2.5
产业经济	**Industrial Economy**						
农 业	**Agriculture**						
农林牧渔业产值结构	Structure of Gross Output Value						
农业	Farming	80.4	58.6	50.1	52.8	52.9	51.3
林业	Forestry	1.4	1.6	1.8	1.8	1.8	1.8
牧业	Animal Husbandry	15.8	23.0	23.2	21.5	18.0	18.4
渔业	Fishery	2.3	16.7	19.9	18.7	21.6	22.4
农林牧渔服务业	Service in Support of Agriculture			5.0	5.1	5.7	6.0
工 业	**Industry**						
工业产值按经济类型分	Grouped by Ownership						
#国有企业	State-owned	61.5	12.7	6.5	4.8	2.2	2.1
集体企业	Collective-owned	31.2	19.0	5.1	1.4	0.6	0.4
港澳台商投资企业	Enterprise Invested by Hong Kong, Macao and Taiwan Funds		9.1	11.8	10.9	11.2	11.0
外商投资企业	Enterprise Invested by Foreign Funds		18.6	28.7	28.8	23.3	22.6
工业产值按轻重分	Grouped by Light and Heavy Industry						
轻工业	Light Industry	52.4	43.2	31.2	26.6	27.4	27.9
重工业	Heavy Industry	47.6	56.8	68.8	73.4	72.6	72.1

1-3 续表2 Continued 2

单位:% (%)

指标	Item	1978	2000	2005	2010	2015	2016
建筑业	**Construction**						
建筑业总产值结构	Structure of Gross Output Value of Construction						
国有经济	State-owned		24.4	19.8	9.7	8.6	8.7
地方	Local-owned		19.9	16.7	5.7	4.8	4.9
部属	Central-owned		4.4	3.1	4.1	3.9	3.8
城镇集体经济	Colletive-owned		24.4	3.5	5.4	5.3	5.5
乡镇企业及其它经济	Rural and Township Industry and Others		51.2	76.7	84.9	86.1	85.8
运输业	**Transportation**						
货运量结构	Structure of Freight Traffic						
#铁路	Railways	22.0	4.5	4.5	3.4	2.4	2.5
公路	Highways	30.7	65.3	67.6	65.5	53.6	54.3
水运	Waterways	44.8	28.6	25.9	25.8	38.0	36.8
对外经济贸易和旅游	**Foreign Trade and Tourism**						
出口商品结构	Structure of Exports						
#亚洲地区	Asia		51.3	45.4	39.2	46.7	46.0
欧洲地区	Europe		20.6	24.8	27.7	19.5	20.9
北美洲	North America		20.9	23.8	23.1	23.1	24.6
海外旅游人数结构	Structure of Tourists						
外国人	Foreigners	76.2	61.0	69.3	72.5	65.8	66.1
港澳同胞	Compatriots from Hongkong, Macao	23.8	16.8	11.9	9.8	4.8	4.9
台湾同胞	Compatriots from Taiwan		22.2	18.8	17.7	29.3	29.0
教育、科技、文化	**Education, Science and Culture**						
教育	**Education**						
在校学生结构	Structure of Student Enrollment						
大学生	College and University Students	0.5	3.8	9.7	16.1	17.0	16.8
中学生	Secondary School Students	30.8	36.2	49.6	45.1	33.4	32.9
小学生	Primary School Students	68.7	60.0	40.6	38.8	49.6	50.3
专任教师结构	Full-time Teachers by Type						
大学	Colleges and Universities	3.0	5.8	10.5	15.1	15.7	15.7
中学	Secondary Schools	37.1	43.7	48.6	47.9	43.7	43.0
小学	Primary Schools	59.9	50.5	40.9	37.0	40.6	41.3
科技	**Science and Technology**						
各类专业技术人员结构	Structure of Scientific and Technical Personnel						

1－3 续表3 Continued 3

单位:% (%)

指 标	Item	1978	2000	2005	2010	2015	2016
工程技术人员	Engineering Personnel	35.3	23.1	14.1	13.5	9.7	9.9
农业技术人员	Agriculture	6.1	2.4	2.1	1.9	2.2	2.1
科学研究人员	Scientific Research	5.5	0.9	1.2	1.1	1.0	0.8
卫生技术人员	Health Care	30.5	11.9	15.8	15.1	19.4	19.8
教学人员	Teaching	22.5	34.1	46.6	47.5	56.9	56.8
生活、卫生	**People's Livelihood and Healthcare**						
生 活	**People's Livelihood**						
城镇居民消费结构	Consumption Structure of Urban Residents						
食品	Food	55.1	41.1	37.2	36.5	28.1	18.4
衣着	Clothing	13.8	9.2	9.3	10.2	7.1	4.5
居住	Residence		8.2	9.2	8.6	22.6	15.3
其他	Others		41.5	44.3	44.7	42.2	61.8
农村居民消费结构	Consumption Structure of Rural Residents						
食品	Food	62.1	43.5	44.0	38.1	31.7	24.2
衣着	Clothing	12.1	5.4	5.4	5.4	6.0	4.6
居住	Residence	13.6	18.9	14.4	17.9	20.6	18.5
其他	Others	12.1	32.2	36.2	38.6	41.7	52.7
卫 生	**Healthcare**						
卫生机构构成	Structure of Health Care Institutions						
#医院卫生院	Hospitals and Commune Hospitals	26.2	19.6	16.2	7.9	8.2	8.5
门诊部	Clinics		0.8	2.4	1.7	3.4	4.0
妇幼保健院	Maternity and Child Care Institutions	0.9	0.9	0.7	0.3	0.3	0.3
疾病预防控制中心	Disease Protection and Controlling Centers	1.2	1.1	1.0	0.4	0.4	0.4
卫生技术人员构成	Structure of Medical Technical Personnels						
#执业医师	Doctors	40.7	45.1	42.3	39.3	38.9	39.6
注册护士	Registered Nurses	12.8	29.1	31.3	37.3	41.9	42.8
卫生机构床位数构成	Hospital Beds by Structures						
医院卫生院	Hospitals	90.1	93.5	94.1	91.7	93.1	93.7
其他卫生机构	Other Sanatation Organization	8.9	3.2	3.4	7.5	6.9	6.3

1-4 国民经济和社会发展比例和效益指标

Indicators on National Economic and Social Development

指标	Item	2012	2013	2014	2015	2016
人口与就业	**Population and Employment**					
出生率 (‰)	Birth Rate (‰)	9.44	9.44	9.45	9.05	9.76
死亡率 (‰)	Death Rate (‰)	6.99	7.01	7.02	7.03	7.03
自然增长率 (‰)	Natural Growth Rate (‰)	2.45	2.43	2.43	2.02	2.73
城镇登记失业率 (%)	Registered Unemployment Rate in Urban Areas (%)	3.14	3.03	3.01	3.00	3.00
国民经济核算	**National Accounting**					
服务业增加值占地区生产总值比重 (%)	Proportion of Value-added of Service Industry to GDP (%)	43.8	45.5	47.0	48.6	50.5
人均地区生产总值 (元)	Per Capita GDP (yuan)	68347	75354	81874	87995	95257
人均地区生产总值 (美元)	Per Capita GDP (USD)	10827	12167	13328	14128	14341
全社会劳动生产率 (元/人)	The Labor Productivity of the Whole Employment (Yuan / person)	113594	125540	136730	147314	159934
固定资产投资	**Investment in Fixed Assets**					
固定资产投资相当于地区生产总值比例 (%)	Proportion of Investment in Fixed Assets to GDP (%)	59.4	60.9	64.4	65.5	64.9
全社会房屋建筑竣工率 (%)	Rate of Total Floor Space of Buildings Completed (%)	35.2	33.0	31.6	35.6	33.9
消费	**Consumption**					
人均社会消费品零售额 (元)	Per Capita Retail Sales of Consumer Goods (yuan)	23278	26329	29508	32442	35940
对外贸易	**Foreign Trade**					
进出口总额相当于地区生产总值比例 (%)	Proportion of Total Value of Imports & Exports to GDP (%)	64.0	56.6	53.2	48.3	44.2
出口总额相当于地区生产总值比例 (%)	Proportion of Total Value of Imports to GDP (%)	38.4	33.8	32.3	30.0	27.7
高新技术产品出口额占出口总额的比重 (%)	Proportion of New and High Technology Product Imports to Imports (%)	40.0	38.9	37.8	38.7	36.6
机电产品出口额占出口总额的比重 (%)	Proportion of Electronic Mechanical Product Imports to Imports (%)	66.2	65.2	64.8	66.4	65.1
一般贸易出口额占出口总额的比重 (%)	Proportion of Ordinary Trade Imports to Imports (%)	42.5	44.3	46.3	45.8	48.7
加工贸易出口额占出口总额的比重 (%)	Proportion of Processing Trade Imports to Imports (%)	48.8	45.6	43.7	43.7	43.5
财政	**Government Finance**					
一般公共预算收入相当于地区生产总值比例 (%)	Proportion of General Public Budget Revenue to GDP (%)	10.8	11.0	11.1	11.5	10.7
一般公共预算支出相当于地区生产总值比例 (%)	Proportion of General Public Budget Expenditure to GDP (%)	13.0	13.1	13.0	13.8	13.1
农业	**Agriculture**					
每公顷播种面积农产品产量 (公斤)	Output of Farm Crops per Hectare of Sown Area (kg)					
粮食	Grain	6320	6385	6493	6565	6380
棉花	Cotton	1292	1348	1210	1240	1164
油料	Oil-bearing Crops	2785	2901	2937	3010	3008
工业	**Industry**					
总资产贡献率 (%)	Ratio of Total Assets to Industrial Output Value (%)	15.42	15.8	15.87	15.57	15.42
资产负债率 (%)	Assets-Liability Ratio (%)	57.26	56.7	54.92	53.14	51.92
流动资产周转次数 (次/年)	Turnover of Working Capital (times/year)	2.57	2.67	2.71	2.72	2.70
成本费用利润率 (%)	Ratio of Profits to Industrial Cost (%)	6.53	6.59	6.71	6.95	7.12
产品销售率 (%)	Proportion of Products Sold (%)	98.82	98.99	98.73	98.37	98.85

指　　标	Item	2012	2013	2014	2015	2016
建筑业	**Construction**					
建筑业劳动生产率　（元/人）	Overall Labor Productivity　（yuan/person）	262833	281085	296918	297437	304925
产值利税率　（%）	Ratio of Pre-tax Profits to Gross Output Value　（%）	7.04	7.13	7.02	7.06	7.08
交通运输业	**Transportation**					
铁路网密度　（公里/万平方公里）	Railway Density　（km/10000 sq. km）	219	238	246	250	254
公路网密度　（公里/万平方公里）	Highway Density　（km/10000 sq. km）	14377	14561	14694	14814	14646
邮电通信业	**Postal and Telecommunication Services**					
电话普及率（含移动电话）　（部/百人）	Access to Telephones（include mobile phone）　（set/100 persons）	125	129	129	129	124
移动电话普及率　（部/百人）	Access to Mobile Phones　（set/100 persons）	95	100	102	103	103
旅游业	**Tourism**					
每一来华游客花费　（美元）	Expenditure per International Tourist in China　（USD）	796	826	1021	1156	1153
国内旅游人均花费　（元）	Expenditure per Domestic Tourist　（yuan）	1304	1347	1377	1416	1468
金融业	**Financial Intermediation**					
金融机构存款相当于地区生产总值比例　（%）	Deposits of Financial Institutions as Percentage of GDP　（%）	139.6	143.3	144.0	153.8	159.2
金融机构贷款相当于地区生产总值比例　（%）	Loans of Financial Institutions as Percentage of GDP　（%）	100.7	103.5	106.9	112.5	119.7
金融机构年末人民币贷、存款余额比例　（%）	Ratio of Loan to Deposit of Financial Institutions at year end　（%）	72.1	72.2	74.2	73.1	75.2
教育	**Education**					
每万人口在校大学生数　（人）	Number of University and College Students per 10000 Population　（person）	228.6	232.7	232.3	234.6	238.4
初中升学率　（%）	Promotion Rate from Junior Secondary Schools to Senior Secondary Schools　（%）	98.0	98.3	100.0	100.0	100.0
小学升学率　（%）	Promotion Rate from Primary Schools to Junior Secondary Schools　（%）	100.0	100.0	100.0	100.0	100.0
学龄儿童入学率　（%）	Enrollment Ratio of Primary Schools　（%）	100.0	100	100.0	100.0	100.0
科技	**Science and Technology**					
研发经费支出相当于地区生产总值比例　（%）	R&D Expenditure as Percentage of GDP　（%）	2.33	2.45	2.54	2.57	2.66
高新技术产业产值占工业总产值比例　（%）	Proportion of New and High Technology Output to Industry　（%）	37.5	38.5	39.5	40.1	41.5
每万人口发明专利拥有量　（件/万人）	Possession of Invention Patent per 10000 Population　（uint/10000 persons）	5.73	7.84	10.22	14.22	18.50
卫生	**Health Care**					
每万人口执业（助理）医师数　（人）	Number of Licensed（Assistant）Doctors per 10000 Population　（person）	19.9	21.4	22.4	23.7	25.6
每万人口医院、卫生院床位数　（张）	Number of Beds of Hospitals and Health Centers per 10000 Population　（bed）	38.8	43.0	45.8	48.3	51.9
医疗机构病床使用率　（%）	Beds Utilization Rate of Medical Organizations　（%）	84.1	84.2	84.0	83.1	82.5
人民生活	**People's Livelihood**					
城镇恩格尔系数　（%）	Engle Coefficient of Urban Household　（%）	35.4	28.4	28.5	28.1	28.0
农村恩格尔系数　（%）	Engle Coefficient of Rural Household　（%）	37.4	31.1	31.4	31.7	29.5
城乡收入比（以农民收入为1）	Income Ratio of Urban and Rural Residents（1 for a Rural Resident）	2.43	2.34	2.30	2.29	2.28
城市市政建设	**Municipal Works**					
用水普及率　（%）	Percentage of Population with Access to Tap Water　（%）	99.7	99.7	99.8	99.8	99.9
燃气普及率　（%）	Percentage of City Population with Access to Gas　（%）	99.4	99.6	99.5	99.6	99.5
人均公园绿地面积　（平方米）	Per Capita Public Green Area　（sq. m）	13.6	14.0	14.4	14.6	14.8

1-5 江苏国民经济占全国的比重（2016年）
Percentage of Jiangsu's National Economy in the Country (2016)

指标	Item	全国 Country	江苏 Jiangsu	江苏占全国的比重(%) Percentage to the Country of Jiangsu(%)
土地面积（万平方公里）	Land Area (10000 sq. km)	960	10.72	1.1
年末总人口（万人）	Year-end Total Population (10000 persons)	138271	7998.60	5.8
地区生产总值（亿元）	Domestic Gross Product (100 million yuan)	744127	76086.17	10.2
第一产业	Primary Industry	63671	4077.18	6.4
第二产业	Secondary Industry	296236	33550.54	11.3
第三产业	Tertiary Industry	384221	38458.45	10.0
人均生产总值（元）	Per Capita GDP (yuan)	53980	95257	高41277元
一般公共预算收入（亿元）	General Public Budget Revenue (100 million yuan)	159552	8121.23	5.1
固定资产投资(含农户)（亿元）	Investment in Fixed Assets(Including Farm Households) (100 million yuan)	606466	49663.21	8.2
#固定资产投资(不含农户)	Investment in Fixed Assets (Excluding Farm Households)	596501	49370.85	8.3
#房地产开发	Real Estate Development	102581	8956.37	8.7
社会消费品零售总额（亿元）	Total Retail Sales of Consumer Goods (100 million yuan)	332316	28707.12	8.6
进出口总额（亿美元）	Total Exports and Imports (USD 100 million)	243386	33634.82	13.8
#出口	Exports	138455	21063.18	15.2
普通高等学校本专科在校生（万人）	Students Enrollment in Institutions of Higher Education (10000 persons)	2696	174.58	6.5
卫生机构床位数（万张）	Number of Beds of Health Care Institutions (10000 units)	741	44.31	6.0
卫生技术人员（万人）	Medical Technical Personnel (10000 persons)	845	51.71	6.1
#执业(助理)医师	Practitioner (Assistant) Doctors	319	20.47	6.4
居民人均可支配收入（元）	Per Capita Disposable Income of Residents (yuan)	23821	32070	高8249元
城镇常住居民人均可支配收入（元）	Per Capita Annual Disposable Income of Urban Permanent Residents (yuan)	33616	40152	高6536元
农村常住居民人均可支配收入（元）	Per Capita Annual Disposable Income of Rural Permanent Residents (yuan)	12363	17606	高5243元
工农业主要产品产量（万吨）	Output of Major Industrial and Agricultural Products (10000 tons)			
粮食	Grain	61624	3466.01	5.6
棉花	Cotton	534	7.38	1.4
油料	Oil-bearing Crops	3613	131.93	3.7
粗钢	Rough Steel	80837	11080.49	13.7
钢材	Rolled Steel	113801	13469.72	11.8
发电量（亿千瓦小时）	Electricity (100 million kW·h)	61425	4667.73	7.6
水泥（亿吨）	Cement (100 million tons)	241353	17989.78	7.5
农用化肥(折100%)	Chemical Fertilizers (convert into 100 %)	7129	207.17	2.9
化学纤维	Chemical Fibers	4944	1458.19	29.5
布（亿米）	Cloth (100 million)	907	91.46	10.1
彩色电视机（万台）	Colour Television Sets (10000 set)	15770	1839.38	11.7
汽车（万辆）	Moter Vehicles (10000 units)	2812	144.89	5.2

1-6 江苏的一天
One Day in Jiangsu

指 标	Item	1978	2000	2005	2010	2015	2016
每天创造的财富	**Daily Production**						
地区生产总值 (亿元)	Gross Domestic Product (100 million yuan)	0.68	23.43	50.96	113.49	192.10	208.46
第一产业	Primary Industry	0.19	2.87	4.00	6.96	10.92	11.17
第二产业	Secondary Industry	0.36	12.15	28.84	59.60	87.79	91.92
第三产业	Tertiary Industry	0.14	8.41	18.12	46.94	93.39	105.37
#工 业	Industry	0.32	10.54	25.86	52.82	76.70	80.93
建筑业	Construction	0.04	1.61	2.97	6.78	11.11	11.43
房地产业	Real Estate	0.02	0.82	2.19	7.13	10.29	11.76
财政收入 (亿元)	Government Revenue (100 million yuan)	0.17	2.37	8.56	32.17	48.88	53.33
粮 食 (万吨)	Grain (10000 tons)	6.58	8.51	7.77	8.86	9.76	9.50
猪牛羊肉 (吨)	Meat (ton)		6230	6633	6135	6499	6239
水产品 (吨)	Aquatic Products (ton)	1089	8460	10648	12615	14304	14333
粗 钢 (万吨)	Steel (10000 tons)	0.15	1.69	9.00	17.10	30.12	30.36
钢 材 (万吨)	Rolled-steel (10000 tons)	0.17	3.84	11.86	24.99	37.15	36.90
发电量 (亿千瓦小时)	Electricity (100 million kW·h)	0.35	2.49	4.90	9.20	11.92	12.79
原 煤 (万吨)	Coal (10000 tons)	4.68	6.79	7.72	5.82	5.26	3.75
水 泥 (万吨)	Cement (10000 tons)	1.22	12.60	26.24	42.87	49.35	49.29
布 (万米)	Cloth (10000 m)	385	924	1479	2424	2621	2506
每天消费量	**Daily Consumption**						
最终消费 (亿元)	Final Consumption (100 million yuan)	0.36	10.17	20.98	47.23	96.00	
居民消费 (亿元)	Resident Consumption (100 million yuan)	0.32	7.71	14.63	29.98	69.16	
城镇居民人均生活消费支出 (元)	Per Living Consumption Expenditure of Urban Residents (yuan)	0.76	14.58	23.62	39.33	68.40	72.42
#食品烟酒	Food, Tobacco and Wine	0.42	6.00	8.78	14.36	19.19	20.24
农村居民人均生活消费支出 (元)	Per Living Consumption Expenditure of Rural Residents (yuan)	0.38	6.40	9.77	17.93	35.29	39.53
#食品烟酒	Food, Tobacco and Wine	0.24	2.79	4.30	6.83	11.17	11.66
政府消费 (亿元)	Government Consumption Expenditure (100 million yuan)	0.04	2.45	6.36	17.25	26.84	
社会消费品零售总额 (亿元)	Total Retail Sales of Consumer Goods (100 million yuan)	0.23	7.97	15.71	37.28	70.90	78.65
每天其他经济活动	**Other Daily Economic Activities**						
货物运输量 (万吨)	Freight Traffic (10000 tons)	40.07	247.77	309.34	516.60	579.86	590.82
旅客运输量 (万人)	Passenger Traffic (10000 persons)	70.19	293.82	397.82	620.90	421.76	368.78
竣工房屋面积 (万平方米)	Floor Space of Housing Completed (10000 sq. m)		58.32	69.57	133.04	210.48	205.45
出版报纸 (万份)	Newspaper Published (10000 copies)	67.12	639.45	734.25	743.05	735.07	638.55
邮寄函件 (万件)	Letters Delivered (10000 pieces)	44.66	157.26	115.34	256.44	133.70	91.23
进出口总额 (万美元)	Total of Imports and Exports (USD 10000)	117	12504	62450	127614	149483	139620
#出口	Export	115	7060	33694	74123	92786	87492
实际使用外资 (万美元)	Actual Use of Foreign Capital (USD 10000)		1760	3611	7808	6651	6724
每天人口变动和婚姻	**Daily Population Changes and Marriages**						
出生人数 (人)	Births (person)	2483	1808	1886	2079	1976	2136
死亡人数 (人)	Deaths (person)	968	1299	1436	1470	1535	1538
结婚对数 (对)	Marriages (couple)		1365	1293	2074	2153	1962
离婚对数 (对)	Divorces (couple)		153	339	439	517	716

1-7 全省人均国民经济主要指标

Major Per Capita Indicators of Jiangsu National Economy

指标	Item	1978	2000	2005	2010	2015	2016
地区生产总值 (元)	Gross Domestic Product (yuan)	430	11765	24616	52840	87995	95257
第一产业	Primary Industry	118	1442	1934	3240	5002	5104
第二产业	Secondary Industry	226	6101	13930	27748	40216	42004
第三产业	Tertiary Industry	85	4222	8751	21852	42777	48149
#工　业	Industry	202	5294	12494	24589	35135	36980
建筑业	Construction	24	808	1436	3159	5090	5225
房地产业	Real Estate	9	410	1058	3318	4713	5374
一般公共预算收入 (元)	General Public Budget Revenue (yuan)	105	617	1751	5204	10076	10192
一般公共预算支出 (元)	General Public Budget Expenditure (yuan)	49	813	2215	6268	12158	10987
全社会固定资产投资 (元)	Total Investment in Fixed Assets (yuan)	38	4120	11567	29573	58039	62327
#房地产开发	Real Estate Development		531	2045	5484	10233	11240
社会消费品零售额 (元)	Total Retail Sales of Consumer Goods (yuan)	146	4001	7591	17115	32475	36027
进出口总额 (美元)	Total Imports and Exports (USD)	7	628	3017	5941	6847	6396
#出　口	Exports	7	354	1628	3451	4250	4008
城镇常住居民可支配收入 (元)	Annual Disposable Income of Urban Residents (yuan)	288	6800	12319	22944	37173	40152
农村常住居民可支配收入 (元)	Annual Disposable Income of Rural Residents (yuan)	155	3595	5276	9118	16257	17606
在校大学生数 (人/万人)	Number of Students Enrollment in Institution of Higher Education (person/10000 persons)	10	65	153	210	215	219
医院病床数 (张/万人)	Hospital Beds (bed/10000 persons)	19	22	24	31	52	56
卫生技术人员数 (人/万人)	Medical Technical Personnel (person/10000 persons)	24	35	34	42	61	65
#执业医师	Doctors	10	16	14	16	23	26
主要工农业产品产量 (千克)	Output of Major Industrial and Agricultural Products (kg)						
粮　食	Grain	414	427	375	413	447	435
棉　花	Cotton	8	4	4	3	1	1
油　料	Oil-Bearing Crops	6	31	29	19	18	17
粗　钢	Steel	9	85	435	796	1380	1391
原　煤	Coal	294	341	373	271	241	172
发电量 (千瓦小时)	Electricity (kW·h)	218	1251	2368	4285	5461	5858

1-8 全省法人单位数及从业人员数
Number of Corporations and Empolyment

项 目	Item	法人单位数(个) Corporation Units (unit)		从业人员(万人) Employees (10000 persons)	
		2015	2016	2015	2016
合 计	**Total**	**1578066**	**1907723**	**4018.84**	**4347.43**
按机构类型分	**Crouped by Type of Organization**				
企业	Enterprises	1414381	1717135	3636.63	3937.92
事业单位	Institutions	39848	39823	182.63	177.44
机关	Agencies & Organizations	10654	10618	61.39	59.29
社会团体	Social Organizations	24735	26721	22.16	23.05
民办非企业单位	Non-enterprise Units Run by NGO	21279	23069	31.30	32.79
基金会	Fund Organizations	401	415	0.21	0.22
居委会	Neighborhood Committee	7564	7732	7.60	7.69
村委会	Village Committee	15293	15266	14.09	14.06
其他组织机构	Others	43911	66944	62.83	94.97
按登记注册类型分	**Grouped by Type of Registration**				
内资	Inner Funded	1544096	1873813	3472.09	3831.58
国有	State-owned	56452	56320	288.55	273.92
集体	Collective-owned	21733	22146	63.22	59.25
股份合作	Share Holding Cooperative	3699	3543	8.94	8.31
联营	Joint Ownership	1867	1832	3.63	3.15
国有联营	State Joint-owned	170	162	0.99	0.58
集体联营	Collective Joint-owned	480	498	0.79	0.78
国有与集体联营	Stale-owned and Collective Joint Funded	136	140	0.67	0.64
其他联营	Other Joint Funded	1081	1032	1.19	1.15
有限责任公司	Limited Liability Co., Ltd.	112936	141652	661.05	755.29
国有独资公司	State-owned Solely Funded Co.	1680	2044	32.45	40.79
其他有限责任公司	Other Responsibility Co., Ltd.	111256	139608	628.60	714.50
股份有限公司	Share Holding Co., Ltd.	12868	13499	165.88	193.19
私营	Private	1177231	1458577	2077.06	2327.40
私营独资	Private Solely Funded	226962	266277	285.30	295.92
私营合伙	Private Partnership	19699	21913	25.31	26.34
私营有限责任公司	Private Responsibility Co., Ltd.	906508	1143835	1682.48	1906.95
私营股份有限公司	Private Responsibility Co., Ltd.	24062	26552	83.97	98.20
其他内资	Others	157310	176244	203.76	211.08

1-8 续表 Continued

项目	Item	法人单位数(个) Corporation Units (unit)		从业人员(万人) Employees (10000 persons)	
		2015	2016	2015	2016
港澳台商投资	Hong Kong, Macao and Taiwan Funded	13592	13739	202.83	203.75
与港澳台商合资经营	Join with Hong Kong, Macao and Taiwan Funded	4121	4088	60.49	58.80
与港澳台商合作经营	Cooperate with Hong Kong, Macao and Taiwan Funded	200	194	3.45	2.12
港澳台商独资	Hong Kong, Macao and Taiwan with Solely Funded	8850	9019	130.01	135.40
港澳台商投资股份有限公司	Hong Kong, Macao and Taiwan Share Holding Co., Ltd.	312	313	8.50	6.71
其他港、澳、台商投资	Others	109	125	0.37	0.72
外商投资	Foreign Funded	20378	20171	343.92	312.10
中外合资经营	Sino-foreign Joint Funded	5925	5792	95.73	87.18
中外合作经营	Sino-foreign Cooperative Funded	313	287	4.10	3.36
外资企业	Foreign Solely Funded	13387	13312	235.12	212.25
外商投资股份有限公司	Foreign Funded Share Holding Co., Ltd.	462	464	8.27	8.19
其他外商投资	Others	291	316	0.69	1.12
按行业分	**Grouped by Sector**				
农、林、牧、渔业	Farming, Forestry, Animal Husbandry and Fishery	45617	56231	65.81	73.91
采矿业	Mining and Quarrying	763	756	13.67	12.20
制造业	Manufacturing	438906	481869	1808.47	1858.59
电力、热力、燃气及水生产和供应业	Production and Supply of Electric Power, Heat Power, Gas and Water	3447	4287	21.17	21.89
建筑业	Construction	78678	104443	744.69	870.91
批发和零售业	Wholesale and Retail Sales	476450	587718	406.22	457.52
交通运输、仓储和邮政业	Transportation, Storage and Post	41171	50401	99.35	110.17
住宿和餐饮业	Hotel and Catering	16648	20393	51.26	51.20
信息传输、软件和信息技术服务业	Informaiton Transfer, Software and IT Services	42515	61674	68.79	82.51
金融业	Banking	7017.00	7550	29.82	29.19
房地产业	Real Estate	41120	48989	82.14	91.87
租赁和商务服务业	Leasing and Commercial Services	146224	190016	151.46	179.52
科学研究、技术服务业	Scientific Research and Technical Services	67730	98989	92.74	114.16
水利、环境和公共设施管理业	Water Coservancy, Environment and Public Facility Management	9235	10268	25.10	27.78
居民服务、修理和其他服务业	Services to Households and Other Services	26909	33190	29.10	32.50
教育	Education	21935	24844	114.22	114.09
卫生和社会工作	Healthcare and Social Welfare	17570	20120	60.47	61.59
文化、体育和娱乐业	Culture, Sports and Recreation	21146	28933	25.52	30.34
公共管理、社会保障和社会组织	Public Management, Social Security and Organizations	74979	77052	128.83	127.48

1－9　个体工商业基本情况（2016 年）
Basic Conditions of Self-employment Business（2016）

行　业	Sector	户数（万户）Households（10000 units）	#城镇 Urban	从业人数（万人）Employees（10000 persons）	#城镇 Urban	资金数额（亿元）Capital（100 million yuan）	#城镇 Urban
总计	**Total**	**438.83**	**324.48**	**801.90**	**616.27**	**4280.61**	**3060.36**
按行业分	**Grouped by Sector**						
农、林、牧、渔业	Agriculture, Forestry, Animal Husbandry and Fishery	10.92	4.48	25.50	10.46	398.08	147.88
采矿业	Mining	0.02	0.01	0.09	0.03	0.58	0.17
制造业	Manufacturing	38.73	22.37	111.93	66.06	537.97	304.96
电力、热力、燃气及水的生产和供应业	Production and Supply of Electricity, Gas and Water	0.08	0.04	0.15	0.09	1.45	0.72
建筑业	Construction	1.97	1.51	5.28	4.20	30.92	23.15
批发和零售业	Wholesale and Retail Trades	40.38	35.00	105.27	95.16	466.06	404.72
交通运输、仓储和邮政业	Transport, Storage and Post	275.29	203.61	421.26	328.34	2204.79	1663.02
住宿和餐饮业	Hotels and Catering Services	1.40	1.08	2.33	1.87	11.06	7.82
信息传输、软件和信息技术服务业	Information Transfer Software and IT Services	11.50	9.16	15.24	12.14	114.37	84.19
金融业	Financial Intermediation	0.02	0.02	0.04	0.04	0.30	0.21
房地产业	Real Estate	1.11	1.05	2.19	2.10	7.96	7.51
租赁和商务服务业	Leasing and Business Services	9.14	7.12	15.85	13.13	92.23	73.56
科学研究、技术服务业	Scientific Research and Technical Service	1.83	1.50	3.86	3.35	16.06	13.57
水利、环境和公共设施管理业	Management of Water Conservancy, Environment and Public Facilities	0.10	0.08	0.31	0.24	1.62	1.17
居民服务、修理和其他服务业	Services to Households and Other Services	41.51	33.25	81.55	69.12	338.05	275.18
教育	Education	0.67	0.61	1.69	1.56	6.71	6.09
卫生和社会工作	Healthcare and Social Welfare	0.43	0.37	1.05	0.96	5.04	4.57
文化、体育和娱乐业	Culture, Sports and Entertainment	3.72	3.20	8.26	7.43	47.30	41.83
其他	Others	0.02	0.01	0.02	0.01	0.06	0.05
按地区分	**by Region**						
南 京 市	Nanjing	43.76	40.26	94.60	87.67	388.16	347.56
无 锡 市	Wuxi	30.94	29.01	60.24	57.22	185.24	175.20
徐 州 市	Xuzhou	40.22	27.95	68.54	49.44	340.42	214.79
常 州 市	Changzhou	28.18	26.95	56.75	53.97	216.22	202.21
苏 州 市	Suzhou	63.86	54.80	126.95	108.64	496.56	425.54
南 通 市	Nantong	48.54	19.19	76.03	32.31	336.47	132.79
连云港市	Lianyungang	18.69	12.54	28.63	18.94	174.55	114.55
淮 安 市	Huaian	24.57	17.40	45.33	33.86	264.71	170.93
盐 城 市	Yancheng	40.63	23.79	55.53	33.60	361.92	218.53
扬 州 市	Yangzhou	26.19	20.73	49.71	39.51	239.90	183.68
镇 江 市	Zhenjiang	19.04	13.83	39.79	28.24	330.24	202.83
泰 州 市	Taizhou	25.59	19.05	50.42	38.04	670.83	504.80
宿 迁 市	Suqian	28.62	18.99	49.38	34.83	275.40	166.97

1－10 私营企业基本情况（2016 年）

行业	Sector	户数（万户）Households (10000 units)	#城镇 Urban
总计	**Total**	**222.91**	**181.72**
按行业分	**Grouped by Sector**		
农、林、牧、渔业	Agriculture, Forestry, Animal Husbandry and Fishery	4.50	1.87
采矿业	Mining	0.05	0.02
制造业	Manufacturing	50.38	31.29
电力、热力、燃气及水的生产和供应业	Production and Supply of Electricity, Gas and Water	0.26	0.18
建筑业	Construction	14.47	12.58
批发和零售业	Wholesale and Retail Trades	1.83	1.66
交通运输、仓储和邮政业	Transport, Storage and Post	71.23	59.98
住宿和餐饮业	Hotels and Catering Services	6.42	5.98
信息传输、软件和信息服务业	Information Transfer, Software and IT Services	5.54	4.56
金融业	Financial Intermediation	0.63	0.57
房地产业	Real Estate	4.74	4.21
租赁和商务服务业	Leasing and Business Services	38.65	37.12
科学研究、技术服务业	Scientific Research and Technical Service	16.06	14.67
水利、环境和公共设施管理业	Management of Water Conservancy, Environment and Public Facilities	0.57	0.43
居民服务、修理和其他服务业	Services to Households and Other Services	4.29	3.54
教育	Education	0.50	0.46
卫生和社会工作	Healthcare and Social Welfare	0.22	0.20
文化、体育和娱乐业	Culture, Sports and Entertainment	2.57	2.38
其他	Others	0.00	0.00
按地区分	**by Region**		
南 京 市	Nanjing	47.87	46.70
无 锡 市	Wuxi	21.59	19.29
徐 州 市	Xuzhou	15.52	11.29
常 州 市	Changzhou	13.30	13.03
苏 州 市	Suzhou	43.37	37.22
南 通 市	Nantong	17.29	8.68
连云港市	Lianyungang	6.77	5.61
淮 安 市	Huaian	7.43	5.19
盐 城 市	Yancheng	14.22	9.13
扬 州 市	Yangzhou	11.26	8.78
镇 江 市	Zhenjiang	7.04	5.05
泰 州 市	Taizhou	8.89	6.32
宿 迁 市	Suqian	8.37	5.41

Basic Conditions of Private Enterprises (2016)

雇工人数 (万人) Employees (10000 persons)	#城镇 Urban	投资者人数 (万人) Investors (10000 persons)	#城镇 Urban	注册资金 (亿元) Registered Capital (100 million yuan)	#城镇 Urban
1930.86	**1363.11**	**381.38**	**317.11**	**98090.69**	**81318.20**
30.00	12.39	6.22	2.81	1321.30	694.51
1.05	0.38	0.08	0.04	63.75	43.71
807.98	480.39	85.51	55.01	22532.34	14950.44
2.85	1.99	0.41	0.29	343.71	267.19
245.42	158.93	24.11	20.70	10560.81	8730.49
331.28	263.04	110.20	94.46	17240.00	14523.29
41.62	31.32	9.05	7.43	1935.10	1619.44
24.30	21.82	2.70	2.45	368.01	317.80
33.51	30.96	11.52	10.86	2038.28	1921.95
5.20	4.41	1.48	1.36	3330.77	3113.73
47.93	40.49	7.84	6.70	5070.71	4242.00
188.42	174.22	78.60	75.68	21329.87	20487.83
113.00	95.56	30.63	27.95	9849.80	8594.80
6.66	4.88	1.03	0.79	405.16	310.86
34.06	26.54	6.69	5.58	741.18	619.30
2.91	2.44	0.81	0.75	74.34	66.03
3.71	3.42	0.36	0.33	151.62	131.62
10.95	9.92	4.15	3.90	733.44	682.76
0.02	0.02	0.00	0.00	0.50	0.44
277.63	249.59	94.05	91.63	16063.21	15209.42
220.99	177.66	41.46	37.12	11165.82	9574.00
114.55	68.79	22.34	16.47	5461.85	4249.35
145.03	136.06	23.44	23.00	6443.91	6252.73
360.78	263.78	80.09	68.05	20860.00	18117.14
184.07	63.08	27.18	13.68	8829.42	5187.19
41.12	29.12	9.07	7.55	2895.36	2354.61
68.39	44.25	10.86	7.85	3934.89	3265.36
125.18	67.89	20.10	13.09	5439.32	3864.52
117.56	83.60	15.97	12.55	5033.74	4020.21
86.47	55.73	11.78	8.45	4627.23	3583.77
102.13	68.96	13.81	9.92	4295.46	3222.76
86.96	54.61	11.22	7.74	3040.46	2417.16

主要统计指标解释

行政区划 指国家对行政区域的划分。根据有关法规规定,我国的行政区域划分如下:(1)全国分为省、自治区、直辖市;(2)省、自治区分为自治州、县、自治县、市;(3)自治州分为县、自治县、市;(4)县、自治县分为乡、民族乡、镇;(5)直辖市和较大的市分为区、县;(6)国家在必要时设立的特别行政区。

平均增长速度 平均增长速度表明社会经济现象在一个较长的时期内逐期平均增长变化的程度,它不能根据各个环比增长速度直接求得,但与平均发展速度之间存在着一定的数量关系:平均增长速度 = 平均发展速度 - 1。

平均发展速度是一种根据环比发展速度计算的序时平均数,由于各时期对比的基础不同,所以计算平均发展速度不能采用一般的序时平均数的计算方法,计算方法分为水平法和累计法。水平法,又称几何平均法,即将环比发展速度按连乘法用几何平均数公式计算。累计法,也称方程法,根据一段时期内各年发展水平总和与基期水平的关系,列出方程式计算平均发展速度。水平法着重考虑最后一年所达到的发展水平;累计法着重考虑整个时期累计发展水平的总量。

本《年鉴》内所列的平均增长速度,均用"水平法"计算。从某年到某年平均增长速度的年份,均不包括基期年在内。如1978年以来的平均增长速度是以1978年为基期计算的,则写为1979—2014年平均增长速度,其余类推。

企业(单位)登记注册类型 是以在工商行政管理机关登记注册的各类企业为划分对象,以工商行政管理部门对企业登记注册的类型为依据,将企业登记注册类型分为内资企业、港澳台商投资企业和外商投资企业三大类。内资企业包括国有企业、集体企业、股份合作企业、联营企业、有限责任公司、股份有限公司、私营公司和其他企业;港澳台商投资企业和外商投资企业分别包括合资经营企业、合作经营企业、独资经营企业和股份有限公司。对不在工商行政管理部门进行登记注册的行政机关、事业单位和社会团体,主要按其经费来源和管理方式进行划分。

国有企业 指企业全部资产归国家所有,并按《中华人民共和国企业法人登记管理条例》规定登记注册的非公司制的经济组织。不包括有限责任公司中的国有独资公司。

集体企业 指企业资产归集体所有,并按《中华人民共和国企业法人登记管理条例》规定登记注册的经济组织。

股份合作企业 指以合作制为基础,由企业职工共同出资入股,吸收一定比例的社会资产投资组建,实行自主经营,自负盈亏,共同劳动,民主管理,按劳分配与按股分红相结合的一种集体经济组织。

联营企业 指两个及两个以上相同或不同所有制性质的企业法人或事业单位法人,按自愿、平等、互利的原则,共同投资组成的经济组织。联营企业包括国有联营企业、集体联营企业、国有与集体联营企业和其他联营企业。

有限责任公司 指根据《中华人民共和国公司登记管理条例》规定登记注册,由两个以上、五十个以下的股东共同出资,每个股东以其所认缴的出资额对公司承担有限责任,公司以其全部资产对其债务承担责任的经济组织。有限责任公司包括国有独资公司以及其他有限责任公司。

股份有限公司 指根据《中华人民共和国公司登记管理条例》规定登记注册,其全部注册资本由等额股份构成并通过发行股票筹集资本,股东以其认购的股份对公司承担有限责任,公司以其全部资产对其债务承担责任的经济组织。

私营企业 指由自然人投资设立或由自然人控股,以雇佣劳动为基础的营利性经济组织。包括按照《公司法》、《合伙企业法》、《私营企业暂行条例》规定登记注册的私营有限责任公司、私营股份有限公司、私营合伙企业和私营独资企业。

其他企业 指上述企业之外的其他内资经济组织。

与港澳台商合资经营企业 指港澳台地区投资者与内地企业依照《中华人民共和国中外合资经营企业法》及有关法律的规定,按合同规定的比例投资设立、分享利润和分担风险的企业。

与港澳台商合作经营企业 指港澳台地区投资者与内地企业依照《中华人民共和国中外合作经营企业法》及有关法律的规定,依照合作合同的约定进行投资或提供条件设立、分配利润和分担风险的企业。

港澳台商独资经营企业 指依照《中华人民共和国外资企业法》及有关法律的规定,在内地由港澳台地区投资者全额投资设立的企业。

港澳台商投资股份有限公司 指根据国家有关规定,经原外经贸部依法批准设立,其中港、澳、台商的股本占公司注册资本的比例达25% 以上的股份有限公司。凡其中港、澳、台商的股本占公司注册资本的比例小于25%的,属于内资企业中的股份有限公司。

中外合资经营企业 指外国企业或外国人与中国内地企业依照《中华人民共和国中外合资经营企业法》及有关法律的规定,按合同规定的比例投资设立、分享利润和分担风险的企业。

中外合作经营企业 指外国企业或外国人与中国内地企业依照《中华人民共和国中外合作经营企业法》及有关法律的规

定,依照合作合同的约定进行投资或提供条件设立、分配利润和分担风险的企业。

外资企业 指依照《中华人民共和国外资企业法》及有关法律的规定,在中国内地由外国投资者全额投资设立的企业。

外商投资股份有限公司 指根据国家有关规定,经原外经贸部依法批准设立,其中外资的股本占公司注册资本的比例达25% 以上的股份有限公司。凡其中外资股本占公司注册资本的比例小于25%的,属于内资企业中的股份有限公司。

行政机关、事业单位和社会团体 参照企业登记注册类型,主要按其经费来源和管理方式划分。具体规定如下:

(1)行政机关:包括国家机关和政党机关,原则上均列为"国有"。但有特殊规定的,如供销社等,则列为"集体"。

(2)事业单位:包括经国家机构编制部门和有关业务主管部门批准成立的各类事业单位,不包括实行企业化管理的事业单位。事业单位的划分办法如下:

①由国家财政预算拨款或列入财政预算外资金管理以及经费主要来源于国有主管部门或国有上级单位的事业单位,列为"国有"。

②经费主要来源于集体单位的事业单位,列为"集体"。

③公民个人(或个人合伙)开办的事业单位,列为"私营"。

④上述以外的其他事业单位,如果其经费来源不明确,按管理方式进行归类。

(3)社会团体:包括经民政部门批准成立以及未纳入社会团体管理条例范围的工会、妇联等各类社会团体。社会团体的划分办法如下:

①未纳入民政部社会团体管理条例范围的工会、妇联、共青团、青联、工商联、科协、侨联等社会团体,国家拨款设立的基金会或基金管理组织以及经费主要来源于国有业务主管部门或国有上级单位的社会团体,列为"国有"。

②经费主要来源于集体单位的社会团体,列为"集体"。

③公民个人(或个人合伙)开办的社会团体,划为"私营"。

④上述以外的其他社会团体,如果其经费来源不明确,改按管理方式进行归类。

Explanatory Notes on Main Statistical Indicators

Divisions of Administrative Areas refers to the division of administrative areas by the State. The relative laws stipulate that 1) the whole country is divided into provinces, autonomous regions and municipalities directly under the Central Government; 2) provinces and autonomous regions are further divided into autonomous prefectures, counties, autonomous counties and cities; 3) autonomous prefectures are further divided into counties, autonomous counties and cities; 4) counties and autonomous counties are further divided into townships, ethnic townships and towns; 5) municipalities directly under the Central Government and large cities are divided into districts and counties, 6) the State shall, when necessary, establish special administrative regions.

Average Annual Growth Rate shows the average growth rate of social and economic development during a longer period. It can not be directly calculated by chain based growth rate. The relation is:

Average Annual Growth Rate = Average Speed of Development - 1

Average speed of development is the time series average of speed which calculated by chain based. Because the reference bases during the different periods are not same, average speed of development can not be calculated by the general method. Level approach and accumulative approach for calculating average speed of development rate are applied. The "level approach", or the method of calculating the geometric average, is derived by the formula of geometric average of the chain-based speeds of development, or comparing the level of the last year of the interval with that of the beginning year; the other is called the "accumulative approach" or the "algebraic average", "equation" method, which is derived by the summation of the actual figure of each year in the interval divided by the figure in the base year. The level approach focuses on the level of the last year, while the accumulative approach emphasizes the aggregate development in the duration.

The average annual growth rates listed in the Yearbook are calculated by the level approach. The base year is not listed in the duration for which average annual growth rates are computed. For instance, the average annual growth rate since 1978 is shown as the average annual growth rate of 1979—2015 without showing the base year 1978.

Registration Status of Enterprises Enterprises are classified into 3 categories, namely domestic-funded enterprises, enterprises with investment from Hong Kong, Macau and Taiwan, and enterprises with foreign investment, according to the registration status of an enterprise in industrial and commercial administration agencies. Domestic-funded enterprises include State-owned enterprises, collective-owned enterprises, cooperative enterprises, joint ownership enterprises, limited liability corporations, share-holding corporations Ltd., private enterprises and other enterprises. Included in the enterprises with investment from Hong Kong, Macau and Taiwan and enterprises with foreign investment are joint-venture enterprises, cooperative enterprises, sole investment enterprises and share-holding corporations Ltd. For government agencies, institutions and social organizations which are not registered in industrial and commercial administration agencies, they are classified mainly by their sources of funding and manner of management.

State-owned Enterprises refer to non-corporation economic units where the entire assets are owned by the State and which have been registered in accordance with the Regulation of the People's Republic of China on the Management of Registration of Corporate Enterprises. Not included from this category are solely State-funded corporations in the limited liability corporations.

Collective-owned Enterprises refer to economic units where the assets are owned collectively and which have been registered in accordance with the Regulation of the People's Republic of China on the Management of Registration of Corporate Enterprises.

Cooperative Enterprises refer to a form of collective economic units (enterprises) where capitals come mainly from employees as their shares, with certain proportion of capital from the outside, where production is organized on the basis of independent operation, independent accounting for profits and losses, joint work, democratic management, and a distribution system that integrates remuneration according to work with dividend according to capital share.

Joint Ownership Enterprises refer to economic units established by two or more corporate enterprises or corporate institutions of the same or different ownership, through joint investment on the basis of voluntary participation, equality, and mutual benefits. They include State joint ownership enterprises; collective joint ownership enterprises; joint State-collective enterprises; and other joint ownership enterprises.

Limited Liability Corporations refer to economic units established with investment from 2—50 investors and registered in accordance with the Regulation of the People's Republic of China on the Management of Registration of Corporations, each investor bearing limited liability to the corporation depending on its share of investment, and the corporation bearing liability to its debt to the maximum of its total assets. Limited liability corporations include solely State-funded limited liability corporations and other limited liability corporations.

Share-holding Corporations Ltd. refer to economic units registered in accordance with the Regulation of the People's Republic of China on the Management of Registration of Corporations, with total registered capital divided into equal shares and raised through issuing stocks. Each investor bears limited liability to the corporation depending on the holding of shares, and the corporation bears liability to its debt to the maximum of its total assets.

Private Enterprises refer to profit-making economic units invested and established by natural persons, or controlled by natural persons using employed labour. Included in this category are private limited liability corporations, private share-holding corporations Ltd., private partnership enterprises and private-funded enterprises registered in accordance with the Company Law, the Law on Partnership Business and Interim Regulations on Private Enterprises .

Other Domestic-funded Enterprises refer to domestic-funded economic units other than those mentioned above.

Joint Venture Enterprises with Funds from Hong Kong, Macau and Taiwan are enterprises established by investors from Hong Kong, Macau and Taiwan with enterprises in the mainland of China in accordance with the Law of the People's Republic of China on Sino-foreign Equity Joint Ventures and other relevant laws, where the establishment of the investment and the sharing of profits and risks are stipulated under joint venture contracts.

Cooperative Enterprises with Funds from Hong Kong, Macau and Taiwan established by investors from Hong Kong, Macau and Taiwan with enterprises in the mainland of China in accordance with the Law of the People's Republic of China on Sino-foreign Contractual Joint Venture and other relevant laws, where the investment or provision of facilities and the sharing of profits and risks are stipulated under cooperative contracts.

Enterprises with Sole (exclusive) Investment from Hong Kong, Macau and Taiwan refer to enterprises established in the mainland of China with exclusive investment from investors from Hong Kong, Macau and Taiwan in accordance with the Law of the People's Republic of China on Wholly Foreign-owned Enterprises and other relevant laws.

Share-holding Corporations Ltd. with Investment from Hong Kong, Macau and Taiwan refer to share-holding corporations Ltd. established with the approval from the former Ministry of Foreign Trade and Economic Relations in line with relevant State regulations, where the share of investment from Hong Kong, Macau or Taiwan businessmen exceeds 25% of the total registered capital of the corporation. In case the share of investment from Hong Kong, Macau or Taiwan is less than 25% of the total registered capital, the enterprise is to be classified as domestic-funded share-holding corporation Ltd.

Joint Venture Enterprises with Foreign Investment refer to enterprises jointly established by foreign enterprises or foreigners with enterprises in the mainland of China in accordance with the Law of the People's Republic of China on Sino-foreign Equity Joint Ventures and other relevant laws, where the sharing of investment, profits and risks is stipulated under contract.

Cooperative Enterprises with Foreign Investment refer to enterprises jointly established by foreign enterprises or foreigners with enterprises in the mainland of China in accordance with the Law of the People's Republic of China on Sino-foreign Contractual Joint Venture and other relevant laws, where the investment or provision of facilities and the sharing of profits and risks are stipulated under cooperative contracts.

Enterprises with Sole (exclusive) Foreign Investment refer to enterprises established in the mainland of China with exclusive investment from foreign investors in accordance with the Law of the People's Republic of China on Wholly Foreign-owned Enterprises and other relevant laws.

Share-holding Corporations Ltd. with Foreign Investment refer to share-holding corporations Ltd. established with the approval from the former Ministry of Foreign Trade and Economic Relations in line with relevant State regulations, where the share of investment from foreign investors exceeds 25% of the total registered capital of the corporation. In case the share of foreign investment is less than 25% of the total registered capital, the enterprise is to be classified as domestic-funded share-holding corporation Ltd.

Government Agencies, Institutions and Social Organizations are classified into the following categories by source of funds and manner of management taking reference of the registration status of enterprises:

(1) Government agencies: include State and party agencies, classified in principle as State-owned. There are exceptions, such as supply and marketing cooperatives which are classified as collective-owned.

(2) Institutions: include institutions of various types established with the approval by organization and staffing departments of the government, but exclude institutions where enterprise management system is introduced. Institutions are further classified as follows:

(a) Institutions for which their main budgets are from government budget appropriations or extra-budget funds, or allocated from the budget of their competent government agencies. Such institutions are classified as state-owned.

(b) Institutions for which their budget mainly come from collective units. Such institutions are classified as collective-owned.

(c) Social institutions established by individual or a group of citizens, which are classified as private.

(d) Institutions other than those mentioned above for which their sources of budget are not clear. Such institutions are classified by the manner of management.

(3) Social organizations: include social organizations established with the approval from the Ministry of Civil Affairs, and organizations that are not covered by social organization management regulations such as trade unions, women's federations etc.. Social organizations are further classified as follows:

(a) Social organizations that are not covered by social organization management regulations of the Ministry of Civil Affairs such as trade unions, women federations, communist youth leagues, youth associations, industrial and commerce associations, scientist associations, overseas Chinese associations, etc., foundations and fund management organizations established with funds from the state, and social organizations whose funds mainly come from the budget of their competent government agencies. Such institutions are classified as State-owned.

(b) Social organizations for which their budget mainly come from collective units. Such institutions are classified as collective-owned.

(c) Social organizations established by individual or a group of citizens, which are classified as private.

(d) Social organizations other than those mentioned above for which their sources of budget are not clear. Such organizations are classified by the manner of management.

2

国民经济核算
National Accounts

简 要 说 明

一、地区生产总值数据是根据不同产业部门、不同支出构成的特点和资料来源情况而采用不同方法计算的。

二、地区生产总值是一个价值量指标，其价值的变化受价格变化和物量变化两大因素影响。不变价地区生产总值是把按当期价格计算的地区生产总值换算成按某个固定期（基期）价格计算的价值，从而使两个不同时期的价值进行比较时，能够剔除价格变化的影响，以反映物量变化，反映生产活动成果的实际变动。地区生产总值指数就是根据两个时期不变价地区生产总值计算得到的。随着经济的不断发展，各行业的价格结构也会不断发生变化，为了更好的反映这种变化对于经济的影响，计算不变价地区生产总值需要每隔若干年调整一次基期。我国自开始核算地区生产总值以来，共有 1952 年、1957 年、1970 年、1980 年、1990 年、2000 年、2005 年、2010 年、2015 年 9 个不变价基期，目前的基期是 2015 年。也就是说，2016 年的不变价地区生产总值是按照 2015 年价格计算的。由于计算不变价地区生产总值采用按不同基期分段计算，因此本年鉴中的不变价地区生产总值数据也按分段方式公布。

三、本年鉴所列分地区的数据来自各地区的国民经济核算资料。由于采取分级核算，各地区数据相加不等于全省总计。

四、本年鉴所列 2013 年数据为第三次全国经济普查核算数。

Brief Introduction

Ⅰ. Data on GDP are computed based on different approaches in the light of the different features of various sectors, various expenditure structures and different data sources.

Ⅱ. Gross Domestic Product (GDP) is a measurement of value which changes depending on changes of price and production. GDP at constant prices converts the gross domestic product based on the current price into a value based on the price of the base period. When adjusted for price changes, the values of two different periods can be compared to reflect changes of both products and production activities. GDP index is derived from the constant-price GDPs of the two periods. As economy grows, changes will take place in the price structures of various industries, and the base period for the measurement of constant-price GDP thus needs to be adjusted every few years in order to better reflect the impact of price change on the economy. Since China started GDP calculation, eight constant-price base periods have been used, i. e., 1952, 1957, 1970, 1980, 1990, 2000, 2005, 2010, and 2015, and the current base period is 2015. That is to say, the 2016 GDP is calculated on the basis of the 2010 prices. As the calculation of constant-price GDP is based on different base periods, the constant-price GDP data in this yearbook shall also be announced in accordance with various periods.

Ⅲ. Regional data in this Yearbook are prepared from the national accounts data provided by the statistical bureaus of provincial cities. The sum of the regional data is not equal to the total provincial due to the decentralized accounting approach.

Ⅳ. Data of 2013 in this Yearbook from The Third Economics Census of Jiangsu.

2-1 主要年份总产出
Total Output in Major Years

本表按当年价格计算 (at current price)

年份 Year	总产出（亿元） Total Output (100 million yuan)	第一产业 Primary Industry	第二产业 Secondary Industry	第三产业 Tertiary Industry	#工业 Industry
1952	81.54	31.87	27.19	22.48	25.53
1955	100.53	36.22	35.77	28.54	32.82
1957	114.15	36.81	44.63	32.71	41.01
1962	133.12	40.15	56.38	36.59	53.36
1965	192.52	57.27	97.49	37.76	88.08
1970	273.85	71.33	149.65	52.87	135.47
1975	412.28	91.66	260.23	60.39	235.28
1976	438.59	100.71	271.19	66.69	247.59
1977	487.98	89.16	326.37	72.45	297.12
1978	566.85	105.87	378.99	81.99	337.65
1979	661.26	145.25	427.36	88.65	386.05
1980	750.12	138.45	515.71	95.96	467.82
1981	816.27	153.62	557.41	105.24	504.94
1982	897.85	188.11	593.52	116.22	534.87
1983	1014.55	206.86	679.67	128.02	600.70
1984	1239.44	253.82	836.02	149.60	745.36
1985	1642.70	288.55	1157.52	196.63	1036.67
1986	1960.44	332.66	1380.16	247.62	1235.38
1987	2472.22	380.25	1771.85	320.12	1590.31
1988	3409.56	497.95	2370.81	540.80	2152.93
1989	3839.67	522.25	2713.50	603.92	2507.42
1990	4208.23	580.53	2978.51	649.19	2764.10
1991	4820.22	580.93	3416.59	822.70	3161.60
1992	6862.87	673.82	5089.59	1099.46	4673.57
1993	10245.27	875.37	7757.28	1612.62	7096.46
1994	14163.89	1358.50	10601.01	2204.38	9826.50
1995	17699.96	1721.35	13053.11	2925.50	11995.30
1996	20304.53	1953.13	14764.02	3587.38	13425.15
1997	22314.78	2096.40	16342.27	3876.11	14703.65
1998	23433.26	2129.05	16967.90	4336.31	15163.56
1999	24578.40	2108.71	17714.22	4755.47	15779.09
2000	27034.80	2115.39	19714.71	5204.71	17653.76
2001	29832.61	2174.81	21753.49	5904.31	19595.68
2002	32550.33	1953.50	23884.16	6712.67	21386.23
2003	38729.25	2115.88	28971.95	7641.42	25882.11
2004	46972.13	2417.63	35900.90	8653.60	32068.53
2005	56754.26	2577.02	43289.06	10888.18	39088.19
2006	67730.81	2707.13	51931.76	13091.92	47205.03
2007	83861.75	3064.84	64753.63	16043.28	59576.71
2008	99579.13	3590.64	76269.91	19718.58	69486.28
2009	107849.20	3772.77	82149.29	21927.14	73871.63
2010	127976.43	4257.14	95967.85	27751.45	86320.41
2011	157421.13	5237.45	116098.73	36084.95	104736.44
2012	170950.28	5808.82	123754.96	41386.50	111202.28
2013	184432.70	5848.42	129984.89	48599.39	116027.76
2014	201066.35	6095.02	139459.67	55511.66	123599.43
2015	218060.09	6630.79	149336.98	62092.32	132838.25
2016	234155.82	6797.40	156980.11	70378.31	140015.65

2－2 主要年份总产出指数

Indices of Total Output in Major Years

按可比价格计算,1952 年＝100 (at constant price with 100 in 1952)

年份 Year	总产出指数 Total Output	第一产业 Primary Industry	第二产业 Secondary Industry	第三产业 Tertiary Industry	#工业 Industry
1952	100.0	100.0	100.0	100.0	100.0
1955	120.0	113.0	134.3	123.6	129.7
1957	127.0	109.1	169.4	132.1	165.9
1962	121.8	93.4	200.8	121.4	208.5
1965	181.6	139.7	372.6	129.2	365.0
1970	263.7	166.3	653.9	179.4	651.2
1975	390.0	204.4	1164.8	207.2	1165.2
1976	420.8	212.3	1267.0	232.1	1285.1
1977	463.9	191.0	1524.5	249.8	1543.0
1978	544.0	232.1	1776.6	285.4	1755.8
1979	598.9	257.4	1983.5	291.2	2000.3
1980	671.6	243.2	2380.5	304.9	2417.9
1981	732.4	262.4	2589.9	342.2	2618.8
1982	802.5	301.5	2796.8	376.6	2820.2
1983	908.5	319.4	3242.2	415.6	3211.5
1984	1090.8	371.9	3955.8	477.5	3959.1
1985	1379.6	383.5	5250.3	599.0	5280.7
1986	1595.5	407.5	6115.4	731.7	6161.6
1987	1912.0	420.2	7474.4	906.9	7631.1
1988	2399.8	448.1	9385.3	1288.2	9590.3
1989	2492.6	449.6	9671.7	1422.0	10036.5
1990	2697.8	460.9	10591.2	1502.8	11042.5
1991	3046.2	455.7	12110.4	1807.0	12642.3
1992	4267.8	515.0	18038.4	2272.0	18864.6
1993	5746.6	573.1	25197.1	2887.9	26795.1
1994	7334.3	642.4	33172.0	3354.0	35831.4
1995	8708.7	730.4	39686.3	3903.8	42818.5
1996	10008.5	803.0	45823.2	4471.4	49213.2
1997	11314.1	856.4	52098.2	5035.8	55704.5
1998	12441.1	885.7	57347.6	5676.1	61113.7
1999	13612.6	925.5	62773.5	6330.8	66941.5
2000	14939.2	959.6	68961.7	7079.4	73797.1
2001	16383.3	988.4	75650.7	7946.8	81472.0
2002	18049.8	1013.1	83613.8	8878.3	89782.1
2003	20560.9	1005.0	96748.4	9976.2	103967.7
2004	23692.0	1065.3	112553.6	11356.7	121434.3
2005	27127.3	1096.2	130562.2	13048.9	141713.8
2006	31413.4	1143.4	152104.9	15071.5	165521.7
2007	36188.3	1178.8	175985.4	17437.7	193991.4
2008	41001.3	1231.9	199039.5	20227.7	220568.2
2009	46167.5	1302.9	224536.5	22853.3	247654.0
2010	52233.8	1404.4	254107.3	26026.1	280780.2
2011	58130.7	1462.5	283540.3	28985.6	314841.1
2012	64234.4	1529.8	314446.2	31884.2	349473.6
2013	70786.3	1598.6	344633.0	36092.9	384421.0
2014	77511.0	1640.2	377028.5	39991.0	419403.3
2015	84487.0	1671.4	410584.0	44030.1	455472.0
2016	91101.7	1678.1	439776.7	48588.3	489278.4

2-3 主要年份地区生产总值
Gross Domestic Product in Major Years

本表按当年价格计算 (at current price)

年份 Year	地区生产总值(亿元) Gross Domestic Product (100 million yuan)	第一产业 Primary Industry	第二产业 Secondary Industry	第三产业 Tertiary Industry	#工业 Industry	#建筑业 Construction	#金融业 Financial Intermediation	#房地产业 Real Estate	人均地区生产总值(元) Per Capita GDP (yuan)
1952	48.41	25.49	8.53	14.39	7.63	0.90			131
1955	58.96	29.69	11.29	17.98	10.06	1.23			150
1957	65.11	29.94	14.40	20.77	12.51	1.89			157
1962	69.20	29.10	17.34	22.76	15.69	1.65			161
1965	95.10	41.20	30.26	23.64	26.87	3.39			208
1970	129.23	51.03	46.16	32.04	42.33	3.83			249
1975	184.16	67.59	79.61	36.96	72.70	6.91			329
1976	187.97	62.38	85.04	40.55	78.48	6.56			332
1977	202.40	53.22	105.35	43.83	97.15	8.20			353
1978	249.24	68.71	131.09	49.44	117.10	13.99	10.43	5.50	430
1979	298.55	104.04	141.14	53.37	126.25	14.89	10.27	5.42	509
1980	319.80	94.24	167.41	58.15	151.22	16.19	11.52	6.08	541
1981	350.02	109.39	178.01	62.62	161.11	16.90	12.32	6.50	586
1982	390.17	135.15	185.52	69.50	168.09	17.43	13.74	7.25	645
1983	437.65	150.41	210.81	76.43	191.52	19.29	14.47	7.64	716
1984	518.85	179.00	250.39	89.46	228.58	21.81	15.52	8.19	843
1985	651.82	195.66	339.56	116.60	307.89	31.67	18.91	11.93	1053
1986	744.94	224.26	376.32	144.36	337.77	38.55	25.56	13.50	1193
1987	922.33	246.86	493.69	181.78	443.23	50.46	25.14	14.59	1462
1988	1208.85	319.18	586.82	302.85	526.92	59.90	47.44	21.25	1891
1989	1321.85	324.18	657.06	340.61	599.91	57.15	65.45	24.72	2038
1990	1416.50	355.17	692.59	368.74	634.13	58.46	72.53	27.02	2109
1991	1601.38	345.14	793.92	462.32	725.83	68.09	77.81	33.51	2353
1992	2136.02	393.82	1119.26	622.94	1017.94	101.32	109.27	43.89	3106
1993	2998.16	490.59	1598.05	909.52	1451.97	146.08	140.04	73.03	4321
1994	4057.39	683.98	2186.77	1186.64	2002.22	184.55	187.37	95.23	5801
1995	5155.25	866.24	2715.26	1573.75	2467.63	247.63	244.65	134.95	7319
1996	6004.21	989.18	3074.12	1940.91	2754.80	319.32	291.71	178.79	8471
1997	6680.34	1035.80	3411.86	2232.68	3016.44	395.42	318.08	211.22	9371
1998	7199.95	1047.16	3640.10	2512.69	3157.69	482.41	322.33	253.14	10049
1999	7697.82	1037.37	3920.15	2740.30	3387.99	532.16	330.25	272.34	10695
2000	8553.69	1048.34	4435.89	3069.46	3848.52	587.37	349.49	298.15	11765
2001	9456.84	1094.48	4907.46	3454.90	4270.90	636.56	353.41	326.74	12879
2002	10606.85	1110.44	5604.49	3891.92	4880.09	724.40	368.86	371.09	14369
2003	12442.87	1162.45	6787.11	4493.31	6004.65	782.46	392.11	447.47	16743
2004	15003.60	1367.58	8437.99	5198.03	7514.39	923.60	440.50	534.17	20031
2005	18598.69	1461.51	10524.96	6612.22	9440.18	1084.78	492.40	799.73	24616
2006	21742.05	1545.05	12282.89	7914.11	11097.64	1185.25	653.25	1017.91	28526
2007	26018.48	1816.31	14471.26	9730.91	13105.24	1366.02	1054.25	1365.71	33837
2008	30981.98	2100.11	16993.34	11888.53	15271.20	1722.14	1298.48	1626.13	40014
2009	34457.30	2261.86	18566.37	13629.07	16464.94	2101.43	1596.98	2025.39	44253
2010	41425.48	2540.10	21753.93	17131.45	19277.65	2476.28	2105.92	2600.95	52840
2011	49110.27	3064.78	25203.28	20842.21	22280.61	2922.67	2600.11	2747.89	62290
2012	54058.22	3418.29	27121.95	23517.98	23908.47	3213.48	3136.51	2992.82	68347
2013	59753.37	3469.86	29086.08	27197.43	25503.86	3590.16	3958.79	3308.40	75354
2014	65088.32	3634.33	30854.50	30599.49	26962.97	3899.47	4723.69	3564.44	81874
2015	70116.38	3986.05	32044.45	34085.88	27996.43	4055.42	5302.93	3755.45	87995
2016	76086.17	4077.18	33550.54	38458.45	29385.87	4173.66	6011.13	4292.79	95257

2-4 主要年份地区生产总值构成

Composition of Gross Domestic Product in Major Years

本表按当年价格计算,单位:% (at current price, %)

年份 Year	地区生产总值 Gross Domestic Product	第一产业 Primary Industry	第二产业 Secondary Industry	第三产业 Tertiary Industry	#工业 Industry	#建筑业 Construction	#金融业 Financial Intermediation	#房地产业 Real Estate
1952	100.0	52.7	17.6	29.7	15.8	1.9		
1955	100.0	50.4	19.1	30.5	17.1	2.1		
1957	100.0	46.0	22.1	31.9	19.2	2.9		
1962	100.0	42.1	25.0	32.9	22.6	2.4		
1965	100.0	43.3	31.8	24.9	28.3	3.6		
1970	100.0	39.5	35.7	24.8	32.8	3.0		
1975	100.0	36.7	43.2	20.1	39.5	3.8		
1976	100.0	33.2	45.2	21.6	41.8	3.5		
1977	100.0	26.3	52.0	21.7	48.0	4.0		
1978	100.0	27.6	52.6	19.8	47.0	5.6	4.2	2.2
1979	100.0	34.8	47.3	17.9	42.3	5.0	3.4	1.8
1980	100.0	29.5	52.3	18.2	47.3	5.1	3.6	1.9
1981	100.0	31.3	50.8	4.8	17.9	46.0	3.5	1.9
1982	100.0	34.6	47.6	17.8	43.1	4.5	3.5	1.9
1983	100.0	34.4	48.2	17.4	43.8	4.4	3.3	1.7
1984	100.0	34.5	48.3	17.2	44.1	4.2	3.0	1.6
1985	100.0	30.0	52.1	17.9	47.2	4.9	2.9	1.8
1986	100.0	30.1	50.5	19.4	45.3	5.2	3.4	1.8
1987	100.0	26.8	53.5	19.7	48.1	5.5	2.7	1.6
1988	100.0	26.4	48.5	25.1	43.6	5.0	3.9	1.8
1989	100.0	24.5	49.7	25.8	45.4	4.3	5.0	1.9
1990	100.0	25.1	48.9	26.0	44.8	4.1	5.1	1.9
1991	100.0	21.5	49.6	28.9	45.3	4.3	4.9	2.1
1992	100.0	18.4	52.4	29.2	47.7	4.7	5.1	2.1
1993	100.0	16.4	53.3	30.3	48.4	4.9	4.7	2.4
1994	100.0	16.9	53.9	29.2	49.3	4.5	4.6	2.3
1995	100.0	16.8	52.7	30.5	47.9	4.8	4.7	2.6
1996	100.0	16.5	51.2	32.3	45.9	5.3	4.9	3.0
1997	100.0	15.5	51.1	33.4	45.2	5.9	4.8	3.2
1998	100.0	14.5	50.6	34.9	43.9	6.7	4.5	3.5
1999	100.0	13.5	50.9	35.6	44.0	6.9	4.3	3.5
2000	100.0	12.2	51.9	35.9	45.0	6.9	4.1	3.5
2001	100.0	11.6	51.9	36.5	45.2	6.7	3.7	3.5
2002	100.0	10.5	52.8	36.7	46.0	6.8	3.5	3.5
2003	100.0	9.3	54.6	36.1	48.3	6.3	3.2	3.6
2004	100.0	9.1	56.3	34.6	50.1	6.2	2.9	3.6
2005	100.0	7.9	56.6	35.6	50.8	5.8	2.6	4.3
2006	100.0	7.1	56.5	36.4	51.0	5.5	3.0	4.7
2007	100.0	7.0	55.6	37.4	50.4	5.3	4.1	5.2
2008	100.0	6.8	54.8	38.4	49.3	5.6	4.2	5.2
2009	100.0	6.5	53.9	39.6	47.8	6.1	4.6	5.9
2010	100.0	6.1	52.5	41.4	46.5	6.0	5.1	6.3
2011	100.0	6.3	51.3	42.4	45.4	5.9	5.3	5.6
2012	100.0	6.3	50.2	43.5	44.2	6.0	5.8	5.5
2013	100.0	5.8	48.7	45.5	42.7	6.0	6.6	5.5
2014	100.0	5.6	47.4	47.0	41.4	6.0	7.3	5.5
2015	100.0	5.7	45.7	48.6	39.9	5.8	7.6	5.4
2016	100.0	5.4	44.1	50.5	38.6	5.5	7.9	5.6

2-5 不变价地区生产总值

Gross Domestic Product at Constant Price

单位:亿元 (100 million yuan)

年份 Year	地区生产总值 Gross Domestic Product	第一产业 Primary Industry	第二产业 Secondary Industry	第三产业 Tertiary Industry	#工业 Industry	#建筑业 Construction
按1980年价格计算 Price Base Year = 1980						
1980	328.21	100.50	169.56	58.15	153.37	16.19
1981	363.85	113.44	181.85	68.56	164.56	17.29
1982	399.66	131.53	192.41	75.72	174.63	17.78
1983	448.78	140.98	221.82	85.98	202.11	19.71
1984	519.29	159.22	261.51	98.56	231.60	29.91
1985	609.14	157.88	334.88	116.38	304.52	30.36
1986	672.32	166.33	367.10	138.89	331.25	35.85
1987	762.72	167.11	433.55	162.06	388.62	44.93
1988	912.08	174.37	510.67	227.04	459.37	51.30
1989	934.74	169.42	512.97	252.35	468.94	44.03
1990	981.59	171.16	540.61	269.82	496.73	43.88
按1990年价格计算 Price Base Year = 1990						
1990	1438.00	358.93	710.33	368.74	651.87	58.46
1991	1557.32	344.81	773.85	438.66	709.30	64.55
1992	1955.77	381.53	1020.73	553.51	928.13	92.60
1993	2342.88	391.25	1258.98	692.65	1143.28	115.70
1994	2728.74	411.73	1545.47	771.54	1410.47	135.00
1995	3148.95	467.66	1795.09	886.20	1626.27	168.82
1996	3533.97	503.88	2016.78	1013.31	1803.53	213.25
1997	3956.46	529.04	2271.40	1156.02	2007.33	264.07
1998	4392.36	540.19	2546.93	1305.24	2224.12	322.81
1999	4835.68	565.06	2834.48	1436.14	2477.67	356.81
2000	5346.92	587.06	3163.06	1596.80	2779.95	383.11
按2000年价格计算 Price Base Year = 2000						
2000	8553.69	1048.34	4435.89	3069.46	3848.52	587.37
2001	9422.01	1079.79	4921.27	3420.95	4291.02	630.25
2002	10521.02	1109.48	5593.98	3817.56	4887.48	706.50
2003	11954.29	1107.82	6557.21	4289.26	5757.45	799.76
2004	13717.60	1174.20	7679.60	4863.80	6782.27	897.33
2005	15703.94	1207.73	8907.14	5589.08	7914.15	992.99
按2005年价格计算 Price Base Year = 2005						
2005	18598.69	1461.51	10524.96	6612.22	9440.18	1084.78
2006	21377.34	1534.28	12205.31	7637.75	11004.68	1200.63
2007	24571.11	1581.10	14097.03	8892.98	12836.96	1260.07
2008	27691.48	1644.32	15960.65	10086.51	14595.62	1365.03
2009	31139.06	1717.84	17963.59	11457.63	16339.82	1623.77
2010	35099.55	1801.27	20311.56	12986.72	18513.90	1797.66
按2010年价格计算 Price Base Year = 2010						
2010	41425.48	2540.10	21753.93	17131.45	19277.65	2476.28
2011	45969.83	2642.02	24296.18	19031.63	21648.83	2647.35
2012	50626.87	2763.55	26982.69	20880.63	24062.67	2920.02
2013	55505.85	2705.56	29680.46	23119.83	26549.80	3138.72
2014	60334.86	2785.40	32115.74	25433.72	28771.53	3352.15
2015	65483.34	2876.19	34780.86	27826.29	31060.36	3728.59
按2015年价格计算 Price Base Year = 2015						
2016	75556.86	4015.21	34151.20	37390.45	29914.37	4245.84

2-6 主要年份地区生产总值指数
Indices of Gross Domestic Product in Major Years

按可比价格计算，上年=100　　　　(at constant price, preceding year=100)

年份 Year	地区生产总值 Gross Domestic Product	第一产业 Primary Industry	第二产业 Secondary Industry	第三产业 Tertiary Industry	#工业 Industry	#建筑业 Construction	#金融业 Financial Intermediation	#房地产业 Real Estate	人均地区生产总值 Per Capita GDP
1952									
1955	111.1	114.7	101.7	107.0	101.9	100.7			108.6
1957	100.4	101.8	100.5	97.6	95.5	130.9			98.2
1962	93.2	101.5	73.5	94.0	72.8	80.8			91.9
1965	107.1	101.3	130.8	103.1	120.8	241.7			104.7
1970	114.9	107.1	136.5	110.1	137.5	130.6			112.3
1975	106.1	102.1	115.6	99.2	117.1	105.4			104.8
1976	101.0	87.3	112.0	111.3	113.7	98.8			99.8
1977	106.3	86.7	123.9	107.1	123.8	125.3			105.1
1978	124.6	132.1	124.6	113.9	123.3	135.7			123.2
1979	112.0	122.9	107.1	105.7	108.0	100.4	96.4	96.5	110.8
1980	104.8	89.5	118.2	101.6	119.7	105.2	104.5	104.7	103.9
1981	110.9	112.9	107.2	117.9	107.3	106.8	117.1	117.1	109.8
1982	109.8	115.9	105.8	110.4	106.1	102.8	111.0	111.0	108.5
1983	112.3	107.2	115.3	113.5	115.7	110.9	108.8	108.7	111.1
1984	115.7	112.9	117.9	114.6	114.6	151.8	114.6	114.7	114.9
1985	117.3	99.2	128.1	118.1	131.5	101.5	101.1	120.9	116.6
1986	110.4	105.4	109.6	119.3	108.8	118.1	130.3	109.1	109.5
1987	113.4	100.5	118.1	116.7	117.3	125.3	91.1	100.2	112.2
1988	119.6	104.3	117.8	140.1	118.2	114.2	158.6	122.4	118.0
1989	102.5	97.2	100.5	111.1	102.1	85.8	136.4	114.9	101.0
1990	105.0	101.0	105.4	106.9	105.9	99.7	109.5	108.1	101.4
1991	108.3	96.1	108.9	119.0	108.8	110.4	104.8	118.3	106.9
1992	125.6	110.6	131.9	126.2	130.9	143.5	133.1	117.9	124.3
1993	119.8	102.5	123.3	125.1	123.2	124.9	113.3	149.8	118.7
1994	116.5	105.2	122.8	111.4	123.4	116.7	111.9	108.1	115.6
1995	115.4	113.6	116.2	114.9	115.3	125.1	118.1	125.0	114.6
1996	112.2	107.7	112.3	114.3	110.9	126.3	115.4	123.7	111.5
1997	112.0	105.0	112.6	114.1	111.3	123.8	113.5	121.5	111.3
1998	111.0	102.1	112.1	112.9	110.8	122.2	103.9	123.8	110.5
1999	110.1	104.6	111.3	110.0	111.4	110.5	104.8	111.2	109.6
2000	110.6	103.9	111.6	111.2	112.2	107.4	109.8	107.5	109.5
2001	110.2	103.0	110.9	111.5	111.5	107.3	102.8	109.7	109.1
2002	111.7	102.8	113.7	111.6	113.9	112.1	105.9	112.6	111.1
2003	113.6	99.9	117.2	112.4	117.8	113.2	106.8	112.0	112.9
2004	114.8	106.0	117.1	113.4	117.8	112.2	107.5	109.5	113.9
2005	114.5	102.9	116.0	114.9	116.7	110.7	118.9	124.6	113.5
2006	114.9	105.0	116.0	115.5	116.6	110.7	121.3	119.3	113.9
2007	114.9	103.1	115.5	116.4	116.7	105.0	138.6	117.3	113.9
2008	112.7	104.0	113.2	113.4	113.7	108.3	112.0	109.0	111.9
2009	112.4	104.5	112.5	113.6	112.0	119.0	128.1	127.3	111.8
2010	112.7	104.9	113.1	113.3	113.3	110.7	117.0	108.9	112.0
2011	111.0	104.0	111.7	111.1	112.3	106.9	106.2	101.1	110.3
2012	110.1	104.6	111.1	109.7	111.1	110.3	114.7	108.6	109.8
2013	109.6	102.9	110.0	109.8	110.3	107.5	112.8	106.2	109.3
2014	108.7	103.0	108.2	110.0	108.4	106.8	116.9	102.1	108.4
2015	108.5	103.3	108.3	109.4	108.0	111.2	111.3	105.7	108.3
2016	107.8	100.7	106.6	109.7	106.9	104.7	112.7	105.7	107.5

2-7 主要年份地区生产总值定基指数
Fixed-base Indices of Gross Domestic Product in Major Years

按可比价格计算 (at constant price)

年份 Year	地区生产总值 Gross Domestic Product	第一产业 Primary Industry	第二产业 Secondary Industry	第三产业 Tertiary Industry	#工业 Industry	#建筑业 Construction	#金融业 Financial Intermediation	#房地产业 Real Estate	人均地区生产总值 Per Capita GDP
1952	100.0	100.0	100.0	100.0	100.0	100.0			100.0
1955	118.9	115.9	133.5	121.6	132.0	142.1			111.3
1957	121.9	111.0	174.3	131.0	166.0	223.2			108.8
1962	103.8	84.6	202.6	118.0	212.1	146.3			89.2
1965	147.6	125.6	375.0	126.4	371.4	396.8			119.1
1970	200.9	148.7	663.6	176.0	671.7	615.8			143.1
1975	277.5	188.4	1179.3	198.1	1216.2	961.1			182.9
1976	280.3	164.4	1320.2	220.4	1382.9	949.5			182.5
1977	297.9	142.5	1636.2	236.0	1711.7	1189.5			191.8
1978	371.3	188.3	2038.8	268.8	2110.7	1613.7	100.0	100.0	236.3
1979	415.9	231.3	2183.9	284.1	2279.2	1620.0	96.4	96.5	261.8
1980	436.0	207.0	2580.8	288.6	2729.0	1704.2	100.8	101.0	272.0
1981	483.3	233.6	2767.9	340.2	2928.1	1820.0	118.0	118.3	298.6
1982	530.9	270.9	2928.6	375.8	3107.3	1871.6	131.0	131.2	323.9
1983	596.1	290.3	3376.3	426.7	3596.3	2074.7	142.4	142.7	360.0
1984	689.8	327.9	3980.4	489.1	4121.0	3148.4	163.3	163.6	413.7
1985	809.2	325.1	5097.1	577.6	5418.5	3195.8	165.1	197.8	482.3
1986	893.1	342.5	5587.5	689.3	5894.1	3773.7	215.1	215.8	528.1
1987	1013.2	344.1	6598.9	804.3	6914.9	4729.5	196.1	216.1	592.7
1988	1211.6	359.1	7772.8	1126.7	8173.8	5400.0	311.0	264.6	699.5
1989	1241.7	348.9	7807.8	1252.4	8344.1	4634.7	424.3	304.2	706.4
1990	1303.9	352.5	8228.5	1339.1	8838.6	4618.9	464.7	328.7	716.5
1991	1412.1	338.6	8964.3	1593.0	9617.3	5100.1	487.2	388.7	765.9
1992	1773.4	374.7	11824.1	2010.0	12584.4	7316.4	648.4	458.2	951.7
1993	2124.4	384.2	14584.0	2515.3	15501.6	9141.5	734.9	686.3	1130.0
1994	2474.3	404.3	17902.7	2801.8	19124.4	10666.4	822.5	741.7	1305.8
1995	2855.3	459.2	20794.3	3218.2	22050.4	13338.5	971.5	926.8	1496.3
1996	3204.5	494.8	23362.4	3679.8	24453.8	16849.0	1121.5	1146.9	1668.6
1997	3587.6	519.5	26311.9	4198.0	27217.1	20864.3	1273.4	1393.8	1857.4
1998	3982.8	530.5	29503.6	4739.9	30156.5	25505.3	1323.5	1726.2	2051.6
1999	4384.8	554.9	32834.6	5215.3	33594.4	28191.7	1387.2	1919.0	2248.4
2000	4848.4	576.5	36640.9	5798.7	37692.9	30269.7	1523.3	2062.3	2461.4
2001	5340.5	593.8	40650.2	6462.7	42026.9	32479.2	1566.0	2262.3	2685.1
2002	5963.5	610.1	46206.8	7212.0	47868.6	36409.2	1658.4	2547.4	2982.4
2003	6775.9	609.2	54163.2	8103.1	56389.2	41215.2	1771.2	2853.1	3366.1
2004	7775.4	645.7	63434.3	9188.5	66426.5	46243.2	1904.3	3124.1	3832.3
2005	8902.8	664.4	73583.7	10557.6	77519.7	51191.3	2264.2	3892.7	4349.7
2006	10229.3	697.7	85357.1	12194.0	90388.0	56668.7	2746.5	4643.9	4956.0
2007	11753.5	719.3	98587.5	14193.8	105482.8	59502.1	3806.6	5447.3	5646.4
2008	13246.1	748.1	111601.0	16095.8	119933.9	64440.8	4263.4	5937.6	6319.6
2009	14895.3	781.5	125606.1	18283.8	134266.2	76655.5	5463.4	7560.6	7066.6
2010	16787.0	819.8	142060.5	20723.8	152123.7	84864.6	6389.5	8233.7	7911.1
2011	18633.6	852.7	158662.2	23022.5	170835.1	90727.2	6785.7	8327.9	8725.9
2012	20515.5	891.9	176273.7	25255.6	189797.8	100072.1	7783.2	9044.1	9581.0
2013	22485.0	917.8	193901.1	27730.7	209347.0	107577.5	8779.4	9604.9	10472.1
2014	24441.2	945.3	209801.0	30503.8	226932.1	114892.8	10263.1	9806.6	11351.7
2015	26518.7	976.5	227214.5	33371.2	245086.7	127760.8	11422.8	10365.6	12293.9
2016	28576.3	983.6	242186.5	36601.8	261918.5	133759.8	12873.5	10956.4	13215.9

2-8 分行业地区生产总值

Gross Domestic Product by Sector

本表按当年价格计算,单位:亿元　　　　(at current price, 100 million yuan)

行业	Sector	2010	2013	2014	2015	2016
地区生产总值	**Gross Domestic Product**	**41425.48**	**59753.37**	**65088.32**	**70116.38**	**76086.17**
按三次产业分	Grouped by Industry					
第一产业	Primary Industry	2540.10	3469.86	3634.33	3986.05	4077.18
第二产业	Secondary Industry	21753.93	29086.08	30854.50	32044.45	33550.54
第三产业	Tertiary Industry	17131.45	27197.43	30599.49	34085.88	38458.45
按行业分	Grouped by Sector					
农、林、牧、渔业	Agriculture, Forestry, Animal Husbandry and Fishery	2540.10	3646.06	3835.16	4209.52	4323.53
农业	Farming	1556.23	2182.66	2314.24	2566.23	2569.37
林业	Forestry	43.90	59.87	66.07	72.36	72.72
畜牧业	Animal Husbandry	373.37	489.12	472.91	515.88	543.57
渔业	Fishery	444.90	738.21	781.11	831.58	891.52
农、林、牧、渔服务业	Services in Support of Agriculture	121.70	176.20	200.83	223.47	246.35
工业	Industry	19277.65	25503.86	26962.97	27996.43	29385.87
采矿业	Mining	275.80	243.96	251.44	186.80	153.87
制造业	Manufacturing	18101.33	24124.67	25484.27	26434.83	27813.27
电力、热力、燃气及水的生产和供应业	Production and Supply of Electric Power, Heat Power, Gas and Water	900.52	1135.23	1227.26	1374.80	1418.73
建筑业	Construction	2476.28	3590.16	3899.47	4055.42	4173.66
批发和零售业	Wholesale and Retail Trades	4447.50	6123.46	6559.03	6992.68	7470.27
交通运输、仓储和邮政业	Transport, Storage and Post	1768.30	2425.11	2591.15	2705.44	2834.56
住宿和餐饮业	Hotels and Catering Services	710.98	1027.97	1094.45	1189.40	1291.32
信息传输、软件和信息技术服务业	Information Transfer, Software and IT Services	605.28	1361.42	1579.55	1870.81	2443.22
金融业	Financial Intermediation	2105.92	3958.79	4723.69	5302.93	6011.13
房地产业	Real Estate	2600.95	3308.40	3564.44	3755.45	4292.79
租赁和商务服务业	Leasing and Business Services	868.34	2033.78	2469.55	2845.33	3451.12
科学研究和技术服务业	Scientific Research and Technical Services	365.17	774.22	884.50	998.71	1097.81
水利、环境和公共设施管理业	Management of Water Conservancy, Environment and Public Facilities	215.34	382.91	428.27	496.67	551.91
居民服务、修理和其他服务业	Services to Households and Other Services	447.86	877.51	1073.53	1259.45	1507.03
教育	Education	1022.72	1680.21	1866.58	2195.15	2426.57
卫生和社会工作	Healthcare and Social Welfare	500.72	887.94	1015.45	1230.89	1410.95
文化、体育和娱乐业	Culture, Sports and Entertainment	220.80	418.85	536.56	635.64	795.79
公共管理、社会保障和社会组织	Public Management, Social Security and Organizations	1251.57	1752.72	2003.97	2376.46	2618.65

2－9　分行业地区生产总值构成

Composition of Gross Domestic Product by Sector

本表按当年价格计算,单位:%　　(at current price,%)

行　业	Sector	2010	2013	2014	2015	2016
地区生产总值	**Gross Domestic Product**	**100.0**	**100.0**	**100.0**	**100.0**	**100.0**
按三次产业分	Grouped by Industry					
第一产业	Primary Industry	6.1	5.8	5.6	5.7	5.4
第二产业	Secondary Industry	52.5	48.7	47.4	45.7	44.1
第三产业	Tertiary Industry	41.4	45.5	47.0	48.6	50.5
按行业分	Grouped by Sector					
农、林、牧、渔业	Agriculture, Forestry, Animal Husbandry and Fishery	6.1	6.1	5.9	6.0	5.7
农业	Farming	3.8	3.7	3.6	3.7	3.4
林业	Forestry	0.1	0.1	0.1	0.1	0.1
畜牧业	Animal Husbandry	0.9	0.8	0.7	0.7	0.7
渔业	Frishery	1.1	1.2	1.2	1.2	1.2
农、林、牧、渔服务业	Services in Support of Agriculture	0.3	0.3	0.3	0.3	0.3
工业	Industry	46.5	42.7	41.4	39.9	38.6
采矿业	Mining	0.7	0.4	0.4	0.3	0.2
制造业	Manufacturing	43.7	40.4	39.2	37.7	36.5
电力、热力、燃气及水的生产和供应业	Production and Supply of Electric Power, Heat Power, Gas and Water	2.2	1.9	1.9	1.9	1.9
建筑业	Construction	6.0	6.0	6.0	5.8	5.5
批发和零售业	Wholesale and Retail Trades	10.7	10.3	10.1	10.0	9.8
交通运输、仓储和邮政业	Transport, Storage and Post	4.3	4.1	4.0	3.9	3.7
住宿和餐饮业	Hotels and Catering Services	1.7	1.7	1.7	1.7	1.7
信息传输、软件和信息技术服务业	Information Transfer, Software and IT Services	1.5	2.3	2.4	2.7	3.2
金融业	Financial Intermediation	5.1	6.6	7.3	7.6	7.9
房地产业	Real Estate	6.3	5.5	5.5	5.4	5.6
租赁和商务服务业	Leasing and Business Services	2.1	3.4	3.8	4.1	4.5
科学研究和技术服务业	Scientific Research and Technical Services	0.9	1.3	1.3	1.4	1.4
水利、环境和公共设施管理业	Management of Water Conservancy, Environment and Public Facilities	0.5	0.6	0.6	0.7	0.7
居民服务、修理和其他服务业	Services to Households and other Services	1.1	1.5	1.6	1.8	2.0
教育	Education	2.5	2.8	2.9	3.1	3.2
卫生和社会工作	Healthcare and Social Welfare	1.2	1.5	1.6	1.7	1.9
文化、体育和娱乐业	Culture, Sports and Entertainment	0.5	0.7	0.8	0.9	1.0
公共管理、社会保障和社会组织	Public Management, Social Security and Organizations	3.0	2.9	3.1	3.4	3.4

2－10　分市分行业地区生产总值(2016年)

本表按当年价格计算,单位:亿元

行业	Sector	南京 Nanjing	无锡 Wuxi	徐州 Xuzhou	常州 Changzhou
地区生产总值	**Gross Domestic Product**	**10503.02**	**9210.02**	**5808.52**	**5773.86**
按三次产业分	Grouped by Industry				
第一产业	Primary Industry	252.54	135.19	542.88	152.67
第二产业	Secondary Industry	4117.32	4346.78	2513.85	2682.46
第三产业	Tertiary Industry	6133.16	4728.05	2751.79	2938.73
按行业分	Grouped by Sector				
农、林、牧、渔业	Agriculture, Forestry, Animal Husbandry and Fishery	265.02	154.74	563.19	163.03
农业	Farming	164.51	91.00	385.97	98.31
林业	Forestry	13.90	10.57	10.89	1.00
畜牧业	Animal Husbandry	18.54	13.39	119.35	14.46
渔业	Fishery	55.59	20.23	26.67	38.90
农、林、牧、渔服务业	Services in Support of Agriculature	12.48	19.55	20.31	10.36
工业	Industry	3581.72	3977.58	2122.58	2428.84
采矿业	Mining	11.35	0.80	128.69	3.75
制造业	Manufacturing	3467.25	3833.20	1933.43	2371.91
电力、热力、燃气及水的生产和供应业	Production and Supply of Electric Power, Heat Power, Gas and Water	103.12	143.58	60.46	53.18
建筑业	Construction	537.06	369.68	393.60	254.20
批发和零售业	Wholesale and Retail Trades	1174.06	1460.27	825.76	791.99
交通运输、仓储和邮政业	Transport, Storage and Post	306.21	195.19	414.78	194.83
住宿和餐饮业	Hotels and Catering Services	183.00	259.90	110.60	140.50
信息传输、软件和信息技术服务业	Information Transfer, Software and IT Services	746.87	210.42	83.36	125.60
金融业	Financial Intermediation	1241.76	686.76	279.53	341.94
房地产业	Real Estate	711.47	467.49	221.86	328.68
租赁和商务服务业	Leasing and Business Services	338.74	444.38	113.34	329.55
科学研究、技术服务业	Scientific Research and Technical Services	347.12	87.93	57.63	71.55
水利、环境和公共设施管理业	Management of Water Conservancy, Environment and Public Facilities	65.05	54.65	22.38	108.03
居民服务、修理和其他服务业	Services to Households and Other Services	136.97	179.59	174.37	114.30
教育	Education	324.07	193.43	130.42	112.59
卫生和社会工作	Healthcare and Social Welfare	150.00	95.53	150.92	52.05
文化、体育和娱乐业	Culture, Sports and Entertainment	101.85	92.28	17.95	92.23
公共管理、社会保障和社会组织	Public Management, Social Security and Organizations	292.05	280.20	126.28	123.95

Composition of Gross Domestic Product by Sector and Region(2016)

(at current price, 100 million yuan)

苏州 Suzhou	南通 Nantong	连云港 Lianyungang	淮安 Huaian	盐城 Yancheng	扬州 Yangzhou	镇江 Zhenjiang	泰州 Taizhou	宿迁 Suqian
15475.09	**6768.20**	**2376.48**	**3048.00**	**4576.08**	**4449.38**	**3833.84**	**4101.78**	**2351.12**
221.81	366.66	301.56	324.61	533.91	251.39	137.78	240.00	275.23
7277.46	3170.30	1049.90	1268.15	2050.02	2197.63	1870.40	1933.89	1139.97
7975.82	3231.24	1025.02	1455.24	1992.15	2000.36	1825.66	1927.89	935.92
247.02	401.08	321.08	330.91	565.86	266.59	157.88	248.99	282.26
117.36	207.73	168.36	227.21	280.78	142.17	92.50	156.58	179.70
13.33	2.67	8.74	8.13	16.96	6.09	5.46	2.40	10.93
16.22	64.59	50.82	54.45	135.45	31.78	17.21	39.39	38.84
74.91	91.67	73.64	34.82	100.72	71.35	22.61	41.63	45.76
25.21	34.42	19.52	6.30	31.95	15.20	20.10	8.99	7.03
6709.02	2633.06	851.82	1071.99	1771.68	1925.92	1728.00	1679.83	976.89
2.43	0.00	7.67	35.60	9.53	65.44	11.82	0.00	5.69
6521.38	2547.23	792.14	1000.08	1726.56	1814.37	1658.97	1658.63	958.82
185.21	85.83	52.01	36.31	35.59	46.11	57.21	21.20	12.38
569.78	539.40	198.08	196.70	280.77	272.30	142.40	255.40	163.48
2047.44	720.40	231.59	241.99	452.60	316.40	380.62	303.05	196.43
478.02	229.08	102.76	106.20	165.75	149.14	142.46	190.42	83.95
439.43	146.61	32.18	83.05	66.09	71.12	81.58	94.65	43.22
390.91	128.40	34.92	53.68	76.70	98.77	73.50	72.32	55.19
1333.77	435.51	106.71	121.84	213.30	234.85	220.00	214.06	107.87
1015.15	490.37	146.81	239.36	283.89	274.08	275.74	293.09	146.90
668.57	242.86	63.99	133.24	76.55	246.83	106.00	171.45	49.97
216.47	88.03	15.47	22.09	26.49	68.66	72.29	33.07	5.87
94.83	29.61	13.42	24.76	25.66	36.96	27.92	30.24	7.72
200.15	142.54	11.89	82.13	131.64	56.67	62.30	105.95	24.19
359.60	180.19	92.27	108.01	126.73	136.60	96.18	100.47	71.00
236.35	104.35	37.92	63.64	89.65	72.79	63.37	61.03	30.85
73.03	49.67	7.95	27.62	21.18	27.47	68.20	34.97	10.40
395.55	207.04	107.62	140.79	201.54	194.23	135.40	212.79	94.93

2-11 三次产业对地区生产总值的贡献率和拉动

本表按可比价格计算

年 份 Year	地 区 生产总值 Gross Domestic Product		第一产业 Primary Industry	
	贡献率(%) Contribution Share(%)	拉动(百分点) Contribution (percentage points)	贡献率(%) Contribution Share(%)	拉动(百分点) Contribution (percentage points)
1990	100.0	5.0	3.7	0.2
1991	100.0	8.3	-11.8	-1.0
1992	100.0	25.6	9.2	2.4
1993	100.0	19.8	2.6	0.5
1994	100.0	16.5	5.3	0.9
1995	100.0	15.4	13.3	2.1
1996	100.0	12.2	9.4	1.2
1997	100.0	12.0	5.9	0.7
1998	100.0	11.0	2.6	0.3
1999	100.0	10.1	5.6	0.6
2000	100.0	10.6	4.3	0.5
2001	100.0	10.2	3.6	0.4
2002	100.0	11.7	2.7	0.3
2003	100.0	13.6	-0.1	0.0
2004	100.0	14.8	3.8	0.6
2005	100.0	14.5	1.7	0.2
2006	100.0	14.9	2.7	0.4
2007	100.0	14.9	1.5	0.2
2008	100.0	12.3	2.1	0.3
2009	100.0	12.4	2.1	0.3
2010	100.0	12.7	2.1	0.3
2011	100.0	11.0	2.2	0.2
2012	100.0	10.1	2.6	0.3
2013	100.0	9.6	1.6	0.1
2014	100.0	8.7	1.7	0.1
2015	100.0	8.5	1.7	0.1
2016	100.0	7.8	0.5	0.0

注:1. 产业贡献率指各产业增加值增量与 GDP 增量之比。
2. 三次产业拉动指 GDP 增长速度与各产业贡献率之乘积。

Contribution Share and Contribution of the Three Strata of Industry to GDP Growth

at constant price

第二产业 Secondary Industry		第三产业 Tertiary Industry		#工 业 Industry	
贡献率(%) Contribution Share(%)	拉动(百分点) Contribution (percentage points)	贡献率(%) Contribution Share(%)	拉动(百分点) Contribution (percentage points)	贡献率(%) Contribution Share(%)	拉动(百分点) Contribution (percentage points)
59.0	2.9	37.3	1.9	59.3	3.0
53.2	4.4	58.6	4.9	48.1	4.0
62.0	15.8	28.8	7.4	54.9	14.1
61.5	12.2	35.9	7.1	55.6	11.0
74.2	12.2	20.5	3.4	69.2	11.4
59.4	9.1	27.3	4.2	51.4	7.9
57.6	7.0	33.0	4.0	46.0	5.6
60.3	7.2	33.8	4.1	48.2	5.8
63.2	6.9	34.2	3.8	49.7	5.5
64.9	6.5	29.5	3.0	57.2	5.8
64.3	6.8	31.4	3.3	59.1	6.3
55.9	5.7	40.5	4.1	51.0	5.2
61.2	7.2	36.1	4.2	54.3	6.3
67.2	9.1	32.9	4.5	60.7	8.3
63.6	9.4	32.6	4.8	58.1	8.6
61.8	9.0	36.5	5.3	57.0	8.3
60.5	9.0	36.8	5.5	56.5	8.4
59.7	8.9	38.8	5.8	57.9	8.6
60.4	7.4	37.4	4.6	57.7	7.1
58.1	7.2	39.8	4.9	50.6	6.3
59.3	7.5	38.6	4.9	54.9	7.0
56.0	6.2	41.8	4.6	52.2	5.7
57.7	5.8	39.7	4.0	51.8	5.2
55.8	5.4	42.6	4.1	51.3	4.9
50.4	4.4	47.9	4.2	46.0	4.0
51.8	4.4	46.5	4.0	44.5	3.8
38.7	3.0	60.8	4.8	35.3	2.7

a) Industrial contribution ration refers to the proportion of the increment of the value-added of each industry to the increment of GDP.

b) Contribution of the three strata of industry to GDP growth refers to the growth rate of GDP multiplied by the contribution share of every industry.

2－12 分市地区生产总值
Gross Domestic Product by Region

本表按当年价格计算，单位：亿元 (at current price, 100 million yuan)

地区	Region	地区生产总值 Gross Domestic Product 2010	2011	2012	2013	2014	2015	2016
按地区分	**by City**							
南 京	Nanjing	5130.65	6145.52	7201.57	8080.21	8820.75	9720.77	10503.02
无 锡	Wuxi	5793.30	6880.15	7568.15	7770.23	8205.31	8518.26	9210.02
徐 州	Xuzhou	2942.14	3551.65	4016.58	4519.82	4963.91	5319.88	5808.52
常 州	Changzhou	3044.89	3580.99	3969.87	4450.00	4901.87	5273.15	5773.86
苏 州	Suzhou	9228.91	10716.99	12011.65	12970.00	13760.89	14504.07	15475.09
南 通	Nantong	3465.67	4080.22	4558.67	5150.01	5652.69	6148.40	6768.20
连云港	Lianyungang	1193.31	1410.52	1603.42	1810.49	1965.89	2160.64	2376.48
淮 安	Huaian	1388.07	1690.00	1920.91	2215.86	2455.39	2745.09	3048.00
盐 城	Yancheng	2332.76	2771.33	3120.00	3490.55	3835.62	4212.50	4576.08
扬 州	Yangzhou	2229.49	2630.30	2933.20	3320.00	3697.91	4016.84	4449.38
镇 江	Zhenjiang	1987.64	2311.45	2630.42	2975.06	3252.44	3502.48	3833.84
泰 州	Taizhou	2048.72	2422.61	2701.67	3064.97	3370.89	3687.90	4101.78
宿 迁	Suqian	1064.09	1320.83	1522.03	1750.28	1930.68	2126.19	2351.12
按区域分	**by Region**							
苏 南	Southern Jiangsu	25185.39	29635.09	33381.66	36245.50	38941.26	41518.73	44795.83
苏 中	Mid Jiangsu	7743.88	9133.14	10193.54	11534.98	12721.49	13853.14	15319.36
苏 北	Northern Jiangsu	8920.37	10744.32	12182.94	13787.01	15151.49	16564.30	18160.20

2－12 续 表1 Continued 1

本表按当年价格计算,单位:亿元 (at current price, 100 million yuan)

地　区 Region		第一产业增加值 Value-added of the Primary Industry						
		2010	2011	2012	2013	2014	2015	2016
按地区分	**by City**							
南　京	Nanjing	142.29	164.28	185.06	195.29	214.25	232.39	252.54
无　锡	Wuxi	104.94	122.98	137.22	130.40	138.13	137.72	135.19
徐　州	Xuzhou	282.82	334.54	382.46	418.88	473.54	504.76	542.88
常　州	Changzhou	99.78	111.78	126.37	130.33	138.46	146.55	152.67
苏　州	Suzhou	155.79	177.75	195.08	193.29	203.98	215.71	221.81
南　通	Nantong	266.22	287.21	319.09	322.31	339.57	354.90	366.66
连云港	Lianyungang	182.60	204.11	232.40	245.26	261.98	282.69	301.56
淮　安	Huaian	195.97	223.46	247.98	267.73	286.99	307.67	324.61
盐　城	Yancheng	374.21	416.83	456.13	464.06	489.50	516.53	533.91
扬　州	Yangzhou	161.37	184.54	205.19	212.79	227.36	241.86	251.39
镇　江	Zhenjiang	81.53	100.77	115.77	111.19	121.45	132.89	137.78
泰　州	Taizhou	151.65	175.11	191.75	198.51	209.25	218.93	240.00
宿　迁	Suqian	187.09	209.72	226.80	230.07	246.37	258.11	275.23
按区域分	**by Region**							
苏　南	Southern Jiangsu	584.33	677.56	759.50	760.50	816.27	865.26	899.99
苏　中	Mid Jiangsu	579.24	646.86	716.03	733.61	776.18	815.69	858.05
苏　北	Northern Jiangsu	1222.69	1388.65	1545.77	1626.00	1758.38	1869.76	1978.19

2-12 续 表2 Continued 2

本表按当年价格计算,单位:亿元 (at current price, 100 million yuan)

地 区 Region		第二产业增加值 Value-added of the Second Industry						
		2010	2011	2012	2013	2014	2015	2016
按地区分	**by City**							
南 京	Nanjing	2327.86	2760.84	3170.78	3462.42	3623.48	3916.77	4117.32
无 锡	Wuxi	3208.79	3728.12	4012.03	4044.93	4095.89	4197.43	4346.78
徐 州	Xuzhou	1490.92	1777.04	1968.52	2139.03	2246.24	2355.06	2513.85
常 州	Changzhou	1683.68	1950.84	2100.76	2273.41	2408.11	2516.04	2682.46
苏 州	Suzhou	5253.81	5957.74	6502.25	6757.81	6892.98	7045.12	7277.46
南 通	Nantong	1908.56	2221.48	2414.11	2658.38	2812.34	2977.53	3170.30
连云港	Lianyungang	545.07	654.28	736.14	816.46	889.68	959.00	1049.90
淮 安	Huaian	647.10	794.18	889.20	1005.60	1085.96	1176.66	1268.15
盐 城	Yancheng	1096.55	1306.26	1472.87	1634.57	1782.41	1923.47	2050.02
扬 州	Yangzhou	1229.34	1427.87	1554.46	1717.29	1885.75	2012.10	2197.63
镇 江	Zhenjiang	1120.63	1272.39	1419.54	1554.80	1631.10	1726.96	1870.40
泰 州	Taizhou	1125.85	1308.21	1434.53	1592.96	1697.45	1811.04	1933.89
宿 迁	Suqian	479.14	614.48	716.85	841.22	933.24	1031.33	1139.97
按区域分	**by Region**							
苏 南	Southern Jiangsu	13594.77	15669.93	17205.36	18093.37	18651.56	19402.32	20294.42
苏 中	Mid Jiangsu	4263.75	4957.56	5403.10	5968.63	6395.54	6800.67	7301.82
苏 北	Northern Jiangsu	4258.78	5146.24	5783.58	6436.87	6937.53	7445.52	8021.89

2-12 续 表3 Continued 3

本表按当年价格计算,单位:亿元 (at current price, 100 million yuan)

地 区 Region		第三产业增加值 Value-added of the Tertiary Industry						
		2010	2011	2012	2013	2014	2015	2016
按地区分	**by City**							
南 京	Nanjing	2660.49	3220.41	3845.73	4422.50	4983.02	5571.61	6133.16
无 锡	Wuxi	2479.57	3029.05	3418.90	3594.90	3971.29	4183.11	4728.05
徐 州	Xuzhou	1168.40	1440.07	1665.60	1961.91	2244.13	2460.07	2751.79
常 州	Changzhou	1261.43	1518.37	1742.74	2046.26	2355.30	2610.56	2938.73
苏 州	Suzhou	3819.31	4581.50	5314.32	6018.90	6663.93	7243.24	7975.82
南 通	Nantong	1290.89	1571.53	1825.47	2169.32	2500.78	2815.97	3231.24
连云港	Lianyungang	465.64	552.13	634.88	748.77	814.23	918.95	1025.02
淮 安	Huaian	545.00	672.36	783.73	942.53	1082.44	1260.76	1455.24
盐 城	Yancheng	862.00	1048.24	1191.00	1391.92	1563.71	1772.50	1992.15
扬 州	Yangzhou	838.78	1017.89	1173.55	1389.92	1584.80	1762.88	2000.36
镇 江	Zhenjiang	785.48	938.29	1095.11	1309.07	1499.89	1642.63	1825.66
泰 州	Taizhou	771.22	939.29	1075.39	1273.50	1464.19	1657.93	1927.89
宿 迁	Suqian	397.86	496.63	578.38	679.00	751.07	836.75	935.92
按区域分	**by Region**							
苏 南	Southern Jiangsu	11006.28	13287.61	15416.80	17391.63	19473.43	21251.15	23601.42
苏 中	Mid Jiangsu	2900.88	3528.72	4074.41	4832.74	5549.77	6236.78	7159.49
苏 北	Northern Jiangsu	3438.90	4209.43	4853.59	5724.13	6455.58	7249.03	8160.12

2-12 续 表4 Continued 4

本表按当年价格计算,单位:亿元 (at current price, 100 million yuan)

地区 Region		全部工业增加值 Value-added of the Industry						
		2010	2011	2012	2013	2014	2015	2016
按地区分	**by City**							
南　京	Nanjing	2005.21	2390.51	2748.46	2997.63	3119.12	3395.26	3581.72
无　锡	Wuxi	2986.52	3463.12	3717.88	3722.62	3747.59	3837.28	3977.58
徐　州	Xuzhou	1268.61	1509.82	1666.62	1807.98	1883.70	1976.57	2122.58
常　州	Changzhou	1530.86	1768.91	1900.55	2052.92	2170.19	2269.99	2428.84
苏　州	Suzhou	4916.49	5555.33	6055.10	6266.07	6360.14	6490.44	6709.02
南　通	Nantong	1568.49	1840.41	1992.11	2192.64	2307.64	2453.38	2633.06
连云港	Lianyungang	431.84	517.82	583.31	647.01	706.89	767.27	851.82
淮　安	Huaian	537.00	661.15	737.20	837.83	903.34	985.66	1071.99
盐　城	Yancheng	935.51	1111.50	1258.22	1399.02	1524.64	1653.90	1771.68
扬　州	Yangzhou	1074.61	1240.87	1344.66	1486.46	1634.48	1749.58	1925.92
镇　江	Zhenjiang	1039.78	1175.63	1309.54	1433.04	1498.41	1588.95	1728.00
泰　州	Taizhou	981.02	1132.27	1237.05	1376.30	1462.03	1565.28	1679.83
宿　迁	Suqian	386.37	502.57	589.82	701.18	780.91	873.04	976.89
按区域分	**by Region**							
苏　南	Southern Jiangsu	12478.86	14353.50	15731.53	16472.28	16895.45	17581.92	18425.16
苏　中	Mid Jiangsu	3624.12	4213.55	4573.82	5055.40	5404.15	5768.24	6238.81
苏　北	Northern Jiangsu	3559.33	4302.86	4835.17	5393.01	5799.48	6256.44	6794.96

2－12 续 表5 Continued 5

本表按当年价计算,单位:元 (at current price, yuan)

地 区 Region		人均地区生产总值(元) Per Capita GDP(yuan)						
		2010	2011	2012	2013	2014	2015	2016
按地区分	**by City**							
南 京	Nanjing	65273	76263	88525	98848	107545	118171	127264
无 锡	Wuxi	92167	107437	117357	120007	126389	130938	141258
徐 州	Xuzhou	34084	41407	46877	52694	57655	61511	66845
常 州	Changzhou	67327	77485	85040	94895	104423	112221	122721
苏 州	Suzhou	93043	102129	114029	123209	129925	136702	145556
南 通	Nantong	48083	56005	62506	70572	77457	84236	92702
连云港	Lianyungang	26987	32119	36470	40984	44277	48416	52987
淮 安	Huaian	28861	35181	39992	46020	50736	56460	62446
盐 城	Yancheng	31640	38222	43172	48150	53115	58299	63278
扬 州	Yangzhou	49786	58950	65691	74296	82654	89647	99151
镇 江	Zhenjiang	64284	73981	83651	94144	102652	110351	120603
泰 州	Taizhou	44118	52396	58378	66171	72706	79479	88330
宿 迁	Suqian	22525	27839	31827	36399	39963	43853	48311
按区域分	**by Region**							
苏 南	Southern Jiangsu	79501	90622	101370	109627	117477	125002	134569
苏 中	Mid Jiangsu	47422	55788	62208	70344	77532	84368	93228
苏 北	Northern Jiangsu	29774	36094	40914	46208	50603	55127	60225

2－13 分市地区生产总值构成
Composition of Gross Domestic Product by Region

本表按当年价格计算,单位:%　　(at current price, %)

地　区 Region		第一产业增加值 Value-added of the Primary Industry						
		2010	2011	2012	2013	2014	2015	2016
按地区分	**by City**							
南　京	Nanjing	2.8	2.7	2.6	2.4	2.4	2.4	2.4
无　锡	Wuxi	1.8	1.8	1.8	1.7	1.7	1.6	1.5
徐　州	Xuzhou	9.6	9.4	9.5	9.3	9.5	9.5	9.3
常　州	Changzhou	3.3	3.1	3.2	2.9	2.8	2.8	2.6
苏　州	Suzhou	1.7	1.7	1.6	1.5	1.5	1.5	1.4
南　通	Nantong	7.7	7.0	7.0	6.3	6.0	5.8	5.4
连云港	Lianyungang	15.3	14.5	14.5	13.5	13.3	13.1	12.7
淮　安	Huaian	14.1	13.2	12.9	12.1	11.7	11.2	10.6
盐　城	Yancheng	16.0	15.0	14.6	13.3	12.8	12.2	11.7
扬　州	Yangzhou	7.2	7.0	7.0	6.4	6.1	6.0	5.7
镇　江	Zhenjiang	4.1	4.4	4.4	3.7	3.7	3.8	3.6
泰　州	Taizhou	7.4	7.2	7.1	6.5	6.2	5.9	5.9
宿　迁	Suqian	17.6	15.9	14.9	13.1	12.8	12.1	11.7
按区域分	**by Region**							
苏　南	Southern Jiangsu	2.3	2.3	2.3	2.1	2.1	2.1	2.0
苏　中	Mid Jiangsu	7.5	7.1	7.0	6.4	6.1	5.9	5.6
苏　北	Northern Jiangsu	13.7	12.9	12.7	11.8	11.6	11.3	10.9

本表按当年价格计算，单位：%　　　　(at current price, %)

地 区 Region		第二产业增加值 Value-added of the Scondary Industry						
		2010	2011	2012	2013	2014	2015	2016
按地区分	**by City**							
南 京	Nanjing	45.4	44.9	44.0	42.9	41.1	40.3	39.2
无 锡	Wuxi	55.4	54.2	53.0	52.1	49.9	49.3	47.2
徐 州	Xuzhou	50.7	50.0	49.0	47.3	45.3	44.3	43.3
常 州	Changzhou	55.3	54.5	52.9	51.1	49.1	47.7	46.5
苏 州	Suzhou	56.9	55.6	54.1	52.1	50.1	48.6	47.0
南 通	Nantong	55.1	54.4	53.0	51.6	49.8	48.4	46.8
连云港	Lianyungang	45.7	46.4	45.9	45.1	45.3	44.4	44.2
淮 安	Huaian	46.6	47.0	46.3	45.4	44.2	42.9	41.6
盐 城	Yancheng	47.0	47.1	47.2	46.8	46.5	45.7	44.8
扬 州	Yangzhou	55.1	54.3	53.0	51.7	51.0	50.1	49.4
镇 江	Zhenjiang	56.4	55.0	54.0	52.3	50.2	49.3	48.8
泰 州	Taizhou	55.0	54.0	53.1	52.0	50.4	49.1	47.1
宿 迁	Suqian	45.0	46.5	47.1	48.1	48.3	48.5	48.5
按区域分	**by Region**							
苏 南	Southern Jiangsu	54.0	52.9	51.5	49.9	47.9	46.7	45.3
苏 中	Mid Jiangsu	55.1	54.3	53.0	51.7	50.3	49.1	47.7
苏 北	Northern Jiangsu	47.7	47.9	47.5	46.7	45.8	44.9	44.2

2-13 续 表2 Continued 2

本表按当年价格计算,单位:% (at current price, %)

地区	Region	第三产业增加值 Value-added of the Tertiary Industry						
		2010	2011	2012	2013	2014	2015	2016
按地区分	**by City**							
南京	Nanjing	51.9	52.4	53.4	54.7	56.5	57.3	58.4
无锡	Wuxi	42.8	44.0	45.2	46.2	48.4	49.1	51.3
徐州	Xuzhou	39.7	40.5	41.5	43.4	45.2	46.2	47.4
常州	Changzhou	41.4	42.4	43.9	46.0	48.1	49.5	50.9
苏州	Suzhou	41.4	42.7	44.2	46.4	48.4	49.9	51.5
南通	Nantong	37.2	38.5	40.0	42.1	44.2	45.8	47.7
连云港	Lianyungang	39.0	39.1	39.6	41.4	41.4	42.5	43.1
淮安	Huaian	39.3	39.8	40.8	42.5	44.1	45.9	47.7
盐城	Yancheng	37.0	37.8	38.2	39.9	40.7	42.1	43.5
扬州	Yangzhou	37.6	38.7	40.0	41.9	42.9	43.9	45.0
镇江	Zhenjiang	39.5	40.6	41.6	44.0	46.1	46.9	47.6
泰州	Taizhou	37.6	38.8	39.8	41.5	43.4	45.0	47.0
宿迁	Suqian	37.4	37.6	38.0	38.8	38.9	39.4	39.8
按区域分	**by Region**							
苏南	Southern Jiangsu	43.7	44.8	46.2	48.0	50.0	51.2	52.7
苏中	Mid Jiangsu	37.5	38.6	40.0	41.9	43.6	45.0	46.7
苏北	Northern Jiangsu	38.6	39.2	39.8	41.5	42.6	43.8	44.9

2－13 续 表3 Continued 3

本表按当年价格计算，单位：%　　（at current price，%）

地　区 Region		全部工业增加值 Value-added of the Tertiary Industry 2010	2011	2012	2013	2014	2015	2016
按地区分	**by City**							
南　京	Nanjing	39.1	38.9	38.2	37.1	35.4	34.9	34.1
无　锡	Wuxi	51.6	50.3	49.1	47.9	45.7	45.0	43.2
徐　州	Xuzhou	43.1	42.5	41.5	40.0	37.9	37.2	36.5
常　州	Changzhou	50.3	49.4	47.9	46.1	44.3	43.0	42.1
苏　州	Suzhou	53.3	51.8	50.4	48.3	46.2	44.7	43.4
南　通	Nantong	45.3	45.1	43.7	42.6	40.8	39.9	38.9
连云港	Lianyungang	36.2	36.7	36.4	35.7	36.0	35.5	35.8
淮　安	Huaian	38.7	39.1	38.4	37.8	36.8	35.9	35.2
盐　城	Yancheng	40.1	40.1	40.3	40.1	39.7	39.3	38.7
扬　州	Yangzhou	48.2	47.2	45.8	44.8	44.2	43.6	43.3
镇　江	Zhenjiang	52.3	50.9	49.8	48.2	46.1	45.4	45.1
泰　州	Taizhou	47.9	46.7	45.8	44.9	43.4	42.4	41.0
宿　迁	Suqian	36.3	38.0	38.8	40.1	40.4	41.1	41.5
按区域分	**by Region**							
苏　南	Southern Jiangsu	49.5	48.4	47.1	45.4	43.4	42.3	41.1
苏　中	Mid Jiangsu	46.8	46.1	44.9	43.8	42.5	41.6	40.7
苏　北	Northern Jiangsu	39.9	40.0	39.7	39.1	38.3	37.8	37.4

2－14 分市地区生产总值指数

Indices of Gross Domestic Product by Region

按可比价格计算，上年＝100　　　　　　　　(at constant price, preceding year＝100)

地区	Region	地区生产总值 Gross Domestic Product						
		2010	2011	2012	2013	2014	2015	2016
按地区分	**by City**							
南　京	Nanjing	113.1	112.0	111.7	111.0	110.1	109.3	108.0
无　锡	Wuxi	113.2	111.6	110.1	109.3	108.2	107.1	107.5
徐　州	Xuzhou	114.0	113.5	113.2	111.8	110.5	109.5	108.2
常　州	Changzhou	113.1	112.2	111.5	110.9	110.1	109.2	108.5
苏　州	Suzhou	113.3	112.0	110.1	109.6	108.3	107.5	107.5
南　通	Nantong	113.0	112.1	111.8	111.8	110.5	109.6	109.3
连云港	Lianyungang	113.6	113.0	112.7	111.8	110.2	110.8	107.8
淮　安	Huaian	113.8	113.2	113.1	112.0	110.9	110.3	109.0
盐　城	Yancheng	113.6	112.8	112.7	112.3	110.9	110.5	108.9
扬　州	Yangzhou	113.5	112.2	111.7	112.0	111.0	110.3	109.4
镇　江	Zhenjiang	113.3	112.3	112.8	112.1	110.9	109.6	109.3
泰　州	Taizhou	113.5	112.1	112.5	111.8	110.8	110.2	109.5
宿　迁	Suqian	113.7	112.8	113.0	112.5	110.8	110.0	109.1
按区域分	**by Region**							
苏　南	Southern Jiangsu	113.2	111.9	110.8	110.2	109.1	108.2	107.9
苏　中	Mid Jiangsu	113.3	112.1	112.0	111.8	110.7	110.0	109.4
苏　北	Northern Jiangsu	113.8	113.1	113.0	112.0	110.6	110.1	109.9

2－14 续 表1 Continued 1

按可比价格计算，上年＝100 （at constant price，preceding year＝100）

地区	Region	第一产业增加值 Value-added of the Primary Industry 2010	2011	2012	2013	2014	2015	2016
按地区分	**by City**							
南京	Nanjing	104.1	104.1	104.9	103.4	103.3	103.4	101.1
无锡	Wuxi	104.3	104.4	104.6	103.0	103.5	99.9	97.6
徐州	Xuzhou	104.2	104.5	105.1	103.3	103.7	103.4	102.0
常州	Changzhou	104.3	103.9	104.7	103.1	103.0	103.1	99.1
苏州	Suzhou	104.1	104.1	104.4	103.0	100.0	103.3	99.0
南通	Nantong	104.0	103.7	104.6	103.1	102.6	102.9	100.7
连云港	Lianyungang	105.1	104.0	105.7	103.1	103.3	103.6	101.6
淮安	Huaian	104.6	104.1	104.3	103.3	103.3	103.6	101.7
盐城	Yancheng	104.3	103.8	104.0	103.2	103.4	103.6	100.9
扬州	Yangzhou	104.5	104.0	105.2	104.6	103.6	103.6	100.0
镇江	Zhenjiang	104.5	105.5	105.2	103.2	103.7	103.6	100.2
泰州	Taizhou	104.5	104.3	104.4	103.1	103.3	103.4	101.4
宿迁	Suqian	105.3	104.3	104.3	103.0	103.3	103.4	102.0
按区域分	**by Region**							
苏南	Southern Jiangsu	104.2	104.3	104.7	103.2	102.5	102.8	99.5
苏中	Mid Jiangsu	104.3	104.0	104.7	103.5	103.0	103.2	100.7
苏北	Northern Jiangsu	104.6	104.1	104.6	103.2	103.4	103.5	101.6

2-14 续 表2 Continued 2

按可比价格计算，上年=100 (at constant price, preceding year=100)

地 区 Region		第二产业增加值 Value-added of the Secondary Industry						
		2010	2011	2012	2013	2014	2015	2016
按地区分	**by City**							
南 京	Nanjing	113.6	112.3	111.9	111.1	108.8	107.3	105.3
无 锡	Wuxi	113.1	111.6	109.3	108.7	106.5	105.0	106.8
徐 州	Xuzhou	115.7	114.6	114.5	112.3	108.9	109.8	108.7
常 州	Changzhou	113.2	112.2	111.7	111.2	109.5	108.5	107.4
苏 州	Suzhou	113.3	111.5	107.8	107.5	106.2	104.8	105.4
南 通	Nantong	113.7	112.4	112.4	112.0	110.3	109.7	109.0
连云港	Lianyungang	116.9	115.6	114.3	113.0	111.5	111.3	107.8
淮 安	Huaian	116.5	115.2	115.4	113.2	111.2	110.9	109.1
盐 城	Yancheng	116.8	114.8	115.2	114.0	111.8	110.5	109.2
扬 州	Yangzhou	114.6	112.6	112.1	112.3	111.0	110.6	108.3
镇 江	Zhenjiang	113.8	112.7	113.1	112.5	110.8	109.5	108.6
泰 州	Taizhou	114.5	112.5	113.1	112.1	110.5	110.2	108.8
宿 迁	Suqian	117.5	116.6	116.9	114.9	112.6	110.9	110.1
按区域分	**by Region**							
苏 南	Southern Jiangsu	113.3	111.8	109.8	109.3	107.6	106.2	106.2
苏 中	Mid Jiangsu	114.2	112.5	112.5	112.1	110.6	110.1	108.7
苏 北	Northern Jiangsu	116.4	115.1	115.1	113.3	110.8	110.5	107.7

2-14 续 表3 Continued 3

按可比价格计算，上年=100 (at constant price, preceding year=100)

地 区	Region	第三产业增加值 Value-added of the Tertary Industry						
		2010	2011	2012	2013	2014	2015	2016
按地区分	**by City**							
南 京	Nanjing	113.0	112.3	111.8	111.3	111.5	111.3	110.3
无 锡	Wuxi	113.7	111.8	111.3	110.3	110.3	109.6	108.6
徐 州	Xuzhou	114.2	114.5	113.4	112.8	113.6	110.2	109.1
常 州	Changzhou	113.6	112.8	111.6	111.2	111.5	110.6	110.1
苏 州	Suzhou	113.7	112.9	113.5	112.7	111.1	110.8	109.7
南 通	Nantong	113.6	113.2	112.3	112.9	112.0	110.5	110.6
连云港	Lianyungang	113.3	113.4	113.3	113.1	110.5	112.3	109.8
淮 安	Huaian	114.1	114.3	113.2	113.3	112.5	111.3	110.6
盐 城	Yancheng	113.6	114.0	112.9	113.4	112.0	112.5	110.8
扬 州	Yangzhou	113.9	113.2	112.1	112.7	112.0	110.7	112.0
镇 江	Zhenjiang	113.4	112.6	113.0	112.2	111.4	110.2	110.7
泰 州	Taizhou	113.9	113.1	113.0	112.7	112.3	111.2	111.4
宿 迁	Suqian	113.0	112.3	112.0	113.0	111.1	111.1	110.2
按区域分	**by Region**							
苏 南	Southern Jiangsu	113.5	112.5	112.3	111.6	111.1	110.6	109.7
苏 中	Mid Jiangsu	113.8	113.2	112.5	112.8	112.1	110.7	111.2
苏 北	Northern Jiangsu	113.8	113.9	113.1	113.1	112.3	111.3	110.1

2-14 续 表4 Continued 4

按可比价格计算，上年=100 (at constant price, preceding year=100)

地 区	Region	全部工业增加值 Value-added of the Industry						
		2010	2011	2012	2013	2014	2015	2016
按地区分	**by City**							
南 京	Nanjing	114.4	112.9	111.0	111.1	109.3	108.0	104.8
无 锡	Wuxi	113.2	111.7	109.0	109.0	106.5	104.8	107.0
徐 州	Xuzhou	116.1	115.6	114.4	113.1	109.2	109.5	109.4
常 州	Changzhou	113.3	112.6	111.7	111.6	109.8	108.3	107.7
苏 州	Suzhou	113.3	111.7	107.4	107.5	106.2	104.4	105.5
南 通	Nantong	114.3	112.9	112.3	112.3	111.1	109.5	109.6
连云港	Lianyungang	117.8	117.3	115.4	113.9	112.8	112.6	108.6
淮 安	Huaian	117.4	116.3	116.1	113.4	112.3	110.9	109.7
盐 城	Yancheng	117.0	115.0	115.7	115.1	112.5	110.7	109.9
扬 州	Yangzhou	114.8	113.0	111.8	113.2	111.5	110.5	108.7
镇 江	Zhenjiang	114.9	113.0	112.7	113.0	111.1	109.3	108.9
泰 州	Taizhou	114.6	112.9	113.2	112.8	110.9	110.0	109.4
宿 迁	Suqian	119.3	118.4	117.5	115.5	113.7	110.9	110.6
按区域分	**by Region**							
苏 南	Southern Jiangsu	113.6	112.1	109.4	109.4	107.7	106.1	106.3
苏 中	Mid Jiangsu	114.5	112.9	112.4	112.7	111.2	109.9	109.3
苏 北	Northern Jiangsu	117.0	116.0	115.4	114.0	111.5	110.6	108.0

2－15　按收入法计算的地区生产总值(2016年)

Income Approach Components of Gross Domestic Product (2016)

本表按当年价格计算,单位:亿元　　(at current price, 100 million yuan)

项　目	Item	增加值 Value Added	劳动者报酬 Compensation of Employees	生产税净额 Net Taxes on Production	固定资产折旧 Depreciation of Fixed Assets	营业盈余 Operating Surplus
地区生产总值	**Gross Domestic Product**	**76086.17**	**33697.24**	**10050.36**	**9676.57**	**22662.00**
按三次产业分	Grouped by Industry					
第一产业	Primary Industry	4077.18	4044.15		33.03	
第二产业	Secondary Industry	33550.54	12047.46	5504.13	4841.42	11157.53
第三产业	Tertiary Industry	38458.45	17605.63	4546.23	4802.12	11504.47
按行业分	Grouped by Sector					
农、林、牧、渔业	Agriculture, Forestry, Animal Husbandry and Fishery	4323.53	4288.50		35.03	
工业	Industry	29385.87	9292.76	4988.41	4744.15	10360.55
采矿业	Mining	153.87	78.48	39.64	54.01	－18.26
制造业	Manufacturing	27813.27	8895.77	4757.87	4252.32	9907.31
电力、热力、燃气及水的生产和供应业	Production and Supply of Electric Power, Heat Power, Gas and Water	1418.73	318.51	190.90	437.83	471.50
建筑业	Construction	4173.66	2756.64	517.98	98.86	800.18
批发和零售业	Wholesale and Retail Trades	7470.27	2941.76	2029.66	244.12	2254.73
交通运输、仓储和邮政业	Transport, Storage and Post	2834.56	1324.20	267.05	549.09	694.21
住宿和餐饮业	Hotels and Catering Services	1291.32	1080.58	67.14	56.93	86.67
信息传输、软件和信息技术服务业	Information Transfer, Software and IT Services	2443.22	892.97	146.77	379.78	1023.70
金融业	Financial Intermediation	6011.13	1527.95	504.49	145.89	3832.78
房地产业	Real Estate	4292.79	534.22	918.74	1780.09	1059.74
租赁和商务服务业	Leasing and Business Services	3451.12	1447.89	331.90	459.01	1212.31
科学研究和技术服务业	Scientific Research and Technical Services	1097.81	579.37	67.46	90.79	360.20
水利、环境和公共设施管理业	Management of Water Conservancy, Environment and Public Facilities	551.91	315.76	20.21	153.41	62.54
居民服务、修理和其他服务业	Services to Households and Other Services	1507.03	864.09	99.66	114.83	428.45

本表按当年价格计算,单位:亿元 (at current price, 100 million yuan)

项目	Item	增加值 Value Added	劳动者报酬 Compensation of Employees	生产税净额 Net Taxes on Production	固定资产折旧 Depreciation of Fixed Assets	营业盈余 Operating Surplus
教育	Education	2426.57	2087.18	8.73	278.12	52.53
卫生和社会工作	Healthcare and Social Welfare	1410.95	1088.71	7.43	133.57	181.24
文化、体育和娱乐业	Culture, Sports and Entertainment	795.79	391.55	57.01	130.99	216.25
公共管理、社会保障和社会组织	Public Management, Social Security and Organizations	2618.65	2283.09	17.73	281.90	35.92
按地区分	Grouped by Region					
南　京	Nanjing	10503.02	3928.14	2045.53	1515.27	3014.08
无　锡	Wuxi	9210.02	3435.49	1989.86	1181.01	2603.66
徐　州	Xuzhou	5808.52	2225.33	1080.52	723.67	1779.01
常　州	Changzhou	5773.86	2148.99	872.69	893.31	1858.87
苏　州	Suzhou	15475.09	5611.06	2800.21	2693.53	4370.30
南　通	Nantong	6768.20	2604.56	1285.50	824.91	2053.23
连云港	Lianyungang	2376.48	1015.44	364.23	316.25	680.56
淮　安	Huaian	3048.00	1356.29	460.25	426.23	805.23
盐　城	Yancheng	4576.08	2136.14	667.35	550.62	1221.97
扬　州	Yangzhou	4449.38	1687.34	697.66	852.79	1211.59
镇　江	Zhenjiang	3833.84	1716.14	477.41	522.41	1117.88
泰　州	Taizhou	4101.78	1809.57	614.43	436.25	1241.53
宿　迁	Suqian	2351.12	945.63	329.88	280.55	795.06

2-16 主要年份按收入法计算的地区生产总值
Income Approach Components of Gross Domestic Product in Major Years

本表按当年价格计算 (at current price)

年 份	地区生产总值(亿元) Gross Domestic Product (100 million yuan)	劳动者报酬 Compensation of Employees	生产税净额 Net Taxes on Production	固定资产折旧 Depreciation of Fixed Assets	营业盈余 Operating Surplus	占地区生产总值比重(%) 劳动者报酬 Compensation of Employees	生产税净额 Net Taxes on Production	固定资产折旧 Depreciation of Fixed Assets	营业盈余 Operating Surplus
1978	249.24	116.91	31.79	19.98	80.56	46.9	12.8	8.0	32.3
1980	319.80	152.29	45.96	23.90	97.65	47.6	14.4	7.5	30.5
1985	651.82	321.08	89.26	48.80	192.68	49.3	13.7	7.5	29.6
1990	1416.50	693.86	192.85	186.92	342.87	49.0	13.6	13.2	24.2
1991	1601.38	731.05	183.38	217.55	469.40	45.7	11.5	13.6	29.3
1992	2136.02	1015.80	268.62	280.87	570.73	47.6	12.6	13.1	26.7
1993	2998.16	1288.09	466.67	322.64	920.76	43.0	15.6	10.8	30.7
1994	4057.39	1827.96	590.40	440.18	1198.86	45.1	14.6	10.8	29.5
1995	5155.25	2427.68	684.68	624.90	1417.99	47.1	13.3	12.1	27.5
1996	6004.21	2840.19	774.39	739.10	1650.53	47.3	12.9	12.3	27.5
1997	6680.34	3162.19	889.95	871.54	1756.66	47.3	13.3	13.0	26.3
1998	7199.95	3372.60	942.41	981.85	1903.09	46.8	13.1	13.6	26.4
1999	7697.82	3531.22	998.28	1083.95	2084.36	45.9	13.0	14.1	27.1
2000	8553.69	3914.44	1107.55	1226.26	2305.44	45.8	12.9	14.3	27.0
2001	9456.84	4332.91	1229.29	1384.14	2510.50	45.8	13.0	14.6	26.5
2002	10606.85	4828.99	1390.24	1516.35	2871.27	45.5	13.1	14.3	27.1
2003	12442.87	5629.45	1732.06	1742.17	3339.18	45.2	13.9	14.0	26.8
2004	15003.60	6056.96	2357.46	2142.36	4446.81	40.4	15.7	14.3	29.6
2005	18598.69	7597.91	2622.82	3034.54	5343.42	40.9	14.1	16.3	28.7
2006	21742.05	8850.32	3370.48	3249.67	6271.58	40.7	15.5	14.9	28.8
2007	26018.48	9684.74	4317.14	3565.59	8451.01	37.2	16.6	13.7	32.5
2008	30981.98	12520.61	4912.90	4141.55	9406.92	40.4	15.9	13.4	30.4
2009	34457.30	15019.10	5420.70	4674.05	9343.45	43.6	15.7	13.6	27.1
2010	41425.48	17141.63	6278.34	5483.65	12521.86	41.4	15.2	13.2	30.2
2011	49110.27	20523.13	7272.03	6588.02	14727.09	41.8	14.8	13.4	30.0
2012	54058.22	22867.66	7862.22	7209.94	16118.40	42.3	14.6	13.3	29.8
2013	59753.37	25785.65	8096.73	7704.71	18166.28	43.2	13.6	12.9	30.3
2014	65088.32	28660.21	8697.30	8235.55	19495.26	44.0	13.4	12.7	29.9
2015	70116.38	31163.93	9146.17	8918.59	20887.69	44.4	13.1	12.7	29.8
2016	76086.17	33697.24	10050.36	9676.57	22662.00	44.3	13.2	12.7	29.8

2－17 按支出法计算的地区生产总值

Gross Domestic Product by Expenditure Approach

本表按当年价格计算，单位：亿元 (at current price, 100 million yuan)

年份 Year	地区生产总值 Gross Domestic Product	最终消费 Final Consumption Expenditures	居民消费 Household Consumption Expenditures	农村居民 Rural Household	城镇居民 Urban Household	政府消费 Government Consumption Expenditures	资本形成总额 Gross Capital Formation	固定资本形成 Fixed Capital Formation	存货增加 Changes in Inventories	货物和服务净出口 Net Export of Goods and Services
1978	249.24	130.55	115.15	76.11	39.04	15.40	77.98	40.40	37.58	40.71
1980	319.80	175.47	154.72	105.13	49.59	20.75	97.44	58.25	39.19	46.89
1985	651.82	353.72	300.86	219.98	80.88	52.86	271.42	193.25	78.17	26.68
1989	1321.85	662.01	557.60	386.40	171.20	104.41	528.44	336.24	192.20	131.40
1990	1416.50	717.36	608.29	403.29	205.00	109.07	588.44	374.12	214.32	110.70
1991	1601.38	835.07	656.99	423.60	233.39	178.08	694.80	461.98	232.82	71.51
1992	2136.02	960.21	735.62	459.99	275.63	224.59	1069.20	747.29	321.91	106.61
1993	2998.16	1251.08	984.44	569.94	414.50	266.64	1589.93	1201.41	388.52	157.15
1994	4057.39	1721.45	1350.89	782.19	568.70	370.56	2018.95	1434.95	584.00	316.99
1995	5155.25	2250.66	1806.43	1029.92	776.51	444.23	2479.30	1756.88	722.42	425.29
1996	6004.21	2721.84	2218.68	1314.01	904.67	503.16	2798.62	2062.17	736.45	483.75
1997	6680.34	3020.94	2417.77	1390.51	1027.26	603.17	2925.28	2295.97	629.31	734.12
1998	7199.95	3161.88	2513.52	1370.53	1142.99	648.36	3321.44	2642.29	679.15	716.63
1999	7697.82	3339.79	2594.18	1328.04	1266.14	745.61	3554.26	2842.65	711.61	803.77
2000	8553.69	3710.72	2815.51	1338.46	1477.05	895.21	4044.78	3225.42	819.36	798.19
2001	9456.84	4141.92	3027.67	1373.31	1654.36	1114.25	4393.21	3543.16	850.05	921.71
2002	10606.85	4801.91	3475.13	1505.92	1969.21	1326.78	4808.67	3994.23	814.44	996.27
2003	12442.87	5484.04	3909.55	1440.63	2468.92	1574.49	6182.38	5480.80	701.58	776.45
2004	15003.60	6227.21	4429.02	1369.38	3059.64	1798.19	7957.76	6972.68	985.08	818.63
2005	18598.69	7658.70	5339.09	1588.27	3750.82	2319.60	9462.30	8888.80	573.45	1477.70
2006	21742.05	9045.90	6236.42	1801.63	4434.79	2809.50	10721.70	10069.30	652.43	1974.40
2007	26018.48	10933.70	7328.19	2079.04	5249.15	3605.50	12504.50	11727.90	776.61	2580.30
2008	30981.98	12843.37	8425.61	2285.87	6139.74	4417.76	15017.72	14038.68	979.04	3120.89
2009	34457.30	14375.40	9235.38	2479.34	6756.04	5140.02	17571.90	17137.99	433.91	2510.00
2010	41425.48	17238.08	10942.82	2676.41	8266.41	6295.26	21173.29	20709.14	464.15	3014.11
2011	49110.27	20649.28	13534.19	3105.75	10428.44	7115.09	25049.05	24522.24	526.81	3411.94
2012	54058.22	22714.57	15385.57	3481.14	11904.43	7329.00	27258.07	26415.45	842.62	4085.58
2013	59753.37	26687.01	18889.19	4252.54	14636.65	7797.82	28920.65	27988.24	932.41	4145.71
2014	65088.32	31067.33	22510.56	4995.08	17515.48	8556.27	29799.68	28796.18	1003.50	4221.31
2015	70116.38	35041.42	25245.17	5556.09	19689.08	9796.25	30600.62	29940.82	659.80	4474.34

2-18 按支出法计算的地区生产总值构成

Composition of Gross Domestic Product by Expenditure Approach

本表按当年价格计算,单位:% (at current price,%)

年份 Year	地区生产总值 Gross Domestic Product	最终消费 Final Consumption Expenditures	居民消费 Household Consumption Expenditures	农村居民 Rural Household	城镇居民 Urban Household	政府消费 Government Consumption Expenditures	资本形成总额 Gross Capital Formation	固定资本形成 Fixed Capital Formation	存货增加 Changes in Inventories	货物和服务净出口 Net Export of Goods and Services
1978	100.0	52.4	46.2	30.5	15.7	6.2	31.3	16.2	15.1	16.3
1980	100.0	54.9	48.4	32.9	15.5	6.5	30.5	18.2	12.2	14.7
1985	100.0	54.3	46.2	33.8	12.4	8.1	41.6	29.6	12.0	4.1
1989	100.0	50.1	42.2	29.2	13.0	7.9	40.0	25.4	14.5	9.9
1990	100.0	50.6	42.9	28.5	14.5	7.7	41.5	26.4	15.1	7.8
1991	100.0	52.1	41.0	26.5	14.6	11.1	43.4	28.8	14.5	4.5
1992	100.0	45.0	34.4	21.5	12.9	10.5	50.1	35.0	15.1	5.0
1993	100.0	41.7	32.8	19.0	13.8	8.9	53.0	40.1	13.0	5.2
1994	100.0	42.4	33.3	19.3	14.0	9.1	49.8	35.4	14.4	7.8
1995	100.0	43.7	35.0	20.0	15.1	8.6	48.1	34.1	14.0	8.2
1996	100.0	45.3	37.0	21.9	15.1	8.4	46.6	34.3	12.3	8.1
1997	100.0	45.2	36.2	20.8	15.4	9.0	43.8	34.4	9.4	11.0
1998	100.0	43.9	34.9	19.0	15.9	9.0	46.1	36.7	9.4	10.0
1999	100.0	43.4	33.7	17.3	16.4	9.7	46.2	36.9	9.2	10.4
2000	100.0	43.4	32.9	15.6	17.3	10.5	47.3	37.7	9.6	9.3
2001	100.0	43.8	32.0	14.5	17.5	11.8	46.5	37.5	9.0	9.7
2002	100.0	45.3	32.8	14.2	18.6	12.5	45.3	37.7	7.7	9.4
2003	100.0	44.1	31.4	11.6	19.8	12.7	49.7	44.0	5.6	6.2
2004	100.0	41.5	29.5	9.1	20.4	12.0	53.0	46.5	6.6	5.5
2005	100.0	41.2	28.7	8.5	20.2	12.5	50.9	47.8	3.1	7.9
2006	100.0	41.6	28.7	8.3	20.4	12.9	49.3	46.3	3.0	9.1
2007	100.0	42.0	28.2	8.0	20.2	13.9	48.1	45.1	3.0	9.9
2008	100.0	41.5	27.2	7.4	19.8	14.3	48.5	45.3	3.2	10.1
2009	100.0	41.7	26.8	7.2	19.6	14.9	51.0	49.7	1.3	7.3
2010	100.0	41.6	26.4	6.5	20.0	15.2	51.1	50.0	1.1	7.3
2011	100.0	42.1	27.6	6.3	21.2	14.5	51.0	49.9	1.1	6.9
2012	100.0	42.0	28.5	6.5	22.0	13.5	50.4	48.9	1.5	7.6
2013	100.0	44.7	31.6	7.1	24.5	13.1	48.4	46.8	1.6	6.9
2014	100.0	47.7	34.6	7.7	26.9	13.1	45.8	44.2	1.5	6.5
2015	100.0	50.0	36.0	7.9	28.1	14.0	43.6	42.7	0.9	6.4

2-19 按支出法计算的地区生产总值指数

Indices of Gross Domestic Product by Expenditure Approach

按可比价格计算,1952 年 = 100 (at constant price with 100 in 1952)

年份 Year	地区生产总值指数 Gross Domestic Product	最终消费 Final Consumption Expenditures	居民消费 Household Consumption Expenditure	农村居民 Rural Household	城镇居民 Urban Household	政府消费 Government Consumption Expenditures	资本形成总额 Gross Capital Formation	固定资本形成 Fixed Capital Formation	存货增加 Changes in Inventories
1952	100.0	100.0	100.0	100.0	100.0	100.0	100.0	100.0	100.0
1978	371.3	367.6	352.3	290.1	607.8	545.3	695.7	593.2	847.1
1980	436.0	468.4	448.7	379.7	732.2	696.3	809.3	811.3	806.4
1985	809.2	824.0	757.4	693.7	1022.5	1595.0	2156.6	2573.0	1541.6
1989	1241.7	1000.3	885.3	757.8	1411.2	2331.2	3610.7	3998.6	3037.7
1990	1303.9	1063.7	949.6	791.9	1601.7	2383.2	4161.1	4791.5	3229.8
1991	1412.1	1162.8	992.5	806.8	1754.9	3246.0	4472.4	5230.2	3389.1
1992	1773.4	1493.5	1253.9	988.1	2337.9	4462.1	5534.2	7583.6	3054.8
1993	2124.4	1787.9	1518.0	1122.8	3114.8	5103.7	6603.7	9239.5	3450.0
1994	2474.3	2095.2	1772.7	1324.5	3585.7	6068.9	7772.3	10860.6	4074.8
1995	2855.3	2422.4	2027.1	1514.1	4102.3	7331.8	9053.4	12381.0	5022.8
1996	3204.5	2670.9	2261.5	1757.6	4311.6	7711.4	10229.2	14289.6	5367.3
1997	3587.6	2944.6	2444.1	1850.0	4851.4	9193.2	11375.3	16021.8	5834.1
1998	3982.8	3250.8	2677.4	1930.6	5686.3	10441.6	12662.2	18662.4	5645.7
1999	4384.8	3593.4	2889.2	1970.4	6573.2	12530.4	13870.1	20698.5	5922.1
2000	4848.4	3970.6	3107.9	1974.7	7632.5	15034.2	15272.9	22421.1	6900.9
2001	5340.5	4420.0	3371.3	2038.8	8640.9	18080.3	16765.7	24392.9	7841.6
2002	5963.5	4993.8	3714.3	2119.8	9963.0	21867.4	18721.5	28445.5	7294.1
2003	6775.9	5667.9	4176.3	2025.7	12455.3	25417.8	21744.0	35873.5	5035.9
2004	7775.4	6452.9	4780.6	1967.3	15489.1	28542.9	25319.8	41206.1	6550.7
2005	8902.8	7391.4	5459.3	2101.1	18199.6	32947.9	28664.5	50217.2	3093.4
2006	10229.3	8581.4	6212.7	2330.1	20929.6	40097.6	32047.0	56193.1	3449.2
2007	11753.5	9963.0	7045.2	2586.4	23943.5	48999.3	35956.7	62823.8	4049.3
2008	13246.1	11328.0	7806.0	2777.8	26840.6	58505.2	39768.1	68603.6	5312.7
2009	14895.3	13038.5	8875.5	3138.9	30598.3	68743.6	45812.9	83010.4	2353.5
2010	16787.0	14889.9	10011.5	3229.9	35677.6	80155.0	51264.6	93137.7	2403.0
2011	18633.6	16870.3	11483.2	3481.9	41707.1	88811.7	56647.4	103010.3	2573.6
2012	20515.5	18861.0	13159.8	3924.0	48046.6	94762.1	62142.2	112796.2	3168.1
2013	22485.0	20973.4	15383.8	4563.7	56214.6	94951.7	67797.1	122947.9	3605.3
2014	24441.2	23091.7	17260.6	5056.6	63297.5	100079.0	73356.5	133029.6	3980.3
2015	26518.7	25470.2	19073.0	5537.0	70070.3	110187.0	78931.6	144603.2	2642.9

主要统计指标解释

可比价格 指计算各种总量指标所采用的扣除了价格变动因素的价格，可进行不同时期总量指标的对比。按可比价格计算总量指标有两种方法：一种是直接用产品产量乘某一年的不变价格计算；另一种是用价格指数进行缩减。

不变价格 指以同类产品某年的平均价格作为固定价格，用于计算各年的产品价值。按不变价格计算的产品价值消除了价格变动因素，不同时期对比可以反映生产的发展速度。新中国成立后，随着工农业产品价格水平的变化，国家统计局先后六次制定了全国统一的工业产品不变价格和农业产品不变价格。从 1952 年到 1957 年使用 1952 年工(农)业产品不变价格，从 1957 年到 1970 年使用 1957 年不变价格，从 1971 年到 1980 年使用 1970 年不变价格，从 1981 年到 1990 年使用 1980 年不变价格，从 1991 年到 2000 年使用 1990 年不变价格，从 2001 年到 2005 年使用 2000 年不变价格，从 2006 年到 2010 年使用 2005 年不变价格，从 2011 年到 2015 年使用 2010 年不变价格，目前使用的是 2015 年不变价格。

国内生产总值(GDP) 指一个国家所有常住单位在一定时期内生产活动的最终成果。国内生产总值有三种表现形态，即价值形态、收入形态和产品形态。从价值形态看，它是所有常住单位在一定时期内生产的全部货物和服务价值超过同期中间投入的全部非固定资产货物和服务价值的差额，即所有常住单位的增加值之和；从收入形态看，它是所有常住单位在一定时期内创造并分配给常住单位和非常住单位的初次收入分配之和；从产品形态看，它是所有常住单位在一定时期内最终使用的货物和服务价值与货物和服务净出口价值之和。在实际核算中，国内生产总值有三种计算方法，即生产法、收入法和支出法。三种方法分别从不同的方面反映国内生产总值及其构成。对于地区，GDP 中文名称为"地区生产总值"。

支出法国内生产总值 指一个国家所有常住单位在一定时期内用于最终消费、资本形成总额，以及货物和服务的净出口总额，它反映本期生产总值的使用及构成。对于地区，名称为"支出法地区生产总值"。

最终消费 指常住单位在一定时期内对于货物和服务的全部最终消费支出，也就是常住单位为满足物质、文化和精神生活的需要，从本国经济领土和国外购买的货物和服务的支出；不包括非常住单位在本国经济领土内的消费支出。最终消费分为居民消费和政府消费。

居民消费 指常住住户对货物和服务的全部最终消费支出。居民消费按市场价格计算，即按居民支付的购买者价格计算。购买者价格是购买者取得货物所支付的价格，包括购买者支付的运输和商业费用。居民消费除了直接以货币形式购买货物和服务的消费之外，还包括以其他方式获得的货物和服务的消费支出，即所谓的虚拟消费支出。居民虚拟消费支出包括以下几种类型：单位以实物报酬及实物转移的形式提供给劳动者的货物和服务；住户生产并由本住户消费了的货物和服务，其中的服务仅指住户的自有住房服务；金融机构提供的金融媒介服务；保险公司提供的保险服务。

政府消费 指政府部门为全社会提供公共服务的消费支出和免费或以较低价格向住户提供的货物和服务的净支出。前者等于政府服务的产出价值减去政府单位所获得的经营收入的价值，政府服务的产出价值等于它的经常性业务支出加上固定资产折旧；后者等于政府部门免费或以较低价格向住户提供的货物和服务的市场价值减去向住户收取的价值。

资本形成总额 指常住单位在一定时期内获得的减去处置的固定资产加存货的变动，包括固定资本形成总额和存货增加。

固定资本形成总额 指常住单位购置、转入和自产自用的固定资产，扣除固定资产的销售和转出后的价值，分有形固定资产形成总额和无形固定资产形成总额。有形固定资产形成总额包括一定时期内完成的建筑工程、安装工程和设备工器具购置(减处置)价值，以及土地改良、新增役、种、奶、毛、娱乐用牲畜和新增经济林木价值。无形固定资产形成总额包括矿藏的勘探、计算机软件、娱乐和文学艺术品原件等获得减处置。

存货增加 指常住单位存货实物量变动的市场价值，即期末价值减期初价值的差额。存货增加可以是正值，也可以是负值；正值表示存货上升，负值表示存货下降。它包括生产单位购进的原材料、燃料和储备物资等存货，以及生产单位生产的产成品、在制品等存货等。

货物和服务净出口 指货物和服务出口减货物和服务进口的差额。出口包括常住单位向非常住单位出售或无偿转让的各种货物和服务的价值；进口包括常住单位从非常住单位购买或无偿得到的各种货物和服务的价值。由于服务活动的提供与使用同时发生，因此服务的进出口业务并不发生出入境现象，一般把常住单位从国外得到的服务作为进口，非常住单位从本国得到的服务作为出口。货物的出口和进口都按离岸价格计算。

Explanatory Notes on Main Statistical Indicators

Comparable Prices refer to prices that are used to remove the factors of price change in calculating economic aggregates, so as to facilitate comparison of aggregates over time. Two methods are used for calculating economic aggregates at comparable prices: 1. Multiplying the output of products by their constant prices of certain year;2. Deflation of data at current prices by relevant price index.

Constant Price refers to the average price of a given product in certain year, which is used for comparison of output value over time. As the output value at constant prices removes the factor of price changes, it reflects the trend of production development over time. Since 1949, with the changes in general price level, National Bureau of Statistics has issued nationally unified constant prices six times: the 1952 constant prices for 1952—1957; the 1957 constant prices for 1957—1970; the 1970 constant prices for 1971—1980; the 1980 constant prices for 1981—1990; the 1990 constant prices for 1991—2000; the 2000 constant prices for 2001—2005; the 2005 constant prices for 2006—2010, the 2010 constant prices for 2011—2015, the 2015 constant prices for now.

Gross Domestic Product(GDP) refers to the final products of all resident units in a country during a certain period of time. Gross domestic product is expressed in three different forms, i. e. value, income, and products respectively. The form of value refers to the total value of all products and services produced by all resident units during a certain period of time minus total value of intimidate input of materials and services of the nature of non-fixed assets or the summation of the value-added of all resident units; the form of income includes all the income created by all resident units and distributed primarily to all resident and non-resident units; the form of products refers to the value of all final goods and services for final use by all resident units plus the value of net exports of goods and services during a given period of time. In the practice of national accounting, gross domestic product is calculated with three approaches, i. e. production approach, income approach, and expenditure approach, which reflect gross domestic product and its composition from different aspects. The Chinese meaning of "GDP" is "Gross Regional Product" as to the certain region.

GDP Calculated with Expenditure Approach refers to total expenditure on final consumption, total capital formation and net export of goods and services by resident units of a country in a certain period of time. It reflects the composition of GDP by its use.

Final Consumption refers to the total expenditure of resident units on final consumption of goods and services in a certain period, namely the expenditure of the resident units for purchases of goods and services from domestic economic territory and abroad to meet the requirements of material, cultural and spiritual life. It excludes the expenditure of non-resident units on consumption in the economic territory of the country. The final consumption is classified into household consumption and government consumption.

Households Consumption refers to the total expenditure of resident households on the final consumption of goods and services. The households consumption is calculated at market prices, namely the purchasers prices which the households pay; the purchasers prices of goods are the prices the households pay when they obtain the goods, including the transport and commercial expenses paid by the households. In addition to the consumption of goods and services bought by the households directly with money, the expenditure on goods and services obtained by the households in other ways, i. e. the so-called imputed expenditure on consumption, is also included in the households consumption. The imputation expenditure of the households on consumption includes the following types: (a) the goods and services provided to the households by the units in the form of payment in kind and transfer in kind; (b) the goods and services produced and consumed by the households themselves, in which the services refer only to the services provided by the residential buildings owned by the households; (c) the services of financial intermediary provided by the financial institutions; (d) the insurance services provided by the insurance companies.

Government Consumption refers to the expenditure on the consumption of the public services provided by the government to the whole society and the net expenditure on the goods and services provided by the government to the households at free charge or lower prices. The former equals to the output value of the government services minus the value of operating income obtained by the government departments. (The output value of the government services equals to its current operating expenditure plus depreciation of fixed assets). The latter equals to the market value of the goods and services provided by the government free of charge or at low prices to the households minus the value received by the government from the households.

Total Capital Formation refers to the fixed assets acquired minus those disposed and the change in inventory, including the total fixed assets formation and the increase in inventory.

Total Fixed Capital Formation refers to the value of fixed assets purchased, transferred in by the resident units and those produced and used by themselves deducting the value of fixed assets sold and transferred out. It can be classified into total tangible assets formation and total intangible assets formation. The total tangible assets formation include the value of the construction projects, installation projects completed and the equipment, apparatus and instruments purchased as well as the value of land improved, the value of draught animals, breeding stock, milk, wool and recreational animals and the newly increased economic forest in a certain period. The total intangible assets formation includes the prospecting of minerals, the acquisition of computer software, the originals of recreational works and works of literature and arts minus the disposal of them. Increase in Inventory refers to the market value of the change in inventory, i. e. the difference of value between the beginning and the end of the period. The increase in inventory can be positive or negative. A positive value indicates the increase in inventory while a negative value indicates the decrease in stock. The inventory includes the raw materials, fuels and reserve materials purchased by the production units as well as the inventory of finished products, semi-finished products, work in progress. etc.

Increase in Inventory refers to the market value of the change in inventory, i. e. The difference of value between the beginning and the end of the period. The increase in inventory can be positive or negative. A positive value indicates the increase in inventory while a negative value indicates the decrease in stock. The inventory includes the materials, fuels and reserve materials purchased by the production units as well as the inventory of finished products, semi-finished products, work-in-progress, ect.

Net Export of Goods and Services refers to the difference of the exports of goods and services minus the imports of goods and services. The imports include the value of various goods and services sold or gratuitously transferred by the resident units to the non-resident units. The imports include the value of various goods and services purchased or gratuitously acquired by the resident units from the non-resident units. Because the provision of services and the use of them happen simultaneously, the import and export of services do not appear to have the phenomena of crossing the border of the country. The acquisition of services by the resident units from abroad is usually treated as import while the acquisition of services by non-resident units in this country is usually treated as export. The export and import of goods are calculated at FOB.

3

人口、就业和工资

Population, Employment and Wages

简　要　说　明

一、本篇资料主要内容

本篇资料反映我省2016年及历年人口就业和职工工资方面的基本情况。

二、本篇资料来源

1. 人口资料：表3－1、表3－2、表3－3为年末主要人口推算数据，其中2001—2009年数据根据第六次人口普查作了修订；表3－4为公安户籍资料；表3－5为六次人口普查主要数据；表3－6为年末常住人口推算数据；表3－7至表3－10为2016年人口抽样调查样本数据。

2. 就业基本情况及分组资料、工资总额等资料，根据《劳动统计报表制度》、《劳动力调查制度》等搜集资料，加工整理。

3. 私营企业及个体工商业就业人员，由工商行政管理部门提供。城镇登记失业人数，由人力资源和社会保障部门整理提供。

三、本篇统计调查方法

1. 人口资料采用抽样调查方法和人口普查资料进行整理。

2. 城镇单位（不含私营个体）统计资料采用全面调查方法；私营企业和个体工商户资料利用行政登记资料进行汇总。

Brief Introduction

I. Main Contents

Data in this chapter show the basic condition of the population, employment and wages in 2016 as well as previous years for the province.

II. Sources of Data

1. Data on population: Data in tables 3－1, 3－2 and 3－3 are estimated from the main population at year-end, figures for 2001—2009 have been revised in line with the data from the sixth National Population Census; data in table 3－4 are household registered population from department of public security; data in table 3－5 present the main results from the sixth National Population Censuses; data in table 3－6 are estimation of permanent population at year-end; data in tables 3－7 to 3－10 are the data of change of population sampling survey in 2016.

2. Data on basic conditions of employment, data by groups, total wage bills of staff and workers are collected and compiled through *The Reporting Form System on Labour Statistics*, *The Sample Survey System on Labour Force*.

3. Data on the number of employed persons in private enterprises and self-employed individuals are provided by the administration for industry and commerce.

III. Methodology of Survey

1. Data on population are collected by sampling survey and compiled according to the population censuses.

2. A complete reporting is used in the employed persons in urban units (excluded private and individual units). Private enterprises and self-employed individuals are collected and compiled on basis of administrative registering records. The sampling survery on wage statistics of private enterprises is conducted by using sampling methods.

3-1 全省人口数、户数(常住)

Population and Households(Permanent)

年 份 Year	总户数(万户) Households (10000 households)	总人口(万人) Total Population (10000 persons)	按性别分 Grouped by Sex 男 Male 人口数(万人) Population (10000 persons)	比重(%) Proportion	女 Female 人口数(万人) Population (10000 persons)	比重(%) Proportion	平均每户人数(人/户) Average Family Size (person/households)	年平均人口(万人) Average Annual Population (10000 persons)	人口密度(人/平方公里) Density of Population (person/sq. km)
1990	1806.78	6766.90	3443.68	50.89	3323.22	49.11	3.75		660
1991	1859.70	6843.70	3451.96	50.44	3391.74	49.56	3.68	6805.30	667
1992	1957.85	6911.20	3483.24	50.40	3427.96	49.60	3.53	6877.45	674
1993	1893.28	6967.27	3513.59	50.43	3453.68	49.57	3.68	6939.24	679
1994	1923.44	7020.54	3534.09	50.34	3486.45	49.66	3.65	6993.91	684
1995	2066.09	7066.02	3589.56	50.80	3476.46	49.20	3.42	7043.28	689
1996	2014.21	7110.16	3610.72	50.78	3499.44	49.22	3.53	7088.09	693
1997	2133.69	7147.86	3628.08	50.76	3519.78	49.24	3.35	7129.01	697
1998	2087.92	7182.46	3643.21	50.72	3539.26	49.28	3.44	7165.16	700
1999	2121.51	7213.13	3656.05	50.69	3557.08	49.31	3.40	7197.80	703
2000	2220.38	7327.24	3710.28	50.64	3616.96	49.36	3.30	7270.19	714
2001	2314.00	7358.52	3724.81	50.62	3633.71	49.38	3.18	7342.88	717
2002	2350.96	7405.50	3752.03	50.67	3653.47	49.33	3.15	7382.01	722
2003	2345.19	7457.70	3775.26	50.62	3682.44	49.38	3.18	7431.60	727
2004	2388.23	7522.95	3811.87	50.67	3711.08	49.33	3.15	7490.33	733
2005	2463.60	7588.24	3795.64	50.02	3792.60	49.98	3.08	7555.59	740
2006	2485.61	7655.66	3829.47	50.02	3826.19	49.98	3.08	7621.95	746
2007	2507.51	7723.13	3863.09	50.02	3860.03	49.98	3.08	7689.40	753
2008	2504.03	7762.48	3883.33	50.03	3879.15	49.97	3.10	7742.81	756
2009	2519.44	7810.27	3908.18	50.04	3902.09	49.96	3.10	7786.38	761
2010	2564.59	7869.34	3964.31	50.38	3905.03	49.62	3.07	7839.80	767
2011	2572.90	7898.80	3977.69	50.36	3921.11	49.64	3.07	7884.07	770
2012	2588.23	7919.98	3987.91	50.35	3932.07	49.65	3.06	7909.40	772
2013	2593.31	7939.49	3997.09	50.34	3942.40	49.66	3.06	7929.74	774
2014	2601.33	7960.06	4007.09	50.34	3952.97	49.66	3.06	7949.78	742
2015	2617.80	7976.30	4014.65	50.33	3961.65	49.67	3.05	7968.18	744
2016	2621.20	7998.60	4025.66	50.33	3972.94	49.67	3.05	7987.45	746

3-2 全省市、镇、乡村人口数及其构成

City, Town, Country Population and It's Composition

单位:万人 (10000 persons)

年 份 Year	总人口数 Total Population	#城镇人口 Urban		市 City		镇 Town		乡村 Rural	
		人口数 Population	占总人口% Proportion	人口数 Population	占总人口% Proportion	人口数 Population	占总人口% Proportion	人口数 Population	占总人口% Proportion
1978	5834.32	800.77	13.7	570.14	9.8	230.63	3.9	5033.55	86.3
1980	5938.19	901.78	15.2	636.41	10.7	265.37	4.5	5036.41	84.8
1985	6213.48	1099.79	17.7	0.00	0.0	0.00	0.0	5113.69	82.3
1990	6766.90	1458.94	21.6	1043.45	15.4	415.49	6.1	5307.96	78.5
1991	6843.70	1587.74	23.2	1163.43	17.0	424.31	6.2	5255.96	76.8
1992	6911.20	1643.72	23.8	1182.59	17.1	461.13	6.7	5267.48	76.2
1993	6967.27	1673.58	24.0	1199.26	17.2	474.32	6.8	5293.69	76.0
1994	7020.54	1733.01	24.7	1255.58	17.9	477.43	6.8	5287.53	75.3
1995	7066.02	1929.09	27.3	1331.30	18.8	597.79	8.5	5136.93	72.7
1996	7110.16	1942.50	27.3	1328.18	18.7	614.32	8.6	5167.66	72.7
1997	7147.86	2133.64	29.9	1465.31	20.5	668.33	9.4	5014.22	70.1
1998	7182.46	2262.47	31.5	1537.05	21.4	725.42	10.1	4919.99	68.5
1999	7213.13	2520.09	34.9	1685.84	23.4	834.25	11.6	4693.04	65.1
2000	7327.24	3040.81	41.5	1868.45	25.5	1172.36	16.0	4286.43	58.5
2001	7358.52	3134.73	42.6	1927.93	26.2	1206.80	16.4	4223.79	57.4
2002	7405.50	3310.25	44.7	2028.37	27.4	1281.89	17.3	4095.25	55.3
2003	7457.70	3487.97	46.8	2137.38	28.7	1350.59	18.1	3969.73	53.2
2004	7522.95	3624.56	48.2	2174.73	28.9	1449.82	19.3	3898.39	51.8
2005	7588.24	3832.06	50.5	2307.80	30.4	1524.26	20.1	3756.18	49.5
2006	7655.66	3973.29	51.9	2392.85	31.3	1580.44	20.6	3682.37	48.1
2007	7723.13	4108.70	53.2	2474.33	32.0	1634.37	21.2	3614.43	46.8
2008	7762.48	4215.17	54.3	2538.45	32.7	1676.72	21.6	3547.31	45.7
2009	7810.27	4342.51	55.6	2619.43	33.5	1723.08	22.1	3467.76	44.4
2010	7869.34	4767.63	60.6	3012.38	38.3	1755.25	22.3	3101.71	39.4
2011	7898.80	4889.36	61.9	3095.45	39.2	1793.91	22.7	3009.44	38.1
2012	7919.98	4990.09	63.0	3160.07	39.9	1830.02	23.1	2929.89	37.0
2013	7939.49	5090.01	64.1	3223.43	40.6	1866.58	23.5	2849.48	35.9
2014	7960.06	5190.76	65.2	3258.18	40.9	1932.58	24.3	2769.30	34.8
2015	7976.30	5305.83	66.5	3286.24	41.2	2019.59	25.3	2670.47	33.5
2016	7998.60	5416.65	67.7	3336.62	41.7	2080.03	26.0	2581.95	32.3

3-3 全省人口自然变动
Natural Change of Population

年　份 Year	出　生 Birth		死　亡 Death		自然增长 Natural Growth	
	人数(万人) Population (10000 persons)	出生率(‰) Birth Rate (‰)	人数(万人) Population (10000 persons)	死亡率(‰) Death Rate (‰)	人数(万人) Population (10000 persons)	自然增长率(‰) Natural Growth Rate (‰)
1978	90.62	15.63	35.32	6.09	55.30	9.54
1979	85.79	14.63	34.31	5.85	51.48	8.78
1980	86.90	14.69	38.87	6.57	48.03	8.12
1981	100.58	16.83	37.18	6.22	63.40	10.61
1982	99.42	16.43	34.77	5.75	64.65	10.68
1983	73.17	11.97	36.39	5.95	36.78	6.02
1984	64.09	10.42	36.32	5.90	27.77	4.52
1985	67.11	10.84	36.35	5.87	30.76	4.97
1986	82.38	13.20	36.19	5.80	46.19	7.40
1987	97.27	15.42	36.50	5.79	60.77	9.63
1988	102.46	16.03	37.65	5.89	64.81	10.14
1989	111.27	17.15	36.31	5.60	74.96	11.55
1990	137.96	20.54	43.86	6.53	94.10	14.01
1991	116.03	17.05	44.23	6.50	71.80	10.55
1992	108.04	15.71	46.49	6.76	61.55	8.95
1993	96.94	13.97	45.87	6.61	51.07	7.36
1994	96.38	13.78	47.98	6.86	48.40	6.92
1995	86.77	12.32	46.20	6.56	40.57	5.76
1996	85.84	12.11	46.64	6.58	39.20	5.53
1997	81.47	11.43	48.76	6.84	32.71	4.59
1998	78.60	10.97	49.01	6.84	29.59	4.13
1999	75.58	10.50	49.95	6.94	25.63	3.56
2000	66.01	9.08	47.40	6.52	18.61	2.56
2001	66.31	9.03	48.61	6.62	17.70	2.41
2002	67.69	9.17	51.60	6.99	16.09	2.18
2003	67.18	9.04	52.24	7.03	14.94	2.01
2004	70.78	9.45	53.93	7.20	16.85	2.25
2005	69.81	9.24	53.12	7.03	16.70	2.21
2006	71.34	9.36	53.96	7.08	17.38	2.28
2007	72.05	9.37	54.36	7.07	17.69	2.30
2008	72.32	9.34	54.51	7.04	17.81	2.30
2009	74.36	9.55	54.43	6.99	19.93	2.56
2010	76.31	9.73	53.94	6.88	22.37	2.85
2011	75.61	9.59	55.03	6.98	20.58	2.61
2012	74.67	9.44	55.29	6.99	19.38	2.45
2013	74.86	9.44	55.59	7.01	19.27	2.43
2014	75.13	9.45	55.81	7.02	19.32	2.43
2015	72.11	9.05	56.02	7.03	16.09	2.02
2016	77.96	9.76	56.15	7.03	21.81	2.73

3-4 全省人口数、户数(户籍)

Population and Households(Registered)

年份 Year	总户数(万户) Households (10000 households)	总人口(万人) Total Population (10000 persons)	按性别分 Grouped by Sex				平均每户人数(人/户) Average Family Size (person/ households)	年平均人口(万人) Average Annual Population (10000 persons)	人口密度(人/平方公里) Density of Population (person/ sq. km)
			男 Male		女 Female				
			人口数(万人) Population (10000 persons)	比重(%) Proportion (%)	人口数(万人) Population (10000 persons)	比重(%) Proportion (%)			
1949	838.00	3512.00	1778.80	50.65	1733.20	49.35	4.19		342
1952	888.00	3739.00	1891.60	50.59	1847.40	49.41	4.21	3697.50	364
1957	985.51	4182.71	2087.06	49.90	2095.65	50.10	4.24	4136.05	408
1962	1089.51	4333.74	2155.01	49.70	2178.73	50.30	3.98	4288.57	422
1965	1110.13	4623.74	2319.92	50.17	2303.82	49.83	4.17	4567.75	451
1970	1215.28	5252.09	2635.02	50.17	2617.07	49.83	4.32	5185.36	512
1975	1315.55	5636.12	2842.86	50.44	2793.26	49.56	4.28	5600.91	549
1980	1471.76	5938.19	3003.75	50.58	2934.44	49.42	4.03	5915.37	579
1985	1633.62	6213.48	3168.25	50.99	3045.23	49.01	3.80	6192.46	606
1990	1956.89	6671.73	3406.33	51.06	3265.40	48.94	3.41	6618.80	650
1991	1987.55	6733.87	3439.29	51.07	3294.58	48.93	3.39	6702.80	656
1992	2015.17	6767.49	3457.77	51.09	3309.72	48.91	3.36	6750.68	660
1993	2034.87	6800.69	3476.26	51.12	3324.43	48.88	3.34	6784.09	663
1994	2055.96	6831.28	3491.72	51.11	3339.56	48.89	3.32	6815.99	666
1995	2085.96	6868.42	3509.59	51.10	3358.83	48.90	3.29	6849.85	669
1996	2113.07	6908.13	3528.95	51.08	3379.19	48.92	3.27	6888.28	673
1997	2146.87	6948.36	3537.04	50.90	3411.32	49.10	3.24	6928.25	677
1998	2186.70	6983.09	3565.55	51.06	3417.54	48.94	3.19	6965.73	681
1999	2221.70	7009.09	3577.71	51.04	3431.37	48.96	3.15	6996.09	683
2000	2268.56	7069.28	3602.92	50.97	3466.36	49.03	3.12	7039.19	689
2001	2300.83	7097.00	3616.16	50.95	3480.84	49.05	3.08	7083.14	692
2002	2323.06	7127.33	3631.10	50.95	3496.23	49.05	3.07	7112.17	695
2003	2344.84	7163.93	3646.60	50.90	3517.33	49.10	3.06	7145.63	698
2004	2359.61	7206.05	3663.62	50.84	3542.43	49.16	3.05	7184.99	702
2005	2382.21	7252.88	3686.09	50.82	3566.79	49.18	3.04	7229.47	707
2006	2390.18	7317.72	3715.24	50.77	3602.48	49.23	3.06	7285.30	713
2007	2390.55	7354.08	3733.67	50.77	3620.41	49.23	3.08	7335.90	717
2008	2399.15	7388.63	3750.38	50.77	3638.25	49.23	3.08	7371.36	720
2009	2403.89	7419.23	3765.32	50.75	3653.91	49.25	3.09	7403.93	723
2010	2417.01	7466.59	3787.73	50.73	3678.86	49.27	3.09	7442.91	728
2011	2425.11	7514.25	3811.84	50.73	3702.41	49.27	3.10	7490.42	732
2012	2416.27	7553.48	3832.55	50.74	3720.93	49.26	3.12	7533.87	736
2013	2423.54	7616.84	3863.48	50.72	3753.36	49.28	3.14	7585.16	742
2014	2435.42	7684.69	3894.09	50.67	3790.60	49.33	3.16	7650.76	714
2015	2439.58	7717.59	3908.27	50.64	3809.32	49.36	3.16	7701.14	718
2016	2453.85	7775.66	3934.87	50.60	3840.79	49.40	3.17	7746.63	725

3-5 全省历次人口普查主要数据

Major Data of All Previous Provincial Population Census

指标	Item	1953	1964	1982	1990	2000	2010	2015
总人口 （万人）	Total Population (10000 persons)	**3767.29**	**4452.21**	**6052.11**	**6705.68**	**7304.36**	**7866.09**	**7973**
男	Male	1888.95	2242.71	3076.75	3412.32	3698.20	3962.67	4013
女	Female	1878.34	2209.50	2975.36	3293.36	3606.16	3903.42	3960
性别比（女性为100）	Sex Ratio (Female = 100)	100.6	101.5	103.4	103.6	102.6	101.5	101.3
家庭户规模 （人/户）	Family Size (person/household)	**4.19**	**4.09**	**3.91**	**3.66**	**3.25**	**2.94**	**2.94**
各年龄组人口 （万人）	Population by Age Group (10000 persons)							
0—14 岁	Aged 0—14	1414.86	1772.66	1753.75	1592.47	1434.20	1023.35	1064
15—64 岁	Aged 15—64	2183.21	2514.48	3962.69	4657.93	5224.32	5986.88	5910
65 岁及以上	Aged 65 and Over	169.22	165.07	335.67	455.28	645.84	855.86	999
民族人口 （万人）	Population by Ethnicity (10000 persons)							
汉族	Han Nationality	3760.92	4443.90	6041.08	6690.37	7278.37	7827.60	7931
占总人口比重 （%）	Proportion (%)	99.8	99.8	99.8	99.8	99.6	99.5	99.5
少数民族	Minority Nationalities	6.37	8.31	11.03	15.28	25.99	38.49	42
占总人口比重 （%）	Proportion (%)	0.2	0.2	0.2	0.2	0.4	0.5	0.5
每十万人拥有的各种受教育程度人口 （人）	Population with Various Education Attainments per 100000 Persons (person)							
大专及以上	Junior College and Above		386	639	1474	3919	10820	15427
高中和中专	Senior Secondary School and Technical Secondary School		1470	6981	8670	13079	16150	17007
初中	Junior Secondary School		5236	20049	26426	36365	38676	34379
小学	Primary School		26588	32613	34791	32882	24196	21874
城乡人口 （万人）	Population by Residence (10000 persons)							
城镇人口	Urban Population	556.81	660.26	957.22	1446.85	3086.24	4737.15	5294
乡村人口	Rural Population	3210.48	3791.95	5094.89	5258.83	4218.12	3128.94	2679
平均预期寿命 （岁）	Average Life Expectancy (age)			**69.49**	**71.62**	**74.13**	**76.63**	**77.51**
男	Male			67.35	69.46	71.88	74.60	75.50
女	Female			71.56	73.82	76.47	78.81	79.52

3-6 按地区分常住人口

Permanent Population by Region

地区 Region		2015			2016		
		总人口（万人） Total Population (10000 persons)	城镇人口（万人） Urban Population (10000 persons)	城镇人口比重（%） Proportion (%)	总人口（万人） Total Population (10000 persons)	城镇人口（万人） Urban Population (10000 persons)	城镇人口比重（%） Proportion (%)
全 省	**Total**	**7976.30**	**5305.83**	**66.5**	**7998.60**	**5416.65**	**67.7**
南京市	Nanjing	823.59	670.40	81.4	827.00	678.14	82.0
无锡市	Wuxi	651.10	490.93	75.4	652.90	494.90	75.8
徐州市	Xuzhou	866.90	529.24	61.1	871.00	543.85	62.4
常州市	Changzhou	470.14	329.10	70.0	470.83	334.29	71.0
苏州市	Suzhou	1061.60	795.14	74.9	1064.74	803.88	75.5
南通市	Nantong	730.00	458.15	62.8	730.20	470.03	64.4
连云港市	Lianyungang	447.37	262.61	58.7	449.64	270.68	60.2
淮安市	Huaian	487.20	283.31	58.2	489.00	291.84	59.7
盐城市	Yancheng	722.85	434.43	60.1	723.50	445.39	61.6
扬州市	Yangzhou	448.36	281.53	62.8	449.14	289.25	64.4
镇江市	Zhenjiang	317.65	215.78	67.9	318.13	220.08	69.2
泰州市	Taizhou	464.16	285.69	61.6	464.58	293.61	63.2
宿迁市	Suqian	485.38	269.53	55.5	487.94	280.71	57.5
苏 南	Southern Jiangsu	3324.08	2501.35	75.3	3333.60	2531.29	75.9
苏 中	Mid Jiangsu	1642.52	1025.37	62.4	1643.92	1052.89	64.0
苏 北	Northern Jiangsu	3009.70	1779.12	59.1	3021.08	1832.47	60.7

3-7 全省人口年龄构成情况(2016年11月1日零时)

Composition of Population Grouped by Age (0 o'clock on November 1, 2016)

单位:人 (person)

年龄组(岁) Age Group	总人口 Total	#女 Female	城镇	乡村 Rural
合 计(Total)	**371096**	**184792**	**246853**	124243
0—4	17771	8188	11709	6062
5—9	19435	8927	12348	7087
10—14	16344	7415	10671	5673
15—19	14743	6727	10401	4342
20—24	21388	10701	15273	6115
25—29	32663	16463	23112	9551
30—34	24911	12816	18692	6219
35—39	24749	12545	18732	6017
40—44	26867	13583	19522	7345
45—49	36541	18474	24078	12463
50—54	34640	17626	22151	12489
55—59	21743	10855	13638	8105
60—64	27181	13539	16294	10887
65—69	19466	9712	11416	8050
70—74	13206	6536	7656	5550
75—79	9359	4792	5427	3932
80—84	6097	3382	3487	2610
85—89	2865	1751	1642	1223
90及以上 (90 and over)	1127	760	604	523

注:本表是2016年人口抽样调查样本数据,抽样比为0.46%(3-8、3-9表同)。

a) Data in this table is 2016 population changes sample survey, sampling ratio 0.46%. (The same as in table 3-8 and table 3-9)

3-8 全省人口受教育程度情况（2016 年 11 月 1 日零时）
Educated Situation of Population (0 o'clock on November 1,2016)

单位:人 (person)

指标	Item	6岁及以上人口 Aged 6 and Over	不识字或识字很少 Illiterate or Nearly Illiterate	学前教育	小学 Primary Shool	初中 Junior Secondary Shool	普通高中	中职	大学专科	大学本科	研究生
合计	**Total**	**349517**	**20660**	**2137**	**85436**	**124760**	**45582**	**17301**	**28359**	**22498**	**2784**
男	Male	174714	4685	1075	38983	65916	26403	9238	15018	11732	1664
女	Female	174803	15975	1062	46453	58844	19179	8063	13341	10766	1120
按城乡分	Grouped by City and Country										
城镇	City	232654	9770	1206	47111	78497	34666	13606	24242	20837	2719
男	Male	116652	2167	637	21329	40621	19443	7200	12783	10843	1629
女	Female	116002	7603	569	25782	37876	15223	6406	11459	9994	1090
乡村	Country	116863	10890	931	38325	46263	10916	3695	4117	1661	65
男	Male	58062	2518	438	17654	25295	6960	2038	2235	889	35
女	Female	58801	8372	493	20671	20968	3956	1657	1882	772	30

3-9 全省 15 岁及以上人口的婚姻状况（2016 年 11 月 1 日零时）
Marriage Status of Population Aged 15 and Over (0 o'clock on November 1,2016)

单位:人 (person)

年龄组(岁) Age Group	未婚 Never Married	有配偶 Married	离婚 Divorce	丧偶 Widowed
合计 (Total)	**45111**	**248463**	**4878**	**19094**
15—19	14522	215	3	3
20—24	16920	4408	47	13
25—29	9025	23247	365	26
30—34	1640	22734	503	34
35—39	569	23429	684	67
40—44	381	25598	727	161
45—49	451	34735	844	511
50—54	360	32700	696	884
55—59	269	20119	363	992
60—64	356	24510	310	2005
65 及以上(65 and over)	618	36768	336	14398

3-10 全省16岁及以上人口经济活动情况(2016年11月1日零时)

Condition of Economic Activities of Age 16 and Above Population(0 o'clock on November 1,2016)

单位:人 (person)

年龄组(岁)	16岁及以上人口 16 aged and Above Population			经济活动人口 Economically Active Population			非经济活动人口 Economically Inactive Population		
Age Group	小计 Total	男 Male	女 Female	小计 Total	男 Male	女 Female	小计 Total	男 Male	女 Female
合计 (Total)	**24937**	**12418**	**12519**	**15692**	**8693**	**6999**	**9245**	**3725**	**5520**
16—19	833	467	366	57	34	23	776	433	343
20—24	1372	722	650	686	378	308	686	344	342
25—29	2021	987	1034	1822	946	876	199	41	158
30—34	1810	884	926	1675	867	808	135	17	118
35—39	2100	1029	1071	1962	1005	957	138	24	114
40—44	2348	1144	1204	2197	1119	1078	151	25	126
45—49	3050	1523	1527	2757	1463	1294	293	60	233
50—54	2938	1448	1490	2100	1333	767	838	115	723
55—59	1870	934	936	1010	718	292	860	216	644
60—64	2390	1182	1208	784	459	325	1606	723	883
65及以上 (65 and over)	4205	2098	2107	642	371	271	3563	1727	1836

注:本表是2016年劳动力抽样调查样本数据,抽样比为0.36‰。

a) Data in the table are the data of change of labour by 0.36‰ sampling survey in 2016.

3－11 就业基本情况
Employment

指标	Item	1995	2000	2005	2010	2015	2016
就业人员合计 （万人）	Total Number of Employed Persons (10000 persons)	4385.17	4418.14	4578.75	4754.68	4758.50	4756.22
第一产业	Primary Industry	2057.08	1890.96	1414.83	1060.29	875.56	841.85
第二产业	Secondary Industry	1407.64	1335.16	1703.29	1996.97	2046.16	2045.17
第三产业	Tertiary Industry	920.45	1192.02	1460.62	1697.42	1836.78	1869.20
就业人员构成 （合计＝100）	Composition of Employed Persons (Total＝100)						
第一产业	Primary Industry	46.9	42.8	30.9	22.3	18.4	17.7
第二产业	Secondary Industry	32.1	30.2	37.2	42.0	43	43.0
第三产业	Tertiary Industry	21.0	27.0	31.9	35.7	38.6	39.3
城镇地区就业人员 （万人）	Urban Employed Persons (10000 persons)	1119.33	1655.00	2133.58	2809.58	3076.22	3126.26
城镇单位就业人员 （万人）	Employed Persons in Urban Units (10000 persons)	926.48	693.09	628.82	763.75	1552.08	1497.30
国有单位	State-owned Units	581.88	421.75	283.75	281.21	294.31	289.86
城镇集体单位	Urban Collective Owned Units	277.71	117.94	38.70	30.31	33.71	32.36
其他单位	Others	66.89	153.41	306.37	452.23	1224.06	1175.08
内资单位	Domestic Funded	29.63	102.03	176.27	243.52	789.10	759.93
股份合作单位	Cooperative Units		17.84	8.31	6.31	4.05	3.65
联营单位	Joint Ownership Units	11.92	5.45	1.78	1.10	1.13	0.97
有限责任公司	Limited Liability Corporations		47.07	88.09	106.90	601.66	576.91
股份有限公司	Share-holding Corporations Ltd.		30.66	52.88	59.27	169.38	165.16
其他	Others		0.99	25.21	69.95	12.88	13.24
港澳台商投资单位	Units with Funds from Hong Kong, Macao & Taiwan	19.27	20.00	50.38	65.03	164.43	155.59
外商投资单位	Foreign Funded Units	17.99	31.38	79.72	143.68	270.53	259.57
城镇私营企业就业人员 （万人）	Employed Persons in Urban Private Enterprises (10000 persons)	65.89	96.57	397.20	958.85	1459.36	1680.22
城镇个体就业人员 （万人）	Urban Self-employed Individuals (10000 persons)		81.18	189.20	338.45	518.33	616.27
在岗职工人数 （万人）	Number of Staff and Workers (10000 persons)	915.98	673.25	602.93	710.58	1467.53	1410.73
国有单位	State-owned Units	576.24	411.40	273.43	263.95	275.97	271.01
城镇集体单位	Urban Collective-owned Units	273.96	114.85	36.84	27.35	30.43	29.51
其他单位	Units of Other Types of Ownership	65.78	147.00	292.67	419.28	1161.13	1110.21
城镇单位女性就业人员 （万人）	Number of Employed Female Persons in Urban Units (10000 persons)	375.50	270.20	264.94	319.03	529.34	510.07
年末城镇登记失业人数 （万人）	Number of Registered Unemployed Persons in Urban Areas (year-end) (10000 persons)	20.13	30.36	41.63	40.65	36.01	35.21
年末城镇登记失业率 （％）	Registered Unemployment Rate in Urban Areas (year-end) (％)	2.0	3.2	3.6	3.16	3.00	3.00

注：从2013年起，原属于乡镇企业的规模以上非私营法人单位纳入城镇单位进行统计。（下同）

a) The non-private legal entities above designated size originally belonged to township enterprises have been taken into urban units since 2013. (The same as in the following tables)

3-12 就业人数

Number of Employed Persons

单位:万人 (10000 persons)

年份 Year	就业人数 Total Number of Employed Persons	#城镇单位职工人数 Number of Staff and Workers in Urban Units	国有单位 State-owned Units	城镇集体单位 Urban Collective-owned Units	其他单位 Other Uuits	#城镇单位其他就业人员 Others Employed Persons in Urban Areas	#城镇私营及个体就业人员 Employed Persons in Urban Private Enterprises and Individual Units
1978	2777.72	581.50	366.37	215.13			1.62
1980	2821.03	644.15	401.98	242.17			2.75
1985	3262.97	782.44	468.80	305.39	8.25		11.86
1989	3519.83	867.55	525.24	324.73	17.58		19.10
1990	4225.02	879.85	536.88	323.34	19.63		23.57
1991	4272.97	899.27	551.52	324.91	22.84		21.92
1992	4315.12	904.09	562.69	313.81	27.59		23.63
1993	4339.81	914.73	574.02	293.57	47.14	12.81	37.11
1994	4362.76	909.83	571.39	277.27	60.67	11.04	52.99
1995	4385.17	915.98	576.24	273.96	65.78	10.50	65.89
1996	4386.97	905.52	575.48	256.91	73.13	10.79	72.80
1997	4388.79	893.74	577.54	239.61	76.59	11.29	90.12
1998	4389.92	752.76	471.52	161.85	119.39	16.41	129.89
1999	4390.71	717.12	445.27	139.03	132.82	18.99	150.34
2000	4418.14	673.25	411.40	114.85	147.00	19.84	177.75
2001	4436.45	625.83	377.40	90.34	158.09	22.35	232.79
2002	4472.84	590.32	329.96	67.11	193.25	25.33	240.61
2003	4499.97	579.10	304.98	52.58	221.54	29.41	352.60
2004	4537.07	575.08	281.03	41.11	252.94	31.77	446.86
2005	4578.75	602.93	273.43	36.83	292.67	25.89	586.40
2006	4628.95	645.71	268.41	33.58	343.72	33.66	722.30
2007	4677.88	667.27	268.54	33.12	365.62	35.41	828.61
2008	4700.96	668.29	264.31	31.45	372.53	39.35	1019.13
2009	4726.54	673.74	263.26	28.15	382.32	47.61	1147.08
2010	4754.68	710.58	263.95	27.35	419.28	53.17	1297.30
2011	4758.23	774.39	276.86	27.77	469.76	36.89	1381.83
2012	4759.53	792.62	280.92	27.59	484.11	38.32	1467.02
2013	4759.89	1418.57	276.26	35.04	1107.27	85.40	1678.55
2014	4760.83	1512.79	281.13	35.34	1196.32	89.61	1776.83
2015	4758.50	1467.53	275.97	30.43	1161.13	84.55	1977.69
2016	4756.22	1410.73	271.01	29.51	1110.21	86.58	2296.49

注:1. 从1990年开始就业人数为推算数。
2. 1998年以前的职工人数包括在岗职工人数和下岗职工人数(下同)。
3. 1998年开始的职工人数为在岗职工人数,不包括离开本单位仍保留劳动关系的职工人数(下同)。

a) Since 1990, the number of employed persons was the estimated figure.
b) Before 1998, the number of staff and workers included employed and laid off personnels. (The same as in the following tables)
c) Since 1998, the number of staff and workers included employed personnels, excluded staff and workers who had left self units, but still remained the labor relationship. (The same as in the following tables)

3－13 分三次产业的就业人数

Number of Employed Persons by Three Types of Industries

单位:万人 （10000 persons）

年 份 Year	就业人数 Total Number of Employed Persons				构 成 （%） Composition （%）		
		第一产业 Primary Industry	第二产业 Secondary Industry	第三产业 Tertiary Industry	第一产业 Primary Industry	第二产业 Secondary Industry	第三产业 Tertiary Industry
1978	2777.72	1937.06	544.57	296.09	69.7	19.6	10.7
1980	2821.03	1987.28	546.48	287.27	70.4	19.4	10.2
1985	3262.97	1738.09	1065.75	459.13	53.2	32.7	14.1
1989	3519.83	1714.69	1215.40	589.74	48.7	34.5	16.8
1990	4225.02	2389.25	1212.58	623.19	56.6	28.7	14.7
1991	4272.97	2405.68	1226.34	640.95	56.3	28.7	15.0
1992	4315.12	2337.93	1270.80	706.39	54.2	29.4	16.4
1993	4339.81	2228.06	1325.38	786.37	51.4	30.5	18.1
1994	4362.76	2131.65	1375.14	855.97	48.9	31.5	19.6
1995	4385.17	2057.08	1407.64	920.45	46.9	32.1	21.0
1996	4386.97	2014.06	1397.25	975.66	45.9	31.9	22.2
1997	4388.79	1981.54	1382.03	1025.22	45.1	31.5	23.4
1998	4389.92	1946.49	1341.12	1102.31	44.3	30.6	25.1
1999	4390.71	1908.64	1330.39	1151.68	43.5	30.3	26.2
2000	4418.14	1890.96	1335.16	1192.02	42.8	30.2	27.0
2001	4436.45	1832.25	1375.30	1228.90	41.3	31.0	27.7
2002	4472.84	1744.41	1453.67	1274.76	39.0	32.5	28.5
2003	4499.97	1615.49	1547.99	1336.49	35.9	34.4	29.7
2004	4537.07	1506.31	1633.35	1397.42	33.2	36.0	30.8
2005	4578.75	1414.83	1703.29	1460.62	30.9	37.2	31.9
2006	4628.95	1323.88	1777.52	1527.55	28.6	38.4	33.0
2007	4677.88	1230.28	1857.12	1590.48	26.3	39.7	34.0
2008	4700.96	1179.94	1889.79	1631.23	25.1	40.2	34.7
2009	4726.54	1120.19	1942.61	1663.74	23.7	41.1	35.2
2010	4754.68	1060.29	1996.97	1697.42	22.3	42.0	35.7
2011	4758.23	1023.02	2017.49	1717.72	21.5	42.4	36.1
2012	4759.53	989.98	2032.32	1737.23	20.8	42.7	36.5
2013	4759.89	956.74	2041.99	1761.16	20.1	42.9	37.0
2014	4760.83	918.84	2047.16	1794.83	19.3	43.0	37.7
2015	4758.50	875.56	2046.16	1836.78	18.4	43.0	38.6
2016	4756.22	841.85	2045.17	1869.20	17.7	43.0	39.3

3－14 分地区就业人数

Number of Employed Persons by Region

单位:万人 (10000 persons)

地 区 Region		2015				2016			
		就业人数 Total Number of Employed Persons	第一产业 Primary Industry	第二产业 Secondary Industry	第三产业 Tertiary Industry	就业人数 Total Number of Employed Persons	第一产业 Primary Industry	第二产业 Secondary Industry	第三产业 Tertiary Industry
全 省	**Total**	**4758.5**	**875.6**	**2046.2**	**1836.8**	**4756.2**	**841.9**	**2045.2**	**1869.2**
按地区分	by Cities								
南 京	Nanjing	455.0	46.7	148.6	259.7	456.0	46.0	148.9	261.1
无 锡	Wuxi	390.0	17.6	219.4	153.0	387.0	17.1	214.9	155.0
徐 州	Xuzhou	482.1	152.8	155.6	173.7	483.4	144.3	159.9	179.2
常 州	Changzhou	281.0	30.7	143.5	106.8	281.4	30.0	142.2	109.2
苏 州	Suzhou	691.4	23.8	414.5	253.1	691.3	23.5	412.1	255.7
南 通	Nantong	460.0	97.2	214.5	148.3	458.0	96.0	213.0	149.0
连云港	Lianyungang	250.3	78.9	80.5	90.9	250.5	78.6	80.7	91.2
淮 安	Huaian	282.5	79.2	88.6	114.7	283.6	78.3	89.6	115.7
盐 城	Yancheng	445.7	114.7	156.9	174.1	446.0	110.2	159.8	176.0
扬 州	Yangzhou	264.5	48.2	117.9	98.4	263.4	46.2	116.4	100.8
镇 江	Zhenjiang	193.1	22.9	88.9	81.3	194.3	22.2	88.1	84.0
泰 州	Taizhou	281.3	63.2	118.0	100.1	278.1	60.1	112.8	105.2
宿 迁	Suqian	281.6	99.6	99.3	82.7	283.2	89.3	106.8	87.1
按区域分	by Regions								
苏 南	Southern Jiangsu	2010.5	141.7	1014.9	853.9	2010.0	138.8	1006.2	865.0
苏 中	Mid Jiangsu	1005.8	208.6	450.4	346.8	999.5	202.3	442.2	355.0
苏 北	Northern Jiangsu	1742.2	525.2	580.9	636.1	1746.7	500.7	596.8	649.2

3-15 城镇非私营单位就业人员数（2016年）
Number of Employed Persons in Urban Units (2016)

单位：万人 (10000 persons)

项目	Item	就业人员年末人数 Number of Employed Persons at Year-end	在岗职工 Employed	其他就业人员 Others
总计	**Total**	**1497.30**	**1410.73**	**86.58**
按登记注册类型分	Grouped by Status of Registration			
国有单位	State-owned Units	289.86	271.01	18.85
城镇集体单位	Urban Collective-owned Units	32.36	29.51	2.85
其他单位	Other Units	1175.08	1110.21	64.88
内资单位	Domestic Funded	759.93	703.68	56.25
股份合作单位	Cooperative Units	3.65	3.47	0.18
联营单位	Joint Ownership Units	0.97	0.89	0.08
有限责任公司	Limited Liability Corporations	576.91	535.08	41.84
股份有限公司	Share-holding Corporations Ltd.	165.16	151.71	13.44
其他	Others	13.24	12.53	0.71
港、澳、台商投资单位	Units with Funds from Hong Kong, Macao and Taiwan	155.59	152.90	2.69
外商投资单位	Foreign Funded Units	259.57	253.63	5.94
按企业、事业、机关分	Grouped by Enterprises, Institutions and Agencies			
企业	Enterprises	1260.98	1189.97	71.01
事业	Institutions	171.16	159.24	11.92
机关	Agencies & Organizations	60.66	57.21	3.44
按国民经济行业分	Grouped by Sector			
农、林、牧、渔业	Agriculture, Forestry, Animal Husbandry and Fishery	5.62	5.32	0.29
采矿业	Mining	8.55	8.40	0.14
制造业	Manufacturing	567.42	557.10	10.32
电力、热力、燃气及水生产和供应业	Production and Supply of Electric Power, Heat Power, Gas and Water	14.51	14.33	0.18
建筑业	Construction	396.77	357.78	39.00
批发和零售业	Wholesale and Retail Trades	56.11	54.28	1.83
交通运输、仓储和邮政业	Traffic, Transport, Storage and Post	49.64	47.87	1.77
住宿和餐饮业	Hotels and Catering Services	16.90	15.10	1.80
信息传输、软件和信息技术服务业	Information Transmission, Computer Services and Software	27.32	26.80	0.52
金融业	Financial Intermediation	38.08	27.06	11.02
房地产业	Real Estate	22.24	21.12	1.13
租赁和商务服务业	Leasing and Business Services	29.44	27.79	1.65
科学研究、技术服务业	Scientific and Fednical Services	21.81	20.93	0.87
水利、环境和公共设施管理业	Management of Water Conservancy, Environment and Public Facilities	15.44	13.47	1.97
居民服务、修理和其他服务业	Services to Households and Other Services	3.21	3.12	0.08
教育	Education	94.97	90.37	4.59
卫生和社会工作	Health and Social Work	49.45	44.81	4.64
文化、体育和娱乐业	Culture, Sports and Entertainment	7.87	7.34	0.53
公共管理、社会保障和社会组织	Public Administralion, Social Secarily and Organization	71.96	67.72	4.24

注：本表城镇单位数据不含私营单位(下相关表同)。

a) Data of employed persons in urban units do not include those fo private enterprises. The same applies to the table following.

3－16 分细行业城镇非私营单位就业人员数（2016 年）
Number of Employed Persons in Urban Units by Sector in Detail(2016)

单位:万人 (10000 persons)

项 目 Item		合 计 Total	#在岗职工 Employed	国有单位 State-owned Units	城镇集体单位 Urban Collective-owned Units	其他单位 Other Units
总 计	**Total**	**1497.30**	**1410.73**	**289.86**	**32.36**	**1175.08**
按企业、事业、机关分	Grouped by Enterprise, Institution and Agenciy					
企业	Enterprises	1260.98	1189.97	70.12	20.71	1170.15
事业	Institutions	171.16	159.24	157.04	11.46	2.66
机关	Agencies & Organizations	60.66	57.21	60.65	0.01	
按国民经济行业分	Grouped by Sector					
农、林、牧、渔业	Agriculture, Forestry, Animal Husbandry and Fishery	5.62	5.32	5.42	0.06	0.14
农业	Farming	4.50	4.25	4.41	0.04	0.05
林业	Forestry	0.28	0.28	0.27		0.01
畜牧业	Animal Husbandry	0.20	0.19	0.18		0.01
渔业	Fishery	0.06	0.06	0.04	0.01	0.01
农、林、牧、渔服务业	Service in Support of Agriculture	0.58	0.55	0.51	0.01	0.06
采矿业	Mining	8.55	8.40	1.27	0.06	7.22
制造业	Manufacturing	567.42	557.10	4.74	6.66	556.02
农副食品加工业	Processing of Food from Agricultural Products	7.95	7.64	0.09	0.02	7.83
食品制造业	Manufacture of Food	5.17	4.99	0.04	5.13	
酒、饮料和精制茶制造业	Manufacture of Beverage	6.41	6.36	0.04	0.01	6.36
烟草制品业	Manufacture of Tobacco	0.60	0.60	0.03		0.57
纺织业	Manufacture of Textile	30.80	30.51	0.30	0.38	30.12
纺织服装、服饰业	Manufacture of Textile Wearing, Apparel, Footwear and Caps	34.47	33.99	0.37	0.14	33.97
皮革、毛皮、羽毛及其制品和制鞋业	Manufacture of Leather, Fur, Feather and Related and saps	6.80	6.75		0.01	6.79
木材加工和木、竹、藤、棕、草制品业	Processing of Timber, Manufacture of Wood, Bamboo, Rattan, Palm and Straw Products	4.60	4.56		0.03	4.58
家具制造业	Manufacture of Furniture	2.45	2.40		0.01	2.44
造纸和纸制品业	Manufacture of Paper and Paper Products	5.70	5.66	0.11	0.07	5.52
印刷和记录媒介复制业	Printing, Reproduction of Recording Media	5.12	5.04	0.11	0.08	4.93
文教、工美、体育和娱乐用品制造业	Manufacture of Articles For Culture, Education and Sport Activities	11.68	11.61		0.17	11.51
石油加工、炼焦和核燃料加工业	Processing of Petroleum, Coking, Processing of Nuclear Fuel	2.50	2.47	0.10	0.01	2.40
化学原料和化学制品制造业	Manufacture of Raw Chemical Materials and Chemical Products	34.25	33.82	0.29	0.36	33.60
医药制造业	Manufacture of Medicines	13.45	13.11			13.45
化学纤维制造业	Manufacture of Chemical Fibers	7.13	7.06		0.01	7.12
橡胶和塑料制品业	Rubber and plastic Products	17.89	17.68	0.03	0.20	17.67
非金属矿物制品业	Manufacture of Non-metallic Mineral Products	14.04	13.88	0.30	0.11	13.64
黑色金属冶炼和压延加工业	Smelting and Pressing of Ferrous Metals	15.40	15.19	0.21	2.14	13.04
有色金属冶炼和压延加工业	Smelting and Pressing of Non-ferrous Metals	6.21	6.15	0.01	0.54	5.65

3-16 续表 1 Continued 1

单位：万人 (10000 persons)

项目	Item	合计 Total	#在岗职工 Employed	国有单位 State-owned Units	城镇集体单位 Urban Collective-owned Units	其他单位 Other Units
金属制品业	Manufacture of Metal Products	18.94	18.59	0.28	0.19	18.47
通用设备制造业	Manufacture of General Purpose Machinery	40.11	39.69	0.40	0.43	39.28
专用设备制造业	Manufacture of Special Purpose Machinery	24.97	24.62	0.20	0.06	24.72
汽车制造业	Manufacture of Automobile	28.36	27.81	0.68	0.04	27.64
铁路、船舶、航空航天和其他运输设备制造业	Manufacture of Railroad, Marihe Aviation and other Transport Equipment	17.42	16.52	0.52	0.14	16.77
电气机械和器材制造业	Manufacture of Electrical Machinery and Equipment	55.19	54.03	0.20	0.43	54.55
计算机、通信和其他电子设备制造业	Manufacture of Communication Equipment, Computer and Other Electronic Equipment	136.84	133.58	0.17	0.75	135.93
仪器仪表制造业	Manufacture of Instrumentation	11.14	11.00	0.29	0.13	10.71
其他制造业	Other Manufacturing	1.16	1.15		0.06	1.09
废弃资源综合利用业	Manufacture of Recycling and Disposal of waste	0.51	0.50	0.01	0.10	0.41
金属制品、机械和设备修理业	Manufacture of Metal Prodults, Machinery and Eauipment Repair	0.17	0.16		0.02	0.15
电力、热力、燃气及水生产和供应业	Production and Supply of Electric Power, Heat Power, Gas and Water	14.51	14.33	6.42	0.18	7.91
电力、热力生产和供应业	Production and Supply of Electric Power and Heat Power	9.53	9.46	5.10	0.08	4.35
燃气生产和供应业	Production and Supply of Gas	1.59	1.57	0.03		1.57
水的生产和供应业	Production and Supply of Water	3.39	3.31	1.29	0.10	1.99
建筑业	Construction	396.77	357.78	8.83	4.78	383.17
房屋建筑业	Housing Construction	318.19	293.61	2.81	3.09	312.30
土木工程建筑业	Civil Engineering Construction	41.33	32.98	5.45	1.10	34.78
建筑安装业	Architectural Installation	19.68	17.30	0.15	0.07	19.45
建筑装饰和其他建筑业	Other Construction	17.58	13.89	0.42	0.51	16.64
批发和零售业	Wholesale and Retail Trades	56.11	54.28	4.06	1.08	50.96
批发业	Wholesale Trade	23.53	23.03	3.26	0.49	19.78
零售业	Retail Trade	32.58	31.25	0.80	0.60	31.19
交通运输、仓储和邮政业	Traffic, Transport, Storage and Post	49.64	47.87	14.62	1.56	33.46
铁路运输业	Railway Transport	2.32	2.22	2.19	0.10	0.04
道路运输业	Road Transport	25.90	24.99	6.11	0.73	19.07
水上运输业	Water Transport	7.73	7.35	0.78	0.39	6.55
航空运输业	Air Transport	1.58	1.47	0.12		1.46
管道运输业	Transport Via Pipeline	1.06	1.06	0.22		0.85
装卸搬运和运输代理业	Handling and Agency	3.42	3.35	0.15	0.32	2.95
仓储业	Storage	1.92	1.89	0.50	0.01	1.40
邮政业	Post	5.71	5.53	4.55	0.02	1.14
住宿和餐饮业	Hotels and Catering Services	16.90	15.10	1.72	0.26	14.92
住宿业	Hotel	7.45	7.01	1.43	0.16	5.86
餐饮业	Catering Services	9.45	8.09	0.29	0.10	9.06
信息传输、软件和信息技术服务业	Information Transfer, Software and IT Services	27.32	26.80	4.28	0.02	23.02
电信、广播电视和卫星传输服务	Telecommunications, Satellites Radio and Television Services	14.04	13.81	4.01	0.01	10.02
互联网和相关服务	Internet and Relatiue Services	2.43	2.28	0.08	0.01	2.34
软件和信息技术服务业	Software and IT Services	10.85	10.71	0.19		10.66

3－16 续表 2 Continued 2

单位：万人 (10000 persons)

项目	Item	合计 Total	#在岗职工 Employed	国有单位 State-owned Units	城镇集体单位 Urban Collective-owned Units	其他单位 Other Units
金融业	Financial Intermediation	38.08	27.06	10.50	2.14	25.44
货币金融服务业	Nonetary and Financial	20.84	20.58	6.63	2.14	12.08
资本市场服务业	Capital Markets	1.07	1.04	0.03		1.04
保险业	Insurance	16.09	5.36	3.81		12.28
其他金融业	Other Financial Activities	0.08	0.07	0.04		0.04
房地产业	Real Estate	22.24	21.12	1.19	0.30	20.76
#房地产开发经营	Development and Management of Real Estate	9.38	9.14	0.40	0.10	8.88
租赁和商务服务业	Leasing and Business Services	29.44	27.79	8.18	2.42	18.84
租赁业	Leasing	0.66	0.64	0.07	0.04	0.55
商务服务业	Business Services	28.78	27.15	8.10	2.38	18.29
科学研究、技术服务业	Scientific and Fednical Services	21.81	20.93	8.58	0.38	12.85
研究和试验发展	Research and Experimental Development	4.60	4.48	3.58	0.03	1.00
专业技术服务业	Professional Technical Services	14.07	13.53	3.99	0.30	9.78
科技推广和应用服务业	Promation and Application of Secscence	3.14	2.92	1.01	0.06	2.07
水利、环境和公共设施管理业	Management of Water Conservancy, Environment and Public Facilities	15.44	13.47	9.09	2.55	3.81
水利管理业	Management of Water Conservancy	3.27	3.08	3.10	0.07	0.10
生态保护和环境治理业	Ecological Protection and Enviromental	0.67	0.57	0.32	0.05	0.30
公共设施管理业	Management of Public Facilities	11.50	9.82	5.67	2.42	3.41
居民服务、修理和其他服务业	Services to Households and Other Services	3.21	3.12	0.51	0.42	2.28
居民服务业	Services to Households	1.24	1.20	0.39	0.30	0.56
机动车、电子产品和日用产品修理业	Vehicle, Electronics and Daiy Maintenance	0.70	0.69	0.05	0.04	0.61
其他服务业	Other Services	1.26	1.24	0.07	0.09	1.11
教育	Education	94.97	90.37	87.77	1.73	5.47
卫生和社会工作	Health and Social Work	49.45	44.81	36.69	7.53	5.24
卫生	Health	48.62	44.03	36.01	7.45	5.16
社会工作	Social Work	0.83	0.78	0.68	0.08	0.08
文化、体育和娱乐业	Culture, Sports and Entertainment	7.87	7.34	4.20	0.21	3.45
新闻和出版业	Journalism and Publishing Activities	1.55	1.47	0.79		0.76
广播、电视、电影和影视录音制作业	Radio, TV, Movie and Video Recording	2.57	2.42	1.61	0.02	0.93
文化艺术业	Cultural and Art Activities	2.06	1.87	1.50	0.17	0.39
体育	Sports Activities	0.53	0.49	0.22		0.31
娱乐业	Entertainment	1.15	1.08	0.08	0.02	1.06
公共管理、社会保障和社会组织	Public Administration, Social Security and Organization	71.96	67.72	71.80	0.03	0.13
中国共产党机关	Organs of Communist Party of China	1.57	1.54	1.57		
国家机构	Government Agencies	68.55	64.41	68.55		
人民政协、民主党派	People's Political Consultative Conference and Democratic Parties	0.30	0.29	0.30		
社会保障	Social Security	0.61	0.58	0.59	0.02	
群众社团、社会团体和其他成员组织	Mass, Society and other Groups	0.82	0.78	0.78	0.01	0.03

3-17 分地区城镇非私营单位就业人员数（2016年）

单位：万人

项目	Item	南京市 Nanjing	无锡市 Wuxi	徐州市 Xuzhou
总计	**Total**	**205.19**	**113.34**	**99.82**
按登记注册类型分	Grouped by Status of Registration			
国有单位	State-owned Units	49.86	19.73	34.88
城镇集体单位	Urban Collective-owned Units	2.22	4.81	3.50
其他单位	Other Units	153.10	88.81	61.45
内资单位	Domestic Funded	113.71	42.07	53.78
股份合作单位	Cooperative Units	0.47	0.37	0.17
联营单位	Joint Ownership Units	0.17		0.06
有限责任公司	Limited Liability Corporations	89.20	28.81	41.05
股份有限公司	Share-holding Corporations Ltd.	21.14	12.27	11.86
其他	Others	2.72	0.62	0.63
港、澳、台商投资单位	Units with Funds from Hong Kong, Macao and Taiwan	12.30	14.36	4.17
外商投资单位	Foreign Funded Units	27.10	32.37	3.50
按企业、事业、机关分	Grouped by Enterprises, Institutions and Agencies			
企业	Enterprises	169.22	95.51	73.64
事业	Institutions	27.36	13.23	18.91
机关	Agencies & Organizations	7.67	4.54	7.07
按国民经济行业分	Grouped by Sector			
农、林、牧、渔业	Agriculture, Forestry, Animal Husbandry and Fishery	0.16	0.14	1.36
采矿业	Mining	0.10		5.84
制造业	Manufacturing	48.44	62.51	22.47
电力、热力、燃气及水生产和供应业	Production and Supply of Electric Power, Heat Power, Gas and Water	1.70	1.00	0.85
建筑业	Construction	40.44	9.11	26.94
批发和零售业	Wholesale and Retail Trades	18.21	5.07	3.57
交通运输、仓储和邮政业	Traffic, Transport, Storage and Post	14.32	3.10	4.73
住宿和餐饮业	Hotels and Catering Services	4.71	2.19	0.48
信息传输、软件和信息技术服务业	Information Transfer, Software and IT Services	14.15	2.66	0.69
金融业	Financial Intermediation	4.44	3.94	2.68
房地产业	Real Estate	5.44	2.01	1.07
租赁和商务服务业	Leasing and Business Services	7.93	1.52	2.04
科学研究和技术服务业	Scientific and Fednical Services	8.20	1.59	1.12
水利、环境和公共设施管理业	Management of Water Conservancy, Environment and Public Facilities	2.35	1.07	1.50
居民服务、修理和其他服务业	Services to Households and Other Services	0.79	0.40	0.14
教育	Education	14.82	6.65	10.49
卫生和社会工作	Health and Social Work	6.71	4.32	5.74
文化、体育和娱乐业	Culture, Sports and Entertainment	2.68	0.65	0.46
公共管理、社会保障和社会组织	Public Administralion, Social Secarily and Organization	9.61	5.40	7.63

Number of Employed Persons in Urban Units by Region(2016)

(10000 persons)

常州市 Changzhou	苏州市 Suzhou	南通市 Nantong	连云港市 Lianyungang	淮安市 Huaian	盐城市 Yancheng	扬州市 Yangzhou	镇江市 Zhenjiang	泰州市 Taizhou	宿迁市 Suqian
68.50	**288.69**	**205.34**	**47.48**	**68.75**	**87.43**	**102.13**	**47.97**	**110.00**	**48.58**
15.98	29.59	20.58	15.80	16.52	23.94	17.91	13.78	14.76	12.60
1.41	4.34	2.33	2.25	1.93	2.06	2.45	1.60	2.86	0.59
51.11	254.76	182.44	29.42	50.29	61.42	81.78	32.58	92.38	35.40
23.25	71.32	149.45	23.38	37.88	51.47	66.66	18.74	79.76	28.33
0.14	0.5	0.59	0.23	0.2	0.19	0.14	0.11	0.26	0.27
0.03	0.04	0.10	0.03	0.06	0.01	0.25	0.20	0.02	
16.57	47.93	113.71	18.17	30.44	40.45	47.82	12.58	70.45	19.74
6.00	21.49	33.71	4.47	6.60	9.81	17.38	5.04	8.27	6.97
0.51	1.36	1.35	0.48	0.58	1.00	1.07	0.81	0.76	1.36
13.95	57.59	12.87	2.21	8.57	3.94	8.11	7.70	4.42	5.39
13.91	125.85	20.12	3.83	3.84	6.02	7.00	6.15	8.21	1.68
54.46	260.71	186.57	34.28	54.65	68.54	88.18	36.53	96.88	37.73
10.31	19.53	13.55	9.74	10.67	13.49	9.13	7.70	9.43	8.12
3.71	6.51	5.01	3.38	3.27	5.22	4.59	3.64	3.47	2.56
0.05	0.02	0.54	0.80	0.51	1.67	0.03	0.08	0.18	0.05
	0.05		0.70	0.37	0.14	0.88	0.10		0.22
32.79	200.77	46.63	10.79	21.82	24.02	26.73	23.90	29.01	17.53
0.57	1.42	0.84	0.66	0.52	0.72	0.66	0.64	0.57	0.41
7.63	12.00	119.30	10.08	22.10	28.80	47.86	4.18	55.31	13.03
2.04	10.44	3.74	1.88	1.76	2.46	1.71	1.43	2.54	1.28
2.02	7.17	2.96	3.12	1.99	2.84	2.47	1.25	2.71	0.96
1.63	3.79	0.55	0.25	0.50	0.84	0.88	0.49	0.38	0.21
0.68	3.87	0.94	0.55	0.60	0.65	0.99	0.39	0.70	0.45
2.37	6.19	4.42	2.37	1.90	3.06	1.79	1.93	2.29	0.69
0.87	5.64	1.21	0.46	1.02	1.07	1.07	1.03	0.84	0.51
1.88	4.38	3.30	1.53	0.91	1.61	1.62	0.98	1.39	0.33
1.12	2.56	1.88	0.77	0.52	0.76	1.28	0.92	0.88	0.20
1.13	1.99	1.13	0.96	1.05	1.07	0.77	0.81	0.69	0.93
0.06	0.65	0.17	0.27	0.15	0.26	0.15	0.05	0.10	0.01
5.54	10.14	7.69	5.19	6.27	7.37	6.02	3.81	4.98	6.01
3.20	6.74	4.11	2.54	2.41	3.70	2.56	2.19	2.93	2.31
0.80	0.90	0.36	0.20	0.26	0.50	0.39	0.29	0.23	0.14
4.11	9.95	5.56	4.37	4.09	5.88	4.26	3.51	4.26	3.31

3－18　分行业城镇非私营单位女性就业人员数(2016年)
Number of Employed Women in Urban Units by Sector (2016)

单位:万人　　　　(10000 persons)

行业	Sector	女性就业人数 Number of Emloyed Women	国有单位 State-owned Units	城镇集体单位 Urban Collective-owned Units	其他单位 Other Units
总计	**Total**	**510.07**	**123.62**	**14.16**	**372.29**
农、林、牧、渔业	Agriculture, Forestry, Animal Husbandry and Fishery	2.22	2.15	0.02	0.05
采矿业	Mining	2.12	0.43	0.01	1.69
制造业	Manufacturing	248.44	1.28	2.83	244.33
电力、热力、燃气及水生产和供应业	Production and Supply of Electric Power, Heat Power, Gas and Water	3.76	1.59	0.04	2.14
建筑业	Construction	25.43	1.02	0.50	23.90
批发和零售业	Wholesale and Retail Trades	31.76	1.43	0.47	29.86
交通运输、仓储和邮政业	Traffic, Transport, Storage and Post	13.37	4.51	0.39	8.47
住宿和餐饮业	Hotels and Catering Services	10.09	0.96	0.16	8.97
信息传输、软件和信息技术服务业	Information Transfer, Software and IT Services	10.50	2.13	0.01	8.36
金融业	Financial Intermediation	20.68	5.54	0.93	14.20
房地产业	Real Estate	9.05	0.44	0.10	8.50
租赁和商务服务业	Leasing and Business Services	9.73	1.85	0.81	7.07
科学研究、技术服务业	Scientific Research and Technical Service	6.72	2.71	0.12	3.89
水利、环境和公共设施管理业	Management of Water Conservancy, Environment and Public Facilities	6.32	3.30	1.40	1.62
居民服务、修理和其他服务业	Services to Households and other Services	1.14	0.15	0.18	0.80
教育	Education	52.81	48.29	1.32	3.20
卫生和社会工作	Health and Social Work	32.18	24.00	4.74	3.45
文化、体育和娱乐业	Culture, Sports and Entertainment	3.66	1.86	0.10	1.71
公共管理、社会保障和社会组织	Public Administration, Social Security and Organization	20.09	19.99	0.02	0.08

3－19 城镇失业人数及失业率

Number of Urban Unemployed Persons and Unemployed Rate

单位:万人　　　　(10000 persons)

年　份 Year	下岗失业人员就业、再就业人数 Re-employment	年末尚有失业人数 Unemployment Registered at Year-end	年末城镇登记失业率(%) Registered Unemployment Rate at Year-end
1979	54.70	34.30	5.4
1980	32.78	20.29	3.1
1985	15.25	7.15	0.9
1990	28.06	22.52	2.4
1991	23.33	18.68	2.0
1992	21.43	18.81	2.0
1993	20.64	19.43	2.0
1994	22.19	19.58	2.0
1995	21.49	20.13	2.0
1996	20.78	22.34	2.2
1997	21.40	23.80	2.4
1998	21.61	24.26	2.6
1999	21.57	26.57	2.9
2000	27.01	30.36	3.4
2001	34.94	36.14	3.6
2002	39.96	42.17	4.2
2003	54.46	41.84	4.1
2004	60.22	42.90	3.9
2005	62.92	41.63	3.6
2006	68.65	40.40	3.4
2007	81.89	39.26	3.19
2008	92.19	41.09	3.25
2009	52.00	40.74	3.22
2010	60.93	40.65	3.16
2011	66.11	41.45	3.22
2012	66.71	40.47	3.14
2013	81.61	37.61	3.03
2014	77.64	36.57	3.01
2015	77.74	36.01	3.00
2016	77.82	35.21	3.00

3-20 在岗职工工资总额及指数

Total Wage Bill of Staff and Workers and Related Index

年份 Year	绝对数(亿元) Total Wage Bill(100 million yuan)				指数(以上年为100) Index (preceding year = 100)			
	全部职工 Total	国有单位 State-owned units	城镇集体单位 Urban Collective-owned units	其他单位 Other Types of Ownership	全部职工 Total	国有单位 State-owned units	城镇集体单位 Urban Collective-owned units	其他单位 Other Types of Ownership
1978	29.05	19.84	9.21		110.7	110.8	110.6	
1979	33.10	22.46	10.64		113.9	113.2	115.5	
1980	41.63	27.99	13.64		125.8	124.6	128.2	
1981	44.13	29.60	14.53		106.0	105.8	106.5	
1982	48.14	32.35	15.79		109.1	109.3	108.7	
1983	50.78	34.41	16.37		105.5	106.4	103.7	
1984	67.28	43.34	23.25	0.69	132.5	126.0	142.0	
1985	86.17	55.10	30.09	0.98	128.1	127.1	129.4	142.0
1986	105.56	67.93	36.28	1.35	122.5	123.3	120.6	137.8
1987	121.26	78.09	41.30	1.87	114.9	115.0	113.8	138.5
1988	152.53	99.17	50.60	2.76	125.8	127.0	122.5	147.6
1989	165.38	108.56	53.05	3.77	108.4	109.5	104.8	136.6
1990	184.60	123.25	56.70	4.65	111.6	113.5	106.9	123.3
1991	204.43	136.26	62.05	6.12	110.7	110.6	109.4	131.6
1992	251.51	170.85	71.64	9.02	123.0	125.4	115.4	147.4
1993	328.21	221.91	85.85	20.45	130.5	129.9	119.8	226.7
1994	450.44	312.56	103.32	34.56	137.2	140.8	120.3	169.0
1995	541.62	369.10	126.57	45.95	120.2	118.1	122.5	132.9
1996	595.72	411.30	128.61	55.81	110.0	111.4	101.6	121.5
1997	635.44	446.95	124.86	63.63	106.7	108.7	97.1	114.0
1998	628.49	422.35	99.49	106.65	103.0	101.8	92.9	131.3
1999	666.28	443.41	91.90	130.97	106.0	105.0	92.4	122.8
2000	705.36	463.63	82.98	158.75	105.9	104.6	90.3	121.2
2001	758.55	498.61	71.42	188.52	107.5	107.5	86.1	118.8
2002	813.09	506.06	60.42	246.61	107.2	101.5	84.6	130.8
2003	917.33	540.59	53.51	323.23	112.8	106.8	88.6	131.1
2004	1050.35	591.38	48.20	410.77	114.5	109.4	90.1	127.1
2005	1252.06	672.70	48.80	530.56	119.2	113.8	101.2	129.2
2006	1520.39	768.86	52.55	698.97	121.4	114.3	107.7	131.7
2007	1806.65	896.36	61.72	848.57	118.8	116.6	117.5	121.4
2008	2132.45	1035.56	72.33	1024.57	118.0	115.5	117.2	120.7
2009	2403.32	1196.05	75.78	1131.49	112.7	115.5	104.8	110.4
2010	2841.33	1344.25	85.33	1411.75	118.2	112.4	112.6	124.8
2011	3548.29	1569.23	102.31	1876.75	124.9	116.7	119.9	132.9
2012	4065.99	1758.24	119.59	2188.16	114.6	112.0	116.9	116.6
2013	8041.98	1914.49	179.22	5948.27	197.8	108.9	149.9	271.8
2014	9174.49	2083.33	190.74	6900.42	114.1	108.8	106.4	116.0
2015	9802.41	2262.27	179.75	7360.39	106.8	108.6	94.2	106.7
2016	10583.16	2570.48	203.71	7808.97	108.0	113.6	113.3	106.1

注：1998年起职工工资为在岗职工工资，不包括离开本单位仍保留劳动关系的职工的生活补助费(下同)。

a) Since 1998, the wage bill of staff and workers was for employed personnels, excluded living expense subsidies of the personnels who had left self units, but still remained labor relationship(the same as in the following tables).

3-21 城镇非私营单位就业人员工资总额(2016年)
Total Wages of Employed Persons in Urban Units (2016)

单位:亿元 (100 million yuan)

项 目	Item	就业人员工资总额 Annual Total Wages	在岗职工 Employed	其他就业人员 Others Employed Persons in Urban Areas
总 计	**Total**	**10583.16**	**10146.97**	**436.19**
按登记注册类型分	**Grouped by Status of Registration**			
国有单位	State-owned Units	2570.48	2492.61	77.87
城镇集体单位	Urban Collective-owned Units	203.71	192.39	11.32
其他单位	Other Units	7808.97	7461.97	347.00
内资单位	Domestic Funded	4865.53	4605.30	260.23
股份合作单位	Cooperative Units	20.98	19.98	1.00
联营单位	Joint Ownership Units	5.27	4.99	0.27
有限责任公司	Limited Liability Corporations	3508.06	3316.00	192.06
股份有限公司	Share-holding Corporations Ltd.	1253.07	1189.43	63.64
其他	Others	78.15	74.90	3.25
港、澳、台商投资单位	Units with Funds from Hong Kong, Macao and Taiwan	1000.33	981.59	18.74
外商投资单位	Foreign Funded Units	1943.11	1875.08	68.03
按企业、事业、机关分	**Grouped by Enterprises, Institutions and Agencies**			
企业	Enterprises	8426.23	8057.25	368.98
事业	Institutions	1521.49	1468.92	52.57
机关	Agencies & Organizations	598.94	585.41	13.54
按国民经济行业分	**Grouped by Sector**			
农、林、牧、渔业	Agriculture, Forestry, Animal Husbandry and Fishery	22.08	21.45	0.63
采矿业	Mining	57.72	57.15	0.57
制造业	Manufacturing	3790.50	3694.88	95.62
电力、热力、燃气及水生产和供应业	Production and Supply of Electric Power, Heat Power, Gas and Water	168.95	168.08	0.88
建筑业	Construction	2222.27	2037.42	184.85
批发和零售业	Wholesale and Retail Trades	379.15	368.57	10.58
交通运输、仓储和邮政业	Transport, Storage and Post	356.86	348.95	7.91
住宿和餐饮业	Hotels and Catering Services	75.48	69.97	5.51
信息传输、软件和信息技术服务业	Information Transfer, Software and IT Services	357.42	354.61	2.80
金融业	Financial Intermediation	442.34	404.35	37.99
房地产业	Real Estate	160.87	155.47	5.40
租赁和商务服务业	Leasing and Business Services	176.94	169.33	7.61
科学研究、技术服务业	Scientific Research and Technical Service	217.44	211.80	5.64
水利、环境和公共设施管理业	Management of Water Conservancy, Environment and Public Facilities	93.67	87.09	6.58
居民服务、修理和其他服务业	Services of Households and other Services	19.15	18.82	0.33
教育	Education	836.23	818.23	18.00
卫生和社会工作	Health and Social Work	448.49	421.76	26.73
文化、体育和娱乐业	Culture, Sports and Entertainment	66.29	64.05	2.24
公共管理、社会保障和社会组织	Public Administration, Social Security and Organization	691.29	674.98	16.31

3－22 制造业城镇非私营单位就业人员工资总额(2016 年)

Total Wages of Manufacturing Employees in Urban Units (2016)

单位:亿元 (100 million yuan)

项目	Item	合计 Total	#在岗职工 Employed	国有单位 State-owned Units	城镇集体单位 Urban Collective-owned Units	其他单位 Other Units
制造业合计	**Total of Manufacturing Industry**	**3790.50**	**3694.88**	**36.80**	**37.71**	**3715.99**
农副食品加工业	Processing of Food from Agricultural Products	46.94	45.18	0.30	0.11	46.52
食品制造业	Manufacture of Food	30.05	29.42	0.01	0.08	29.96
酒、饮料和精制茶制造业	Manufacture of Beverage	31.89	31.56	0.17	0.03	31.69
烟草制品业	Manufacture of Tobacco	9.40	9.40	0.27		9.13
纺织业	Manufacture of Textile	172.18	170.27	2.37	2.14	167.66
纺织服装、服饰业	Manufacture of Textile Wearing, Apparel, Footwear and Caps	180.74	177.63	0.98	0.57	179.19
皮革、毛皮、羽毛及其制品和制鞋业	Manufacture of Leather, Fur, Feather and Related and saps	33.14	32.81	0.05	0.03	33.06
木材加工和木、竹、藤、棕、草制品业	Processing of Timber, Manufacture of Wood, Bamboo, Rattan, Palm and Straw Products	23.24	22.95		0.07	23.17
家具制造业	Manufacture of Furniture	14.61	14.16		0.05	14.57
造纸和纸制品业	Manufacture of Paper and Paper Products	47.24	46.43	1.24	0.29	45.71
印刷和记录媒介复制业	Printing, Reproduction of Recording Media	30.98	30.28	0.48	0.26	30.23
文教、工美、体育和娱乐用品制造业	Manufacture of Articles For Culture, Education and Sport Activities	62.06	61.53		1.01	61.05
石油加工、炼焦和核燃料加工业	Processing of Petroleum, Coking, Processing of Nuclear Fuel	19.87	19.56	0.67	0.05	19.15
化学原料和化学制品制造业	Manufacture of Raw Chemical Materials and Chemical Products	262.77	256.63	3.12	2.02	257.63
医药制造业	Manufacture of Medicines	105.30	103.25			105.30
化学纤维制造业	Manufacture of Chemical Fibers	43.73	43.21	0.01	0.03	43.69
橡胶和塑料制品业	Rubber and Plastic Products	116.91	114.29	0.12	0.82	115.98
非金属矿物制品业	Manufacture of Non-metallic Mineral Products	84.79	83.29	2.53	0.55	81.71
黑色金属冶炼和压延加工业	Smelting and Pressing of Ferrous Metals	108.02	106.37	1.28	12.33	94.42
有色金属冶炼和压延加工业	Smelting and Pressing of Non-ferrous Metals	42.59	41.83	0.08	4.04	38.47
金属制品业	Manufacture of Metal Products	123.96	121.44	1.71	1.10	121.15
通用设备制造业	Manufacture of General Purpose Machinery	300.13	294.30	5.03	2.22	292.88
专用设备制造业	Manufacture of Special Purpose Machinery	183.06	178.70	0.98	0.23	181.85
汽车制造业	Manufacture of Automobile	222.97	216.15	5.41	0.22	217.33
铁路、船舶、航空航天和其他运输设备	Manufacture of Railroad, Marine Aviation and other Transport Equipment	119.13	115.80	4.01	0.61	114.50
电气机械和器材制造业	Manufacture of Electrical Machinery and Equipment	398.05	386.46	1.49	1.66	394.90
计算机、通信和其他电子设备制造业	Manufacture of Communication Equipment, Computers and other Electronic Equipment	876.82	843.82	1.45	5.50	869.87
仪器仪表制造业	Manufacture of Instrumentation	89.83	88.28	3.00	0.74	86.09
其他制造业	Other	6.32	6.27		0.31	6.00
废弃资源综合利用业	Manufacture of Recycling and Disposal of Waste	2.97	2.80	0.03	0.58	2.36
金属制品、机械和设备修理业	Manufacture of Metal Prodults, Machinery and Eauipment Repair	0.83	0.79		0.07	0.76

3-23 在岗职工平均工资及指数

Average Wage of Staff and Workers and Related Indices

年份 Year	绝对数（元） Absolute Figure (yuan)				指数（以上年为100） Index (preceding year = 100)			
	全部职工 Total	国有单位 State-owned Units	城镇集体单位 Urban Collective-owned Units	其他单位 Others	全部职工 Total	国有单位 State-owned Units	城镇集体单位 Urban Collective-owned Units	其他单位 Others
1978	513	563	432		108.2	108.9	107.5	
1979	565	618	478		110.3	109.8	110.9	
1980	667	721	578		117.8	116.7	120.7	
1981	672	718	594		100.7	99.6	102.8	
1982	703	748	626		104.6	104.2	105.4	
1983	723	768	643		102.8	102.7	102.7	
1984	931	1003	820	1012	128.8	130.6	127.5	
1985	1135	1211	1015	1237	121.9	120.7	123.8	122.2
1986	1327	1430	1166	1468	116.9	118.1	114.9	118.7
1987	1471	1581	1295	1639	110.9	110.6	111.1	111.6
1988	1796	1936	1564	2059	122.1	122.5	120.8	125.6
1989	1918	2082	1639	2185	106.8	107.5	104.8	106.1
1990	2129	2331	1776	2444	111.0	111.9	108.4	111.9
1991	2302	2501	1932	2773	108.1	107.3	108.8	113.5
1992	2800	3057	2292	3370	121.6	122.2	118.6	121.5
1993	3615	3896	2937	4434	129.1	127.4	128.1	131.6
1994	4974	5491	3728	5827	137.6	140.9	126.9	131.4
1995	5943	6441	4621	7137	119.5	117.3	124.0	122.5
1996	6603	7186	4990	7740	111.1	111.6	108.0	108.4
1997	7108	7745	5183	8376	107.6	107.8	103.9	108.2
1998	8256	8872	6033	8867	105.7	106.3	101.3	102.5
1999	9171	9855	6452	9763	111.1	111.1	106.9	110.1
2000	10299	11109	6962	10698	112.3	112.7	107.9	109.6
2001	11842	12917	7543	11790	115.0	116.3	108.3	110.2
2002	13509	15030	8638	12633	114.1	116.4	114.5	107.2
2003	15712	17502	9836	14656	116.3	116.4	113.9	116.0
2004	18202	20876	11350	16346	115.8	119.3	115.4	111.5
2005	20957	24659	13064	18468	115.1	118.1	115.1	113.0
2006	23782	28722	15550	20691	113.5	116.5	119.0	112.0
2007	27374	33411	18837	23641	115.1	116.3	121.1	114.3
2008	31667	39325	22929	27067	115.7	117.7	121.7	114.5
2009	35890	45446	27022	29901	113.3	115.6	117.9	110.5
2010	40505	51245	31502	34260	112.9	112.8	116.6	114.6
2011	45987	57002	37302	40028	113.5	111.2	118.4	116.8
2012	51279	62913	43835	45008	111.5	110.4	117.5	112.4
2013	57985	70114	51757	55117	113.1	111.4	118.1	122.5
2014	61783	74673	54993	58913	106.5	106.5	106.3	106.9
2015	67200	82355	59629	63790	108.8	110.3	108.4	108.3
2016	72684	92412	65536	68024	108.2	112.2	109.9	106.6

3-24 在岗职工平均工资指数
Average Wage Indices of Staff and Workers

1978 年 = 100 (100 in 1978)

年 份 Year	全部职工 Total		国有单位 State-owned Units		城镇集体单位 Urban Collective-owned Units		其他单位 Others	
	平均货币工资指数 Index of Average Wage	平均实际工资指数 Index of Average Real Wage	平均货币工资指数 Index of Average Wage	平均实际工资指数 Index of Average Real Wage	平均货币工资指数 Index of Average Wage	平均实际工资指数 Index of Average Real Wage	平均货币工资指数 Index of Average Wage	平均实际工资指数 Index of Average Real Wage
1978	100.0	100.0	100.0	100.0	100.0	100.0		
1979	110.3	109.5	109.8	109.0	110.9	110.1		
1980	130.0	121.7	128.1	119.9	133.8	125.3		
1981	130.0	118.3	128.1	116.6	133.8	121.7		
1982	137.0	122.3	132.9	118.7	144.9	129.4		
1983	140.9	132.7	136.4	128.4	148.8	140.1		
1984	181.5	154.9	178.2	152.0	189.8	161.9	100.0	100.0
1985	221.2	174.9	215.1	170.0	235.0	185.8	122.2	111.5
1986	258.7	189.2	254.0	185.8	269.9	197.4	145.1	124.4
1987	286.7	189.7	280.8	185.8	299.8	198.4	162.0	125.7
1988	350.1	189.0	343.9	185.7	362.0	195.5	203.5	128.8
1989	373.9	174.1	369.8	172.2	379.4	176.6	215.9	117.8
1990	415.0	189.8	414.0	189.3	411.1	188.0	241.5	127.4
1991	448.7	190.5	444.2	188.6	447.2	189.9	274.0	134.2
1992	545.8	213.2	543.0	212.1	530.6	207.3	333.0	149.9
1993	704.7	231.9	692.0	227.7	679.9	223.7	438.1	166.1
1994	969.6	254.6	675.3	256.1	863.0	226.6	575.8	174.2
1995	1158.5	261.7	1144.0	258.5	1069.7	241.7	705.2	183.6
1996	1287.1	262.5	1276.4	260.3	1155.1	235.5	764.8	179.7
1997	1385.6	278.9	1375.7	276.9	1199.8	241.5	827.7	192.0
1998	1609.4	324.1	1575.8	317.3	1396.5	281.2	876.2	203.4
1999	1787.7	365.1	1750.4	357.5	1493.5	305.0	964.7	227.1
2000	2007.6	410.1	1973.2	403.0	1611.6	329.2	1057.1	215.9
2001	2308.4	471.0	2294.3	468.1	1746.1	356.3	1165.0	237.7
2002	2545.6	525.2	2669.6	550.8	1999.5	412.5	1248.3	257.5
2003	3062.8	629.6	3108.7	639.0	2276.9	468.0	1448.2	297.7
2004	3548.2	703.3	3708.0	735.0	2627.3	520.8	1615.2	320.2
2005	4085.2	793.1	4379.9	850.3	3024.1	587.1	1824.9	354.3
2006	4635.9	885.8	5101.6	974.8	3599.5	687.8	2044.6	390.7
2007	5336.1	980.5	5934.5	1090.4	4360.4	801.2	2336.1	429.2
2008	6172.9	1078.0	6984.9	1219.9	5307.6	926.9	2674.6	467.1
2009	6996.1	1226.7	8072.1	1415.4	6255.1	1096.7	2954.6	518.1
2010	7895.7	1336.3	9102.1	1540.6	7292.1	1234.1	3385.4	573.0
2011	8964.3	1443.5	10124.7	1630.5	8634.7	1390.4	3955.3	637.0
2012	9995.9	1568.8	11174.6	1754.0	10147.0	1592.5	4447.4	698.1
2013	11303.1	1734.1	12453.6	1910.8	11980.8	1838.0	5446.3	835.7
2014	12043.5	1807.9	13263.4	1992.1	12729.9	1916.2	5821.4	871.3
2015	13099.4	1933.5	14627.9	2160.3	13803.0	2043.0	6303.4	927.7
2016	14168.4	2042.3	16414.2	2367.3	15170.4	2192.8	6721.7	966.1

注：其他单位以 1984 年为 100。
a) Other units with 100 in 1984.

3-25 城镇非私营单位就业人员平均工资(2016年)
Average Wage of Employed Persons in Urban Units (2016)

单位:元 (yuan)

项 目	Item	就业人员年平均工资 Annual Average Wage	在岗职工平均工资 Annual Average Wage of Staff and Workers	其他就业人员年均工资 Annual Average Wage of Others
总 计	**Total**	**71574**	**72684**	**52810**
按登记注册类型分	**Grouped by Type of Registreration**			
国有单位	State-owned Units	89222	92412	42388
城镇集体单位	Urban Collective-owned Units	63175	65536	39185
其他单位	Other Units	67418	68024	56572
内资单位	Inner Funded	65375	66620	49127
股份合作单位	Share Holding Cooperative Units	58000	58149	55169
联营单位	Joint-owned Co., Ltd.	52212	53735	34457
有限责任公司	Responsibility Co., Ltd.	61864	62954	47624
股份有限公司	Share Holding Co., Ltd.	78553	80465	54393
其他	Others	59930	60602	47725
港、澳、台商投资单位	Hong Kong, Macao and Taiwan Funded	64503	64355	73349
外商投资单位	Foreign Funded	75033	74068	117063
按企业、事业、机关分	**Grouped by Character of the Units**			
企业	Enterprises	67763	68499	54892
事业	Institutions	89344	92663	44655
机关	Government Agencies	99162	102726	39659
按国民经济行业分	**Grouped by Sector**			
农、林、牧、渔业	Farming, Forestry, Animal Husbandry and Fishery	37953	38858	21194
采矿业	Mining and Quarrying	62330	62797	35650
制造业	Manufacturing	66994	66468	96545
电力、热力、燃气及水生产和供应业	Production and Supply of Electric Power, Heat Power, Gas and Water	116629	117547	46677
建筑业	Construction	58172	59102	49569
批发和零售业	Wholesale and Retail Trade	67127	67423	58236
交通运输、仓储和邮政业	Transportation, Storage and Post	71773	72826	43837
住宿和餐饮业	Hotel and Catering Industry	45013	46514	31927
信息传输、软件和信息技术服务业	Information Transfer, Software and IT Services	130501	131872	56375
金融业	Banking	122648	151615	40430
房地产业	Real Estate	72680	74088	46985
租赁和商务服务业	Leasing and Commercial Services	60258	61083	46332
科学研究、技术服务业	Scientific Research and Technical Service	100375	101897	64304
水利、环境和公共设施管理业	Management of Water Conservancy, Environment and Public Facilities	60723	64760	33280
居民服务、修理和其他服务业	Services of Households and other Services	57905	58345	40404
教育	Education	88282	90661	40264
卫生和社会工作	Health and Social Work	92202	95727	58316
文化、体育和娱乐业	Culture, Sports and Recreation	84242	87087	43589
公共管理、社会保障和社会组织	Public Administralion, Social Secarily and Organization	96402	100010	38676

3-26 分地区城镇非私营单位就业人员平均工资
Average Wage of Employed Persons in Urban Units by Region

单位:元 (yuan)

地　区	Region	2011	2012	2013	2014	2015	2016
全　省	Total	45487	50639	57177	60867	66196	71574
苏　南	Southern Jiangsu	51234	56749	62126	67663	73792	81053
苏　中	Mid Jiangsu	41227	45838	53421	58337	62901	66331
苏　北	Northern Jiangsu	36377	41061	44196	48301	52866	56905
南京市	Nanjing	53753	59375	64811	70507	78946	87559
无锡市	Wuxi	50376	55381	61744	68187	74556	80251
徐州市	Xuzhou	38525	43130	45310	48770	52580	55750
常州市	Changzhou	49263	55027	60802	66852	70144	75946
苏州市	Suzhou	52504	58267	61995	67381	72656	80187
南通市	Nantong	44180	49063	57546	61383	65957	69654
连云港市	Lianyungang	37954	43195	45097	50224	54402	59208
淮安市	Huaian	36262	41072	45055	49204	53612	58111
盐城市	Yancheng	34928	39384	43052	47200	52389	57374
扬州市	Yangzhou	39778	44142	52582	58190	63168	66706
镇江市	Zhenjiang	42190	47064	53447	56733	62240	67581
泰州市	Taizhou	37717	42223	46190	52341	56613	59685
宿迁市	Suqian	31595	36159	41929	46236	51796	54466

3-27 分细行业城镇非私营单位就业人员平均工资(2016年)

Average Wage of Employed Persons in Urban Units by Sector in Detail(2016)

单位:元 (yuan)

项目	Item	合计 Total	#在岗职工 Employed	国有单位 State-owned Units	城镇集体单位 Urban Collective-owned Units	其他单位 Other Units
总计	**Total**	**71574**	**72684**	**89222**	**63175**	**67418**
按企业、事业、机关分	**Grouped by Enterprise, Institution and Agency**					
企业	Enterprises	67763	68499	77537	56956	67368
事业	Institutions	89344	92663	90694	74350	74379
机关	Agencies & Organizations	99162	102726	99166	77856	
按国民经济行业分	**Grouped by Sector**					
农、林、牧、渔业	Agriculture, Forestry, Animal Husbandry and Fishery	37953	38858	37763	51531	39775
农业	Farming	35376	36263	35106	51369	46322
林业	Forestry	39858	40521	40048		34217
畜牧业	Animal Husbandry	39596	40074	39443	60333	39980
渔业	Fishery	56847	57492	61620	51920	38181
农、林、牧、渔服务业	Service in Support of Agriculture	55449	56561	57826	50653	35450
采矿业	Mining	62330	62797	62445	34771	62506
制造业	Manufacturing	66994	66468	77131	56177	67038
电力、热力、燃气及水生产和供应业	Production and Supply of Electric Power, Heat Power, Gas and Water	116629	117547	139279	69823	99369
电力、热力生产和供应业	Production and Supply of Electric Power and Heat Power	137985	138680	158118	87655	115294
燃气生产和供应业	Production and Supply of Gas	81450	82171	73605	64867	81598
水的生产和供应业	Production and Supply of Water	72767	73480	64974	55716	78561
建筑业	Construction	58172	59102	57937	42453	58379
房屋建筑业	Housing Construction	58705	59440	53078	40075	58940
土木工程建筑业	Civil Engineering Construction	52802	54263	59130	44610	52049
建筑安装业	Architectural Installation	64023	64306	88366	49816	63897
建筑装饰和其他建筑业	Other Construction	55005	57272	59181	51296	55014
批发和零售业	Wholesale and Retail Trades	67127	67423	73957	37006	67220
批发业	Wholesale Trade	89466	89192	81022	34519	92169
零售业	Retail Trade	50857	51286	45034	39016	51232
交通运输、仓储和邮政业	Transport, Storage and Post	71773	72826	79209	49104	69608

3－27 续 表 Continued 1

单位:元 (yuan)

项 目	Item	合 计 Total	#在岗职工 Employed	国有单位 State-owned Units	城镇集体单位 Urban Collective-owned Units	其他单位 Other Units
铁路运输业	Railway Transport	105180	107053	107177	49576	133123
道路运输业	Road Transport	65179	66222	70803	51201	63926
水上运输业	Water Transport	67196	68768	77097	40253	67604
航空运输业	Air Transport	133128	137311	123927		133922
管道运输业	Transport Via Pipeline	90871	91002	85301		92275
装卸搬运和运输代理业	Handling and agency	70866	70998	72614	52072	72744
仓储业	Storage	68536	68469	67472	61905	69010
邮政业	Post	75598	76384	77280	94689	69297
住宿和餐饮业	Hotels and Catering Services	45013	46514	49245	41925	44580
住宿业	Hotel	49350	49784	49272	44543	49502
餐饮业	Catering Services	41517	43660	49113	37479	41315
信息传输、软件和信息技术服务业	Information Transfer, Software and IT Services	130501	131872	82386	79138	139512
电信、广播电视和卫星传输服务	Telecommunications, Satellites Radio and Television Services	106423	107069	79693	78403	117225
互联网和相关服务	Internet and Relatiue Services	113656	118640	181098	79678	111815
软件和信息技术服务业	Software and IT Services	165980	167235	99623	75250	167192
金融业	Financial Intermediation	122648	151615	102348	118951	131683
货币金融服务业	Nonetary and Financial	158478	159696	129091	118983	181790
资本市场服务业	Capital Markets	198854	203086	202196	67077	198931
保险业	Insurance	64514	108375	51240		68834
其他金融业	Other Financial Activities	207649	213672	75315		344820
房地产业	Real Estate	72680	74088	74150	52998	72876
#房地产开发经营	Development and Management of Real Estate	107224	107661	79332	60368	108963
租赁和商务服务业	Leasing and Business Services	60258	61083	51980	49812	65161
租赁业	Leasing	67588	67283	46603	50715	71532
商务服务业	Business Services	60087	60937	52030	49798	64968
科学研究、技术服务业	Scientific and Fednical Services	100375	101897	106930	75449	96721
研究和试验发展	Research and Experimental Development	132906	133642	137485	54166	118459
专业技术服务业	Professional Technical Services	96557	97689	87924	72708	100841

单位:元 (yuan)

项 目	Item	合 计 Total	#在岗职工 Employed	国有单位 State-owned Units	城镇集体单位 Urban Collective-owned Units	其他单位 Other Units
科技推广和应用服务业		70178	73069	75739	99530	66631
水利、环境和公共设施管理业	Management of Water Conservancy, Environment and Public Facilities	60723	64760	67110	42656	57376
水利管理业	Management of Water Conservancy	80351	82629	79503	116369	79830
生态保护和环境治理业	Ecological Protection and Enviromental	66415	71864	67384	23129	72591
公共设施管理业	Management of Public Facilities	54805	58744	60372	40780	55371
居民服务、修理和其他服务业	Services to Households and Other Services	57905	58345	75951	45156	56299
居民服务业	Services to Households	57546	58222	79780	42841	50017
机动车、电子产品和日用产品修理业	Vehicle, Electronics and Daiy Maintenance	73317	73595	50372	46391	76997
其他服务业	Other Services	50448	50786	74082	52491	49001
教育	Education	88282	90661	89580	81171	69533
卫生和社会工作	Health and Social Work	92202	95727	97803	81721	68344
卫生	Health	92456	95996	98126	81901	68509
社会工作	Social Work	77554	80608	81155	64524	55705
文化、体育和娱乐业	Culture, Sports and Entertainment	84242	87087	93103	73310	74139
新闻和出版业	Journalism and Publishing Activities	92237	94711	84687		99978
广播、电视、电影和影视录音制作业	Radio, TV, Movie and Video Recording	101006	104320	112761	122655	79751
文化艺术业	Cultural and Art Activities	75308	79093	78858	67397	65171
体育	Sports Activities	67197	68448	78870	114588	58402
娱乐业	Entertainment	59869	60437	82095	57956	58310
公共管理、社会保障和社会组织	Public Administration, Social Security and Organization	96402	100010	96445	80191	76106
中国共产党机关	Organs of Communist Party of China	105946	107054	105946		
国家机构	Government Agencies	96127	99814	96127		
人民政协、民主党派	People's Political Consultative Conference and Democratic Parties	121436	122855	121436		
社会保障	Social Security	83594	85955	84046	66778	126000
群众社团、社会团体和其他成员组织	Mass, Society and other Groups	105126	108279	105893	104607	84915

3－28 制造业城镇非私营单位就业人员平均工资（2016年）

Average Wage of Employed Persons in Manufacturing of Urban Units（2016）

单位:元 (yuan)

项目	Item	合计 Total	#在岗职工 Employed	国有单位 State-owned Units	城镇集体单位 Urban Collective-owned Units	其他单位 Other Units
制造业合计	**Total of Manufacturing Industry**	**66994**	**66468**	**77131**	**56177**	**67038**
农副食品加工业	Processing of Food from Agricultural Products	59014	58992	33114	53841	59329
食品制造业	Manufacture of Food	59004	59821	26022	23339	59281
酒、饮料和精制茶制造业	Manufacture of Beverage	49091	49015	42055	38107	49147
烟草制品业	Manufacture of Tobacco	156064	156064	105291		158364
纺织业	Manufacture of Textile	55626	55563	78440	55241	55403
纺织服装、服饰业	Manufacture of Textile Wearing, Apparel, Footwear and Caps	52119	51969	26276	42531	52439
皮革、毛皮、羽毛及其制品和制鞋业	Manufacture of Leather, Fur, Feather and Related and Saps	48320	48207	109045	30255	48308
木材加工和木、竹、藤、棕、草制品业	Processing of Timber, Manufacture of Wood, Bamboo, Rattan, Palm and Straw Products	50607	50482		24571	50758
家具制造业	Manufacture of Furniture	59962	59215		30698	60142
造纸和纸制品业	Manufacture of Paper and Paper Products	82720	81813	112104	38381	82732
印刷和记录媒介复制业	Printing, Reproduction of Recording Media	61424	60954	44504	34510	62225
文教、工美、体育和娱乐用品制造业	Manufacture of Articles For Culture, Education and Sport Activities	52296	52130		60052	52184
石油加工、炼焦和核燃料加工业	Processing of Petroleum, Coking, Processing of Nuclear Fuel	78838	78560	65754	88018	79369
化学原料和化学制品制造业	Manufacture of Raw Chemical Materials and Chemical Products	76909	76104	107272	56767	76861
医药制造业	Manufacture of Medicines	79240	79674			79240
化学纤维制造业	Manufacture of Chemical Fibers	60755	60592	24000	31220	60811
橡胶和塑料制品业	Rubber and Plastic Products	65182	64552	37263	41537	65495
非金属矿物制品业	Manufacture of Non-metallic Mineral Products	60144	59879	85359	48029	59699
黑色金属冶炼和压延加工业	Smelting and Pressing of Ferrous Metals	69485	69374	54078	57501	71713
有色金属冶炼和压延加工业	Smelting and Pressing of Non-ferrous Metals	68611	68121	83990	70494	68392
金属制品业	Manufacture of Metal Products	64784	64529	64103	57425	64868
通用设备制造业	Manufacture of General Purpose Machinery	74687	74030	124830	51486	74428
专用设备制造业	Manufacture of Special Purpose Machinery	73965	73303	48664	41384	74247
汽车制造业	Manufacture of Automobile	81316	80381	82168	45851	81358
铁路、船舶、航空航天和其他运输设备	Manufacture of Railroad, Marine Aviation and other Transport Equipment	69233	70514	75596	45486	69223
电气机械和器材制造业	Manufacture of Electrical Machinery and Equipment	72548	71820	72102	37444	72836
计算机、通信和其他电子设备制造业	Manufacture of Communication Equipment, Computers and Other Electronic Equipment	64409	63394	86946	73509	64331
仪器仪表制造业	Manufacture of Instrumentation	81799	81409	100620	55622	81599
其他制造业	Other	52534	52468	62750	50603	52634
废弃资源综合利用业	Manufacture of Recycling and Disposal of Waste	58927	57595	43500	60788	58759
金属制品、机械和设备修理业	Manufacture of Metal Prodults, Machinery and Eauipment Repair	49727	49906		43681	50366

3-29 城镇私营单位就业人员平均工资
Average Wage of Employed Persons in Urban Private Units

单位:元 (yuan)

行业	Sector	2011	2012	2013	2014	2015	2016
总计	**Total**	**27500**	**32069**	**36308**	**39975**	**43689**	**47156**
农、林、牧、渔业	Farming, Forestry, Animal Husbandry and Fishery	23187	26974	32509	33060	35768	37048
采矿业	Mining	24032	27956	31952	35613	38081	39749
制造业	Manufacturing	27684	32020	36209	39661	44082	48133
电力、热力、燃气及水生产和供应业	Production and Supply of Electric Power, Heat Power, Gas and Water	28316	30331	34937	37951	39841	43928
建筑业	Construction	29461	32435	37086	41457	44776	48351
批发和零售业	Wholesale and Retail Trade	26315	31261	34243	37335	39986	41803
交通运输、仓储和邮政业	Transportation, Storage and Post	27615	31778	37581	40785	43236	47241
住宿和餐饮业	Hotel and Catering Industry	25388	28282	32203	33819	35818	36197
信息传输、软件和信息技术服务业	Information Transfer, Software and IT Services	31875	38178	48079	51238	52318	52879
金融业	Banking	29360	34809	37342	38444	43725	46658
房地产业	Real Estate	29256	32984	36671	36768	41083	42121
租赁和商务服务业	Leasing and Commercial Services	27860	33849	36304	40240	43948	46631
科学研究、技术服务业	Scientific Research and Technical Service	31947	37866	43454	44305	46993	50933
水利、环境和公共设施管理业	Management of Water Conservancy, Environment and Public Facilities	26504	31329	41626	43240	45312	45393
居民服务、修理和其他服务业	Services of Households and other Services	26183	30309	36246	40699	41195	42302
教育	Education	27662	32264	42977	44023	44600	45802
卫生和社会工作	Health and Social Work	30710	33202	34448	38292	41992	46492
文化、体育和娱乐业	Culture, Sports and Recreation	26187	29752	32697	36443	39839	43600

主要统计指标解释

人口数 指一定时点、一定地区范围内的有生命的个人的总和。

年度统计的年末人口数指每年12月31日24时的人口数。年度统计的全国人口总数内未包括台湾省和港澳同胞以及海外华侨人数。

城镇人口和乡村人口

1952—1989年城镇人口是指市辖区内和县辖镇的全部人口;乡村人口是指县辖乡人口。

1990—1999年城镇人口是指设区的市的区人口和不设区的市所辖的街道人口以及不设区的市所辖镇的居民委员会人口和县辖镇的居民委员会人口;乡村人口是除上述两种人口以外的全部人口。

2000—2005年人口普查和2000年以后城镇人口:市人口是指设区市的人口密度在1500人/平方公里以上的市区人口和人口密度不足1500人的区政府驻地和区辖其他街道人口,以及政府驻地的城市建设延伸到的周边乡镇人口;不设区市的市政府驻地和市辖其他街道人口,以及政府驻地的城市建设延伸到的乡镇人口。镇人口是指镇政府驻地和镇辖其他居委会人口,以及镇政府驻地的城区建设延伸到周边村民委员会人口。乡村人口是指除上述人口以外的全部人口。

2006年至今的城镇人口分为城区人口和镇区人口。其中,城区人口,包括街道办事处所辖的居民委员会(社区委员会),及城市公共设施、居住设施等连接到的其他居民委员会(社区委员会)和村民委员会的人口。镇区人口,包括镇所辖的居民委员会(社区委员会),镇的公共设施、居住设施等连接到的村民委员会,以及常住人口在3000人以上独立的工矿区、开发区、科研单位、大专院校、农场、林场等特殊区域中的人口。乡村人口是指除上述人口以外的全部人口。

出生率(又称粗出生率) 指在一定时期内(通常为一年)一定地区的出生人数与同期内平均人数(或期中人数)之比。一般用千分率表示。本资料中的出生率指年出生率,其计算公式为:

出生率 = 年出生人数/年平均人数 × 1000‰

式中:出生人数指活产婴儿,即胎儿脱离母体时(不管怀孕月数),有过呼吸或其他生命现象。年平均人数指年初、年底人口数的平均数,也可用年中人口数代替。

死亡率(又称粗死亡率) 指在一定时期内(通常为一年)一定地区的死亡人数与同期内平均人数(或期中人数)之比,一般用千分率表示。本资料中的死亡率指年死亡率,其计算公式为:

死亡率 = 年死亡人数/年平均人数 × 1000‰

人口自然增长率 指在一定时期内(通常为一年)人口自然增加数(出生人数减死亡人数)与该时期内平均人数(或期中人数)之比,一般用千分率表示。计算公式为:

人口自然增长率 = (本年出生人数—本年死亡人数)/年平均人数 × 1000‰

就业人员 指从事一定社会劳动并取得劳动报酬或经营收入的人员,包括在岗职工、再就业的离退休人员、私营业主、个体户主、私营和个体就业人员、乡镇企业就业人员、农村就业人员、其他就业人员(包括民办教师、宗教职业者、现役军人等)。这一指标反映了一定时期内全部劳动力资源的实际利用情况,是研究我国基本国情国力的重要指标。

单位就业人员 指在各类法人单位工作,并由单位支付劳动报酬的人员,包括在岗职工和其他就业人员。在岗职工指在本单位工作且与本单位签订劳动合同,并由单位支付各项工资和社会保险、住房公积金的人员,以及上述人员中由于学习、病伤、产假等原因暂未工作仍由单位支付工资的人员。其他就业人员指在本单位工作,不能归到在岗职工、劳务派遣人员中的人员。此类人员是实际参加本单位生产或工作并从本单位取得劳动报酬的人员。具体包括:非全日制人员、聘用的正式离退休人员、兼职人员和第二职业者等,以及在本单位中工作的外籍和港澳台方人员。

城镇私营和个体就业人员 城镇私营就业人员指在工商管理部门注册登记,其经营地址设在县城关镇(含城关镇)以上的私营企业就业人员;包括私营企业投资者和雇工。城镇个体就业人员指在工商管理部门注册登记,并持有城镇户口或在城镇长期居住,经批准从事个体工商经营的就业人员;包括个体经营者和在个体工商户劳动的家庭帮工和雇工。

城镇登记失业人员 指在劳动年龄(16周岁至退休年龄)内,有劳动能力无业而要求就业,并在当地就业服务机构进行失业登记的城镇常住人员。

国有单位就业人员 指在国有经济单位及其附属机构工作,并由其支付工资的各类人员。

城镇集体单位就业人员 指在城镇集体经济单位及其管理部门工作,并由其支付工资的各类人员。

其他单位就业人员 指在联营经济、股份制经济、外商投资经济、港、澳、台投资经济单位工作,并由其支付工资的各类人员。

工资总额 根据《关于工资总额组成的规定》,工资总额是指本单位在报告期内(季度或年度)直接支付给本单位人员的劳动报酬总额。包括计时工资、计件工资、奖金、津贴和补贴、加班加点工资、特殊情况下支付的工资。工资总额是税前工资,包括单位从个人工资中直接为其代扣或代缴的房费、个人所得税、水费、电费、住房公积金和社会保险基金个人缴纳部分等。工资总额不论是计入成本的还是不计入成本的,不论是以货币形式支付的还是以实物形式支付的,均应列入工资总额的计算范围。工资总额由基本工资、绩效工资、工资性津贴和补贴、其他工资四部分组成。工资总额不包括病假、事假等情况的扣款。

平均工资 指在报告期内单位发放工资的人均水平。计算公式为:

平均工资 = 报告期工资总额/报告期平均人数

在岗职工平均工资指数 指报告期在岗职工平均工资与基期在岗职工平均工资的比率,是反映不同时期在岗职工货币工资水平变动情况的相对数。计算公式为:

在岗职工平均工资指数 = 报告期平均工资/基期平均工资 × 100%

在岗职工平均实际工资指数 在岗职工平均实际工资指扣除物价变动因素后的在岗职工平均工资。在岗职工平均实际工资指数是反映实际工资变动情况的相对数,表明在岗职工实际工资水平提高或降低的程度。计算公式为:

在岗职工平均实际工资指数 = 报告期平均工资指数/报告期城镇居民消费价格指数 × 100%。

Explanatory Notes on Main Statistical Indicators

Total Population refers to the total number of people alive at a certain point of time within a given area.

The annual statistics on total population is taken at midnight, the 31st of December, not including residents in Taiwan province, Chinese compatriots in Hong Kong and Macao and overseas Chinese.

Urban Population and Rural Population

From 1952 to 1989 urban population refers to the population of municipal districts and towns under the administration of counties; rural population refers to the population of townships under the administration of counties. From 1990 to 1999 rural population is composed of the population of districts of cities divided into districts, the population of sub-district offices under the cities not divided into districts, the population of neighborhoods of towns under the administration of cities not divided into districts and the population of neighborhoods of towns under the administration of counties; rural population is the population other than those mentioned above. Rural population from 2000 to 2005: city population is composed of the population of districts of cities divided into districts with population density at more than 1500 people per square kilometer, the population of places where the district governments are stationed and other sub-district offices under the administration of the district with population density at less than 1500 people per square kilometer, and the population of circumjacent townships where are the extending areas of city construction of the places where the governments are stationed; the population of places where the city (not divided into districts) governments are stationed and other sub-district offices under the administration of the city, and the population of circumjacent townships where are the extending areas of city construction of the places where the governments are stationed. Town population refers to the population of places where town governments are stationed and other neighborhood committees under the administration of the towns, and the population of circumjacent villagers' committees where are the extending areas of town construction of the places where the town governments are stationed. Rural population is the population other than those mentioned above. From 2006 to now urban population is composed of city population and town population. City population includes the population of neighborhood committees (community committees) under the administration of sub-district offices and the population of other neighborhood committees (community committees) and villagers' committees connected through city common facilities and residence facilities. Town population includes the population of neighborhood committees (community committees) under the administration of towns and the population of villagers' committees connected through town common facilities and residence facilities, and the population of special areas with more than 3000 permanent residents, such as independent mining areas, development zones, research institutes, universities and colleges, farms, forestry centers and so on. Rural population is the population other than those mentioned above.

Birth Rate or (Crude Birth Rate) refers to the ratio of the number of births to the average population (or mid-period population) during a certain period of time (usually a year) which is often expressed in ‰. Birth rate in the chapter refers to annual birth rate. The following formula is used: Birth Rate = Number of Births/Average Number of Population × 1000‰

Number of births refers to live births i. e. the births when babies had showed any vital phenomena regardless of the length of pregnancy.

Annual Average Number of Population is the average of the number of population at the beginning of the year and that at the end of the year. Sometimes it is substituted for with the mid year population.

Death Rate(or Crude Death Rate) refers to the ratio of the number of deaths to the average population(or mid-period population) during a certain period of time(usually a year) which is often expressed in ‰. Death rate in the chapter refers to annual death rate. The following formula is used:

Death Rate = Number of Deaths/Annual Average Number of Population × 1000‰

Natural Growth Rate of Population refers to the ratio of natural increase in population(number of births minus number of deaths) in a certain period of time(usually a year) to the average population(or mid-period population) of the same period which is often expressed in ‰. The following formulas are applied:

Natural Growth of Population = (Number of Births – Number of Deaths)/Average Number of Population × 1000‰

Natural Growth Rate of Population = Birth Rate-Death Rate

Illiteracy Rate refers to the percentage of illiterate population to total aged 15 and over of resilent population.

Employed Persons refer to the persons who are engaged in social working and receive remuneration payment or earn business income, including total staff and workers, re-employed retirees, employers of private enterprises, self-employed workers, employees in private enterprises and individual economy, employees in township enterprises, employed persons in the rural areas, and other employed persons(including teachers in the schools run by the local people, people engaged in religious profession and the servicemen, etc.). This indicator reflects the actual utilization of total labour force during a certain period of time and is often used for the research on China's economic situation and national power.

Persons Employed in Various Units refer to all the persons working in government agencies of various levels, political and party organization, social organizations, enterprises and institutions, and receiving wages or other forms of payment. They include fully-employed staff and workers, re-employed retirees, teachers in schools run by the local people, foreigners and Chinese compatriots from Hong Kong, Macao, and Taiwan working in various units, part-time employees, employees of other units working temporarily at current posts, and employees holding the second job, but exclude staff and workers who have left their working units while keeping their labour contract(employment relation) unchanged. This indicator reflects the total number of laborers actually engaged in production or other operations in various units.

Persons Employed in Private Enterprises and Self-Employed Individuals in Urban Areas Persons employed in private enterprises refer to the persons employed in the private enterprises which have been registered at the departments of industrial and commercial administration and are situated at urban areas or townships for business operation or at urban areas with the level higher than a county town. The self-employed individuals in urban areas refer to persons who hold the certificates of residence in urban areas or have resided in the urban areas for a long time and have been registered at the departments of industrial and commercial administration and approved to be engaged in individual industrial or commercial business, including self-employed persons as well as helpers and hired labourers who work in the individual households engaged in industrial or commercial business.

Registered Urban Unemployed Persons The registered unemployed persons in urban areas refer to the persons who are registered as permanent residents in the urban areas, aged within the range of working age, capable to labour, unemployed but desirous to be employed and have been registered at the local employment service agencies to apply for a job.

Staff and Workers in State-owned Economic Units refer to the persons who work in the state-owned economic units or their attached units and are listed in their payrolls.

Staff and Workers of Collective Owned Units in Urban Areas refer to the persons who work in collective owned units in urban areas and their administration departments and receive payment therefrom.

Staff and Workers in Units of Other types of Ownership refer to those who work in (and receive payment therefrom) enterprises and institutions of joint ownership, share holding, foreign ownership, and ownership by entrepreneurs from Hong Kong, Macao, and Taiwan.

Total Wages of Staff and Workers refer to the total remuneration payment to staff and workers in various units during a certain period of time. The calculation of total wages is based on the total remuneration payment to the staff and workers. Therefore, all the wages and salaries and other payments to staff and workers are included in the total wages regardless of their sources, category, and forms (in kind or cash). (Total wages of staff and workers in this yearbook include only total wages of fully employed staff and workers, excluding the living allowances distributed to those who have left their working units while keeping their labor contract/employment relation unchanged).

Average Wage of Staff and Workers refers to the average wage in money terms per person during a certain period of time for staff and workers in enterprises, institutions, and government agencies, which reflects the general level of wage income during a certain period of time and is calculated as follows:

Average Wage of Staff and Workers = Total Wages of Staff and Workers at the Report Period/Average Number of Staff and Workers at the Report Period.

Average Wage Indices of Employed Staff and Workers refers to the ratio of average wage of staff and workers in the report period to that in the base period, which reflects the change of wage of staff and workers at the different period. It is calculated as follows:

Average Wage Indices of Staff and Workers = Average Wage of Staff and Workers at the Report Period/Average Wage of Staff and Workers at the Base Period × 100%

Average Real Wage Indices of Employed Staff and Workers average real wage of staff and workers refers to the average wage of staff and workers after removing the effects of the price changes and average real wage indices of staff and workers refers to the change of real wage, which reflects the relative increasing or decreasing level of real wage of staff and workers, which is calculated as follows:

Average Real Wage Indices of Staff and Workers = Average Wage Indices of Staff and Workers at the Report Period/Urban Consumer Price Indices at the Report Period × 100%

价格指数

Price Indices

简 要 说 明

一、本篇资料的主要内容

本篇价格指数资料，反映生产、流通、消费与投资等环节的价格变动趋势和变动幅度。主要包括居民消费价格指数、商品零售价格指数、农业生产资料价格指数、工业生产者价格指数、固定资产投资价格指数和房地产价格指数等。

二、本篇的资料来源

价格指数编制由国家统计局江苏调查总队组织实施。各市、县调查队依据国家统计局统一制定的价格统计调查制度向基层采集原始数据汇总后上报。

三、居民消费、商品零售价格指数

编制居民消费、商品零售价格指数的资料采用抽样调查和重点调查相结合的方法取得，即在全省选择不同经济区域和分布合理的地区，以及有代表性的商品作为样本，对其市场价格进行定期调查，以样本推断总体。编制过程按下列几个步骤进行：

1. 选择调查地区和调查点。调查地区按照经济区域和地区分布合理等原则，选出具有代表性的大、中、小城市和县作为国家的调查地区，在此基础上选定经营规模大、商品种类多的商场（包括集市和服务网点）作为调查点。

2. 选择代表商品和代表规格品。代表商品是选择那些消费量大、价格变动有代表性的商品；代表规格品的确定是根据商品零售资料和城市居民、农村居民的消费支出记帐资料，按照有关规定筛选的。筛选原则：(1)与社会生产和人民生活关系密切；(2)消费（销售）数量（金额）大；(3)市场供应稳定；(4)价格变动趋势有代表性；(5)所选的代表规格品之间差异大。

目前，居民消费价格调查按用途划分为 8 大类，262 个基本分类，各地每月调查 600 种以上规格产品价格；商品零售价格按用途划分为 16 个大类，197 个基本分类，各地每月调查 500 种以上的规格产品价格。

3. 价格调查方式。采用派员直接到调查点登记调查，同时聘请辅助调查员协助登记调查。

4. 权数的确定。商品零售价格指数的计算权数主要根据社会商品零售额资料确定；居民消费价格指数的计算权数根据城乡居民家庭消费支出构成确定。

四、工业生产者价格指数

工业生产者价格包括工业企业产品第一次出售时的出厂价格（下简称工业生产者出厂价格）和原材料、燃料、动力购进价格（下简称工业生产者购进价格）。

工业生产者价格调查采用重点调查与典型调查相结合的调查方法。重点调查将全部年主营业务收入 2000 万元以上（2010 年以前为 500 万元以上）的企业列为调查对象；典型调查是把年主营业务收入 2000 万元以下（2010 年以前为 500 万元以下）的企业作为抽样对象。

1. 代表企业的选择原则：(1)按工业行业选择调查企业，各中类行业原则上都要有调查企业。(2)大型企业应尽量都选上（或占相当大比重）。(3)选择生产稳定、正常的企业作为调查对象。

2. 代表产品的选择原则：(1)按工业行业选择基本分类和代表产品。(2)选择对国计民生影响大的产品。(3)选择生产较为稳定的产品。(4)选择有发展前景的产品。(5)选择具有地方特色的产品。

目前《工业生产者出厂价格调查目录》包括 20000 多种工业产品，并将其划分为 1638 个基本分类。工业生产者购进价格调查项目由上述出厂调查目录的大部分和部分农副产品两部分组成，包括 10000 多种调查产品，确定为 981 个基本分类。

3. 价格调查方式。采用企业报表形式。

4. 权数的确定。工业生产者出厂价格统计中，小类及小类以上的权数资料来源于工业统计中分行业工业销售产值数据资料；基本分类的权数资料来源于独立的工业企业产品权数调查。工业生产者购进价格统计中，基本分类及以上分类的权数资料主要来源于独立的工业企业产品权数调查，小类及小类以上的权数还可以参照相应行业的出厂权数和分行业的投入产出数据资料。权数一般五年更换一次。

五、固定资产投资价格指数

固定资产投资价格调查采用重点调查与典型调查相结合的方法。固定资产投资价格调查所涉及的价格是构成固定资产投资额实体的实际购进价格或结算价格。调查的内容包括构成当年建筑工程实体的钢材、木材、水泥、地方建材（如砖、瓦、灰、沙、石等)、化工材料(如油漆等)等主要建筑材料价格;作为活劳动投入的劳动力价格(单位工资)和建筑机械使用费;设备工器具购置和其他费用投资价格。

固定资产投资价格调查样本的选择遵循以下原则:

1. 选择建筑安装工程调查点的原则:(1)样本单位应具有一定覆盖面;(2)投资经济活动代表性强;(3)兼顾不同经济类型;(4)选择重点工程;(5)兼顾国民经济各门类及不同工程类别。

2. 选择其他费用调查点的原则:在选择其他费用调查点时,所遵循的原则与建筑安装工程调查点的原则基本相同,特别是要注意选择那些投资额大的工程。但由于其他费用不易取得,所以在实际操作过程中,应同时在建设单位、施工单位开展重点调查,并辅以典型调查(从管理部门取得资料)。

3. 价格调查方式。采用企业报表和调查员走访相结合的方式。

4. 权数的确定。固定资产投资价格指数的计算权数是建筑安装工程、设备工器具购置和其他费用三者前两年投资完成额的平均比重。

六、房地产价格指数

住宅销售价格包括新建住宅和二手住宅两部分。

新建住宅价格调查,在2010年以前采用重点调查与典型调查相结合的方法,从2011年开始,采用全面调查的方法。二手住宅价格调查采用重点调查与典型调查相结合的方法。

调查方式采用报表与走访相结合的方式。

Brief Introduction

Ⅰ. Main Contents

Data on price indices in this chapter show the changing trends and the change rates in the prices of production, trade, consumption and investment, including mainly consumer price indices, retail price indices, price indices for means of agricultural production, producer price indices for farm products, price indices for investment in fixed assets, and price indices for real estate.

Ⅱ. Sources of Data

Compilation of statistics on price indices is organized by the Survey Office of the National Bureau of Statistics in Jiangsu. The selected cities and counties collect data from the grassroots units in accordance with the scheme of price survey system stipulated by the NBS, tabulate them and report them to the higher agencies.

Ⅲ. Consumer Price Indices and Retail Price Indices

Data for compilation of the consumer price indices and the retail price indices in Jiangsu are collected through a combination of sample surveys and surveys of key units. Areas distributed in different economic regions are selected as the sample areas and representative commodities are selected as the sample commodities. Regular surveys are conducted to collect data on their market prices. Population parameters are inferred on the basis of the sample data. Following are major steps in the process of calculation of the price indices:

(1) The selection of areas and survey points: Based on such principles as regional economic features and reasonable geographic distribution, representative sample areas for the national survey are selected which include large, medium and small cities and counties. When the sample areas have been selected, large-scale shops and markets (including fairs and service outlets) with wide variety of commodities are selected as survey points.

(2) The selection of representative commodities and their specifications or varieties: The representative commodities selected are those consumed in large quantity and representative in price changes. The representative specifications or varieties are determined according to the data on the retail sales of commodities and the consumption expenditure account data of the residents of urban households and rural households; and selection follows the related instructions. The principles for selection are: (a) The commodities are closely related to so-

cial production and people's living conditions; (b) They are consumes (or sold) in large quantities (or large values); (c) The market supply is stable; (d) The changes of their prices are representative in trend; (e) There is great heterogeneity among the specifications or varieties selected.

At present, data are collected on 600 and more specifications each month under 262 basic headings in 8 categories in the consumer price surveys. For the retail price surveys, data are collected on more than 500 specifications each month under 229 basic headings in 16 categories.

(3) Method of data collection: Enumerators are sent to the survey points to take the records of the prices. Assistant enumerators are recruited to assist the survey work.

(4) Determination of the weights: The weights for calculation of the retail price indices are determined mainly according to the total retail sales of commodities. The weights for calculation of the consumer price indices are determined according to the composition of the consumption expenditures of urban and rural households.

Ⅳ. Producer Price Indices for Industrial Products

Producer prices for manufactured goods refer to the ex-factory price of manufactured goods when they are first sold. The survey program is a combined use of the key units' survey and typical units' survey methods. Key units refer to those non-State-owned industrial enterprises with annual revenue above 20 million yuan. (Before 2010, it was above 5 nillion yuan) Typical units refer to the industrial enterprises with annual sale revenue below 20 million yuan. (Before 2010, it was below 5 million yuan).

(1) Principles for selecting the representative enterprises:

(a) Enterprises to be covered in the survey are selected by industrial sectors. In principle, every branch should have enterprises selected; (b) All (or a majority of) large-sized enterprises should be selected; (c) Enterprises selected should be those with normal and stable production; (d) Different types of ownership should be considered in selecting enterprises.

(2) Principle for the selection of representative goods:

(a) The goods are selected by industrial sectors; (b) The selected goods should have great impact on the national economy and people's living conditions; (c) The production of the goods selected are relatively more stable; (d) The prospects of the goods selected are promising; (e) The goods selected are typical to the place in question.

The *survey catalog of Producer Prices for Industrial Products* includes over 20000 goods, and they are divided into 1638 basic classification; *Survey catalog of Purchasing Price for Industrial Producers* includes over 10000 goods, and they are divided into 981 basic classifications.

(3) Method of data collection: The method of reporting forms by enterprises is adopted.

(4) Determination of the weights: The weights for calculation of the producer price indices for manufactured goods are determined according to the total sales value of manufactured goods. Data from the industrial census are used for the calculation. If census data are not available for the reference year, industrial statistical data and statistical data from other agencies will be used to estimate the weights. The weights are replaced every five years.

Ⅴ. Price Indices for Investment in Fixed Assets

Data on prices of investment in fixed assets are collected by a program involving the combined use of surveys on key units and surveys on typical units. The prices collected in the surveys of investment in fixed assets are the actual purchasing prices or settlement prices of entities of investment in fixed assets. The survey content includes the prices of main construction materials that constitute the architectural engineering entity in the year, such as steel, timber, cement, local construction materials (such as brick, tile, calcareous ashes, sand, stone, etc.), chemical materials (such as oil paint, etc.), the price of labor force as input (wages), prices for renting of building machinery and equipment, the purchasing price of equipment, tools and instruments and the prices of others investments.

The following principles should be followed in selecting the sample for the price survey of investment in fixed assets:

(1) Principles for selecting the survey points of construction and installation: (a) Sample units should have a good coverage; (b) The economic activity of investment should have strong representativeness; (c) Different economic types of ownership should be considered; (d) key projects should be selected; (e) Attention should be given to various sectors of the national economy and types of projects.

(2) Principles for selecting price survey points of other fees: The principles for selecting survey points of others fees is in general the same as that of construction and installation, with special attention being paid to selecting projects with huge investment value. Since it is not easy to obtain the other fees, during the actual data gathering operations, survey on key construction owner units and building units is to conducted concurrently with survey on typical units (with information from administration units)

(3) Method of price survey: A combination of enterprises reporting system and enumerator visits method.

(4) Determination of the weights: The weights for calculation of the price indices for investment in fixed assets are determined according to the average proportion of construction and installation, purchase of equipment, tools and instruments and other investments in the 2 preceding years.

Ⅵ. Price Indices for Real Estate

Sale prices of houses include the prices for commercialized houses and for second-hand houses.

New housing price Survey before 2010 using the key survey and typical method of combining. Beginning of 2011, take a comprohensive survey. Second-hand housing prices using a combiration of approaches fouse on investigation and sampling surveys. The mothod including reports and visition.

4-1 各种价格指数
Price Indices

上年=100　　(preceding year=100)

年　份 Year	居民消费价格指数 Consumer Price Index	城市 Urban	农村 Rural	商品零售价格指数 Retail Price Index	工业生产者出厂价格指数 Producer Price Index for Industrial Products	工业生产者购进价格指数 Purchasing Price Index for Industrial Products	固定资产投资价格指数 Price Index for Investment in Fixed Assets
1979	101.0	100.7	101.3	101.3			
1980	105.6	105.7	105.6	105.8			
1981	101.5	102.3	100.9	101.4			
1982	100.9	100.9	101.0	100.9			
1983	100.4	100.8	100.0	100.1			
1984	103.0	104.1	102.1	102.5			
1985	109.5	109.6	109.4	109.5			
1986	107.1	106.4	107.7	107.1			
1987	109.2	110.5	107.7	109.3			
1988	121.9	122.6	121.4	122.3			
1989	117.1	116.0	118.5	116.8			
1990	103.2	103.4	103.0	102.3			
1991	104.9	107.7	101.9	104.8	103.2	107.0	104.5
1992	106.6	108.8	104.4	105.1	103.8	110.2	112.1
1993	118.2	118.7	117.3	115.9	118.5	125.7	138.8
1994	123.2	125.3	121.7	123.6	121.4	120.1	114.6
1995	115.8	116.2	115.3	114.3	114.2	117.3	107.4
1996	109.3	110.8	107.1	106.8	100.6	103.9	103.2
1997	101.7	101.3	102.0	99.3	97.9	97.9	99.2
1998	99.4	100.0	99.0	98.2	94.5	91.4	98.8
1999	98.7	98.6	98.8	96.9	96.1	94.4	98.3
2000	100.1	100.0	100.1	98.6	101.1	107.1	101.2
2001	100.8	100.1	101.5	98.9	99.1	99.5	100.8
2002	99.2	98.4	100.2	98.4	97.6	98.6	101.3
2003	101.0	100.9	101.2	99.8	102.3	106.5	104.3
2004	104.1	103.7	104.6	102.2	106.5	116.3	109.3
2005	102.1	102.0	102.4	100.3	102.6	107.6	100.9
2006	101.6	101.6	101.7	100.8	101.5	106.4	101.2
2007	104.3	104.1	104.8	102.9	102.6	105.0	104.9
2008	105.4	105.2	105.6	104.9	104.6	115.0	110.0
2009	99.6	99.6	99.5	98.9	95.2	91.9	97.7
2010	103.8	103.6	104.3	103.2	107.3	112.8	105.1
2011	105.3	105.1	105.9	104.6	106.2	108.9	106.8
2012	102.6	102.6	102.6	102.1	97.1	95.8	98.6
2013	102.3	102.3	102.5	101.4	98.0	97.1	100.5
2014	102.2	102.2	102.2	101.6	98.3	97.0	101.1
2015	101.7	101.7	101.5	100.6	95.3	92.1	96.2
2016	102.3	102.4	101.8	100.8	98.1	98.0	98.8

4-2 各种价格定基指数
Fixed-base Price Indices

年份 Year	居民消费价格指数（1978年=100） Consumer Price Index (1978=100)	城市 Urban	农村 Rural	商品零售价格指数（1978年=100） Retail Price Index (1978=100)	工业生产者出厂价格指数（1990年=100） Producer Price Index for Industrial Products (1990=100)	工业生产者购进价格指数（1990年=100） Purchasing Price Index for Industrial Products (1990=100)	固定资产投资价格指数（1990年=100） Price Index for Investment in Fixed Assets (1990=100)
1979	101.0	100.7	101.3	101.3			
1980	106.7	106.4	107.0	107.7			
1981	108.3	108.9	107.9	108.7			
1982	109.2	109.9	109.0	109.7			
1983	109.7	110.7	109.0	109.8			
1984	113.0	115.3	111.3	112.5			
1985	123.7	126.4	121.8	123.2			
1986	132.5	134.4	131.1	131.9			
1987	144.7	148.6	141.2	144.2			
1988	176.3	182.1	171.5	176.4			
1989	206.5	211.3	203.2	206.0			
1990	213.1	218.5	209.3	210.7			
1991	223.5	235.3	213.3	220.9	103.2	107.0	104.5
1992	238.3	256.0	222.6	232.1	107.1	117.9	117.1
1993	281.7	303.9	261.2	269.0	126.9	148.2	162.6
1994	347.0	380.7	317.8	332.5	154.1	178.0	186.3
1995	401.8	442.4	366.5	380.1	176.0	208.8	200.1
1996	439.2	490.2	392.5	405.9	177.0	216.9	206.5
1997	446.7	496.6	400.3	403.1	173.3	212.4	204.9
1998	444.0	496.6	396.3	395.8	163.8	194.1	202.4
1999	438.2	489.6	391.6	383.5	157.4	183.3	199.0
2000	438.7	489.6	392.0	378.1	159.1	196.3	201.4
2001	442.2	490.1	397.8	373.9	157.7	195.3	203.0
2002	438.6	482.2	398.6	368.0	153.9	192.6	205.6
2003	443.0	486.5	403.4	367.3	157.4	205.2	214.4
2004	461.2	504.5	422.0	375.4	167.6	238.6	234.3
2005	470.9	514.6	432.1	376.5	171.9	256.8	236.4
2006	478.4	522.8	439.5	379.5	174.5	273.2	239.2
2007	499.0	544.3	460.6	390.5	179.0	286.7	250.9
2008	525.9	572.6	486.4	409.6	187.2	329.7	276.0
2009	523.8	570.3	484.0	405.1	178.2	303.0	269.7
2010	543.7	590.8	504.8	418.1	191.2	341.8	283.5
2011	572.7	621.1	534.7	437.4	203.1	372.2	302.8
2012	587.4	637.0	548.5	446.4	197.2	356.6	298.6
2013	601.2	651.6	562.2	452.7	193.3	346.3	300.1
2014	614.4	666.0	574.5	459.8	190.0	335.9	303.4
2015	624.7	677.4	583.2	462.5	181.1	309.4	291.9
2016	638.7	693.3	593.0	466.2	177.7	303.2	288.4

4－3 居民消费价格分类指数（2016年）

Consumer Price Indices by Category（2016）

上年＝100　　(preceding year＝100)

类别	Item	全省 Total	城市 Urban	农村 Rural
总指数	**General Index**	**102.3**	**102.4**	**101.8**
消费品价格指数	Consumer Price Index	101.8	101.7	102.0
服务价格指数	Service Item Price Index	103.0	103.4	101.3
食品烟酒	Food or smoke wine	103.8	103.6	104.3
食品	Food	104.7	104.6	105.4
粮食	Grain	100.2	100.3	100.0
薯类	Tubers	110.7	110.9	110.0
豆类	Beans	99.8	100.2	98.9
食用油	Oil	100.9	101.2	100.0
菜	Vegetables	110.3	109.6	113.3
#鲜菜	Fresh Vegetables	111.3	110.4	114.8
畜肉类	Meat	111.1	110.9	111.9
#猪肉	Pork	116.0	115.8	116.3
禽肉类	Poultry	101.2	101.0	102.1
水产品	Aquatic Products	106.7	106.8	106.3
蛋类	Eggs	96.3	96.4	96.0
奶类	Dairy	100.1	100.1	99.9
干鲜瓜果类	Dried and Fresh Melons and Fruits	97.0	97.1	96.5
#鲜瓜果	Fresh Fruits	96.1	96.2	95.9
糖果糕点类	Cake, Biscuit and Bread	100.5	100.2	101.1
调味品	Flavoring	103.5	103.8	102.2
其他食品类	Other Foods	101.3	101.7	100.6
茶及饮料	Tea and Beverages	100.3	100.3	100.6
烟酒	Tobacco and Wine	101.3	101.2	101.5
烟草	Tobacco	102.1	102.1	102.0
酒类	Liquor	99.9	99.8	100.4
在外餐饮	Dining Out	102.8	102.7	103.3
衣着	Clothing	101.8	101.8	102.0
服装	Garments	101.6	101.5	101.9
服装材料	Clothing Material	103.3	103.3	103.3
其他衣着及配件	Other Clothing and Accessories	101.4	101.3	101.6
衣着加工服务费	Clothing Manufacturing Services	102.0	101.5	103.8

4-3 续 表 Continued

上年=100 (preceding year=100)

类 别	Item	全省 Total	城市 Urban	农村 Rural
鞋类	Footwear	102.7	102.8	102.3
居住	Residence	101.2	101.5	100.3
租赁房房租	Renting	101.8	101.8	101.5
住房保养维修及管理	Maintenance and management of housing	101.1	101.4	100.4
水电燃料	Water, Electricity and Fuels	100.4	101.1	98.1
自有住房	Private Housing	101.5	101.5	101.1
生活用品及服务	Daily Necessities and Services	101.6	101.7	101.0
家具及室内装饰品	Furniture and Interior Decorations	101.1	101.2	100.9
家用器具	Household Appliances	100.7	100.7	100.6
家用纺织品	Daily Use Textile	101.1	101.4	100.3
家庭日用杂品	Daily Use Household Articles	100.8	100.7	101.1
个人护理用品	Personal Articles	101.6	101.7	101.2
家庭服务	Household Services	107.6	107.9	104.8
交通和通信	Transportation and Communication	98.8	98.7	99.1
交通	Transportation	98.3	98.2	98.6
通信	Communication	99.8	99.8	99.9
教育文化和娱乐	Education and Culture Articles	100.9	100.9	100.7
教育	Education	101.6	101.8	101.2
文化娱乐	Culture and Recreational Articles	100.0	100.0	99.3
文娱耐用消费品	Durable Consumer Goods for Cultural and Recreational Use and Services	96.6	96.7	95.9
文化娱乐服务	Cultural and Recreational Services	100.2	100.2	100.6
旅游	Touring and Outing	101.0	101.0	101.5
医疗保健	Health Care	109.1	111.2	102.6
药品及医疗器具	Medicine and Medical Instrument	99.7	99.0	102.8
医疗服务	Medical Services	113.7	117.9	102.5
其他用品和服务	Other Supplies and Services	102.7	102.8	102.5
其他用品类	Other Supplies	104.0	104.4	102.4
其他服务类	Other Services	101.7	101.6	102.7

4－4 商品零售价格分类指数（2016 年）

Retail Price Indices by Categories（2016）

上年＝100　　　　（preceding year＝100）

类　别	Item	全省 Total	城市 Urban	农村 Rural
商品零售价格指数	**Retail Price Index**	**100.8**	**100.7**	**101.3**
食品	Food	104.2	104.1	105.0
饮料、烟酒	Beverages, Tobacco and Liquor	101.0	101.0	101.2
服装、鞋帽	Garments, Shoes, Hats	102.0	102.0	102.1
纺织品	Textiles	101.6	101.6	101.2
家用电器及音像器材	Household Appliances, Music and Video Equipment	99.5	99.5	99.4
文化办公用品	Cultural and Office Appliances	97.9	97.9	97.7
日用品	Articles for Daily Use	101.0	101.0	100.9
体育娱乐用品	Sports and Recreation Arcticles	100.7	100.7	100.2
交通、通信用品	Transportation and Communicatior Appliances	99.6	99.6	99.8
家具	Furniture	101.3	101.3	100.6
化妆品	Cosmetics	102.0	102.0	101.4
金银饰品	Gold and Silver Ornaments	105.9	106.1	104.7
中西药品及医疗保健用品	Traditional Chinese and Western Medicines and Health Care Articles	99.0	98.6	102.7
书报杂志及电子出版物	Books, Newspapers, Magazines and Electronic Publications	100.5	100.4	101.6
燃料	Fuels	96.8	96.9	95.6
建筑材料及五金电料	Building Materials and Hardware	100.2	100.2	100.0
农业生产资料类	**Means of Agricultural Production General Price Index**	**99.9**		
农用手工工具	Farm Handtools	100.1		
饲料	Forage	95.1		
仔畜幼禽及产品畜	Young Animal Production Livestock	129.3		
半机械化农具	Semi-mechanized Farm Tools	100.5		
机械化农具	Mechanized Farm Machinery	100.0		
化学肥料	Chemical Fertilizer	96.0		
农药及农药器械	Pesticide and Its Appliances	100.4		
化学农药	Chemical Pesticide	100.3		
农药器械	Pesticide Appliances	101.1		
农机用油	Oil for Farm Machinery	94.6		
其他农用生产资料	Other Means of Agricultural Production	100.9		
农业生产服务	Service for Agricultural Prodcution	102.8		

4-5 工业生产者出厂价格指数

Producer Price Indices for Industrial Products

上年=100 (preceding year=100)

类别	Item	2000	2005	2010	2015	2016
工业生产者出厂价格指数	**Producer Price Indices for Industrial Products**	**101.1**	**102.6**	**107.3**	**95.3**	**98.1**
轻工业	Light Industry	97.9	100.3	104.9	98.3	98.9
以农产品为原料	Using Farm Products as Raw Materials	97.1	100.9	107.3	99.1	100.2
以非农产品为原料	Using Non-Farm Products as Raw Materials	99.5	100.1	103.6	97.0	97.4
重工业	Heavy Industry	102.8	105.4	109.7	94.3	97.8
采掘	Mining and Quarrying	102.2	121.6	125.0	80.8	93.1
原料	Raw Materials	110.9	109.7	113.8	91.1	96.5
加工	Manufacturing	96.7	102.1	107.4	95.4	98.3
生产资料	Means of Production	103.0	103.2	108.2	94.4	97.8
采掘	Mining and Quarrying	101.9	121.9	124.4	80.8	93.1
原料	Raw Materials	110.8	108.9	114.3	90.5	96.3
加工	Manufacturing	97.3	100.9	106.3	95.6	98.2
生活资料	Consumer Goods	96.6	100.5	103.1	99.6	99.3
食品	Food	89.6	99.9	105.6	99.1	100.4
衣着	Clothing	100.9	102.9	103.2	100.6	101.3
一般日用品	Daily-use Articles	98.5	101.2	102.1	99.3	99.3
耐用消费品	Durable Consumer Goods	95.6	98.2	100.8	99.5	97.1

4-6 分部门工业生产者出厂价格指数

Producer Price Indices for Industrial Products by Industry

上年=100 (preceding year=100)

类别	Item	2000	2005	2010	2015	2016
工业生产者出厂价格指数	**Producer Price Indices for Industrial Products**	**101.1**	**102.6**	**107.3**	**95.3**	**98.1**
冶金工业	Metallurgical Industry	104.1	103.5	112.6	86.5	98.3
电力工业	Power Industry	106.1	106.0	100.5	100.7	96.3
煤炭及炼焦工业	Coal Industry	94.0	116.1	116.8	81.6	100.1
石油工业	Petroleum Industry	144.4	119.6	127.3	80.0	91.6
化学工业	Chemical Industry	105.2	105.8	113.8	91.1	97.0
机械工业	Machine Building Industry	95.8	100.0	102.9	98.7	98.0
建筑材料工业	Building Materials Industry	99.2	95.4	105.5	94.5	98.2
森林工业	Timber Industry	97.1	103.0	101.3	101.0	100.3
食品工业	Food Industry	89.4	99.6	105.1	98.7	100.3
纺织工业	Textile Industry	101.8	101.5	111.7	98.3	99.5
缝纫工业	Tailoring Industry	102.0	103.3	103.2	100.6	101.2
皮革工业	Leather Industry	102.5	101.5	101.8	99.6	100.4
造纸工业	Paper Industry	104.9	101.8	107.9	99.4	99.5
文教艺术用品工业	Cultural, Educational and Handicrafts Articles	103.4	102.2	101.1	100.3	101.6
其他工业	Others	102.6	100.8	104.0	100.4	99.7

4-7 分行业工业生产者出厂价格指数
Producer Price Indices for Industrial Products by Sector

上年=100 (preceding year=100)

行业	Sector	2012	2013	2014	2015	2016
工业生产者出厂价格指数	**Producer Price Indices for Industrial Products**	**97.1**	**98.0**	**98.3**	**95.3**	**98.1**
煤炭开采和洗选业	Mining and Washing of Coal	91.1	85.7	86.8	79.8	90.1
石油和天然气开采业	Extraction of Petroleum and Natural Gas	98.6	94.2	94.6	54.9	84.9
黑色金属矿采选业	Mining and Processing of Ferrous Metal Ores	84.4	97.3	78.7	63.2	80.9
有色金属矿采选业	Mining and Processing of Non-Ferrous Metal Ores	86.3	91.1	98.1	96.0	91.1
非金属矿采选业	Mining and Processing of Nonmetal Ores	104.3	100.5	100.1	99.6	100.7
农副食品加工业	Processing of Food from Agricultural Products	100.2	98.6	97.6	98.0	100.6
食品制造业	Manufacture of Food	101.7	101.8	101.1	99.8	99.5
酒、饮料和精制茶制造业	Manufacture of Beverage	103.6	100.2	100.0	99.0	99.0
烟草制品业	Manufacture of Tobacco	101.9	100.4	100.0	100.5	100.0
纺织业	Manufacture of Textile	95.9	99.5	99.0	98.4	99.5
纺织服装、服饰业	Manufacture of Textile Wearing, Apparel, Footwear and Caps	104.6	101.6	100.1	101.1	101.6
皮革、毛皮、羽毛及其制品和制鞋业	Manufacture of Textile, Fur, Feather and footwear Products	103.0	103.2	100.4	99.2	99.9
木材加工和木、竹、藤、棕、草制品业	Processing of Timber, Manufacture of Wood, Bamboo, Rattan, Palm and Straw Products	103.8	100.3	100.8	101.1	100.3
家具制造业	Manufacture of Furniture	102.5	100.7	101.5	99.7	100.4
造纸和纸制品业	Manufacture of Paper and Paper Products	97.6	97.7	100.8	99.4	99.4
印刷和记录媒介复制业	Printing, Reproduction of Recording Media	100.2	99.7	99.8	99.9	99.4
文教、工美、体育和娱乐用品制造业	Manufacture of Culture, Education, Arts, Crafts Sports and Enterfaiment Supplies	102.0	100.7	99.8	100.7	101.9
石油加工、炼焦和核燃料加工业	Processing of Petroleum, Coking, Processing of Nuclear Fuel	101.4	96.5	94.8	78.1	94.0

4－7 续 表 Continued

上年＝100 （preceding year＝100）

行业	Item	2012	2013	2014	2015	2016
化学原料和化学制品制造业	Manufacture of Raw Chemical Materials and Chemical Products	94.1	97.0	98.6	89.2	96.5
医药制造业	Manufacture of Medicines	94.4	99.2	99.5	98.9	99.8
化学纤维制造业	Manufacture of Chemical Fibers	87.7	96.3	93.1	87.7	94.9
橡胶和塑料制品业	Manufacture of Rubber and Plastics	99.4	99.6	99.3	96.0	98.1
非金属矿物制品业	Manufacture of Non-ferrous Metals	96.9	98.7	100.8	95.2	98.1
黑色金属冶炼和压延加工业	Smelting and Pressing of Ferrous Metals	90.3	92.7	92.5	81.1	99.3
有色金属冶炼和压延加工业	Smelting and Pressing of Non－ferrous Metals	92.2	95.1	96.4	91.7	94.7
金属制品业	Manufacture of Metal Products	98.4	98.0	99.2	96.4	98.1
通用设备制造业	Manufacture of General Purpose Machinery	99.6	99.9	99.7	99.1	98.7
专用设备制造业	Manufacture of Special Purpose Machinery	100.9	101.8	99.9	99.2	99.0
汽车制造业	Manufacturing of Transport Equipment	99.7	99.0	99.0	98.7	97.5
铁路、船舶、航空航天和其他运输设备制造业	Manufacture of Railroad, Marine, Aviation and other Transport Equipment	99.2	98.7	99.3	99.9	99.7
电气机械和器材制造业	Manufacture of Electrical Machinery and Equipment	95.9	97.1	98.7	97.4	97.5
计算机、通信和其他电子设备制造业	Manufacture of Computer Communications and other Electronic Equipment	98.1	97.7	98.7	98.9	97.7
仪器仪表制造业	Manufacture of Instrumentation	100.8	99.8	100.0	99.6	99.6
其他制造业	Other Manufacturing	103.8	102.0	103.5	103.2	102.9
废弃资源综合利用业	Manufacture of Recycling and Disposal of Waste	95.2	92.8	83.9	86.0	101.5
金属制品、机械和设备修理业	Manufacture of Metal Products, Machinery and Equipment Repair	102.0	98.7	98.1	99.4	99.7
电力、热力生产和供应业	Production and Supply of Electric Power and Heat Power	101.2	99.6	100.1	101.2	95.2
燃气生产和供应业	Production and Supply of Gas	100.7	101.6	106.4	102.8	91.4
水的生产和供应业	Production and Supply of Water	101.0	102.2	100.9	102.4	103.5

4-8 工业生产者购进价格指数
Purchasing Price Indices for Industrial Products

上年=100 (preceding year=100)

类别	Item	2012	2013	2014	2015	2016
工业生产者购进价格指数	**Purchasing Price Indices for Industrial Products**	**95.8**	**97.1**	**97.0**	**92.1**	**98.0**
燃料动力类	Fuel and Power	99.1	95.8	96.0	85.1	96.7
黑色金属材料类	Ferrous Metal	92.1	94.7	94.9	87.8	98.4
有色金属材料和电线类	Non-Ferrous Metal and Wire	91.8	95.3	95.3	90.2	95.9
化工原料类	Chemical Materials	91.6	97.3	97.8	91.1	97.3
木材及纸浆类	Timber and Pulp	101.9	99.8	98.7	102.5	99.0
建筑材料及非金属矿类	Construction Materials and Non-Metal Mining Industry	96.0	95.7	99.0	91.7	96.5
其他工业原材料、半成品类	Other Industrial Raw Materials and Semi-Finished Products	97.0	97.6	97.8	96.7	98.7
农副产品类	Farm and Sideline Products	101.3	102.3	97.7	93.5	100.3
纺织原料类	Textile Raw Materials	97.9	99.4	97.7	98.0	100.3

4-9 固定资产投资价格指数
Price Indices for Investment in Fixed Assets

上年=100 (preceding year=100)

类别	Item	2000	2005	2010	2015	2016
总指数	**General Index**	**101.2**	**100.9**	**105.1**	**96.2**	**98.8**
建筑安装工程	Construction and Installation	102.4	99.6	106.9	93.4	98.3
设备、工器用具购置	Purchase of Equipment and Instruments	97.8	100.5	101.7	99.5	98.7
其他费用	Others	102.6	106.5	105.6	101.8	102.1

4-10 房地产价格指数
Real Estate Price Indices

上年=100 (preceding year=100)

类别	Item	2012	2013	2014	2015	2016
新建住宅	New Residential					
南京	Nanjing	98.5	108.6	104.2	100.2	129.0
无锡	Wuxi	99.2	103.4	100.6	96.4	115.7
徐州	Xuzhou	99.0	106.4	102.6	96.7	103.9
扬州	Yangzhou	99.3	103.9	102.4	95.2	103.9
二手住宅	Second-hand Residential					
南京	Nanjing	96.8	105.4	103.4	100.9	121.6
无锡	Wuxi	100.1	101.9	99.8	96.9	107.9
徐州	Xuzhou	97.7	102.2	99.3	96.3	102.0
扬州	Yangzhou	96.9	100.8	100.9	97.9	101.7

主要统计指标解释

商品零售价格指数 是反映城乡商品零售价格变动趋势的一种经济指数。零售物价的调整变动直接影响到城乡居民的生活支出和国家的财政收入,影响居民购买力和市场供需平衡,影响消费与积累的比例。因此,计算零售价格指数,可以从一个侧面对上述经济活动进行观察和分析。

居民消费价格指数 是反映一定时期内城乡居民所购买的生活消费品价格和服务项目价格变动趋势和程度的相对数,是对城市居民消费价格指数和农村居民消费价格指数进行综合汇总计算的结果。利用居民消费价格指数,可以观察和分析消费品的零售价格和服务价格变动对城乡居民实际生活费支出的影响程度。

城市居民消费价格指数 是反映城市居民家庭所购买的生活消费品价格和服务项目价格变动趋势和程度的相对数。城市居民消费价格指数可以观察和分析消费品的零售价格和服务价格变动对职工货币工资的影响,作为研究职工生活和确定工资政策的依据。

农村居民消费价格指数 是反映农村居民家庭所购买的生活消费品价格和服务项目价格变动趋势和程度的相对数。农村居民消费价格指数可以观察农村消费品的零售价格和服务价格变动对农村居民生活消费支出的影响,直接反映农民生活水平的实际变化情况,为分析和研究农村居民生活问题提供依据。

工业生产者价格指数 是反映工业产品价格变化趋势和变动幅度的统计指标,是工业企业的产品价格在不同时间和空间条件下平均变动的相对数。工业生产者价格包括工业品第一次出售时的出厂价格和企业作为中间投入的原材料、燃料、动力购进价格,简称为工业生产者出厂价格和工业生产者购进价格。工业生产者价格指数是进行国民经济核算和经济管理的重要依据。

固定资产投资价格指数 是反映固定资产投资价格变动趋势和程度的相对数。固定资产投资额由建筑安装工程投资完成额,设备、工器具购置投资完成额和其他费用投资完成额三部分组成。编制固定资产投资价格指数应首先分别编制上述三部分投资的价格指数,然后采用加权算术平均法求出固定资产投资价格总指数。

编制固定资产投资价格指数可以准确地反映固定资产投资中涉及的各类商品和取费项目价格变动趋势和变动幅度,消除按现价计算的固定资产投资指标中的价格变动因素,真实地反映固定资产投资的规模、速度、结构和效益,为国家制定、检查固定资产投资计划并提高宏观调控水平,为完善国民经济核算体系提供科学的、可靠的依据。

Explanatory Notes on Main Statistical Indicators

Retail Price Indices reflects the general change in retail prices of commodities. The change and adjustment in retail prices directly affect the living expenditure of urban and rural residents, government revenue, purchasing power of residents and the equilibrium of market supply and demand, and the ratio of consumption to accumulation. Therefore, the calculation of retail price index is useful to analyze the changes of the above economic activities.

Consumer Price Indices reflects the trend of changes in prices of consumer goods and services purchased by urban and rural residents, and is a composite index derived from the urban consumer price index and the rural consumer price index. Consumer price index can be used to analyze the impact of consumer price change on actual expenditure for living cost of urban and rural residents.

Urban Consumer Price Indices reflects the trend and degree of changes in prices of consumer goods and services purchased by urban households. It can be used to observe and analyze the impact of price changes in consumer goods and services on money wages ot staff and workers, and provide basis for policy making concerning the living cost and wages of staff and workers.

Rural Consumer Price Indices reflects the trend and degree of changes in prices of consumer goods and services purchased by rural households. It can be used to observe the impact of change in retail prices of consumer goods and service prices in rural areas on living expenditure of rural households, and to show the changes in the living standard of peasants. It provides basis for analysis and research on condition of life in rural areas.

Producer Price Indices for Industrial Products reflects the trend and manitude of response changes in the prices of industrial prouducts. It is the price of the industrial enterprises in the different time and space in relative number. This index including industrial products for the first time and as an intermediate input of raw materials full and power purchase. It is an important basis for the national accounts and economic management.

Price Indices for Investment in Fixed Assets reflects the trend and degree of changes in prices of investment in fixed assets. The investment in fixed assets consists of three componen, namely the investment in construction and installation, the investment in purchases of equipment and instrument, and the investment in other items. Price index of investment in fixed assets is calculated as the weighted arithmetic mean of the price indices of the three components of investment in fixed assets.

5

人民生活
People's Living Conditions

简 要 说 明

一、本篇资料的主要内容

本篇资料反映江苏人民生活现状及变化情况。

居民生活状况的数据来源于住户调查，是对居民家庭抽样调查汇总的结果。主要内容包括居民现金和实物收支情况、住户成员及劳动力从业情况、居民家庭食品和能源消费情况、住房和耐用消费品拥有情况、家庭经营和生产投资情况、社区基本情况以及其他民生状况等。

二、住户样本抽选方法

住户调查的样本抽选包括抽样方法设计、调查网点代表性评估、调查小区抽选以及摸底调查、调查住宅抽选、调查户落实等现场抽样工作。

住户调查的样本量按满足以下代表性需求的标准确定：在 95% 的置信度下，居民及分城乡居民人均可支配收入、消费支出以及主要收入项和消费项的抽样误差控制在 3% 以内。

三、住户调查方法

住户调查采用日记账和问卷调查相结合的方式采集基础数据。其中，居民现金收入与支出、实物收入与支出等内容主要使用记账方式采集。住户成员及劳动力从业情况、住房和耐用消费品拥有情况、家庭经营和生产投资情况、社区基本情况及其他民生状况等资料使用问卷调查方式采集。

四、城乡一体化住户调查

从 2013 年开始，经国务院同意，国家统计局对长期分开进行的城镇住户调查和农村住户调查实施了一体化改革。按照城乡常住人口现状，统一调查指标、统一抽样方法、统一调查过程、统一数据处理和统一数据发布，建立了城乡一体化住户收支调查制度，并在全国统一实施。指标名称、城乡划分范围和指标口径同时发生了变化。

Brief Introduction

Ⅰ. Main Contents

Data in this chapter show the people's living conditions in Jangsu.

Data on resident's living conditions are collected through a sample survey on households, consisting of income and expenditure of cash and real object, household members, employed persons, food and energy consumption, residence condition, ownership of durable consumer goods, household business and production investment, basic situation of community and so on.

Ⅱ. Method for Household Sampling

Samples selection consist of sampling method design, representative evaluation of surevey site, survey area selection, suvey for basic conditon, investigated residence selection, investigated household verification.

Samples of household survey meet the standards: under the confidence level of 95%, the sampling errors of income of income of residents, income of urban and rural residents, consumption expenditure, main income and consumption are controlled within 3%.

Ⅲ. Method for Household Survey

Basic data are collected by journal and questionnaire, among this ways, cash income and expenditure, real objects income and expenditure are mainly collected by account. Data on people's livelihood consist of household members, employed persons, ownership of housing and durable consumer, household business and production investment, basic situation of community are collected by questionnaire.

Ⅳ. Urban and Rural Household Survey

From 2013, the State Council agreed that the National Bureau of Statistics can carry out the integration of rural household and urban household survey. According to the current situation of urban and rural resident population, investigation index, sampling methods, investigation process, data processing and data release were all unified, the unified urban and rural household income and expenditure survey system has been established and carried out nationwide, name of index name, rage of urban and rural areas and standards of some indicators were changed at the same time.

5-1 人民生活水平情况

Basic Statistics on People's Living Standard

指　　标	Item	2013	2014	2015	2016
就业	**Employment**				
农村平均每户家庭从业人口 (人)	Number of Employed Persons per Rural Household (person)	2.14	2.07	1.92	1.95
每一农村就业人口负担人数 (人)	Number of Dependents per Labor of Rural (person)	1.44	1.44	1.54	1.53
城镇平均每户家庭从业人口 (人)	Number of Employed Persons per Urban Household (person)	1.72	1.71	1.65	1.66
每一城镇就业人口负担人数 (人)	Number of Dependents per Labor of Urban (person)	1.74	1.75	1.80	1.79
城镇登记失业率 (%)	Registered Urban Unemployment Rate (%)	3.03	3.01	3.00	3.00
收入与支出 (元)	**Income and Expenditure (yuan)**				
居民人均可支配收入	Per Capita Disposable Income of Residents	24776	27173	29539	32070
居民生活消费支出	Per Capita Consumption Expanditure of Residents	17926	19164	20556	22130
城镇常住居民人均可支配收入	Per Capita Disposable Income of Urban Permanent Residents	31585	34346	37173	40152
城镇常住居民人均生活消费支出	Per Capita Consumption Expanditure of Urban Permanent Residents	22262	23476	24966	26433
农村常住居民人均可支配收入	Per Capita Disposable Income of Rural Permanent Residents	13521	14958	16257	17606
农村常住居民人均生活消费支出	Per Capita Consumption Expanditure of Rural Permanent Residents	10759	11820	12883	14428
职工年平均工资	Annual Average Wage of Workers and Staff	57985	61783	67200	72684
生活质量	**Life Quality**				
居民家庭恩格尔系数 (%)	Household's Engle Coefficient (%)	29.0	29.2	28.9	28.3
城镇居民	Urban	28.4	28.5	28.1	28.0
农村居民	Rural	31.1	31.4	31.7	29.5
人均住房面积 (平方米)	Per Capita Floor Space of Residential Building (sq. m)	44.2	44.9	45.2	46.3
城镇人均现住房建筑面积	Per Capita Existing Residential Building Space in Urban Areas	39.3	39.5	39.6	40.3
农村人均现住房建筑面积	Per Capita Existing Residential Building Space in Rural Areas	52.4	54.2	55.0	56.9
交通状况	**Traffic**				
城市每万人拥有公共汽(电)车 (辆)	Number of Public Transportation Vehicles Per 10000 Persons (unit)	12.7	14.1	15.1	15.5
城市人均拥有道路面积 (平方米)	Per Capita Area of Road in Urban Areas (sq. m)	23.2	23.9	24.4	25.4
城镇每百户拥有家用汽车 (辆)	Number of Automabiles Per 100 Urban Households (unit)	30.8	34.6	39.1	45.8
农村每百户拥有摩托车 (辆)	Number of Motor－cycles Per 100 Rural Households (unit)	44.9	47.8	43.7	42.1

5－1 续表1 Continued 1

指 标	Item	2013	2014	2015	2016
邮电通信水平	**Level of Postal and Telecommunication**				
每一邮政局所服务面积（平方公里）	Average Area Served by Every Post Office (sq. km)	42.50	42.80	44.95	45.02
固定电话普及率 （部/百人）	Popularization Rate of Fixed Telephones (unit/100 persons)	28.84	26.90	25.10	21.42
移动电话普及率 （部/百人）	Rate Popularization of Mobil-telephones (unit/100 persons)	100.03	101.70	103.40	102.79
城市公用事业	**Public Utilities in Urban Areas**				
用水普及率 （%）	Coverage Rate of Urban Population with Access to Tap Water (%)	99.7	99.8	99.8	99.9
燃气普及率 （%）	Coverage Rate of Urban Population with Access to Gas (%)	99.6	99.5	99.6	99.5
人均公园绿地面积（平方米）	Per Capita Public Green Land Area (sq. m)	14.0	14.4	14.6	14.79
文化、教育和卫生	**Culture, Education and Healthcare**				
文化	Culture				
广播综合人口覆盖率 （%）	Radio Coverage of Population (%)	99.99	99.99	100.0	100.0
电视综合人口覆盖率 （%）	TV Coverage of Population (%)	99.88	99.88	100.0	100.0
城镇每百户拥有彩色电视机（台）	Numberof Color TV Sets Owned per 100 Househo0lds in Urban Areas (unit)	164.5	166.9	170.6	173.9
农村每百户拥有彩色电视机（台）	Numberof Color TV Sets Owned per 100 Households in Rural Areas (unit)	145.0	141.7	146.8	154.5
每百户家用电脑拥有量（台）	Number of Computers Owned per 100 Households (unit)	65.8	67.4	73.4	76.6
城镇	Urban Areas	89.7	91.7	91.4	94.2
农村	Rural Areas	36.5	37.7	42.3	45.0
居民家庭文教娱乐支出比重（%）	Percentage of Household Expenditure on Culture, Recreation and Education (%)	11.88	11.68	11.79	11.36
城镇	Urban Areas	12.27	12.09	12.25	11.97
农村	Rural Areas	10.54	10.28	10.25	9.37
教育	Education				
升学率 （%）	Enrollment Rate (%)				
学龄儿童入学率	Enrollment Rate of School-age Chidren	100.0	100.0	100.0	100.0
小学毕业生升学率	Enrollment Rate of Primary School Graduates	100.0	100.0	100.0	100.0
每万人口在校学生数 （人）	Number of Students per 10000 Persons (person)				
大学生数	University (or college) Students	232.7	232.3	234.6	238.5

5－1 续表2 Continued 2

指 标	Item	2013	2014	2015	2016
中学生数	Secondary School Students	374.7	362.6	356.7	362.7
小学生数	Primary School Students	549.7	592.3	626.4	652.9
平均每一教师负担学生（人）	Average Number of Students Supported by a Teacher (person)				
大学	University (or college)	16.9	17.7	17.5	17.4
中学	Secondary School	11.7	11.4	10.6	11.3
小学	Primary School	16.9	17.4	18.0	18.1
卫生	Public Health				
每万人拥有病床（张）	Number of Hospital Beds per 10000 Persons (unit)	43.0	45.8	48.3	51.9
每万人拥有医生数（人）	Number of Doctors per 10000 Persons (person)	21.4	22.4	23.7	25.6
居民家庭医疗保健支出比重(%)	Percentage of Household Expenditure on Medicine and Healthcare (%)	6.73	6.95	6.86	6.57
城镇	Urban Areas	6.51	6.89	6.39	6.15
农村	Rural Areas	7.51	7.15	8.45	7.96
社会保障、社区服务和治安	**Social Security, Community Service and Public Security**				
社会保障	Social Security				
参加基本养老保险职工人数（万人）	Number of Workers Joining Basic Pension Insurance (10000 persons)	2582.1	2698.9	2653.6	2725.9
参加失业保险人数（万人）	Number of Workers Joining Unemployment Insurance (10000 persons)	1389.3	1442.7	1490.9	1538.2
参加基本医疗保险人数（万人）	Number of Workers Joining Basic Medicine Insurance (10000 persons)	2274.7	2361.8	2429.0	2490.5
参加新型农村合作医疗人数（万人）	Number of Persons Joining New-type Rural Cooperative Medical Treatment (10000 persons)	4055	4076	3997	3395
城镇居民最低生活保障人数（万人）	Number of Urban Residents Supported by Lowest Life Security Line (10000 persons)	33.75	30.68	27.98	24.84
农村居民最低生活保障人数（万人）	Number of Rural Residents Supported by Lowest Life Security Line (10000 persons)	130.14	119.10	114.79	109.89
社区服务	Community Service				
城镇社区服务设施（个）	Number of Urban Community Service Facilities (unit)	12289	33085	38975	39767
城镇便民利民服务网点（个）	Number of Convenience Stores in Urban Area (unit)	56314	44351	31832	13716
社会治安	Social Public Security				
公安机关刑事案件立案数（起）	Number of Criminal Cases Registered (file)	398214	395440	364437	401507
公安机关治安案件受理数（起）	Number of Public Security Cases Accepted by Public Security Organs (case)	780562	682620	674236	696432
交通事故发生数（起）	Number of Traffic Accidents (times)	13395	13187	12999	13293
火灾事故发生数（起）	Number of Fire Accidents (times)	30513	32416	28600	25012

注:从2013年开始,农村居民家庭人均纯收入调整为农村常住居民人均可支配收入,城镇居民家庭人均可支配收入调整为城镇常住居民人均可支配收入,其它相关指标口径同时作相应调整。

a) Since 2013, per capita net income of rural households is per capita disposable income of rural permanent residents, per capita disposable of urban households is per capita disposable income of urban permanent residents, and the other related standards of index are adjusted at the same time.

5-2 农村居民家庭人均收入及恩格尔系数
Per Capita Annual Income and Engle Coefficient of Rural Households

年 份 Year	农村居民家庭人均纯收入 Per Capita Net Income of Rural Houselds				农村居民家庭恩格尔系数 (%) Engle Coefficient of Rural Households	城乡居民收入比(以农民收入为1) Income Ratio of Urban and Rural Residents (1 for a Rural Resident)
	绝对数 (元) Value (yuan)	名义增长 (%) Nominal Growth Rate(%)	实际增长 (%) Real Growth Rate(%)	实际增长指数 (1978=100) Real Income Index(100 in 1978)		
1978	155			100.0	62.3	1.86
1979	200			127.5	59.9	
1980	218			150.1	58.0	1.99
1981	258	18.4	17.3	176.1	56.9	1.74
1982	309	19.8	18.6	208.9	55.5	1.57
1983	357	15.4	15.4	241.1	55.3	1.40
1984	448	25.6	21.0	291.7	53.0	1.40
1985	493	10.0	0.5	293.2	52.1	1.55
1986	561	13.9	6.7	312.8	49.5	1.62
1987	627	11.6	3.7	324.4	48.4	1.60
1988	797	27.2	4.8	340.0	46.1	1.53
1989	876	9.9	-7.3	315.1	50.2	1.57
1990	884	0.9	6.3	335.0	52.3	1.66
1991	921	4.2	-5.8	315.6	56.1	1.76
1992	1061	15.2	10.3	348.1	54.7	2.02
1993	1267	19.4	3.0	358.5	50.2	2.19
1994	1832	44.6	6.0	380.0	54.8	2.06
1995	2457	34.1	9.5	416.1	54.8	1.89
1996	3029	23.3	12.6	468.6	51.2	1.71
1997	3270	7.9	4.4	489.2	48.9	1.76
1998	3377	3.3	4.5	511.2	47.8	1.78
1999	3495	3.5	5.3	538.3	44.7	1.87
2000	3595	2.9	3.5	557.1	43.5	1.89
2001	3785	5.3	4.0	579.4	42.6	1.95
2002	3996	5.6	5.9	613.6	40.0	2.05
2003	4239	6.1	5.2	645.5	41.4	2.18
2004	4754	12.1	7.2	692.0	44.2	2.20
2005	5276	11.0	8.4	750.1	44.0	2.33
2006	5813	10.2	8.4	813.1	41.8	2.42
2007	6561	12.9	7.7	875.7	41.6	2.50
2008	7357	12.1	6.2	930.0	41.3	2.54
2009	8004	8.8	9.4	1017.4	39.2	2.57
2010	9118	13.9	9.2	1111.0	38.1	2.52
2011	10805	18.5	11.9	1243.2	38.5	2.44
2012	12202	12.9	10.1	1368.4	37.4	2.43
2013	13598	11.4	8.7	1487.5	36.3	2.39

5-3 城镇居民家庭人均收入及恩格尔系数
Per Capita Annual Income and Engle Coefficient of Urban Households

年份 Year	城镇居民家庭人均可支配收入 Per Capita Disposal Income of Urban Households				城镇居民家庭恩格尔系数（%） Engle Coefficient of Urban Households（%）
	绝对数（元） Value（yuan）	名义增长（%） Nominal Growth Rate（%）	实际增长（%） Real Growth Rate（%）	实际增长指数（1978=100） Real Income Index（100 in 1978）	
1978	288			100.0	55.1
1979					
1980	433			141.4	55.1
1981	448	3.4	1.0	142.8	55.9
1982	484	8.0	7.1	152.9	58.2
1983	498	2.9	2.1	156.2	58.6
1984	626	25.7	20.7	188.5	56.3
1985	766	22.3	11.6	210.4	52.5
1986	910	18.8	11.8	235.1	51.2
1987	1005	10.4	-0.1	234.8	52.0
1988	1218	21.2	-1.1	232.2	50.8
1989	1372	12.6	-2.9	225.5	53.9
1990	1464	6.7	3.2	232.6	55.5
1991	1623	10.9	3.0	239.5	55.7
1992	2138	31.8	21.1	290.0	53.9
1993	2774	29.7	9.3	316.9	49.4
1994	3779	36.2	8.8	344.7	50.1
1995	4634	22.6	5.5	363.7	51.9
1996	5186	11.9	1.0	367.3	51.0
1997	5765	11.2	9.7	403.1	47.7
1998	6018	4.4	4.4	420.8	45.1
1999	6538	8.6	10.2	463.7	44.1
2000	6800	4.0	4.0	482.3	41.1
2001	7375	8.5	8.3	522.5	39.7
2002	8178	10.9	12.7	588.8	40.4
2003	9263	13.3	12.3	661.0	38.3
2004	10482	13.2	9.1	721.3	40.0
2005	12319	17.5	15.2	831.1	37.2
2006	14084	14.3	12.5	935.2	36.0
2007	16378	16.3	11.7	1044.7	36.7
2008	18680	14.1	8.5	1133.5	37.9
2009	20552	10.0	10.5	1252.5	36.3
2010	22944	11.6	7.8	1350.2	36.5
2011	26341	14.8	9.2	1474.4	36.1
2012	29677	12.7	9.9	1620.4	35.4
2013	32538	9.6	7.1	1735.4	34.7

5－4 居民家庭基本情况
Basic Conditions of Residents

指标	Item	全体居民 All Residents 2015	全体居民 All Residents 2016	城镇常住居民 Urban Residents 2015	城镇常住居民 Urban Residents 2016	农村常住居民 Rural Resident 2015	农村常住居民 Rural Resident 2016
基本情况	**Basic Conditions**						
调查户数 （户）	Number of Households Surveyed (household)	6600	6600	4200	4200	2400	2400
平均每户家庭常住人口 （人）	Number of Permanent Residents per Household (person)	2.97	2.97	2.98	2.97	2.96	2.98
平均每户就业人口 （人）	Average Number of Employed Persons Per Household (person)	1.75	1.76	1.65	1.66	1.92	1.95
平均每一就业人口负担人数 （人）	Number of Dependents per Employee (person)	1.70	1.69	1.80	1.79	1.54	1.53
平均每户就业面 （%）	Proportion of Employment per Household (%)	58.99	59.25	55.55	55.82	64.98	65.37
平均每人现住房建筑面积 （平方米）	Average Existing Building Space per Capita (sq. m)	45.22	46.26	39.62	40.32	54.95	56.88
人均可支配收入（元）	**Per Capita Disposable Income (yuan)**	**29539**	**32070**	**37173**	**40152**	**16257**	**17606**
#工资性收入	Income from Wages and Salaries	17188	18664	22460	24214	8015	8732
经营净收入	Net Income from Operations	4467	4724	4134	4411	5046	5283
财产净收入	Net Income from Properties	2537	2880	3682	4151	545	606
转移净收入	Net Income from Transfers	5348	5802	6897	7375	2651	2985
#低收入户	Low Income Households	8485	9436	14234	15989	5529	5804
中等偏下户	Lower Middle Income Households	16614	18581	24632	27057	10199	11404
中等收入户	Middle Income Households	25122	27670	33252	36456	14352	15819
中等偏上户	Upper Middle Income Households	36374	40363	44566	48646	19574	21520
高收入户	Highest Income Households	68590	73201	79350	84072	34802	37610
人均生活消费支出（元）	**Per Capita Consumption Expanditure (yuan)**	**20556**	**22130**	**24966**	**26433**	**12883**	**14428**
食品烟酒	Food, Tobacco and Wine	5936	6266	7004	7389	4078	4255
衣着	Clothing	1415	1453	1781	1810	778	816
居住	Residence	4552	5107	5645	6141	2650	3258
生活用品及服务	Articles for Daily Use and Services	1238	1363	1517	1616	754	910
交通通信	Transport and Communications	2985	3372	3620	3952	1880	2334
教育文化娱乐	Education, Culture and Recreation	2424	2515	3058	3164	1320	1352
医疗保健	Healthcare and Medical Services	1410	1454	1594	1624	1088	1148
其他用品和服务	Other Articles and Services	597	600	747	737	334	356

5-5 不同收入组城镇常住居民家庭基本情况(2016年)
Basic Conditions of Urban Residents by Income(2016)

指标	Item	全省调查户平均水平 Average	低收入户 Low Income Households	中低收入户 Lower Middle Income Households	中等收入户 Middle Income Households	中高收入户 Upper Middle Income Households	高收入户 Highest Income Households
平均每户常住人口(人)	Number of Permanent Residents per Household (person)	2.97	3.35	3.24	2.93	2.80	2.51
平均每户就业人口(人)	Number of Employed Persons per Household (person)	1.66	1.69	1.83	1.69	1.63	1.44
平均每一就业人口负担人数(人)	Number of Dependents per Labor (person)	1.79	1.98	1.77	1.73	1.72	1.75
人均可支配收入(元)	**Per Capita Disposable Income (yuan)**	**40152**	**15989**	**27057**	**36456**	**48646**	**84072**
工资性收入	Income from Wages and Salaries	24214	9541	17862	23642	29644	46570
经营净收入	Net Income from Operations	4411	2463	3041	2421	4301	11216
财产净收入	Net Income from Properties	4151	1398	2188	3352	5074	10253
转移净收入	Net Income from Transfers	7375	2587	3965	7041	9627	16033
人均生活消费支出(元)	**Per Capita Consumption Expanditure (yuan)**	**26433**	**13112**	**18117**	**24565**	**31398**	**51548**
食品烟酒	Food,Tobacco and Wine	7389	4195	5844	7488	9054	11667
食品	Food	4868	3199	4109	5059	5772	6839
烟酒	Tobacco and Wine	849	444	677	867	1061	1352
饮料	Beverage	122	57	88	125	142	227
饮食服务	Catering Service	1550	494	970	1437	2078	3250
衣着	Clothing	1810	829	1332	1647	2300	3374
衣类	Dressing	1447	653	1041	1300	1817	2788
鞋类	Shoes	363	176	291	347	484	586
居住	Residence	6141	3034	4154	5635	7052	12413
#租赁房房租	Rent	192	115	168	200	259	242
住房维修及管理	Housing Maintenance and Management	770	405	485	703	805	1664
水电燃料及其他	Water and Electric Energy for Fuel and the Other	878	582	722	845	906	1479
生活用品及服务	Articles for Daily Use and Services	1616	802	991	1369	1838	3548
家具及室内装饰品	Furniture and Articles for Interior Decoration	266	167	112	201	231	709
家用器具	Household Appliances	417	185	256	372	462	937
家用纺织品	Household Textile	118	59	67	108	161	226
家庭日用杂品	Household Articles for Daily Use	432	241	320	412	502	777
个人用品	Personal Articles	274	127	195	233	364	522
家庭服务	Household Services	109	23	40	43	119	377
交通通信	Transport an Communication	3952	1611	2527	3923	4456	8382
交通	Transport	2925	1036	1712	2840	3245	6746
通信	Communication	1028	575	816	1083	1211	1635
教育文化娱乐	Education,Culture and Recreation	3164	1588	1946	2577	3802	6807
教育	Education	1430	1116	1103	1286	1393	2481
文化娱乐	Culture and Recreation	1734	472	844	1291	2409	4326
医疗保健	Healthcare and Medical Services	1624	776	808	1277	2015	3778
医疗器具及药品	Medical Instrument and Drug	496	272	255	378	649	1075
医疗服务	Medical Services	1128	504	553	899	1367	2703
其他用品和服务	Other Goods and Services	737	276	514	649	880	1579
其他用品	Other Goods	414	115	309	385	512	875
其他服务	Other Services	322	161	205	264	369	704

5-6 不同收入组农村常住居民家庭基本情况(2016年)
Basic Conditions of Rural Residents by Income(2016)

指标	Item	全省调查户平均水平 Average	低收入户 Low Income Households	中低收入户 Lower Middle Income Households	中等收入户 Middle Income Households	中高收入户 Upper Middle Income Households	高收入户 Highest Income Households
平均每户常住人口（人）	Number of Permanent Residents per Household (person)	2.98	3.09	3.26	3.11	2.91	2.54
平均每户就业人口（人）	Number of Employed Persons per Household (person)	1.95	1.73	1.93	2.05	2.12	1.90
平均每一就业人口负担人数（人）	Number of Dependents per Labor (person)	1.53	1.78	1.69	1.51	1.37	1.33
人均可支配收入（元）	**Per Capita Disposable Income (yuan)**	**17606**	**5804**	**11404**	**15819**	**21520**	**37610**
工资性收入	Income from Wages and Salaries	8732	2816	6239	9979	12051	13796
经营净收入	Net Income from Operations	5283	1443	2813	3212	5083	15880
第一产业经营净收入	Primary Industry	2815	1223	2016	2058	2381	7198
#农业	Agriculture	2023	1457	1712	1787	1841	3610
林业	Forestry	141	90	83	84	112	379
牧业	Animal Husbandry	388	-121	186	116	324	1674
渔业	Fishery	263	-202	35	72	104	1535
第二产业经营净收入	Secondary Industry	862	12	196	165	648	3846
第三产业经营净收入	Tertiary Industry	1606	208	602	988	2053	4837
财产净收入	Net Income from Properties	606	161	215	262	602	2073
转移净收入	Net Income from Transfers	2985	1384	2136	2366	3784	5860
人均生活消费支出（元）	**Per Capita Consumption Expanditure (yuan)**	**14428**	**8330**	**11287**	**14410**	**17117**	**22815**
食品烟酒	Food, Tobacco and Wine	4255	2545	3283	4218	5073	6687
食品	Food	2860	1927	2370	2839	3300	4145
烟酒	Tobacco and Wine	763	420	535	756	914	1310
饮料	Beverage	77	38	55	79	94	130
饮食服务	Catering Service	555	160	324	545	766	1102
衣着	Clothing	816	408	635	802	998	1351

5－6 续 表 1 Continued 1

指	标 Item	全省调查户平均水平 Average	低收入户 Low Income Households	中低收入户 Lower Middle Income Households	中等收入户 Middle Income Households	中高收入户 Upper Middle Income Households	高收入户 Highest Income Households
衣类	Dressing	634	309	499	619	773	1062
鞋类	Shoes	182	99	136	183	225	289
居住	Residence	3258	1955	2456	3258	3909	5124
#租赁房房租	Rent	67	15	45	60	103	122
住房维修及管理	Housing Maintenance and Management	685	443	456	621	860	1151
水电燃料及其他	Water and Electric Energy for Fuel and the Other	615	445	484	583	692	942
生活用品及服务	Articles for Daily Use and Services	910	499	610	993	1177	1389
家具及室内装饰品	Furniture and Articles for Interior Decoration	165	85	68	216	212	274
家用器具	Household Appliances	292	152	199	322	401	417
家用纺织品	Household Textile	66	31	35	72	96	105
家庭日用杂品	Household Articles for Daily Use	253	169	205	248	290	380
个人用品	Personal Articles	105	50	81	101	147	163
家庭服务	Household Services	29	12	23	33	30	51
交通通信	Transport an Communication	2334	991	1825	2252	2893	4079
交通	Transport	1694	605	1320	1596	2134	3114
通信	Communication	639	385	505	656	759	964
教育文化娱乐	Education, Culture and Recreation	1352	934	1328	1413	1468	1686
教育	Education	795	695	932	913	727	676
文化娱乐	Culture and Recreation	557	239	396	500	741	1009
医疗保健	Healthcare and Medical Services	1148	836	927	1094	1133	1895
医疗器具及药品	Medical Instrument and Drug	298	297	254	252	296	415
医疗服务	Medical Services	850	539	673	842	837	1480
其他用品和服务	Other Goods and Services	356	163	223	380	467	605
其他用品	Other Goods	202	86	113	202	268	380
其他服务	Other Services	154	77	110	178	199	225

5-7 居民家庭平均每人主要消费品消费量
Per Capita Consumption on Major Consumer Goods of Residents

单位:公斤 (kg)

指标	Item	全体居民 All Residents		城镇常住居民 Urban Residents		农村常住居民 Rural Resident	
		2015	2016	2015	2016	2015	2016
粮食	Grain	122.0	116.9	107.6	107.4	147.2	133.9
#小麦	Wheat	29.3	29.8	27.3	29.4	32.7	30.6
稻谷	Rice	75.8	69.5	63.4	60.5	97.3	85.5
油脂类	Oil and Fat	12.5	12.1	12.3	12.3	13.0	11.8
蔬菜及菜制品	Vegetable and Vegetable Productions	104.1	104.8	110.2	111.9	93.4	92.0
肉类	Meat	26.1	25.9	28.0	28.0	22.7	22.3
#猪肉	Pork	19.6	19.1	20.6	20.1	17.9	17.2
牛肉	Beef	1.7	1.8	2.0	2.2	1.0	1.1
羊肉	Mutton	0.8	1.0	0.9	1.1	0.7	0.8
禽类	Poultry	9.9	11.1	11.0	12.3	8.1	9.1
水产品	Aquatic Products	17.4	17.9	19.6	20.2	13.7	14.0
蛋类及蛋制品	Eggs and Egg Productions	10.2	10.3	10.6	10.9	9.5	9.2
奶和奶制品	Milk and Milk Productions	16.4	15.8	19.3	18.6	11.5	10.8
干鲜瓜果类	Dried and Fresh Melons and Fruits	40.4	43.7	47.1	49.5	28.9	33.2
糖果糕点类	Sugars and Cakes	6.4	6.2	7.0	6.7	5.5	5.4
茶叶	Tea	0.2	0.2	0.2	0.2	0.2	0.1
酒	Wine	8.0	8.4	6.5	7.0	10.6	10.8

5-8 不同收入组城镇常住居民家庭平均每人主要消费品消费量(2016年)

Per Capita Consumption on Major Consumer Goods of Urban Residents by Income(2016)

单位:公斤 (kg)

指标	Item	全省调查户平均水平 Average	低收入户 Low Income Households	中低收入户 Lower Middle Income Households	中等收入户 Middle Income Households	中高收入户 Upper Middle Income Households	高收入户 Highest Income Households
粮食	Grain	107.4	113.0	111.5	105.6	104.1	100.6
#小麦	Wheat	29.4	35.2	28.5	28.0	26.3	28.0
稻谷	Rice	60.5	60.4	65.8	60.5	60.1	54.3
油脂类	Oil and Fat	12.3	11.5	12.5	13.4	12.0	12.4
蔬菜及菜制品	Vegetable and Vegetable Productions	111.9	95.2	107.3	115.5	123.8	122.7
肉类	Meat	28.0	22.3	26.9	30.2	31.7	30.1
#猪肉	Pork	20.1	16.3	20.0	21.7	22.4	20.9
牛肉	Beef	2.2	1.4	1.9	2.3	2.8	2.8
羊肉	Mutton	1.1	0.8	0.9	1.2	1.5	1.3
禽类	Poultry	12.3	8.6	11.4	13.4	15.1	14.0
水产品	Aquatic Products	20.2	14.7	18.5	22.2	23.7	23.4
蛋类及蛋制品	Eggs and Egg Productions	10.9	10.1	10.3	11.6	11.4	11.6
奶和奶制品	Milk and Milk Productions	18.6	13.0	16.1	17.9	23.0	25.1
干鲜瓜果类	Dried and Fresh Melons and Fruits	49.5	36.0	42.3	51.4	58.2	64.7
糖果糕点类	Sugars and Cakes	6.7	4.8	5.7	7.1	7.7	9.1
茶叶	Tea	0.2	0.1	0.2	0.2	0.3	0.4
酒	Wine	7.0	6.8	6.9	6.9	7.5	7.0

5－9 不同收入组农村常住居民家庭平均每人主要消费品消费量(2016 年)

Per Capita Consumption on Major Consumer Goods of Rural Residents by Income(2016)

单位:公斤 (kg)

指标	Item	全省调查户平均水平 Average	低收入户 Low Income Households	中低收入户 Lower Middle Income Households	中等收入户 Middle Income Households	中高收入户 Upper Middle Income Households	高收入户 Highest Income Households
粮食	Grain	133.9	127.5	122.3	132.5	141.1	149.8
#小麦	Wheat	30.6	36.7	32.2	30.0	26.7	26.2
稻谷	Rice	85.5	71.5	74.1	85.4	96.2	105.0
油脂类	Oil and Fat	11.8	9.6	10.7	12.5	12.7	14.2
蔬菜及菜制品	Vegetable and Vegetable Productions	92.0	74.0	78.9	89.3	107.0	117.1
肉类	Meat	22.3	15.2	19.0	22.6	26.2	30.1
#猪肉	Pork	17.2	11.8	14.8	17.0	20.3	23.4
牛肉	Beef	1.1	0.6	0.9	1.2	1.2	1.6
羊肉	Mutton	0.8	0.5	0.7	0.9	0.9	1.2
禽类	Poultry	9.1	5.7	7.2	8.9	10.8	13.8
水产品	Aquatic Products	14.0	10.0	11.2	14.0	16.1	19.8
蛋类及蛋制品	Eggs and Egg Productions	9.2	7.4	8.4	8.9	10.8	10.9
奶和奶制品	Milk and Milk Productions	10.8	8.2	9.8	11.0	12.3	13.4
干鲜瓜果类	Dried and Fresh Melons and Fruits	33.2	25.7	30.8	33.0	37.8	40.5
糖果糕点类	Sugars and Cakes	5.4	4.2	5.5	5.0	6.1	6.3
茶叶	Tea	0.1	0.0	0.1	0.1	0.2	0.3
酒	Wine	10.8	8.5	9.6	11.6	11.7	13.0

5-10 居民家庭平均购买商品数量
Annual Purchases of Commodities of Residents

指标	Item	全体居民 All Residents 2015	全体居民 All Residents 2016	城镇常住居民 Urban Residents 2015	城镇常住居民 Urban Residents 2016	农村常住居民 Rural Resident 2015	农村常住居民 Rural Resident 2016
平均每人购买	**Per Capita Purchases**						
粮食 （公斤）	Grain （kg）	73.3	75.2	78.4	79.9	64.4	66.7
食用植物油 （公斤）	Edible Vegetable Oil （kg）	10.9	10.9	11.7	11.8	9.5	9.3
动物油 （公斤）	Animal Oil （kg）	0.2	0.2	0.2	0.1	0.2	0.2
鲜菜 （公斤）	Fresh Vegetable （kg）	76.5	79.3	97.2	99.6	40.4	43.0
猪肉 （公斤）	Pork （kg）	19.5	19.0	20.5	20.1	17.7	17.0
牛羊肉 （公斤）	Red Meat （kg）	2.5	2.7	3.0	3.2	1.6	1.8
禽类 （公斤）	Poultry （kg）	9.4	10.7	10.9	12.2	6.9	8.0
水产品 （公斤）	Aquatic Products （kg）	17.1	17.6	19.5	20.0	13.1	13.3
蛋类 （公斤）	Egg （kg）	9.2	9.3	10.3	10.6	7.4	7.0
奶类 （公斤）	Milk （kg）	16.4	15.8	19.2	18.6	11.5	10.8
干鲜瓜果类 （公斤）	Dried and Fresh Melons and Fruits （kg）	40.1	43.4	47.0	49.5	28.2	32.6
糖果糕点类 （公斤）	Sugars and Cakes （kg）	6.4	6.2	7.0	6.7	5.5	5.4
平均每百户购买	**Per 100 Households Purchases**						
洗衣机 （台）	Washing Machine （set）	5.7	6.4	5.8	6.7	5.6	5.9
电冰箱(柜) （台）	Refrigerator （set）	5.5	5.8	5.7	5.0	5.2	7.1
空调器 （台）	Air Conditioner （set）	6.4	9.0	6.6	8.7	6.0	9.4
吸尘器 （台）	Cleaner （set）	0.9	1.1	1.3	1.5	0.3	0.5
抽油烟机 （台）	Smoke Exhaust Ventilator （set）	2.5	2.9	3.1	3.5	1.3	1.8
微波炉 （台）	Microwave Oven （set）	2.7	3.0	3.2	3.5	1.9	2.1
非太阳能热水器 （台）	Non - Solar Water Heater （set）	3.1	3.8	4.0	4.2	1.7	3.0
太阳能热水器 （台）	Solar Water Heater （set）	1.3	1.1	1.0	0.8	2.0	1.7
燃气炉具 （台）	Gas - fired Stove （set）	4.0	4.0	3.7	4.3	4.4	3.5
太阳能炉具 （台）	Solar Stove （set）	0.1	0.1	0.2	0.1	0.1	0.1
洗碗机 （台）	Dish - washing Machine （set）	0.3	0.2	0.3	0.2	0.3	0.3
汽车 （辆）	Car （unit）	2.3	2.7	2.5	2.8	2.1	2.5
摩托车 （辆）	Motorcycle （unit）	0.6	0.3	0.5	0.3	0.8	0.5
自行车 （辆）	Bicycle （unit）	3.5	2.6	3.6	3.1	3.2	1.6
电动自行车 （辆）	Electrical Bicycle （unit）	11.2	12.0	10.2	10.5	13.1	14.7
移动电话机 （部）	Mobile Telephone （set）	41.1	42.4	41.6	43.3	40.2	40.8

5-11 不同收入组城镇常住居民家庭平均购买商品数量(2016年)
Annual Purchases of Commodities of Urban Residents by Income(2016)

指 标	Item	全省调查户平均水平 Average	低收入户 Low Income Households	中低收入户 Lower Middle Income Households	中等收入户 Middle Income Households	中高收入户 Upper Middle Income Households	高收入户 Highest Income Households
平均每人购买	**Per Capita Purchases**						
粮食 (公斤)	Grain (kg)	79.9	75.4	82.3	81.1	80.7	80.8
食用植物油 (公斤)	Edible Vegetable Oil (kg)	11.8	10.5	11.9	13.0	11.7	12.1
动物油 (公斤)	Animal Oil (kg)	0.1	0.1	0.2	0.2	0.1	0.1
鲜菜 (公斤)	Fresh Vegetable (kg)	99.6	76.6	94.7	104.9	113.9	114.3
猪肉 (公斤)	Pork (kg)	20.1	16.2	20.0	21.7	22.4	20.9
牛羊肉 (公斤)	Red Meat (kg)	3.2	2.1	2.7	3.4	4.2	4.1
禽类 (公斤)	Poultry (kg)	12.2	8.4	11.3	13.2	15.0	13.9
水产品 (公斤)	Aquatic Products (kg)	20.0	14.6	18.3	22.1	23.6	23.3
蛋类 (公斤)	Egg (kg)	10.6	9.5	9.9	11.2	11.3	11.6
奶类 (公斤)	Milk (kg)	18.6	13.0	16.1	17.9	23.0	25.1
干鲜瓜果类 (公斤)	Dried and Fresh Melons and Fruits (kg)	49.5	36.0	42.2	51.4	58.2	64.7
糖果糕点类 (公斤)	Sugars and Cakes (kg)	6.7	4.8	5.7	7.1	7.7	9.1
平均每百户购买	**Per 100 Households Purchases**						
洗衣机 (台)	Washing Machine (set)	6.7	6.2	4.0	6.7	8.0	8.7
电冰箱(柜) (台)	Refrigerator (set)	5.0	4.0	3.8	4.4	5.2	7.8
空调器 (台)	Air Conditioner (set)	8.7	4.8	6.3	9.2	8.5	14.8
吸尘器 (台)	Cleaner (set)	1.5	0.6	1.4	0.4	1.6	3.6
抽油烟机 (台)	Smoke Exhaust Ventilator (set)	3.5	2.6	3.3	2.8	4.3	4.7
微波炉 (台)	Microwave Oven (set)	3.5	1.5	3.2	3.0	5.1	4.9
非太阳能热水器 (台)	Non-Solar Water Heater (set)	4.2	3.3	3.5	3.9	5.6	4.7
太阳能热水器 (台)	Solar Water Heater (set)	0.8	1.2	0.6	0.6	0.9	0.7
燃气炉具 (台)	Gas-fired Stove (set)	4.3	4.3	4.5	3.9	5.2	3.3
太阳能炉具 (台)	Solar Stove (set)	0.1	0.2	0.0	0.1	0.2	0.0
洗碗机 (台)	Dish-washing Machine (set)	0.2	0.0	0.2	0.3	0.4	0.2
汽车 (辆)	Car (unit)	2.8	1.3	1.9	2.8	2.9	4.9
摩托车 (辆)	Motorcycle (unit)	0.3	0.4	0.1	0.2	0.2	0.5
自行车 (辆)	Bicycle (unit)	3.1	2.5	1.9	2.9	3.8	4.3
电动自行车 (辆)	Electrical Bicycle (unit)	10.5	9.5	12.2	13.3	9.1	8.2
移动电话机 (部)	Mobile Telephone (set)	43.3	32.2	44.6	46.9	43.9	48.7

5－12 不同收入组农村常住居民家庭平均购买商品数量(2016年)
Annual Purchases of Commodities of Rural Residents by Income(2016)

指标	Item	全省调查户平均水平 Average	低收入户 Low Income Households	中低收入户 Lower Middle Income Households	中等收入户 Middle Income Households	中高收入户 Upper Middle Income Households	高收入户 Highest Income Households
平均每人购买	**Per Capita Purchases**						
粮食 (公斤)	Grain (kg)	66.7	58.6	60.4	65.0	73.2	78.9
食用植物油 (公斤)	Edible Vegetable Oil (kg)	9.3	7.2	8.1	9.7	10.0	11.8
动物油 (公斤)	Animal Oil (kg)	0.2	0.1	0.2	0.2	0.3	0.2
鲜菜 (公斤)	Fresh Vegetable (kg)	43.0	27.2	37.5	44.6	48.5	61.1
猪肉 (公斤)	Pork (kg)	17.0	11.8	14.6	16.9	20.1	22.7
牛羊肉 (公斤)	Red Meat (kg)	1.8	1.1	1.5	1.9	2.0	2.7
禽类 (公斤)	Poultry (kg)	8.0	4.8	6.3	8.1	9.7	11.9
水产品 (公斤)	Aquatic Products (kg)	13.3	9.7	10.8	13.4	15.5	18.3
蛋类 (公斤)	Egg (kg)	7.0	5.3	6.5	7.1	8.5	7.9
奶类 (公斤)	Milk (kg)	10.8	8.2	9.8	11.0	12.3	13.4
干鲜瓜果类 (公斤)	Dried and Fresh Melons and Fruits (kg)	32.6	25.5	30.3	32.5	36.7	39.6
糖果糕点类 (公斤)	Sugars and Cakes (kg)	5.4	4.2	5.5	5.0	6.1	6.3
平均每百户购买	**Per 100 Households Purchases**						
洗衣机 (台)	Washing Machine (set)	5.9	4.4	5.4	7.1	7.0	5.9
电冰箱(柜) (台)	Refrigerator (set)	7.1	5.1	8.2	6.7	9.3	6.0
空调器 (台)	Air Conditioner (set)	9.4	4.3	7.7	7.6	13.4	14.2
吸尘器 (台)	Cleaner (set)	0.5	0.0	0.3	1.0	1.1	0.0
抽油烟机 (台)	Smoke Exhaust Ventilator (set)	1.8	1.5	0.5	2.0	2.9	2.2
微波炉 (台)	Microwave Oven (set)	2.1	1.5	2.0	2.0	2.5	2.5
非太阳能热水器 (台)	Non-Solar Water Heater (set)	3.0	1.0	1.0	5.9	2.3	4.7
太阳能热水器 (台)	Solar Water Heater (set)	1.7	2.1	1.4	2.4	1.3	1.5
燃气炉具 (台)	Gas-fired Stove (set)	3.5	1.7	2.5	3.2	3.6	6.4
太阳能炉具 (台)	Solar Stove (set)	0.1	0.0	0.0	0.3	0.0	0.1
洗碗机 (台)	Dish-washing Machine (set)	0.3	0.0	0.0	0.3	0.8	0.3
汽车 (辆)	Car (unit)	2.5	0.6	2.6	2.6	3.5	3.2
摩托车 (辆)	Motorcycle (unit)	0.5	0.3	0.3	1.1	0.2	0.5
自行车 (辆)	Bicycle (unit)	1.6	1.8	1.6	1.5	1.5	1.7
电动自行车 (辆)	Electrical Bicycle (unit)	14.7	16.2	13.9	16.7	15.0	11.8
移动电话机 (部)	Mobile Telephone (set)	40.8	34.6	42.4	43.9	39.6	43.6

5-13 居民家庭平均每百户年末耐用品拥有量
Ownership of Major Durable Consumer Goods per 100 Residents at Year-end

指 标		Item		全体居民 All Residents		城镇常住居民 Urban Residents		农村常住居民 Rural Resident	
				2015	2016	2015	2016	2015	2016
家用汽车	（辆）	Family Car	（unit）	29.5	36.1	39.1	45.8	13.0	18.7
摩托车	（辆）	Motorcycle	（unit）	27.7	24.4	18.4	14.7	43.7	42.1
助力车	（台）	Moped	（set）	111.9	118.3	107.5	110.7	119.5	131.8
洗衣机	（台）	Washing Machine	（set）	96.7	98.9	99.4	100.4	91.9	96.2
电冰箱（柜）	（台）	Refrigerator	（set）	99.0	102.5	101.1	103.0	95.2	101.5
微波炉	（台）	Microwave Stove	（set）	78.7	81.9	88.7	89.8	61.5	67.7
彩色电视机	（台）	Color Television	（set）	161.9	166.9	170.6	173.9	146.8	154.5
#接入有线电视		Connected to the CATV Network		138.3	141.0	148.6	149.2	120.5	126.5
空调器	（台）	Air Conditioner	（set）	162.6	177.1	194.3	206.0	107.7	125.2
热水器	（台）	Water Heater	（set）	98.4	101.2	104.5	106.0	87.7	92.7
#太阳能热水器		Solar Water Heater		63.2	63.3	55.0	54.4	77.4	79.5
消毒碗柜	（台）	Sterilized Cupboard	（set）	5.4	5.6	7.8	7.9	1.2	1.4
洗碗机	（台）	Dish-washing Machine	（set）	1.3	1.3	1.8	1.8	0.4	0.4
抽油烟机	（台）	Smoke Exhaust Ventilator	（set）	63.2	66.2	81.5	82.8	31.6	36.2
固定电话	（线）	Fixed-line Telephone	（line）	63.5	56.3	64.4	57.1	61.8	54.8
移动电话机	（部）	Mobile Telephone	（set）	228.6	239.3	234.9	241.0	217.6	236.2
#接入互联网		Connected to the Internet		124.4	144.2	140.6	158.9	96.2	117.8
计算机	（台）	Computer	（set）	73.4	76.6	91.4	94.2	42.3	45.0
#接入互联网		Connected to the Internet		65.8	68.8	83.2	86.1	35.8	37.8
摄像机	（台）	Vidicon	（set）	6.1	5.5	8.9	7.8	1.2	1.3
照相机	（台）	Camera	（set）	27.7	25.4	38.2	34.9	9.5	8.3
中高档乐器	（架）	Medium-High Grade Instrument	（set）	4.1	4.2	5.9	5.9	1.0	1.1
健身器材	（台）	Fitness Equipment	（set）	5.5	5.5	7.3	7.3	2.4	2.1
组合音响	（套）	music center	（unit）	9.9	8.2	12.2	10.0	5.9	4.9

5-14 不同收入组城镇常住居民家庭平均每百户年末耐用品拥有量(2016年) Ownership of Major Durable Consumer Goods per 100 Urban Residents by Income at Year-end(2016)

指标		Item		全省调查户平均水平 Average	低收入户 Low Income Households	中低收入户 Lower Middle Income Households	中等收入户 Middle Income Households	中高收入户 Upper Middle Income Households	高收入户 Highest Income Households
家用汽车	(辆)	Family Car	(unit)	45.8	22.9	36.8	45.1	55.4	69.1
摩托车	(辆)	Motorcycle	(unit)	14.7	18.7	20.3	14.8	12.2	7.4
助力车	(台)	Moped	(set)	110.7	128.4	132.5	116.8	102.1	73.8
洗衣机	(台)	Washing Machine	(set)	100.4	97.1	99.4	100.8	101.5	103.1
电冰箱(柜)	(台)	Refrigerator	(set)	103.0	99.8	101.2	102.9	104.4	106.8
微波炉	(台)	Microwave Stove	(set)	89.8	78.2	89.9	94.5	93.7	92.5
彩色电视机	(台)	Color Television	(set)	173.9	149.4	171.1	176.2	183.9	188.7
#接入有线电视		Connected to the CATV Network		149.2	124.1	142.6	157.8	156.4	164.8
空调器	(台)	Air Conditioner	(set)	206.0	146.9	180.8	209.8	231.9	260.4
热水器	(台)	Water Heater	(set)	106.0	95.1	101.6	105.6	112.8	114.8
#太阳能热水器		Solar Water Heater		54.4	70.2	63.8	51.0	49.6	37.2
消毒碗柜	(台)	Sterilized Cupboard	(set)	7.9	1.8	5.0	4.6	10.3	17.9
洗碗机	(台)	Dish-washing Machine	(set)	1.8	0.7	1.0	1.5	1.7	4.2
抽油烟机	(台)	Smoke Exhaust Ventilator	(set)	82.8	60.1	79.4	88.4	91.3	94.9
固定电话	(线)	Fixed-line Telephone	(line)	57.1	46.5	52.1	59.5	59.2	68.2
移动电话机	(部)	Mobile Telephone	(set)	241.0	231.2	252.4	247.9	240.6	232.8
#接入互联网		Connected to the Internet		158.9	132.1	158.8	165.0	165.3	173.5
计算机	(台)	Computer	(set)	94.2	66.9	82.8	95.3	102.9	123.2
#接入互联网		Connected to the Internet		86.1	59.4	74.5	88.5	93.3	114.6
摄像机	(台)	Vidicon	(set)	7.8	2.2	4.0	5.7	10.0	17.1
照相机	(台)	Camera	(set)	34.9	13.7	28.1	33.7	43.6	55.3
中高档乐器	(架)	Medium-High Grade Instrument	(set)	5.9	2.0	4.2	4.9	7.1	11.6
健身器材	(台)	Fitness Equipment	(set)	7.3	2.5	3.5	7.7	9.4	13.5
组合音响	(套)	music center	(unit)	10.0	3.2	8.8	9.5	9.5	19.0

5-15 不同收入组农村常住居民家庭平均每百户年末耐用品拥有量(2016年)

Ownership of Major Durable Consumer Goods per 100 Rural Residents by Income at Year-end(2016)

指标		Item		全省调查户平均水平 Average	低收入户 Low Income Households	中低收入户 Lower Middle Income Households	中等收入户 Middle Income Households	中高收入户 Upper Middle Income Households	高收入户 Highest Income Households
家用汽车	(辆)	Family Car	(unit)	18.7	8.5	13.1	15.6	25.5	30.6
摩托车	(辆)	Motorcycle	(unit)	42.1	34.3	42.1	49.6	41.0	43.4
助力车	(台)	Moped	(set)	131.8	123.4	128.5	140.8	148.2	118.4
洗衣机	(台)	Washing Machine	(set)	96.2	91.5	93.1	101.6	100.3	94.4
电冰箱(柜)	(台)	Refrigerator	(set)	101.5	92.0	99.1	103.6	108.9	104.0
微波炉	(台)	Microwave Stove	(set)	67.7	46.8	63.0	71.4	80.1	77.4
彩色电视机	(台)	Color Television	(set)	154.5	133.1	146.2	160.1	171.9	161.0
#接入有线电视		Connected to the CATV Network		126.5	99.0	113.3	135.5	144.2	140.3
空调器	(台)	Air Conditioner	(set)	125.2	91.3	108.6	127.6	145.1	153.4
热水器	(台)	Water Heater	(set)	92.7	80.7	90.9	97.5	100.0	94.4
#太阳能热水器		Solar Water Heater		79.5	72.6	83.3	80.7	83.5	77.5
消毒碗柜	(台)	Sterilized Cupboard	(set)	1.4	0.1	0.2	0.8	3.0	3.0
洗碗机	(台)	Dish-washing Machine	(set)	0.4	0.0	0.0	0.7	0.8	0.5
抽油烟机	(台)	Smoke Exhaust Ventilator	(set)	36.2	16.4	29.1	39.1	45.4	51.0
固定电话	(线)	Fixed-line Telephone	(line)	54.8	43.6	52.0	57.9	64.3	56.2
移动电话机	(部)	Mobile Telephone	(set)	236.2	218.1	230.6	248.0	252.4	231.9
#接入互联网		Connected to the Internet		117.8	92.9	106.3	128.5	137.5	123.9
计算机	(台)	Computer	(set)	45.0	32.4	39.6	43.9	56.9	52.1
#接入互联网		Connected to the Internet		37.8	24.1	33.5	37.2	49.9	44.2
摄像机	(台)	Vidicon	(set)	1.3	0.2	1.6	0.8	2.1	1.9
照相机	(台)	Camera	(set)	8.3	2.8	5.5	7.9	10.5	14.8
中高档乐器	(架)	Medium-High Grade Instrument	(set)	1.1	0.5	0.8	0.9	0.9	2.4
健身器材	(台)	Fitness Equipment	(set)	2.1	0.7	0.4	1.8	2.5	5.3
组合音响	(套)	music center	(unit)	4.9	1.7	2.7	4.3	7.0	8.8

5－16 分地区城镇常住居民家庭基本情况(2016 年)

指标	Item	苏南 Southern Jiangsu	苏中 Mid Jiangsu	苏北 Northern Jiangsu
基本情况	**Basic Conditions**			
调查户数 (户)	Number of Households Surveyed (household)	4449	2021	3840
平均每户家庭人口 (人)	Average Household Size (person)	3.01	3.14	3.20
平均每户就业人口 (人)	Number of Employed Persons per Household (person)	1.77	1.88	1.77
平均每一就业人口负担人数 (人)	Number of Dependents per Employee (person)	1.70	1.67	1.80
平均每户就业面 (%)	Proportion of Employment per Household (%)	58.9	59.9	55.4
平均每人现住房建筑面积 (平方米)	Existing Building Space per Capita (sq. m)	42.6	47.8	43.8
人均可支配收入 (元)	**Per Capita Disposable Income (yuan)**	**49920**	**37585**	**28515**
工资性收入	Income from Wages and Salaries	32172	22622	16380
经营净收入	Net Income from Household Operations	5131	5804	5376
财产净收入	Net Income from Properties	5856	3421	2141
转移净收入	Net Income from Transfers	6761	5738	4618
人均生活消费支出 (元)	**Per Capita Consumption Expanditure (yuan)**	**30444**	**23311**	**17163**
食品烟酒	Food, Tobacco and Wine	8184	6826	5384
衣着	Clothing	2230	1878	1469
居住	Living	6649	5197	3251
生活用品及服务	Articles for Daily Use and Services	1738	1294	1094
交通通信	Transport and Communications	4663	3061	1906
教育文化娱乐	Education, Culture and Recreation	4472	2909	2579
医疗保健	Healthcare and Medical Services	1615	1443	1028
其他用品和服务	Other Articles and Services	893	703	452

Basic Conditions of Urban Residents by Region(2016)

南京 Nanjing	无锡 Wuxi	徐州 Xuzhou	常州 Changzhou	苏州 Suzhou	南通 Nantong	连云港 Lianyun gang	淮安 Huaian	盐城 Yancheng	扬州 Yangzhou	镇江 Zhenjiang	泰州 Taizhou	宿迁 Suqian
1470	695	975	639	1155	794	562	831	1038	600	490	627	434
2.82	3.00	3.01	2.93	3.15	3.10	3.13	3.30	3.30	3.03	3.17	3.29	3.35
1.57	1.73	1.71	1.65	1.93	1.90	1.71	1.91	1.70	1.77	2.06	1.95	1.92
1.80	1.73	1.76	1.78	1.63	1.63	1.83	1.73	1.94	1.71	1.54	1.69	1.74
55.7	57.7	56.7	56.3	61.2	61.3	54.6	57.9	51.5	58.4	65.0	59.3	57.4
36.7	46.7	41.4	44.3	43.3	47.8	46.1	44.2	43.1	46.4	44.7	49.0	46.7
49997	**48628**	**28421**	**46058**	**54341**	**39247**	**27853**	**30335**	**30496**	**35659**	**41794**	**36828**	**24086**
31083	33305	17060	28559	35074	22766	15195	18206	16921	21538	27314	23389	13267
5382	4479	4315	6516	4676	7018	5458	5871	5932	5099	5470	4613	5880
5335	4109	1973	4062	8604	3272	2316	2634	2451	3423	3828	3645	1234
8197	6735	5073	6921	5987	6191	4884	3624	5192	5599	5182	5181	3705
29772	**31438**	**17255**	**27080**	**33305**	**25217**	**18344**	**16912**	**17546**	**21064**	**24388**	**22480**	**15521**
7642	8818	5182	7357	8882	7227	5924	5054	5532	6551	6939	6470	5390
2192	2729	1442	2017	2084	1913	1612	1485	1526	1664	2054	2020	1274
6514	6574	3597	5600	7540	5790	3450	3432	3021	4255	5456	5159	2557
1792	1748	1256	1629	1796	1468	1124	977	1028	1180	1496	1136	995
3710	4760	2078	4168	5918	3620	1736	1644	2294	2380	3268	2837	1416
5311	3923	1900	3848	4728	2827	3042	3001	2776	3328	3227	2651	2640
1734	1886	1371	1780	1411	1635	1031	819	828	1116	1128	1452	925
877	1000	429	681	946	737	425	500	541	590	820	755	324

5－17 分地区农村常住居民家庭基本情况(2016 年)

指 标	Item	苏 南 Southern Jiangsu	苏 中 Mid Jiangsu	苏 北 Northern Jiangsu
基本情况	**Basic Conditions**			
调查户数 (户)	Number of Households Surveyed (household)	1893	1419	2901
平均每户家庭人口 (人)	Average Household Size (person)	3.33	3.05	3.22
平均每户就业人口 (人)	Number of Employed Persons per Household (person)	2.31	2.09	1.94
平均每一就业人口负担人数 (人)	Number of Dependents per Employee (person)	1.44	1.45	1.66
平均每户就业面 (%)	Proportion of Employment per Household (%)	69.4	68.8	60.2
平均每人现住房建筑面积 (平方米)	Existing Building Space per Capita (sq. m)	60.7	60.3	50.9
人均可支配收入 (元)	**Per Capita Disposable Income (yuan)**	**24638**	**18320**	**15102**
工资性收入	Income from Wages and Salaries	15455	10757	7285
经营净收入	Net Income from Household Operations	4557	4199	5166
财产净收入	Net Income from Properties	1831	549	322
转移净收入	Net Income from Transfers	2795	2815	2329
人均生活消费支出 (元)	**Per Capita Consumption Expanditure (yuan)**	**17423**	**13460**	**10929**
食品烟酒	Food,Tobacco and Wine	4956	4022	3525
衣着	Clothing	1154	797	847
居住	Living	3748	2752	1973
生活用品及服务	Articles for Daily Use and Services	1017	800	677
交通通信	Transport and Communications	2760	2246	1311
教育文化娱乐	Education,Culture and Recreation	2102	1524	1672
医疗保健	Healthcare and Medical Services	1129	863	735
其他用品和服务	Other Articles and Services	555	455	189

Basic Conditions of Rural Residents by Region(2016)

南京 Nanjing	无锡 Wuxi	徐州 Xuzhou	常州 Changzhou	苏州 Suzhou	南通 Nantong	连云港 Lianyun gang	淮安 Huaian	盐城 Yancheng	扬州 Yangzhou	镇江 Zhenjiang	泰州 Taizhou	宿迁 Suqian
380	286	635	322	529	530	431	587	865	507	376	382	382
3.30	3.10	3.30	3.00	3.70	2.90	3.20	3.10	3.10	3.20	3.30	3.10	3.40
2.50	2.00	2.10	2.10	2.50	2.10	2.00	2.00	1.70	2.10	2.50	2.10	1.90
1.30	1.60	1.60	1.40	1.50	1.40	1.60	1.60	1.80	1.60	1.30	1.50	1.70
74.2	64.2	63.1	70.0	67.0	72.4	62.2	63.3	54.8	64.4	75.4	67.7	57.4
56.6	56.4	53.3	64.7	65.6	61.5	48.7	51.2	50.9	54.2	57.7	64.0	47.8
21156	**26158**	**15274**	**23780**	**27691**	**18741**	**13932**	**14319**	**17172**	**18057**	**20922**	**17861**	**13929**
14456	16618	7274	14562	16364	10945	6462	7848	7701	10545	13460	10631	7015
3331	4494	5940	5326	5243	4105	4855	3522	6135	4442	4525	4104	4455
1001	2247	211	451	3067	485	190	266	582	433	767	750	320
2368	2799	1849	3441	3017	3206	2425	2683	2754	2637	2170	2376	2139
15773	**18463**	**11059**	**16567**	**18820**	**13440**	**10113**	**9633**	**13145**	**13722**	**15925**	**13250**	**9395**
4745	5502	3475	5102	4832	3923	3298	3055	4159	4185	4547	4025	3358
902	1662	857	1225	1058	672	616	540	1346	892	971	900	605
3000	3840	2071	3325	4468	2852	1995	1704	2342	2786	3702	2571	1481
994	949	863	1028	1084	775	642	619	564	837	968	805	603
2421	2779	1545	2003	3484	2594	1008	954	1682	1756	2153	2167	968
2334	1830	1175	1843	2171	1352	1855	1699	2134	1949	2197	1396	1678
864	1294	892	1380	1194	790	539	884	672	933	895	908	552
513	607	181	660	529	482	160	178	246	384	492	478	150

5－18 农村常住居民家庭房屋情况
Housing Conditions of Rural Residents

指标		Item		2015	2016
平均每人住房		**Per Capita Housing Conditons**			
现住房建筑面积	（平方米）	Existing Residential Building Space	（sq. m）	54.95	56.88
按居住空间样式	**（平方米）**	**by Spatial Style**	**（sq. m）**		
单栋楼房		Independent Bulding		30.09	59.10
单栋平房		Independent House		22.28	37.15
主要建筑材料	**（%）**	**Main Building Materials**	**（%）**		
#钢筋混凝土		Reinforced Concrete Structure		11.75	13.62
砖混材料		Brick-mixed		58.26	60.22
砖瓦砖木		Brick-Block or Brick-Wood Structure		28.89	25.98

主要统计指标解释

可支配收入　指调查户在调查期内获得的、可用于最终消费支出和储蓄的总和,即调查户可以用来自由支配的收入。可支配收入既包括现金,也包括实物收入。按照收入的来源,可支配收入包含四项:工资性收入、经营净收入、财产净收入和转移净收入。计算公式为:

可支配收入 = 工资性收入 + 经营净收入 + 财产净收入 + 转移净收入

工资性收入　指就业人员通过各种途径得到的全部劳动报酬和各种福利,包括受雇于单位或个人、从事各种自由职业、兼职和零星劳动得到的全部劳动报酬和福利。

经营净收入　指住户或住户成员从事生产经营活动所获得的净收入,是全部经营收入中扣除经营费用、生产性固定资产折旧和生产税之后得到的净收入。计算公式具体为:经营净收入 = 经营收入 - 经营费用 - 生产性固定资产折旧 - 生产税

财产净收入　指住户或住户成员将其所拥有的金融资产、住房等非金融资产和自然资源交由其他机构单位、住户或个人支配而获得的回报并扣除相关的费用之后得到的净收入。财产净收入包括利息净收入、红利收入、储蓄性保险净收益、转让承包土地经营权租金净收入、出租房屋净收入、出租其他资产净收入和自有住房折算净租金等。

转移净收入　计算公式为:转移净收入 = 转移性收入 - 转移性支出

其中:转移性收入是指国家、单位、社会团体对住户的各种经常性转移支付和住户之间的经常性收入转移。包括政府、非行政事业单位、社会团体对居民转移的养老金或退休金、社会救济和补助、惠农补贴、政策性生活补贴、救灾款、经常性捐赠和赔偿以及报销医疗费等;住户之间的赡养收入、经常性捐赠和赔偿以及农村地区(村委会)在外(含国外)工作的本住户非常住成员寄回带回的收入等。转移性支出是指调查户对国家、单位、住户或个人的经常性或义务性转移支付。包括缴纳的税款、各项社会保障支出、赡养支出、经常性捐赠和赔偿支出以及其他经常转移。

消费支出　指住户用于满足家庭日常生活消费需要的全部支出,包括用于消费品的支出和用于服务性消费的支出。根据用途不同,消费支出可划分为食品烟酒、衣着、居住、生活用品及服务、交通通信、教育文化娱乐、医疗保健、其他用品及服务八大类。根据来源不同,消费支出可划分为现金消费支出、实物消费支出(含自产自用、来自单位、来自政府和其他社会组织)。

Explanatory Notes on Main Statistical Indicators

Disposable Income　refers to the sum of final consumption expenditure and saving deposits which is gotten during survey period. it's the income which can be freely allocated by sample households. It includes income both in cash and in kind from four categories: income from wages and salaries, net income from operations, net income from properties and net income from transfers. Using the following formula:

Disposable Income = Income from Wages and Salaries + Net Income from Operations + Net Income from Properties + Net Income from Transfers.

Income from Wages and Salaries　refers to all the payment of labor and welfare earned by employee through various means, including members who are employed by units or individuals, self - employed and part - time and so on.

Net Income from Operations　refers to the net income earned by the households or members of households who engage in production or operation activities. It is obtained from all operating income deducted operating costs, production of fixed assets depreciation and production tax. Using the following formula: Net Income from Operations = Income from Operations - Operating Costs - Production of Fixed Assets Depreciation - Production Tax

Net Income from Properties　refers to the net income obtained in return and deduction of the expenses, earned by the households or members of households who make the financial assets, housing and other non - financial assets or natural resources dominated by other institutional units, households or individuals. Net income from operation contains net interest income, bonus, net income from saving insurance, net income from rent of transferring contracted land use rights, net income from rent of tenanted housing, net income from rent of tenanted other properties and net rent from ownership housing.

Net Income from Transfers　Using the following formula: Net Income from Transfers = Income from Transfers - Transfer Expenditure

Among: Income from Transfer refers to the recurrent transfer payments of household from the the country, units and social groups, and the recurrent income transfer between households. It contains pensions, social relief and aid, agriculture subsidy, policy allowance, disaste donation, recurrent donation and free medical treatment of households from governments, non – executive public institutions and social groups; alimony payments between households, recurrent donation, compensation and postal income from the the non – permanent residents of rural households. Transfer Expenditure refers to the recurrent or obligatory transfer payment of household from the country, unit, household and individual, including tax payment, social security expenditure, recurrent donation, compensation and so on.

Consumption Expenditure refers to all the expenditures of households for consumption in daily life, including expenditures for consumer goods and services. It includes expenditure in cash and in kind on eight categories by use: food; clothing; housing; household appliances and sevices; transport and communications; education, cultural and recreational activities; medical care and the other appliances and services. It includes expenditure in cash and in kind (including self – produced and self – used expenditure and expenditures of units, government and the other social organization) by source.

固定资产投资
Investment in Fixed Assets

简 要 说 明

一、本篇资料的主要内容

本篇资料通过对一定时期全社会建造和购置固定资产活动的数量方面的描述，反映报告期内固定资产投资的规模和速度、固定资产投资的结构和比例关系、固定资产投资的资金来源及固定资产投资的效果等。

二、本篇资料的统计范围

固定资产投资统计的范围包括：城乡建设项目投资，房地产开发投资。

三、本篇的资料来源

固定资产投资统计调查。

四、本篇的统计调查方法

全面统计报表。

Brief Introduction

Ⅰ. Main Contents

Statistics in this chapter describe activities on the construction and purchase of fixed assets of the whole country during a given period of time, and reflect the size, growth, structure, ratio, financing and results of the investment in fixed assets during the reference period.

Ⅱ. Scope of Statistics

Statistics on the investment in fixed assets cover investments in capital construction projects in urban and rural areas, investments in real estate development.

Ⅲ. Sources of Data

Data on investments in fixed assets are from surveys conducted.

Ⅳ. Methodology of Data Collection

Data on investments in fixed assets are collected by the system of reporting form with complete enumeration.

6－1 固定资产投资主要指标

Major Indicators of Investment in Fixed Assets

指　　标	Item	2012	2013	2014	2015	2016
投资总额　　（亿元）	**Total Investment　（100 million yuan）**	**31706.58**	**35982.52**	**41552.75**	**45905.17**	**49370.85**
按经济类型分	Grouped by Ownership					
国有经济	State Owned Units	6022.51	6865.27	8308.13	8901.58	8236.65
集体经济	Collective Owned Units	1393.13	1639.37	1835.30	1872.50	806.51
私营个体经济	Private Individuals	12074.90	14955.56	18185.36	21252.12	23417.12
联营经济	Joint-ownership	74.66	82.69	66.04	52.32	42.52
股份制经济	Share-holding Economy	1645.86	1567.00	1376.93	1210.16	1176.19
有限责任公司	Limited Liability Corporations	5738.63	5924.45	6792.92	7752.74	10481.14
港澳台投资经济	Funds from Hong Kong, Macao and Taiwan	1599.75	1597.74	1679.36	1648.71	2306.36
外商投资经济	Foreign Investment	2218.49	2315.26	2476.57	2253.73	2386.47
其他经济	Others	938.66	1035.18	832.16	961.31	517.88
按资金来源分	Grouped by Sources of Funds					
国家预算内资金	State Budget	448.05	529.19	627.26	806.89	990.43
国内贷款	Domestic Loans	4658.42	5091.04	5360.60	4810.95	5778.54
利用外资	Foreign Investment	1216.78	1127.55	1152.05	926.17	599.88
自筹资金	Self-raising Fund	25824.05	29444.25	33325.52	36305.15	36257.99
其他资金来源	Others	5262.67	6822.96	6232.21	7206.37	10830.18
按构成分	Grouped by Composition of Funds					
建筑安装工程	Construction and Installation	17913.03	20821.56	24686.18	27570.90	28989.35
设备工器具购置	Purchase of Equipments and Instruments	9756.39	10903.11	12327.57	14225.16	15368.57
其他费用	Others	4037.16	4257.84	4539.00	4109.11	5012.94
按产业分	Grouped by Industry					
#住宅	Residential Buildings	4842.52	5646.33	6367.41	6527.16	6971.13
第一产业	Primary Industry	205.23	195.71	206.97	232.24	293.11
第二产业	Secondary Industry	16631.07	18412.48	20298.45	22890.96	24673.81
第三产业	Tertiary Industry	14870.28	17374.32	21047.33	22781.97	24403.93
新增固定资产　　（亿元）	**Newly Increased Fixed Assets（100 million yuan）**	**23327.46**	**26434.29**	**32156.36**	**36648.83**	**33963.72**
房屋建筑面积（万平方米）	**Floor Space of Building　（10000 sq. m）**					
施工面积	Floor Space Under Construction	93565.19	100944.93	109353.56	98850.04	93782.52
#住宅	Residential Buildings	37150.80	42305.79	44641.13	45370.63	45254.99
竣工面积	Floor Space Completed	32938.72	33342.59	34562.35	36541.38	24665.24
#住宅	Residential Buildings	9301.97	9251.55	8426.35	9349.36	8335.47
商品房销售面积（万平方米）	**Floor Space of Commercializ Buildings Sold　（10000 sq. m）**	**9019.18**	**11454.77**	**9846.84**	**11414.05**	**13962.09**

注：1. 自筹投资中含发行债券部分（下同）。
　　2. 从2003年开始，资金来源为可用于投资的资金到位数（下同）。
　　3. 从2004年开始，水利业投资从第一产业调到第三产业（下同）。
　　4. 从2010年开始，投资总额中不含农户投资（下同）。

a) Fund raising included bond publishing(so did as follows).
b) Since 2003, the sources of finance was available for investment(so did as follows).
c) Since 2004, the investment for water conservancy was transferred from primary industry to tertiary industry(so did as follows).
d) Since 2010, the investment of farm households was not included in the total investment(so did as follows).

6-2 固定资产投资额
Investment in Fixed Assets

单位:亿元 (100 million yuan)

年 份 Items	投资额 Investment	#工业投资 Industrial Investment	#房地产开发 Real Estate Development	#国有经济 State-owned	#集体经济 Collective-owned	#私营个体 Private Individuals	#外商及港澳台商投资 Hong Kong, Macao, Taiwan and Foreign Funds
1978	21.75			20.70	1.05		
1980	34.73			34.73	3.08		
"六五"时期 The Period of the Sixth Five-year plan	**564.89**			**242.73**	**156.57**		
"七五"时期 The Period of the Seventh Five-year plan	**1606.75**			**642.46**	**377.21**		
"八五"时期 The Period of the Eighth Five-year plan	**5307.18**		**554.92**	**1944.32**	**1788.50**		
1991	439.98		17.22	172.09	109.87		
1992	711.70		30.42	288.00	276.16		
1993	1144.20		114.01	403.67	493.12		
1994	1331.13		152.42	477.86	418.27		
1995	1680.17		240.85	602.70	491.08		300.22
"九五"时期 The Period of the Ninth Five-year plan	**12426.20**		**1463.68**	**4912.01**	**2288.90**		**2124.97**
1996	1949.53		232.62	708.60	465.21		399.99
1997	2203.09		241.55	826.60	447.94		437.25
1998	2535.50		300.24	1031.96	457.36		514.23
1999	2742.65		330.55	1144.84	462.53	148.23	410.28
2000	2995.43		358.72	1200.01	455.86	326.08	363.22
"十五"时期 The Period of the Tenth Five-year plan	**28055.30**	**10495.83**	**4583.38**	**8790.13**	**2018.49**	**6453.90**	**4719.01**
2001	3302.96	684.83	414.36	1285.71	400.36	528.38	378.17
2002	3849.24	905.69	544.13	1422.06	297.56	769.90	568.77
2003	5335.80	1667.65	809.96	1998.19	456.98	932.11	972.88
2004	6827.59	2104.28	1269.78	2006.20	418.43	1599.91	1230.56
2005	8739.71	5133.38	1545.15	2077.97	445.16	2623.60	1568.63
"十一五"时期 The Period of the Eleventh Five-year plan	**79534.10**	**42558.47**	**15124.96**	**14898.12**	**3136.70**	**27735.48**	**12592.54**
2006	10071.42	5347.13	1906.71	2144.93	441.57	3049.30	1756.83
2007	12268.07	6599.08	2515.91	2092.57	453.28	4125.86	2301.12
2008	15060.45	8246.27	3064.46	2494.77	539.99	5268.79	2838.43
2009	18949.88	10167.44	3338.50	3677.11	753.73	6872.67	2681.77
2010	23184.28	12342.54	4299.38	4488.74	948.13	8418.86	3014.39
2010(新口径)(New Statistical Scale)	21643.02	11442.06	4299.38	4348.46	902.95	7778.03	2969.94
"十二五"时期 The Period of the Twelveth Five-year plan	**181461.67**	**91701.18**	**35409.39**	**35102.31**	**7873.25**	**76164.81**	**19093.01**
2011	26314.66	13771.12	5567.94	5004.82	1132.95	9696.87	3303.41
2012	31706.58	16544.02	6206.10	6022.51	1393.13	12074.90	3818.24
2013	35982.52	18369.54	7241.45	6865.27	1639.37	14955.56	3913.00
2014	41552.75	20259.05	8240.22	8308.13	1835.30	18185.36	4155.92
2015	45905.17	22757.45	8153.68	8901.58	1872.50	21252.12	3902.44
"十三五"时期 The Period of the Thirteen Five-year plan							
2016	49370.85	24544.40	8956.37	8236.65	806.51	23417.12	4692.83

注:房地产开发投资统计制度从1990年开始建立,城乡私营个体投资统计制度从1999年开始建立。

a) The statitistical system of real estate development investment was established in 1990, while that of the urban and rural private and individual investment was established in 1999.

6-3 按登记注册类型分固定资产投资
Investment in Fixed Assets by Registration Status

单位:亿元 (100 million yuan)

类别	Item	2015 投资额 Investment	2015 #工业投资 Industrial Investment	2016 投资额 Investment	2016 #工业投资 Industrial Investment
总计	**Total**	**45905.17**	**22757.45**	**49370.85**	**24544.40**
内资企业	Domestic Funded Enterprises	41912.57	20194.55	44617.85	21257.35
国有企业	State-owned Enterprises	8031.45	1307.58	6551.63	644.36
集体企业	Collective-owned Enterprises	1767.39	137.16	752.12	51.95
股份合作企业	Cooperative Enterprises	91.72	67.14	43.42	20.88
联营企业	Joint Ownreship Enterprises	119.64	19.34	156.27	31.00
国有联营	State Joint Ownership Enterprises	53.93	9.80	102.78	10.78
集体联营	Collective Joint Ownership Enterprises	13.39	6.41	10.97	4.12
国有与集体联营	Joint State-collective Enterprises	15.81	0.73	15.50	13.90
其他联营企业	Other Joint Ownership Enterprises	36.51	2.40	27.02	2.20
有限责任公司	Limited Liability Corporations	8568.94	3069.47	12063.38	3975.86
国有独资公司	State Sole Funded Corporations	816.20	119.46	1582.24	190.35
其他有限责任公司	Other Limited Liability Corporations	7752.74	2950.01	10481.14	3785.51
股份有限公司	Share-holding Corporations Ltd.	1210.16	649.29	1176.19	664.64
私营企业	Private Enterprises	21161.96	14632.30	23356.95	15644.85
其他企业	Others Enterprises	961.31	312.28	517.88	223.82
港、澳、台商投资企业	Enterprises with Funds from Hong Kong, Macao and Taiwan	1648.71	780.47	2306.36	1319.55
合资经营企业	Joint-venture Enterprises	509.09	238.10	822.99	510.28
合作经营企业	Cooperative Enterprises	15.45	7.70	31.22	17.91
独资企业	Enterprises with Sole Fund	1045.86	491.31	1345.73	719.96
股份有限公司	Share-holding Corporations Ltd.	66.19	37.29	101.65	71.12
其他港澳台商投资	Other Hong Kong, Macao Taiwan Investment	12.12	6.07	4.78	0.29
外商投资企业	Foreign Funded Enterprises	2253.73	1761.78	2386.47	1952.04
合资经营企业	Joint-venture Enterprises	661.18	498.58	984.99	804.69
合作经营企业	Cooperative Enterprises	31.13	10.78	35.69	18.92
独资企业	Enterprises with Sole Fund	1501.32	1220.80	1299.79	1069.88
股份有限公司	Share-holding Corporations Ltd.	29.58	27.51	58.14	50.94
其他外商投资	Others	30.53	4.11	7.85	7.61
个体经营	Individuals	90.15	20.66	60.17	15.46
个体户	Self-employed Individuals	86.13	18.67	54.91	15.09
个人合伙	Partnership Individuals	4.03	1.99	5.26	0.36

6-4 按资金来源和构成分固定资产投资
Investment in Fixed Assets by Sources of Finance and Use of Funds

年　份 Year	按资金来源分 Grouped by Sources of Funds				
	国家预算内资金 State Budget	国内贷款 Domestic Loans	利用外资 Foreign Investment	自筹资金 Self-raising	其他资金来源 Others
投资额(亿元) **Investment (100 million yuan)**					
1985	17.25	36.79	3.98	64.45	69.46
1986	18.74	43.52	12.71	73.27	92.99
1987	21.46	63.15	19.15	85.66	127.71
1988	17.23	69.94	27.77	106.30	150.63
1989	16.80	41.74	19.91	91.66	150.12
1990	15.02	45.47	15.92	106.47	173.42
1991	16.38	84.77	20.41	290.13	28.29
1992	24.73	189.49	40.56	378.30	78.62
1993	17.85	253.80	89.48	649.95	133.12
1994	17.54	242.93	151.96	744.20	174.50
1995	25.83	270.16	228.89	880.02	275.27
1996	24.01	282.88	335.16	1001.29	306.19
1997	29.63	293.66	390.59	1199.29	289.92
1998	49.46	331.83	413.66	1406.39	334.16
1999	62.91	399.36	309.02	1639.01	332.35
2000	73.42	489.04	281.17	1827.79	324.01
2001	69.97	524.51	326.22	1977.97	404.29
2002	54.48	735.30	421.21	2237.73	400.52
2003	92.61	1141.99	579.51	2999.19	587.42
2004	81.30	1233.07	641.66	4201.29	928.38
2005	67.60	1264.49	836.19	5826.89	1205.90
2006	66.59	1445.16	874.82	6800.90	1590.15
2007	135.20	1561.06	1255.85	8522.18	2398.08
2008	153.86	1818.06	1394.98	10624.51	2210.27
2009	278.79	2774.45	1114.78	14064.93	4350.16
2010	282.11	3343.47	1154.87	17553.37	4912.63
2010(新口径)(New Statistical Scale)	273.00	3231.05	1135.69	16186.61	4839.81
2011	344.87	3751.24	1241.65	20652.57	4394.19
2012	448.05	4658.42	1216.78	25824.05	5262.67
2013	529.19	5091.04	1127.55	29444.25	6822.96
2014	627.26	5360.60	1152.05	33325.52	6232.21
2015	806.89	4810.95	926.17	36305.15	7206.37
2016	990.43	5778.54	599.88	36257.99	10830.18
构成(%) **Composition(%)**					
1985	9.0	19.1	2.1	33.6	36.2
1990	4.2	12.8	4.5	29.9	48.6
1995	1.5	16.1	13.6	52.4	16.4
2000	2.5	16.3	9.4	61.0	10.8
2005	0.7	13.8	9.1	63.3	13.1
2006	0.6	13.4	8.1	63.1	14.8
2007	1.0	11.3	9.0	61.4	17.3
2008	0.9	11.2	8.6	65.6	13.6
2009	1.2	12.3	4.9	62.3	19.3
2010	1.0	12.3	4.2	64.4	18.0
2010(新口径)(New Statistical Scale)	1.1	12.6	4.4	63.1	18.9
2011	0.9	10.6	3.7	53.3	15.9
2012	1.1	12.3	4.1	68.0	14.5
2013	1.2	11.8	2.6	68.5	15.9
2014	1.3	11.5	2.5	71.4	13.3
2015	1.6	9.6	1.9	72.5	14.4
2016	1.8	10.6	1.1	66.6	19.9

年 份 Year	按构成分 Grouped by Use of Funds		
	建筑安装工程 Construction and Installation	设备工器具购置 Purchases of Equipments and Instruments	其他费用 Others
投资额(亿元) **Investment (100 million yuan)**			
1985	149.40	34.41	8.12
1986	187.33	43.82	10.08
1987	240.92	60.61	15.60
1988	281.34	73.71	16.82
1989	256.23	52.25	11.75
1990	284.24	53.70	18.36
1991	347.72	71.33	20.93
1992	408.59	257.45	45.66
1993	651.17	395.34	97.69
1994	775.84	437.87	117.42
1995	983.24	536.48	160.45
1996	1151.16	600.59	197.78
1997	1307.24	688.66	207.19
1998	1503.62	755.02	276.86
1999	1682.72	746.75	313.18
2000	1817.08	867.74	310.61
2001	1901.68	967.21	434.07
2002	2091.15	1160.08	598.01
2003	2906.59	1510.59	918.62
2004	3886.52	1928.66	1012.41
2005	4879.72	2544.36	1315.63
2006	5624.16	2944.50	1502.76
2007	6804.65	3558.53	1904.89
2008	8310.70	4587.89	2161.86
2009	10454.05	5901.61	2594.22
2010	12601.51	7054.33	3528.44
2010(新口径)(New Statistical Scale)	11804.76	6436.57	3401.70
2011	14569.44	8112.05	3633.17
2012	17913.03	9756.39	4037.16
2013	20821.56	10903.11	4257.84
2014	24686.18	12327.57	4539.00
2015	27570.90	14225.16	4109.11
2016	28989.35	15368.57	5012.94
构成(%) Composition(%)			
1985	77.9	17.9	4.2
1990	80.0	15.1	4.9
1995	58.5	31.9	9.6
2000	60.6	29.0	10.4
2005	55.8	29.1	15.1
2006	55.9	29.2	14.9
2007	55.5	29.0	15.5
2008	55.2	30.5	14.3
2009	55.2	31.1	13.7
2010	54.4	30.4	15.2
2010(新口径)(New Statistical Scale)	54.5	29.7	15.7
2011	44.9	24.5	12.9
2012	55.4	30.8	13.8
2013	57.9	30.3	11.8
2014	59.4	29.7	10.9
2015	60.1	31.0	9.0
2016	58.7	31.1	10.2

6－5 按构成分固定资产投资（2016年）
Investment in Fixed Assets by Use of Funds(2016)

单位:亿元 (100 million yuan)

行业	Sector	投资额 Investment	建筑工程 Construction	安装工程 Installation	设备工器具购置 Purchase of Equipment and Instruments	其他 Others
总计	**Total**	**49370.85**	**25704.74**	**3284.60**	**15368.57**	**5012.94**
农、林、牧、渔业	Agriculture, Forestry, Animal Husbandry and Fishery	410.46	251.62	29.00	87.72	42.12
农业	Farming	166.39	105.01	11.65	34.80	14.94
林业	Forestry	13.64	7.05	1.22	2.77	2.60
畜牧业	Animal Husbandry	79.76	42.47	5.92	22.21	9.16
渔业	Fishery	33.32	20.98	3.51	5.57	3.26
农、林、牧、渔服务业	Service in Support of Agriculture	117.35	76.12	6.69	22.38	12.16
采矿业	Mining	72.94	22.44	7.95	32.53	10.03
煤炭开采和洗选业	Mining and Washing of Coal	14.04	1.39	2.54	10.08	0.04
石油和天然气开采业	Extraction of Petroleum and Natural Gas	17.28	4.98	0.83	4.69	6.79
黑色金属矿采选业	Mining and Processing of Ferrous Metal Ores	14.41	5.87	1.76	5.83	0.95
有色金属矿采选业	Mining and Processing of Non-ferracs Metal Ores	2.78	0.93	0.44	1.42	
非金属矿采选业	Mining and Processing of Nonmetal Ores	23.85	9.28	2.36	9.96	2.25
开采辅助活动	Auxiliary Mining	0.57	0.00	0.01	0.56	0.00
其他采矿业	Mining of Other Ores					
制造业	Manufacturing	22869.69	8058.83	1571.87	12189.18	1049.81
农副食品加工业	Processing of Food from Agricultural Products	609.39	231.85	56.74	287.28	33.52
食品制造业	Manufacture of Food	353.72	144.79	27.21	161.38	20.33
酒、饮料和精制茶制造业	Manufacture of Beverage	141.95	60.41	8.75	68.31	4.48
烟草制品业	Manufacture of Tobacco	11.92	3.16	1.68	6.72	0.36
纺织业	Manufacture of Textile	1211.63	358.98	62.78	745.95	43.92
纺织服装、服饰业	Manufacture of Textile Wearing, Apparel, Footwear and Caps	613.37	241.25	40.85	303.59	27.69
皮革、毛皮、羽毛及其制品和制鞋业	Manufacture of Leather, Fur, Feather and Related Products	160.07	63.33	15.51	73.64	7.60
木材加工和木、竹、藤、棕、草制品业	Processing of Timber, Manufacture of Wood, Bamboo, Rattan, Palm and Straw Products	433.03	188.03	22.43	197.94	24.63
家具制造业	Manufacture of Furniture	271.73	106.98	14.31	131.05	19.38
造纸和纸制品业	Manufacture of Paper and Paper Products	249.03	84.98	17.26	138.26	8.53
印刷和记录媒介复制业	Printing, Reproduction of Recording Media	195.58	67.32	9.99	110.44	7.83
文教、工美、体育和娱乐用品制造业	Manufacture of Articles For Culture, Education and Sport Activities	325.12	126.94	19.57	163.09	15.52
石油加工、炼焦和核燃料加工业	Processing of Petroleum, Coking, Processing of Nuclear Fuel	147.14	52.16	13.52	75.32	6.14
化学原料和化学制品制造业	Manufacture of Raw Chemical Materials and Chemical Products	1879.68	667.26	188.19	910.85	113.37
医药制造业	Manufacture of Medicines	678.36	262.04	61.66	313.25	41.41
化学纤维制造业	Manufacture of Chemical Fibers	240.38	65.63	8.78	161.29	4.68
橡胶和塑料制品业	Rubber and Plastic	787.43	250.36	54.18	454.74	28.15
非金属矿物制品业	Manufacture of Non - metallic Mineral Products	1251.40	470.56	93.62	625.70	61.52
黑色金属冶炼和压延加工业	Smelting and Pressing of Ferrous Metals	454.30	145.60	36.48	260.56	11.66
有色金属冶炼和压延加工业	Smelting and Pressing of Non-ferrous Metals	372.36	135.22	28.48	193.68	14.97

6-5 续 表 1 Continued 1

单位:亿元 (100 million yuan)

行业	Sector	投资额 Investment	建筑工程 Construction	安装工程 Installation	设备工器具购置 Purchase of Equipment and Instruments	其他 Others
金属制品业	Manufacture of Metal Products	1460.32	492.80	89.93	817.95	59.64
通用设备制造业	Manufacture of General Purpose Machinery	2361.80	768.00	153.80	1351.70	88.30
专用设备制造业	Manufacture of Special Purpose Machinery	2151.39	805.71	133.34	1127.12	85.22
汽车制造业	Manufacture of Automobile	1293.03	521.13	77.28	628.01	66.61
铁路、船舶、航空航天和其他运输设备制造业	Manufacture of Railroad, Marine Aviation and other Transport Equipment	456.45	173.13	34.04	216.46	32.82
电气机械和器材制造业	Manufacture of Electrical Machinery and Equipment	2349.53	832.73	153.23	1256.14	107.43
计算机、通信和其他电子设备制造业	Manufacture of Communication Equipment, Computers and Other Electronic Equipment	1711.72	455.79	103.65	1073.80	78.49
仪器仪表制造业	Manufacture of Instrumentation	414.49	147.60	23.97	224.86	18.07
其他制造业	Other Manufacturing	164.81	88.18	11.56	53.20	11.88
废弃资源综合利用业	Manufacture of Recycling and Disposal of Waste	101.24	40.40	7.54	49.24	4.06
金属制品、机械和设备修理业	Manufacture of Metal Products, Machinery and Equipment Repair	17.31	6.50	1.52	7.68	1.62
电力、热力、燃气及水生产和供应业	Production and Supply of Electric Power, Heat Power, Gas and Water	1619.65	525.17	181.34	759.86	153.27
电力、热力生产和供应业	Production and Supply of Electric Power and Heat Power	1327.62	375.86	151.57	656.17	144.02
燃气生产和供应业	Production and Supply of Gas	77.90	29.69	11.61	34.17	2.42
水的生产和供应业	Production and Supply of Water	214.13	119.62	18.15	69.52	6.83
建筑业	Construction	129.41	81.88	8.57	31.74	7.22
房屋建筑业	Housing Construction	28.53	16.35	2.10	9.00	1.07
土木工程建筑业	Civil Engineering Construction	56.37	43.85	2.19	7.90	2.43
建筑安装业	Building Installation	17.44	10.72	1.79	4.06	0.88
建筑装饰和其他建筑业	Other Construction	27.08	10.96	2.49	10.78	2.84
批发和零售业	Wholesale and Retail Trades	1640.53	990.07	105.53	409.07	135.85
批发业	Wholesale Trades	858.23	517.06	50.50	239.48	51.20
零售业	Retail Trades	782.29	473.01	55.04	169.60	84.65
交通运输、仓储和邮政业	Transport, Storage and Post	2542.29	1662.64	99.76	423.44	356.44
铁路运输业	Railway Transport	93.85	41.91	2.72	0.22	49.00
道路运输业	Road Transport	1408.80	962.18	44.11	192.17	210.35
水上运输业	Water Transport	287.10	164.12	10.74	91.29	20.94
航空运输业	Air Transport	20.02	15.45	0.56	2.09	1.92
管道运输业	Transport Via Pipelines	35.94	24.61	2.06	9.09	0.18
装卸搬运和运输代理业	Loading, Unloading and Other Transport Services	82.88	47.84	2.70	26.39	5.95
仓储业	Storage	581.79	385.25	34.47	96.52	65.54
邮政业	Post	31.92	21.28	2.42	5.66	2.56
住宿和餐饮业	Hotels and Catering Services	455.91	308.38	32.87	77.72	36.94
住宿业	Hotels	231.01	157.92	16.48	37.64	18.97
餐饮业	Catering Services	224.90	150.46	16.39	40.09	17.97
信息传输、软件和信息技术服务业	Information Transfer、Software and IT Services	635.48	307.77	96.37	204.81	26.54
电信、广播电视和卫星传输服务	Telecommunications、Satellites Radio and Television Services	134.04	32.39	49.74	48.66	3.25
互联网和相关服务	Internet and Relatiue Services	84.47	37.42	6.79	36.03	4.23
软件和信息技术服务业	Software and IT Services	416.97	237.96	39.84	120.12	19.06

6-5 续 表 2 Continued 2

单位:亿元 (100 million yuan)

行 业	Sector	投资额 Investment	建筑工程 Constru-ction	安装工程 Installa-tion	设备工器具购置 Purchase of Equipment and Instr-uments	其他 Others
金融业	Financial Intermediation	141.65	107.19	9.58	17.22	7.65
货币金融服务	Monetary and Financial	71.29	48.88	6.37	12.51	3.54
资本市场服务	Capital Markets	38.79	31.15	2.31	2.32	3.01
保险业	Insurance	3.47	2.39	0.25	0.63	0.19
其他金融业	Other Financial Activities	28.10	24.77	0.66	1.76	0.91
房地产业	Real Estate	10277.09	6992.43	744.58	197.75	2342.34
房地产业	Real Estate	10277.09	6992.43	744.58	197.75	2342.34
租赁和商务服务业	Leasing and Business Services	1545.71	1160.20	74.38	142.97	168.16
租赁业	Leasing	48.14	27.27	1.84	16.55	2.47
商务服务业	Business Services	1497.57	1132.92	72.54	126.42	165.69
科学研究和技术服务业	Scientific Research and Technical Services	639.21	374.09	41.64	179.86	43.63
研究和试验发展	Research and Experimental Development	174.88	90.51	10.39	55.31	18.67
专业技术服务业	Professional Technical Services	259.57	157.48	19.55	68.61	13.93
科技推广和应用服务业	Promation and Application of Science	204.76	126.10	11.70	55.93	11.03
水利、环境和公共设施管理业	Management of Water Conservancy, Environment and Public Facilities	3965.38	3171.43	156.40	283.84	353.71
水利管理业	Management of Water Conservancy	398.21	303.26	8.67	29.40	56.87
生态保护和环境治理业	Ecological Protection and Enviromental	123.21	74.43	9.22	31.76	7.80
公共设施管理业	Management of Public Facilities	3443.96	2793.74	138.51	222.68	289.04
居民服务、修理和其他服务业	Services to Households and Other Services	260.86	178.60	15.33	54.26	12.67
居民服务业	Services to Households	158.87	118.08	8.44	24.41	7.93
机动车、电子产品和日用产品修理业	Vehicle、Electronics and Dairy Maintenance	57.60	35.98	2.39	16.60	2.63
其他服务业	Other Services	44.39	24.54	4.49	13.25	2.11
教育	Education	590.09	439.62	23.77	59.09	67.61
教育	Education	590.09	439.62	23.77	59.09	67.61
卫生和社会工作	Health and Social Work	446.43	311.71	21.58	75.15	37.99
卫生	Health	379.36	268.93	14.26	65.52	30.64
社会工作	Social Work	67.07	42.78	7.32	9.63	7.34
文化、体育和娱乐业	Culture, Sports and Entertainment	642.24	367.00	40.02	98.31	136.91
新闻和出版业	Journalism and Publishing Activities	2.71	1.92	0.21	0.43	0.14
广播、电视、电影和影视录音制作业	Broadcasting, Movies, Television and Audiovisual Activities	55.79	26.45	1.94	25.86	1.54
文化艺术业	Cultural and Art Activities	294.80	143.87	14.75	23.93	112.26
体育	Sports Activities	135.10	100.39	11.56	17.85	5.29
娱乐业	Entertainment	153.84	94.38	11.55	30.23	17.67
公共管理、社会保障和社会组织	Public Management and Social Organization	485.82	393.66	24.06	44.04	24.06
中国共产党机关	Organs of Communist Party of China	2.26	2.23	0.01	0.00	0.01
国家机构	Government Agencies	407.35	325.97	21.27	39.01	21.09
人民政协、民主党派	People's Political Cousultative Conference and Remocratic Parlies					
社会保障	Social Security	2.48	2.19	0.12	0.05	0.12
群众团体、社会团体和其他成员组织	Non-governmental Organizations, Social Organizations and Relighion Organizations	24.35	18.91	1.86	2.02	1.57
基层群众自治组织	Grass Roots Self-governing Organizataions	49.39	44.36	0.81	2.96	1.26

6-6 按建设性质分固定资产投资（2016年）
Investment in Fixed Assets by Type of Construction(2016)

单位：亿元 (100 million yuan)

行业	Sector	投资额 Investment	#新建 New Construction	#扩建 Expansion	#改建 Reconstruction
总计	**Total**	**40414.48**	**21064.65**	**8049.64**	**8967.07**
农、林、牧、渔业	Agriculture, Forestry, Animal Husbandry and Fishery	410.46	321.88	63.81	23.10
农业	Farming	166.39	131.40	26.29	7.93
林业	Forestry	13.64	11.73	1.56	0.35
畜牧业	Animal Husbandry	79.76	59.55	16.52	3.59
渔业	Fishery	33.32	29.51	2.77	1.04
农、林、牧、渔服务业	Service in Support of Agriculture	117.35	89.68	16.68	10.19
采矿业	Mining	72.94	36.48	7.50	28.39
煤炭开采和洗选业	Mining and Washing of Coal	14.04	1.92	2.84	9.29
石油和天然气开采业	Extraction of Petroleum and Natural Gas	17.28	7.01	0.00	10.27
黑色金属矿采选业	Mining and Processing of Ferrous Metul Ores	14.41	11.15	2.77	0.49
有色金属矿采选业	Mining and Processing of Non-ferrous Metal Ores	2.78	1.63	0.00	1.16
非金属矿采选业	Mining and Processing of Nonmetal Ores	23.85	14.77	1.89	6.62
开采辅助活动	Auxiliary Mining	0.57	0.00	0.00	0.57
其他采矿业	Mining of Other Ores				
制造业	Manufacturing	22869.69	8648.42	4945.36	7530.47
农副食品加工业	Processing of Food from Agricultural Products	609.39	263.10	121.08	216.78
食品制造业	Manufacture of Food	353.72	167.74	59.99	114.74
酒、饮料和精制茶制造业	Manufacture of Beverage	141.95	61.75	24.09	53.92
烟草制品业	Manufacture of Tobacco	11.92	1.07	8.38	2.47
纺织业	Manufacture of Textile	1211.63	346.04	339.96	449.79
纺织服装、服饰业	Manufacture of Textile Wearing, Apparel, Footwear and Caps	613.37	233.35	160.56	193.38
皮革、毛皮、羽毛及其制品和制鞋业	Manufacture of Leather, Fur, Feather and Related Products	160.07	68.85	39.02	47.68
木材加工和木、竹、藤、棕、草制品业	Processing of Timber, Manufacture of Wood, Bamboo, Rattan, Palm and Straw Products	433.03	208.37	122.44	89.88
家具制造业	Manufacture of Furniture	271.73	153.52	46.01	59.97
造纸和纸制品业	Manufacture of Paper and Paper Products	249.03	90.30	52.26	84.40
印刷和记录媒介复制业	Printing, Reproduction of Recording Media	195.58	57.36	54.27	69.54
文教、工美、体育和娱乐用品制造业	Manufacture of Articles for Culture, Education and Sport Activities	325.12	102.55	96.33	116.61
石油加工、炼焦和核燃料加工业	Processing of Petroleum, Coking, Processing of Nuclear Fuel	147.14	95.22	12.20	35.68
化学原料和化学制品制造业	Manufacture of Raw Chemical Materials and Chemical Products	1879.68	680.77	309.44	796.00
医药制造业	Manufacture of Medicines	678.36	348.26	103.09	190.91
化学纤维制造业	Manufacture of Chemical Fibers	240.38	51.96	94.59	79.19
橡胶和塑料制品业	Rubber and Plastic	787.43	241.28	202.24	249.58
非金属矿物制品业	Manufacture of Non-metallic Mineral Products	1251.40	578.95	250.26	367.80
黑色金属冶炼和压延加工业	Smelting and Pressing of Ferrous Metals	454.30	181.61	70.33	185.16
有色金属冶炼和压延加工业	Smelting and Pressing of Non-ferrous Metals	372.36	143.34	83.36	121.45

单位:亿元 (100 million yuan)

行业	Sector	投资额 Investment	#新建 New Construction	#扩建 Expansion	#改建 Reconstruction
金属制品业	Manufacture of Metal Products	1460.32	550.91	365.63	447.48
通用设备制造业	Manufacture of General Purpose Machinery	2361.80	749.33	578.40	816.34
专用设备制造业	Manufacture of Special Purpose Machinery	2151.39	860.32	401.49	709.84
汽车制造业	Manufacture of Automobile	1293.03	505.72	304.27	366.49
铁路、船舶、航空航天和其他运输设备制造业	Manufacture of Railroad, Marine Aviation and other Transport Equipment	456.45	188.68	109.43	127.98
电气机械和器材制造业	Manufacture of Electrical Machinery and Equipment	2349.53	916.48	490.28	760.00
计算机、通信和其他电子设备制造业	Manufacture of Communication Equipment, Computers and Other Electronic Equipment	1711.72	513.24	316.90	556.04
仪器仪表制造业	Manufacture of Instrumentation	414.49	126.85	87.63	152.73
其他制造业	Other Manufacturing	164.81	108.42	21.75	28.80
废弃资源综合利用业	Manufacture of Recycling and Disposal of Waste	101.24	45.66	16.97	32.88
金属制品、机械和设备修理业	Manufacture of Metal Products, Machinery and Equipment Repair	17.31	7.43	2.75	6.96
电力、热力、燃气及水生产和供应业	Production and Supply of Electric Power, Heat Power, Gas and Water	1619.65	882.82	380.07	334.51
电力、热力生产和供应业	Production and Supply of Electric Power and Heat Power	1327.62	725.75	320.28	264.15
燃气生产和供应业	Production and Supply of Gas	77.90	26.76	18.21	31.67
水的生产和供应业	Production and Supply of Water	214.13	130.32	41.58	38.68
建筑业	Construction	129.41	83.23	21.45	14.10
房屋建筑业	Housing Construction	28.53	14.64	5.52	4.17
土木工程建筑业	Civil Engineering Construction	56.37	43.09	8.67	3.02
建筑安装业	Building Installation	17.44	12.20	2.41	2.28
建筑装饰和其他建筑业	Other Construction	27.08	13.31	4.84	4.64
批发和零售业	Wholesale and Retail Trades	1640.53	988.94	462.21	126.45
批发业	Wholesale Trades	858.23	477.57	271.83	69.59
零售业	Retail Trades	782.29	511.37	190.38	56.85
交通运输、仓储和邮政业	Transport, Storage and Post	2542.29	1869.93	379.16	186.96
铁路运输业	Railway Transport	93.85	87.88	0.68	0.29
道路运输业	Road Transport	1408.80	1013.44	238.75	103.82
水上运输业	Water Transport	287.10	199.91	29.10	29.71
航空运输业	Air Transport	20.02	11.37	8.34	0.30
管道运输业	Transport Via Pipelines	35.94	17.20	9.16	9.58
装卸搬运和运输代理业	Loading, Unloading and Other Transport Services	82.88	53.44	19.30	3.31
仓储业	Storage	581.79	466.11	64.14	39.42
邮政业	Post	31.92	20.56	9.69	0.53
住宿和餐饮业	Hotels and Catering Services	455.91	314.87	97.84	28.77
住宿业	Hotels	231.01	178.28	33.24	12.29
餐饮业	Catering Services	224.90	136.60	64.60	16.48
信息传输、软件和信息技术服务业	Information Transfer、Software and IT Services	635.48	448.02	92.76	44.78
电信、广播电视和卫星传输服务	Telecommunications、Satellites Radio and Television Services	134.04	99.02	20.08	13.93
互联网和相关服务	Internet and Relatiue Services	84.47	50.87	14.98	5.47
软件和信息技术服务业	Software and IT Services	416.97	298.12	57.70	25.38

单位:亿元 (100 million yuan)

行 业	Sector	投资额 Investment	#新 建 New Construction	#扩 建 Expansion	#改 建 Recons-truction
金融业	Financial Intermediation	141.65	110.72	15.86	6.37
货币金融服务	Monetary and Financial	71.29	49.12	10.86	5.09
资本市场服务	Capital Markets	38.79	32.58	3.92	0.48
保险业	Insurance	3.47	1.70	0.29	0.79
其他金融业	Other Financial Activities	28.10	27.31	0.79	0.00
房地产业	Real Estate	1320.73	1080.92	178.23	33.87
房地产业	Real Estate	1320.73	1080.92	178.23	33.87
租赁和商务服务业	Leasing and Business Services	1545.71	1252.20	191.18	70.13
租赁业	Leasing	48.14	31.56	8.20	3.85
商务服务业	Business Services	1497.57	1220.65	182.99	66.28
科学研究和技术服务业	Scientific Research and Technical Services	639.21	410.98	132.59	58.27
研究和试验发展	Research and Experimental Development	174.88	121.58	33.77	13.23
专业技术服务业	Professional Technical Serrices	259.57	158.58	51.08	21.98
科技推广和应用服务业	Promation and Application of Science	204.76	130.81	47.74	23.06
水利、环境和公共设施管理业	Management of Water Conservancy, Environment and Public Facilities	3965.38	2781.49	742.12	362.61
水利管理业	Management of Water Conservancy	398.21	274.21	90.49	28.14
生态保护和环境治理业	Ecological Protection and Enviromental	123.21	77.03	22.07	20.69
公共设施管理业	Management of Public Facilities	3443.96	2430.25	629.55	313.79
居民服务、修理和其他服务业	Services to Households and Other Services	260.86	187.44	43.11	17.57
居民服务业	Services to House Holds	158.87	120.04	22.41	10.15
机动车、电子产品和日用产品修理业	Vehicle、Electronics and Dairy Maintenance	57.60	32.66	15.37	5.11
其他服务业	Othe Services	44.39	34.75	5.34	2.31
教育	Education	590.09	448.18	94.60	18.57
教育	Education	590.09	448.18	94.60	18.57
卫生和社会工作	Health and Social Work	446.43	288.49	75.90	27.41
卫生	Health	379.36	249.53	62.61	14.35
社会工作	Social Work	67.07	38.97	13.29	13.07
文化、体育和娱乐业	Culture, Sports and Entertainment	642.24	534.10	68.83	22.68
新闻和出版业	Journalism and Publishing Activities	2.71	1.57	0.58	0.00
广播、电视、电影和影视录音制作业	Broadcasting, Movies, Television and Audiovisual Activities	55.79	45.74	4.35	2.02
文化艺术业	Cultural and Art Activities	294.80	250.83	28.40	9.33
体育	Sports Activities	135.10	115.90	10.37	6.65
娱乐业	Entertainment	153.84	120.06	25.14	4.68
公共管理、社会保障和社会组织	Public Management and Social Organization	485.82	375.54	57.05	32.06
中国共产党机关	Organs of Communist Party of China	2.26	2.18	0.00	0.08
国家机构	Government Agencies	407.35	322.74	36.47	27.07
人民政协、民主党派	People's Political Cousultative Conference and Remocratic Parlies				
社会保障	Social Security	2.48	2.20	0.28	0.00
群众团体、社会团体和其他成员组织	Non-governmental Organizations, Social Organizations and Religion Organizations	24.35	14.23	8.38	1.74
基层群众自治组织	Grass Roots Self-governing Organizations	49.39	34.20	11.92	3.17

6-7 按隶属关系和注册类型分固定资产投资(2016年)

单位:亿元

行业	Sector	投资额 Investment	中央 Central Investment	地方 Local Investment
总计	**Total**	**49370.85**	**912.23**	**48458.62**
农、林、牧、渔业	Agriculture, Forestry, Animal Husbandry and Fishery	410.46	9.33	401.14
农业	Farming	166.39	8.73	157.66
林业	Forestry	13.64	0.15	13.49
畜牧业	Animal Husbandry	79.76	0.00	79.76
渔业	Fishery	33.32	0.36	32.96
农、林、牧、渔服务业	Service in Support of Agriculture	117.35	0.09	117.26
采矿业	Mining	72.94	12.32	60.62
煤炭开采和洗选业	Mining and Washing of Coal	14.04	0.00	14.04
石油和天然气开采业	Extraction of Petroleum and Natural Gas	17.28	12.17	5.11
黑色金属矿采选业	Mining and Processing of Ferrous Metul Ores	14.41	0.00	14.41
有色金属矿采选业	Mining and Processing of Non-ferrous Metal Ores	2.78	0.00	2.78
非金属矿采选业	Mining and Processing of Nonmetal Ores	23.85	0.10	23.76
开采辅助活动	Auxiliary Mining	0.57	0.05	0.52
其他采矿业	Mining of Other Ores			
制造业	Manufacturing	22869.69	144.42	22725.27
农副食品加工业	Processing of Food from Agricultural Products	609.39	3.11	606.28
食品制造业	Manufacture of Food	353.72		353.72
酒、饮料和精制茶制造业	Manufacture of Beverage	141.95		141.95
烟草制品业	Manufacture of Tobacco	11.92		11.92
纺织业	Manufacture of Textile	1211.63	0.36	1211.27
纺织服装、服饰业	Manufacture of Textile Wearing, Apparel, Footwear and Caps	613.37	0.46	612.91
皮革、毛皮、羽毛及其制品和制鞋业	Manufacture of Leather, Fur, Feather and Related Products	160.07		160.07
木材加工和木、竹、藤、棕、草制品业	Processing of Timber, Manufacture of Wood, Bamboo, Rattan, Palm and Straw Products	433.03	2.75	430.28
家具制造业	Manufacture of Furniture	271.73		271.73
造纸和纸制品业	Manufacture of Paper and Paper Products	249.03		249.03
印刷和记录媒介复制业	Printing, Reproduction of Recording Media	195.58		195.58
文教、工美、体育和娱乐用品制造业	Manufacture of Articles For Culture, Education and Sport Activities	325.12		325.12
石油加工、炼焦和核燃料加工业	Processing of Petroleum, Coking, Processing of Nuclear Fuel	147.14	30.73	116.42
化学原料和化学制品制造业	Manufacture of Raw Chemical Materials and Chemical Products	1879.68	29.58	1850.10
医药制造业	Manufacture of Medicines	678.36		678.36
化学纤维制造业	Manufacture of Chemical Fibers	240.38	4.23	236.16
橡胶和塑料制品业	Rubber and Plastic	787.43	5.01	782.42
非金属矿物制品业	Manufacture of Non-metallic Mineral Products	1251.40	0.65	1250.75
黑色金属冶炼和压延加工业	Smelting and Pressing of Ferrous Metals	454.30	2.20	452.10
有色金属冶炼和压延加工业	Smelting and Pressing of Non-ferrous Metals	372.36		372.36

Investment in Fixed Assets by Jurisdiction of Management and Registration Status(2016)

(100 million yuan)

内 资 Domestic Funds	港澳台商投资 Funds from Hong Kong, Macao and Taiwan	外商投资 Foreign Funded	国有控股 State-holding	集体控股 Collective-holding	私人控股 Private-holding
44617.85	**2306.36**	**2386.47**	**11241.10**	**1471.57**	**29680.29**
389.91	13.31	2.24	93.71	27.37	262.20
159.64	3.95	0.00	33.77	6.71	121.32
13.64	0.00	0.00	3.69	0.06	9.70
67.97	9.35	1.85	1.96	1.14	62.49
31.85			5.18	0.60	22.14
116.81		0.39	49.11	18.86	46.55
72.14	0.80		19.71	1.18	47.28
14.04			0.50		13.55
17.28			16.80		0.48
14.41					14.41
2.78			1.14		1.16
23.05	0.80		1.22	1.18	17.17
0.57			0.05		0.52
19775.48	1169.19	1909.56	786.35	147.67	18464.74
557.15	18.40	32.96	12.65	2.45	539.78
287.62	35.78	30.32	6.18	0.47	271.81
119.86	0.34	20.89	6.07	0.22	111.76
11.92			11.43		0.49
1120.80	58.50	31.48	9.13	0.89	1109.40
572.89	17.16	21.54	2.69	7.75	546.32
150.74	4.73	4.60	2.75		145.54
413.15	8.39	10.68	6.69	0.10	399.79
250.90	12.31	8.43	1.30	0.35	238.75
226.63	5.09	17.02	5.30	0.56	215.77
183.80	6.92	4.40	1.76	1.85	169.05
299.46	6.28	18.99	0.42	4.48	297.32
139.85	2.41	4.88	46.23		89.44
1477.59	207.75	193.88	107.46	36.30	1259.84
573.29	26.11	78.97	35.89	3.61	504.56
194.13	26.38	19.88	5.61	0.51	188.25
674.24	34.19	79.00	6.78	3.30	644.75
1176.64	36.70	37.05	31.84	7.30	1121.45
422.37	26.41	5.52	5.25	4.95	388.74
350.73	5.80	15.84	1.52	0.69	347.85

单位:亿元

行业	Sector	投资额 Investment	中央 Central Investment	地方 Local Investment
金属制品业	Manufacture of Metal Products	1460.32	1.80	1458.52
通用设备制造业	Manufacture of General Purpose Machinery	2361.80	9.91	2351.89
专用设备制造业	Manufacture of Special Purpose Machinery	2151.39	4.23	2147.16
汽车制造业	Manufacture of Automobile	1293.03	13.19	1279.84
铁路、船舶、航空航天和其他运输设备制造业	Manufacture of Railroad, Marine Aviation and other Transport Equipment	456.45	14.79	441.66
电气机械和器材制造业	Manufacture of Electrical Machinery and Equipment	2349.53	5.88	2343.65
计算机、通信和其他电子设备制造业	Manufacture of Communication Equipment, Computers and Other Electronic Equipment	1711.72	12.16	1699.57
仪器仪表制造业	Manufacture of Instrumentation	414.49	2.17	412.32
其他制造业	Other Manufacturing	164.81		164.81
废弃资源综合利用业	Manufacture of Recycling and Disposal of Waste	101.24	1.22	100.02
金属制品、机械和设备修理业	Manufacture of Metal Products, Machinery and Equipment Repair	17.31		17.31
电力、热力、燃气及水生产和供应业	Production and Supply of Electric Power, Heat Power, Gas and Water	1619.65	379.47	1240.18
电力、热力的生产和供应业	Production and Supply of Electric Power and Heat Power	1327.62	365.81	961.82
燃气生产和供应业	Production and Supply of Gas	77.90	3.01	74.89
水的生产和供应业	Production and Supply of Water	214.13	10.66	203.47
建筑业	Construction	129.41	2.60	126.81
房屋建筑业	Housing Construction	28.53		28.53
土木工程建筑业	Civil Engineering Construction	56.37	2.08	54.29
建筑安装业	Building Installation	17.44	0.53	16.92
建筑装饰和其他建筑业	Other Construction	27.08		27.08
批发和零售业	Wholesale and Retail Trades	1640.53	4.79	1635.74
批发业	Wholesale Trades	858.23	2.73	855.50
零售业	Retail Trades	782.29	2.06	780.24
交通运输、仓储和邮政业	Transport, Storage and Post	2542.29	34.69	2507.60
铁路运输业	Railway Transport	93.85	0.30	93.55
道路运输业	Road Transport	1408.80	8.21	1400.59
水上运输业	Water Transport	287.10	14.01	273.08
航空运输业	Air Transport	20.02		20.02
管道运输业	Transport Via Pipelines	35.94	8.52	27.43
装卸搬运和运输代理业	Loading, Unloading and Other Transport Services	82.88	0.29	82.59
仓储业	Storage	581.79	3.36	578.42
邮政业	Post	31.92		31.92
住宿和餐饮业	Hotels and Catering Services	455.91	0.52	455.39
住宿业	Hotels	231.01	0.52	230.49
餐饮业	Catering Services	224.90		224.90
信息传输、软件和信息技术服务业	Information Transfer、Software and IT Services	635.48	39.69	595.79
电信、广播电视和卫星传输服务	Telecommunications、Satellites Radio and Television Services	134.04	34.76	99.28
互联网和相关服务	Internet and Relatiue Services	84.47		84.47
软件和信息技术服务业	Software and IT Services	416.97	4.94	412.04

6－7 Continued 1

(100 million yuan)

内　资 Domestic Funds	港澳台商投资 Funds from Hong Kong, Macao and Taiwan	外商投资 Foreign Funded	国有控股 State-holding	集体控股 Collective-holding	私人控股 Private-holding
1348.76	56.93	50.81	19.57	4.98	1289.48
2159.76	64.66	136.80	41.08	7.69	2085.94
1933.43	91.88	125.64	31.09	9.03	1873.46
998.62	48.32	245.74	93.53	6.13	916.42
396.33	23.19	36.93	36.16	2.10	364.76
2087.30	84.05	177.18	127.47	14.26	1859.86
1037.73	224.69	448.85	102.72	18.31	917.10
358.36	15.94	39.24	9.65	2.66	348.57
155.83	3.51	5.47	14.01	4.66	132.68
78.29	16.39	6.57	3.65	2.09	68.93
17.31			0.48		16.84
1427.62	149.56	42.48	820.04	19.38	525.93
1174.27	128.57	24.79	697.37	8.59	417.77
51.38	14.66	11.86	9.32	1.41	45.89
201.97	6.33	5.83	113.35	9.38	62.27
129.41			52.09	5.13	65.65
28.53			10.35	0.64	16.14
56.37			36.42	2.78	14.00
17.44			3.39	0.51	13.05
27.08			1.92	1.20	22.47
1587.66	25.37	20.07	103.34	22.43	1403.46
832.16	12.88	11.85	44.28	8.32	765.35
755.50	12.49	8.22	59.05	14.11	638.12
2401.50	92.95	40.25	1367.35	73.06	894.97
93.85			90.85	0.43	2.57
1395.69	7.38	5.74	958.41	16.36	393.68
263.57	12.73	3.19	139.70	25.83	90.61
20.02			16.60		3.42
29.20	4.77	1.97	23.99		11.46
78.67	3.73	0.48	14.45	0.47	63.07
488.58	64.33	28.87	115.28	29.48	306.78
31.92			8.07	0.48	23.36
427.96	8.08	4.02	55.70	8.41	352.18
218.39	7.17	2.42	34.14	6.66	160.23
209.56	0.91	1.60	21.56	1.75	191.95
621.07	10.73	3.68	205.97	9.47	382.09
124.87	9.17		122.23	0.50	2.99
84.32	0.15		13.22	0.02	63.48
411.88	1.41	3.68	70.52	8.96	315.62

单位:亿元

行业	Sector	投资额 Investment	中央 Central Investment	地方 Local Investment
金融业	Financial Intermediation	141.65	5.99	135.66
货币金融服务	Monetary and Financial	71.29	4.43	66.86
资本市场服务	Capital Markets	38.79		38.79
保险业	Insurance	3.47		3.47
其他金融业	Other Financial Activities	28.10	1.56	26.54
房地产业	Real Estate	10277.10	170.20	10106.89
房地产业	Real Estate	10277.10	170.20	10106.89
租赁和商务服务业	Leasing and Business Services	1545.71	10.40	1535.31
租赁业	Leasing	48.14		48.14
商务服务业	Business Services	1497.57	10.40	1487.17
科学研究和技术服务业	Scientific Research and Technical Services	639.21	28.04	611.17
研究和试验发展	Research and Experimental Developmant	174.88	19.61	155.27
专业技术服务业	Professional Technical Serrices	259.57	8.43	251.14
科技推广和应用服务业	Promation and Application of Science	204.76	0.00	204.76
水利、环境和公共设施管理业	Management of Water Conservancy, Environment and Public Facilities	3965.38	35.47	3929.91
水利管理业	Management of Water Conservancy	398.21	5.61	392.60
生态保护和环境治理业	Ecological Protection and Enviromental	123.21		123.21
公共设施管理业	Management of Public Facilities	3443.96	29.87	3414.10
居民服务、修理和其他服务业	Services to Households and Other Services	260.86	7.90	252.96
居民服务业	Services to Households	158.87		158.87
机动车、电子产品和日用产品修理业	Vehicle、Electronics and Dairy Maintenance	57.60		57.60
其他服务业	Other Services	44.39	7.90	36.49
教育	Education	590.09	17.15	572.94
教育	Education	590.09	17.15	572.94
卫生和社会工作	Health and Social Work	446.43	3.33	443.10
卫生	Health	379.36	2.35	377.01
社会工作	Social Work	67.07	0.98	66.09
文化、体育和娱乐业	Culture, Sports and Entertainment	642.24	1.72	640.52
新闻和出版业	Journalism and Publishing Activities	2.71		2.71
广播、电视、电影和影视录音制作业	Broadcasting, Movies, Television and Audiovisual Activities	55.79		55.79
文化艺术业	Cultural and Art Activities	294.80	1.37	293.43
体育	Sports Activities	135.10	0.00	135.10
娱乐业	Entertainment	153.84	0.35	153.48
公共管理、社会保障和社会组织	Public Management and Social Organization	485.82	4.18	481.64
中国共产党机关	Organs of Communist Party of China	2.26		2.26
国家机构	Government Agencies	407.35	3.85	403.50
人民政协、民主党派	People's Political Cousultative Conference and Remocratic Parlies			
社会保障	Social Security	2.48		2.48
群众团体、社会团体和其他成员组织	Non-governmental Organizations, Social Organizations and Religion Organizations	24.35		24.35
基层群众自治组织	Grass Roots Self-governing Organizations	49.39	0.33	49.06

(100 million yuan)

内 资 Domestic Funds	港澳台商投资 Funds from Hong Kong, Macao and Taiwan	外商投资 Foreign Funded	国有控股 State-holding	集体控股 Collective-holding	私人控股 Private-holding
141.23	0.42		79.27	4.52	45.23
70.87	0.42		37.09	2.54	24.90
38.79			19.44		14.72
3.47			2.02	0.48	0.97
28.10			20.72	1.51	4.64
9200.42	754.23	322.44	2280.54	332.21	5267.36
9200.42	754.23	322.44	2280.54	332.21	5267.36
1506.55	29.18	9.47	666.44	134.58	614.88
47.84	0.20		13.80	0.40	33.63
1458.71	28.98	9.47	652.64	134.18	581.25
610.85	11.18	16.99	123.82	65.89	400.46
161.53	5.76	7.58	39.73	5.34	106.94
250.89	3.35	5.15	57.60	42.55	148.71
198.43	2.07	4.26	26.49	18.00	144.80
3941.24	19.97	2.18	2987.35	443.37	397.39
398.21			308.00	50.32	22.28
116.16	6.06	0.99	56.10	10.73	40.29
3426.86	13.91	1.19	2623.24	382.31	334.82
252.19		4.60	112.04	19.95	115.34
150.92		4.15	85.42	18.42	41.79
57.07		0.40	6.77		50.58
44.20		0.05	19.85	1.53	22.97
586.09	1.36	2.49	452.91	36.04	85.72
586.09	1.36	2.49	452.91	36.04	85.72
441.49	0.88	3.40	295.00	41.53	98.02
374.89	0.88	3.40	264.03	37.47	66.84
66.59			30.97	4.06	31.18
619.75	19.15	2.29	331.37	31.03	245.12
2.71			2.18		0.53
55.79			7.54	0.40	47.40
291.40	3.23		221.59	20.61	35.67
124.44	10.17		52.20	3.07	76.34
145.42	5.75	2.29	47.87	6.96	85.19
485.31		0.32	408.11	48.36	12.26
2.26			2.26		
407.35			373.51	20.94	4.48
2.48			2.48		
23.83		0.32	10.51	5.82	3.79
49.39			19.34	21.60	4.00

6-8 按行业分施工投产项目个数（2016年）
Number of Projects Under Construction and Put into Use by Sector(2016)

行业	Sector	施工项目（个）Number of Projects under Construction (unit)	#新开工 Number of Proiects Started this Year	全部建成投产项目（个）Number of Projects Completed and Put into Use (unit)	项目建成投产率（%）Rate of Construction Projects Completed and Put into Use(%)
总　计	**Total**	**60983**	**50343**	**47709**	**78.23**
农、林、牧、渔业	Agriculture, Forestry, Animal Husbandry and Fishery	1005	866	796	79.20
农业	Farming	422	358	332	78.67
林业	Forestry	41	38	38	92.68
畜牧业	Animal Husbandry	172	142	114	66.28
渔业	Fishery	75	61	63	84.00
农、林、牧、渔服务业	Service in Support of Agriculture	295	267	249	84.41
采矿业	Mining	83	67	62	74.70
煤炭开采和洗选业	Mining and Washing of Coal	5	4	4	80.00
石油和天然气开采业	Exctraction of Petroleum and Natural Gas	28	26	19	67.86
黑色金属矿采选业	Mining and Processing of Ferrous Metal Ores	5	1	3	60.00
有色金属矿采选业	Mining and Processing of Non-ferrous Metal Ores	3	2	3	100.00
非金属矿采选业	Mining and Processing of Nonmetal Ores	40	32	32	80.00
开采辅助活动	Auxiliary Mining	2	2	1	50.00
其他采矿业	Mining of Other Ores				
制造业	Manufacturing	34496	28805	27259	79.02
农副食品加工业	Processing of Food from Agricultural	957	811	769	80.36
食品制造业	Manufacture of Food	518	426	413	79.73
酒、饮料和精制茶制造业	Manufacture of Beverage	212	169	174	82.08
烟草制品业	Manufacture of Tobacco	8	5	4	50.00
纺织业	Manufacture of Textile	2642	2306	2255	85.35
纺织服装、服饰业	Manufacture of Textile Wearing, Apparel, Footwear and Caps	1302	1136	1075	82.57
皮革、毛皮、羽毛及其制品和制鞋业	Manufacture of Leather, Fur, Feather and Related Products	326	275	268	82.21
木材加工和木、竹、藤、棕、草制品业	Processing of Timber, Manufacture of Wood, Bamboo, Rattan, Palm and Straw Products	768	643	605	78.78
家具制造业	Manufacture of Furniture	494	408	334	67.61
造纸和纸制品业	Manufacture of Paper and Paper Products	460	388	381	82.83
印刷和记录媒介复制业	Printing, Reproduction of Recording Media	369	308	298	80.76
文教、工美、体育和娱乐用品制造业	Manufacture of Articles For Culture, Education and Sport Activities	629	548	511	81.24
石油加工、炼焦及核燃料加工业	Processing of Petroleum, Coking, Processing of Nuclear Fuel	111	84	85	76.58
化学原料和化学制品制造业	Manufacture of Raw Chemical Materials and Chemical Products	2155	1739	1590	73.78
医药制造业	Manufacture of Medicines	659	495	481	72.99
化学纤维制造业	Manufacture of Chemical Fibers	332	269	245	73.80
橡胶和塑料制品业	Rubber and Plastic	1403	1195	1136	80.97
非金属矿物制品业	Manufacture of Non-metallic Mineral Products	1857	1489	1417	76.31
黑色金属冶炼和压延加工业	Smelting and Pressing of Ferrous Metals	588	469	444	75.51
有色金属冶炼和压延加工业	Smelting and Pressing of Non-ferrous Metals	562	452	414	73.67

6－8 续 表1 Continued 1

行业	Sector	施工项目（个）Number of Projects under Construction (unit)	#新开工 Number of Projects Started this Year	全部建成投产项目（个）Number of Projects Completed and Put into Use (unit)	项目建成投产率（%）Rate of Construction Projects Completed and Put into Use(%)
金属制品业	Manufacture of Metal Products	2561	2213	2162	84.42
通用设备制造业	Manufacture of General Purpose Machinery	4319	3701	3537	81.89
专用设备制造业	Manufacture of Special Purpose Machinery	3412	2805	2689	78.81
汽车制造业	Manufacture of Automobile	1387	1114	1002	72.24
铁路、船舶、航空航天和其他运输设备制造业	Manufacture of Railroad, Marine Aviation and other Transport Equipment	660	546	520	78.79
电气机械和器材制造业	Manufacture of Electrical Machinery and Equipment	3017	2513	2324	77.03
计算机、通信和其他电子设备制造业	Manufacture of Communication Equipment, Computers and Other Electronic Equipment	1709	1395	1305	76.36
仪器仪表制造业	Manufacture of Instrumentation	656	550	484	73.78
其他制造业	Other Manufacturing	260	212	213	81.92
废弃资源综合利用业	Manufacture of Recycling and Disposal of Waste	132	113	96	72.73
金属制品、机械和设备修理业	Manufacture of Metal Products, Machinery and Equipment Repair	31	28	28	90.32
电力、热力、燃气及水生产和供应业	Production and Supply of Elcctric Power, Heat Power, Gas and Water	1242	912	815	65.62
电力、热力生产和供应业	Production and Supply of Electric Power and Heat Power	783	563	505	64.50
燃气生产和供应业	Production and Supply of Gas	106	87	74	69.81
水的生产和供应业	Production and Supply of Water	353	262	236	66.86
建筑业	Construction	347	303	220	63.40
房屋建筑业	Housing Construction	72	63	46	63.89
土木工程建筑业	Civil Engineering Construction	164	142	88	53.66
建筑安装业	Building Installation	41	37	36	87.80
建筑装饰和其他建筑业	Other Construction	70	61	50	71.43
批发和零售业	Wholesale and Retail Trades	3313	2926	2891	87.26
批发业	Wholesale Trades	1871	1691	1663	88.88
零售业	Retail Trades	1442	1235	1228	85.16
交通运输、仓储和邮政业	Transport, Storage and Post	2358	1777	1653	70.10
铁路运输业	Railway Transport	22	16	9	40.91
道路运输业	Road Transport	1355	1050	1016	74.98
水上运输业	Water Transport	198	125	122	61.62
航空运输业	Air Transport	20	17	12	60.00
管道运输业	Transport Via Pipelines	27	20	20	74.07
装卸搬运和运输代理业	Loading, Unloading and Other Transport Services	133	107	96	72.18
仓储业	Storage	552	400	349	63.22
邮政业	Post	51	42	29	56.86
住宿和餐饮业	Hotels and Catering Services	809	669	658	81.33
住宿业	Hotels	330	247	231	70.00
餐饮业	Catering Services	479	422	427	89.14
信息传输、软件和信息技术服务业	Information Transfer、Software and IT Services	895	761	695	77.65
电信、广播电视和卫星传输服务	Telecommunications、Satellites Radio and Television Services	143	125	117	81.82
互联网和相关服务	Internet and Relatiue Services	134	108	119	88.81
软件和信息技术服务业	Software and IT Services	618	528	459	74.27

6-8 续 表2 Continued 2

行业 Sector		施工项目(个) Number of Projects under Construction (unit)	#新开工 Number of Proiects Started this Year	全部建成投产项目(个) Number of Projects Completed and Put into Use (unit)	项目建成投产率(%) Rate of Construction Projects Completed and Put into Use(%)
金融业	Financial Intermediation	161	112	109	67.70
货币金融服务	Monetary and Financial	85	63	63	74.12
资本市场服务	Capital Markets	44	33	25	56.82
保险业	Insurance	10	5	10	100.00
其他金融业	Other Financial Activities	22	11	11	50.00
房地产业	Real Estate	1346	946	973	72.29
房地产业	Real Estate	1346	946	973	72.29
租赁和商务服务业	Leasing and Business Services	1978	1516	1461	73.86
租赁业	Leasing	75	66	63	84.00
商务服务业	Business Services	1903	1450	1398	73.46
科学研究和技术服务业	Scientific Research and Technical Services	1142	986	907	79.42
研究和试验发展	Research and Experimental Developmant	323	271	233	72.14
专业技术服务业	Professional Technical Serrices	449	401	370	82.41
科技推广和应用服务业	Promation and Application of Science	370	314	304	82.16
水利、环境和公共设施管理业	Management of Water Conservancy, Environment and Public Facilities	7756	6474	6067	78.22
水利管理业	Management of Water Conservancy	655	553	498	76.03
生态保护和环境治理业	Ecological Protection and Enviromental	248	202	200	80.65
公共设施管理业	Management of Public Facilities	6853	5719	5369	78.35
居民服务、修理和其他服务业	Services to Households and Other Services	586	522	513	87.54
居民服务业	Services to Households	364	326	315	86.54
机动车、电子产品和日用产品修理业	Vehicle、Electronics and Dairy Maintenance	135	122	123	91.11
其他服务业	Other Services	87	74	75	86.21
教育	Education	973	746	695	71.43
教育	Education	973	746	695	71.43
卫生和社会工作	Health and Social Work	602	473	427	70.93
卫生	Health	469	362	320	68.23
社会工作	Social Work	133	111	107	80.45
文化、体育和娱乐业	Culture, Sports and Entertainment	800	639	618	77.25
新闻和出版业	Journalism and Publishing Activities	7	2	4	57.14
广播、电视、电影和影视录音制作业	Broadcasting, Movies, Television and Audiovisual Activities	116	102	96	82.76
文化艺术业	Cultural and Art Activities	248	175	165	66.53
体育	Sports Activities	189	166	147	77.78
娱乐业	Entertainment	240	194	206	85.83
公共管理、社会保障和社会组织	Public Management and Social Organization	1091	843	890	81.58
中国共产党机关	Organs of Communist Party of China	6	5	3	50.00
国家机构	Government Agencies	812	642	654	80.54
人民政协、民主党派	People's Political Cousultative Conference and Remocratic Parlies				
社会保障	Social Security	8	7	5	62.50
群众团体、社会团体和其他成员组织	Non-governmental Organizations, Social Organizations and Religion Organizations	57	53	46	80.70
基层群众自治组织	Grass Roots Self-governing Organizations	208	136	182	87.50

6-9 国有单位固定资产投资
Investment of State-owned Units in Capital Construction

指标	Item	2014 合计 Total	2014 #房地产开发 Real Estate Development	2015 合计 Total	2015 #房地产开发 Real Estate Development	2016 合计 Total	2016 #房地产开发 Real Estate Development
建设项目	**Construction Projects**						
施工项目（个）	Number of Projects Under Construction (unit)	7377		8331		11544	
全部建成投产项目（个）	Total Projects Completed and Put into Use (unit)	5004		6337		8762	
建成项目投产率（%）	Rate of Projects Completed and Put into Use (%)	67.8		76.1		75.9	
建设周期（年）	Construction Cycle (year)	1.47		1.31		1.32	
资金来源（亿元）	**Sources of Funds (100 million yuan)**						
国家预算内资金	State Budget	553.52		696.20		909.93	
国内贷款	Domestic Loans	1464.42	246.34	1163.21	237.19	1138.44	305.18
利用外资	Foreign Investment	7.46		1.16	0.01	8.41	
自筹资金	Self-raising Funds	6415.83	270.27	6737.29	331.33	5260.19	293.25
其他资金	Others	453.42	196.99	426.73	242.68	713.56	385.16
投资总额（亿元）	**Total Investment (100 million yuan)**	**8308.13**	**534.54**	**8901.58**	**636.85**	**8236.65**	**684.57**
按构成分	Grouped by Use of Funds						
#建筑工程	Construction	5948.03	414.53	6281.17	453.93	6032.51	478.48
安装工程	Installation	312.53	24.86	473.06	31.87	415.79	50.29
设备工具器具购置	Purchase of Equipment and Instruments	1118.93	6.16	1252.76	7.55	847.22	9.12
按产业分	Grouped by Industry						
第一产业	Primary Industry	14.72		32.08		83.16	
第二产业	Secondary Industry	1235.54		1499.09		892.86	
第三产业	Tertiary Industry	7057.86	534.54	7370.42	636.85	7260.64	684.57
#住宅	Residential Buildings	642.30	389.70	734.21	515.48	673.43	499.81
按建设性质分	Grouped by Type of Construction						
#新建	New Construction	5421.98		5650.23		5579.29	
扩建	Expension	1749.73		1765.31		1133.88	
改建	Reconstruction	341.38		575.52		625.43	
房屋建筑面积（万平方米）	**Floor Space of Buildings (10000 sq. m)**						
施工面积	Floor Space Under Construction	14111.35	4473.26	11755.05	3970.56	10040.16	4045.07
#住宅	Residential Buildings	5226.29	3534.14	4735.94	3303.14	4238.80	3077.81
竣工面积	Floor Space Completed	5591.00	1219.47	4889.70	1012.49	2725.63	543.76
#住宅	Residential Buildings	1698.26	1012.05	1606.01	911.58	902.27	413.05

注：建设周期按项目个数计算。

a) Construction cycle was calculated by the number of construction projects.

6－10 分市固定资产投资(2016 年)

指标	Item	南京 Nanjing	无锡 Wuxi	徐州 Xuzhou	常州 Changzhou
投资总额 (亿元)	**Total Investment (100 million yuan)**	**5533.56**	**4793.69**	**4797.33**	**3605.08**
按经济类型分	Grouped by Ownership				
国有经济	State Owned Units	1326.25	859.91	804.58	600.38
集体经济	Collective Owned Units	89.97	182.70	39.41	75.87
私营个体经济	Private Individuals	1470.81	1909.46	2949.90	2339.40
联营经济	Joint-ownership	7.16	0.71	3.81	
股份制经济	Share Holding Co. Lid.	178.72	104.07	99.32	37.80
有限责任公司	Limited Liability Corporations	1820.89	1044.23	559.24	212.72
港澳台投资经济	Funds from Hong Kong, Macao and Taiwan	276.99	320.89	146.22	186.52
外商投资经济	Foreign lnvestment	326.61	364.46	76.82	145.94
其他经济	Others	36.15	7.26	118.03	6.46
按资金来源分	Grouped by Sources of Funds				
国家预算内资金	State Budget	86.51	54.56	138.58	97.43
国内贷款	Domestic Loans	1032.08	345.46	649.22	619.66
利用外资	Foreign Investment	11.03	265.31	8.97	48.17
自筹资金	Self-raising Fund	3608.87	3276.16	3509.12	2414.41
其他资金来源	Others	2621.70	886.92	546.04	593.03
按构成分	Grouped by Composition of Funds				
建筑安装工程	Construction and Installation	3205.17	2836.63	2851.24	2062.48
设备工器具购置	Purchase of Equipments and Instruments	1071.19	1586.93	1646.81	1226.07
其他费用	Others	1257.20	370.13	299.28	316.52
按产业分	Grouped by Industry				
#住宅	Residential Buildings	1445.55	709.78	447.09	338.54
第一产业	Primary Industry	40.78	7.10	40.37	3.94
第二产业	Secondary Industry	1784.22	2046.74	2668.61	1919.62
#工业	Industry	1761.65	2043.63	2664.93	1918.48
第三产业	Tertiary Industry	3708.57	2739.85	2088.35	1681.52
新增固定资产 (亿元)	**Newly Increased Fixed Assets (100million yuan)**	**3019.53**	**3730.42**	**3321.67**	**2645.73**
房屋建筑面积 (万平方米)	**Floor Space of Building (10000 sq. m)**				
施工面积	Floor Space Under Construction	10813.19	7893.18	7770.89	6045.36
#住宅	Residential Buildings	5706.60	4391.96	3570.02	2477.25
竣工面积	Floor Space Completed	1960.41	2231.93	2299.29	2000.66
#住宅	Residential Buildings	1018.04	1067.37	551.89	474.67
商品房销售面积 (万平方米)	**Floor Space of Commercializ Buildings Sold (10000 sq. m)**	**1558.18**	**1276.41**	**1071.43**	**933.20**

Investment by Region (2016)

苏州 Suzhou	南通 Nantong	连云港 Lianyungang	淮安 Huaian	盐城 Yancheng	扬州 Yangzhou	镇江 Zhenjiang	泰州 Taizhou	宿迁 Suqian
5648.49	**4811.95**	**2385.16**	**2535.19**	**3882.83**	**3288.68**	**2873.43**	**3155.87**	**2059.58**
938.72	573.08	373.32	299.70	682.93	533.90	542.95	408.95	291.96
141.26	19.68	13.43	20.35	33.31	58.60	36.09	65.83	30.02
1801.93	2559.12	1246.74	1340.00	1656.09	1789.47	1429.45	1580.88	1343.86
0.39	10.45		1.94	3.78	0.96	2.03	10.81	0.49
110.93	73.82	43.20	57.67	113.80	92.08	65.26	117.90	81.62
1544.08	1050.10	559.46	635.62	1120.74	567.14	445.22	706.54	215.17
408.05	258.44	72.63	99.10	93.38	145.96	135.32	104.57	58.28
680.20	241.01	61.45	49.53	103.16	93.52	145.18	72.78	25.80
22.93	26.23	14.94	31.28	75.63	7.05	71.93	87.60	12.39
133.97	191.51	27.40	29.99	55.87	37.04	34.87	15.10	87.60
1122.68	273.95	271.09	119.90	457.80	180.25	441.78	161.21	103.46
157.18	26.92	14.18	8.41	22.44	1.07	3.68	5.83	26.71
3289.67	4001.46	1798.17	2073.56	3124.41	2879.99	1899.41	2678.46	1704.30
3251.24	557.54	215.30	296.00	326.22	406.27	521.62	364.63	243.68
3077.27	2562.32	1447.20	1558.38	2521.31	2251.75	1823.78	1743.49	1048.31
1570.97	2033.10	696.72	762.62	1166.95	769.82	740.34	1182.92	914.15
1000.25	216.54	241.24	214.18	194.57	267.12	309.31	229.46	97.12
1723.42	481.27	202.43	243.09	286.01	308.99	351.98	202.98	230.01
0.91	8.87	42.58	51.86	41.31	16.84	5.34	6.84	26.38
1987.31	2406.95	1492.23	1551.82	2299.01	1714.93	1515.95	1955.66	1330.76
1982.29	2406.36	1487.34	1518.49	2291.98	1714.43	1475.13	1950.99	1328.70
3660.27	2396.13	850.35	931.51	1542.51	1556.91	1352.14	1193.38	702.44
3682.31	**3240.33**	**1541.93**	**1612.42**	**2960.76**	**2263.68**	**1794.13**	**2680.51**	**1470.29**
15857.37	11629.98	3883.01	3922.14	5380.78	4152.39	4962.35	4973.26	6498.62
8994.12	4137.09	1761.19	2240.14	2366.23	2134.92	2527.70	1910.74	3037.03
3111.69	3316.97	978.03	866.72	1547.50	1190.36	1048.31	1896.74	2216.61
1481.76	866.96	260.47	310.82	441.91	572.48	372.43	487.68	429.01
2494.05	**1200.80**	**524.44**	**869.80**	**842.55**	**734.76**	**996.50**	**694.87**	**765.10**

6－11 房地产开发投资主要指标
Major Indicaotrs of Real Estate Investment

指 标	Item	2000	2005	2010	2015	2016
投资完成额 （亿元）	**Investment Completed This Year (100 million yuan)**	**358.72**	**1545.15**	**4299.38**	**8153.68**	**8956.37**
按构成分	Grouped by Use of Funds					
#建筑安装工程	Construction and Installation Projects	255.81	1091.29	2897.21	6186.30	6604.18
设备工器具购置	Purchase of Equipment and Instruments	3.34	12.53	41.09	118.93	141.68
按工程用途分	Grouped by Use of Project					
#住宅	Residential Buidlings	260.79	1133.06	3158.46	6080.21	6628.87
#90 平方米以下	Below 90 Square Meters			733.15	1773.41	2073.60
#140 平方米以上	Above 140 Square Meters			744.76	1248.38	1465.68
办公楼	Office Buildings	21.59	54.27	154.61	344.07	363.17
商业营业用房	Houses for Business Use	48.48	217.02	611.08	1130.91	1246.13
其他	Others	27.86	140.81	375.23	598.50	718.20
按资金来源分	Grouped by Sources of Funds					
国内贷款	Domesitc Loans	88.01	392.73	1515.66	1877.93	2299.18
利用外资	Foreign Investment	5.82	33.16	92.76	44.91	8.29
自筹投资	Self-raising Funds	101.34	614.76	2031.38	3416.80	3172.21
其他投资	Others	195.48	998.18	4382.54	6700.36	10021.40
房屋建筑面积 （万平方米）	**Floor Space of Building (10000 sq. m)**					
施工面积	Floor Space Under Construction	4268.45	15619.26	35106.90	58118.44	58761.73
#住宅	Residential Buidlings	3348.36	12385.98	26347.13	42315.98	43002.93
竣工面积	Floor Space Completed	2143.22	5500.12	8696.28	10296.96	10073.96
#住宅	Residential Buildings	1774.80	4497.68	6553.53	7930.21	7602.69
商品房销售情况 （万平方米）	**Sale of Commercialized Buildings (10000 sq. m)**					
房屋销售面积	Floor Space of Commercialized Buildings	1740.93	5135.55	9485.47	11414.05	13962.09
#住宅	Residential Buildings	1555.97	4523.14	8112.37	10275.95	12657.66
#90 平方米以下	Below 90 Square Meters			1583.11	1896.76	2054.14
#140 平方米以上	Above 140 Square Meters			1816.86	1533.98	2144.43

注：1. 本表资金来源为资金到位数。
2. 从2011年开始，将140平方米及以上住宅改为144平方米及以上。

a) The funds sources of this table were all available for investment.

b) The high－grade residential area standard has been changed to 144 square meters and above from 2011.

6－12 房地产开发企业经营情况
Operating Statistics on Enterprises for Real Estate Development

指　　标	Item	2000	2005	2010	2015	2016
企业个数　（个）	**Number of Enterprises (unit)**	**1930**	**3810**	**6070**	**6642**	**6626**
内资	Domestic Funded	1636	3384	5450	6056	6053
#国有	State-owned Enterprises	585	248	252	201	55
集体	Collective-owned Enterprises	482	192	124	35	29
港澳台商投资	Enterprises with Funds from Hong Kong, Macao and Taiwan	197	277	352	396	395
外商投资	Foreign Funded	97	149	268	190	178
平均从业人数　（万人）	**Average Number of Employed Persons (10000 persons)**	**5.74**	**8.47**	**13.17**	**17.96**	**17.34**
内资	Domestic Funded		7.54	11.61	15.85	15.48
#国有	State-owned Enterprises		0.63	0.59	0.70	0.69
集体	Collective-owned Enterprises		0.33	0.19	0.09	0.08
港澳台商投资	Enterprises with Funds from Hong Kong, Macao and Taiwan		0.59	0.87	1.41	1.23
外商投资	Foreign Funded		0.34	0.69	0.70	0.63
土地开发及购置（万平方米）	**Land Development and Purchase (10000 sq. m)**					
本年土地成交价款（亿元）	Total Value of Land Purchased (100 million yuan)		319.02	613.85	530.42	845.47
待开发土地面积	Land Space Pending Development	928.335	3981.34	3798.79	4044.91	3445.47
本年购置土地面积	Land Space Purchased This Year	1395.98	2848.80	2055.71	1693.35	1736.90
资产负债　（亿元）	**Assets and Liabilities (100 million yuan)**					
实收资本	Capital Held		953.90	4061.51	8815.06	8868.63
资产总计	Total Assets	1201.82	5679.81	19791.32	46749.11	51534.57
累计折旧	Total Depreciation	13.25	34.48	128.74	264.16	279.84
#本年折旧	Depreciation This Year	2.75	8.45	33.70	52.22	51.51
负债总计	Total Liabilities	958.47	4343.07	14233.81	35200.59	39415.82
所有者权益	Owners' Equity	243.36	1336.74	5557.51	11548.52	12118.75

6－13 按登记注册类型分房地产开发投资(2016年)

项目		总计 Total	内资 Domestic Funds	国有 State-owned	集体 Collective-owned
企业个数 (个)	**Number of Enterprises (unit)**	**6626**	**6053**	**55**	**29**
本年完成投资 (亿元)	**Investment Completed This Year (100 million yuan)**	**8956.37**	**7885.48**	**240.54**	**14.60**
按构成分	Grouped by Use of Funds				
建筑工程	Construction Projects	5898.39	5177.69	174.75	12.15
安装工程	Installation Projects	705.79	598.15	11.73	0.58
设备工器具购置	Pruchase of Equipment and Instruments	141.68	126.03	3.31	0.84
其他费用	Others Expenses	2210.50	1983.62	50.75	1.04
按构成用途分	Grouped by Use of Project				
住宅	Residential Buildings	6628.87	5842.79	188.48	12.61
#90平方米以下	Below 90 Square Meters	2073.60	1835.34	79.61	8.40
140平方米以上住房	Above 140 Square Meters	1465.68	1247.52	16.26	1.22
别墅、高档公寓	Villas, High-grade Apartments	485.17	420.98	3.28	
办公楼	Office Buidings	363.17	322.52	2.49	0.06
商业营业用房	Buidings for Business Use	1246.13	1082.89	21.25	1.01
其他	Others	718.20	637.27	28.33	0.92
本年新增固定资产 (亿元)	**Newly Increased Fixed Assets This Year (100 million yuan)**	**4581.13**	**3922.75**	**38.85**	**0.98**
资金来源	**Sources of Funds**				
本年资金来源合计	Total of Funds This Year	20152.95	16639.17	414.18	14.06
上年末结余资金	Balance of Founds Last Year	4651.87	3440.57	120.85	1.31
本年资金来源小计	Subtotal Funds This Year	15501.08	13198.61	293.33	12.75
国内贷款	Domestic Loans	2299.18	2023.86	104.00	2.00
利用外资	Foreign Investment	8.29	4.00		
自筹资金	Self-raising Funds	3172.21	2872.34	68.71	9.00
#自有资金	Self-owned	1206.15	1071.87	26.17	7.23
其他资金来源	Others	10021.40	8298.40	120.62	1.75
#定金及预收款	Bargain Money and Pre-received Money	5442.87	4507.10	50.17	1.04

Investment in Real Estate Development by Registration Status(2016)

股份合作 Cooperative Enterprises	联营 Joint Ownership	国有独资公司 State Sole Funded	其它有限责任公司 Other Limited Liability Corporations	股份有限公司 Share Holding Co., Ltd.	私营 Private	其它 Other
1		**151**	**2162**	**205**	**3448**	**2**
5.55		**444.03**	**3660.85**	**207.99**	**3296.50**	**15.42**
3.26		303.73	2314.68	154.67	2207.33	7.12
1.14		38.56	253.15	17.10	275.68	0.21
0.14		5.81	59.42	5.11	50.81	0.59
1.00		95.93	1033.61	31.11	762.67	7.51
4.54		311.34	2714.21	173.77	2423.60	14.25
2.23		135.34	869.00	56.31	678.23	6.21
0.62		50.82	565.80	31.70	577.59	3.50
		22.78	219.01	12.59	160.06	3.26
		36.39	160.45	4.24	118.89	0.00
0.08		50.78	484.17	22.02	502.93	0.66
251.09	0.51	0.94		45.52	302.02	7.96
0.00		**156.61**	**2001.75**	**127.46**	**1592.13**	**4.97**
11.57		982.25	7870.72	512.44	6816.64	17.32
0.40		292.00	1615.82	99.91	1310.01	0.27
11.17		690.25	6254.90	412.53	5506.63	17.05
6.64		201.17	1069.21	63.72	575.31	1.80
					4.00	
0.60		224.54	1210.62	72.12	1281.46	5.29
		81.60	429.35	36.23	488.89	2.41
3.93		264.53	3975.07	276.69	3645.85	9.95
2.35		152.73	2167.20	138.18	1987.60	7.83

指　　标 Iteam		港澳台商投资 Funds from Hong Kong, Macao and Taiwan	合资经营 Joint-venture Enterprises	合作经营 Cooperative Enterprises
企业个数　（个）	**Number of Enterprises　(unit)**	**395**	**132**	**11**
本年完成投资　（亿元）	**Investment Completed This Year (100 million yuan)**	**748.80**	**234.75**	**9.41**
按构成分	Grouped by Use of Funds			
建筑工程	Construction Projects	508.40	161.36	7.51
安装工程	Installation Projects	82.16	31.10	1.09
设备工器具购置	Pruchase of Equipment and Instruments	9.79	3.99	
其他费用	Others Expenses	148.46	38.30	0.81
按构成用途分	Grouped by Use of Project			
住宅	Residential Buildings	532.51	150.23	8.39
#90 平方米以下	Below 90 Square Meters	148.03	38.69	1.52
140 平方米以上住房	Above 140 Square Meters	149.59	51.05	2.91
别墅、高档公寓	Villas, High-grade Apartments	42.22	15.96	26.26
办公楼	Office Buidings	33.75	12.70	20.56
商业营业用房	Buidings for Business Use	135.23	49.35	0.96
其他	Others	47.32	22.46	0.06
本年新增固定资产　（亿元）	**Newly Increased Fixed Assets This Year (100 million yuan)**	**474.31**	**106.07**	
资金来源	**Sources of Funds**			
本年资金来源合计	Total of Funds This Year	2263.08	555.68	42.22
上年末结余资金	Balance of Founds Last Year	671.02	108.95	7.55
本年资金来源小计	Subtotal Funds This Year	1592.06	446.74	34.67
国内贷款	Domestic Loans	200.88	66.11	
利用外资	Foreign Investment			2.07
自筹资金	Self-raising Funds	230.79	69.26	10.07
#自有资金	Self-owned	118.09	45.04	
其他资金来源	Others	1158.31	311.36	24.60
#定金及预收款	Bargain Money and Pre-received Money	596.23	141.11	12.93

独资公司 Enterprises with Sole Fund	股份有限公司 Share Holding Co., Ltd.	其他港澳台商投资 Other Funds from Hong Kong, Macao and Taiwan	外商投资 Foreign Inveslment	合资经营 Joint-venture Enterprises	合作经营 Cooperative Enterprises	独资公司 Enterprises with Sole Fund	股份有限公司 Share Holding Co., Ltd.	其他外商投资 Other Foreign Inveslment
242	**8**	**2**	**178**	**73**	**8**	**94**	**1**	**2**
476.13	**28.52**		**322.08**	**132.09**	**12.99**	**177.01**		
315.19	24.34		212.31	78.39	10.85	123.07		
46.71	3.26		25.49	7.00	1.48	17.01		
5.80			5.86	1.47		4.40		
108.43	0.92		78.42	45.23	0.66	32.53		
350.61	23.28		253.56	103.99	11.82	137.75		
93.96	13.86		90.23	42.04	4.02	44.17		
93.13	2.50		68.57	22.92	6.08	39.58		
		21.96	2.18	1.20	18.58			
0.49		6.90	3.21	3.69				
81.01	3.90		28.01	6.94	0.72	20.35		
23.95	0.84		33.61	17.95	0.45	15.21		
350.87	**17.38**		**184.06**	**95.53**		**88.54**		
1600.57	64.61		1250.70	489.08	72.04	689.03	0.54	
528.71	25.81		540.28	226.66	19.81	293.77	0.04	
1071.86	38.80		710.41	262.43	52.23	395.26	0.50	
129.83	4.94		74.43	26.42		48.01		
2.07			2.22	0.45		1.77		
151.46			69.08	22.76		46.21	0.10	
73.05			16.19	5.14		10.95	0.10	
788.49	33.85		564.69	212.80	52.23	299.26	0.40	
429.50	12.69		339.53	95.26	24.23	219.94	0.10	

6－14 分市房地产开发投资(2016 年)

指　　标	Item	南京 Nanjing	无锡 Wuxi	徐州 Xuzhou	常州 Changzhou
企业个数　(个)	Number of Enterprises (unit)	582	707	417	395
平均从业人数　(万人)	Average Number of Employed Persons (10000 persons)	2.10	1.73	1.24	0.97
本年购置土地面积 (万平方米)	Land Space Purchased This Year (10000 sq. m)	283.19	146.09	116.59	26.19
投资完成额　(亿元)	Investment Completed This Year (100 million yuan)	1845.60	1033.62	549.13	446.70
按构成分	Grouped by Use of Funds				
#建筑安装工程	Construction and Installation Projects	1057.77	796.98	464.51	394.87
设备工器具购置	Purchase of Equipment and Instruments	34.26	16.63	20.70	4.88
按工程用途分	Grouped by Use of Project				
住宅	Residential Buidlings	1392.76	684.42	415.04	316.48
办公楼	Office Buildings	96.68	37.41	25.52	23.06
商业营业用房	Houses for Business Use	195.05	213.48	84.77	58.84
其他	Others	161.11	98.30	23.81	48.32
按资金来源分	Grouped by Sources of Funds				
国内贷款	Domesitc Loans	687.75	214.79	76.36	57.61
利用外资	Foreign Investment	0.00	6.02	0.00	0.00
自筹投资	Self-raising Funds	562.63	390.22	203.58	118.85
其他投资	Others	2531.04	817.87	432.32	517.79
本年新增固定资产　(亿元)	Newly Increased Fixed Assets This Year (100 million yuan)	685.80	734.05	199.70	276.16
房屋建筑面积 (万平方米)	Floor Space of Building (10000 sq. m)				
施工面积	Floor Space Under Construction	7691.41	5986.76	4290.41	3388.87
#住宅	Residential Buidlings	5247.76	4281.47	3334.84	2345.65
竣工面积	Floor Space Completed	1241.33	1325.22	601.79	626.28
#住宅	Residential Buildings	911.63	970.64	488.73	430.26
商品房销售情况 (万平方米)	Sale of Commercialized Buildings (10000 sq. m)				
房屋销售面积	Floor Space of Commercialized Buildings	1558.18	1276.41	1071.43	933.20
#住宅	Residential Buildings	1406.29	1168.43	917.89	810.80

Real Estate Investment by Region (2016)

苏州 Suzhou	南通 Nantong	连云港 Lianyungang	淮安 Huaian	盐城 Yancheng	扬州 Yangzhou	镇江 Zhenjiang	泰州 Taizhou	宿迁 Suqian
1281	580	300	352	530	390	355	339	398
2.92	1.21	0.69	1.05	1.37	1.07	1.13	0.83	1.02
558.52	83.38	34.61	61.90	81.09	106.47	127.54	57.16	54.16
2163.24	584.14	235.41	321.41	358.57	410.18	448.64	249.96	309.76
1459.19	502.12	200.79	237.21	312.12	328.49	368.19	201.01	280.93
12.57	8.78	6.17	10.40	11.81	3.65	7.03	1.81	3.01
1655.24	425.88	192.92	222.99	273.02	289.28	341.45	194.31	225.10
79.71	33.31	14.18	15.93	8.44	12.98	10.73	1.81	3.41
227.82	87.09	17.60	70.04	62.40	75.80	49.76	38.83	64.66
200.48	37.86	10.73	12.46	14.71	32.11	46.70	15.02	16.59
733.88	172.68	31.04	33.12	35.71	67.58	104.45	31.80	52.432
0.02	0.00	1.27	0.71	0.00	0.00	0.08	0.20	0.00
796.71	205.61	102.67	139.21	150.46	174.93	115.29	85.96	126.09
3139.20	548.99	170.59	231.52	254.50	351.10	476.35	326.10	224.03
1142.84	368.92	100.34	126.16	172.39	260.17	188.83	204.17	121.59
12124.10	5102.27	2147.12	2872.10	3011.13	2752.89	3177.73	2307.45	3909.47
8554.74	3765.55	1729.01	2178.44	2319.93	2013.48	2440.07	1804.60	2987.38
1882.07	1049.29	289.55	370.66	518.06	731.88	446.66	524.36	466.81
1402.80	755.01	237.87	275.75	406.78	533.29	359.24	436.16	394.53
2494.05	1200.80	524.44	869.80	842.55	734.76	996.50	694.87	765.10
2258.60	1115.64	503.30	749.08	751.32	682.21	947.93	641.76	704.42

主要统计指标解释

固定资产投资 是以货币表现的建造和购置固定资产活动的工作量,它是反映固定资产投资规模、速度、比例关系和使用方向的综合性指标。全社会固定资产投资按登记注册类型可分为国有、集体、个体、联营、股份制、外商、港澳台商、其他等。全社会固定资产投资总额分为城镇项目投资、农村建设项目投资和房地产开发投资三个部分。

城镇和农村建设项目投资 指城镇和农村各种登记注册类型的企业、事业、行政单位及个体户进行的计划总投资500万元及500万元以上建设项目的投资。

房地产开发投资 指房地产开发公司、商品房建设公司及其他房地产开发法人单位和附属于其他法人单位实际从事房地产开发或经营的活动单位统一开发的包括统代建、拆迁还建的住宅、厂房、仓库、饭店、宾馆、度假村、写字楼、办公楼等房屋建筑物和配套的服务设施,土地开发工程(如道路、给水、排水、供电、供热、通讯、平整场地等基础设施工程)的投资;不包括单纯的土地交易活动。

固定资产投资的资金来源 根据固定资产投资的资金来源不同,分为国家预算内资金、国内贷款、利用外资、自筹资金和其他资金来源。

(1) 国家预算内资金:分为财政拨款和财政安排的贷款两部分。包括中央财政的基本建设基金、专项支出、收回再贷、贴息资金,财政安排的挖潜改造和新产品试制支出、城建支出、商业部门简易建筑支出、不发达地区发展基金等资金中用于固定资产投资的资金;地方财政中由国家统筹安排的资金等。

(2) 国内贷款:指报告期内企、事业单位向银行及非银行金融机构借入的用于固定资产投资的各种国内借款。包括银行利用自有资金及吸收的存款发放的贷款、上级主管部门拨入的国内贷款、国家专项贷款(包括煤代油贷款、劳改煤矿专项贷款等)、地方财政专项资金安排的贷款、国内储备贷款、周转贷款等。

(3) 利用外资:指报告期收到的用于固定资产建造和购置投资的境外资金(包括设备、材料、技术在内)。计算利用外资时,需要折算成人民币,折算中所使用的外汇汇率按现汇计算,即按使用外汇时的汇率计算。包括外商直接投资、对外借款及外商其他投资。不包括我国自有外汇资金。

(4) 自筹资金:指固定资产投资单位报告期收到的,由各地区、各部门及企业、事业单位筹集用于固定资产投资的预算外资金,包括中央各部门、各级地方和企业、事业单位的自有资金。

(5) 其他资金:指在报告期收到的除以上各种资金之外其他用于固定资产投资的资金。包括社会集资、个人资金、无偿捐赠的资金及其他单位拨入的资金等。

固定资产投资按国民经济行业分 按建设项目建成投产后的主要产品或主要用途及社会经济活动性质来确定。一般情况下,一个建设项目或一个企业、事业单位只能属于一种国民经济行业。

固定资产投资按建设性质分 建设项目的性质一般分为新建、扩建、改建、迁建、恢复。

(1) 新建:一般是指从无到有、"平地起家"新开始建设的单位。有的单位原有的基础很小,经过建设后其新增加的固定资产价值超过原有固定资产价值(原值)三倍以上的也算新建。

(2) 扩建:一般是指为扩大原有产品的生产能力,在厂内或其他地点增建主要生产车间(或主要工程)、独立的生产线或分厂的企业;事业单位和行政单位在原单位增建业务用房(如学校增建教学用房、医院增建门诊部或病床用房、行政机关增建办公楼等)也作为扩建。

(3) 改建:一般是指现有企业、事业单位为了技术进步,提高产品质量,增加花色品种,促进产品升级换代,降低消耗和成本,加强资源综合利用和三废治理、劳保安全等,采用新技术、新工艺、新设备、新材料等对现有设施、工艺条件进行技术改造或更新(包括相应配套的辅助性生产、生活福利设施)。有的企业为充分发挥现有生产能力,进行填平补齐而增建不增加本单位主要产品生产能力的车间等,也属于改建。

固定资产投资按构成分 固定资产投资活动按其工作内容和实现方式分为建筑安装工程,设备、工具、器具购置,其他费用三个部分。

(1) 建筑安装工程(建筑安装工作量):指各种房屋、建筑物的建造工程和各种设备、装置的安装工程。包括各种房屋建造工程,各种用途设备基础和各种工业窑炉的砌筑工程;为施工而进行的各种准备工作和临时工程以及完工后的清理工作等;铁路、道路的铺设,矿井的开凿及石油管道的架设等;水利工程;防空地下建筑等特殊工程;以及各种机械设备的安装工程;为测定安装工程质量,对设备进行的试运工作。在安装工程中,不包括被安装设备本身的价值。

(2) 设备、工具、器具购置:指购置或自制达到固定资产标准的设备、工具、器具的价值,固定资产的标准按财务部门规定。新建单位、扩建单位的新建车间按照设计和计划要求购置或自制的全部设备、工具、器具,不论是否达到固定资产标准均计入"设备、工具、器具购置"中。

（3）其他费用：指在固定资产建造和购置过程中发生的，除建筑安装工程和设备、工具、器具购置以外的各种应摊入固定资产的费用。

施工项目 指报告期内曾进行建筑或安装工程施工活动的建设项目，包括报告期内新开工项目、报告期以前开工跨入报告期继续施工的项目以及报告期施过工并在报告期内全部建成投产或停缓建的项目。

全部建成投产项目 工业项目是指设计文件规定形成生产能力的主体工程及其相应配套的辅助设施全部建成，经负荷试运转，证明具备生产设计规定合格产品的条件，并经过验收鉴定合格或达到竣工验收标准，与生产性工程配套的生活福利设施可以满足近期正常生产的需要，正式移交生产的建设项目。非工业项目是指设计文件规定的主体工程和相应的配套工程全部建成，能够发挥设计规定的全部效益，经验收鉴定合格或达到竣工验收标准，正式移交使用的建设项目。

房屋建筑面积 指从房屋外墙线算起的各层平面面积的总和，包括可供使用的有效面积和房屋结构（如柱、墙）占用的面积。多层建筑按各层（包括地下室）面积总和计算。

住宅建筑面积 指施工和竣工房屋建筑面积中供居住用的施工和竣工房屋建筑面积。

施工面积 指报告期内施工的全部房屋建筑面积。包括本期新开工的面积、上期跨入本期继续施工的房屋面积、上期停缓建在本期恢复施工的房屋面积、本期竣工的房屋面积及本期施工后又停缓建的房屋面积。

竣工面积 指在报告期内房屋建筑按照设计要求已全部完工，达到住人和使用条件，经验收鉴定合格，正式移交使用单位的建筑面积。

房屋建筑面积竣工率 指一定时期内房屋竣工面积占同期房屋施工面积的比率。它是从房屋建筑施工速度的角度反映投资效果和建筑业经济效益的指标。

新增固定资产 指通过投资活动所形成的新的固定资产价值，包括已经建成投入生产或交付使用的工程价值和达到固定资产标准的设备、工具、器具的价值及有关应摊入的费用。它是以价值形式表示的固定资产投资成果的综合性指标，可以综合反映不同时期、不同部门、不同地区的固定资产投资成果。

建设项目投产率 指一定时期内全部建成投入生产项目个数与同期正式施工项目个数的比率。它是从项目建设速度的角度反映投资效果的指标。

建设周期 是指报告期（年）所有正式施工项目全部建成平均需要的时间，它是从宏观角度反映建设速度的指标。建设周期的计算方法有两种：

（1）按建设项目计算：建设周期＝报告期正式施工项目个数/报告期全部建成投产项目个数

（2）按投资额计算：建设周期＝报告期正式施工项目计划总投资之和/报告期正式施工项目完成投资之和。

Explanatory Notes on Main Statistical Indicators

Investment in Fixed Assets refers to the volume of activities in construction and purchases of fixed assets of the whole country expressed in monetary terms, it is a comprehensive indicator which shows the size, pace, proportional relations and use direction of the investment in fixed assets. Total investment in fixed assets in the whole country includes, by type of ownership, the investment by State-owned units, collective-owned units, individuals, joint ownership units, share-holding units, as well as investments by entrepreneurs from foreign countries and from Hong Kong, Macao and Taiwan, and by other units. The investment in fixed assets in the whole country is classified into the following three parts: investment in urban projects, rural construction projects and real estate development.

Urban and Rural Investment in Construction Projects refers to construction projects involving a total planned investment of 5 million yuan and over by enterprises of various types of ownership, institutions, administrative units and individuals in urban and rural areas.

Investment in Real Estate Development It includes the investment by the real estate development companies, commercial buildings construction companies and other real estate development units of various types of ownership in the construction of house buildings, such as residential buildings, factory buildings, warehouses, hotels, guesthouses, holiday villages, office buildings, and the complementary service facilities and land development projects, such as roads, water supply, water drainage, power supply, heating, telecommunications, land leveling and other projects of infrastructure. It excludes the activities in simple land transactions.

Sources of Funds for Investment in Fixed Assets state budgetary appropriation, domestic loans, foreign investment, self-raised funds, and others.

(1) Fund from the State budget consists of budgetary appropriation and loans from the State budget. More specifically, it includes, from the budget of the central government, capital construction fund, special expenses, loans from repayment, discount fund, expenses on innovation and trial production of new products, expenses on urban construction, expenses on temporary construction from

business departments, development fund for less developed areas, as well as local budgetary fund transferred from the central budget.

(2) Domestic loans refer to various funds borrowed by enterprises and institutions from banks and non-bank financial institutions during the reference period for the purpose of investment in fixed assets, including loans issued by banks from their self-owned funds and deposit, loans appropriated by higher responsible authorities, special loans by government (including loan for replacing petroleum with coal, special loan for reform through labor coal mines), loans arranged by local government from special funds, domestic reserve loan, and working loan, etc.

(3) Foreign investment refers to foreign funds received during the reference period for the construction and purchase of investment in fixed assets (covering equipment, materials and technology). In calculating the utilization of foreign capital, foreign currencies are converted into Chinese RMB applying the current exchange rate when the foreign capitals are actually used. It includes foreign borrowings (loans from foreign governments and international financial institutions, export credit, commercial loans from foreign banks, issue of bonds and stocks overseas), foreign direct investment and other foreign investments.

(4) Self-raised funds refer to extra-budgetary funds for investment in fixed assets received during the reference period by investing units from central government ministries, local governments, enterprises and institutions, including their self-raised funds.

(5) Others refer to funds for investment in fixed assets received from sources other than those listed above, including funds raised from society and individuals, donations, and funds transferred from other units.

Investment in Fixed Assets by Sector In general, one project or one enterprise or institution can only be classified into one sector.

Investment in Fixed Assets by Types of Construction The construction projects in general can be classified by the type of construction into new construction, expansion, reconstruction, moving and resumption.

(1) New construction in general refers to newly constructed units. In the case in which the value of the original fixed assets is quite small, and the value of newly added fixed assets exceeds the original ones by three times, the expansion construction is considered as new construction.

(2) Expansion refers to construction of new major production workshop or independent production line within a factory or in other locations, or construction of a branch factory so as to increase the production capacity of the original products. Newly constructed business houses in institutions and administrative organizations (such as the newly constructed teaching buildings in schools, clinics or bed building in hospitals, and office buildings in administrative agencies, etc.) are also classified as expansion.

(3) Reconstruction refers to technical innovation and transformation of the existing equipment and technical conditions undertaken by enterprises and institutions for the purposes of technological advancement, improvement in product quality, enlarging variety of products, promoting new generation of products, reducing production consumption and cost, promoting comprehensive utilization of resources, strengthening treatment of waste gas, waste water and solid wastes, and safety in production, etc. through application of new technologies and techniques, use of new equipment and new materials (including accessory facilities for production or for living and welfare purposes). Construction of new workshops for improving existing production capacity rather than increasing production capacity is also considered as reconstruction.

Investment in Fixed Assets by Structure refers to the three major parts of investment activities, i. e. construction and installation, purchase of equipment and instrument, and other expenses.

(1) Construction and installation (work volume of construction and installation) refers to the construction of various houses and buildings and installation of various kinds of equipment and instruments, including construction of various houses, equipment foundations and industrial kilns and stoves, preparation works for project construction, and clearing up works post project construction, pavement of railways and roads, drilling of mines and putting up of oil pipes, construction of projects of water conservancy, construction of underground air-raid shelters and construction of other special projects, installation of various machinery equipment, testing operation for pretesting the quality of installation projects. The value of equipment installed is not included in the value of installation projects.

(2) Purchase of equipment and instruments refers to the total value of equipment, tools, and vessels purchased or self-produced which come up to standards for fixed assets. Equipment, tools and vessels purchased or self produced for new workshops by newly established or expanded units are categorized as "purchase of equipment and instruments" no matter whether they come up to the standards for fixed assets or not.

(3) Other expenses refer to expenses occurring during the construction or purchase of fixed assets other than construction, installation or purchase of equipment and instruments.

Projects under Construction refer to projects having construction and installation activities undertaken in the reference period, including projects started in the reference period, or continued from the previous pound, or completed and put into production or suspended in the reference period.

Projects Completed and Put into Use Industrial projects refer to the major projects and accessory facilities completed which result in forming production capacity and have been checked and accepted while the living and welfare facilities have been completed and can ensure normal production and formally put into production. Non-industrial projects refer to the major projects and accessory facilities completed which possess the designed capacity and have been checked, accepted and formally put into production.

Floor Space of Buildings under Construction refers to total floor space in each story of buildings calculated from the outside line of building walls, including both usable space and the space occupied by constructions like pillars or walls. The floor space of multi-story buildings includes the total floor space of each story (including basement).

Floor Space of Residential Buildings refers to the floor space of the residential buildings among the total space of buildings under construction or completed.

Floor Space under Construction refers to total floor space of all buildings under construction during the reference period, including floor space of newly started buildings during the reference period, floor space of construction extended from the previous period to the current period, floor space of construction suspended during the previous period and resumed in the current period, floor space of construction completed in the current period, and floor space of construction started and then suspended in the current period.

Floor Space of Buildings Completed refers to the floor space of buildings completed in the reference period, which have come up to the designed standards and have been put into use.

Completion Rate of Floor Space of Buildings refers to the ratio of the floor space of buildings completed in certain period of time to the floor space of buildings under construction in the same period which reflects the investment result and economic efficiency of the construction industry from the angle of the speed of project construction.

Newly Increased Fixed Assets refer to the newly increased value of fixed assets through investment, including the value of projects completed and put into production, the value of equipment, tools, and vessels considered as fixed assets, as well as the relevant expenses as investment in fixed assets. This is a comprehensive indicator of investment in fixed assets, reflecting the achievements of investment in fixed assets in different periods, different sectors, and different regions.

Rate of Construction Projects Completed and Put into Use refers to the ratio of the number of construction projects completed and put into use in certain period of time to the number of projects under construction in the same period. This reflects the investment efficiency from the angle of the speed of projects construction.

Construction cycle refers to how longtime it will be taken in average that all the projects formally under construction can be completed in reference year. This indicator reflect the speed of construction in view of macrocosm.

There are two formulas in calculating the construction cycle:

(1) By the number of construction projects

Construction cycle = number of projects formally under construction in reference period (year) / number of all the projects are completed and put in production in reference period (year)

(2) By the value of investment

Construction cycle = total investment plan for the projects formally under construction in reference period (year) / total fulfihnent of investment on the projects formally under construction in reference period (year).

7

财政、金融

Government Finance, Financial Intermediation

简 要 说 明

本篇主要反映财政收支的基本情况及金融、证券和保险业的发展情况。

一、财政部分的主要内容、资料来源和口径说明

财政统计资料主要内容：一是财政收支历年统计数据；二是财政收支的主要构成项目。

资料来源：财政相关统计资料由江苏省财政厅提供，资料基础为财政决算表。其中，有关财政收支方面的资料根据财政决算收支总表、财政决算收入明细表、财政决算支出明细表的数据加工整理编制。

财政统计资料口径变动说明：财政预算外资金从1982年开始建立统计制度，1993年实施新的财务通则和会计准则，国营企业更新改造资金、大修理基金等不再作为预算外资金。从1997年起，财政部将政府预算收支科目分为两部分，即：将纳入预算管理的政府性基金收支及原属预算外的地方税费附加收支称为财政基金预算收支，原来的财政预算收支改称为财政一般预算收支。2007年财政收支科目实施了较大改革，特别是财政支出项目口径变化很大。

二、金融部分的主要内容和资料来源

金融统计资料主要内容：反映我省金融、证券和保险业发展情况。由四个部分构成：一是金融机构金融活动情况，二是金融机构、人员情况，三是保险业务情况，四是直接融资情况。

资料来源：金融机构金融活动情况和金融机构、人员情况由人民银行南京分行提供；保险业务情况由中国保险监督管理委员会江苏监管局提供；直接融资情况由中国证券监督管理委员会江苏监管局提供。

Brief Introduction

The data in this chapter present the government revenue and expenditure situation. Also present the development of financial, securities and insurance industries.

Ⅰ. Main Contents, Sources of Data and Diameter Description of Government Revenue

Financial Statistics main including the revenue and expenditure statistics over the years, the main component of revenue and expenditure project.

The data is provided by of the Finance Department of Jiangsu province. The base data from the financial statement sheets. Among them, information about revenue and expenditure of the total balance sheet based on final accounts, final accounts of income schedule, schedule of expenditures of final accounts data processing order preparation.

Data on the extra-budgetary funds have been collected in accordance with the statistical reporting scheme since 1982. In 1993, new general financial rules and accounting standards were implemented. As a result, the innovation fund and the major repair fund in the state-owned enterprises were no longer listed as extra-budgetary funds. Starting from 1997, government funds have been reclassified into budget management and have not been included in the extra-budgetary revenue and expenditure.

In 2007, financial renvenve and expenditure subject a large reform especially the caliber charges of financial support for projects.

Ⅱ. Main Contents and Sources of Data of Finance

Data in this chapter show the development of Jiangsu province's financial, securities and insurance industries. (1) the financial activities of the financial institutions; (2) the Situation of Financial Institutions and Personnel; (3) the situation regarding the insurance business ; (4) the situation regarding direct financing.

Financial situation of financial institutions and institutions, personnel provided by the People's Bank of China, Nanjing Branch. Major indicator of Insurance Business provided by China Insurance Regulatory Commission ,Jiangsu Branch. Basic Information of direct finacing provided b by the China Securities Regulatory Commission, Jiangsu province.

7-1 历年财政收支

Financial Revenue and Expenditure over the Years

单位:亿元 (100 million yuan)

年份 Year	财政总收入 Government Revenue	#一般公共预算收入 General Public Budget Revenue	#税收收入 Taxes	一般公共预算支出 General Public Budget Expenditure	财政总收入占地区生产总值的比重(%) Percentage of Government Revenue to GDP(%)	一般公共预算收入占地区生产总值的比重(%) Percentage of Budget Revenue to GDP(T)
1978	61.09	61.09	35.93	28.38	24.5	24.5
1979	59.28	59.28	38.33	32.06	19.9	19.9
1980	62.45	62.45	41.36	28.95	19.5	19.5
1981	63.04	63.04	44.64	23.79	18.0	18.0
1982	66.61	66.61	49.84	24.63	17.1	17.1
1983	73.63	73.63	54.57	32.29	16.8	16.8
1984	76.28	76.28	61.79	39.15	14.7	14.7
1985	89.00	89.00	80.32	50.53	13.7	13.7
1986	98.73	98.73	87.29	66.16	13.3	13.3
1987	107.17	107.17	94.96	68.00	11.6	11.6
1988	117.96	117.96	107.74	81.45	9.8	9.8
1989	126.39	126.39	122.82	92.25	9.6	9.6
1990	136.20	136.20	130.96	100.97	9.6	9.6
1991	143.29	143.29	125.91	128.18	8.9	8.9
1992	152.31	152.31	145.49	125.86	7.1	7.1
1993	221.30	221.30	220.05	163.87	7.4	7.4
1994	293.41	136.62	121.05	200.17	7.2	3.4
1995	350.08	172.64	146.39	253.49	6.8	3.3
1996	427.99	223.17	184.65	310.94	7.1	3.7
1997	512.93	255.59	210.56	364.36	7.7	3.8
1998	579.90	296.58	244.20	424.90	8.1	4.1
1999	680.23	343.36	314.26	484.65	8.8	4.5
2000	865.00	448.31	409.14	591.28	10.1	5.2
2001	1064.99	572.15	523.84	729.64	11.3	6.1
2002	1483.68	643.70	565.30	860.25	14.0	6.1
2003	1968.92	798.11	690.53	1047.68	15.8	6.4
2004	2216.41	980.43	833.64	1312.04	14.8	6.5
2005	3124.83	1322.68	1107.27	1673.40	16.8	7.1
2006	3935.87	1656.68	1389.13	2013.25	18.1	7.6
2007	5591.29	2237.73	1894.77	2553.72	21.5	8.6
2008	7109.72	2731.41	2278.71	3247.49	22.9	8.8
2009	8404.99	3228.78	2654.75	4017.36	24.4	9.4
2010	11743.22	4079.86	3312.61	4914.06	28.3	9.8
2011	14119.85	5148.92	4124.62	6221.72	28.8	10.5
2012	14843.89	5860.69	4782.59	7027.67	27.5	10.8
2013	17328.80	6568.46	5419.49	7798.47	29.3	11.1
2014	18201.33	7233.14	6006.05	8472.45	28.0	11.1
2015	17841.60	8028.59	6610.12	9687.58	25.4	11.5
2016	19464.48	8121.23	6531.83	9981.96	25.6	10.7

注:财政总收入为一般公共预算收入、基金收入、上划中央四税之和。

a) Provincial financial revenue is the sum of general public budget revenue, fund revenue and four kinds of taxes to the central government.

7-2 公共财政收支

Public Financial Budget Revenue and Expenditure

单位:亿元 (100 million yuan)

指标	Item	2012	2013	2014	2015	2016
一般公共预算收入	**General Public Budget Revenue**	**5860.69**	**6568.46**	**7233.14**	**8028.59**	**8121.23**
税收收入	Taxes	4782.59	5419.49	6006.05	6610.12	6531.83
增值税	Value Added Tax	708.75	859.26	987.54	1046.92	1974.58
营业税	Business Taxes	1659.67	1872.41	2084.66	2442.82	1325.14
企业所得税	Company Income Tax	745.88	763.66	821.04	917.58	978.81
个人所得税	Personal Income Tax	224.22	264.88	306.33	360.89	382.37
城市维护建设税	Urban Maintenance and Development Tax	309.93	339.53	376.15	421.46	433.98
房产税	Tax on Real Estates	160.88	192.84	228.73	248.01	256.60
土地增值税	Value Added Tax on Land	317.17	405.79	444.89	437.01	480.58
耕地占用税	Tax on Use of Arable Land	57.96	42.91	34.74	31.76	26.63
契税	Tax on Contracts	332.84	383.75	401.69	370.11	335.40
其他各项税收	Others	265.29	294.46	320.27	333.56	337.74
非税收收入	Non-tax Income	1078.10	1148.98	1227.10	1418.47	1589.40
专项收入	Special Project Income	179.34	193.11	209.33	463.64	484.42
行政事业性收费收入	Income from Administrative Fees	375.31	389.60	426.52	390.01	410.47
罚没收入	Penalty and Cofiscatory Income	98.51	118.54	120.63	131.66	132.52
国有资本经营收入	Profit from State-owned Assets	234.91	241.10	242.34	0.00	0.00
其他各项收入	Other Income	190.03	206.62	228.27	433.16	561.99
上划中央收入	**Turn Over Revenue to the Central Government**	**3922.35**	**4167.00**	**4583.29**	**5005.17**	**5295.43**
消费税	Consumption Tax	453.30	506.78	577.83	676.98	709.15
增值税	Value Added Tax	2080.03	2178.15	2377.62	2484.31	2622.23
企业所得税	Company Income Tax	1052.69	1084.76	1168.33	1302.55	1390.49
个人所得税	Personal Income Tax	336.34	397.32	459.50	541.33	573.56
一般公共预算支出	**General Public Budget Expenditure**	**7027.67**	**7798.47**	**8472.45**	**9687.58**	**9981.96**
一般公共服务	General Public Service	820.43	859.41	856.70	845.68	920.93
公共安全	Public Security	407.78	452.99	473.83	519.92	634.76
教育	Education	1350.61	1434.99	1504.86	1746.22	1842.94
科学技术	Science and Technology	257.24	302.59	327.10	371.96	381.02
文化体育与传媒	Culture, Sports and Media	150.90	173.54	190.86	196.06	193.28
社会保障和就业	Social Security and Employment	557.77	631.15	709.59	838.06	897.93
医疗卫生	Medical Treatment and Healthcare	418.14	475.86	560.93	649.31	712.77
节能环保	Envionment Protection	193.83	229.18	237.78	308.45	285.11
城乡社区事务	Operating Expenses of Urban and Rural Communities	858.13	1006.80	1221.64	1535.59	1440.12
农林水事务	Operating Expenses of Agriculture, Forestry and Water	754.09	868.34	899.31	1008.60	985.62
交通运输	Transport	436.58	448.58	496.93	547.81	511.81
资源勘探电力信息等事务	Operating Expenses of Industry, Commerce and Financial Intermediation	283.18	345.89	364.33	448.45	437.26
其他各项支出	Others	538.99	569.15	628.59	671.47	738.41

7－3 分市财政收支(2016 年)

单位:亿元

指　标	Item	南京 Nanjing	无锡 Wuxi	徐州 Xuzhou	常州 Changzhou
一般公共预算收入	**General Public Budget Revenue**	**1142.60**	**875.00**	**516.06**	**480.29**
税收收入	Taxes	956.62	706.04	390.30	383.19
增值税	Value Added Tax	296.63	262.52	82.63	132.50
营业税	Business Taxes	158.19	121.33	104.69	55.22
企业所得税	Company Income Tax	141.41	103.65	25.93	51.30
个人所得税	Personal Income Tax	77.27	49.51	12.47	27.48
城市维护建设税	Urban Maintenance and Development Tax	78.35	54.18	29.40	26.89
房产税	Tax on Real Estates	33.39	33.06	12.40	17.98
土地增值税	Value Added Tax on Land	95.42	19.17	52.58	10.10
耕地占用税	Tax on Use of Arable Land	1.37	2.01	2.01	1.88
契税	Tax on Contracts	35.83	24.10	33.33	32.82
其他各项税收	Others	38.76	36.51	34.86	27.02
非税收收入	Non-tax Income	185.98	168.96	125.76	97.10
专项收入	Special Project Income	91.28	51.87	29.65	24.23
行政事业性收费收入	Income from Administrative Fees	24.74	29.08	29.11	25.05
罚没收入	Penalty and Cofiscatory Income	15.64	13.46	18.94	8.05
国有资本经营收入	Profit from State-owned Assets	0.00	0.00	0.00	0.00
其他各项收入	Other Income	54.32	74.55	48.06	39.77
上划中央收入	**Turn Over Revenue to the Central Government**	**1055.94**	**595.13**	**285.95**	**306.01**
消费税	Consumption Tax	346.29	16.89	114.91	9.33
增值税	Value Added Tax	381.64	348.50	113.45	178.51
企业所得税	Company Income Tax	212.11	155.48	38.89	76.95
个人所得税	Personal Income Tax	115.90	74.27	18.70	41.22
一般公共预算支出	**General Public Budget Expenditure**	**1173.84**	**867.36**	**797.99**	**508.11**
一般公共服务	General Public Service	93.65	68.85	62.36	50.05
公共安全	Public Security	80.22	55.13	43.69	33.35
教育	Education	202.86	137.34	165.33	83.69
科学技术	Science and Technology	53.13	37.24	20.76	24.02
文化体育与传媒	Culture, Sports and Media	30.88	14.08	8.89	7.54
社会保障和就业	Social Security and Employment	121.19	70.63	83.60	54.54
医疗卫生	Medical Treatment and Healthcare	75.15	50.46	59.58	44.75
节能环保	Envionment Protection	49.69	37.74	19.86	11.74
城乡社区事务	Operating Expenses of Urban and Rural Communities	201.46	196.73	119.47	82.56
农林水事务	Operating Expenses of Agriculture, Forestry and Water	65.76	47.34	117.68	49.58
交通运输	Transport	50.37	51.76	21.96	15.07
资源勘探电力信息等事务	Operating Expenses of Industry, Commerce and Financial Intermediation	58.12	44.00	24.14	7.74
其他各项支出	Others	91.36	56.06	50.67	43.48

Financial Revenue and Expenditure by Region (2016)

(100 million yuan)

苏州 Suzhou	南通 Nantong	连云港 Lianyungang	淮安 Huaian	盐城 Yancheng	扬州 Yangzhou	镇江 Zhenjiang	泰州 Taizhou	宿迁 Suqian
1730.04	**590.18**	**211.47**	**315.51**	**415.18**	**345.30**	**293.01**	**321.18**	**238.08**
1505.82	456.77	170.80	235.15	324.67	267.16	231.40	257.62	186.27
553.11	116.58	47.71	47.87	69.36	79.96	66.08	85.38	40.46
165.79	105.90	44.49	76.90	109.67	50.70	60.89	58.74	49.56
276.13	51.75	18.23	12.32	22.96	27.85	22.16	24.93	18.15
105.02	32.10	5.47	6.68	14.00	10.19	11.64	12.15	5.96
103.63	26.38	10.83	18.12	19.84	17.74	15.94	17.62	9.99
71.12	17.80	4.49	8.55	15.51	9.70	8.28	7.57	14.50
110.90	34.54	10.60	28.14	25.16	38.92	14.52	18.14	22.31
3.91	3.14	0.16	1.07	2.38	2.49	1.74	3.82	0.64
49.91	37.28	11.97	22.28	27.03	14.46	18.22	14.71	13.46
66.30	31.30	16.85	13.22	18.76	15.15	11.93	14.56	11.24
224.22	133.41	40.67	80.36	90.51	78.14	61.61	63.56	51.81
113.11	29.12	14.44	16.38	22.89	23.24	16.81	20.42	10.10
37.92	33.79	12.71	27.58	17.13	21.28	18.48	15.03	10.23
15.13	9.37	6.73	8.15	7.20	4.81	5.36	7.39	9.44
0.00	0.00	0.00	0.00	0.00	0.00	0.00	0.00	0.00
58.06	61.13	6.79	28.25	43.29	28.81	20.96	20.72	22.04
1346.86	**289.10**	**103.63**	**167.62**	**182.06**	**184.15**	**143.69**	**180.55**	**110.73**
28.85	10.92	5.46	77.99	35.93	20.78	5.45	16.35	20.00
746.28	152.41	62.61	61.12	90.70	106.30	87.54	108.59	54.57
414.20	77.62	27.35	18.48	34.43	41.77	33.24	37.39	27.23
157.53	48.15	8.21	10.03	21.00	15.29	17.46	18.22	8.93
1617.11	**749.22**	**373.12**	**483.47**	**730.33**	**478.97**	**362.94**	**448.93**	**424.57**
146.16	87.62	42.99	51.67	77.27	57.50	36.50	53.16	32.12
116.13	47.95	20.86	24.23	33.09	30.85	25.65	29.33	18.24
262.32	154.87	73.76	77.83	129.76	84.73	67.05	75.59	69.20
95.20	22.83	10.03	9.29	32.36	12.28	13.48	11.65	8.63
37.57	12.34	4.94	5.89	12.50	9.55	9.57	6.36	9.35
142.39	78.70	36.68	48.23	76.83	40.52	32.84	42.83	46.36
93.63	69.59	28.42	43.69	69.76	37.80	23.34	39.65	37.53
43.97	12.18	10.85	11.25	13.77	21.48	16.72	10.88	12.48
354.05	96.01	48.94	54.20	71.23	60.04	58.79	51.47	43.45
89.36	74.83	46.08	66.65	97.28	50.19	34.17	56.74	83.95
61.68	13.85	18.81	11.09	19.86	11.74	7.41	11.21	12.40
57.61	18.90	5.54	44.19	45.82	27.98	11.54	23.22	21.92
117.04	59.55	25.22	35.26	50.80	34.31	25.88	36.84	28.94

7-4 历年金融机构存贷款

The Balance of Deposits of Financial Institutions over the Years

单位:亿元 (100 million yuan)

年 份 Year	金融机构各项存款余额(本外币) The Balance of Deposits of Financial Institutions(RMB and Foreign Currency)	#储蓄存款 Saving Deposit	金融机构各项贷款余额(本外币) Financial Institutions, the LoanBalance (RMB and Foreign Currency)	金融机构各项存款余额(人民币) The Balance of Deposits of Financial Institutions (RMB)	#储蓄存款 Saving Deposit	金融机构各项贷款余额(人民币) Financial Institutions, the Loan Balance (RMB)
1978				60.72	12.40	115.29
1979				78.31	16.68	129.70
1980				95.55	23.72	159.11
1981				124.54	30.42	195.33
1982				146.21	40.60	217.87
1983				171.12	56.93	242.28
1984				221.68	74.76	333.40
1985				247.12	99.35	387.06
1986				372.62	139.59	528.83
1987				443.44	193.68	659.29
1988				517.81	231.85	742.10
1989				640.84	331.86	835.56
1990				860.33	471.18	1013.45
1991				1136.51	617.61	1230.49
1992				1422.61	766.11	1480.80
1993				1797.33	964.22	1777.80
1994				2481.10	1352.57	2218.15
1995				3500.49	1922.33	2875.39
1996				4706.36	2581.06	3840.74
1997				5674.94	3101.89	4452.46
1998				6578.80	3656.46	5063.57
1999				7470.43	4131.98	5535.15
2000				8400.75	4456.83	5967.66
2001				9700.68	5172.83	6671.74
2002				11881.19	6276.20	8234.58
2003				15378.49	7638.18	11299.55
2004				18211.02	8863.10	13480.98
2005	22821.57	10860.60	16282.60	22001.44	10581.27	15396.59
2006	26722.83	12454.90	19383.65	25860.47	12183.47	18485.02
2007	31337.99	13213.11	23265.83	30450.54	13014.92	22092.10
2008	38063.38	16916.74	27081.06	37017.48	16721.18	26160.72
2009	50061.85	20303.67	36846.34	48850.29	20080.63	35296.73
2010	60583.07	23533.13	44180.21	58984.14	23334.48	42121.04
2011	67638.75	26111.82	50283.52	65723.56	25914.74	47868.30
2012	78109.00	30285.44	57652.84	75481.51	30057.19	54412.30
2013	88302.07	34072.84	64908.22	85604.08	33823.90	61836.53
2014	96939.01	36847.53	72490.02	93735.61	36580.59	69572.67
2015	111329.86	40951.02	81169.72	107873.03	40562.97	78866.34
2016	125576.94	44544.05	92957.02	121106.58	43900.50	91107.60

注:2015 年人民银行调整金融报表项目及归属,取消储蓄存款,本表 2015 年往后数据为住户存款。

a) In 2015, the People's Bank of China to adjust the financial statement of the project and attribation, the abolition of Savings deposits, the data in 2015 for household deposits.

7-5 金融机构存贷款年末余额(2016)

Deposits and Loans of Financial Institutions at Year-end(2016)

		本外币(亿元) RMB and Foreign Currency (100 million yuan)	人民币(亿元) RMB (100 million yuan)	外汇(亿美元) Foreign Currency (USD 100 million)
各项存款	**The Deposits**	**125576.94**	**121106.58**	**644.42**
境内存款	Domestic Deposit	125234.79	120828.32	635.21
住户存款	Household Deposits	44544.05	43900.50	92.77
活期存款	Demand Deposits	14204.65	13860.55	49.60
定期及其他存款	Regular and Other Deposits	30339.40	30039.95	43.17
非金融企业存款	Non Financial Enterprise Deposit	48870.53	45277.91	517.89
活期存款	Demand Deposits	19029.97	17249.58	256.65
定期及其他存款	Regular and Other Deposits	29840.56	28028.33	261.24
广义政府存款	General Government Deposits	25103.68	24982.85	17.42
财政性存款	Fiscal Deposits	1519.94	1519.94	
机关团体存款	Government Organs, Social Groups, Enterprises Deposits	23583.74	23462.91	17.42
非银行业金融机构存款	Non Banking Financial Institutions Deposit	6716.53	6667.06	7.13
境外存款	Offshore Deposits	342.15	278.26	9.21
各项贷款	**Loans**	**92957.02**	**91107.60**	**266.60**
境内贷款	Domestic Loans	92748.28	91021.06	248.99
住户贷款	Household Loans	27128.51	27126.04	0.36
短期贷款	Short-term Loans	5015.84	5013.56	0.33
消费贷款	Consumer Loans	1847.57	1845.28	0.33
经营贷款	Operating Loan	3168.28	3168.28	
中长期贷款	Medium and Long Term Loans	22112.67	22112.48	0.03
消费贷款	Consumer Loans	20552.83	20552.65	0.03
经营贷款	Business Loans	1559.84	1559.84	
非金融企业及机关团体贷款	Non Financial Enterprise and Institution Loan	65608.99	63884.25	248.63
短期贷款	Short-term Loans	25953.17	24716.16	178.32
中长期贷款	Long-term Loans	33232.86	32761.09	68.01
票据融资	Bill Financing	5495.36	5495.20	0.02
融资租赁	Finance Leases	814.78	814.78	
各项垫款	The Advances	112.82	97.02	2.28
非银行业金融机构贷款	Non Banking Financial Institution Loans	10.78	10.78	
境外贷款	Overseas Loan	208.73	86.54	17.62

7-6 分地区金融机构本外币存贷款年末余额(2016 年)

单位:亿元

指标	Item	南京 Nanjing	无锡 Wuxi	徐州 Xuzhou	常州 Changzhou
各项存款	**The Deposits**	**28355.89**	**14612.00**	**5640.76**	**8850.03**
境内存款	Domestic Deposit	28297.75	14582.56	5637.48	8841.37
住户存款	Household Deposits	6095.08	4957.02	3108.34	3415.31
活期存款	Demand Deposits	2363.83	1470.32	1109.86	1008.75
定期及其他存款	Regular and Other Deposits	3731.25	3486.71	1998.48	2406.55
非金融企业存款	Non Financial Enterprise Deposit	11483.72	6429.48	1534.28	3384.57
活期存款	Demand Deposits	4685.48	2280.27	674.05	1166.74
定期及其他存款	Regular and Other Deposits	6798.24	4149.21	860.23	2217.83
广义政府存款	General Government Deposits	7585.47	2525.28	988.89	1322.24
财政性存款	Fiscal Deposits	521.76	135.22	110.55	37.25
机关团体存款	Government Organs, Social Groups, Enterprises Deposits	7063.71	2390.06	878.34	1284.99
非银行业金融机构存款	Non Banking Financial Institutions Deposit	3133.49	670.77	5.96	719.25
境外存款	Offshore Deposits	58.13	29.45	3.28	8.66
各项贷款	**Loans**	**22268.94**	**10517.75**	**3630.85**	**6081.37**
境内贷款	Domestic Loans	22147.85	10513.92	3630.46	6080.31
住户贷款	Household Loans	6533.72	2043.62	1231.41	1460.26
短期贷款	Short-term Loan	1015.35	264.95	275.01	311.27
消费贷款	Consumer Loans	710.55	133.89	55.81	68.78
经营贷款	Operating Loan	304.80	131.05	219.19	242.49
中长期贷款	Medium and Long Term Loans	5518.36	1778.68	956.40	1148.99
消费贷款	Consumer Loans	5256.14	1660.19	846.10	1059.26
经营贷款	Operating Loan	262.23	118.49	110.30	89.73
非金融企业及机关团体贷款	Non Financial Enterprise and Institution Loan	15603.36	8470.30	2399.06	4620.04
短期贷款	Short-term Loan	3880.86	3652.23	1103.49	2371.08
中长期贷款	Medium and Long Term Loans	10245.90	3893.96	908.98	1809.93
票据融资	Bill Financing	836.23	910.27	347.39	310.28
融资租赁	Finance Leases	627.97	0.14	18.73	120.41
各项垫款	The Advances	12.39	13.70	20.47	8.34
非银行业金融机构贷款	Non Banking Financial Institution Loans	10.78			
境外贷款	Overseas Loan	121.09	3.83	0.38	1.07

Deposits and Loans of Financial Institutions at Year-end by Region (RMB and Foreign Currency) (2016)

(100 million yuan)

苏州 Suzhou	南通 Nantong	连云港 Lianyungang	淮安 Huaian	盐城 Yancheng	扬州 Yangzhou	镇江 Zhenjiang	泰州 Taizhou	宿迁 Suqian
27727.55	**11330.14**	**2555.48**	**3121.81**	**5471.02**	**5448.23**	**4824.88**	**5406.35**	**2232.80**
27519.29	11314.90	2554.42	3119.16	5468.32	5444.31	4820.28	5402.98	2231.98
8068.20	5597.93	1179.91	1367.16	2693.14	2585.52	1899.19	2487.93	1089.31
3079.01	1032.16	487.30	535.26	707.51	701.47	510.43	656.57	542.18
4989.19	4565.77	692.61	831.91	1985.63	1884.05	1388.76	1831.36	547.14
12028.00	3808.78	866.31	1097.12	1846.46	1820.76	1805.64	2056.17	709.24
4476.09	1455.47	382.47	661.02	699.01	716.41	699.14	810.86	322.96
7551.91	2353.30	483.85	436.10	1147.45	1104.35	1106.50	1245.31	386.28
6131.07	1527.96	483.92	653.49	878.81	1011.59	805.66	795.02	394.28
418.86	53.93	54.19	52.35	38.20	29.85	22.15	20.63	25.02
5712.21	1474.04	429.73	601.14	840.61	981.73	783.51	774.39	369.26
1292.02	380.24	24.27	1.39	49.91	26.44	309.78	63.86	39.14
208.26	15.24	1.06	2.65	2.70	3.92	4.60	3.37	0.82
22752.22	**6896.58**	**2093.90**	**2312.94**	**3718.40**	**3526.36**	**3472.35**	**3720.85**	**1964.51**
22699.32	6869.66	2093.76	2312.91	3717.43	3525.83	3471.69	3720.75	1964.39
7427.89	1468.21	792.93	935.06	1147.80	1176.16	894.07	1010.67	1006.71
766.08	466.16	213.04	242.05	303.56	303.41	158.64	325.13	371.20
369.59	94.83	60.71	50.50	79.48	62.49	34.68	63.05	63.20
396.49	371.33	152.33	191.55	224.08	240.91	123.96	262.08	308.00
6661.81	1002.05	579.90	693.01	844.23	872.75	735.43	685.54	635.51
6289.58	889.92	529.89	633.91	748.02	788.63	685.84	590.14	575.20
372.23	112.13	50.01	59.10	96.21	84.12	49.59	95.39	60.31
15271.43	5401.45	1300.83	1377.85	2569.63	2349.67	2577.62	2710.08	957.67
6440.24	2226.08	491.96	539.11	1168.50	1043.96	1278.93	1252.91	503.84
7424.17	2813.17	680.12	733.85	941.63	1057.61	1119.63	1238.10	365.82
1332.89	356.21	125.67	104.40	457.56	246.25	169.46	212.07	86.67
47.53								
26.60	6.00	3.09	0.49	1.94	1.85	9.60	7.00	1.34
52.90	26.92	0.13	0.03	0.97	0.53	0.66	0.10	0.12

7-7 分地区金融机构人民币存贷款年末余额（2016 年）

单位:亿元

指　　标	Item	南京 Nanjing	无锡 Wuxi	徐州 Xuzhou	常州 Changzhou
各项存款	**The Deposits**	**27633.55**	**14101.40**	**5495.31**	**8540.82**
境内存款	Domestic Deposit	27591.34	14077.07	5492.13	8533.12
住户存款	Household Deposits	5894.47	4867.43	3090.21	3366.85
活期存款	Demand Deposits	2262.56	1428.47	1099.67	983.48
定期及其他存款	Regular and Other Deposits	3631.91	3438.96	1990.54	2383.37
非金融企业存款	Non Financial Enterprise Deposit	11070.07	6030.44	1408.89	3125.48
活期存款	Demand Deposits	4435.05	2016.51	627.66	998.89
定期及其他存款	Regular and Other Deposits	6635.02	4013.93	781.23	2126.60
广义政府存款	General Government Deposits	7515.89	2518.25	987.08	1322.03
财政性存款	Fiscal Deposits	521.76	135.22	110.55	37.25
机关团体存款	Government Organs, Social Groups, Enterprises Deposits	6994.14	2383.03	876.52	1284.79
非银行业金融机构存款	Non Banking Financial Institutions Deposit	3110.90	660.95	5.95	718.75
境外存款	Offshore Deposits	42.21	24.33	3.18	7.71
各项贷款	**Loans**	**21681.28**	**10382.93**	**3620.21**	**6043.15**
境内贷款	Domestic Loans	21663.52	10381.02	3620.11	6042.40
住户贷款	Household Loans	6532.82	2043.36	1231.35	1460.11
短期贷款	Short-term Loan	1014.59	264.68	274.97	311.12
消费贷款	Consumer Loans	709.79	133.62	55.77	68.63
经营贷款	Operating Loan	304.80	131.05	219.19	242.49
中长期贷款	Medium and Long Term Loans	5518.23	1778.68	956.39	1148.99
消费贷款	Consumer Loans	5256.00	1660.19	846.08	1059.26
经营贷款	Operating Loan	262.23	118.49	110.30	89.73
非金融企业及机关团体贷款	Non Financial Enterprise and Institution Loan	15119.92	8337.67	2388.76	4582.29
短期贷款	Short-term Loan	3660.03	3533.29	1095.79	2334.75
中长期贷款	Medium and Long Term Loans	9986.54	3880.52	906.49	1808.68
票据融资	Bill Financing	836.18	910.27	347.39	310.28
融资租赁	Finance Leases	627.97	0.14	18.73	120.41
各项垫款	The Advances	9.20	13.44	20.36	8.18
非银行业金融机构贷款	Non Banking Financial Institution Loans	10.78			
境外贷款	Overseas Loan	17.76	1.91	0.11	0.75

Deposits and Loans of Financial Institutions at Year-end by Region(RMB)(2016)

(100 million yuan)

苏州 Suzhou	南通 Nantong	连云港 Lianyungang	淮安 Huaian	盐城 Yancheng	扬州 Yangzhou	镇江 Zhenjiang	泰州 Taizhou	宿迁 Suqian
25864.26	**11097.74**	**2501.84**	**3066.00**	**5255.06**	**5361.55**	**4705.99**	**5275.62**	**2207.43**
25686.33	11091.78	2500.91	3064.73	5252.41	5357.84	4701.66	5272.38	2206.63
7913.85	5554.89	1168.71	1360.51	2682.46	2560.98	1879.10	2474.71	1086.33
2988.74	1007.26	480.32	530.87	700.63	689.30	500.31	649.14	539.81
4925.11	4547.63	688.39	829.64	1981.83	1871.68	1378.79	1825.57	546.52
10397.64	3634.57	824.06	1049.81	1641.31	1758.90	1711.03	1938.83	686.87
3819.24	1338.20	346.13	623.62	678.28	676.79	627.22	747.98	314.04
6578.41	2296.37	477.93	426.20	963.03	1082.11	1083.81	1190.86	372.84
6090.62	1527.67	483.88	653.02	878.75	1011.54	804.83	795.01	394.28
418.86	53.93	54.19	52.35	38.20	29.85	22.15	20.63	25.02
5671.76	1473.75	429.70	600.67	840.55	981.69	782.68	774.38	369.26
1284.22	374.65	24.26	1.39	49.90	26.42	306.69	63.83	39.14
177.93	5.96	0.93	1.27	2.65	3.72	4.34	3.24	0.80
21924.44	**6835.46**	**2046.93**	**2304.22**	**3699.32**	**3508.13**	**3444.36**	**3656.79**	**1960.37**
21884.73	6811.72	2046.80	2304.18	3698.34	3507.60	3443.70	3656.69	1960.25
7427.20	1468.09	792.91	935.03	1147.77	1176.08	894.00	1010.62	1006.70
765.39	466.04	213.02	242.03	303.53	303.34	158.58	325.09	371.19
368.90	94.71	60.69	50.48	79.45	62.43	34.62	63.01	63.19
396.49	371.33	152.33	191.55	224.08	240.91	123.96	262.08	308.00
6661.81	1002.04	579.90	693.01	844.23	872.75	735.43	685.53	635.51
6289.58	889.91	529.88	633.91	748.02	788.63	685.84	590.13	575.20
372.23	112.13	50.01	59.10	96.21	84.12	49.59	95.39	60.31
14457.53	5343.63	1253.88	1369.15	2550.58	2331.52	2549.69	2646.08	953.55
5725.02	2199.93	475.96	530.41	1152.23	1026.65	1262.75	1218.19	501.16
7330.00	2784.20	649.25	733.85	938.85	1056.76	1110.02	1211.56	364.38
1332.89	356.11	125.67	104.40	457.56	246.25	169.45	212.07	86.67
47.53								
22.09	3.39	3.01	0.49	1.94	1.85	7.48	4.26	1.34
39.71	23.75	0.13	0.03	0.97	0.53	0.66	0.10	0.12

7－8　分地区金融机构外汇存贷款年末余额（2016 年）

单位:亿元

指　标	Item	南京 Nanjing	无锡 Wuxi	徐州 Xuzhou	常州 Changzhou
各项存款	**The Deposits**	**104.13**	**73.61**	**20.97**	**44.57**
境内存款	Domestic Deposit	101.83	72.87	20.95	44.44
住户存款	Household Deposits	28.92	12.92	2.61	6.99
活期存款	Demand Deposits	14.60	6.03	1.47	3.64
定期及其他存款	Regular and Other Deposits	14.32	6.88	1.14	3.34
非金融企业存款	Non Financial Enterprise Deposit	59.63	57.52	18.08	37.35
活期存款	Demand Deposits	36.10	38.02	6.69	24.20
定期及其他存款	Regular and Other Deposits	23.53	19.50	11.39	13.15
广义政府存款	General Government Deposits	10.03	1.01	0.26	0.03
财政性存款	Fiscal Deposits				
机关团体存款	Government Organs, Social Groups, Enterprises Deposits	10.03	1.01	0.26	0.03
非银行业金融机构存款	Non Banking Financial Institutions Deposit	3.26	1.41	0.00	0.07
境外存款	Offshore Deposits	2.30	0.74	0.01	0.14
各项贷款	**Loans**	**84.71**	**19.44**	**1.53**	**5.51**
境内贷款	Domestic Loans	69.82	19.16	1.49	5.46
住户贷款	Household Loans	0.13	0.04	0.01	0.02
短期贷款	Short-term Loan	0.11	0.04	0.01	0.02
消费贷款	Consumer Loans	0.11	0.04	0.01	0.02
经营贷款	Operating Loan				
中长期贷款	Medium and Long Term Loans	0.02	0.00	0.00	0.00
消费贷款	Consumer Loans	0.02	0.00	0.00	0.00
经营贷款	Operating Loan				
非金融企业及机关团体贷款	Non Financial Enterprise and Institution Loan	69.69	19.12	1.48	5.44
短期贷款	Short-term Loan	31.83	17.14	1.11	5.24
中长期贷款	Medium and Long Term Loans	37.39	1.94	0.36	0.18
票据融资	Bill Financing	0.01			
融资租赁	Finance Leases				
各项垫款	The Advances	0.46	0.04	0.02	0.02
非银行业金融机构贷款	Non Banking Financial Institution Loans				
境外贷款	Overseas Loan	14.89	0.28	0.04	0.05

Deposits and Loans of Financial Institutions at Year-end by Region (Foreign Currency) (2016)

(100 million yuan)

苏州 Suzhou	南通 Nantong	连云港 Lianyungang	淮安 Huaian	盐城 Yancheng	扬州 Yangzhou	镇江 Zhenjiang	泰州 Taizhou	宿迁 Suqian
268.60	**33.50**	**7.73**	**8.04**	**31.13**	**12.49**	**17.14**	**18.85**	**3.66**
264.23	32.16	7.71	7.85	31.12	12.47	17.10	18.83	3.65
22.25	6.20	1.62	0.96	1.54	3.54	2.90	1.91	0.43
13.01	3.59	1.01	0.63	0.99	1.76	1.46	1.07	0.34
9.24	2.61	0.61	0.33	0.55	1.78	1.44	0.83	0.09
235.02	25.11	6.09	6.82	29.57	8.92	13.64	16.91	3.22
94.69	16.91	5.24	5.39	2.99	5.71	10.37	9.06	1.29
140.33	8.21	0.85	1.43	26.58	3.21	3.27	7.85	1.94
5.83	0.04	0.01	0.07	0.01	0.01	0.12	0.00	0.00
5.83	0.04	0.01	0.07	0.01	0.01	0.12	0.00	0.00
1.12	0.81	0.00	0.00	0.00	0.00	0.45	0.00	
4.37	1.34	0.02	0.20	0.01	0.03	0.04	0.02	0.00
119.33	**8.81**	**6.77**	**1.26**	**2.75**	**2.63**	**4.03**	**9.23**	**0.60**
117.43	8.35	6.77	1.26	2.75	2.63	4.03	9.23	0.60
0.10	0.02	0.00	0.00	0.00	0.01	0.01	0.01	0.00
0.10	0.02	0.00	0.00	0.00	0.01	0.01	0.01	0.00
0.10	0.02	0.00	0.00	0.00	0.01	0.01	0.01	0.00
0.00		0.00	0.00	0.00	0.00	0.00	0.00	
0.00		0.00	0.00	0.00	0.00	0.00	0.00	
117.33	8.34	6.77	1.25	2.75	2.62	4.03	9.23	0.59
103.10	3.77	2.31	1.25	2.34	2.49	2.33	5.00	0.39
13.57	4.18	4.45		0.40	0.12	1.39	3.83	0.21
0.00	0.01					0.00		
0.65	0.38	0.01				0.31	0.40	
1.90	0.46							

7－9 分行业金融机构贷款年末余额

行　业	Sector	本外币(亿元) RMB and Foreign Currency (100 million yuan)				
		2012	2013	2014	2015	2016
总　计	**Total**	**55900.17**	**62805.68**	**69262.46**	**76605.13**	**87656.54**
农、林、牧、渔业	Agriculture, Forestry, Animal Husbandry and Fishery	915.00	1270.13	1500.84	1488.50	1482.38
采矿业	Mining	62.65	105.39	100.46	107.36	119.51
制造业	Manufacturing	15821.34	16509.63	16275.43	15839.77	15263.76
电力、热力、燃气及水生产和供应业	Production and Supply of Electric Power, Heat Power, Gas and Water	1612.77	1655.21	1691.56	1994.42	2347.16
建筑业	Construction	2374.62	2766.82	3112.24	3418.13	3335.06
批发和零售业	Wholesale and Retail Trades	5229.39	5875.73	5930.97	6049.68	5869.39
交通运输、仓储和邮政业	Transport, Storage and Post	3377.03	3549.03	3824.00	3993.95	4003.88
住宿和餐饮业	Hotels and Catering Services	353.83	458.04	480.30	474.14	434.08
信息传输、软件和信息技术服务业	Information Transfer, Software and IT Services	168.67	202.27	207.46	270.62	253.76
金融业	Financial Intermediation	293.03	246.78	342.71	654.48	826.34
房地产业	Real Estate	3749.14	4620.55	5531.26	6080.13	6083.06
租赁和商务服务业	Leasing and Business Services	4107.14	4707.19	6229.98	7630.99	10062.03
科学研究和技术服务业	Scientific and Technical Services	104.34	136.20	168.82	209.01	264.92
水利、环境和公共设施管理业	Management of Water Conservancy, Environment and Public Facilities	3520.44	3956.03	5042.38	6005.49	8118.76
居民服务、修理和其他服务业	Services to Households and Other Services	150.84	158.45	174.54	156.97	163.61
教育	Education	404.51	413.00	426.72	405.50	359.86
卫生和社会工作	Health and Social Work	349.60	409.74	507.90	590.84	580.72
文化、体育和娱乐业	Culture, Sports and Entertainment	204.90	267.78	351.26	434.79	420.16
公共管理、社会保障和社会组织	Public Management and Social Organization	167.16	177.96	209.21	347.47	325.01

注：本表不含票据融资、非银行金融机构的委托贷款以及外资银行的数据。

Loans of Financial Institutions at Year-end by Sector

人民币(亿元) RMB (100 million yuan)					外汇(亿美元) Foreign Currency (USD 100 million)				
2012	2013	2014	2015	2016	2012	2013	2014	2015	2016
52659.87	**59738.11**	**66345.80**	**74261.76**	**85770.22**	**515.52**	**503.14**	**476.66**	**360.87**	**271.92**
914.49	1268.70	1499.32	1487.37	1482.30	0.08	0.23	0.25	0.17	0.01
61.91	103.10	99.16	106.81	119.21	0.12	0.38	0.21	0.08	0.04
13590.36	14410.26	14267.71	14287.81	13923.27	354.94	344.33	328.11	239.00	193.24
1545.92	1599.08	1639.79	1916.77	2258.01	10.64	9.21	8.46	11.96	12.85
2372.22	2761.16	3106.85	3412.38	3330.98	0.38	0.93	0.88	0.89	0.59
4583.52	5202.70	5304.84	5607.48	5628.34	102.76	110.39	102.33	68.10	34.75
3335.86	3511.98	3776.49	3950.83	3979.91	6.55	6.08	7.76	6.64	3.46
353.83	458.04	480.30	474.14	434.08					
167.83	201.64	206.74	268.02	251.00	0.13	0.10	0.12	0.40	0.40
258.57	246.74	342.71	611.37	783.15	5.48	0.01		6.64	6.23
3748.51	4620.24	5530.95	6079.54	6083.06	0.10	0.05	0.05	0.09	
4084.06	4688.80	6202.23	7621.83	10052.54	3.67	3.02	4.54	1.41	1.37
103.79	135.97	168.73	208.20	263.50	0.09	0.04	0.01	0.12	0.21
3505.41	3955.63	5042.17	6005.29	8118.55	2.39	0.07	0.03	0.03	0.03
147.81	156.81	172.65	155.84	159.28	0.48	0.27	0.31	0.17	0.62
404.51	413.00	426.72	405.50	359.86					
348.15	407.94	506.46	589.62	579.65	0.23	0.30	0.24	0.19	0.15
204.90	267.78	350.65	434.10	420.09			0.10	0.11	0.01
167.01	177.96	209.21	347.47	325.01	0.02				

a) This table does not include bill financing, trust loans of non-banking financial institutions and data from foreign banks.

7－10 分市分行业金融机构本外币贷款年末余额（2016年）

行业	Sector	南京 Nanjing	无锡 Wuxi	徐州 Xuzhou	常州 Changzhou
总计	**Total**	**21539.37**	**9610.48**	**3283.46**	**5777.59**
农、林、牧、渔业	Agriculture, Forestry, Animal Husbandry and Fishery	129.78	351.16	39.22	145.20
采矿业	Mining	35.88	8.18	49.58	3.78
制造业	Manufacturing	2000.94	2791.98	523.93	1217.00
电力、热力、燃气及水生产和供应业	Production and Supply of Electric Power, Heat Power, Gas and Water	602.33	179.13	122.09	123.45
建筑业	Construction	743.74	176.55	123.23	270.55
批发和零售业	Wholesale and Retail Trades	1336.27	598.98	387.03	494.37
交通运输、仓储和邮政业	Transport, Storage and Post	2026.23	275.01	60.38	145.80
住宿和餐饮业	Hotels and Catering Services	79.80	38.35	24.86	29.03
信息传输、软件和信息技术服务业	Information Transfer, Software and IT Services	113.19	44.95	7.20	7.31
金融业	Financial Intermediation	342.04	104.54	12.94	113.78
房地产业	Real Estate	2380.34	506.48	182.89	304.49
租赁和商务服务业	Leasing and Business Services	2122.95	1374.15	271.80	774.94
科学研究和技术服务业	Scientific and Technical Services	79.95	27.86	1.97	19.73
水利、环境和公共设施管理业	Management of Water Conservancy, Environment and Public Facilities	2353.44	982.15	168.30	518.07
居民服务、修理和其他服务业	Services to Households and Other Services	16.41	12.00	2.73	17.20
教育	Education	98.83	15.45	22.48	23.92
卫生和社会工作	Health and Social Work	220.19	34.65	33.62	45.22
文化、体育和娱乐业	Culture, Sports and Entertainment	102.04	27.46	5.08	54.34
公共管理、社会保障和社会组织	Public Management and Social Organization	94.38	13.99	12.32	8.10
国际组织	International Organization				
对境外贷款	Overseas Loans	121.09	3.83	0.38	1.07
个人贷款及透支	Personal Loans and Overdrafts	6539.55	2043.62	1231.41	1460.26

注：本表不含票据融资、非银行金融机构的委托贷款数据，含外资银行数据。

Deposits and Loans of Financial Institutions at Year-end by Region and Sector (2016)

苏州 Suzhou	南通 Nantong	连云港 Lianyungang	淮安 Huaian	盐城 Yancheng	扬州 Yangzhou	镇江 Zhenjiang	泰州 Taizhou	宿迁 Suqian
21493.95	**6540.37**	**1968.23**	**2208.59**	**3264.88**	**3280.11**	**3302.89**	**3508.78**	**1877.84**
490.96	86.84	21.05	28.04	60.99	33.60	39.88	34.14	21.53
3.28		5.21	4.53	0.80	1.08	7.16	0.04	
4308.94	1026.60	195.12	237.64	558.95	526.88	919.09	717.58	239.12
476.85	284.07	131.40	68.35	153.36	37.90	48.48	75.25	44.49
460.44	656.96	67.38	78.95	135.73	248.42	133.39	182.89	56.83
1156.41	560.34	95.06	148.64	246.08	204.19	214.92	297.26	129.84
761.42	156.09	230.80	33.56	85.12	74.29	42.56	93.19	19.44
137.10	27.86	2.86	9.83	25.34	24.88	12.74	17.49	3.94
43.51	14.69	0.71	2.51	1.40	7.56	4.15	3.98	2.61
147.90	14.86	5.34	6.60	24.24	13.36	7.74	18.15	14.83
1422.96	499.44	52.86	101.54	113.95	165.81	156.83	146.19	49.28
2666.35	835.37	156.40	206.24	388.12	277.97	373.30	491.81	122.63
92.57	4.75	4.13	0.77	6.98	5.91	8.08	11.08	1.14
1426.06	752.60	150.31	296.99	233.69	418.39	352.94	344.53	121.29
59.87	6.14	2.63	4.21	5.37	5.48	9.68	17.22	4.68
51.17	39.31	16.97	17.02	17.88	18.61	10.33	19.11	8.78
73.96	21.71	21.22	19.99	28.65	18.79	26.60	22.74	13.36
167.67	17.70	10.74	1.95	5.95	5.63	14.68	2.34	4.57
65.73	39.90	4.98	6.15	23.50	14.66	25.61	3.03	12.66
52.90	26.92	0.13	0.03	0.97	0.53	0.66	0.10	0.12
7427.89	1468.21	792.93	935.06	1147.80	1176.16	894.07	1010.67	1006.71

a) This table contains data from foreign banks and does not contain bill financing and trust loans of non-banking institutions.

7－11 金融机构人员情况表
Number of Institutions and Staff and Workers of Banking Organizations

项　　目	Item	2012	2013	2014	2015	2016
机构数　（家）	**Number of Institutions (unit)**	**12029**	**12330**	**12686**	**13024**	**13227**
#国有商业银行	State-owned Commercial Banks	4768	4849	4839	4822	4774
政策性银行	Banks of Budgetary Subsidies	93	93	93	93	93
股份制商业银行	Joint-stock Commercial Banks	832	915	1074	1183	1325
农村商业银行	Rural Commercial Banks	2692	2932	3034	3132	3287
农村信用社	Rural Credit Cooperatives	269	146	135	109	1
财务公司	Financial Companies	9	11	12	13	14
信托投资公司	Trusted Investment Agencies	4	4	4	4	4
租赁公司	Rent Companies	1	1	1	3	5
职工人数　（人）	**Number of Staff and Workers (person)**	**204366**	**215558**	**226183**	**236576**	**241768**
#国有商业银行	State-owned Commercial Banks	99346	100229	102718	103548	102764
政策性银行	Banks of Budgetary Subsidies	2254	2341	2333	2331	2393
股份制商业银行	Joint-stock Commercial Banks	30973	34570	37513	39932	41533
农村商业银行	Rural Commercial Banks	36592	41065	43469	46054	48774
农村信用社	Rural Credit Cooperatives	3989	2293	2090	1682	542
财务公司	Financial Companies	227	292	325	360	381
信托投资公司	Trusted Investment Agencies	285	336	400	428	461
租赁公司	Rent Companies	112	121	118	228	388

注：机构数为营业网点数。
a) The Insititution means business department.

7－12 保险业务主要指标
Major Indicators of Insurance Business

指　标	Item	2012	2013	2014	2015	2016
保费收入（亿元）	**Premium（100 million yuan）**	**1301.28**	**1446.08**	**1683.76**	**1989.91**	**2690.25**
财产险	Property Insurance	440.92	518.61	606.29	672.19	733.43
#企业财产保险	Enterprise Property Insurance	36.71	39.77	41.48	41.85	41.10
家庭财产保险	Household Property Insurance	2.36	2.65	2.53	4.33	4.99
机动车辆保险	Motor Vehicle Insurance	328.91	393.49	465.69	531.15	587.92
人身意外伤害险	Accident Injury Insurance	35.20	41.88	48.47	54.22	61.32
健康险	Health Insurance	59.29	76.41	112.27	179.58	388.53
寿险	Life Insurance	765.87	809.17	916.72	1083.92	1506.96
各项赔款和给付（亿元）	**Claim and Payment（100 million yuan）**	**386.97**	**527.02**	**616.78**	**732.59**	**915.13**
财产险	Property Insurance	240.08	303.23	336.30	403.04	437.66
#企业财产保险	Enterprise Property Insurance	16.91	25.05	18.46	35.33	22.84
家庭财产保险	Household Property Insurance	0.59	0.53	0.57	1.92	2.39
机动车辆保险	Motor Vehicle Insurance	191.94	246.34	277.02	315.95	356.70
人身意外伤害险	Accident Injury Insurance	10.02	11.18	13.45	15.26	17.64
健康险	Health Insurance	17.85	24.00	35.16	46.09	55.89
寿险	Life Insurance	119.03	188.62	231.87	268.21	403.95
保险公司数（家）	**Number of Insurance Co.（unit）**	**90**	**90**	**93**	**95**	**99**
#财产保险公司	Property Insurance Co.	39	39	39	40	41
人寿保险公司	Life Insurance Co.	51	51	54	55	58
#中资保险公司	Chinese-Funded Co.	63	63	62	64	67
外资保险公司	Foreign-Funded Co.	27	27	31	31	32
保险公司分支机构（家）	**Branches of Insurance Co.（unit）**	**5718**	**5743**	**5900**	**5894**	**6253**
从业人员数（万人）	**Number of Staff and Workers（10000 persons）**	**22.80**	**23.49**	**27.34**	**39.64**	**53.83**

7－13 江苏辖区证券市场基本情况
Basic Information of Securities Markets within Jiangsu

项 目	Item	2012	2013	2014	2015	2016
上市公司数 （家）	Number of Listed Companies (unit)	236	235	254	276	317
#A 股	A Shares	231	230	252	275	316
#B 股	B Shares	5	5	5	4	4
辅导企业数 （家）	Number of Guidance Enterprises (unit)	244	206	175	193	197
证券公司数 （家）	Number of Securities Companies (unit)	6	6	6	6	6
证券营业部数 （家）	Number of Securities Business Departments (unit)	365	540	624	683	805
期货经纪公司 （家）	Number of Futures Broker Companies (unit)	11	10	10	10	10
期货经纪公司营业部 （个）	Number of Trading Offices of Futures Broker Companies (unit)	101	119	125	135	140
证券投资咨询机构数 （家）	Number of Securities Investment Consultative Institutions (unit)	2	2	3	3	3
证券从业人员数 （人）	Number of Staff and Workers in Securities (person)	11280	9333	9391	10908	11201
期货从业人员数 （人）	Number of Staff and Workers in Futures (person)	2336	2636	2468	2279	1155
证券投资者开户数 （万户）	Number of Accounts of Securities Investors (10000 accounts)	737	767	811	1075	1325
期货投资者开户数 （户）	Number of Accounts of Futures Investors (account)	195338	210026	223885	242964	178432
上市公司募集资金总额 （亿元）	Total Capital Volume Collected by Listed Companies (100 million yuan)	343.55	284	701	1213.98	2254.62
发行	Issuing	135.08	0	93	108	250
配股	Share Right Issued	5.71	0.00	4.70	9.93	0.00
增发	Adding Shares Issue	82.46	79.84	550.43	1061.31	1452.69
公司债	Debenture	120.30	203.90	53.32	35.05	551.50
上市公司总资产 （亿元）	Total Assets of Listed Companies (100 million yuan)	12489.34	10848.16	22963.26	30964.62	57063.33
上市公司净资产 （亿元）	Net Assets of Listed Companies (101 million yuan)	4360.70	5373.23	7008.93	8768.52	12855.78
上市公司总股本 （亿股）	Total Capital Shares of Listed Companies (100 million yuan)	1250.60	1379.89	1596.57	2153.45	2838.48
市价总值 （亿元）	Total Market Value (100 million yuan)	11394.27	12787.24	19630.99	36720.48	37171.14
上市公司净利润 （亿元）	Net Profit of Listed Companies (100 million yuan)	525.25	424.42	587.80	738.74	1097.29
上市公司每股收益 （元）	Per Share Income of Listed Companies (yuan)	0.42	0.36	0.35	0.33	0.37
证券经营机构证券交易量 （亿元）	Trading Volume of Securities Business Institutions (100 million yuan)	41877.16	62452.24	98654.91	351317.58	196825.91
期货经营机构代理交易量 （亿元）	Proxy Trading Volume of Futures Business Institutions (100 million yuan)	197158.93	212668.01	196768.34	305574.82	148889.90

主要统计指标解释

财政收入 指国家财政参与社会产品分配所取得的收入，是实现国家职能的财力保证。按我省口径，财政总收入为公共财政预算收入、基金收入和上划中央四税之和。

财政支出 国家财政将筹集起来的资金进行分配使用，以满足经济建设和各项事业的需要。

存款 指企业、机关、团体或居民根据资金必须收回的原则，把货币资金存入银行或其他信用机构保管并取得一定利息的一种信用活动形式。根据存款对象的不同可划分为企业存款、财政存款、机关团体存款、基本建设存款、城镇储蓄存款、农村存款等科目。它是银行信贷资金的主要来源。

贷款 指银行或其他信用机构根据资金必须归还的原则，按一定利率，为企业、个人等提供资金的一种信用活动形式。我国银行贷款分为流动资金贷款、固定资产贷款、城乡个体工商户贷款以及农业贷款等科目。

保险公司 经保险监管机构批准设立，并依法登记注册经营保险业务的公司。

保险金额 保险人承担赔偿或者给付保险金责任的最高限额。

保费 投保人为取得保险保障，按保险合同约定向保险人支付的费用。

赔款 保险人对保险事故造成的损失，根据合同约定向被保险人或受益人给予的经济补偿。

给付 人身保险合同中，保险人向被保险人或受益人给付保险金的行为。包括死伤医疗给付、满期给付和年金给付。死伤医疗给付指因人寿保险及长期健康保险业务的被保险人在保险期内发生保险责任范围内的保险事故，保险公司按保险合同约定支付给被保险人（或受益人）的保险金。满期给付指因人寿保险业务的被保险人生存至保险期满，保险公司按保险合同约定支付给被保险人的满期保险金。年金给付指保险公司因年金保险业务的被保险人生存至规定的年龄，按保险合同约定支付给被保险人的给付金额。

Explanatory Notes on Main Statistical Indicators

Government Revenue refers to income for the government finance through participating in the distribution of social products. It is the financial guarantee to ensure government functioning. In our province, total financial revenue is the sum of General public budgetary revenue, funds budgetary revenue and four taxes turned over to central government.

Government Expenditure refers to the distribution and use of the funds which the government finance has raised, so as to meet the needs of economic construction and various causes.

Deposit is a form of credit by which enterprises, institutions, organizations or residents can put money into banks and other credit institutions for safekeeping and interest earning under the principle of freedrawal. Deposits are major sources of credit funds of banks.

Loan is a form of credit by which banks and other credit institutions provide funds at certain interest rate to enterprises and individual in the light of the principle of unconditional repayment.

Insurance Companies refer to commercial insurance companies of various forms registered by law and established with the approval of insurance regulatory agencies.

Amount Insured refers to the maximum that the insurant will get for the claim of the case insured.

Premium is the fee paid by the insurant to the insurer to obtain the obligation of compensation from the insurance within the agreed terms.

Settled Claim is the compensation paid by the insurer to the insurant or beneficiary for the loss of the insurance accident in accordance with the insurance contract.

Payment is the behavior that the insurer pays insured amount to the insurant or the beneficiary according to the personal insurance contract. It includes payment for death, injury or medical treatment, payment at maturity and annuity payment. Payment for death, injury or medical treatment refers to the money paid to the insurant (or the beneficiary) in accordance with the life or health insurance contract when the insurant encounters accidents within the insured period covered in the contract. Payment at maturity refers to the payment to the insurant in accordance with the life insurance contract at the end of the insured period. Annuity payment refers to the payment to the insurant in accordance with the life insurance contract when the insurant under the annuity insurance lives to the specified age.

对外经济贸易

Foreign Trade and Economic Cooperation

简要说明

本篇资料综合反映江苏的对外贸易、利用外资、对外直接投资、对外经济合作的历年概况，重点反映对外经济贸易的近期发展状况。

一、对外贸易部分

对外贸易统计的主要内容包括：进出口货物的品种、数（重）量、金额、国别（地区）、经营单位、境内目的地、境内货源地、贸易方式、关别等项目。

对外贸易统计的资料来源于海关总署，调查方法是全面调查。

历年出口商品分类金额和历年进口商品分类金额按照联合国《国际贸易标准分类》（SITC）进行统计。

对各国（地区）进出口总额表中，出口货物按中华人民共和国关境外最终目的国（地区），进口货物按中华人民共和国关境外原产国（地区）统计。进出口总额分别按境内经营单位所在地和目的地、货源地列示。经营单位所在地是指江苏省境内进出口企业报关注册的登记地；境内货源地是指出口货物在江苏省境内的产地或原始发货地。

二、利用外资统计部分

利用外资统计的主要内容包括：对外借款、外商直接投资和外商其他投资、外商投资企业登记注册情况。

统计范围是凡经工商行政管理机关核准登记，在江苏省境内所有利用外资的单位和部门，经批准设立的中外合资经营企业、合作经营企业、外资企业、外商投资股份制企业、合作开发项目等具有法人资格的独立核算企业（包括港澳台地区投资企业），在华从事经营活动的外国及港澳台地区企业及外国公司在江苏境内设立的分支机构。

利用外资统计的资料来源于商务部门，其中，外商投资企业的登记注册情况资料来源于工商行政管理部门，调查方法是全面调查。

三、对外经济合作部分

对外经济合作统计的主要内容包括：对外承包工程、对外劳务合作的合同数、合同金额、完成营业额等。

统计范围是对外承包工程、对外劳务合作。

该制度统计单位是经各级商务主管部门批准的从事对外承包和劳务合作业务并具有法人地位的对外承包劳务企业。

资料来源是商务部门，调查方法是全面调查。

四、对外直接投资部分

对外直接投资统计的内容主要包括：境内投资主体的基本情况、境外企业的基本情况等。

统计范围主要包括境内投资主体通过直接投资在境外设立的各类公司型企业和非公司型企业。

资料来源是商务部门，调查方法是全面调查。

五、其他

历年人民币对美元、日元、港币的年平均汇价，资料来源于国家外汇管理局，各年的年平均汇价是根据当年国家外汇管理局公布的每日汇价进行加权平均计算而得出的。

Brief Introduction

Data in this chapter provide summary data of Jiangsu's foreign trade, utilization of foreign capital, overseas direct investment, contracted projects and labour cooperation with foreign countries or territories over the years, focusing on the recent situation of foreign trade and economic cooperation.

Ⅰ. Foreign Trade

Data on foreign trade include: varieties of imports and exports, amount (weight), value, countries (regions), imports and exports corporations, destination within territory, origin of goods within territory, mode of trade, types of tariffs and so on.

Sources of data on foreign trade are from the General Administration of Customs of the People's Republic of China through a comprehensive reporting system.

Customs statistics in value terms for both imports and exports are compiled according to the classifications of *UN Standard International Trade Classification* (*SITC*).

In the table on total imports and exports with related countries and regions, the export commodities are calculated at the Customs of the countries (regions) of destination and the import commodities are calculated at the Customs of the countries (regions) of origin. The total values of the import and export commodities are calculated respectively at the provinces where the import or export corporations are situated and at the provinces of destination or provinces of origin within the border of Jiangsu. The province where the import or export corporations are situated refers to the province where the import or export corporations have applied to and have been registered at the Customs. The province of origin within the border of Jiangsu refers to the province where the export commodities are produced or originally delivered.

Ⅱ. Statistics on Utilization of Foreign Capitals

Utilization of foreign capitals includes: foreign loans, foreign direct investments and other foreign investments, and the basic condition of registration of foreign funded enterprises.

The statistics cover all the units and departments which have utilized foreign capital and all the Sino-foreign joint ventures, Sino-foreign cooperative enterprises, ventures exclusively with foreign investment, foreign-funded stock companies, Sino-foreign cooperative development projects and other corporate enterprises (including the enterprises funded by the entrepreneurs from Hong Kong, Macao and Taiwan) with independent accounting system which have been approved by the Chinese government to set up in the boundary of Jiangsu.

Data on utilization of foreign capitals are from departments of commerce, of which, data on basic condition of registration of foreign funded enterprises are from industrial and commercial administrations through comprehensive reporting system.

Ⅲ. Foreign Economic Cooperation

Data on foreign economic cooperation include: number of contracted foreign projects and foreign labour services cooperation, contracted volume, complete business turnover and so on.

The statistics cover contracted projects, labour services cooperation.

The statistical unit in the scheme is the corporate enterprise engaged in contracted projects and labour services cooperation with foreign countries and has been approved by the department of commerce at various levels.

Data on foreign economic cooperation are from departments of commerce through a comprehensive reporting system.

Ⅳ. Overseas Direct Investment

Contents of statistics on overseas direct investment include basic situation of domestic investors and overseas enterprises they invest in.

The statistics cover overseas corporate and non-corporate enterprises of various forms established by domestic investors through their investment operation.

Data on foreign economic cooperation are from departments of commerce through a comprehensive reporting system.

Ⅴ. Others

The average exchange rates of RMB yuan to US dollar, Japanese yen and Hong Kong dollar over the years come from the State Administration of Exchange Control. The annual average exchange rate is calculated as the weighted mean of the daily exchange rates provided by the State Administration of Foreign Exchange in the year.

8－1 对外经济主要指标
Major Indicators of Foreign Trade and Economic Cooperation

单位:亿美元 (USD 100 million)

指标	Item	2012	2013	2014	2015	2016
进出口总额	**Total Imports and Exports**	**5480.93**	**5508.44**	**5637.62**	**5456.14**	**5096.12**
进口总额	Total Import	2195.55	2219.88	2218.93	2069.45	1902.68
初级产品	Primary Goods	329.81	346.21	330.39	253.40	233.26
工业制成品	Manufactured Goods	1816.88	1831.55	1840.54	1749.47	1591.87
出口总额	Total Exports	3285.38	3288.57	3418.69	3386.68	3193.44
初级产品	Primary Goods	54.86	52.56	56.01	50.99	51.38
工业制成品	Manufactured Goods	3189.55	3193.96	3321.42	3285.58	3077.73
协议注册外资项目 (个)	**Agreement Registered Foreign Investment Projects (unit)**	**4156**	**3453**	**3031**	**2580**	**2859**
协议注册外资	**Agreement Registered Foreign**	**571.41**	**472.68**	**431.87**	**393.61**	**431.39**
实际使用外资	**Actual Use of Foreign Capital**	**357.60**	**332.59**	**281.74**	**242.75**	**245.43**
外商投资企业基本情况	**Registered Foreign-funded Enterprises**					
年底登记户数 (户)	Number of Registered Enterprises (unit)	50461	50514	51634	53551	55938
投资总额	Total Investment	6250.00	6663.76	7181.31	7821.54	8798.68
注册资本	Registered Capital	3301.38	3542.82	3839.34	4229.01	4718.23
对外经济合作	**Economic Cooperation with Foreign Countries & Regions**					
对外承包工程	Contracted Projects					
合同金额	Contracted Value	71.98	86.57	96.61	77.96	72.87
完成营业额	Value of Turnover Fulfilled	64.68	72.63	79.54	87.61	91.11
对外劳务合作	Labor Services					
新签劳务人员合同工资总额	Total Contract Wages of New Signed Labor	6.20	7.57	12.08	5.19	4.53
劳务人员实际收入总额	Total Real Income of Signed Labor	7.74	8.88	8.54	7.46	6.96
境外投资情况	**Overseas Investment**					
新批项目数 (个)	Newly Approved projects (unit)	572	605	736	880	1067
贸易型项目	Trade	243	210	277	315	286
非贸易型项目	Nontrade	329	395	459	565	781
中方协议金额 (万美元)	Protocol Fund from China (USD 10000)	504547	614272	721571	1030460	1422365
贸易型项目	Trade	154336	128831	167014	225716	242426
非贸易型项目	Nontrade	350210	485441	554557	8047444	1179940

注:本表进出口额按 HS 统计,初级产品、工业制成品按 SITC 统计。

a) Data of imports and exports are counted by HS, data of Primary goods and manufactured goods are counted by SITC.

8-2 人民币对主要外币年平均汇价(中间价)
Average Exchange Rate of RMB Yuan Against Main Convertible Currencies (Middle Price)

单位:人民币元 (RMB yuan)

年份 Year	100美元 100 US Dollars	100日元 100 Japanese Yen	100港元 100 Hong Kong Dollars	100欧元 100 Euro
1985	293.66	1.2457	37.57	
1986	345.28	2.0694	44.22	
1987	372.21	2.5799	47.74	
1988	372.21	2.9082	47.70	
1989	376.51	2.7360	48.28	
1990	478.32	3.3233	61.39	
1991	532.33	3.9602	68.45	
1992	551.46	4.3608	71.24	
1993	576.20	5.2020	74.41	
1994	861.87	8.4370	111.53	
1995	835.10	8.9225	107.96	
1996	831.42	7.6352	107.51	
1997	828.98	6.8600	107.09	
1998	827.91	6.3488	106.88	
1999	827.83	7.2932	106.66	
2000	827.84	7.6864	106.18	
2001	827.70	6.8075	106.08	
2002	827.70	6.6237	106.07	800.58
2003	827.70	7.1466	106.24	936.13
2004	827.68	7.6552	106.23	1029.00
2005	819.17	7.4484	105.30	1019.53
2006	797.18	6.8570	102.62	1001.90
2007	760.40	6.4632	97.46	1041.75
2008	694.51	6.7427	89.19	1022.27
2009	683.10	7.2986	88.12	952.70
2010	676.95	7.7279	87.13	897.25
2011	645.88	8.1050	82.97	900.11
2012	631.25	7.9037	81.38	810.67
2013	619.32	6.3323	79.85	822.19
2014	614.28	5.8196	79.22	816.51
2015	622.84	5.1553	80.34	691.41
2016	664.23	6.1243	85.58	734.26

8－3　对外贸易进出口总额
Total Imports and Exports

单位:亿美元　　　　(USD 100 million)

年　份 Year	海关进出口总额(经营单位) Total Import and Export Value by Customs (Running Unit)			海关进出口总额(目源地) Total Import and Export Value by Customs (Goods Destination or Original Place)		
	合　计 Total	进　口 Imports	出　口 Exports	合　计 Total	进　口 Imports	出　口 Exports
1985	19.87	4.01	15.86			
1986	24.12	5.42	18.70			
1987	28.73	7.56	21.17			
1988	34.58	10.41	24.17			
1989	38.43	13.07	25.36			
1990	41.39	11.95	29.44			
1991	53.10	18.85	34.25			
1992	69.62	29.60	40.02			
1993	91.29	44.77	46.52	107.75	59.81	47.94
1994	117.59	50.73	66.86	122.47	52.86	69.61
1995	162.78	64.96	97.82	180.05	79.42	100.63
1996	206.88	90.87	116.01	222.17	102.92	119.25
1997	236.21	95.32	140.89	252.93	108.82	144.11
1998	264.26	107.75	156.51	281.66	122.09	159.57
1999	312.61	129.52	183.09	328.62	142.80	185.82
2000	456.38	198.68	257.70	491.98	228.17	263.81
2001	513.55	224.77	288.78	544.84	250.91	293.93
2002	703.05	318.25	384.80	745.09	354.80	390.29
2003	1136.70	545.30	591.40	1213.37	617.26	596.11
2004	1708.57	833.60	874.97	1794.72	913.67	881.05
2005	2279.41	1049.59	1229.82	2384.86	1138.75	1246.11
2006	2839.95	1235.77	1604.19	2990.58	1360.67	1629.91
2007	3496.71	1459.38	2037.33	3723.93	1646.19	2077.74
2008	3922.68	1542.32	2380.36	4304.81	1852.62	2452.19
2009	3388.32	1395.89	1992.43	3659.94	1585.99	2073.95
2010	4657.93	1952.42	2705.50	4987.59	2173.02	2814.58
2011	5397.59	2271.36	3126.23	5813.74	2568.98	3244.77
2012	5480.93	2195.55	3285.38	5887.95	2545.48	3342.47
2013	5508.44	2219.88	3288.57	5932.74	2594.53	3338.21
2014	5637.62	2218.93	3418.69	6093.14	2587.38	3505.75
2015	5456.14	2069.45	3386.68	5810.72	2321.73	3488.99
2016	5096.12	1902.68	3193.44	5475.16	2162.05	3313.11

8－4 按贸易方式和经济类型分的进口额
Total Imports by Type of Trade and Ownership

单位:万美元 (USD 10000)

项目	Item	2012	2013	2014	2015	2016
总值	**Total**	**21955510.1**	**22198752**	**22189296**	**20694533**	**19026827**
按贸易方式分	**Grouped by Type of Trade**					
#一般贸易	Ordinary Trade	7973301	8769215	9019211	8357709	8851895
来料加工装配贸易	Assembling Trade with Provided Raw Material	2070277	2057496	2291253	2269538	2043741
进料加工贸易	Processing Trade with Raw Material	6544109	6301517	6356784	5901943	5663378
加工贸易进口设备	Processing and Assembling with Equipments Provided	7228	2437	9074	10133	5392
外商投资企业作为投资进口的设备、物品	Import Equipments as Investment	402209	307201	256193	279724	111102
出料加工贸易	Processing Trade Providing Raw Material	3938	5463	7757	7310	2554
易货贸易	Barter Trade					
保税监管场所进出境货物	Bonded Inbounded and Outbound Goods	1382722	1197681	1286375	965732	750163
海关特殊监管区域物流货物	Areas under Special Customs Supervision Logistics Goods	3326683	3325124	2698992	2667406	1406523
按经济类型分	**Grouped by Ownership**					
#国有企业	State-owned Enterprises	1701424	1791109	1622396	1422078	1256832
集体企业	Collective-owned Enterprises	644130	626162	476376	359797	274659
私营企业	Private Enterprise	4274827	5183857	4954444	4558828	3552933
外商投资企业	Foreign-funded Enterprises	15320624	14514309	15110980	14343335	13936555
#中外合作	Sino-Foreign Cooperative	155013	177934	188642	166033	161503
中外合资	Sino-Foreign Joint Funded	4119048	3555275	3354028	3261222	3125533
外商独资	Foreign Funded	11046563	10781100	11568310	10916081	10649519

8－5 按贸易方式和经济类型分的出口额
Total Exports by Type of Trade and Ownership

单位:万美元 (USD 10000)

项目	Item	2012	2013	2014	2015	2016
出口总额	**Total**	**32853789**	**32885683**	**34186898**	**33866822**	**31934422**
按贸易方式分	**Grouped by Type of Trade**					
#一般贸易	Ordinary Trade	13954791	14552930	15834354	15524922	15543673
来料加工装配贸易	Assembling Trade with Provided Raw Material	2140849	1774011	1645108	1643571	1365992
进料加工贸易	Processing Trade with Raw Material	13879105	13232056	13276771	13151944	12527006
出料加工贸易	Processing Trade Providing Raw Material	3674	3542	4102	4112	1732
易货贸易	Barter Trade					
保税监管场所进出境货物	Bonded Inbounded and Outbound Goods	275183	305545.7	458701.9	429799	68289
海关特殊监管区域物流货物	Areas under Special Customs Supervision Logistics Goods	2471844	2917852	2872483	3029687	2076507
按经济类型分	**Grouped by Ownership**					
#国有企业	State-owned Enterprises	2758608	2876115	3061824	3073976	2870634
集体企业	Collective-owned Enterprises	692981	593346	660632	695249	567301
私营企业	Private Enterprise	8908287	9967602	10546177	10681755	9814912
外商投资企业	Foreign-funded Enterprises	20468393	19422155	19879858	19388612	18654352
#中外合作	Sino-foreign Cooperative	103405	116745	104072	100879	118985
中外合资	Sino-foreign Joint Funded	4548370	4354884	4466909	4010918	3775668
外商独资	Foreign Funded	15816618	14950527	15308876	15276815	14759699

8－6 进口商品分类总额
Total Value of Imports by Category of Commodities

单位：万美元 (USD 10000)

项	目 Item	2012	2013	2014	2015	2016
进口总额	**Total**	**21466875**	**21777542**	**21709293**	**20028665**	**18251304**
初级产品	**Primary Goods**	**3298097**	**3462069**	**3303915**	**2534000**	**2332628**
#食品及活动物	Food and Live Animals	151494	153986	155875	161218	150263
饮料及烟类	Beverages and Tobacco	5286	6663	8186	9732	8924
非食用原料(燃料除外)	Non-edible Raw Materials	2505048	2538023	2341037	1820600	1646873
矿物燃料、润滑油及有关原料	Mineral Fuels, Lubricants and Related Materials	462749	624094	674811	415774	394491
动植物油、脂及蜡	Animal and Vegetable Oils, Fats and Wax	173522	139303	124005	126677	132076
工业制成品	**Manufactured Goods**	**18168778**	**18315473**	**18405378**	**17494665**	**15918676**
#化学成品及有关产品	Chemicals and Related Products	3708609	3823328	3904546	3379824	3088347
按原料分类的制成品	Manufactured Goods Grouped by Raw Materials	1725394	1661021	1719625	1516499	1439096
机械及运输设备	Machinery and Transport Equipments	9814610	10110878	10112676	9898339	8996813
杂项制品	Miscellaneous Products	2911090	2646724	2663858	2695754	2384025

注：本表按 SITC 分类统计(8－7 表、8－8 表同)。

a) Data in this table are complied according to the classifications of SITC(The same applies to the table 8－7 and 8－8).

8－7 出口商品分类总额
Total Value of Exports by Category of Commodities

单位：万美元 (USD 10000)

项	目 Item	2012	2013	2014	2015	2016
出口总额	**Total**	**32444163**	**32465195**	**33774301**	**33365671**	**31291098**
初级产品	**Primary Goods**	**548632**	**525635**	**560070**	**509857**	**513846**
#食品及活动物	Food and Live Animals	207354	213710	251286	231475	243947
饮料及烟类	Beverages and Tobacco	528	833	1545	1902	3681
非食用原料(燃料除外)	Non-edible Raw Materials	209821	218957	228779	215152	211974
矿物燃料、润滑油及有关原料	Mineral Fuels, Lubricants and Related Materials	122658	84308	72199	55414	48339
动植物油、脂及蜡	Animal and Vegetable Oils, Fats and Wax	8272	7828	6262	5915	5904
工业制成品	**Manufactured Goods**	**31895531**	**31939561**	**33214231**	**32855814**	**30777253**
#化学成品及有关产品	Chemicals and Related Products	2160801	2289492	2494298	2315512	2325642
按原料分类的制成品	Manufactured Goods Grouped by Raw Materials	5105959	5262112	5697069	5454410	5154069
机械及运输设备	Machinery and Transport Equipments	18079423	18132848	18717293	18898514	17396215
杂项制品	Miscellaneous Products	6547831	6253457	6303895	6185859	5893657

8-8 进出口商品细分类总额(2016年)

Value of Imports and Exports by Category of Commodities (2016)

单位:万美元　　(USD 10000)

项　　目	Item	进出口总额 Total Improts and Exports Value	进　口 Imports	出　口 Exports
总　计	**Total**	**49542402**	**18251304**	**31291098**
初级产品	**Primary Goods**	**2846473**	**2332628**	**513846**
食品及活动物	**Food and Live Animal**	**394210**	**150263**	**243947**
活动物	Live Animals	1579	334	1245
肉及肉制品	Meat and Related Products	60295	57830	2466
乳品及蛋品	Dairy Products and Eggs	11636	11402	234
鱼、甲壳及软体类动物及其制品	Fish, Shellfish Products	16391	1393	14998
谷物及其制品	Cereals and Related Products	15274	5498	9776
蔬菜及水果	Vegetables and Fruits	172867	48378	124489
糖、糖制品及蜂蜜	Sugar, Sugar Products and Natural Honey	12048	1745	10303
咖啡、茶、可可、调味料及其制品	Coffee, Tea, Cocoa, Spices and Related Products	18148	10037	8111
饲料(不包括未碾磨谷物)	Forage	33026	4825	28200
杂项食品	Miscellaneous Food	52948	8822	44126
饮料及烟类	**Beverages and Tobacco**	**12605**	**8924**	**3681**
#饮料	Beverages	10320	8924	1396
非食用原料(燃料除外)	**Non-edible Materials**	**1858847**	**1646873**	**211974**
生皮及生毛皮	Raw Hides and Raw Furs	15631	15578	53
油籽及含油果实	Oil Seeds and Oil-bearing Fruits	15538	15480	58
生橡胶(包括合成橡胶及再生橡胶)	Raw Rubber	98136	81247	16889
软木及木材	Cork and Wood	208860	199040	9821
纸浆及废纸	Paper Pulp and Paper Waste	300618	299450	1168
纺织纤维(羊毛条除外)及其废料	Textile Fiber and Waste	320783	217098	103685
天然肥料及矿物(煤、石油及宝石除外)	Natural Fertilizers and Minerals	43828	35998	7831
金属矿砂及金属废料	Metallic Ore and Metallic Waste	769676	762251	7425
其他动、植物原料	Other Raw Materials of Animals and Plants	85778	20733	65046
矿物燃料、润滑油及有关原料	**Mineral Fuels, Lubricants and Related Materials**	**442830**	**394491**	**48339**
煤、焦炭及煤砖	Coal, Coke and Coal Brick	55860	49807	6053
石油、石油产品及有关原料	Petroleum, Petroleum Products and Related Materials	208081	165992	42089
天然气及人造气	Natural Gas and Man-made Gas	178890	178692	198
动植物油、脂及蜡	**Animal and Vegetable Oils, Fats and Wax**	**137981**	**132076**	**5904**
动物油、脂	Animal Oil, Fat	5466	1891	3575
植物油、脂	Vegetable Oil, Fat	128120	127016	1105
已加工的动植物油、脂及动植物蜡	Processed Animal and Vegetable Oils, Fats and Wax	4395	3169	1225

8－8 续表 Continued

单位:万美元 (USD 10000)

指标	Item	进出口总额 Total Improts and Exports Value	进口 Imports	出口 Exports
工业制成品	**Manufactured Goods**	**46695929**	**15918676**	**30777253**
化学成品及有关产品	**Chemicals and Related Products**	**5413989**	**3088347**	**2325642**
有机化学品	Organic Chemicals	2266752	1396925	869827
无机化学品	Inorganic Chemicals	262680	132447	130233
染料、鞣料及着色料	Dye, Tanning Material and Colouring Materials	159828	58356	101473
医药品	Pharmaceutical Products	422527	230863	191664
精油、香料及盥洗、光洁制品	Essential Oils, Perfumed Materials, Toilet Preparations, Bright and clean products	135174	42524	92651
制成肥料	Finished Fertilizers	63480	13972	49508
初级形状的塑料	Primary Shaped Plastics	829482	524817	304664
非初级形状的塑料	Non-primary Shaped Plastics	527414	312495	214919
其他化学原料及产品	Other Chemical Materials and Related Products	746652	375948	370704
按原料分类的制成品	**Manufactured Goods Grouped by Materials**	**6593165**	**1439096**	**5154069**
皮革、皮革制品及已鞣毛皮	Leather and Related Products and Tanned Furs	38541	20532	18009
橡胶制品	Rubber and Related Products	233465	70039	163426
软木及木制品(家具除外)	Cork and Wooden Products	283671	16048	267623
纸及纸板;纸浆、纸及纸板制品	Paper and Paperboard; Articles of Paper Pulp, of Paper or Paperboard	320841	57635	263206
纺纱、织物、制成品及有关产品	Textile Fabrics, Textile Materials and Related Products	2217429	214605	2002824
非金属矿物制品	Non-metalic Mineral Products	438607	154419	284188
钢铁	Iron and Steel	1230782	279031	951752
有色金属	Nonferrous Metal	594175	353988	240188
金属制品	Metallic Products	1235654	272800	962853
机械及运输设备	**Machinery and Transport Equipment**	**26393028**	**8996813**	**17396215**
动力机械及设备	Power-driven Machinery and Related Equipment	934547	284553	649993
特种工业专用机械	Special Industrial Machinery of Particular Use	1423341	650907	772434
金工机械	Metalworking Machinery	367806	240572	127234
通用工业机械设备及零件	Equipment and Accessories for General Industrial	2339218	756888	1582330
办公用机械及自动数据处理设备	Machinery for Office Use and Automatic Data-processing Equipment	4723533	685479	4038054
电信及声音的录制及重放装置设备	Telecommunication and Recorders	4110792	582456	3528336
电力机械、器具及其电气零件	Electronic Machinery, Equipment and Accessories	10522598	5421857	5100741
陆路车辆(包括气垫式)	Overland Vehicles	1270594	331764	938831
其他运输设备	Other Transport Equipment	700599	42337	658262
杂项制品	**Miscellaneous Products**	**8277682**	**2384025**	**5893657**
活动房屋;卫生、水道、供热及照明装置	Movable Houses, Public Health, Waterway, Heat Supply and Lighting Installation	192470	12714	179756
家具及其零件;褥垫及类似填充制品	Furniture and Accessories, Beddings and Filler Products and Similar Products for Stuffing	602280	21735	580544
旅行用品、手提包及类似品	Travel Articles, Handbag and Similar Articles	139032	3590	135442
服装及衣着附件	Garments and Clothing Accessories	2302813	45766	2257046
鞋靴	Parts of Footwear	298435	94776	203658
专业、科学及控制用仪器和装置	Instruments and Equipment for Professional, Scientific and Control Use	2811868	1602704	1209164
摄影器材、光学物品及钟表	Photographic and Optical Equipment and Clocks	597851	349070	248781
杂项制品	Miscellaneous Products	1332935	253670	1079265

8-9 进出口商品细分类总额(RMB)(2016年)
Value of Imports and Exports by Category of Commodities(RMB)(2016)

单位:万元 (10000)

项目	Item	进出口总额 Total Improts and Exports Value	进口 Imports	出口 Exports
总计	**Total**	**326984094**	**120595373**	**206388721**
初级产品	**Primary Goods**	**18801222**	**15415104**	**3386117**
食品及活动物	**Food and Live Animal**	**2600551**	**991377**	**1609174**
活动物	Live Animals	10437	2206	8231
肉及肉制品	Meat and Related Products	397794	381550	16244
乳品及蛋品	Dairy Products and Eggs	76873	75329	1543
鱼、甲壳及软体类动物及其制品	Fish, Shellfish Products	108220	9229	98991
谷物及其制品	Cereals and Related Products	100773	36198	64575
蔬菜及水果	Vegetables and Fruits	1140377	318824	821553
糖、糖制品及蜂蜜	Sugar, Sugar Products and Natural Honey	79443	11505	67938
咖啡、茶、可可、调味料及其制品	Coffee, Tea, Cocoa, Spices and Related Products	119516	66213	53303
饲料(不包括未碾磨谷物)	Forage	217476	31890	185586
杂项食品	Miscellaneous Food	349643	58433	291210
饮料及烟类	**Beverages and Tobacco**	**83718**	**59175**	**24542**
#饮料	Beverages	68404	59175	9228
非食用原料(燃料除外)	**Non-edible Materials**	**12270494**	**10874498**	**1395996**
生皮及生毛皮	Raw Hides and Raw Furs	102963	102610	353
油籽及含油果实	Oil Seeds and Oil-bearing Fruits	102303	101925	379
生橡胶(包括合成橡胶及再生橡胶)	Raw Rubber	648651	537359	111292
软木及木材	Cork and Wood	1377810	1313052	64758
纸浆及废纸	Paper Pulp and Paper Waste	1983736	1976030	7706
纺织纤维(羊毛条除外)及其废料	Textile Fiber and Waste	2114974	1432366	682608
天然肥料及矿物(煤、石油及宝石除外)	Natural Fertilizers and Minerals	289073	237250	51822
金属矿砂及金属废料	Metallic Ore and Metallic Waste	5084995	5036858	48137
其他动、植物原料	Other Raw Materials of Animals and Plants	565989	137048	428941
矿物燃料、润滑油及有关原料	**Mineral Fuels, Lubricants and Related Materials**	**2931811**	**2614478**	**317332**
煤、焦炭及煤砖	Coal, Coke and Coal Brick	370702	330863	39839
石油、石油产品及有关原料	Petroleum, Petroleum Products and Related Materials	1372366	1096179	276187
天然气及人造气	Natural Gas and Man-made Gas	1188743	1187436	1307
动植物油、脂及蜡	**Animal and Vegetable Oils, Fats and Wax**	**914649**	**875577**	**39073**
动物油、脂	Animal Oil, Fat	35969	12448	23521
植物油、脂	Vegetable Oil, Fat	849583	842127	7456
已加工的动植物油、脂及动植物蜡	Processed Animal and Vegetable Oils, Fats and Wax	29097	21002	8095

8-9 续表 Continued

单位:万元 (10000)

指标	Item	进出口总额 Total Improts and Exports Value	进口 Imports	出口 Exports
工业制成品	**Manufactured Goods**	**308182872**	**105180268**	**203002604**
化学成品及有关产品	**Chemicals and Related Products**	**35728273**	**20400589**	**15327683**
有机化学品	Organic Chemicals	14958059	9225849	5732210
无机化学品	Inorganic Chemicals	1733411	874967	858444
染料、鞣料及着色料	Dye, Tanning Material and Colouring Materials	1054447	385671	668775
医药品	Pharmaceutical Products	2792903	1525786	1267117
精油、香料及盥洗、光洁制品	Essential Oils, Perfumed Materials, Toilet Preparations, Bright and clean products	892297	280761	611535
制成肥料	Finished Fertilizers	414959	91404	323555
初级形状的塑料	Primary Shaped Plastics	5472722	3467252	2005470
非初级形状的塑料	Non-primary Shaped Plastics	3483163	2066329	1416833
其他化学原料及产品	Other Chemical Materials and Related Products	4926313	2482570	2443743
按原料分类的制成品	**Manufactured Goods Grouped by Materials**	**43485770**	**9509378**	**33976392**
皮革、皮革制品及已鞣毛皮	Leather and Related Products and Tanned Furs	254866	135561	119305
橡胶制品	Rubber and Related Products	1539114	463068	1076047
软木及木制品(家具除外)	Cork and Wooden Products	1869383	105966	1763417
纸及纸板;纸浆、纸及纸板制品	Paper and Paperboard; Articles of Paper Pulp, of Paper or Paperboard	2115358	380874	1734484
纺纱、织物、制成品及有关产品	Textile Fabrics, Textile Materials and Related Products	14616796	1417691	13199105
非金属矿物制品	Non-metalic Mineral Products	2897175	1020406	1876769
钢铁	Iron and Steel	8114986	1843051	6271934
有色金属	Nonferrous Metal	3923858	2339641	1584217
金属制品	Metallic Products	8154234	1803120	6351114
机械及运输设备	**Machinery and Transport Equipment**	**174190408**	**59438692**	**114751717**
动力机械及设备	Power-driven Machinery and Related Equipment	6168925	1884258	4284667
特种工业专用机械	Special Industrial Machinery of Particular Use	9379613	4289504	5090109
金工机械	Metalworking Machinery	2425321	1586503	838818
通用工业机械设备及零件	Equipment and Accessories for General Industrial	15433452	5000735	10432717
办公用机械及自动数据处理设备	Machinery for Office Use and Automatic Data-processing Equipment	31168880	4528344	26640536
电信及声音的录制及重放装置设备	Telecommunication and Recorders	27157906	3854464	23303442
电力机械、器具及其电气零件	Electronic Machinery, Equipment and Accessories	69456800	35822235	33634565
陆路车辆(包括气垫式)	Overland Vehicles	8381752	2193055	6188697
其他运输设备	Other Transport Equipment	4617761	279595	4338165
杂项制品	**Miscellaneous Products**	**54657679**	**15762286**	**38895393**
活动房屋;卫生、水道、供热及照明装置	Movable Houses, Public Health, Waterway, Heat Supply and Lighting Installation	1272505	84411	1188094
家具及其零件;褥垫及类似填充制品	Furniture and Accessories, Beddings and Filler Products and Similar Products for Stuffing	3972290	143688	3828602
旅行用品、手提包及类似品	Travel Articles, Handbag and Similar Articles	917572	23696	893876
服装及衣着附件	Garments and Clothing Accessories	15199025	302770	14896256
鞋靴	Parts of Footwear	1972033	626838	1345195
专业、科学及控制用仪器和装置	Instruments and Equipment for Professional, Scientific and Control Use	18578704	10597339	7981364
摄影器材、光学物品及钟表	Photographic and Optical Equipment and Clocks	3947726	2308800	1638926
杂项制品	Miscellaneous Products	8797825	1674745	7123080

8-10 进出口商品主要国家和地区
Imports and Exports Value by Country and Region

单位:万美元 (USD 10000)

国家(地区)	Country (Region)	2015 进出口 Imports and Exports	2015 进口 Imports	2015 出口 Exports	2016 进出口 Imports and Exports	2016 进口 Imports	2016 出口 Exports
亚　洲	**Asia**	**30355414**	**14555096**	**15800319**	**27595198**	**13194534**	**14400664**
#巴林	Bahrain	12831	3762	9069	9979	2304	7675
孟加拉国	Bangladesh	288883	5401	283483	294679	5825	288854
缅甸	Myanmar	66321	744	65577	77278	1628	75650
柬埔寨	Cambodia	84656	11506	73150	91638	14030	77608
塞浦路斯	Cyprus	13199	19	13179	14972	45	14927
中国香港	Hong Kong, China	3524518	45555	3478963	2789854	62922	2726932
印度	India	1089289	126288	963001	1091724	99185	992540
印度尼西亚	Indonesia	745603	255650	489954	765010	249764	515247
伊朗	Iran	212165	61238	150927	196825	34401	162424
以色列	Israel	128461	32735	95726	126051	28653	97398
日本	Japan	5281906	2473708	2808198	5006702	2408686	2598016
科威特	Kuwait	105384	67766	37618	61030	26902	34128
中国澳门	Macao, China	20561	207	20355	10892	274	10618
马来西亚	Malaysia	1198194	669363	528831	1143064	632689	510376
巴基斯坦	Pakistan	161616	15359	146257	170573	9721	160852
菲律宾	Philippines	555582	251884	303697	605986	284472	321514
卡塔尔	Qatar	122527	83810	38717	93871	70291	23580
沙特阿拉伯	Saudi Arabia	534354	287755	246599	385842	199464	186378
新加坡	Singapore	1243447	519578	723869	979513	386313	593200
韩国	Korea, Rep.	5849986	4182164	1667822	5421156	3752512	1668644
斯里兰卡	Sri Lanka	44746	4427	40319	46893	5700	41193
叙利亚	Syria	7855	55	7801	8554	40	8514
泰国	Thailand	1144950	533141	611809	1206156	544977	661179
土耳其	Turkey	314344	21760	292585	305509	18127	287381
阿拉伯联合酋长国	United Arab Emirates	435557	57264	378293	413673	76506	337168
越南	Vietnam	910393	206841	703553	983470	238776	744694
中国台湾	Taiwan, China	4344067	2965719	1378348	3756786	2758346	998440
非　洲	**Africa**	**1025487**	**155410**	**870077**	**926501**	**155925**	**770577**
#喀麦隆	Cameroon	15955	7987	7968	10593	4411	6183
埃及	Egypt	111683	2001	109682	106444	1146	105298
加蓬	Gabon	8151	6000	2151	7447	5597	1850
摩洛哥	Morocco	30522	3357	27166	35183	4928	30255
尼日利亚	Nigeria	115818	6157	109661	77250	8438	68813
南非	South Africa	248598	58716	189883	236534	63916	172618
欧　洲	**Europe**	**9258347**	**2644028**	**6614319**	**9046009**	**2512704**	**6533305**
#比利时	Belgium	354705	92480	262225	340289	91583	248706
丹麦	Denmark	118479	27955	90524	116961	29046	87915
英国	United Kindom	1076308	185545	890763	1005785	160478	845307

单位：万美元 (USD 10000)

国别（地区）	Country (Region)	2015 进出口 Imports and Exports	2015 进口 Imports	2015 出口 Exports	2016 进出口 Imports and Exports	2016 进口 Imports	2016 出口 Exports
德国	Germany	2098657	1004265	1094392	2058395	932319	1126076
法国	France	595682	188677	407005	580088	190343	389745
爱尔兰	Ireland	59874	13554	46321	47471	11611	35860
意大利	Italy	581531	186073	395457	560301	180013	380288
荷兰	Netherlands	1412581	127685	1284897	1353573	93947	1259627
希腊	Greece	74137	3273	70865	72712	1857	70856
葡萄牙	Portugal	41247	6532	34715	79552	8087	71465
西班牙	Spain	403555	86320	317235	425336	94103	331234
奥地利	Austria	109242	72612	36631	121866	83556	38311
芬兰	Finland	124222	55658	68564	108048	49467	58581
匈牙利	Hungary	142451	31565	110886	142814	38925	103889
挪威	Norway	106379	49581	56798	90999	36168	54831
波兰	Poland	278772	24964	253809	272590	26579	246011
罗马尼亚	Romania	72080	10979	61101	83268	11915	71353
瑞典	Sweden	288481	181241	107240	267789	166995	100794
瑞士	Switzerland	165188	100103	65085	169498	96728	72770
俄罗斯联邦	Russia Fed.	410778	63371	347408	467069	80913	386156
乌克兰	Ukraine	68367	29166	39201	84465	32285	52180
捷克	Czech Rep.	245795	52265	193530	242378	53103	189275
拉丁美洲	**Latin America**	**2800262**	**906979**	**1893283**	**2638599**	**948219**	**1690380**
#阿根廷	Argentina	186011	75363	110649	190570	94607	95963
巴西	Brazil	1010193	551116	459077	938124	564537	373587
智利	Chile	246664	74115	172550	245358	70130	175228
哥伦比亚	Colombia	105917	3571	102345	95538	1330	94208
危地马拉	Guatemala	27057	3702	23355	25141	3458	21683
墨西哥	Mexico	653509	78504	575005	667090	105856	561234
巴拿马	Panama	81223	48	81175	81706	55	81651
秘鲁	Peru	121448	26734	94714	109110	23279	85831
乌拉圭	Uruguay	65232	36698	28534	49502	28230	21272
委内瑞拉	Venezuela	27728	1481	26247	24028	5544	18484
北美洲	**North America**	**9485545**	**1647856**	**7837689**	**9139071**	**1441506**	**7697566**
#加拿大	Canada	796430	251221	545210	730458	213650	516808
美国	United States	8676316	1396635	7279681	8400748	1227817	7172931
大洋洲	**Oceania**	**1633275**	**782139**	**851136**	**1614297**	**772365**	**841932**
#澳大利亚	Australia	1328826	683275	645551	1302733	668056	634678
新西兰	New Zealand	132483	62595	69888	149164	72587	76577
巴布亚新几内亚	Papua New Guinea	23161	17034	6128	23227	18443	4784
附：东南亚国家联盟	Association of Southeast-Asia Nations	5965438	2454704	3510734	5867436	2356850	3510585
欧洲联盟	European Union	8473473	2394898	6078575	8210844	2262865	5947979
亚太经济合作组织	Asia-Pacific Economic Cooperation	38823474	16385804	22437670	35990265	15032352	20957913

8-11 进出口商品主要国家和地区(RMB)
Imports and Exports Value by Country and Region(RMB)

单位:万元 (10000)

国家（地区）	Country (Region)	2015 进出口 Imports and Exports	2015 进口 Imports	2015 出口 Exports	2016 进出口 Imports and Exports	2016 进口 Imports	2016 出口 Exports
亚　洲	**Asia**	**188480041**	**90372638**	**98107403**	**182169018**	**87186590**	**94982428**
#巴林	Bahrain	79332	23164	56168	65762	15150	50612
孟加拉国	Bangladesh	1792478	33528	1758950	1940827	38568	1902259
缅甸	Myanmar	411732	4635	407096	509919	10785	499133
柬埔寨	Cambodia	525268	71492	453776	603934	92508	511426
塞浦路斯	Cyprus	83058	121	82938	98295	297	97998
中国香港	Hong Kong, China	21943584	282847	21660737	18411339	416424	17994915
印度	India	6761065	783576	5977490	7200204	655095	6545109
印度尼西亚	Indonesia	4626170	1584788	3041382	5052572	1653271	3399301
伊朗	Iran	1316732	379576	937157	1298600	227875	1070726
以色列	Israel	796258	202758	593500	831163	189057	642106
日本	Japan	32785668	15353565	17432103	33053449	15915491	17137957
科威特	Kuwait	652931	419597	233334	401814	176816	224998
中国澳门	Macao, China	128567	1281	127286	72445	1809	70636
马来西亚	Malaysia	7437085	4156942	3280142	7551782	4186003	3365779
巴基斯坦	Pakistan	1003777	95190	908587	1124349	64421	1059928
菲律宾	Philippines	3450203	1564189	1886013	4001054	1882974	2118080
卡塔尔	Qatar	760173	520720	239452	623955	468805	155150
沙特阿拉伯	Saudi Arabia	3310847	1782471	1528376	2544102	1317087	1227016
新加坡	Singapore	7712038	3219951	4492087	6467496	2552382	3915113
韩国	Korea, Rep.	36333875	25984303	10349572	35789091	24780111	11008980
斯里兰卡	Sri Lanka	277943	27499	250444	309459	37704	271755
叙利亚	Syria	48871	342	48530	56423	260	56163
泰国	Thailand	7110921	3311744	3799177	7965796	3605255	4360541
土耳其	Turkey	1948949	135206	1813743	2012024	119760	1892264
阿拉伯联合酋长国	United Arab Emirates	2697084	352167	2344917	2729795	508431	2221364
越南	Vietnam	5652120	1284282	4367838	6499302	1581662	4917641
中国台湾	Taiwan, China	26938588	18407979	8530609	24798348	18219298	6579050
非　洲	**Africa**	**6359397**	**963521**	**5395876**	**6107066**	**1029588**	**5077479**
#喀麦隆	Cameroon	98829	49494	49335	69864	29192	40672
埃及	Egypt	692294	12340	679954	701353	7541	693812
加蓬	Gabon	50628	37265	13362	49093	36940	12153
摩洛哥	Morocco	190074	20846	169228	231882	32444	199438
尼日利亚	Nigeria	718303	38002	680300	509207	55803	453404
南非	South Africa	1541877	364306	1177572	1560748	422773	1137974
欧　洲	**Europe**	**57488837**	**16427804**	**41061033**	**59694999**	**16607593**	**43087407**
#比利时	Belgium	2200468	574621	1625847	2245498	605712	1639786
丹麦	Denmark	734683	174158	560525	771633	191921	579712
英国	United Kindom	6682080	1151925	5530156	6635717	1059930	5575787

单位：万元 (10000)

国别（地区）	Country (Region)	2015 进出口 Imports and Exports	2015 进口 Imports	2015 出口 Exports	2016 进出口 Imports and Exports	2016 进口 Imports	2016 出口 Exports
德国	Germany	13037249	6243179	6794071	13590375	6163901	7426474
法国	France	3697929	1172410	2525519	3829385	1259153	2570231
爱尔兰	Ireland	370857	83929	286928	312894	76460	236434
意大利	Italy	3609339	1156475	2452864	3694627	1189167	2505460
荷兰	Netherlands	8773270	792951	7980319	8928376	620657	8307719
希腊	Greece	460589	20236	440354	479488	12258	467229
葡萄牙	Portugal	256108	40481	215627	524092	53570	470522
西班牙	Spain	2504991	535742	1969249	2807916	622689	2185227
奥地利	Austria	679448	451765	227683	804720	551820	252900
芬兰	Finland	771019	345496	425523	712958	326747	386211
匈牙利	Hungary	884860	196380	688481	942873	257499	685374
挪威	Norway	659709	308181	351528	598470	237620	360850
波兰	Poland	1731040	155200	1575840	1799206	175509	1623696
罗马尼亚	Romania	447704	68230	379474	549505	78871	470634
瑞典	Sweden	1788115	1123730	664386	1767581	1103310	664271
瑞士	Switzerland	1029156	624628	404528	1118274	639090	479184
俄罗斯联邦	Russia Fed.	2551168	392051	2159117	3083736	534887	2548849
乌克兰	Ukraine	423471	180070	243401	557564	213322	344242
捷克	Czech Rep.	1527062	324665	1202396	1599073	351103	1247970
拉丁美洲	**Latin America**	**17369809**	**5640442**	**11729367**	**17397113**	**6254065**	**11143048**
#阿根廷	Argentina	1157447	471497	685950	1260076	628346	631730
巴西	Brazil	6264564	3425422	2839142	6179854	3714956	2464898
智利	Chile	1529312	459760	1069552	1617912	462781	1155131
哥伦比亚	Colombia	655979	22048	633931	629058	8734	620324
危地马拉	Guatemala	167842	23104	144739	165513	22785	142728
墨西哥	Mexico	4052393	487850	3564543	4400784	700412	3700371
巴拿马	Panama	507087	300	506788	536800	361	536439
秘鲁	Peru	754530	166813	587718	720114	153774	566339
乌拉圭	Uruguay	404982	228337	176645	327287	187343	139944
委内瑞拉	Venezuela	171516	9085	162430	158764	36718	122045
北美洲	**North America**	**58859039**	**10216531**	**48642507**	**60311041**	**9524790**	**50786252**
#加拿大	Canada	4938157	1557797	3380360	4816585	1407449	3409135
美国	United States	53839984	8658732	45181252	55442448	8117088	47325360
大洋洲	**Oceania**	**10130441**	**4845321**	**5285120**	**10658563**	**5103422**	**5555141**
#澳大利亚	Australia	8243536	4232850	4010687	8603942	4415410	4188533
新西兰	New Zealand	821305	387654	433650	984730	478616	506114
巴布亚新几内亚	Papua New Guinea	143601	105708	37893	153437	121847	31590
附：东南亚国家联盟	Association of Southeast-Asia Nations	37027156	15235380	21791776	38752815	15592368	23160447
欧洲联盟	European Union	52615130	14880143	37734987	54184047	14957896	39226150
亚太经济合作组织	Asia-Pacific Economic Cooperation	241028913	101723800	139305112	237590585	99325717	138264869

8－12 主要商品进口数量和金额
Major Import Commodities in Volume and Value

商品名称		Item		2015 数量 Volume	2015 金额（千美元）Value (USD 1000)	2016 数量 Volume	2016 金额（千美元）Value (USD 1000)
冻鱼	（吨）	Frozen Fish	(ton)	1334	4847	8815	21648
鲜、干水果及坚果	（吨）	Fresh, Dried Fruits and Nuts	(ton)	69179	54279	59887	40141
谷物及谷物粉	（万吨）	Cereals and Cereal Powder	(10000 tons)	146	429850	93	238673
大豆	（万吨）	Soybean	(ton)	1154	4836189	1474	5960792
食用植物油	（万吨）	Edible Vegetable Oil	(10000 tons)	89	648537	92	649605
食糖	（万吨）	Sugar	(10000 tons)	4	16697	1	4359
酒类	（千升）	Alcohol	(kiloliter)	43822	91509	35579	82399
饲料用鱼粉	（万吨）	Fish Powder for Forage	(10000 tons)	1	16690	1	14988
纸烟	（万条）	Cigarette	(10000 carton)				
天然橡胶（包括胶乳）	（万吨）	Natural Rubber	(10000 tons)	13	193505	13	174571
合成橡胶（包括胶乳）	（吨）	Synthetic Rubber	(ton)	264435	548071	361289	635735
原木	（万立方米）	Log	(10 kilostere)	737	1299357	838	1286289
锯材	（万立方米）	Wood Sawn	(10 kilostere)	199	521125	217	502766
胶合板及类似多层板	（万立方米）	Veneer	(10 kilostere)	1	3379	1	4867
纸浆	（万吨）	Paper Pulp	(10000 tons)	449	2885979	402	2338017
羊毛	（吨）	Wool	(ton)	177073	1360700	159563	1327659
毛条	（吨）	Woolen Yarn	(ton)	1844	19610	966	8530
棉花	（万吨）	Cotton	(10000 tons)	38	656949	23	393598
二醋酸纤维丝束	（吨）	Acetate	(ton)	353	2128	263	1439
纺织用合成纤维	（万吨）	Synthietic Fibre for Spinning	(10000 tons)	9	225952	9	175124
人造纤维短纤	（吨）	Man-made Fibre	(ton)	32906	66087	25249	58601
铁矿砂及其精矿	（万吨）	Iron Ores	(10000 tons)	9890	6279782	10819	6568325
锰矿砂及其精矿	（万吨）	Manganese Ores	(10000 tons)	12	14118	26	31347
铜矿砂及其精矿	（万吨）	Copper Ores	(10000 tons)	9	123238	4	45206
铬矿砂及其精矿	（万吨）	Chrome Ores	(10000 tons)	33	62713	26	38375
氧化铝	（万吨）	Alumina	(10000 tons)	93	333207	45	128738
煤及褐煤	（万吨）	Coal and Brown Coal	(10000 tons)	506	392273	572	497976
成品油	（万吨）	Petroleum Products Refined	(10000 tons)	125	961360	134	888891
液化石油气及其他烃类气	（万吨）	Liquefied Petroleum Gas	(10000 tons)	304	1810010	463	1786918
甲苯	（吨）	Toluene	(ton)	233736	166107	216858	132794
二甲苯	（万吨）	Xylene	(10000 tons)	312	2639679	362	2828985

商 品 名 称 Item		2015		2016	
		数 量 Volume	金 额（千美元）Value（USD 1000）	数 量 Volume	金 额（千美元）Value（USD 1000）
苯乙烯 （吨）	Styrene （ton）	2079402	2330025	1792643	1861138
乙二醇 （吨）	Glycol （ton）	5250958	4200021	3493448	2238226
异氰酸酯 （吨）	Isocyanic Ester （ton）	21640	65948	18991	64328
对苯二甲酸 （吨）	Telephthalic Acid （ton）	198418	124449	38794	22186
己内酰胺 （吨）	Caprolactam （ton）	75771	118274	87445	109337
医药品 （吨）	Pharmaceuticals （ton）	8431	2170385	11774	2308628
美容化妆品及护肤品 （吨）	Cosmetics and Skin Care Products （ton）	5302	97589	5315	100298
肥料 （万吨）	Fertilizer （10000 tons）	23	78196	53	135628
合成有机染料 （吨）	Synthetic Organic Dyeing （ton）	3057	32028	3066	32859
钛白粉 （吨）	Titanium Dioxide （ton）	7832	24688	6793	19575
聚合物油漆及清漆 （吨）	Polymer Paint and Varnish （ton）	25972	143592	25092	125613
感光材料	Sensitization Material		41605		39239
初级形状的塑料 （万吨）	Primary-shape Plastic （10000 tons）	299	5404619	281	4934420
初级形状的聚乙烯 （吨）	Primary-shape Polythene （ton）	571374	767998	511978	635634
初级形状的线型低密度聚乙烯（吨）	Primary-shape Line-type Low-density Polythene （ton）	196424	259359	211079	258977
初级形状的聚丙烯 （吨）	Primary-shape Polypropylene （ton）	344613	445329	332714	381240
初级形状的聚苯乙烯聚合物（吨）	Primary-shape Polystyrene （ton）	388118	631610	385320	567429
ABS 树脂 （吨）	ABS Colophony （ton）	163229	290523	158743	249154
初级形状的聚氯乙烯 （吨）	Primary-shape PVC （ton）	158591	165516	127798	141087
初级形状的聚酯 （吨）	Primary-shape Polyester （ton）	400430	627577	253393	512919
聚酯切片 （吨）	Polyester Slice （ton）	54177	71604	56532	70586
聚酰胺切片 （吨）	Polyamide Slice （ton）	95716	246972	81784	182560
非泡沫塑料的板、片、膜、箔 （吨）	Non-foam Plastic Board, Slice, Film and Foil （ton）	219915	2047664	215698	2137064
废塑料 （万吨）	Waste Plastic （10000 tons）	55	328311	62	313752
杀虫剂、除草剂及类似品 （吨）	Insecticide、Herbicide and the Like （ton）	18987	313883	18645	249206
牛皮革及马皮革 （吨）	Cowskin and Horse Leather （ton）	48321	219197	40833	165780
废纸 （万吨）	Waste Paper （10000 tons）	378	724023	362	656482
纸及纸板（未切成形的） （万吨）	Paper and Paper Board （10000 tons）	43	509037	46	517484
纺织纱线、织物及制品	Textile Yarn, Textile and Their Products		2419874		2160787
服装及衣着附件	Garments and Clothing Accessories		394424		461180
玻璃纤维及其制品 （吨）	Fiberglass （ton）	65283	273791	48593	242993
钻石 （千克）	Diamond （kg）	39	213	2	144
废金属 （万吨）	Waste Metal （10000 tons）	45	392192	23	211956
钢坯及粗锻件 （万吨）	Billet and Crude Forgings （10000 tons）	12	60301	8	33187

商 品 名 称	Item	2015 数 量 Volume	2015 金 额（千美元）Value（USD 1000）	2016 数 量 Volume	2016 金 额（千美元）Value（USD 1000）
钢材 （万吨）	Rolled Steel （10000 tons）	195	2386240	213	2262520
钢铁制标准紧固件 （吨）	Iron and Steel Standard Solidity Articles （ton）	50791	498121	53561	511136
未锻造的铜及铜材 （吨）	Copper and its Material （ton）	268932	2072795	246277	1768396
未锻造的铝及铝材 （吨）	Aluminium and its Material （ton）	152089	943744	149136	890177
钢铁或铝制结构体及其部件（吨）	Iron and Steel and Aluminium Units and Parts （ton）	31620	118726	23045	72353
蒸汽锅炉及过热水锅炉 （台）	Steam Boiler （set）	15	5113	36	4310
活塞式内燃机的零件 （吨）	Parts of Piston Internal-combustion Engine （ton）	20664	440094	25056	458307
液泵及液体提升机 （台）	Hydraulic Pumps and Lifters （set）	36721839	651585	22257634	649293
制冷设备用压缩机 （万台）	Compressors for Refrigerating Equipment （10000 sets）	161	162801	167	113798
空气调节器 （台）	Air Conditioners （set）	2685	21954	5349	7260
冷冻机和制冷设备 （台）	Refrigerating Equipment （set）	227074	472808	157498	324321
非家用型水的过滤、净化机器 （台）	Non-household Water Purify Machines （set）	22909	60576	16774	47727
饮料及液体食品灌装设备 （台）	Beverage Filling Equipment （set）	78	48685	47	24087
机械提升搬运装卸设备及零件	Machine Lifting, Transporting and Loading and Unloading Equipment and Accessories		911176		635301
建筑及采矿用机械及零件	Construction and Mining Machinery and Spare Parts		321969		273072
食品、饮料工业用加工机械及零件	Food Processing Machinery and Spare Parts		68252		49791
制造纸及纸制品用机械及零件	Paper and Related Articles Production Machinery		123271		119387
印刷、装订机械及零件	Printing and Bookbinding Machinery		775928		645340
纺织机械及零件	Textile Machinery		866761		733582
工业用缝纫机 （台）	Industrial Use Sewing Machine （set）	2346	8364	3493	10862
金属加工机床 （台）	Machine Tools （set）	20313	2201223	18356	1876060
加工中心 （台）	Machining Center （set）	8615	797208	6291	683450
金属轧机及零件	Metal Rolling Machine and Accessories		55462		27883
橡胶或塑料加工机械及零件	Rubber and Plastic Processing Machinery		625459		617038
型模及金属铸造用型箱 （吨）	Metal Forging Molds （ton）	3980	342276	2984	271546
阀门 （万套）	Valves （10000 sets）	7134	917707	11004	823652
自动数据处理设备及其部件（万台）	Automatic Data Processing Machines and Accessories （10000 sets）	10985	3104821	9625	3418650
自动数据处理设备的零件 （吨）	Accessories of Automatic Data Processing Machines （ton）	16807	2677466	15883	2922877
制造单晶柱或晶圆用的机器及装置 （台）	Crystal Pole Making Machine （set）	581	108810	655	113855
制造半导体器件或集成电路用的机器及装置 （台）	Semiconductor and IC Making Machine （set）	1439	898899	1489	524653
制造平板显示器用的机器及装置 （台）	Flat Display Making Machine （set）	1638	1567062	1080	707885
电动机及发电机 （万台）	Electric Motors and Generators （10000 sets）	8339	612397	5202	580279
发电机组及旋转式变流机 （台）	Electric Moter Set and Converters （set）	1029	187821	1093	118224
变压、整流、电感器及零件	Transformer, Recitifier, Inductance and Accessories		1511747		1568355

商品名称	Item	2015 数量 Volume	2015 金额(千美元) Value (USD 1000)	2016 数量 Volume	2016 金额(千美元) Value (USD 1000)
蓄电池 (万个)	Accumulator (10000 units)	51164	912154	57193	977900
电话机 (台)	Telephone (set)	396674	9602	44990	3095
数字式程控电话或电报交换机(台)	Digital Program-controlled Telephone or Telegraph Exchange (set)	64	268	37	371
无线电导航雷达及遥控设备(台)	Radio Navigation Radar and Remote Device (set)	1269747	88718	2372044	82308
电视摄像机、数字照相机及视频摄录一体机 (万台)	TV Camera, Digital Camera and Video Creator (10000 sets)	7330	1076842	7160	858423
声音录制或重放设备 (万台)	Audio Recorder and Playback Device (10000 sets)	3	1495	11	5735
收音设备(包括收录音组合机及整套散件) (万台)	Radio Device (10000 sets)	2	1286	3	6244
彩色电视机(包括整套散件)	TV set		490		414
电视、收音机及无线电讯设备的零附件 (吨)	TV sets, Radio and Spare Parts of Wireless Dispatch Equipments (ton)	4801	1383043	4985	1463046
电容器 (吨)	Capacitor (ton)	8113	1354792	8565	1491164
电阻器 (吨)	Resistor (ton)	2306	353657	2510	370444
印刷电路 (万块)	Printing Circuits (10000 board)	999006	2227992	1075223	2000364
通断保护电路装置及零件	Electrical Apparatus and Spare Parts for Switching or Protecting Electrical Cursuits		3147673		3160791
电视显像管 (万只)	Kinescope (10000 units)				
彩色数据/图形显示管 (万只)	Color Digital/Graph Display (10000 units)				
二极管及类似半导体器件(百万个)	Diodes and Similar Semi Conductors (million)	97010	3603034	113154	3538505
集成电路 (百万个)	IC (million)	80810	44513289	84555	37000264
电线和电缆 (吨)	Electric Wire and Cable (ton)	29678	654184	30649	635231
汽车(包括整套散件) (辆)	Automobile (set)	1586	102481	3362	218139
装有引擎的汽车底盘 (辆)	Moter Underpan with Engine (set)	578	43666	699	50341
汽车零件	Parts of Motor Vehicles		2556689		3131450
航空器零件 (吨)	Aerostat Parts (ton)	345	62834	387	62129
船舶 (艘)	Watercrafts (unit)	31	12908	35	10849
液晶显示板 (万个)	Liquid Crystal Display Panel (10000 board)	58415	11333131	44093	8381819
医疗仪器及器械	Medical Instruments and Appliances		504463		593042
计量检测分析自控仪器及器具	Automatic Instruments of Measuring, Examining and Analysing and Related Apparatus		4431512		4671751
手表 (万只)	Watch (10000 sets)	8	3811	9	787
印刷品 (吨)	Printed Matter (ton)	4417	110673	3836	84447
塑料制品 (吨)	Plastic Products (ton)	82482	1021398	85207	1003534
农产品	Agricultural Products		11473411		11891230
机电产品	Electronic Mechanical Products		126822544		114374881
高新技术产品	New and High Technology Products		90761188		78726044

8-13 主要商品进口数量和金额(RMB)
Major Import Commodities in Volume and Value(RMB)

商品名称		Item		2015		2016	
				数量 Volume	金额(千元) Value(USD 1000)	数量 Volume	金额(千元) Value(USD 1000)
冻鱼	(吨)	Frozen Fish	(ton)	1334	30314	8815	144417
鲜、干水果及坚果	(吨)	Fresh, Dried Fruits and Nuts	(ton)	69179	336157	59887	263966
谷物及谷物粉	(万吨)	Cereals and Cereal Powder	(10000 tons)	146	2665057	93	1567496
大豆	(万吨)	Soybean	(ton)	1154	30101807	1474	39378813
食用植物油	(万吨)	Edible Vegetable Oil	(10000 tons)	89	4017905	92	4303142
食糖	(万吨)	Sugar	(10000 tons)	4	103002	1	28539
酒类	(千升)	Alcohol	(kiloliter)	43822	571288	35579	546169
饲料用鱼粉	(万吨)	Fish Powder for Forage	(10000 tons)	1	103524	1	98492
纸烟	(万条)	Cigarette	(10000 carton)				
天然橡胶(包括胶乳)	(万吨)	Natural Rubber	(10000 tons)	13	1200354	13	1152479
合成橡胶(包括胶乳)	(吨)	Synthetic Rubber	(ton)	264435	3402973	361289	4206801
原木	(万立方米)	Log	(10 kilostere)	737	8042267	838	8478782
锯材	(万立方米)	Wood Sawn	(10 kilostere)	199	3224350	217	3322389
胶合板及类似多层板	(万立方米)	Veneer	(10 kilostere)	1	20834	1	32172
纸浆	(万吨)	Paper Pulp	(10000 tons)	449	17900637	402	15435461
羊毛	(吨)	Wool	(ton)	177073	8426974	159563	8758192
毛条	(吨)	Woolen Yarn	(ton)	1844	121716	966	56125
棉花	(万吨)	Cotton	(10000 tons)	38	4055567	23	2599106
二醋酸纤维丝束	(吨)	Acetate	(ton)	353	13175	263	9506
纺织用合成纤维	(万吨)	Synthietic Fibre for Spinning	(10000 tons)	9	1405124	9	1154565
人造纤维短纤	(吨)	Man-made Fibre	(ton)	32906	409642	25249	388270
铁矿砂及其精矿	(万吨)	Iron Ores	(10000 tons)	9890	38926376	10819	43403106
锰矿砂及其精矿	(万吨)	Manganese Ores	(10000 tons)	12	87754	26	205890
铜矿砂及其精矿	(万吨)	Copper Ores	(10000 tons)	9	769084	4	298783
铬矿砂及其精矿	(万吨)	Chrome Ores	(10000 tons)	33	389725	26	252545
氧化铝	(万吨)	Alumina	(10000 tons)	93	2062118	45	850119
煤及褐煤	(万吨)	Coal and Brown Coal	(10000 tons)	506	2426872	572	3308012
成品油	(万吨)	Petroleum Products Refined	(10000 tons)	125	5958638	134	5858789
液化石油气及其他烃类气	(万吨)	Liquefied Petroleum Gas	(10000 tons)	304	11200382	463	11874361
甲苯	(吨)	Toluene	(ton)	233736	1030526	216858	874330
二甲苯	(万吨)	Xylene	(10000 tons)	312	16374714	362	18666006

商品名称 Item		2015		2016	
		数量 Volume	金额（千元）Value (USD 1000)	数量 Volume	金额（千元）Value (USD 1000)
苯乙烯 （吨）	Styrene （ton）	2079402	14446786	1792643	12286663
乙二醇 （吨）	Glycol （ton）	5250958	25999686	3493448	14776902
异氰酸酯 （吨）	Isocyanic Ester （ton）	21640	409762	18991	424648
对苯二甲酸 （吨）	Telephthalic Acid （ton）	198418	770731	38794	146282
己内酰胺 （吨）	Caprolactam （ton）	75771	733861	87445	719877
医药品 （吨）	Pharmaceuticals （ton）	8431	13479679	11774	15257863
美容化妆品及护肤品 （吨）	Cosmetics and Skin Care Products （ton）	5302	607718	5315	661042
肥料 （万吨）	Fertilizer （10000 tons）	23	483787	53	887441
合成有机染料 （吨）	Synthetic Organic Dyeing （ton）	3057	198724	3066	217038
钛白粉 （吨）	Titanium Dioxide （ton）	7832	153336	6793	129471
聚合物油漆及清漆 （吨）	Polymer Paint and Varnish （ton）	25972	891468	25092	830075
感光材料	Sensitization Material		257659		259220
初级形状的塑料 （万吨）	Primary-shape Plastic （10000 tons）	299	33525167	281	32597337
初级形状的聚乙烯 （吨）	Primary-shape Polythene （ton）	571374	4759177	511978	4200477
初级形状的线型低密度聚乙烯 （吨）	Primary-shape Line-type Low-density Polythene （ton）	196424	1609557	211079	1712035
初级形状的聚丙烯 （吨）	Primary-shape Polypropylene （ton）	344613	2762528	332714	2517832
初级形状的聚苯乙烯聚合物 （吨）	Primary-shape Polystyrene （ton）	388118	3912240	385320	3746544
ABS 树脂 （吨）	ABS Colophony （ton）	163229	1800239	158743	1646422
初级形状的聚氯乙烯 （吨）	Primary-shape PVC （ton）	158591	1027056	127798	932664
初级形状的聚酯 （吨）	Primary-shape Polyester （ton）	400430	3894954	253393	3386403
聚酯切片 （吨）	Polyester Slice （ton）	54177	444012	56532	464900
聚酰胺切片 （吨）	Polyamide Slice （ton）	95716	1530798	81784	1205988
非泡沫塑料的板、片、膜、箔 （吨）	Non-foam Plastic Board, Slice, Film and Foil （ton）	219915	12721490	215698	14131186
废塑料 （万吨）	Waste Plastic （10000 tons）	55	2034834	62	2075185
杀虫剂、除草剂及类似品 （吨）	Insecticide、Herbicide and the Like （ton）	18987	1943743	18645	1638147
牛皮革及马皮革 （吨）	Cowskin and Horse Leather （ton）	48321	1360457	40833	1093252
废纸 （万吨）	Waste Paper （10000 tons）	378	4493326	362	4324841
纸及纸板（未切成形的） （万吨）	Paper and Paper Board （10000 tons）	43	3158492	46	3419195
纺织纱线、织物及制品	Textile Yarn, Textile and Their Products		15016808		14274780
服装及衣着附件	Garments and Clothing Accessories		2448021		3050934
玻璃纤维及其制品 （吨）	Fiberglass （ton）	65283	1698739	48593	1606419
钻石 （千克）	Diamond （kg）	39	1317	2	955
废金属 （万吨）	Waste Metal （10000 tons）	45	2427519	23	1407911
钢坯及粗锻件 （万吨）	Billet and Crude Forgings （10000 tons）	12	374472	8	217571

商品名称		Item		2015 数量 Volume	2015 金额（千元）Value（USD 1000）	2016 数量 Volume	2016 金额（千元）Value（USD 1000）
钢材	（万吨）	Rolled Steel	（10000 tons）	195	14800523	213	14946329
钢铁制标准紧固件	（吨）	Iron and Steel Standard Solidity Articles	（ton）	50791	3095467	53561	3381012
未锻造的铜及铜材	（吨）	Copper and its Material	（ton）	268932	12862969	246277	11683894
未锻造的铝及铝材	（吨）	Aluminium and its Material	（ton）	152089	5859357	149136	5885074
钢铁或铝制结构体及其部件	（吨）	Iron and Steel and Aluminium Units and Parts	（ton）	31620	740263	23045	476463
蒸汽锅炉及过热水锅炉	（台）	Steam Boiler	（set）	15	32991	36	28478
活塞式内燃机的零件	（吨）	Parts of Piston Internal-combustion Engine	（ton）	20664	2729457	25056	3034326
液泵及液体提升机	（台）	Hydraulic Pumps and Lifters	（set）	36721839	4037291	22257634	4298215
制冷设备用压缩机	（万台）	Compressors for Refrigerating Equipment	（10000 sets）	161	1008059	167	751687
空气调节器	（台）	Air Conditioners	（set）	2685	136410	5349	47939
冷冻机和制冷设备	（台）	Refrigerating Equipment	（set）	227074	2936915	157498	2143452
非家用型水的过滤、净化机器	（台）	Non-household Water Purify Machines	（set）	22909	376494	16774	315204
饮料及液体食品灌装设备	（台）	Beverage Filling Equipment	（set）	78	301438	47	158518
机械提升搬运装卸设备及零件		Machine Lifting, Transporting and Loading and Unloading Equipment and Accessories			5651758		4190016
建筑及采矿用机械及零件		Construction and Mining Machinery and Spare Parts			1992653		1807226
食品、饮料工业用加工机械及零件		Food Processing Machinery and Spare Parts			427237		332179
制造纸及纸制品用机械及零件		Paper and Related Articles Production Machinery			764395		783046
印刷、装订机械及零件		Printing and Bookbinding Machinery			4819905		4258366
纺织机械及零件		Textile Machinery			5403980		4861804
工业用缝纫机	（台）	Industrial Use Sewing Machine	（set）	2346	51729	3493	71541
金属加工机床	（台）	Machine Tools	（set）	20313	13676847	18356	12365730
加工中心	（台）	Machining Center	（set）	8615	4939225	6291	4495856
金属轧机及零件		Metal Rolling Machine and Accessories			343751		184049
橡胶或塑料加工机械及零件		Rubber and Plastic Processing Machinery			3889431		4081368
型模及金属铸造用型箱	（吨）	Metal Forging Molds	（ton）	3980	2127348	2984	1795143
阀门	（万套）	Valves	（10000 sets）	7134	5706478	11004	5446077
自动数据处理设备及其部件	（万台）	Automatic Data Processing Machines and Accessories	（10000 sets）	10985	19320802	9625	22588054
自动数据处理设备的零件	（吨）	Accessories of Automatic Data Processing Machines	（ton）	16807	16637771	15883	19306771
制造单晶柱或晶圆用的机器及装置	（台）	Crystal Pole Making Machine	（set）	581	672858	655	746059
制造半导体器件或集成电路用的机器及装置	（台）	Semiconductor and IC Making Machine	（set）	1439	5570875	1489	3464490
制造平板显示器用的机器及装置	（台）	Flat Display Making Machine	（set）	1638	9754533	1080	4608153
电动机及发电机	（万台）	Electric Motors and Generators	（10000 sets）	8339	3800831	5202	3839699
发电机组及旋转式变流机	（台）	Electric Moter Set and Converters	（set）	1029	1166285	1093	778876
变压、整流、电感器及零件		Transformer, Recitifier, Inductance and Accessories			9387090		10367670

商 品 名 称 Item		2015		2016	
		数 量 Volume	金 额（千元）Value（USD 1000）	数 量 Volume	金 额（千元）Value（USD 1000）
蓄电池 （万个）	Accumulator （10000 units）	51164	5661140	57193	6454012
电话机 （台）	Telephone （set）	396674	59428	44990	20453
数字式程控电话或电报交换机（台）	Digital Program-controlled Telephone or Telegraph Exchange （set）	64	1662	37	2467
无线电导航雷达及遥控设备（台）	Radio Navigation Radar and Remote Device （set）	1269747	549907	2372044	543712
电视摄像机、数字照相机及视频摄录一体机 （万台）	TV Camera, Digital Camera and Video Creator （10000 sets）	7330	6688461	7160	5673381
声音录制或重放设备 （万台）	Audio Recorder and Playback Device （10000 sets）	3	9517	11	37864
收音设备（包括收录音组合机及整套散件） （万台）	Radio Device （10000 sets）	2	8013	3	41764
彩色电视机（包括整套散件）	TV set		3097		2802
电视、收音机及无线电讯设备的零附件 （吨）	TV sets, Radio and Spare Parts of Wireless Dispatch Equipments （ton）	4801	8571480	4985	9673639
电容器 （吨）	Capacitor （ton）	8113	8435527	8565	9922948
电阻器 （吨）	Resistor （ton）	2306	2195846	2510	2449579
印刷电路 （万块）	Printing Circuits （10000 board）	999006	13836915	1075223	13213847
通断保护电路装置及零件	Electrical Apparatus and Spare Parts for Switching or Protecting Electrical Cursuits		19554533		20901917
电视显像管 （万只）	Kinescope （10000 units）				
彩色数据/图形显示管 （万只）	Color Digital/Graph Display （10000 units）				
二极管及类似半导体器件（百万个）	Diodes and Similar Semi Conductors （million）	97010	22350145	113154	23424177
集成电路 （百万个）	IC （million）	80810	276454408	84555	244318275
电线和电缆 （吨）	Electric Wire and Cable （ton）	29678	4062419	30649	4198258
汽车（包括整套散件） （辆）	Automobile （set）	1586	635820	3362	1433534
装有引擎的汽车底盘 （辆）	Moter Underpan with Engine （set）	578	271398	699	331187
汽车零件	Parts of Motor Vehicles		15898000		20726397
航空器零件 （吨）	Aerostat Parts （ton）	345	390488	387	409557
船舶 （艘）	Watercrafts （unit）	31	79332	35	70578
液晶显示板 （万个）	Liquid Crystal Display Panel （10000 board）	58415	70436030	44093	55417692
医疗仪器及器械	Medical Instruments and Appliances		3139185		3920091
计量检测分析自控仪器及器具	Automatic Instruments of Measuring, Examining and Analysing and Related Apparatus		27540895		30856122
手表 （万只）	Watch （10000 sets）	8	23807	9	5173
印刷品 （吨）	Printed Matter （ton）	4417	685978	3836	558435
塑料制品 （吨）	Plastic Products （ton）	82482	6346620	85207	6631731
农产品	Agricultural Products		71240985		78543517
机电产品	Electronic Mechanical Products		787836043		755734235
高新技术产品	New and High Technology Products		563760616		519963505

8-14 主要商品出口数量和金额

Major Export Commodities in Volume and Value

商品名称	Item	2015 数量 Volume	2015 金额（千美元）Value (USD 1000)	2016 数量 Volume	2016 金额（千美元）Value (USD 1000)
冻鸡（吨）	Frozen Chicken (ton)				
水海产品（万吨）	Aquatic and Seawater Products (10000 tons)	5	279371	4	265315
谷物及谷物粉（万吨）	Cereals and Cereal Powder (10000 tons)		3220		8608
蔬菜（万吨）	Vegetables (10000 tons)	61	766864	56	903685
鲜、干水果及坚果（万吨）	Fresh, Dried Fruits and Nuts (10000 tons)	1	10538	1	10435
食用油籽（万吨）	Edible Oil Seeds (10000 tons)		2983		2548
食用植物油（吨）	Edible Vegetable Oil (ton)	1555	2767	9109	10702
食糖（吨）	Sugar (ton)	110	154	1254	1134
天然蜂蜜（吨）	Natural Honey (ton)	13839	25874	13480	26727
茶叶（吨）	Tea (ton)	1251	17109	979	7124
猪肉罐头（吨）	Canned Pork (ton)	1483	4151	1450	3651
蘑菇罐头（吨）	Canned Mushroom (ton)	3995	6620	2620	3399
啤酒（万升）	Beer (10 kiloliter)	190	1143	113	662
肠衣（吨）	Casings (ton)	34224	329123	36764	451958
填充用羽毛;羽绒（吨）	Feathers and Down for Stuffing (ton)	7660	92833	4916	66922
中药材及中式成药（吨）	Chinese Medical Materials and Medicaments of Chinese Type (ton)	10299	43452	3748	33857
肥料（万吨）	Fertilizer (10000 tons)	328	705258	320	536187
锯材（万立方米）	Wood Sawn (10 kilostere)	1	3968	1	5684
胶合板及类似多层板（万立方米）	Veneer (10 kilostere)	428	1789737	438	1684241
印刷品（吨）	Printed Matter (ton)	36878	204489	36285	194794
生丝（吨）	Raw Silk (ton)	1557	71569	1747	78837
煤及褐煤（万吨）	Coal and Brown Coal (10000 tons)	1	970	2	2864
成品油（万吨）	Petroleum Products Refined (10000 tons)	38	217783	45	197925
氧化铝（吨）	Alumina (ton)	264080	103134	80644	30343
氧化锌及过氧化锌（吨）	Zinc Oxide and Zinc Peroxide (ton)	1014	2045	797	1725
合成有机染料（吨）	Synthetic Organic Dyeing (ton)	58537	422207	60652	399785
医药品（吨）	Pharmaceuticals (ton)	112081	1614045	117115	1916637
美容化妆品及护肤品（吨）	Cosmctics and Skin Care Products (ton)	8127	98515	9990	97438
口腔及牙齿清洁剂（吨）	Mouth and Teech Detergent (ton)	6397	27540	9090	32558
洗衣粉（吨）	Detergent Powder (ton)	13399	9024	11618	5944
烟花、爆竹（吨）	Firework and Cracker (ton)	941	2559	739	1748

商品名称	Item	2015 数量 Volume	2015 金额（千美元）Value (USD 1000)	2016 数量 Volume	2016 金额（千美元）Value (USD 1000)
新的充气橡胶轮胎（万条）	New Pneumatic Rubber Tyres (10000 units)	3627	1309057	3368	1084855
家用或装饰用木制品（万吨）	Wooden Products for Domestic Use and Decoration (10000 tons)	2	62227	2	57973
纸及纸板（未切成形的）（万吨）	Paper and Paper Board (10000 tons)	164	1794513	182	1890730
纺织纱线、织物及制品	Textile Yarn Thread, Woven Goods and Related Products		20127602		20138990
水泥及水泥熟料（万吨）	Cement (10000 tons)	130	58839	135	60997
平板玻璃（万平方米）	Plate Glass (10 kilostere)	1023	47669	1083	40631
玻璃制品（吨）	Glass Products (ton)	249237	485535	274051	519747
家用陶瓷（万吨）	Pottery Ware for Household Use (10000 tons)	10	352492	9	238908
珍珠、钻石、宝石及半宝石	Pearl, Gem and Semi-gem		61573		12172
生铁及镜铁（万吨）	Pig Iron and Spiegeleisen (10000 tons)				134
铁合金（万吨）	Ferroalloy (10000 tons)	3	54760	3	43486
钢坯及粗锻件（万吨）	Billet and Crude Forgings (10000 tons)		1302	1	5488
钢材（万吨）	Rolled Steel (10000 tons)	1964	11068208	1866	9449732
废钢（吨）	Waste Steel (ton)	34	9	17	20
未锻造的铜及铜材（吨）	Copper and Its Material (ton)	71829	547319	70385	487300
未锻造的铝及铝材（万吨）	Aluminium and Its Material (10000 tons)	68	2025030	62	1741416
未锻造的锰（吨）	Manganese (ton)	385	1198	721	1435
钢铁或铜制标准紧固件（万吨）	Standard Infrangible Articles made of Steel or Copper (10000 tons)	25	598749	25	566011
不锈钢厨具、餐具等家用器具（吨）	Kitchenware, Tableware and Home Appliances Made of Stainless Steel (ton)	12195	101306	13628	94430
餐桌、厨房及其他家用搪瓷器（吨）	Porcelain and Pottery Ware for Table, Kitchen and Other Household Use (ton)	3741	9299	4338	13243
手用或机用工具（万吨）	Hand Tools and Tools for Machines (10000 tons)	20	1407834	20	1378708
电扇（万台）	Electric Fans (10000 sets)	2249	191614	2387	202193
空气调节器（万台）	Air Conditioners (10000 sets)	235	524459	238	492401
冰箱（万台）	Refrigerators (10000 sets)	419	921258	387	846131
洗衣机（万台）	Washing Machines (10000 sets)	752	1922576	794	1701003
纺织机械及零件	Textile Machinery		790875		717605
家用型缝纫机（万台）	Ordinary Sewing Machines (10000 sets)	79	43871	77	38530
工业用缝纫机（万台）	Industrial Sewing Machines (10000 sets)	10	44274	9	41176
金属加工机床（万台）	Machine Tools for Processing Metal (10000 sets)	243	646901	266	647505
电子计算器（包括具有计算功能的袖珍数据记录重现机）（万台）	Electron Calculators (10000 sets)	366	5047	166	3585
自动数据处理设备及其部件（万台）	Automatic Data Processing Machines and Accessories (10000 sets)	26902	35820876	26460	33015541

商品名称	Item	2015 数量 Volume	2015 金额(千美元) Value (USD 1000)	2016 数量 Volume	2016 金额(千美元) Value (USD 1000)
自动数据处理设备的零件(万吨)	Accessories of Automatic Data Processing Machines (10000 tons)	6	6978886	6	6573711
打印机(包括多功能一体机)(万台)	Printers (including Multi Function Printers) (10000 sets)	133	1776196	117	1573631
液晶显示板 (万个)	Liquid Crystal Display Panel (10000 board)	43669	8850991	29154	6521343
轴承 (万套)	Bearings (10000 sets)	73574	564203	72604	573642
电动机及发电机 (万台)	Electric Motors and Generators (10000 sets)	36399	1887393	21885	1771273
变压器 (万个)	Transformers (10000)	8222	276170	11047	320119
静止式变流器 (万个)	Static Converters (10000 sets)	140974	2181853	158852	2114527
原电池 (万个)	Primary Cells and Batteries (10000 sets)	72437	40296	74635	45795
蓄电池 (万个)	Accumulator (10000 sets)	31415	1629208	30390	1812125
电话机 (万台)	Telephone (10000 sets)	4828	6442286	5065	8177291
扬声器 (万个)	Loudspeakers (10000 sets)	27334	681487	27132	722034
激光唱机 (万台)	Laser Phonographs (10000 sets)	1	1435	6	7198
录、放像机 (万台)	Video Cassette Recorders (10000 sets)	220	189984	191	224763
声音录制或重放设备 (万台)	Audio Recorder and Playback Device (10000 sets)	113	21859	174	37888
收音设备(包括收录音组合机及整套散件) (万台)	Radio Device (10000 sets)	203	171614	371	174802
彩色电视机(包括整套散件) (万台)	TV-sets (10000 sets)	774	1481433	942	1757684
录放音、像机及唱机的零附件	Accessories of Videorecorder, Camera and Gramophone		59285		34616
电视、收音机及无线电讯设备的零附件 (吨)	TV-sets, Radio and Spare Parts of Wireless Dispatch Equipments (ton)	77382	1635977	85209	1721005
电容器 (吨)	Capacitor (ton)	18739	1614474	17500	1288178
印刷电路 (百万块)	Printing Circuits (million board)	6509	2869658	6248	2884816
通断保护电路装置及零件	Electrical Apparatus and Spare Parts for Switching or Protecting Electrical Cursuits		3717597		3942017
节能灯 (百万只)	Energy-saving Lights (million)	84	78399	57	55902
二极管及类似半导体器件 (百万个)	Diodes and Similar Semi Conductors (million)	109368	8783188	109712	7804405
集成电路 (百万个)	IC (million)	59059	23343830	52564	15359736
电线和电缆 (万吨)	Electric Wire and Cable (ton)	29	2557817	33	2645557
集装箱 (万个)	Containers (million)	49	2398675	36	1467213
汽车和汽车底盘 (万辆)	Motor Vehicles and Chassis (10000 sets)	4	689021	5	502180
汽车零件	Parts of Motor Vehicles		5732334		5948533
摩托车 (万辆)	Motorcycles (10000 sets)	101	512187	144	628212

商品名称 Item		2015 数量 Volume	2015 金额（千美元）Value（USD 1000）	2016 数量 Volume	2016 金额（千美元）Value（USD 1000）
自行车 （万辆）	Bicycles （10000 sets）	922	867049	860	744478
摩托车及自行车的零件	Parts of Motorcycles and Bicycles		733375		711197
船舶 （万艘）	Watercrafts （unit）		7472056		5866121
照相机 （万架）	Cameras （10000 sets）	971	761869	834	577896
医疗仪器及器械	Medical Instruments and Appliances		1535490		1535211
手表 （万只）	Watches （10000 sets）	698	62952	718	78553
日用钟 （万只）	Clocks （10000 sets）	371	14066	429	15168
家具及其零件	Furniture and its Parts		3632093		3616465
床垫、寝具及类似品	Beddings, Bedclothing and Similar Products		2192444		2188979
灯具、照明装置及类似品	Lamps and Lanterns, Lighting Installation and Similar Products		1888573		1538147
旅行用品及箱包 （千克）	Travel Articles, Suitcases and Handbags and Similar Articles （kg）	151315194	1448186	152396693	1332583
体育用具及设备	Physical Appliances and Equipments		1130086		1129785
服装及衣着附件	Garments and Clothing Accessories		23931127		23285098
鞋类 （吨）	Footware （ton）	206388	2156296	202281	2084978
塑料制品 （万吨）	Plastic Products （10000 tons）	148	4174463	177	4527163
玩具	Toys		1131829		1205879
游戏机及零附件 （万台）	Recreational Machines （ton）	2086	1277489	3676	2425203
圣诞用品 （吨）	Christmas Articles （ton）	10667	121179	10385	109969
足球、篮球、排球 （万个）	Footballs, Basketballs and Volleyballs （10000 units）	4046	78696	4653	84292
打火机 （百万个）	Lighters （million）	27	3384	24	2583
艺术品、收藏品及古董	Artworks, Collections and Antiques		19681		6777
贵金属或包贵金属的首饰	Noble Metals		9171		1476
伞 （万把）	Umbrellas （10000 units）	1045	55711	1355	69594
竹编结品 （吨）	Bamboo-work （ton）	353	2467	224	1754
藤编结品 （吨）	Bine-work （ton）	12	230	36	367
草编结品 （吨）	Grass-work （ton）	727	3669	698	5200
柳编结品 （吨）	Wickerwork （ton）	985	10811	1016	13215
农产品	Farm Products		3368466		3591991
机电产品	Electronic Mechanical Products		224751602		208003938
高新技术产品	New and High Technology Products		131089251		116977714

8-15 主要商品出口数量和金额(RMB)

Major Export Commodities in Volume and Value(RMB)

商品名称		Item		2015 数量 Volume	2015 金额(千元) Value (USD 1000)	2016 数量 Volume	2016 金额(千元) Value (USD 1000)
冻鸡	(吨)	Frozen Chicken	(ton)				
水海产品	(万吨)	Aquatic and Seawater Products	(10000 tons)	5	1736456	4	1748579
谷物及谷物粉	(万吨)	Cereals and Cereal Powder	(10000 tons)		20356		57368
蔬菜	(万吨)	Vegetables	(10000 tons)	61	4757924	56	5966921
鲜、干水果及坚果	(万吨)	Fresh, Dried Fruits and Nuts	(10000 tons)	1	66348	1	69208
食用油籽	(万吨)	Edible Oil Seeds	(10000 tons)		18598		16778
食用植物油	(吨)	Edible Vegetable Oil	(ton)	1555	17238	9109	72317
食糖	(吨)	Sugar	(ton)	110	955	1254	7362
天然蜂蜜	(吨)	Natural Honey	(ton)	13839	160464	13480	176205
茶叶	(吨)	Tea	(ton)	1251	106567	979	46996
猪肉罐头	(吨)	Canned Pork	(ton)	1483	25651	1450	24005
蘑菇罐头	(吨)	Canned Mushroom	(ton)	3995	41066	2620	22241
啤酒	(万升)	Beer	(10 kiloliter)	190	7114	113	4348
肠衣	(吨)	Casings	(ton)	34224	2042852	36764	2982515
填充用羽毛;羽绒	(吨)	Feathers and Down for Stuffing	(ton)	7660	572755	4916	439669
中药材及中式成药	(吨)	Chinese Medical Materials and Medicaments of Chinese Type	(ton)	10299	272288	3748	223443
肥料	(万吨)	Fertilizer	(10000 tons)	328	4356258	320	3504886
锯材	(万立方米)	Wood Sawn	(10 kilostere)	1	24791	1	37802
胶合板及类似多层板	(万立方米)	Veneer	(10 kilostere)	428	11089738	438	11093314
印刷品	(吨)	Printed Matter	(ton)	36878	1272403	36285	1287771
生丝	(吨)	Raw Silk	(ton)	1557	443640	1747	519629
煤及褐煤	(万吨)	Coal and Brown Coal	(10000 tons)	1	5934	2	18992
成品油	(万吨)	Petroleum Products Refined	(10000 tons)	38	1348507	45	1301455
氧化铝	(吨)	Alumina	(ton)	264080	638308	80644	192324
氧化锌及过氧化锌	(吨)	Zinc Oxide and Zinc Peroxide	(ton)	1014	12570	797	11377
合成有机染料	(吨)	Synthetic Organic Dyeing	(ton)	58537	2615692	60652	2632947
医药品	(吨)	Pharmaceuticals	(ton)	112081	10011551	117115	12671166
美容化妆品及护肤品	(吨)	Cosmetics and Skin Care Products	(ton)	8127	611386	9990	643222
口腔及牙齿清洁剂	(吨)	Mouth and Teech Detergent	(ton)	6397	171058	9090	214808
洗衣粉	(吨)	Detergent Powder	(ton)	13399	56172	11618	39216
烟花、爆竹	(吨)	Firework and Cracker	(ton)	941	15769	739	11533

8－15 续 表 1 Continued 1

商品名称 Item		2015		2016	
		数量 Volume	金额(千元) Value (USD 1000)	数量 Volume	金额(千元) Value (USD 1000)
新的充气橡胶轮胎 (万条)	New Pneumatic Rubber Tyres (10000 units)	3627	8110267	3368	7136535
家用或装饰用木制品 (万吨)	Wooden Products for Domestic Use and Decoration (10000 tons)	2	386751	2	383355
纸及纸板(未切成形的) (万吨)	Paper and Paper Board (10000 tons)	164	11123857	182	12448313
纺织纱线、织物及制品	Textile Yarn Thread, Woven Goods and Related Products		124913936		132722197
水泥及水泥熟料 (万吨)	Cement (10000 tons)	130	365211	135	398975
平板玻璃 (万平方米)	Plate Glass (10 kilostere)	1023	295934	1083	269135
玻璃制品 (吨)	Glass Products (ton)	249237	3015566	274051	3427091
家用陶瓷 (万吨)	Pottery Ware for Household Use (10000 tons)	10	2210623	9	1588115
珍珠、钻石、宝石及半宝石	Pearl, Gem and Semi-gem		384899		79269
生铁及镜铁 (万吨)	Pig Iron and Spiegeleisen (10000 tons)				884
铁合金 (万吨)	Ferroalloy (10000 tons)	3	339831	3	286408
钢坯及粗锻件 (万吨)	Billet and Crude Forgings (10000 tons)		8186	1	36160
钢材 (万吨)	Rolled Steel (10000 tons)	1964	68516511	1866	62272788
废钢 (吨)	Waste Steel (ton)	34	54	17	129
未锻造的铜及铜材 (吨)	Copper and Its Material (ton)	71829	3393101	70385	3214065
未锻造的铝及铝材 (万吨)	Aluminium and Its Material (10000 tons)	68	12547552	62	11477995
未锻造的锰 (吨)	Manganese (ton)	385	7437	721	9427
钢铁或铜制标准紧固件 (万吨)	Standard Infrangible Articles made of Steel or Copper (10000 tons)	25	3717073	25	3735673
不锈钢厨具、餐具等家用器具(吨)	Kitchenware, Tableware and Home Appliances Made of Stainless Steel (ton)	12195	633244	13628	624812
餐桌、厨房及其他家用搪瓷器(吨)	Porcelain and Pottery Ware for Table, Kitchen and Other Household Use (ton)	3741	57766	4338	86966
手用或机用工具 (万吨)	Hand Tools and Tools for Machines (10000 tons)	20	8734734	20	9091544
电扇 (万台)	Electric Fans (10000 sets)	2249	1187905	2387	1332971
空气调节器 (万台)	Air Conditioners (10000 sets)	235	3242170	238	3234794
冰箱 (万台)	Refrigerators (10000 sets)	419	5707178	387	5577342
洗衣机 (万台)	Washing Machines (10000 sets)	752	11908118	794	11180864
纺织机械及零件	Textile Machinery		4916383		4735248
家用型缝纫机 (万台)	Ordinary Sewing Machines (10000 sets)	79	272282	77	253937
工业用缝纫机 (万台)	Industrial Sewing Machines (10000 sets)	10	274911	9	271327
金属加工机床 (万台)	Machine Tools for Processing Metal (10000 sets)	243	4014413	266	4269034
电子计算器(包括具有计算功能的袖珍数据记录重现机)(万台)	Electron Calculators (10000 sets)	366	31310	166	23846
自动数据处理设备及其部件(万台)	Automatic Data Processing Machines and Accessories (10000 sets)	26902	222541880	26460	217796192

8-15 续 表 2 Continued 2

商品名称 Item		2015		2016	
		数量 Volume	金额(千元) Value (USD 1000)	数量 Volume	金额(千元) Value (USD 1000)
自动数据处理设备的零件(万吨)	Accessories of Automatic Data Processing Machines (10000 tons)	6	43303136	6	43399021
打印机(包括多功能一体机)(万台)	Printers (including Multi Function Printers) (10000 sets)	133	11002042	117	10359399
液晶显示板 (万个)	Liquid Crystal Display Panel (10000 board)	43669	54998325	29154	43063711
轴承 (万套)	Bearings (10000 sets)	73574	3502340	72604	3782901
电动机及发电机 (万台)	Electric Motors and Generators (10000 sets)	36399	11706081	21885	11681870
变压器 (万个)	Transformers (10000)	8222	1714202	11047	2110399
静止式变流器 (万个)	Static Converters (10000 sets)	140974	13545015	158852	13950334
原电池 (万个)	Primary Cells and Batteries (10000 sets)	72437	250461	74635	301939
蓄电池 (万个)	Accumulator (10000 sets)	31415	10119578	30390	11968113
电话机 (万台)	Telephone (10000 sets)	4828	40082942	5065	54145334
扬声器 (万个)	Loudspeakers (10000 sets)	27334	4242784	27132	4773314
激光唱机 (万台)	Laser Phonographs (10000 sets)	1	9088	6	47622
录、放像机 (万台)	Video Cassette Recorders (10000 sets)	220	1181100	191	1483437
声音录制或重放设备 (万台)	Audio Recorder and Playback Device (10000 sets)	113	136188	174	251402
收音设备(包括收录音组合机及整套散件) (万台)	Radio Device (10000 sets)	203	1065216	371	1157181
彩色电视机(包括整套散件) (万台)	TV-sets (10000 sets)	774	9204320	942	11595028
录放音、像机及唱机的零附件	Accessories of Videorecorder, Camera and Gramophone		368139		228404
电视、收音机及无线电讯设备的零附件 (吨)	TV-sets, Radio and Spare Parts of Wireless Dispatch Equipments (ton)	77382	10152460	85209	11350944
电容器 (吨)	Capacitor (ton)	18739	10095216	17500	8508611
印刷电路 (百万块)	Printing Circuits (million board)	6509	17805144	6248	19031148
通断保护电路装置及零件	Electrical Apparatus and Spare Parts for Switching or Protecting Electrical Cursuits		23063281		26021074
节能灯 (百万只)	Energy-saving Lights (million)	84	486245	57	370128
二极管及类似半导体器件 (百万个)	Diodes and Similar Semi Conductors (million)	109368	54621053	109712	51396562
集成电路 (百万个)	IC (million)	59059	145006278	52564	101228032
电线和电缆 (万吨)	Electric Wire and Cable (ton)	29	15886492	33	17445039
集装箱 (万个)	Containers (million)	49	14833008	36	9650349
汽车和汽车底盘 (万辆)	Motor Vehicles and Chassis (10000 sets)	4	4267924	5	3314799
汽车零件	Parts of Motor Vehicles		35557365		39229796
摩托车 (万辆)	Motorcycles (10000 sets)	101	3178986	144	4143575

商品名称 Item		2015		2016	
		数量 Volume	金额(千元) Value (USD 1000)	数量 Volume	金额(千元) Value (USD 1000)
自行车 (万辆)	Bicycles (10000 sets)	922	5364651	860	4899674
摩托车及自行车的零件	Parts of Motorcycles and Bicycles		4552254		4691667
船舶 (万艘)	Watercrafts (unit)		46287086		38625890
照相机 (万架)	Cameras (10000 sets)	971	4727253	834	3824440
医疗仪器及器械	Medical Instruments and Appliances		9533520		10134958
手表 (万只)	Watches (10000 sets)	698	392431	718	516443
日用钟 (万只)	Clocks (10000 sets)	371	88017	429	101029
家具及其零件	Furniture and its Parts		22553889		23849974
床垫、寝具及类似品	Beddings, Bedclothing and Similar Products		13608076		14436048
灯具、照明装置及类似品	Lamps and Lanterns, Lighting Installation and Similar Products		11772183		10161805
旅行用品及箱包 (千克)	Travel Articles, Suitcases and Handbags and Similar Articles (kg)	151315194	8998059	152396693	8794585
体育用具及设备	Physical Appliances and Equipments		7013469		7445336
服装及衣着附件	Garments and Clothing Accessories		148445702		153674286
鞋类 (吨)	Footware (ton)	206388	13398353	202281	13771447
塑料制品 (万吨)	Plastic Products (10000 tons)	148	25923165	177	29874730
玩具	Toys		7030604		7976684
游戏机及零附件 (万台)	Recreational Machines (ton)	2086	8003065	3676	15984448
圣诞用品 (吨)	Christmas Articles (ton)	10667	752965	10385	727644
足球、篮球、排球 (万个)	Footballs, Basketballs and Volleyballs (10000 units)	4046	488597	4653	555184
打火机 (百万个)	Lighters (million)	27	20964	24	17028
艺术品、收藏品及古董	Artworks, Collections and Antiques		121959		44956
贵金属或包贵金属的首饰	Noble Metals		58249		9768
伞 (万把)	Umbrellas (10000 units)	1045	345792	1355	459539
竹编结品 (吨)	Bamboo-work (ton)	353	15283	224	11598
藤编结品 (吨)	Bine-work (ton)	12	1446	36	2414
草编结品 (吨)	Grass-work (ton)	727	22889	698	34392
柳编结品 (吨)	Wickerwork (ton)	985	67245	1016	87463
农产品	Farm Products		20902547		23693763
机电产品	Electronic Mechanical Products		1395552246		1372108135
高新技术产品	New and High Technology Products		814292138		771803425

8－16　协议注册外资项目
Agreement Registered Foreign Investment Project

单位:个　　　　(unit)

指　　标　　Item		2016年止累计 2016 Year end Accumulated	2011	2012	2013	2014	2015	2016
合　计	**Total**	**118290**	**4496**	**4156**	**3453**	**3031**	**2580**	**2859**
合资经营企业	Joint Venture Enterprises	50779	932	721	632	709	606	776
合作经营企业	Cooperative Enterprises	3066	29	15	14	2	3	15
独资经营企业	Foreign Solely Funded	64382	3531	3414	2806	2316	1963	2062
外商投资股份制企业	Share Holding with Foreign Investment	63	4	6	1	4	8	6

8－17　协议注册外资
Agreement Registered Foreign

单位:万美元　　　　(USD 10000)

指　　标　　Item		2016年止累计 2016 Year end Accumulated	2011	2012	2013	2014	2015	2016
合　计	**Total**	**78107103**	**5955372**	**5714109**	**4726816**	**4318685**	**3936089**	**4313941**
合资经营企业	Joint Venture Enterprises	14535533	980904	743004	561458	661894	610010	851874
合作经营企业	Cooperative Enterprises	1607386	34123	32100	26282	9808	19050	95114
独资经营企业	Foreign Solely Funded	61342533	4889203	4869617	4128148	3512530	3222822	3315933
外商投资股份制企业	Share Holding with Foreign Investment	621260	51142	69388	10928	134453	84207	51020

8-18 实际使用外资
Actual Use of Foreign Capital

单位:万美元 (USD 10000)

指标	Item	1985~2016	1990	2000	2005	2010
合计	**Total**	**39937112**	**14110**	**642358**	**1318339**	**2849777**
合资经营企业	Joint Venture Enterprises	8597790	13787	227369	248652	474350
合作经营企业	Cooperative Enterprises	693077	249	35755	19130	24697
独资经营企业	Foreign Solely Funded	28100770	74	378946	1041074	2283780
外商投资股份制企业	Share Holding with Foreign Investment	454588		288	9483	66950

8-18 续表 Continued

单位:万美元 (USD 10000)

指标	Item	2012	2013	2014	2015	2016
合计	**Total**	**3575956**	**3325922**	**2817416**	**2427469**	**2454296**
合资经营企业	Joint Venture Enterprises	577193	590073	429339	460420	545032
合作经营企业	Cooperative Enterprises	19118	20102	9508	14383	22837
独资经营企业	Foreign Solely Funded	2887099	2692125	2322693	1856173	1825448
外商投资股份制企业	Share Holding with Foreign Investment	92546	23622	55876	96493	60979

8-19 按行业分外商直接投资(2016年)
Foreign Direct Investment Grouped by Sector(2016)

单位:万美元 (USD 10000)

行业	Sector	项目(个) Number of Projects(unit)	协议注册外资 Agreement Registered Foreign	实际使用外资 Actual Use of Foreign Capital
总计	**Total**	**2859**	**4313941**	**2454296**
农、林、牧、渔业	Agriculture, Forestry, Animal Husbandry and Fishery	98	117289	48024
采矿业	Mining	2	819	1907
制造业	Manufacturing	902	1653436	1046039
农副食品加工业	Processing of Food from Agricultural Products	14	25604	9469
食品制造业	Manufacture of Food	27	25888	19304
饮料制造业	Manufacture of Beverage	9	26327	13147
烟草制品业	Manufacture of Tobacco			
纺织业	Manufacture of Textile	18	24542	13921
纺织服装、鞋、帽制造业	Manufacture of Textile Wearing, Apparel, Footwear and Caps	36	33259	36497
皮革、毛皮、羽毛(绒)及其制品业	Manufacture of Leather, Fur, Feather and Related Products	6	3852	686
木材加工及木、竹、藤、棕、草制品业	Processing of Timber, Manufacture of Wood, Bamboo, Rattan, Palm and Straw Products	8	4720	1777
家具制造业	Manufacture of Furniture	17	30081	14791
造纸及纸制品业	Manufacture of Paper and Paper Products	9	8920	12235
印刷业和记录媒介的复制	Printing, Reproduction of Recording Media	1	716	2439
文教体育用品制造业	Manufacture of Articles For Culture, Education and Sport Activities	10	14337	2851
石油加工、炼焦及核燃料加工业	Processing of Petroleum, Coking, Processing of Nuclear Fuel		2846	6976
化学原料及化学制品制造业	Manufacture of Raw Chemical Materials and Chemical Products	37	115817	93722
医药制造业	Manufacture of Medicines	18	57135	107234
化学纤维制造业	Manufacture of Chemical Fibers	3	25606	3002
橡胶制品业	Manufacture of Rubber	5	4698	7905
塑料制品业	Manufacture of Plastics	31	31141	23642
非金属矿物制品业	Manufacture of Non-metallic Mineral Products	30	55804	29028
黑色金属冶炼及压延加工业	Smelting and Pressing of Ferrous Metals	1	10104	2100
有色金属冶炼及压延加工业	Smelting and Pressing of Non-ferrous Metals	3	29153	27298
金属制品业	Manufacture of Metal Products	55	101509	68077

8－19 续 表 Continued

单位:万美元 (USD 10000)

行业	Sector	项 目(个) Number of Projects(unit)	协议注册外资 Agreement Registered Foreign	实际使用外资 Actual Use of Foreign Capital
通用设备制造业	Manufacture of General Purpose Machinery	141	212772	97866
专用设备制造业	Manufacture of Special Purpose Machinery	113	109457	54362
交通运输设备制造业	Manufacture of Transport Equipment	76	138048	97518
电气机械及器材制造业	Manufacture of Electrical Machinery and Equipment	94	162043	100293
通信设备、计算机及其他电子设备制造业	Mafacture of Communication Equipment, Computers and Other Electronic Equipment	94	330245	171190
仪器仪表及文化、办公用机械制造业	Manufacture of Measuring Instruments and Machinery for Cultural Activity and Office Work	15	17692	8504
工艺品及其他制造业	Manufacture of Artwork and Other Manufacturing	25	45662	18884
废弃资源和废旧材料回收加工业	Recycling and Disposal of Waste	7	5458	1315
电力、热力、燃气及水的生产和供应业	Production and Supply of Electric Power, Heat Power, Gas and Water	77	162084	40419
建筑业	Construction	76	395449	171651
交通运输、仓储和邮政业	Transport, Storage and Post	50	126544	65722
信息传输、计算机服务和软件业	Information Transmission, Computer Services and Software	117	80854	22396
批发和零售业	Wholesale and Retail Trades	790	662952	265669
住宿和餐饮业	Hotels and Catering Services	61	12910	5781
金融业	Financial Intermediation	31	102786	74483
房地产业	Real Estate	60	209192	304135
租赁和商务服务业	Leasing and Business Services	284	458189	294560
科学研究、技术服务和地质勘查业	Scientific Research, Technical Service and Geologic Prospecting	217	221192	68437
水利、环境和公共设施管理业	Management of Water Conservancy, Environment and Public Facilities	18	50522	24530
居民服务和其他服务业	Services to Households and Other Services	25	21699	3305
教育	Education	8	8558	6289
卫生、社会保障和社会福利业	Health, Social Security and Social Welfare	7	15252	8435
文化、体育和娱乐业	Culture, Sports and Entertainment	34	14214	2514

8－20 按国家或地区分外商直接投资

Foreign Direct Investment by Country or Region

单位:万美元　　　　(USD 10000)

国家(地区) Country(Region)		2015			2016		
		项目(个) Number of Projects (unit)	协议注册外资 Agreement Registered Foreign	实际使用外资 Actual Use of Foreign Capital	项目(个) Number of Projects (unit)	协议注册外资 Agreement Registered Foreign	实际使用外资 Actual Use of Foreign Capital
合　　计	**Total**	**2580**	**3936089**	**2427469**	**2859**	**4313941**	**2454296**
亚　洲	**Asia**	**1815**	**2994322**	**1762865**	**2027**	**3068833**	**1919350**
#中国香港	Hong Kong, China	905	2412862	1428006	1084	2545820	1534202
中国澳门	Macao, China	7	8761	1856	14	15007	8315
中国台湾	Taiwan, China	364	136043	41550	419	246126	82938
印度尼西亚	Indonesia	9	17654	9202	3	1436	6247
日本	Japan	109	126151	104383	86	38716	84564
马来西亚	Malaysia	24	22782	35988	16	14567	15223
菲律宾	Philippines	4	325	315	4	10393	3609
新加坡	Singapore	88	144803	70418	96	26974	99846
韩国	Korea, Rep.	245	113349	64183	236	130625	77466
泰国	Thailand	4	2186	1020	1	25	77
非　洲	**Africa**	**62**	**28167**	**15811**	**60**	**27987**	**12711**
欧　洲	**Europe**	**258**	**175276**	**190022**	**264**	**204788**	**93746**
#比利时	Belgium	3	400	309	10	3505	362
丹麦	Dermark	4	－1498	1551	2	1420	1175
英国	United Kindom	48	33974	27572	35	56905	14852
德国	Germany	77	32050	31489	76	33989	21139
法国	France	20	45500	76909	24	14755	8568
爱尔兰	Ireland	1	1026	1215	2	2245	1226
意大利	Italy	27	1223	3824	29	13354	6827
卢森堡	Luxemboury	1	7682	4327	5	2791	780
荷兰	Netherlands	15	11311	9310	10	34144	5706
希腊	Greece	0	0	5	0	0	0
葡萄牙	Portugal	0	0	201	1	30	0
西班牙	Spain	10	2170	2098	9	1965	4490
芬兰	Finland	3	686	3164	8	4332	379
瑞士	Switzerland	14	11812	7254	7	12521	14156
北美洲	**North America**	**236**	**159393**	**67116**	**240**	**172100**	**114857**
#加拿大	Canada	54	17070	4728	66	46825	6973
美国	United States	181	125628	43829	172	119472	104069
大洋洲	**Oceania**	**142**	**124389**	**73061**	**122**	**86138**	**55553**
#澳大利亚	Australia	54	47469	9540	43	19608	7003
南美洲	**South America**	**60**	**103891**	**165307**	**73**	**227681**	**120582**

8-21 年末登记外商投资企业行业分布情况(2016年)

Sector Distribution Registered of Foreign-funded Enterprises at Year-end(2016)

行业	Sector	企业数(个) Number of Registered Enterprises (unit)	投资总额(万美元) Total Investment (USD 10000)	注册资本(万美元) Registered Capital (USD 10000)	#外方 Capital Invested by Foreign Partner
总计	**Total**	**55938**	**87986813**	**47182292**	**39522865**
农、林、牧、渔业	Agriculture, Forestry, Animal Husbandry and Fishery	862	942121	665903	616178
采矿业	Mining	16	140924	66865	60378
制造业	Manufacturing	28055	51959277	25802086	21968711
电力、热力、燃气及水的生产和供应业	Production and Supply of Electricity, Gas and Water	568	2027423	782060	538334
建筑业	Construction	717	2209770	1452328	1224952
批发和零售业	Wholesale and Retail Trades	8856	4053899	2484072	2313187
交通运输、仓储和邮政业	Transport, Storage and Post	972	2269068	1091814	881875
住宿和餐饮业	Hotels and Catering Services	3049	434292	278432	243019
信息传输、软件和信息技术服务业	Information Transfor Software and IT Services	1991	707177	412432	338131
金融业	Financial Intermediation	1055	828849	642115	393268
房地产业	Real Estate	1831	10802994	5873783	4823718
租赁和商务服务业	Leasing and Business Services	3197	3486817	3149114	2628722
科学研究、技术服务业	Scientific Research and Technical Service	3838	6869743	3727650	2889197
水利、环境和公共设施管理业	Management of Water Conservancy, Environment and Public Facilities	146	499739	296683	203236
居民服务、修理和其他服务业	Services to Households and Other Services	402	307582	174370	153941
教育	Education	43	15165	10160	8301
卫生和社会工作	Healthcare and Social Welfare	38	174336	86512	78046
文化、体育和娱乐业	Culture, Sports and Entertainment	283	245152	178192	152599
其他	Other	19	12484	7722	7071

8－22 对外承包工程
Contracted Projects with Foreign Countries

年 份 Year	合 同 数(份) Number of Contracts (unit)	合同金额(万美元) Contracted Value (USD 10000)	实际完成营业额(万美元) Value of Business Fulfilled (USD 10000)	年末在外人数(人) Number of Persons Abroad at the Year-end(person)
1985	13	262		
1990	32	3571	3521	881
1995	101	19495	19774	2946
1996	148	24040	22725	3298
1997	239	34599	31011	5997
1998	224	38224	34878	5784
1999	273	52110	34636	7403
2000	306	58544	49722	8616
2001	513	71200	62747	8320
2002	587	133743	105403	10992
2003	642	174201	142671	13449
2004	3317	213267	188958	21073
2005	1853	290079	251095	30211
2006	4975	426788	376509	38432
2007	922	400569	344919	41268
2008	791	432043	388434	34945
2009	727	449596	433249	36739
2010	968	544726	519838	35987
2011	891	594909	599171	35484
2012	1009	719844	646755	35615
2013	1021	865653	726299	36266
2014	1067	966108	795426	36552
2015	875	779596	876128	37907
2016	1543	728708	911122	32403

注：合同数口径2007年起调整，在国内承包的外资项目不再作为对外承包工程。

a) "Contracted projects" are adjusted from 2007, foreign funded projects contracted in domestic are no longer "contracted projects with foreign countries".

8－23 对外劳务合作

Labor Services Cooperation with Foreign Countries

年 份 Year	新签劳务人员合同工资总额（万美元） Total Contract Wages of New Signed Labor (USD 10000)	劳务人员实际收入总额（万美元） Tatal Real Income of Singned Labor (USD 10000)	年末在外人数(人) Number of Persons Abroad at the Year-end(person)
1985	2704		
1990	475	525	390
1995	8591	6120	5260
1996	12253	6287	9068
1997	13022	7454	9049
1998	24250	17271	17439
1999	29286	26538	25012
2000	39394	30293	34426
2001	48689	45316	56852
2002	37401	49989	62670
2003	33444	53984	65576
2004	31322	56974	69984
2005	40451	68056	70049
2006	41243	58843	73984
2007	51874	71087	75924
2008	56072	71304	66240
2009	53793	74555	63045
2010	76040	76864	59778
2011	64883	73590	53864
2012	62021	77438	51234
2013	75680	88826	51748
2014	120789	85351	59850
2015	51941	74550	63911
2016	45319	69634	55371

8－24 境外投资情况
Information of Overseas Investment

指　　标	Item	2012	2013	2014	2015	2016
新批项目数　（个）	**Number of Newly Approved Projects（unit）**	**572**	**605**	**736**	**880**	**1067**
按项目类型	By Broject Type					
企业	Enterprise	528	550	698	851	1049
子公司	Sub-enterprise	501	522	685	806	990
独资子公司	Joint Venture Enterprise	390	414	517	621	759
合资子公司	Solely Funded Enterprise	111	108	168	184	231
联营公司	Joint Ownership Enterprise	27	28	13	45	59
机构	Institution	44	55	38	29	18
按主体类型	By Subject Type					
国有及国有控股企业	State-owned Enterprise	60	58	58	52	95
集体企业	Collective-owned Enterprise	4	3	1	3	6
民营企业	Private Enterprise	383	426	554	693	814
外资企业	Foreign Funded Enterprise	125	118	123	132	152
按业务类型	By Business Type					
#参股并购类项目	Projects of Share Participating and Merging	83	80	110	170	220
风险投资类项目	Venture Investment Projects	13	10	7	7	2
贸易型项目	Trade Projects	243	210	277	315	286
非贸易型项目	Nontrade Projects	329	395	459	565	781
#境外加工贸易项目	Projects of Overseas Processing Trade	33	38	61	65	76
境外资源开发项目	Projects of Overseas Resource Development	33	9	10	18	7
中方协议金额　（万美元）	**Protocol Fund from China　（USD 10000）**	**504547**	**614272**	**721571**	**1030460**	**1422365**
按项目类型	By Project Type					
企业	Enterprise	504089	611917	721154	1030123	1422194
子公司	Sub-enterprise	491387	579871	712482	996893	1373375
独资子公司	Joint Venture Enterprise	393106	488365	543147	798599	1137147
合资子公司	Solely Funded Enterprise	98281	91506	169335	198294	236228
联营公司	Joint Ownership Enterprise	12702	32046	8672	33230	48820
机构	Institution	458	2356	417	337	171
按主体类型	By Subject Type					
国有及国有控股企业	State-owned Enterprise	84488	46418	65224	59895	180317
集体企业	Collective-owned Enterprise	2185	974	9998	38164	4641
民营企业	Private Enterprise	320725	434218	547679	795137	999928
外资企业	Foreign Funded Enterprise	97149	132663	98669	137264	237479
按业务类型	By Business Type					
#参股并购类项目	Projects of Share Participating and Merging	99294	126803	110347	199902	306426
风险投资类项目	Venture Investment Projects	13522	28342	17973	7753	897
贸易型项目	Trade Projects	154336	128831	167014	225716	242426
非贸易型项目	Nontrade Projects	350210	485441	554557	804744	1179940
#境外加工贸易项目	Projects of Overseas Processing Trade	34988	34307	57923	112433	150458
境外资源开发项目	Projects of Overseas Resource Development	61756	24100	22658	73734	30808

8-25 境外投资主要国别地区情况

Information of Overseas Investment to Main Countries or Regions

国家(地区) Country(Region)		2015		2016	
		新批项目数(个) Number of Newly Approved Projects (unit)	中方协议投资(万美元) Protocol Fund from China (USD 10000)	新批项目数(个) Number of Newly Approved Projects (unit)	中方协议投资(万美元) Protocol Fund from China (USD 10000)
全　部	**Total**	**880**	**1030460**	**1067**	**1422365**
亚洲	**Asia**	**469**	**594900**	**558**	**813219**
巴林	Bahrain				
孟加拉国	Bangladesh	5	1765	5	1705
缅甸	Burma	7	12501	22	7926
柬埔寨	Cambodia	16	4680	18	1306
塞浦路斯	Cyprus				
朝鲜	North Korea	1	278	1	9
中国香港	Hong Kong, China	240	335883	275	505401
印度	India	15	2651	17	37072
印度尼西亚	Indonesia	17	74627	24	84480
伊朗	Iran			2	9925
以色列	Israel	3	6133	3	1100
日本	Japan	21	21494	39	4022
老挝	Laos	2	1350	3	2480
中国澳门	Macao, China	4	813		
马来西亚	Malaysia	17	23549	15	30427
蒙古	Mongolia	4	16776	3	287
尼泊尔	Nepal			1	450
巴基斯坦	Pakistan	6	28000	9	26136
菲律宾	Philippines	3	2057	1	250
卡塔尔	Qatar				
沙特阿拉伯	Saudi Arabia	5	23	2	250
新加坡	Singapore	27	2386	26	19497
韩国	Korea	21	-452	20	1835
斯里兰卡	Sri Lanka	1	3400	4	2700
泰国	Thailand	9	25179	17	22451
土耳其	Tether			3	4649
阿拉伯联合酋长国	United Arab Emirates	6	2022	5	7632
越南	Vietnam	8	2581	18	24842
中国台湾	Taiwan, China	10	2481	12	1737
东帝汶	East Timor				
哈萨克斯坦	Kazakhstan	6	16678	6	13182
吉尔吉斯斯坦	Kyrgyzstan	2	3561		
土库曼斯坦	Turkmenistan				
乌兹别克斯坦	Uzbekistan	6	1270	1	130
其他	Other				

8－25 续 表 1 Contiued 1

国家(地区)	Country(Region)	2015		2016	
		新批项目数(个) Number of Newly Approved Projects (unit)	中方协议投资(万美元) Protocol Fund from China (USD 10000)	新批项目数(个) Number of Newly Approved Projects (unit)	中方协议投资(万美元) Protocol Fund from China (USD 10000)
非洲	**Africa**	**41**	**71453**	**55**	**80158**
阿尔及利亚	Airily	2	1	5	14021
安哥拉	Angola	2	750	1	660
喀麦隆	Cameroon				
乍得	Chad				
刚果	Congo			3	11102
埃及	Egypt			1	5
赤道几内亚	Guinea	2	2100	1	500
埃塞俄比亚	Ethiopia	5	7671	19	29472
加蓬	Gabon				
几内亚	Guinea	2	11970		
肯尼亚	Kenya	3	1100	2	650
毛里塔尼亚	Mauritania				
毛里求斯	Mauritius				
莫桑比克	Mozambique	5	3607	1	
纳米比亚	Namibia	1		1	408
尼日利亚	Nigeria	6	13592	3	4999
塞内加尔	Senegal				
塞舌尔	Seychelles	4	4330	1	405
南非	South Africa	1	1000	1	4000
苏丹	Sudan				
坦桑尼亚	Tanzania	3	20850	6	3946
乌干达	Uganda				
赞比亚	Zambia	3	625	4	5726
津巴布韦	Zimbabwe			3	860
欧洲	**Europe**	**78**	**47991**	**107**	**137630**
比利时	Belgium	1	130	2	86
丹麦	Denmark	1	215	2	338
英国	United Kingdom	9	3910	15	26994
德国	Germany	16	5300	34	40250
法国	France	11	1844	14	2107
意大利	Italy	5	1109	8	41722
卢森堡	Luxembourg	1	4000	1	1

8-25 续 表 2 Contiued 2

国家(地区) Country(Region)		2015		2016	
		新批项目数(个) Number of Newly Approved Projects (unit)	中方协议投资(万美元) Protocol Fund from China (USD 10000)	新批项目数(个) Number of Newly Approved Projects (unit)	中方协议投资(万美元) Protocol Fund from China (USD 10000)
荷兰	Netherlands	9	4410	10	5818
西班牙	Spain	2	1404	3	1038
阿尔巴尼亚	Albania				
奥地利	Austria				
保加利亚	Bulgaria	1	169		
芬兰	Finland	3	71	2	8506
匈牙利	Hungary	2	350		
挪威	Norway			1	180
波兰	Poland	1	1000	1	
罗马尼亚	Romania				
瑞典	Sweden	2	6000	1	307
瑞士	Switzerland	1	10	3	1152
俄罗斯联邦	the Russian Federation	8	17505	7	8635
乌克兰	Ukraine			1	280
克罗地亚	Croatia				
捷克	Czech				
塞尔维亚	Serbia				
拉丁美洲	**Latin America**	**55**	**117250**	**60**	**86379**
阿根廷	Argentina			1	4
巴西	Brazil	7	12989	5	17230
开曼群岛	Cayman Islands	21	35151	31	33070
智利	Chili	3	1070	2	300
古巴	Cuba				
厄瓜多尔	Ecuador	1	50	1	75
墨西哥	Mexico	1	9950	4	3381
秘鲁	Peru			1	300
英属维尔京群岛	British Virgin Islands	17	56912	15	32018
北美洲	**North America**	**200**	**127332**	**240**	**198528**
加拿大	Canada	12	15755	24	13932
美国	United States	185	107655	210	182098
其他	Other	3	3922	6	2497
大洋洲	**Oceania**	**37**	**71483**	**47**	**106452**
澳大利亚	Australia	33	64663	36	95537
斐济	Fiji	1	6000		
瓦努阿图	Vanuatu			1	20
新西兰	New Zealand	2	810	6	8715
萨摩亚	Samoa	1	10	3	1700

8-26 分行业境外投资情况
Information of Overseas Investment by Sector

行业	Sector	2015 新批项目数（个）Number of Newly Approved Projects (unit)	2015 中方协议投资（万美元）Protocol Fund from China (USD 10000)	2016 新批项目数（个）Number of Newly Approved Projects (unit)	2016 中方协议投资（万美元）Protocol Fund from China (USD 10000)
全部	**Total**	**880**	**1030460**	**1067**	**1422365**
第一产业	**Primary Industry**	**20**	**12406**	**27**	**48227**
农、林、牧、渔业	Farming, Forestry, Animal Husbandry and Fishery	20	12406	27	48227
农业	Farming	6	1940	16	39783
林业	Forestry	3	2599	3	13001
畜牧业	Animal Husbandry				
渔业	Fishery	3	1664	2	3175
农、林、牧、渔服务业	Services of Farming, Forestry, Animal Husbandry and Fishery	8	6204	6	-7732
第二产业	**Secondary Industry**	**287**	**388572**	**396**	**529713**
采矿业	Mining	13	72696	15	60036
煤炭开采和洗选业	Mining and Washing of Coal	5	28000	4	33425
黑色金属矿采选业	Mining and Processing of Ferrous Metal Ores			1	11000
有色金属矿采选业	Mining and Processing of Non-ferrous Metal Ores	6	43866	6	13609
非金属矿采选业	Mining and Processing of Nonmetal Ores	1	650	1	300
其他采矿业	Other Mining	1	180	3	1702
制造业	Manufacturing	222	256947	316	386615
农副食品加工业	Processing of Food from Agricultural Products	2	678		
食品制造业	Manufacture of Food	5	7804	5	3097
饮料制造业	Manufacture of Beverage	2	99		
纺织业	Manufacture of Textile	13	14275	14	16129
纺织服装、鞋、帽制造业	Manufacture of Textile Wearing, Apparel, Footwear and Caps	18	10801	35	24568
皮革、毛皮、羽毛（绒）及其制品业	Manufacture of Textile, Fur, Feather and Related Products	2	538		
木材加工及木、竹、藤、棕、草制品业	Processing of Timber, Manufacture of Wood, Bamboo, Rattan, Palm and Straw Products	4	1310	4	5863
家具制造业	Manufacture of Furniture	2	1852	4	8985
造纸及纸制品业	Manufacture of Paper and Paper Products	2	237	1	500
印刷业和记录媒介的复制	Printing, Reproduction of Recording Media	2	118	2	413
文教体育用品制造业	Manufacture of Articles For Culture, Education and Sport Activities			1	2
石油加工、炼焦及核燃料加工业	Processing of Petroleum, Coking, Processing of Nuclear Fuel			1	350

行业	Sector	2015 新批项目数（个） Number of Newly Approved Projects (unit)	2015 中方协议投资（万美元） Protocol Fund from China (USD 10000)	2016 新批项目数（个） Number of Newly Approved Projects (unit)	2016 中方协议投资（万美元） Protocol Fund from China (USD 10000)
化学原料及化学制品制造业	Manufacture of Raw Chemical Materials and Chemical Products	9	5132	13	20121
医药制造业	Manufacture of Medicines	19	10840	17	15811
化学纤维制造业	Manufacture of Chemical Fibers			3	2353
橡胶制品业	Manufacture of Rubber	5	2350	8	9160
塑料制品业	Manufacture of Plastics	8	4154	5	2054
非金属矿物制品业	Manufacture of Non-metallic Mineral Products	5	24016	3	1709
黑色金属冶炼及压延加工业	Smelting and Pressing of Ferrous Metals	1	2550	3	10701
有色金属冶炼及压延加工业	Smelting and Pressing of Non-ferrous Metals	6	45273	8	39827
金属制品业	Manufacture of Metal Products	13	9940	23	40565
通用设备制造业	Manufacture of General Purpose Machinery	13	18050	24	9918
专用设备制造业	Manufacture of Special Purpose Machinery	37	23429	35	32620
交通运输设备制造业	Manufacture of Transport Equipment	8	12411	24	22309
电气机械及器材制造业	Manufacture of Electrical Machinery and Equipment	18	49842	24	75859
通信设备、计算机及其他电子设备制造业	Manufacture of Communication Equipment, Computers and Other Electronic Equipment	20	7187	38	35676
仪器仪表及文化、办公用机械制造业	Manufacture of Measuring Instruments and Machinery for Cultural Activity and Office Work	2	150	6	1377
工艺品及其他制造业	Manufacture of Artwork and Other Manufacturing	5	3525	12	2847
废弃资源和废旧材料回收加工业	Recycling and Disposal of Waste			3	3800
电力、热力、燃气及水的生产和供应业	Production and Supply of Electric Power, Heat Power, Gas and Water	16	17550	13	20995
电力、热力的生产和供应业	Production and Supply of Electric Power and Heat Power	15	17381	13	20995
建筑业	Construction	36	41379	52	62067
房屋和土木工程建筑业	Construction of Building & Civil Engineering	20	24554	27	11658
建筑安装业	Building Installation	1	520	4	6450
建筑装饰业	Building Decoration	9	14660	12	7828
其他建筑业	Other Construction	6	1645	9	36131
第三产业	**Tertiary Industry**	**573**	**629432**	**644**	**844425**
交通运输、仓储和邮政业	Transport, Storage and Post	16	14920	9	1313

行 业	Sector	2015		2016	
		新批项目数（个）Number of Newly Approved Projects (unit)	中方协议投资（万美元）Protocol Fund from China (USD 10000)	新批项目数（个）Number of Newly Approved Projects (unit)	中方协议投资（万美元）Protocol Fund from China (USD 10000)
道路运输业	Road Transport			1	800
水上运输业	Warter Transport	8	13420	1	152
装卸搬运和其他运输服务业	Loading, Unloading and Other Transport Services	3	80	2	154
仓储业	Storage	5	1420	3	171
邮政业	Post			1	5
信息传输、计算机服务和软件业	Information Transmission, Computer Services and Software	42	26370	53	32853
电信和其他信息传输服务业	Information Transmission	6	12378	7	2464
计算机服务业	Computer Services	18	7346	28	10188
软件业	Software	18	6647	18	20202
批发和零售业	Wholesale and Retail Trades	263	214429	269	290119
批发业	Wholesale Trades	236	193909	245	261881
零售业	Retail Trads	27	20520	24	28238
住宿和餐饮业	Hotels and Catering Services	8	2753	10	2737
住宿业	Hotels	2	2099	1	1000
餐饮业	Catering Services	6	654	9	1737
金融业	Financial Intermediation			10	19856
房地产业	Real Estate	33	117456	32	91205
房地产业	Real Estate	33	117456	32	91205
租赁和商务服务业	Leasing and Business Services	137	209296	153	246799
租赁业	Leasing	8	5365	7	2305
商务服务业	Business Services	129	203931	146	244494
科学研究、技术服务和地质勘查业	Scientific Research, Technical Services and Geologic Prospecting	41	18987	74	100898
研究与试验发展	Research and Experimental Development	22	10986	40	39407
专业技术服务业	Professional Technical Services	9	5424	20	32565
科技交流和推广服务业	Services of Science and Technology Exchanges and Promotion	10	2577	14	28926
水利、环境和公共设施管理业	Management of Water Conservancy, Environment and Public Facilities	5	2250	8	10960
生态保护和环境治理业	Ecological Protection and Environment	5	2250	7	9760
居民服务和其他服务业	Services to Households and Other Services	17	23029	12	12627
居民服务业	Households Services	4	9272	3	7337
其他服务业	Other Services	13	13757	9	5290
教育	Education	2	1480	6	4214
教育	Education	2	1480	6	4214
文化、体育和娱乐业	Culture, Sports and Entertainment	9	3462	8	30845
新闻出版业	Journalism and Publishing Activities				
广播、电视、电影和音像业	Broadcasting, Movies, Television and Audiovisual Activities	6	2800	1	150
文化艺术业	Cultural and Art Activities	1	550	5	1307

8－27 分地区境外投资情况

Information of Overseas Investment by Region

地　　区 Region		2015		2016	
		新批项目数（个）Number of Newly Approved Projects（unit）	中方协议投资（万美元）Protocol Fund from China（USD 10000）	新批项目数（个）Number of Newly Approved Projects（unit）	中方协议投资（万美元）Protocol Fund from China（USD 10000）
全　省	**Total**	**880**	**1030460**	**1067**	**1422365**
苏　南	Southern Jiangsu	648	683111	775	947409
苏　中	Middle Jiangsu	141	168086	197	236251
苏　北	Northern Jiangsu	91	179263	95	238706
南京市	Nanjing	170	206155	175	300680
无锡市	Wuxi	115	174764	142	209661
徐州市	Xuzhou	31	73526	24	76490
常州市	Changzhou	67	75530	91	96631
苏州市	Suzhou	252	204754	333	320896
南通市	Nantong	78	113910	112	120891
连云港市	Lianyungang	23	50962	24	70969
淮安市	Huaian	6	6660	15	3883
盐城市	Yancheng	25	46295	26	56044
扬州市	Yangzhou	25	38859	47	57685
镇江市	Zhenjiang	44	21908	34	19541
泰州市	Taizhou	38	15317	38	57675
宿迁市	Suqian	6	1821	6	31319

主要统计指标解释

进出口总额 海关进出口总额指实际进出我国国境的货物总金额。包括对外贸易实际进出口货物,来料加工装配进出口货物,国家间、联合国及国际组织无偿援助物资和赠送品,华侨、港澳台同胞和外籍华人捐赠品,租赁期满归承租人所有的租赁货物,进料加工进出口货物,边境地方贸易及边境地区小额贸易进出口货物(边民互市贸易除外),中外合资企业、中外合作经营企业、外商独资经营企业进出口货物和公用物品,到、离岸价格在规定限额以上的进出口货样和广告品(无商业价值、无使用价值和免费提供出口的除外),从保税仓库提取在中国境内销售的进口货物,以及其他进出口货物。进出口总额用以观察一个国家在对外贸易方面的总规模。我国规定出口货物按离岸价格统计,进口货物按到岸价格统计。

商品经营单位所在地进、出口额 指所在地海关注册登记的有进出口经营权的企业实际进、出口额。

商品目的地进口额和商品货源地出口额 目的地进口额指进口货物的消费、使用或最终抵运地的实际进口额,货源地出口额是指出口货物的产地或原始发货地的实际出口额。

实际使用外资 指外国企业和经济组织或个人(包括华侨、港澳台胞以及我国在境外注册的企业)按我国有关政策、法规,用现汇、实物、技术等在我国境内开办外商独资企业、与我国境内的企业或经济组织共同举办中外合资经营企业、合作经营企业或合作开发资源的投资(包括外商投资收益的再投资)。

对外承包工程 指各对外承包公司以招标议标承包方式承揽的下列业务:(1)承包国外工程建设项目,(2)承包我国对外经援项目,(3)承包我国驻外机构的工程建设项目,(4)承包我国境内利用外资进行建设的工程项目,(5)与外国承包公司合营或联合承包工程项目时我国公司分包部分,(6)对外承包兼营的房屋开发业务。对外承包工程的营业额是以货币表现的本期内完成的对外承包工程的工作量,包括以前年度签订的合同和本年度新签订的合同在报告期内完成的工作量。

对外劳务合作 指以收取工资的形式向业主或承包商提供技术和劳动服务的活动。我国对外承包公司在境外开办的合营企业,中国公司同时又提供劳务的,其劳务部分也纳入劳务合作统计。劳务合作营业额按报告期内向雇主提交的结算数(包括工资、加班费和奖金等)统计。

Explanatory Notes on Main Statistical Indicators

Total Imports and Exports at Customs refer to the value of commodities imported into and exported from the boundary of China. They include the actual imports and exports through foreign trade, imported and exported goods under the processing and assembling trades and materials, supplies and gifts as aid given gratis between governments and by the United Nations and other international organizations, and contributions donated by overseas Chinese, compatriots in Hong Kong and Macao and Chinese with foreign citizenship, leasing commodities owned by tenant at the expiration of leasing period, the imported and exported commodities processed with imported materials, commodities trading in border areas (excluding mutual exchange goods), the imported and exported commodities and articles for public use of the Sino-foreign joint ventures, cooperative enterprises and ventures exclusively with foreign own investment. Also included are import or export of samples and advertising goods for whose CIF or FOB value are beyond the permitted ceiling (excluding goods of no trading or use value and free commodities for export), imported goods sold in China from bonded warehouses and other imported or exported goods. The indicator of the total imports and exports at customs can be used to observe the total size of external trade in a country. In accordance with the stipulation of the Chinese government, imports are calculated at CIF, while exports are calculated at FOB.

Import Export Value by Location of Chinas Foreign Trade Managing Units refers to actual value of imports and exports carried out by corporations which have been registered by the local customhouse and are vested with fight to run import export business.

Import Value of Commodities by the Places of their Destination and Export Value of Commodities by the Places of their Origin in China: The former indicator refers to the value of import commodities of the places of their consumption, utilization or the places of their final destination. The latter indicator refers to the value of export commodities of the places of their origin or the places of the commodities dispatched.

Actual Use of Foreign Capital refers to the investments inside China by foreign enterprises and economic organizations or individuals (including overseas Chinese, compatriots from Hong Kong and Macao, and Chinese enterprises registered abroad), following the relevant policies and laws of China, for the establishment of ventures exclusively with foreign own investment, Sino-foreign joint ventures and cooperative enterprises or for co-operative exploration of resources with enterprises or economic organizations in China. It includes the re investment of the foreign entrepreneurs with the profits gained from the investment. Foreign direct investment of 2005 was the volume affirmed by the Commercial Department.

Contracted Projects with Foreign Countries refer to projects undertaken by Chinese contractors (project contracting companies) through bidding process. They include: (1) overseas civil engineering construction projects financed by foreign investors; (2) overseas projects financed by the Chinese government through its foreign aid programs; (3) construction projects of Chinese diplomatic missions, trade offices and other institutions stationed abroad; (4) construction projects in China financed by foreign investment; (5) sub-contracted projects to be taken by Chinese contractors through a joint umbrella project with foreign contractor(s); (6) housing development projects. The business income from international contracted projects is the work volume of contracted projects completed during the reference period, expressed in monetary terms, including completed work on projects signed in previous years.

Service Cooperation with Foreign Countries refers to the activities of providing technology and labor services to employers or contractors in the forms of receiving salaries and wages. Labor services providing by contractual joint ventures of Chinese international contracting corporations should be included in the statistics of service co-operation with foreign countries. The business income of labor service co operation is the income in the form of wages and salaries, overtime pay, bonuses and other remuneration received from the employers during the reference period.

9

能源、资源、环境

Energy, Resource and Environment

简 要 说 明

一、本篇资料的主要内容

本篇主要反映江苏自然资源、能源消费、电力运行、环境保护事业发展情况。

自然资源包括水资源、气象等数据资料。

能源消费包括综合能源平衡表、规模以上工业企业主要能源品种消费量等。

电力运行包括电网生产经营情况、用电量、主要电厂发电量等。

环境保护事业发展情况主要包括污染排放与处理情况、生态环境保护情况等。

二、本篇资料的统计范围

本篇资料的统计范围为全社会。

三、本篇的资料来源

气象、水资源、环境保护事业发展情况分别由气象、水利、环保等部门提供。

电力运行数据来源于省电力公司。

能源消费数据来自历年能源平衡表及相关能源统计年报。

Brief Introduction

I. Main Contents

This chapter contains information that reflects natural resource conditions, energy consumption, power operation and the development of environment protection.

Data on natural resource cover water resource and meteorological phenomena, etc.

Data on energy cover aggregate balance sheet of energy and major energy consumption of above designated industrial enterprises, etc.

Data on power operation Including power grid production and operation, use of electricity, the main power plant power generation, etc.

Data on the development of environment protection mainly include discharge and treatment of pollution, ecological and environmental protection, etc.

II. Sources of Data

The scope of data in this chapter is the whole country.

III. Sources of Data

Data on meteorological phenomena, water resources, development of environment protection are provided respectively by meteorology, water conservancy and environment protection ministry.

Power operation data from the Jiangsu Electric Power Company.

Data on energy consumption are from the energy balance sheets over the years and relevant energy statistics annals.

9-1 主要城市月平均气温（2016年）
Monthly Average Temperature of Major Cities (2016)

单位:摄氏度 (℃)

城市 City	1月 Jan	2月 Feb	3月 Mar	4月 Apr	5月 May	6月 June	7月 July	8月 Aug	9月 Sept	10月 Oct	11月 Nov	12月 Dec	年平均气温 Yearly Average
南京市 Nanjing	3.1	6.7	11.2	17.3	20.1	24.1	28.9	29.1	24.1	18.3	11.3	7.3	16.8
无锡市 Wuxi	3.8	6.7	11.2	17.3	20.6	24.5	30.0	29.8	24.5	19.6	12.3	8.1	17.4
徐州市 Xuzhou	0.3	4.4	11.2	17.7	20.7	25.5	28.1	28.2	24.1	16.6	9.2	4.7	15.9
常州市 Changzhou	3.4	6.6	11.1	17.5	20.5	24.5	29.4	29.6	24.5	19.0	11.8	7.6	17.1
苏州市 Suzhou	4.2	7.2	11.4	17.4	20.8	24.4	30.1	29.9	24.7	19.9	12.8	8.9	17.6
南通市 Nantong	3.2	5.9	10.0	16.2	19.8	23.9	28.8	29.0	24.0	19.2	12.0	7.6	16.6
连云港市 Lianyungang	-0.2	3.1	8.4	15.8	19.5	23.7	27.2	27.6	23.4	16.9	9.2	4.1	14.9
淮安市 Huaian	1.0	4.3	9.6	16.2	19.4	23.9	27.5	27.6	22.5	16.7	9.3	4.9	15.2
盐城市 Yancheng	1.7	4.5	9.4	15.8	19.5	24.0	27.8	28.2	23.7	18.2	10.5	6.0	15.8
扬州市 Yangzhou	2.3	5.4	10.8	17.2	20.2	24.3	29.0	29.0	24.0	18.2	10.7	6.1	16.4
镇江市 Zhenjiang	3.2	6.6	11.1	17.4	20.3	24.3	29.1	29.5	24.5	18.7	11.4	7.5	17.0
泰州市 Taizhou	2.2	5.1	9.9	16.3	19.6	24.0	28.4	28.4	23.6	18.4	10.8	6.5	16.1
宿迁市 Suqian	0.9	4.5	10.3	17.0	20.2	24.5	27.9	27.9	23.5	16.6	9.5	5.3	15.7

9-2 主要城市月降水量（2016年）
Monthly Precipitation of Major Cities (2016)

单位:毫米 (mm)

城市 City	1月 Jan	2月 Feb	3月 Mar	4月 Apr	5月 May	6月 June	7月 July	8月 Aug	9月 Sept	10月 Oct	11月 Nov	12月 Dec	全年累计 Yearly Total
南京市 Nanjing	62.8	31.1	40.0	155.4	119.6	186.2	477.3	78.7	187.4	308.0	95.4	65.8	1807.7
无锡市 Wuxi	64.1	21.5	42.9	220.3	186.8	353.6	234.0	27.7	292.6	314.8	83.4	48.7	1890.4
徐州市 Xuzhou	8.2	14.1	7.3	33.4	84.9	106.8	136.1	78.8	40.3	174.4	29.5	53.0	766.8
常州市 Changzhou	64.7	19.9	34.5	143.9	188.2	335.9	433.4	56.8	397.0	341.0	95.5	54.3	2165.1
苏州市 Suzhou	71.9	30.0	46.3	186.9	192.5	400.9	283.6	31.9	260.0	282.9	131.8	55.6	1974.3
南通市 Nantong	55.1	22.9	33.4	139.0	147.9	470.1	399.2	23.1	234.2	345.9	63.8	37.6	1972.2
连云港市 Lianyungang	5.7	30.3	9.7	30.6	61.4	123.1	135.3	217.4	33.2	200.5	11.2	42.8	901.2
淮安市 Huaian	8.5	20.2	26.3	68.4	113.5	194.0	164.9	60.8	51.7	226.6	34.5	37.3	1006.7
盐城市 Yancheng	25.4	10.9	32.8	86.4	137.9	127.4	362.1	97.5	210.8	263.7	52.6	52.8	1460.3
扬州市 Yangzhou	62.4	23.5	39.5	111.5	194.8	258.3	385.1	138.5	266.3	326.3	112.7	73.2	1992.1
镇江市 Zhenjiang	64.1	26.0	30.9	135.4	162.9	181.4	380.5	94.6	315.2	416.6	121.8	66.7	1996.1
泰州市 Taizhou	48.3	18.7	26.9	100.2	211.5	256.0	322.0	97.1	268.0	427.0	122.1	75.4	1973.2
宿迁市 Suqian	6.0	26.8	20.0	28.8	98.1	219.5	131.9	134.0	20.2	300.0	16.2	52.2	1053.7

9－3 水资源总量（2016 年）
Water Resources (2016)

单位:亿立方米 (100 million cu. m)

项目	Item	水资源总量 Total	地表水资源量 Surface Water Volume	地下水资源量 Underground Water Volume	地下水与地表水重复计算量 Duplicated Computation Volume of Surface Water and Underground Water	年降水量 Annual Precipitation
合计	**Total**	**741.8**	**605.8**	**164.0**	**28.0**	**1438.0**
按流域区域分	**by Drainage Area**					
淮河流域	Drainage Area of Huaihe River	315.1	230.1	102.2	17.3	714.0
王家坝至中渡区	from Wangjiaba to Zhongdu	39.3	25.1	15.2	1.0	93.0
中渡以下	below Zhongdu	187.0	160.5	34.3	7.7	399.0
沂沭泗河区	Yishusi River District	88.8	44.5	52.8	8.6	221.0
长江流域	Drainage Area of Yangtze River	426.7	375.6	61.8	10.7	724.0
湖口以下干流	below Hukou	195.9	165.9	31.6	1.7	352.0
太湖流域	Drainage Area of Taihu Lake	230.8	209.7	30.2	9.1	373.0
按行政区域分	**by Administrative Areas**					
南京市	Nanjing	68.8	60.3	10.2	1.7	119.0
无锡市	Wuxi	61.2	56.6	10.4	5.7	92.0
徐州市	Xuzhou	45.7	19.0	29.8	3.1	97.0
常州市	Changzhou	65.7	61.5	4.5	0.3	96.0
苏州市	Suzhou	81.8	72.5	11.2	1.9	151.0
南通市	Nantong	88.2	75.0	13.9	0.7	168.0
连云港市	Lianyungang	20.9	12.2	10.4	1.7	61.0
淮安市	Huaian	47.8	32.6	18.6	3.4	109.0
盐城市	Yancheng	85.0	68.6	23.1	6.7	187.0
扬州市	Yangzhou	49.9	44.8	6.3	1.1	105.0
镇江市	Zhenjiang	43.2	39.0	5.0	0.7	72.0
泰州市	Taizhou	52.9	44.4	8.8	0.3	98.0
宿迁市	Suqian	30.6	19.4	11.8	0.6	83.0

9－4 农村自然灾害情况
Basic Siatistics on Rural Natural Disaster

单位:千公顷 (1000 hectares)

指标	Item	2000	2010	2012	2013	2014	2015	2016
受灾面积	Area Covered	3411.68	1070.93	1406.45	487.36	407.69	615.46	332.10
#旱灾	Drought	1196.87	522.99	219.46	222.28	320.57		31.53
水灾	Flood	175.59	316.37	156.86	98.37	2.28	224.77	87.79

9-5 规模以上工业企业主要能源消费量
Major Energy Consumption of above Designated Industrial Enterprises

单位:万吨 (10000 tons)

名称	Item	2005	2009	2010	2012	2013	2014	2015	2016
原煤	Coal	15154.25	19726.52	22159.36	24627.54	25927.40	25646.36	24601.86	25775.42
焦炭	Coke	1562.66	2519.04	2784.16	3169.66	3210.61	3558.65	3588.63	3840.22
原油	Crude Oil	2250.86	2652.49	2992.16	2942.17	3382.97	3498.79	3810.32	4078.99
汽油	Gasoline	32.07	44.60	47.54	38.37	36.51	37.46	38.31	37.12
煤油	Kerasene	3.75	2.24	2.53	1.97	1.51	1.32	1.20	1.79
柴油	Diesel Oil	117.88	108.36	111.37	96.13	94.32	93.87	79.61	73.61
燃料油	Fuel Oil	212.52	116.47	110.60	70.71	61.43	54.27	38.74	47.76
液化石油气	LPG	53.40	44.64	38.03	33.39	41.86	34.19	33.85	47.51

9-6 规模以上工业企业平均每天主要能源消费量
Average Daily Energy Consumption of above Designated Industrial Enterprises

单位:吨 (ton)

名称	Item	2005	2009	2010	2012	2013	2014	2015	2016
原煤	Coal	415185	540453	607106	674727	710340	702640	674024	704247
焦炭	Coke	42813	69015	76278	86840	87962	97497	98319	104924
原油	Crude Oil	61667	72671	81977	80607	92684	95857	104392	111448
汽油	Gasoline	879	1222	1302	1051	1000	1026	1050	1014
煤油	Kerasene	103	61	69	54	41	36	33	49
柴油	Diesel Oil	3230	2969	3051	2634	2584	2572	2181	2011
燃料油	Fuel Oil	5822	3191	3030	1937	1683	1487	1061	1305
液化石油气	LPG	1463	1223	1042	915	1147	937	927	1298

9－7　综合能源平衡表

单位：万吨标准煤

项　　目	Item	2000	2005	2006	2007
可供消费的能源总量	**Total Energy**				
一次能源生产量	Primary Energy Output	1996.86	2267.63	2516.29	2405.84
回收能	Retrieved	136.24	356.07	675.51	641.62
进口量	Imported	708.45	2315.38	2249.05	2441.19
出口量	Exported	48.20	186.52	179.67	70.43
年初年末库存差额	Stock Changes in the Year	13.21	－19.73	124.81	－128.23
能源消费总量	**Total Energy Consumption**	**8612.43**	**17167.39**	**18742.19**	**20948.04**
在总量中：	of This Total：				
农、林、牧、渔、水利业	Farming Forestry，Animal Husbandry，Fishery and Water Conservancy	400.39	321.59	327.97	330.16
工业	Industry	6743.95	14020.33	15401.34	17307.23
建筑业	Construction	41.34	204.68	218.02	227.77
交通运输、仓储及邮电通讯业	Transportantion，Storage，Post and Telecommunication	358.52	899.45	957.00	1058.69
批发和零售贸易餐饮业	Wholesale and Retail and Catering Trade	169.94	249.86	260.27	293.51
其他	Others	209.38	373.21	416.19	476.52
生活消费	Residential Consumption	688.91	1098.27	1161.40	1254.16
在总量中：	of This Total：				
终端消费	Final Consumption	8220.49	16311.17	17860.58	20008.61
#工业	Industry	6352.00	13164.12	14519.73	16367.80
损失量	Loss	269.36	653.43	691.48	748.50

Aggregate Balance Sheet of Energy

(10000 tons standardized coal)

2008	2009	2010	2012	2013	2014	2015	2016
2489.40	2618.54	2771.96	2751.62	2720.88	3096.99	2893.58	2471.20
883.24	1039.79	884.86	1045.78	1348.41	1572.05	1590.94	1693.32
2226.54	2806.18	3267.83	3226.63	3941.23	3717.27	4301.50	4695.14
97.34	205.33	176.89	164.53	241.15	312.12	352.39	412.89
-200.66	-26.50	-377.43	149.22	26.35	-88.72	160.00	731.21
22232.23	**23709.28**	**25773.70**	**27821.11**	**29205.38**	**29863.03**	**30235.30**	**31053.89**
330.89	360.96	394.68	389.48	440.98	462.61	516.32	534.04
18133.51	19260.23	20597.82	21917.80	22548.91	23080.21	23119.51	23456.02
232.93	249.09	281.22	343.43	397.04	415.54	377.84	349.66
1201.71	1254.10	1462.56	1676.40	1835.07	2014.31	2125.45	2200.99
341.13	366.74	400.80	485.63	529.46	531.53	531.92	571.63
538.59	628.20	753.80	911.28	1028.91	1031.45	1101.72	1196.69
1453.47	1589.96	1882.82	2097.09	2425.01	2327.38	2462.54	2744.86
21245.30	22667.03	24267.83	27112.25	29219.75	29753.16	30247.39	31395.38
17146.59	18218.00	19976.78	21208.94	22563.28	22970.34	23131.60	23797.51
803.13	826.90	954.20	973.52	659.18	853.34	809.79	673.95

9－8 江苏电网生产经营综合情况

指 标 名 称	Item	2005	2006	2007
发电装机 （万千瓦）	Power Generation Capacity （10000 kW）	4270	5304	5599
发电量 （亿千瓦时）	Power Generation （100 million kW·h）	2120.00	2536.56	2825.33
统调发电最高负荷（万千瓦）	Maximum Controlled Power Generation Load （10000 kW）	3215.7	3853.6	4392.5
统调发电平均负荷率 （%）	Average Controlled Power Generation Load Rate （%）	89.67	89.88	89.72
全社会用电量 （亿千瓦时）	Total Electricity Consumption （100 million kW·h）	2193.45	2569.75	2952.02
第一产业	Primary Industry （100 million kW·h）	29.12	24.92	24.47
第二产业	Secondary Industry （100 million kW·h）	1793.34	2110.55	2439.13
第三产业	Tertiary Industry （100 million kW·h）	1771.28	2088.68	2415.45
#工业	Industry （100 million kW·h）	170.27	200.00	233.06
统调用电最高负荷（万千瓦）	Maximum Controlled Electricity Consumption Load （10000 kW）	3319.3	3827.6	4562.4
统调用电平均负荷率 （%）	Average Controlled Electricity Consumption Load Rate （%）	88.94	89.66	90.03
电源固定资产投资 （亿元）	Investment in Fixed Assets in Power Supply （100 million yuan）	289.02	208.79	125.52
电网固定资产投资 （亿元）	Investment in Fixed Assets in Power Grid （100 million yuan）	166.02	225.94	226.25
新增110千伏及以上输电能力 （公里）	Newly Increased Capacity of 110 kV and above Power Transmission （km）	5188	5197	5119
新增110千伏及以上变电能力 （万千伏安）	Newly Increased Capacity of 110 kV and above Power Transformation （10000 kW）	1863	1721	1979
新投发电装机 （万千瓦）	Newly Increased Power Generation Capacity （10000 kW）	1450.50	1044.90	406.45

General Production and Business of Jiangsu Power Grid

2008	2009	2010	2012	2013	2014	2015	2016
5442	5650	6458	7532	8229	8599	9529	10148
2887.26	2984.31	3499.29	4158.37	4404.94	4347.82	4425.96	4753.67
4328.2	4479.5	5302.6	5820.0	6400.8	6429.1	6870.3	7360.1
89.30	90.36	90.99	91.39	91.66	91.62	91.47	91.84
3118.32	3313.99	3864.37	4580.90	4956.62	5012.54	5114.70	5458.95
23.34	25.45	28.36	37.96	43.40	46.62	52.51	4081.42
2529.68	2660.16	3085.35	3605.58	3844.47	3926.70	3952.57	61.87
2502.70	2631.28	3052.12	3562.48	3794.18	3873.35	3903.61	4126.55
269.57	304.44	361.04	468.51	521.67	542.35	580.42	650.98
4726.7	5229.7	6033.7	6856.6	7738.2	7863.0	8118.3	8886.2
89.00	89.61	90.22	90.97	91.55	91.97	91.78	91.60
59.08	93.06	103.89	220.05	201.65	163.73	76.15	89.12
300.46	321.29	296.95	368.70	378.71	309.82	328.61	383.71
[illegible]	5987	5210	6726	3145	3678	2841	2573
3750	4091	4061	3432	1773	1933	2198	2322
349.16	303.90	864.80	670.84	778.23	398.18	961.43	667.76

9－9　全社会用电情况

单位:亿千瓦小时

项　　目	Item	2005	2006	2007	2008
全社会用电量	**Total**	**2193.45**	**2569.75**	**2952.02**	**3118.32**
按产业分	Grouped by Type of Industry				
第一产业	Primary Industry	29.12	24.92	24.47	23.34
第二产业	Secondary Industry	1793.34	2110.55	2439.13	2529.68
第三产业	Tertiary Industry	170.27	200.00	233.06	269.57
按行业分	Grouped by Sector				
农林牧渔水利业	Farming, Forestry, Animal Husbandry, Fishery and Water Conservancy	29.12	24.92	24.47	23.34
#排灌	Irrigation	12.05	8.97	8.92	7.56
工业	Industry	1771.28	2088.68	2415.45	2502.70
#轻工业	Light Industry	519.99	578.06	615.90	612.33
重工业	Heavy Industry	1251.29	1510.62	1799.55	1890.37
#制造业	Manufacturing	1745.07	1645.82	1928.80	1998.23
#纺织业	Manufacture of Textile	228.39	269.24	309.72	298.69
化学原料及化学制品制造业	Chemical Raw Materials and Chemical Products	210.26	241.77	275.81	282.74
非金属矿物制品业	Manufacture of Non-metallic Mineral Products	118.77	133.43	146.18	151.02
黑色金属冶炼及压延加工业	Smelting and Pressing of Ferrous Metals	224.90	279.92	336.90	341.65
通用及专用设备制造业	Ordinary and Special Purpose Equipment	67.39	81.07	107.02	124.09
建筑业	Construction	22.06	21.87	23.68	26.98
交通运输、仓储和邮政业	Transportation, Post and Telecommunication	16.45	16.90	19.50	22.89
信息传输、计算机服务和软件业	Information Transmission, Computer Service and Software	9.01	10.99	13.12	15.25
商业、住宿和餐饮业	Commerce, Hotel and Catering Industry	55.52	64.57	73.47	83.42
金融、房地产、商务及居民服务业	Banking, Real Estate, Commercial and Residents' Service	27.72	35.88	43.78	53.62
公共事业及管理组织	Public Undertaking and Management Organizations	61.58	71.66	83.20	94.38
城乡居民生活用电	Electricity Consumption by Urban and Rural Residents	200.72	234.29	255.35	295.74
城镇居民	Urban Area	102.18	118.51	127.17	146.17
乡村居民	Rural Area	98.54	115.77	128.19	149.57

Basic Situation of Total Electricity Consumption

(100 million kW · h)

2009	2010	2012	2013	2014	2015	2016
3313.99	**3864.37**	**4580.90**	**4956.62**	**5012.54**	**5114.70**	**5458.95**
25.45	28.36	37.96	43.40	46.62	52.51	61.87
2660.16	3085.35	3605.58	3844.47	3926.70	3952.57	4126.55
304.44	361.04	468.51	521.67	542.35	580.42	650.98
25.45	28.36	37.96	43.40	46.62	52.51	61.87
8.44	8.94	10.85	11.12	12.06	12.53	14.39
2631.28	3052.12	3562.48	3794.18	3873.35	3903.61	4081.42
640.56	725.64	867.46	924.66	949.31	985.17	1031.63
1990.73	2326.48	2695.02	2869.52	2924.03	2918.44	3049.79
2090.27	2447.56	2902.94	3137.53	3278.71	3331.02	3426.38
309.01	340.06	398.56	419.09	417.38	434.64	443.12
287.34	311.38	371.35	372.34	403.27	430.41	443.94
154.33	172.91	186.99	195.92	201.62	188.47	192.52
343.37	388.12	428.99	498.99	508.81	488.21	452.63
132.72	178.23	225.89	256.83	279.38	278.60	301.70
28.88	33.23	43.09	50.29	53.35	48.96	45.13
25.40	31.01	47.24	52.26	57.23	62.72	70.12
17.70	20.80	30.00	33.88	37.73	43.34	48.02
93.64	108.25	137.28	150.74	155.08	161.94	180.55
62.66	78.92	110.36	125.60	132.07	141.82	161.54
105.05	122.05	143.63	159.18	160.24	170.60	190.74
323.93	389.62	468.86	547.08	496.87	529.20	619.54
159.26	194.26	230.64	264.52	239.17	257.46	303.95
164.67	195.36	238.22	282.56	257.70	271.74	315.59

9－10 分地区全社会用电量

单位:亿千瓦小时

地 区	Region	2005	2006	2007	2008
全 省	**Total**	**2193.45**	**2569.75**	**2952.02**	**3118.32**
苏 南	**Southern Jiangsu**	**1429.59**	**1681.27**	**1925.13**	**2000.92**
南京市	Nanjing	246.67	270.57	299.13	310.79
镇江市	Zhenjiang	97.18	110.54	126.80	137.69
常州市	Changzhou	182.66	212.68	230.62	237.33
无锡市	Wuxi	337.05	400.99	461.31	466.69
苏州市	Suzhou	566.04	686.49	807.27	848.42
苏 中	**Mid Jiangsu**	**316.61**	**371.29**	**433.96**	**466.10**
扬州市	Yangzhou	82.04	94.22	108.94	116.99
泰州市	Taizhou	95.74	113.47	134.02	145.57
南通市	Nantong	138.83	163.60	191.01	203.55
苏 北	**Northern Jiangsu**	**322.18**	**376.49**	**435.75**	**483.61**
徐州市	Xuzhou	120.18	139.99	160.30	172.00
淮安市	Huaian	59.05	65.49	77.71	89.70
宿迁市	Suqian	25.90	32.07	38.79	45.60
盐城市	Yancheng	76.26	89.78	106.21	118.39
连云港市	Lianyungang	40.80	49.17	52.74	57.92

注：各市用电量中未包括网损、大厂厂用电量和沙河抽水电量(下同)。

Electricity Consumption by Region

(100 million kW · h)

2009	2010	2012	2013	2014	2015	2016
3313.99	**3864.37**	**4580.90**	**4956.62**	**5012.54**	**5114.70**	**5458.95**
2097.90	**2403.82**	**2737.87**	**2935.47**	**2941.26**	**3031.71**	**3208.38**
337.05	373.66	424.96	462.67	470.50	495.18	524.79
144.92	164.22	193.47	212.20	209.41	216.27	232.41
255.41	291.19	351.51	390.98	395.06	408.04	429.93
480.57	550.64	578.01	606.40	598.18	600.50	638.67
879.94	1024.10	1189.93	1263.21	1268.12	1311.72	1382.58
502.04	**577.40**	**686.72**	**746.08**	**769.89**	**788.16**	**839.70**
129.16	151.09	173.63	197.38	204.36	211.50	225.37
155.43	176.61	211.31	222.55	232.30	227.46	239.55
217.45	249.70	301.79	326.15	333.23	349.19	374.79
549.83	**672.60**	**908.96**	**1031.48**	**1066.44**	**1099.23**	**1141.38**
202.44	246.01	318.57	336.42	332.47	344.19	353.91
95.82	111.77	134.78	148.39	151.53	156.54	163.20
53.89	72.69	114.34	136.58	146.38	151.24	168.83
131.64	158.63	225.31	275.16	278.55	280.58	289.29
66.03	83.52	115.97	134.94	157.51	166.68	166.15

a) Begion Electricity consumption are not included network losses, point plant and river pumping pouser consumption.

9－11 分地区工业用电量

单位:亿千瓦小时

地 区	Region	2005	2006	2007	2008
全 省	**Total**	**1771.28**	**2088.68**	**2415.45**	**2502.70**
苏 南	**Southern Jiangsu**	**1168.80**	**1384.62**	**1596.21**	**1624.04**
南京市	Nanjing	173.53	187.04	207.11	207.70
镇江市	Zhenjiang	79.96	90.83	105.32	112.48
常州市	Changzhou	145.20	175.00	190.80	192.09
无锡市	Wuxi	286.55	343.34	397.24	393.45
苏州市	Suzhou	483.56	588.41	695.73	718.32
苏 中	**Mid Jiangsu**	**243.06**	**287.85**	**339.81**	**359.33**
扬州市	Yangzhou	60.32	69.10	81.03	85.49
泰州市	Taizhou	77.59	92.10	109.39	117.64
南通市	Nantong	105.15	126.65	149.39	156.19
苏 北	**Northern Jiangsu**	**234.35**	**275.53**	**322.25**	**351.66**
徐州市	Xuzhou	91.61	109.26	126.33	132.69
淮安市	Huaian	45.10	49.23	59.07	68.47
宿迁市	Suqian	15.87	20.35	25.23	29.41
盐城市	Yancheng	54.34	63.50	76.58	84.71
连云港市	Lianyungang	27.43	33.18	35.04	36.37

Industrial Electricity Consumption by Region

(100 million kW · h)

2009	2010	2012	2013	2014	2015	2016
2631.28	**3052.12**	**3562.48**	**3794.18**	**3873.35**	**3903.61**	**4081.42**
1685.72	**1916.54**	**2142.30**	**2265.03**	**2289.15**	**2337.80**	**2429.39**
223.75	242.66	265.64	286.71	289.02	300.54	310.81
117.14	131.81	151.62	163.38	162.44	165.33	173.77
205.41	231.82	277.88	308.06	316.09	325.49	334.78
400.88	455.00	464.51	476.28	477.47	472.24	493.73
738.54	855.25	982.66	1030.61	1044.14	1074.20	1116.30
383.84	**436.74**	**510.97**	**542.52**	**571.50**	**578.06**	**598.45**
93.72	109.96	123.20	139.13	147.89	152.49	156.60
124.71	138.94	164.81	169.02	180.73	172.53	176.20
165.41	187.84	222.96	234.38	242.89	253.05	265.65
397.50	**488.30**	**661.87**	**743.04**	**777.74**	**792.14**	**784.10**
156.85	191.90	246.08	252.97	247.48	254.36	250.22
71.28	81.75	95.50	102.30	106.89	108.89	106.70
34.61	48.81	79.90	94.86	103.90	106.04	115.81
93.42	111.86	164.49	204.19	209.02	206.28	201.37
41.34	53.99	75.91	88.73	110.44	116.57	110.00

9－12 主要发电厂发电情况
Electricity Production of Major Power Plants

厂 名 Item		2015 装机容量（万千瓦）Installed Capacity (10000 kW)	2015 发电量（亿千瓦时）Electricity Production (100 million kW·h)	2016 装机容量（万千瓦）Installed Capacity (10000 kW)	2016 发电量（亿千瓦时）Electricity Production (100 million kW·h)
全省总计	**Total**	**9529**	**4425.96**	**10148**	**4753.67**
#统调发电厂	Unified Planning Power Plant	8505	3999.66	9013	4318.46
非统调发电厂	Non-unified Planning Power Plant	1023	426.30	1135	435.21
（一）中国华能集团公司	**State Grid Xinyuan Co.**				
华能南京金陵发电有限公司	Nanjing Jinling Power Co.,Ltd of Huaneng Group	200	117.28	200	127.66
华能南通发电厂	Nantong Power Plant of Huaneng Group	140	61.67	140	61.29
华能淮阴第二发电有限责任公司	Huaiyin Second Power Co.,Ltd of Huaneng Group	132	58.13	132	55.70
华能太仓发电有限责任公司	Taichang Power Co.,Ltd of Huaneng Group	126	68.97	126	69.35
华能南京燃机发电有限公司	Nanjing Combustion Generating Power Co., Ltd of Huaneng Group	78	25.81	78	17.17
华能南京发电厂	Nanjing Power Plant of Huaneng Group	64	27.36	64	30.01
华能（苏州工业园区）发电有限责任公司	Suzhou Industrial Park Power Co., Ltd of Huaneng Group	64	31.84	64	35.72
华能金陵燃机热电有限公司	Jinling Combustion Generating Power Co., Ltd of Huaneng Group	36	17.11	36	18.01
华能苏州热电有限公司	Suzhou Thermal Power Co.,Ltd of Huaneng			12	7.84
（二）中国大唐集团公司	**China Datang Group Co.**				
江苏大唐国际吕四港发电有限责任公司	Jiangsu Datang Lvsi Power Co.,Ltd	264	131.76	264	141.89
大唐南京发电厂	Datang Nanjing Power Plant	132	74.22	132	77.04
江苏徐塘发电有限公司	jiangsu Xutang Power Co.,Ltd	130	44.81	130	40.73
大唐苏州热电有限责任公司	Datang Suzhou Thermal Power Co.,Ltd	36	16.20	36	14.04
（三）中国华电集团公司	**China Huadian Group Co.**				
江苏华电句容发电有限公司	Jiangsu Huadian Jurong Power Co.,Ltd			200	116.10
江苏华电戚墅堰发电有限公司	Jiangsu Huadian Qishuyan Power Co.,Ltd	173	33.88	173	37.87
中国华电集团公司望亭发电厂	Jiangsu Huadian Wangting Natural Power Plant	132	65.66	132	82.96
江苏华电集团望亭天然气发电有限公司	Jiangsu Huadian Wangting Natural Gaspower Co.,Ltd	78	25.44	78	17.49
江苏华电扬州发电有限公司	Jiangsu Huandian Yangzhou Power Co.,Ltd	66	26.69	66	28.96
江苏华电仪征热电有限公司	Jiangsu Yizheng Thermal Power Co.,Ltd	66	29.50	66	23.76
上海华电电力发展有限公司	Shanghai Huadian Power Co.,Ltd	64	30.73	64	29.45
江苏华电戚墅堰热电有限公司	Jiangsu Huadian Qishuyan Thermal Power Co.,Ltd	40	18.01	40	14.81
江苏华电吴江热电有限公司	Jiangsu Huadian Qishuyan Thermal Power Co.,Ltd	36	12.90	36	18.72
（四）中国国电集团公司	**China Guodian Group Co.**				
国电泰州发电有限公司	China Guodian Taizhou Power Co.,Ltd	300	136.12	400	229.02
中国国电集团谏壁发电厂	China Guodian Jianbi Power Plant	299	161.90	299	162.88
国电常州发电有限公司	China Guodian Changzhou Power Co.,Ltd	126	70.56	126	75.06
国电江苏谏壁发电有限公司	China Guodian Jiangsu Jianbi Power Co.,Ltd	66	15.27	66	27.32
天生港发电有限公司	Tianshenggang Power Co.,Ltd	66	32.05	66	32.04
江阴苏龙热电有限公司	Jiangyin Sulong Thermal Power Co.,Ltd	122	62.46	122	67.77
国电宿迁热电有限公司	China Guodian Suqian Thermal Power Co.,Ltd	27	15.26	27	15.38
（五）中国电力投资集团公司	**China Power Investment Group Co.**				
江苏常熟发电有限公司	Jiangsu Changshu Power Co.,Ltd	332	166.98	332	179.22
江苏阚山发电有限公司	Jiangsu Kanshan Power Co.,Ltd	120	64.29	120	59.87
（六）华润电力控股有限公司	**China Resources Power Holdings Co., Ltd.**				
铜山华润电力有限公司	Tongshan Huarun Power Co.,Ltd	200	119.42	200	116.14
华润电力（常熟）有限公司	Huarun(Changshu) Power Co.,Ltd	195	105.12	195	105.80

厂	名 Item	2015		2016	
		装机容量（万千瓦）Installed Capacity（10000 kW）	发电量（亿千瓦时）Electricity Production（100 million kW·h）	装机容量（万千瓦）Installed Capacity（10000 kW）	发电量（亿千瓦时）Electricity Production（100 million kW·h）
徐州华润电力有限公司	Xuzhou Huarun Power Co.,Ltd	128	50.17	128	48.66
江苏镇江发电有限公司	Jiangsu Zhenjiang Power Co.,Ltd	153	75.74	153	76.40
江苏南热发电有限责任公司	Jiangsu Huanan Thermal Power Co.,Ltd	120	67.01	120	70.12
南京华润热电有限公司	Nanjing Huarun Thermal Power Co.,Ltd	66	26.62	66	32.06
徐州华鑫发电有限公司	Xuzhou Huaxin Power Co.,Ltd	66	27.21	66	31.57
南京化学工业园热电有限公司	Nanjing Chemical Industry Park Thermal Power Co.,Ltd	60	37.14	71	46.89
宜兴华润热电有限公司	Yixin Huarun Thermal Power Co.,Ltd			12	7.42
（七）神华国华电力公司	**Shenhua Guohua Power Company**				
国华徐州发电有限公司	Xuzhou Guohua Power Co.,Ltd	200	119.01	200	103.87
江苏国华陈家港发电有限公司	Jiangsu Guohua Chenjiagang Power Co.,Ltd	132	74.59	132	68.80
国华太仓发电有限公司	Guohua Taichang Power Co.,Ltd	126	68.67	126	66.03
（八）江苏省国信集团公司	**Jiangsu Province Gguoxin Group Co.**				
江苏新海发电有限公司	Jiangsu Xinhai Power Co.,Ltd	166	80.97	266	119.84
江苏国信靖江发电有限公司	Jinjiang Power Co.,Ltd of Jiangsu Province Gguoxin Group			132	62.51
江苏射阳港发电有限责任公司	Jiangsu Sheyanggang Power Co.,Ltd	132	67.03	132	70.89
扬州第二发电有限责任公司	Yangzhou No.2 Power Co.,Ltd	126	58.88	126	60.00
江苏国信扬州发电有限责任公司	Yangzhou Power Co.,Ltd of Jiangsu Province Gguoxin Group	126	62.91	126	65.94
国信宜兴燃机	Guoxin Yixing Power Co.,Ltd			84	42.00
江苏淮阴发电有限责任公司	Jiangsu Huaiyin Power Co.,Ltd	66	28.18	66	24.36
江苏国信淮安燃气发电有限责任公司	Huaian Natrual Power Co.,Ltd of Jiangsu Province Gguoxin Group	36	17.45	36	18.00
盐城发电有限公司	Yancheng Power Co.,Ltd	27	9.64	27	9.58
江苏国信协联能源有限公司	Jiangsu Guoxin Energy Co., Ltd			27	19.82
（九）国网新能源公司	**State Grid Xinyuan Co.**				
华东宜兴抽水蓄能有限公司	East China Yixing Pumped Storage Power Co.,Ltd	100	9.37	100	14.97
（十）省内其他电厂	**Other**				
江阴利港发电股份有限公司	Jiangyin Ligang Power Co.,Ltd	250	109.29	250	132.22
江苏南通发电有限公司	Jiangsu Nantong Power Co.,Ltd			200	112.35
江苏核电有限公司	Jiangsu Nucleat Power Co.,Ltd	200	166.16	200	153.49
江苏利港电力有限公司	Jiangsu Ligang Power Co.,Ltd	144	55.31	144	57.89
太仓港协鑫发电有限公司	Taichanggang Xiexin Power Co.,Ltd	130	72.04	130	77.34
张家港沙洲电力有限公司	Zhangjiagang Shazhou Power Co.,Ltd	126	67.05	126	72.91
张家港华兴电力有限公司	Zhangjiagang Huaxing Power Co.,Ltd	78	25.75	78	17.17
苏州工业园区蓝天燃气热电有限公司	Suzhou Lantian Interna-combustion Thermal Power Co.,Ltd	36	17.72	36	18.72
苏州北部燃机热电有限公司	Suzhou North Gasturbine Co., Ltd.			36	18
苏美热电	Sumei Thermal Power Co.,Ltd			70	28.02
江苏徐矿综合利用发电有限公司	Jiangsu Xukuang Comprehensive Utilization Power Co.,Ltd	60	22.76	60	21.02
徐州坨城电力有限责任公司	Xuzhou Tuocheng Power Co., Ltd.			27	8.2
无锡蓝天燃机热电有限公司	Wuxi Lantian Thermal Power Co.,Ltd			36	13.32

9－13 环境保护基本情况

Basic Statistics on Environmental Protection

项　　　目	Item	2011	2012	2013	2014	2015
污染排放与处理利用情况	**Discharge and Treatment of Pollution**					
废水	**Waster Water**					
工业废水排放量（亿吨）	Industrial Waste Water Emission (100 million tons)	24.63	23.61	22.06	20.49	20.64
城镇生活污水排放量（亿吨）	Volume of Urban Domestic Sewage Emission (100 million tons)	34.63	36.18	37.35	39.59	41.45
集中式治理设施污水排放量（亿吨）	Volume of Centralized Sewage Treatment Facilities (100 million tons)	0.02	0.03	0.03	0.03	0.04
化学需氧量排放量（万吨）	Volume of COD (10000 tons)	124.62	119.7	114.89	110.00	105.46
#工业源	Industry	23.93	23.14	20.92	20.44	20.13
农业源	Agriculture	39.93	38.77	37.61	36.41	35.07
城镇生活源	Urban Life	60.23	57.25	55.87	52.79	49.96
集中式治理设施	Centralized Sewage Treatment Facilities	0.53	0.54	0.49	0.37	0.29
氨氮排放量（万吨）	Ammonia Emissions (10000 tons)	15.72	15.31	14.74	14.25	13.77
#工业源	Industry	1.67	1.63	1.44	1.37	1.35
农业源	Agriculture	3.99	3.91	3.82	3.75	3.62
城镇生活源	Urban Life	9.99	9.7	9.43	9.08	8.76
集中式治理设施	Centralized Sewage Treatment Facilities	0.07	0.07	0.05	0.05	0.03
废气	**Waste Gas**					
二氧化硫排放量（万吨）	Volume of Sulphur Dioxide Emission (10000 tons)	105.38	99.2	94.17	90.47	83.51
#工业源	Industry	102.50	95.92	90.95	87.02	79.47
城镇生活源	Urban Life	2.85	3.25	3.20	3.43	4.03
集中式治理设施	Centralized Sewage Treatment Facilities	0.02	0.03	0.03	0.03	0.01
氮氧化物排放量（万吨）	Oxynitride Emissions (10000 tons)	153.57	147.96	133.80	123.26	106.76
#工业源	Industry	119.56	113.36	98.53	88.82	75.36
城镇生活源	Urban Life	0.62	0.65	0.61	0.64	0.86

项 目	Item	2011	2012	2013	2014	2015
机动车	Motor	33.35	33.9	34.62	33.74	30.50
集中式治理设施	Centralized Sewage Treatment Facilities	0.04	0.05	0.04	0.05	0.05
烟(粉)尘排放量(万吨)	Volume of Soot Emission (10000 tons)	52.74	44.32	50.00	76.37	65.45
#工业源	Industry	48.64	39.6	45.56	72.05	61.22
城镇生活源	Urban Life	1.2	1.85	1.71	1.82	1.94
机动车	Motor	2.88	2.85	2.7	2.48	2.27
集中式治理设施	Centralized Sewage Treatment Facilities	0.02	0.02	0.03	0.03	0.02
工业固体废物	**Industrial Solid Waste**					
一般工业固体废物产生量(万吨)	General Industrial Solid Waste (10000 tons)	10475.50	10224.44	10855.87	10924.73	10701.01
一般工业固体废物综合利用量 (万吨)	Comprehensive Utilization of General Industrial Solid Waste (10000 tons)	9997.24	9341.57	10501.86	10577.77	10206.98
#综合利用往年贮存量	Storage Capacity Utilization in Previous years	59.61	34.32	113.87	114.30	11.32
一般工业固体废物综合利用率 (%)	Comprehensive Rate of General Industrial Solid Waste (%)	94.89	91.06	95.73	95.82	95.28
一般工业固体废物处置量(万吨)	Greneral Industrial solido waste Disposnl (10000 tons)	334.56	630.40	286.79	278.92	407.37
#处置往年贮存量	Disposal in previous years	17.44	16.10	16.04	0.70	0.12
一般工业固体废物贮存量(万吨)	General Industrial Solide Waste Storage (10000 tons)	220.02	302.87	197.14	182.75	98.09
自然生态保护与建设情况	**Natural Ecological Protection**					
自然保护区个数 (个)	Number of Natural Reserves (unit)	31	31	31	31	31
#国家级自然保护区	Natural	3	3	3	3	3
自然保护区面积 (万公顷)	Areas of Natural Reserves (10000 hectares)	56.64	56.64	56.64	56.64	56.64
自然保护区面积占辖区面积(%)	Rate of area (%)	5.5	5.5	5.5	5.5	5.5

主要统计指标解释

水资源 水在自然界中以固体、液体和气态三种聚集状态存在，分布于海洋、陆地(包括土壤)以及大气之中，通过水循环形成水资源。水资源包括经人类控制并直接可供灌溉、发电、给水、航运、养殖等用途的地表水和地下水，以及江河、湖泊、井、泉、潮汐、港湾和养殖水域等。水资源是发展国民经济不可缺少的重要自然资源。

地表水和地下水 陆地上的水因空间分布不同，分为地表水和地下水。地表水指分别存在于河流、湖泊、沼泽、冰川和冰盖等水体中水分的总称，又称陆地水。地下水指储存在地面以下饱和岩土孔隙、裂隙及溶洞中的水。

矿产保有储量 指探明的矿产储量(包括工业储量和远景储量)，扣除已开采部分和地下损失量后的年末实有储量。

气温 指空气的温度，我国一般以摄氏度(℃)为单位表示。气象观测的温度表是放在离地面约1.5米处通风良好的百叶箱里测量的，因此，通常说的气温指的是离地面1.5米处百叶箱中的温度。其统计计算方法为：

月平均气温是将全月各日的平均气温相加，除以该月的天数而得。

年平均气温是将12个月的月平均气温累加后除以12而得。

降水量 指从天空降落到地面的液态或固态(经融化后)水，未经蒸发、渗透、流失而在地面上积聚的深度。其统计计算方法为：

月降水量是将全月各日的降水量累加而得。

年降水量是将12个月的月降水量累加而得。

能源生产总量 指一定时期内，全国一次能源生产量的总和。该指标是观察全国能源生产水平、规模、构成和发展速度的总量指标。一次能源生产量包括原煤、原油、天然气、水电、核能及其他动力能(如风能、地热能等)发电量，不包括低热值燃料生产量、生物质能、太阳能等的利用和由一次能源加工转换而成的二次能源产量。

能源消费总量 指一定时期内，全国各行业和居民生活消费的各种能源的总和。该指标是观察能源消费水平构成和增长速度的总量指标。能源消费总量包括原煤和原油及其制品、天然气、电力，不包括低热值燃料生产量、生物质能、太阳能等的利用。能源消费总量分为终端能源消费量、能源加工转换损失量和能源损失量三部分。

(1) 终端能源消费量：指一定时期内，全国生产和生活消费的各种能源在扣除了用于加工转换二次能源消费量和损失量以后的数量。

(2) 能源加工转换损失量：指一定时期内，全国投入加工转换的各种能源数量之和与产出各种能源产品之和的差额。它是观察能源在加工转换过程中损失量变化的指标。

(3) 能源损失量：指一定时期内，能源在输送、分配、储存过程中发生的损失和由客观原因造成的各种损失量，不包括各种气体能源放空、放散量。

工业废水排放量 指报告期内经过企业厂区所有排放口排到企业外部的工业废水量。包括生产废水、外排的直接冷却水、超标排放的矿井地下水和与工业废水混排的厂区生活污水，不包括外排的间接冷却水(清污不分流的间接冷却水应计算在废水排放量内)。

城镇生活污水排放量 指报告期内城镇居民排放生活污水的量。城镇生活包括“住宿业与餐饮业、居民服务和其他服务业、医院和独立燃烧设施以及城镇生活污染源”。

集中式治理设施污水排放量 指报告期内集中式治理设施的渗滤液排放量。集中式治理设施包括垃圾处理场(厂)和危险废物(医疗废物)集中处置厂。

化学需氧量排放量 指报告期内工业、农业、城镇生活和集中式治理设施排放的废水中COD排放量之和。

氨氮排放量 指报告期内工业、农业、城镇生活和集中式治理设施排放的废水中氨氮排放量之和。

二氧化硫排放量 指报告期内工业、城镇生活和集中式治理设施SO_2排放量之和。

氮氧化物排放量 指报告期内工业、城镇生活、机动车和集中式治理设施氮氧化物排放量之和。

烟(粉)尘排放量 指报告期内工业、城镇生活、机动车和集中式治理设施烟(粉)尘排放量之和。

一般工业固体废物产生量 指未被列入《国家危险废物名录》或者根据国家规定的危险废物鉴别标准(GB5085)、固体废物浸出毒性浸出方法(GB5086)及固体废物浸出毒性测定方法(GB/T 15555)鉴别方法判定不具有危险特性的工业固体废物。

一般工业固体废物综合利用量 指报告期内企业通过回收、加工、循环、交换等方式，从固体废物中提取或者使其转化为可以利用的资源、能源和其他原材料的固体废物量(包括当年利用的往年工业固体废物累计贮存量)。如用作农业肥料、生产建筑材料、筑路等。

综合利用往年贮存量 指企业在报告期内对往年贮存的工业固体废物进行综合利用的量。

Explanatory Notes on Main Statistical Indicators

Water Resource Water exists in the nature in solid, liquid and gaseous states, is distributed in the ocean, land (including earth) and air, and constitutes the water resource through the circulation of water. Water resource includes the surface water and underground water that is controlled by the human being for irrigation, power-generation, water supply, navigation and cultivation. It also includes rivers, lakes, wells, springs, tides, gulf and water area for cultivation. Water resource as an important natural resource is indispensable for the development of the national economy.

Surface Water and Underground Water Water on earth can be divided into surface water and underground water according to its distribution. Surface water refers to moisture exists in rivers, lakes, swamps, glaciers, icecaps and so on. It is also called land water. The underground water refers to water deposited underground in the cranny and the hole of saturated rock soil and in the water-eroded cave.

Mineral Reserves refer to the proven mineral reserves (including industrial reserves and prospective reserves), and the reserves at the end of the year after deduction of the mined and underground losses.

Temperature refers to the air temperature. China uses centigrade as the unit. The thermometry used for weather observation is put in a breezy shutter, which is 1.5 meters high from the ground. Therefore, the commonly used temperature refers to the temperature in the breezy shutter 1.5 meters away from the ground. The calculation method is as follows:

Monthly average temperature is the summation of average daily temperature of one month divided by the actual days of that particular month.

Annual average temperature is the summation of monthly average of a year divided by 12 months.

Volume of Precipitation refers to the deepness of liquid state or solid state (thawed) water falling from the sky to the ground that has not been evaporated, infiltrated or run off. The calculation method is as follows:

Monthly precipitation is the summation of daily precipitation of a month.

Annual precipitation is the summation of 12 months precipitation of a year.

Total Energy Production refers to the total production of primary energy by all energy producing enterprises in the country (region) in a given period of time. It is a comprehensive indicator to show the level, scale, composition and pace of development of energy production of the country (region). The production of primary energy includes that of coal, crude oil, natural gas, hydro-power and electricity generated by nuclear energy and other means such as wind power and geothermal power. However, it does not include the secondary energy converted from primary energy.

Total Energy Consumption refers to the total consumption of energy of various kinds by the production sectors and the households in the country (region) in a given period of time. Total energy consumption can be divided into three parts: end-use energy consumption; loss during the process of energy conversion; and energy loss.

(1) End-use Energy Consumption: It refers to the total energy consumption by the production sectors and the households in the country (region) in a given period of time. It does not include the consumption during the conversion of primary energy into secondary energy and the loss in the process of energy conversion.

(2) Loss During the Process of Energy Conversion: It refers to the total input of various kinds of energy for conversion, minus the total output of various kinds of energy in the country (region) in a given period of time. It is an indicator to show the loss that occurs during the process of energy conversion.

(3) Energy Loss: It refers to the total of the loss of energy during the course of energy transport, distribution and storage and the loss caused by any objective reason in a given period of time. The loss of various kinds of gas due to gas discharges and stocktaking is not included.

Waste Water Discharged by Industry refer to the volume of waste water discharged by industrial enterprises through all their outlets during the period, including waste water from production process, directly cooled water, groundwater from mining wells which does not meet discharge standards and sewage from households mixed with waste water produced by industrial activities, but excluding indirectly cooled water discharged (It should be included if the discharge is not separated with waste water).

Urban Domestic Sewage Emission refer to the volume of sewage discharged by urban living during the period. Urban living contain hotels and catering services, residential service and others, hospital, Independent burning facilities and so on.

Volume of Centralized Sewage Treatment Facilities refer to the volume of leachate discharged by centralized treatment facilities during the period, such as waste treatment plants, hazardous waste treatment plants and medical waste plants.

Volume of COD refer to the sum of COD discharged by industry, agriculture, urban living and centralized sewage treatment facilities during the period.

Ammonia Emissions refer to the sum of ammonia emissions in waste water discharged by industry, agriculture, urban living and centralized sewage treatment facilities during the period.

Sulphur Dioxide Emission refer to the sum of sulphur dioxide discharged by industry, urban living and centralized treatment facilities during the period.

Oxynitride Emissions refer to the sum of Oxynitridede discharged by industry, urban living, motor vehicles and centralized treatment facilities during the period.

Soot Emissions refer to the sum of soot discharged by industry, urban living, motor vehicles and centralized treatment facilities during the period.

Common Industrial Solid Waste Produce refer to the industrial solid wastes that are not listed in the National Catalogue of Hazardous Wastes, or not regarded as hazardous according to the national hazardous waste identification standards (GB5085), solid waste-Extraction procedure for leaching toxicity (GB5086) and solid waste-Extraction procedure for leaching toxicity (GB/T 15555).

Common Industrial Solid Wastes Comprehensively Utilized refer to volume of solid wastes from which useful materials can be extracted or which can be converted into usable resources, energy or other materials by means of reclamation, processing recycling and exchange(including utilizing in the year the stocks of industrial solid wastes of the previous year) during the report period, e. g. being used as agricultural fertilizers, building materials or as material for paving road. Examples of such utilizations include fertilizers, building materials and road materials.

Storage Capacity Utilization in Previous Years refer to the volume of comprehensive utilization of industrial solid wastes stored in previous.

10

农　业

Agriculture

简　要　说　明

一、本篇资料的主要内容及统计范围

本篇资料反映我省农业生产和农村经济的基本情况,内容主要包括农业机械拥有量、农林牧渔业产值、主要农产品产量、国营农场基本情况等方面的统计资料。

农业统计范围包括全社会除军马生产及农业科研机构进行的农业生产以外的所有农业生产活动。包括:农村各种经济组织和农户经营的农林牧渔业生产活动;各种专业性农、林、牧、渔场的农业生产活动;国家各级机关、团体、学校、部队进行的农业生产活动;集体所有制的乡、镇、村办农场的农业生产活动;以及工矿企业经营的农、林、牧、渔业生产活动。

1. 农业:指对各种农作物的种植活动。包括谷物、豆类、薯类、棉花、油料、糖料、麻类、烟叶、蔬菜、园艺作物、水果、坚果、饮料和香料作物、中草药及其他作物的种植。

2. 林业:包括林木的栽培(不包括茶园、桑园和果园的栽培、管理和收获等活动),木材和竹材的采运,林产品的采集。

3. 畜牧业:包括牲畜饲养和放牧,家禽饲养以及野生动物的捕猎和饲养。

4. 渔业:包括水生动物和海藻类植物的养殖和捕捞。

5. 农、林、牧、渔服务业:指对农、林、牧、渔业生产活动进行的各种支持性服务,但不包括各种科学技术和专业性技术服务活动。

二、本篇的资料来源及统计调查方法

1. 农业生产基本情况:根据《农林牧渔业统计调查制度》、《农业产值与增加值核算统计报表制度》、《县域社会经济基本情况统计报表制度》的有关资料整理提供。

《农林牧渔业统计调查制度》为全面报表,由各级统计部门根据当地实际情况,采取抽样调查、重点调查或全面调查的办法搜集资料并逐层上报,或利用同级业务部门统计资料上报。如林业生产情况、渔业生产情况等指标取自同级业务部门的统计资料。

《县域社会经济基本情况统计报表制度》主要对县、乡、村基本情况每年进行一次全面调查。

2. 国营农场基本情况资料主要取材于农垦系统汇总的统计报表,统计方法为逐级上报、全面汇总。

Brief Introduction

Ⅰ. Main Contents and Statistical Scopes

The data in this chapter show the basic conditions of agricultural production and rural economy, including mainly quantity of agricultural machinery, output of agriculture, forestry, animal husbandry and fishery, output of major products, basic conditions of State-owned farms.

Statistics on agriculture cover all agricultural production activities except horse raising for military purpose and agricultural production activities undertaken by agriculture research institutions. Including agriculture, forestry, animal husbandry and fishery production activities undertaken by rural economic units of various types and by rural households; production activities of farms specializing in agriculture, forestry, animal husbandry and fishery; production activities in agriculture undertaken by government agencies, institutions, schools and military units; production activities in agriculture undertaken by collective farms run by townships and villages; and production activities in agriculture, forestry, animal husbandry and fishery undertaken by manufacturing and mining enterprises.

(1) Agriculture: refers to cultivation of farm crops, including cereals, beans, tuber crops, cotton, oil-bearing crops, sugar crops, hemp, tobacco leaves, vegetables, gardening plants, fruits, nuts, crops for beverages and spices, medicinal herbs and other farm crops.

(2) Forestry: includes the planting of trees

(excluding the operations of planting, management and harvesting on tea plantations, mulberry fields and orchards), cutting and transport of timber and bamboo and collection of forest products.

(3) Animal husbandry: includes the raising and grazing of domestic animals and poultry, and the hunting and raising of wild animals.

(4) Fishery: includes cultivation and catching of aquatic animals and seaweed.

(5) Services of agriculture, forestry, animal husbandry and fishery: include supporting services to production activities in agriculture, forestry, animal husbandry and fishery but do not include activities of science and technology and professional services.

Ⅱ. Data Sources and Survey Methods

(1) Data on agricultural production come from the *Statistical Reporting System on Agriculture, Forestry, Animal Husbandry and Fishery*; the *Statistical Reporting System on Agricultural Output and Value-added Accounting*; *Statistical Reporting System on Basical Social Economy of Country*.

Statistical Reporting System on Agriculture, Forestry, Animal Husbandry and Fishery is a comprehensive reporting program. Data required in this reporting program are collected by statistical offices at all levels by means of sample surveys, surveys of key units or complete enumeration depending on the local circumstances, or estimated by using information from other government agencies at the same level. For instance, some data on forestry and fishery are obtained from statistics data collected by other government agencies at the same level.

Statistical Reporting System on Basical Social Econorny of Country is conducted every year to collect information on the basic conditions of all towns, townships and villages, and a complete enumeration in administratively designated towns.

(2) Data on the basic conditions of the State-owned farms come from the statistical reports tabulated by the Bureau of Reclamation. Data are collected from the grassroots units in accordance with the statistical reporting scheme whereby reporting is done level by level for aggregation.

10－1 农业基本情况
Basic Statistics of Agriculture

指 标 Item		2012	2013	2014	2015	2016
乡村户数 （万户）	Rural Households （10000 units）	1444.65	1436.59	1430.61	1428.78	1419.44
乡村劳动力 （万人）	Rural Laborers （10000 persons）	2620.82	2613.96	2604.86	2600.75	2594.78
按性别分	Grouped by Sex					
男	Male	1373.68	1368.96	1365.53	1364.55	1359.60
女	Female	1247.14	1245.00	1239.33	1236.20	1235.18
按行业分	Grouped by Sector					
农林牧渔业	Agriculture, Forestry, Animal Husbandry, Fishery	796.03	776.05	762.00	747.41	736.12
#农业	Farming	643.16	622.56	608.98	598.87	592.17
工业	Industry	798.46	807.46	820.25	829.56	832.27
建筑业	Construction	377.65	383.69	383.60	383.60	383.10
交通运输、仓储业和邮电通讯业	Transport, Storage, Post and Telecommunication	114.55	114.56	114.29	114.50	113.94
批发、零售贸易业、餐饮业	Wholesale, Retail Sales and Catering Services	213.40	217.76	217.37	219.47	220.95
金融、保险业	Banking and Insurance	9.69	10.07	10.72	11.22	11.75
房地产、社会服务业	Real Estate and Social Services	37.35	37.61	36.95	36.41	36.67
卫生、体育、社会福利业	Healthcare, Sports and Social Welfare	13.90	14.00	14.29	14.69	15.12
教育、文化、艺术和广播电视事业	Education, Culture, Arts, Broadcasting and Television	17.09	17.27	17.30	17.58	17.76
科学研究和综合技术服务事业	Scientific Research and Ploytechnical Services	3.65	3.75	4.08	4.31	4.60
乡经济组织管理	Rural Economic Management	12.23	12.33	12.47	12.76	13.00
其他	Others	226.82	219.41	211.54	209.24	209.50
农作物总播种面积 （千公顷）	Sown Area of Farm Crops （1000 hectares）	7651.57	7683.64	7678.63	7745.04	7676.93
#粮食	Grain Crops	5336.57	5360.78	5376.07	5424.64	5432.70
主要农产品产量 （万吨）	Output of Major Farm Products （10000 tons）					
粮食	Grain	3372.48	3422.98	3490.62	3561.34	3466.01
棉花	Cotton	22.04	20.93	15.95	11.69	7.38
油料	Oil-bearing	146.95	150.37	146.60	143.11	131.93
肉类产量	Meat	396.52	383.23	379.46	369.43	355.63
水产品产量	Aquatic Products	493.74	509.38	518.84	522.11	523.15

10－2　农业现代化情况
Statistics on Agricultural Modernization

指　　标	Item	2012	2013	2014	2015	2016
农业机械化情况	**Statistics on Agricultural Machinery**					
农业机械总动力　（万千瓦）	Total Power of Agricultural Machinery　(10000 kW)	4214.64	4405.78	4649.98	4825.49	4906.55
机耕面积　（千公顷）	Ploughed Area by Tractors　(1000 hectares)	5845.67	5947.94	6100.16	6066.15	5939.63
机播面积　（千公顷）	Sown Area by Tractors　(1000 hectares)	3887.94	4371.78	4437.83	4576.06	4663.12
#机播小麦面积	Sown Area of Wheat by Tractors	2026.10	2099.42	2117.97	2148.19	2158.20
机械植保面积　（千公顷）	Planting Protection Area by Tractors　(1000 hectares)	5400.50	6732.05	5736.80	5649.06	5699.61
机械收获面积　（千公顷）	Harvest Area by Tractors　(1000 hectares)	4896.87	5114.39	5549.26	5142.77	5199.94
农村电气化情况	**Electrification of Rural Area**					
农村用电量　（亿千瓦小时）	Electricity Consumed in Rural Areas　(100 million kW·h)	1696.41	1801.86	1834.93	1836.19	1869.27
农用物资使用情况	**Agricultural Product Material Used**					
化肥施用量(折纯量)　（万吨）	Consumption of Chemical Fertilizers (pure)　(10000 tons)	330.94	326.82	323.61	319.99	312.52
每亩耕地施用化肥(折纯量)　（千克）	Per Mu Consumption of Chemical Fertilizers(pure)　(kg)	48.03	47.43	47.00	46.54	45.46
农用塑料薄膜使用量　（万吨）	Plastic Film　(10000 tons)	11.26	11.68	11.98	11.32	11.39
农用柴油使用量　（万吨）	Diesel Oil　(10000 tons)	102.97	106.80	107.45	108.58	108.71
农药使用量　（万吨）	Agricultural Chemical Insecticides　(10000 tons)	8.37	8.12	7.95	7.81	7.62
农田水利情况	**Irrigation and Water Conservancy**					
有效灌溉面积　（千公顷）	Effective Irrigation Area　(1000 hectares)	3704.17	3785.27	3890.53	3952.50	4054.07
节水灌溉面积　（千公顷）	Water-saving Irrigated Area　(1000 hectares)	1923.37	2005.43	2189.54	2336.09	2422.57
除涝面积　（千公顷）	Flooded or Waterlogged Area　(1000 hectares)	2812.02	2853.25	2961.97	3017.69	3125.61
水土流失治理面积　（千公顷）	Area of Soil Erosion under Control　(1000 hectares)	717.31	886.97	899.66	893.82	907.89
堤防长度　（公里）	Total Length of Dikes　(km)	55105	55403	55387	55654	55797
堤防保护面积　（千公顷）	Area of Land Protected by Dikes　(1000 hectares)	3257.81	3519.38	2767.32	2826.85	2885.60

10－3 主要年份农林牧渔业总产值

Gross Output Value of Agriculture, Forestry, Animal Husbandry and Fishery in Major Years

当年价格,单位:亿元 (at current price,100 million yuan)

年 份 Year	农林牧渔业总产值 Total	农 业 Farming	林 业 Foresty	畜牧业 Animal Husbandry	渔 业 Fishery	农林牧渔服务业 Services of Agriculture, Forestry, Animal Husbandry and Fishery
1949	22.59	19.41	…	3.02	0.16	
1952	31.87	26.14	0.03	5.00	0.70	
1957	36.81	30.10	0.22	5.25	1.24	
1962	40.15	34.19	0.32	4.48	1.16	
1965	57.27	47.02	0.63	8.25	1.37	
1970	71.33	57.08	0.85	11.76	1.64	
1975	91.66	72.17	1.47	15.55	2.47	
1976	100.71	82.53	1.31	14.86	2.01	
1977	89.16	73.05	1.25	12.90	1.96	
1978	105.87	85.17	1.48	16.78	2.44	
1979	145.25	114.26	2.03	25.77	3.19	
1980	138.45	105.98	1.94	26.65	3.88	
1981	153.62	119.90	2.00	27.11	4.61	
1982	188.11	145.69	1.96	35.80	4.66	
1983	206.86	160.38	3.30	36.66	6.52	
1984	253.82	193.28	4.33	47.17	9.04	
1985	288.55	201.85	4.63	66.54	15.53	
1986	332.66	235.07	5.15	69.83	22.61	
1987	380.25	257.90	6.02	87.95	28.38	
1988	497.95	310.20	7.29	140.49	39.97	
1989	522.25	325.02	7.02	148.13	42.08	
1990	580.53	362.46	7.94	160.78	49.35	
1991	580.93	354.42	7.55	168.30	50.66	
1992	673.82	411.33	9.93	188.64	63.92	
1993	875.37	518.55	14.61	236.81	105.40	
1994	1335.23	777.94	18.38	390.70	148.21	
1995	1686.78	986.15	21.42	475.67	203.54	
1996	1693.76	1062.39	23.48	368.54	239.35	
1997	1816.37	1085.26	22.56	430.57	277.98	
1998	1849.20	1096.88	24.16	435.51	292.65	
1999	1837.43	1095.13	26.13	413.95	302.22	
2000	1869.73	1096.02	30.17	430.53	313.01	
2001	1956.10	1142.66	30.76	448.51	334.17	
2002	2011.48	1165.49	36.29	456.02	353.68	
2003	1952.20	981.25	31.49	458.87	371.56	109.03
2004	2417.63	1242.41	40.16	563.44	449.47	122.15
2005	2576.98	1291.06	45.27	599.14	511.86	129.65
2006	2718.61	1416.91	54.26	544.48	543.39	159.57
2007	3064.72	1542.53	58.88	704.38	579.00	179.94
2008	3590.64	1746.83	64.92	916.46	665.75	196.69
2009	3816.02	1948.20	70.79	873.97	719.25	203.81
2010	4297.14	2269.56	78.12	923.25	805.25	220.95
2011	5237.45	2640.95	92.81	1190.50	1060.44	252.74
2012	5808.81	2966.72	99.74	1226.18	1235.40	280.77
2013	6158.03	3167.78	107.30	1222.22	1351.11	309.60
2014	6443.37	3362.81	118.18	1182.69	1426.74	352.95
2015	7030.76	3722.10	129.09	1262.09	1517.51	399.97
2016	7235.06	3714.64	129.33	1331.55	1621.88	437.67

10－4 主要年份农林牧渔业总产值指数
Indices of Gross Output Value of Agriculture, Forestry, Animal Husbandry and Fishery in Major Years

按可比价格计算，上年＝100　　　　(at constant price with 100 in preceding year)

年 份 Year	农林牧渔业总产值指数 Total	农 业 Farming	林 业 Forestry	畜牧业 Animal Husbandry	渔 业 Fishery	农林牧渔服务业 Services of Agriculture, Forestry, Animal Husbandry and Fishery
1949						
1952	117.4	110.0		141.9	306.1	
1957	103.4	99.2	553.8	128.4	106.9	
1962	101.1	97.5	98.2	135.2	94.9	
1965	105.7	100.5	168.0	141.7	95.6	
1970	107.2	107.1	67.2	109.4	124.2	
1975	100.9	99.5	98.0	107.1	104.0	
1976	103.9	105.1	121.1	93.4	94.4	
1977	89.9	89.5	99.2	93.0	101.9	
1978	121.5	123.4	84.5	115.6	98.8	
1979	110.9	108.5	105.0	131.8	110.3	
1980	94.5	91.9	99.5	102.1	118.2	
1981	107.9	109.7	95.3	99.3	115.4	
1982	114.9	113.0	106.0	123.8	105.2	
1983	105.9	107.2	110.8	98.2	99.6	
1984	116.4	106.3	117.8	118.2	124.1	
1985	103.1	99.0	107.9	117.1	126.3	
1986	106.3	106.6	97.3	100.6	134.9	
1987	103.1	103.3	104.8	101.2	108.1	
1988	106.6	104.8	93.8	114.4	108.9	
1989	100.3	100.6	94.4	99.5	101.7	
1990	102.5	101.1	97.4	106.7	107.9	
1991	98.9	95.9	90.0	105.2	101.2	
1992	113.0	113.7	119.1	110.5	115.6	
1993	111.3	106.2	124.1	114.0	134.8	
1994	112.1	108.0	112.4	117.5	119.0	
1995	113.6	112.9	117.0	110.8	124.0	
1996	107.4	108.7	107.4	103.1	111.8	
1997	107.7	106.4	92.6	110.9	109.5	
1998	104.0	103.0	109.9	104.2	107.2	
1999	105.2	105.9	100.0	103.5	106.5	
2000	105.0	103.1	119.9	107.5	107.4	
2001	104.5	105.0	99.1	102.4	106.7	
2002	103.8	102.3	115.8	103.9	108.0	
2003	101.0	94.3	120.0	102.8	106.6	130.0
2004	107.8	113.8	109.4	97.7	109.7	107.0
2005	103.7	101.1	107.5	103.6	110.7	104.0
2006	104.9	105.4	115.7	101.2	106.8	106.0
2007	103.1	102.6	109.9	100.7	104.4	108.3
2008	104.5	103.2	104.7	107.1	105.4	102.6
2009	104.6	103.3	105.2	106.6	105.2	104.0
2010	104.4	103.8	105.6	105.3	104.5	105.1
2011	104.2	104.3	104.0	102.7	104.4	107.6
2012	104.8	104.5	102.8	105.3	104.4	107.8
2013	102.6	103.3	103.9	96.9	105.3	107.1
2014	103.1	104.0	105.8	98.9	102.5	111.9
2015	102.6	103.3	106.1	97.7	102.5	111.6
2016	100.8	100.5	104.2	98.9	101.2	107.5

10-5 主要年份农林牧渔业总产值定基指数
Fixed-base Indices of Gross Output Value of Agriculture, Forestry, Animal Husbandry and Fishery in Major Years

按可比价格计算,1949年=100 (at constant price with 100 in 1949)

年份 Year	农林牧渔业总产值指数 Total	农业 Farming	林业 Forestry	畜牧业 Animal Husbandry	渔业 Fishery	农林牧渔服务业 Services of Agriculture, Forestry, Animal Husbandry and Fishery
1949	100.0	100.0		100.0	100.0	
1952	144.2	135.7	100.0	166.5	612.2	
1957	157.4	151.4	900.0	159.0	563.4	
1962	134.7	134.1	1387.5	106.8	407.3	
1965	201.4	190.7	2162.5	224.6	534.1	
1970	239.7	232.5	1487.5	255.0	575.6	
1975	294.7	281.6	2487.5	322.3	819.5	
1976	306.2	296.1	3012.5	301.1	773.2	
1977	275.4	264.9	2987.0	280.1	787.8	
1978	334.6	326.8	2525.0	323.9	778.0	
1979	371.1	354.7	2650.0	426.8	858.5	
1980	350.7	326.0	2637.5	435.8	1014.6	
1981	378.4	357.7	2512.5	432.6	1170.7	
1982	434.8	404.2	2662.5	535.6	1231.7	
1983	460.6	433.3	2950.0	525.9	1226.8	
1984	536.3	460.6	3475.0	621.5	1522.0	
1985	553.1	456.1	3750.0	727.9	1922.0	
1986	587.7	486.4	3650.0	732.5	2592.7	
1987	605.9	502.4	3825.0	741.1	2802.4	
1988	646.1	526.3	3587.5	847.5	3051.2	
1989	648.3	529.4	3387.5	843.1	3102.4	
1990	664.6	535.2	3300.5	899.3	3346.3	
1991	657.1	513.3	2971.7	946.3	3385.3	
1992	742.5	583.6	3538.2	1045.7	3913.7	
1993	826.4	619.6	4391.5	1191.6	5275.3	
1994	926.3	668.9	4936.8	1400.2	6278.5	
1995	1052.7	755.4	5774.3	1551.0	7785.4	
1996	1130.6	821.0	6204.0	1599.2	8707.8	
1997	1217.1	873.5	5746.0	1773.5	9532.8	
1998	1265.6	899.4	6313.9	1847.5	10219.7	
1999	1331.1	952.4	6312.3	1911.5	10883.6	
2000	1397.9	981.6	7566.8	2055.1	11688.1	
2001	1461.5	1030.6	7500.2	2103.9	12474.9	
2002	1516.9	1053.8	8681.6	2186.3	13475.4	100.0
2003	1532.8	994.0	10415.4	2248.1	14369.5	130.0
2004	1653.0	1131.5	11389.9	2196.7	15768.3	139.1
2005	1714.2	1143.9	12245.5	2275.4	17448.0	144.6
2006	1798.2	1205.6	14168.0	2302.7	18634.5	153.3
2007	1853.2	1236.7	15569.2	2319.0	19458.1	166.1
2008	1936.8	1276.4	16294.7	2483.0	20510.8	170.5
2009	2024.9	1318.4	17144.7	2646.0	21573.2	177.4
2010	2113.6	1368.5	18104.8	2786.9	22552.0	186.5
2011	2201.6	1427.5	18836.2	2863.4	23554.6	200.8
2012	2307.0	1491.7	19371.5	3015.0	24591.8	216.5
2013	2365.9	1540.6	20123.0	2922.6	25885.6	231.7
2014	2438.9	1602.8	21282.6	2889.3	26521.5	259.2
2015	2502.5	1656.0	22578.0	2821.7	27184.4	289.3
2016	2522.6	1664.0	23520.3	2789.3	27497.6	310.9

10-6 农林牧渔业分项产值
Gross Output Value of Agriculture, Forestry, Animal Husbandry and Fishery by Branch

按当年价格计算,单位:亿元　　(at current price,100 million yuan)

指标	Item	2012	2013	2014	2015	2016
农林牧渔业总产值	**Total**	**5808.81**	**6158.03**	**6443.37**	**7030.76**	**7235.06**
农业产值	**Farming**	**2966.72**	**3167.78**	**3362.81**	**3722.10**	**3714.64**
谷物及其他作物	Planting	1261.04	1285.32	1335.94	1400.96	1295.35
#谷物	Cereal	948.87	996.38	1056.01	1116.71	1033.67
薯类	Tubers	41.27	37.79	35.08	38.36	36.26
豆类	Soybeans	39.55	36.67	36.58	42.55	38.41
棉花	Cotton	93.78	79.12	69.27	50.47	38.12
油料	Oil-bearing	89.43	84.34	84.21	86.80	78.72
蔬菜园艺作物	Vegetables and Gardening Crops	1440.13	1592.70	1696.70	1930.70	2021.12
#蔬菜(含菜用瓜、食用菌)	Vegetable (include Melons、Edible Mushroom)	1265.38	1392.49	1474.56	1691.44	1852.89
水果、坚果、饮料和香料作物	Fresh Fruits, Nuts, Beverage and Perfume Crops	254.31	280.24	319.75	377.50	382.48
#水果、坚果(含果用瓜)	Fresh Fruits, Nuts (include Melons)	213.57	240.42	270.82	327.97	328.54
中药材	Chinese Herbal Medicine	11.25	9.52	10.42	12.94	15.70
林业产值	**Forestry**	**99.74**	**107.30**	**118.18**	**129.09**	**129.33**
林木的培育和种植	Afforestation	73.65	76.85	84.62	91.44	92.38
竹木采运	Cutting and Transportation of Bamboo and Timber	16.01	19.86	22.64	25.61	23.73
林产品	Forest Products	10.08	10.58	10.92	12.05	13.21
牧业产值	**Animal Husbandry**	**1226.18**	**1222.22**	**1182.69**	**1262.09**	**1331.55**
牲畜饲养	Livestock Raising	92.56	98.52	97.21	94.53	96.96
#牛	Cattle and Buffaloes	11.86	12.10	12.67	13.36	12.66
羊	Sheep and Goats	46.44	52.09	51.80	50.68	55.45
猪的饲养	Hogs Raising	464.84	467.51	434.91	517.33	593.15
家禽饲养	Poultry Raising	540.46	501.37	491.54	484.28	480.30
#肉禽	Live Animal and Poultry Products	326.65	284.00	273.61	270.16	266.38
禽蛋	Poultry Eggs	210.05	214.44	214.89	211.03	210.88
狩猎和捕捉动物	Hunting	1.96	1.98	1.88	2.00	1.60
其他畜牧业	Other Animal Husbandry	126.36	152.85	157.14	163.94	159.54
渔业产值	**Fishery**	**1235.40**	**1351.11**	**1426.74**	**1517.51**	**1621.88**
海水产品	Seawater Aquatic Products	344.21	370.70	383.57	416.91	453.47
内陆水域水产品	Freshwater Aquatic Products	891.19	980.42	1043.17	1100.59	1168.40
农林牧渔服务业产值	**Services in Support of Agriculture**	**280.77**	**309.60**	**352.95**	**399.97**	**437.67**

10－7　农作物播种面积

单位:千公顷

年　份 Year	总播种面积 Total Sown Areas	粮食作物 Grain Crops	#小　麦 Wheat	#稻　谷 Rice	#薯　类 Tubers	#玉　米 Corn	#大　豆 Sonja
1978	8582.74	6310.93	1412.82	2661.18	478.29	445.01	345.36
1980	8248.93	6090.25	1519.47	2676.15	332.02	386.21	236.47
1985	8557.84	6432.44	2170.39	2431.11	282.45	659.62	317.93
1989	8384.33	6454.51	2353.54	2419.67	248.16	501.15	309.39
1990	8259.18	6363.02	2399.19	2454.44	221.65	461.01	244.67
1991	8091.70	6202.77	2364.93	2351.40	214.51	426.44	177.81
1992	8234.63	6180.77	2366.23	2447.27	192.59	421.14	192.28
1993	8032.29	6029.66	2281.66	2278.44	201.00	472.37	270.67
1994	7861.76	5748.78	2114.26	2168.36	179.46	458.95	255.41
1995	7909.01	5755.15	2150.35	2250.31	166.71	461.98	201.32
1996	7914.10	5877.42	2216.26	2335.91	180.59	467.83	179.49
1997	7966.78	5994.43	2341.37	2377.62	169.61	439.00	217.44
1998	8058.28	5946.26	2314.95	2369.70	162.67	473.49	220.83
1999	8023.43	5828.52	2251.70	2398.45	156.89	454.31	210.41
2000	7944.87	5304.31	1954.60	2203.46	158.26	423.16	249.19
2001	7777.42	4886.66	1712.81	2010.25	146.01	429.81	244.37
2002	7797.40	4882.58	1715.85	1982.05	143.75	436.53	243.44
2003	7681.49	4659.47	1620.45	1840.93	134.20	451.90	241.68
2004	7668.98	4774.59	1601.17	2112.90	114.17	389.11	216.42
2005	7641.20	4909.48	1684.44	2209.33	100.16	370.24	214.80
2006	7385.16	5110.80	1912.67	2216.00	76.27	378.17	213.00
2007	7407.73	5215.59	2039.12	2228.07	67.73	391.21	222.73
2008	7510.27	5267.10	2073.12	2232.55	66.17	398.51	232.77
2009	7558.15	5272.04	2077.61	2233.24	66.55	399.84	232.98
2010	7619.58	5282.36	2093.07	2234.16	61.26	403.70	226.90
2011	7663.25	5319.20	2112.41	2248.63	59.43	414.34	219.71
2012	7651.57	5336.57	2132.56	2254.22	60.15	418.90	210.46
2013	7683.64	5360.78	2146.93	2265.67	58.47	426.38	209.36
2014	7678.63	5376.07	2159.94	2271.69	55.11	436.10	203.37
2015	7745.04	5424.64	2178.83	2291.59	53.02	451.68	201.54
2016	7676.93	5432.70	2189.85	2294.82	53.45	444.21	201.73

Total Sown Areas of Farm Crops

(1000 hectares)

经济作物 Economic Crops	#棉　花 Cotton	#油菜籽 Rape-seeds	#花　生 Peanuts	#芝　麻 Sesame	#黄红麻 Jute and Ambary Hemp	#甘　蔗 Sugar-cane	#甜　菜 Beet-roots	#烤　烟 Flue-cured Tobacco	其他作物 Others
905.84	589.99	156.46	65.49	10.60	20.71	0.75	6.91	7.05	1365.97
957.04	631.00	169.58	83.79	4.61	11.51	0.35	5.78	2.17	1201.64
1302.77	592.24	442.64	134.11	12.85	24.78	4.11	4.39	3.47	822.63
1194.62	535.19	459.12	116.39	6.29	5.14	3.92	2.09	9.47	735.20
1188.41	572.13	440.81	108.71	5.85	5.16	3.35	2.23	5.63	707.75
1202.48	550.61	482.80	102.95	4.79	4.57	3.18	0.73	5.16	686.45
1350.29	673.43	483.78	107.36	7.14	3.99	3.83	0.70	7.39	703.57
1143.39	517.65	458.30	125.42	8.65	5.20	5.50	1.31	2.02	859.24
1225.86	534.57	516.59	146.52	6.65	2.15	4.57	0.70	0.87	887.12
1268.75	564.90	530.66	148.66	7.54	1.31	3.95	0.17	1.17	885.11
1132.24	485.91	498.00	123.55	9.19	0.89	3.66	0.87	1.44	904.44
1063.10	438.74	473.93	117.25	13.66	0.79	3.46	1.51	2.61	909.25
1063.32	416.16	468.94	141.39	16.23	0.54	3.25	0.52	0.09	1048.70
1006.41	261.99	518.83	177.25	20.62	0.41	4.20	0.15	0.01	1188.50
1227.97	295.27	650.50	227.90	18.20	0.20	5.16	0.07	0.02	1412.59
1347.53	383.99	681.04	230.21	15.53	0.36	5.75	0.40	…	1543.23
1255.19	311.35	668.08	223.63	15.00	0.32	6.08	0.38	…	1659.63
1315.37	369.50	683.03	214.52	12.70	0.31	5.98	0.29	…	1706.65
1356.65	409.62	689.86	218.59	11.91	0.16	4.89	0.12	…	1537.74
1237.36	368.27	660.50	174.29	11.92	0.18	4.10	0.02		1494.36
1007.48	330.40	525.47	130.60	11.38	0.04	1.39	0.01		1266.88
876.25	326.93	434.36	95.71	10.59	0.02	1.18	0.00		1315.89
883.86	300.47	454.49	101.58	11.26	0.02	1.59	0.00	0.02	1359.31
862.07	252.34	476.27	105.50	11.44	0.05	2.00	0.02	0.04	1424.04
824.77	235.68	460.08	103.39	10.80		1.70	0.08	0.24	1512.45
806.93	239.25	441.28	100.21	10.71	0.02	1.63		0.04	1537.12
712.58	170.63	421.31	95.90	10.39		1.62	0.03	0.03	1602.42
690.79	155.22	413.87	94.21	10.06		1.57	0.02	0.02	1632.07
649.94	131.81	398.08	91.64	9.39		1.63	0.01	0.02	1652.62
588.43	94.29	375.66	90.59	9.12		1.54	0.03	0.02	1731.97
518.86	63.40	336.04	93.87	8.66		1.47	0.01		1725.37

10-8 主要农作物种植结构
Planting Structure of Major Farm Crops

单位:% (%)

项目	Item	2012	2013	2014	2015	2016
农作物总播种面积	**Total Sown Area of Farm Crops**	**100.00**	**100.00**	**100.00**	**100.00**	**100.00**
粮食作物	**Grain Crops**	**69.74**	**69.77**	**70.01**	**70.04**	**70.77**
谷物	Cereal	64.76	64.91	65.31	65.42	66.08
稻谷	Rice	29.46	29.49	29.58	29.59	29.89
小麦	Wheat	27.87	27.94	28.13	28.13	28.53
玉米	Corn	5.47	5.55	5.68	5.83	5.79
其它谷物	Other Cereal	1.96	1.93	1.92	1.87	1.87
豆类	Soybeans	4.19	4.10	3.99	3.94	3.99
#大豆	Sonja	2.75	2.72	2.65	2.60	2.63
杂豆	Miscellaneous Beans	0.17	0.16	0.16	1.34	1.36
薯类	Tubers	0.79	0.76	0.72	0.68	0.70
油料作物	**Oil-bearing Crops**	**6.90**	**6.75**	**6.50**	**6.14**	**5.71**
#花生	Peanuts	1.25	1.23	1.19	1.17	1.22
油菜籽	Rapeseeds	5.51	5.39	5.18	4.85	4.38
芝麻	Sesame	0.14	0.13	0.12	0.12	0.11
棉花	**Cotton**	**2.23**	**2.02**	**1.72**	**1.22**	**0.83**
麻类	**Fiber Crops**	**0.01**	**0.01**	**0.01**	**0.01**	**0.00**
糖料	**Sugar Crops**	**0.02**	**0.02**	**0.02**	**0.02**	**0.02**
#甘蔗	Sugarcane	0.02	0.02	0.02	0.02	0.02
烟叶	**Tobacco**	…	…	…	…	…
药材	**Medicinal Materials**	**0.15**	**0.19**	**0.22**	**0.21**	**0.19**
蔬菜、瓜类	**Vegetables and Melon**	**19.17**	**19.52**	**19.82**	**20.58**	**20.68**
#蔬菜	Vegetables	17.30	17.63	17.87	18.48	18.63
其他农作物	**Other Farm Crops**	**1.78**	**1.72**	**1.70**	**1.78**	**1.80**
#青饲料	Succulence	0.38	0.39	0.39	0.38	0.37

10－9 主要农作物播种面积和产量(2016 年)
Total Sown Areas of Farm Crops and Output (2016)

指 标	Item	播种面积(千公顷) Sown Area (1000 hectares)	单位面积产量(千克/公顷) Per Hectare Output (kg/hectare)	总产量(吨) Total Output (ton)
农作物总播种面积	**Total Sown Area of Farm Crops**	**7676.93**		
粮食作物	**Total Grain and Soybeans**	**5432.70**	**6380**	**34660068**
夏粮	Summer Grain	2423.17	5020	12165340
小麦	Wheat	2189.85	5112	11195516
元麦	Hull-less Barley	2.49	3645	9088
大麦	Barley	139.07	5313	738819
蚕豌豆	Horsebean and Pea	91.76	2418	221917
秋粮	Autumn Grain	3009.53	7474	22494728
稻谷	Rice	2294.82	8416	19313939
#中稻和一季晚稻	Rice and Late Season Rice	2294.82	8416	19313939
#籼稻	Long-grained Nonglutinous Rice	252.62	7900	1995653
玉米	Corn	444.21	5266	2339281
高粱	Sorghum	0.22	7250	1595
谷子	Millet	0.15	1387	208
薯类	Tubers	53.45	6135	327952
大豆	Sonja	201.73	2336	471148
其他秋粮	Others	14.95	2716	40605
经济作物	**Economic Crops**	**518.86**		
棉花	Cotton	63.4	1165	73849
油料	Oil-bearing Crops	438.63	3008	1319336
#花生	Peanuts	93.87	3910	366989
油菜籽	Rapeseed	336.04	2785	936013
芝麻	Sesame	8.66	1869	16189
麻类	Fiber Crops	0.3	2737	821
#黄麻	Jute			
苎 麻	Ramee	0.3	2737	821
糖类	Sugar Crops	1.48	60980	90251
#甘蔗	Sugarcane	1.47	61327	90151
烟叶	Tobacco Crops			
药材	Medicinal Materials	14.83		
其他经济作物	Others	0.22	491	108
#薄荷	Mint	0.22	491	108
其他农作物	**Others**	**1725.37**		
#蔬菜	Vegetable	1430.36	39108	55939133
瓜果类	Melon and Fruits Crops	157.08	37987	5966956
绿肥	Organic Fertilizer	6.57		

10－10 主要农产品产量
Output of Major Farm Crops

单位:万吨 (10000 tons)

年 份 Year	粮 食 Grain	夏 粮 Summer Grain	秋 粮 Autumn Grain	棉 花 Cotton	油 料 Oil-bearing Crops	#花 生 Peanuts	#油菜籽 Rape-seeds
1952	997.55	277.85	719.70	9.28	21.68	14.38	6.00
1957	1063.60	274.85	788.75	15.01	25.07	19.81	4.93
1962	965.35	280.65	684.70	8.21	10.27	6.38	3.52
1965	1442.75	379.85	1062.90	26.44	21.68	13.87	7.41
1970	1705.15	415.50	1289.65	32.82	21.67	10.31	10.87
1975	2056.85	524.40	1532.45	45.48	29.64	11.73	17.63
1978	2400.65	677.30	1723.35	47.54	37.44	13.60	23.06
1980	2417.95	873.60	1544.35	41.81	38.64	14.50	23.93
1985	3126.52	1064.46	2062.06	47.91	108.78	34.13	73.11
1989	3282.80	1033.00	2249.80	48.47	99.91	31.25	67.72
1990	3264.15	1143.46	2120.69	46.42	112.39	30.12	81.41
1991	3035.51	1032.43	2003.08	55.71	114.06	28.12	85.32
1992	3320.55	1251.19	2069.36	52.74	127.33	30.51	95.88
1993	3279.70	1152.60	2127.10	42.90	125.71	37.66	87.04
1994	3124.05	1105.29	2018.76	45.71	133.59	44.80	87.77
1995	3286.30	1073.46	2212.84	56.16	159.46	48.43	109.54
1996	3476.35	1200.95	2275.40	53.75	147.50	39.65	106.34
1997	3563.79	1226.91	2336.88	50.75	141.93	39.53	100.53
1998	3415.12	864.22	2550.90	46.19	115.63	48.90	64.26
1999	3559.03	1195.96	2363.07	24.60	184.04	63.25	117.89
2000	3106.63	899.75	2206.88	31.45	225.65	79.75	142.99
2001	2942.05	821.44	2120.61	46.05	232.53	84.09	145.81
2002	2907.05	758.18	2148.87	36.28	217.03	83.71	130.81
2003	2471.85	729.29	1742.56	29.10	199.45	51.57	145.74
2004	2829.06	807.24	2021.82	50.28	238.38	69.12	167.32
2005	2834.59	844.42	1990.17	32.27	215.99	55.46	158.67
2006	3096.03	1017.12	2078.91	35.52	176.47	45.51	129.00
2007	3132.24	1070.70	2061.54	34.75	145.08	33.84	109.46
2008	3175.49	1094.50	2080.99	32.60	150.29	35.57	112.81
2009	3230.10	1103.20	2126.90	25.55	162.23	38.67	121.69
2010	3235.10	1105.33	2129.77	26.08	151.97	37.70	112.44
2011	3307.76	1117.18	2190.58	24.68	144.05	37.00	105.25
2012	3372.48	1143.52	2228.97	22.04	146.95	36.02	109.13
2013	3422.98	1195.83	2227.15	20.93	150.37	35.28	113.26
2014	3490.62	1254.68	2235.94	15.95	146.60	34.82	110.06
2015	3561.34	1271.67	2289.67	11.69	143.11	35.07	106.33
2016	3466.01	1216.53	2249.47	7.38	131.93	36.70	93.60

10-11 人均占有主要农产品产量
Per Capita Output of Major Farm Products

单位:千克/人 (kg/person)

年 份 Year	粮食产量 Grain	棉花产量 Cotton	油料产量 Oil-bearing Grops	生猪饲养量（头/人） Output of Raising Hogs (head/person)	猪、牛、羊肉产量 Output of Pork, Beef and Mutton	水产品产量 Output of Aquatic Products
1952	270.0	2.5	5.9	0.24		4.6
1957	257.0	3.7	6.1	0.34		6.9
1962	225.0	1.9	2.4	0.22		4.5
1965	316.0	5.8	4.8	0.46		5.5
1970	329.0	6.4	4.2	0.50		5.2
1975	367.0	8.1	5.3	0.60		6.5
1978	414.0	8.2	6.5	0.60		6.9
1980	408.5	7.1	6.6	0.70	18.1	7.2
1985	505.0	7.8	17.6	0.64	22.4	10.9
1989	506.1	7.5	15.4	0.60	23.3	17.0
1990	486.0	6.9	16.7	0.59	23.6	17.6
1991	446.1	8.2	16.8	0.59	24.0	17.3
1992	482.8	7.7	18.5	0.61	25.1	19.6
1993	472.6	6.2	18.1	0.62	25.8	22.7
1994	446.7	6.5	19.1	0.65	28.5	25.8
1995	466.6	8.0	22.6	0.69	30.9	31.2
1996	490.4	7.6	20.8	0.51	24.7	34.7
1997	499.9	7.1	19.9	0.57	26.2	37.3
1998	476.6	6.4	16.1	0.63	29.2	39.4
1999	494.5	3.4	25.6	0.63	29.9	41.2
2000	427.3	4.3	31.0	0.66	31.3	42.5
2001	400.8	6.3	31.7	0.67	32.2	43.7
2002	394.6	4.9	29.5	0.67	32.6	45.4
2003	334.4	3.9	27.0	0.68	33.1	46.4
2004	381.3	6.8	32.1	0.66	32.7	49.3
2005	380.3	4.3	29.0	0.66	32.5	52.1
2006	412.1	4.7	23.5	0.63	28.4	53.0
2007	412.8	4.6	19.1	0.52	25.5	53.9
2008	415.1	4.3	19.6	0.56	26.7	55.4
2009	419.5	3.3	21.1	0.59	28.0	57.6
2010	415.0	3.3	19.5	0.59	28.7	59.1
2011	419.6	3.1	18.3	0.59	28.8	60.4
2012	426.4	2.8	18.6	0.61	30.3	62.4
2013	431.7	2.6	19.0	0.61	30.4	64.3
2014	439.1	2.0	18.4	0.61	30.6	65.3
2015	446.9	1.5	18.0	0.60	29.8	65.5
2016	433.9	0.9	16.5	0.57	28.5	65.5

10－12 蚕、茶、果生产情况

Statistics on Silkworm Cocoons, Tea and Fruits

单位：万吨　　　　　　　　　　　　　　　　(10000 tons)

指标		Item		2012	2013	2014	2015	2016
蚕茧产量	(万吨)	Silkworm Cocoons	(10000 tons)	6.83	5.90	5.69	4.97	3.95
茶叶产量	(万吨)	Tea	(10000 tons)	1.54	1.39	1.46	1.45	1.40
红毛茶		Black Tea		0.25	0.20	0.23	0.24	0.25
绿毛茶		Green Tea		1.27	1.19	1.23	1.20	1.13
其他茶		Others		0.02	…	…	…	0.02
水果产量	(万吨)	Fruits	(10000 tons)	281.22	274.58	306.17	300.03	296.31
#苹果		Apples		60.12	54.18	59.77	59.95	56.41
柑桔		Citrus		5.80	4.73	4.82	4.32	3.27
梨		Pears		74.82	69.45	83.11	77.98	75.83
葡萄		Grapes		48.57	51.35	58.69	63.24	61.00
桃子		Peaches		55.57	50.81	61.44	61.75	63.47
红枣		Dates		1.34	1.06	1.13	1.10	0.90
柿子		Persimmons		14.62	14.31	14.94	13.88	11.56
桑园面积	(千公顷)	Area of Mulberry Plantations	(1000 hectares)	53.17	49.07	42.62	38.06	33.35
茶园面积	(千公顷)	Area of Tea Plantations	(1000 hectares)	34.04	33.98	34.28	33.77	33.78
#当年采摘面积		Picked Area in the Year		28.82	28.42	28.47	30.30	30.57
果园	(千公顷)	Area of Orchards	(1000 hectares)	209.83	222.05	214.29	209.42	209.97
#苹果园		Apples		34.33	32.95	31.95	32.10	30.89
柑桔园		Citrus		3.54	3.02	2.89	2.67	2.54
梨园		Pears		39.42	39.14	39.35	39.92	39.04
葡萄园		Grapes		31.15	34.11	37.55	37.98	34.91

10－13　林业生产情况
Statistics on Forestry

指　　标　Item		2012	2013	2014	2015	2016
造林面积　（千公顷）	Area of Forestation　(1000 hectares)	57.34	65.26	58.12	42.58	27.21
用材林	Timber Forests	10.12	7.85	6.84	6.73	4.56
经济林	By-product Forests	10.01	11.45	11.83	7.86	6.81
防护林	Protection Forests	36.82	43.92	40.10	27.34	15.37
其他林	Others	0.39	2.04	1.09	0.65	0.47
林产品产量　（吨）	Output of Forestry Products　(ton)					
油茶籽	Tea-oil Seeds	61	62	299	256	263
竹笋干	Bamboo Shoots	3140	3200	7178	721	852
板栗	Chestnut	26065	26905	28585	24237	21388
白果	Ginkgo	39455	59908	61921	26711	48584
育苗面积　（千公顷）	Area of Seedlings　(1000 hectares)	86.96	121.29	106.46	140.66	142.86
当年苗木产量　（亿株）	Output of Seedlings in the Year (100 million units)	50.24	54.41	56.87	50.92	54.23
林木种子采集量　（吨）	Output of Forestry Seeds Picking (ton)	1602	3889	3636	7347	8639
木材采伐量　（万立方米）	Output of Timber Cutting (10000 cu. m)	173.00	144.00	141.33	148.86	178.47
竹材采伐量　（万根）	Bamboo Cutting　(10000 units)	627.00	408.00	404.43	408.00	387.83
四旁植树　（万株）	Planting　(10000 units)	10964	10696	9229	7180	5585

10－14 畜牧业生产情况
Statistics on Livestock

指　　标	Item	2012	2013	2014	2015	2016
牲畜年末头数　（万头）	**Livestock (Year-end) (10000 units)**					
大牲畜	Large Animals	36.40	34.53	34.54	34.15	33.54
牛	Cattle and Buffaloes	32.06	30.41	30.59	30.70	30.30
#奶牛	Cows	20.87	20.41	20.51	19.98	19.88
马	Horses	0.31	0.29	0.28	0.25	0.21
驴	Donkeys	2.98	2.82	2.77	2.44	2.34
骡	Mules	1.05	1.01	0.90	0.76	0.69
猪	Hogs	1775.17	1787.26	1799.50	1780.30	1690.56
羊	Sheep and Goats	400.61	403.07	413.80	417.50	404.30
山羊	Goats	391.24	393.59	404.10	407.64	394.84
绵羊	Sheep	9.37	9.48	9.70	9.86	9.46
畜禽产品产量	**Output of Livestock and Poultry Products**					
猪牛羊出栏头数　（万头）	Hogs, Sheep and Goats (10000 units)					
当年肉猪出栏头数	Hogs	3043.12	3049.56	3073.60	2978.32	2847.27
当年出售和自宰的肉用牛	Cattle and Buttaloes Sold and Killed in the Year	18.82	17.29	17.60	17.40	16.97
当年出售和自宰的肉用羊（万只）	Sheep and Goats Sold and Killed in the Year (10000 units)	687.96	703.87	719.45	730.24	739.27
肉类产量　（万吨）	Output of Meat (10000 tons)	396.52	383.23	379.46	369.43	355.63
猪肉	Pork	228.84	229.86	232.35	225.84	216.36
牛肉	Beef	3.47	3.19	3.27	3.22	3.11
羊肉	Mutton	7.61	7.79	8.01	8.14	8.26
禽肉	Poultry	146.08	131.93	125.40	122.02	118.13
其他畜禽产品产量　（吨）	Others (ton)					
牛奶产量	Milk	612980	598912	607200	595900	590100
绵羊毛产量	Sheep's Wool	340	344	359	366	348
山羊毛产量	Goat's Wool	9	10	10	10	11
蜂蜜	Honey	3975	4058	4521	4844	4423
禽蛋　（万吨）	Poultry Eggs (10000 tons)	197.20	200.07	196.97	198.81	201.15

10－15 水产品产量
Output of Aquatic Products

指标	Item	2012	2013	2014	2015	2016
水产品产量（万吨）	**Output of Aquatic Products (10000 tons)**	**493.74**	**509.38**	**518.84**	**522.11**	**523.15**
海水产品	Seawater Aquatic Products	148.48	151.20	150.47	149.24	149.72
按生产性质分	Grouped by Nature					
天然生产	Naturally Grown	57.98	57.33	56.88	59.89	59.30
人工养殖	Artificially Cultured	90.50	93.87	93.59	89.35	90.42
按类别分	Grouped by Category					
鱼类	Fish	40.89	40.75	40.41	38.87	38.39
甲壳类	Shrimp, Prawn and Crab	22.21	25.93	27.28	27.53	27.38
贝类	Shellfish	76.04	76.13	74.90	70.43	71.58
藻类	Algae	2.42	3.09	2.83	2.93	3.01
按主要品种分	Among Seawater Aquatic					
大黄鱼	Big Yellow Croaker	0.06	0.05	0.05	0.05	0.05
小黄鱼	Little Yellow Croaker	3.54	3.07	2.95	2.96	2.96
带鱼	Hairtail	5.73	5.67	5.42	5.53	5.59
鱿鱼	Sleeve-fish	1.24	0.99	1.70	3.18	3.24
淡水产品	Freshwater Aquatic Products	345.26	358.18	368.37	372.86	373.43
按生产性质分	Grouped by Nature					
天然生产	Naturally Grown	33.42	32.85	32.58	32.54	31.71
人工养殖	Artificially Cultured	311.84	325.33	335.79	340.32	341.72
按类别分	Grouped by Category					
鱼类	Fish	253.80	264.64	269.92	272.47	273.16
甲壳类	Shrimp, Prawn and Crab	75.27	78.18	83.52	85.63	85.74
贝类	Shellfish	12.23	11.55	11.17	11.15	10.93
水产养殖面积（千公顷）	**Aquatic Raise Areas (1000 hectares)**	**771.18**	**765.28**	**761.04**	**753.44**	**753.16**
淡水养殖面积	Freshwater Area for Breeding	571.83	571.47	572.38	571.61	567.88
海水养殖面积	Seawater Area for Breeding	199.35	193.81	188.66	181.83	185.28

10－16 主要农业机械和农产品加工机械年底拥有量

年 份 Year	农业机械总动力 （万千瓦） Total Power of Agricultural Machinery (10000 kW)	农用小型及手扶拖拉机（万台） Small and Walking Agricultural Tractors (10000 units)	农用排灌动力机械（万千瓦） Machinery for Agricultural Drainage and Irrigation (10000 kW)	农用水泵 （万台） Agricultural Water Pumps (10000 units)
1978	855.16	19.25	363.73	29.20
1980	1113.05	25.61	442.48	36.18
1985	1675.06	49.16	450.27	37.75
1989	2212.37	70.02	475.95	40.29
1990	2004.77	71.65	490.83	39.63
1991	1966.61	72.64	492.88	40.73
1992	2016.07	72.41	494.57	41.55
1993	2081.75	73.52	501.35	41.59
1994	2161.40	74.98	507.66	42.63
1995	2226.95	75.04	508.91	43.36
1996	2297.43	76.53	515.99	44.84
1997	2499.69	83.32	538.66	50.63
1998	2594.83	83.87	553.73	52.20
1999	2767.89	86.78	577.99	54.07
2000	2925.29	88.89	576.25	65.62
2001	2957.93	89.42	618.72	58.09
2002	2983.89	89.75	604.04	59.74
2003	3029.10	87.46	567.79	58.81
2004	3052.51	86.71	599.71	56.88
2005	3135.33	90.11	609.08	61.93
2006	3278.53	91.37	606.00	62.00
2007	3392.44	89.95	431.40	59.09
2008	3630.86	120.44	601.83	59.80
2009	3810.57	123.32	612.87	60.42
2010	3937.34	122.84	630.46	59.29
2011	4106.11	123.41	642.41	63.49
2012	4214.64	98.71	664.80	66.29
2013	4405.78	92.53	687.98	66.53
2014	4649.98	88.16	695.79	65.99
2015	4825.49	81.86	693.46	65.92
2016	4906.55	76.05	706.72	67.61

Agricultural Machinery and Machinery for Processing Farm Products at Year-end

联合收割机（台） Combine Harvesters (unit)	机动脱粒机（万台） Motorized Huller (10000 units)	机动喷雾（粉）器（万部） Motorized Duster (10000 units)	大中型拖拉机配套农具（万件） Large and Mediumsized Tractor Towing Farm Machinery (10000 units)	小型拖拉机配套农具（万件） Small Tractor Towing Farm Machinery (10000 units)
295	32.96	2.01	2.45	33.99
478	40.99	4.33	3.23	53.58
687	68.51	5.51	3.38	111.15
1821	86.36	7.08	3.29	112.49
2411	89.42	9.49	3.42	118.26
3583	92.29	11.35	3.91	122.40
5964	93.37	12.37	4.16	122.33
7279	94.80	12.63	4.30	124.66
8604	98.32	13.28	4.37	125.50
12063	105.22	17.08	4.69	127.74
20074	105.01	19.64	5.68	129.22
27656	121.42	26.55	7.00	138.63
33343	123.80	29.10	7.69	143.08
42266	124.52	31.59	8.51	148.41
48821	129.69	33.26	8.62	152.45
52025	120.16	35.17	8.39	151.48
56151	111.45	34.54	8.17	145.02
58645	93.56	34.99	7.84	145.70
61115	91.45	34.88	7.52	144.45
69569	73.95	37.41	8.08	143.64
77100	75.00	39.50	8.37	144.68
78498	59.00	41.39	9.13	143.07
85327	43.62	50.27	11.01	163.43
90979	38.00	53.50	13.29	170.91
98511	33.19	57.32	16.41	168.83
103500	20.92	61.92	19.17	173.59
118078	18.39	67.11	19.83	155.64
136619	16.44	68.60	22.28	149.98
149503	14.95	68.85	26.53	147.04
159115	10.50	67.04	30.25	140.59
169641	8.93	65.97	33.71	131.86

10－17 农业主要经济效益指标

Main Indicators on Economic Benefit of Agriculture

指标	Item	2012	2013	2014	2015	2016
每个农林牧渔业劳动力创造的	**Per Labor Creating**					
农林牧渔业总产值（元）	Gross Output Value of Agriculture, Forestry, Animal Husbandry and Fishery (yuan)	71814.83	78342.40	83786.17	93159.05	97538.49
粮食产量（公斤）	Output of Grain (kg)	4169.42	4354.72	4539.02	4718.85	4672.65
棉花产量（公斤）	Output of Cotton (kg)	27.25	26.63	20.75	15.49	9.95
油料产量（公斤）	Output of Oil-bearing Crops (kg)	181.67	191.30	190.63	189.63	177.86
肉类产量（公斤）	Output of Meat (kg)	490.22	487.54	493.43	489.50	479.44
水产品产量（公斤）	Output of Aquatic Products (kg)	610.42	648.03	674.67	691.81	705.28
每亩耕地创造的	**Per Mu Cultivated Land Creating**					
农林牧渔业总产值（元）	Gross Output Value of Agriculture, Forestry, Animal Husbandry and Fishery (yuan)	8431.00	8936.98	9357.17	10210.19	10523.81
农林牧渔业增加值（元）	Value Added of Agriculture, Forestry, Animal Husbandry and Fishery (yuan)	4961.36	5291.43	5569.52	6113.12	6288.81

注:产值、增加值均为现行价格。

a) Both output value and value-added are caculated at current prices.

10-18 国有农场基本情况
Basic Statistics on State Farms

指　标	Item	2012	2013	2014	2015	2016
农场数　（个）	Number of Farms (unit)	18	17	17	18	18
职工人数　（万人）	Number of Staff and Workers (10000 persons)	6.19	5.72	5.51	5.33	5.03
耕地面积　（千公顷）	Cultivated Area (1000 hectares)	71.43	67.67	71.08	70.82	65.53
农业机械总动力（万千瓦）	Total Power of Agricultural Machinery (10000 kW)	45.22	43.55	44.33	49.06	51.78
农业机械拥有量（台、辆）	Ownership of Agricultural Machinery (unit)					
大中型农用拖拉机	Large and Medium-sized Agricultural Tractors	3475	3369	3470	3796	3538
小型及手扶拖拉机	Small and Walking Agricultural Tractors	1528	1357	1090	989	847
农用排灌动力机械	Machinery for Agricultural Drainage and Irrigation	702	842	909	663	793
联合收割机	Combine Harvesters	1933	1975	1815	1795	1571
农用载重汽车	Trucks for Agricultural Use	151	101	111	71	41
农用化肥施用量（万吨）	Consumption of Chemical Fertilizers (10000 tons)	13.80	13.79	14.26	15.94	14.10
农业总产值　（亿元）	Gross Agricultural Output Value (100 million yuan)	53.40	58.95	61.17	60.98	59.91
农作物总播种面积（千公顷）	Sown Area of Farm Crops (1000 hectares)	148.36	124.12	141.66	155.24	155.46
粮食作物	Grain	123.22	116.08	134.19	149.65	151.52
棉　花	Cotton	0.23	0.14	0.07	0.04	
油　料	Oil-bearing Crops	0.05	0.03	0.02	0.09	0.06
年底实有桑园面积（公顷）	Area of Mulberry Plantations (year-end) (hectare)	231	231	213	213	202
年底实有果园面积（公顷）	Area of Orchards (year-end) (hectare)	260	126	183	134	257
主要农产品产量	Output of Major Farm Products					
粮食作物　（万吨）	Grain (10000 tons)	94.34	88.61	101.17	116.61	120.65
棉　花　（万吨）	Cotton (10000 tons)	0.22	0.20	0.07	0.06	
油　料　（万吨）	Oil-bearing Crops (10000 tons)	0.14	0.10	0.09	0.05	0.01
水　果　（万吨）	Fruits (10000 tons)	0.28	0.19	0.24	0.23	0.25
畜牧业、渔业生产	Production of Animal Husbandry and Fishery					
大牲畜年底头数（万头）	Number of Large Animals (year-end) (10000 heads)	0.57	0.43	0.54	0.75	0.79
猪年底头数（万头）	Number of Hogs (10000 heads)	8.42	7.55	7.32	6.75	9.29
羊年底只数（万只）	Number of Sheep and Goats Sheep (10000 heads)	1.22	1.95	1.51	1.09	1.31
畜产品产量　（万吨）	Output of Livestock Products (10000 tons)					
猪牛羊肉	Pork, Beef and Mutton	7.69	6.76	6.26	5.51	4.53
#猪　肉	Pork	2.10	2.06	1.76	1.54	1.56
牛　奶	Milk	0.88	1.06	1.32	2.62	3.15
禽　蛋	Poultry Eggs	1.48	1.35	1.34	1.77	1.79
羊　毛	Sheep Wool					
水产品总产量（万吨）	Output of Aquatic Products (10000 tons)	4.78	4.85	4.76	4.81	5.35

注：本表为农垦系统数据。

a) Data in this table are from farming system.

10-19 分市农业基本情况(2016 年)

指　标	Item	南京市 Nanjing	无锡市 Wuxi	徐州市 Xuzhou
乡村户数　(万户)	Rural Households　(10000 units)	63.25	59.91	175.79
乡村劳动力　(万人)	Rural Laborers　(10000 persons)	116.97	109.81	358.55
#农林牧渔业	Agriculture, Forestry, Animal Husbandry, Fishery	23.21	16.30	130.56
工业	Industry	36.65	67.21	104.30
建筑业	Construction	23.81	6.39	51.80
交通运输、仓储业和邮电通讯业	Transport, Storage, Post and Telecommunication	7.14	3.34	15.63
批发、零售贸易业、餐饮业	Wholesale, Retail Sales and Catering Services	12.49	8.20	32.53
农业机械总动力　(万千瓦)	Total Power of Agricultural Machinery　(10000 kW)	227.61	99.22	712.33
化肥施用量　(万吨)	Consumption of Chemical Fertilizers　(10000 tons)	7.39	5.18	60.46
农村用电量　(亿千瓦小时)	Electricity Consumed in Rural Areas　(100 million kW·h)	32.08	394.38	66.11
农作物总播种面积　(千公顷)	Sown Area of Farm Crops　(1000 hectares)	289.25	160.31	1154.55
#粮食	Grain Crops	153.05	94.06	737.77
主要农产品产量　(万吨)	Output of Major Farm Products　(10000 tons)			
粮食	Grain	108.04	59.16	469.16
棉花	Cotton	0.31		2.07
油料	Oil-bearing	7.43	0.81	13.45
肉类产量	Meat	9.81	7.35	90.77
#猪牛羊肉	Pork, Beef and Mutton	5.66	5.20	44.91
水产品产量	Aquatic Products	22.31	12.67	18.88
农林牧渔业总产值　(亿元)	Gross Output Value of Agriculture, Forestry, Animal Husbandry and Fishery　(100 million yuan)	451.16	249.98	1046.76
农业	Farming	258.75	140.30	650.95
林业	Forestry	24.26	18.53	18.47
畜牧业	Animal Husbandry	46.83	27.46	301.90
渔业	Fishery	99.36	35.36	43.22
农林牧渔服务业	Services in Support of Agriculture	21.97	28.32	32.21

Basic Statistics of Agriculture by Region (2016)

常州市 Changzhou	苏州市 Suzhou	南通市 Nantong	连云港市 Lianyun gang	淮安市 Huaian	盐城市 Yancheng	扬州市 Yangzhou	镇江市 Zhenjiang	泰州市 Taizhou	宿迁市 Suqian
72.68	87.50	198.67	93.07	99.50	183.00	100.85	57.57	119.19	108.46
128.05	171.89	299.48	177.97	211.79	299.92	181.49	101.27	212.34	225.25
23.22	21.83	63.55	80.84	86.13	107.93	33.22	21.68	42.93	84.72
59.45	103.57	86.19	31.00	42.36	60.76	64.44	50.14	63.08	63.12
17.36	9.66	62.50	31.30	31.91	36.68	34.69	11.64	36.42	28.94
5.18	5.48	15.58	8.08	6.79	13.71	7.61	3.65	13.34	8.41
9.20	14.79	34.46	12.44	13.68	19.12	16.96	5.48	22.42	19.18
146.25	163.89	398.28	588.06	622.60	679.12	270.19	145.72	275.52	577.77
6.04	7.11	22.24	34.57	38.85	50.56	20.03	5.36	16.12	38.59
156.59	609.78	170.31	34.28	16.00	80.30	61.14	77.44	124.44	46.42
209.20	241.40	824.10	631.90	797.17	1399.86	507.16	233.75	575.18	718.03
132.79	145.01	518.87	501.53	659.99	981.57	418.85	174.02	435.05	579.41
93.74	97.68	325.20	360.80	458.55	687.31	300.30	118.74	313.03	384.54
0.04	0.05	2.38	0.05	0.01	1.13	0.11	0.09	0.18	0.06
3.41	1.34	35.82	11.40	8.80	24.30	6.87	5.83	12.20	4.65
13.52	9.76	45.73	29.50	30.39	81.40	18.01	7.95	26.65	32.86
6.88	6.38	28.32	23.75	19.45	54.60	10.12	5.04	21.57	19.58
16.64	25.49	89.03	75.30	26.10	119.43	40.12	9.85	39.64	27.11
283.97	424.67	691.55	589.42	602.72	1104.93	477.95	240.71	415.96	517.24
152.43	178.81	294.61	275.56	373.23	480.98	221.18	134.13	228.85	298.51
1.97	24.76	4.60	16.54	13.59	27.95	12.02	9.08	3.60	18.09
39.43	37.39	159.06	119.01	139.93	303.65	78.05	31.52	78.94	102.14
72.98	136.08	163.99	143.24	64.63	214.72	140.97	34.91	83.30	84.90
17.18	47.62	69.29	35.07	11.34	77.64	25.73	31.07	21.27	13.61

主要统计指标解释

农林牧渔业总产值 指以货币表现的农、林、牧、渔业全部产品和对农业生产进行各种支持性服务活动的总量，它反映一定时期内农业生产总规模和总成果。从2003年开始农林牧渔业总产值执行新的国民经济行业分类标准，包括农业、林业、牧业、渔业、农林牧渔服务业，不再包括农民兼营商品性工业。农林牧渔业总产值中的农、林、牧、渔四业的计算方法通常是按农、林、牧、渔业产品及其副产品的产量分别乘以各自单位产品价格求得，现行价格从2003年开始使用生产价格调查的价格；少数生产周期较长，当年没有产品或产品产量不易统计的，则采用间接方法匡算其产值；然后将四业产品产值与农林牧渔服务业相加即为农林牧渔业总产值。

粮食产量 指全社会的产量。包括国有经济经营的、集体统一经营的和农民家庭经营的粮食产量，还包括工矿企业办的农场和其他生产单位的产量。粮食除包括稻谷、小麦、玉米、高粱、谷子及其他杂粮外，还包括薯类和豆类。其产量计算方法，豆类按去豆荚后的干豆计算（作为蔬菜食用的青豆列入蔬菜统计）；薯类（包括甘薯和马铃薯，不包括芋头和木薯）1963年以前按每4公斤鲜薯折1公斤粮食计算，从1964年开始改为按5公斤鲜薯折1公斤粮食计算。经请示国家统计局同意，目前江苏的马铃薯已全部列入蔬菜统计，不再作为粮食统计，产量按鲜品计算。其他粮食一律按脱粒后的原粮计算。

棉花产量 指全社会的产量。包括春播棉和夏播棉。产量按皮棉计算。

油料产量 指全部油料作物的生产量。包括花生、油菜籽、芝麻、向日葵籽、胡麻籽（亚麻籽）和其他油料。不包括大豆、木本油料和野生油料。花生以带壳干花生计算。

水产品产量 指人工养殖的水产品和天然生长的水产品的捕捞量。包括海水的鱼类、虾蟹类、贝类和藻类以及内陆水域的鱼类、虾蟹类和贝类，不包括淡水水生植物。

猪、牛、羊肉产量 指当年出栏并已屠宰、除去头蹄下水后带骨肉（即胴体重）的重量。

期初（末）畜禽存栏头（只）数 指报告期初（末）农村各种合作经济组织和国营农场、农民个人、机关、团体、学校、工矿企业、部队等单位以及城镇居民饲养的大牲畜、猪、羊、家禽等畜禽的存栏数。

耕地面积 是指年初可用来种植农作物并经常进行耕种、能够正常收获的土地。包括当年实际耕种的熟地、当年新开荒地、休闲不满三年随时可以复耕的地和当年休闲地以及以种植农作物为主并附带种植桑树、茶树、果树和其他林木的土地、沿海、沿湖地区已围垦利用的"海涂"、"湖田"等面积。不包括临时种植农作物的坡度在25度以上的陡坡地、在河套、湖畔、库区临时开发的成片或零星土地，属于专业性的桑园、茶园、果园、果木苗圃、林地、芦苇地、天然或人工草地面积、也不包括已列为国家和省（区、市）退耕计划但临时耕种的土地。

农作物播种面积 指实际播种或移植有农作物的面积。凡是实际种植有农作物的面积，不论种植在耕地上还是种植在非耕地上，均包括在农作物播种面积中。在播种季节基本结束后，因遭灾而重新改种和补种的农作物面积，也包括在内。

有效灌溉面积 指具有一定的水源，地块比较平整，灌溉工程或设备已经配套，在一般年景下当年能够进行正常灌溉的耕地面积。在一般情况下，有效灌溉面积应等于灌溉工程或设备已经配备，能够进行正常灌溉的水田和水浇地面积之和。

农用化肥施用量 指本年内实际用于农业生产的化肥数量，包括氮肥、磷肥、钾肥和复合肥。化肥施用量要求按折纯量计算数量。折纯量是指把氮肥、磷肥、钾肥分别按含氮、含五氧化二磷、含氧化钾的百分之一百成份进行折算后的数量。复合肥按其所含主要成分折算。

农业机械总动力 指主要用于农、林、牧、渔业的各种动力机械的动力总和。包括耕作机械、排灌机械、收获机械、农用运输机械、植物保护机械、牧业机械、林业机械、渔业机械和其他农业机械[内燃机按引擎马力折成瓦（特）计算、电动机按功率折成瓦（特）计算]。不包括专门用于乡、镇、村、组办工业、基本建设、非农业运输、科学试验和教学等非农业生产方面用的动力机械与作业机械。

农林牧渔业劳动力 指全社会直接参加农林牧渔业生产活动的劳动力。

Explanatory Notes on Main Statistical Indicators

Gross Output Value of Farming, Forestry, Animal Husbandry and Fishery refers to the total value of products of farming, forestry, animal husbandry and fishery and various supporting service activities for agricultural production, which reflects the total scale and result of agricultural production during a given period. Since 2003, the total output value of farming, forestry, animal husbandry and fishery is counted with new classified standard of the national economy, including the service industry serving for agricultural production, while excluding the output value of commercialized handicraft products. Gross output value of farming, forestry, animal husbandry, fishery and the value of service industry is obtained by first multiplying the output of each product with its price, resulting in the output value of each single item. Since 2003, the current price is used by the investigated production price. For a small number of products, annual output of which is not available or difficult to get due to the long production growing process involved, the output value is estimated through an indirect approach. The sum of output value of all products of farming, forestry, animal husbandry, fishery and service activities for them is then equal to the gross output value of agriculture. Prior to 1957, gross agricultural output value included barnyard manure and handicraft products for self consumption (clothes, shoes, stockings, and initial grain processing undertaken by peasants). Since 1958, cutting and felling of bamboo and trees by villages and other cooperative organizations under villages have been included in forestry; value of barnyard manure has been excluded from animal husbandry; self consumed handicrafts has been excluded from sideline occupations, while the output value of industries run by villages and cooperative organizations under village had been included in sideline occupations and the output value of fish catches by motor fishing boats has been added to fishery. Since 1980, the value of handicraft products made for sale by individuals in households had been added to sideline occupations. Since 1984, industries run by villages and under villages have been included in the sector of industry. Since 1993, the subdivision of sideline occupations has been canceled, and the hunting of wild animals has been classified into animal husbandry, and the gathering of wild plants and commodity industryrun by rural household have been included infarming. Since 2003, the output value of commercialized handicraft products, as the farmer's household sideline occupation, don't include in farming anymore. The first agriculture census of China in 1996 revealed some discrepancy between the production of animal products from the annual reports and that from the census. Efforts were made by the Rural Socio-economic Survey Organization of NBS to adjust the output value of animal husbandry to make the figures from the annual reports consistent with the census data.

Grain Output refers to the grain production in the whole country including grains produced by state farms, collective units, industrial enterprises and mines. Grain includes rice, wheat, corn, sorghum, millet and other miscellaneous grains as well as tubers and beans. Output of beans refers to dry beans without pods. The output of tubers (sweet potatoes and potatoes, not including taros and cassava) was converted into that of grain at the ratio 4: 1, e. 4 kilograms of fresh tubers was equivalent to 1 kilogram of grain up to 1963. Since 1964 the ratio for conversion has been 5: 1. Tubers supplied as vegetables (such as potatoes) in cities and suburbs are calculated as fresh vegetables and their output is not included in the output of grain. Output of all other grains refers to husked grain.

Cotton Output refers to the cotton production in the whole country including cotton sown in spring and in autumn. Output is measured as the weight of ginned cotton.

Output of Oil-bearing Crops refers to the total production of oil bearing crops of various kinds, including peanuts, (dry, in shell) rapeseeds, sesame, sunflower seeds, flax seeds, and other oil bearing crops. Soybeans, oil-bearing woody plants, and wild oil-bearing crops are not included.

Output of Aquatic Products refers to catches of both artificially cultured and naturally grown aquatic products, including fish, shrimps, crabs and shellfish in sea and inland water as well as seaweed. Freshwater plants are not included.

Output of Pork, Beef, and Mutton refers to the meat of slaughtered hogs, cattle, sheep and goats with head, feet, and offal taken away.

Number of Livestock or Poultry in Stock at Beginning (or End) refers to the total number of large animals, pigs, sheep, fowls, etc. raised by rural cooperative organizations, state farms, rural individuals, government agencies, schools, industrial and mining enterprises, army, and urban residents at the beginning (or end) of the reference period.

Regularly Cultivated Land refers to farmland among the total land resources which is exclusively used for farming and is under regular cultivation with harvest in normal years. Included are currently cultivated land, land that has been abandoned or put in idle for less than 3 years and could be re-used for cultivation at any time, and new-claimed land that has been put into cultivation for more than 3 years. Excluded under this category are steep slope land over 25 degrees under temporary cultivation, land (large or small plots) that is claimed along river bends, lake sides or banks of reservoirs, as well as land that has been designated under the "Green for Grain" programmes of the state and provincial governments but is still temporarily under cultivation.

Sown Area of Crops refers to area of land sown or transplanted with crops regardless of being in cultivated area or non cultivated area. Area of land re-sown due to natural disasters is also included.

Irrigated Area refers to areas that are effectively irrigated, level land which has water source and complete sets of irrigation facilities to lift and move adequate water for irrigation purpose under normal conditions. Under normal conditions, irrigated area is the sum of watered fields and irrigated fields where irrigation systems or equipment have been installed for regular irrigation purpose.

Consumption of Chemical Fertilizers in Agriculture refers to the quantity of chemical fertilizers applied in agriculture in the year, including nitrogenous fertilizer, phosphate fertilizer, potash fertilizer, and compound fertilizer. The consumption of chemical fertilizers is required in calculation to convert the gross weight into weight containing 100% effective component(e. g. 100% nitrogen content in nitrogenous fertilizer, 100% phosphorous pentoxide contents in phosphate fertilizer, 100% potassium oxide contents in potash fertilizer). Compound fertilizer is converted with its major component.

Total Power of Farm Machinery refers to total mechanical power of machinery used in farming, forestry, animal husbandry, and fishery, including ploughing, irrigation and drainage, harvesting, transport, plant protection, stock breeding, forestry and fishery. The power of internal combustion engines is required to convert horsepower into watts and the power of electric motors is required to beconverted into watts. Machinery employed for non agricultural purposes, such as the machines used in township run and village-run industry, construction, non agricultural transport, scientific experiments and teaching, is excluded.

Labour Force Engaged in Farming, Forestry, Animal Husbandry and Fishery refers to the total laborers who are directly engaged in production of farming, forestry, animal husbandry and fishery.

11

工　业

Industry

简 要 说 明

一、本篇资料的主要内容

本篇资料反映我省工业经济方面的基本情况，包括：

1. 全省规模以上工业企业主要经济指标，以及按企业登记注册类型、轻重工业、企业规模、工业行业大类分组的主要经济指标和经济效益指标；

2. 国有及国有控股、私营、外商投资和港澳台商投资工业企业按工业行业大类分组的主要经济指标和经济效益指标；

3. 大中型工业企业按工业行业大类分组的主要经济指标和经济效益指标；

4. 主要工业产品产量等。

二、本篇资料的统计范围

本篇资料的统计范围1998年至2006年为全部国有及年主营业务收入在500万元以上非国有工业企业，2007至2010年为年主营业务收入在500万元以上工业企业，2011年起为年主营业务收入2000万元以上工业企业（即规模以上工业企业）。本篇资料中工业行业分类按2011年《国民经济行业分类》标准划分；企业大中小微型划分按2011年《统计上大中小微型企业划分办法》标准执行。

三、本篇的资料来源和统计调查方法

本篇工业企业统计数据主要是根据工业统计进度报表中有关年度资料整理汇总的。

Brief Introduction

I. Main Contents

Data in this chapter reflect the basic conditions of the industrial sector in Jiangsu:

(1) Main economic indicators of industrial enterprises above designated size; as well as their main economic indicators and efficiency indicators classified by type of registration, by light and heavy industries, by size of enterprise, by branch of industry .

(2) Main economic indicators and efficiency indicators of State-owned industrial enterprises and enterprises where the State holds the majority of shares; private industrial enterprises, foreign-funded industrial enterprises and enterprises funded by entrepreneurs from Hong Kong, Macao and Taiwan classified by branch of industry.

(3) Main economic indicators and efficiency indicators of large and medium-sized industrial enterprises classified by branch of industry.

(4) Output of key industrial products.

II. Scopes of Statistics

The scopes of industrial statistics are all State-owned industrial enterprises and non-State-owned industrial enterprises with revenue from principal business over 5 million yuan from 1998 to 2006. From 2007 to 2010, the scopes of industrial statistics are all industrial enterprises with revenue from principal business over 5 million yuan, since 2011, the scope is adjusted to all industrial enterprises with revenue from principal above 20 million. (or the industrial enterprises above designated size).

Data by branch of industry this chapter are based on the *2011's National Industrial Classification of all Economic Activities*, and data by size of enterprise are based on the *2011's Preliminary Standards of Enterprises by Size*.

III. Sources of Data and Methods of Survey

The data on enterprises statistics in this Chapter are collected mainly based on the annual relevant data in the month industrial statistics reporting forms.

11－1 1998—2016年规模以上工业企业主要经济指标

Main Indicators of Industrial Enterprises above Designated Size(1998—2016)

单位:亿元 (100 million yuan)

年份 Year 地区 Region	企业单位数(个) Number of Enterprises (unit)	工业总产值 Gross Industrial Output Value	主营业务收入 Revenue from Principal Business	利润总额 Total Profits	应收账款净额 Accounts Receivalble	产成品 Finished Goods
1998	17957	8053.03	7375.45	151.51	1238.11	584.21
1999	18001	8915.44	8256.12	234.07	1360.48	617.49
2000	18309	10452.87	9971.01	370.03	1496.80	666.81
2001	19684	11747.83	11247.52	419.85	1583.56	707.66
2002	21476	13865.86	13534.77	554.21	1848.48	734.00
2003	23862	18034.60	18019.97	793.98	2420.45	845.99
2004	27123	24836.47	24492.28	1111.42	3025.34	1164.41
2005	32224	32707.09	32098.48	1384.64	4056.66	1298.38
2006	36319	41410.40	41015.28	1906.91	4954.52	1527.95
2007	41841	53316.38	52594.30	2765.77	6287.46	1916.52
2008	45818	67798.68	66481.84	3972.93	7239.07	2484.95
2009	60817	73200.03	71724.90	4099.58	8316.41	2676.61
2010	64136	92056.48	91077.41	5970.56	10261.18	3042.05
2011	43368	107680.68	107030.09	7074.44	11885.97	3655.22
2012	45859	120124.91	119286.78	7250.20	13577.65	3986.09
2013	48787	134080.91	133605.91	8379.50	15212.05	4214.89

单位:亿元 (100 million yuan)

年份 Year 地区 Region	企业单位数(个) Number of Enterprises (unit)	工业总产值 Gross Industrial Output Value	主营业务收入 Revenue from Principal Business	利润总额 Total Profits	应收账款净额 Accounts Receivalble	产成品 Finished Goods
2014	48708	143016.94	141955.99	9057.17	16341.30	4525.64
2015	48488	149841.41	147074.45	9686.84	17500.33	4596.18
2016	47900	157640.23	156591.04	10574.40	19022.03	4787.06
南京市 Nanjing	2661	12945.02	12442.36	959.35	1904.88	378.20
无锡市 Wuxi	4888	14352.96	14120.24	968.02	2850.04	766.11
徐州市 Xuzhou	2992	13644.36	13947.04	1108.89	765.50	240.72
常州市 Changzhou	4139	12096.82	12435.86	725.27	1690.21	434.66
苏州市 Suzhou	9616	30713.99	30380.18	1772.74	6175.53	1341.83
南通市 Nantong	5071	14525.72	14650.80	1118.27	1269.40	388.14
连云港市 Lianyungang	1815	5974.81	5946.41	496.53	367.66	102.09
淮安市 Huaian	2609	6951.32	7014.24	404.81	353.83	112.45
盐城市 Yancheng	3185	9180.84	8870.47	475.83	582.45	192.68
扬州市 Yangzhou	2686	9661.65	9502.36	593.15	761.72	158.43
镇江市 Zhenjiang	2635	8722.84	8632.13	582.17	898.25	245.12
泰州市 Taizhou	3018	12170.80	12139.45	938.67	1073.92	302.23
宿迁市 Suqian	2599	4096.70	3896.33	391.93	365.18	135.84

11－2 规模以上工业企业单位数和产销总值(2016 年)
Number of Industrial Enterprises above Designated Size and Their Total Value of Gross Output and Sales (2016)

单位:亿元 (100 million yuan)

项 目	Item	企业单位数(个) Number of Enterprises (unit)	工业总产值(现价) Gross Industrial Output Value (current price)	#新产品产值 Output Value of New Products	工业销售产值(现价) Value of Industrial Products Seld (current price)	#出口交货值 Delivery Value for Export
总 计	**Total**	**47900**	**157640.23**	**28598.31**	**155820.09**	**23299.50**
按登记注册类型分	**Grouped by Status of Registration**					
内资企业	Domestic Funded Enterprises	37845	104695.74	16582.72	103581.43	5762.88
国有企业	State-owned Enterprises	77	3250.47	164.27	3243.42	23.60
集体企业	Collective-owned Enterprises	192	553.71	41.39	549.21	9.89
股份合作企业	Cooperative Enterprises	63	148.11	10.67	144.68	4.41
联营企业	Joint Ownership Enterprises	11	18.42	3.53	18.76	0.18
有限责任公司	Limited Liability Corporations	6027	25714.25	4964.80	25533.37	1524.68
#国有独资	State Sole Funded Corporatios	190	2509.15	498.88	2480.79	102.63
股份有限公司	Share-holding Corporations Ltd.	1293	9720.46	2651.98	9450.13	871.74
私营企业	Private Enterprises	30122	65186.20	8740.22	64539.01	3320.89
其他企业	Other Enterprises	60	104.12	5.86	102.85	7.48
港、澳、台商投资企业	Enterprises with Funds from Hong Kong, Macao and Taiwan	3612	17384.85	3722.98	17152.50	4080.68
外商投资企业	Foreign Funded Enterprises	6443	35559.64	8292.61	35086.16	13455.94
按轻重工业分	**Grouped by Light & Heavy Industries**					
轻工业	Light Industry	17710	43986.98		43425.98	6312.98
重工业	Heavy Industry	30190	113653.25		112394.11	16986.52
按企业规模分	**Grouped by Size of Enterprises**					
大型企业	Large Enterprises	1249	57474.68	15669.90	56785.28	14422.51
中型企业	Medium-sized Enterprises	6018	39928.40	7523.78	39599.85	5242.86
小微型企业	Small Enterprises	40633	60237.15	5404.62	59434.96	3634.12
按行业分	**Grouped by Sector**					
采矿业	**Mining**	**130**	**588.52**	**41.72**	**586.27**	**1.13**
煤炭开采和洗选业	Mining and Washing of Coal	12	191.41	0.49	192.28	

单位:亿元 (100 million yuan)

项 目	Item	企业单位数(个) Number of Enterprises (unit)	工业总产值(现价) Gross Industrial Output Value (current price)	#新产品产值 Output Value of New Products	工业销售产值(现价) Value of Industrial Products Seld (current price)	#出口交货值 Delivery Value for Export
石油和天然气开采业	Extraction of Petroleum and Natural Gas	2		0.14		
黑色金属矿采选业	Mining and Processing of Ferrous Metal Ores	12	38.18	12.94	39.77	
有色金属矿采选业	Mining and Processing of Non - ferrous Metals Ores	6	8.82	1.30	8.78	
非金属矿采选业	Mining and Processing of Non-metal Ores	97	311.22	26.85	306.47	1.13
开采辅助活动	Support Activities for Mining	1		0.00		
其他采矿业	Mining of Other Ores					
制造业	**Manufacturing**	**47208**	**151934.14**	**28537.62**	**150132.65**	**23291.55**
农副食品加工业	Processing of Food from Agricultural Products	1679	5076.24	345.79	5073.24	112.12
食品制造业	Manufacture of Food	429	1181.98	100.89	1152.39	114.73
酒、饮料和精制茶制造业	Manufacture of Liquor, Beverages and Refined Tea	189	1187.29	169.00	1158.53	5.07
烟草制品业	Manufacture of Tobacco	6	542.46	6.17	530.20	0.19
纺织业	Manufacture of Textile	4454	7280.16	779.09	7163.73	827.41
纺织服装、服饰业	Manufacture of Textile, Wearing Apparel and Accessories	2393	4619.83	570.64	4573.09	910.31
皮革、毛皮、羽毛及其制品和制鞋业	Manufacture of Leather, Fur, Feather and Related Products and Footwear	606	1121.38	72.31	1099.19	179.27
木材加工和木、竹、藤、棕、草制品业	Processing of Timber, Manufacture of Wood, Bamboo, Rattan, Palm and Straw Products	1299	2615.74	214.41	2594.17	150.07
家具制造业	Manufacture of Furniture	296	397.93	55.57	393.71	93.86
造纸和纸制品业	Manufacture of Paper and Paper Products	556	1634.17	387.55	1633.00	107.34
印刷和记录媒介复制业	Printing, Reproduction of Recording Media	654	895.59	85.04	883.24	75.22
文教、工美、体育和娱乐用品制造业	Manufacture of Articles for Culture, Education, Arts and Crafts, Sport and Entertainment Activities	1340	2336.47	224.38	2322.53	539.61
石油加工、炼焦和核燃料加工业	Processing of Petroleum, Coking, Processing of Nuclear Fuel	146	2074.02	43.44	2056.11	11.82
化学原料和化学制品制造业	Manufacture of Raw Chemical Materials and Chemical Products	3657	17850.13	3016.59	17707.77	1315.73

11－2 续 表 2 Continued 2

单位:亿元 (100 million yuan)

项 目	Item	企业单位数(个) Number of Enterprises (unit)	工业总产值(现价) Gross Industrial Output Value (current price)	#新产品产值 Output Value of New Products	工业销售产值(现价) Value of Industrial Products Seld (current price)	#出口交货值 Delivery Value for Export
医药制造业	Manufacture of Medicines	703	3933.97	928.68	3838.94	217.15
化学纤维制造业	Manufacture of Chemical Fibers	737	2850.79	589.96	2786.86	234.32
橡胶和塑料制品业	Manufacture of Rubber and Plastics Products	2099	3196.69	414.36	3159.23	416.37
非金属矿物制品业	Manufacture of Non-metallic Mineral Products	2780	5187.47	490.61	5129.70	200.59
黑色金属冶炼和压延加工业	Smelting and Pressing of Ferrous Metals	1249	9055.63	1149.01	8954.96	504.38
有色金属冶炼和压延加工业	Smelting and Pressing of Non-ferrous Metals	1035	4064.79	471.03	4034.17	175.00
金属制品业	Manufacture of Metal Products	3089	6461.34	863.02	6367.55	579.30
通用设备制造业	Manufacture of General Purpose Machinery	4132	9203.60	1959.32	9088.57	1178.28
专用设备制造业	Manufacture of Special Purpose Machinery	3042	6470.63	1194.51	6451.61	751.47
汽车制造业	Manufacture of Automobiles	1742	7910.63	1729.57	7790.50	452.68
铁路、船舶、航空航天和其他运输设备制造业	Manufacture of Railway, Ship, Aerospace and Other Transport Equipments	870	3799.84	1175.94	3770.80	777.83
电气机械和器材制造业	Manufacture of Electrical Machinery and Apparatus	4124	17420.15	4556.41	17216.82	2311.02
计算机、通信和其他电子设备制造业	Manufacture of Computers, Communication and Other Electronic Equipment	2676	19199.77	6096.23	18864.38	10592.93
仪器仪表制造业	Manufacture of Measuring Instruments and Machinery	899	3727.26	798.01	3711.33	407.07
其他制造业	Other Manufacture	166	331.30	36.12	325.09	49.95
废弃资源综合利用业	Utilization of Waste Resources	138	267.77	13.11	262.95	0.36
金属制品、机械和设备修理业	Repair Service of Metal Products, Machinery and Equipment	23	39.12	0.86	38.29	0.12
电力、热力、燃气及水的生产和供应业	**Production and Supply of Electric Power, Heat Power, Gas and Water**	**562**	**5117.57**	**18.97**	**5101.17**	**6.83**
电力、热力的生产和供应业	Production and Supply of Electric Power and Heat Power	332	4500.11	14.86	4489.06	
燃气生产和供应	Production and Supply of Gas	101	452.72	1.28	449.44	6.83
水的生产和供应业	Production and Supply of Water	129	164.74	2.83	162.66	

11－3 分市规模以上工业总产值(2016 年)

单位:亿元

项目	Item	南京市 Nanjing	无锡市 Wuxi	徐州市 Xuzhou
总　计	**Total**	**12945.02**	**14352.96**	**13644.36**
按登记注册类型分	**Grouped by Status of Registration**			
内资企业	Domestic Funded Enterprises	7554.24	9108.05	12442.52
国有企业	State-owned Enterprises	190.38	118.05	5.03
集体企业	Collective-owned Enterprises	42.04	173.62	18.14
股份合作企业	Cooperative Enterprises	2.96	2.33	0.91
联营企业	Joint Ownership Enterprises	9.95		
有限责任公司	Limited Liability Corporations	2937.54	1854.84	2294.26
#国有独资	State Sole Funded Corporatios	489.32	100.21	668.55
股份有限公司	Share-holding Corporations Ltd.	1955.10	1076.29	637.31
私营企业	Private Enterprises	2395.14	5881.11	9483.31
其他企业	Other Enterprises	21.14	1.81	3.56
港、澳、台商投资企业	Enterprises with Funds from Hong Kong, Macao and Taiwan	1027.53	1736.45	704.21
外商投资企业	Foreign Funded Enterprises	4363.25	3508.46	497.64
按轻重工业分	**Grouped by Light & Heavy Industries**			
轻工业	Light Industry	2958.57	3642.34	4610.4
重工业	Heavy Industry	9986.45	10710.62	9033.96
按企业规模分	**Grouped by Size of Enterprises**			
大型企业	Large Enterprises	5933.04	6417.27	2689.15
中型企业	Medium-sized Enterprises	2891.58	3316.92	5294.56
小微型企业	Small Enterprises	4120.40	4618.76	5660.65
按行业分	**Grouped by Sector**			
采矿业	**Mining**	**18.44**		**302.48**
煤炭开采和洗选业	Mining and Washing of Coal			190.52

Gross Industrial Output Value above Designated Size by Region (2016)

(100 million yuan)

常州市 Changzhou	苏州市 Suzhou	南通市 Nantong	连云港市 Lianyungang	淮安市 Huaian	盐城市 Yancheng	扬州市 Yangzhou	镇江市 Zhenjiang	泰州市 Taizhou	宿迁市 Suqian
12096.82	**30713.99**	**14525.72**	**5974.81**	**6951.32**	**9180.84**	**9661.65**	**8722.84**	**12170.8**	**4096.7**
8106.11	10845.61	10010.92	4707.38	5758.55	7104.81	6938.27	5925.14	9775.98	3679.11
1.65	13.81	9.84	3.91	37.84	3.09	32.41	76.11	3.05	13.67
	7.05	12.69	0.38	17.2	8.6	70.49	31.99	167.37	4.14
5.36	20.33	48.05	1.42	3.29	1.23	18.18	0.59	43.47	
	3.21	1.66			0.31	3.29			
1003.17	4007.21	1654.83	997.37	1448.95	2032.7	1656.9	1601.76	3563.94	666.09
36.32	162.3	97.47	48.57	200.06	114.25	383.62	107.52	99.47	1.48
290.6	1557.4	960.53	227.14	294.76	545.85	513.76	518.63	746.61	393.44
6798.9	5214.27	7322.57	3477.16	3951.44	4512.26	4634.67	3680.01	5239.22	2596.46
6.43	22.34	0.75		5.07	0.77	8.56	16.05	12.33	5.31
2008.34	5233.58	1693.67	244.41	872.33	386.37	1149.4	1320.76	793.76	290.36
1982.36	14634.8	2821.13	1023.02	320.43	1689.66	1573.98	1476.94	1601.06	127.22
2773.03	7695.83	4554.61	2052.49	2964.07	3143.63	2501.77	1535.87	3407.52	2146.85
9323.78	23018.16	9971.11	3922.32	3987.25	6037.21	7159.88	7186.98	8763.28	1949.85
4690.67	16464.17	3598.49	1893.56	1320.66	1898.88	2785.62	2997.58	3473.07	670.62
3167.63	6496.86	3885.71	1405.3	1215.58	2383.36	3379.68	3178.71	2665.27	672.5
4238.52	7752.96	7041.52	2675.96	4415.08	4898.6	3496.35	2546.55	6032.46	2753.58
7.93	**1.88**		**65.48**	**90.99**	**2.34**	**48.15**	**26.88**	**0.23**	**15.61**
						0.88			

单位:亿元

项 目	Item	南京市 Nanjing	无锡市 Wuxi	徐州市 Xuzhou
石油和天然气开采业	Extraction of Petroleum and Natural Gas			
黑色金属矿采选业	Mining and Processing of Ferrous Metal Ores	1.95		13.62
有色金属矿采选业	Mining and Processing of Non - ferrous Metals Ores	2.31		
非金属矿采选业	Mining and Processing of Non-metal Ores	14.18		98.33
开采辅助活动	Support Activities for Mining			
其他采矿业	Mining of Other Ores			
制造业	**Manufacturing**	**12661.22**	**14096.56**	**13172.19**
农副食品加工业	Processing of Food from Agricultural Products	140.28	16.62	936.26
食品制造业	Manufacture of Food	130.78	65.02	165.25
酒、饮料和精制茶制造业	Manufacture of Liquor, Beverages and Refined Tea	57.12	50.5	421.47
烟草制品业	Manufacture of Tobacco	202.59		207.5
纺织业	Manufacture of Textile	81.33	784.49	713.34
纺织服装、服饰业	Manufacture of Textile, Wearing Apparel and Accessories	380.76	608.77	211.44
皮革、毛皮、羽毛及其制品和制鞋业	Manufacture of Leather, Fur, Feather and Related Products and Footwear	80.85	5.71	102.72
木材加工和木、竹、藤、棕、草制品业	Processing of Timber, Manufacture of Wood, Bamboo, Rattan, Palm and Straw Products	18.71	18.19	1293.38
家具制造业	Manufacture of Furniture	37.58	10.71	98.2
造纸和纸制品业	Manufacture of Paper and Paper Products	46.05	68.7	88.73
印刷和记录媒介复制业	Printing, Reproduction of Recording Media	57.56	134.61	41.38
文教、工美、体育和娱乐用品制造业	Manufacture of Articles for Culture, Education, Arts and Crafts, Sport and Entertainment Activities	126.38	43.68	155.68
石油加工、炼焦和核燃料加工业	Processing of Petroleum, Coking, Processing of Nuclear Fuel	632.37	138.78	202.95
化学原料和化学制品制造业	Manufacture of Raw Chemical Materials and Chemical Products	1755.44	1374.1	1868.85

(100 million yuan)

常州市 Changzhou	苏州市 Suzhou	南通市 Nantong	连云港市 Lianyungang	淮安市 Huaian	盐城市 Yancheng	扬州市 Yangzhou	镇江市 Zhenjiang	泰州市 Taizhou	宿迁市 Suqian
0.18			0.37	1.75		20.08		0.23	
			4.87				1.63		
7.76	1.88		56.64	89.24	2.34		25.24		15.61
11957.05	**30193.41**	**14304.75**	**5786.2**	**6777.91**	**9016.36**	**9520.18**	**8547.95**	**12016.85**	**4030.86**
28.73	280.61	521.4	460.78	737.02	482.89	182.62	231.5	734.48	323.04
56.12	256.49	59.21	145.95	57.8	40.19	15.51	28.42	81.75	79.52
8.8	51.22	24.28	89.62	41.76	54.96	14.64	12.96	48.1	311.86
	1.07	11.48		119.83					
680.04	1309.88	1375.59	48.87	322.21	905.43	241.9	126.33	342.05	348.7
262.75	739.66	523.86	154.16	366.14	326	409.78	156.85	231.04	248.62
31.88	45.78	96.06	32.9	248.14	131.39	214.96	67.08	27.5	36.43
85.97	53.62	12.06	78.43	188.95	42.02	29.71	226.01	14.09	554.6
5.12	91.5	36.74	18.24	12.1	4.45	6.11	5.53	35.47	36.18
61.59	540.2	72.13	23.7	163.5	92.96	123.31	294.52	33.91	24.86
34.58	216.08	29.84	49.86	112.53	17.33	33.98	34.93	11.14	121.78
167.08	240.53	626.54	89.18	191.13	144.9	204.36	74.36	116.62	156.03
115.38	131.69	28.39	237.29	110.39	38.2	27.04	131.48	279.68	6.07
2011.9	1956.21	1909.74	1008.61	485.78	1185.04	1001.16	1700.61	1372.41	220.75

单位:亿元

项 目	Item	南京市 Nanjing	无锡市 Wuxi	徐州市 Xuzhou
医药制造业	Manufacture of Medicines	284.72	234.48	576.83
化学纤维制造业	Manufacture of Chemical Fibers	49.65	487.78	119.24
橡胶和塑料制品业	Manufacture of Rubber and Plastics Products	180.08	325.73	345.2
非金属矿物制品业	Manufacture of Non-metallic Mineral Products	362.41	233.97	779.93
黑色金属冶炼和压延加工业	Smelting and Pressing of Ferrous Metals	585.78	1104.86	786.72
有色金属冶炼和压延加工业	Smelting and Pressing of Non-ferrous Metals	292.31	969.52	322.68
金属制品业	Manufacture of Metal Products	423.39	803.23	390.36
通用设备制造业	Manufacture of General Purpose Machinery	489.90	784.15	610.37
专用设备制造业	Manufacture of Special Purpose Machinery	292.05	651.97	596.05
汽车制造业	Manufacture of Automobiles	1898.07	793.72	87.84
铁路、船舶、航空航天和其他运输设备制造业	Manufacture of Railway, Ship, Aerospace and Other Transport Equipments	347.21	282.63	139.86
电气机械和器材制造业	Manufacture of Electrical Machinery and Apparatus	960.45	2052.6	905.62
计算机、通信和其他电子设备制造业	Manufacture of Computers, Communication and Other Electronic Equipment	2329.93	1915.28	388.38
仪器仪表制造业	Manufacture of Measuring Instruments and Machinery	383.18	125.48	571.94
其他制造业	Other Manufacture	1.15	7.63	23.84
废弃资源综合利用业	Utilization of Waste Resources	26.25	3.66	15.59
金属制品、机械和设备修理业	Repair Service of Metal Products, Machinery and Equipment	6.88		4.59
电力、热力、燃气及水的生产和供应业	**Production and Supply of Electric Power, Heat Power, Gas and Water**	**265.36**	**256.4**	**169.69**
电力、热力的生产和供应业	Production and Supply of Electric Power and Heat Power	175.74	184.91	156.22
燃气生产和供应	Production and Supply of Gas	62.60	55.58	8.67
水的生产和供应业	Production and Supply of Water	27.02	15.9	4.8

(100 million yuan)

常州市 Changzhou	苏州市 Suzhou	南通市 Nantong	连云港市 Lianyun gang	淮安市 Huaian	盐城市 Yancheng	扬州市 Yangzhou	镇江市 Zhenjiang	泰州市 Taizhou	宿迁市 Suqian
162.88	305.57	349.28	559.56	100.06	313.93	113.79	43.26	860.55	29.06
53.89	1040.51	385.4	4.78	46.15	214.09	208.85	6.83	49.64	183.98
149.79	857.8	207.03	70.36	222.41	173.49	171.61	104.83	257.92	130.44
421.01	454.06	404.82	632.67	401.12	452.13	215.35	403.46	215.75	210.79
1611.74	2434.86	238.99	718.46	276.76	243.24	350.52	202.44	475.14	73.54
362.35	538.62	204.97	147.23	179.91	284.42	186.46	297.46	164.11	114.73
496.73	772.84	808.04	272.65	233.5	209.47	414.44	437.33	1153.7	70.12
699.38	1952.05	1208.34	113.48	378.85	1039.11	497.93	406.17	899.44	124.94
649.46	1028.13	711.01	168.9	215.34	522.85	514.81	283.2	797.6	39.26
355.31	1545.18	177.3	57.4	160.43	1250.96	1013.96	292.9	250.36	30.45
414.38	272.3	378.38	113.5	28.57	20.4	263.22	406.08	1172.09	21.92
2057.53	2715.52	2261.36	283.98	461.43	482.7	1946.87	1571.62	1485.01	240.33
743.96	9947.91	944.79	151.59	775.95	151.88	462.09	524.81	603.07	260.12
175.12	368.69	683.54	4.52	61.61	159.27	483.53	420.79	278.19	11.4
0.57	5.9	5.44	8.61	48.94	1.53	162.76	36.38	15.37	13.2
48.9	38.94	5.52	40.96	29.6	17.33	8.91	19.71	5.32	7.08
4.09		3.22			13.83		0.09	5.36	1.06
131.83	**518.7**	**220.98**	**123.13**	**82.42**	**162.14**	**93.32**	**148.02**	**153.72**	**50.23**
85.91	344.68	160.8	108.34	62.02	143.32	71.88	120.1	104.64	39.9
30.88	135.77	42.36	10.68	12.96	9.78	14.79	20.84	39.69	8.14
15.04	38.26	17.81	4.11	7.44	9.04	6.65	7.08	9.4	2.19

11-4 规模以上工业企业主要经济指标(2016年)

单位:亿元

项目	Item	流动资产合计 Current Assets	应收账款 Accounts Receivalble
总计	**Total**	**59354.58**	**19022.03**
按登记注册类型分	**Grouped by Status of Registration**		
内资企业	Domestic Funded Enterprises	37648.30	11169.11
国有企业	State-owned Enterprises	616.71	95.94
集体企业	Collective-owned Enterprises	255.22	58.18
股份合作企业	Cooperative Enterprises	47.42	15.78
联营企业	Joint Ownership Enterprises	7.96	1.09
有限责任公司	Limited Liability Corporations	11956.53	3467.56
#国有独资	State Sole Funded Corporatios	2273.83	557.63
股份有限公司	Share-holding Corporations Ltd.	5908.94	1518.00
私营企业	Private Enterprises	18808.59	6002.91
其他企业	Other Enterprises	46.91	9.65
港、澳、台商投资企业	Enterprises with Funds from Hong Kong, Macao and Taiwan	6862.63	2396.42
外商投资企业	Foreign Funded Enterprises	14843.65	5456.50
按轻重工业分	**Grouped by Light & Heavy Industries**		
轻工业	Light Industry	15420.33	4018.33
重工业	Heavy Industry	43934.25	15003.70
按企业规模分	**Grouped by Size of Enterprises**		
大型企业	Large Enterprises	24522.70	7230.84
中型企业	Medium-sized Enterprises	14485.98	4627.50
小微型企业	Small Enterprises	20345.90	7163.69
按行业分	**Grouped by Sector**		
采矿业	**Mining**	**322.92**	**52.58**
煤炭开采和洗选业	Mining and Washing of Coal	171.17	33.44
石油和天然气开采业	Extraction of Petroleum and Natural Gas		
黑色金属矿采选业	Mining and Processing of Ferrous Metal Ores	19.82	4.04
有色金属矿采选业	Mining and Processing of Non-ferrous Metals Ores	3.60	-0.35
非金属矿采选业	Mining and Processing of Non-metal Ores	104.33	13.45
开采辅助活动	Support Activities for Mining		
其他采矿业	Mining of Other Ores		
制造业	**Manufacturing**	**57341.04**	**18718.55**
农副食品加工业	Processing of Food from Agricultural Products	892.30	207.98

Main Economic Indicators of above Designated Size Industrial Enterprises(2016)

(100 million yuan)

存货 Inventory	#产成品 Finished Goods	固定资产合计 Original Value	资产总计 Total Assets	负债合计 Total Liabilities
12526.29	**4787.06**	**38880.97**	**114536.32**	**59466.56**
8137.98	3169.97	25979.61	75590.64	40527.56
63.71	14.13	2474.20	3813.49	2262.87
38.02	21.80	89.20	412.87	235.09
13.45	8.07	19.87	75.37	36.39
2.23	1.06	9.99	18.44	4.46
2579.20	940.25	8461.74	24541.40	14263.36
615.18	151.21	1727.08	4824.06	2822.78
1306.31	430.44	3085.48	11267.14	5210.62
4130.22	1751.64	11818.35	35378.85	18459.86
4.84	2.58	20.79	83.07	54.91
1352.00	513.38	4615.93	13063.35	6382.89
3036.30	1103.72	8285.42	25882.33	12556.10
3693.32	1456.08	9232.79	28783.21	14098.61
8832.97	3330.98	29648.18	85753.11	45367.94
5217.33	1762.17	16100.19	48758.57	25888.86
3105.11	1263.46	10285.44	28421.06	14460.48
4203.85	1761.44	12495.34	37356.69	19117.22
50.71	**20.20**	**636.38**	**1216.69**	**720.92**
30.05	11.09	335.16	680.03	414.30
4.21	1.36	18.39	40.37	27.19
0.79	0.51	5.18	10.06	7.57
13.31	6.14	148.61	294.59	156.27
12364.20	**4760.29**	**32730.03**	**104200.47**	**53239.36**
286.12	120.56	762.75	1908.19	1002.25

单位:亿元

项 目 Item		流动资产合计 Current Assets	应收账款 Accounts Receivalble
食品制造业	Manufacture of Food	362.31	105.88
酒、饮料和精制茶制造业	Manufacture of Liquor, Beverages and Refined Tea	654.98	94.99
烟草制品业	Manufacture of Tobacco	476.18	22.77
纺织业	Manufacture of Textile	2408.57	641.53
纺织服装、服饰业	Manufacture of Textile, Wearing Apparel and Accessories	1455.50	316.88
皮革、毛皮、羽毛及其制品和制鞋业	Manufacture of Leather, Fur, Feather and Related Products and Footwear	215.67	63.42
木材加工和木、竹、藤、棕、草制品业	Processing of Timber, Manufacture of Wood, Bamboo, Rattan, Palm and Straw Products	446.52	96.59
家具制造业	Manufacture of Furniture	175.54	38.37
造纸和纸制品业	Manufacture of Paper and Paper Products	807.13	226.93
印刷和记录媒介复制业	Printing, Reproduction of Recording Media	382.00	138.22
文教、工美、体育和娱乐用品制造业	Manufacture of Articles for Culture, Education, Arts and Crafts, Sport and Entertainment Activities	531.00	139.05
石油加工、炼焦和核燃料加工业	Processing of Petroleum, Coking, Processing of Nuclear Fuel	435.07	81.03
化学原料和化学制品制造业	Manufacture of Raw Chemical Materials and Chemical Products	5365.02	1543.35
医药制造业	Manufacture of Medicines	1500.45	464.80
化学纤维制造业	Manufacture of Chemical Fibers	1116.47	161.26
橡胶和塑料制品业	Manufacture of Rubber and Plastics Products	1274.31	500.81
非金属矿物制品业	Manufacture of Non-metallic Mineral Products	1946.23	789.49
黑色金属冶炼和压延加工业	Smelting and Pressing of Ferrous Metals	2968.34	410.74
有色金属冶炼和压延加工业	Smelting and Pressing of Non-ferrous Metals	1215.76	351.88
金属制品业	Manufacture of Metal Products	2379.26	841.24
通用设备制造业	Manufacture of General Purpose Machinery	4674.01	1724.02
专用设备制造业	Manufacture of Special Purpose Machinery	3282.90	1176.97
汽车制造业	Manufacture of Automobiles	3319.54	1226.30

11－4 Continued 1

(100 million yuan)

存货 Inventory	#产成品 Finished Goods	固定资产合计 Original Value	资产总计 Total Assets	负债合计 Total Liabilities
84.52	38.01	272.56	783.35	362.00
249.51	48.76	339.28	1170.85	469.03
233.60	4.09	62.80	601.52	66.56
673.37	293.70	1523.46	4528.64	2430.38
383.14	190.98	774.33	2716.30	1371.32
55.66	20.44	138.23	414.33	185.78
111.62	48.14	414.02	993.85	379.47
34.53	13.40	101.24	309.84	150.99
112.87	44.93	584.90	1702.61	868.19
70.62	30.48	266.03	724.19	341.15
141.79	68.89	358.16	1023.00	495.81
142.87	52.23	431.04	990.34	570.53
1172.32	477.60	4507.59	11579.04	5586.44
304.69	127.50	812.38	2826.06	1024.38
270.35	122.82	871.68	2313.85	1304.03
275.43	120.95	817.45	2325.15	989.58
298.20	129.73	1389.87	3756.79	2032.15
787.86	288.29	2659.62	6601.97	3992.68
292.11	112.46	528.56	2099.00	1189.65
533.91	221.28	1286.80	4290.81	2168.21
1013.17	420.94	2043.64	7832.77	3938.23
733.60	255.27	1381.51	5363.59	2731.24
559.68	253.34	1534.94	5574.78	3343.00

单位:亿元

项 目	Item	流动资产合计 Current Assets	应收账款 Accounts Receivalble
铁路、船舶、航空航天和其他运输设备制造业	Manufacture of Railway, Ship, Aerospace and Other Transport Equipments	2040.86	476.92
电气机械和器材制造业	Manufacture of Electrical Machinery and Apparatus	8034.16	3175.59
计算机、通信和其他电子设备制造业	Manufacture of Computers, Communication and Other Electronic Equipment	7267.69	3146.93
仪器仪表制造业	Manufacture of Measuring Instruments and Machinery	1569.18	518.81
其他制造业	Other Manufacture	76.89	17.80
废弃资源综合利用业	Utilization of Waste Resources	57.68	14.12
金属制品、机械和设备修理业	Repair Service of Metal Products, Machinery and Equipment	9.52	3.88
电力、热力、燃气及水的生产和供应业	**Production and Supply of Electric Power, Heat Power, Gas and Water**	**1690.62**	**250.90**
电力、热力的生产和供应业	Production and Supply of Electric Power and Heat Power	951.84	212.40
燃气生产和供应	Production and Supply of Gas	241.76	22.86
水的生产和供应业	Production and Supply of Water	497.02	15.63
按地区分	**by Region**		
南京市	Nanjing	5995.95	1904.88
无锡市	Wuxi	9218.06	2850.04
徐州市	Xuzhou	2589.67	765.50
常州市	Changzhou	5217.24	1690.21
苏州市	Suzhou	17149.91	6175.53
南通市	Nantong	4154.74	1269.40
连云港市	Lianyungang	1347.86	367.66
淮安市	Huaian	1238.31	353.83
盐城市	Yancheng	2056.19	582.45
扬州市	Yangzhou	2381.08	761.72
镇江市	Zhenjiang	2899.80	898.25
泰州市	Taizhou	3602.58	1073.92
宿迁市	Suqian	1632.65	365.18

(100 million yuan)

存货 Inventory	#产成品 Finished Goods	固定资产合计 Original Value	资产总计 Total Assets	负债合计 Total Liabilities
594.04	127.48	880.69	3431.90	1904.20
1185.43	534.47	2904.53	12718.58	6753.25
1421.60	481.02	4222.26	12632.15	6230.15
312.71	102.04	720.55	2662.43	1192.37
16.91	5.94	59.75	157.26	77.28
9.87	4.07	67.12	143.88	77.08
2.14	0.49	12.27	23.47	11.98
111.37	**6.58**	**5514.56**	**9119.15**	**5506.28**
82.45	3.72	4731.91	7325.42	4388.57
13.75	1.64	218.56	591.32	303.72
15.17	1.23	564.10	1202.41	813.99
1257.81	378.20	3806.84	11448.85	6166.10
1925.87	766.11	3616.06	15095.63	8085.84
596.12	240.72	3489.44	6952.73	3159.11
1103.97	434.66	2588.10	8942.07	4945.73
3462.83	1341.83	7624.80	28356.50	14838.02
978.48	388.14	3009.52	8801.91	4423.65
262.20	102.09	1539.05	3650.60	1856.14
319.82	112.45	1383.22	3071.44	1370.93
442.90	192.68	2569.58	5261.84	2768.18
497.40	158.43	1758.72	4678.72	2430.70
537.98	245.12	2018.97	5858.18	3171.09
818.74	302.23	2115.84	6653.84	3405.33
382.61	135.84	1315.32	3346.13	1337.44

单位:亿元

项 目	Item	所有者权益合计 Owners' Equities	#实收资本 Paid-in Capital
总 计	**Total**	**54939.31**	**26361.83**
按登记注册类型分	**Grouped by Status of Registration**		
内资企业	Domestic Funded Enterprises	34947.27	14614.88
国有企业	State-owned Enterprises	1548.19	984.42
集体企业	Collective-owned Enterprises	177.22	74.81
股份合作企业	Cooperative Enterprises	38.98	6.49
联营企业	Joint Ownership Enterprises	13.98	9.01
有限责任公司	Limited Liability Corporations	10263.65	4468.47
#国有独资	State Sole Funded Corporatios	2002.51	685.17
股份有限公司	Share-holding Corporations Ltd.	6050.88	2229.07
私营企业	Private Enterprises	16831.84	6833.51
其他企业	Other Enterprises	22.52	9.10
港、澳、台商投资企业	Enterprises with Funds from Hong Kong, Macao and Taiwan	6670.46	3688.29
外商投资企业	Foreign Funded Enterprises	13321.57	8058.67
按轻重工业分	**Grouped by Light & Heavy Industries**		
轻工业	Light Industry	14644.47	6368.65
重工业	Heavy Industry	40294.85	19993.18
按企业规模分	**Grouped by Size of Enterprises**		
大型企业	Large Enterprises	22869.71	9551.68
中型企业	Medium-sized Enterprises	13962.10	6654.52
小微型企业	Small Enterprises	18107.50	10155.64
按行业分	**Grouped by Sector**		
采矿业	**Mining**	**492.84**	**262.68**
煤炭开采和洗选业	Mining and Washing of Coal	265.70	61.88
石油和天然气开采业	Extraction of Petroleum and Natural Gas		
黑色金属矿采选业	Mining and Processing of Ferrous Metal Ores	12.77	12.69
有色金属矿采选业	Mining and Processing of Non-ferrous Metals Ores	2.49	1.43
非金属矿采选业	Mining and Processing of Non-metal Ores	135.85	64.23
开采辅助活动	Support Activities for Mining		
其他采矿业	Mining of Other Ores		
制造业	**Manufacturing**	**50835.14**	**23827.78**
农副食品加工业	Processing of Food from Agricultural Products	896.87	369.34

(100 million yuan)

主营业务收入 Revenue from Principal Business	主营业务成本 Cost of Principle Business	利润总额 Total Profits	平均用工人数（万人） The Average Number of Employment (10000 Persons)
156591.04	**134083.08**	**10574.40**	**1111.84**
104548.00	89487.24	6851.25	723.95
3234.91	3071.54	82.32	8.19
587.93	517.11	35.45	4.52
144.10	122.96	11.27	1.03
18.80	16.53	0.79	0.19
25844.30	21628.96	1612.31	165.65
2535.23	1798.57	183.82	18.49
9587.47	7591.53	888.61	64.88
65030.17	56451.45	4214.53	478.83
100.31	87.16	5.96	0.66
17346.26	14922.52	1318.04	146.20
34696.78	29673.31	2405.11	241.70
43641.87	36406.25	3078.14	393.87
112949.17	97676.83	7496.26	717.98
57641.93	49361.19	3717.92	359.46
40134.65	33930.43	3142.97	312.16
58814.46	50791.45	3713.51	440.22
606.00	**519.93**	**－29.87**	**10.20**
196.68	150.01	7.05	6.02
39.79	35.67	0.17	0.32
10.39	9.68	－0.28	0.12
312.45	266.05	18.12	2.76
150898.52	**129143.93**	**10080.62**	**1086.72**
5100.74	4488.09	325.18	22.56

单位:亿元

项　目 Item		所有者权益合计 Owners' Equities	#实收资本 Paid-in Capital
食品制造业	Manufacture of Food	420.37	210.06
酒、饮料和精制茶制造业	Manufacture of Liquor, Beverages and Refined Tea	701.58	221.96
烟草制品业	Manufacture of Tobacco	534.96	22.52
纺织业	Manufacture of Textile	2080.75	1007.38
纺织服装、服饰业	Manufacture of Textile, Wearing Apparel and Accessories	1342.60	490.28
皮革、毛皮、羽毛及其制品和制鞋业	Manufacture of Leather, Fur, Feather and Related Products and Footwear	226.88	89.84
木材加工和木、竹、藤、棕、草制品业	Processing of Timber, Manufacture of Wood, Bamboo, Rattan, Palm and Straw Products	602.73	201.46
家具制造业	Manufacture of Furniture	158.77	86.09
造纸和纸制品业	Manufacture of Paper and Paper Products	833.90	652.95
印刷和记录媒介复制业	Printing, Reproduction of Recording Media	381.78	169.57
文教、工美、体育和娱乐用品制造业	Manufacture of Articles for Culture, Education, Arts and Crafts, Sport and Entertainment Activities	525.47	224.97
石油加工、炼焦和核燃料加工业	Processing of Petroleum, Coking, Processing of Nuclear Fuel	419.10	228.81
化学原料和化学制品制造业	Manufacture of Raw Chemical Materials and Chemical Products	5987.85	3194.26
医药制造业	Manufacture of Medicines	1801.41	557.62
化学纤维制造业	Manufacture of Chemical Fibers	1009.36	566.41
橡胶和塑料制品业	Manufacture of Rubber and Plastics Products	1333.46	696.46
非金属矿物制品业	Manufacture of Non-metallic Mineral Products	1719.27	888.33
黑色金属冶炼和压延加工业	Smelting and Pressing of Ferrous Metals	2602.07	996.58
有色金属冶炼和压延加工业	Smelting and Pressing of Non-ferrous Metals	903.36	435.83
金属制品业	Manufacture of Metal Products	2118.55	1046.74
通用设备制造业	Manufacture of General Purpose Machinery	3882.29	1670.76
专用设备制造业	Manufacture of Special Purpose Machinery	2623.42	1176.54
汽车制造业	Manufacture of Automobiles	2225.84	1346.11

(100 million yuan)

主营业务收入 Revenue from Principal Business	主营业务成本 Cost of Principle Business	利润总额 Total Profits	平均用工人数(万人) The Average Number of Employment (10000 Persons)
1162.85	910.91	82.71	9.51
1154.51	844.74	178.96	7.89
533.47	113.92	85.42	0.62
7244.84	6444.18	381.87	80.76
4641.92	3988.50	312.58	70.40
1092.30	954.09	62.17	14.11
2584.21	2249.55	186.47	18.67
396.91	340.41	25.39	5.49
1637.92	1405.90	97.49	10.73
875.52	725.86	71.62	11.12
2349.83	2017.52	157.57	27.93
2113.41	1737.66	111.32	3.78
17957.37	15377.07	1303.15	71.69
3870.28	2502.18	419.34	22.53
2778.87	2500.70	124.40	17.21
3169.42	2674.53	216.63	34.75
5097.54	4407.46	319.83	40.67
9447.20	8486.73	400.13	35.61
4149.75	3785.65	182.54	16.42
6355.02	5495.34	390.16	50.56
9117.19	7555.55	705.87	77.64
6449.34	5317.17	484.83	54.44
7470.38	6192.32	589.94	45.69

单位:亿元

项 目	Item	所有者权益合计 Owners' Equities	#实收资本 Paid-in Capital
铁路、船舶、航空航天和其他运输设备制造业	Manufacture of Railway, Ship, Aerospace and Other Transport Equipments	1525.72	566.18
电气机械和器材制造业	Manufacture of Electrical Machinery and Apparatus	5956.76	2717.78
计算机、通信和其他电子设备制造业	Manufacture of Computers, Communication and Other Electronic Equipment	6392.74	3476.66
仪器仪表制造业	Manufacture of Measuring Instruments and Machinery	1469.28	437.01
其他制造业	Other Manufacture	79.73	29.00
废弃资源综合利用业	Utilization of Waste Resources	66.80	45.32
金属制品、机械和设备修理业	Repair Service of Metal Products, Machinery and Equipment	11.49	4.95
电力、热力、燃气及水的生产和供应业	**Production and Supply of Electric Power, Heat Power, Gas and Water**	**3611.33**	**2271.37**
电力、热力的生产和供应业	Production and Supply of Electric Power and Heat Power	2936.37	1923.81
燃气生产和供应	Production and Supply of Gas	286.85	117.16
水的生产和供应业	Production and Supply of Water	388.10	230.40
按地区分	**by Region**		
南京市	Nanjing	5275.07	2731.63
无锡市	Wuxi	6994.78	3314.37
徐州市	Xuzhou	3764.27	1019.96
常州市	Changzhou	3996.24	1877.62
苏州市	Suzhou	13502.06	7560.59
南通市	Nantong	4373.01	1913.46
连云港市	Lianyungang	1794.11	781.92
淮安市	Huaian	1692.11	808.39
盐城市	Yancheng	2466.99	1132.46
扬州市	Yangzhou	2243.06	2734.15
镇江市	Zhenjiang	2682.40	1328.63
泰州市	Taizhou	3245.38	1043.91
宿迁市	Suqian	2000.25	802.76

(100 million yuan)

主营业务收入 Revenue from Principal Business	主营业务成本 Cost of Principle Business	利润总额 Total Profits	平均用工人数(万人) The Average Number of Employment (10000 Persons)
3680.22	3129.28	311.66	31.31
17185.11	14742.03	1223.68	106.04
18881.07	17042.64	964.59	169.65
3774.83	3162.73	329.57	22.97
324.79	284.60	18.94	4.17
265.55	235.54	14.06	1.49
36.15	31.07	2.56	0.32
5086.52	**4419.21**	**523.65**	**14.92**
4488.40	3959.57	435.58	10.30
436.50	353.83	64.04	1.62
161.62	105.81	24.03	3.00
12442.36	10182.08	959.35	74.44
14120.24	12097.75	968.02	117.89
13947.04	11725.51	1108.89	81.07
12435.86	10880.58	725.27	85.68
30380.18	26169.61	1772.74	286.58
14650.80	12711.66	1118.27	101.55
5946.41	4867.53	496.53	31.45
7014.24	6079.35	404.81	46.75
8870.47	7701.78	475.83	56.64
9502.36	8300.95	593.15	70.59
8632.13	7419.44	582.17	55.56
12139.45	10133.65	938.67	59.68
3896.33	3278.80	391.93	40.85

11－5 规模以上工业企业主要经济效益指标（2016年）

单位：%

项 目	Item	企业亏损面 Percentage of Loss Making Enterprises
总 计	**Total**	**11.29**
按登记注册类型分	**Grouped by Status of Registration**	
内资企业	Domestic Funded Enterprises	9.25
国有企业	State-owned Enterprises	23.38
集体企业	Collective-owned Enterprises	7.29
股份合作企业	Cooperative Enterprises	7.94
联营企业	Joint Ownership Enterprises	9.09
有限责任公司	Limited Liability Corporations	12.18
#国有独资	State Sole Funded Corporatios	18.95
股份有限公司	Share-holding Corporations Ltd.	12.14
私营企业	Private Enterprises	8.53
其他企业	Other Enterprises	5.00
港、澳、台商投资企业	Enterprises with Funds from Hong Kong, Macao and Taiwan	17.75
外商投资企业	Foreign Funded Enterprises	19.68
按轻重工业分	**Grouped by Light & Heavy Industries**	
轻工业	Light Industry	9.97
重工业	Heavy Industry	12.07
按企业规模分	**Grouped by Size of Enterprises**	
大型企业	Large Enterprises	6.57
中型企业	Medium-sized Enterprises	9.29
小微型企业	Small Enterprises	11.73
按行业分	**Grouped by Sector**	
采矿业	**Mining**	**12.31**
煤炭开采和洗选业	Mining and Washing of Coal	8.33
石油和天然气开采业	Extraction of Petroleum and Natural Gas	
黑色金属矿采选业	Mining and Processing of Ferrous Metal Ores	25.00
有色金属矿采选业	Mining and Processing of Non-ferrous Metals Ores	33.33
非金属矿采选业	Mining and Processing of Non-metal Ores	8.25
开采辅助活动	Support Activities for Mining	
其他采矿业	Mining of Other Ores	
制造业	**Manufacturing**	**11.31**
农副食品加工业	Processing of Food from Agricultural Products	5.78

Main Indicators on Economic Benefit of above Designated Size Industrial Enterprises(2016)

(%)

资产负债率 Assets Liability Ratio	流动资产周转次数(次/年) Times of Turnover of Circulating Funds (times/year)	成本费用利润率 Ratio of Profits to Industrial Cost	产品销售率 Proportion of Products Sold	总资产贡献率 Ratio of Total Assets to Industrial Output Value
51.92	**2.70**	**7.12**	**98.85**	**15.42**
53.61	2.86	6.88	98.94	16.18
59.34	5.29	2.61	99.78	6.39
56.94	2.31	6.42	99.19	15.36
48.28	3.05	8.47	97.68	26.05
24.20	2.37	4.42	101.80	10.30
58.12	2.29	6.37	99.30	12.88
58.51	1.56	5.99	98.87	14.36
46.25	1.69	10.02	97.22	14.56
52.18	3.51	6.86	99.01	20.03
66.11	2.14	6.33	98.78	13.03
48.86	2.58	8.09	98.66	14.45
48.51	2.37	7.38	98.67	13.69
48.98	2.88	7.53	98.72	18.52
52.91	2.64	6.97	98.89	14.38
53.10	2.46	6.68	98.80	13.33
50.88	2.81	8.40	99.18	17.32
51.17	2.92	6.71	98.67	16.70
59.25	**3.18**	**-2.92**	**99.62**	**2.23**
60.92	3.56	1.18	100.46	4.51
67.35	2.11	0.42	104.15	3.24
75.23	2.91	-2.59	99.54	0.80
53.05	3.02	6.15	98.48	12.84
51.09	**2.69**	**7.07**	**98.81**	**16.09**
52.52	5.73	6.83	99.94	26.59

11－5 续 表1

单位:%

项　　目 Item		企业亏损面 Percentage of Loss Making Enterprises
食品制造业	Manufacture of Food	11.42
酒、饮料和精制茶制造业	Manufacture of Liquor, Beverages and Refined Tea	12.70
烟草制品业	Manufacture of Tobacco	0.00
纺织业	Manufacture of Textile	9.90
纺织服装、服饰业	Manufacture of Textile, Wearing Apparel and Accessories	9.90
皮革、毛皮、羽毛及其制品和制鞋业	Manufacture of Leather, Fur, Feather and Related Products and Footwear	7.92
木材加工和木、竹、藤、棕、草制品业	Processing of Timber, Manufacture of Wood, Bamboo, Rattan, Palm and Straw Products	2.62
家具制造业	Manufacture of Furniture	10.14
造纸和纸制品业	Manufacture of Paper and Paper Products	10.43
印刷和记录媒介复制业	Printing, Reproduction of Recording Media	12.69
文教、工美、体育和娱乐用品制造业	Manufacture of Articles for Culture, Education, Arts and Crafts, Sport and Entertainment Activities	7.61
石油加工、炼焦和核燃料加工业	Processing of Petroleum, Coking, Processing of Nuclear Fuel	10.96
化学原料和化学制品制造业	Manufacture of Raw Chemical Materials and Chemical Products	10.50
医药制造业	Manufacture of Medicines	8.96
化学纤维制造业	Manufacture of Chemical Fibers	19.54
橡胶和塑料制品业	Manufacture of Rubber and Plastics Products	11.15
非金属矿物制品业	Manufacture of Non-metallic Mineral Products	14.93
黑色金属冶炼和压延加工业	Smelting and Pressing of Ferrous Metals	13.37
有色金属冶炼和压延加工业	Smelting and Pressing of Non-ferrous Metals	14.01
金属制品业	Manufacture of Metal Products	11.01
通用设备制造业	Manufacture of General Purpose Machinery	11.79
专用设备制造业	Manufacture of Special Purpose Machinery	12.79
汽车制造业	Manufacture of Automobiles	12.06

11－5　Continued 1

(%)

资产负债率 Assets Liability Ratio	流动资产周转次数(次/年) Times of Turnover of Circulating Funds (times/year)	成本费用利润率 Ratio of Profits to Industrial Cost	产品销售率 Proportion of Products Sold	总资产贡献率 Ratio of Total Assets to Industrial Output Value
46.21	3.23	7.57	97.50	17.25
40.06	1.77	18.25	97.58	22.85
11.07	1.38	33.26	97.74	77.83
53.67	3.07	5.47	98.40	15.31
50.48	3.29	7.01	98.99	19.20
44.84	5.07	6.07	98.02	27.20
38.18	5.80	7.81	99.18	31.24
48.73	2.27	6.83	98.94	13.71
50.99	2.06	6.24	99.93	9.72
47.11	2.31	8.85	98.62	15.73
48.47	4.45	7.18	99.40	25.12
57.61	4.88	6.13	99.14	40.42
48.25	3.39	7.78	99.20	18.38
36.25	2.59	12.16	97.58	23.72
56.36	2.56	4.56	97.76	10.10
42.56	2.50	7.33	98.83	14.99
54.09	2.63	6.69	98.89	15.20
60.48	3.43	4.16	98.89	11.16
56.68	3.57	4.42	99.25	14.56
50.53	2.74	6.40	98.55	15.63
50.28	2.06	7.95	98.75	14.35
50.92	2.00	8.04	99.71	14.51
59.97	2.30	8.55	98.48	18.24

单位:%

项 目 Item		企业亏损面 Percentage of Loss Making Enterprises
铁路、船舶、航空航天和其他运输设备制造业	Manufacture of Railway, Ship, Aerospace and Other Transport Equipments	12.07
电气机械和器材制造业	Manufacture of Electrical Machinery and Apparatus	11.35
计算机、通信和其他电子设备制造业	Manufacture of Computers, Communication and Other Electronic Equipment	16.48
仪器仪表制造业	Manufacture of Measuring Instruments and Machinery	10.01
其他制造业	Other Manufacture	6.63
废弃资源综合利用业	Utilization of Waste Resources	18.84
金属制品、机械和设备修理业	Repair Service of Metal Products, Machinery and Equipment	13.04
电力、热力、燃气及水的生产和供应业	**Production and Supply of Electric Power, Heat Power, Gas and Water**	**9.25**
电力、热力的生产和供应业	Production and Supply of Electric Power and Heat Power	8.13
燃气生产和供应	Production and Supply of Gas	5.94
水的生产和供应业	Production and Supply of Water	14.73
按地区分	**by Region**	
南京市	Nanjing	14.54
无锡市	Wuxi	18.47
徐州市	Xuzhou	3.81
常州市	Changzhou	13.14
苏州市	Suzhou	19.32
南通市	Nantong	7.32
连云港市	Lianyungang	5.73
淮安市	Huaian	6.98
盐城市	Yancheng	6.53
扬州市	Yangzhou	7.11
镇江市	Zhenjiang	9.72
泰州市	Taizhou	6.10
宿迁市	Suqian	4.23

(%)

资产负债率 Assets Liability Ratio	流动资产周转次数(次/年) Times of Turnover of Circulating Funds (times/year)	成本费用利润率 Ratio of Profits to Industrial Cost	产品销售率 Proportion of Products Sold	总资产贡献率 Ratio of Total Assets to Industrial Output Value
55.49	1.82	9.18	99.24	13.34
53.10	2.17	7.58	98.83	14.87
49.32	2.62	5.35	98.25	10.31
44.79	2.43	9.45	99.57	17.91
49.14	4.23	6.24	98.12	21.95
53.57	4.62	5.58	98.20	17.01
51.04	3.82	7.70	97.86	19.68
60.38	**3.10**	**11.04**	**99.68**	**9.45**
59.91	4.82	10.46	99.75	10.14
51.36	1.92	15.89	99.28	13.15
67.70	0.39	13.53	98.74	3.39
53.86	2.12	8.43	98.02	16.77
53.56	1.65	6.80	98.22	9.78
45.44	5.75	8.19	101.00	28.37
55.31	2.43	6.12	98.57	13.81
52.33	1.81	6.06	98.69	9.03
50.26	3.57	8.22	99.50	20.37
50.84	4.43	9.12	99.21	21.14
44.63	5.70	6.18	98.78	23.45
52.61	4.38	5.64	97.78	18.10
51.95	4.00	6.71	98.45	22.20
54.13	3.00	7.24	98.83	15.84
51.18	3.39	8.39	99.03	23.41
39.97	2.41	11.07	97.77	17.04

11-6 国有控股工业企业主要经济指标（2016年）

单位：亿元

项目	Item	企业单位数（个） Number of Enterprises (unit)	流动资产合计 Current Assets	应收账款 Accounts Receivalble
总　计	**Total**	**1013**	**7348.13**	**2027.87**
按登记注册类型分	**Grouped by Status of Registration**			
内资企业	Domestic Funded Enterprises	895	6514.42	1826.89
国有企业	State-owned Enterprises	77	616.71	95.94
集体企业	Collective-owned Enterprises			
股份合作企业	Cooperative Enterprises			
联营企业	Joint Ownership Enterprises	7	7.28	0.84
有限责任公司	Limited Liability Corporations	697	4717.84	1363.82
#国有独资	State Sole Funded Corporatios	190	2273.83	557.63
股份有限公司	Share-holding Corporations Ltd.	114	1172.59	366.30
私营企业	Private Enterprises			
其他企业	Other Enterprises			
港、澳、台商投资企业	Enterprises with Funds from Hong Kong, Macao and Taiwan	47	118.24	30.48
外商投资企业	Foreign Funded Enterprises	71	715.47	170.49
按轻重工业分	**Grouped by Light & Heavy Industries**			
轻工业	Light Industry	262	1354.54	134.06
重工业	Heavy Industry	751	5993.59	1893.80
按企业规模分	**Grouped by Size of Enterprises**			
大型企业	Large Enterprises	122	4747.77	1317.68
中型企业	Medium-sized Enterprises	276	1442.92	365.75
小微型企业	Small Enterprises	615	1157.44	344.43
按行业分	**Grouped by Sector**			
采矿业	**Mining**	**26**	**267.02**	**40.98**
煤炭开采和洗选业	Mining and Washing of Coal	5	161.63	30.80
石油和天然气开采业	Extraction of Petroleum and Natural Gas	2		
黑色金属矿采选业	Mining and Processing of Ferrous Metal Ores	1		
有色金属矿采选业	Mining and Processing of Non-ferrous Metals Ores	2		
非金属矿采选业	Mining and Processing of Non-metal Ores	16	75.89	5.16
开采辅助活动	Support Activities for Mining			
其他采矿业	Mining of Other Ores			
制造业	**Manufacturing**	**772**	**5994.77**	**1837.66**
农副食品加工业	Processing of Food from Agricultural Products	37	41.40	3.17
食品制造业	Manufacture of Food	17	24.17	7.99
酒、饮料和精制茶制造业	Manufacture of Liquor, Beverages and Refined Tea	12	115.74	34.48
烟草制品业	Manufacture of Tobacco	6	476.18	22.77
纺织业	Manufacture of Textile	22	47.10	8.10
纺织服装、服饰业	Manufacture of Textile, Wearing Apparel and Accessories	33	35.29	2.69

Main Economic Indicators of State Shareholding Industrial Enterprises(2016)

(100 million yuan)

存货 Inventory	#产成品 Finished Goods	固定资产合计 Original Value	资产总计 Total Assets	负债合计 Total Liabilities
1625.99	**426.13**	**8715.56**	**19521.06**	**11527.66**
1479.80	383.52	7733.87	17440.58	10400.05
63.71	14.13	2474.20	3813.49	2262.87
2.13	1.00	4.46	12.20	3.85
1115.67	299.75	3910.87	10631.54	6579.42
615.18	151.21	1727.08	4824.06	2822.78
298.29	68.65	1344.34	2983.35	1553.91
33.90	10.43	218.61	391.44	237.78
112.30	32.18	763.08	1689.04	889.83
393.63	52.88	854.58	2529.41	1166.62
1232.36	373.26	7860.97	16991.65	10361.05
1156.25	266.71	5630.65	12970.26	7523.76
293.15	91.26	1851.24	3794.88	2280.23
176.60	68.16	1233.66	2755.92	1723.67
41.77	**15.73**	**571.12**	**1069.78**	**651.23**
28.99	10.27	324.54	659.87	405.92
10.14	4.22	109.00	203.63	120.01
1505.53	**409.45**	**3636.50**	**11392.26**	**6535.05**
13.00	4.35	29.04	77.00	55.67
7.38	2.18	26.48	71.52	33.92
48.51	7.77	49.62	180.01	99.25
233.60	4.09	62.80	601.52	66.56
22.58	9.56	58.29	112.49	65.00
3.23	1.17	14.85	55.95	20.87

单位:亿元

项 目 Item		企业单位数(个) Number of Enterprises (unit)	流动资产合计 Current Assets	应收账款 Accounts Receivalble
皮革、毛皮、羽毛及其制品和制鞋业	Manufacture of Leather, Fur, Feather and Related Products and Footwear	1		
木材加工和木、竹、藤、棕、草制品业	Processing of Timber, Manufacture of Wood, Bamboo, Rattan, Palm and Straw Products	1		
家具制造业	Manufacture of Furniture			
造纸和纸制品业	Manufacture of Paper and Paper Products	5	20.50	0.97
印刷和记录媒介复制业	Printing, Reproduction of Recording Media	19	14.24	5.25
文教、工美、体育和娱乐用品制造业	Manufacture of Articles for Culture, Education, Arts and Crafts, Sport and Entertainment Activities	5	7.45	1.93
石油加工、炼焦和核燃料加工业	Processing of Petroleum, Coking, Processing of Nuclear Fuel	10	109.74	17.90
化学原料和化学制品制造业	Manufacture of Raw Chemical Materials and Chemical Products	78	568.74	97.47
医药制造业	Manufacture of Medicines	19	63.35	15.47
化学纤维制造业	Manufacture of Chemical Fibers	12	80.40	6.67
橡胶和塑料制品业	Manufacture of Rubber and Plastics Products	11	16.86	2.54
非金属矿物制品业	Manufacture of Non-metallic Mineral Products	66	168.50	49.01
黑色金属冶炼和压延加工业	Smelting and Pressing of Ferrous Metals	14	144.30	25.72
有色金属冶炼和压延加工业	Smelting and Pressing of Non-ferrous Metals	17	35.66	2.82
金属制品业	Manufacture of Metal Products	28	126.08	48.63
通用设备制造业	Manufacture of General Purpose Machinery	56	856.53	386.75
专用设备制造业	Manufacture of Special Purpose Machinery	53	324.05	172.73
汽车制造业	Manufacture of Automobiles	52	750.67	233.41
铁路、船舶、航空航天和其他运输设备制造业	Manufacture of Railway, Ship, Aerospace and Other Transport Equipments	40	409.06	92.92
电气机械和器材制造业	Manufacture of Electrical Machinery and Apparatus	68	662.74	351.06
计算机、通信和其他电子设备制造业	Manufacture of Computers, Communication and Other Electronic Equipment	59	589.73	130.11
仪器仪表制造业	Manufacture of Measuring Instruments and Machinery	25	294.57	114.67
其他制造业	Other Manufacture			
废弃资源综合利用业	Utilization of Waste Resources	4	6.42	1.34
金属制品、机械和设备修理业	Repair Service of Metal Products, Machinery and Equipment	2		
电力、热力、燃气及水的生产和供应业	**Production and Supply of Electric Power, Heat Power, Gas and Water**	**215**	**1086.35**	**149.23**
电力、热力的生产和供应业	Production and Supply of Electric Power and Heat Power	127	588.71	133.55
燃气生产和供应	Production and Supply of Gas	25	92.58	7.04
水的生产和供应业	Production and Supply of Water	63	405.06	8.65

11-6 Continued 1

(100 million yuan)

存货 Inventory	#产成品 Finished Goods	固定资产合计 Original Value	资产总计 Total Assets	负债合计 Total Liabilities
3.30	0.99	14.08	39.72	18.90
2.70	0.71	13.40	32.44	9.32
1.98	0.73	3.02	11.46	5.62
67.55	11.64	177.75	334.50	208.79
160.55	50.60	634.68	1477.98	723.33
12.60	6.55	42.19	143.63	47.93
21.91	8.61	90.21	201.50	71.26
5.49	2.98	17.15	37.82	21.08
20.44	10.01	152.99	367.57	239.21
31.79	7.72	261.09	514.49	357.77
19.72	5.44	18.51	61.17	42.32
38.15	16.04	63.61	206.79	116.02
181.61	107.73	260.57	1468.57	922.06
67.23	22.35	93.07	463.37	377.34
89.78	45.38	313.05	1247.65	889.40
157.01	11.29	179.73	704.71	474.20
89.29	41.42	140.80	887.66	558.20
162.19	24.60	836.39	1618.06	844.17
41.14	2.94	76.07	450.41	250.77
0.01	0.01	4.45	13.99	9.01
78.69	**0.95**	**4507.93**	**7059.02**	**4341.38**
60.32	0.02	3946.95	5853.00	3557.91
7.51	0.22	116.97	247.92	121.74
10.87	0.72	444.01	958.10	661.73

单位:亿元

项 目	Item	所有者权益合计 Owners' Equities	#实收资本 Paid-in Capital
总 计	**Total**	**7987.87**	**4422.52**
按登记注册类型分	**Grouped by Status of Registration**		
内资企业	Domestic Funded Enterprises	7036.70	3663.64
国有企业	State-owned Enterprises	1548.19	984.42
集体企业	Collective-owned Enterprises		
股份合作企业	Cooperative Enterprises		
联营企业	Joint Ownership Enterprises	8.35	3.79
有限责任公司	Limited Liability Corporations	4050.91	1930.35
#国有独资	State Sole Funded Corporatios	2002.51	685.17
股份有限公司	Share-holding Corporations Ltd.	1429.25	745.08
私营企业	Private Enterprises		
其他企业	Other Enterprises		
港、澳、台商投资企业	Enterprises with Funds from Hong Kong, Macao and Taiwan	151.97	114.93
外商投资企业	Foreign Funded Enterprises	799.20	643.96
按轻重工业分	**Grouped by Light & Heavy Industries**		
轻工业	Light Industry	1359.80	430.53
重工业	Heavy Industry	6628.07	3991.99
按企业规模分	**Grouped by Size of Enterprises**		
大型企业	Large Enterprises	5446.50	2868.36
中型企业	Medium-sized Enterprises	1514.64	818.89
小微型企业	Small Enterprises	1026.73	2273.73
按行业分	**Grouped by Sector**		
采矿业	**Mining**	**418.51**	**221.61**
煤炭开采和洗选业	Mining and Washing of Coal	253.91	59.51
石油和天然气开采业	Extraction of Petroleum and Natural Gas		
黑色金属矿采选业	Mining and Processing of Ferrous Metal Ores		
有色金属矿采选业	Mining and Processing of Non-ferrous Metals Ores		
非金属矿采选业	Mining and Processing of Non-metal Ores	83.63	39.98
开采辅助活动	Support Activities for Mining		
其他采矿业	Mining of Other Ores		
制造业	**Manufacturing**	**4852.05**	**2480.31**
农副食品加工业	Processing of Food from Agricultural Products	19.98	13.99
食品制造业	Manufacture of Food	37.21	16.07
酒、饮料和精制茶制造业	Manufacture of Liquor, Beverages and Refined Tea	80.77	28.51
烟草制品业	Manufacture of Tobacco	534.96	22.52
纺织业	Manufacture of Textile	46.75	36.41
纺织服装、服饰业	Manufacture of Textile, Wearing Apparel and Accessories	35.07	8.49

11－6 Continued 2

(100 million yuan)

主营业务收入 Revenue from Principal Business	主营业务成本 Cost of Principle Business	利润总额 Total Profits	平均用工人数（万人） The Average Number of Employment (10000 Persons)
15090.90	**12423.13**	**1099.08**	**67.24**
12646.06	10497.24	766.94	59.78
3234.91	3071.54	82.32	8.19
8.00	6.68	0.20	0.11
6857.00	5494.10	452.08	41.42
2535.23	1798.57	183.82	18.49
2546.15	1924.91	232.34	10.06
417.35	364.31	36.78	1.99
2027.49	1561.58	295.37	5.46
1686.82	1026.62	187.06	13.55
13404.08	11396.52	912.02	53.69
10000.59	8243.11	549.49	42.23
2951.95	2447.79	304.97	16.44
2138.36	1732.24	244.62	8.57
328.97	**284.85**	**-49.34**	**8.18**
165.70	124.80	4.12	5.74
113.07	97.71	2.98	1.24
10580.76	**8410.37**	**789.28**	**48.26**
156.18	141.20	4.63	0.50
103.92	76.52	10.89	0.80
79.56	41.35	24.12	0.96
533.47	113.92	85.42	0.62
105.12	97.01	1.84	1.78
36.67	26.95	1.89	1.63

单位:亿元

项 目	Item	所有者权益合计 Owners' Equities	#实收资本 Paid-in Capital
皮革、毛皮、羽毛及其制品和制鞋业	Manufacture of Leather, Fur, Feather and Related Products and Footwear		
木材加工和木、竹、藤、棕、草制品业	Processing of Timber, Manufacture of Wood, Bamboo, Rattan, Palm and Straw Products		
家具制造业	Manufacture of Furniture		
造纸和纸制品业	Manufacture of Paper and Paper Products	20.82	14.65
印刷和记录媒介复制业	Printing, Reproduction of Recording Media	23.12	12.14
文教、工美、体育和娱乐用品制造业	Manufacture of Articles for Culture, Education, Arts and Crafts, Sport and Entertainment Activities	5.84	1.74
石油加工、炼焦和核燃料加工业	Processing of Petroleum, Coking, Processing of Nuclear Fuel	125.71	101.43
化学原料和化学制品制造业	Manufacture of Raw Chemical Materials and Chemical Products	755.88	484.51
医药制造业	Manufacture of Medicines	95.69	22.04
化学纤维制造业	Manufacture of Chemical Fibers	130.24	80.14
橡胶和塑料制品业	Manufacture of Rubber and Plastics Products	16.69	10.63
非金属矿物制品业	Manufacture of Non-metallic Mineral Products	128.40	78.71
黑色金属冶炼和压延加工业	Smelting and Pressing of Ferrous Metals	156.72	124.14
有色金属冶炼和压延加工业	Smelting and Pressing of Non-ferrous Metals	18.85	15.93
金属制品业	Manufacture of Metal Products	90.77	67.49
通用设备制造业	Manufacture of General Purpose Machinery	544.82	97.56
专用设备制造业	Manufacture of Special Purpose Machinery	86.03	79.24
汽车制造业	Manufacture of Automobiles	358.25	325.53
铁路、船舶、航空航天和其他运输设备制造业	Manufacture of Railway, Ship, Aerospace and Other Transport Equipments	228.71	173.82
电气机械和器材制造业	Manufacture of Electrical Machinery and Apparatus	329.05	112.70
计算机、通信和其他电子设备制造业	Manufacture of Computers, Communication and Other Electronic Equipment	773.89	489.00
仪器仪表制造业	Manufacture of Measuring Instruments and Machinery	199.64	56.45
其他制造业	Other Manufacture		
废弃资源综合利用业	Utilization of Waste Resources	4.98	3.27
金属制品、机械和设备修理业	Repair Service of Metal Products, Machinery and Equipment		
电力、热力、燃气及水的生产和供应业	**Production and Supply of Electric Power, Heat Power, Gas and Water**	**2717.31**	**1720.60**
电力、热力的生产和供应业	Production and Supply of Electric Power and Heat Power	2295.09	1501.92
燃气生产和供应	Production and Supply of Gas	126.18	53.31
水的生产和供应业	Production and Supply of Water	296.05	165.36

(100 million yuan)

主营业务收入 Revenue from Principal Business	主营业务成本 Cost of Principle Business	利润总额 Total Profits	平均用工人数（万人） The Average Number of Employment (10000 Persons)
41.68	36.36	2.48	0.34
20.70	17.24	1.97	0.68
10.46	8.53	0.43	0.18
913.11	653.08	54.10	0.99
1668.24	1338.51	142.96	5.78
103.60	72.98	11.30	1.21
248.04	201.06	23.91	1.56
37.16	32.42	1.02	0.43
298.45	255.31	15.89	1.89
300.38	278.06	3.65	0.97
301.21	292.41	3.47	0.50
203.85	181.56	5.65	1.37
698.09	576.70	35.38	5.33
222.14	193.16	-31.37	2.00
2054.65	1644.44	231.17	5.53
483.59	427.36	14.02	3.21
846.71	723.45	71.54	3.23
750.04	657.24	47.49	5.43
331.55	296.45	22.69	1.23
26.52	22.12	2.68	0.05
4181.17	**3727.91**	**359.14**	**10.80**
3904.76	3524.79	321.97	7.88
163.90	131.39	23.73	0.63
112.50	71.73	13.45	2.29

11－7　国有控股工业企业主要经济效益指标（2016 年）

单位：%

项　目	Item	企业亏损面 Percentage of Loss Making Enterprises
总　计	**Total**	**19.35**
按登记注册类型分	**Grouped by Status of Registration**	
内资企业	Domestic Funded Enterprises	19.22
国有企业	State-owned Enterprises	23.38
集体企业	Collective-owned Enterprises	
股份合作企业	Cooperative Enterprises	
联营企业	Joint Ownership Enterprises	14.29
有限责任公司	Limited Liability Corporations	19.80
#国有独资	State Sole Funded Corporatios	18.95
股份有限公司	Share-holding Corporations Ltd.	13.16
私营企业	Private Enterprises	
其他企业	Other Enterprises	
港、澳、台商投资企业	Enterprises with Funds from Hong Kong, Macao and Taiwan	23.40
外商投资企业	Foreign Funded Enterprises	18.31
按轻重工业分	**Grouped by Light & Heavy Industries**	
轻工业	Light Industry	18.70
重工业	Heavy Industry	19.57
按企业规模分	**Grouped by Size of Enterprises**	
大型企业	Large Enterprises	13.93
中型企业	Medium-sized Enterprises	18.12
小微型企业	Small Enterprises	20.98
按行业分	**Grouped by Sector**	
采矿业	**Mining**	**26.92**
煤炭开采和洗选业	Mining and Washing of Coal	20.00
石油和天然气开采业	Extraction of Petroleum and Natural Gas	
黑色金属矿采选业	Mining and Processing of Ferrous Metal Ores	
有色金属矿采选业	Mining and Processing of Non-ferrous Metals Ores	
非金属矿采选业	Mining and Processing of Non-metal Ores	12.50
开采辅助活动	Support Activities for Mining	
其他采矿业	Mining of Other Ores	
制造业	**Manufacturing**	**21.89**
农副食品加工业	Processing of Food from Agricultural Products	27.03
食品制造业	Manufacture of Food	0.00
酒、饮料和精制茶制造业	Manufacture of Liquor, Beverages and Refined Tea	41.67
烟草制品业	Manufacture of Tobacco	0.00
纺织业	Manufacture of Textile	27.27
纺织服装、服饰业	Manufacture of Textile, Wearing Apparel and Accessories	18.18

Main Indicators on Economic Benefit of State Shareholding Industrial Enterprises(2016)

(%)

资产负债率 Assets Liability Ratio	流动资产周转次数(次/年) Times of Turnover of Circulating Funds (times/year)	成本费用利润率 Ratio of Profits to Industrial Cost	产品销售率 Proportion of Products Sold	总资产贡献率 Ratio of Total Assets to Industrial Output Value
59.05	**2.24**	**7.49**	**98.97**	**13.36**
59.63	2.14	6.11	98.98	11.95
59.34	5.29	2.61	99.78	6.39
31.56	1.10	2.51	102.73	5.29
61.89	1.70	6.26	99.28	11.31
58.51	1.56	5.99	98.87	14.36
52.09	2.24	10.70	97.17	21.34
60.74	3.65	9.35	100.11	14.79
52.68	2.93	16.99	98.68	27.63
46.12	1.38	13.80	98.48	25.24
60.98	2.43	6.85	99.03	11.59
58.01	2.34	5.53	99.29	13.36
60.09	2.09	11.24	98.75	12.85
62.54	1.99	12.02	97.99	14.06
60.88	**2.80**	**-6.45**	**99.45**	**-0.70**
61.51	3.57	0.72	100.88	3.90
58.93	1.52	2.64	96.82	5.20
57.36	**1.90**	**7.93**	**98.63**	**17.38**
72.30	3.78	3.13	101.59	9.97
47.42	4.36	11.66	98.68	25.36
55.13	0.69	45.62	92.53	21.86
11.07	1.38	33.26	97.74	77.83
57.78	2.51	1.58	100.50	5.01
37.31	1.06	5.32	99.24	7.37

单位:%

项 目 Item		企业亏损面 Percentage of Loss Making Enterprises
皮革、毛皮、羽毛及其制品和制鞋业	Manufacture of Leather, Fur, Feather and Related Products and Footwear	
木材加工和木、竹、藤、棕、草制品业	Processing of Timber, Manufacture of Wood, Bamboo, Rattan, Palm and Straw Products	
家具制造业	Manufacture of Furniture	
造纸和纸制品业	Manufacture of Paper and Paper Products	40.00
印刷和记录媒介复制业	Printing, Reproduction of Recording Media	15.79
文教、工美、体育和娱乐用品制造业	Manufacture of Articles for Culture, Education, Arts and Crafts, Sport and Entertainment Activities	0.00
石油加工、炼焦和核燃料加工业	Processing of Petroleum, Coking, Processing of Nuclear Fuel	10.00
化学原料和化学制品制造业	Manufacture of Raw Chemical Materials and Chemical Products	21.79
医药制造业	Manufacture of Medicines	10.53
化学纤维制造业	Manufacture of Chemical Fibers	16.67
橡胶和塑料制品业	Manufacture of Rubber and Plastics Products	9.09
非金属矿物制品业	Manufacture of Non-metallic Mineral Products	28.79
黑色金属冶炼和压延加工业	Smelting and Pressing of Ferrous Metals	35.71
有色金属冶炼和压延加工业	Smelting and Pressing of Non-ferrous Metals	23.53
金属制品业	Manufacture of Metal Products	21.43
通用设备制造业	Manufacture of General Purpose Machinery	19.64
专用设备制造业	Manufacture of Special Purpose Machinery	26.42
汽车制造业	Manufacture of Automobiles	26.92
铁路、船舶、航空航天和其他运输设备制造业	Manufacture of Railway, Ship, Aerospace and Other Transport Equipments	15.00
电气机械和器材制造业	Manufacture of Electrical Machinery and Apparatus	23.53
计算机、通信和其他电子设备制造业	Manufacture of Computers, Communication and Other Electronic Equipment	22.03
仪器仪表制造业	Manufacture of Measuring Instruments and Machinery	16.00
其他制造业	Other Manufacture	
废弃资源综合利用业	Utilization of Waste Resources	25.00
金属制品、机械和设备修理业	Repair Service of Metal Products, Machinery and Equipment	
电力、热力、燃气及水的生产和供应业	**Production and Supply of Electric Power, Heat Power, Gas and Water**	**9.30**
电力、热力的生产和供应业	Production and Supply of Electric Power and Heat Power	5.51
燃气生产和供应	Production and Supply of Gas	12.00
水的生产和供应业	Production and Supply of Water	15.87

(%)

资产负债率 Assets Liability Ratio	流动资产周转次数(次/年) Times of Turnover of Circulating Funds (times/year)	成本费用利润率 Ratio of Profits to Industrial Cost	产品销售率 Proportion of Products Sold	总资产贡献率 Ratio of Total Assets to Industrial Output Value
47.58	2.04	6.22	98.79	11.42
28.73	1.54	9.67	98.13	9.73
49.03	1.42	4.24	101.67	7.56
62.42	8.33	8.01	99.01	91.51
48.94	2.97	9.74	99.78	21.09
33.37	1.64	12.14	97.04	11.89
35.36	3.15	10.47	100.04	17.54
55.73	2.22	2.79	101.20	7.24
65.08	1.78	5.55	98.46	8.65
69.54	2.26	1.14	99.58	2.70
69.18	10.21	0.97	92.55	10.43
56.11	1.63	2.85	98.11	6.32
62.79	1.33	3.17	97.34	4.61
81.43	0.70	-13.66	101.29	-4.09
71.29	2.81	12.80	99.16	31.22
67.29	1.20	2.94	96.49	4.92
62.88	1.29	9.03	98.96	11.91
52.17	1.29	6.42	98.28	4.67
55.68	1.14	7.04	95.23	7.14
64.41	4.14	11.29	100.06	22.82
61.50	**3.97**	**9.07**	**99.77**	**9.01**
60.79	6.79	8.76	99.87	9.94
49.11	1.92	15.31	98.40	11.79
69.07	0.34	10.39	98.70	2.63

11－8　私营工业企业主要经济指标（2016 年）

单位:亿元

项　　目	Item	企业单位数（个） Number of Enterprises (unit)	流动资产合计 Current Assets	应收账款 Accounts Receivalble
总　计	**Total**	**30122**	**18808.59**	**6002.91**
按登记注册类型分	**Grouped by Status of Registration**			
私营独资企业	Private Solely Funds Enterprises	1931	448.04	160.56
私营合伙企业	Private Partnership Enterprises	128	34.38	11.71
私营有限责任公司	Private Limited Liabieity Corporations	26929	16318.32	5249.49
私营股份有限公司	Private Share Holding Co., Ltd.	1134	2007.85	581.15
按轻重工业分	**Grouped by Light & Heavy Industries**			
轻工业	Light Industry	11609	5162.61	1408.06
重工业	Heavy Industry	18513	13645.98	4594.86
按企业规模分	**Grouped by Size of Enterprises**			
大型企业	Large Enterprises	294	4345.52	929.76
中型企业	Medium-sized Enterprises	2651	4322.34	1326.61
小微型企业	Small Enterprises	27177	10140.73	3746.54
按行业分	**Grouped by Sector**			
采矿业	**Mining**	**73**	**18.56**	**3.71**
煤炭开采和洗选业	Mining and Washing of Coal	4	0.78	0.17
石油和天然气开采业	Extraction of Petroleum and Natural Gas			
黑色金属矿采选业	Mining and Processing of Ferrous Metal Ores	5	0.90	0.16
有色金属矿采选业	Mining and Processing of Non-ferrous Metals Ores	2		
非金属矿采选业	Mining and Processing of Non-metal Ores	62	15.62	3.89
开采辅助活动	Support Activities for Mining			
其他采矿业	Mining of Other Ores			
制造业	**Manufacturing**	**29939**	**18682.01**	**5970.38**
农副食品加工业	Processing of Food from Agricultural Products	1240	374.29	87.94
食品制造业	Manufacture of Food	222	97.71	20.80
酒、饮料和精制茶制造业	Manufacture of Liquor, Beverages and Refined Tea	87	55.92	13.03
烟草制品业	Manufacture of Tobacco			
纺织业	Manufacture of Textile	3334	1326.01	370.42
纺织服装、服饰业	Manufacture of Textile, Wearing Apparel and Accessories	1457	711.54	144.54
皮革、毛皮、羽毛及其制品和制鞋业	Manufacture of Leather, Fur, Feather and Related Products and Footwear	385	95.57	30.88
木材加工和木、竹、藤、棕、草制品业	Processing of Timber, Manufacture of Wood, Bamboo, Rattan, Palm and Straw Products	1102	262.32	62.37
家具制造业	Manufacture of Furniture	184	55.99	12.65
造纸和纸制品业	Manufacture of Paper and Paper Products	366	169.01	56.62

Main Economic Indicators of Private Industrial Enterprises(2016)

(100 million yuan)

存货 Inventory	#产成品 Finished Goods	固定资产合计 Original Value	资产总计 Total Assets	负债合计 Total Liabilities
4130.22	**1751.64**	**11818.35**	**35378.85**	**18459.86**
85.83	44.17	418.74	969.78	448.38
6.08	3.43	32.28	71.43	37.60
3635.65	1526.30	10315.85	30555.39	16129.63
402.66	177.74	1051.49	3782.27	1844.24
1310.38	602.26	3681.39	10236.14	5254.54
2819.84	1149.37	8136.97	25142.71	13205.32
1052.59	380.44	2451.19	8243.41	4593.88
953.68	437.28	3176.29	8611.58	4349.36
2123.95	933.92	6190.87	18523.87	9516.62
2.93	**2.02**	**26.25**	**56.37**	**19.58**
0.13	0.13	2.19	2.97	0.94
0.40	0.20	1.85	3.31	1.63
1.99	1.31	22.08	48.58	15.23
4118.96	**1748.08**	**11622.64**	**34955.26**	**18254.21**
120.15	63.57	415.14	889.84	388.48
27.34	13.67	84.80	206.80	101.47
16.29	9.10	60.14	135.76	61.13
352.55	164.76	833.57	2466.36	1393.99
201.52	94.45	362.80	1282.51	664.92
23.27	9.25	62.36	177.67	89.32
62.15	26.22	315.27	665.54	208.31
15.44	7.63	52.00	123.05	59.08
38.42	16.29	136.92	336.48	194.44

11-8 续 表 1

单位:亿元

项 目	Item	企业单位数(个) Number of Enterprises (unit)	流动资产合计 Current Assets	应收账款 Accounts Receivalble
印刷和记录媒介复制业	Printing, Reproduction of Recording Media	451	189.75	69.14
文教、工美、体育和娱乐用品制造业	Manufacture of Articles for Culture, Education, Arts and Crafts, Sport and Entertainment Activities	836	254.31	72.89
石油加工、炼焦和核燃料加工业	Processing of Petroleum, Coking, Processing of Nuclear Fuel	82	81.82	19.86
化学原料和化学制品制造业	Manufacture of Raw Chemical Materials and Chemical Products	1995	1688.63	494.18
医药制造业	Manufacture of Medicines	333	277.26	66.50
化学纤维制造业	Manufacture of Chemical Fibers	573	404.32	71.81
橡胶和塑料制品业	Manufacture of Rubber and Plastics Products	1290	461.00	195.79
非金属矿物制品业	Manufacture of Non-metallic Mineral Products	1959	1035.89	462.28
黑色金属冶炼和压延加工业	Smelting and Pressing of Ferrous Metals	932	1094.59	225.85
有色金属冶炼和压延加工业	Smelting and Pressing of Non-ferrous Metals	715	656.73	197.12
金属制品业	Manufacture of Metal Products	2150	1182.74	422.67
通用设备制造业	Manufacture of General Purpose Machinery	2602	1260.63	466.70
专用设备制造业	Manufacture of Special Purpose Machinery	1898	1289.78	425.42
汽车制造业	Manufacture of Automobiles	893	682.16	245.68
铁路、船舶、航空航天和其他运输设备制造业	Manufacture of Railway, Ship, Aerospace and Other Transport Equipments	488	682.20	169.09
电气机械和器材制造业	Manufacture of Electrical Machinery and Apparatus	2592	2677.60	1025.77
计算机、通信和其他电子设备制造业	Manufacture of Computers, Communication and Other Electronic Equipment	1060	983.53	358.89
仪器仪表制造业	Manufacture of Measuring Instruments and Machinery	497	550.51	159.79
其他制造业	Other Manufacture	116	45.86	11.73
废弃资源综合利用业	Utilization of Waste Resources	87	29.27	8.20
金属制品、机械和设备修理业	Repair Service of Metal Products, Machinery and Equipment	13	5.09	1.75
电力、热力、燃气及水的生产和供应业	**Production and Supply of Electric Power, Heat Power, Gas and Water**	**110**	**108.02**	**28.82**
电力、热力的生产和供应业	Production and Supply of Electric Power and Heat Power	85	95.58	26.97
燃气生产和供应	Production and Supply of Gas	13	7.68	1.17
水的生产和供应业	Production and Supply of Water	12	4.76	0.68

(100 million yuan)

存货 Inventory	#产成品 Finished Goods	固定资产合计 Original Value	资产总计 Total Assets	负债合计 Total Liabilities
41.32	18.99	131.37	358.37	189.89
65.64	30.88	200.65	531.43	258.48
15.89	6.55	33.98	139.12	86.38
371.29	144.27	1280.25	3535.81	1810.35
51.97	23.35	264.04	725.08	286.24
105.88	42.76	390.64	903.02	542.84
91.15	39.67	251.43	797.10	410.07
145.33	66.52	718.07	1990.30	1108.27
322.12	135.23	943.07	2258.86	1289.05
140.29	49.28	234.45	1124.55	665.14
253.27	101.51	687.83	2197.32	1209.90
300.07	124.25	786.02	2335.43	1132.43
290.71	110.24	625.49	2162.68	1075.81
128.92	60.52	273.75	1073.92	632.37
210.69	62.74	345.61	1173.45	702.82
434.78	204.68	1225.16	4451.39	2220.04
172.29	75.76	482.08	1715.71	925.57
100.14	38.49	355.69	1020.70	465.12
12.14	4.70	36.60	98.32	43.20
6.77	2.52	26.90	66.34	33.27
1.15	0.23	6.57	12.36	5.81
8.34	**1.53**	**169.47**	**367.22**	**186.07**
6.95	0.58	162.61	345.85	175.71
0.75	0.60	2.03	10.75	5.51
0.64	0.35	4.84	10.62	4.85

单位:亿元

项目	Item	所有者权益合计 Owners' Equities	#实收资本 Paid-in Capital
总 计	**Total**	**16831.84**	**6833.51**
按登记注册类型分	**Grouped by Status of Registration**		
私营独资企业	Private Solely Funds Enterprises	512.94	163.44
私营合伙企业	Private Partnership Enterprises	33.49	9.34
私营有限责任公司	Private Limited Liabieity Corporations	14349.71	6047.49
私营股份有限公司	Private Share Holding Co., Ltd.	1935.71	613.24
按轻重工业分	**Grouped by Light & Heavy Industries**		
轻工业	Light Industry	4957.24	1949.89
重工业	Heavy Industry	11874.61	4883.62
按企业规模分	**Grouped by Size of Enterprises**		
大型企业	Large Enterprises	3649.53	1054.89
中型企业	Medium-sized Enterprises	4262.22	1446.74
小微型企业	Small Enterprises	8920.10	4331.88
按行业分	**Grouped by Sector**		
采矿业	**Mining**	**35.99**	**15.69**
煤炭开采和洗选业	Mining and Washing of Coal	2.02	0.70
石油和天然气开采业	Extraction of Petroleum and Natural Gas		
黑色金属矿采选业	Mining and Processing of Ferrous Metal Ores	1.26	1.25
有色金属矿采选业	Mining and Processing of Non-ferrous Metals Ores		
非金属矿采选业	Mining and Processing of Non-metal Ores	32.96	13.34
开采辅助活动	Support Activities for Mining		
其他采矿业	Mining of Other Ores		
制造业	**Manufacturing**	**16614.70**	**6688.79**
农副食品加工业	Processing of Food from Agricultural Products	495.49	162.01
食品制造业	Manufacture of Food	104.81	40.81
酒、饮料和精制茶制造业	Manufacture of Liquor, Beverages and Refined Tea	74.39	29.40
烟草制品业	Manufacture of Tobacco		
纺织业	Manufacture of Textile	1062.44	482.70
纺织服装、服饰业	Manufacture of Textile, Wearing Apparel and Accessories	615.68	211.59
皮革、毛皮、羽毛及其制品和制鞋业	Manufacture of Leather, Fur, Feather and Related Products and Footwear	87.39	34.89
木材加工和木、竹、藤、棕、草制品业	Processing of Timber, Manufacture of Wood, Bamboo, Rattan, Palm and Straw Products	445.61	147.33
家具制造业	Manufacture of Furniture	63.88	27.73
造纸和纸制品业	Manufacture of Paper and Paper Products	141.53	66.96

11－8 Continued 2

(100 million yuan)

主营业务收入 Revenue from Principal Business	主营业务成本 Cost of Principle Business	利润总额 Total Profits	平均用工人数（万人） The Average Number of Employment (10000 Persons)
65030.17	**56451.45**	**4214.53**	**478.83**
2963.61	2601.10	196.87	20.14
196.15	167.42	13.74	1.53
57507.44	49988.20	3684.27	428.36
4362.98	3694.73	319.65	28.80
20135.15	17525.68	1255.66	187.13
44895.02	38925.77	2958.87	291.70
11586.05	10111.01	757.13	71.45
17196.55	14724.83	1278.84	128.89
36247.57	31615.62	2178.57	278.49
189.74	**160.74**	**14.50**	**1.15**
17.22	14.80	1.32	0.09
8.57	6.87	0.80	0.03
157.46	132.65	12.60	1.02
64699.79	**56184.69**	**4176.66**	**476.80**
2804.12	2463.26	179.81	13.82
417.17	358.86	29.34	3.70
252.71	210.26	23.75	1.41
4241.06	3768.56	223.55	48.55
2316.60	2007.03	163.08	34.36
558.33	489.16	31.42	7.10
1935.07	1690.69	147.23	13.80
245.28	213.33	15.25	2.68
587.48	509.78	31.77	4.63

单位:亿元

项 目 Item		所有者权益合计 Owners' Equities	#实收资本 Paid-in Capital
印刷和记录媒介复制业	Printing, Reproduction of Recording Media	168.07	65.47
文教、工美、体育和娱乐用品制造业	Manufacture of Articles for Culture, Education, Arts and Crafts, Sport and Entertainment Activities	272.05	100.50
石油加工、炼焦和核燃料加工业	Processing of Petroleum, Coking, Processing of Nuclear Fuel	52.04	28.58
化学原料和化学制品制造业	Manufacture of Raw Chemical Materials and Chemical Products	1721.32	637.61
医药制造业	Manufacture of Medicines	438.75	132.88
化学纤维制造业	Manufacture of Chemical Fibers	360.06	165.51
橡胶和塑料制品业	Manufacture of Rubber and Plastics Products	385.91	178.09
非金属矿物制品业	Manufacture of Non – metallic Mineral Products	878.41	411.70
黑色金属冶炼和压延加工业	Smelting and Pressing of Ferrous Metals	964.19	345.00
有色金属冶炼和压延加工业	Smelting and Pressing of Non-ferrous Metals	453.48	161.86
金属制品业	Manufacture of Metal Products	982.76	464.93
通用设备制造业	Manufacture of General Purpose Machinery	1197.04	578.67
专用设备制造业	Manufacture of Special Purpose Machinery	1077.97	433.15
汽车制造业	Manufacture of Automobiles	441.16	184.79
铁路、船舶、航空航天和其他运输设备制造业	Manufacture of Railway, Ship, Aerospace and Other Transport Equipments	470.44	169.78
电气机械和器材制造业	Manufacture of Electrical Machinery and Apparatus	2223.90	927.28
计算机、通信和其他电子设备制造业	Manufacture of Computers, Communication and Other Electronic Equipment	786.62	324.54
仪器仪表制造业	Manufacture of Measuring Instruments and Machinery	554.79	137.73
其他制造业	Other Manufacture	54.89	15.37
废弃资源综合利用业	Utilization of Waste Resources	33.07	19.06
金属制品、机械和设备修理业	Repair Service of Metal Products, Machinery and Equipment	6.55	2.88
电力、热力、燃气及水的生产和供应业	**Production and Supply of Electric Power, Heat Power, Gas and Water**	**181.15**	**129.04**
电力、热力的生产和供应业	Production and Supply of Electric Power and Heat Power	170.14	123.59
燃气生产和供应	Production and Supply of Gas	5.24	3.56
水的生产和供应业	Production and Supply of Water	5.77	1.89

(100 million yuan)

主营业务收入 Revenue from Principal Business	主营业务成本 Cost of Principle Business	利润总额 Total Profits	平均用工人数（万人） The Average Number of Employment (10000 Persons)
513.88	436.07	34.91	5.94
1386.66	1188.36	95.84	14.70
308.17	282.85	10.72	0.84
7017.61	6105.70	484.99	31.62
1203.11	997.60	99.94	6.82
1465.05	1342.64	52.56	8.21
1570.69	1361.17	94.17	16.07
3234.37	2813.22	207.39	24.38
4747.27	4233.64	230.14	19.13
2347.47	2145.25	106.51	9.10
4139.94	3603.81	249.77	29.82
4229.80	3602.75	284.83	35.05
3596.77	3005.57	265.85	27.96
1536.88	1308.35	98.49	15.89
1697.18	1444.65	130.24	12.95
7493.55	6475.39	523.67	47.66
2606.55	2220.06	183.13	26.13
1866.40	1574.02	156.02	10.73
233.80	206.73	13.17	2.77
125.32	107.59	7.63	0.81
21.49	18.37	1.48	0.17
140.65	**106.02**	**23.36**	**0.89**
118.99	87.83	21.45	0.74
14.89	13.13	1.01	0.06
6.77	5.06	0.91	0.08

11－9 私营工业企业主要经济效益指标（2016年）

单位：%

项目	Item	企业亏损面 Percentage of Loss Making Enterprises
总计	**Total**	**8.53**
按登记注册类型分	**Grouped by Status of Registration**	
私营独资企业	Private Solely Funds Enterprises	2.54
私营合伙企业	Private Partnership Enterprises	2.34
私营有限责任公司	Private Limited Liabieity Corporations	8.93
私营股份有限公司	Private Share Holding Co., Ltd.	9.79
按轻重工业分	**Grouped by Light & Heavy Industries**	
轻工业	Light Industry	7.58
重工业	Heavy Industry	9.12
按企业规模分	**Grouped by Size of Enterprises**	
大型企业	Large Enterprises	2.38
中型企业	Medium-sized Enterprises	4.79
小微型企业	Small Enterprises	8.96
按行业分	**Grouped by Sector**	
采矿业	**Mining**	**5.48**
煤炭开采和洗选业	Mining and Washing of Coal	0.00
石油和天然气开采业	Extraction of Petroleum and Natural Gas	
黑色金属矿采选业	Mining and Processing of Ferrous Metal Ores	20.00
有色金属矿采选业	Mining and Processing of Non-ferrous Metals Ores	
非金属矿采选业	Mining and Processing of Non-metal Ores	3.23
开采辅助活动	Support Activities for Mining	
其他采矿业	Mining of Other Ores	
制造业	**Manufacturing**	**8.53**
农副食品加工业	Processing of Food from Agricultural Products	3.95
食品制造业	Manufacture of Food	6.76
酒、饮料和精制茶制造业	Manufacture of Liquor, Beverages and Refined Tea	4.60
烟草制品业	Manufacture of Tobacco	
纺织业	Manufacture of Textile	8.40
纺织服装、服饰业	Manufacture of Textile, Wearing Apparel and Accessories	6.86
皮革、毛皮、羽毛及其制品和制鞋业	Manufacture of Leather, Fur, Feather and Related Products and Footwear	3.64
木材加工和木、竹、藤、棕、草制品业	Processing of Timber, Manufacture of Wood, Bamboo, Rattan, Palm and Straw Products	1.45
家具制造业	Manufacture of Furniture	5.43
造纸和纸制品业	Manufacture of Paper and Paper Products	5.74

Main Indicators on Economic Benefit of Private Industrial Enterprises(2016)

(%)

资产负债率 Assets Liability Ratio	流动资产周转次数(次/年) Times of Turnover of Circulating Funds (times/year)	成本费用利润率 Ratio of Profits to Industrial Cost	产品销售率 Proportion of Products Sold	总资产贡献率 Ratio of Total Assets to Industrial Output Value
52.18	**3.51**	**6.86**	**99.01**	**20.03**
46.24	6.62	7.16	98.41	34.18
52.65	5.72	7.57	98.39	31.79
52.79	3.58	6.77	99.07	20.36
48.76	2.20	7.84	98.56	13.54
51.33	3.95	6.59	98.84	21.02
52.52	3.34	6.98	99.08	19.63
55.73	2.83	6.61	99.30	14.98
50.51	4.01	8.02	99.61	24.30
51.37	3.59	6.40	98.64	20.30
34.73	**10.22**	**8.41**	**98.82**	**46.23**
31.84	22.09	8.35	93.93	79.49
49.37	9.51	10.45	100.91	40.83
31.34	10.08	8.85	99.19	46.63
52.22	**3.52**	**6.83**	**99.01**	**20.11**
43.66	7.50	6.90	99.80	32.40
49.07	4.28	7.59	98.49	23.50
45.03	4.54	10.47	99.24	28.81
56.52	3.23	5.54	98.15	17.00
51.85	3.46	7.13	98.69	21.03
50.27	5.85	6.00	98.50	31.62
31.30	7.38	8.29	99.10	35.76
48.02	4.39	6.68	97.53	22.06
57.79	3.49	5.72	99.72	16.76

单位:%

项 目	Item	企业亏损面 Percentage of Loss Making Enterprises
印刷和记录媒介复制业	Printing, Reproduction of Recording Media	10.86
文教、工美、体育和娱乐用品制造业	Manufacture of Articles for Culture, Education, Arts and Crafts, Sport and Entertainment Activities	4.90
石油加工、炼焦和核燃料加工业	Processing of Petroleum, Coking, Processing of Nuclear Fuel	6.10
化学原料和化学制品制造业	Manufacture of Raw Chemical Materials and Chemical Products	7.22
医药制造业	Manufacture of Medicines	6.91
化学纤维制造业	Manufacture of Chemical Fibers	19.37
橡胶和塑料制品业	Manufacture of Rubber and Plastics Products	7.36
非金属矿物制品业	Manufacture of Non-metallic Mineral Products	11.89
黑色金属冶炼和压延加工业	Smelting and Pressing of Ferrous Metals	12.12
有色金属冶炼和压延加工业	Smelting and Pressing of Non-ferrous Metals	12.59
金属制品业	Manufacture of Metal Products	8.88
通用设备制造业	Manufacture of General Purpose Machinery	9.61
专用设备制造业	Manufacture of Special Purpose Machinery	9.22
汽车制造业	Manufacture of Automobiles	6.94
铁路、船舶、航空航天和其他运输设备制造业	Manufacture of Railway, Ship, Aerospace and Other Transport Equipments	11.89
电气机械和器材制造业	Manufacture of Electrical Machinery and Apparatus	9.38
计算机、通信和其他电子设备制造业	Manufacture of Computers, Communication and Other Electronic Equipment	10.19
仪器仪表制造业	Manufacture of Measuring Instruments and Machinery	7.24
其他制造业	Other Manufacture	5.17
废弃资源综合利用业	Utilization of Waste Resources	13.79
金属制品、机械和设备修理业	Repair Service of Metal Products, Machinery and Equipment	7.69
电力、热力、燃气及水的生产和供应业	**Production and Supply of Electric Power, Heat Power, Gas and Water**	**8.18**
电力、热力的生产和供应业	Production and Supply of Electric Power and Heat Power	8.24
燃气生产和供应	Production and Supply of Gas	15.38
水的生产和供应业	Production and Supply of Water	0.00

(%)

资产负债率 Assets Liability Ratio	流动资产周转次数(次/年) Times of Turnover of Circulating Funds (times/year)	成本费用利润率 Ratio of Profits to Industrial Cost	产品销售率 Proportion of Products Sold	总资产贡献率 Ratio of Total Assets to Industrial Output Value
52.99	2.73	7.26	98.50	16.68
48.64	5.48	7.44	99.26	29.46
62.09	3.79	3.62	98.87	14.67
51.20	4.21	7.36	99.67	22.48
39.48	4.34	9.10	99.08	22.27
60.11	3.75	3.59	98.21	11.85
51.45	3.42	6.40	98.54	20.53
55.68	3.13	6.87	98.78	18.35
57.07	4.51	4.97	97.93	18.10
59.15	3.75	4.56	99.25	15.48
55.06	3.62	6.25	98.90	20.17
48.49	3.37	7.24	98.41	21.44
49.74	2.85	7.86	100.36	20.45
58.88	2.27	6.82	97.78	15.86
59.89	2.50	8.36	99.58	17.37
49.87	2.82	7.48	99.04	18.91
53.95	2.67	7.55	99.58	17.51
45.57	3.43	9.07	100.21	22.67
43.94	5.10	6.01	97.93	24.19
50.15	4.29	6.51	98.01	20.19
47.01	4.25	7.43	97.27	20.91
50.67	**1.36**	**18.74**	**99.03**	**9.02**
50.80	1.31	20.51	99.08	8.82
51.28	1.96	7.20	99.22	11.79
45.68	1.48	14.77	97.80	12.74

11－10 外商投资和港澳台商投资工业企业主要经济指标（2016 年）

单位：亿元

项　目	Item	企业单位数（个）Number of Enterprises (unit)	流动资产合计 Current Assets	应收账款 Accounts Receivalble
总　计	**Total**	**10055**	**21706.28**	**7852.92**
按登记注册类型分	**Grouped by Status of Registration**			
与港澳台商合资经营	Joint-venture Enterprises with Hong Kong Macao and Taiwan	1298	2229.80	599.49
与港澳台商合作经营	Cooperative Enterprises with Hong Kong, Macao and Taiwan	41	95.65	25.51
港澳台商独资	Enterprises with Sole Funds from Hong Kong, Macao and Taiwan	2177	4217.92	1676.25
港澳台商投资股份有限公司	Share Holding with Hong Kong, Macao and Taiwan Investment	80	292.36	86.85
其他港澳台投资	Other Share Hold with Hong Kong. Macao and Taiwan Investment	16	26.90	8.31
中外合资经营	Joint-venture Enterprises with Foreign Funded	1818	4392.71	1266.84
中外合作经营	Chinese-foreign Cooperative Enterprises	72	123.13	46.04
外资企业	Foreign Solely Funded	4438	9767.58	3976.96
外商投资股份有限公司	Share Holding with Foreign Investment	81	533.11	156.99
其他外商投资	Others	34	27.11	9.67
按轻重工业分	**Grouped by Light & Heavy Industries**			
轻工业	Light Industry	3502	5266.65	1598.38
重工业	Heavy Industry	6553	16439.63	6254.53
按企业规模分	**Grouped by Size of Enterprises**			
大型企业	Large Enterprises	606	9677.80	3662.28
中型企业	Medium-sized Enterprises	2177	6183.46	2180.86
小微型企业	Small Enterprises	7272	5845.02	2009.78
按行业分	**Grouped by Sector**			
采矿业	**Mining**	**8**	**16.99**	**2.41**
煤炭开采和洗选业	Mining and Washing of Coal			
石油和天然气开采业	Extraction of Petroleum and Natural Gas			
黑色金属矿采选业	Mining and Processing of Ferrous Metal Ores	3	11.80	0.19
有色金属矿采选业	Mining and Processing of Non-ferrous Metals Ores			
非金属矿采选业	Mining and Processing of Non-metal Ores	4	3.24	1.46
开采辅助活动	Support Activities for Minin	1		
其他采矿业	Mining of Other Ores			
制造业	**Manufacturing**	**9899**	**21274.26**	**7793.43**
农副食品加工业	Processing of Food from Agricultural Products	161	318.71	58.61
食品制造业	Manufacture of Food	103	168.42	47.93
酒、饮料和精制茶制造业	Manufacture of Liquor, Beverages and Refined Tea	60	82.98	26.80
烟草制品业	Manufacture of Tobacco			
纺织业	Manufacture of Textile	625	626.86	172.73
纺织服装、服饰业	Manufacture of Textile, Wearing Apparel and Accessories	614	287.41	84.02

Main Economic Indicators of Industrial Enterprises with Hong Kong, Macao, Taiwan and Foreign Funds (2016)

(100 million yuan)

存货 Inventory	#产成品 Finished Goods	固定资产合计 Original Value	资产总计 Total Assets	负债合计 Total Liabilities
4388.31	**1617.10**	**12901.36**	**38945.68**	**18939.00**
480.65	185.79	1910.94	4936.98	2660.64
11.33	4.13	98.48	214.19	89.11
818.10	308.27	2445.52	7327.29	3423.09
36.90	13.74	153.00	546.47	194.23
5.03	1.46	8.00	38.43	15.82
879.06	325.55	3111.43	8578.88	4261.93
30.71	11.04	68.53	244.46	106.50
2040.60	737.98	4888.41	15958.88	7771.37
79.43	26.37	200.91	1051.35	392.13
6.50	2.78	16.14	48.76	24.17
1137.06	454.12	2925.82	9392.13	4530.46
3251.25	1162.97	9975.53	29553.55	14408.53
1776.50	619.73	5760.81	17448.79	8562.76
1335.83	501.15	3895.04	11284.92	5506.65
1275.97	496.22	3245.50	10211.96	4869.58
3.75	**1.18**	**17.80**	**36.47**	**23.10**
2.98	0.78	9.27	22.06	15.84
0.14	0.08	6.11	10.03	4.11
4357.79	**1614.62**	**12035.51**	**37312.83**	**18072.07**
115.68	37.22	179.87	571.33	341.96
31.25	11.76	116.86	376.72	162.05
24.44	7.03	110.57	214.24	104.24
177.63	72.62	355.62	1090.40	545.33
70.43	31.56	188.33	551.76	241.22

11－10 续 表 1

单位:亿元

项 目	Item	企业单位数（个）Number of Enterprises (unit)	流动资产合计 Current Assets	应收账款 Accounts Receivalble
皮革、毛皮、羽毛及其制品和制鞋业	Manufacture of Leather, Fur, Feather and Related Products and Footwear	146	99.60	25.82
木材加工和木、竹、藤、棕、草制品业	Processing of Timber, Manufacture of Wood, Bamboo, Rattan, Palm and Straw Products	64	64.46	16.46
家具制造业	Manufacture of Furniture	65	52.36	20.46
造纸和纸制品业	Manufacture of Paper and Paper Products	104	566.22	148.92
印刷和记录媒介复制业	Printing, Reproduction of Recording Media	97	99.42	34.28
文教、工美、体育和娱乐用品制造业	Manufacture of Articles for Culture, Education, Arts and Crafts, Sport and Entertainment Activities	344	188.41	50.07
石油加工、炼焦和核燃料加工业	Processing of Petroleum, Coking, Processing of Nuclear Fuel	22	81.34	19.45
化学原料和化学制品制造业	Manufacture of Raw Chemical Materials and Chemical Products	879	2025.65	670.06
医药制造业	Manufacture of Medicines	153	551.50	152.53
化学纤维制造业	Manufacture of Chemical Fibers	70	217.51	27.98
橡胶和塑料制品业	Manufacture of Rubber and Plastics Products	536	588.42	229.23
非金属矿物制品业	Manufacture of Non-metallic Mineral Products	340	411.51	155.59
黑色金属冶炼和压延加工业	Smelting and Pressing of Ferrous Metals	148	476.60	84.69
有色金属冶炼和压延加工业	Smelting and Pressing of Non-ferrous Metals	159	264.11	89.71
金属制品业	Manufacture of Metal Products	509	647.72	222.46
通用设备制造业	Manufacture of General Purpose Machinery	886	1552.98	545.72
专用设备制造业	Manufacture of Special Purpose Machinery	680	1275.86	453.73
汽车制造业	Manufacture of Automobiles	593	1685.39	587.01
铁路、船舶、航空航天和其他运输设备制造业	Manufacture of Railway, Ship, Aerospace and Other Transport Equipments	200	750.80	157.26
电气机械和器材制造业	Manufacture of Electrical Machinery and Apparatus	803	2576.09	1073.95
计算机、通信和其他电子设备制造业	Manufacture of Computers, Communication and Other Electronic Equipment	1253	5191.26	2479.79
仪器仪表制造业	Manufacture of Measuring Instruments and Machinery	224	382.31	150.35
其他制造业	Other Manufacture	33	27.17	4.99
废弃资源综合利用业	Utilization of Waste Resources	26	12.29	2.28
金属制品、机械和设备修理业	Repair Service of Metal Products, Machinery and Equipment	2		
电力、热力、燃气及水的生产和供应业	**Production and Supply of Electric Power, Heat Power, Gas and Water**	**148**	**415.03**	**57.08**
电力、热力的生产和供应业	Production and Supply of Electric Power and Heat Power	62	199.86	34.21
燃气生产和供应	Production and Supply of Gas	57	169.60	18.51
水的生产和供应业	Production and Supply of Water	29	45.57	4.36

11－10 Continued 1

(100 million yuan)

存货 Inventory	#产成品 Finished Goods	固定资产合计 Original Value	资产总计 Total Assets	负债合计 Total Liabilities
26.97	8.87	54.34	187.87	73.49
18.63	10.12	41.77	114.61	49.31
13.65	4.11	29.86	93.35	35.39
61.96	23.88	385.07	1189.37	595.65
15.27	6.01	64.47	181.64	71.11
51.51	26.52	110.37	339.22	156.39
26.26	15.51	104.25	196.64	94.80
452.60	196.68	1900.10	4456.79	2039.24
117.83	56.97	224.44	907.70	360.99
46.21	20.40	197.63	488.21	227.94
132.95	55.58	435.29	1113.78	418.08
70.86	29.87	277.46	758.08	345.33
140.04	43.27	519.86	1163.38	695.49
71.59	28.64	144.44	459.60	225.16
151.16	63.54	314.06	1088.78	463.23
351.31	110.68	626.23	2387.93	1074.84
289.65	89.87	478.98	1997.34	967.99
296.58	125.99	927.72	2975.44	1638.01
190.95	39.51	269.48	1243.25	557.47
335.50	129.86	885.70	3895.69	2112.43
980.32	338.92	2911.99	8613.04	4178.65
91.18	28.18	149.66	576.49	252.56
3.61	0.92	20.38	50.97	30.62
1.57	0.53	10.55	28.14	12.10
26.77	**1.30**	**848.05**	**1596.38**	**843.82**
12.50	0.60	544.74	944.00	500.50
9.40	0.67	180.23	454.89	231.64
4.87	0.03	123.08	197.49	111.68

单位:亿元

项目	Item	所有者权益合计 Owners' Equities	#实收资本 Paid-in Capital
总计	**Total**	**19992.04**	**11746.95**
按登记注册类型分	**Grouped by Status of Registration**		
与港澳台商合资经营	Joint-venture Enterprises with Hong Kong Macao and Taiwan	2274.09	1142.14
与港澳台商合作经营	Cooperative Enterprises with Hong Kong, Macao and Taiwan	124.83	61.88
港澳台商独资	Enterprises with Sole Funds from Hong Kong, Macao and Taiwan	3900.90	2326.26
港澳台商投资股份有限公司	Share Holding with Hong Kong, Macao and Taiwan Investment	348.03	149.31
其他港澳台投资	Other Share Hold with Hong Kong. Macao and Taiwan Investment	22.61	8.69
中外合资经营	Joint-venture Enterprises with Foreign Funded	4314.31	2572.13
中外合作经营	Chinese-foreign Cooperative Enterprises	137.97	39.90
外资企业	Foreign Solely Funded	8185.74	5107.46
外商投资股份有限公司	Share Holding with Foreign Investment	659.22	319.01
其他外商投资	Others	24.34	20.16
按轻重工业分	**Grouped by Light & Heavy Industries**		
轻工业	Light Industry	4853.29	2871.73
重工业	Heavy Industry	15138.75	8875.23
按企业规模分	**Grouped by Size of Enterprises**		
大型企业	Large Enterprises	8886.03	4597.53
中型企业	Medium-sized Enterprises	5779.79	3423.55
小微型企业	Small Enterprises	5326.21	3725.87
按行业分	**Grouped by Sector**		
采矿业	**Mining**	**13.36**	**14.78**
煤炭开采和洗选业	Mining and Washing of Coal		
石油和天然气开采业	Extraction of Petroleum and Natural Gas		
黑色金属矿采选业	Mining and Processing of Ferrous Metal Ores	6.22	10.49
有色金属矿采选业	Mining and Processing of Non-ferrous Metals Ores		
非金属矿采选业	Mining and Processing of Non-metal Ores	5.92	2.75
开采辅助活动	Support Activities for Mining		
其他采矿业	Mining of Other Ores		
制造业	**Manufacturing**	**19226.58**	**11307.66**
农副食品加工业	Processing of Food from Agricultural Products	229.37	121.51
食品制造业	Manufacture of Food	214.66	129.77
酒、饮料和精制茶制造业	Manufacture of Liquor, Beverages and Refined Tea	109.99	86.78
烟草制品业	Manufacture of Tobacco		
纺织业	Manufacture of Textile	539.28	357.07
纺织服装、服饰业	Manufacture of Textile, Wearing Apparel and Accessories	310.21	144.96

11－10 Continued 2

(100 million yuan)

主营业务收入 Revenue from Principal Business	主营业务成本 Cost of Principle Business	利润总额 Total Profits	平均用工人数(万人) The Average Number of Employment (10000 Persons)
52043.03	**44595.83**	**3723.16**	**387.89**
6451.05	5532.69	501.86	41.44
209.37	172.47	23.04	1.38
9994.48	8646.88	723.42	97.81
647.07	536.03	64.66	5.16
44.29	34.46	5.06	0.41
11279.42	9514.81	913.15	60.86
312.07	262.86	27.77	2.05
22142.65	19150.52	1362.11	171.34
909.67	700.21	100.44	6.90
52.97	44.92	1.65	0.54
13080.68	10874.29	954.38	121.47
38962.35	33721.55	2768.78	266.43
25390.65	22191.87	1709.02	175.61
14350.06	12002.26	1155.38	119.67
12302.32	10401.70	858.75	92.62
34.15	**30.07**	**1.38**	**0.12**
23.05	21.31	0.08	0.03
7.49	5.91	0.88	0.05
51262.61	**43998.42**	**3566.23**	**384.86**
1188.47	1051.28	81.15	3.96
475.62	334.81	33.02	3.22
254.97	196.29	25.24	1.51
1454.16	1276.61	82.69	15.63
1267.58	1109.12	72.56	21.43

单位:亿元

项 目 Item		所有者权益合计 Owners' Equities	#实收资本 Paid-in Capital
皮革、毛皮、羽毛及其制品和制鞋业	Manufacture of Leather, Fur, Feather and Related Products and Footwear	113.79	42.15
木材加工和木、竹、藤、棕、草制品业	Processing of Timber, Manufacture of Wood, Bamboo, Rattan, Palm and Straw Products	65.30	31.66
家具制造业	Manufacture of Furniture	57.96	40.29
造纸和纸制品业	Manufacture of Paper and Paper Products	593.72	529.97
印刷和记录媒介复制业	Printing, Reproduction of Recording Media	109.67	66.12
文教、工美、体育和娱乐用品制造业	Manufacture of Articles for Culture, Education, Arts and Crafts, Sport and Entertainment Activities	182.62	91.78
石油加工、炼焦和核燃料加工业	Processing of Petroleum, Coking, Processing of Nuclear Fuel	101.84	34.44
化学原料和化学制品制造业	Manufacture of Raw Chemical Materials and Chemical Products	2416.60	1678.51
医药制造业	Manufacture of Medicines	546.71	243.58
化学纤维制造业	Manufacture of Chemical Fibers	260.27	183.71
橡胶和塑料制品业	Manufacture of Rubber and Plastics Products	694.85	428.11
非金属矿物制品业	Manufacture of Non-metallic Mineral Products	411.72	276.51
黑色金属冶炼和压延加工业	Smelting and Pressing of Ferrous Metals	467.89	282.57
有色金属冶炼和压延加工业	Smelting and Pressing of Non-ferrous Metals	234.37	189.67
金属制品业	Manufacture of Metal Products	626.93	348.27
通用设备制造业	Manufacture of General Purpose Machinery	1311.40	666.22
专用设备制造业	Manufacture of Special Purpose Machinery	1031.94	517.80
汽车制造业	Manufacture of Automobiles	1337.43	823.64
铁路、船舶、航空航天和其他运输设备制造业	Manufacture of Railway, Ship, Aerospace and Other Transport Equipments	685.77	186.24
电气机械和器材制造业	Manufacture of Electrical Machinery and Apparatus	1783.26	983.85
计算机、通信和其他电子设备制造业	Manufacture of Computers, Communication and Other Electronic Equipment	4428.66	2656.82
仪器仪表制造业	Manufacture of Measuring Instruments and Machinery	323.93	140.28
其他制造业	Other Manufacture	20.35	12.66
废弃资源综合利用业	Utilization of Waste Resources	16.04	12.54
金属制品、机械和设备修理业	Repair Service of Metal Products, Machinery and Equipment		
电力、热力、燃气及水的生产和供应业	**Production and Supply of Electric Power, Heat Power, Gas and Water**	**752.09**	**424.52**
电力、热力的生产和供应业	Production and Supply of Electric Power and Heat Power	443.02	265.67
燃气生产和供应	Production and Supply of Gas	223.25	97.34
水的生产和供应业	Production and Supply of Water	85.81	61.51

(100 million yuan)

主营业务收入 Revenue from Principal Business	主营业务成本 Cost of Principle Business	利润总额 Total Profits	平均用工人数(万人) The Average Number of Employment (10000 Persons)
419.30	360.58	26.85	5.75
257.18	219.18	17.51	1.93
99.48	83.68	6.04	1.94
814.79	687.48	53.13	4.04
186.82	146.76	17.00	2.75
683.18	586.51	47.73	10.01
396.91	339.83	35.12	0.86
6248.85	5382.94	453.90	17.94
995.12	533.03	158.68	6.54
423.04	349.34	42.32	3.24
1159.19	941.46	92.65	14.32
791.57	676.59	41.64	7.67
1804.71	1627.75	74.82	5.65
719.93	651.82	30.86	3.04
1318.72	1131.66	85.51	12.53
2664.38	2118.82	270.36	23.00
1814.57	1465.30	149.91	17.80
4209.41	3370.25	417.65	20.38
1060.39	874.38	134.69	10.47
5191.34	4484.04	366.24	34.36
14328.83	13124.05	662.81	126.96
923.61	781.59	78.45	6.58
67.56	57.62	4.17	1.11
41.03	33.93	3.55	0.22
746.27	**567.35**	**155.54**	**2.92**
393.39	289.10	94.23	1.20
321.44	257.66	52.24	1.23
31.43	20.58	9.07	0.48

11－11 外商投资和港澳台商投资工业企业主要经济效益指标(2016 年)

单位:%

项　　目	Item	企业亏损面 Percentage of Loss Making Enterprises
总　计	**Total**	**18.99**
按登记注册类型分	**Grouped by Status of Registration**	
与港澳台商合资经营	Joint-venture Enterprises with Hong Kong Macao and Taiwan	16.10
与港澳台商合作经营	Cooperative Enterprises with Hong Kong, Macao and Taiwan	14.63
港澳台商独资	Enterprises with Sole Funds from Hong Kong, Macao and Taiwan	18.74
港澳台商投资股份有限公司	Share Holding with Hong Kong, Macao and Taiwan Investment	17.50
其他港澳台投资	Other Share Hold with Hong Kong. Macao and Taiwan Investment	25.00
中外合资经营	Joint-venture Enterprises with Foreign Funded	14.80
中外合作经营	Chinese-foreign Cooperative Enterprises	11.11
外资企业	Foreign Solely Funded	21.72
外商投资股份有限公司	Share Holding with Foreign Investment	20.99
其他外商投资	Others	29.41
按轻重工业分	**Grouped by Light & Heavy Industries**	
轻工业	Light Industry	17.05
重工业	Heavy Industry	20.02
按企业规模分	**Grouped by Size of Enterprises**	
大型企业	Large Enterprises	7.76
中型企业	Medium-sized Enterprises	13.69
小微型企业	Small Enterprises	21.51
按行业分	**Grouped by Sector**	
采矿业	**Mining**	**12.50**
煤炭开采和洗选业	Mining and Washing of Coal	
石油和天然气开采业	Extraction of Petroleum and Natural Gas	
黑色金属矿采选业	Mining and Processing of Ferrous Metal Ores	33.33
有色金属矿采选业	Mining and Processing of Non-ferrous Metals Ores	
非金属矿采选业	Mining and Processing of Non-metal Ores	0.00
开采辅助活动	Support Activities for Mining	
其他采矿业	Mining of Other Ores	
制造业	**Manufacturing**	**19.15**
农副食品加工业	Processing of Food from Agricultural Products	11.80
食品制造业	Manufacture of Food	26.21
酒、饮料和精制茶制造业	Manufacture of Liquor, Beverages and Refined Tea	25.00
烟草制品业	Manufacture of Tobacco	
纺织业	Manufacture of Textile	17.28
纺织服装、服饰业	Manufacture of Textile, Wearing Apparel and Accessories	15.31

Main Indicators on Economic Benefit of Industrial Enterprises with Hong Kong, Macao, Taiwan and Foreign Funds (2016)

(%)

资产负债率 Assets Liability Ratio	流动资产周转次数(次/年) Times of Turnover of Circulating Funds (times/year)	成本费用利润率 Ratio of Profits to Industrial Cost	产品销售率 Proportion of Products Sold	总资产贡献率 Ratio of Total Assets to Industrial Output Value
48.63	**2.44**	**7.62**	**98.67**	**13.94**
53.89	3.01	8.16	98.31	15.83
41.60	2.20	12.26	95.29	16.22
46.72	2.39	7.75	99.04	13.38
35.54	2.23	11.01	97.51	15.33
41.16	1.65	12.94	100.83	16.99
49.68	2.62	8.73	98.71	16.96
43.56	2.56	9.65	101.71	17.63
48.70	2.30	6.49	98.62	11.89
37.30	1.72	12.23	98.17	13.64
49.58	1.98	3.19	99.17	9.29
48.24	2.52	7.79	98.88	15.47
48.75	2.41	7.56	98.60	13.46
49.07	2.66	7.16	98.11	13.80
48.80	2.37	8.58	99.21	14.99
47.69	2.14	7.42	99.19	13.03
63.35	**2.11**	**4.06**	**104.13**	**5.99**
71.81	2.10	0.32	106.07	0.11
40.99	2.31	13.60	100.47	14.92
48.43	**2.45**	**7.40**	**98.65**	**13.99**
59.85	3.76	7.28	99.65	20.67
43.02	2.85	7.28	96.61	14.08
48.66	3.13	10.92	96.46	20.07
50.01	2.37	5.94	98.97	12.72
43.72	4.42	6.10	99.39	23.01

单位:%

项 目 Item		企业亏损面 Percentage of Loss Making Enterprises
皮革、毛皮、羽毛及其制品和制鞋业	Manufacture of Leather, Fur, Feather and Related Products and Footwear	17.81
木材加工和木、竹、藤、棕、草制品业	Processing of Timber, Manufacture of Wood, Bamboo, Rattan, Palm and Straw Products	17.19
家具制造业	Manufacture of Furniture	24.62
造纸和纸制品业	Manufacture of Paper and Paper Products	26.92
印刷和记录媒介复制业	Printing, Reproduction of Recording Media	25.77
文教、工美、体育和娱乐用品制造业	Manufacture of Articles for Culture, Education, Arts and Crafts, Sport and Entertainment Activities	10.47
石油加工、炼焦和核燃料加工业	Processing of Petroleum, Coking, Processing of Nuclear Fuel	22.73
化学原料和化学制品制造业	Manufacture of Raw Chemical Materials and Chemical Products	17.52
医药制造业	Manufacture of Medicines	11.11
化学纤维制造业	Manufacture of Chemical Fibers	21.43
橡胶和塑料制品业	Manufacture of Rubber and Plastics Products	21.64
非金属矿物制品业	Manufacture of Non-metallic Mineral Products	29.71
黑色金属冶炼和压延加工业	Smelting and Pressing of Ferrous Metals	22.30
有色金属冶炼和压延加工业	Smelting and Pressing of Non-ferrous Metals	22.64
金属制品业	Manufacture of Metal Products	19.65
通用设备制造业	Manufacture of General Purpose Machinery	17.27
专用设备制造业	Manufacture of Special Purpose Machinery	22.79
汽车制造业	Manufacture of Automobiles	18.89
铁路、船舶、航空航天和其他运输设备制造业	Manufacture of Railway, Ship, Aerospace and Other Transport Equipments	14.00
电气机械和器材制造业	Manufacture of Electrical Machinery and Apparatus	16.94
计算机、通信和其他电子设备制造业	Manufacture of Computers, Communication and Other Electronic Equipment	22.43
仪器仪表制造业	Manufacture of Measuring Instruments and Machinery	15.18
其他制造业	Other Manufacture	15.15
废弃资源综合利用业	Utilization of Waste Resources	34.62
金属制品、机械和设备修理业	Repair Service of Metal Products, Machinery and Equipment	
电力、热力、燃气及水的生产和供应业	**Production and Supply of Electric Power, Heat Power, Gas and Water**	**8.11**
电力、热力的生产和供应业	Production and Supply of Electric Power and Heat Power	14.52
燃气生产和供应	Production and Supply of Gas	0.00
水的生产和供应业	Production and Supply of Water	10.34

(%)

资产负债率 Assets Liability Ratio	流动资产周转次数(次/年) Times of Turnover of Circulating Funds (times/year)	成本费用利润率 Ratio of Profits to Industrial Cost	产品销售率 Proportion of Products Sold	总资产贡献率 Ratio of Total Assets to Industrial Output Value
39.12	4.22	6.89	96.92	25.34
43.02	4.02	7.36	100.13	25.71
37.91	1.92	6.36	103.19	9.56
50.08	1.47	6.78	100.25	7.32
39.15	1.89	10.00	99.35	14.23
46.10	3.66	7.47	100.03	22.12
48.21	4.89	9.83	100.86	25.78
45.76	3.12	7.78	98.80	15.13
39.77	1.82	19.00	96.77	26.90
46.69	1.98	10.98	98.58	13.33
37.54	1.99	8.65	99.84	12.28
45.55	1.95	5.51	100.85	10.27
59.78	4.22	3.94	96.06	11.15
48.99	2.75	4.45	100.59	11.37
42.55	2.06	6.85	98.22	12.08
45.01	1.73	11.23	99.85	15.00
48.46	1.45	8.92	99.11	10.52
55.05	2.57	10.97	98.52	23.68
44.84	1.43	14.23	99.99	13.77
54.22	2.05	7.47	99.19	13.36
48.52	2.78	4.83	97.88	9.53
43.81	2.45	9.17	99.96	18.22
60.07	2.49	6.69	98.29	15.66
43.01	3.38	9.45	100.26	17.09
52.86	**1.90**	**24.13**	**99.53**	**13.12**
53.02	2.02	29.64	99.53	14.17
50.92	2.02	17.84	99.81	13.89
56.55	0.89	26.81	96.67	6.29

11－12 大中型工业企业主要经济指标(2016 年)

单位:亿元

项目	Item	企业单位数(个) Number of Enterprises (unit)	流动资产合计 Current Assets	应收账款 Accounts Receivalble
总计	**Total**	**7267**	**39008.68**	**11858.34**
按登记注册类型分	**Grouped by Status of Registration**			
内资企业	Domestic Funded Enterprises	4484	23147.42	6015.20
国有企业	State-owned Enterprises	29	493.79	84.10
集体企业	Collective-owned Enterprises	26	184.15	36.12
股份合作企业	Cooperative Enterprises	7	16.48	3.58
联营企业	Joint Ownership Enterprises	1		
有限责任公司	Limited Liability Corporations	1057	8755.73	2423.85
#国有独资	State Sole Funded Corporatios	88	2121.00	517.07
股份有限公司	Share-holding Corporations Ltd.	415	5022.84	1208.34
私营企业	Private Enterprises	2945	8667.86	2256.37
其他企业	Other Enterprises	4	5.97	2.65
港、澳、台商投资企业	Enterprises with Funds from Hong Kong, Macao and Taiwan	1017	4975.04	1751.19
外商投资企业	Foreign Funded Enterprises	1766	10886.22	4091.95
按轻重工业分	**Grouped by Light & Heavy Industries**			
轻工业	Light Industry	2728	9998.68	2360.63
重工业	Heavy Industry	4539	29010.00	9497.72
按行业分	**Grouped by Sector**			
采矿业	**Mining**	**30**	**293.77**	**43.61**
煤炭开采和洗选业	Mining and Washing of Coal	5	168.31	32.81
石油和天然气开采业	Extraction of Petroleum and Natural Gas	2		
黑色金属矿采选业	Mining and Processing of Ferrous Metal Ores	2		
有色金属矿采选业	Mining and Processing of Non-ferrous Metals Ores	1		
非金属矿采选业	Mining and Processing of Non-metal Ores	20	83.97	5.68
开采辅助活动	Support Activities for Mining			
其他采矿业	Mining of Other Ores			
制造业	**Manufacturing**	**7148**	**37845.56**	**11700.56**
农副食品加工业	Processing of Food from Agricultural Products	133	347.66	74.81
食品制造业	Manufacture of Food	72	177.67	45.40
酒、饮料和精制茶制造业	Manufacture of Liquor, Beverages and Refined Tea	41	548.20	71.42
烟草制品业	Manufacture of Tobacco	4	473.53	22.68
纺织业	Manufacture of Textile	523	1209.80	266.36
纺织服装、服饰业	Manufacture of Textile, Wearing Apparel and Accessories	554	1074.80	204.68
皮革、毛皮、羽毛及其制品和制鞋业	Manufacture of Leather, Fur, Feather and Related Products and Footwear	118	107.34	28.04
木材加工和木、竹、藤、棕、草制品业	Processing of Timber, Manufacture of Wood, Bamboo, Rattan, Palm and Straw Products	117	169.92	32.64
家具制造业	Manufacture of Furniture	44	54.56	16.75
造纸和纸制品业	Manufacture of Paper and Paper Products	60	607.68	145.17

Main Economic Indicators of Big and Medium Size Industrial Enterprises (2016)

(100 million yuan)

存货 Inventory	#产成品 Finished Goods	固定资产合计 Original Value	资产总计 Total Assets	负债合计 Total Liabilities
8322.44	**3025.62**	**26385.63**	**77179.63**	**40349.34**
5210.10	1904.75	16729.78	48445.92	26279.93
55.83	10.39	2413.74	3608.28	2114.20
28.47	17.42	63.43	306.99	168.58
5.67	4.35	9.39	28.05	14.37
1987.42	696.48	5948.67	17948.36	10549.30
595.23	144.94	1497.50	4357.02	2512.57
1124.40	357.57	2654.12	9675.87	4478.19
2006.27	817.71	5627.48	16854.99	8943.24
1.73	0.59	12.71	22.38	11.23
967.24	352.36	3515.60	9677.80	4815.67
2145.10	768.51	6140.25	19055.92	9253.74
2388.36	872.57	5664.85	18591.71	8841.14
5934.08	2153.06	20720.78	58587.92	31508.20
45.87	**17.12**	**572.83**	**1104.09**	**670.74**
29.36	10.50	331.58	673.26	410.92
10.70	4.67	98.18	205.10	120.44
8204.24	**3007.22**	**21720.24**	**69629.74**	**35754.51**
114.03	44.68	309.69	749.15	418.97
37.27	14.23	146.34	427.88	198.63
210.88	33.43	222.17	916.03	348.09
233.22	4.08	54.71	589.56	64.95
339.16	137.28	783.15	2378.73	1181.50
286.82	151.67	503.42	1961.98	1020.57
27.36	9.77	60.78	203.76	86.25
56.89	24.67	137.29	355.34	164.06
14.39	3.67	36.38	106.40	43.34
74.34	30.81	453.04	1313.48	666.43

单位:亿元

项 目	Item	企业单位数(个) Number of Enterprises (unit)	流动资产合计 Current Assets	应收账款 Accounts Receivalble
印刷和记录媒介复制业	Printing, Reproduction of Recording Media	63	135.30	49.48
文教、工美、体育和娱乐用品制造业	Manufacture of Articles for Culture, Education, Arts and Crafts, Sport and Entertainment Activities	218	239.56	50.03
石油加工、炼焦和核燃料加工业	Processing of Petroleum, Coking, Processing of Nuclear Fuel	26	301.83	49.59
化学原料和化学制品制造业	Manufacture of Raw Chemical Materials and Chemical Products	467	3250.16	853.76
医药制造业	Manufacture of Medicines	164	1180.02	374.04
化学纤维制造业	Manufacture of Chemical Fibers	100	878.53	96.52
橡胶和塑料制品业	Manufacture of Rubber and Plastics Products	249	537.28	201.11
非金属矿物制品业	Manufacture of Non-metallic Mineral Products	229	648.40	189.20
黑色金属冶炼和压延加工业	Smelting and Pressing of Ferrous Metals	168	2420.53	236.86
有色金属冶炼和压延加工业	Smelting and Pressing of Non-ferrous Metals	112	563.26	141.19
金属制品业	Manufacture of Metal Products	324	1139.22	363.32
通用设备制造业	Manufacture of General Purpose Machinery	507	2927.52	1067.64
专用设备制造业	Manufacture of Special Purpose Machinery	397	1771.00	628.25
汽车制造业	Manufacture of Automobiles	379	2432.61	843.66
铁路、船舶、航空航天和其他运输设备制造业	Manufacture of Railway, Ship, Aerospace and Other Transport Equipments	170	1656.20	348.02
电气机械和器材制造业	Manufacture of Electrical Machinery and Apparatus	744	5632.10	2213.83
计算机、通信和其他电子设备制造业	Manufacture of Computers, Communication and Other Electronic Equipment	930	6187.04	2726.71
仪器仪表制造业	Manufacture of Measuring Instruments and Machinery	194	1111.23	344.82
其他制造业	Other Manufacture	29	51.67	10.54
废弃资源综合利用业	Utilization of Waste Resources	9	8.48	3.19
金属制品、机械和设备修理业	Repair Service of Metal Products, Machinery and Equipment	3	2.45	0.86
电力、热力、燃气及水的生产和供应业	**Production and Supply of Electric Power, Heat Power, Gas and Water**	**89**	**869.35**	**114.17**
电力、热力的生产和供应业	Production and Supply of Electric Power and Heat Power	44	562.31	99.71
燃气生产和供应	Production and Supply of Gas	15	61.45	7.91
水的生产和供应业	Production and Supply of Water	30	245.59	6.55

(100 million yuan)

存货 Inventory	#产成品 Finished Goods	固定资产合计 Original Value	资产总计 Total Assets	负债合计 Total Liabilities
24.59	10.53	81.96	248.02	101.95
66.99	34.84	151.18	462.07	224.88
115.82	40.12	378.31	758.49	459.56
738.86	275.56	2990.12	7421.68	3618.82
225.20	86.31	548.67	2139.11	721.35
214.22	94.00	711.08	1874.35	1049.19
125.29	55.63	409.86	1056.66	362.54
111.06	45.07	556.68	1373.45	732.93
658.54	228.12	2321.50	5557.43	3419.57
149.70	52.70	309.88	1122.86	627.82
262.00	103.78	555.40	2084.60	1053.64
591.80	266.09	1125.28	4818.48	2503.76
387.52	132.66	709.84	2893.15	1496.63
401.88	187.06	1089.39	4070.39	2472.08
495.57	97.84	679.44	2773.46	1556.73
798.58	372.03	2071.31	9036.76	4834.98
1211.24	393.06	3749.75	10903.16	5398.38
218.43	72.73	505.46	1891.04	850.65
9.69	3.71	40.86	99.40	50.44
2.22	0.92	22.26	34.68	20.81
0.65	0.15	5.04	8.18	5.02
72.32	**1.29**	**4092.57**	**6445.81**	**3924.09**
55.80	0.59	3563.14	5478.89	3313.54
7.57	0.25	94.60	198.08	108.39
8.95	0.45	434.83	768.84	502.16

单位:亿元

项 目	Item	所有者权益合计 Owners' Equities	#实收资本 Paid-in Capital
总 计	**Total**	**36831.81**	**16206.19**
按登记注册类型分	**Grouped by Status of Registration**		
内资企业	Domestic Funded Enterprises	22165.99	8185.11
国有企业	State-owned Enterprises	1494.08	954.03
集体企业	Collective-owned Enterprises	138.40	61.88
股份合作企业	Cooperative Enterprises	13.68	1.65
联营企业	Joint Ownership Enterprises		
有限责任公司	Limited Liability Corporations	7399.05	2807.33
#国有独资	State Sole Funded Corporatios	1844.44	539.56
股份有限公司	Share-holding Corporations Ltd.	5197.68	1854.21
私营企业	Private Enterprises	7911.75	2501.64
其他企业	Other Enterprises	11.15	4.30
港、澳、台商投资企业	Enterprises with Funds from Hong Kong, Macao and Taiwan	4862.12	2485.66
外商投资企业	Foreign Funded Enterprises	9803.70	5535.42
按轻重工业分	**Grouped by Light & Heavy Industries**		
轻工业	Light Industry	9750.57	3810.83
重工业	Heavy Industry	27081.24	12395.36
按行业分	**Grouped by Sector**		
采矿业	**Mining**	**433.34**	**229.72**
煤炭开采和洗选业	Mining and Washing of Coal	262.34	60.91
石油和天然气开采业	Extraction of Petroleum and Natural Gas		
黑色金属矿采选业	Mining and Processing of Ferrous Metal Ores		
有色金属矿采选业	Mining and Processing of Non-ferrous Metals Ores		
非金属矿采选业	Mining and Processing of Non-metal Ores	84.66	37.19
开采辅助活动	Support Activities for Mining		
其他采矿业	Mining of Other Ores		
制造业	**Manufacturing**	**33876.74**	**14404.82**
农副食品加工业	Processing of Food from Agricultural Products	330.18	106.17
食品制造业	Manufacture of Food	229.25	108.54
酒、饮料和精制茶制造业	Manufacture of Liquor, Beverages and Refined Tea	567.94	144.97
烟草制品业	Manufacture of Tobacco	524.61	11.92
纺织业	Manufacture of Textile	1197.23	533.55
纺织服装、服饰业	Manufacture of Textile, Wearing Apparel and Accessories	941.41	320.28
皮革、毛皮、羽毛及其制品和制鞋业	Manufacture of Leather, Fur, Feather and Related Products and Footwear	117.51	35.81
木材加工和木、竹、藤、棕、草制品业	Processing of Timber, Manufacture of Wood, Bamboo, Rattan, Palm and Straw Products	191.28	48.45
家具制造业	Manufacture of Furniture	63.06	32.44
造纸和纸制品业	Manufacture of Paper and Paper Products	647.05	537.63

(100 million yuan)

主营业务收入 Revenue from Principal Business	主营业务成本 Cost of Principle Business	利润总额 Total Profits	平均用工人数（万人） The Average Number of Employment (10000 Persons)
97776.58	**83291.62**	**6860.89**	**671.62**
58035.87	49097.49	3996.48	376.34
3157.15	3003.49	78.43	7.51
350.99	310.76	21.52	2.66
54.65	47.30	4.47	0.35
17623.09	14569.67	1081.82	111.75
2375.20	1669.12	172.68	17.21
8032.53	6300.45	771.64	53.52
28782.60	24835.84	2035.97	200.34
33.04	28.57	2.50	0.17
13258.07	11403.66	1044.56	113.61
26482.65	22790.48	1819.85	181.67
25126.04	20327.67	1953.21	224.10
72650.54	62963.95	4907.68	447.52
363.88	**311.49**	**-43.71**	**8.86**
175.54	132.27	5.52	5.88
116.14	96.94	6.91	1.71
93360.94	**79359.31**	**6555.77**	**652.28**
1987.50	1726.08	139.51	8.52
666.96	494.15	49.18	5.24
808.95	553.67	152.27	6.05
530.05	112.15	84.90	0.58
3340.61	2962.45	191.36	38.75
2877.52	2442.78	213.11	44.36
522.64	447.96	33.60	7.91
906.40	783.96	59.82	6.61
138.03	117.30	8.38	2.44
993.29	843.84	66.77	5.36

单位:亿元

项 目 Item		所有者权益合计 Owners' Equities	#实收资本 Paid-in Capital
印刷和记录媒介复制业	Printing, Reproduction of Recording Media	146.07	52.10
文教、工美、体育和娱乐用品制造业	Manufacture of Articles for Culture, Education, Arts and Crafts, Sport and Entertainment Activities	237.18	92.34
石油加工、炼焦和核燃料加工业	Processing of Petroleum, Coking, Processing of Nuclear Fuel	298.93	159.12
化学原料和化学制品制造业	Manufacture of Raw Chemical Materials and Chemical Products	3802.86	1952.50
医药制造业	Manufacture of Medicines	1417.76	355.59
化学纤维制造业	Manufacture of Chemical Fibers	825.16	459.59
橡胶和塑料制品业	Manufacture of Rubber and Plastics Products	694.12	316.04
非金属矿物制品业	Manufacture of Non-metallic Mineral Products	640.52	284.90
黑色金属冶炼和压延加工业	Smelting and Pressing of Ferrous Metals	2137.86	723.07
有色金属冶炼和压延加工业	Smelting and Pressing of Non-ferrous Metals	495.05	192.48
金属制品业	Manufacture of Metal Products	1032.48	416.08
通用设备制造业	Manufacture of General Purpose Machinery	2314.71	792.14
专用设备制造业	Manufacture of Special Purpose Machinery	1396.52	511.96
汽车制造业	Manufacture of Automobiles	1598.31	913.32
铁路、船舶、航空航天和其他运输设备制造业	Manufacture of Railway, Ship, Aerospace and Other Transport Equipments	1216.73	390.01
电气机械和器材制造业	Manufacture of Electrical Machinery and Apparatus	4201.78	1722.31
计算机、通信和其他电子设备制造业	Manufacture of Computers, Communication and Other Electronic Equipment	5504.78	2921.38
仪器仪表制造业	Manufacture of Measuring Instruments and Machinery	1040.39	250.58
其他制造业	Other Manufacture	48.96	14.29
废弃资源综合利用业	Utilization of Waste Resources	13.86	4.45
金属制品、机械和设备修理业	Repair Service of Metal Products, Machinery and Equipment	3.16	0.78
电力、热力、燃气及水的生产和供应业	**Production and Supply of Electric Power, Heat Power, Gas and Water**	**2521.72**	**1571.66**
电力、热力的生产和供应业	Production and Supply of Electric Power and Heat Power	2165.35	1382.40
燃气生产和供应	Production and Supply of Gas	89.69	29.73
水的生产和供应业	Production and Supply of Water	266.68	159.52

(100 million yuan)

主营业务收入 Revenue from Principal Business	主营业务成本 Cost of Principle Business	利润总额 Total Profits	平均用工人数（万人） The Average Number of Employment (10000 Persons)
288.70	231.66	27.82	4.36
1043.24	892.40	69.18	14.21
1649.28	1317.50	94.68	2.83
10903.96	9291.50	859.85	40.45
2794.62	1630.74	324.76	15.56
1987.53	1796.45	87.43	12.00
1243.71	1020.32	104.76	16.03
1640.36	1401.20	120.53	14.54
7668.83	6908.53	308.80	25.36
1927.82	1750.08	86.42	8.52
2733.33	2358.01	181.39	22.37
4556.71	3693.47	412.00	38.54
3284.10	2666.80	275.90	25.78
5245.02	4366.09	380.30	29.22
2755.82	2334.27	253.91	22.90
11528.66	9836.68	876.79	68.89
16576.70	15067.49	838.15	147.01
2453.64	2039.72	236.21	14.65
192.44	169.34	10.66	2.63
104.09	93.66	6.60	0.49
10.44	9.06	0.75	0.12
4051.76	**3620.82**	**348.83**	**10.48**
3816.82	3454.68	313.25	7.63
150.07	114.05	25.08	0.87
84.87	52.09	10.50	1.98

11－13 大中型工业企业主要经济效益指标（2016 年）

单位：%

项目	Item	企业亏损面 Percentage of Loss Making Enterprises
总 计	**Total**	**8.82**
按登记注册类型分	**Grouped by Status of Registration**	
内资企业	Domestic Funded Enterprises	6.60
国有企业	State-owned Enterprises	20.69
集体企业	Collective-owned Enterprises	0.00
股份合作企业	Cooperative Enterprises	14.29
联营企业	Joint Ownership Enterprises	
有限责任公司	Limited Liability Corporations	11.45
#国有独资	State Sole Funded Corporatios	12.50
股份有限公司	Share-holding Corporations Ltd.	8.19
私营企业	Private Enterprises	4.55
其他企业	Other Enterprises	0.00
港、澳、台商投资企业	Enterprises with Funds from Hong Kong, Macao and Taiwan	11.60
外商投资企业	Foreign Funded Enterprises	12.85
按轻重工业分	**Grouped by Light & Heavy Industries**	
轻工业	Light Industry	8.21
重工业	Heavy Industry	9.19
按行业分	**Grouped by Sector**	
采矿业	**Mining**	**20.00**
煤炭开采和洗选业	Mining and Washing of Coal	0.00
石油和天然气开采业	Extraction of Petroleum and Natural Gas	
黑色金属矿采选业	Mining and Processing of Ferrous Metal Ores	
有色金属矿采选业	Mining and Processing of Non-ferrous Metals Ores	
非金属矿采选业	Mining and Processing of Non-metal Ores	15.00
开采辅助活动	Support Activities for Mining	
其他采矿业	Mining of Other Ores	
制造业	**Manufacturing**	**8.81**
农副食品加工业	Processing of Food from Agricultural Products	1.50
食品制造业	Manufacture of Food	5.56
酒、饮料和精制茶制造业	Manufacture of Liquor, Beverages and Refined Tea	21.95
烟草制品业	Manufacture of Tobacco	0.00
纺织业	Manufacture of Textile	8.03
纺织服装、服饰业	Manufacture of Textile, Wearing Apparel and Accessories	9.93
皮革、毛皮、羽毛及其制品和制鞋业	Manufacture of Leather, Fur, Feather and Related Products and Footwear	8.47
木材加工和木、竹、藤、棕、草制品业	Processing of Timber, Manufacture of Wood, Bamboo, Rattan, Palm and Straw Products	1.71
家具制造业	Manufacture of Furniture	18.18
造纸和纸制品业	Manufacture of Paper and Paper Products	10.00

Main Indicators on Economic Benefit of Big and Medium Size Industrial Enterprises (2016)

(%)

资产负债率 Assets Liability Ratio	流动资产周转次数(次/年) Times of Turnover of Circulating Funds (times/year)	成本费用利润率 Ratio of Profits to Industrial Cost	产品销售率 Proportion of Products Sold	总资产贡献率 Ratio of Total Assets to Industrial Output Value
52.28	**2.59**	**7.37**	**98.95**	**14.80**
54.25	2.62	7.17	99.27	15.11
58.59	6.45	2.55	99.80	6.55
54.92	1.91	6.53	99.71	11.99
51.22	3.32	8.88	98.68	27.97
58.78	2.17	6.19	99.69	12.61
57.67	1.60	5.93	99.07	15.39
46.28	1.67	10.45	97.43	14.94
53.06	3.42	7.43	99.49	19.74
50.20	5.54	8.14	99.89	17.10
49.76	2.72	8.39	98.56	15.11
48.56	2.47	7.31	98.47	13.84
47.55	2.58	8.32	98.78	18.45
53.78	2.59	7.05	99.02	13.64
60.75	**2.67**	**-5.49**	**100.16**	**0.12**
61.03	3.49	0.96	101.22	4.15
58.72	1.41	6.13	97.33	8.16
51.35	**2.54**	**7.41**	**98.91**	**15.52**
55.93	5.72	7.60	101.03	28.99
46.42	3.80	7.79	97.17	18.88
38.00	1.48	22.98	97.66	24.15
11.02	1.38	33.48	97.67	79.29
49.67	2.87	5.85	98.27	14.28
52.02	2.81	7.61	99.18	17.65
42.33	4.88	6.92	97.31	29.51
46.17	5.36	7.07	100.03	30.33
40.73	2.55	6.44	100.49	12.48
50.74	1.67	7.03	100.53	8.41

单位:%

项 目	Item	企业亏损面 Percentage of Loss Making Enterprises
印刷和记录媒介复制业	Printing, Reproduction of Recording Media	6.35
文教、工美、体育和娱乐用品制造业	Manufacture of Articles for Culture, Education, Arts and Crafts, Sport and Entertainment Activities	4.59
石油加工、炼焦和核燃料加工业	Processing of Petroleum, Coking, Processing of Nuclear Fuel	7.69
化学原料和化学制品制造业	Manufacture of Raw Chemical Materials and Chemical Products	7.28
医药制造业	Manufacture of Medicines	6.10
化学纤维制造业	Manufacture of Chemical Fibers	16.00
橡胶和塑料制品业	Manufacture of Rubber and Plastics Products	8.03
非金属矿物制品业	Manufacture of Non-metallic Mineral Products	9.61
黑色金属冶炼和压延加工业	Smelting and Pressing of Ferrous Metals	8.33
有色金属冶炼和压延加工业	Smelting and Pressing of Non-ferrous Metals	8.04
金属制品业	Manufacture of Metal Products	8.33
通用设备制造业	Manufacture of General Purpose Machinery	7.30
专用设备制造业	Manufacture of Special Purpose Machinery	8.82
汽车制造业	Manufacture of Automobiles	10.55
铁路、船舶、航空航天和其他运输设备制造业	Manufacture of Railway, Ship, Aerospace and Other Transport Equipments	8.24
电气机械和器材制造业	Manufacture of Electrical Machinery and Apparatus	6.59
计算机、通信和其他电子设备制造业	Manufacture of Computers, Communication and Other Electronic Equipment	14.95
仪器仪表制造业	Manufacture of Measuring Instruments and Machinery	4.64
其他制造业	Other Manufacture	0.00
废弃资源综合利用业	Utilization of Waste Resources	0.00
金属制品、机械和设备修理业	Repair Service of Metal Products, Machinery and Equipment	33.33
电力、热力、燃气及水的生产和供应业	**Production and Supply of Electric Power, Heat Power, Gas and Water**	**5.62**
电力、热力的生产和供应业	Production and Supply of Electric Power and Heat Power	0.00
燃气生产和供应	Production and Supply of Gas	6.67
水的生产和供应业	Production and Supply of Water	13.33

(%)

资产负债率 Assets Liability Ratio	流动资产周转次数(次/年) Times of Turnover of Circulating Funds (times/year)	成本费用利润率 Ratio of Profits to Industrial Cost	产品销售率 Proportion of Products Sold	总资产贡献率 Ratio of Total Assets to Industrial Output Value
41.11	2.16	10.59	98.96	17.00
48.67	4.40	7.06	99.99	24.49
60.59	5.47	6.91	100.18	47.39
48.76	3.40	8.52	99.33	18.88
33.72	2.38	13.15	97.30	24.26
55.98	2.34	4.44	97.41	8.80
34.31	2.33	9.17	99.27	14.77
53.36	2.55	7.88	98.82	15.29
61.53	3.46	3.90	99.08	10.36
55.91	3.57	4.50	99.69	13.43
50.54	2.53	6.76	98.68	14.06
51.96	1.72	8.94	99.25	12.74
51.73	1.91	8.98	100.70	14.67
60.73	2.19	7.83	98.27	16.94
56.13	1.68	10.05	99.51	12.87
53.50	2.08	8.11	98.99	14.59
49.51	2.70	5.29	98.16	10.00
44.98	2.24	10.47	99.92	17.54
50.74	3.73	5.92	97.64	20.08
60.02	12.28	6.79	97.27	28.77
61.33	4.26	7.81	99.32	17.95
60.88	**4.76**	**9.17**	**99.88**	**9.50**
60.48	6.88	8.80	99.91	10.27
54.72	2.65	18.23	99.68	14.90
65.31	0.45	9.94	98.70	2.66

11－14 主要年份工业主要产品产量
Output of Main Industrial Products in Major Years

年份 Year	原煤 (万吨) Coal (100000 tons)	发电量 (亿千瓦时) Electricity (100 million kW·h)	钢材 (万吨) Rolled Steel (10000 tons)	水泥 (万吨) Cement (10000 tons)	农用化肥 (万吨) Chemical Fertilizer (10000 tons)	布 (亿米) Cloth (100 million m)	化学纤维 (万吨) Chemical Fiber (10000 tons)	汽车 (辆) Motor Vehicles (units)
1949	81.49	1.98	0.03	3.10	0.38	2.32		
1952	113.21	4.10	0.19	36.90	1.32	6.10		
1957	193.11	7.08	0.27	80.70	3.63	6.97		
1962	462.70	15.43	6.19	58.60	10.09	3.20		452
1965	485.66	25.78	18.48	103.00	20.25	6.76	0.54	2350
1970	699.17	49.96	18.36	163.12	28.21	9.60	0.52	7472
1975	1143.75	81.80	44.09	274.16	41.82	11.68	0.88	13932
1978	1707.02	126.42	60.31	444.10	72.18	14.06	2.11	15079
1980	1690.00	156.32	104.87	629.00	111.61	17.97	3.26	19624
1985	2193.85	234.48	145.18	1116.90	121.71	21.05	12.52	24474
1990	2407.79	404.47	203.01	1532.89	145.90	28.91	40.76	46291
1991	2470.55	441.20	247.76	1823.18	147.33	27.01	48.15	64045
1992	2457.76	481.15	387.51	2275.59	144.63	29.04	55.09	101009
1993	2505.53	536.84	466.02	2660.50	133.69	30.19	66.18	124334
1994	2503.44	631.90	674.19	3087.38	153.09	32.71	78.09	129957
1995	2650.72	700.41	787.89	3966.42	191.85	48.90	102.20	125197
1996	2606.52	756.87	795.58	4040.28	184.30	34.55	105.94	110157
1997	2506.01	777.00	856.79	4031.73	187.98	40.46	139.11	104801
1998	2378.53	754.27	933.63	3856.30	170.12	31.72	140.94	89828
1999	2291.97	787.06	1170.25	4378.32	171.27	31.76	170.06	91300
2000	2479.02	909.69	1401.83	4599.52	192.38	33.74	190.99	90636
2001	2451.14	986.64	1754.13	5135.59	187.62	32.91	219.75	97682
2002	2593.58	1116.56	2274.56	6035.29	205.02	37.28	261.22	168248
2003	2760.40	1277.88	2876.80	7225.14	190.90	37.61	303.76	212566
2004	2747.03	1539.49	3749.91	7993.22	227.22	42.74	377.81	243750
2005	2817.56	1789.53	4328.32	9579.15	284.63	53.97	458.49	305726
2006	3047.53	2216.40	5816.26	10880.77	254.66	64.95	665.14	274820
2007	2480.20	2674.43	7276.33	11787.42	259.93	64.20	803.35	269387
2008	2428.09	2776.85	7364.13	12683.21	255.83	74.55	790.67	330257
2009	2397.44	2928.21	7859.69	14434.14	317.34	78.97	894.50	506188
2010	2122.48	3358.98	9122.95	15647.46	241.96	88.46	1027.19	728700
2011	2100.27	3755.63	9994.01	14899.69	243.70	67.73	1123.80	803758
2012	2104.16	3928.35	10989.18	16777.87	267.15	80.34	1274.95	886959
2013	2011.18	4288.91	13038.96	18646.40	260.21	101.28	1372.89	1117137
2014	2019.20	4347.07	13255.21	19439.06	230.70	91.26	1312.17	1257161
2015	1918.90	4351.78	13560.81	18013.66	203.76	95.68	1430.62	1217487
2016	1367.91	4667.73	13469.72	17989.78	207.17	91.46	1458.19	1448947

11－15 规模以上工业企业主要产品生产、销售、库存（2016年）
Main Indicators on Economic Benefit of above Designated Size Industrial Enterprises(2016)

单位：万吨 （10000 tons）

产品名称	Item	年初库存 Stock at Year-beginning	本年生产 Production This Year	本年销售 Sales This Year	年末库存 Stock at Year-end
原煤	Coal	11.03	1367.91	278.38	4.06
天然原油	Crude Petroleum Oil	1.93	166.02	159.00	1.57
铁矿石原矿	Iron Ore	0.13	98.35		0.19
原盐	Salt	78.15	910.66	923.22	65.60
精制食用植物油	Refined Edible Vegetable Oil	35.30	749.06	759.88	24.48
乳制品	Dairy products	2.70	160.21	160.19	2.71
白酒(折65度,商品量)(万千升)	Liquor (65 fold, Quantity) (Million Liters)	9.51	106.89	104.02	12.16
软饮料	Soft Drink	43.86	560.29	552.97	40.00
卷烟(亿支)	Cigarettes (100 Million Pieces)	14.53	1027.68	1016.65	25.49
纱	Yarn	38.75	536.86	531.09	40.15
布(亿米)	Cloth (100 Million m)	4.52	91.46	89.05	6.33
服装(亿件)	Clothing (100 Million Units)	2.15	47.71	47.32	2.41
机制纸及纸板(外购原纸加工除外)	Machine Made Paper and Paperboard (except paper processing outsourcing)	59.55	1319.83	1330.70	46.16
汽油	Gasoline	6.10	698.65	697.82	6.92
煤油	Kerosene	5.18	434.35	433.92	5.53
燃料油	Fuel Oil	7.32	365.01	360.27	11.87
焦炭	Coke	114.36	2527.46	1553.68	93.25
硫酸(折100%)	Sulfuric Acid (100%)	6.03	349.66	335.76	9.58
烧碱(折100%)	Sodium Hydroxide(100%)	19.56	487.83	436.91	19.16
纯碱(碳酸钠)	Sodium Carhonate(Soda Ash)	2.92	311.13	307.57	5.62
乙烯	Ethylene	0.41	162.95	9.78	0.30
合成氨(无水氨)	Synthetic Ammonia(anhydrous ammonia)	1.12	356.02	127.27	1.90
农用氮、磷、钾化学肥料总计	Chemical Fertilizers	5.70	207.17	204.31	5.18
氮肥(折含N100%)	Nitrogen(N100%)	4.58	196.04	193.04	4.25
磷肥(折五氧化二磷100%)	Phosphate(P_2O_5 100%)	1.03	10.10	10.24	0.85
化学农药原药(折有效成分100%	Chemical Pesticides(100% effectiveness)	7.33	120.55	117.80	6.18
涂料	Coating	12.71	227.26	223.19	15.78

单位:万吨 (10000 tons)

产品名称	Item	年初库存 Stock at Year-beginning	本年生产 Production This Year	本年销售 Sales This Year	年末库存 Stock at Year-end
初级形态的塑料	Primary Plastic	71.63	1319.50	1315.54	67.25
合成橡胶	Synthetic Rubber	3.92	150.66	150.98	3.59
合成洗涤剂	Synthetic Detergents	0.15	13.46	13.45	0.16
化学药品原药	Chemical Medicines	1.66	32.67	32.02	1.94
化学纤维	Chemical Fiber	75.71	1458.19	1442.03	65.48
橡胶轮胎外胎(万条)	Tires (10000 Tires)	908.33	9440.30	9648.03	677.50
塑料制品	Plastic Product	42.56	552.71	545.26	48.29
水泥	Cement	491.56	17989.78	17933.75	547.38
平板玻璃(万重量箱)	Plain Glass (10000 Weight Cases)	433.15	2997.31	3157.17	272.90
生铁	Pig Iron	21.62	7174.08	2517.71	15.55
粗钢	Crude Steel	122.60	11080.49	3201.59	150.89
钢材	Rolled Steel	453.56	13469.72	13180.97	483.29
十种有色金属	Ten Kinds of Nonferrous Metals	0.35	33.87	33.78	0.38
金属切削机床(万台)	Metal-cutting Machine Tools (10000 Units)	0.77	10.34	10.57	0.54
挖掘机(万台)	Excavating Machinery (10000 Units)	0.35	2.84	2.61	0.59
基本型乘用车(轿车)(万辆)	Basic Passenger Cars (Cars) (10000 Vehicles)	1.49	72.17	72.75	0.87
运动型多用途车(SUV)(万辆)	Sport Utility Vehicle (SUV) (10000 Vehicles)	0.47	36.35	35.57	1.22
载货汽车(万辆)	Truck (10000 Vehicles)	0.51	9.59	9.75	0.36
新能源汽车(万辆)	New Energy Vehicles (10000 Vehicles)	0.12	3.11	3.09	0.14
民用钢质船舶(万载重吨)	Civilian Steel Ships (10000 DWT)	30.97	1646.30	1656.18	21.09
发电机组(发电设备)(万千瓦)	Generator Sets (Power Generation Equipment) (10000 kw)	28.29	623.72	628.68	23.32
家用电冰箱(万台)	Home Refrigerators (10000 Sets)	37.84	868.96	866.11	40.53
房间空气调节器(万台)	Air Conditioners (10000 Sets)	27.36	454.10	436.27	45.18
家用洗衣机(万台)	Household Washing Machines (10000 Units)	75.67	1849.64	1835.48	89.64
电子计算机整机(万台)	Computer Complete Machine (10000 Units)	82.59	5614.82	5637.34	60.06
移动通信手持机(手机)(万台)	Mobile Telephones (10000 Sets)	178.94	5352.44	5421.99	109.38
彩色电视机(万台)	Color Television Sets (10000 Sets)	30.60	1752.78	1756.51	26.33
集成电路(亿块)	Integrated Circuits (100 Million Units)	10.16	453.96	453.28	10.47

主要统计指标解释

工业 指从事自然资源的开采,对采掘品和农产品进行加工和再加工的物质生产部门。具体包括:(1)对自然资源的开采,如采矿、晒盐、森林采伐等(但不包括禽兽捕猎和水产捕捞);(2)对农副产品的加工、再加工,如粮油加工、食品加工、缫丝、纺织、制革等;(3)对采掘品的加工、再加工,如炼铁、炼钢、化工生产、石油加工、机器制造、木材加工等,以及电力、自来水、煤气的生产和供应等;(4)对工业品的修理、翻新,如机器设备的修理、交通运输工具(包括小卧车)的修理等。

1984 年以前农村的村及村以下办工业归属农业,1984 年以后划归工业。

国有及国有控股企业 指国有企业加上国有控股企业。国有企业是指企业全部资产归国家所有,并按《中华人民共和国企业法人登记管理条例》规定登记注册的非公司制的经济组织。1957 年以前的公私合营和私营工业,后均改造为国营工业,1992 年改为国有工业,这部分工业的资料不单独分列时,均包括在国有企业内。国有控股企业是对混合所有制经济的企业进行的"国有控股"分类。它是指这些企业的全部资产中国有资产(股份)相对其他所有者中的任何一个所有者占资(股)最多的企业。该分组反映了国有经济控股情况。

集体企业 指企业资产归集体所有,并按《中华人民共和国企业法人登记管理条例》规定登记注册的经济组织。是社会主义公有制经济的组成部分。包括城乡所有使用集体投资举办的企业,以及部分个人通过集资自愿放弃所有权并依法经工商行政管理机关认定为集体所有制的企业。

股份合作企业 指以合作制为基础,由企业职工共同出资入股,吸收一定比例的社会资产投资组建,实行自主经营,自负盈亏,共同劳动,民主管理,按劳分配与按股分红相结合的一种集体经济组织。

联营企业 指两个及两个以上相同或不同所有制性质的企业法人或事业单位法人,按自愿、平等、互利的原则,共同投资组成的经济组织。联营企业包括:国有联营企业指国有企业与国有企业间的联营;集体联营企业指集体企业与集体企业间的联营;国有与集体联营企业指国有企业与集体企业间的联营。

有限责任公司 指根据《中华人民共和国公司登记管理条例》规定登记注册,由两个以上,五十个以下的股东共同出资,每个股东以其所认缴的出资额对公司承担有限责任,公司以其全部资产对其债务承担责任的经济组织。

有限责任公司包括国有独资公司以及其他有限责任公司。

股份有限公司 指根据《中华人民共和国企业法人登记管理条例》规定登记注册,其全部注册资本由等额股份构成并通过发行股票筹集资本,股东以其认购的股份对公司承担有限责任,公司以其全部资产对其债务承担责任的经济组织。

私营企业 指由自然人投资设立或由自然人控股,以雇佣劳动为基础的营利性经济组织。包括按照《公司法》、《合伙企业法》、《私营企业暂行条例》规定登记注册的私营有限责任公司、私营股份有限公司、私营合伙企业和私营独资企业。

港、澳、台商投资企业 指企业注册登记类型中的港、澳、台资合资、合作、独资经营企业和股份有限公司之和。

外商投资企业 指企业注册登记类型中的中外合资、合作经营企业、外资企业和外商投资股份有限公司之和。

"三资"企业 系指港、澳、台商投资企业和外资企业的简称。

轻工业 指主要提供生活消费品和制作手工工具的工业。按其所使用的原料不同,可分为两大类:(1) 以农产品为原料的轻工业,是指直接或间接以农产品为基本原料的轻工业。主要包括食品制造、饮料制造、烟草加工、纺织、缝纫、皮革和毛皮制作、造纸以及印刷等工业;(2) 以非农产品为原料的轻工业,是指以工业品为原料的轻工业。主要包括文教体育用品、化学药品制造、合成纤维制造、日用化学制品、日用玻璃制品、日用金属制品、手工工具制造、医疗器械制造、文化和办公用机械制造等工业。

重工业 是指为国民经济各部门提供物质技术基础的主要生产资料的工业。按其生产性质和产品用途,可以分为下列三类:(1) 采掘(伐)工业,是指对自然资源的开采,包括石油开采、煤炭开采、金属矿开采、非金属矿开采和木材采伐等工业;(2) 原材料工业,指向国民经济各部门提供基本材料、动力和燃料的工业。包括金属冶炼及加工、炼焦及焦炭、化学、化工原料、水泥、人造板以及电力、石油和煤炭加工等工业;(3) 加工工业,是指对工业原材料进行再加工制造的工业。包括装备国民经济各部门的机械设备制造工业、金属结构、水泥制品等工业,以及为农业提供的生产资料如化肥、农药等工业。

根据上述划分原则,修理业中以重工业产品为修理作业对象的划为重工业,反之划为轻工业。

工业总产值 是以货币表现的工业企业在一定时期内生产的已出售或可供出售工业产品总量,它反映一定时间内工业生产的总规模和总水平。它包括:在本企业内不再进行加工,经检验、包装入库(规定不需包装的产品除外)的成品价值,对外加工费收入,自制半成品、在产品期末初差额价值。工业总产值采用"工厂法"计算,即以工业企业作为一个整体,按企业工业生产活动的最终成果来计算,企业内部不允许重复计算,不能把企业内部各个车间(分厂)生产的成果相加。但在企业之间、行业之间、地区之间存在着重复计算。

轻重工业总产值的划分是按"工厂法"计算的,即一个工业企业生产的主要产品性质属于轻工业,则该企业的全部总产值作为轻工业总产值;如它的主要产品性质属于重工业,则该企业的全部总产值作为重工业总产值。

工业增加值 是指工业行业在报告期内以货币表现的工业生产活动的最终成果。

实收资本 指企业实际收到的投资人投入的资本。按投资主体可分为国家资本、集体资本、法人资本、个人资本、港澳台资本和外商资本等。

资产总计 指企业拥有或控制的能以货币计量的经济资源。包括各种财产、债权和其他权利。资产按其流动性划分为流动资产、长期投资、固定资产、无形及递延资产和其他资产。

(1) 流动资产 指企业可以在一年内或者超过一年的一个生产周期内变现或耗用的资产合计。包括现金及各种存款、短期投资、应收及预付款项、存货等。

(2) 固定资产 指企业固定资产净值、固定资产清理、在建工程、待处理固定资产损失所占用的资金合计。

(3) 无形资产 指企业长期使用而没有实物形态的资产。包括专利权、非专利技术、商标权、著作权、土地使用权、商誉等。

负债合计 指企业承担的能以货币计量,将以资产或劳务偿付的债务。负债一般按偿还期长短分为流动负债和长期负债、递延税项等。

(1)流动负债 指企业在一年内或者超过一年的一个营业周期内需要偿还的债务合计,其中包括短期借款、应付及预收款项、应付工资、应交税金和应交利润等。

(2)长期负债 指企业在一年以上或者超过一年的一个营业周期以上需要偿还的债务合计,其中包括长期借款、应付债务、长期应付款项等。

所有者权益 指企业投资人对企业净资产的所有权。企业净资产等于企业全部资产减去全部负债后的余额,其中包括投资者对企业的最初投入,以及资本公积金、盈余公积金和未分配利润,对股份制企业即为股东权益。

Explanatory Notes on Main Statistical Indicators

Industry refers to the material production sector which is engaged in extraction of natural resources and processing or reprocessing of minerals and agricultural products, including(1) extraction of natural resources, such as mining, salt production, logging(but not including hunting and fishing); (2) processing and reprocessing of farm and sideline produces, such as rice husking, flour milling, wine making, oil pressing, cotton ginning, silk reeling, spinning and weaving, and leather making; (3) manufacture of industrial products, such as steel making, iron smelting, chemicals manufacturing, petroleum processing, machine building, timber processing; water and gas production and electricity generation and supply; (4) repairing of industrial products such as the repairing of machinery and means of transport(including cars).

Prior to 1984, the rural industry runed by villages and cooperative organizations under village was classified into agriculture. Since 1984, it has been grouped into industry.

(1) **State-owned and State-share holding Enterprises** State-owned enterprises refer to industrial enterprises where the means of production are all owned by the state. Joint state-private industries and private industries, which existed before 1957, have been transformed into state run industries. Statistics on these enterprises has been included in the state-owned industries since 1992 when separation of data was no longer necessary. State-share holding Enterprises refers to classification of "state-share holding" to the mixed-owned enterprises, which indicate that among the total assets of enterprises, the state assets(share) occupying the most part (share) than any other enterprises. Such group reflects the condition of share-holding of the state-owned economy.

(2) **Collective-owned Enterprises** refer to industrial enterprises where the means of production are owned collectively. It is part of sociolist public economy. It including urban and rural enterprises invested by collectives and some enterprises which were formerly owned privately but have been registered in industrial and commercial administration agency as collective units through raising fund from the public.

(3) **Share-holding Cooperative Enterprises** refer to economic units set up on cooperative basis, with funding partly from members of the enterprise and partly from outside investment, where the operation and management is decided by the members who also participate in the production. And the distribution of income is based both on work(labour input) and on shares(capital input).

(4) **Joint-operation enterprises** refer to economic units that established by joint investment by two or more corporate enterprises or institutions of the same or different types of ownership on voluntary, equal and mutual-beneficial basis. They include:

a) state-owned joint-operation enterprises(joint operation between state-owned enterprises);

b) collective joint-operation enterprises(joint operation between collective enterprises);

c) state-collective joint-operation enterprises (joint operation between state and collective enterprises).

(5) **Limited Liability Corporations** refer to economic units registered in accordance with the Regulation of the People's Republic of China on the Management of Registration of Corporations, with capitals from 2 to 49 investors, each investor bears limited liability to the corporation depending on the holding of shares, and the corporation bears liability to its debt to the maximum of its total assets. Limited Liability corporations State-owned Enterprises and othe limited liabliliy corporations.

(6) **Share-holding Corporations Ltd.** refer to economic units registered in accordance with the Regulation of the People's Republic of China on the Management of Registration of Corporate Enterprises, with total registered capitals divided into equal shares and raised through issuing stocks. Each investor bears limited liability to the corporation depending on the holding of shares, and the corporation bears liability to its debt to the maximum of its total assets.

(7) **Private Enterprises** refer to economic units invested or controlled (by holding the majority of the shares) by natural persons who hire labours for profit-making activities. Included in this category are private limited liability corporations, private share-holding corporations Ltd., private partnership enterprises and private sole investment enterprises registered in accordance with the Corporation Law, Partnership Enterprise Law and Tentative Regulation on Private Enterprises.

(8) **Enterprises with Funds form Hong Kong, Macao and Taiwan** refers to all industrial enterprises registered as the joint-venture, cooperative, sole (exclusive) investment industrial enterprises and limited liability corporations with funds from Hong Kong, Macao and Taiwan.

(9) **Foreign Funded Enterprises** refers to all industrial enterprises registered as the joint-venture, cooperative, sole (exclusive) investment industrial enterprises and limited liability corporations with foreign funds.

Light Industry refers to the industry that produces consumer goods and hand tools. It consists of two categories, depending on the materials used:

(1) Industries using farm products as raw materials. These are branches of light industry which directly or indirectly use farm products as basic raw materials, including the manufacture of food and beverages, tobacco processing, textile, clothing, fur and leather manufacturing, paper making, printing, etc.

(2) Industries using non farm products as raw materials. These are branches of light industry which use manufactured goods as raw-materials, including the manufacture of cultural, educational articles and sports goods, chemicals, synthetic fiber, chemical products for daily use, glass products for daily use, metal products for daily use, hand tools, medical apparatus and instruments, and the manufacture of cultural and clerical machinery.

Heavy Industry refers to the industry which produces capital goods, and provides various sectors of the national economy with necessary material and technical basis. It consists of the following three branches according to the purpose of production or the use of products:

(1) Mining, quarrying and logging industry refers to the industry that extracts natural resources. Including extraction of petroleum, coal, metal and non-metal ores and logging.

(2) Raw materials industry refers to the industry that provides various sectors of the national economy with raw materials, fuels and power. It includes smelting and processing of metals, coking and coke chemistry, chemical materials and building materials such as cement, plywood, and power, petroleum refining and coal dressing.

(3) Manufacturing industry refers to the industry that processes raw materials. It includes machine building industry which equips sectors of the national economy, industries of metal structure and cement products, industries producing means of agricultural production, such as chemical fertilizers and pesticides.

According to the above principle of classification, the repairing trades which are engaged primarily in repairing products of heavy industry are classified into heavy industry while these engaged in repairing products of light in-dustry are classified into light industry.

Gross Industrial Output Value is the total volume of industrial products sold or available for sale in value terms which reflects the total achievements and overall scale of industrial production during a given period. It includes the value of the finished products, which are not to be further processed in the enterprises and have been inspected, packed and put in storage, the value of industrial services rendered to other units, and the changes in the value of the semi-finished products and products in process between the be ginning and closing of the period. The gross industrial output value is calculated with "factory method". No double calculations are to be made within the same enterprise. However, double counting does occur among different enterprises.

Output value of light and heavy industries is based on the "factory" method. If the major products of an industrial enterprise are classified as light industry products, the entire gross output value of that enterprise is classified into the light industry; the same principle applies to heavy industry.

Acctually Received Capital refer main management capital actually received by enterprises used for long-term circulation, including state capital, collective capital, individual capital, Hong Kong Macao Taiwan capital and foreign capital.

Total Assets refer to all economic resources, owned or controlled by enterprises, that could be measured in monetary terms, including properties, creditors equity and other economic rights of all forms. Classified by the degree of equitability, total assets include current assets, long term investment, fixed assets, intangible assets and deferred assets, and other assets.

(1) Current assets (working capital) refer to assets which can be cashed in or spent or consumed in an operating cycle of one year or over one year, including cash, all kinds of deposits, short term investment, receivables, advance payment, stock, etc.

(2) Fixed assets refer to the net value of fixed assets, elearance of fixed assets, project under construction, fixed assets losses in suspense. These are corporations' fund holdings.

(3) Intangible assets refer to the assets without material form used by enterprises over a long time, such as patents, non-patent technologies, trade marks, copyright, land use right, business reputation, etc.

Total Liabilities refer to the debts, measured in monetary terms, that enterprises are responsible for repayment in the form of cash, assets or labour. Classified by terms of repayment, liability include liquid liabilities and long-term liabilities.

(1) Liquid liabilities (also called quick liabilities or immediate liabilities) refer to enterprises' total debt payable within an operating cycle of one year or over one year, including short term loans, payable and advance payments, wages payable, taxes payable and profit payable, etc.

(2) Long term liabilities refers to total debt payable within an operating cycle of one year or over one year, including long-term loans, payable liabilities, long-term payable, etc.

Creditors' Equity refers to investors ownership of net assets of the enterprise. It is equal to the total assets of the enterprise minus its total liabilities, including the primary input from investors, capital accumulation fund, surplus accumulation fund and undistributed profit. It is the shareholder's equity in share-holdting companies.

12

建筑业

Construction

简 要 说 明

一、本篇资料的主要内容

本篇资料反映我省建筑业概况和发展情况。包括建筑业企业基本情况和生产经营情况。主要指标有企业个数、从业人员数、建筑业总产值、房屋建筑面积、劳动生产率等。

二、本篇资料的统计范围

根据建筑业发展的实际情况，建筑业统计范围从2002年年报起由原具有建筑业资质等级四级及四级以上的独立核算的建筑业企业调整为具有总承包和专业承包建筑业企业资质的独立核算建筑业企业。

三、本篇的资料来源及统计调查方法

本篇建筑业企业统计数据是根据国家统计局制定的《建筑业统计报表制度》整理汇总的。建筑业统计报表是各级统计部门根据当地实际情况采取全面调查的方法布置、收集，由辖区内各资质内建筑业企业通过联网直报上报统计数据。

Brief Introduction

I. Main Contents

Data in this chapter show the general situation and the development of the construction industry in Jiangsu. They cover the situation of production and management of the construction enterprises, including the number of enterprises; number of employed persons; gross output value of the construction industry; floor space of buildings under construction and labour productivity etc.

II. Scope of Statistics

In view of the development of the construction industry, starting from 2002 the scope of construction statistics has been adjusted to include all the construction enterprises of various types of ownership with qualification certificates and independent accounting systems, replacing the previous criteria that required general contract and specilized construction enterprises of various types of ownership to have qualification certificates at or above Class 4 with independent accounting systems.

III. Sources of Data and Methods of Survey

Data on construction enterprises are collected in accordance with the *Reporting Form System of Construction Statistics* stipulated by the National Bureau of Statistics. The construction statistical reports are deployed and collected through comprehensive survey by each Bureau of statistics in accordance with real conditions of the enterprises, they are directly reported by qualified construction enterprises through internet.

12－1 建筑施工企业概况

Basic Statistics on Construction Enterprises

项　　目 Item	总　计 Total	国有经济 State-owned	地　方 Local-owned	部　属 Central-owned	城镇集体经　济 Urban Collective-owned	乡镇企业及其它经济 Rural and Township Enterprises and Others
企业单位个数（个） Number of Enterprises (unit)						
1985	2360	114	86	28	148	2098
1989	2408	175	144	31	204	2029
1990	2284	162	138	24	201	1921
1991	2316	173	147	26	209	1934
1992	2417	203	176	27	251	1963
1993	2810	308	273	35	429	2073
1994	3348	389	353	36	513	2446
1995	3426	406	370	36	505	2515
1996	3528	589	554	35	868	2071
1997	3546	564	525	39	884	2098
1998	3587	573	535	38	881	2133
1999	3994	550	514	36	980	2464
2000	3948	529	485	44	903	2516
2001	3872	469	424	45	631	2772
2002	4084	489	438	51	440	3155
2003	4267	358	322	36	326	3583
2004	5241	318	279	39	266	4657
2005	5909	556	524	32	220	5133
2006	6371	444	439	5	206	5721
2007	7017	453	449	4	204	6360
2008	8389	413	380	33	213	7763
2009	8664	391	362	29	181	8092
2010	8949	375	347	28	392	8182
2011	9164	392	359	33	380	8392
2012	9254	383	350	33	324	8547
2013	9560	383	348	35	399	8778
2014	9220	368	332	36	354	8498
2015	9149	361	327	34	330	8458
2016	9023	355	322	33	320	8348
从事主营业务活动的从业人员平均人数（万人） The Average Number of Employees Engaged in Principal Business (10000 persons)						
1985	124.09	17.60	13.82	3.78	14.05	92.44
1989	128.55	22.08	15.10	6.98	20.30	86.17
1990	124.31	21.53	15.24	6.29	23.94	78.44
1991	126.44	22.06	15.83	6.23	25.46	78.92
1992	143.44	24.67	17.66	7.01	30.07	88.70
1993	175.06	34.58	27.50	7.08	34.00	106.48
1994	212.17	44.60	31.60	13.00	34.37	133.20
1995	232.94	45.42	38.58	6.84	51.56	135.96
1996	220.71	59.55	52.14	7.41	55.26	105.90
1997	215.69	51.20	44.57	6.63	61.70	102.78
1998	232.32	50.52	42.22	8.30	83.97	97.83

项目 Item	总计 Total	国有经济 State-owned	地方 Local-owned	部属 Central-owned	城镇集体经济 Urban Collective-owned	乡镇企业及其它经济 Rural and Township Enterprises and Others
1999	222.80	46.30	38.85	7.45	63.59	112.91
2000	221.48	43.85	36.41	7.44	59.73	117.9
2001	239.52	41.74	35.33	6.41	44.11	153.67
2002	251.36	45.96	39.26	6.70	30.27	175.13
2003	277.91	30.37	23.85	6.52	23.62	223.92
2004	305.64	30.06	23.31	6.75	15.84	259.74
2005	342.24	60.77	53.98	6.79	13.50	267.97
2006	379.77	50.24	48.44	1.80	17.49	312.04
2007	437.10	54.50	52.81	1.69	16.08	366.52
2008	488.67	44.49	34.90	9.60	22.22	421.96
2009	540.52	40.43	28.30	12.13	17.25	482.84
2010	598.98	40.23	31.09	9.14	34.48	524.27
2011	607.55	38.41	29.09	9.33	37.65	531.48
2012	700.96	40.23	29.74	10.49	38.89	621.84
2013	782.36	62.79	47.54	15.25	42.48	677.09
2014	828.27	51.71	34.17	17.54	43.35	733.21
2015	833.31	51.82	34.67	17.15	37.96	743.53
2016	845.84	51.18	35.88	15.30	40.67	753.99
建筑业总产值 （亿元） Gross Output Value of Construction Enterprises (100 million yuan)						
1985	82.63	14.32	10.92	3.39	10.80	57.52
1989	142.05	30.94	9.52	11.42	23.97	87.14
1990	147.23	32.00	21.49	10.51	29.76	85.47
1991	176.21	37.84	26.04	11.80	34.35	104.02
1992	265.80	58.20	40.07	18.12	55.99	151.62
1993	449.99	104.73	82.40	22.33	86.87	258.40
1994	738.60	171.60	131.04	40.56	178.46	388.53
1995	998.11	257.36	207.39	49.97	259.76	480.98
1996	1049.42	377.92	318.79	59.13	253.63	417.88
1997	1102.12	352.86	294.21	58.65	308.08	441.18
1998	1224.42	335.16	272.55	62.61	387.29	501.97
1999	1338.46	343.12	282.03	61.09	346.97	648.37
2000	1546.17	376.59	308.3	68.29	377.31	792.27
2001	1859.41	414.58	339.7	74.88	284.9	1159.93
2002	2199.52	492.90	414.84	78.06	222.35	1484.27
2003	2794.94	345.39	258.10	87.29	194.75	2254.80
2004	3656.66	436.40	299.08	137.32	134.09	3086.17
2005	4368.95	865.07	727.50	137.57	154.46	3349.42
2006	5424.85	812.35	770.02	42.33	190.51	4421.99
2007	7010.57	1075.79	1038.81	36.98	222.50	5712.28
2008	8547.94	917.82	620.31	297.51	328.16	7301.96
2009	10264.92	981.35	618.32	363.03	291.15	8992.42
2010	12405.90	1206.68	703.69	502.99	668.42	10530.80
2011	15122.74	1411.67	799.54	612.13	955.45	12755.61
2012	18423.55	1595.37	951.82	643.55	1081.19	15746.99
2013	21990.84	1867.61	1036.00	831.61	1328.73	18794.50
2014	24592.93	2070.42	1129.97	940.45	1369.41	21153.10
2015	24785.81	2143.55	1186.93	956.62	1313.76	21328.50
2016	25791.76	2238.45	1256.88	981.57	1427.29	22126.02

12－1 续表 2 Continued 2

项 目 Item	总 计 Total	国有经济 State-owned	地 方 Local-owned	部 属 Central-owned	城镇集体经济 Urban Collective-owned	乡镇企业及其它经济 Rural and Township Enterprises and Others
房屋建筑施工面积 （万平方米） Housing Construction Area （10000 sq. m）						
1985	5570.32	619.94	536.58	83.36	690.92	4259.46
1989	5447.40	672.60	547.40	125.20	927.70	3847.10
1990	5240.98	699.10	580.30	118.80	1070.40	3471.48
1991	5711.13	778.71	660.44	118.27	1143.12	3789.30
1992	7780.32	1049.90	901.00	148.90	1688.30	5042.12
1993	10229.96	1801.32	1573.13	228.19	2045.54	6383.10
1994	13201.21	2356.00	2062.20	293.90	3269.60	7575.61
1995	16646.14	3470.96	3135.28	335.68	4621.48	8553.70
1996	15672.95	5032.00	4663.09	368.91	3723.69	6917.26
1997	16191.85	4407.38	4031.04	376.34	4344.53	7439.94
1998	17803.33	3831.67	3593.61	238.06	5887.35	8084.31
1999	18748.25	3830.22	3633.96	196.26	4710.61	10207.42
2000	21287.10	4096.75	3871.42	225.33	4982.85	12207.50
2001	24319.01	3706.55	3380.84	325.71	4060.51	16551.95
2002	27753.39	3669.91	3301.01	368.90	3113.95	20969.53
2003	33949.95	1893.32	1503.56	389.76	2369.63	29687.00
2004	43170.57	2815.09	2273.46	541.63	1655.20	38700.28
2005	52242.23	7706.17	7383.99	322.18	1966.09	42569.97
2006	63140.49	6553.90	6329.13	224.77	2248.13	54338.46
2007	79901.63	9386.76	9092.19	294.57	2833.32	67681.55
2008	90144.64	5437.75	4655.54	782.21	4115.15	80591.74
2009	99659.92	3580.73	2684.79	895.94	3416.26	92662.93
2010	119035.52	4465.90	3273.48	1192.42	5966.74	108602.88
2011	145451.48	6273.08	4486.17	1786.91	8661.59	130516.81
2012	166779.12	7006.79	5281.84	1724.95	8567.65	151204.68
2013	196739.85	9070.57	6661.60	2408.97	8845.73	178823.55
2014	213038.78	11454.23	8453.47	3100.76	8907.73	192676.82
2015	215591.97	11763.27	8034.19	3729.08	8935.35	194893.35
2016	221493.57	13235.38	8963.95	4271.43	9866.43	198391.76
房屋建筑竣工面积 （万平方米） Buildings Completed （10000 sq. m）						
1985	3527.20	272.55	245.03	27.52	382.94	2871.71
1989	3446.50	284.50	246.40	38.10	502.10	2659.90
1990	3307.93	354.40	302.20	52.20	617.00	2336.53
1991	3422.75	361.35	322.27	39.08	618.49	2442.91
1992	4387.99	446.60	395.90	50.70	837.40	3103.99
1993	5767.78	772.59	705.11	67.48	1077.09	3918.10
1994	9336.28	903.20	838.60	64.60	1620.00	6813.08
1995	8739.38	1304.03	1243.04	60.99	2056.55	5378.80
1996	8252.13	1946.38	1872.36	74.02	2141.69	4164.06
1997	8787.36	1678.84	1601.39	77.46	2600.34	4508.18
1998	9958.90	1748.46	1686.40	62.05	3497.35	4713.10
1999	10558.22	1692.42	1636.92	55.50	2751.61	6114.19
2000	12329.65	1961.86	1896.93	64.93	2986.11	7381.68

项　　目 Item	总　　计 Total	国有经济 State-owned	地　　方 Local-owned	部　　属 Central-owned	城镇集体经　济 Urban Collective-owned	乡镇企业及其它经　济 Rural and Township Enterprises and Others
2001	14268.89	1822.02	1718.15	103.87	2622.17	9824.70
2002	15478.58	1877.94	1773.00	104.94	1867.91	11732.73
2003	17730.02	879.14	786.81	92.33	1490.80	15360.08
2004	21756.82	1246.57	1084.82	161.75	1040.82	19469.43
2005	25391.86	3696.89	3526.71	170.18	1113.19	20581.78
2006	28715.39	2517.69	2448.11	69.58	1244.15	24953.55
2007	34992.20	3610.75	3505.88	104.87	1580.78	29800.67
2008	40272.98	2182.40	1948.24	234.16	2350.51	35740.07
2009	43307.52	1294.73	1063.59	231.15	1763.20	40249.59
2010	48560.07	1388.19	1034.71	353.48	2826.55	44345.33
2011	54650.20	1505.31	1291.08	214.23	4139.90	49004.99
2012	61241.69	1788.25	1539.63	248.62	3922.45	55530.99
2013	69010.15	2675.97	2238.06	437.91	3727.99	62606.19
2014	76795.04	2962.05	2350.28	611.77	3460.80	70372.19
2015	76823.92	3119.41	2580.11	539.30	2738.63	70965.88
2016	74990.29	3816.67	3094.29	722.38	2874.84	68298.78
房屋建筑面积竣工率（%） **Rate of Buildings Completed（%）**						
1985	66.2	44.0	45.7	33.0	55.4	67.4
1989	63.3	42.3	45.0	30.4	54.1	69.1
1990	63.1	50.7	52.1	43.9	57.6	67.3
1991	59.9	46.4	48.8	33.0	54.1	64.5
1992	56.4	42.5	43.9	34.0	49.6	61.6
1993	56.4	42.9	44.8	29.6	52.7	61.4
1994	70.7	38.3	40.7	22.0	49.5	89.9
1995	52.5	34.9	39.6	18.2	44.5	62.9
1996	52.7	38.7	40.2	20.1	57.5	60.2
1997	54.3	38.1	39.7	20.6	59.9	60.6
1998	55.9	45.6	46.9	26.1	59.4	58.3
1999	56.3	44.2	45.0	28.3	58.4	59.9
2000	57.9	47.9	49.0	28.8	59.9	60.5
2001	58.7	49.2	50.8	31.9	64.6	59.4
2002	55.8	51.2	53.7	28.4	60.0	56.0
2003	52.2	46.4	52.3	23.7	62.9	51.7
2004	50.4	44.3	47.7	29.9	62.9	50.3
2005	48.6	48.0	47.8	52.8	56.6	48.3
2006	45.5	38.4	38.7	31.0	55.3	45.9
2007	43.8	38.5	38.6	35.6	55.8	44.0
2008	44.7	40.1	41.8	29.9	57.1	44.3
2009	43.5	36.2	39.6	25.8	51.6	43.4
2010	40.8	31.1	31.6	29.6	47.4	40.8
2011	37.6	24.0	28.8	12.0	47.8	37.5
2012	36.7	25.5	29.1	14.4	45.8	36.7
2013	35.1	29.5	33.6	18.2	42.1	35.0
2014	36.0	25.9	27.8	19.7	38.9	36.5
2015	35.6	26.5	32.1	14.5	30.6	36.4
2016	33.9	28.8	34.5	16.9	29.1	34.4

12－2 建筑业企业主要经济指标
Main Economic Indicators on Construction Enterprises

指　　标	Item	2012	2013	2014	2015	2016
施工企业个数（个）	Number of Construction Enterprises (unit)	9254	9560	9220	9149	9023
建筑业总产值（亿元）	Gross Product of Construction Industry (100 million yuan)	18423.55	21990.84	24592.93	24785.81	25791.76
#建筑工程	Construction	17298.82	20512.05	23164.48	23278.24	24268.36
安装工程	Installation	983.17	1290.11	1253.41	1321.50	1343.79
固定资产折旧（亿元）	Depreciation of Fixed Assets (100 million yuan)	115.67	115.37	112.10	117.76	118.42
本年应付职工薪酬（亿元）	Workers Salary Paid in this Year (100 million yuan)	2802.85	3579.05	3917.02	3986.74	4209.45
主营业务税金及附加（亿元）	Taxes and Other Charges on Principle Business (100 million yuan)	531.08	638.74	709.84	721.82	591.08
竣工产值（亿元）	Output Value of Completion (100 million yuan)	13857.12	16640.07	18917.21	20431.39	21270.41
房屋建筑施工面积（万平方米）	Floor Space of Buildings under Construction (10000 sq. m)	166779.12	196739.85	213038.78	215591.97	221493.57
#本年新开工	Newly Started Projects this Year	75120.88	86375.22	84670.18	75967.02	84035.71
房屋建筑竣工面积（万平方米）	Floor Space of Completed Buildings (10000 sq. m)	61241.69	69010.15	76795.04	76823.92	74990.29
从事主营业务活动的从业人员平均人数（万人）	The Average Number of Employees Engaged in Principal Business (10000 persons)	700.96	782.36	828.27	833.31	845.84
全员劳动生产率（元/人）	Overall Labor Productivity (yuan/person)	262833	281085	296918	297437	304925
利润总额（亿元）	Total Profits (100 million yuan)	727.17	899.24	980.82	985.46	992.63
利税总额（亿元）	Total Pre-tax Profits (100 million yuan)	1297.41	1568.90	1726.16	1749.99	1826.14

12－3 按登记注册类型分建筑业企业主要经济指标(2016 年)

指 标 Item		合 计 Total	内资企业 Domestic	国有 State-owned	集体 Collective-owned	股份合作 Cooperative
施工企业个数 (个)	Number of Construction Enterprises (unit)	9023	8937	140	101	15
#亏损企业个数	Number of Loss-making Enterprises	544	524	8	4	
年末从业人员数 (万人)	Number of Employed Persons at Year-end (10000 persons)	763.75	760.69	8.94	4.59	0.42
建筑业总产值 (亿元)	Gross Output Value of Construction (100 million yuan)	25791.76	25693.66	439.15	129.99	8.91
#建筑工程	Construction	24268.36	24196.62	405.97	126.19	6.60
安装工程	Installation	1343.79	1317.57	29.16	3.13	2.17
竣工产值 (亿元)	Output Value of Completed Building (100 million yuan)	21270.41	21202.97	284.12	114.59	7.00
房屋建筑施工面积 (万平方米)	Floor Space of Building under Construction (10000 sq. m)	221493.57	221194.38	923.21	678.74	38.13
#本年新开工	Newly Started Projects in this Year	84035.71	83970.77	465.79	374.80	32.74
房屋建筑竣工面积 (万平方米)	Floor Space of Building Completed (10000 sq. m)	74990.29	74908.81	387.00	353.33	31.21
从事主营业务活动的从业人员平均人数 (万人)	(10000 persons)	845.84	843.12	11.37	5.02	0.41
全员劳动生产率 (元/人)	Overall Labor Productivity (yuan/person)	304925	304744	386106	258688	216067

Main Economic Indicators on Construction Enterprises by Registration Status (2016)

联营 Joint Ownership Enterprises	有限责任公司 Limited Liabilit Corporations	股份有限公司 Share-holding Corporations Limited	私营 Private Enterprises	其他 Others	港澳台商投资企业 Enterprises with Funds from Hong Kong, Macao and Taiwan	外商投资企业 Foreign Funded Enterprises
6	2471	438	5755	11	42	44
1	107	15	388	1	9	11
0.19	339.11	71.05	335.97	0.41	1.13	1.93
64.16	12545.44	2613.88	9878.04	14.10	49.10	49.00
63.74	11850.52	2503.41	9226.31	13.88	35.61	36.13
0.42	609.63	103.23	569.63	0.22	13.47	12.74
1.18	10272.89	2164.85	8341.20	17.14	33.23	34.22
	117647.17	24680.46	77151.79	74.88	120.44	178.75
	42063.10	9453.48	31566.90	13.98	22.38	42.56
	37242.04	7319.09	29507.21	68.93	34.42	47.06
0.19	370.04	73.73	381.81	0.54	1.58	1.14
3398338	339032	354504	258714	260752	311313	430055

12－4　按登记注册类型分建筑业企业财务状况(2016年)

单位:亿元

指标	Item	合计 Total	内资企业 Domestic Funded	国有 State-owned	集体 Collective-owned	股份合作 Cooperative Enterprises
资本金合计	Total Capital Assets	2948.95	2916.80	73.00	17.56	2.61
流动资产合计	Circulating Funds	14793.36	14657.71	466.50	78.18	7.91
#存货	Stock	3450.64	3426.53	88.28	15.94	0.92
固定资产合计	Total Fixed Asstes	1558.70	1546.42	39.80	10.82	2.07
固定资产原价合计	Total Original Value of Fixed Assets	2015.54	1999.34	65.20	16.21	2.98
累计折旧	Accumulated Depreciation	835.00	828.47	33.53	7.23	0.93
#本年折旧	Depreciation this Year	119.10	117.47	3.86	0.91	0.08
在建工程	Project under Construction	190.51	189.11	4.25	0.92	0.02
资产总计	Total Assets	17982.62	17810.54	553.30	97.84	10.77
流动负债合计	Liquid Liability	9667.46	9576.54	327.36	49.68	5.48
非流动负债合计	Total Non-current Liabilities	492.70	485.05	54.16	1.39	0.28
负债合计	Total Liabilities	10357.58	10258.44	387.49	54.48	6.10
所有者权益合计	Owners Equity	7618.66	7545.90	165.82	43.20	4.67
主营业务收入	Revenue from Principal Business	22256.20	22153.86	470.83	102.32	8.83
主营业务成本	Cost of Principle Business	19761.79	19674.44	416.99	86.19	7.42
主营业务税金及附加	Taxes and Other Charges on Principle Business	591.08	589.67	9.53	3.29	0.37
其他业务利润	Profits from Other Businesses	17.44	17.36	0.52	0.30	
销售费用	Selling Expenses	83.11	82.17	0.89	0.47	0.04
管理费用	Management Expenses	630.91	624.42	17.70	4.50	0.63
#税金	Taxes	27.43	27.11	0.47	0.24	0.02
财务费用	Financial Cost	151.63	151.05	-0.58	0.46	0.02
营业利润	Operating Profit	990.04	983.93	14.51	4.59	0.35
利润总额	Total Profits	992.63	986.16	15.15	4.66	0.35
应交所得税	Payable Income Taxes	223.54	221.88	3.75	1.23	0.11
本年应付职工薪酬	Workers Salary Paid in this Year	4209.45	4198.46	52.34	22.85	2.11

Financial Indicators on Construction Enterprises by Registration Status (2016)

(100 million yuan)

联营 Joint Ownership Enterprises	有限责任公司 Limited Liability Corporations	股份有限公司 Share-holding Corporations Limited	私营 Private Enterprises	其他 Others	港澳台商投资企业 Enterprises with Funds from Hong Kong, Macao and Taiwan	外商投资企业 Foreign Funded Enterprises
1.47	1043.85	225.10	1550.55	2.66	14.79	17.36
47.34	6553.85	1464.49	6031.62	7.83	79.53	56.12
3.29	1562.12	310.20	1444.00	1.78	15.45	8.66
5.81	633.78	186.10	665.55	2.48	5.92	6.37
5.45	857.76	170.27	878.27	3.20	8.70	7.50
2.37	367.75	66.35	349.40	0.90	3.54	3.00
0.21	49.00	10.73	52.51	0.16	0.49	1.14
2.57	85.35	22.40	73.60		0.21	1.18
56.32	7676.72	1998.31	7406.64	10.64	90.50	81.58
9.88	4322.64	1102.06	3754.99	4.45	53.83	37.09
0.05	193.42	68.64	167.11	0.00	3.91	3.75
52.14	4569.86	1178.29	4005.63	4.45	57.82	41.33
4.18	3105.61	820.02	3396.22	6.18	32.68	40.08
50.58	10596.80	2250.63	8659.97	13.91	49.97	52.37
48.68	9473.52	2001.56	7628.25	11.82	43.26	44.09
0.67	274.72	50.78	249.98	0.33	0.86	0.54
0.01	8.10	2.63	5.81		0.03	0.04
0.01	24.97	9.97	45.67	0.15	0.49	0.45
1.10	272.45	57.55	269.74	0.75	2.77	3.72
0.01	10.49	2.46	13.41	0.01	0.09	0.23
-0.14	68.35	10.95	71.90	0.10	0.42	0.15
-0.28	457.20	118.28	388.46	0.82	2.33	3.77
-0.31	459.19	118.62	387.68	0.82	2.37	4.10
0.07	103.98	24.28	88.27	0.20	0.66	1.01
3.20	1943.36	458.49	1713.90	2.22	5.96	5.03

12-5 按行业分建筑业企业主要经济指标和财务状况(2016年)
Main Economic Indicators on Construction Enterprises by Sector (2016)

单位:亿元 (100 million yuan)

指标	Item	房屋建筑业 Housing Industry	土木工程建筑业 Civil Engineering	建筑安装业 Construction Installation	建筑装饰和其他建筑业 Building Decoration and Other Construction	建筑装饰业 Construction Decoration
企业个数 (个)	Number of Construction Enterprises (unit)	3601	2063	1478	1881	1223
#亏损企业	Number of Loss-making Enterprises	142	130	126	146	90
建筑业总产值	Gross Output Value of Construction	19158.29	3559.67	1604.64	1469.16	1171.55
#建筑工程	Construction	18811.93	3414.93	657.84	1383.66	1140.21
安装工程	Installation	219.51	110.00	939.69	74.59	26.53
竣工产值	Output Value of Completed Building	16282.48	2568.67	1241.63	1177.63	953.19
房屋建筑施工面积 (万平方米)	Floor Space of Building under Construction (10000 sq. m)	215264.71	3744.31	2140.09	344.47	2.02
#本年新开工	Newly Started Projects in this Year	81102.10	2021.76	827.16	84.68	2.02
房屋建筑竣工面积 (万平方米)	Floor Space of Building Completed (10000 sq. m)	72214.24	1904.49	714.97	156.58	0.87
从事主营业务活动的从业人员平均人数 (万人)	the Average Number of Employees Engaged in Principal Business (10000 persons)	639.33	99.90	55.89	50.71	40.30
全员劳动生产率 (元/人)	Overall Labor Productivity (yuan/person)	299660	356317	287087	289721	290710
资本金合计	Total Capital Assets	1586.97	813.67	273.59	274.73	178.36
流动资产合计	Circulating Funds	8482.16	3871.43	1264.02	1175.76	851.15
#存货	Stock	2307.95	716.42	250.49	175.78	111.41
固定资产合计	Total Fixed Asstes	936.13	383.33	122.11	117.13	67.99
固定资产原价合计	Total Original Value of Fixed Assets	1069.53	616.71	172.21	157.10	89.67
累计折旧	Accumulated Depreciation	398.06	300.75	73.11	63.09	34.05
#本年折旧	Depreciation this Year	58.42	39.07	11.09	10.52	5.35
在建工程	Project Under Construction	135.66	32.09	12.13	10.64	7.18
资产总计	Total Assets	10193.50	4693.35	1652.24	1443.53	1017.51
流动负债合计	Liquid Liability	5424.45	2638.41	865.53	739.07	541.86
非流动负债合计	Total Non-current Liabilities	274.59	182.51	14.40	21.19	12.56
负债合计	Total Liabilities	5775.42	2907.48	894.13	780.55	564.74
所有者权益合计	Owners Equity	4414.53	1784.23	757.10	662.80	452.66
主营业务收入	Revenue from Principal Business	15411.84	3713.91	1670.47	1459.98	1136.89
主营业务成本	Cost of Principle Business	13792.79	3265.00	1459.76	1244.23	973.12
主营业务税金及附加	Taxes and Other Charges on Principle Business	436.26	86.27	37.68	30.86	22.74
其他业务利润	Profits from Other Businesses	8.07	4.08	3.62	1.67	0.94
销售费用	Selling Expenses	40.57	15.65	10.39	16.50	13.85
管理费用	Management Expenses	330.53	146.35	84.69	69.34	49.00
#税金	Taxes	15.51	6.13	3.26	2.54	1.69
财务费用	Financial Cost	106.57	30.65	6.24	8.17	6.40
营业利润	Operating Profit	651.59	176.48	75.19	86.78	67.71
利润总额	Total Profits	651.09	177.46	76.62	87.46	68.28
应交所得税	Payable Income Taxes	148.59	39.18	17.82	17.96	13.45
本年应付职工薪酬	Workers Salary Paid in this Year	3285.59	447.75	248.39	227.73	179.85

12－6 按地区分建筑业企业主要指标
Main Indicators on Construction Enterprises by Region

地 区 Region		建筑施工企业个数(个) Number of Construction Enterprises (unit)					年末从业人员数(万人) Number of Employed Persons by the Final(10000 persons)				
		2012	2013	2014	2015	2016	2012	2013	2014	2015	2016
全 省	Total	9254	9560	9220	9149	9023	740.20	764.81	788.27	752.48	763.75
南京市	Nanjing	1605	1638	1487	1478	1458	77.39	81.61	90.82	83.96	83.77
无锡市	Wuxi	574	585	577	576	550	25.48	26.68	23.68	20.18	19.15
徐州市	Xuzhou	390	442	413	411	436	46.70	50.31	51.70	49.69	51.85
常州市	Changzhou	594	644	633	621	612	43.41	47.40	48.34	47.07	46.64
苏州市	Suzhou	1476	1460	1438	1424	1396	54.79	54.40	53.61	50.56	46.26
南通市	Nantong	946	937	892	895	900	157.27	156.76	165.50	153.74	159.84
连云港市	Lianyungang	231	304	301	292	288	24.60	27.14	29.53	24.94	24.57
淮安市	Huaian	579	658	611	586	547	48.33	46.66	53.40	48.09	47.48
盐城市	Yancheng	709	739	751	771	776	51.43	48.68	48.26	48.78	46.50
扬州市	Yangzhou	763	744	735	717	686	79.14	88.38	83.65	83.22	87.80
镇江市	Zhenjiang	381	396	391	381	367	14.66	16.26	16.86	16.98	13.16
泰州市	Taizhou	673	666	634	635	633	79.76	82.65	88.12	92.68	106.33
宿迁市	Suqian	333	347	357	362	374	37.24	37.90	34.79	32.60	30.40
苏 南	Southern Jiangsu	4630	4723	4526	4480	4383	215.73	226.34	233.32	218.74	208.97
苏 中	Middle Jiangsu	2382	2347	2261	2247	2219	316.17	327.78	337.26	329.64	353.97
苏 北	Northern Jiangsu	2242	2490	2433	2422	2421	208.30	210.68	217.68	204.10	200.80

12－6　续表 1　Continued 1

地　区	Region	建筑业总产值(亿元) Gross Output Value of Construction (100 million yuan)					房屋建筑施工面积(万平方米) Floor Space of Building under Construction (10000 sq. m)				
		2012	2013	2014	2015	2016	2012	2013	2014	2015	2016
全　省	Total	18423.55	21990.84	24592.93	24785.81	25791.76	166779.12	196739.85	213038.78	215591.97	221493.57
南京市	Nanjing	2647.31	3112.48	3217.80	3028.32	3094.65	16636.91	18114.76	19565.64	19496.84	19228.82
无锡市	Wuxi	570.69	662.15	650.48	601.62	633.52	4430.64	4445.15	4250.19	3530.38	3133.48
徐州市	Xuzhou	881.66	1109.27	1321.04	1361.22	1387.79	7702.88	10147.90	11606.80	11718.43	11880.35
常州市	Changzhou	1050.20	1161.27	1284.03	1288.52	1273.35	8765.07	10132.24	10747.96	10050.99	9236.17
苏州市	Suzhou	1743.71	2003.55	2116.98	1955.62	1855.90	10999.47	11995.89	11803.55	10881.77	9681.78
南通市	Nantong	4423.51	5439.92	6281.21	6144.55	6619.39	54420.45	65837.01	68200.55	68382.30	71731.81
连云港市	Lianyungang	431.53	556.83	583.31	629.68	648.73	3451.11	5015.52	5341.67	5267.66	5309.08
淮安市	Huaian	838.99	1028.01	1225.95	1323.70	1337.29	8054.09	9687.80	11969.79	13016.11	12889.05
盐城市	Yancheng	945.45	1122.05	1286.63	1343.76	1422.73	8942.53	10450.32	10536.04	11785.75	12769.72
扬州市	Yangzhou	2241.78	2625.53	2944.71	3167.39	3346.48	17651.69	21150.92	24684.57	25288.31	26807.86
镇江市	Zhenjiang	370.91	495.17	555.46	541.46	530.67	1904.81	2186.58	2412.24	2362.29	2406.84
泰州市	Taizhou	1751.16	2021.62	2385.82	2662.55	2924.44	18977.08	21592.44	24851.81	26882.13	30128.84
宿迁市	Suqian	526.66	652.98	739.53	737.42	716.82	4842.38	5983.33	7067.96	6929.00	6289.76
苏　南	Southern Jiangsu	6382.81	7434.63	7824.74	7415.54	7388.10	42736.91	46874.62	48779.58	46322.28	43687.10
苏　中	Middle Jiangsu	8416.46	10087.07	11611.73	11974.50	12890.31	91049.22	108580.37	117736.94	120552.75	128668.51
苏　北	Northern Jiangsu	3624.28	4469.14	5156.46	5395.77	5513.35	32992.99	41284.86	46522.27	48716.95	49137.96

12-6 续表2 Continued 2

地 区 Region		房屋建筑竣工面积(万平方米) Floor Space of Building Completed (10000 sq. m)				
		2012	2013	2014	2015	2016
全 省	Total	61241.69	69010.15	76795.04	76823.92	74990.29
南京市	Nanjing	5076.74	6096.80	6315.87	6850.05	5012.89
无锡市	Wuxi	1852.81	1705.58	1761.79	1471.09	1308.62
徐州市	Xuzhou	3247.33	3943.48	5274.97	4970.80	4613.18
常州市	Changzhou	3067.89	3525.74	3811.33	3448.59	3575.17
苏州市	Suzhou	4056.02	4414.82	4006.64	4014.44	3569.78
南通市	Nantong	16294.79	17017.36	20199.21	18345.14	19160.04
连云港市	Lianyungang	1584.53	2739.21	2608.14	2085.47	2306.10
淮安市	Huaian	3316.22	3460.89	4364.40	3968.49	3676.99
盐城市	Yancheng	3979.24	4144.53	4366.78	4299.72	4954.27
扬州市	Yangzhou	7507.02	8690.45	9332.67	10619.79	10094.65
镇江市	Zhenjiang	772.88	784.13	954.19	926.97	878.01
泰州市	Taizhou	8317.65	9789.56	10897.85	12308.02	12845.86
宿迁市	Suqian	2168.58	2697.63	2901.19	3515.33	2994.74
苏 南	Southern Jiangsu	14826.34	16527.06	16849.81	16711.15	14344.48
苏 中	Middle Jiangsu	32119.45	35497.36	40429.74	41272.96	42100.55
苏 北	Northern Jiangsu	14295.89	16985.73	19515.48	18839.81	18545.26

主要统计指标解释

建建筑业统计单位　指从事房屋、构筑物建造、装饰装修、设备安装活动和工程准备、提供施工设备服务等其他建筑活动的具有建筑业资质的法人企业。建筑业法人企业应同时具备的条件是:①依法成立,有自己的名称、组织机构和场所,能够承担民事责任;②独立拥有和使用资产,承担负债,有权与其他单位签订合同;③独立核算盈亏,能够编制资产负债表。

建建筑业总产值(即自行完成施工产值)　是以货币表现的建筑业企业在一定时期内生产的建筑业产品和服务的总和。建筑业总产值包括:

(1)建筑工程产值:指列入建筑工程预算内的各种工程价值。

(2)安装工程产值:指设备安装工程价值,不包括被安装设备本身价值。

(3)其他产值:指建筑业总产值中除建筑工程、安装工程以外的产值。包括房屋、构筑物修理所完成的产值(不包括被修理的房屋、构筑物本身的价值)、非标准设备制造产值、总包企业向分包企业收取的管理费和不能明确划分的施工活动所完成的产值。

建房屋建筑施工面积　指在报告期内施过工的全部房屋建筑面积,包括本期新开工的房屋面积、上期跨入本期继续施工的房屋面积、上期停缓建在本期恢复施工的房屋面积、本期竣工的房屋面积及本期施工后又停缓建的房屋面积。

建房屋建筑竣工面积　指在报告期内房屋建筑按照设计要求全部完工,达到了住人和使用条件,经检查验收鉴定合格的房屋建筑面积。

建自有施工机械设备年末总台数　指归本企业(或单位)所有,属于本企业(或单位)固定资产的直接用于工程施工的各种机械设备年末总台数。但不包括附属辅助生产机械设备、运输机械设备、生产试验机械设备的台数。

建自有施工机械设备年末总功率　指本企业(或单位)自有施工机械设备年末总功率,按设定能力或查定能力计算。包括机械本身的动力和为该机械服务的单独动力设备,如电动机等。计算单位用千瓦,动力换算可按 1 马力 =0.735 千瓦折合成千瓦数。电焊机、变压器、锅炉不计算动力。

建营业收入　指企业经营主要业务和其他业务所确认的收入总额,包括主营业务收入和其他业务收入。计算公式为:

营业收入 = 主营业务收入 + 其他业务收入

建主营业务收入　指企业确认的销售商品、提供劳务等主营业务的收入。对建筑业企业而言,主营业务收入指企业承包工程实现的工程价款结算收入,以及向发包单位收取的除工程价款以外按规定列作营业收入的各种款项,如临时设施费、劳动保险费、施工机械调迁费等以及向发包单位收取的各种索赔款。

建营业利润　指企业从事生产经营活动所取得的利润。执行 2006 年《企业会计准则》的企业,营业利润为营业收入减去营业成本、营业税金及附加、销售费用、管理费用、财务费用、资产减值损失,再加上公允价值变动收益和投资收益。未执行 2006 年《企业会计准则》的企业,营业利润为主营业务收入减去主营业务成本、主营业务税金及附加,加上其他业务利润后,再减去销售费用、管理费用、财务费用后的金额。

建利润总额　指企业在一定会计期间的经营成果,是生产经营过程中各种收入扣除各种耗费后的盈余,反映企业在报告期内实现的盈亏总额。执行 2006 年《企业会计准则》的企业,利润总额为营业利润加上营业外收入,减去营业外支出后的金额;未执行 2006 年《企业会计准则》的企业,利润总额为营业利润加上投资收益、补贴收入、营业外收入,再减去营业外支出后的金额。

建从事主营业务活动的从业人员平均人数　指建筑业企业(或单位)报告期实际拥有的、与建筑施工活动有关的人员的平均人数,包括参加本企业(或单位)建筑施工活动的非本企业(或单位)人员,但不包括企业内部社会服务性机构的人员以及由本企业支付工资但所从事的工作与本企业生产基本无关的人员。

Explanatory Notes on Main Statistical Indicators

Statistical Unit in Construction　refers to corporate enterprise engaged in the construction of buildings、structures in the installation of equipment and with constrution qualifications. A corporate constrnction enterprise should meet the following 3 requirements: ①being set up in line with relevant legal basis, having its full name, organization and location, and capable of taking civil liabilities; ②independently possessing and using its assets and assuming its liabilities, and entitled to sign contracts with other institutions; ③making independent accounts of its profits and losses, and capable of compiling its own balance sheet.

Gross Output Value of Construction (Output Value of Projects Under Construction)　refers to total of construction products and services expressed in money terms, completed by construction enterprises during a given period of time. It includes:

(1) Output: value of construction projects, that is the value of projects covered by the project budgets;

(2) Output value of installation projects, that is the value of the installation of equipment (excluding the value of the equipment to be installed);

(3) Other Output Value refers to the total output of construction industry except the output value of constrution projects, output value of installation projects. It covered the output value of buildings and strucutres repairing (excluding the value of buildings and structures being repaired); output value of manufactured non-standard equipment; management expenses collected by general contracted enterprises from branch contracted enterprises, and the output value of const ruction activities which can't to be divided definitely.

Housing Construction area refers to floor space of buildings under construction during the reference period, including newly started buildings, buildings started earlier and continued during the reference period, and buildings suspended earlier but restarted during the reference period, buildings completed during the reference period, and buildings under construction and then suspended during the reference period.

Buildings Completed refers to the floor space of buildings that are completed in the reference period in accordance with the requirements of the design, up to the standard for putting them into use, and have been checked and accepted by concerned departments as qualified ones.

Total Number of Machinery and Equipment Owned by the End of Year refers to the number of machines and equipment owned by the enterprises, directly used the prodution by the end of the year, but not including auailiary, transport and test equipment.

Total Power of Machinery and Equipment Owned by the End of Year refers to the total power of machinery and equipment owned by the enterprises, including machinery and equipment for construction. The power of the machinery is calculated on basis of the designed or verified capacity, covering the power of the machinery/equipment and the separate power equipment serving the machinery/equipment (such as electric motors), but excluding welders, transformers and boilers. The unit used for the calculation of power is kilowatt, with horsepower converted to kilowatt by 1 horsepower = 0.735 kilowatt.

Operation Revenue refers to the sum of income from principal business and other business, including revenue from principal business and other business income. namely:

operating income = revenue from principle business + revenue from other business

Income from Principal Business refers to the revenue from principal business such as sales of products, service provided and so on. for construction enterprises, income from principal business refers to the income received by the construction enterprise from the contracted project through settlement procedures, and other charges to the contractors as operational costs in addition to the value of the project, such as temporary facility fee, labour insurance premium, moving cost of construction equipment, as well as various types of claims to the contractors.

Operating Profit refers to the profit from production and managing movement of the corporation. Enterprises in accordance with Accounting Criteria for Business Enterprises (2006), their operating profit is operating income which is subtracted operating cost, business tariff and annex, selling expense, administration expense , financial cost and devaluation lost of assets, then added changes in fair value of the proceeds and investment income. Enterprises which don't follow Criteria for Business Enterprises (2006), their operating profit is income from principal business which is subtracted main business cost, main business tariff and annex, selling expense, administration expense and financial cost, then added other business income.

Total Profit refers to the profits gained by the enterprises during a accounting period. It reflect profit and loss during report period. Enterprises in accordance with Accounting Criteria for Business Enterprises (2006), their total profit is operating profit which is added nonbusiness income, and subtracted nonbusiness expenditure; Enterprises which don't follow Criteria for Business Enterprises (2006), their total profit is operating profit which is added investment income, subsidize revenue, nonbusiness income, and subtracted nonbusiness expenditure.

The average number of employees engaged in principal Business refers to the average personnels actually held by construction enterprises (units) and related to construction activities in the reference period, including the personnels of other enterprises, who took part in the construction activities of these enterprises, but excluding the personnels of the inner social service institutions, and the personnels their wages were paid by the enterprises but did not take part in the construction activities basically.

13

运输、邮电和服务业

Transport,Postal and Telecommunication Services,Service Industry

简 要 说 明

本篇反映我省交通运输业和邮政、电信业发展情况。

一、交通运输邮政电信业部分的主要内容

1. 交通运输业资料主要包括：五种运输方式的线路里程、各种运输方式完成的货物运输量和旅客运输量，全社会港口码头泊位和通过能力，主要港口吞吐量以及民用车辆拥有量等资料。

2. 邮政电信业资料主要包括：邮电业务总量、业务收入情况，电信主要通信能力，邮电主要业务完成情况，邮政电信发展水平等资料。

3. 规模以上服务业资料主要内容包括：按企业登记注册类型、按行业门类和按地区分组的主要经济指标。

二、交通运输邮政电信业部分的资料来源和相关说明

1. 铁路资料：由上海铁路局提供。范围是江苏境内国家铁路（含控股合资）、地方铁路和非控股合资铁路运营情况，不含军用铁路及由厂矿企事业单位自建的铁路专用线和专用铁道。

2. 公路、水运、港口资料：由江苏省交通运输厅以及南京港、连云港、南通港、苏州港提供。(1)公路和水路线路里程为年末通车和通航里程数，不含未正式投入使用的公路和航道里程；(2)民用车辆拥有量及机动车和汽车驾驶员人数，根据江苏省公安厅交通管理局登记注册的车辆资料和驾驶员资料整理，不含军用车辆，不含拖拉机数量。(3) 公路营运汽车拥有量，根据各地区道路运输主管部门登记注册的从事公路运输的营业性运输车辆资料整理，从2010年起，不含出租车数量；(4) 营业性运输船舶拥有量，根据各地区交通运输主管部门登记注册的从事水上客、货运输的营业性船舶资料整理，不含非运输船舶及农业、渔业生产船舶；(5) 公路、水路客货运输量资料，由省交通运输厅负责收集整理；(6) 公路、水路运输量统计包括全面调查和非全面调查两种方式，统计范围是在各地区交通运输主管部门登记注册的从事公路、水路客、货运输的营业性的车辆和船舶所完成的运输量，由交通部门组织实施。(7) 规模以上港口的统计范围为年通过能力在1000万吨以上的沿海港口和200万吨以上的内河港口，以及从事外贸、集装箱装卸的港口，具体范围由交通运输部划定。江苏港口数量为15个，沿海1个，内河港口14个。

3. 管道运输资料：由中国石油化工股份有限公司徐州管道储运分公司提供。包括输原油、输成品油、输天然气及输其他气体的运输量。

4. 民航运输资料：由中国民航江苏安全监督管理局提供。统计对象为在江苏省境内注册从事民用航空运输飞行和通用飞行的航空运输企业和民用航空机场。统计范围为民航运输企业及东航公司从事国内运输、港澳台运输、国际运输的定期航班航线条数及里程、运输量及运营情况，飞行完成情况等。

5. 邮政电信资料：由江苏省邮政管理局和江苏省通信管理局提供。包括邮政企业和年业务收入200万元以上快递企业，以及所有从事电信运营的企业（即中国电信、中国移动、中国联通三家基础电信企业），不含专用网业务资料。邮电业务量按业务种类分为邮政业务量和电信业务量；按业务范围分为国内业务量和国际及港澳业务量（对台业务量统计在港澳中）。

6. 规模以上服务业资料：根据规模以上服务业统计年度报表中有关资料汇总整理。统计范围为：(1) 辖区内年营业收入1000万元及以上，或年末从业人员50人及以上服务业法人单位。包括：交通运输、仓储和邮政业，信息传输、软件和信息技术服务业，租赁和商务服务业，科学研究和技术服务业，水利、环境和公共设施管理业，教育，卫生和社会工作；以及物业管理、房地产中介服务等行业。(2) 辖区内年营业收入500万元及以上，或年末从业人员50人及以上服务业法人单位。包括：居民服务、修理和其他服务业，文化、体育和娱乐业。

Brief Introduction

Data in this chapter present the development of transportation, post and telecommunications and above scale seruice industry in Jiangsu Province.

Ⅰ. Main Contents in This Article

1. Data on transport cover mainly the length of the routes of five means of transportation, freight traffic and passenger traffic accomplished by various means of transportation, number of berths and traffic capacity in all ports, volume of freight and passenger handled at major ports, and number of civil motor vehicles.

2. Data on business volume of post and telecommunication services, revenue from post and telecommunication services, telephone lines, telegraph lines and the possession of telecommunication facilities; business volume of postal and telecommunication services achieved; and the level of development of postal and telecommunication services.

3. Date of Above scale service industry include: index of Enterprise registration type、industry categorg and provincial cities.

Ⅱ. Scope of Statistics in This Article

1. Data on railway transportation: from Shanghai Railway Bureau. Including the operation and management of the national, local and joint-venture railways in Jiangsu Province but not including railways for military purpose, lines built by industrial and mining enterprises and special railways.

2. Data on highways, waterways and ports: from Jiangsu Provincial Communications Department and Nanjing, Lianyungang, Nantong. (1) The length of highways and waterways refer to the length open to traffic or navigation at the end of the year, but not including the highways and waterways under construction or not officially having been put into use. (2) Data on the possession of civil motor vehicles and the number of drivers are provided by the divisions of vehicle management under the provincial departments of public security, subordinate to the Traffic Management Bureau, Ministry of Public Security, but not including vehicles for military use. (3) Data on possession of highway vehicles are provided by the divisions of vehicle management under provincial departments of public security, which are subordinate to the Traffic Management Bureau, Ministry of Public Security, including vehicles for business use and non-business use. From 2010, possession of taxies are not included. (4) Data on possession of ships are provided by the divisions of navigation or ports management under municipal departments of communications, which are subordinate to the Ministry of Transport. However, fishing boats, boats for constructions in water and boats for military use are not included. (5) Data on passenger traffic and freight traffic by highways and waterways are collected and prepared by Jiangsu Provincial Communications Department. (6) Data on highway and waterway transportation are collected through both comprehensive reporting system and non-comprehensive reporting system. The statistical scope encompasses all the enterprises, institutional units and individuals (including joint-households) registered in municipal departments of communications and engaged in highway or waterway freight or passenger transport business. (7) Data on production capacity and handling capacity include the seaports handling cargo more than 1 million tons, inland river ports with turnover over 2 million tons and ports with operation in foreign trade and containing shipping. The specific scope are decided by the Administration of Transportation. There are 15ports in Jiangsu Province: 1

coastal port and 14 ports of inland rivers.

3. Data on pipeline transport: Data are from Xuzhou PSTC of China Petroleum & Chemical Corporation. The data on pipeline transport cover the volume transported of petroleum (crude oil) pipelines, petroleum products pipelines, natural gas pipelines and other gas pipelines.

4. Data on civil aviation transport: Data are from Jiangsu Provincial Bureau of Safety Administration of Civil Aviation. The targets of statistical collection are enterprises registered for engagement in civil aviation transport flights and flights for general purposes and civil airports in Jiangsu Province. The scope of statistics encompasses number of lines, mileage flown, transport volume, composition of the fleets operational situation of the airlines, performance of general purpose flights in respect of domestic transport, transport between China mainland and Hong Kong, Macao and Taiwan, and international transport.

5. Data on post and telecommunications: Data are from JiangSu Provincial Postal Administration and Jiangsu Communication Administration. Data in this category include postal enterprises express delivery company with revenue above 2 million yuan and all telecommunication enterprises (i. e. the three major enterprises of telecommunication China Telecom, China Mobile and China Unicom), but exclude services provided through dedicated networks. The business volume of post and telecommunications is classified by type of business into postal and telecommunication services, and by customers into domestic service, international service, and service between the Mainland and Hong Kong, Macao (business volume of the service to Taiwan is covered in that for Hong Kong and Macao).

6. Date of Above Scale service industry according to statistical annual report. (1) Within the jurisdiction of 10 million yuan or more, 50 people and above at the end of year. The scope conclude: Transport, Storage and post, Information Transmmission, Computer Service and Sofeware, Leasing and Business Services, Scientific Research. Technical Services and Geologic Prospecting, Management of Water Conservancy, Environment and Public Facilities, Education, Healtheare and Social work, Property, Real estate agency. (2) Within the jurisdiction of 5 million yuan or more, 50 people and above at the end of year. The scope conclude Resident service repair, Cluture、Sports and Entertainment.

13－1　交通运输基本情况
Basic Statistics of Transport

指　标	Item	2012	2013	2014	2015	2016
运输线路长度（公里）	**Length of Transport Routes (km)**					
铁路营业里程	Railways in Operation	2348	2554	2632	2679.2	2721.9
铁路正线延展长度	Extended Raitways	3725	4125	4200	4569.7	4676.7
公路通车里程	Highways in Operation	154118	156094	157521	158805	157304
#等级公路里程	Expressway and ClassⅠ to Ⅳ Highway	146100	148263	149845	151459	154405
#高速公路	Expressways	4371	4443	4488	4539	4657
一级公路	ClassⅠ Highways	10476	11283	12015	12687	12955
二级公路	ClassⅡ Highways	22144	22677	22790	22945	23054
内河航道里程	Navigable Inland Waterways	24280	24315	24342	23559	24366
输油管道里程	Petroleum Pipelines	6264	6299	6116	6116	6338
公路桥梁（座）	Highway Bridges (unit)	67159	68306	68774	69925	69823
公路桥梁长度（米）	Length of Highway Bridges (m)	3050891	3174281	3204617	3376516	3438053
客运量总计（万人）	**Total Passenger Traffic (10000 persons)**	**268371**	**152172**	**156016**	**153943**	**134605**
铁路	Railways	11757	13435	15374	16116	17814
公路	Highways	255358	135555	137270	134553	113493
水运	Waterways	594	2454	2563	2392	2272
民用航空	Civil Aviation	662	728	809	882	1025
旅客周转量(亿人公里)	**Total Passenger-kilometers (100 million person-km)**	**1949.80**	**1451.14**	**1550.60**	**1566.40**	**1591.93**
货运量总计（万吨）	**Total Freight Traffic (10000 tons)**	**231295**	**194048**	**208623**	**211648**	**215651**
铁路	Railways	7223	6806	6090	5066	5335
公路	Highways	153696	103709	114449	113351	117166
水运	Waterways	58639	70909	75328	80343	79314
民用航空	Civil Aviation	6.69	6.67	7.10	7.00	7.61
输油管道	Petroleum Pipelines	11730	12617	12749	12881	13828
货物周转量(亿吨公里)	**Total Freight Ton-kilometers (100 million ton-km)**	**8474.63**	**10536.84**	**11028.50**	**8887.71**	**8290.69**
民用车辆拥有量(万辆)	**Possession of Civil Motor Vehicles (10000 coaches)**	**1604.18**	**1725.34**	**1782.09**	**1699.46**	**1733.70**
#民用汽车拥有量	Civil Vehicles	813.12	954.38	1103.97	1247.86	1434.52
#载客汽车	Passenger Vehicles	706.27	840.52	991.13	1143.57	1326.73
载货汽车	Trucks	89.29	96.79	97.17	90.39	94.17
#营运汽车(含公交出租车辆)	Motor Vehicles in Operation(Include Bus and Taxi)	82.15	86.75	93.46	85.16	88.67
#私人汽车	Private Vehicles	657.27	790.13	935.71	1076.90	1252.20
民用运输船舶拥有量（万艘）	**Possession of Civil Transport Vessels (10000 units)**	**4.88**	**4.77**	**4.62**	**4.32**	**4.14**
机动船	Motor Vessels	3.96	3.93	3.84	3.63	3.49
驳船	Barges	0.92	0.84	0.78	0.69	0.65
港口货物吞吐量(万吨)	**Volume of Freight Handled at Ports (10000 tons)**	**195417**	**213987**	**226049**	**233289**	**241487**
#外贸	Foreign Trade	31390	35160	37991	39766	44780

注:1. 公路客运量2013年以来不包括公交车和出租车的运输量;
2. 公路货运量2013年以来不包含农用车和拖拉机的运输量;
3. 2014年民用车辆总数中包含拖拉机103.27万辆;
4. 2015年民用车辆拥有量中不包含拖拉机数量。
5. 根据2015年度全国公路水路运输量小样本抽样调查结果,对2015年公路、内河客货运输量、周转量统计值有所修正,与2014年值不具可比性。

a) From 2013, road passanger traffic volume doos not include transpotation by buses and taxis.
b) From 2013, road freight volume does not include transpotation by agricultraul vehiles and tractors.
c) In 2014, the total number of civilian vehicles including trators.
d) Based on the Small sample sampling survey results of 2015 national highway water traffic, amend some statistics, cover highway water passenger traffic, highway water passenger-kilometers, highway water freight traffic, highway water freight ton-kilometers, it's can't compare with the 2014 figures.

13-2 客 运 量
Passenger Traffic

单位:万人 (10000 persons)

年份 Year	总计 Total	铁路 Railway	公路 Highway	水运 Waterway	民用航空 Civil Aviation
1978	25621	2752	18694	4175	
1980	34002	3364	26463	4175	
1980	34002	3364	26463	4175	
1985	53935	4819	45751	3365	
1990	48339	4788	41850	1701	
1991	50264	4932	43764	1568	
1992	55400	5035	48748	1617	
1993	59666	5533	53331	797	5
1994	61104	5471	54930	677	26
1995	84803	5185	78947	623	48
1996	91870	4502	86801	499	68
1997	93684	4433	88826	341	84
1998	97033	4451	92215	273	94
1999	101000	4824	95564	504	108
2000	107244	4891	101713	514	126
2001	110713	5029	105105	430	149
2002	115889	5297	110139	284	170
2003	123462	5104	118046	147	165
2004	128516	5997	122218	91	210
2005	145204	6658	138287	37	222
2006	161425	7293	153824	27	280
2007	187241	7658	179206	27	350
2008	208237	8846	199008	32	351
2009	201262	9167	191001	686	408
2010	226627	9711	215850	590	476
2011	247405	10598	235673	579	555
2012	268371	11757	255358	594	662
2013	152172	13435	135555	2454	728
2014	156016	15374	137270	2563	809
2015	153943	16116	134553	2392	882
2016	134605	17814	113493	2272	1025

注:民用航空客运量仅指省内航空公司完成数。

a) The passenger traffic by civil aviation only referred to the fulfillment in our province.

13－3 旅 客 周 转 量
Turnover Volume of Passenger Traffic

单位:亿人公里 (100 million person-km)

年 份 Year	总 计 Total	铁 路 Railway	公 路 Highway	水 运 Waterway	民用航空 Civil Aviation
1978	105.29	46.35	49.93	9.01	
1980	140.15	61.60	68.25	10.30	
1985	273.76	107.46	156.30	10.00	
1990	324.94	124.13	195.24	5.57	
1991	342.12	132.57	204.11	5.44	
1992	515.08	147.53	361.28	6.27	
1993	520.86	161.36	355.50	3.42	0.58
1994	541.09	166.94	367.98	3.28	2.89
1995	630.56	163.69	459.08	3.42	4.37
1996	647.73	143.85	495.70	2.51	5.67
1997	657.93	144.68	504.05	1.64	7.56
1998	680.02	141.15	527.62	1.12	10.13
1999	725.66	157.65	554.04	1.40	12.57
2000	776.25	165.87	594.48	1.45	14.45
2001	874.63	173.40	682.25	1.06	17.93
2002	924.31	183.80	719.08	0.70	20.71
2003	978.03	182.88	774.11	0.50	20.53
2004	1109.19	226.73	855.41	0.27	26.78
2005	1222.03	245.37	948.10	0.11	28.45
2006	1366.95	267.99	1062.61	0.10	36.25
2007	1596.06	309.83	1241.13	0.33	44.77
2008	1766.00	319.14	1400.80	0.37	45.69
2009	1423.33	311.29	1058.01	1.29	52.74
2010	1604.00	351.00	1196.59	1.50	54.00
2011	1777.80	398.10	1307.30	1.50	70.90
2012	1949.80	446.40	1418.40	1.40	83.60
2013	1451.14	505.88	847.28	3.97	94.01
2014	1550.64	589.60	852.00	3.04	106.00
2015	1566.40	613.50	835.00	2.70	115.20
2016	1591.93	672.65	779.98	2.39	136.91

13-4 货 运 量
Freight Traffic

单位:万吨 (10000 tons)

年 份 Year	总 计 Total	铁 路 Railway	公 路 Highway	水 运 Waterway	内 河 Inland Waterway	沿海、远洋 Seashipping	民用航空 Civil Aviation	输油管道 Petroleum Pipeline
1978	14626	3224	4488	6557	6557			357
1980	16527	3420	4427	6482	6452	30		2198
1985	46842	4037	23255	18117	18067	50		1433
1990	49399	4235	27904	15908	15809	99		1352
1991	49298	4078	27948	16064	15884	180		1208
1992	56953	4343	30730	20751	20533	218		1129
1993	66339	4344	35060	25915	25610	305		1020
1994	69470	4318	36899	27279	26920	359		974
1995	81830	4143	49578	27161	26728	433		948
1996	84666	4361	50571	28819	28429	390		915
1997	82290	4131	52441	24826	24424	402		892
1998	80429	3793	54328	21363	21059	304		945
1999	81529	3941	54803	21596	20045	1551		1188
2000	90436	4077	59056	25902	24275	1627		1395
2001	87505	4239	59058	22583	21030	1553		1622
2002	88588	4407	60299	22411	20681	1730		1468
2003	93511	4462	64321	23320	20845	2475		1405
2004	100093	4665	69058	24812	21239	3573		1554
2005	112909	5090	76301	29277	25061	4216		2236
2006	125114	5169	84319	32862	25779	7083		2759
2007	143805	5177	97473	37858	29567	8291	5.32	3292
2008	166322	5118	110302	42799	27154	15645	4.68	8098
2009	160967	6137	104002	42016	30221	11795	4.44	8807
2010	188558	6374	123500	48702	35713	12989	5.46	9977
2011	212594	7282	140803	54012	37783	16229	6.08	10491
2012	231295	7223	153696	58639	41007	17632	6.69	11730
2013	194048	6806	103709	70909	47559	23350	6.67	12617
2014	208623	6090	114449	75328	51603	23725	7.10	12749
2015	211648	5066	113351	80343	58065	22278	7.00	12881
2016	215651	5335	117166	79314	56656	22658	7.61	13828

注:1. 民用航空货运量仅指省内航空公司完成数。
2. 水运货物周转量数据为全社会、全口径数据。
3. 根据2015年度全国公路水路运输量小样本抽样调查结果,对2015年公路、内河客货运输量、周转量统计值有所修正,与2014年值不具可比性。

a) The turnover volume of freight traffic by civil aviation only referred to the fulfillment in our province.
b) The data coverage of highway freight ton-kilometers is comprehensive.
c) Based on the Small sample sampling survey results of 2015 national highway water traffic, amend some statistics, cover highway water passenger traffic, highway water passenger-kilometers, highway water freight traffic, highway water freight ton-kilometers, it's can't compare with the 2014 figures.

13－5　货物周转量
Turnover Volume of Freight Traffic

单位：亿吨公里　　　　　　(100 million ton-km)

年份 Year	总计 Total	铁路 Railway	公路 Highway	水运 Waterway	内河 Inland Waterway	沿海、远洋 Seashipping	民用航空 Civil Aviation	输油管道 Petroleum Pipeline
1978	283.85	172.72	11.24	87.97	87.97			11.92
1980	382.77	186.31	11.45	93.56	91.51	2.05		91.45
1985	575.58	240.48	81.30	205.90	194.83	11.07		47.90
1990	730.22	297.44	154.01	233.65	209.53	24.12		45.12
1991	788.41	301.73	166.21	280.59	240.23	40.36		39.88
1992	963.94	333.85	179.92	400.78	361.87	38.91		49.39
1993	1193.87	346.49	235.07	578.01	520.51	57.50		34.30
1994	1246.12	372.13	243.33	598.02	523.21	74.81		32.64
1995	1376.88	393.51	281.04	670.75	585.84	84.91		31.58
1996	1412.56	380.09	289.44	712.33	635.20	77.13		30.70
1997	1370.63	355.73	303.40	681.42	617.18	64.24		30.08
1998	1353.23	343.41	316.14	661.85	579.51	82.34		31.71
1999	1400.55	342.65	319.75	704.01	436.89	267.12		33.91
2000	1505.57	371.32	340.72	746.39	463.17	283.22		46.84
2001	1524.96	371.97	340.73	757.58	489.01	268.57		54.37
2002	1549.12	377.17	351.95	770.03	395.05	374.98		49.63
2003	1817.44	408.69	365.01	995.34	444.98	550.36		47.97
2004	2398.64	434.72	386.91	1523.63	468.13	1055.50		52.87
2005	3068.88	480.49	459.18	2056.90	631.98	1424.92		71.73
2006	3644.79	497.42	542.09	2515.09	583.94	1931.15		89.54
2007	4099.16	424.00	638.59	2930.08	634.65	2295.43	0.74	105.75
2008	4707.74	346.50	723.60	3179.30	598.29	2581.01	0.67	457.67
2009	5154.46	323.90	971.13	3372.05	638.45	2733.60	0.64	486.74
2010	6111.57	336.86	1149.10	4095.70	694.11	3401.59	0.78	529.13
2011	7513.99	398.57	1315.27	5236.91	748.30	4488.61	0.84	562.40
2012	8474.64	391.53	1452.45	6052.95	823.60	5229.35	0.91	576.80
2013	10536.84	373.17	1790.40	7753.02	1336.55	6416.46	0.95	619.30
2014	11028.47	346.10	1978.50	8087.07	1505.20	6581.87	1.10	615.70
2015	7374.00	303.70	2072.96	5886.75	1871.18	4015.57	1.00	623.30
2016	8290.69	282.46	2140.33	5224.60	1863.70	3360.90	1.09	642.20

注：1. 民用航空货物周转量仅指省内航空公司完成数。
2. 水运货物周转量数据为全社会、全口径数据。
3. 根据2015年度全国公路水路运输量小样本抽样调查结果，对2015年公路、内河客货运输量、周转量统计值有所修正，与2014年值不具可比性。

a) The freight traffic by civil aviation only referred to the fulfillment in our province.
b) The data coverage of highway freight ton-kilometers is comprehensive.
c) Based on the Small sample sampling survey results of 2015 national highway water traffic, amend some statistics, cover highway water passenger traffic, highway water passenger-kilometers, highway water freight traffic, highway water freight ton-kilometers, it's can't compare with the 2014 figures.

13－6 全社会港口码头泊位和通过能力

指标	Item	2012 合计 Total	2012 沿海港口 Coastal Ports	2012 内河港口 Ports of Inland Rivers	2013 合计 Total	2013 沿海港口 Coastal Ports	2013 内河港口 Ports of Inland Rivers
生产用码头泊位	Number of Berths of Ports						
泊位个数 （个）	Number of Berths (unit)	7300	136	7164	7546	133	7413
泊位长度 （米）	Length of Ports Line (m)	443396	18697	424699	466125	19830	446295
泊位年通过能力	Comprehensive Traffic Capacity						
货物 （万吨）	Freight (10000 tons)	148097	12364	135733	159563	13369	146194
旅客 （万人）	Passenger (10000 persons)	992			992		
非生产用码头泊位	Ports for Nonproductive Use						
泊位个数 （个）	Number of Berths (unit)	53			56		
泊位长度 （米）	Length of Ports Line (m)	3175			3569		

13－7 主要港口吞吐量

港口名称	Ports	2012 旅客吞吐量（万人）Passenger (10000 persons)	2012 货物吞吐量（万吨）Freight (10000 tons)	2013 旅客吞吐量（万人）Passenger (10000 persons)	2013 货物吞吐量（万吨）Freight (10000 tons)
总　计	**Total**	**12.19**	**195417.07**	**12.18**	**213986.54**
沿海港口	Coastal Ports	12.19	23245.41	12.18	26919.33
#连云港	Lianyungang	12.19	18527.53	12.18	20165.06
内河港口	Ports of Inland Rivers		172171.66		187067.21
#长江干流水系	Yangtze River Mainstream System		126369.77		135756.00
长江支流水系	Yangtze River Tributary System		9906.08		10383.39
京杭运河水系	Jinghang Canal System		26445.54		29323.95
淮河水系	Huaihe River System		6807.42		8994.85

Number of Berths and Traffic Capacity in All Ports

2014			2015			2016		
合　计 Total	沿海港口 Coastal Ports	内河港口 Ports of Inland Rivers	合　计 Total	沿海港口 Coastal Ports	内河港口 Ports of Inland Rivers	合　计 Total	沿海港口 Coastal Ports	内河港口 Ports of Inland Rivers
7474	152	7322	7279	158	7121	7278	162	7116
478201	23735	454466	474881	25993	448888	482461	26935	455526
168987	17163	151824	171565	18969	152596	181,389	19146	162,243
639			630			602		602
47			56			81		
2967			3254			4827		

Volume of Freight and Passenger Handled at Major Ports

2014		2015		2016	
旅客吞吐量（万人）Passenger (10000 persons)	货物吞吐量（万吨）Freight (10000 tons)	旅客吞吐量（万人）Passenger (10000 persons)	货物吞吐量（万吨）Freight (10000 tons)	旅客吞吐量（万人）Passenger (10000 persons)	货物吞吐量（万吨）Freight (10000 tons)
9.26	**226049.20**	**7.00**	**233289.00**	**4.92**	**241486.92**
9.26	28706.16	7.00	30181.55	4.92	31630.25
9.26	21007.88	7.00	21074.95	4.92	22134.97
	197343.04		203107.45		209856.67
	142325.70		148746.23		156532.94
	10739.97		12972.32		11008.81
	31461.59		28081.35		28069.17
	12140.17		13307.92		14245.75

13-8 全省民用车辆拥有量(2016 年)
Number of Civil Motor Vehicles(2016 年)

单位:辆 (coach)

指标	Item	总计 Total	#营运 Working	#进口 Import	#个人 Individual
合计	**Total**	**17337006**	**1211196**	**729237**	**15400764**
汽车	Civil Vehicles	14345156	886747	724764	12522020
载客汽车	Passenger Vehicles	13267338	194715	722498	11971733
#大型	Large Scale	107571	78755	614	419
中型	Medium Scale	51274	6182	1777	14141
小型	Small Scale	12997427	109761	705421	11851633
#轿车	Cars	9629571	105255	373705	8920721
载货汽车	Trucks	941706	639878	1770	462165
#重型	Heavy Scale	374462	342595	1092	143165
中型	Medium Scale	108904	78941	8	47067
轻型	Light Scale	457310	218121	670	271085
#普通载货	Ordinary Trucks	453686	248345	637	266754
其他汽车	Other Vehicles	136112	52154	496	88122
#三轮汽车	Tricycle Motors	48796	35785		47940
低速货车	Lowspeed Trucks	17215	8596		15754
摩托车	Motor	2875337	209274	4400	2842801
#普通	Ordinary Motor	2843827	209132	4391	2811336
轻便	Light Motors	31510	142	9	31465
挂车	Freight Trailers	116498	115173	73	35941
其他类型车	Other Motor Vehicles	15	2		2
拖拉机	Tractors				

注:合计数中不含拖拉机数量

a) Total do not include number of tractors.

13-9 个人车辆拥有量
Number of Private-owned Vehicles

单位:辆 (coach)

指标	Item	2012	2013	2014	2015	2016
合计	**Total**	**13624122**	**14744726**	**14999357**	**15180121**	**15400764**
民用汽车	Civil Vehicles	6572682	7901333	9357126	10768671	12522020
载客汽车	Passenger Vehicles	6005133	7294560	8754968	10222220	11971733
#大型	Large Scale	1910	1379	987	613	419
轿车	Cars	4559240	5546187	6656432	7738857	8920721
载货汽车	Ordinary Trucks	443303	488352	496554	455539	462165
#重型	Large Scale	124053	141035	148377	142698	143165
其他汽车	Other	124246	118421	105604	90912	88122
摩托车	Motors	7025815	6814148	5611553	4378953	2842801
挂车	Freight Trailers	25625	29238	30691	32492	35941

13－10 全省公路运输汽车拥有量
Number of Transport Motor Vehicles

单位：辆 (coach)

指标	Item	2012	2013	2014	2015	2016
合计	**Total**	**659825**	**774126**	**791921**	**774189**	**807012**
载客汽车	Passenger Vehicles					
辆数	Number	44221	44005	45306	46685	48126
客位 （万客位）	Seats （10000 seats）	164	162	167	162	164
载货汽车	Trucks					
辆数	Number	615604	727784	746615	727504	758886
#普通载货汽车	Ordinary Trucks	535764	559093	584748	558814	571127
吨位 （万吨）	Tonnages （10000 tons）	525	579	614	622	686
#普通载货汽车	Ordinary Trucks	402	439	468	461	501

13－11 全社会运输船舶拥有量
Number of Transport Vessels

指标	Item	2015			2016		
		数量（艘） Number （unit）	载客量（客位） Passenger Capacity	净载重量（万吨位） Dead Weight Tonnage (10000 tons)	数量（艘） Number （unit）	载客量（客位） Passenger Capacity （seat）	净载重量（万吨位） Dead Weight Tonnage (10000 tons)
总计	**Total**	**43261**	**45158**	**4379.65**	**41353**	**50957**	**4459.09**
#内河船舶	Inland Waterway Vessels	41799	45058	3134.94	39922	50857	3236.82
沿海船舶	Coastal Vessels	1354	100	872.89	1325	100	821.25
远洋船舶	Oceanic Vessels	108		405.68	106		401.03
#机动船	Motor Vessels	36339	45158	3987.33	34888	50957	4031.44
客船	Passenger Ships	333	22072	3.06	328	30777	1.89
客货船	Passenger Cargo Ships	57	23086	2.61	64	20180	2.62
货船	Cargo Ships	34762		3981.66	33374		4026.93
拖轮	Tugboats	1187			1122		
驳船	Cargo Barges	6922		392.32	6465		427.65

13－12 分市交通运输基本情况（2016 年）

指　　标	Item	南京市 Nanjing	无锡市 Wuxi	徐州市 Xuzhou	常州市 Changzhou
运输线路	**Transport Routes**				
公路通车里程　（公里）	Highways in Operation　(km)	11211	7695	16277	9031
#等级公路里程	Expressway and Class Ⅰ to Ⅳ Highway	10991	7695	15405	9031
#高速公路	Expressways	555	274	459	306
一级公路	Class Ⅰ Highways	1050	886	1214	1074
二级公路	Class Ⅱ Highways	1470	1720	1530	1240
内河航道里程　（公里）	Navigable Inland Waterways　(km)	630	1578	1033	1080
公路桥梁　（座）	Highway Bridges　(unit)	2248	3888	4974	2996
公路桥梁长度　（米）	Length of Highway Bridges　(m)	225077	253357	230039	207632
客运量	**Passenger Traffic**				
公路　（万人）	Highways　(10000 persons)	8490	5785	13217	5423
水运　（万人）	Waterways　(10000 persons)	19	511		
民用航空　（万人）	Civil Aviation　(10000 persons)	2236	556	149	196
货运量	Freight Traffic　(10000 tons)				
公路　（万吨）	Highways　(10000 tons)	12463	13225	17586	11095
水运　（万吨）	Waterways　(10000 tons)	13814	2521	5801	2191
民用航空　（吨）	Civil Aviation　(tons)	341267	95984	9088	15690
机动车拥有量　（万辆）	**(10000 coaches)**	**239.48**	**181.24**	**146.64**	**121.62**
#机动汽车拥有量	Civil Vehicles	221.68	160.01	101.61	109.80
#载客汽车	Passenger Vehicles	210.42	151.12	87.80	102.01
载货汽车	Trucks	10.21	8.25	11.57	7.39
#营运汽车（含公交出租车辆）	Motor Vehicles in Operation	12.02	8.20	12.30	6.70
#私人汽车	Private Vehicles	192.71	134.08	92.64	93.93
全社会船舶拥有量（万艘）	**Number of Transport Vessels (10000 units)**	**1783**	**1437**	**4158**	**2099**
机动船	Motor Vessels	1720	1406	1305	2064
驳船	Barges	63	31	2853	35
港口货物吞吐量　（万吨）	**Volume of Freight Handled at Ports (10000 tons)**	**22768**	**18815**	**9122**	**9091**
#外贸	Foreign Trade	2369	2404	0	569

Basic Statistics of Transport by Region (2016)

苏州市 Suzhou	南通市 Nantong	连云港市 Lianyungang	淮安市 Huaian	盐城市 Yancheng	扬州市 Yangzhou	镇江市 Zhenjiang	泰州市 Taizhou	宿迁市 Suqian
12681	18427	12027	13351	19568	9546	7354	9635	10500
12681	18427	12027	12589	19303	9166	7354	9628	10110
598	334	354	401	396	271	182	284	245
1749	1501	613	632	1393	581	820	898	545
4100	1782	1886	1541	2531	1205	918	1381	1750
2786	3522	1114	1483	4346	2297	597	2550	980
9754	8329	3027	3734	15615	4434	1236	6333	3255
550356	351894	216035	198028	488133	191946	94176	272540	158841
31589	8204	4654	7226	8283	3840	3574	7300	5909
[illegible]	561	473	5	3			11	
		154	85	86	121	144		
12287	11535	8378	5663	5076	6546	6950	2577	3785
1221	8311	1837	6548	10860	5778	1458	16736	2238
	35371	1245	4638	5118	7715			
328.29	**181.20**	**82.33**	**81.32**	**109.46**	**88.24**	**65.96**	**93.36**	**88.21**
312.60	134.95	47.85	45.27	75.57	63.53	49.20	61.91	48.67
297.44	126.60	40.15	40.04	67.32	57.94	45.90	57.30	40.99
13.99	7.63	6.36	4.52	6.77	4.99	3.00	3.99	5.37
13.74	5.85	5.16	4.35	5.12	5.44	2.79	4.20	5.19
267.03	120.41	43.16	40.31	67.55	56.27	43.68	55.54	44.88
360	**1533**	**1443**	**3322**	**10286**	**2706**	**522**	**9229**	**2475**
324	1429	1255	2986	8930	2674	451	9195	1149
36	104	188	336	1356	32	71	34	1326
64727	**26932**	**23064**	**9051**	**11356**	**10893**	**14887**	**19200**	**1582**
15142	5811	11233	0	2139	803	2750	1560	

13 - 13 邮电业务基本情况
Basic Conditions of Post and Telecommunication Services

指标	Item	2012	2013	2014	2015	2016
邮电业务总量 （亿元）	Business Volume of Postal & Telecommunication Services (100 million yuan)	1120.37	1252.18	1680.80	2280.60	3431.23
邮政行业业务总量	Postal Services	205.75	269.60	359.00	516.02	663.69
电信业务总量	Telecommunicatoin Services	914.62	982.58	1321.80	1764.60	2767.54
邮电业务收入 （亿元）	Revenue from Post and Telecommunication Services (100 million yuan)	1000.48	1107.62	1153.40	1244.30	1345.35
邮政行业业务收入	Postal Revenue	178.75	233.10	299.50	407.22	463.33
电信业务收入	Telecommunication Revenue	821.73	874.52	853.90	837.08	882.02
函件 （亿件）	Letters (100 million pcs)	8.95	7.61	6.26	4.88	3.33
包件 （万件）	Parcels (10000 pcs)	416.80	407.20	273.90	220.30	165.30
快递 （亿件）	Special Express (100 million pcs)	6.39	9.84	14.84	22.90	28.38
报刊期发数 （万份）	Newspapers and Magazines Circulation (10000 pcs)	1168.04	1243.86	1192.00	1104.06	1062.97
长途电话通话量 （万分钟）	Long-distance Calls (10000 minutes)	433597	360575	350016	349125	325727
移动短信业务量 （亿条）	Short Message Services (100 million messages)	633.31	581.54	523.00	512.00	619.69
年末固定电话用户 （万户）	Fixed Telephone Subscribers at Year-end (10000 subscribers)	2387.20	2289.81	2133.61	1972.99	1708.33
#城市	Urban	1341.00	1275.85	1222.91	1217.98	1096.96
乡村	Rural	1046.20	1013.95	910.70	755.01	611.37
年末移动电话用户（万户）	Mobile Telephone Subscribers at Year-end (10000 subscribers)	7471.40	7941.95	8070.35	8227.33	8198.75
固定宽带接入用户（万户）	Fixed Broadband Users (10000 subscribers)	1406.40	1431.35	1523.35	2183.06	2685.24
邮政局所（个）	Number of Post Offices (unit)	2470	2414	2399	2385	2381

13－13　续表 Continued

指　标	Item	2012	2013	2014	2015	2016
邮路及农村投递路线总长度　（万公里）	Length of Postal Routes and Rural Delivery Routes (10000 km)	33.32	32.98	34.90	35.15	37.17
#汽车邮路	Highway Routes	6.11	6.70	8.93	9.07	11.59
铁路邮路	Railway Routes	0.58	0.12	0.00	0.00	0.00
移动电话交换机容量　（万户）	Capacity of Mobile Telephone Exchanges (10000 subscribers)	9666	10357	10473	10633	10863
固定长途电话交换机容量　（万路端）	Capacity of Long-distance Fixed Telephone Exchanges (10000 circuits)	110	38	38	38	38
长途光缆线路长度　（公里）	Length of Long Distance Optical Cable Lines (km)	32820	35864	36249	38841	2939498
每局所服务面积　（平方公里）	Per Bureau (Office) Service Area (sq. km)	41.53	42.50	42.77	44.95	45.02
人均邮电业务量　（元/人）	Per Capita Business Volume of Post (yuan/person)	1414.61	1577.15	2111.56	2859.22	579.26
每百人平均函件量　（件/百人）	Number of Letters Mailed Per 100 Persons (unit/100 persons)	1053.89	958.49	786.43	611.42	4.00
每百人平均订阅报刊量　（份/百人）	Number of Newspaper and Magazine Subscribed Per 100 Persons (unit/100 persons)	13.76	15.66	15.00	13.84	13.00
每百人平均包件（件/百人）	Number of Parcels Per 100 Persons (unit/100 persons)	5.25	5.12	4.11	2.76	2.00
每百人移动短信量　（条/百人）	Number of Short Messages Per 100 Persons (unit/person)	79964	73251	65873	5535	77692
电话普及率　（部/百人）	Popularization Rate of Telephones (unit/100 persons)	125.00	128.87	128.52	128.50	124.21
固定电话普及率	Popularization Rate of Fixed Telephones	30.00	28.84	26.87	24.80	21.42
移动电话普及率	Popularization Rate of Mobile Telephones	95.00	100.03	101.65	103.40	102.79

注:2008 年起邮政行业业务总量、邮政行业业务收入及快递包含国有、民营、外资各类企业的快递业务活动;2011 年起,电信由 2000 年不变单价调整为 2010 年不变单价。

a) Postal services, postal revenue and express services contain express state-owned, services of private and foreign enterprises from 2008; telecommunication revenue is caculated at 2010 constant prices ratner than 2000 constant prices.

13－14 分市邮电业务基本情况(2016 年)

指 标	Item	南京市 Nanjing	无锡市 Wuxi	徐州市 Xuzhou	常州市 Changzhou
邮电业务总量 (亿元)	Business Volume of Postal & Telecommunication Services (100 million yuan)	525.27	368.86	246.69	231.95
邮政行业业务总量	Postal Services	102.89	84.02	39.30	40.57
电信业务总量	Telecommunicatoin Services	422.38	284.84	207.39	191.39
邮电业务收入 (亿元)	Revenue from Post and Telecommunication Services (100 million yuan)	211.02	155.24	84.55	96.35
邮政行业业务收入	Postal Revenue	78.79	56.86	23.77	33.87
电信业务收入	Telecommunication Revenue	132.23	98.39	60.78	62.48
函件 (亿件)	Letters (100 million pcs)	0.68	0.37	0.09	0.10
包件 (万件)	Parcels (10000 pcs)	31.82	13.69	10.78	8.72
快递 (万件)	Special Express (10000 pcs)	47229.59	34752.75	17377.70	16435.78
报刊期发数 (万份)	Newspapers and Magazines Circulation (10000 pcs)	132.93	129.12	64.84	71.11
年末固定电话用户 (万户)	Fixed Telephone Subscribers at Year-end (10000 subscribers)	243.50	168.09	115.78	123.49
年末移动电话用户 (万户)	Mobile Telephone Subscribers at Year-end (10000 subscribers)	1114.72	799.86	762.01	539.94
固定宽带接入用户 (万户)	Fixed Broadband Users (10000 subscribers)	373.66	269.95	223.61	195.15
邮政局所 (个)	Number of Post Offices (unit)	181.00	141.00	235.00	150.00
邮路及农村投递路线总长度 (万公里)	Length of Postal Routes and Rural Delivery Routes (10000 km)	4.24	2.72	3.33	2.48
#汽车邮路	Highway Routes	2.89	0.79	1.09	1.09
邮政通信水平	Level of Postal and Telecommunication				
每局所服务面积 (平方公里)	Per Bureau (Office) Service Area (sq. km)	36.39	32.82	50.06	29.15
人均邮电业务量 (元/人)	Per Capita Business Volume of Post (yuan/person)	952.71	870.82	272.94	719.43
每百人平均函件量 (件/百人)	Number of Letters Mailed Per 100 Persons (unit/100 persons)	8.00	5.00	0.00	2.00
每百人平均订阅报刊量 (份/百人)	Number of Newspaper and Magazine Subscribed Per 100 Persons (unit/100 persons)	16.00	19.00	7.00	15.00
每百人平均包件 (件/百人)	Number of Parcels Per 100 Persons (unit/100 persons)	3.85	2.10	1.24	1.85
电话普及率 (部/百人)	Popularization Rate of Telephones (unit/100 persons)	164.92	148.66	101.26	141.11
固定电话普及率	Popularization Rate of Fixed Telephones	29.57	25.82	13.36	26.27
移动电话普及率	Popularization Rate of Mobile Telephones	135.35	122.85	87.90	114.85

Basic Conditions of Post and Telecommunication Services by Region (2016)

苏州市 Suzhou	南通市 Nantong	连云港市 Lianyungang	淮安市 Huaian	盐城市 Yancheng	扬州市 Yangzhou	镇江市 Zhenjiang	泰州市 Taizhou	宿迁市 Suqian
789.21	261.92	119.96	126.06	173.17	155.88	109.87	131.20	130.21
193.61	56.14	17.38	21.04	22.65	26.61	16.62	18.25	24.63
595.60	205.77	102.58	105.03	150.52	129.27	93.25	112.96	105.58
335.20	102.33	41.93	45.31	62.97	61.53	42.60	51.47	43.17
134.14	37.41	11.18	14.53	15.19	19.25	12.41	14.44	11.49
201.06	64.92	30.75	30.78	47.78	42.29	30.19	37.03	31.68
1.38	0.22	0.04	0.07	0.07	0.12	0.11	0.08	0.01
59.73	7.14	4.17	2.16	3.98	9.27	4.41	4.50	4.93
85093.28	21627.96	7527.34	9812.99	8560.49	10736.31	6920.60	6591.61	11156.83
165.56	109.81	35.17	77.79	74.54	49.15	39.42	77.20	36.33
314.20	179.98	71.20	57.06	98.80	108.59	75.79	104.85	47.00
1447.59	678.69	368.05	383.34	584.97	437.36	305.89	404.76	371.56
471.80	225.34	114.94	111.15	174.43	146.95	107.69	134.75	105.72
240.00	311.00	129.00	171.00	227.00	183.00	105.00	174.00	134.00
5.58	5.41	1.45	1.91	3.19	1.97	1.33	2.15	1.41
2.21	1.21	0.24	0.43	0.54	0.34	0.21	0.30	0.25
36.07	33.92	59.03	58.65	74.59	36.02	36.57	33.26	63.61
1262.43	512.29	248.60	297.19	209.98	428.49	390.22	310.84	235.39
13.00	3.00	0.00	1.00	0.00	2.00	3.00	1.00	0.00
15.00	15.00	7.00	15.00	10.00	10.00	12.00	16.00	7.00
5.62	0.98	0.93	0.44	0.55	2.06	1.39	0.97	1.01
165.96	117.63	98.18	90.40	94.59	121.77	120.16	109.79	86.23
29.60	24.66	15.91	11.71	13.67	24.22	23.86	22.59	9.68
136.36	92.97	82.27	78.68	80.93	97.55	96.30	87.20	76.55

13－15 规模以上服务业企业主要经济指标

单位:亿元

指标	Item	单位数(个) Number of Enterprises(unit) 2015	2016
总计	**Total**	**16541**	**17557**
按登记注册类型分	**Grouped by Status of Registration**		
内资企业	Domestic Funded Enterprises	15920	16920
国有企业	State-owned Enterprises	551	505
集体企业	Collective-owned Enterprises	311	297
股份合作企业	Cooperative Enterprises	39	40
联营企业	Joint Ownership Enterprises	9	7
有限责任公司	Limited Liability Corporations	4777	4974
#国有独资公司	State Sole Funded Corporatios	432	493
股份有限公司	Share-holding Corporations Ltd.	582	609
私营企业	Private Enterprises	8760	9617
其他企业	Other Enterprises	891	871
港、澳、台商投资企业	Enterprises with Funds from Hong Kong, Macao and Taiwan	244	268
外商投资企业	Foreign Funded Enterprises	377	369
按行业门类分	**Grouped by Sector**		
交通运输、仓储和邮政业	Traffic, Transport, Storage and Post	4626	4848
信息传输、软件和信息技术服务业	Information Transfer, Software and IT Services	1428	1587
租赁和商务服务业	Leasing and Business Services	3647	3732
科学研究和技术服务业	Scientific Research and Technical Service	2658	2801
水利、环境和公共设施管理业	Management of Water Conservancy, Environment and Public Facilities	647	728
居民服务、修理和其他服务业	Services to Households and other Services	607	605
教育	Education	438	501
卫生和社会工作	Health and Social Work	431	492
文化、体育和娱乐业	Health, Social Security and Social Welfare	709	833
房地产业	Real Estate	1350	1430
按地区分	**Grouped by Cities**		
南京市	Nanjing	2674	2891
无锡市	Wuxi	1013	1046
徐州市	Xuzhou	983	1204
常州市	Changzhou	1295	1363
苏州市	Suzhou	2756	2629
南通市	Nantong	2031	2067
连云港市	Lianyungang	570	622
淮安市	Huaian	1117	1156
盐城市	Yancheng	1253	1488
扬州市	Yangzhou	918	912
镇江市	Zhenjiang	655	657
泰州市	Taizhou	758	860
宿迁市	Suqian	518	662

Main Indicators of Service Industrial Enterprises above Designated Size

(100 million yuan)

资产总计 Total Assets		负债合计 Total Liabilities		营业收入 Operation Revenue		主营业务收入 Income from Principal Business	
2015	2016	2015	2016	2015	2016	2015	2016
46939.4	**53228.9**	**26358.9**	**30379.3**	**11570.9**	**13129.6**	**11329.7**	**12727.9**
44759.2	50680.9	25208.1	29050.4	10512.7	11923.3	10287.2	11550.4
4107.9	3900.0	2439.7	2499.0	767.0	688.3	740.1	654.0
436.5	505.6	304.1	366.3	95.7	114.3	94.4	111.8
91.8	59.3	59.7	42.3	25.3	15.0	25.3	14.9
1.8	1.8	0.4	0.3	2.1	2.2	2.1	2.1
30926.3	35904.1	17429.8	20447.6	4496.3	5160.2	4364.3	4968.4
16454.4	19897.5	8904.6	10974.2	1110.8	1262.7	1044.7	1182.6
4146.1	4403.6	2119.3	2213.6	1387.4	1458.4	1364.9	1401.3
4774.2	5608.7	2714.4	3329.2	3487.8	4215.9	3446.2	4132.3
274.5	297.9	140.7	152.1	251.0	268.8	249.9	265.7
966.1	1123.2	577.6	683.2	343.1	381.1	334.4	367.9
1214.1	1424.8	573.3	645.7	715.1	825.2	708.1	809.6
9600.7	10723.7	5651.2	6190.6	3476.6	3766.1	3387.7	3652.5
3218.5	3647.0	1762.5	1983.5	2321.6	2714.5	2267.2	2643.9
27332.3	30159.4	15029.8	17217.8	3106.8	3462.0	3047.2	3345.5
2607.5	2984.7	1432.9	1623.0	1385.0	1607.0	1373.1	1563.0
2120.4	3414.9	1221.4	1951.7	349.7	473.8	344.3	461.1
132.6	132.1	87.2	82.7	126.5	144.3	124.8	141.4
138.8	163.0	68.4	80.8	93.6	107.8	92.2	105.1
270.7	321.5	179.1	203.3	196.6	229.7	195.0	226.0
994.4	1080.4	568.0	636.9	270.1	319.1	260.8	300.9
523.5	602.3	358.3	408.7	244.4	305.2	237.4	288.5
15522.8	17361.5	8454.0	9417.0	4025.6	4549.4	3961.1	4427.9
3597.3	3995.7	2294.0	2564.6	719.7	825.5	700.3	800.6
1566.3	1690.6	834.9	890.2	528.8	634.8	521.6	587.6
2040.4	2503.5	1255.4	1627.4	769.8	799.4	759.2	784.9
8636.0	9543.9	4773.8	5268.3	2070.3	2343.7	2021.5	2280.9
3373.5	2945.0	2049.1	1667.7	903.9	1011.9	894.0	984.8
3261.2	4424.8	1743.9	2543.7	466.0	550.6	447.7	508.5
742.0	905.0	345.8	440.6	406.2	431.8	403.2	420.8
2004.4	2611.6	1164.8	1522.1	476.3	597.1	447.3	589.2
1833.0	1885.1	1039.2	1089.2	376.5	401.8	368.4	383.3
1869.0	1400.9	1017.8	840.1	300.6	359.1	295.9	349.6
1915.9	3311.1	1061.7	2142.8	332.5	407.7	318.2	398.2
577.6	650.4	324.5	365.6	194.6	216.8	191.5	211.5

主要统计指标解释

铁路营业里程　又称营业长度(包括正式营业和临时营业里程),指办理客货运输业务的铁路正线总长度。凡是全线或部分建成双线及以上的线路,以第一线的实际长度计算;复线、站线、段管线、岔线和特殊用途线以及不计算运费的联络线都不计算营业里程。铁路营业里程是反映铁路运输业基础设施发展水平的重要指标,也是计算客货周转量、运输密度和机车车辆运用效率等指标的基础资料。

铁路正线延展里程　指正线第一线、第二线、第三线和其他正线建筑里程之和,不包括站线、段管线、岔线及特殊用途线的延展里程。它是作为计算铁路线上钢轨、枕木及路基砂石需要量的主要依据。

公路里程　指在一定时期内实际达到《公路工程技术标准 JTJ01－88》规定的等级公路,并经公路主管部门正式验收交付使用的公路里程数。包括大中城市的郊区公路以及通过小城镇街道部分的公路里程和桥梁、渡口的长度,不包括大中城市的街道、厂矿、林区生产用道和农业生产用道的里程。两条或多条公路共同经由同一路段,只计算一次,不得重复计算里程长度。它是反映公路建设发展规模的重要指标,也是计算运输网密度等指标的基础资料。

内河航道里程　也称内河通航里程,指在一定时期内,能通航运输船舶及排筏的天然河流、湖泊水库、运河及通航渠道的长度。包括全年季节性通航累计三个月以上的航道,不包括仅供零散流放竹、木排的河道。它是反映内河水运网规模、水平和发展情况的主要指标。

输油(气)管道长度　也称输油(气)里程,指油品(或天然气)的实际输送距离,一般按输油(气)管道的单线长度计算。若包括复线和备用线长度则称为输油(气)管道延展长度,是指管道铺设的实际长度。我们通常使用的是不包括复线的"输油(气)管道里程",它是反映管道运输发展规模和水平的主要指标。

货(客)运量　指在一定时期内,各种运输工具实际运送的货物(旅客)数量。它是反映运输业为国民经济和人民生活服务的数量指标,也是制定和检查运输生产计划、研究运输发展规模和速度的重要指标。货运按吨计算,客运按人计算。货物不论运输距离长短、货物类别,均按实际重量统计。旅客不论行程远近或票价多少,均按一人一次客运量统计;半价票、小孩票也按一人统计。

货物(旅客)周转量　指在一定时期内,由各种运输工具运送的货物(旅客)数量与其相应运输距离的乘积之总和。它是反映运输业生产总成果的重要指标,也是编制和检查运输生产计划,计算运输效率、劳动生产率以及核算运输单位成本的主要基础资料。计算货物周转量通常按发出站与到达站之间的最短距离,也就是计费距离计算。计算公式为:

$$\text{货物(旅客)周转量} = \sum \text{货物(旅客)运输量} \times \text{运输距离}$$

沿海主要港口货物吞吐量　指经水运进出沿海主要港区范围,并经过装卸的货物数量,包括邮件及办理托运手续的行李、包裹以及补给运输船舶的燃、物料和淡水。货物吞吐量按货物流向分为进口、出口吞吐量,按货物交流性质分为外贸货物吞吐量和国内贸易货物吞吐量。货物吞吐量的货类构成及其流向,是衡量港口生产能力大小的重要指标。

邮电业务总量　指以价值量形式表现的邮电通信企业为社会提供各类邮电通信服务的总数量。邮电业务量按专业分类包括函件、包件、汇票、报刊发行、邮政快件、特快专递、邮政储蓄、集邮、公众电报、用户电报、传真、长途电话、出租电路、无线寻呼、移动电话、分组交换数据通信、出租代维等。计算方法为各类产品乘以相应的平均单价(不变价)之和,再加上出租电路和设备、代用户维护电话交换机和线路等的服务收入。它综合反映了一定时期邮电业务发展的总成果,是研究邮电业务量构成和发展趋势的重要指标。计算公式为:

$$\text{邮电业务总量} = \sum(\text{各类邮电业务量} \times \text{不变单价}) + \text{出租代维及其他业务收入}$$

无线寻呼用户　无线寻呼是指电话用户通过无线寻呼中心,在规定范围内向携带小型寻呼机的用户发出声音、数字或文字显示信息。在寻呼台办理登记手续携带小型寻呼机的用户,称为无线寻呼用户。

移动电话用户　是指通过移动电话交换机进入移动电话网、占用移动电话号码的电话用户。用户数量以报告期末在移动电话营业部门实际办理登记手续进入移动电话网的户数进行计算,一部移动电话统计为一户。

电话用户　指接入国家公众固定电话网,并按固定电话业务进行经营管理的电话用户。1997 年以前,电话用户分为市内电话用户和农村电话用户。"市内电话用户"是指接入县城及县以上城市的电话网上的电话用户;"农村电话用户"是指接入县邮电局农话台及县以下农村电话交换点,以县城为中心(除市话用户外)联通县、乡(镇)、行政村、村民小组的用户。从1997 年起,电话用户数分组调整为以用户所在区域划分为"城市电话用户"和"乡村电话用户",与过去的按市内电话和农村电话划分方法不同。而电话用户总数、电话机总部数统计范围不变。

城市电话用户　指直辖市、地区、地级市、县级市的市区、市郊区及县城(包括县人民政府所在地的县城关区或行政建制相当于县人民政府所在地的镇)范围内接入局用交换机的电话用户数,包括分布在农村地区的独立工矿区、林区、驻军等接入局用交换机的电话用户数。

乡村电话用户　指县城关区以下的集镇和农村接入局用交换机的电话用户数。

住宅电话用户　是指安装在居民住宅或农民家里并按照住宅电话用户登记注册和收费的电话用户。包括私人付费、单位付费和按规定免费安装的住宅电话用户。

局用交换机容量　是指安装在本地电信运营商内用于接续本地固定电话的电话交换机容量,有倍增设备按倍增后的数量计数。包括现用和备用的人工或自动交换机的全部容量。

Explanatory Notes on Main Statistical Indicators

Length of Railways in Operation refers to the total length of the trunk line under passenger and freight transportation(including both full operation and temporary operation). The calculation is based on the actual length of the first line even if this line has a full or partial double track or more tracks,excluding double tracks,station sidings,tracks under the charge of stations,branch lines,special-purpose lines and the non-payable connecting lines. The length of railways in operation is an important indicator to show the development of the infrastructure for the railway transport,and also the essential data to calculate volume of passenger freight transport, traffic density and utilization efficiency of the locomotives and carriages.

Extenuation Length of Trunk Lines refers to the sum of the first,the second,the third lines and other constructed length of the trunk railways,excluding the extenuation length of the station lines,lines under the jurisdiction depots,siding and lines for special purpose. It provides important information for the calculation of the needs for rails,sleepers,sand and stone for the construction ot railways.

Length of Highways refers to the length of highways which are built in conformity with the grades specified by the highway engineering standard formulated by the Ministry of Communications,and have been formally checked and accepted by the departments of highways and put into use. The length of highways includes that of the suburb highways at large and medium-sized cities,highways passing through streets at small cities and towns,and also the length of bridges and ferries. It does not include the length of streets in big and medium-sized cities and highways built for the production purpose at factories,mines,forest areas and agricultural areas. If two or more highways go the same section of the way,the length of the section is only calculated for once and no duplication is allowed. The length of highways is an important indicator to show the development of the highway construction and to provide essential information to calculate the transport network density.

Length of Navigable Inland Waterways an indicator reflecting the size and development of inland water network,it refers to the length of the natural rivers,lakes,reservoirs,canals,and ditches open to navigation during a given period,which enables the transport by ships and rafts. It includes the channels open to navigation for over an accumulative 3 months in a year,yet this does not include the river courses which are only used to float odd logs and bamboo rafts.

Length of Oil(Gas)Pipelines used as an indicator to show the development,scale and level of the pipeline transportation,it refers to the actual transport distance of oil (or gas) products,and is in general calculated in the length of single pipe line. If the length of the double pipelines and alternate pipeline are included,it is called the extension length of the oil (gas)pipelines,which indicates the actual length of the pipelines built,excluding double pipelines.

Freight(Passenger)Traffic refers to the volume of freight (passenger) transported with various means. Freight transport is calculated in tons and passenger traffic is calculated in the number of persons. Despite the type of freight and travelling distance,the freight transport is calculated in the actual weight of the goods;and despite the travelling distance and ticket price,the passenger traffic is calculated by the principle that one person can be counted only once in one travel. The passenger who travel with a half price ticket or a child ticket is also calculated as one person. The freight(passenger) traffic provides a quantitative measure to show how the transport industry serves the national economy and people,and is also an important indicator for planning the transport industry and for studying the development scale and speed of the transport industry.

Freight Ton-kilometers (Passenger-kilometers) refer to the sum of the products of the volume of transported cargo (passengers) multiplying by the transport distance,usually using ton-kilometer and passenger-kilometer as units for measurement. Normally,the shortest distance between the departure station and the destination station(i. e. ,the payable distance) is the basis to calculate the freight ton-kilometers. This is an important indicator to show the total results of the transport industry,to prepare and examine the transport plan and to measure the efficiency,the labour productivity and the unit cost of transport. The formula is as follows:

Freight Ton-kilometers(Passenger-kilometers) = {fFreight(Passenger) Traffic × Distance of Transportation}

Volume of Freight Handled in Major Coastal Ports refers to the volume of cargo passing in and out the harbor area of the major coastal ports and having been loaded and unloaded. The volume includes that of the postal matters, registered luggage and fuels, materials and fresh water as supplies of the ships. The volume of freight handled may be classified by direction of flow as freight for import and freight for export, or by nature of cargo as freight for domestic trade and freight for foreign trade. As an important indicator, the volume of freight handled by type of cargo and by main flow direction reflects the production capacity of ports.

Business Volume of Post and Telecommunications refers to the total amount of post and telecommunications services, expressed in value terms, provided by the post and telecommunications departments for the society. Post and telecommunication services can be classified as letters, parcels, remittance, issue of newspapers and magazines, fast mail service, express mail service, savings deposits, stamps for collection, public and individual telegraph service, facsimiles, long-distance telephone service, leasing of telephone lines, urban paging service, mobile telephone service, data transfer and transmission, etc. The accounting approach is to multiply the service products of all types with their average unit price (constant price) to get sum of business value, plus income from other services such as leasing of telephone lines and equipment, maintenance of telephone switchboards and lines on behalf of customers. This indicator reflects the overall results of post and telecommunications service during a given period, and is important to study the composition of business service and the development of post and telecommunications service. The formula is as follows:

Business Volume of Post and Telecommunications = $\sum$ (Transaction of Post and Telecommunication Service × Constant Price) + Income from Leasing, Maintenance and other Services.

Mobile Telephone Subscribers refer to the persons who own mobile telephone numbers and are connected with the mobile telephone communication network through the mobile telephone switchboards. The number of subscribers is calculated by the subscribers who have completed registration at mobile communication business centers and entered into the mobile telephone network. One mobile telephone is taken as a subscriber.

Fixed Telephone Subscribers refer to subscribers that are connected to the public line telephone network provided with telephone services. Before 1997, telephone subscribers were classified as city subscribers and village subscribers. City subscribers referred to those connected to city telephone networks in county towns and cities, while village subscribers referred to those connected to village telephone stations at and below counties. Since 1997, the classification of telephone subscribers was modified on the basis of physical location of the subscribers as rban telephone subscribers and ural telephone subscribers, which is different from the previous classification of catgorizing local telephones and ural telephones, while the definition of total subscribers and total number of telephones remain unchanged.

Urban Telephone Subscribers refer to subscribers telephone subscribers, located at municipalities, cities under the jurisdiction of province, cities at prefectural level, downtown and suburb of city at county level town and county towns (including country towns where county government located, and towns of county level according to the administrative organizational system), that are connected to the public line telephone network, including rural mineral area, forest area, military area.

Rural Telephone Subscribers refer to telephone subscribers, located at towns under county town and country, that are connected to the public line telephone network.

Household Telephone Subscribers refer to telephone sets installed in the dwelling units of urban or rural residents, and registered as residence subscribers for payment, including 3 types of payment for the service: private payment, public payment and free service.

Capacity of Office Telephone Exchanges refers to the capacity (measured in gate) of telephone exchanges installed in the offices of local telecommunication service providers for communication between fixed telephones. It includes the capacity of both manual and automatic exchanges in use and for stand-by purpose. Equipment with expansion function is to be counted by the expanded capacity.

14

批发零售、住宿餐饮和旅游

Wholesale and Retail Trade, Hotels, Catering Services and Tourism

简要说明

一、本篇资料的主要内容

本篇资料主要反映江苏消费品市场、批发和零售业、住宿和餐饮业以及旅游业的发展状况。主要内容包括社会消费品零售总额;批发和零售业、住宿和餐饮业全行业经营情况;限额以上批发和零售业、住宿和餐饮业的基本情况、财务状况、连锁经营情况;亿元以上商品交易市场基本情况和成交情况;旅行社、星级饭店基本情况;入境旅游人数、国内居民旅游人数以及国际、国内旅游收入。

二、本篇资料的统计范围

社会消费品零售总额的统计范围为参与市场商品零售或餐饮经营活动的各行业法人企业、产业活动单位和个体经营户;批发和零售业、住宿和餐饮业全行业经营情况的统计范围为全部批发和零售业、住宿和餐饮业法人企业、产业活动单位和个体经营户;限额以上批发和零售业基本情况、财务状况和连锁经营情况的统计范围为年主营业务收入达到2000万元及以上的批发业、年主营业务收入达到500万元及以上的零售业法人企业、产业活动单位和个体经营户;限额以上住宿和餐饮业基本情况、财务状况和连锁经营情况的统计范围为年主营业务收入达到200万元及以上的住宿和餐饮业法人企业、产业活动单位和个体经营户;亿元以上商品交易市场基本情况和成交情况统计范围为年商品成交额达到亿元及以上的现货商品交易市场;旅行社和星级饭店基本情况、入境旅游人数、国内居民旅游人数以及国际、国内旅游收入的统计范围为全省范围内的旅行社、星级饭店和旅游者。

三、本篇资料的来源

本篇资料中社会消费品零售总额以及批发和零售业、住宿和餐饮业发展情况根据《批发和零售业统计报表制度》《住宿和餐饮业统计报表制度》规定的有关统计内容进行加工整理;旅游业发展情况根据旅游局提供的有关资料编制。

四、本篇资料的统计调查方法

本篇资料中社会消费品零售总额以及批发和零售业、住宿和餐饮业发展情况方面资料涉及限额以上法人企业、产业活动单位和个体经营户以及亿元及以上商品交易市场的采用全面调查方法;涉及限额以下法人企业、产业活动单位和个体经营户的采用抽样调查方法推算。旅游业发展情况数据中国际、国内旅游收入和国内居民旅游人数等指标采用抽样调查方法,其余数据均为全面调查统计取得。

Brief Introduction

Ⅰ. Main Contents

Data in this chapter reflect the development of markets of consumer goods, wholesale and retail trades, hotels and catering services and tourism. Main contents include the total sales of consumer goods, the operation of wholesale and retail trades and hotel and catering services, the basic conditions, financial status and chain operation of the wholesale and retail trades and hotel and catering services above designated size, the basic condition and turnover of large commodity transaction markets with transaction over 100 million yuan, the basic conditions of travel agencies and star-rated hotels, number of international tourists and Chinese residents going abroad, number of domestic tourists and income from international and domestic tourism.

Ⅱ. Scope of Statistics

The scope of statistics of the total sales of consumer goods include corporate enterprises, establishments, and self-employed individuals involved in wholesale and retail trades and hotels and catering services. The scope of statistics of the operation of wholesale and retail trades and hotel and catering services include all corporate enterprises, establishments, and self-employed individuals involved in wholesale and retail trades and hotels and catering services. The scope of statistics of the basic conditions, financial status and chain operation of the wholesale and retail trades above designated size include corporate enterprises, establishments, and self-employed individuals involved in wholesale trade with annual principal business sales over 20 million yuan, retail trade with annual principal business sales over 5 million yuan. The scope of statistics of the basic conditions, financial status and chain operation of the hotel and catering services above designated size include corporate enterprises, establishments, and self-employed individuals involved in the hotel and catering services with annual principal business sales over 2 million yuan. The scope of statistics of the basic condition and turnover of large commodity transaction markets with transaction over 100 million yuan include all transaction markets with the total sales value of commodities over 100 million yuan. The scope of statistics of the basic conditions of travel agencies and star-rated hotels, number of international tourists and Chinese residents going abroad, number of domestic tourists and income from international and domestic tourism include all travel agencies, star-rated hotels and tourists in Jiangsu Province.

Ⅲ. Sources of Data

The total sales of consumer goods and the development of wholesale and retail trades, hotels and catering services are collected and processed in accordance with The Statistical Reporting Form System on Wholesale and Retail Trades and The Satistical Reporting Form System on Hotels and Catering Services. The data on tourism are from the Ministry of Public Security and State Tourism Administration.

Ⅳ. Methods of Survey

Data on corporate enterprises above designated

size, establishments, self-employed individuals and commodity transaction markets with transaction over 100 million yuan are collected through comprehensive reporting system. Data on enterprises and self-employed individuals below the designated size are collected by sample surveys. Data on tourism are from the comprehensive reporting form system except those on the earnings from international and domestic tourism and number of domestic tourists going abroad from sample surveys.

14－1 国内贸易基本情况
Basic Conditions of Domestic Trade

指　　标	Item	2012	2013	2014	2015	2016
限额以上法人企业　（个）	**Number of Corporation Enterprises above Designated Size　(unit)**	**16358**	**25175**	**22683**	**22165**	**22514**
批发业	Wholesale Trade	7871	13050	11388	10753	10852
零售业	Retail Trade	5740	8681	8147	8290	8571
住宿业	Hotels	935	1042	1026	1057	1061
餐饮业	Catering Services	1812	2402	2122	2065	2030
限额以上产业活动单位（个）	**Industry Activity Units　(unit)**	**28452**	**39672**	**36544**	**36099**	**36611**
批发业	Wholesale Trade	11221	16009	13474	12734	12437
零售业	Retail Trade	13052	18645	18395	18635	19436
住宿业	Hotels	1072	1178	1156	1203	1203
餐饮业	Catering Services	3107	3840	3519	3527	3535
限额以上企业(单位)从业人数　（人）	**Engaged Persons　(person)**	**1229898**	**1442376**	**1372467**	**1316192**	**1288982**
批发业	Wholesale Trade	347101	462293	426460	414793	404339
零售业	Retail Trade	515393	605001	589719	573752	561763
住宿业	Hotels	144273	134364	127611	129100	126789
餐饮业	Catering Services	223131	240718	228677	198547	196091
限额以上批发和零售业	**Wholesale and Retail Trades**					
商品购进总额　（亿元）	Total Purchases　(100 million yuan)	32972.76	42377.61	41554.17	40149.81	43797.28
商品销售总额　（亿元）	Total Sales　(100 million yuan)	35792.88	46399.82	46152.51	42772.98	47801.39
商品库存总额　（亿元）	Total Stock　(100 million yuan)	2108.28	2496.86	2582.84	2471.78	2928.76
社会消费品零售总额（亿元）	**Total Retail Sales of Consumer Goods　(100 million yuan)**	**18411.11**	**20878.20**	**23458.07**	**25876.77**	**28707.12**
商品交易市场数　（个）	**Number of Commodity Exchange Markets　(unit)**	**3890**	**2625**	**2826**	**2861**	**2817**
消费品市场	Markets of Consumer Goods	3492	2204	2438	2466	2448
生产资料市场	Markets of Production Material	398	421	388	395	369

14－2 按行业分社会消费品零售总额
Total Retail Sales of Consumer Goods by Sector

单位:亿元 (100 million yuan)

年 份 Year	社会消费品零售总额 Total Retail Sales of Consumer Goods	批发和零售业 Wholesale and Retail Sales Trade	住 宿 业 Hotel	餐 饮 业 Catering Services	其他行业 Others
1978	84.79	79.18		3.24	2.37
1979	99.16	91.61		3.90	3.65
1980	122.56	114.35		4.72	3.49
1981	134.79	125.16		5.17	4.46
1982	150.01	138.87		5.49	5.65
1983	169.12	156.28		6.14	6.70
1984	205.05	188.80		7.61	8.64
1985	262.57	240.69		10.45	11.43
1986	304.58	279.25		12.53	12.80
1987	360.74	329.31		15.84	15.59
1988	471.83	432.06		20.33	19.44
1989	509.56	467.11		22.47	19.98
1990	515.43	472.72		24.17	18.54
1991	578.12	529.94		27.86	20.32
1992	704.52	644.61		33.64	26.27
1993	967.77	888.24		44.74	34.79
1994	1359.61	1238.30		71.44	49.87
1995	1741.92	1573.01		95.21	73.70
1996	2080.44	1901.47		135.64	43.33
1997	2300.61	2082.71		167.92	49.99
1998	2453.84	2208.24		192.52	53.08
1999	2649.56	2367.59		227.58	54.39
2000	2908.46	2583.19		269.59	55.69
2001	3233.35	2845.89		326.71	60.76
2002	3656.57	3179.23		410.83	66.52
2003	4194.50	3613.67		510.94	69.88
2004	4892.18	4333.18	41.67	496.10	21.22
2005	5735.50	5051.70	49.81	583.09	50.91
2006	6706.19	5898.79	67.68	678.83	60.89
2007	7985.90	7023.48	82.48	810.56	69.38
2008	9905.10	8890.30	99.80	826.10	88.90
2009	11487.72	10312.81	107.66	957.23	110.02
2010	13606.34	12207.18	127.15	1147.99	124.02
2011	16058.31	14320.87	161.94	1359.27	216.23
2012	18411.11	16448.83	178.42	1588.08	195.78
2013	20878.20	18694.85	173.23	1788.44	221.68
2014	23458.07	21229.55	187.67	2040.85	
2015	25876.77	23414.30	198.91	2263.56	
2016	28707.12	25899.14	216.73	2591.25	

注:1. 2003 年前住宿业包括在餐饮业和其他行业中。
2. 2004 年为第一次经普数据,1993—2003 年原则根据原各年环比发展速度和 2004 年经济普查数据调整。
3. 2008 年为第二次经普数据,2005—2007 年根据趋势离差法和 2008 年经济普查数据调整。
4. 2013 年为第三次经普数据,2014 年为按经普口径统计数据,2009—2012 年根据趋势离差法和 2013 年经济普查数据调整。

a) Before 2003, the hotel includes in the catering industry and other industries.

b) In 2004, it was first Economic Census data, the data in 1993—2003 was accordance with the principles of the original development rate of the economy and 2004 Economic Census data adjustment.

c) In 2008, it was second Economic Census data, the data in 2005—2007 was according to the trend of the deviation from the law and 2008 Economic Census data adjustment.

d) In 2013, it was third Economic Census data, the data in 2014 Economic Census data adjustment, the data in 2009—2012 was according to the trend of the deviation from the law and the 2013 Economic Census data adjustment.

14－3 按地区分社会消费品零售总额(2016年)
Total Retail Sales of Consumer Goods by Region (2016)

单位:亿元 (100 million yuan)

年份 Year		社会消费品零售总额 Total Retail Sales of Consumer Goods	批发和零售业 Wholesale and Retail Sales Trade	住宿业 Hotel	餐饮业 Catering Services
苏南	Southern Jiangsu	16584.16	14965.42	206.38	1412.36
苏中	Mid Jiangsu	5110.01	4573.11	47.41	489.50
苏北	Northern Jiangsu	7012.94	6321.27	103.06	588.62
南京市	Nanjing	5088.20	4638.45	87.16	362.58
无锡市	Wuxi	3119.56	2880.94	23.99	214.62
徐州市	Xuzhou	2659.39	2433.52	42.10	183.77
常州市	Changzhou	2202.83	2016.06	17.16	169.61
苏州市	Suzhou	4936.79	4343.02	64.09	529.68
南通市	Nantong	2632.87	2406.78	12.18	213.91
连云港市	Lianyungang	933.31	829.64	13.86	89.80
淮安市	Huaian	1083.83	978.30	12.41	93.12
盐城市	Yancheng	1630.88	1465.26	16.96	148.66
扬州市	Yangzhou	1358.80	1201.39	22.02	135.40
镇江市	Zhenjiang	1236.78	1086.95	13.97	135.87
泰州市	Taizhou	1118.34	964.94	13.21	140.19
宿迁市	Suqian	705.54	614.55	17.73	73.26

注:因分行业计算方法问题,分行业零售额全省数与各市之和有所不等。
Note: Because the method of calculation of industry, the province total retail sales by industry is not equal to 13 cities.

14－4 限额以上批发和零售业基本情况(2016年)

Basic Conditions of Enterprises above Designated Size in Wholesale and Retail Trades(2016)

项目	Item	法人企业(个) Number of Corporation Enterprises (unit)	产业活动单位数(个) Number of Establishments (unit)	零售营业面积(平方米) Floor Space of Retail Business (sq. m)	从业人员(人) Persons Engaged (person)
总计	**Total**	**19423**	**31873**	**29929774**	**966102**
#国有控股	State-owned and State Share Holding	855	4166	4128508	102975
批发业	**Wholesale Trade**	**10852**	**12437**	**4860476**	**404339**
#国有控股	State-owned and State Share Holding	539	1173	1574357	57527
按登记注册类型分	**Grouped by Status of Registration**				
内资企业	Domestic Funded Enterprises	10463	11912	3987835	346759
国有企业	State-owned Enterprises	217	309	86901	20479
集体企业	Collective-owned Enterprises	44	60	36133	1454
股份合作企业	Cooperative Enterprises	5	5	1028	344
联营企业	Joint Ownership Enterprises				
国有联营企业	State Joint Ownership Enterprises				
集体联营企业	Collective Joint Ownership Enterprise				
国有与集体联营企业	Joint State-collective Enterprises				
其他联营企业	Other Joint Ownership Enterprises				
有限责任公司	Limited Liability Corporations	2102	2622	1448213	106459
国有独资公司	State Solely Funded Corporations	65	197	574469	8013
其他有限责任公司	Other Limited Liability Corporations	2037	2425	873744	98446
股份有限公司	Share-holding Corporations Ltd.	165	525	212423	29195
私营企业	Private Enterprises	7649	8106	2031953	173733
私营独资企业	Private-funded Enterprises	83	97	79519	2060
私营合伙企业	Private Partnership Enterpises	9	9	454	269
私营有限责任公司	Private Limited Liability Corporations	7364	7803	1809660	165218
私营股份有限公司	Private Share-holding Corporations Ltd.	193	197	142320	6186
其他企业	Other Enterprises	281	285	171184	15095
港、澳、台商投资企业	Enterprises with Funds from Hong Kong, Macao and Taiwan	171	273	40051	21330
合资经营企业	Joint-venture Enterprises	28	38	9965	3554
合作经营企业	Cooperative Enterprises				
独资经营企业	Enterprises with Sole Fund	138	227	29986	17315
港、澳、台商投资股份有限公司	Share-holding Corporations Ltd.	5	8	100	461
其他港澳台投资	Other Funds from Hong Kong, Macao and Taiwan				
外商投资企业	Foreign Funded Enterprises	218	252	832590	36250
合资经营企业	Joint-venture Enterprises	39	48	717875	2663
合作经营企业	Cooperative Enterprises	2	3	50	229
独资经营企业	Enterprises with Sole Fund	173	189	111564	31500
外商投资股份有限公司	Share-holding Corporations Ltd.		1	100	589
其他外商投资	Other Foreign Funds	4	11	3001	1269

14－4 续 表 1 Continued 1

项 目	Item	法人企业(个) Number of Corporation Enterprises (unit)	产业活动单位数(个) Number of Establishments (unit)	零售营业面积(平方米) Floor Space of Retail Business (sq. m)	从业人员(人) Persons Engaged (person)
按行业分	**Grouped by Sector**				
农、林、牧产品批发	Wholesale of Farm Products and Livestock Products	663	724	287187	25029
食品、饮料及烟草制品批发	Wholesale of Food, Beverages and Tobaccos	854	1001	458866	64237
纺织、服装及日用品批发	Wholesale of Textiles, Garments and Daily Consumer Articals	1643	1779	363825	94462
文化、体育用品及器材批发	Wholesale of Culture, Sports Appliances and Equipment	289	310	105681	15589
医药及医疗器材批发	Wholesale of Medicines and Medical Appliances	315	379	232791	45972
矿产品、建材及化工产品批发	Wholesale of Mineral Products, Building Material and Chemical Products	4980	6024	2750489	96656
机械设备、五金交电及电子产品批发	Wholesale of Machinery, Hardware and Electronic Equipment	1554	1628	481377	50926
贸易经纪与代理	Trade Broker and Agency	157	157	22902	2651
其他批发	Others	397	435	157358	8817
零售业	**Retail Trade**	**8571**	**19436**	**25069298**	**561763**
#国有控股	State-owned and State Share Holding	316	2993	2554151	45448
按登记注册类型分	**Grouped by Status of Registration**				
内资企业	Domestic Funded Enterprises	8349	17961	20296676	444834
国有企业	State-owned Enterprises	51	84	122175	4517
集体企业	Collective-owned Enterprises	111	202	168521	3569
股份合作企业	Cooperative Enterprises	12	16	11480	260
联营企业	Joint Ownership Enterprises	5	10	14767	553
国有联营企业	State Joint Ownership Enterprises	1	2	2826	412
集体联营企业	Collective Joint Ownership Enterprise	4	8	11941	141
国有与集体联营企业	Joint State-collective Enterprises				
其他联营企业	Other Joint Ownership Enterprises				
有限责任公司	Limited Liability Corporations	1919	7143	7605968	157878
国有独资公司	State Solely Funded Corporations	29	183	81796	1860
其他有限责任公司	Other Limited Liability Corporations	1890	6960	7524172	156018
股份有限公司	Share-holding Corporations Ltd.	206	2047	2480627	33446
私营企业	Private Enterprises	5781	8184	9675722	232624
私营独资企业	Private-funded Enterprises	345	377	302585	5894
私营合伙企业	Private Partnership Enterpises	41	44	25320	477
私营有限责任公司	Private Limited Liability Corporations	5192	7437	8943050	216076
私营股份有限公司	Private Share-holding Corporations Ltd.	203	326	404767	10177
其他企业	Other Enterprises	264	275	217416	11987

项　　目	Item	法人企业(个) Number of Corporation Enterprises (unit)	产业活动单位数(个) Number of Establishments (unit)	零售营业面积(平方米) Floor Space of Retail Business (sq. m)	从业人员(人) Persons Engaged (person)
港、澳、台商投资企业	Enterprises with Funds from Hong Kong, Macao and Taiwan	128	477	2560605	70904
合资经营企业	Joint-venture Enterprises	31	40	461664	7865
合作经营企业	Cooperative Enterprises				
独资经营企业	Enterprises with Sole Fund	94	429	2075505	62121
港、澳、台商投资股份有限公司	Share-holding Corporations Ltd.	3	5	22180	867
其他港澳台投资	Other Funds from Hong Kong, Macao and Taiwan		3	1256	51
外商投资企业	Foreign Funded Enterprises	94	998	2212017	46025
合资经营企业	Joint-venture Enterprises	27	843	1329688	25493
合作经营企业	Cooperative Enterprises	1	4	20400	237
独资经营企业	Enterprises with Sole Fund	63	142	842332	19830
外商投资股份有限公司	Share-holding Corporations Ltd.	2	8	18597	435
其他外商投资	Other Foreign Funds	1	1	1000	30
按行业分	**Grouped by Sector**				
综合零售	Integrated Retail	856	3453	9875205	191737
食品、饮料及烟草制品专门零售	Retail of Food, Beverages and Tobaccos	1048	2943	847691	42496
纺织、服装及日用品专门零售	Retail of Textiles, Garments and Daily Consumer Articles	590	961	1032038	43355
文化、体育用品及器材专门零售	Retail of Culture, Sports Appliances and Equipment	577	990	846650	25199
医药及医疗器材专门零售	Retail of Medicines and Medica Appliances	491	3269	716473	42630
汽车、摩托车、燃料及零配件专门零售	Retail of Motor Vehicles, Motorcycles, Fuel and Parts	2844	4943	8197249	130325
家用电器及电子产品专门零售	Special Retail of Household Electric Appliances and Electronic Products	1013	1600	1947099	45451
五金、家具及室内装饰材料专门零售	Special Retail of Hardware, Furniture and Decoration Materials	661	719	911758	18765
货摊无店铺及其他零售业	Non-shop and Other Retail	491	558	695135	21805
按经营方式分	**Grouped by Business Mode**				
独立商店	Independent Stores	7062	9339	16696967	335223
连锁商店总店	Chain Stores	220	6472	4537258	105813
连锁商店分店	Branches of Chain Stores	237	1863	2358384	48054
其他	Others	1052	1762	1476689	72673
按零售业态分	**Grouped by Store Type**				
有店铺零售	Retail Store	8190	19049	24680131	538239
食杂店	Grocery Store	60	211	43107	2562
便利店	Convenience Store	81	441	232498	5068

项 目 Item		法人企业(个) Number of Corporation Enterprises (unit)	产业活动单位数(个) Number of Establishments (unit)	零售营业面积(平方米) Floor Space of Retail Business (sq. m)	从业人员(人) Persons Engaged (person)
折扣店	Discount Store	9	13	43549	569
超市	Supermarket	341	823	622411	28179
大型超市	Large Supermarket	199	1717	5119573	108589
仓储会员店	Store Member Store	12	12	68148	646
百货店	Department Store	437	827	4267524	66729
专业店	Specialty Stores	4551	10863	8016952	184035
专卖店	Franchised Stores	2045	3610	4930262	113018
家具建材商店	Furniture Building Material Shop	168	179	401983	7602
购物中心	Shopping Mall	40	91	598720	8872
厂家直销中心	Factory Direct Soles Center	247	259	334684	11931
无店铺零售	No Shop Retail	381	387	389167	23524
电视购物	TV Shopping	4	4	130	1145
邮购	Mail Order Shopping	2	3	3550	1039
网上商店	Online Commodity	270	273	306578	17767
自动售货亭	Vending Machine	1	3	1258	71
电话购物	Telephone Shopping	5	5	1456	206
其他		99	99	76195	3296
在总计中:	**In the Total**				
南京市	Nanjing	2593	5908	6190468	239968
无锡市	Wuxi	1543	2802	2866115	90250
徐州市	Xuzhou	2392	2854	2616738	81873
常州市	Changzhou	1912	2829	1928898	66782
苏州市	Suzhou	3228	5834	5710300	186695
南通市	Nantong	2217	3417	3418814	74134
连云港市	Lianyungang	522	808	555529	27731
淮安市	Huaian	907	1053	1144645	32321
盐城市	Yancheng	1436	1742	1240499	42454
扬州市	Yangzhou	714	1556	1216891	33075
镇江市	Zhenjiang	548	759	965427	27834
泰州市	Taizhou	865	1382	1368496	38960
宿迁市	Suqian	546	929	706954	24025

注:产业活动单位数包括本省限额上批零住餐法人所属的全部(包括在外省的)产业活动单位和其他行业及外省法人所属在本省的限额以上批发和零售业产业活动单位。营业面积、从业人数为法人在地口径。

a) The number of establishments include the number of enterprises above designated size in wholesale and retail trades of Jiangsu and other province eatablished in Jiangsu. The data of persons engaged and floor space of retail business base on the data of corporation enterprises.

14－5 批发和零售业商品购销存总额(2016年)
Total Value of Commodity Purchasing, Sales and Inventory of Enterprises above Designated Size in Wholesale and Retail Sale Trade(2015)

单位:亿元 (100 million yuan)

项目	Item	商品购进总额 Total Purchaes Value	商品销售总额 Total Sales Value	批发 Whole-sale Value	零售 Retail Sale Value	商品库存总额 Stock
总计	**Total**		**111205.89**	**85425.58**	**25780.31**	
限额以上企业和单位	**Above Designated Size Enterprises and Units**	**43797.28**	**47801.39**	**35079.51**	**12721.88**	**2928.76**
#国有控股	State-owned and State Share Holding	7974.08	9278.27	7385.37	1892.90	548.57
批发业	**Wholesale Trade**	**33447.47**	**35840.96**	**33871.04**	**1969.92**	**1891.48**
#国有控股	State-owned and State Share Holding	6439.91	7481.52	6952.62	528.89	391.42
按登记注册类型分	**Grouped by Status of Registration**					
内资企业	Domestic Funded Enterprises	30732.15	32252.37	30438.90	1813.46	1688.37
国有企业	State-owned Enterprises	1022.71	1617.66	1496.43	121.23	93.92
集体企业	Collective-owned Enterprises	78.91	84.28	74.90	9.38	3.26
股份合作企业	Cooperative Enterprises	93.51	94.34	94.34		1.10
联营企业	Joint Ownership Enterprises					
国有联营企业	State Joint Ownership Enterprises					
集体联营企业	Collective Joint Ownership Enterprise					
国有与集体联营企业	Joint State-collective Enterprises					
其他联营企业	Other Joint Ownership Enterprises					
有限责任公司	Limited Liability Corporations	11328.99	12262.39	11590.08	672.31	615.02
国有独资公司	State Solely Funded Corporations	905.48	961.44	906.36	55.07	42.59
其他有限责任公司	Other Limited Liability Corporations	10423.51	11300.95	10683.71	617.24	572.43
股份有限公司	Share-holding Corporations Ltd.	4260.58	3127.50	2873.86	253.64	256.26
私营企业	Private Enterprises	13746.82	14836.57	14120.45	716.12	711.90
私营独资企业	Private-funded Enterprises	52.89	58.46	46.93	11.53	2.00
私营合伙企业	Private Partnership Enterprises	17.85	20.68	15.31	5.37	0.13
私营有限责任公司	Private Limited Liability Corporations	13370.94	14416.29	13743.26	673.03	683.71
私营股份有限公司	Private Share-holding Corporations Ltd.	305.14	341.14	314.95	26.19	26.06
其他企业	Other Enterprises	200.64	229.62	188.84	40.78	6.91
港、澳、台商投资企业	Enterprises with Funds from Hong Kong, Macao and Taiwan	1063.07	1270.25	1227.89	42.36	65.17
合资经营企业	Joint-venture Enterprises	210.28	246.07	239.19	6.88	11.42
合作经营企业	Cooperative Enterprises					
独资经营企业	Enterprises with Sole Fund	840.80	1010.47	977.03	33.44	53.34
港、澳、台商投资股份有限公司	Share-holding Corporations Ltd.	11.99	13.70	11.67	2.03	0.41
其他港澳台投资	Other Funds from Hong Kong, Macao and Taiwan					
外商投资企业	Foreign Funded Enterprises	1652.24	2318.35	2204.24	114.10	137.94

单位:亿元 (100 million yuan)

项目	Item	商品购进总额 Total Purchaes Value	商品销售总额 Total Sales Value	批发 Whole-sale Value	零售 Retail Sale Value	商品库存总额 Stock
合资经营企业	Joint-venture Enterprises	558.01	578.45	567.28	11.17	12.57
合作经营企业	Cooperative Enterprises	4.38	5.63	5.63		0.36
独资经营企业	Enterprises with Sole Fund	1082.12	1715.59	1616.10	99.49	111.48
外商投资股份有限公司	Share-holding Corporations Ltd.	2.16	2.76	2.75	0.01	0.00
其他外商投资	Other Foreign Funds	5.58	15.92	12.49	3.43	13.52
按行业分	**Grouped by Sector**					
农、林、牧产品批发	Wholesale of Farm Products and Livestock Products	695.40	770.93	713.11	57.82	67.17
食品、饮料及烟草制品批发	Wholesale of Food, Beverages and Tobaccos	1997.88	2538.52	2328.42	210.10	135.84
纺织、服装及日用品批发	Wholesale of Textiles, Garments and Daily Consumer Articals	7328.47	7190.70	6886.33	304.37	568.55
文化、体育用品及器材批发	Wholesale of Culture, Sports Appliances and Equipment	518.89	601.90	564.94	36.96	60.79
医药及医疗器材批发	Wholesale of Medicines and Medical Appliances	1148.90	1414.55	1289.22	125.33	139.40
矿产品、建材及化工产品批发	Wholesale of Mineral Products, Building Material and Chemical Products	17712.53	18820.66	17823.88	996.78	665.31
机械设备、五金交电及电子产品批发	Wholesale of Machinery, Hardware and Electronic Equipment	3176.30	3549.13	3368.17	180.96	219.19
贸易经纪与代理	Trade Broker and Agency	333.73	367.90	361.18	6.72	5.70
其他批发	Others	535.37	586.66	535.78	50.88	29.54
零售业	**Retail Trade**	**10349.81**	**11960.43**	**1208.47**	**10751.96**	**1037.28**
#国有控股	State-owned and State Share Holding	1534.17	1796.75	432.74	1364.00	157.14
按登记注册类型分	**Grouped by Status of Registration**					
内资企业	Domestic Funded Enterprises	8870.81	10209.66	880.04	9329.62	875.55
国有企业	State-owned Enterprises	98.88	106.82	6.92	99.90	43.61
集体企业	Collective-owned Enterprises	109.10	115.84	23.19	92.65	4.90
股份合作企业	Cooperative Enterprises	1.99	2.92	0.27	2.64	0.22
联营企业	Joint Ownership Enterprises	18.63	18.97	0.04	18.93	0.04
国有联营企业	State Joint Ownership Enterprises	17.86	18.16		18.16	0.00
集体联营企业	Collective Joint Ownership Enterprise	0.77	0.81	0.04	0.77	0.04
国有与集体联营企业	Joint State-collective Enterprises					
其他联营企业	Other Joint Ownership Enterprises					
有限责任公司	Limited Liability Corporations	3112.86	3512.81	356.40	3156.41	291.55
国有独资公司	State Solely Funded Corporations	75.58	77.91	11.98	65.93	5.00
其他有限责任公司	Other Limited Liability Corporations	3037.28	3434.90	344.43	3090.47	286.56
股份有限公司	Share-holding Corporations Ltd.	1128.88	1461.01	247.84	1213.17	75.75

单位:亿元 (100 million yuan)

项 目	Item	商品购进总额 Total Purchaes Value	商品销售总额 Total Sales Value	批发 Whole-sale Value	零售 Retail Sale Value	商品库存总额 Stock
私营企业	Private Enterprises	4341.01	4910.44	236.63	4673.81	457.74
私营独资企业	Private-funded Enterprises	78.88	92.58	3.98	88.60	3.77
私营合伙企业	Private Partnership Enterpises	9.44	11.11	0.37	10.74	0.83
私营有限责任公司	Private Limited Liability Corporations	4095.48	4624.66	225.49	4399.17	441.13
私营股份有限公司	Private Share-holding Corporations Ltd.	157.21	182.09	6.79	175.31	12.01
其他企业	Other Enterprises	59.46	80.84	8.74	72.11	1.74
港、澳、台商投资企业	Enterprises with Funds from Hong Kong, Macao and Taiwan	808.67	975.73	194.73	781.00	108.07
合资经营企业	Joint-venture Enterprises	106.62	133.55	5.67	127.88	31.19
合作经营企业	Cooperative Enterprises					
独资经营企业	Enterprises with Sole Fund	686.96	825.33	185.83	639.50	75.73
港、澳、台商投资股份有限公司	Share-holding Corporations Ltd.	14.26	15.89	3.22	12.66	1.07
其他港澳台投资	Other Funds from Hong Kong, Macao and Taiwan	0.84	0.96		0.96	0.08
外商投资企业	Foreign Funded Enterprises	670.33	775.04	133.71	641.33	53.65
合资经营企业	Joint-venture Enterprises	387.42	399.93	120.40	279.54	25.88
合作经营企业	Cooperative Enterprises	6.10	7.97		7.97	0.39
独资经营企业	Enterprises with Sole Fund	263.72	353.45	13.17	340.28	25.84
外商投资股份有限公司	Share-holding Corporations Ltd.	11.49	11.69	0.14	11.54	1.32
其他外商投资	Other Foreign Funds	1.61	2.01		2.01	0.22
按行业分	**Grouped by Sector**					
综合零售	Integrated Retail	2007.85	2505.67	306.98	2198.70	184.35
食品、饮料及烟草制品专门零售	Retail of Food, Beverages and Tobaccos	417.39	503.47	58.07	445.39	33.53
纺织、服装及日用品专门零售	Retail of Textiles, Garments and Daily Consumer Articles	365.67	452.05	32.62	419.43	50.59
文化、体育用品及器材专门零售	Retail of Culture, Sports Appliances and Equipment	418.60	482.87	46.90	435.97	84.67
医药及医疗器材专门零售	Retail of Medicines and Medica Appliances	863.12	916.96	180.47	736.49	110.23
汽车、摩托车、燃料及零配件专门零售	Retail of Motor Vehicles, Motorcycles, Fuel and Parts	4462.99	5028.51	417.52	4610.99	381.46
家用电器及电子产品专门零售	Special Retail of Household Electric Appliances and Electronic Products	851.61	968.87	87.30	881.56	61.80
五金、家具及室内装修材料专门零售	Special Retail of Hardware, Furniture and Decoration Materials	476.67	513.96	53.17	460.79	105.57
货摊、无店铺及其他零售业	Non-shop and Other Retail	485.91	588.08	25.45	562.63	25.08

14－5 续 表 3 Continued 3

单位:亿元 (100 million yuan)

项 目	Item	商品购进总额 Total Purchaes Value	商品销售总额 Total Sales Value	批发 Wholesale Value	零售 Retail Sale Value	商品库存总额 Stock
按经营方式分	**Grouped by Business Mode**					
独立商店	Independent Stores	6783.71	7883.72	489.82	7393.90	711.03
连锁商店总店	Chain Stores	1327.42	1459.80	344.26	1115.54	122.76
连锁商店分店	Branches of Chain Stores	648.73	778.35	101.89	676.45	61.88
其他	Others	1589.95	1838.57	272.50	1566.07	141.60
按零售业态分	**Grouped by Store Type**					
有店铺零售	Retail Store	9792.20	11278.84	1159.66	10119.18	981.35
食杂店	Grocery Store	22.36	27.88	3.08	24.80	2.89
便利店	Convenience Store	52.08	88.54	22.82	65.72	2.79
折扣店	Discount Store	4.77	8.16	0.31	7.85	0.41
超市	Supermarket	191.51	208.34	8.91	199.43	20.98
大型超市	Large Supermarket	1087.52	1217.30	279.80	937.50	120.31
仓储会员店	Store Member Store	16.38	18.49	0.04	18.45	1.10
百货店	Department Store	794.55	1165.98	25.17	1140.82	59.88
专业店	Specialty Stores	4272.56	4845.88	496.66	4349.22	389.25
专卖店	Franchised Stores	2800.13	3078.78	210.63	2868.15	269.94
家具建材商店	Furniture Building Material Shop	207.10	219.06	44.47	174.59	90.63
购物中心	Shopping Mall	105.70	127.56	1.96	125.59	4.22
厂家直销中心	Factory Direct Soles Center	219.92	254.77	65.80	188.97	18.93
无店铺零售	No Shop Retail	557.62	681.59	48.81	632.78	55.93
电视购物	TV Shopping	2.88	18.21	0.16	18.05	0.17
邮购	Mail Order Shopping	2.52	4.87		4.87	0.27
网上商店	Online Commodity	469.16	563.62	24.68	538.94	48.24
自动售货亭	Vending Machine	0.53	0.62		0.62	0.05
电话购物	Telephone Shopping	0.75	1.04	0.12	0.92	0.25
其他		81.77	93.23	23.86	69.38	6.96
限额以下企业(单位)和个体	**Enterprises (units) below Designated Size and Individuals**		63404.50	50346.07	13058.43	

14-6 限额以上批发和零售业企业财务状况(2016年)

单位:亿元

项目	Item	资产总计 Total Assets	#流动资产 Crculating Assets	#固定资产 Fixed Assets
总 计	**Total**	**19990.69**	**15273.90**	**1521.57**
#国有控股	State-owned and State Share Holding	4656.68	3498.05	360.59
批发业	**Wholesale Trade**	**13112.18**	**10799.27**	**665.08**
#国有控股	State-owned and State Share Holding	3567.67	2679.18	232.92
按登记注册类型分	**Grouped by status of Registration**			
内资企业	Domestic Funded Enterprises	11645.26	9558.85	599.35
国有企业	State-owned Enterprises	818.20	685.99	66.94
集体企业	Collective-owned Enterprises	35.00	23.93	7.65
股份合作企业	Cooperative Enterprises	11.49	10.29	0.19
联营企业	Joint Ownership Enterprises			
国有联营企业	State Joint Ownership Enterprises			
集体联营企业	Collective Joint Ownership Enterprise			
国有与集体联营企业	Joint State-collective Enterprises			
其他联营企业	Other Joint Ownership Enterprises			
有限责任公司	Limited Liability Corporations	4419.20	3594.38	235.50
国有独资公司	State Solely Funded Corporations	428.14	299.39	29.82
其他有限责任公司	Other Limited Liability Corporations	3991.06	3294.99	205.68
股份有限公司	Share-holding Corporations Ltd.	2213.74	1758.58	50.32
私营企业	Private Enterprises	4076.84	3430.75	225.88
私营独资企业	Private-funded Enterprises	13.13	8.11	4.44
私营合伙企业	Private Partnership Enterprises	0.85	0.60	0.24
私营有限责任公司	Private Limited Liability Corporations	3956.08	3338.07	213.57
私营股份有限公司	Private Share-holding Corporations Ltd.	106.78	83.97	7.63
其他企业	Other Enterprises	70.78	54.93	12.87
港、澳、台商投资企业	Enterprises with Funds from Hong Kong, Macao and Taiwan	745.05	594.45	38.98
合资经营企业	Joint-venture Enterprises	188.42	125.46	11.54
合作经营企业	Cooperative Enterprises			
独资经营企业	Enterprises with Sole Fund	554.38	467.15	27.39
港、澳、台商投资股份有限公司	Share-holding Corporations Ltd.	2.24	1.85	0.05
其他港澳台投资	Other Funds from Hong Kong, Macao and Taiwan			
外商投资企业	Foreign Funded Enterprises	721.88	645.97	26.75
合资经营企业	Joint-venture Enterprises	83.49	75.81	2.74
合作经营企业	Cooperative Enterprises	6.80	6.37	0.01
独资经营企业	Enterprises with Sole Fund	600.55	535.68	23.20
外商投资股份有限公司	Share-holding Corporations Ltd.			
其他外商投资	Other Foreign Funds	31.03	28.11	0.81

Financial Indicators of Enterprises above Designated Size in Wholesale and Retail Trade(2016)

(100 million yuan)

负债合计 Total Liabilities	所有者权益合计 Owner's Equities	主营业务收入 Revenue from Principal Business	主营业务成本 Cost of Principle Business	其他业务利润 Profits from Other Business	营业利润 Profit from Major Business	利润总额 Total Profits
13997.57	**5993.11**	**40240.23**	**36801.18**	**135.48**	**1115.56**	**1149.82**
2886.90	1769.78	7849.04	7121.32	12.49	309.74	327.17
9327.87	**3784.31**	**30204.64**	**27923.17**	**40.29**	**795.47**	**827.25**
2151.45	1416.22	6324.66	5730.89	5.78	268.95	285.72
8476.93	3168.33	27782.78	26024.62	32.28	655.74	678.56
266.62	551.58	1308.74	1015.06	0.86	127.85	133.65
21.78	13.22	70.92	64.07		4.23	4.45
10.83	0.66	80.51	79.52	0.10	0.00	0.11
3484.10	935.10	10567.80	10050.80	21.06	168.30	180.19
312.76	115.38	859.20	847.59	1.25	4.01	6.92
3171.34	819.72	9708.60	9203.21	19.81	164.29	173.26
1555.93	657.81	2976.35	2776.88	3.68	83.35	87.94
3087.28	989.56	12580.82	11869.06	6.57	255.83	256.33
7.49	5.64	52.47	44.83		3.95	3.89
0.44	0.41	17.84	14.97		2.29	2.29
3009.11	946.97	12221.35	11548.92	6.26	240.70	241.00
70.24	36.54	289.16	260.33	0.31	8.88	9.15
50.39	20.40	197.64	169.23	0.00	16.17	15.90
422.20	322.85	1066.67	863.10	2.21	64.46	68.92
99.07	89.35	206.57	187.21	0.23	14.29	13.60
321.80	232.59	854.86	671.65	1.98	49.67	54.83
1.34	0.91	5.23	4.24	0.00	0.50	0.49
428.74	293.13	1355.19	1035.45	5.80	75.28	79.78
39.00	44.49	411.36	381.89	0.33	17.18	17.17
4.29	2.51	3.13	2.47	0.01	0.02	0.02
377.65	222.90	925.24	641.52	5.27	55.40	59.92
7.80	23.23	15.46	9.56	0.20	2.67	2.66

单位:亿元

项 目	Item	资产总计 Total Assets	#流动资产 Crculating Assets	#固定资产 Fixed Assets
按行业分	**Grouped by Sector**			
农、林、牧产品批发	Wholesale of Farm Products and Livestock Products	382.84	279.01	63.22
食品、饮料及烟草制品批发	Wholesale of Food, Beverages and Tobaccos	1225.90	1028.18	96.23
纺织、服装及日用品批发	Wholesale of Textiles, Garments and Daily Consumer Articals	3367.75	2875.36	93.48
文化、体育用品及器材批发	Wholesale of Culture, Sports Appliances and Equipment	438.11	298.47	14.49
医药及医疗器材批发	Wholesale of Medicines and Medical Appliances	688.88	612.99	28.74
矿产品、建材及化工产品批发	Wholesale of Mineral Products, Building Material and Chemical Products	5200.98	4151.75	295.13
机械设备、五金交电及电子产品批发	Wholesale of Machinery, Hardware and Electronic Equipment	1522.24	1319.02	53.40
贸易经纪与代理	Trade Broker and Agency	89.91	77.03	3.69
其他批发	Others	195.57	157.47	16.69
零售业	**Retail Trade**	**6878.50**	**4474.63**	**856.49**
#国有控股	State-owned and State Share Holding	1089.00	818.87	127.67
按登记注册类型分	**Grouped by Status of Registration**			
内资企业	Domestic Funded Enterprises	6133.17	4036.20	712.18
国有企业	State-owned Enterprises	51.74	44.12	4.14
集体企业	Collective-owned Enterprises	25.51	11.05	7.31
股份合作企业	Cooperative Enterprises	1.33	0.92	0.18
联营企业	Joint Ownership Enterprises	0.34	0.18	0.09
国有联营企业	State Joint Ownership Enterprises	0.06	0.03	0.03
集体联营企业	Collective Joint Ownership Enterprise	0.28	0.15	0.06
国有与集体联营企业	Joint State-collective Enterprises			
其他联营企业	Other Joint Ownership Enterprises			
有限责任公司	Limited Liability Corporations	1666.78	1129.59	256.46
国有独资公司	State Solely Funded Corporations	151.83	98.85	11.57
其他有限责任公司	Other Limited Liability Corporations	1514.94	1030.74	244.88
股份有限公司	Share-holding Corporations Ltd.	2314.88	1575.11	154.10
私营企业	Private Enterprises	2047.48	1264.32	281.20
私营独资企业	Private-funded Enterprises	22.89	9.87	9.34
私营合伙企业	Private Partnership Enterpises	2.06	1.11	0.63
私营有限责任公司	Private Limited Liability Corporations	1917.10	1182.05	259.97
私营股份有限公司	Private Share-holding Corporations Ltd.	105.43	71.28	11.26
其他企业	Other Enterprises	25.12	10.91	8.71

(100 million yuan)

负债合计 Total Liabilities	所有者权益合计 Owner's Equities	主营业务收入 Revenue from Principal Business	主营业务成本 Cost of Principle Business	其他业务利润 Profits from Other Business	营业利润 Profit from Major Business	利润总额 Total Profits
266.64	116.21	701.36	640.42	0.68	27.34	33.26
577.99	647.91	2203.04	1747.42	2.91	213.39	217.16
2464.49	903.26	5764.05	5139.58	6.54	190.37	202.87
236.68	201.43	515.15	464.18	0.93	17.66	19.62
547.07	141.81	1224.00	1026.85	17.50	17.23	19.31
3861.72	1339.26	15821.96	15215.36	6.41	222.52	229.22
1173.09	349.16	3121.34	2890.67	4.88	84.79	83.23
70.66	19.25	327.56	310.30	0.07	6.74	6.42
129.55	66.02	526.18	488.39	0.38	15.44	16.16
4669.70	**2208.81**	**10035.60**	**8878.02**	**95.19**	**320.09**	**322.56**
735.45	353.56	1524.38	1390.43	6.71	40.80	41.45
4167.71	1965.46	8664.83	7683.70	61.70	298.88	302.06
42.13	9.61	85.36	79.01	0.33	1.62	2.11
9.20	16.31	69.86	60.69	0.08	4.73	4.69
0.46	0.87	2.55	2.11	0.00	0.21	0.21
0.10	0.24	1.47	1.24		0.15	0.15
0.00	0.06	0.78	0.74		0.02	0.02
0.09	0.19	0.70	0.50		0.13	0.13
1225.38	441.40	3013.23	2686.63	25.00	70.21	74.56
84.64	67.19	67.10	59.34	0.36	3.47	3.09
1140.74	374.21	2946.13	2627.29	24.64	66.74	71.47
1515.37	799.51	1183.08	1056.94	10.64	48.26	48.58
1367.63	679.85	4235.28	3741.91	25.60	162.02	160.29
9.37	13.52	79.77	65.70	0.00	8.05	7.93
0.88	1.17	8.85	6.75		1.51	1.51
1310.36	606.74	3987.63	3528.78	24.40	141.62	140.43
47.01	58.42	159.02	140.68	1.19	10.83	10.41
7.45	17.67	73.99	55.16	0.04	11.69	11.47

单位:亿元

项　　目	Item	资产总计 Total Assets	#流动资产 Crculating Assets	#固定资产 Fixed Assets
港、澳、台商投资企业	Enterprises with Funds from Hong Kong, Macao and Taiwan	426.22	246.94	97.21
合资经营企业	Joint-venture Enterprises	83.40	31.68	38.26
合作经营企业	Cooperative Enterprises			
独资经营企业	Enterprises with Sole Fund	337.62	211.42	58.31
港、澳、台商投资股份有限公司	Share-holding Corporations Ltd.	5.21	3.85	0.64
其他港澳台投资	Other Funds from Hong Kong, Macao and Taiwan			
外商投资企业	Foreign Funded Enterprises	319.11	191.49	47.11
合资经营企业	Joint-venture Enterprises	120.28	86.73	15.17
合作经营企业	Cooperative Enterprises	0.06	0.05	0.01
独资经营企业	Enterprises with Sole Fund	188.10	98.95	31.62
外商投资股份有限公司	Share-holding Corporations Ltd.	9.24	4.34	0.30
其他外商投资	Other Foreign Funds	1.43	1.41	0.02
按行业分	**Grouped by Sector**			
综合零售	Integrated Retail	1427.95	773.94	302.67
食品、饮料及烟草制品专门零售	Retail of Food, Beverages and Tobaccos	195.44	109.16	46.02
纺织、服装及日用品专门零售	Retail of Textiles, Garments and Daily Consumer Articles	314.54	192.46	35.19
文化、体育用品及器材专门零售	Retail of Culture, Sports Appliances and Equipment	266.67	189.83	28.41
医药及医疗器材专门零售	Retail of Medicines and Medica Appliances	408.51	347.76	24.63
汽车、摩托车、燃料及零配件专门零售	Retail of Motor Vehicles, Motorcycles, Fuel and Parts	1855.04	1321.98	294.59
家用电器及电子产品专门零售	Special Retail of Household Electric Appliances and Electronic Products	1729.66	1190.67	60.67
五金、家具及室内装修材料专门零售	Special Retail of Hardware, Furniture and Decoration Materials	479.85	190.90	35.92
货摊、无店铺及其他零售业	Non-shop and Other Retail	200.84	157.93	28.37
按经营方式分	**Grouped by Business Mode**			
独立商店	Independent Stores	3764.54	2286.90	611.66
连锁商店总店	Chain Stores	2066.41	1429.32	104.64
连锁商店分店	Branches of Chain Stores	357.11	257.13	52.10
其他	Others	690.44	501.29	88.10
按零售业态分	**Grouped by Store Type**			
有店铺零售	Retail Store	6614.77	4261.34	840.85
食杂店	Grocery Store	8.92	3.97	1.98

(100 million yuan)

负债合计 Total Liabilities	所有者权益合计 Owner's Equities	主营业务收入 Revenue from Principal Business	主营业务成本 Cost of Principle Business	其他业务利润 Profits from Other Business	营业利润 Profit from Major Business	利润总额 Total Profits
313.94	112.28	825.03	709.89	13.46	5.97	5.30
45.40	38.00	103.12	90.54	3.18	1.81	1.62
264.35	73.27	708.30	606.85	9.85	3.89	3.41
4.20	1.01	13.60	12.50	0.42	0.27	0.27
188.04	131.06	545.74	484.42	20.03	15.23	15.21
81.50	38.78	330.97	302.33	13.77	5.87	6.20
0.01	0.05	0.09	0.05		0.01	0.01
97.49	90.61	208.10	176.02	6.24	8.94	8.58
7.77	1.47	5.23	4.78	0.03	0.41	0.42
1.28	0.15	1.36	1.24		0.01	0.01
1005.51	422.45	2029.99	1744.55	54.53	51.00	53.73
108.29	87.15	395.50	315.11	1.13	40.06	39.91
210.76	103.79	363.38	287.40	1.27	17.31	17.00
170.96	95.71	387.69	324.21	2.66	24.06	24.48
311.67	96.84	800.55	719.66	2.32	21.10	20.28
1304.47	550.56	4339.21	4004.20	23.81	98.90	99.70
1133.68	595.98	799.11	703.13	5.86	25.57	25.32
272.40	207.45	429.82	353.41	1.85	30.54	30.17
151.96	48.88	490.36	426.35	1.75	11.54	11.98
2476.06	1288.47	6693.23	5934.53	58.04	251.42	253.65
1452.53	613.89	1262.72	1116.30	25.54	7.43	7.98
253.71	103.41	573.94	503.62	7.16	11.73	11.16
487.40	203.04	1505.71	1323.57	4.44	49.51	49.78
4457.37	2157.40	9475.82	8391.83	94.17	309.30	311.56
3.80	5.11	22.76	18.79	0.01	1.68	1.74

单位:亿元

项目	Item	资产总计 Total Assets	#流动资产 Crculating Assets	#固定资产 Fixed Assets
便利店	Convenience Store	32.26	16.00	14.98
折扣店	Discount Store	8.76	1.80	0.24
超市	Supermarket	72.48	42.89	17.42
大型超市	Large Supermarket	413.14	261.10	84.83
仓储会员店	Store Member Store	6.13	4.59	1.09
百货店	Department Store	1104.29	573.26	211.86
专业店	Specialty Stores	3282.88	2279.40	310.88
专卖店	Franchised Stores	1121.70	826.02	155.36
家具建材商店	Furniture Building Material Shop	382.20	134.96	18.11
购物中心	Shopping Mall	80.19	34.61	10.36
厂家直销中心	Factory Direct Soles Center	101.82	82.73	13.74
无店铺零售	No Shop Retail	263.74	213.30	15.64
电视购物	TV Shopping	15.06	13.20	0.24
邮购	Mail Order Shopping	2.32	1.72	0.08
网上商店	Online Commodity	188.64	153.89	6.62
自动售货亭	Vending Machine	0.58	0.08	0.41
电话购物	Telephone Shopping	0.55	0.54	0.01
其他	Others	56.57	43.86	8.28
在总计中:	**In the Total**			
南京市	Nanjing	7227.10	5440.03	351.48
无锡市	Wuxi	2284.90	1885.15	171.80
徐州市	Xuzhou	783.96	554.58	161.77
常州市	Changzhou	1620.70	1162.05	89.32
苏州市	Suzhou	4033.95	3255.46	265.49
南通市	Nantong	1117.29	846.15	119.10
连云港市	Lianyungang	240.05	168.67	31.63
淮安市	Huaian	292.36	175.42	62.84
盐城市	Yancheng	482.55	330.18	80.89
扬州市	Yangzhou	393.02	279.46	46.53
镇江市	Zhenjiang	413.47	288.04	50.56
泰州市	Taizhou	645.14	513.86	55.68
宿迁市	Suqian	456.21	374.84	34.50

(100 million yuan)

负债合计 Total Liabilities	所有者权益合计 Owner's Equities	主营业务收入 Revenue from Principal Business	主营业务成本 Cost of Principle Business	其他业务利润 Profits from Other Business	营业利润 Profit from Major Business	利润总额 Total Profits
21.40	10.86	76.69	66.44	0.14	2.66	2.80
6.44	2.32	5.91	4.98	0.23	-0.08	-0.08
69.02	3.46	171.63	144.86	1.60	1.49	2.15
389.11	24.03	1014.52	889.11	29.01	-0.38	-0.45
3.93	2.20	17.88	16.35		0.48	0.39
640.02	464.27	910.97	761.41	24.56	53.40	54.67
2142.09	1140.79	4131.18	3665.88	19.85	162.82	162.93
834.98	286.72	2612.82	2393.88	16.04	57.46	57.36
216.98	165.22	172.93	136.72	1.78	11.64	11.53
58.75	21.44	114.19	95.86	0.41	4.59	5.03
70.84	30.98	224.34	197.57	0.53	13.55	13.49
212.33	51.41	559.77	486.18	1.02	10.79	11.00
8.29	6.77	16.19	12.35	0.49	0.28	0.34
1.22	1.10	3.99	1.42		0.43	0.43
153.42	35.22	454.24	396.43	0.15	8.10	8.33
0.43	0.15	0.53	0.33	0.03	-0.04	-0.04
0.27	0.28	0.91	0.57	0.01	0.04	0.04
48.70	7.88	83.90	75.06	0.34	1.98	1.91
5093.41	2133.69	9281.00	8580.13	55.61	171.17	185.58
1748.76	536.14	5416.64	5074.85	14.72	91.21	92.56
462.35	321.60	2785.03	2446.52	3.49	154.54	151.70
1082.49	538.21	3133.60	2907.46	10.80	77.21	79.56
2970.91	1063.04	9808.38	8989.50	24.41	186.63	208.61
739.06	378.23	3178.74	2954.20	10.99	92.35	92.31
159.94	80.11	681.85	613.77	0.59	20.80	20.61
157.66	134.70	759.77	652.72	2.74	55.36	55.85
297.30	185.25	1242.71	1081.74	1.86	73.19	74.08
218.53	174.50	1051.34	940.93	3.30	46.40	46.18
285.91	127.56	1057.63	964.00	2.31	41.67	36.32
447.09	198.05	1211.68	1095.30	3.68	22.17	25.68
334.17	122.04	631.85	500.08	0.98	82.87	80.79

14－7 限额以上住宿和餐饮业基本情况(2016 年)
Basic Conditions of Enterprises above Designated Size in Hotel and Catering Trade(2016)

项 目	Item	法人企业(个) Number of Corporation Enterprises (unit)	产业活动单位数(个) Number of Establishments(unit)	餐饮营业面积(平方米) Floor Space of Catering Service (sq. m)	从业人员(人) Persons Engaged (person)
总 计	**Total**	**3091**	**4738**	**6868577**	**322880**
#国有控股	State-owned and State Share Holding	273	328	849332	45175
住宿业	**Hotel Service**	**1061**	**1203**	**2556078**	**126789**
#国有控股	State-owned and State Share Holding	192	215	618997	34070
按登记注册类型分组	**Grouped by Status of Registration**				
内资企业	Domestic Funded Enterprises	992	1106	2293305	110341
国有企业	State-owned Enterprises	80	96	221303	13837
集体企业	Collective-owned Enterprises	20	21	30358	1540
股份合作企业	Cooperative Enterprises		2	3930	564
联营企业	Joint Ownership Enterprises	2	2	5000	138
国有联营企业	State Joint Ownership Enterprises	1	1	2000	73
集体联营企业	Collective Joint Ownership Enterprise	1	1	3000	65
国有与集体联营企业	Joint State-collective Enterprises				
其他联营企业	Other Joint Ownership Enterprises				
有限责任公司	Limited Liability Corporations	319	354	989640	45727
国有独资公司	State Solely Funded Corporations	27	28	95973	5970
其他有限责任公司	Other Limited Liability Corporations	292	326	893667	39757
股份有限公司	Share-holding Corporations Ltd.	38	53	129507	7006
私营企业	Private Enterprises	527	570	900887	40996
私营独资企业	Private-funded Enterprises	46	50	63871	2373
私营合伙企业	Private Partnership Enterpises	5	6	7700	391
私营有限责任公司	Private Limited Liability Corporations	441	478	772390	34384
私营股份有限公司	Private Share-holding Corporations Ltd.	35	36	56926	3848
其他企业	Other Enterprises	6	8	12680	533
港、澳、台商投资企业	Enterprises with Funds from Hong Kong, Macao and Taiwan	35	44	107822	7822
合资经营企业	Joint-venture Enterprises	16	20	59359	4876
合作经营企业	Cooperative Enterprises				
独资经营企业	Enterprises with Sole Fund	19	23	48303	2911

项 目	Item	法人企业(个) Number of Corporation Enterprises (unit)	产业活动单位数(个) Number of Establishments (unit)	餐饮营业面积(平方米) Floor Space of Catering Service (sq. m)	从业人员(人) Persons Engaged (person)
港、澳、台商投资股份有限公司	Share-holding Corporations Ltd.				
其他港澳台投资	Other Funds from Hong Kong, Macao and Taiwan		1	160	35
外商投资企业	Foreign Funded Enterprises	34	53	154951	8626
合资经营企业	Joint-venture Enterprises	11	18	80859	3104
合作经营企业	Cooperative Enterprises		0		
独资经营企业	Enterprises with Sole Fund	21	33	70692	5162
外商投资股份有限公司	Share-holding Corporations Ltd.	2	2	3400	360
其他外商投资	Other Foreign Funds				
按行业分组	**Grouped by Sector**				
旅游饭店	Tourist Restaurants	648	748	2158468	108190
一般旅馆	Ordinary Hotels	376	416	352339	16047
其他住宿服务	Other Hotel Service	37	39	45271	2552
按星级等级分组	**Grouped by Star Glass**				
一星	One-star Class	2	3	4296	317
二星	Two-star Class	39	42	61071	2039
三星	Three-star Class	183	197	390267	15204
四星	Four-star Class	144	156	545994	27176
五星	Five-star Class	78	107	454375	31872
其他	Others	615	698	1100075	50181
餐饮业	**Catering Service**	**2030**	**3535**	**4312499**	**196091**
#国有控股	State-owned and State Share Holding	81	113	230335	11105
按登记注册类型分组	**Grouped by Status of Registration**				
内资企业	Domestic Funded Enterprises	1959	2368	3737749	139918
国有企业	State-owned Enterprises	26	57	85894	3413
集体企业	Collective-owned Enterprises	14	15	14423	780
股份合作企业	Cooperative Enterprises	2	3	6400	149
联营企业	Joint Ownership Enterprises		1	150	40
国有联营企业	State Joint Ownership Enterprises				

项 目	Item	法人企业（个）Number of Corporation Enterprises (unit)	产业活动单位数（个）Number of Establishments (unit)	餐饮营业面积（平方米）Floor Space of Catering Service (sq. m)	从业人员（人）Persons Engaged (person)
集体联营企业	Collective Joint Ownership Enterprise				
国有与集体联营企业	Joint State-collective Enterprises				
其他联营企业	Other Joint Ownership Enterprises		1	150	40
有限责任公司	Limited Liability Corporations	413	501	924729	41550
国有独资公司	State Solely Funded Corporations	20	20	51002	2627
其他有限责任公司	Other Limited Liability Corporations	393	481	873727	38923
股份有限公司	Share-holding Corporations Ltd.	32	48	147295	3697
私营企业	Private Enterprises	1456	1715	2513010	89008
私营独资企业	Private-funded Enterprises	308	326	397912	10512
私营合伙企业	Private Partnership Enterpises	19	21	26339	803
私营有限责任公司	Private Limited Liability Corporations	1084	1299	1993004	74308
私营股份有限公司	Private Share-holding Corporations Ltd.	45	69	95755	3385
其他企业	Other Enterprises	16	28	45848	1281
港、澳、台商投资企业	Enterprises with Funds from Hong Kong, Macao and Taiwan	39	253	152991	12356
合资经营企业	Joint-venture Enterprises	13	128	60729	4351
合作经营企业	Cooperative Enterprises	3	3	6600	226
独资经营企业	Enterprises with Sole Fund	22	118	74957	7514
港、澳、台商投资股份有限公司	Share-holding Corporations Ltd.		2	503	21
其他港澳台投资	Other Funds from Hong Kong, Macao and Taiwan	1	2	10202	244
外商投资企业	Foreign Funded Enterprises	32	914	421759	43817
合资经营企业	Joint-venture Enterprises	9	402	149154	22059
合作经营企业	Cooperative Enterprises	1	2	4600	202
独资经营企业	Enterprises with Sole Fund	21	504	266832	21440
外商投资股份有限公司	Share-holding Corporations Ltd.	1	4	923	80
其他外商投资	Other Foreign Funds		2	250	36

项 目	Item	法人企业（个）Number of Corporation Enterprises (unit)	产业活动单位数（个）Number of Establishments (unit)	餐饮营业面积（平方米）Floor Space of Catering Service (sq. m)	从业人员（人）Persons Engaged (person)
按行业分组	**Grouped by Sector**				
正餐服务	Dinner Service	1865	2192	3659027	132936
快餐服务	Snack Service	95	1146	540467	50857
饮料及冷饮服务	Beverage and Cool Drink Service	13	92	45436	3148
其他餐饮服务	Other Catering Service	57	105	67569	9150
按经营方式分组	**Grouped by Business Mode**				
独立商店	Independent Stores	1809	2004	3328380	122096
连锁商店总店	Chain Stores	55	1166	554407	51374
连锁商店分店	Branches of Chain Stores	69	257	207450	10865
其他	Others	97	108	222262	11756
在总计中：	**In the Total**				
南京市	Nanjing	577	1238	1550872	72486
无锡市	Wuxi	255	499	764725	44638
徐州市	Xuzhou	259	270	393265	13096
常州市	Changzhou	158	290	548175	32450
苏州市	Suzhou	397	852	1066749	67143
南通市	Nantong	224	278	430969	15278
连云港市	Lianyungang	102	116	187537	6695
淮安市	Huaian	218	224	329085	10963
盐城市	Yancheng	315	324	475685	16787
扬州市	Yangzhou	203	239	364396	15688
镇江市	Zhenjiang	121	132	255671	10922
泰州市	Taizhou	171	181	321870	11711
宿迁市	Suqian	91	95	179578	5023

14－8 住宿和餐饮业经营情况(2016 年)

单位:万元

项目	Item	营业额 Business Revenue	客房收入 Hotel Rooms
总 计	**Total**	**42255058**	
限额以上企业和单位	**Above Designated Size Enterprises and Units**	**7095335**	**1682183**
#国有控股	State-owned and State Share Holding	960301	329436
住宿业	**Hotel Service**	**2765582**	**1257967**
#国有控股	State-owned and State Share Holding	741784	285256
按登记注册类型分组	**Grouped by Status of Registration**		
内资企业	Domestic Funded Enterprises	2384496	1072383
国有企业	State-owned Enterprises	269975	108806
集体企业	Collective-owned Enterprises	33652	10745
股份合作企业	Cooperative Enterprises	20026	10285
联营企业	Joint Ownership Enterprises	4239	1778
国有联营企业	State Joint Ownership Enterprises	3410	1539
集体联营企业	Collective Joint Ownership Enterprise	829	240
国有与集体联营企业	Joint State-collective Enterprises		
其他联营企业	Other Joint Ownership Enterprises		
有限责任公司	Limited Liability Corporations	950844	420984
国有独资公司	State Solely Funded Corporations	93635	39008
其他有限责任公司	Other Limited Liability Corporations	857209	381976
股份有限公司	Share-holding Corporations Ltd.	233706	88471
私营企业	Private Enterprises	861286	425865
私营独资企业	Private-funded Enterprises	55937	24992
私营合伙企业	Private Partnership Enterprises	11174	3085
私营有限责任公司	Private Limited Liability Corporations	716274	364486
私营股份有限公司	Private Share-holding Corporations Ltd.	77901	33303
其他企业	Other Enterprises	10768	5449
港、澳、台商投资企业	Enterprises with Funds from Hong Kong, Macao and Taiwan	164622	76437
合资经营企业	Joint-venture Enterprises	106484	46156
合作经营企业	Cooperative Enterprises		
独资经营企业	Enterprises with Sole Fund	57896	30039
港、澳、台商投资股份有限公司	Share-holding Corporations Ltd.		
其他港澳台投资	Other Funds from Hong Kong, Macao and Taiwan	242	242
外商投资企业	Foreign Funded Enterprises	216465	109147
合资经营企业	Joint-venture Enterprises	57632	24748
合作经营企业	Cooperative Enterprises		
独资经营企业	Enterprises with Sole Fund	144888	78180
外商投资股份有限公司	Share-holding Corporations Ltd.	13945	6218
其他外商投资	Other Foreign Funds		
按行业分组	**Grouped by Sector**		
旅游饭店	Tourist Restaurants	2371997	1000494
一般旅馆	Ordinary Hotels	343055	227652
其他住宿服务	Other Hotel Service	50530	29821
按星级等级分组	**Grouped by Star Glass**		
一星	One-star Class	2314	1253

Business of Enterprises of Hotels and Catering Services(2016)

(10000 yuan)

餐费收入 Catering Service	商品销售收入 Sales of Commodities	其他收入 Other Revenue	年末拥有床位数(个) Number of Bedsat Year-end (unit)	年末拥有餐位数(位) Number of Dining-seats at Year-end (unit)
4910753	**242570**	**259829**	**379078**	**1713833**
484747	46994	99124	71666	214918
1240957	**78704**	**187955**	**267706**	**526145**
331828	37757	86943	61258	141354
1067332	75957	168824	237221	473914
133952	4132	23085	24778	59501
20798	545	1565	3561	7991
9349		393	784	1051
2134	39	288	504	1350
1544	39	288	372	950
590			132	400
438192	22860	68809	87478	192828
42324	2416	9888	9448	20865
395868	20444	58921	78030	171963
82052	26583	36600	15080	31514
376660	21564	37196	103856	176459
26066	3029	1850	6316	13024
7909	163	18	806	2113
303238	15521	33029	89425	147336
39449	2851	2299	7309	13986
4196	235	888	1180	3220
79801	797	7587	14463	29355
53679	438	6211	8190	19622
26122	359	1376	6110	9733
			163	
93824	1950	11544	16022	22876
28023	1292	3569	6045	10320
59968	393	6347	9392	11194
5833	265	1628	585	1362
1131203	69140	171159	198904	464310
94115	8350	12938	61706	52969
15638	1214	3858	7096	8866
1034	27		572	500

单位:万元

项目	Item	营业额 Business Revenue	客房收入 Hotel Rooms
二星	Two-star Class	41692	14428
三星	Three-star Class	269043	100220
四星	Four-star Class	518401	206483
五星	Five-star Class	848165	344663
其他	Others	1085968	590920
餐饮业	**Catering Service**	**4329753**	**424217**
#国有控股	State-owned and State Share Holding	218517	44180
按登记注册类型分组	**Grouped by Status of Registration**		
内资企业	Domestic Funded Enterprises	3071181	393950
国有企业	State-owned Enterprises	94716	12944
集体企业	Collective-owned Enterprises	13691	2307
股份合作企业	Cooperative Enterprises	5331	109
联营企业	Joint Ownership Enterprises	870	363
国有联营企业	State Joint Ownership Enterprises		
集体联营企业	Collective Joint Ownership Enterprise		
国有与集体联营企业	Joint State-collective Enterprises		
其他联营企业	Other Joint Ownership Enterprises	870	363
有限责任公司	Limited Liability Corporations	839851	160122
国有独资公司	State Solely Funded Corporations	48865	11301
其他有限责任公司	Other Limited Liability Corporations	790986	148821
股份有限公司	Share-holding Corporations Ltd.	129119	6543
私营企业	Private Enterprises	1961467	207198
私营独资企业	Private-funded Enterprises	266368	16585
私营合伙企业	Private Partnership Enterprises	25815	2011
私营有限责任公司	Private Limited Liability Corporations	1588644	178948
私营股份有限公司	Private Share-holding Corporations Ltd.	80641	9655
其他企业	Other Enterprises	26136	4364
港、澳、台商投资企业	Enterprises with Funds from Hong Kong, Macao and Taiwan	294416	22188
合资经营企业	Joint-venture Enterprises	89160	7641
合作经营企业	Cooperative Enterprises	2133	576
独资经营企业	Enterprises with Sole Fund	195820	10830
港、澳、台商投资股份有限公司	Share-holding Corporations Ltd.	792	
其他港澳台投资	Other Funds from Hong Kong, Macao and Taiwan	6511	3142
外商投资企业	Foreign Funded Enterprises	964156	8078
合资经营企业	Joint-venture Enterprises	342646	545
合作经营企业	Cooperative Enterprises	5283	369
独资经营企业	Enterprises with Sole Fund	611057	7165
外商投资股份有限公司	Share-holding Corporations Ltd.	3597	
其他外商投资	Other Foreign Funds	1572	
按行业分组	**Grouped by Sector**		
正餐服务	Dinner Service	2942428	418059
快餐服务	Snack Service	1089145	1075
饮料及冷饮服务	Beverage and Cool Drink Service	112508	
其他餐饮服务	Other Catering Service	185672	5082
按经营方式分组	**Grouped by Business Mode**		
独立商店	Independent Stores	2730337	391124
连锁商店总店	Chain Stores	1057626	881
连锁商店分店	Branches of Chain Stores	276401	13087
其他	Others	265390	19125
限额以下企业(单位)和个体	**Enterprises(units) below Designated Size and Individuals**	**35159723**	

14－8 Continued

(10000 yuan)

餐费收入 Catering Service	商品销售收入 Sales of Commodities	其他收入 Other Revenue	年末拥有床位数(个) Number of Bedsat Year-end (unit)	年末拥有餐位数(位) Number of Dining-seats at Year-end (unit)
22360	934	3969	4869	11889
141062	6196	21565	33875	89196
263580	11537	36801	46818	138895
402681	34853	65969	46903	114607
410239	25157	59652	134669	171058
3669796	**163867**	**71874**	**111372**	**1187688**
152919	9237	12181	10408	73564
2483899	126090	67242	105560	1021302
70416	4011	7345	4156	37391
9137	424	1823	941	4099
5196	26		74	2680
507			85	120
507			85	120
629672	25048	25009	39944	246239
33480	2232	1852	2046	18142
596192	22816	23157	37898	228097
115799	4575	2202	2010	30908
1631738	91838	30693	57087	688208
226513	21255	2016	4613	106094
20967	2421	417	813	8237
1328485	64221	16990	48554	549472
55774	3943	11269	3107	24405
21433	169	170	1263	11657
267280	1034	3914	4033	36543
79142	155	2222	1171	12614
1492	64		200	1320
182665	806	1520	2062	21885
792				130
3188	9	172	600	594
918618	36742	718	1779	129843
341891	34	176	436	49633
4727	184	3	180	2122
566850	36504	539	1163	77572
3577	20			361
1572				155
2355435	112789	56145	109801	959526
1050911	24534	12625	435	169429
96283	14310	1915		12690
167167	12234	1188	1136	46043
2173135	115114	50964	102670	876656
1015164	38841	2740	354	170897
258090	4036	1188	3419	55183
223406	5876	16982	4929	84952

14-9 限额以上住宿和餐饮业企业财务状况(2016 年)

单位:亿元

项目	Item	资产总计 Total Assets	#流动资产 Crculating Assets	#固定资产 Fixed Assets
总　计	**Total**	**1228.43**	**404.26**	**517.03**
#国有控股	State-owned and State Share Holding	341.23	78.03	168.19
住宿业	**Hotel Service**	**767.34**	**222.65**	**350.24**
#国有控股	State-owned and State Share Holding	309.20	68.30	150.86
按登记注册类型分组	**Grouped by Status of Registration**	**0.00**	**0.00**	**0.00**
内资企业	Domestic Funded Enterprises	650.44	192.46	291.31
国有企业	State-owned Enterprises	97.73	20.83	55.78
集体企业	Collective-owned Enterprises	7.92	3.70	2.53
股份合作企业	Cooperative Enterprises			
联营企业	Joint Ownership Enterprises	0.16	0.11	0.02
国有联营企业	State Joint Ownership Enterprises	0.10	0.06	0.01
集体联营企业	Collective Joint Ownership Enterprise	0.06	0.05	0.01
国有与集体联营企业	Joint State-collective Enterprises			
其他联营企业	Other Joint Ownership Enterprises			
有限责任公司	Limited Liability Corporations	310.64	83.38	139.33
国有独资公司	State Solely Funded Corporations	39.40	8.16	24.54
其他有限责任公司	Other Limited Liability Corporations	271.24	75.22	114.79
股份有限公司	Share-holding Corporations Ltd.	72.50	22.41	35.67
私营企业	Private Enterprises	161.31	61.88	57.96
私营独资企业	Private-funded Enterprises	8.63	5.11	2.91
私营合伙企业	Private Partnership Enterpises	0.70	0.20	0.41
私营有限责任公司	Private Limited Liability Corporations	138.06	52.23	49.56
私营股份有限公司	Private Share-holding Corporations Ltd.	13.93	4.34	5.09
其他企业	Other Enterprises	0.19	0.15	0.04
港、澳、台商投资企业	Enterprises with Funds from Hong Kong, Macao and Taiwan	62.82	18.88	25.19
合资经营企业	Joint-venture Enterprises	44.39	13.75	15.24
合作经营企业	Cooperative Enterprises			
独资经营企业	Enterprises with Sole Fund	18.43	5.12	9.95
港、澳、台商投资股份有限公司	Share-holding Corporations Ltd.			
其他港澳台投资	Other Funds from Hong Kong, Macao and Taiwan			
外商投资企业	Foreign Funded Enterprises	54.07	11.31	33.74
合资经营企业	Joint-venture Enterprises	9.64	3.86	4.86
合作经营企业	Cooperative Enterprises			
独资经营企业	Enterprises with Sole Fund	41.58	7.15	27.57
外商投资股份有限公司	Share-holding Corporations Ltd.	2.86	0.30	1.31
其他外商投资	Other Foreign Funds			

Financial Indicators of Enterprises above Designated Size in Hotel and Catering Industry (2016)

(100 million yuan)

负债合计 Total Liabilities	所有者权益合计 Owner's Equities	主营业务收入 Revenue from Principal Business	主营业务成本 Cost of Principle Business	其他业务利润 Profits from Other Business	营业利润 Profit from Major Business	利润总额 Total Profits
904.83	**323.61**	**590.52**	**279.34**	**3.48**	**-1.77**	**-1.08**
204.52	136.71	83.33	34.68	0.97	-8.68	-7.76
568.47	**198.87**	**219.61**	**87.51**	**2.26**	**-16.64**	**-15.78**
176.46	132.74	66.12	27.11	0.96	-7.74	-6.91
0.00	0.00	0.00	0.00	0.00	0.00	0.00
463.00	187.44	194.47	79.40	2.06	-10.59	-9.86
54.26	43.47	20.49	8.04	0.60	-2.59	-2.19
6.49	1.43	3.01	1.30	0.05	-0.15	-0.09
0.20	-0.04	0.41	0.10	0.00	0.03	0.03
0.17	-0.07	0.33	0.08		0.03	0.03
0.03	0.02	0.08	0.02	0.00	0.00	0.00
209.20	101.44	80.58	28.31	0.48	-4.42	-4.51
20.01	19.38	8.70	2.58	0.15	-1.66	-1.52
189.18	82.06	71.88	25.73	0.33	-2.76	-2.99
52.30	20.21	20.35	10.76	0.06	-2.13	-1.94
140.37	20.94	69.24	30.74	0.88	-1.33	-1.16
7.54	1.09	3.79	2.13		-0.03	-0.03
0.53	0.17	1.04	0.61	0.00	0.08	0.08
123.76	14.30	57.11	24.39	0.83	-1.73	-1.58
8.54	5.38	7.30	3.60	0.05	0.35	0.37
0.20	-0.01	0.39	0.16		-0.01	0.01
66.31	-3.48	12.69	3.66	0.04	-3.72	-3.64
48.26	-3.87	7.68	2.39	0.01	-1.74	-1.66
18.05	0.39	5.01	1.27	0.03	-1.98	-1.98
39.16	14.91	12.45	4.45	0.15	-2.33	-2.29
7.64	2.00	2.98	1.18	0.00	0.14	-0.18
29.95	11.63	8.14	3.01	0.15	-2.30	-2.22
1.57	1.28	1.34	0.25		0.11	0.11

14－9 续 表 1

单位:亿元

项 目	Item	资产总计 Total Assets	#流动资产 Crculating Assets	#固定资产 Fixed Assets
按行业分组	**Grouped by Sector**			
旅游饭店	Tourist Restaurants	715.62	203.94	330.93
一般旅馆	Ordinary Hotels	46.45	16.57	17.56
其他住宿服务	Other Hotel Service	5.27	2.14	1.76
按星级等级分组	**Grouped by Star Glass**			
一星	One-star Class	0.07	0.05	0.01
二星	Two-star Class	4.34	1.12	2.81
三星	Three-star Class	57.21	26.83	19.38
四星	Four-star Class	176.91	47.82	68.32
五星	Five-star Class	283.25	71.66	141.59
其他	Others	245.55	75.16	118.14
餐饮业	**Catering Service**	**461.09**	**181.61**	**166.78**
#国有控股	State-owned and State Share Holding	32.03	9.73	17.33
按登记注册类型分组	**Grouped by Status of Registration**	**0.00**	**0.00**	**0.00**
内资企业	Domestic Funded Enterprises	402.89	164.10	149.69
国有企业	State-owned Enterprises	8.74	2.77	5.15
集体企业	Collective-owned Enterprises	1.70	0.86	0.66
股份合作企业	Cooperative Enterprises	0.12	0.05	0.07
联营企业	Joint Ownership Enterprises			
国有联营企业	State Joint Ownership Enterprises			
集体联营企业	Collective Joint Ownership Enterprise			
国有与集体联营企业	Joint State-collective Enterprises			
其他联营企业	Other Joint Ownership Enterprises			
有限责任公司	Limited Liability Corporations	157.91	70.79	55.24
国有独资公司	State Solely Funded Corporations	5.46	2.22	2.18
其他有限责任公司	Other Limited Liability Corporations	152.45	68.57	53.06
股份有限公司	Share-holding Corporations Ltd.	14.52	8.98	3.64
私营企业	Private Enterprises	218.65	80.45	84.07
私营独资企业	Private-funded Enterprises	20.01	7.53	10.03
私营合伙企业	Private Partnership Enterpises	0.89	0.45	0.40
私营有限责任公司	Private Limited Liability Corporations	191.99	70.07	71.53
私营股份有限公司	Private Share-holding Corporations Ltd.	5.76	2.40	2.10
其他企业	Other Enterprises	1.25	0.19	0.87

14－9 Continued 1

(100 million yuan)

负债合计 Total Liabilities	所有者权益合计 Owner's Equities	主营业务收入 Revenue from Principal Business	主营业务成本 Cost of Principle Business	其他业务利润 Profits from Other Business	营业利润 Profit from Major Business	利润总额 Total Profits
526.82	188.80	186.82	72.37	2.09	－16.32	－15.56
37.06	9.39	28.16	13.14	0.16	－0.25	－0.14
4.60	0.67	4.63	2.00	0.01	－0.08	－0.08
0.04	0.03	0.17	0.11	0.00	0.02	0.02
4.17	0.17	3.87	1.98	0.00	0.20	0.19
40.77	16.45	24.87	11.80	0.21	－0.05	－0.27
97.96	78.95	47.54	19.36	0.98	－1.49	－1.66
221.18	62.07	60.78	22.18	0.30	－8.32	－7.74
204.36	41.19	82.39	32.08	0.77	－7.01	－6.33
336.35	**124.74**	**370.90**	**191.83**	**1.22**	**14.87**	**14.71**
28.06	3.97	17.21	7.57	0.01	－0.94	－0.85
0.00	0.00	0.00	0.00	0.00	0.00	0.00
305.11	97.78	266.62	143.72	1.11	7.40	7.87
7.58	1.16	5.26	2.54	0.02	0.01	0.07
1.49	0.21	1.30	0.64	0.00	0.00	－0.01
0.06	0.06	0.10	0.06	0.00	0.01	0.00
124.67	33.24	74.53	33.52	0.35	－0.33	－0.01
7.40	－1.93	4.69	2.33	0.00	－0.18	－0.23
117.27	35.17	69.84	31.19	0.34	－0.15	0.23
10.88	3.64	7.14	3.50	0.05	0.16	0.16
159.56	59.09	176.89	102.58	0.69	7.51	7.63
7.32	12.69	23.52	15.63	0.02	2.65	2.58
0.23	0.67	1.86	1.14		0.27	0.27
147.61	44.37	145.31	82.61	0.64	4.39	4.58
4.41	1.35	6.20	3.20	0.03	0.20	0.20
0.87	0.39	1.40	0.87		0.04	0.03

单位:亿元

项目	Item	资产总计 Total Assets	#流动资产 Crculating Assets	#固定资产 Fixed Assets
港、澳、台商投资企业	Enterprises with Funds from Hong Kong, Macao and Taiwan	27.41	9.82	9.52
合资经营企业	Joint-venture Enterprises	7.52	3.79	1.22
合作经营企业	Cooperative Enterprises	0.86	0.10	0.05
独资经营企业	Enterprises with Sole Fund	18.75	5.66	8.25
港、澳、台商投资股份有限公司	Share-holding Corporations Ltd.			
其他港澳台投资	Other Funds from Hong Kong, Macao and Taiwan	0.27	0.27	
外商投资企业	Foreign Funded Enterprises	30.80	7.69	7.57
合资经营企业	Joint-venture Enterprises	8.60	0.81	2.61
合作经营企业	Cooperative Enterprises	0.22	0.11	0.08
独资经营企业	Enterprises with Sole Fund	21.88	6.75	4.82
外商投资股份有限公司	Share-holding Corporations Ltd.	0.10	0.03	0.07
其他外商投资	Other Foreign Funds			
按行业分组	**Grouped by Sector**			
正餐服务	Dinner Service	410.69	162.72	154.66
快餐服务	Snack Service	37.31	11.90	9.10
饮料及冷饮服务	Beverage and Cool Drink Service	4.30	2.03	0.80
其他餐饮服务	Other Catering Service	8.79	4.96	2.22
按经营方式分组	**Grouped by Business Mode**			
独立商店	Independent Stores	368.52	136.92	147.23
连锁商店总店	Chain Stores	44.90	15.98	9.73
连锁商店分店	Branches of Chain Stores	25.65	16.73	3.22
其他	Others	22.02	11.99	6.60
在总计中:	**In the Total**			
南京市	Nanjing	220.53	82.81	85.81
无锡市	Wuxi	131.73	39.21	61.04
徐州市	Xuzhou	42.72	15.99	19.36
常州市	Changzhou	61.97	25.33	19.34
苏州市	Suzhou	374.29	107.65	167.53
南通市	Nantong	71.63	25.18	26.50
连云港市	Lianyungang	20.57	5.54	7.37
淮安市	Huaian	47.95	21.57	20.24
盐城市	Yancheng	67.18	28.32	28.30
扬州市	Yangzhou	65.65	15.56	29.02
镇江市	Zhenjiang	38.96	11.40	13.06
泰州市	Taizhou	50.95	17.40	22.34
宿迁市	Suqian	34.31	8.30	17.12

14－9 Continued 2

(100 million yuan)

负债合计 Total Liabilities	所有者权益合计 Owner's Equities	主营业务收入 Revenue from Principal Business	主营业务成本 Cost of Principle Business	其他业务利润 Profits from Other Business	营业利润 Profit from Major Business	利润总额 Total Profits
17.11	10.30	25.28	9.30	0.09	-0.20	-0.75
2.74	4.78	7.97	3.04	0.08	0.23	0.20
0.44	0.42	0.18	0.10		-0.14	-0.14
13.74	5.02	16.50	6.07	0.00	-0.41	-0.93
0.20	0.08	0.62	0.09		0.13	0.13
14.14	16.66	79.01	38.81	0.03	7.67	7.58
4.18	4.42	33.74	17.28	0.00	3.65	3.69
0.15	0.08	0.35	0.16		0.02	0.02
9.77	12.10	44.84	21.33	0.03	3.97	3.84
0.04	0.06	0.07	0.04		0.02	0.02
307.49	103.20	251.10	132.45	0.99	5.17	5.45
22.38	14.93	99.00	47.60	0.13	8.40	8.10
2.14	2.16	2.42	1.13	0.05	0.02	0.02
4.34	4.45	18.39	10.64	0.05	1.27	1.14
267.94	100.58	231.98	124.81	0.94	6.22	6.29
27.64	17.26	101.45	47.27	0.11	8.39	8.05
21.06	4.59	16.08	7.16	0.09	-0.27	-0.19
19.72	2.31	21.39	12.58	0.08	0.53	0.55
153.22	67.31	151.72	66.15	1.47	4.72	4.84
128.23	3.50	68.11	29.30	0.29	-5.54	-5.54
24.72	18.01	40.15	26.72	0.05	3.41	3.39
58.38	3.59	48.03	19.90	0.31	-0.88	-1.02
261.83	112.46	121.26	50.16	0.68	-5.60	-5.34
40.15	31.48	29.25	15.10	0.13	1.13	1.34
11.19	9.38	11.37	6.54	0.05	0.23	0.24
32.93	15.02	19.63	11.44	0.14	1.34	1.23
51.20	15.98	31.43	18.37	0.08	1.54	1.82
50.01	15.64	23.67	10.29	0.23	-1.58	-1.39
30.22	8.74	20.96	11.61	0.04	0.25	0.06
38.73	12.21	18.51	10.18	0.04	-0.60	-0.58
24.02	10.29	6.44	3.57	-0.01	-0.19	-0.11

14－10 批发和零售业、住宿和餐饮业连锁总店经营情况（2016年）

项目	Item	连锁总店数（个）Number of Chain Shops (unit)	连锁门店数（个）Number of Chain Stores (unit)
总计	**Total**	**195**	**19707**
批发和零售业	**Retail Trade**	**172**	**18172**
#外商及港澳台投资	Enterprises Prisese with Funds from Hong Kong, Macao Taiwan and Foreign Fanded	21	2524
按零售业态分	Grouped by Store Type		
百货商店	Department Store	7	1201
超级市场	Supermarket	41	4011
专业店	Specialty Store	99	11722
专卖店	Franchised Store	14	1065
便利店	Convenience Store	9	170
家居建材店	Building Material Store	2	3
其他	Other Store		
住宿业和餐饮业	**Hotel Service and Catering Service**	**23**	**1535**
#外商及港澳台投资	Enterprises Prisese with Funds from Hong Kong, Macao Taiwan and Foreign Fanded	11	1402
住宿业	**Hotel Service**	**2**	**8**
餐饮业	**Catering Service**	**21**	**1527**
按行业分	Grouped by Sector		
正餐	Dinner	6	66
快餐	Fast Food Snack	10	1385
其他	Others	5	76

Management Conditions of General Chain Stores of Wholesale and Retail Sale Trade, Hotel and Catering Trade Service (2016)

商品销售总额（或营业总收入）（亿元）Total Sales of Commodities (100 million yuan)	#商品零售额 Retail Sales	零售或餐饮营业面积（万平方米）Business Area for Retail and Catering Service (10000 sq. m)	从业人员（万人）Employees (10000 persons)
4789.61	**2187.85**	**2447.03**	**36.40**
4695.61	**2094.38**	**2397.88**	**31.80**
978.29	674.92	991.79	9.42
223.72	170.04	566.91	2.81
1011.07	718.61	515.97	10.49
3432.34	1179.91	1297.54	17.87
15.17	13.84	8.71	0.50
11.03	9.76	5.39	0.12
2.27	2.22	3.35	0.01
94.00	**93.47**	**49.15**	**4.60**
89.06	88.82	43.84	4.33
0.33	**0.01**	**0.04**	**0.01**
93.67	**93.46**	**49.11**	**4.59**
2.46	2.46	3.75	0.11
87.74	87.72	42.50	4.27
3.47	3.28	2.86	0.21

14－11 亿元以上商品交易市场基本情况（2016 年）

项　　目	Item	市场个数（个）Number of Markets (unit)	年末摊位数（个）Number of Booths at Year-end (unit)
总　计	**Total**	**501**	**392772**
按经营环境分	**Grouped by Business Environment**		
露天式	Open Air	51	23239
封闭式	Close	379	319330
其他	Others	71	50203
按经营方式分	**Grouped by Business Mode**		
以批发为主	Whole-sale	274	265549
以零售为主	Retail-sale	227	127223
按市场类别分	**Grouped by Catergary of Market**		
综合市场	Integrated Market	118	108595
综合贸易市场	Integrated Trade Market	118	108595
生产资料综合市场	Integrated Production Material Market	4	10875
工业消费品综合市场	Integrated Industrial Consumer Goods Market	19	32345
农产品综合市场	Integrated Farm Products Market	72	43997
其他综合市场	Others	23	21378
专业市场	Specialty Market	383	284177
生产资料市场	Production Goods Market	89	62243
农业生产用具市场	Agricultural Production Appliances Market	1	328
农用生产资料市场	Means of Agricultural Production	2	253
煤炭市场	Coal		
木材市场	Wood	8	5123
建材市场	Building Material	31	24904
化工材料及制品市场	Chemical Material and Products	8	8371
金属材料市场	Matel Materials	32	18709
机械设备市场	Machinery	5	3456
其他生产资料市场	Others	2	1099
农产品市场	Farm Products Market	107	54341
粮油市场	Grain and Oil	13	6695
肉禽蛋市场	Meat, Poultry and Eggs	26	9219
水产品市场	Aquatic Products	22	8653
蔬菜市场	Vegetables	14	7962
干鲜果品市场	Dried and Fresh Fruits	9	6285
棉麻土畜、烟叶市场	Cotton, Hemp, Livestock and Tobacco Leaf	2	2440

Basic Condition of Transaction Markets with Transaction Value over 100 Million Yuan (2016)

年末已出租摊位（个）Number of Rented Booths at Year-end (unit)	商品成交额（亿元）Transaction Value (100 million yuan)	营业面积（万平方米）Business Area (10000 sq. m)	交易业主从业人员（万人）Persons Engaged by Transaction Proprietor (10000 persons)
344084	**16900.81**	**3211.56**	**98.39**
19580	1172.53	233.53	8.23
280530	12382.49	2437.74	80.52
43974	3345.79	540.29	9.64
231308	15121.83	2372.96	72.80
112776	1778.98	838.60	25.59
93427	2944.54	751.78	25.84
93427	2944.54	751.78	25.84
8949	84.19	133.21	1.28
29781	661.49	210.06	8.18
37214	1701.88	266.88	10.62
17483	496.98	141.63	5.76
250657	13956.27	2459.78	72.55
49476	5474.39	719.45	12.07
328	5.11	5.27	0.10
231	23.17	11.05	0.14
4577	106.32	60.93	0.45
19400	277.23	255.96	4.83
7594	1282.50	47.14	0.91
13956	3630.11	310.70	4.66
2397	133.06	25.62	0.82
993	16.89	2.78	0.16
48349	1938.73	335.04	16.34
5516	373.09	84.38	0.99
7668	382.50	33.51	1.94
7538	273.54	74.82	3.04
7613	219.83	44.97	5.57
5207	194.52	33.77	1.07
2411	250.00	43.05	1.26

项 目 Item		市场个数（个）Number of Markets (unit)	年末摊位数（个）Number of Booths at Year-end (unit)
其他农产品市场	Others	21	13087
食品、饮料及烟酒市场	Food, Beverage, Tobacco and Alcohol Market	15	5430
食品饮料市场	Food and Beverage	3	790
茶叶市场	Tea		
烟酒市场	Tobacco and Alcohol	1	200
其他食品、饮料及烟酒市场	Others	11	4440
纺织、服装、鞋帽市场	Textile Products, Garment, Footware and Headgear Market	34	86028
布料及纺织品市场	Cloth and Testile Products	8	22945
服装市场	Garment	11	35371
鞋帽市场	Footware and Headgear	3	2898
其他纺织服装鞋帽市场	Others	12	24814
日用品及文化用品市场	Commodity and Culture Articles Market	9	6347
小商品市场	Small Commodities	5	4975
箱包市场	Boxes and Bags		
玩具市场	Toyes		
文具市场	Stationeries	1	300
图书、报刊杂志市场	Books, Newspapers and Magazines		
音像制品及电子出版物市场	Audio and Video Products and E-journal	1	328
体育用品市场	Sports Goods		
其他日用品及文化用品市场	Others	2	744
黄金、珠宝、玉器等首饰市场	Gold, Jewelry and Jade Article Market	2	1500
黄金、珠宝、玉器等首饰市场	Gold, Jewelry and Jade Article Market	2	1500
电器、通讯器材、电子设备市场	Electrical Appliances, Communications Equipments and Electronic Equipment Market	9	3869
家电市场	Electric Household Appliances	1	400
通讯器材市场	Communications Equipments	1	1604
照相、摄像器材市场	Photographic and Video Equipments		
计算机及辅助设备市场	Computers and Ancillary Equipments	6	1740
其他电器、通讯器材、电子设备市场	Others	1	125
医药、医疗用品及器材市场	Medicine, Medical Articles and Appliances		
中药材市场	Chinese Traditional Medicine Material		

14－11　Continued 1

年末已出租摊位（个）Number of Rented Booths at Year-end (unit)	商品成交额（亿元）Transaction Value (100 million yuan)	营业面积（万平方米）Business Area (10000 sq. m)	交易业主从业人员（万人）Persons Engaged by Transaction Proprietor (10000 persons)
12396	245.24	20.55	2.47
4515	109.15	36.47	1.00
687	23.19	9.57	0.10
188	3.19	0.32	0.04
3640	82.76	26.58	0.86
80281	4474.08	393.43	26.55
22306	2671.94	180.96	9.77
31803	1444.44	131.81	11.00
2747	45.83	16.22	0.54
23425	311.88	64.43	5.25
6227	110.22	20.71	1.57
4914	101.93	13.96	1.20
250	1.89	4.00	0.13
328	2.74	1.10	0.12
735	3.67	1.65	0.12
1440	97.18	6.00	0.55
1440	97.18	6.00	0.55
3451	39.82	9.71	0.92
385	5.42	1.10	0.05
1604	5.01	4.42	0.32
1337	27.42	3.99	0.52
125	1.96	0.20	0.03

项 目	Item	市场个数（个）Number of Markets (unit)	年末摊位数（个）Number of Booths at Year-end (unit)
其他医药、医疗用品及器材市场	Others		
家具、五金及装饰材料市场	Furniture, Hardware and Decorating Material Market	91	52619
家具市场	Furniture	26	15185
装饰材料市场	Decorating Material	37	18045
灯具市场	Lamps and Lanterns	1	3000
厨具、盥洗设备市场	Kitchenware and Toilet Facility		
五金材料市场	Hardware Material	17	10780
其他装修市场	Others	10	5609
汽车、摩托车及零配件市场	Motor Vehicles, Motorcycles and Spare Parts Market	16	5535
汽车市场	Motor Vehicles	11	2568
摩托车市场	Motorcycles		
机动车零配件市场	Spare Parts for Motor-driven Vehicles	5	2967
花、鸟、鱼、虫市场	Flowers, Birds, Fish and Insects Market	3	3994
花卉市场	Flowers	3	3994
鸟市场	Birds		
观赏鱼市场	Display Fish		
其他花鸟鱼虫市场	Others		
旧货市场	Secondhand Goods	1	73
古玩、古董、字画市场	Antiques, Calligraphy and Painting		
邮票、硬币市场	Stamps and Coins		
其他旧货市场	Others	1	73
其他专业市场	Other Speciality Markets	7	2198
按地区分	**by City**		
南京市	Nanjing	37	34848
无锡市	Wuxi	53	45314
徐州市	Xuzhou	28	40951
常州市	Changzhou	56	43708
苏州市	Suzhou	82	84729
南通市	Nantong	80	46752
连云港市	Lianyungang	24	16062
淮安市	Huaian	18	11506
盐城市	Yancheng	22	10466
扬州市	Yangzhou	56	21038
镇江市	Zhenjiang	14	7379
泰州市	Taizhou	24	17691
宿迁市	Suqian	7	12328

14－11 Continued 2

年末已出租摊位（个）Number of Rented Booths at Year-end (unit)	商品成交额（亿元）Transaction Value (100 million yuan)	营业面积（万平方米）Business Area (10000 sq. m)	交易业主从业人员（万人）Persons Engaged by Transaction Proprietor (10000 persons)
46918	885.12	682.11	9.98
12437	187.29	200.22	1.73
16821	289.55	280.17	3.99
2940	95.21	41.10	0.80
9223	174.59	85.44	1.48
5497	138.48	75.18	1.98
4233	530.31	171.08	2.21
2038	464.63	137.38	1.33
2195	65.67	33.70	0.88
3658	224.91	63.30	0.64
3658	224.91	63.30	0.64
70	2.00	2.50	0.01
70	2.00	2.50	0.01
2039	70.38	19.97	0.71
33519	959.74	242.98	6.84
39901	3207.04	489.44	11.66
32148	763.31	252.12	8.65
36650	2065.80	515.72	11.89
77306	6056.62	600.18	24.44
42372	1801.81	287.22	11.31
14962	262.02	92.85	2.70
9189	85.81	72.11	3.00
9177	81.17	88.35	2.26
19917	706.25	167.47	7.70
6614	383.09	111.56	1.86
15209	328.61	178.09	2.66
7120	199.54	113.47	3.44

14-12 省外批发和零售业、住宿和餐饮业连锁总店在江苏分店经营情况(2016)

Management Conditions of Branch Stores of Wholesale and Retail Sale Trade Hotel and Catering Trade of General Chain Stores of Other Province in Jiangsu(2016)

项　　目	Item	连锁门店数(个) Number of Chain Stores (unit)	商品销售总额(或营业总收入)(亿元) Total Sales of Commodities (100 million yuan)	#商品零售额 Retail Sales	零售或餐饮营业面积(万平方米) Business Area for Retail and Catering Service (10000 sq. m)	从业人员(万人) Employees (10000 persons)
总　计	**Total**	**99**	**78.47**	**66.49**	**36.01**	**0.87**
批发和零售业	**Retail Trade**	**50**	**70.92**	**59.34**	**33.61**	**0.64**
#外商及港澳台投资	Enterprisese with Funds from Hong Kong, Macao Taiwan and Foreign Fanded	26	46.03	34.70	18.17	0.36
按零售业态分	Grouped by Store Type					
百货商店	Department Store	3	0.62	0.62	2.80	0.13
超级市场	Supermarket	21	38.55	38.28	15.42	0.42
专业店	Specialty Store	8	2.09	2.09	1.35	0.02
专卖店	Franchised Store	13	13.29	10.56	6.18	0.11
便利店	Convenience Store					
家居建材店	Building Material Store					
其他	Other Store	5	16.37	7.52	10.48	0.07
住宿和餐饮业	**Hotel Service and Catering Service**	**49**	**7.55**	**7.15**	**2.40**	**0.23**
#外商及港澳台投资	Enterprisese with Funds from Hong Kong, Macao, Taiwan and Foreign Funded	29	6.25	6.19	1.61	0.18
住宿业	**Hotel Service**	**8**	**0.43**	**0.03**	**0.06**	**0.02**
餐饮业	**Catering Service**	**41**	**7.12**	**7.12**	**2.34**	**0.21**
按行业分	Grouped by Sector					
正餐	Dinner	20	2.16	2.16	1.24	0.10
快餐	Fast Food Snack	7	0.94	0.94	0.31	0.05
其他	Others	14	4.02	4.02	0.79	0.06

14－13 旅游业主要指标

Main Indicators of Tourism

项　目	Item	2012	2013	2014	2015	2016
旅行社数（个）	**Number of Travel Agencies (unit)**	**2117**	**2204**	**2251**	**2336**	**2469**
南京市	Nanjing City	539	557	576	572	609
无锡市	Wuxi City	152	156	165	171	186
徐州市	Xuzhou City	187	194	191	196	200
常州市	Changzhou City	122	127	129	139	145
苏州市	Suzhou City	257	267	288	314	354
南通市	Nantong City	132	137	140	150	162
连云港市	Lianyungang City	114	113	113	109	110
淮安市	Huaian City	89	100	103	110	110
盐城市	Yancheng City	129	133	136	136	139
扬州市	Yangzhou City	134	141	126	132	138
镇江市	Zhenjiang City	95	104	103	109	109
泰州市	Taizhou City	111	115	114	124	128
宿迁市	Suqian City	56	60	67	74	79
星级饭店数（个）	**Number of Star-rated Hotel (unit)**	**890**	**970**	**873**	**791**	**696**
南京市	Nanjing City	114	117	102	96	91
无锡市	Wuxi City	65	64	55	49	42
徐州市	Xuzhou City	81	117	123	94	73
常州市	Changzhou City	65	72	68	56	42
苏州市	Suzhou City	150	154	132	124	116
南通市	Nantong City	96	120	96	87	80
连云港市	Lianyungang City	59	60	44	39	34
淮安市	Huaian City	38	39	48	48	48
盐城市	Yancheng City	58	55	49	50	36
扬州市	Yangzhou City	60	67	63	60	48
镇江市	Zhenjiang City	51	52	38	34	34
泰州市	Taizhou City	29	29	29	29	28
宿迁市	Suqian City	24	24	26	25	24
国内旅游接待人数（万人次）	**Number of Domestic Visitors (10000 person-times)**	**46437.41**	**51539.20**	**57113.32**	**61933.65**	**67779.99**
南京市	Nanjing City	7950.45	8674.01	9419.31	9992.66	10657.32
无锡市	Wuxi City	6365.25	6993.57	7573.72	8043.33	8586.03
徐州市	Xuzhou City	2752.56	3087.15	3566.61	4005.31	4515.48
常州市	Changzhou City	3958.27	4425.71	4989.34	5443.00	5989.56
苏州市	Suzhou City	8624.43	9416.33	10028.84	10605.45	11300.37
南通市	Nantong City	2407.46	2716.00	3066.34	3387.24	3792.11
连云港市	Lianyungang City	1894.27	2136.03	2415.03	2682.74	3011.08
淮安市	Huaian City	1610.73	1833.20	2089.60	2323.79	2610.54
盐城市	Yancheng City	1536.80	1754.36	2014.67	2266.34	2573.70
扬州市	Yangzhou City	3572.47	3965.36	4545.88	5027.21	5622.02
镇江市	Zhenjiang City	3502.86	3895.00	4385.48	4802.68	5348.34
泰州市	Taizhou City	1457.04	1640.46	1848.68	2037.34	2282.32
宿迁市	Suqian City	804.82	1002.02	1169.82	1316.56	1491.12

项 目	Item	2012	2013	2014	2015	2016
国内旅游收入（亿元）	**Earnings from Domestic Tourism (100 million yuan)**	**6055.80**	**6940.05**	**7863.51**	**8769.31**	**9952.47**
南京市	Nanjing City	1169.01	1317.48	1470.00	1612.15	1803.45
无锡市	Wuxi City	974.92	1100.40	1229.85	1356.25	1518.91
徐州市	Xuzhou City	311.82	360.47	423.46	485.99	565.90
常州市	Changzhou City	481.96	557.39	639.98	718.35	820.04
苏州市	Suzhou City	1254.38	1419.09	1574.81	1728.79	1932.50
南通市	Nantong City	299.29	348.16	400.60	453.04	521.98
连云港市	Lianyungang City	221.59	257.25	297.42	338.70	391.58
淮安市	Huaian City	172.65	200.12	231.63	264.02	305.64
盐城市	Yancheng City	142.79	166.09	195.21	226.27	265.56
扬州市	Yangzhou City	392.50	454.42	525.21	592.00	681.91
镇江市	Zhenjiang City	410.14	474.53	543.93	614.12	706.19
泰州市	Taizhou City	160.88	186.19	213.63	241.54	278.22
宿迁市	Suqian City	63.85	98.47	117.79	138.08	160.60
接待海外旅游者人数（人次）	**Number of Overseas Tourists Received (person-times)**	**7915366**	**2880287**	**2970956**	**3050104**	**3297735**
南京市	Nanjing City	1627142	518568	566202	588100	637846
无锡市	Wuxi City	981947	391185	403116	391343	439185
徐州市	Xuzhou City	199488	25849	29485	33776	34105
常州市	Changzhou City	455706	109958	120423	126952	145896
苏州市	Suzhou City	2492157	1442138	1453273	1512029	1612849
南通市	Nantong City	440788	216943	187185	172999	180156
连云港市	Lianyungang City	144684	24228	22972	20345	22624
淮安市	Huaian City	34699	10565	13607	14675	18223
盐城市	Yancheng City	80077	26048	42164	49110	53059
扬州市	Yangzhou City	660160	47783	53539	51229	58561
镇江市	Zhenjiang City	663075	36675	44986	52956	54934
泰州市	Taizhou City	101323	26644	29979	31891	36068
宿迁市	Suqian City	34120	3703	4025	4699	4229
旅游外汇收入（万美元）	**Foreign Exchange Earnings from International Tourism (USD 10000)**	**629972**	**237989**	**303271**	**352729**	**380362**
南京市	Nanjing City	136216	40063	55293	63999	67617
无锡市	Wuxi City	68138	26985	32994	35783	38954
徐州市	Xuzhou City	21045	2193	2975	3861	3938
常州市	Changzhou City	47439	7590	10160	12066	13147
苏州市	Suzhou City	164723	135687	170463	200183	216708
南通市	Nantong City	42995	11196	10792	11668	12482
连云港市	Lianyungang City	14434	1668	1876	2064	2281
淮安市	Huaian City	3056	888	1313	1558	1705
盐城市	Yancheng City	6477	2533	4511	5866	6419
扬州市	Yangzhou City	55921	3711	4919	5588	6280
镇江市	Zhenjiang City	55819	3130	4640	5992	6479
泰州市	Taizhou City	10855	1990	2791	3255	3631
宿迁市	Suqian City	2854	355	546	846	721

14-14 接待海外旅游者人数和收入
Number of Overseas Tourists Received and Earnings

项目	Item	2012	2013	2014	2015	2016
接待人数(人次)	**Number of Received Tourists (person-times)**	**7915366**	**2880287**	**2970956.405**	**3050104**	**3297735**
外国人	Foreigners	5752148	1934356	1970417	2008386	2179954
#亚洲	Asia					
#日本	Japan	1219303	439400	419280	397104	414889
菲律宾	Philippines	45548	28269	23584	23506	28284
新加坡	Singapore	270166	67429	68558	66501	68466
泰国	Thailand	99093	30296	21030	21403	25793
印度尼西亚	Indonesia	95112	41472	35002	32332	33158
马来西亚	Malaysia	267864	94160	98686	93550	91107
韩国	Korea	649399	327453	348682	358214	407723
北美洲	America					
#美国	United States	651505	184712	196864	209899	225373
加拿大	Canada	247105	63359	66324	75996	78812
欧洲	Europe					
#英国	United Kingdom	230102	52147	53943	54009	59919
法国	France	159688	45511	43588	44066	46447
德国	Germany	347216	92110	98626	98979	103154
意大利	Italy	115336	30156	31183	32146	34374
瑞士	Switzerland	32419	8261	8634	8026	8574
瑞典	Sweden	36151	14014	13397	11568	12112
俄罗斯	Russia Fed.	54369	16486	17380	17694	21253
西班牙	Spain	36986	15591	17974	16338	18927
大洋洲	Oceania					
#澳大利亚	Australia	212149	50570	53490	53500	60124
香港同胞	Chinese Compatriots from Hong Kong	715111	129068	144170	140427	153754
澳门同胞	Chinese Compatriots from Macao	81436	5071	6150	7071	8219
台湾同胞	Chinese Compatriots from Taiwan	1366671	811792	850219	894220	955808
接待人天数(人天)	**Number of Received (person-days)**	**33912453**	**10424885**	**10964550.31**	**11415317**	**12338457**
外国人	Foreigners	24287413	6457922	6799370	6952408	7526609
香港同胞	Chinese Compatriots from Hong Kong	3321504	321902	364773	351052	380831
澳门同胞	Chinese Compatriots from Macao	266955	12179	15136	17146	19760
台湾同胞	Chinese Compatriots from Taiwan	6036581	3632882	3785271	4094711	4411257
旅游外汇收入(万美元)	**Foreign Exchange Earnings From Tourism (USD 10000)**	**629972**	**237989**	**303271**	**352729**	**380362**

主要统计指标解释

社会消费品零售总额 指企业(单位、个体户)通过交易直接售给个人、社会集团非生产、非经营用的实物商品金额,以及提供餐饮服务所取得的收入金额。个人包括城乡居民和入境人员,社会集团包括机关、社会团体、部队、学校、企事业单位、居委会或村委会等。

批发和零售业商品购、销、存总额 指各种登记注册类型的批发和零售企业、产业活动单位、个体经营者以本单位为总体的商品购进、销售、库存总额。

商品购进总额 指从本单位以外的单位和个人购进(包括从境外直接进口)作为转卖或加工后转卖的商品总额。

商品销售总额 指对本单位以外的单位和个人出售(包括对境外直接出口)本单位经营的商品总额(含增值税)。

商品批发额 指商品零售额以外的一切商品销售额。包括售给生产经营单位用于生产或经营用的商品销售额;售给批发和零售业、餐饮业用于转卖或加工后转卖的商品销售额;直接向国(境)外出口和委托外贸部门代理出口的商品销售额。

商品零售额 指售给城乡居民用于生活消费、售给社会集团用公款购买用作非生产、非经营使用的商品销售额。

商品库存总额 指报告期末各种登记注册类型的批发和零售业企业、产业活动单位、个体经营者已取得所有权的商品。

商品交易市场 指有固定场所、设施,有若干经营者入场实行集中、公开交易各类实物商品的市场。

商品交易市场成交额 指商品交易市场内所有经营者所实现的商品销售金额。商品交易市场包括消费品市场和生产资料市场。

旅游者人数

(1)入境国际旅游者人数:指来中国参观、访问、旅行、探亲、访友、休养、考察、参加会议和从事经济、科技、文化、教育、宗教等活动的外国人、华侨、港澳同胞和台湾同胞的人数。不包括外国在我国的常驻机构,如使领馆、通讯社、企业办事处的工作人员;来我国常住的外国专家、留学生以及在岸逗留不过夜人员。

(2)出境居民人数:指大陆居民因公务活动或私人事务短期出境的人数。公务活动出境居民人数包括在国际交通工具上的中国服务员工,因私出境居民人数不包括在国际交通工具上的中国服务员工。

(3)国内旅游者人数:指我国大陆居民和在我国常住1年以上的外国人、华侨、港澳台同胞离开常住地在境内其他地方的旅游设施内至少停留一夜,最长不超过6个月的人数。

国际旅游(外汇)收入 指入境旅游的外国人、华侨、港澳同胞和台湾同胞在中国大陆旅游过程中发生的一切旅游支出,对于国家来说就是国际旅游(外汇)收入。

Explanatory Notes on Main Statistical Indicators

Wholesale Trade refers to the activities of selling wholesale commodities for daily use and capital goods to enterprises of wholesale and retail trades (including self-employed individuals) and other enterprises, institutions and government organs and organizations, and the activities of engaging in import and export and acting as a trade agent. The wholesaler may have the ownership of the commodities for wholesale and trade in the name of its own (a company), and the wholesaler can act as commission agent or commodity broker without the ownership of commodities. Also included are the wholesale activities at the fixed stalls in wholesale market and the acquisition for sales purpose.

Purchase, Sales and Stock of Commodities by Wholesale and Retail Trade refers to the purchase, sales and stock of commodities by wholesale and retail enterprises, industrial activity units and individual sellers of different status of registration.

Total Purchases of Commodities refers to the total value of purchases of commodities by the establishments from other establishments or individuals (including direct import from abroad) for the purpose of re-selling.

Total Sales of Commodities refers to the total value (included added tax) of commodities sold by the establishments to other establishments and individuals(including direct export).

Wholesale of Commodities refers to all the total sales of commodities except the retail sales of consumer goods. Included the sales of commodities to production or operation units for the purpose of production and operation; the sales of commodities to wholesale and retail sale trade and catering industry for the purpose of re-selling or re-selling after further processing; the sales of commodities for direct export to abroad or export on a commission basis by entrusted the foreign trade department.

Retail Sale of Commodities refers to the commodities sold to urban and rural residents for their daily use, to social groups for the use of non-production and non-operation and purchased by public money of the social groups.

Total Value of Commodity Stock refers to the total commodities owned by wholesale and retail sale enterprises, economic active units and individual sellers of various types of registration status at the end of the reference period.

Commodity Transaction Markets refers to the markets provided with fixed place and equipments, and there are some operators who engaged in transaction of various substantial commodities in the markets by public and concentrating transaction.

Value of Transaction at Transaction Markets refers to the total sales value of commodities realized by the operators in the transaction market. Commodity transaction markets include consumer good markets and means of production markets.

Number of Tourists

(1) International tourists refer to foreigners, overseas Chinese, Chinese compatriots from Hong Kong, Macao and Taiwan coming to China for sight-seeing, visits, tours, family reunions, vacations, study tours, conferences and other activities of a business, scientific and technological, cultural, educational and religious nature. It does not include representatives and employees of resident institutions of foreign countries in China such as embassies, consulates, news agencies and offices of foreign companies and organizations, nor does it include long-term foreign experts or students residing in China, or persons in transition without spending a night in China.

(2) Chinese residents going abroad refer to Chinese residents going abroad for short terms for either public business or private purposes. Chinese employees working on international transport carriers are included in those going abroad for public business purpose, not in those for private purpose.

(3) Domestic tourists refer to residents of the mainland of China who stay for one night at least but no more than 6 months at tourist facilities in other places than their permanent residence within the territory of the mainland China, including foreigners, overseas Chinese and Chinese compatriots from Hong Kong, Macao and Taiwan who have resided in China for over one year.

Foreign Exchange Earnings from International Tourism refer to the total expenditures of foreigners, overseas Chinese, Chinese compatriots from Hong Kong, Macao and Taiwan during their stay in the mainland of China, which are earnings of foreign exchange from international tourism from the point of view from China.

15

科技、教育

Science and Technology，Education

简 要 说 明

一、本篇资料的主要内容

本篇主要反映科技、专利、教育情况等内容。

科技部分主要包括科技活动、研究与发展课题情况，县级以上政府部门所属研究与开发机构情况，大中型工业企业、高等学校科技活动情况；人才部分包括工程、农业、科研、卫生等各类专业技术人员数；专利部分主要包括三种专利申请受理量，三种专利授权量；教育事业部分包括各级各类教育事业情况，各级各类学校招生、在校生、专任教师人数等情况。

二、本篇的资料来源

根据各部门制定的统计报表制度汇总加工整理而成。科技资料主要来自省科技厅、省教育厅、省统计局；人才资料来自省人力资源和社会保障厅；专利资料来自省知识产权局；教育事业资料来自省教育厅。

Brief Introduction

Ⅰ. Main Contents

Data in this chapter show statistics on science and technology, patents, education.

Data on technology mainly include: data on scientific and technical activities, research and development (R&D) projects, state-owned R&D institutions above county level, large and medium-sized industrial enterprises, scientific and technical activities of institutions of higher education; data on talents mainly include: number of scientific and technical personnel of engineering, agriculture, scientific research, health care and so on, all kinds of human resources; data on patents mainly include: application of three kinds of patents accepted, three kinds of patents granted; data on education consist of education by level and type, new student enrollment, student enrollment full-time teachers of all kinds of school.

Ⅱ. Sources of Data

Data are collected and tabulated in accordance with the statistic reporting schemes stipulated by the departments concerned. Data on scientific and technical are mainly from Provincial Science and Technology Department, Education Department and Statistics Bureau; data on talents are from Provincial Human Resources and Social Security Department; data on patents are provided by Provincial Intellectual Property Office, data on product quality supervision are from Provincial Pledges Inspect Bureau; data on education are from Provincial Education Department.

15－1 科技活动基本情况
Basic Statistics on Scientific and Technical Activities

指 标	Item	2012	2013	2014	2015	2016
科技机构数 （个）	Number of Scientific and Technical Institutions (unit)	17776	19393	21844	23101	25402
科研单位	Research Institutions	148	143	144	142	135
规模以上工业企业	Industrial Engineers above Designated Size	16417	17996	20411	21542	23564
#大中型工业企业	Large and Medium-sized Industrial Enterprises	7395	7231	7538	7432	7816
高等院校	Institutions of Higher Education	761	801	854	971	1055
其他	Others	450	453	435	446	648
科技活动人员数 （万人）	Persons Engaged in Scientific and Technical Activities (10000 persons)	98.23	109.46	115.00	111.99	117.00
#大学本科及以上学历	Bechelor and Above Education Regree	44.96	49.09	53.61	54.84	70.16
研究与发展经费内部支出 （亿元）	Internal Expenses of Research and Development (100 million yuan)	1288.02	1487.45	1652.82	1801.23	2026.87
研究与发展经费支出占地区生产总值比重 （%）	Ratio of Internal Expenses of Research and Development to GDP (%)	2.33	2.45	2.54	2.57	2.66

注：规模以上工业企业科技统计从2011年开始实施。
a) Statistics of science and technology of industry enterprises above designated size is implemented from 2011.

15－2 研究与发展课题情况
Research and Development Projects

单位:项 (unit)

指 标	Item	2012	2013	2014	2015	2016
研究与发展课题	Research and Development Projects	97602	107690	118467	122629	138251
#科研单位	Research Institutions	4831	5430	5657	6490	6817
高等院校	Institutes of Higher Education	44383	48980	55018	59887	67670
规上工业企业	Industrial Enterprises above Designated Size	44575	48559	53117	51720	59535
#大中型工业企业	Large and Medium-sized Industrial Enterprises	24545	25966	26778	24782	26847
其他	Others	3813	4721	4675	4532	4229
#基础研究	Basic Research	19736	22669	25432	28340	32168
应用研究	Applied Research	25708	28227	31285	33295	36787
试验发展	Experiment al Development	52158	56794	61750	60994	69296

15－3 县级以上政府部门所属研究与开发机构(2016年)

项目	Item	机构数(个) Institutions (unit)	从业人员总数(人) Employees (person)
总计	**Total**	**124**	**20678**
按隶属关系分	by Administrative Relationship		
地方部门属	Local Departments	107	15494
省级部门属	Provincial Departments	51	13484
副省级部门属	Departments of Municipalities Directly under the Central Government in Plan	8	374
地市级部门属	Departments of City and Region Under Province	48	1636
中央部门属	Central Departments	17	5184
#中国科学院	Academy of Science of China	7	2011
按国民经济行业分	by Sector		
农、林、牧、渔业	Agriculture, Forestry, Animal Husbandry and Fishery	31	3707
农业	Farming	20	2521
林业	Forestry	2	398
畜牧业	Animal Husbandry	2	234
渔业	Fishery	5	470
农、林、牧、渔服务业	Service in Support of Agriculture	2	84
制造业	Manufacturing	12	5216
纺织服装、服饰业	Manufacture of Textile, Wearing Apparel and Accessories		
印刷业和记录媒介的复制业	Printing and Reproduction of Recording Media	1	28
化学原料和化学制品制造业	Manufacture of Raw Chemical Material and Chemical Products	1	198
医药制造业	Manufacture of Medicines	5	1576
非金属矿物制品业	Mining and Processing of Nonmental Ores	1	9
通用设备制造业	Manufacture of General Purpose Machinery	1	2966
专用设备制造业	Manufacture of Special Purpose Machinery	1	292
电气机械和器材制造业	Manufacture of Electrical Machinery and Apparatus		
计算机、通信和其他电子设备制造业	Manufacture of Computers, Communication and Other Electronic Equipment	1	128
仪器仪表制造业	Manufacture of Measuring Instruments and Machinery	1	19
电力、热力、燃气及水生产和供应业	Production and Supply of Electricity, Gas and Water	2	60
电力、热力的生产和供应业	Production and Supply of Electric Power and Heat Power	2	60
建筑业	Construction	2	128
房屋建筑业	Housing Construction	1	52
土木工程建筑业	Civil Engineering Construction	1	76
交通运输、仓储和邮政业	Transport, Storage and Post	1	318
道路运输业	Road Transport	1	318
信息传输、软件和信息技术服务业	Information Transfer、Software and IT Services	2	353
互联网和相关服务	Internet and Relatiue Services	1	343
软件和信息技术服务业	Software and IT Services	1	10
科学研究和技术服务业	Scientific Research and Technical Services	38	5414
研究与试验发展	Research and Experimental Development	15	2401
专业技术服务业	Professional Technology Service	20	2715
科技推广和应用服务业	Promation and Application of Science	3	298
水利、环境和公共设施管理业	Water Conservancy, Environment and Public Facility Management	15	1784
水利管理业	Water Conservancy Management	6	1364
生态保护和环境治理业	Ecological Protection and Enviromental	8	385
公共设施管理业	Public Facility Management	1	35
教育	Education	2	71
教育	Education	2	71
卫生和社会工作	Healthcare and Social Work	16	3531
卫生	Healthcare	16	3531
文化、体育和娱乐业	Culture, Sports and Recreation	3	96
文化艺术业	Cultural and Artistic Industry	2	49
体育	Sports	1	47

State-owned Research and Development Institutions above County Level(2016)

#单位在职科技活动人员 Personnels Engaged in Scientific and Technical Activities	经费收入总额（万元） Total Funds Revenue (10000 yuan)	#政府资金 Government Appropriated	经费支出总额（万元） Total Expenditure (10000 yuan)	#科技经费支出 Expenditure for Science & Technology
14473	**1349493**	**720625**	**1256675**	**775464**
9828	881508	439921	817952	452690
8244	792476	402551	744847	403091
255	12548	10846	11101	8561
1329	76484	26524	62004	41038
4645	467985	280705	438722	322774
1980	174711	147711	153742	134073
2938	234951	193323	194520	157220
2035	180745	147159	147147	124619
294	14212	12623	13820	11584
182	7663	6444	7621	5938
364	29547	25071	23538	13211
63	2784	2027	2394	1868
2497	231973	133800	226980	147735
28	644	556	644	602
188	10187	7793	9607	5812
939	88636	13548	89268	19110
9	98	10	100	81
904	104166	90484	102138	97516
292	16636	15349	17900	17894
128	11112	6060	6785	6235
9	495		538	485
59	836	436	1792	1792
59	836	436	1792	1792
128	13244		8901	7937
52	1231		978	978
76	12013		7924	6960
305	50986	6405	64700	29680
305	50986	6405	64700	29680
271	3771	1550	6619	5968
262	3677	1490	6475	5824
9	94	60	144	144
4899	378020	268066	341545	267048
2310	187588	157493	160079	134394
2298	180346	105181	174040	130414
291	10087	5392	7426	2239
1530	125574	64866	122178	99961
1152	109073	54842	105797	86074
363	15730	9309	15384	13221
15	770	715	997	666
64	3777	3770	3824	2172
64	3777	3770	3824	2172
1689	301146	43799	279396	50742
1689	301146	43799	279396	50742
93	5215	4608	6219	5209
47	2210	1982	2654	1803
46	3006	2626	3565	3406

15－4 县级以上政府部门所属研究与开发机构课题情况（2016 年）

项目	Item	课题数（个）Number of Projects（unit）	#R&D 课题 R&D Projects	课题经费内部支出（万元）Intramural Expenditures on Projects（10000 yuan）
总计	**Total**	**8064**	**6435**	**352158.6**
中央政府部门下达课题	Projects Assigned by Central Governmental Departments	3072	2715	159077.4
国家重大科技专项	Major National Science and Technology and Special	152	131	16536.7
自然科学基金课题	Natural Scientific Foundation	1416	1416	38254.1
863 计划课题	863 Plan	29	26	2747.7
国家科技支撑(攻关)计划课题	National S&T Support Plan	73	54	6840
国家重点研发计划课题	National Torch Plan	41	33	1951.4
国家发改委产业化示范工程	National Spark Plan	2	2	81
国家 973 计划课题	National 973 Plan	35	35	2568.4
公益性行业科研专项	Public Welfare Industry Research Speical	102	59	9294.1
国家社会科学基金课题	National Social Scientific Fundation	25	24	1216.5
其它课题	Other Projects	1197	935	79587.6
地方政府部门下达课题	Projects Assigned by Local Governmental Depurtments	3146	2335	134328.8
地方自然科学基金课题	Local Natural Scientific Fundation	428	417	13486.3
地方科技攻关计划课题	Local Key Tackling Plan Items	298	237	18224.3
地方火炬计划课题	Local Torch Plan	1		66.8
地方星火计划课题	Local Spark Plan			
地方社会科学基金课题	Local Social Scientific Fundation	41	34	5567.7
其它课题	Other Projects	2378	1647	96983.6
企业委托课题	Projects Entrusted by Enterprises	1003	638	33427.4
自选课题	Optional	490	453	11864.9
国际合作课题	International Coorperation	29	26	1454.8
其它课题	Others	324	268	12005.4

Projects of State-owned Research and Development Institutions above County Level(2016)

#政府资金 Government Appropriation	#R&D 课题经费 Funds for R&D Projects	课题投入人员(人年) Project Personnels (person-years)	#R&D 人员 R&D Personnels
254284.1	**267195.3**	**9920**	**6996**
138485.8	132322.5	4065	3033
12231.3	12724.4	259	194
35615.7	38254.1	1711	1388
1183.2	2595	148	49
6178.5	4401.7	207	112
1527.3	1702	66	51
81	81	3	3
2543.7	2568.4	41	33
7705.1	6443.2	200	127
742.1	1124.5	32	29
70677.9	62428.1	1399	1047
96719.9	98080.1	4238	2883
11447.2	13234.1	667	481
9804	16241	694	336
66.8		2	2
4864.7	4708.2	72	57
70537.1	63896.8	2802	2008
1837.8	14650.3	550	355
9663.1	10917.9	378	335
449.7	1361.8	25	16
7127.8	9862.6	665	372

15－5　县级以上政府部门所属研究与开发机构基本情况
Basic Statistics on State-owned Research and Development Institutions above County Level

指　　标	Item	2012	2013	2014	2015	2016
机构数　（个）	Number of Institutions　(unit)	136	131	132	130	124
职工总数　（人）	Employees　(person)	16797	17442	18342	18119	20678
#大学本科及以上学历	Bachelor Degree or Above	10360	11043	11758	11558	12439
经费收入总额　（亿元）	Funds Revenue　(100 million yuan)	89.75	101.27	109.06	112.07	134.95
#政府拨款	Government Appropriations	49.52	52.68	57.76	54.94	72.06
经费支出总额　（亿元）	Expenditures　(100 million yuan)	87.63	91.45	102.16	103.55	125.67
#科研基建支出	Expenditures for Capital Construction	6.29	5.40	8.52	6.26	11.12

15－6　县级以上政府部门所属研究与开发机构成果
Achievements of State-owned Research and Development Institutions above County Level

年　份 Year	科学著作(种) Scientific Works (kind)	科学论文(篇) Scientific Papers (piece)
1978	2138(万字)	2532
1978	2138(万字)	2532
1989	1717(万字)	3263
1990	2540(万字)	3728
1991	2454(万字)	3392
1992	2086(万字)	3962
1993	2273(万字)	4629
1994	2783(万字)	4049
1995	4196(万字)	4662
1996	107(部)	4378
1997	93	4906
1998	92	4798
1999	139	4782
2000	113	4774
2001	139	4872
2002	129	5502
2003	116	5463
2004	106	5214
2005	110	4306
2006	153	4920
2007	169	5396
2008	147	6259
2009	240	6779
2010	145	6919
2011	167	7020
2012	135	7877
2013	163	8021
2014	162	8443
2015	133	7970
2016	207	9966

15－7 规上工业企业研发情况

Basic Statistics on Scientific and Technical Research Activities of above Designated Size Industrial Enterprises

单位:亿元 (100 million yuan)

指标	Item	2012	2013	2014	2015	2016
企业数 (个)	Number of Enterprise (unit)	45859	48771	48708	48488	47899
#有 R&D 活动的企业数	Quantity of R&D Enterprise	11133	12283	14150	18872	19186
企业办研发机构数 (个)	R&D Institutions of Enterprise (unit)	16528	17996	20411	21542	23564
从事科技活动的人员数 (万人)	Number of Persons Engaged in Scientific and Technological Activities (10000 persons)	77.69	82.93	88.53	84.98	87.26
#科技机构中的人员	Personnel of Scientific and Technological Activities	48.82	53.22	56.66	57.19	59.34
#大学本科及以上学历的人员	University Degree and Above	30.23	32.65	36.94	45.48	45.24
R&D 经费内部支出总额	R&D Internal Expenditure	1080.31	1239.57	1376.54	1506.51	1657.54
经常性支出	Recurrent Expenditure	931.97	1073.13	1193.02	1328.54	1460.53
#R&D 人员劳务费	Service Fee of R&D	280.77	339.69	391.20	434.77	485.89
资产性支出	Capital Expenditure	148.34	166.45	183.52	177.96	197.01
#土建工程	Civil Engineering	4.51	4.36	4.61	4.01	3.62
仪器设备	Intruments and Apparatuses	143.83	162.08	178.91	173.96	193.39
R&D 经费来源	Sources of R&D Funds					
#政府资金	Loans from Financial Institutions	22.05	24.07	24.33	24.96	25.53
企业资金	Seff-raised Funds by Enterprise	1036.65	1192.33	1328.79	1456.27	1610.06
境外资金	Offshore Funds	8.21	6.40	7.99	7.91	7.75
其它资金	Others Funds	13.39	16.79	15.43	17.38	14.20
R&D 经费外部支出经费	External Expenditure of R&D Funds	36.83	39.40	68.74	55.56	55.40
技术引进支出总额	Technological Introduction	57.44	52.46	45.46	36.21	33.27
用于消化吸收的经费	Funds for Digestion and Absorption	25.92	20.44	24.87	12.47	9.49
购买国内技术用款	Funds for Purchasing Domestic Fechnd-ogy	29.46	41.32	34.44	20.16	17.38
技术改造支出总额	Technological Fransformation	717.89	642.14	603.13	507.20	521.95
研发活动产出	R&D Output					
新产品销售收入	Sale Revenue of New Products	17845.42	19714.21	23540.93	24463.27	28084.67
企业专利申请数 (件)	Total Number of Owning Inventive Patents (unit)	84876	93518	115616	102002	131284
#发明专利数	Number of Invention Patents	27820	33090	39858	37407	49229
企业拥有有效发明专利数 (件)	Total Number of Owning Effective Inventive Patents (unit)	45120	52718	73252	85287	117912

15－8　大中型工业企业研发情况

Basic Statistics on Scientific and Technical Research Activities of Large and Medium-sized Industrial Enterprises

单位:亿元　　　　(100 million yuan)

指　　标	Item	2012	2013	2014	2015	2016
企业数(个)	Number of Enterprise (unit)	7128	7316	7346	7249	7301
#有 R&D 活动的企业数	Quantity of R&D Enterprise	4503	4574	4740	5833	5750
企业办研发机构数(个)	Science and Technology Institutions of Enterprises (unit)	7395	7231	7538	7432	7816
从事科技活动的人员数(万人)	Number of Persons Engaged in Scientific and Technological Activities (10000 persons)	56.70	58.21	59.89	56.02	55.81
#科技机构中的人员	Personnel of Scientific and Technological Activities	34.78	36.42	37.06	36.14	36.77
#大学本科及以上学历的人员	University Degree and Above	21.80	22.41	23.65	29.84	29.44
R&D 经费内部支出总额	R&D Internal Expenditure	802.73	891.16	969.19	1032.79	1091.59
经常性支出	Recurrent Expenditure	698.03	776.80	848.11	920.46	971.25
#R&D 人员劳务费	Service Fee of R&D	209.22	247.07	280.02	304.67	328.59
资产性支出	Capital Expenditure	104.70	114.36	121.08	112.33	120.34
#土建工程	Civil Engineering	3.22	2.97	3.17	2.50	2.04
仪器设备	Intruments and Apparatuses	101.48	111.40	117.91	109.83	118.30
R&D 经费来源	Sources of R&D Funds					
#政府资金	Loans from Firancial Institutions	16.19	16.50	16.98	17.42	16.99
企业资金	Seff-raised Funds by Enterprise	768.78	856.74	934.52	996.02	1057.85
境外资金	Offshore Funds	7.17	4.60	6.31	6.74	6.39
其它资金	Others Funds	10.59	13.33	11.37	12.58	10.36
R&D 经费外部支出经费	External Expenditure of R&D Funds	31.04	32.03	53.18	43.35	41.98
技术引进支出总额	Technological Introduction	53.48	47.64	39.62	26.59	24.23
用于消化吸收的经费	Funds for Digestion and Absorption	23.43	17.33	21.10	10.04	7.45
购买国内技术用款	Funds for Purchasing Domestic Fechndogy	24.61	35.22	28.83	15.36	13.97
技术改造支出总额	Technological Fransformation	583.63	499.76	486.91	394.24	422.64
研发活动产出	R&D Output					
新产品销售收入(亿元)	Sale Revenue of New Products	15486.97	16735.09	19691.06	20126.82	22801.22
企业专利申请数(件)	Total Number of Owning Inventive Patents (unit)	47397	50776	63240	55022	62744
#发明专利数	Number of Invention Patents	15247	18052	22168	20820	25212
企业拥有有效发明专利数(件)	Total Number of Owning Effective Inventive Patents (unit)	28202	31602	42804	47952	65151

15-9 规上工业企业研究与发展经费内部支出
Basic Statistics on Intramural R&D Expenditure of above Designated Size Industrial Enterprises

单位:亿元 (100 million yuan)

指标	Item	2012	2013	2014	2015	2016
总计	**Total**	**1080.31**	**1239.57**	**1376.54**	**1506.51**	**1657.54**
按登记注册类型分	**Grouped by Statys of Registration**					
内资企业	Domestic Funded Enterprises	681.80	820.65	928.23	1030.27	1149.26
国有企业	State-owned Enterprises	42.39	13.81	12.58	16.29	10.24
集体企业	Collective-owned Enterprises	4.65	4.13	4.99	4.89	3.22
股份合作企业	Cooperative Enterprises	3.29	1.32	0.90	1.53	0.65
联营企业	Joint Ownership Enterprises	0.47	0.42	0.31	0.34	0.62
有限责任公司	Limited Liability Corporations	195.07	251.44	277.47	310.09	320.03
#国有独资	State Solely Funded Corporatios	29.38	34.43	34.32	34.05	33.44
股份有限公司	Share-holding Corporations Ltd.	91.29	127.61	141.55	141.54	168.25
私营企业	Private Enterprises	336.89	420.26	489.21	554.14	645.64
其他企业	Other Enterprises	7.74	1.66	1.22	1.45	0.62
港、澳、台商投资企业	Enterprises with Funds from Hong Kong, Macao and Taiwan	128.88	148.14	152.62	169.83	182.92
外商投资企业	Foreign Funded Enterprises	269.64	270.79	295.69	306.41	325.36
按企业规模分	**Grouped by Size of Enterprises**					
大型企业	Large Enterprises	488.52	530.08	568.11	600.90	602.09
中型企业	Medium-sized Enterprises	314.25	360.81	401.08	431.89	489.49
小微型企业	Small Enterprises	277.54	348.68	407.35	473.71	565.96
按行业分	**Grouped by Sector**					
采矿业	**Mining**	**8.24**	**7.65**	**6.48**	**9.14**	**6.19**
煤炭开采和洗选业	Mining and Washing of Coal	4.55	3.75	2.92	5.58	2.51
石油和天然气开采业	Extraction of Petroleum and Natural Gas	1.97	2.51	1.54	1.16	1.35
黑色金属矿采选业	Mining and Processing of Ferrous Metal Ores	0.07	0.03	0.10	0.20	0.53
有色金属矿采选业	Mining and Processing of Non-ferrous Metals Ores	0.19	0.12	0.11	0.11	0.06
非金属矿采选业	Mining and Processing of Nonmetal Ores	1.37	1.24	1.80	2.08	1.73
开采辅助活动	Support Activities for Mining	0.09	0.00	0.01	0.00	0.00
其他矿采业	Mining of Other Ores					
制造业	**Manufacturing**	**1068.34**	**1226.98**	**1359.75**	**1483.41**	**1641.42**
农副食品加工业	Processing of Food from Agricultural Products	9.22	12.25	13.24	17.87	23.05
食品制造业	Manufacture of Food	5.40	7.04	8.05	9.71	9.74
酒、饮料和精制茶制造业	Manufacture of Liquor, Beverages and Refined Tea	5.67	6.40	8.76	7.14	7.61
烟草制品业	Manufacture of Tobacco	0.29	0.34	0.15	0.32	0.26
纺织业	Manufacture of Textile	39.63	43.40	47.12	54.12	59.28
纺织服装、服饰业	Manufacture of Textile, Wearing Apparel and Accessories	20.25	24.79	23.37	28.73	30.76
皮革、毛皮、羽毛及其制品和制鞋业	Manufacture of Textile,Fur,Feather and Footwear Products and Footwear	3.30	3.07	3.12	4.53	5.73
木材加工及木、竹、藤、棕、草制品业	Processing of Timber,Manufacture of Wood, Bamboo,Rattan,Palm and Straw Products	6.68	11.18	12.51	16.34	20.52

15-9 续表 Continued

单位:亿元 (100 million yuan)

指标	Item	2012	2013	2014	2015	2016
家具制造业	Manufacture of Furniture	1.04	1.23	1.74	2.18	3.45
造纸和纸制品业	Manufacture of Paper and Paper Products	10.57	9.12	12.73	16.96	18.72
印刷业和记录媒介的复制	Printing, Reproduction of Recording Media	4.73	6.71	5.07	5.75	7.72
文教、工美、体育和娱乐用品制造业	Manufacture of Articles for Culture, Education, Arts and Crafts, Sport and Entertainment Activities	9.74	13.09	15.19	18.47	21.80
石油加工、炼焦及核燃料加工业	Processing of Petroleum, Coking, Processing of Nuclear Fuel	4.88	5.44	4.44	5.57	5.13
化学原料及化学制品制造业	Manufacture of Raw Chemical Materials and Chemical Products	122.96	149.27	161.17	162.20	176.21
医药制造业	Manufacture of Medicines	46.14	50.59	54.62	62.95	76.09
化学纤维制造业	Manufacture of Chemical Fibers	25.07	26.13	31.05	35.28	31.68
橡胶和塑料制品业	Manufacture of Rubber and Plastics	19.27	23.54	27.01	31.04	38.25
非金属矿物制品业	Manufacture of Non-metallic Mineral Products	25.70	28.92	32.38	35.43	41.31
黑色金属冶炼及压延加工业	Smelting and Pressing of Ferrous Metals	67.97	69.87	79.30	76.75	69.15
有色金属冶炼及压延加工业	Smelting and Pressing of Non-ferrous Metals	17.14	20.70	22.95	26.82	35.23
金属制品业	Manufacture of Metal Products	37.88	49.09	54.15	58.41	67.83
通用设备制造业	Manufacture of General Purpose Machinery	91.89	102.42	120.83	124.89	140.21
专用设备制造业	Manufacture of Special Purpose Machinery	64.32	82.62	92.11	98.06	113.16
汽车制造业	Manufacture of Automobiles	42.74	45.26	50.52	71.10	85.36
铁路、船舶、航空航天和其他运输设备制造业	Manufacture of Railway, Ship, Aerospace and Other Transport Equipment	32.27	40.71	35.81	51.13	51.48
电气机械及器材制造业	Manufacture of Electrical Machinery and Equipment	166.26	191.10	221.18	237.91	252.22
计算机、通信和其他电子设备制造业	Manufacture of Computers, Communication and Other Electronic Equipment	146.88	156.62	167.03	170.80	188.54
仪器仪表制造业	Manufacture of Measuring Instruments and Machinery	39.11	44.37	52.31	49.92	57.40
其他制造业	Other Manufacturing	0.79	0.91	0.80	2.08	2.15
废弃资源综合利用业	Utilization of Waste Resources	0.32	0.60	0.86	0.68	1.09
金属制品、机械和设备修理业	Repair Service of Metal Products, Machinery and Equipment	0.22	0.20	0.18	0.28	0.30
电力、热力、燃气及水的生产和供应业	**Production and Supply of Electric Power, Heat Power, Gas and Water**	**3.73**	**4.94**	**10.30**	**13.95**	**9.93**
电力、热力的生产和供应业	Production and Supply of Electric Power and Heat Power	2.61	3.45	8.87	12.57	7.69
燃气生产和供应	Production and Supply of Gas	0.65	0.37	0.45	0.37	0.87
水的生产和供应业	Production and Supply of Water	0.47	1.12	0.98	1.02	1.38

15-10 大中型工业企业研究与发展经费内部支出
Basic Statistics on Intramural R&D Expenditure of Large and Medium-sized Industrial Enterprises

单位:亿元 (100 million yuan)

指标	Item	2012	2013	2014	2015	2016
总计	**Total**	**802.73**	**891.16**	**969.19**	**1032.79**	**1091.59**
按登记注册类型分	**Grouped by Statys of Registration**					
内资企业	Domestic Funded Enterprises	471.16	550.91	611.86	648.35	698.41
国有企业	State-owned Enterprises	39.88	13.11	12.31	15.99	10.16
集体企业	Collective-owned Enterprises	2.61	3.16	3.94	3.55	1.99
股份合作企业	Cooperative Enterprises	1.95	0.60	0.46	0.40	0.27
联营企业	Joint Ownership Enterprises	0.13	0.03	0.05	0.02	0.02
有限责任公司	Limited Liability Corporations	164.86	200.72	220.79	238.95	235.50
#国有独资	State Solely Funded Corporatios	29.08	29.49	33.12	31.67	31.76
股份有限公司	Share-holding Corporations Ltd.	79.43	110.32	121.36	115.66	137.71
私营企业	Private Enterprises	177.86	222.41	252.60	273.31	312.56
其他企业	Other Enterprises	4.44	0.56	0.36	0.48	0.19
港、澳、台商投资企业	Enterprises with Funds from Hong Kong, Macao and Taiwan	105.18	117.06	118.59	135.07	138.46
外商投资企业	Foreign Funded Enterprises	226.38	223.19	238.74	249.37	254.72
按行业分	**Grouped by Sector**					
采矿业	**Mining**	**7.73**	**7.29**	**6.06**	**8.38**	**5.30**
煤炭开采和洗选业	Mining and Washing of Coal	4.55	3.75	2.92	5.58	2.40
石油和天然气开采业	Extraction of Petroleum and Natural Gas	1.97	2.51	1.54	1.16	1.35
黑色金属矿采选业	Mining and Processing of Ferrous Metal Ores	0.07	0.03	0.10	0.10	0.53
有色金属矿采选业	Mining and Processing of Non-ferrous Metals Ores	0.19	0.12	0.11	0.11	0.06
非金属矿采选业	Mining and Processing of Nonmetal Ores	0.94	0.88	1.38	1.43	0.95
其他矿采选业	Mining of Other Ores					
制造业	**Manufacturing**	**792.87**	**880.31**	**955.80**	**1014.47**	**1080.21**
农副食品加工业	Processing of Food from Agricultural Products	3.27	4.69	6.25	6.58	11.09
食品制造业	Manufacture of Food	3.78	4.06	4.64	5.86	5.66
饮料制造业	Manufacture of Beverage	4.35	4.72	7.29	5.56	5.97
烟草制品业	Manufacture of Tobacco	0.29	0.34	0.15	0.31	0.26
纺织业	Manufacture of Textile	30.29	32.04	33.15	35.67	34.81
纺织服装、鞋、帽制造业	Manufacture of Textile Wearing, Apparel, Footwear and Caps	17.57	20.88	18.72	22.29	24.53
皮革、毛皮、羽毛(绒)及其制品业	Manufacture of Textile, Fur, Feather and Related Products	2.81	2.55	2.39	3.29	4.09
木材加工及木、竹、藤、棕、草制品业	Processing of Timber,Manufacture of Wood, Bamboo,Rattan,Palm and Straw Products	4.21	7.68	8.63	10.72	13.51

15－10 续 表 Continued

单位:亿元 (100 million yuan)

指标	Item	2012	2013	2014	2015	2016
家具制造业	Manufacture of Furniture	0.52	0.71	1.29	1.02	1.75
造纸及纸制品业	Manufacture of Paper and Paper Products	9.48	7.45	10.93	13.91	14.61
印刷业和记录媒介的复制	Printing, Reproduction of Recording Media	3.47	4.52	2.56	2.56	4.02
文教体育用品制造业	Manufacture of Articles for Culture, Education and Sport Activities	6.36	8.23	9.07	10.94	12.54
石油加工、炼焦及核燃料加工业	Processing of Petroleum, Coking, Processing of Nuclear Fuel	3.87	3.91	2.82	3.54	2.66
化学原料及化学制品制造业	Manufacture of Raw Chemical Materials and Chemical Products	79.63	92.70	104.35	98.55	107.17
医药制造业	Manufacture of Medicines	34.50	38.65	41.34	45.57	55.02
化学纤维制造业	Manufacture of Chemical Fibers	22.21	22.03	26.30	28.23	24.22
橡胶制品业	Manufacture of Rubber	25.34	14.89	15.98	17.53	18.85
塑料制品业	Manufacture of Plastics	0.00	0.00	0.00	14.76	15.93
非金属矿物制品业	Manufacture of Non-metallic Mineral Products	13.50	15.79	16.18	64.19	54.98
黑色金属冶炼及压延加工业	Smelting and Pressing of Ferrous Metals	59.39	62.84	68.32	15.15	19.49
有色金属冶炼及压延加工业	Smelting and Pressing of Non-ferrous Metals	9.70	12.14	11.11	32.89	37.77
金属制品业	Manufacture of Metal Products	23.67	30.65	31.63	73.05	77.96
通用设备制造业	Manufacture of General Purpose Machinery	56.96	63.87	71.92	51.83	57.82
专用设备制造业	Manufacture of Special Purpose Machinery	37.42	48.50	51.02	52.21	62.81
交通运输设备制造业	Manufacture of Transport Equipment	67.64	69.68	62.74	39.67	38.73
电气机械及器材制造业	Manufacture of Electrical Machinery and Equipment	132.26	145.14	169.58	180.52	180.69
通信设备、计算机及其他电子设备制造业	Manufacture of Communication Equipment, Computers and Other Electronic Equipment	126.26	132.43	141.26	142.65	153.73
仪器仪表及文化、办公用机械制造业	Manufacture of Measuring Instruments and Machinery for Cultural Activity and Office Work	26.71	28.29	35.43	33.68	37.89
工艺品及其他制造业	Manufacture of Artwork and Other Manufacturing	0.75	0.71	0.46	1.49	1.34
废弃资源和废旧材料回收加工业	Recycling and Disposal of Waste	0.05	0.17	0.24	0.15	0.21
金属制品、机械和设备修理业	Manufacture of Metal Products, Machinery and Equipment Repair	0.11	0.02	0.04	0.10	0.11
电力、燃气及水的生产和供应业	**Production and Supply of Electricity, Gas and Water**	**2.12**	**3.55**	**7.33**	**9.94**	**6.07**
电力、热力的生产和供应业	Production and Supply of Electric Power and Heat Power	1.36	2.34	6.45	9.14	4.91
燃气生产和供应	Production and Supply of Gas	0.41	0.21	0.14	0.09	0.26
水的生产和供应业	Production and Supply of Water	0.35	1.00	0.74	0.72	0.90

15－11 高等学校科技活动情况
Basic Statistics on Scientific and Technical Activities of Institutions of Higher Education

项 目	Item	2012	2013	2014	2015	2016
参加科技统计的高校（所）	**Institutions of Higher Education in Statistics (unit)**	**102**	**111**	**117**	**142**	**146**
从事科技活动人数（人）	**Personnel in Scientific and Technical Activities (person)**	**61939**	**65116**	**68815**	**73204**	**75776**
教 师	Teachers	42185	44799	46645	48423	49622
其他技术人员	Other Technical Persons	19754	20317	22170	24781	26154
辅助人员	Assistants	731	740	1148	568	509
从事研究与发展活动人员（人）	**Perssonnel in Research and Development (person)**	**42185**	**44799**	**46645**	**48423**	**71468**
#正教授	Professors	6545	7035	7534	7929	8311
副教授	Vice-professors	13350	14475	15403	16321	17058
讲 师	Lecturers	18446	19639	20112	20759	20912
助 教	Assistants	3767	3551	3488	3353	3217
研究与发展机构（个）	**Institution of Research and Development (unit)**	**521**	**557**	**606**	**635**	**702**
机构中研究与发展人员（人）	Personnel (person)	15266	16778	18505	19034	21653
当年研究与开发经费收入（万元）	**Funds Revenue of Research and Development (10000 yuan)**	**1211365**	**1339448**	**1417795**	**1449858**	**1600660**
#科技事业费	Scientific and Technical Funds	57310	55326	57263	62760	71435
主管部门专项费	Speical Funds of Responsible Department for the Work	177115	208425	219284	241007	343371
国务院各部门专项费	Speical Funds of State Council Department	168465	187936	217147	212947	101067
省专项费	Provincial Special Foundation	80368	90773	99058	104529	110453
企事业单位委托经费	Entrusting Funds of Enterprises and Institutions	524513	575251	562054	549983	502037
国家自然科学基金	State Natural Sciences Foundation	136205	139787	152835	173960	204841
各种收入转入科研经费	Funds from Other Revenues	64777	79158	99524	97252	119620
研究与发展课题（项）	**Projects of Research and Development (unit)**	**33489**	**37596**	**40765**	**42988**	**48734**
#基础研究	Fundamental Research	10181	12022	13376	15509	18333
应用研究	Applied Research	11740	12154	13678	13567	16153
试验发展	Experimental Development	3069	3189	3673	3484	4548
研究与发展成果	**Achievements of Research and Development**					
出版科学专著（部）	Published Scientific Works (book)	212	275	267	370	418
发表学术论文（篇）	Published Papers (piece)	77244	79321	81844	86525	86037
#国外发表	Abroad	25592	25998	29247	34201	37319
科技成果转让（项）	**Scientific Achievements Transfered (unit)**	**1573**	**1703**	**1666**	**1432**	**2349**
获奖成果数（项）	**Prized Achievements (unit)**	**480**	**539**	**547**	**394**	**385**
#国家级	National Level	32	30	32	28	33
部省级	Provincial Level	280	330	346	279	218

15－12 高新技术产业产值
Output Value in High-tech Industry

单位:亿元 (100 million yuan)

项 目	Item	2012	2013	2014	2015	2016
总计	**Total**	**45041.48**	**51899.10**	**57277.28**	**61373.61**	**67124.65**
按行业分	**Grouped by Sector**					
航空航天制造业	Aviation and Aircrafts Manufacturing	218.30	263.65	294.68	316.28	335.07
电子计算机及办公设备制造业	Electronic Computers and Office Equipments	2260.06	2548.86	2349.71	2375.86	2882.60
电子及通信设备制造业	Electronic and Communication Equipments	11367.89	12288.74	13621.74	13955.09	14693.38
生物医药制造业	Medical and Pharmaceutical Products	2651.73	3184.23	3586.55	4170.23	4716.59
仪器仪表制造业	Manufactune of Special purpose Scientific Equipment	1084.99	1190.99	1291.54	1393.42	3874.04
高端装备制造业	Manufacture of Eleetrical Machinary & Equipment	12123.94	15561.06	17376.23	18182.56	18649.01
新材料制造业	Manufacture of New Material	12214.01	13602.31	15378.60	17289.21	18348.33
新能源制造业	Manufacture of New Energy	3120.55	3259.25	3378.23	3690.95	3625.64
按地区分	**Grouped by Region**					
南京市	Nanjing City	4739.55	5402.73	5740.94	5918.94	5902.61
无锡市	Wuxi City	5665.21	6346.30	6110.66	6211.38	6548.72
徐州市	Xuzhou City	3016.11	4013.63	4047.74	4505.26	5177.46
常州市	Changzhou City	3555.22	4471.83	4805.99	4975.62	5453.78
苏州市	Suzhou City	11888.80	14178.77	13644.87	13962.32	14470.32
南通市	Nantong City	3822.80	5115.92	5404.03	6048.45	7072.89
连云港市	Lianyungang City	1144.58	1426.58	1669.25	1936.90	2178.43
淮安市	Huaian City	956.49	1244.63	1473.86	1687.22	1909.00
盐城市	Yancheng City	1302.54	1830.27	2044.97	2455.42	3044.15
扬州市	Yangzhou City	3106.72	3650.80	3880.85	4032.30	4520.07
镇江市	Zhenjiang City	2814.42	3560.56	3900.80	4337.49	4586.86
泰州市	Taizhou City	2639.27	3772.74	3888.13	4528.76	5310.75
宿迁市	Suqian City	389.76	572.70	665.19	773.55	949.61

注:2012 年起,高新技术产业行业目录调整。

a) Industry direction of high-tech industry has been adjusted since 2012.

15－13 各类专业技术人员数
Number of Scientific and Technical Personnels

单位:万人　　(10000 persons)

年份　地区 Year　Region	各类专业技术人员 Total	#工程技术人员 Engineering	#农业技术人员 Agriculture	#科学研究人员 Scientific Research	#卫生技术人员 Health Care	#教学人员 Teaching
1980	43.87	9.63	1.13	1.47	9.02	17.13
1985	83.41	20.70	1.76	1.59	13.35	35.90
1990	158.86	31.84	2.35	1.84	13.87	44.50
1995	184.97	28.38	2.65	0.60	15.48	50.72
2000	194.24	44.84	4.61	1.81	23.04	66.15
2001	186.05	40.11	4.18	1.75	23.19	66.95
2002	175.79	35.79	3.74	1.56	22.96	67.56
2003	163.20	29.19	3.74	1.82	22.07	68.01
2004	147.23	22.16	3.25	1.77	20.86	69.25
2005	148.67	20.96	3.18	1.83	23.45	69.33
2006	142.20	20.54	3.11	1.69	21.35	69.27
2007	142.18	20.03	2.92	1.64	21.86	69.00
2008	142.26	19.72	3.06	1.68	22.04	69.89
2009	141.61	19.67	2.99	1.64	21.88	69.48
2010	140.53	19.00	2.72	1.53	21.21	66.69
2011	140.51	19.82	2.85	1.71	22.04	69.09
2012	140.65	19.79	2.69	1.77	22.30	68.93
2013	117.11	10.99	2.58	0.82	22.37	66.95
2014	117.98	11.20	2.63	0.87	23.01	67.38
2015	118.43	11.46	2.59	1.21	23.01	67.43
2016	118.42	11.77	2.44	1.00	23.46	67.27
南京市 Nanjing	10.23	1.22	0.11	0.05	2.48	5.29
无锡市 Wuxi	9.08	0.93	0.09	0.03	2.07	4.87
徐州市 Xuzhou	11.78	0.77	0.25	0.03	2.16	7.79
常州市 Changzhou	6.57	0.46	0.11	0.05	1.83	3.39
苏州市 Suzhou	13.59	1.46	0.17	0.06	3.38	7.35
南通市 Nantong	9.52	1.01	0.23	0.03	1.95	5.50
连云港市 Lianyungang	7.13	0.69	0.20	0.04	1.16	4.32
淮安市 Huaian	6.22	0.45	0.18	0.03	1.09	4.00
盐城市 Yancheng	9.38	0.63	0.31	0.02	1.72	5.80
扬州市 Yangzhou	6.05	0.51	0.14	0.02	1.24	3.52
镇江市 Zhenjiang	4.77	0.53	0.14	0.02	1.08	2.48
泰州市 Taizhou	6.48	0.52	0.23	0.02	1.43	3.77
宿迁市 Suqian	5.38	0.51	0.12	0.04	0.22	4.15

注：本表数据含辖区内的全民所有制单位和集体所有制单位。

a) Figures in the table are the data of state-owned and collective-owned units.

15－14 三种专利申请受理量
Application for Three Kinds of Patents Accepted

单位:件 (unit)

项目	Item	2000	2010	2012	2013	2014	2015	2016
申请受理量合计	**Applications Accepted**	**8210**	**235873**	**472656**	**504500**	**421907**	**428337**	**512429**
#发 明	Inventions	1159	50298	110091	141259	146660	154608	184632
实用新型	Utility Models	4590	51436	107091	128898	124980	154281	192636
外观设计	Designs	2461	134139	255474	234343	150267	119448	135161
#非职务	Non-official	4530	97222	135058	145244	125796		119677
职 务	Official	3680	138651	337598	359256	296111		392752
大专院校	Universities and Colleges	212	11290	23329	26818	26771	33550	42303
科研机构	Scientific Resarch Institutions	129	1743	4086	4631	4919	5148	5846
企业	Industrial and Mineral Enterprises	3296	125089	308801	325090	260501	275249	338726
机关团体	Government Agencies and Organizations	43	529	1382	2717	3920	4677	5877

15－15 三种专利授权量
Three Kinds of Patents Granted

单位:件 (unit)

项目	Item	2000	2010	2012	2013	2014	2015	2016
授权量合计	**Patents Granted**	**6432**	**138382**	**269944**	**239645**	**200032**	**250290**	**231033**
#发 明	Inventions	341	7210	16242	16790	19671	36015	40952
实用新型	Utility Models	4095	41161	77944	98246	100810	119513	117827
外观设计	Designs	1996	90011	175758	124609	79551	94762	72254
#非职务	Non-official	3125	59588	68424	50663	52031		48082
职务	Official	3307	78794	201520	188982	148001		182951
大专院校	Universities and Colleges	139	6038	11234	12116	13003	19209	19848
科研机构	Scientific Resarch Institutions	106	688	1128	1822	1840	2377	2366
企业	Industrial and Mineral Enterprises	3022	71781	186220	172787	131966	166445	157887
机关团体	Government Agencies and Organizations	40	287	2938	2257	1192	3027	2850

15-16 全省产品质量监督检查情况（2016 年）
Results of Sampling Check on the Quality of Products under Provincial Supervision (2016)

产品名称	Item	监督检查批次数（批次）Batches of Supervision and Inspection (batch)	监督检查合格批次数（批次）Qualified Batches (batch)	批次合格率（%）Rate of Batch-times Qualified (%)
合计	**Total**	**5965**	**5612**	**94.1**
食品相关产品	**Food Related Products**	**825**	**819**	**99.3**
餐具洗涤剂	Tableware Detergent	17	16	94.1
食品用塑料包装容器工具产品	Plastic Packaging Containers for Food Products	796	791	99.4
日用消费品	**Consumer Goods**	**2005**	**1844**	**92.0**
电动自行车	Electric Bicycle	17	15	88.2
羽绒服	Doun Jaket	102	88	86.3
休闲服装	Casual Clothe	199	172	86.4
雪地靴	Snow Boots	100	96	96.0
卫生纸	Toilet Paper	51	46	90.2
纸巾纸	Tissue	49	34	69.4
建筑装饰装修材料	**Building Raw Materials**	**865**	**812**	**93.9**
木家具	Wood Furniture	100	96	96.0
地板	Floor	100	91	91.0
塑料管材	Plastic Pipe	71	66	93.0
水泥	Cement	167	166	99.4
管材	Pipe	40	36	90.0
内墙涂料	Interior Wall Paint	96	93	96.9
工业生产资料	**Industrial Production**	**1744**	**1636**	**93.8**
电力电缆	Power Cable	266	258	97.0
阀门	Valve	25	23	92.0
农业生产资料	**Aqricultural Production**	**526**	**501**	**95.2**
肥料	Manure	253	235	92.9
农药	Pesticides	199	195	98.0

15－17 教育事业基本情况
Basic Statistics on Education

指 标	Item	2012	2013	2014	2015	2016
学校数 （所）	**Number of Schools （unit）**					
普通高等学校	Regular Institutions of Higher Education	128	131	134	137	141
普通中等学校	Secondary Schools	2903	2886	2875	2885	2908
中等专业学校	Specialized Schools	168	169	174	174	165
普通中学	Regular Secondary Schools	2660	2651	2644	2660	2692
#高 中	Senior Secondary Shools	594	578	567	569	571
职业高中	Vocational Senior Secondary Schools	75	66	57	51	51
小 学	Primary Schools	4128	4020	4023	4068	4036
特殊教育	Special Schools	107	107	106	106	101
专任教师 （万人）	**Number of Fulltime Teachers （10000 persons）**					
普通高等学校	Regular Institutions of Higher Education	10.60	10.83	10.45	10.72	10.98
普通中等学校	Secondary Schools	31.94	31.51	31.15	30.84	31.09
中等专业学校	Specialized Schools	2.80	2.97	3.03	3.04	2.98
普通中学	Regular Secondary Schools	27.95	27.43	27.13	26.88	27.17
#高 中	Senior Secondary Shools	9.72	9.73	9.65	9.54	9.51
职业高中	Vocational Senior Secondary Schools	1.19	1.11	0.99	0.92	0.95
小 学	Primary Schools	25.26	25.82	27.02	27.79	28.92
特殊教育	Special Schools	0.31	0.32	0.32	0.33	0.33
招生数 （万人）	**New Student Enrollment （10000 persons）**					
普通高等教育	Regular Higher Education	48.13	48.75	49.40	49.96	50.58
研究生	Postgraduates	4.62	4.80	4.91	5.10	5.31
本专科生	University and College Students	43.50	43.95	44.49	44.86	45.27
普通中等学校	Secondary Schools	126.37	119.63	114.97	116.74	122.26
中等专业学校	Specialized Secondary Schools	19.70	18.51	17.40	17.72	17.55
普通中学	Regular Secondary Schools	101.72	96.00	93.75	95.38	101.98
#高 中	Senior Secondary Shools	37.69	42.59	31.98	31.95	31.82
职业高中	Vocational Senior Secondary Schools	4.95	5.12	3.82	3.64	2.73
小 学	Primary Schools	79.48	85.13	88.89	91.96	93.46
特殊教育	Special Schools	0.35	0.35	0.34	0.38	0.40
在校学生 （万人）	**Students Enrollment （10000 persons）**					
普通高等教育	Regular Higher Education	181.07	183.04	184.93	187.13	190.74
研究生	Postgraduates	13.95	14.59	15.07	15.56	16.15
本专科生	University and College Students	167.12	168.45	169.86	171.57	174.58
普通中等学校	Secondary Schools	398.58	369.10	354.79	347.43	350.50
中等专业学校	Specialized Secondary Schools	63.12	56.68	54.00	51.89	51.13
普通中学	Regular Secondary Schools	317.89	296.74	288.62	284.52	290.10
#高 中	Senior Secondary Shools	120.87	110.99	103.42	97.80	95.15
职业高中	Vocational Senior Secondary Schools	17.57	15.68	12.17	11.02	9.27
小 学	Primary Schools	422.76	435.37	471.48	499.64	522.20
特殊教育	Special Schools	2.47	2.31	2.24	2.31	2.47
毕业生数 （万人）	**Graduates （10000 persons）**					
普通高等教育	Regular Higher Education	50.86	51.41	52.04	52.69	52.52
研究生	Postgraduates	3.84	4.03	4.17	4.28	4.37
本专科生	University and College Students	47.03	47.38	47.87	48.41	48.16
普通中等学校	Secondary Schools	141.67	138.52	124.98	120.18	116.25
中等专业学校	Specialized Secondary Schools	15.45	21.36	18.40	18.06	17.06
普通中学	Regular Secondary Schools	119.69	110.11	101.12	98.09	95.47
#高 中	Senior Secondary Shools	44.48	42.59	39.67	36.88	33.87
职业高中	Vocational Senior Secondary Schools	6.53	7.05	5.46	4.03	3.72
小 学	Primary Schools	64.51	63.94	62.19	64.69	72.18
特殊教育	Special Schools	0.33	0.34	0.30	0.35	0.33

15－18　各级各类教育事业(2016 年)
Basic Statistics on Education by Level and Type (2016)

单位:人　　　　　　　　　　　　　　　　　　　　　　　　　　　(person)

指　标	Item	学校数(所) Number of Schools (unit)	毕业生数 Graduates	招生数 New Student Enrollment	在校学生数 Students Enrollment in schools	教职工数 Teachers and Staff	#专任教师 Full-time Teachers
普通高等教育	Regular Higher Education	198	525237	505755	1907377	165722	109846
研究生	Postgraduates	42	43683	53054	161530		
本专科学生	Undergraduate and Specialized Courses	166	481554	452701	1745847		
普通中等专业学校	Regular Specialized Secondary Schools	165	170612	175501	511287	35152	29770
普通中学	Regular Secondary Schools	2692	954692	1019818	2900981	348313	271667
高　中	Senior Secondary Schools	571	338683	318236	951525	348313	95070
初　中	Junior Secondary Schools	2121	616009	701582	1949456		176597
职业高中	Vocational Senior Secondary Schools	51	37153	27313	92727	10665	9458
技工学校	Technical Schools	121	74980	101975	243271	18882	14629
小　学	Primary Schools	4036	721757	934578	5222018	270886	289202
特殊教育学校	Special Education	101	3282	3964	24662	3959	3346
幼儿园	Kindergartens	6867	843086	901912	2572212	235229	137730
成人高等教育	Adult Higher Education	8	173567	187340	435299	1132	648
#广播电视大学	Radio and TV Universities	2	4266	3318	14530	535	232
管理干部学院	Colleges for Training Managerial Personnel	2	2921	1100	2650	363	270
职工高等学校	Schools of Higher Education for Staff	3	64	89	202	98	65
教育学院	Pedagogical College	1	1497	1398	2903	136	81
成人中等专业学校	Specialized Secondary Schools for Adults	19	21900	18125	48485	1839	951
成人中学	Secondary Schools for Adults	337	4439		4938	900	629
网络教育	Internet-based Education		24302	30708	69234		

15－19 全省研究生数
Number of Postgraduates

单位:人 (person)

指　标	Item	2012	2013	2014	2015	2016
高等学校	**Institutions of Higher Education**					
招生数	New Student Enrollment	45807	47588	48937	50841	52885
在读人数	Student Enrollment	138284	144699	150135	155017	160978
#女　性	Female	66868	67069	69849	72285	76576
毕业生数	Graduates	37998	39936	41512	42601	43526
研究所(院)	**Research Institutions (Academies)**					
招生数	New Student Enrollment	407	397	168	174	169
在读人数	Student Enrollment	1245	1248	555	543	552
#女　性	Female	440	442	174	156	159
毕业生数	Graduates	354	351	167	162	157

15－20 各级各类学校女在校学生和女专任教师数
Number of Female Students Enrollment and Teachers by Level and Type of Schools

指　标	Item	2012	2013	2014	2015	2016
女在校学生数（万人）	**Number of Female Students in Schools (10000 persons)**					
普通高等教育本、专科	Regular Institutions of Higher Education	82.68	83.16	84.45	85.28	86.66
普通中等专业学校	Regular Specialized Secondary Schools	31.12	28.00	26.35	25.00	24.22
普通中学	Regular Secondary Schools	147.80	138.70	134.89	132.81	135.50
职业高中	Vocational Senior Secondary Schools	7.97	6.85	5.44	5.03	4.39
小　学	Primary Schools	192.28	198.53	214.43	227.47	238.19
女在校学生占在校学生总数（%）	**Percentage of Female Students in Schools to Total Students (%)**					
普通高等教育本、专科	Regular Institutions of Higher Education	49.4	49.4	49.7	49.7	49.6
普通中等专业学校	Regular Specialized Secondary Schools	49.3	49.4	48.8	48.2	47.4
普通中学	Regular Secondary Schools	46.5	46.7	46.7	46.7	46.7
职业高中	Vocational Senior Secondary Schools	45.3	43.7	44.7	45.6	47.4
小　学	Primary Schools	45.5	45.6	45.5	45.5	45.6
女专任教师数（万人）	**Number of Full Time Female Teachers (10000 persons)**					
普通高等学校	Regular Institutions of Higher Education	4.77	4.91	4.74	4.87	5.00
普通中等专业学校	Regular Specialized Secondary Schools	1.50	1.59	1.62	1.64	1.63
普通中学	Regular Secondary Schools	13.42	13.37	13.39	13.46	13.76
职业高中	Vocational Senior Secondary Schools	0.57	0.54	0.49	0.47	0.48
小　学	Primary Schools	15.40	16.00	17.13	18.08	19.20
女专任教师占专任教师总数（%）	**Percentage of Full Time Female Teachers to Total Teachers (%)**					
普通高等学校	Regular Institutions of Higher Education	44.9	45.3	45.4	45.4	45.5
普通中等专业学校	Regular Specialized Secondary Schools	53.4	53.5	53.6	54.1	54.9
普通中学	Regular Secondary Schools	48.0	48.8	49.4	50.1	50.7
职业高中	Vocational Senior Secondary Schools	47.9	48.8	49.8	50.5	50.6
小　学	Primary Schools	61.0	62.0	63.4	65.1	66.4

15-21 普通高等教育分科学生数(2016年)
Student Enrollment in Regular Higher Education by Field of Study (2016)

单位:人 (person)

项 目	Item	毕业生数 Graduates	招生数 New Enrollment	在校生数 Total Enrollment
本科合计	**Undergraduate**	**244215**	**290333**	**1068951**
#女生	Female	128144	147846	546243
哲 学	Philosophy	90	137	511
经济学	Economics	14469	16610	62222
法 学	Law	6571	7317	28356
教育学	Education	5917	8813	29085
文 学	Literature	20751	23998	85769
#外语	Foreign Language	10873	12455	44141
#艺术	Art	604	589	2425
历史学	History	15810	17496	66863
理 学	Science	100485	122880	449131
工 学	Engineering	3306	3608	13506
农 学	Agriculture	12471	15088	64038
医 学	Medicine	47772	52847	191402
管理学	Management	15969	20950	75643
专科合计	**Specialist**	**237339**	**240924**	**676896**
#女生	Female	118839	114297	320361
农林牧渔大类	Animou Husbandry and Fishery	5836	6519	17459
交通运输大类	Transportation	1971	1836	5359
生化与药品大类	Biochemical and Drug	1600	1328	4448
资源开发与测绘大类	Resource Develpment and Mapping	24110	20575	62565
材料与能源大类	Material and Energy	75	88	302
土建大类	Civil Construction	41860	40568	118550
水利大类	Water Conservation	3786	2503	9064
制造大类	Manufacture	2911	2406	7018
电子信息大类	Electronic Information	4766	5710	15510
环保、气象与安全大类	Meteorology and Environmental Safety	8238	12355	30797
轻纺食品大类	Textile, Food	29472	31020	83121
财经大类	Finance and Economices	13197	18248	43732
医药卫生大类	Medicine and Health	49575	51910	146522
旅游大类	Tourism	7490	8749	23554
公共事业大类	Public Utilities	16145	14443	48584
文化教育大类	Public Education	2066	1946	5989
艺术设计传媒大类	Art Design and Media	21768	18624	47607
公安大类	Public Security	961	723	2011
法律大类	Law	1512	1373	4704

注:招生数含五年制高职、专转本学生。

a) The enrollment number include five years higher vocational enducation and upgraded students.

15－22 分市教育事业基本情况(2016 年)

指 标	Item	南京市 Nanjing	无锡市 Wuxi	徐州市 Xuzhou	常州市 Changzhou
学校数 (所)	**Number of Schools (unit)**				
普通高等学校	Regular Institutions of Higher Education	44	12	10	10
普通中等学校	Secondary Schools	249	205	358	171
中等专业学校	Specialized Schools	22	20	11	11
普通中学	Regular Secondary Schools	227	183	337	160
#高 中	Senior Secondary Shools	53	44	88	34
职业高中	Vocational Senior Secondary Schools	0	2	10	0
小 学	Primary Schools	346	197	928	201
特殊教育	Special Schools	12	7	12	5
专任教师 (人)	**Number of Fulltime Teachers (persons)**				
普通高等学校	Regular Institutions of Higher Education	48854	6144	8217	5557
普通中等学校	Secondary Schools	26649	24108	37390	16543
中等专业学校	Specialized Schools	3667	3973	1821	2483
普通中学	Regular Secondary Schools	22982	19991	33695	14060
#高 中	Senior Secondary Shools	8046	6909	12144	4793
职业高中	Vocational Senior Secondary Schools	0	144	1874	0
小 学	Primary Schools	23644	20119	42716	14173
特殊教育	Special Schools	478	261	428	127
招生数 (人)	**New Student Enrollment (persons)**				
普通高等教育	Regular Higher Education	201244	33469	38942	30620
研究生	Postgraduates	35805	2206	4026	701
本专科生	University and College Students	165439	31263	34916	29919
普通中等学校	Secondary Schools	96927	92860	151945	70065
中等专业学校	Specialized Secondary Schools	18607	15523	12349	11576
普通中学	Regular Secondary Schools	78320	76152	130494	58489
#高 中	Senior Secondary Shools	25597	22989	37699	16896
职业高中	Vocational Senior Secondary Schools	0	1185	9102	0
小 学	Primary Schools	69143	65010	161368	48937
特殊教育	Special Schools	323	321	792	111
在校学生 (人)	**Students Enrollment (persons)**				
普通高等教育	Regular Higher Education	827773	113732	140825	104140
研究生	Postgraduates	110387	6735	11991	1864
本专科生	University and College Students	717386	106997	128834	102276
普通中等学校	Secondary Schools	279502	263571	434935	200380
中等专业学校	Specialized Secondary Schools	54954	44284	36290	35041
普通中学	Regular Secondary Schools	224548	215413	361022	165339
#高 中	Senior Secondary Shools	75641	66044	118972	49952
职业高中	Vocational Senior Secondary Schools	0	3874	37623	0
小 学	Primary Schools	375445	361282	905360	281099
特殊教育	Special Schools	1998	1557	4679	947
毕业生数 (人)	**Graduates (persons)**				
普通高等教育	Regular Higher Education	232303	34009	36166	28695
研究生	Postgraduates	29214	1806	3360	574
本专科生	University and College Students	203089	32203	32806	28121
普通中等学校	Secondary Schools	90336	84634	146495	64767
中等专业学校	Specialized Secondary Schools	17836	12436	13242	11787
普通中学	Regular Secondary Schools	72500	69000	117142	52980
#高 中	Senior Secondary Shools	24957	22032	45684	17875
职业高中	Vocational Senior Secondary Schools	0	3198	16111	0
小 学	Primary Schools	52221	53583	95912	41861
特殊教育	Special Schools	347	172	434	137

Basic Statistics on Education by Region (2016)

苏州市 Suzhou	南通市 Nantong	连云港市 Lianyungang	淮安市 Huaian	盐城市 Yancheng	扬州市 Yanzhou	镇江市 Zhenjiang	泰州市 Taizhou	宿迁市 Suqian
22	8	4	7	6	6	6	3	3
318	220	188	206	292	180	121	198	202
21	5	9	16	5	10	10	9	16
292	206	174	188	277	166	110	186	186
68	46	37	31	51	35	20	37	27
5	9	5	2	10	4	1	3	0
391	322	451	252	329	203	111	149	156
12	7	7	7	10	7	5	5	5
12143	4937	2128	3797	3543	4780	5690	3134	922
32478	28234	22442	22427	29585	18826	11671	20696	19846
4296	602	1511	2942	794	1723	1561	1655	2742
27726	24493	19959	19454	26634	16467	10088	19014	17104
9218	9255	6985	6264	9087	6135	3531	6986	5717
456	3139	972	31	2157	636	22	27	0
35770	19636	23614	21067	26548	13593	9632	14108	24582
373	318	191	188	330	201	135	152	164
63104	24788	10238	19789	15483	22234	24589	16730	4525
4168	799	77	46	0	2134	3092	0	0
58936	23989	10161	19743	15483	20100	21497	16730	4525
133545	100797	97110	91961	110174	71672	39939	68155	97482
20753	16492	13734	15017	6756	13269	6572	8117	16736
112302	80860	80877	75606	95478	58403	33345	59232	80260
30491	24850	25806	24227	29892	20748	10804	20614	27623
490	3445	2499	1338	7940	0	22	806	486
133006	57112	77416	58029	73548	34514	24924	37598	93973
454	221	218	245	458	299	132	209	181
219271	87482	38647	69653	61164	80450	87481	59201	17558
12477	2172	193	104	0	6033	9574	0	0
206794	85310	38454	69549	61164	74417	77907	59201	17558
370969	294975	275517	262265	316239	217382	114228	194746	280286
59135	50022	37474	43401	20840	41803	18965	21291	47787
309824	235907	230091	215227	269984	175579	95204	170830	232013
84676	77347	74489	72163	92437	64196	31561	61427	82620
2010	9046	7952	3637	25415	0	59	2625	486
693657	327060	432004	350503	450232	212554	143830	219965	469027
2735	1787	1192	1917	2575	2390	926	1029	930
58774	22988	10722	19053	17103	22715	22408	15632	4657
3588	630	0	25	0	1823	2651	0	0
55186	22358	10722	19028	17103	20892	19757	15632	4657
109824	101902	88560	89221	112071	76091	36920	66839	94797
16975	16824	10162	15529	8584	14505	5388	6996	20348
92143	82468	74667	72171	94365	61559	31518	59730	74449
25633	30256	26187	26785	34832	23416	10995	22525	27506
706	2610	3731	1521	9122	27	14	113	0
89873	56212	56281	52534	69492	38321	22725	39388	53354
558	210	124	254	296	337	105	184	124

15－23　每万人口在校学生数和中小学升学情况
Number of Students Per 10000 Population and Enrollment Rate of Secondary and Primary Schools

年　份 Year	平均每万人口中 Number of Students per 10000 Population			小学学龄儿童入学率（%）Enrollment Rate of School-age Children（%）	小学毕业生升学率（%）Primary school Graduates Entering into Junior Secondary Schools（%）	初中毕业生升学率（%）Junior Secondary Graduates Entering into Senior Secondary Schools（%）
	大学生（人）University and College Students（person）	中学生（人）Secondary School Students（person）	小学生（人）Primary School Students（person）			
1978	10.4	667.9	1489.3	96.7	90.3	42.3
1980	14.2	553.8	1409.4	97.1	81.3	28.4
1985	19.2	492.3	1091.1	99.5	74.2	29.5
1989	23.0	426.4	980.9	98.8	79.8	38.2
1990	21.7	460.3	904.8	99.9	82.0	39.6
1991	21.1	467.4	869.1	99.3	84.2	40.0
1992	22.1	476.6	846.5	99.5	85.9	41.8
1993	25.9	481.3	853.9	99.4	88.0	45.4
1994	28.7	503.8	877.7	99.4	93.5	51.1
1995	29.5	530.5	912.5	99.8	96.6	56.8
1996	31.0	549.1	967.4	99.8	96.6	61.2
1997	33.4	547.9	1024.6	99.8	97.1	63.8
1998	38.0	550.3	1046.8	99.8	97.5	62.4
1999	49.8	565.8	1027.6	99.8	97.2	65.1
2000	61.7	592.3	980.7	99.8	97.2	68.5
2001	79.6	643.1	933.4	98.7	97.9	73.9
2002	94.9	710.7	860.6	99.6	98.2	78.6
2003	116.1	761.3	782.3	99.6	98.7	83.2
2004	133.8	795.3	710.7	99.7	98.8	84.8
2005	155.2	793.3	649.6	99.8	99.8	89.6
2006	173.0	775.1	603.7	99.9	100.0	93.5
2007	193.1	740.8	562.9	99.6	100.0	95.7
2008	204.9	697.7	531.6	99.9	100.0	96.0
2009	214.0	642.6	512.7	99.9	100.0	97.3
2010	209.6	588.1	506.8	99.9	100.0	97.5
2011	227.1	430.2	518.6	99.9	100.0	97.7
2012	228.6	401.4	533.8	100.0	100.0	98.0
2013	232.7	374.7	549.7	100.0	100.0	98.3
2014	232.3	362.6	592.3	100.0	100.0	100.0
2015	234.8	357.1	627.0	100.0	100.0	100.0
2016	238.4	362.6	652.9	100.0	100.0	100.0

15－24　各级学校教师负担学生数
Student-teacher Ratio by Level of School

年　份 Year	普通高等学校 Institutions of Regular Higher Education		普通中等学校 Regular Secondary Schools		小　学 Primary Schools	
	教师数（万人）Number of Teachers (10000 persons)	平均每个教师负担学生数（人）Student-teacher Ratio (person)	教师数（万人）Number of Teachers (10000 persons)	平均每个教师负担学生数（人）Student-teacher Ratio (person)	教师数（万人）Number of Teachers (10000 persons)	平均每个教师负担学生数（人）Student-teacher Ratio (person)
1978	1.34	4.5	16.75	23.3	27.07	32.1
1980	1.59	5.3	16.83	19.5	27.97	29.9
1985	2.30	5.2	16.53	18.5	25.91	26.2
1989	2.79	5.3	19.00	16.0	26.74	23.6
1990	2.76	5.3	19.63	15.9	26.95	22.7
1991	2.76	5.2	20.06	15.9	27.00	22.0
1992	2.70	5.7	20.32	16.2	26.66	21.9
1993	2.70	6.7	20.71	16.2	25.59	23.2
1994	2.73	7.4	21.28	16.6	26.95	22.9
1995	2.73	7.6	22.16	16.9	27.35	23.6
1996	2.74	8.1	22.82	17.1	27.96	24.6
1997	2.79	8.6	23.26	16.8	28.32	25.9
1998	2.86	9.6	23.57	16.8	28.20	26.7
1999	3.04	11.8	24.10	16.9	28.41	26.1
2000	3.31	13.7	25.02	17.3	28.90	24.9
2001	3.80	15.4	25.96	18.2	28.84	23.8
2002	4.43	15.8	27.38	19.2	27.95	22.7
2003	4.98	18.3	28.74	19.6	26.84	21.6
2004	5.90	18.0	30.19	19.6	29.22	19.9
2005	6.73	18.4	31.14	19.0	26.16	18.6
2006	7.84	17.8	31.92	18.3	26.05	17.5
2007	8.86	17.7	32.30	17.5	25.83	16.6
2008	9.63	17.4	32.51	16.5	25.47	16.0
2009	9.99	17.7	32.54	15.3	25.47	15.6
2010	10.20	17.4	32.36	14.3	24.96	16.0
2011	10.39	17.3	32.14	13.2	25.01	16.4
2012	10.60	17.1	31.94	12.5	25.26	16.7
2013	10.83	16.9	31.51	11.7	25.82	16.9
2014	10.45	17.7	31.15	11.4	27.02	17.4
2015	10.72	17.5	30.84	11.2	27.79	18.0
2016	10.98	17.4	31.48	11.3	28.92	18.1

主要统计指标解释

科技活动 指在自然科学、农业科学、医药科学、工程与技术科学、人文与社会科学领域(简称科学技术领域)中,与科技知识的产生、发展、传播和应用密切相关的有组织的活动。可分为研究与试验发展(R&D)、研究与试验发展成果应用及相关的科技服务三类活动。

科技活动人员 指直接从事科技活动、以及专门从事科技活动管理和为科技活动提供直接服务的人员。累计从事科技活动的实际工作时间占全年制度工作时间10%及以上的人员。(1)直接从事科技活动的人员包括:在独立核算的科学研究与技术开发机构、高等学校、各类企业及其他事业单位内设的研究室、实验室、技术开发中心及中试车间(基地)等机构中从事科技活动的研究人员、工程技术人员、技术工人及其它人员;虽不在上述机构工作,但编入科技活动项目(课题)组的人员;科技信息与文献机构中的专业技术人员;从事论文设计的研究生等。(2)专门从事科技活动管理和为科技活动提供直接服务的人员包括:独立核算的科学研究与技术开发机构、科技信息与文献机构、高等学校、各类企业及其他事业单位主管科技工作的负责人,专门从事科技活动的计划、行政、人事、财务、物资供应、设备维护、图书资料管理等工作的各类人员,但不包括保卫、医疗保健人员、司机、食堂人员、茶炉工、水暖工、清洁工等为科技活动提供间接服务的人员。**研究与试验发展(R&D)** 指在科学技术领域,为增加知识总量、以及运用这些知识去创造新的应用而进行的系统的创造性的活动,包括基础研究、应用研究、试验发展三类活动。

基础研究 指为了获得关于现象和可观察事实的基本原理的新知识(揭示客观事物的本质、运动规律,获得新发现、新学说)而进行的实验性或理论性研究,它不以任何专门或特定的应用或使用为目的。其成果以科学论文和科学著作为主要形式。

应用研究 指为获得新知识而进行的创造性研究,主要针对某一特定的目的或目标。应用研究是为了确定基础研究成果可能的用途,或是为达到预定的目标探索应采取的新方法(原理性)或新途径。其成果形式以科学论文、专著、原理性模型或发明专利为主。

试验发展 指利用从基础研究、应用研究和实际经验所获得的现有知识,为产生新的产品、材料和装置,建立新的工艺、系统和服务,以及对已产生和建立的上述各项作实质性的改进而进行的系统性工作。其成果形式主要是专利、专有技术、具有新产品基本特征的产品原型或具有新装置基本特征的原始样机等。在社会科学领域,试验发展是指把通过基础研究、应用研究获得的知识转变成可以实施的计划(包括为进行检验和评估实施示范项目)的过程。人文科学领域没有对应的试验发展活动。

研究与试验发展人员 指参与研究与试验发展项目研究、管理和辅助工作的人员,包括项目(课题)组人员,企业科技行政管理人员和直接为项目(课题)活动提供服务的辅助人员。

研究与试验发展人员全时当量 指全时人员数加非全时人员按工作量折算为全时人员数的总和。例如:有两个全时人员和三个非全时人员(工作时间分别为20%、30%和70%),则全时当量为2+0.2+0.3+0.7=3.2人年。

专业技术人员 指从事专业技术工作和专业技术管理工作的人员,即企事业单位中已经聘任专业技术职务从事专业技术工作和专业技术管理工作的人员,以及未聘任专业技术职务,现在专业技术岗位上工作的人员。包括工程技术人员,农业技术人员,科学研究人员,卫生技术人员,教学人员,经济人员,会计人员,统计人员,翻译人员,图书资料、档案、文博人员,新闻出版人员,律师、公证人员,广播电视播音人员,工艺美术人员,体育人员,艺术人员及企业政治思想工作人员,共十七个专业技术职务类别。

科技活动经费筹集 指从各种渠道筹集到的计划用于科技活动的经费,包括政府资金、企业资金、事业单位资金、金融机构贷款、国外资金和其他资金等。

政府资金 指从各级政府部门获得的计划用于科技活动的经费,包括科学事业费、科技三项费、科研基建费、科学基金、教育等部门事业费中计划用于科技活动的经费以及政府部门预算外资金中计划用于科技活动的经费等。

企业资金 指从自有资金中提取或接受其他企业委托的、科研院所和高校等事业单位接受企业委托获得的,计划用于科研和技术开发的经费。不包括来自政府、金融机构及国外的计划用于科技活动的资金。

金融机构贷款 指从各类金融机构获得的用于科技活动的贷款。

科技活动经费内部支出 指报告年内用于科技活动的实际支出包括劳务费、科研业务费、科研管理费,非基建投资购建的固定资产、科研基建支出以及其他用于科技活动的支出。不包括生产性活动支出、归还贷款支出及转拨外单位支出。

劳务费 指以货币或实物形式直接或间接支付给从事科技活动人员的劳动报酬及各种费用。包括各种形式的工资、津贴、奖金、福利、离退休人员费用、人民助学金等。

固定资产购建费 指报告年内使用非基建投资购建的固定资产和用于科研基建投资的实际支出额,即固定资产实际支出和科研基建投资实际完成额之和。固定资产是指长期使用而不改变原有实物形态的主要物资设备、图书资料、实验材料和标本以及其他设备和家具、房屋、建筑物。

新产品 指采用新技术原理、新设计构思研制、生产的全新产品，或在结构、材质、工艺等某一方面比原有产品有明显改进，从而显著提高了产品性能或扩大了使用功能的产品。既包括政府有关部门认定并在有效期内的新产品，也包括企业自行研制开发，未经政府有关部门认定，从投产之日起一年之内的新产品。

专利 是专利权的简称，是对发明人的发明创造经审查合格后，由专利局依据专利法授予发明人和设计人对该项发明创造享有的专有权。包括发明、实用新型和外观设计。

发明 指对产品、方法或者其改进所提出的新的技术方案。

实用新型 指对产品的形状、构造或者其结合所提出的适于实用的新的技术方案。

外观设计 指对产品的形状、图案、色彩或者其结合所作出的富有美感并适于工业上应用的新设计。

普通高等学校 指按照国家规定的设置标准和审批程序批准举办，通过国家统一招生考试，招收高中毕业生为主要培养对象，实施高等学历教育的全日制大学、独立设置的学院和高等专科学校、高等职业学校和其他机构。

成人高等学校 指按照国家规定的设置标准和审批程序举办的，通过全国成人高等教育统一招生考试，招收具有高中毕业或同等学历的人员为主要培养对象，利用脱产、业余或函授等多种形式对其实施高等学历教育的学校。包括广播电视大学、职工高等学校、农民高等学校、管理干部学院、教育学院、独立函授学院、其他机构。

小学学龄儿童入学率 指调查范围内已入小学学习的学龄儿童占校内外学龄儿童总数（包括弱智儿童，不包括盲聋哑儿童）的比重。计算公式为：

小学学龄儿童入学率 = 已入学的小学学龄儿童数/校内外小学学龄儿童总数 ×100%

Explanatory Notes on Main Statistical Indicators

Scientific and Technological Activities(S&T Activities) refer to organized activities which are closely related to the creation, development, dissemination and application of the scientific and technical knowledge in the fields of natural sciences, agricultural science, medical science, engineering and technological science, humanities and social sciences (referred to as scientific and technological fields). S&T activities can be classified in to 3 categories: research and development(R&D) activities, application of R&D results, and related S&T services.

Personnel Engaged in S&T Activities refer to personnel directly engaged in S&T activities, in the management of S&T activ—ities, and in providing direct service to S&T activities, who spend over 10% of the total working hours in a year in S&T activities. (1) Personnel directly engaged in S&T activities include researchers, engineers, technicians and other related personnel engaged in S&T activities in independent—accounting R&D institutions, institutions of higher learning, and in research institutes, laboratories, technology development centers and central experiment workshops under enterprises and institutions. Also included are people working in S&T research project teams, professional and technical personnel working in S&T information archiving institutes, and graduate students working on the design of their thesis. (2) Personnel engaged in the management of S&T activities and in providing direct service to S&T activities include senior management people responsible for S&T activities in independent-accounting R&D institutions, S&T infor-mation archiving institutes, institutions of higher learning, and in enterprises and institutions where S&T activities are undertaken. Also included are people responsible for the planning, administration, personnel management, financial management, logistics supply, equipment maintenance, information and library management that are related with S&T activities. People providing indirect services are excluded, such as security, medical service, drivers, plumbers, cleaners and those providing catering and related service.

Scientists and Engineers refer to persons engaged in S&T activities who have obtained titles of senior and middle level professional positions, and those without such position but have completed university or higher education.

Research and Development(R&D) refers to systematic and creative activities in the field of science and technology aiming at increasing the knowledge and using the knowledge for new application. R&D includes 3 categories of activities: basic research, applied research and experiments and development.

Basic Research refers to empirical or theoretical research aiming at obtaining new knowledge on the fundamental principles of phenomena of observable facts to reveal the nature and law of movement of objects and to acquire new discoveries or new theories. Basic research takes no specific or designated application as the aim of the research. Results of basic research are mainly released or disseminated in the form of scientific papers or monographs.

Applied research refers to creative research aiming at obtaining new knowledge on a specific objective or target. Purpose of the applied research is to identify the possible use of results from basic research, or to explore new (fundamental) methods or new approaches. Results of applied research are expressed in the form of scientific papers, monographs, fundamental models or invention patents.

Experiments and Development refer to systematic activities aiming at using the knowledge from basic and applied researches or from practical experience to develop new products, materials and equipment, to establish new production process, systems and services, or to make substantial improvement on the existing products, process or services. Results of experiment and development activities are embodied in patents, exclusive technology, monotype of new products or equipment. In social sciences, experiment and development activities refer to the process of converting the knowledge from basic or applied researches into feasible programmes (including conduct of demonstration projects for assessment and evaluation). There is no experiment and development activities in the science of humani-ties. R&D Personnel refer to persons engaged in research, management and supporting activities of R&D, including persons in the project teams, persons engaged in the management of S&T activities of enterprises and supporting staff providing direct service to the research projects.

R&D Personnel refer to persons engaged in reasearch, management and supporting activities of R&D, including persons in project teams, persons engaged in management of S&T activities of enterprises and supporting staff providing direct service to the research projects.

Full-time Equivalent of R&D Personnel refers to the sum of the full-time persons and the full-time equivalent of part-time persons converted by workload. For instance, if there are 2 full-time persons and 3 part-time workers (20%, 30% and 70% of working hours respectively on R&D activities), the full-time equivalent is 2 + 0.2 + 0.3 + 0.7 = 3.2 person-years.

Professional and Technical Personnel refer to person engaged in professional and technical work or in the management of professional and technical activities, i.e., people with professional or technical positions who are engaged in professional and technical work or in the management of professional and technical activities, and people without professional or technical positions but are working on professional or technical posts. They include professionals and technicians working in 17 categories of technical occupations including engineering, agriculture, scientific researches, medical service, teaching, economic research and application, accounting, statistics, translation, libraries, archives, cultural and museum service, journalism and publication, lawyers, notarization service, radio and television broadcasting, handicraft and fine arts, sports, performing art, and political workers in enterprises.

Funding for S&T Activities refers to funds obtained from various sources for S&T activities, including government funds, self-raised funds by enterprises, self-raised funds by institutions, loans from financial institutions, foreign funds and other funds.

Government Funds refer to funds obtained from government agencies at all levels to be used for S&T activities, including fund for scientific undertakings, 3 kinds of fund for S&T activities, fund for capital construction for scientific researches, science fund, funds from education expenditures by education departments for S&T activities, and extra-budget fund from government agencies for S&T activities.

Self-raised Funds by Enterprises refers to self-raised funds by enterprises from their own expenditure or from other enterprises and funds received by universities or research institutions from enterprises for scientific research or technical development projects. Excluded in this category are funds from government agencies, financial institutions or from foreign institutions. Loans from Financial Institutions refer to loans from various financial institutions for S&T activities.

Loans from Financial Institutions refer to loans from various financial institutions for S&T activities.

Total Internal Expenditure of Funds on R&D refers to the real expenditure of surveyed units on their own R&D activities (basic research, application study, test and development) including direct expenditure on R&D activities, indirect expendure of management and services on R&D activities, expenditure on capital construction and material processing by others. Excluding the expenditure on production activities, return of loan, and fees transferred to cooperated and entrusted agencies on R&D activities.

Service Fees refer to direct or indirect payment, in cash or in kind, made to personnel engaged in S&T activities as remuneration and other fees. They include, in various forms, salaries, subsidies, bonus, benefits, retirement pension, stipend, etc.

Purchase or Construction of Fixed Assets refers to the fixed assets purchased or constructed using funds other than the investment in capital construction, and the actual expenditure on capital construction for scientific researches. In other words, it is the sum of the actual expenditure on fixed assets and the accomplished investment in capital construction for scientific researches. Fixed assets refer to main materials and equipment, literatures and documents in libraries, materials for experiments, specimen, instruments, furniture, buildings and constructions that can be used for a long time without changing the form and shape of those articles or constructions.

New Products refer to new products produced with new technology and new design, or products that represent noticeable improvement in terms of structure, material, or production process so as to improve significantly the character or function of the older versions. They include new products certified by relevant government agencies within the period of certification, as well as new products designed and produced by enterprises within a year without certification by government agencies.

Patent is an abbreviation for the patent right and refers to the exclusive right of ownership by the inventors or designers for the creation or inventions, given from the patent offices after due process of assessment and approval in accordance with the Patent Law.

Patents are granted for inventions, utility models and designs.

Inventions refer to the new technical proposals to the products or methods or their modifications.

Utility Models refer to the practical and new technical proposals on the shape and structure of the product or the combination of both.

Designs refer to the aesthetics and industrially applicable new designs for the shape, pattern and color of the product, or their combinations.

Regular Institutions of Higher Learning refer to educational establishments set up according to the government evaluation and approval procedures, enrolling graduates from senior secondary schools and providing higher education courses and training for senior professionals. They include full-time universities, colleges, high professional schools, high vocatoinal universities and other institutions.

Institutions of Higher Learning for Adults refer to educational establishments, set up in line with the government evalution and approval procedures, enrolling personnels with senior secondary school or equivalent education as main training objects, and providing higher education courses in many forms of full time, spare time, or correspondence for adults. Institutions of higher learning for adults include Radio and TV universities, schools of high education for staff and workers and peasants, colleges for management cadres, pedagogical colleges, independent correspondence colleges and other institutions.

Enrollment Rate of Primary School Age Children refers to the proportion of school age children enrolled at schools to the total number of school age children both in and outside schools (including retarded children, but excluding blind, deaf and mute children). The formula is:

Enrollment Rate of Primary School-age Children = (Total Primary School—age Children at Schools) (Total Primary School age Children Both at and outside Schools) 100%

16

文化、体育、卫生

Culture, Sports and Public Health

简 要 说 明

一、本篇资料的主要内容

本篇主要反映文化、新闻出版、广播电影电视、体育、卫生事业的发展情况。

文化部分主要包括文化艺术和文物机构人员情况，群众艺术馆、文化馆站、公共图书馆业务活动及经费情况，文化产业发展展情况；新闻出版部分包括报纸、期刊、图书出版情况；广播电影电视部分包括广播、电视事业发展情况，广播、电视节目制作时间；体育部分主要内容包括体育系统职工人数，等级运动员、裁判员人数，运动员在各级比赛中获奖牌情况；卫生部分主要内容有卫生机构、人员、床位数，医院诊疗人次及入院人数，传染病的发病及死亡等情况。

二、本篇的资料来源

根据各部门制定的统计报表制度汇总加工整理而成。文化艺术业、文物业、图书馆业、群众文化服务业的资料主要来自省文化厅；文化产业的资料来自省统计局；新闻出版、广播、电视资料来自省新闻出版广电局；体育资料来自省体育局；卫生部分的资料来自省卫生计生委。

Brief Introduction

I. Main Contents

Data in this chapter mainly reflect the development of culture; news and publication; radio broadcasting; films and television; sports; and public health.

Data on culture cover mainly information on institution and personnel of cultural and cultural relics; mass art centers; cultural centers (stations); facilities, services and expenditures of public libraries; Cultural industry development. Press and Publication section includes newspaper, periodicals and books published; Part of Radio, Film and TV includes broadcasting and television stations; production of broadcasting and TV programs.

Data on sports cover number of staff and workers in sports commissions, athletes and referees in grades and awards for athletes in competitions of all levels.

Data on public health include mainly the number of institutions; personnel, hospital beds; number of patients treated and in-patients; the incidence of and the deaths caused by infections diseases.

II. Sources of Data

Data are collected and tabulated in accordance with the statistic reporting schemes stipulated by the departments concerned. Data on cultural and arts, Cultural relics, libraries and mass culture are mainly from Jiangsu Provincial Department of Culture; data on culture industry are from Jiangsu Bureau of Statistics; data on journalism broadcasting and television are from Provincial Administration of Press Radio, Film and Television; data on sports are from Province Sports Bureau; data on public heath are from Jiangsu Provincial Commission of Health and Family Planning.

16－1 文化艺术和文物事业机构、人员情况
Number of Cultural Institution and Personnel

项目	Item	机构数(个) Institution (unit)		从业人数(人) Personnel (person)	
		2015	2016	2015	2016
总计	**Total**	**20263**	**21506**	**167883**	**169337**
艺术业	Art	653	744	16441	161532
#艺术展览、创作机构	Art Exhibition and Creation Mechanism	77	77	683	734
#艺术表演团体	Art Performance Troupes	369	444	10529	11163
话剧、儿童剧、滑稽剧类	Drama, Plays for Children and Comedy Troupes	45	65	793	810
歌舞、音乐类	Song and Dance	81	72	1782	2034
京剧、昆曲类	Peking Opera and Kunqu	11	11	341	301
地方戏曲类	Local Drama	100	107	3652	2915
杂技、魔术、马戏类	Acrobatics, Magic and Circus	29	37	848	970
曲艺类	Art Class	19	27	354	577
综合性艺术表演团体	Compenhensive Art Performing Groups	84	124	2759	3516
#艺术表演场馆	Art Centers	207	223	5229	5796
#剧场、影剧院	Theaters and Music Halls	135	146	2822	2831
图书馆业	Libraries	114	114	3183	3439
#少儿图书馆	Children's Libraries	8	7	98	102
群众文化服务业	Mass Culture	1396	1395	6980	7215
群众艺术馆、文化馆	Mass Art Centers	115	113	2125	2144
文化站	Cultural Stations	1281	1282	4855	5071
#乡镇文化站	Township Cultural Stations	912	909	3443	3495
艺术教育业	Art Education	14	13	887	804
中等专业学校	Secondary Art Schools	8	7	700	603
其他教育机构	Others	6	6	187	201
文化市场经营单位	Business Units Deding in Cultural Market	17240	18831	96708	105409
文艺科研	Art Research Institutions	9	8	93	101
其他文化类	Others	299	218	33122	29318
文物业	Cultural Relic Industry	423	426	7406	7805
文物保护管理机构	Agencies of Historical Relics Preservation	51	50	391	456
文物科研及其他文物机构	Research and Other Historical Relics Agencies	52	51	628	629
博物馆	Museums	312	317	6181	6524
综合性	Comprehensive	78	78	2749	2890
历史类	History	143	142	2478	2686
艺术类	Arts	61	63	701	679
自然科技类	Natural Science and Technology	8	9	59	71
其他	Other	22	25	194	198
文物商店	Cultural Relics Shops	8	8	206	196

16-2 群众艺术馆、文化馆站业务活动及经费情况（2016年）

Basic Statistics on Activities and Expenditures of Mass Art Centers and Cultural Centers (2016)

项目	Item	总计 Total	群众艺术馆、文化馆 Mass Art Centers	文化站 Cultural Stations
单位数 （个）	Number of Units (unit)	1395	113	1282
举办展览 （个）	Number of Exhibitions (unit)	8785	1510	7275
组织文艺活动 （次）	Number of Cultural Activities (times)	58503	11970	46533
举办训练班班次 （次）	Number of Training Classes (times)	25686	7781	17905
举办训练班结业人次 （万人次）	Number of Persons Completing Courses (10000 person-times)	199.000	46.00	153.000
由群众艺术馆、文化馆(站)指导的单位	Units Responsible for Guiding Mass Art Center and Cultural Centers	19559	5213	14346
馆办文艺团体 （个）	Art Groups Run by Cultural Centers (unit)	416	416	
馆办老年大学 （个）	Colleges for Senior Citizens Run by Cultural Centers (unit)	44	44	
群众业余文艺团队 （个）	Part-time Art Groups (unit)	19099	4753	14346
总支出 （万元）	Total Expenditures (10000 yuan)	139878	59973	79905

注：本表仅为文化系统内。

a) Data in this table only refer to those under the administration of the cultural departments.

16-3 公共图书馆业务活动及经费情况（2016年）

Facilities, Services and Expenditures of Public Libraries (2016)

项目	Item	总计 Total	#省级公共图书馆 Public Libraries at Provincial Level	#县(市、区)级公共图书馆 Public Libraries at County Level
总藏量 （万册、件）	Total Collections (10000 volumes)	7602.00	1139.00	4292.00
书架单层总长度 （万米）	Total Length of Bookshelves (10000 m)	131.00	26.00	44.00
累计发放有效借书证数 （万个）	Number of Library Cards Distributed Accumulately (10000 units)	1100.00	61.00	371.00
书刊文献外借人次 （万人次）	Total Number of Circulation Borrowed by the Readers (10000 person-times)	2888.00	125.00	1884.00
书刊文献外借册次 （万册次）	Number of Books Borrowed by the Readers (10000 volume-times)	5088.00	153.00	3111.00
组织各类讲座次数 （次）	Number of Activities Provided for Readers (times)	3393	107	2275
参加人数 （万人次）	Number of Readers Involved in Activities (10000 person-times)	65.00	3.00	37.00
举办展览 （个）	Number of Exhibition (unit)	1237	61	809
参观人次 （万人次）	Visitors (10000 person-times)	384.00	118.00	183.00
举办培训班 （个）	Number of Training Classes (unit)	2086	430	1350
培训人次 （万人次）	Training Persons (10000 person-times)	10.00		8.00
总支出 （万元）	Total Expenditures (10000 yuan)	103891	18129	43136
#新增藏量购置费	Purchase Expenses	15626	3336	7070
本年新购藏量 （万册、件）	Number of Books Purchased During the Year (10000 volumes)	584.00	46.00	368.00
公用房屋建筑面积 （万平方米）	Floor Space of Public Buildings (10000 sq. m)	116.00	10.00	72.00
#书库	Stack Rooms	17.00	1.00	9.00
阅览室座席 （个）	Seating Capacity of Reading Rooms (seats)	54037	2747	35033

16－4 报纸、期刊出版情况（2016年）

Basic Statistics on Newspaper and Periodicals Published (2016)

指标	Item	种数（种）Number of Publications (kind)	总印数（万册、万份）Printed Copies (10000 volumes)	总印张（万印张）Printed Sheets (10000 sheets)
报纸	**Newspapers**	**143**	**233072**	**813521**
期刊	**Periodicals**	**444**	**11954**	**52332**
综合	Comprehensiveness	18	101	521
哲学、社会科学	Philosophy and Social Sciences	90	4370	19184
自然科学、技术	Natural Sciences and Technology	252	2676	10989
文化、教育	Culture and Education	56	4079	18172
文学、艺术	Literature and Art	28	728	3466
画刊	**Pictorials**	**1**	**10**	**35**
少年儿童读物	**Children's Reading Material**	**2121**	**3455**	**17855**

16－5 图书出版情况(2016年)

Basic Statistics on Books Published (2016)

指标	Item	出版图书种数（种）Number of Publications (kind)	总印数（万册）Printed Copies (10000 volumes)	总印张（万印张）Printed Sheets (10000 sheets)
总计	**Total**	**27473**	**62415.13**	**450214.67**
马列主义、毛泽东思想	Marxism-leninism, Mao Zedong Thought	34	13.57	178.69
哲学	Philosophy	400	326.01	4068.68
社会科学总论	General Social Sciences	185	141.58	1806.53
政治、法律	Politics and Law	394	329.56	3589.19
军事	Military Affairs	20	73.66	688.67
经济	Economics	785	214.30	3284.99
文化、科学、教育、体育	Culture, Science, Education and Sports	16452	54218.23	363109.52
语言、文字	Languages	750	376.53	4951.91
文学	Literature	2725	3114.68	36012.26
艺术	Arts	1965	1910.79	9878.82
历史、地理	History and Geography	770	451.72	6173.59
自然科学总论	General Natural Sciences	27	10.36	76.08
数理科学、化学	Mathematics and Chemistry	298	110.59	1452.77
天文学、地理科学	Astronomy and Geology	86	26.93	294.91
生物科学	Biology	61	51.64	500.57
医药、卫生	Medicine and Health Care	691	443.57	5616.51
农业科学	Agricultural Science	123	50.59	339.63
工业技术	Industrial Technology	1414	451.28	6894.76
交通运输	Transportation	126	31.90	500.16
航空、航天	Aeronautics and Aerospace	3	1.80	11.45
环境科技	Environmental Science	65	14.14	147.81
综合性图书	General Books	99	51.72	637.17

注：该表为使用中国标准书刊号部分。

a) In this table, the data were used according to the standard serial number of China.

16－6 分地区公共图书馆基本情况（2016 年）

指标	Item	南京市 Nanjing	无锡市 Wuxi	徐州市 Xuzhou	常州市 Changzhou
公共图书馆 （个）	Number of Public Library (unit)	14	8	8	5
总藏量 （万册件）	Total Collections (10000 copies)	624.00	710.00	330.00	452.00
人均拥有公共图书馆藏量 （册）	Collections of Public Libraries Owned Per Person (copy)	2.00	1.00		1.00
有效借书证数 （个）	Accumulative Number of Library Cards Distributed (unit)	32	24	12	24
总流通人次 （万人次）	Number of Circulation (10000 person-times)	579.00	675.00	189.00	237.00
#书刊文献外借人次	Borrowing from Libraries	258.00	187.00	165.00	144.00
书刊文献外借册次 （万册次）	Books and Periodicals Lent to Readers (10000 copies-times)	442.00	678.00	198.00	204.00
阅览室座席数 （个）	Seats of Reading Room (unit)	6251	6242	1920	2928
每万人拥有公共图书馆建筑面积 （平方米）	Floor Space of Buildings of Public Libraries Owned per 10000 Population (sq. m)	259	149	81	134
组织各类讲座次数 （次）	Number of Lectures (time)	426	513	191	122
参加讲座人次 （万人次）	Attending Lectures (10000person-times)	12.00	6.00	7.00	2.00
举办展览 （个）	Exhibitions Held (unit)	143	109	58	44
参观展览人次 （万人次）	Visiting Exhibitions (10000 person-times)	31.00	89.00	18.00	12.00
举办培训班 （个）	Training Classes Held (unit)	194	196	39	26
参加培训人次 （万人次）	Attending Training (10000 person-times)	1.00	1.00		
计算机 （台）	Computers (set)	948	1011	499	452
#电子阅览室终端数	Terminals in Electronic Media Reading Rooms	647	637	371	139

Statistics on Public Libraries by Region (2016)

苏州市 Suzhou	南通市 Nantong	连云港市 Lianyungang	淮安市 Huaian	盐城市 Yancheng	扬州市 Yangzhou	镇江市 Zhenjiang	泰州市 Taizhou	宿迁市 Suqian
11	10	8	9	11	7	9	7	6
1878.00	500.00	265.00	286.00	335.00	354.00	315.00	271.00	144.00
2.00	1.00	1.00	1.00		1.00	1.00	1.00	
802	29	11	10	21	26	15	16	15
2536.00	329.00	275.00	120.00	364.00	165.00	261.00	286.00	110.00
907.00	157.00	107.00	84.00	190.00	100.00	182.00	190.00	91.00
1609.00	312.00	228.00	165.00	253.00	218.00	232.00	240.00	155.00
9210	4023	2324	2428	4468	4374	2710	3104	1308
168	111	137	176	130	138	129	130	108
501	226	197	172	207	209	253	148	121
7.00	4.00	3.00	2.00	3.00	3.00	6.00	3.00	4.00
269	94	61	28	91	80	58	46	95
25.00	13.00	9.00	2.00	21.00	18.00	8.00	14.00	5.00
581	94	56	27	52	124	63	159	45
3.00	1.00			1.00	1.00	1.00	1.00	
2093	741	462	460	668	615	675	388	411
1139	482	287	286	403	355	372	246	285

16－7 广播、电视事业发展情况
Basic Statistics on Broadcasting and Television Stations

项　目	Item	2012	2013	2014	2015	2016
职工人数（人）	Number of Staff and Workers (person)	51291	52089	53699	52664	53531
中短波发射台及转播台（座）	Number of Transmission and Relaying Stations of Medium and Short Ware Broadcast (set)	21	21	21	21	21
中短波发射机功率（千瓦）	Power of Transmitters of Medium and Short Ware Broadcast (kW)	618	718	734	735	735
广播人口覆盖率（%）	Radio Coverage of Population (%)	99.99	99.99	99.99	100.00	100.00
广播电台（座）	Radio (set)				8	8
电视台(座)	Television Station (set)				8	8
广播电视台(座)	Radio and Television (set)				71	71
调频电视发射及转播台（座）	Launch and FM TV Station (set)				98	104
调频发射机功率(千瓦)	FM Transmitter Power (kW)				168.20	175.8
电视发射机功率(千瓦)	TV Transmitter Power (kW)				510.15	512.95
电视人口覆盖率（%）	TV Coverage of Population (%)	99.88	99.88	99.88	100.00	100.00
有线电视用户数（万户）	Users of Cable TV (10000 households)	2178	2249	2291	2226	2069
数字电视用户数（万户）	Users of Digital TV (10000 households)	1450	1662	1787	1761	1754
有线电视入户率（%）	Cable TV Coverage of Households (%)	89.8	93.1	94.6	91.4	84.8

16－8 广播、电视节目制作时间
Time of Production of Broadcasting and TV Programs

单位:小时　　(hour)

项　目	Item	2012	2013	2014	2015	2016
广播节目制作	**Production of Broadcasting Programs**	**582066**	**600722**	**603551**	**589282**	**608779**
#新闻	News Programs	106333	108120	106702	101840	104118
专题	Special Subject Programs	151635	147833	156862	136748	151160
文艺(综艺)	General Entertainment Programs	138443	149552	148263	158768	155311
广告	Advertising Programs	84744	87249	81997	76548	73031
电视节目制作	**Production of TV Programs**	**205738**	**217672**	**193135**	**189429**	**195036**
#新闻	News Programs	58072	61432	58391	58367	59534
专题	Special Subject Programs	50250	54437	46047	44822	43939
文艺(综艺)	General Entertainment Programs	23289	23194	20557	20610	19597
广告	Advertising Programs	48722	46610	36617	32668	33796

16－9 分地区规模以上文化及相关产业法人单位数（2016 年底）
Number of Legal Persons of Culture and Relavant Industry above Ddesignated Size by Region at Year-end (2016)

地 区	Region	法人单位数(个) Legal Persons (unit)	文化制造业 Cultual Manufacturing	文化批发和零售业 Wholesale and Retail of Culture	文化服务业 Services of Culture
全 省	Province	7578	2836	1181	3561
南京市	Nanjing	1327	155	207	965
无锡市	Wuxi	630	294	87	249
徐州市	Xuzhou	418	104	156	158
常州市	Changzhou	853	301	111	441
苏州市	Suzhou	1022	455	151	416
南通市	Nantong	842	369	113	360
连云港市	Lianyungang	245	157	42	46
淮安市	Huaian	362	126	37	199
盐城市	Yancheng	533	186	117	230
扬州市	Yangzhou	327	158	38	131
镇江市	Zhenjiang	385	184	45	156
泰州市	Taizhou	291	114	51	126
宿迁市	Suqian	343	233	26	84

16-10 分地区规模以上文化制造业企业基本情况（2016 年）
Basic Conditions of Cultural Manufacturing Enterprises above Designated Size by Region (2016)

单位:万元 (10000 yuan)

地区	Region	企业单位数（个）Number of Enterprises (unit)	年末从业人员(人) Engaged Persons at Year-end (person)	资产总计 Total Assets	营业收入 Business Revenue	营业税金及附加 Taxes and Extra Charges on Business	营业利润 Operating Profit	应交增值税 Value-added Tax Payable
全省	Province	2836	755058	57094315	89527100	364299	5558699	2156430
南京市	Nanjing	155	34376	2734732	9559842	14675	300892	148890
无锡市	Wuxi	294	80158	7139196	10563952	26839	555024	159426
徐州市	Xuzhou	104	19768	999357	2894532	19293	259297	115005
常州市	Changzhou	301	100782	6042404	8274048	38611	647484	263101
苏州市	Suzhou	455	220038	20823800	22198264	71328	1397218	381784
南通市	Nantong	369	81784	4572938	8171106	33384	561649	291855
连云港市	Lianyungang	157	22747	1252090	2948777	27685	213913	56986
淮安市	Huaian	126	21832	1133106	3607264	22003	206900	86342
盐城市	Yancheng	186	38016	2520236	4688420	28985	252949	153094
扬州市	Yangzhou	158	39103	1714227	4654577	16424	305159	116826
镇江市	Zhenjiang	184	40507	4917973	5593325	18401	361008	138064
泰州市	Taizhou	114	19138	1307629	3478459	26454	265999	155943
宿迁市	Suqian	233	36809	1936626	2894534	20218	231206	89115

16－11 分地区限额以上文化批发和零售业企业基本情况（2016 年）
Basic Conditions of Enterprises of Wholesale and Retail of Culture above Designated Size by Region (2016)

单位：万元 (10000 yuan)

地区	Region	企业单位数（个）Number of Enterprises (unit)	年末从业人员（人）Engaged Persons at Year-end (person)	资产总计 Total Assets	营业收入 Business Revenue	营业税金及附加 Taxes and Extra Charges on Business	营业利润 Operating Profit	应交增值税 Value-added Tax Payable
全省	Province	1181	70193	18755317	31051078	65148	773488	289510
南京市	Nanjing	207	31791	13812926	19568045	18991	271359	134251
无锡市	Wuxi	87	4508	932780	2219190	2485	22365	16942
徐州市	Xuzhou	156	5085	293976	836479	8086	65920	24925
常州市	Changzhou	111	6091	533772	1923999	6197	108000	30862
苏州市	Suzhou	151	9632	1458851	3633631	9995	75407	47438
南通市	Nantong	113	3153	272747	493018	4630	36145	7852
连云港市	Lianyungang	42	1100	124934	281449	1451	9729	2637
淮安市	Huaian	37	910	91168	209279	1462	20530	3029
盐城市	Yancheng	117	2304	192936	433038	4276	41471	10291
扬州市	Yangzhou	38	997	138229	171112	1777	6999	2451
镇江市	Zhenjiang	45	1022	132701	479733	3999	27855	4277
泰州市	Taizhou	51	1838	171695	376670	1034	17913	3337
宿迁市	Suqian	26	1762	598604	425435	766	69796	1222

16－12 分地区重点文化服务业企业基本情况（2016年）
Basic Conditions of Major Enterprises of Services of Culture by Region (2016)

单位:万元 (10000 yuan)

地区	Region	企业单位数（个）Number of Enterprises (unit)	年末从业人员(人) Engaged Persons at Year-end (person)	资产总计 Total Assets	营业收入 Business Revenue	营业税金及附加 Taxes and Extra Charges on Business	营业利润 Operating Profit	应交增值税 Value-added Tax Payable
全省	Province	3561	380001	53187240	23597629	242807	2048651	431017
南京市	Nanjing	965	126757	19740381	11028138	82524	781363	202314
无锡市	Wuxi	249	32539	7587070	2184342	16205	211342	44084
徐州市	Xuzhou	158	10662	1018586	418316	7292	43707	8773
常州市	Changzhou	441	65914	7816863	3065856	43235	472481	44722
苏州市	Suzhou	416	64553	7515767	3183813	23496	216697	67909
南通市	Nantong	360	19254	2018305	970246	22187	60498	16035
连云港市	Lianyungang	46	4570	540061	132089	1538	6089	2068
淮安市	Huaian	199	7973	464889	505817	8252	46688	6251
盐城市	Yancheng	230	11730	892776	428510	8435	57125	6976
扬州市	Yangzhou	131	10294	905297	302273	6216	8505	6251
镇江市	Zhenjiang	156	9159	2770892	599930	8337	86234	12351
泰州市	Taizhou	126	11105	1250388	473895	12313	31044	7027
宿迁市	Suqian	84	5491	665965	304406	2777	26879	6257

16－13 体育系统职工人数（2016年）
Number of Staff and Workers in Sports Commissions（2016）

单位：人 （person）

项目	Item	总计 Total	体育行政机关 Sports Adminis-tration	优秀运动队 Excellent Sports Teams	体育运动学校 Physical Education and Sports Schools	业余体校 Spare-time Sports Schools	体育场馆 Public Stadiums and Gym-nasiums	其他 Others
总计	**Total**	**9022**	**1016**	**1484**	**1026**	**1148**	**1009**	**3339**
公务员	Civil Servant	940	940					
教练员	Coaches	1479		186	436	522	104	231
运动员	Athletes	1461		1030		1	1	429
科研人员	Scientific and Technical Personnel	92			11	2	2	77
医务人员	Medical Personnel	66		16	9	2	2	37
文化教师	Teachers	993		1	256	211	2	523
管理人员	Administrative Staff	1566		205	126	183	412	640
其他人员	Others	2425	76	46	188	227	486	1402

16－14 等级运动员、裁判员人数
Number of Athletes and Referees in Grades

单位：人 （person）

项目	Item	2012	2013	2014	2015	2016
等级运动员发展人数	**Number of Athletes in Grades**					
运动健将	Master of Sports	155	122	189	152	159
一级	First Grade	507	692	825	581	515
二级	Second Grade	1915	2517	1568	1230	1583
等级裁判员发展人数	**Number of Referees in Grades**					
国家（际）级	National（International）Referees	53	80	40		17
一级	First Grade	465	761	632	792	1327
二级	Second Grade	3740	3788	4848	4491	5298

注：2011年始运动健将包含国际运动健将。

a）From the 2011，Athlete inculdes World-Class.

16－15 运动员在各级比赛中获奖牌情况（2016年）
Awards for Athletes in Competitions of All Levels（2016）

单位：个 （unit）

项目	Item	冠军 Champion	亚军 Second Place	季军 Third Place
世界最高比赛	World Highest Competition	22	11	18
亚洲最高比赛	Asian Highest Competition	7	15	4
全国最高比赛	National Highest Competition	55	49	33

16－16　卫生事业基本情况（2016 年）

Basic Statistics on Health Care（2016）

项　　目	Item	机构数（个）Institutions (unit)	床位数（张）Hospital Beds (bed)	卫　生工作人员（人）Personnel (person)	#卫生技术人员 Medical Technical Personnel	#医师 Doctors
总　计	**Total**	**32135**	**443100**	**654210**	**517065**	**204687**
医　院	**Total Hospitals**	**1679**	**356228**	**397939**	**332678**	**111971**
综合医院	General Hospitals	1033	224834	261802	222874	75114
中医医院	Hospitals Specialized in Traditional Chinese Medicine	111	43781	54705	47217	17262
中西结合医院	Hospitals of Integrated Traditional Chinese and Western Medicine	27	6329	8178	6833	2646
专科医院	Specialized Hospitals	403	61125	65398	51664	16117
护理院	Nursing Hospitals	105	20159	7856	4090	832
基层医疗卫生机构	**Primary Health Care Institutions**	**29116**	**77546**	**212852**	**155894**	**81286**
社区卫生服务中心(站)	Health Service Center for Community	2660	18480	44447	37674	16151
卫生院	Township Hospitals	1041	58803	79787	67002	30562
村卫生室	Village Health Stations	15481		48417	15893	14629
门诊部	Outpatient Departments	1300	157	16892	13317	6576
诊所、卫生所、医务室	County (District) Chinics, Sanitation Offices and Medical Matter Centers Sanitation Service Station	8634	106	23309	22008	13368
专业公共卫生机构	**Professional Public Health Agencies**	**1059**	**6495**	**36528**	**24801**	**9978**
疾病预防控制中心	Disease Prevention and Controlling Centers	117		7956	6135	3734
专科疾病防治院(所、站)	Specilized Disease Prevention and Treatment Institutes	42	1079	1507	1141	509
健康教育所(站、中心)	Health Education Centers	6		99	38	12
妇幼保健院(所、站)	Maternity and Child Care Centers	110	5411	13096	10640	4412
急救中心(站)	Emergency Treatment Centers (Stations)	43	5	1541	651	355
采供血机构	Blood Collection and Supply Institutions	30		2166	1520	132
卫生监督所(中心)	Sanitation Supervision Agenicies	106		3447	3064	
计划生育技术服务机构	Family Planning Technical Services Institutions	605		6716	1612	824
其他卫生机构	**Other Health Care Institutions**	**281**	**2831**	**6891**	**3692**	**1452**
疗养院	Sanatoriums	15	2831	1367	761	294
医学科学研究机构	Institutions of Medical Sciences Research	9		402	188	111
医学在职培训机构	In-service Training of Medical Science	29		966	202	88
临床检验中心(所、站)	Clinical Laboratory Center and Stations	32		1654	904	61
统计信息中心	Statistical Information Center	4		55	6	2
其他	Other	192		2447	1631	896

注:本表人员合计中包括乡村医生 31179 人和卫生员 1345 人。

a) Total personnel in this table contain 31179 rural doctors and 1345 health workers.

16－17 卫生机构数
Number of Health Care Institutions

单位:个 (unit)

年份 地区 Year Region	总 计 Total	#医 院 Hospitals	#卫生院 Township Hospitals	#门诊部 Clinics	#妇幼保健院(所、站) Maternity and Child Care Conters	#专科疾病防治院(所、站) Specialized Disease Prevention and Treatment Institutes	#疾病预防控制中心(防疫站) Disease Prevention and Controlling Centers
1978	9277	2428			84	9	107
1980	9943	2457			99	17	119
1985	11515	2460			105	84	127
1990	12366	2491			114	108	135
1995	12039	2534			117	122	141
2000	12813	634	1877	106	112	118	142
2001	13208	662	1771	119	112	113	147
2002	12368	891	1625	293	111	80	145
2003	12733	920	1602	313	106	59	136
2004	14447	995	1493	371	107	45	143
2005	15324	1014	1472	372	107	49	154
2006	17143	1061	1407	395	107	48	153
2007	19129	1087	1384	458	106	49	166
2008	13451	1093	1448	474	104	49	170
2009	13388	1112	1440	484	105	47	170
2010	30961	1157	1276	535	103	46	130
2011	31680	1283	1223	708	106	53	129
2012	31054	1426	1117	813	110	48	128
2013	31005	1490	1066	921	109	45	124
2014	32000	1524	1046	992	110	43	123
2015	31925	1581	1035	1100	109	44	120
2016	32135	1679	1041	1300	110	42	117
南京市 Nanjing	2383	209	16	124	14	5	17
无锡市 Wuxi	2308	159	32	178	7	6	7
徐州市 Xuzhou	4584	131	160	55	13	1	11
常州市 Changzhou	1267	56	58	107	7	2	7
苏州市 Suzhou	3175	206	77	311	7	4	11
南通市 Nantong	3131	216	105	69	7	3	9
连云港市 Lianyungang	2726	80	91	76	9	1	9
淮安市 Huaian	2237	57	128	10	9	4	9
盐城市 Yancheng	3233	151	135	66	10	4	10
扬州市 Yangzhou	1787	69	73	150	8	4	7
镇江市 Zhenjiang	976	47	50	55	7	3	7
泰州市 Taizhou	1963	67	116	73	6	4	7
宿迁市 Suqian	2365	231	0	26	6	1	6

注:从 2010 年起卫生机构数包括村卫生室的数字(以下表同)。

a) From 2010, the number of health care institutions have involved the figure of village health stations (the same below).

16－18　卫生机构人员数

Number of Persons Engaged in Health Care Institutions

单位:万人　　　　(10000 persons)

年份地区 Year　Region	卫生工作人员 Medical Personnel	卫生技术人员 Medical Technical Personnel	#执业(助理)医师 Doctors	#注册护士 Registered Nurses	每万人拥有医师数(人) Number of Doctors per 10000 Population (person)
1978	17.45	14.00	5.70	1.79	9.7
1980	19.03	15.04	6.10	2.08	10.2
1985	23.68	18.28	7.65	3.61	12.3
1990	27.58	21.35	9.94	5.34	14.6
1995	31.57	24.55	11.22	6.44	15.9
2000	32.18	25.36	11.44	7.39	15.6
2001	32.08	25.36	11.46	7.54	16.2
2002	30.08	24.00	10.22	7.25	14.3
2003	30.37	24.37	10.40	7.37	14.5
2004	30.95	25.01	10.60	7.70	14.7
2005	31.61	25.97	11.13	8.05	15.0
2006	33.45	27.54	11.46	8.59	15.7
2007	35.53	28.62	11.87	9.45	16.1
2008	36.13	29.16	11.97	10.09	15.6
2009	37.76	30.65	12.32	11.06	15.9
2010	45.93	32.84	12.90	12.26	16.4
2011	48.18	35.05	13.47	13.56	17.1
2012	52.02	39.61	15.80	15.53	19.9
2013	55.12	42.90	16.97	17.42	21.4
2014	58.96	45.85	17.86	18.88	22.4
2015	61.89	48.70	18.92	20.40	23.7
2016	65.42	51.71	20.47	22.12	25.6
南京市 Nanjing	8.63	7.07	2.53	3.21	30.6
无锡市 Wuxi	5.84	4.75	1.81	2.05	27.7
徐州市 Xuzhou	7.60	5.55	2.18	2.43	25.1
常州市 Changzhou	3.78	3.12	1.24	1.35	26.4
苏州市 Suzhou	8.93	7.22	2.77	3.07	26.0
南通市 Nantong	5.48	4.36	1.80	1.82	24.6
连云港市 Lianyungang	3.54	2.62	1.10	1.09	24.4
淮安市 Huaian	4.02	3.15	1.24	1.43	25.3
盐城市 Yancheng	4.97	3.95	1.81	1.48	25.1
扬州市 Yangzhou	3.18	2.53	1.04	1.04	23.2
镇江市 Zhenjiang	2.42	1.94	0.79	0.83	24.8
泰州市 Taizhou	3.33	2.61	1.13	1.02	24.3
宿迁市 Suqian	3.72	2.84	1.03	1.28	21.2

16－19　卫生机构床位数

Number of Beds in Health Care Institutions

单位:万张　　　　　　　　　　　　　　　　　　　　　　　　　　　　　　　　　(10000 beds)

年份　地区 Year　Region	总　计 Total	#医　院 Hospitals	#卫生院 Township Hospitals	#社区卫生服务中心 Health Service Center for Community	#专科疾病防治院(所、站) Specialized Disease Prevention and Treatment Institutes	每万人拥有医院、卫生院床位数(张) Number of Hospital Beds per 10000 Population (bed)
1978	12.29	11.07				19.0
1980	12.75	11.62				19.6
1985	14.29	12.65				20.4
1990	16.45	14.54				21.5
1995	17.46	15.48				21.9
2000	17.31	10.01	6.18		0.13	22.1
2001	17.32	10.14	6.13		0.09	22.9
2002	17.45	11.38	5.58		0.10	23.8
2003	17.99	11.54	5.63		0.08	24.0
2004	18.90	12.31	5.42		0.14	24.6
2005	20.01	13.18	5.41		0.10	25.6
2006	21.16	14.27	5.31		0.10	26.8
2007	22.00	15.15	5.30	0.92	0.10	27.8
2008	23.51	16.39	5.70	0.82	0.07	28.8
2009	25.15	17.76	5.71	1.07	0.07	30.4
2010	26.97	19.55	5.20	1.58	0.09	31.5
2011	29.64	22.17	5.13	1.57	0.11	34.6
2012	33.31	25.59	5.18	1.67	0.13	38.8
2013	36.83	28.62	5.51	1.81	0.12	43.0
2014	39.23	30.93	5.56	1.85	0.11	45.8
2015	41.36	32.85	5.64	1.90	0.11	48.3
2016	44.31	35.62	5.88	1.82	0.11	51.9
南京市 Nanjing	49857	44776	419	3368	222	54.6
无锡市 Wuxi	39732	35354	796	2324	109	55.4
徐州市 Xuzhou	52247	38223	10703	2436	0	56.2
常州市 Changzhou	25370	19724	3684	1189	40	49.7
苏州市 Suzhou	63241	56697	4150	2128	20	57.2
南通市 Nantong	39147	30551	7603	817	160	52.3
连云港市 Lianyungang	23281	16606	4840	646	200	47.7
淮安市 Huaian	27529	17574	7926	908	81	52.2
盐城市 Yancheng	38663	28714	8425	843	100	51.3
扬州市 Yangzhou	20683	15261	3160	1391	125	41.0
镇江市 Zhenjiang	14585	10823	1891	1113	0	40.0
泰州市 Taizhou	23324	16659	5206	962	22	47.1
宿迁市 Suqian	25441	25266	0	50	0	51.8

注:分市数计量单位为张。

a) The units of measurement is bed by region.

16-20 医疗机构门诊情况（2016年）

Service of Health Institutions (2016)

指标	Item	诊疗人次（万人次）Total Number of Patients Treated (10000 person-times)	#门诊 Out-patients Service	#急诊 Emergency Patients
总计	**Total**	**55216.00**	**50279.55**	**3395.24**
医院	**Hospitals**	**24754.70**	**21801.14**	**2466.95**
综合医院	General Hospitals	16966.00	14842.21	1840.79
中医医院	Hospitals Specialized in Traditional Chinese Medicine	4141.00	3719.13	303.41
中西医结合医院	Hospitals of Integrated Traditional Chinese and Western Medicine	526.60	463.44	57.80
专科医院	Specialized Hospitals	3092.70	2760.24	264.82
基层医疗卫生机构	**Primary Health Care Institutions**	**29116.30**	**27332.54**	**814.02**
社区卫生服务中心(站)	Health Service Center for Commnunity	7794.10	7101.91	365.05
卫生院	Township Hospitals	8290.50	7686.90	448.97
乡镇卫生院	Rural Township Hospitals	8288.60	7686.16	448.97
村卫生室	Village Health Stations	9145.70	8800.86	0.00
门诊部	Outpatient Departments	1024.30	938.00	0.00
诊所、卫生所、医务室	County(District) Chinics, Sanitation Offices and Medical Matter Centers Sanitation Service Station		2804.87	0.00
专业公共卫生机构	**Professional Public Health Agencies**	**1297.60**	**1109.50**	**113.19**
专科疾病防治院(所、站)	Specialized Disease Prevention and Treatment Institutes	125.60	112.44	0.23
妇幼保健院(所、站)	Maternity and Child Care Centers	1112.70	997.07	53.57
急救中心(站)	Emergency Treatment Centers (Stations)		0.00	59.39
其他机构	**Other Health Care Institutions**	**47.30**	**36.37**	**1.07**
疗养院	Sanatoriums	30.00	19.06	1.07

16－21 医疗机构住院服务、病床使用情况（2016年）

Situation of Hospitalization Service and Beds Utilization of Health Institutions (2016)

指标	Item	病床使用率（%） Utilization Rate of Beds (%)			入院人数（万人） Hospital Admissions (10000 persons)			每百门急诊人次的入院人数（人） Hospital Admissions per 100 Patient-times (person)
		合计 Total	非营利 Non-profit	营利 Profit	合计 Total	非营利 Non-profit	营利 Profit	
总计	**Total**	**82.46**	**84.04**	**60.67**	**1309.00**	**1238.16**	**70.84**	**3.19**
医院	**Hospitals**	**87.31**	**89.72**	**60.59**	**1077.58**	**1008.28**	**69.30**	**4.44**
综合医院	General Hospitals	88.72	90.83	65.97	782.47	730.34	52.12	4.69
中医医院	Hospitals Specialized in Traditional Chinese Medicine	89.68	90.10	64.21	145.51	144.02	1.49	3.62
中西医结合医院	Hospitals of Integrated Traditional Chinese and Western Medicine	79.28	82.40	65.81	18.13	15.10	3.02	3.48
专科医院	Specialized Hospitals	84.58	89.15	46.02	126.19	113.99	12.20	4.17
基层医疗卫生机构	**Primary Health Care Institutions**	**60.77**	**60.79**	**0.00**	**198.22**	**198.15**	**0.07**	**1.27**
社区卫生服务中心	Health Service Center for Community	51.38	51.44	0.00	34.59	34.59	0.00	0.46
卫生院	Township Hospitals	63.58	63.58	0.00	163.44	163.44	0.00	2.01
乡镇卫生院	Rural Township Hospitals	63.59	63.59	0.00	163.38	163.38	0.00	2.01
专业公共卫生机构	**Professional Public Health Agencies**	**84.34**	**84.01**	**92.29**	**24.64**	**23.35**	**1.28**	**2.12**
专科疾病防治院（所、站）	Specialized Disease Prevention and Treatment Institutes	70.25	70.25	0.00	0.82	0.82	0.00	0.73
妇幼保健院（所、站）	Maternity and Child Care Centers	87.15	86.89	92.29	23.81	22.53	1.28	2.27
其他机构	**Other Health Care Institutions**	**52.26**	**53.72**	**15.10**	**8.57**	**8.38**	**0.18**	**22.87**
疗养院	Sanatoriums	52.26	53.72	15.10	8.57	8.38	0.18	42.53

16－22　法定报告传染病发病及死亡情况（2016 年）
Legal Report on Infection Disease Incidence and Death（2016）

病　名	Item	发病率（1/10 万）Incidence（1/100 thousand）	死亡率（1/10 万）Rate of Death（1/100 thousand）	病死率（%）Rate of Death from illness（%）
鼠疫	Pestilence			
霍乱	Cholera	0.0100		
传染性非典型肺炎	SARS			
艾滋病	AIDS	2.0200	0.2800	14.02
病毒性肝炎	Viral Hepatitis	28.4600	0.0100	0.02
脊髓灰质炎	Polio			
人感染高致病性禽流感	Highly Pathogenic Avian Influenza to Humans			
麻疹	Measles	0.9400		
流行性出血热	Hemorrhage Fever	0.4100	0.0100	2.42
狂犬病	Hydrophobia	0.0600	0.0600	100.00
流行性乙型脑炎	Epidemic Encephalitis B	0.0200		
登革热	Pengue	0.0200		
炭疽	Anthrax			
细菌性和阿米巴性痢疾	Dysentery	4.0500		
肺结核	Pulmonary Tuberculosis	35.9300	0.1200	0.34
伤寒、副伤寒	Typhoid and Paralyphoid Fever	0.4000		
流行性脑脊髓膜炎	Epidemic Cerebrospinal Meningitis	0.0100		
百日咳	Pertussis	0.0200		
白喉	Diphtheria			
新生儿破伤风	Newborn Tetanus			
猩红热	Scarlet Fever	2.8000		
布鲁氏菌病	Brucellosis	0.1800		
淋病	Gonorrhea	9.0300		
梅毒	Syphilis	29.7000		
钩端螺旋体病	Leptospirosis			
血吸虫病	Bilharziasis	0.0100		
疟疾	Malaria	0.3800		
人感染 H7N9 禽流感	Avian Influenza H7N9 Infection	0.1300	0.0300	25.24

16－23　孕产妇及婴儿死亡率
Death Rate of Pregnant Women and Babies

指　标	Item	2012	2013	2014	2015	2016
孕产妇死亡率　（1/10 万）	Death Rate of Pregnant Women（1/100 thousand）	5.28	4.99	4.65	4.64	4.47
婴儿死亡率　（‰）	Death Rate of Babies　（‰）	3.81	3.79	3.36	3.30	3.05
5 岁以下儿童死亡率（‰）	Death Rate of Children Aged 5 and Below（‰）	4.91	4.82	4.39	4.33	4.13

主要统计指标解释

文化事业机构 指从事专业文化工作和为专业文化工作服务的独立建制的单位。不包括这些单位另外举办独立核算的其他机构和各部门的业余文化组织。

艺术表演团体 指从事戏曲、音乐、舞蹈、杂技等专业艺术表演,有独立帐户的单位,不包括半工半艺、半农半艺和民间职业剧团。

等级运动员人数 指经考核正式批准授予等级运动员称号的人数。运动员等级分为国际级运动健将、运动健将、一级运动员、二级运动员、三级运动员、少年级运动员。

等级裁判员人数 指经考核正式批准授予等级裁判员称号的人数。裁判员等级分为国际裁判、国家级裁判、一级裁判、二级裁判、三级裁判。

卫生机构 指从卫生计生行政部门取得《医疗机构执业许可证》,或从民政、工商行政、机构编制管理部门取得法人单位登记证书,为社会提供医疗保障、疾病控制、卫生监督服务或从事医学科研和教育等工作的单位。

卫生技术人员 指卫生事业机构支付工资的全部职工中现任职务为卫生技术工作的专业人员,包括执业医师、执业助理医师、注册护士、药剂人员、检验人员和其他卫生技术人员。

执业(助理)医师和注册护士 指领取医师执业证书和注册护士证书的人员。

Explanatory Notes on Main Statistical Indicators

Cultural Institutions refer to units which have their own organizational system and independent accounting system and specilize in or serve cultural development. They exclude other establishment runed by these cultural institutions and amateur groups established by various departments.

Art Troupe refer to the troupe which is engaged in drama, opera, music, dance, acrobatics or other art performance, opens independent accounts with banks and has self-accounting system; excluding the troupes which are engaged partly in industrial or agricultural activities, partly in art performance and the professional troupes organized by the people.

Number of Athletes in Grades refers to the number of athletes who have been given titles through examination. The titles of athlets include international masters of sports, masters of sports, first grade, second grade and third grade sportsmen and young athletes.

Number of Referees in Grades refers to the number of referees who have been given titles after examination. They are classified as international referees, national referees and referees of the first, second and third grades.

Health Care Institutions refers to the units which have received the "Practitioner Licence Certification of Medical and Health Institutions" from health administration, or the registered certification of corporation units from the civil, industrial and commercial, and establishment administration. They provide the services of medical security, disease controlling, health supervision, or engaged in medical scientific research and education.

Medical Technical Personnel refer to all medical staff and workers employed by medical institutions, including doctor of Chinese and Western medicine, senior doctors who integrated traditional Chinese therapeutics with Western therapeutics in practice, senior nurses, pharmacists of Chinese and Western medicine, laboratory specialists, other specialists, paramedics of Chinese and Western medicine, nurses, midwives, druggists in Chinese and Western medicine, laboratory technicians, other technicians, other practitioners of Chinese medicine, nursing attendants, pharmacological workers of Chinese and Western medicine, laboratory workers and other primary medical personnel.

Practitioner(Assistant) Doctor and Registered Nurse refer to the doctors and nurses who have received the practitioner doctor certification and registered nurse certification respectively.

17

公共管理、社会保障和社会组织

Public Management, Social Services and Social Organizations

简 要 说 明

一、本篇资料的主要内容

本篇主要反映档案、民政、残疾人、社会保障、工会妇联、公检法司情况等内容。

档案部分主要包括档案机构人员，档案馆档案资料馆藏和利用情况；民政事业部分主要包括民政行业单位情况，民政事业经费情况，收养类单位情况，办理结婚、离婚情况；社会保障部分主要包括社会保险基本情况，社会保险基金收支及累计结余情况；公检法司部分主要包括公安机关的刑事案件立案情况和治安案件查处情况，交通、火灾事故情况，人民检察院的办案情况，人民法院审理案件和收结案情况，以及律师、公证、调解工作等情况。

二、本篇的资料来源

根据各部门制定的统计报表制度汇总加工整理而成。档案资料来自省档案局；民政事业资料来自省民政厅；残疾人事业资料来自省残疾人联合会；社会保障资料来自省人力资源和社会保障厅；工会妇联资料分别来自省妇女联合会和省总工会；公检法司资料分别来自省公安厅、省人民检察院、省高级人民法院、省司法厅。

Brief Introduction

I. Main Contents

Data in this chapter show statistics on archives, civil affairs, disabled persons, social security, labour union, woman's federation, public security, procuratorial, legal and judicial affairs and so on.

Data on archives cover mainly information on persons and institutions of archives, conditions of files stored and used in archives; data on civil affairs include: basic conditions of affairs agencies, expenses for civil administration, statistics on adoptive homes, marriages and divorces; data on social security cover information such as basic statistics of social insurance, revenue, expenses and balance of social insurance fund; data on public security, procuratorial, legal and judicial affairs covering information on criminal cases registered and offense cases handled by the public security agencies, traffic or fire accidents, cases handled by procuratorate's offices, cases accepted and settled by the people's courts, and statistics on lawyers, notarization and mediation.

II. Sources of Data

Data are collected and tabulated in accordance with the statistic reporting schemes stipulated by the departments concerned; data on archives are provided by the Province Archives; data on civil affairs are from Provincial Department of Civil Affairs; data on disabled persons are from Province Disabled Persons' Federation; data on social security are from Provincial Department of Human Resources and Social Security; data on labour union and woman's federation are respectively from Province Women's Federation and Federation of Trade Unions; data on public security, procuratorial, legal and judicial affairs are respectively from Provincial Public Security Bureau, People's Procuratorate, Higher people's court and Justice Department.

17－1 档案事业机构人员数（2016 年）
Number of Persons and Institutions of Archives（2016）

项 目	Item	机构数（个）Number of Institutions (unit)	专职人员数（人）Full-time Personnel (person)	#女 性 Female	#大专以上文化程度 College and Higher Level
总 计	**Total**	3750	5865	3879	5577
档案行政管理部门	Administrative Department of Archives	110	1396	631	1350
档案馆	Archives	116	492	297	478
档案室（处、科）	Archives Offices（Sections）	3524	3977	2951	3749

17－2 档案馆档案资料馆藏和利用情况
Conditions of Files Stored and Used in Archives

项 目	Item	2012	2013	2014	2015	2016
馆藏档案	**Archives Stored**					
全 宗 （个）	Whole Volume （unit）	18771	19463	22019	22427	20724
案 卷 （万卷/万件）	Files （10000 volumes）	2226	2590	2433	4298	1975
录音录像影片档案 （盘）	Records, Films of Videotape Files （copy）	81210	84706	93002	102026	80109
照片档案 （万张）	Photos （10000 pieces）	127	131	297	330	175
馆藏资料 （万册）	**Number of Material Stored （10000 volumes）**	**141**	**145**	**163**	**166**	**155**
档案馆面积 （平方米）	**Areas of Archives （sq. m）**	**532830**	**547802**	**746920**	**800936**	**769284**
#库房面积	Areas of Storerooms	195364	200630	281333	301124	282623
档案资料利用	**Use of Material**					
利用档案人次 （万人次）	Number of Person-times Using Files Material （10000 person-times）	42	39	68	71	44
利用档案卷次 （万卷/万件次）	Number of Archives Used （10000 volume-times）	85.4	97	115	151	72
利用资料 （册/件次）	Number of Data Used （volumes-times）	2.81	2.70	3.60	2.12	2.13
开放档案	**Opening archives**					
全 宗 （个）	Whole Volume （unit）	10940	11313	11702	11647	11812
案 卷 （万卷/万件）	Files （10000 volumes）	261	302	229	218	227

注：本表档案馆指综合档案馆。
a) Archives in this table refer to comprehensive archives.

17－3 律师、公证及调解工作基本情况

Basic Statistics on Lawyers, Notarization and Mediation

项目	Item	2010	2012	2013	2014	2015	2016
律师工作	**Lawyers**						
律师事务所 （个）	Number of Lawyer Offices (unit)	1112	1238	1288	1385	1512	1612
律师所工作人员 （人）	Number of Lawyers (person)	11903	13874	15475	16708	18235	19140
担任法律顾问 （家）	Number of Units with Legal Advisors (unit)	57670	74212	80298	105755	90137	94244
民事案件诉讼代理 （件）	Agent of Civil Cases (case)	180151	196469	232835	248517	289806	367380
刑事诉讼辩护及代理 （件）	Defender and Agent of Criminal Cases (case)	28472	33310	37677	35135	37765	40995
非诉讼法律事务 （件）	Agent of Non-litigious Legal Affairs (case)	31780	45630	58463	73217	80327	86381
解答法律咨询 （人次）	Agent of Legal Advisory Services (person-times)	317252	313569	308575	256990	331423	377846
代写法律事务文书 （件）	Agent of Legal Document Written on Behalf of Clients (case)	29612	34242	28488	32459	33265	37052
行政诉讼 （件）	Administrative Lawsuit (case)	2703	2364	2202	3169	4650	6762
公证工作	**Notarization**						
公证处 （个）	Number of Notary Offices (unit)	110	109	106	104	104	104
公证人员 （人）	Notarial Personnel (person)	1230	1312	1402	1445	1504	1549
#公证员	Notaries	574	614	632	632	666	643
助理公证员	Assistant Notaries	343	384	417	462	487	570
办理国内公证文书 （件）	Number of Domestic Notarized Documents (case)	570380	507842	540186	477759	520165	643237
人民调解工作	**People's Mediation**						
人民调解委员会 （个）	Number of People's Mediation Committees (unit)	32189	33233	36048	34533	29566	33412
调解人员 （人）	Number of Mediators (person)	226714	170141	160403	154560	150618	138361

17－4 国内公证文书分类

Domestic Notarial Documents by Type

单位:件 (case)

指标	Item	2015	2016
总　计	**Total**	**520165**	**643237**
合同(协议)	Contract (Agreement)	74710	84101
继承	Inheritance	58260	64011
单方法律行为	Unilateral Legal Act	187270	260429
现场监督	Field Supervision	13562	14996
保全证据	Preservation of Evidence	16310	23133
公司章程	Articles of Association of the Company	45	39
组织资格	Organization Qualification	469	253
财产权	Property	146	24
身份	Identity	1404	2249
收养关系	Child Adoption	77	119
婚姻状况	Marital Status	1324	568
亲属关系	Kinship Confirmation	3472	2513
有无违法犯罪记录	No Criminal Record	1850	2851
其他有法律意义事实	Other Legal Facts	2192	3008
证书(执照)	Certificate (License)	2780	6162
签名(印鉴)	Signature (Seal)	49574	62257
文本相符	Confirmation of Copies and Photo-offset Copies to Orignals	19991	26534
赋予执行效力	Give Effect to Execution	25143	23049
执行证书	Execution Certificate	1430	1267
抵押登记	Mortgage Registration	374	255
提存	Drawing	34	58
保管	Safekeeping	24	3
其他	Others	35020	65358

17－5 涉外公证文书分类

Foreign-related Notarial Documents by Type

单位:件 (case)

指标	Item	2012	2013	2014	2015	2016
总　计	**Total**	**192882**	**214405**	**231881**	**246455**	**240234**
出　生	Births	25622	26930	31466	35320	29586
学　历	Schooling	19573	14781	17568	19879	17404
经　历	Personal Histories	1217	2543	1314	802	1025
生存、居住	Survival and Residence	826	1490	1550	1583	1811
死　亡	Deaths	382	226	211	206	286
收　养	Child Adoption	392	77	277	248	148
亲属关系	Kinship Confirmation	16560	18158	20466	24381	21537
婚姻状况	Marital Status	5401	6018	6562	6626	5137
继承权	Rights of Inheritance	30	13	20	9	28
遗　嘱	Testaments	155	13	2	1	3
委托书	Proxy	2480	2459	2315	2362	2920
声明书	Announcement	4451	4615	3756	3168	4172
受、未受刑事处分	Criminal Records	23567	24897		28152	26881
文本相符	Confirmation of Copies and Photo-offset Copies to Originals	43282	43960	39654	33084	36959
其　他	Others	26388	32762	22494	47470	52229

17－6 民政行业单位基本情况
Basic Conditions of Affairs Agencies

指 标	Item	单位数(个) Number of Institutions (unit)		职工人数(人) Number of Staff and Workers(person)	
		2015	2016	2015	2016
民政行业单位	**Civil Affairs Agencies**	**110356**	**114248**	**986544**	**975865**
民政行政机关	Civil Affairs Administrative Departments	121	118	3491	3475
民政事业单位	Civil Affairs Institutions	5920	6045	68273	69591
优抚安置单位	Agencies for Serviceman	232	223	2034	1991
救灾储备单位	Salvation and Institutions	6	2	13	100
社区服务中心	Community Service Centers	2667	2777	25543	25763
婚姻登记服务类单位	Marriage Registration Institutions	86	81	584	500
提供住宿的社会服务机构	Soual Service Institutions Providing Accommodation	2464	2510	34076	36800
殡仪类单位	Funeral and Interment Institutions	255	250	4358	2800
福利彩票发行单位	Welfare Lottery Issuing Institutions	79	78	849	900
老龄事业单位	Aging Population Institutions	60	56	244	200
其他事业单位	Other Institutions	71	68	572	537
社会组织	Non-governmental Organizations	80385	84094	574738	569500
社会团体	Social Organization	35137	34952	236898	220000
基金会	Fund Organization	543	608	2115	2400
民办非企业单位	Non-enterprise Units Run by NGO	44705	48534	335725	347100
基层群众自治组织	Grass Roots Autonomy Organizations	21495	21556	111048	111600
社区居委会	Neighborhood Committee	7009	7079	38471	39000
村委会	Village Committee	14486	14477	72577	72600
福利企业	Social Welfare Enterprises	2435	2435	228994	221699

备注:提供住宿的社会服务机构在2014年为收养类单位,2015年改为提供住宿的社会服务机构,指标口径有所调整。

a) Residential mstitutions have bee replaced with soual service mstitutions providing accommodation from 2015.

17－7 民政事业费支出情况
Operating Expenses for Civil Administration

单位:万元 (10000 yuan)

年 份 Year	民政事业费实际支出 Actual Operating Expenses for Civil Administration	#抚恤事业费 Commiserate	#社会救济福利事业费 Subsidies of Social Welfare	#自然灾害救济费 Subsidies of Natural Calamity
1980	15208	5138	7188	2882
1985	24095	11115	10976	2004
1989	27647	9098	7396	4203
1990	46657	20676	20333	5648
1991	69567	20530	27005	22032
1992	60808	22548	23267	14993
1993	60972	25920	27448	7605
1994	72276	31933	34078	6265
1995	87470	38966	39544	8961
1996	104278	48874	46470	8935
1997	119396	57247	52304	9846
1998	141192	67183	63207	10803
1999	157082	78084	69053	9945
2000	175738	86088	78046	11604
2001	187786	89952	87732	10102
2002	205763	54223	72244	8918
2003	255690	58221	91748	27724
2004	309196	72157	117935	13954
2005	419996	103882	178157	14999
2006	502744	118955	229594	17130
2007	632560	137177	274117	17801
2008	811832	161662	372348	13468
2009	996449	200052	450462	8037
2010	1265312	238040	559834	15339
2011	1726189	290324	926602	14140
2012	1970956	346611	748848	23477
2013	2335260	400631	966893	21365
2014	2460508	423763	1022106	16524
2015	2672006	463209	1142715	24696
2016	2872253	484847	1481146	60224

注:社会救济福利事业费包含:城乡低保、农村社会救济、其他城镇社会救济、社会福利。

a) Subsidies of social welfare consists of urban and rural low, sucial relief of country, other town social relief and social welfare.

17－8 提供住宿的社会服务机构基本情况（2016年）

Basic Statistics of Provide Accommodation Social service Agencies(2016)

项目	Item	院数（个）	工作人员（人）	床位（张）	年末收养人员（人）
总计	**Total**	**2475**	**36757**	**428469**	**219431**
为老年人与残疾人提供服务的机构	**Institutions Providing Services for the Elderly and the Disabled**	**2342**	**33458**	**410501**	**209694**
城市养老服务机构	Urban Pension Service Instituions	867	16851	163137	73294
农村养老服务机构	Rural Pension Service Instituions	1271	12098	207839	115464
社会福利院	Social Welfare Centers	62	3006	26764	10547
光荣院	Nursing Homes for Elderly Revolutionaries and Relatives	9	86	470	290
荣誉军人康复医院	Rehabilitation Hospitals for Honorary soldiers	1	264	220	191
复员军人疗养院	Nursing Homes for Demobilization Soldiers	4	83	340	253
军休所	Homes for Soldiers	128	1070	11731	9655
为智障与精神病人提供服务的机构	**Institutions Providing Services for Retarded Pepole and Psychiatric Patients**	**11**	**1717**	**6456**	**5571**
社会福利医院	Social Welfare Hospitals	10	1448	5334	4450
复退军人精神病院	Mental Hospital for Demobilization Soldiers	1	269	1122	1121
为儿童提供收养救助服务的机构	**Adoptive Institutions Providing Services for children**	**32**	**631**	**4287**	**2116**
儿童福利机构	Children Welfare Institutions	13	564	3265	2075
未成年人救助保护中心	Minors Rescue and Protection Centers	19	67	1022	41
其他提供住宿的社会服务机构	**Other Social Service Institutions Providing Accommodation**	**90**	**951**	**7225**	**2050**
生活无着人员救助站	Rescue Stations for Helpless Pepole	69	716	4590	1469
军供站	Army supply stations	16	199	1662	0
其他收留抚养机构	Other Adoptive Institutions	5	36	973	581

17－9 残疾人事业基本情况(2016)

Basic Statistics of People with Disabilities(2016)

项 目	Item	绝对数(人)
康复	**Rehabilitation**	
视力残疾康复	Rehabilitation of Persons with Visual Disability	16274
白内障复明手术	Sight-restoring Surgeries for Cataract Patients	1224
盲杖及其辅助器具	Blind Stick and Auxiliary Device	7762
盲人定向行走及适应训练	Directional Walking and Adaptive Training for Blind Persons	3857
中途盲者支持性服务	Blind Persons Receiving Orientation Skill Training	1576
听力残疾康复	Rehabilitation of Persons with Hearing and Speech Disability	7265
人工耳蜗植入手术及服务(0—6 岁儿童)	Cochlear Implants Surgery and Services (0—6 year olds)	260
助听器适配及适应训练(0—6 岁儿童)	Hearing Aid Adaptation and Training (0—6 year olds)	1095
肢体残疾康复	Rehabilitation of Persons with Physical Disability	64967
矫治手术(0—6 岁儿童)	Corrective surgery (0—6 year olds)	169
辅助器具适配及服务	Assistive Devices Adaptation and Services	53894
支持性服务	Supporting Services	13956
智力残疾康复	Rehabilitation of Persons with Intellectual Disability	7350
认知及适应训练	Cognitive and Adaptive Training	7054
支持性服务	Supporting Services	5057
精神残疾康复	Rehabilitation of Persons with Mental Illness	49472
沟通及适应训练(0—17 岁)	Communication and Adaptation Training (0—17 years old)	3039
支持性服务	Supporting Services	27523
精神疾病治疗	Psychiatric Treatmen	44704
精神障碍作业疗法训练	Mental Disorders Occupational Therapy Training	18073
教育	**Education**	
新入园残疾儿童(彩票公益金助学项目)	New Admission Disabled Children (Lottery Public Welfare Scholarship Program)	186
特殊教育普通高中在校生	Students at Special Education Senior High Schools	521

17－9 续表 Continued

项　　目 Item		绝对数(人)
残疾人中等职业教育在校生	Disabled Secondary Vocational Education Students	1225
普通高等院校录取残疾考生	Disable Students Admitted to Higher Education Institutions	415
就业	**Employment**	
残疾人就业合计	Total Employment of Disabled Persons	366019
务农及种养大户	Farmer and Breeding Large Family	121367
灵活就业及居家就业	Flexible Employment and Home Employment	68192
按比例就业	Proportional Employment	66426
集中就业	Centralized Employment	50403
自主创业	Self-employed	8115
社区基层就业及公益性岗位	Community Employment at the Basic Level and Public Welfare Posts	3387
辅助性就业	Auxiliary Employment	7111
农村劳动力转移	Rural Labor Transfer	5278
基地就业	Base Employment	3085
其他	Other	32655
社会保障	**Social Security**	
60 周岁以下参保残疾居民	Under 60 years of age Insured Disabled Residents	641310
#重度残疾人	Severely Disabled	208706
非重度残疾人	Non-severely Disabled	432604
扶贫	**Poverty Alleviation**	
残疾人实用技术培训（人次）	Practical Technical Training for Disabled Person (person-times)	
实用技术培训	Practical Technical Training	14335
#扫盲教育	Anti-illiteracy Education	2740
农村贫困残疾人危房改造	Dilapidated House Renovation for Poor PWDs	
危房改造（户）	Dilapidated House Renovation (households)	921
受益残疾人	PWDs Benefited	1000
残联组织建设	**Federation of Disabled Persons Organization Development**	
省市县乡残联实有人员	Actual Personnel of Province - City - County - Township Federation of Disabled Persons	4973

17－10 婚姻登记和离婚情况
Number of Marriages and Divorces

年份 Year 地区 Region	结婚登记对数(万对) Total Number of Registered Marriages (10000 couples)	内地居民登记结婚(万人) Registered Marriages in the Mainland (10000 persons)	涉外及港澳台居民登记结婚(万人) Registered Marriages with Foreigner or the Citizen of Hong Kong, Macao, Taiwan (10000 persons)	初婚(万人) First Marriages (10000 persons)	再婚(万人) Re-marriages (10000 persons)	离婚(万对) Divorces (10000 couples)
1985	43.01	86.01	0.01	84.51	1.51	2.11
1990	52.72	105.40	0.04	102.88	2.56	4.63
1995	57.51	114.93	0.10	112.00	3.03	6.76
2000	49.81	99.50	0.12	94.43	4.95	8.19
2001	44.42	88.60	0.13	83.25	5.35	8.62
2002	48.14	96.15	0.13	89.41	6.60	9.70
2003	46.15	92.17	0.13	85.84	6.20	9.65
2004	51.64	103.13	0.14	93.98	9.00	11.74
2005	47.20	94.26	0.14	84.94	9.66	12.38
2006	59.23	118.30	0.16	105.70	12.76	13.80
2007	57.14	114.11	0.17	99.93	14.36	16.04
2008	62.47	123.64	0.17	110.60	14.30	13.55
2009	73.09	145.99	0.17	129.51	16.66	14.37
2010	75.71	151.42	0.16	137.41	14.02	16.02
2011	86.75	173.34	0.17	152.53	20.97	16.68
2012	88.76	177.18	0.17	159.03	18.50	18.12
2013	90.38	180.42	0.33	158.20	22.55	21.66
2014	83.45	166.58	0.32	141.84	25.06	21.84
2015	78.60	156.88	0.32	132.21	25.00	22.93
2016	71.61	143.22	0.28	116.28	26.94	26.13
南京市 Nanjing	7.98	15.96		10.80	5.16	5.09
无锡市 Wuxi	3.63	7.26		6.06	1.21	1.59
徐州市 Xuzhou	9.54	19.08		15.99	3.09	2.89
常州市 Changzhou	3.06	6.12		4.98	1.15	1.29
苏州市 Suzhou	4.81	9.62		7.28	2.34	2.14
南通市 Nantong	5.56	11.12		8.82	2.30	1.89
连云港市 Lianyungang	4.91	9.82		8.12	1.69	1.65
淮安市 Huaian	5.99	11.98		10.13	1.85	1.77
盐城市 Yancheng	6.99	13.98		11.54	2.44	2.32
扬州市 Yangzhou	4.40	8.80		7.46	1.34	1.23
镇江市 Zhenjiang	2.38	4.76		3.77	0.98	0.98
泰州市 Taizhou	5.52	11.04		9.56	1.48	1.32
宿迁市 Suqian	6.70	13.40		11.58	1.81	1.96

17－11 社会保险基本情况
Basic Statistics of Social Insurance

单位:万人 (10000 persons)

年份 Year 地区 Region	失业保险 Unemployment Insurance			城镇职工基本医疗保险 Basic Medical Care Insurance		工伤保险 Work Injury Insurance		年末参加生育保险人数 Maternity Insurance Contributors at Year-end
	年末参保人数 Contributors at Year-end	全年发放失业保险金人数 Beneficiaries of Unemployment Insurance Fund	全年发放失业保险金(亿元) Unemployment Relief (100 million yuan)	年末参保职工人数 Contributors at Year-end	年末参保退休人员 Retirees Contributors at Year-end	年末参保人数 Contributors at Year-end	年末享受工伤待遇的人数 Beneficiaries at Year-end	
2001	750.90	53.70	9.16	367.64	122.65	473.94	0.79	483.46
2002	733.87	76.71	13.00	507.69	183.24	480.00	1.44	486.06
2003	761.62	88.25	13.92	608.41	226.67	503.02	1.68	504.06
2004	797.09	85.98	14.73	715.11	261.62	577.20	2.28	552.68
2005	838.48	67.02	12.03	821.07	303.02	680.21	3.22	630.92
2006	901.08	51.63	9.36	935.77	338.51	812.69	5.06	711.49
2007	968.48	48.65	9.37	1070.34	365.45	920.98	5.84	794.11
2008	1052.24	48.83	11.57	1213.90	390.35	1055.71	7.90	907.23
2009	1079.14	49.98	14.17	1282.50	418.63	1118.10	9.34	962.46
2010	1153.78	46.51	13.95	1405.06	443.20	1205.52	9.79	1086.44
2011	1238.16	57.70	19.83	1541.55	470.89	1327.46	10.66	1199.21
2012	1332.18	64.14	28.73	1646.53	508.94	1420.74	12.29	1276.25
2013	1389.34	68.70	31.69	1731.09	543.64	1487.27	13.57	1355.62
2014	1441.56	67.93	35.71	1784.86	576.95	1540.11	14.28	1374.56
2015	1490.91	68.30	40.63	1818.20	610.80	1594.14	14.66	1471.68
2016	1538.22	70.54	47.17	1849.36	641.16	1633.93	15.08	1510.32
南京市 Nanjing	259.76	18.30	13.75	304.16	96.04	265.10	2.13	251.74
无锡市 Wuxi	204.25	9.71	6.75	232.91	81.62	198.55	1.99	199.01
徐州市 Xuzhou	88.97	3.10	2.16	110.32	46.71	86.96	1.42	79.51
常州市 Changzhou	111.57	5.61	3.56	143.31	50.26	119.87	1.03	113.85
苏州市 Suzhou	354.93	15.34	8.68	416.85	121.82	357.62	3.37	366.69
南通市 Nantong	103.30	5.57	3.40	135.74	52.19	129.77	1.22	109.97
连云港市 Lianyungang	39.86	0.97	0.56	53.58	21.53	51.24	0.29	43.10
淮安市 Huaian	64.30	1.35	0.77	58.99	22.43	51.66	0.35	50.00
盐城市 Yancheng	74.37	2.21	1.26	93.09	36.59	85.35	0.67	71.09
扬州市 Yangzhou	65.49	3.18	1.69	92.31	31.88	79.88	0.78	65.04
镇江市 Zhenjiang	52.87	2.13	1.38	64.71	25.34	60.52	0.63	56.77
泰州市 Taizhou	65.52	2.02	1.19	88.86	32.83	82.40	0.89	59.19
宿迁市 Suqian	32.08	0.62	0.36	42.99	12.76	47.00	0.22	33.23

17-12 社会保险基金收支及累计结余
Revenue, Expenses and Balance of Social Insurance Fund

单位:亿元 (100 million yuan)

年份 Year	合计 Total	企业职工基本养老保险 Enterprise Basic Pension Insurance	失业保险 Unemployment Insurance	城镇职工基本医疗保险 Urban Workers Basic Medical Care Insurance	工伤保险 Work Injury Insurance	生育保险 Maternity Insurance
基金收入 Revenue						
2001	205.03	148.53	18.28	33.43	2.18	2.61
2002	271.46	194.12	20.10	51.27	2.67	3.30
2003	344.49	238.86	24.97	73.32	3.32	4.01
2004	413.75	283.40	26.69	94.40	4.25	5.01
2005	519.83	356.23	31.63	117.99	6.66	7.32
2006	667.93	456.36	39.23	154.62	9.05	8.67
2007	874.11	598.45	48.71	203.65	12.12	11.19
2008	1107.35	749.30	62.88	264.07	16.12	14.98
2009	1251.93	865.28	63.00	291.67	15.74	16.24
2010	1450.34	999.80	72.46	339.90	18.77	19.41
2011	1854.94	1269.20	105.71	421.94	32.29	25.80
2012	2295.10	1566.17	121.63	531.60	43.70	32.00
2013	2513.41	1674.81	134.20	611.10	57.00	36.30
2014	2815.97	1889.12	114.86	698.60	73.35	40.04
2015	3141.11	2114.01	130.07	783.16	79.06	34.81
2016	3358.18	2259.27	112.44	869.39	78.13	38.95
基金支出 Expenses						
2001	187.12	145.79	16.50	21.60	1.48	1.75
2002	251.47	192.36	20.09	35.42	1.68	1.92
2003	289.96	207.41	22.05	55.55	2.80	2.15
2004	339.98	243.75	21.13	69.35	2.82	2.92
2005	401.03	281.85	20.22	90.60	4.01	4.34
2006	493.45	355.28	20.06	107.73	5.41	4.96
2007	586.98	419.36	19.81	133.83	7.05	6.93
2008	751.91	524.33	31.00	178.56	9.85	8.17
2009	913.13	617.65	40.77	231.80	11.92	10.99
2010	1075.78	737.91	41.37	270.26	13.94	12.29
2011	1337.14	884.20	74.92	338.01	24.19	15.82
2012	1615.07	1078.06	57.35	418.74	38.70	22.22
2013	1943.66	1309.63	62.85	496.12	48.12	26.94
2014	2305.80	1553.78	70.16	586.60	61.08	34.18
2015	2640.03	1792.82	76.13	666.98	61.08	43.02
2016	2967.09	2006.70	109.77	735.25	55.24	60.13
累计结余 Balance at Year-end						
2001	104.48	56.99	18.46	18.37	6.08	4.59
2002	124.37	58.74	18.37	34.22	7.07	5.97
2003	178.03	90.25	20.37	52.00	7.59	7.83
2004	249.39	127.58	25.83	77.05	9.02	9.91
2005	368.71	201.96	37.76	104.44	11.66	12.89
2006	550.51	305.40	58.26	154.95	15.31	16.59
2007	837.51	484.54	87.16	224.57	20.38	20.85
2008	1192.97	709.52	119.04	310.08	26.67	27.66
2009	1531.68	957.14	141.18	369.95	30.50	32.91
2010	1906.24	1219.03	172.27	439.60	35.32	40.03
2011	2424.02	1604.03	203.03	523.52	43.42	50.02
2012	3104.13	2092.14	267.30	636.40	48.50	59.79
2013	3667.81	2457.32	332.57	751.42	57.35	69.15
2014	4184.06	2792.66	383.36	863.42	69.61	75.01
2015	4685.13	3113.84	437.31	979.59	87.59	66.80
2016	5074.12	3366.42	439.97	1111.79	110.49	45.61

17－13 工会、妇联基本情况
Basic Statistics on Labour Union and Women's Federation

单位：个　　(unit)

项　目	Item	2012	2013	2014	2015	2016
工会基本情况	**Basic Condition of Labour Union**					
基层工会组织数	Number of Grassroot Labour Unions	431393	461681	491172	517723	168000
职工人数　(万人)	Number of Staff and Workers (10000 persons)	1962.39	2085.53	2192.56	2390.29	2439.19
#女职工人数	Women Workers	819.81	874.36	918.76	978.58	1009.84
会员人数　(万人)	Number of Members (10000 persons)	1887.40	2012.32	2122.68	2265.32	2352.60
#女会员人数	Women Members	792.69	849.42	897.07	956.25	987.79
女职工工作委员会	Number of Women Workers Working Committees	99924	109128	114188	118775	151102
建立工会经费审查组织	Number of Units Established with Funds Examing by Labour Union	103453	109904	112003	111587	123978
建立职工代表大会制度的单位	Number of Units Established with Workers Delegating Congress System	117272	122424	130714	138554	342643
实行厂务公开的单位	Number of Units Carried Out the Factory Business to Public	111380	115605	123285	127829	326637
建立工会劳动保护监督检查委员会	Number of Units Established with Labour Protection, Supervisting and Examing Committees	80085	90250	103690	108013	111130
建立工会劳动法律监督组织	Number of Organizations Established with Law of Labour Supervising Committees by Labour Union	81421	93340	104568	110347	115432
建立劳动争议调解委员会的单位	Number of Units Established with Mediating Committee of Labour Disputes	78524	85574	98139	102907	105841
建有职工技协组织	Number of Organizations Established with Technical Association of Staff and Workers	5024	4526	5028	6966	9014
职工董事人数　(人)	Staff Sensible (person)	8490	8849	8609	8162	7931
#女性	Female	3125	3289	3388	2900	2777
职工监事人数　(人)	Staff Supervisor (person)	8289	6801	6389	7010	6520
#女性	Female	2886	2408	2551	2660	2483
妇联基本情况	**Basic Condition of Women's Federation**					
基层妇代会数	Number of Grassroot Dlegating Congress	23740	21410	20920	20631	14477
妇联干部数　(人)	Number of Cadres of Women's Federation (person)	3006	2542	2565	2636	2673
按年龄分	Grouped by Age					
35岁以下	Aged 35 and Below	1051	1070	1018	986	1004
36—45岁	Aged 36—45	1053	1014	1005	1071	1086
46—55岁	Aged 46—55	790	434	510	543	546
56岁以上	Aged 56 and Above	112	24	32	36	37
按文化程度分	Grouped by Educational Attainment					
研究生	Postgraduates	153	239	294	355	392
大学本科、大专学历	University or College	2719	2157	2184	2189	2200
高中、中专及以下	Senior Middle School, Specialized Secondary School and Below	134	146	87	92	81

注：2011年起，基层妇代会包括乡镇街道、村社区；干部人数统计到县、乡镇街道，含行政、事业和其他。

a) From 2011, Grassroots Women's Congress inluding township and village communities; the number of cadres statistics to country, township, including administrative, institution and others.

17－14 公安机关立案的刑事案件情况
Criminal Cases Registered in Public Security Organs

案 件 类 别	Category of Cases	立 案 (起) Number of Cases Registered(case)		构 成 (%) Composition(%)	
		2015	2016	2015	2016
合 计	**Total**	**364437**	**401507**	**100**	**100**
杀 人	Homicide	317	285	0.08	0.07
伤 害	Injury	4337	4519	1.06	1.13
抢 劫	Robbery	1374	1098	0.34	0.27
强 奸	Rape	1392	1328	0.34	0.33
拐卖妇女儿童	Bduction	29	21	0.01	0.01
盗 窃	Larceny	291551	287401	71.31	71.58
诈 骗	Fraud	65388	60380	15.99	15.04
走 私					
伪造、变造货币，出售、购买、运输、持有、使用假币	Holding and Using Counterfeit Money	49	130	0.01	0.03
毒品刑事犯罪			5126		1.28
抢 夺			1397		0.35
信用卡诈骗			2569		0.64
其 他	Others	44389	37253	10.86	9.27

17－15 公安机关受理、查处治安案件情况
Offense Cases Against Public Order Handled by Public Security Organs

单位：件 (case)

案 件 类 别	Category of Cases	2015		2016	
		受 理 Number of Cases Accepted to be Treated	查 处 Number of Cases Investigated and Treated	受 理 Number of Cases Accepted to be Treated	查 处 Number of Cases Investigated and Treated
合 计	**Total**	**674236**	**661097**	**696432**	**675468**
扰乱公共场所秩序	Disturbing the Orders in Public Places	13834	13831	12006	11688
寻衅滋事	Causing Quarrels and Making Troubles	4536	4515	4957	4792
非法携带枪支、弹药、管制刀具	Violation of Firearms Control Regulations	1756	1777	1754	1762
违反危险物质管理规定	Violation of Provisions of Risk Material Management	443	440	411	408
殴打他人	Battering Other Persons	196680	194492	217309	212233
盗 窃	Stealing Property	221543	214641	206523	197569
诈骗、抢夺、敲诈勒索	Swindling, Robbery and Racketeering	26249	25325	25716	23996
伪造、变造、倒卖有价票证、凭证	Forge, Alter, Scalp Valuable Coupons or Certificates	148	140	216	201
利用迷信活动危害社会	Endangering the Society through Superstition	310	310	176	167
卖淫、嫖娼	Prostitution or Soliciting Prostitutes	6097	6203	6318	6353
赌 博	Gambling	18413	18449	17492	17502
其 他	Others	184227	180974	203554	198797

17－16　交通事故情况(2016 年)

Basic Statistics on Traffic Accidents (2016)

类　别　Type		发生数（起）Number of Traffic Accidents (case)	死亡人数（人）Number of Deaths (person)	受伤人数（人）Number of Injuries (person)	直接经济损失（万元）Losses Coverted into Cash (10000 yuan)
总计	**Total**	**13293**	**4601**	**11999**	**6383.13**
特别重大事故	Accident with More Than Three Persons' Death at one Time				
重大事故	Accident with More Than Three Persons' Death at one Time				
较大事故	Accident with More Than Three Persons' Death at one Time	18	59	52	120.83
机动车	Vehicles	10402	3886	9120	5053.26
#汽车	Motor Vehicles	8559	3333	7220	4604.41
摩托车	Motorcycles	1577	442	1725	389.26
拖拉机	Non-motor-driven Vehicles	266	111	175	59.59
#电动自行车	Bicycles	1960	355	2086	829.69

17－17　火灾事故情况(2016 年)

Basic Statistics on Fire Accidents (2016)

项　目　Item		合计 Total	按事故发生程度分 By Degree	
			重　大 Serious	一　般 Ordinary
发生数（起）	Number of Fire Accidents (case)	25012	0	25012
死亡人数（人）	Number of Deaths (person)	109	0	109
受伤人数（人）	Number of Injuries (person)	103	0	103
直接财产损失（万元）	Direct Property Losses (10000 yuan)	31878	0	31878
人口火灾发生率（1/10 万人）	( )	39.96	0.00	40.00
平均每起事故损失（万元）	Average Loss per Fire (10000 yuan)	1.27	0.00	1.27

17－18 人民检察院直接立案侦查案件情况（2016年）
Cases under Direct Investigation by People's Procuratorate(2016)

案件分类	Category of Cases	受案（件）Cases Accepted (case)	立案件数（件）Number of Cases Registered (case)	立案人数（人）Person of Cases Registered (person)	#要案 Key Case	结案件数（件）Number of Cases Settled (case)	结案人数（人）Person of Cases Settled (person)
合计	**Total**	3712	1530	1996	122	1394	1819
贪污贿赂案件	**Sub-total of Cases on Corruption and Bribery**						
贪污	Corruption	765	212	328	8	200	304
贿赂	Bribery	1719	838	997	88	748	890
挪用公款	Misappropriation of Public Funds	209	139	183	4	144	178
集体私分	Collective Illegal Possession of Public Funds	12	2	4	1	1	1
巨额财产来源不明	Unstated Source of Large Properities	28	1	1	1	1	1
其他	Others	49	3	3	0	5	5
渎职案件	**Sub-total of Cases on Abuse and Dereliction of Duty**						
滥用职权	Abuse of Power	515	193	303	19	168	271
玩忽职守	Dereliction of Duty	251	98	115	0	81	96
徇私舞弊	Fraudulent Practice	98	12	15	1	13	15
其他	Others	66	32	47	0	33	58

注:结案中含上年旧存（以下各表同）。

a) Data of cases settled include cases turned over from previous year. (The same as in the following tables).

17－19 人民检察院审查批准、决定逮捕犯罪嫌疑人和提起公诉被告人情况（2016年）
Arrests of Criminal Suspects and Defendants under Public Prosecution Approved by People's Procuratorate(2016)

案件分类	Category of Cases	批捕、决定逮捕 Total of Arrests		决定起诉 Total of Public Prosecutions	
		件 (case)	人 (person)	件 (case)	人 (person)
合计	**Total**	**26776**	**35557**	**75667**	**101752**
公安、安全、监狱机关提请	**Sub-total of Requests by Departments of State and Public Security and Prisons**				
危害国家安全案	Offences Against State Security	2	2	2	2
危害公共安全案	Offences Against Public Security	1785	1877	21846	22128
破坏社会主义市场经济秩序案	Offences Against Socialist Economic Order	1842	2993	4511	9073
侵犯公民人身、民主权利案	Offences Against Citizens' Personal and Democratic Rights	4104	5069	7415	10039
侵犯财产案	Offences Against Properties	11405	14903	24991	32516
妨害社会管理秩序案	Offences Against Social Management of Order	6545	9566	14413	24840
危害国防利益案	Offences Against National Defense	11	19	11	14
检察机关直接立案侦查案件	**Sub -total of Cases Directly Handled by Procuratorate officess**				
贪污贿赂案	Offences on Corruption and Bribery	493	511	990	1233
渎职案	Offences on Abuse and Dereliction of Duty	50	55	251	339

17－20 人民检察院处理申诉案件情况（2016 年）
Appeals Handled by People's Procuratorate(2016)

单位:件 (case)

案件分类	Category of Cases	受案 Cases Accepted	立案复查 Cases Registered for Reinvestigation	结案 Cases Settled	#改变原决定 Original Decision Changed
合计	**Total**	**870**	**166**	**137**	**4**
不服检察机关处理决定	Appeals against Decision of Procurator's Offices	96	71	57	3
不服不批捕	Appeals against Rejection of Arrest	10	2	2	0
不服不起诉	Appeals against Rejection of Prosecuting	82	68	54	3
不服撤案	Appeals against Withdrawal of the Case	4	1	1	0
不服原免予起诉	Appeals against Original Exemption of Lawsuit	0	0	0	0
其他	Others	0	0	0	0
不服法院刑事判决裁定	Appeals against Judgment of Criminal Case	774	95	80	1
刑罚执行中被害人申诉	Appeals of the Victim at the Punishment	143	27	25	0
刑罚执行中被告人申诉	Appeals of the Defendant at the Punishment	196	24	22	0
刑罚执行完毕后被害人申诉	Appeals of the Victim after the Punishment	62	15	15	0
刑罚执行完毕后被告人申诉	Appeals of the Defendant after the Punishment	373	29	18	1

17－21 人民法院审理刑事一审案件收结案情况
First Trial Criminal Cases Accepted and Settled by Courts

单位:件 (case)

项目	Item	2014 收案 Cases Accepted	2014 结案 Cases Settled	2015 收案 Cases Accepted	2015 结案 Cases Settled	2016 收案 Cases Accepted	2016 结案 Cases Settled
合 计	**Total**	**68152**	**67008**	**76378**	**72831**	**75289**	**75801**
危害公共安全罪	Offences Against Public Security	18191	18136	21219	20567	22082	22270
破坏社会主义市场经济秩序罪	Offences Against Socialist Economic Order	3961	3796	4039	3578	4399	4285
侵犯公民人身权利民主权利罪	Offences Against Citizens's Personal and Democratic Rights	8877	8668	8707	8401	7989	8008
侵犯财产罪	Offences Against Properties	23417	23122	24743	23764	25233	25568
妨害社会管理秩序罪	Offences Against Social Management of Order	12221	11932	16230	15575	14308	14109
危害国防利益罪	Offences Against National Defense	24	21	14	18	10	10
贪污贿赂罪	Offences on Corruption and Bribery	1234	1120	1189	752	1036	1309
渎职罪	Offences on Dereliction of Duty	225	210	228	171	229	235
其他	Others	2	3	9	5	3	7
合计中含自诉案件	Private Prosecution Among the Total	531	519	806	760	683	696

注:结案含上年旧存(下同)。

a) Data of cases settled include cases turned over from previous year (The same as the following tables).

17-22 人民法院审理婚姻家庭、继承一审案件收结案情况（2016年）

First Trial Civil Cases of Marriages, Family Affairs and Inheritance Accepted and Settled by Courts(2016)

单位:件 (case)

项 目	Item	收案 Cases Accepted	结案 Cases Settled	调解 Mediation	判决 Judgement	驳回 Reject	撤诉 With-drawal	其他 Other
合计	**Total**	**120288**	**120438**	**45583**	**43583**	**674**	**29619**	**979**
婚姻家庭	Marriages and Family Affairs	115539	115731	42824	42389	637	28944	937
离婚	Divorce	97089	97365	34901	36326	491	24944	703
赡养纠纷	Support Disputes	1933	1974	642	772	11	509	40
抚养、扶养关系纠纷	Upbringing Disputes	3618	3606	2175	770	16	625	20
抚育费纠纷	Upbringing Fee Disputes	3052	3018	1027	1193	24	741	33
其他	Others	9847	9768	4079	3328	95	2125	141
继承	Inheritance	4749	4707	2759	1194	37	675	42
法定继承	Legal Inheritance	1941	2036	1334	414	16	260	12
遗嘱继承	Testament Inheritance	420	463	237	155	5	64	2
其他	Others	2388	2208	1188	625	16	351	28

17-23 人民法院审理合同纠纷一审案件收结案情况（2016年）

First Trial Cases of Contracts Disputes Accepted and Settled by Courts (2016)

单位:件 (case)

项 目	Item	收案 Cases Accepted	结案 Cases Settled	调解 Mediation	判决 Judgement	驳回 Reject	撤诉 With-drawal	其他 Other
合计	**Total**	**542666**	**533941**	**136670**	**261455**	**8458**	**121153**	**6205**
借款合同	Loan Contracts	211308	207855	46598	126947	2419	30355	1536
买卖合同	Trade Contracts	94908	92666	27273	39808	1066	23255	1264
电信合同	Telecom Contracts	200	215	30	52	9	123	1
租赁合同	Lease Contracts	23910	23854	7214	10678	492	5214	256
劳动争议	Work Disputes	52576	53531	20605	22526	1563	8258	579
劳务合同	Service contracts	12165	11804	4785	5012	100	1722	185
房地产合同	Real Estate Contracts	18872	18484	4620	7893	437	5336	198
供用动力合同	Labor Contracts	262	271	51	106	9	104	1
建设工程合同	Construction Contracts	16967	16724	4097	8109	404	3674	440
农村承包合同	Rural Contracts	557	593	142	231	36	176	8
承揽合同	Contracts for Work	12876	12994	4166	5110	124	3322	272
保险合同	Insurance Contracts	9318	9386	3005	4751	157	1403	70
服务合同	Service Contracts	48128	46969	6622	9828	701	29702	116
信用卡纠纷	Credit Card Dispute	8794	8765	985	6373	90	1297	20
经营合同	Work Disputes	3963	3846	746	1756	152	987	205
其他	Others	27862	25984	5731	12275	699	6225	1054

17－24 人民法院审理权属、侵权纠纷及其他民事一审收结案情况（2016年）
First Trial Cases of Disputes of Right, Infringement of Right and Other Civil Affairs Accepted and Settled by Courts(2016)

单位：件 (case)

项 目	Item	收 案 Cases Accepted	结 案 Cases Settled	调 解 Mediation	判 决 Judgement	驳 回 Reject	撤 诉 With-drawal	其 他 Other
合计	**Total**	**187676**	**187114**	**55598**	**73864**	**3585**	**35557**	**18510**
所有权及其相关权利	Ownership and Related Rights	21440	20913	3769	8853	1355	6571	365
票据、证券权益纠纷	Disputes of Bill, Securities and Stocks	1621	1467	127	951	24	340	25
股东权纠纷	Stockholder's Right Disputes	3162	2990	485	1365	196	790	154
知识产权案件	Intellectual Rights	9440	9524	1221	2712	118	5403	70
人身权纠纷	Personal Rights	113178	113792	46453	51172	290	15512	365
特殊侵权纠纷	Disputes of Special Infringement of Right	12406	11976	2876	4096	197	4652	155
不当得利	Unjustified Enrichment	2786	2798	511	1193	122	896	76
特别程序	Special Proceedings	21282	21521	18	2437	1010	871	17185
其他	Others	2361	2133	138	1085	273	522	115

17－25 人民法院行政一审案件收结案情况（2016年）
First Trial Administrative Cases Accepted and Settled by Courts(2016)

单位：件 (case)

项 目	Item	收 案 Cases Accepted	结 案 Cases Settled	维持 Affirmation of Original Judgement	撤销 Cancel	驳 回 Reject	撤 诉 With-drawal	单独赔偿 Separate Compen-sation	其 他 Other
合计	**Total**	**13617**	**13714**	**349**	**388**	**3388**	**3459**	**26**	**6104**
土地等资源	Land	1355	1258	21	35	398	257	5	542
公安	Public Security	1503	1477	44	3	261	390	0	779
城建	City Construction	2970	2783	60	106	1001	673	16	927
交通运输	Traffic and Transport	88	84	0	3	19	25	0	37
工商	Industry and Commerce	327	287	1	24	50	106	0	106
环保	Environment Protection	109	122	5	2	17	45	0	53
计划生育	Family Planning	22	16	1	0	3	7	0	5
税务	Tax	92	76	0	2	14	25	0	35
卫生	Health	50	51	0	0	6	19	0	26
乡政府	Townships Government	467	466	4	16	139	104	2	201
劳动和社会保障	Labour and Social Security	1793	1848	57	37	229	576	0	949
其他	Other	4841	5246	156	160	1251	1232	3	2444

主要统计指标解释

民政事业费支出 指报告期内本辖区各项民政事业费实际支出的总数额。包括抚恤事业费、军队移交地方安置的离退休人员费用、社会救济福利事业费、救灾支出以及其它民政事业费。

城镇居民最低生活保障人数 指在报告期末家庭平均收入在当地规定的最低生活保障线以下的城镇居民数。包括“三无”对象、失业人员和在职、下岗、退休人员等。

农村居民最低生活保障人数 指报告期末在建立农村最低生活保障制度的地区，得到当地政府或集体给予最低生活保障的农业人口数。

农村传统救济人数 指未开展最低生活保障制度的农村地区，仍沿用传统救济制度救济贫困人口数。

收养性福利单位 指荣誉军人康复医院、复员军人疗养院、复退军人精神病院、光荣院、社会福利院、儿童福利院、精神病福利院、城镇老年福利机构、农村老年福利机构以及其它收养性单位的总称。

社会福利企业 指以集中安置有一定劳动能力的残疾人就业为目的（残疾职工占生产人员10%以上）、带有社会福利性质的特殊企业的总称。

律师 指受聘参加法律顾问处工作，担任法律顾问、刑（民）事代理人、刑事辩护人，办理非诉讼事件、解答法律询问，代写法律事务文书等主要从事律师业务的专职法律工作者和兼职律师。

公证人员 指在国家公证机关依法办理公证事务的司法人员，包括公证员、助理公证员和在公证处工作的其他人员。

办理公证文书 指公证处在一定时期内办结的公证文书件数。公证文书按司法部规定或批准的格式制作，包括国内公证和涉外公证两部分。国内公证分为经济合同公证和民事法律关系公证两大类。

调解人员 指在人民调解委员会担负调解民间一般民事纠纷和轻微违法行为引起纠纷的工作人员，包括调解委员会的委员和调解小组的调解员。

调解民间纠纷 指调解委员会依照法律规定，根据自愿原则，用说服教育的方法调解民间发生的有关民事权利和义务的争执，促成当事双方达到协议和谅解，解决纠纷。包括婚姻家庭纠纷，财产权益纠纷等，不包括法院受理调解的民事案件数。

受理劳动争议案件数 指劳动争议仲裁委员会根据国家有关规定，对劳动争议当事人的申请予以审查，符合受理条件而正式立案、准备处理的劳动争议案件数。

决定逮捕 指检察机关对直接受理、自行侦查的案件，认为需要逮捕犯罪嫌疑人时，依据法律作出的逮捕决定。

批准逮捕 指检察机关对公安机关、国家安全机关、监狱管理机关提出逮捕的犯罪嫌疑人进行审查，根据事实，依法作出逮捕决定。

决定起诉 指检察机关对公安机关、国家安全机关、监狱管理机关和检察机关内设机构反贪污贿赂部门移送起诉的刑事犯罪嫌疑人进行审查，根据事实，依法向人民法院提起公诉。

Explanatory Notes on Main Statistical Indicators

Operation Expenses for Civil Adiministration refer to the total actual expenditures for all the operating expenses of civil administration in this jurisdiction district at reference period, including pensions, settlement allowance for the retirees who are transfered from P. L. A. units to the local government to be settled down, social welfare, disaster relief and other civil administration expenses.

Number of Persons Receiving Lowest-Lost-Living in Urban Area refer to the number of urban residents their family average income is below the lowest living standard insurance line at the year end, according to the local regulation; including "three proverty-striken people", unemployment, employees, laid off and retired personnels.

Number of Persons Receiving Lowest-Cost-Living in Rural Area refer the number of rural population in rural area with the system of lowest living standard insurance has been established, they are being insured by the local government and collective units.

Number of Traditional Relief Persons in Rural Areas refer to the rural areas which has not been established the system of lowest living standard insurance, the poor people are still succoured according to the traditional relief system.

Adopting Social Welfare Institutions refer to the all names of social welfare homes and adopting social welfare institutions, including homes for disabled soldiers, convalescent homes for demobilized soldiers, psychopathy welfare homes for demobilized soldiers, homes for disabled veterancs, social welfare homes, children welfare homes, urban eldery welfare units, rural elderly welfare units.

Social Welfare Enterprises refer the all names of special enterprises with the social welfare character, for the aim of employment of the disabled persons who still provide certain labor capacity, and are settled down concentratively (10% above are disabled staff and workers).

Lawyers are legal workers who are employed full time by legal counseling firms to act as a legal adivisers, agents in criminal civil lawsuits or defenders in criminal lawsuits, or to handle non-liligious legal affairs, to advise on matters of law or to write legal papers for others. Both full time and part time lawyers are included.

Notary Personnel refer to judicial workers of the state notary offices handling notarization work according to law. They include notaries and other people working for notary offices.

Notarized Documents refer to documents settled by notary offices in a year. The notary documents are drawn up in accordance with the regulations of the Ministry of Justice, including domestic documents and foreign-related documents. Domestic documents are divided into two major categories, documents on economic contracts and documents on civil legal relation.

Mediators refer to workers on peoples mediation committees responsible for mediating in civil disputes and cases of slight infraction of the law. They include members of the mediation committees and mediators of mediation groups.

Mediatoin of Civil Disputes refers to mediation committees work in mediating in civil disputes concerning civil rights and duties through persuasion and education in accordance with the provisions of law on a voluntary basis, so as to solve disputes by helping the parties involved come to an agreement and understanding. These disputes include divora cases and disputes over property ownership, but exclude the civil cases to be handled by the court.

Number of Labour Dispute Cases Accepted refer to the number of cases of labour dispute submitted that, after being reviewed by the labour dispute arbitraction committees in line with relevant state regulations, are accepted and registered for treatment.

Decision on Arrest refers to decision made by procurators office, in accordance:e with laws, to arrest the suspect(s) in the cases that are accepted and to be investigated by procurators office.

Approval for Arrest refers to the decision made b procurators office, in accordance with laws and relevant facts, to approve the arrest of the suspect(s) that is proposed by the public security departments or authority of prisons.

Decision on Prosecution refers to the decision made by procurators office, in accordance with laws and relevent facts, to institute proeedings to the people court against the suspect(s) of criminal cases handed by the public security departments, state security departments or authority of prisons, or by the anti-corruption departments within the procurators office.

18

城市经济与建设

Urban Economy and Construction

简 要 说 明

一、本篇资料的主要内容

本篇资料反映城市建设基本情况、城市经济社会发展情况。

二、资料来源

城市建设数据来自住房与城乡建设部门及交通运输部门，城市经济社会发展统计数据来自市县社会经济基本情况统计年报。

Brief Introduction

I. Main Contents

Data in this chapter reflect the basic situation of cities construction, cities economic and social development.

II. Date Source

Data of city construction provided by Ministry of Housing and Urban-rural Development, Ministry of communications. Data of City economic and social development come from cities and counties in basic socio-economic statistics annual report.

18－1 城市公用事业基本情况
Basic Statisics on Urban Public Utilities

指 标	Item	2012	2013	2014	2015	2016
城市基本情况	**Basic Condition of City**					
建成区面积 (平方公里)	Areas of Built Districts (sq. km)	3655	3809	4020	4189	4299
城市人口密度 (人/平方公里)	Population Density of City Districts (person/sq. km)	2002	2016	2038	2034	2057
供水、供气	**Water Supply and Gas Supply**					
自来水年供水量 (亿吨)	Annual Supply of Tap Water (100million tons)	49.28	48.93	48.81	50.68	53.31
#生活用水量	Residential Consumption	21.90	22.01	22.73	23.09	24.67
平均每人日生活用水 (升)	Daily Per Capita Residential Tap Water Comsuption (litre)	215.44	209.76	209.62	210.74	215.39
用水普及率 (%)	Coverage Rate of Urban Population with Access to Tap Water (%)	99.7	99.7	99.8	99.8	99.9
煤气(天燃气)供气量 (亿立方米)	Gaswork Gas and Natural Gas Supply (100 million cu. m)	69.67	76.98	84.27	96.98	96.25
#家庭用量	Residential Use	12.59	14.28	14.84	17.32	19.33
煤气(天燃气)管道长度 (公里)	Length of Gas Pipelines (km)	44567	50457	55864	61125	66599
液化气家庭用量 (万吨)	Residential Consumption of Liquefied Gas (10000 tons)	50.23	69.85	64.98	59.12	31.45
燃气普及率 (%)	Population with Access to Gas (%)	99.4	99.6	99.5	99.6	99.5
市政工程	**Municipal Engineering**					
年末实有道路长度 (公里)	Length of Paved Roads at Year-end (km)	34966	36975	39070	40749	44999
平均每万人拥有道路长度 (公里)	Length of Paved Roads Per 10000 Persons (km)	12.52	12.82	13.12	13.26	14.32
年末实有道路面积 (万平方米)	Area of Paved Roads at Year-end (10000 sq. m)	62438	66970	71151	75052	79733
人均拥有道路面积 (平方米)	Per Capita Area of Paved Roads (sq. m)	22.35	23.22	23.89	24.42	25.37
排水管道长度 (公里)	Length of Sewer Pipelines (km)	56887	62194	66256	70048	72823
建成区排水管道密度 (公里/平方公里)	Density of Drainage Pipelines (km/sq. km)	15.56	16.33	16.48	16.72	16.94
公共交通	**Public Traffic**					
公共汽(电)车总数 (辆)	Operating Public Transportation Vehicles (unit)	32105	34176	36665	39729	39855
平均每万人拥有公共汽(电)车 (辆)	Number of Public Transportation Vehicles Per 10000 Persons (unit)	11.7	12.7	14.1	15.1	15.5
出租汽车 (万辆)	Taxis (10000 units)	5.45	5.68	6.07	6.11	5.45
城市绿化	**Landscaping in Cities**					
公园绿地面积 (公顷)	Area of Parks and Green Land (hectare)	38069	40413	42901	44713	46476
人均公园绿地面积 (平方米)	Per Capita Area of Parks and Green Land (sq. m)	13.63	14.01	14.40	14.55	14.79
公园面积 (公顷)	Area of Parks (hectare)	16465	18707	21879	25935	29076
环境卫生	**Sanitation and Hygiene**					
清运生活垃圾 (万吨)	Garbage Disposal (10000 tons)	1210.07	1202.69	1352.44	1456.07	1562.31
清运粪便 (万吨)	Disposal of Night Soil (10000 tons)	72.92	81.70	82.40	72.49	65.85
每万人拥有公厕 (座)	Public Restrooms Per 10000 Persons (unit)	3.59	3.62	3.75	3.82	3.86

注：2011 年起，煤气、天燃气供气量统计口径调整。
a) From 2011, gaswork gas, natural gas supply statistical adjustment.

18-2 城市自来水情况

Basic Statistics on Tap Water Supply in Cities

年份 Year 城市 City	综合生产能力（万吨/日）General Production Capacity (10000 tons/day)	全年供水总量（万吨）Total Aunual Supply of Tap Water (10000 tons)	#生产用水量 Productive Use	#生活用水量 Residential Use	用水人口（万人）Residents with Access to Tap Water (10000 persons)	人均日生活用水量（升）Daily Per Capita Residential Tap Water Comsuption (liter)	城市人口用水普及率（%）Population with Access to Tap Water (%)
1978	112.3	35056	20073	12013	347.2	94.8	83.6
1980	142.6	45221	26005	16323	463.0	89.0	92.2
1985	218.9	76609	40908	29280	585.4	137.0	89.0
1989	856.3	233848	167472	54326	896.6	166.0	88.3
1990	941.7	256664	181543	62369	968.0	176.4	91.3
1991	1056.1	282691	201088	68287	1049.2	178.3	93.8
1992	1191.4	317812	224575	77010	1158.6	182.1	96.0
1993	1299.5	342780	239520	83041	1238.6	183.7	97.1
1994	1368.9	358696	243332	93030	1212.3	210.2	98.7
1995	1388.7	382325	190471	105192	1277.5	225.6	98.9
1996	1424.4	349423	192948	135429	1300.7	285.3	99.0
1997	1457.1	343106	189889	131650	1346.1	267.9	99.3
1998	1543.6	358999	199055	137663	1388.0	271.8	99.2
1999	1585.5	339066	173487	138264	1425.4	265.8	99.1
2000	1641.6	353366	172552	145707	1503.1	265.6	99.2
2001	1698.5	332155	156019	156717	1745.2	246.0	91.0
2002	1803.7	380991	182591	168929	2048.7	225.9	89.0
2003	1835.0	380395	174834	171830	2167.7	217.2	91.9
2004	1871.4	392462	179602	179068	2273.7	215.8	94.0
2005	1977.6	390460	161320	185906	2408.5	211.5	96.3
2006	2166.8	472128	225805	164928	2209.1	204.6	99.2
2007	2334.7	452628	198647	167341	2300.9	199.5	99.5
2008	2356.9	436597	187915	173506	2331.5	205.0	99.9
2009	2534.1	449037	185461	183641	2443.9	207.2	99.7
2010	2714.7	482821	204878	197408	2515.6	220.4	99.6
2011	2757.2	477044	198830	206120	2660.5	212.3	99.6
2012	2749.8	492791	200532	219008	2785.1	215.4	99.7
2013	2902.6	489286	194884	220130	2875.2	209.8	99.7
2014	2961.6	488062	184371	227293	2970.7	209.6	99.8
2015	3104.1	506807	193679	236039	3068.6	210.7	99.8
2016	3369.7	533098	201351	246698	3138.0	215.4	99.9
南京市区 Nanjing	655.4	132652	45077	71735	627.2	313.4	100.0
无锡市区 Wuxi	280.0	43838	17745	19781	251.1	215.9	100.0
徐州市区 Xuzhou	137.0	26199	8995	8301	182.5	124.6	99.8
常州市区 Changzhou	203.0	30825	11995	15906	187.7	232.2	100.0
苏州市区 Suzhou	417.7	78279	36527	33929	312.2	297.7	100.0
南通市区 Nantong	331.5	29277	12219	10835	164.3	180.7	100.0
连云港市区 Lianyungang	65.6	14298	5146	6367	105.2	165.9	100.0
淮安市区 Huaian	122.6	17831	8751	7591	161.8	128.5	100.0
盐城市区 Yancheng	59.8	10953	1911	6986	135.7	141.0	100.0
扬州市区 Yangzhou	115.2	19376	4881	9013	116.6	211.7	100.0
镇江市区 Zhenjiang	59.0	17710	8110	6328	89.0	194.7	100.0
泰州市区 Taizhou	42.0	10238	2508	4738	94.3	137.7	100.0
宿迁市区 Suqian	37.0	8064	2837	4229	73.1	158.6	100.0

18-3 城市煤气、液化石油气情况

Basic Statistics on Supply of Gas and Liquefied Petroleum Gas in Cities

年份 Year 城市 City	全年供气总量 Total Gas Supply			家庭用气量 Residential Use			用气人口(万人) Population with Access to Gas (10000 persons)			燃气普及率(%)
	煤气(万立方米) Gaswork Gas (10000 cu. m)	天然气(万立方米) Natural Gas (10000 cu. m)	液化石油气(吨) Liquefied Petroleum Gas(ton)	煤气(万立方米) Gaswork Gas (10000 cu. m)	天然气(万立方米) Natural Gas (10000 cu. m)	液化石油气(吨) Liquefied Petroleum Gas(ton)	煤气 Gaswork Gas	天然气 Natural Gas	液化石油气 Liquefied Petroleum Gas	Percentage of Population Using Gas for Household Use (%)
1978	11756		23666	1592		22043	15.7		48.4	15.7
1980	11401		32591	2215		31350	20.0		69.6	17.8
1985	13155		42495	3851		38834	39.9		76.2	17.9
1989	140497		190471	13429		105671	93.0		186.1	32.5
1990	142681		216936	15902		122691	101.2		219.3	36.8
1991	142665		252342	17750		137780	116.3		261.2	41.9
1992	147625		337456	20943		190861	131.0		373.1	53.3
1993	153994		442089	23774		258003	150.6		498.0	63.5
1994	184552		574191	26281		337126	180.3		558.8	74.1
1995	282227		436131	30877		361990	213.4		637.3	81.8
1996	271852		543989	35837		468838	243.3		701.2	86.6
1997	274853		468106	34055		392574	244.1		746.2	87.8
1998	331580		620344	34797		430131	271.1		798.3	93.0
1999	350299		667556	41206		427971	323.9		814.1	94.9
2000	362606		705010	39141		492377	324.7		882.9	95.8
2001	376025		780527	44685		523600	373.2		1200.3	82.0
2002	788537		1252001	38761		632199	361.1		1600.0	85.2
2003	802430		1357710	47369		687358	405.8		1673.5	88.6
2004	1027886		1226675	40926		708033	333.8		1712.1	92.0
2005	1290834		1110300	27831		649936	234.1		1720.0	93.3
2006	1420015	155940	1042278	18120	22710	591415	177.1	574.9	1408.8	97.1
2007	1633281	254507	999243	13228	39383	548113	146.1	699.8	1407.3	97.4
2008	1554953	299726	931734	12518	62207	578762	123.2	841.7	1328.2	98.2
2009	1728890	343544	865663	11741	53244	531023	135.5	1029.6	1248.1	98.4
2010	1931995	472309	766586	9664	79160	471731	89.8	1299.7	1115.0	99.1
2011	10310	591493	766635	9270	99133	464117	45.8	1557.5	1042.6	99.0
2012	4889	691763	735757	3883	121988	502258	27.5	1743.6	1006.5	99.4
2013	3940	765869	700765	2270	140471	458823	9.0	1906.6	956.6	99.6
2014	612	842071	651779	470	147899	390403	9.0	2125.0	828.9	99.5
2015		969799	593577		173196	358045		2345.7	714.6	99.6
2016		962542	515611		193326	314482		2505.6	622.3	99.5
南京市区 Nanjing		116394	84795		37299	44344		483.6	140.6	99.5
无锡市区 Wuxi		93030	39446		17521	18901		235.2	15.9	100.0
徐州市区 Xuzhou		31629	20925		8375	13103		152.8	26.5	98.0
常州市区 Changzhou		90685	9450		11214	3061		183.9	3.8	100.0
苏州市区 Suzhou		117130	35905		24185	14117		293.8	18.5	100.0
南通市区 Nantong		24440	19737		5578	9158		141.0	23.3	100.0
连云港市区 Lianyungang		13716	11383		6275	9891		74.0	30.0	98.9
淮安市区 Huaian		17766	29588		8350	25160		105.7	54.6	99.0
盐城市区 Yancheng		17377	25428		10012	20110		100.6	34.5	99.5
扬州市区 Yangzhou		21627	16814		7867	11523		103.5	12.6	99.6
镇江市区 Zhenjiang		38058	19909		4300	10346		64.9	24.2	100.0
泰州市区 Taizhou		26687	13079		3744	9609		59.9	34.4	99.9
宿迁市区 Suqian		15261	8555		2831	8102		51.0	22.1	100.0

18－4 城市市政工程情况

Basic Statistics on Municipal Engineering in Cities

年份 Year 城市 City	年末实有道路长度（公里） Length of Paved Roads at Year-end (km)	年末实有道路面积（万平方米） Area of Paved Roads at Year-end (10000 sq. m)	排水管道长度（公里） Length of Drainage Pipelines (km)	城市污水日处理能力（万吨） Day Capacity of Sewerage Disposal (10000 tons)	城市路灯盏数（千盏） Number of Street Light (1000 units)	人均拥有道路面积（平方米） Per Capita Area of Paved Roads (sq. m)	建成区排水管道密度（公里/平方公里） Density of Drainage Pipelines (km/sq. km)	污水处理率（%） Rate of Sewerage Disposal (%)
1978	1893	1154	1503					
1980	1881	1160	1650	0.1	48	2.3		0.2
1985	2437	1623	2277	1.8	71	2.5	5.3	0.6
1989	5272	6607	3782	91.3	122	7.7	5.7	23.0
1990	5812	5672	4099	103.5	129	6.3	5.7	16.4
1991	5658	5216	4872	133.2	144	5.8	5.4	13.4
1992	6781	6587	5721	155.5	165	7.0	5.6	16.7
1993	7090	7581	6653	160.7	194	7.4	4.7	22.9
1994	6150	7094	7019	236.7	194	7.1	6.0	31.8
1995	8163	8669	8262	273.5	215	8.3	7.5	38.7
1996	8552	9711	8860	390.3	256	8.9	7.5	42.7
1997	9440	10438	8812	434.3	290	9.3	7.1	47.5
1998	9618	11336	9574	589.3	328	9.8	7.6	49.3
1999	10066	12283	10382	632.9	381	10.2	8.0	58.1
2000	11011	13357	11097	712.9	437	10.6	8.0	61.8
2001	16702	20309	13974	736.7	549	10.6	9.0	65.3
2002	22656	26987	16744	800.4	753	11.7	8.6	66.0
2003	25541	31859	20343	906.6	971	13.5	9.6	69.9
2004	26598	35596	25537	1017.8	1169	14.7	11.3	76.1
2005	28674	40830	28568	1084.7	1296	16.3	12.0	77.7
2006	27058	41623	31215	1224.9	1501	18.7	12.1	81.8
2007	28456	44595	34050	1184.1	1701	19.3	12.6	84.4
2008	28761	47330	38062	1432.2	1660	20.3	13.1	84.1
2009	30003	50075	42826	1411.2	1982	20.4	14.1	85.4
2010	31899	53723	46867	1590.0	2174	21.3	14.3	87.6
2011	32491	58405	51735	1555.5	2331	21.9	14.8	89.9
2012	34966	62438	56887	1564.5	2727	22.4	15.6	90.7
2013	36975	66970	62194	1606.5	2877	23.2	16.3	92.1
2014	39070	71151	66256	1622.4	3198	23.9	19.5	93.5
2015	40749	75052	70048	1673.2	3391	24.4	16.7	93.9
2016	44999	79733	72823	1742.9	3510	25.4	16.9	94.6
南京市区 Nanjing	8012	14649	8657	488.1	483	23.4	11.2	96.0
无锡市区 Wuxi	3715	6679	13105	157.1	326	26.6	39.5	97.1
徐州市区 Xuzhou	2550	4463	2196	61.0	294	24.4	8.4	93.6
常州市区 Changzhou	2553	4880	5880	109.8	252	26.0	22.5	96.3
苏州市区 Suzhou	7166	10681	8678	269.3	431	34.2	18.8	95.2
南通市区 Nantong	2770	5064	4493	74.3	236	30.8	20.8	94.1
连云港市区 Lianyungang	1432	2506	2156	33.1	98	23.8	10.1	87.2
淮安市区 Huaian	2026	3506	2514	42.1	132	21.7	14.1	93.2
盐城市区 Yancheng	1353	3122	2157	38.2	239	23.0	14.6	90.5
扬州市区 Yangzhou	1616	2559	2596	48.3	130	21.9	17.4	94.4
镇江市区 Zhenjiang	1405	2313	2016	48.0	97	26.0	14.5	94.5
泰州市区 Taizhou	1234	2525	1877	39.1	109	26.8	16.4	91.2
宿迁市区 Suqian	898	1995	1617	36.0	65	27.3	18.8	94.5

18－5　城市园林绿化情况

Basic Statistics on Parks, Gardens and Green Areas in Cities

年　份　Year 城　市　City	园　林 绿地面积 （公顷） Total Area of Parks, Gardens and Green Areas in Cities (hectare)	#公　园 绿　地 Parks and Green Land	建成区绿化覆盖面积 （公顷） Coverage Space of Green Areas Developed (hectare)	公　园　Park 个　数 （个） Number (unit)	面　积 （公顷） Area (hectare)	人均公园绿地面积 （平方米） Per Capita Area of Parks and Green Land (sq. m)	建成区面积（平方公里） Areas of Built Districts (sq. km)	建成区绿化覆盖率 （%） Coverage Rate of Green Area Developed (%)
1978	7303			59	786			
1980	6582	1341		72	944	2.7		19.3
1985	7998	1450		83	1030	2.3		20.6
1989	18148	3214	12804	172	2725	3.7		19.2
1990	20337	3447	14112	184	2991	3.8		19.5
1991	19096	3841	16423	201	3071	4.3		18.4
1992	20898	4283	21726	217	2958	4.5		21.4
1993	30174	5882	31133	242	5179	5.8		22.1
1994	33089	6124	34728	241	5396	6.1		29.6
1995	48564	7226	34093	264	5648	6.9		30.8
1996	50558	7528	35964	283	5263	6.9		30.3
1997	52349	8175	38356	287	4831	7.3		30.9
1998	54756	8891	40513	295	4920	7.7		32.3
1999	57386	9581	43725	303	5027	8.0		33.7
2000	60064	10248	45925	313	5159	8.1		33.2
2001	94175	12724	49456	374	5549	6.6	1549	31.9
2002	137702	16252	68413	403	6374	7.1	1939	35.3
2003	145956	18743	74929	446	7317	7.9	2120	35.4
2004	172563	21617	85367	489	9098	8.9	2253	37.9
2005	189070	25687	94778	539	9924	10.3	2379	39.8
2006	152885	25868	107752	492	10608	11.6	2583	41.7
2007	180784	29125	116157	601	11787	12.6	2714	42.8
2008	195460	30645	123801	628	13026	13.1	2904	42.6
2009	214989	32403	127930	590	13740	13.2	3046	42.0
2010	227584	33585	137623	584	12433	13.3	3271	44.1
2011	237486	35634	147157	701	15687	13.3	3494	42.1
2012	247001	38069	154135	783	16465	13.6	3655	42.2
2013	256263	40413	161671	842	18707	14.0	3810	42.4
2014	265543	42901	171265	883	21879	14.4	4020	42.6
2015	274071	44713	179411	942	25935	14.6	4189	42.8
2016	281855	46476	184591	1074	29076	14.8	4299	42.9
南京市区 Nanjing	91674	9624	34625	141	7301	15.3	774	44.8
无锡市区 Wuxi	18905	3744	14270	54	3814	14.9	332	43.0
徐州市区 Xuzhou	15983	2879	11436	74	1810	15.7	261	43.8
常州市区 Changzhou	11320	2713	11256	39	1080	14.5	261	43.1
苏州市区 Suzhou	22184	4592	19385	167	2110	14.7	462	42.0
南通市区 Nantong	9638	3035	9332	37	561	18.5	216	43.3
连云港市区 Lianyungang	22460	1542	8609	25	632	14.7	214	40.2
淮安市区 Huaian	8166	2267	7506	20	1176	14.0	179	42.1
盐城市区 Yancheng	6844	1731	6141	56	1194	12.8	148	41.5
扬州市区 Yangzhou	7540	2167	6525	89	1762	18.6	149	43.8
镇江市区 Zhenjiang	8445	1689	5975	24	627	19.0	139	42.9
泰州市区 Taizhou	4538	1008	4809	23	580	10.7	115	42.0
宿迁市区 Suqian	9115	1116	3693	20	943	15.3	86	42.9

18－6 城市环境卫生情况

Basic Statistics on Urban Environmental Sanitation

年份 Year 城市 City	清扫面积（万平方米）Sweeping Areas (10000 sq. m)	生活垃圾清运量（万吨）Residential Garbages Disposal Cleared (10000 tons)	粪便清运量（万吨）Night Soil Disposal Cleared (10000 tons)	无害化处理厂日处理能力（吨）Day Disposal Capacities of No Harmful Disposal Factory (ton)	垃圾粪便年处理量（万吨）Annual Garbages and Night Soil Disposal Cleared (10000 tons)	环卫机械（辆）Machines of Environment Sanitation (unit)	公共厕所（座）Public Toilet (unit)
1978	503	79	229			223	3545
1980	601	158	232			296	3712
1985	1078	159	147	20		734	4700
1989	2136	262	260	162		1735	7910
1990	2445	288	221	385		1322	8072
1991	3068	341	271	1588	357.3	1604	9974
1992	3432	409	419	7622	531.7	1785	9265
1993	4095	408	441	14014	654.1	1998	9162
1994	4240	360	388	16442	658.8	1736	7095
1995	5429	398	209	13810	532.5	2072	7263
1996	6252	426	198	13125	523.9	2144	6932
1997	7085	479	196	15813	606.0	2351	7675
1998	7589	486	302	18570	721.4	2407	7486
1999	8221	505	310	43419	756.0	2458	7337
2000	8773	515	309	17392	762.9	2569	7393
2001	10971	634	338	17324	868.1	3800	9532
2002	16101	723	400.1	19997	985.9	4573	11016
2003	20874	775	405.5	20728	1060.9	4456	10660
2004	22505	808	388.6	23569	1106.6	4494	10260
2005	27101	835	388.4	24000	1030.5	5094	10591
2006	29409	851	126.9	24545	915.7	5447	9165
2007	31072	898	140.2	24192	942.8	5589	8520
2008	35418	934	159.9	27985	1024.8	5939	9050
2009	36160	957	116.1	34570	1048.4	6923	9654
2010	44088	1017	84.9	37637	1064.3	7481	9475
2011	46162	1120	95.2	42170	1142.0	7984	10134
2012	48098	1210	72.9	43113	1258.4	8709	10035
2013	52029	1203	81.7	40723	1250.3	9865	10438
2014	55132	1352	82.4	50574	1400.7	11227	11178
2015	57992	1456	72.5	52816	1518.2	12175	11739
2016	62827	1562	65.9	55403	1634.3	13482	12136
南京市区 Nanjing	8557	213	4.9	8950	215.8	1925	1249
无锡市区 Wuxi	4700	142	13.1	2950	142.4	1083	1500
徐州市区 Xuzhou	2786	92	1.2	2700	93.6	840	813
常州市区 Changzhou	3435	84	1.7	3910	90.5	657	927
苏州市区 Suzhou	11437	246	1.6	10197	261.6	2977	1016
南通市区 Nantong	3423	72	3.6	500	74.5	573	314
连云港市区 Lianyungang	3154	40	2.8	1300	40.4	510	808
淮安市区 Huaian	2602	55	2.0	2400	56.8	336	486
盐城市区 Yancheng	2299	46	1.6	1800	48.2	299	618
扬州市区 Yangzhou	2029	66	4.0	2110	71.7	326	504
镇江市区 Zhenjiang	1580	41	0.9	1450	41.8	211	216
泰州市区 Taizhou	2182	31	2.4	1000	33.0	659	416
宿迁市区 Suqian	2028	28	1.9	1050	29.7	374	361

18-7 城市公共汽(电)车、出租汽车情况
Basic Statistics on Buses (Trolley Buses) and Taxis in Cities

年份 Year 城市 City	年末实有公共汽(电)车营运车辆(辆) Operating Public Transit Vehicles at Year-end (unit)	实有公共汽(电)车营运标准车台(标台) Operating Standard Public Transit Vehicles (Standardized) (unit)	公共汽(电)车营运线路长度(公里) Length of Public Transit Route (km)	公共汽(电)车客运总量(万人次) Passengers Carried by Transit (10000 person-times)	每万人拥有公共交通车辆(标台) Public Transit Vehicales Per 10000 Population (Standard sets)	出租汽车营运车数(辆) Operating Taxis (unit)
1978	1407		1772			
1980	1605		1920	100671		150
1985	2237		2904	143146		605
1989	2826	3167	4603	135947	3.7	4555
1990	2827	3210	3991	130641	3.6	5775
1991	2968	3727	4229	124409	4.1	5005
1992	4578	4855	6939	120282	5.1	8133
1993	6384	5954	7570	109248	5.8	9838
1994	7367	6808	10127	110921	6.8	12307
1995	8019	7215	13642	95362	7.1	18073
1996	7962	7144	3544	104583	6.6	25403
1997	9665	7916	5684	124805	7.0	32493
1998	12411	10080	5198	157600	8.9	34661
1999	14136	11625	5858	191831	9.7	36613
2000	14838	13341	6896	246314	10.6	36603
2001	16244	14871	7296	224582	7.8	41480
2002	16902	15874	12397	245227	6.9	41933
2003	17822	17015	14696	233586	7.2	40073
2004	19079	19098	15888	263088	7.9	40746
2005	22197	22484	18077	283760	9.1	41476
2006	22002	22898	12121	304669	10.4	42032
2007	23874	26419	16133	322230	11.6	44993
2008	25369	28664	14657	352597	12.4	44708
2009	30432	34335	18881	389293	11.7	52282
2010	28687	32927	44941	391856	11.9	52957
2011	30867	35715	50971	424699	12.0	53409
2012	32105	37743	52887	444148	11.7	54464
2013	34176	40463	53903	453366	12.7	56785
2014	36665	43815	57734	461348	14.1	60712
2015	39729	47138	63623	474984	15.1	61120
2016	39855	48090	63982	448734	15.5	54521
南京市区 Nanjing	9208	11465	10245	94447	23.7	14297
无锡市区 Wuxi	4562	5429	7962	52724	18.4	5141
徐州市区 Xuzhou	2907	3537	4802	39631	15.8	5313
常州市区 Changzhou	3106	3733	4764	33512	21.3	3680
苏州市区 Suzhou	7710	9378	13002	87698	19.1	9012
南通市区 Nantong	2439	2849	6208	20629	21.7	2529
连云港市区 Lianyungang	1168	1437	1829	12957	16.3	1814
淮安市区 Huaian	1257	1550	1625	21431	11.6	1473
盐城市区 Yancheng	1340	1657	2480	15385	16.3	1833
扬州市区 Yangzhou	2046	2462	2738	22736	22.7	3399
镇江市区 Zhenjiang	1793	1955	3385	18754	17.2	2635
泰州市区 Taizhou	1327	1462	3352	15795	13.7	2627
宿迁市区 Suqian	992	1176	1592	13037	16.8	768

18－8 主要城市土地面积、人口情况（2016年）
Land Area and Population of Major Cities(2016)

城市 City		土地面积（平方公里）Land Area (sq. km)	年末户籍人口（万人）Registered Population at Year-end (10000 persons)	#女 Female	当年出生人口（万人）Births (10000 persons)	当年死亡人口（万人）Deaths (10000 persons)	年末常住人口（万人）Permanent Population at Year-end (10000 persons)
南京市区	Nanjing	6587	662.79	331.93	8.03	3.72	827.00
无锡市区	Wuxi	1643	253.06	128.40	2.40	1.51	363.31
徐州市区	Xuzhou	3063	338.09	164.72	3.28	0.66	326.89
常州市区	Changzhou	2838	294.95	150.03	2.90	1.91	394.67
苏州市区	Suzhou	4653	348.02	176.80	4.33	2.08	551.03
南通市区	Nantong	2140	213.57	109.23	1.75	1.63	234.72
连云港市区	Lianyungang	3012	222.69	107.31	2.55	0.58	208.78
淮安市区	Huaian	4476	335.75	163.52	3.73	1.21	305.67
盐城市区	Yancheng	5129	243.34	119.08	2.59	1.54	237.22
扬州市区	Yangzhou	2306	232.47	117.14	2.00	1.71	242.75
镇江市区	Zhenjiang	1088	103.42	52.13	0.83	0.57	123.13
泰州市区	Taizhou	1567	163.98	81.83	1.58	1.31	162.60
宿迁市区	Suqian	2154	176.14	85.50	2.77	0.63	159.74

18－9 主要城市就业情况（2016年）
Employment of Major Cities(2016)

单位:万人 (10000 persons)

城市 City		年末就业人员 Employment at Year-end	#城镇私营企业就业人员 Number of Employed Persons Private Enterprises	#城镇个体就业人员 Number of Self-employed Individuals	就业人员按三次产业分 Employment Grouped by Type of Industry		
					第一产业 Primary Industry	第二产业 Secondary Industry	第三产业 Tertiary Industry
南京市区	Nanjing	456.00	371.68	94.60	46.00	148.90	261.10
无锡市区	Wuxi	214.09	129.20	34.32	3.62	113.51	96.96
徐州市区	Xuzhou	156.82	45.63	28.80	33.34	48.89	74.58
常州市区	Changzhou	231.56	142.29	47.35	18.44	116.73	96.39
苏州市区	Suzhou	347.41	184.21	59.17	10.81	200.21	136.39
南通市区	Nantong	135.80	43.51	20.52	17.25	58.75	59.80
连云港市区	Lianyungang	109.60	27.62	12.61	26.39	39.01	44.20
淮安市区	Huaian	176.93	34.99	22.55	43.88	58.23	74.82
盐城市区	Yancheng	143.08	40.99	16.70	26.46	54.01	62.61
扬州市区	Yangzhou	137.15	67.00	24.89	13.17	62.04	61.94
镇江市区	Zhenjiang	69.74	28.27	13.51	5.52	26.97	37.25
泰州市区	Taizhou	97.50	42.93	16.23	14.30	39.70	43.50
宿迁市区	Suqian	101.15	22.23	15.76	28.62	38.43	34.10

18－10　主要城市地区生产总值及指数（2016 年）
Gross Domestic Product of Major Cities(2016)

城　市 City		地区生产总值(亿元) Gross Domestic Product (100 million yuan)	第一产业 Primary Industry	第二产业 Secondary Industry	第三产业 Tertiary Industry	人均地区生产总值(元) Per Capita GDP (yuan)	地区生产总值指数(上年=100) GDP Index (preceding year =100)
南京市区	Nanjing	10503.02	252.54	4117.32	6133.16	127264	108.0
无锡市区	Wuxi	4749.02	42.11	1956.28	2750.63	130935	107.7
徐州市区	Xuzhou	3072.18	109.01	1442.79	1520.39	94402	106.0
常州市区	Changzhou	4985.66	104.37	2291.09	2590.20	126424	108.4
苏州市区	Suzhou	8008.45	80.88	3685.44	4242.13	145576	107.5
南通市区	Nantong	2475.03	59.97	1113.84	1301.22	105599	109.2
连云港市区	Lianyungang	1307.59	118.67	575.43	613.49	62788	107.7
淮安市区	Huaian	2062.33	180.66	890.03	991.64	67635	108.9
盐城市区	Yancheng	1884.64	160.69	951.98	771.97	80122	109.0
扬州市区	Yangzhou	2900.30	91.21	1420.61	1388.48	119578	109.3
镇江市区	Zhenjiang	1711.60	29.33	829.74	852.53	139126	109.3
泰州市区	Taizhou	1718.27	60.95	863.57	793.75	105789	110.5
宿迁市区	Suqian	860.43	63.11	423.53	373.79	54078	109.6

18－11　主要城市固定资产投资（2016 年）
Investment in Fixed Assets of Major Cities(2016)

单位:亿元　　(100 million yuan)

城　市 City		固定资产投资 Investment in Fixed Assers	房地产开发投资 Investment in Real Estate Development	#住宅 Resdential Building	新增固定资产 Newly Increased Fixed Assets	商品房屋销售建筑面积(万平方米) Construction Floor Space of Commercial House Sold (10000 sq. m)	#住宅 Resdential Building
南京市区	Nanjing	5533.56	1845.60	1392.76	3019.53	1558.18	1406.29
无锡市区	Wuxi	3124.91	663.82	419.29	2554.07	908.23	836.46
徐州市区	Xuzhou	2352.23	326.39	232.66	1573.19	483.96	405.52
常州市区	Changzhou	3118.52	402.64	280.97	2310.20	857.66	739.31
苏州市区	Suzhou	3156.39	1381.20	1060.20	1784.23	1272.75	1147.67
南通市区	Nantong	1878.80	351.37	243.40	1192.78	676.56	621.95
连云港市区	Lianyungang	1564.32	165.86	129.91	907.44	344.63	331.99
淮安市区	Huaian	1653.71	240.04	173.23	934.62	603.22	543.78
盐城市区	Yancheng	1658.29	209.37	157.24	1048.70	435.83	386.73
扬州市区	Yangzhou	1989.33	315.84	208.16	987.87	449.08	409.95
镇江市区	Zhenjiang	1693.52	239.59	169.67	1152.88	329.93	312.38
泰州市区	Taizhou	1557.00	125.45	98.39	1267.67	378.09	355.52
宿迁市区	Suqian	784.91	120.80	85.96	521.02	286.92	261.64

18－12 主要城市工业基本情况（2016 年）
Basic Statistics on Industry of Major Cities(2016)

单位:亿元 (100 million yuan)

城市 City		工业企业单位数(个) Number of Industrial Enterprises (unit)	#大中型企业 Enterprises of Large and Medium Size	资产总计 Total Assets	负债合计 Total Liabilities	主营业务收入 Major Business Income	利润总额 Total Profits
南京市区	Nanjing	2661	510	11448.85	6166.10	12442.36	959.35
无锡市区	Wuxi	2664	384	6547.51	3182.08	6280.65	493.08
徐州市区	Xuzhou	779	212	4615.69	2315.80	5888.95	488.16
常州市区	Changzhou	3746	495	7997.81	4304.61	11086.35	646.19
苏州市区	Suzhou	4358	932	11988.01	5998.26	11725.75	758.36
南通市区	Nantong	1515	200	3367.16	1685.69	4688.23	332.71
连云港市区	Lianyungang	798	77	2708.96	1436.46	3627.12	323.48
淮安市区	Huaian	1481	131	2138.44	913.41	4623.62	301.67
盐城市区	Yancheng	1204	192	2298.20	1249.27	3791.86	202.25
扬州市区	Yangzhou	1385	374	2891.00	1514.09	5775.55	334.19
镇江市区	Zhenjiang	906	146	2465.13	1265.82	3464.56	256.80
泰州市区	Taizhou	1210	129	2711.41	1405.59	5394.22	407.02
宿迁市区	Suqian	643	80	1338.15	595.83	1185.78	156.38

18－13 主要城市工业总产值（2016 年）
Gross Output Value of Industry of Major Cities(2016)

单位:亿元 (100 million yuan)

城市 City		工业总产值 Tatal Output Value of Industry	内资企业 Inner Funded Enterprises	外商港澳台投资企业 Foreign, Hong Kong, Macao and Taiwan Funded Enterprises	#国有控股企业 State-owned Share Holding Enterprises	#大中型企业 Large and Medium-sized Enterprises	#制造业 Manufacturing
南京市区	Nanjing	12945.02	7554.24	5390.78	4920.80	8824.62	12654.34
无锡市区	Wuxi	6388.09	2805.23	3582.86	537.95	4269.48	6321.33
徐州市区	Xuzhou	5701.27	4999.47	701.80	860.44	4286.46	5379.14
常州市区	Changzhou	10733.40	7127.29	3606.11	400.60	6699.83	10607.49
苏州市区	Suzhou	12046.53	3643.57	8402.96	304.54	8786.00	11847.14
南通市区	Nantong	4771.88	2719.32	2052.55	437.11	2766.38	4679.92
连云港市区	Lianyungang	3663.54	2453.97	1209.57	340.15	2594.41	3547.13
淮安市区	Huaian	4557.09	3522.15	1034.94	331.19	1807.91	4406.12
盐城市区	Yancheng	3932.36	2450.59	1481.76	178.16	2469.97	3878.79
扬州市区	Yangzhou	5918.50	4193.99	1724.51	551.96	3936.22	5803.45
镇江市区	Zhenjiang	3421.62	1869.55	1552.07	461.47	2507.00	3297.97
泰州市区	Taizhou	5489.57	4321.77	1167.80	445.26	3016.22	5403.02
宿迁市区	Suqian	1267.78	1031.40	236.38	65.04	736.17	1254.64

18－14 主要城市财政、金融（2016年）

Government Revenue and Expenditures of Major Cities(2016)

单位:亿元 (100 million yuan)

城市 City		一般公共预算收入 General Public Budget Revenue	#税收收入 Taxes	一般公共预算支出 General Public Budget Expenditure	存款余额 Deposits Balance	#住户存款 Household Deposits	贷款余额 Loans Balance
南京市区	Nanjing	1142.60	956.62	1173.84	27633.55	5894.47	21681.28
无锡市区	Wuxi	536.44	423.62	523.68	8688.75	2829.11	6300.99
徐州市区	Xuzhou	268.56	201.42	350.13	3372.86	1649.21	2383.41
常州市区	Changzhou	421.29	336.45	438.67	7546.00	2888.34	5244.21
苏州市区	Suzhou	919.82	805.59	888.72	15705.43	4025.00	13993.25
南通市区	Nantong	263.54	201.73	294.55	5064.90	2005.85	3302.70
连云港市区	Lianyungang	144.91	115.24	217.35	1743.70	470.61	1480.37
淮安市区	Huaian	233.75	169.45	322.87	2298.81	889.05	1722.04
盐城市区	Yancheng	198.42	156.94	299.37	2835.08	1072.21	2108.63
扬州市区	Yangzhou	235.63	173.45	306.71	3724.09	1632.92	2548.23
镇江市区	Zhenjiang	154.48	114.07	191.74	2457.48	748.20	1487.41
泰州市区	Taizhou	174.41	138.43	226.10	2742.07	1053.58	1952.97
宿迁市区	Suqian	101.24	80.91	170.41	1125.67	375.58	953.40

18－15 主要城市贸易、外经(2016年)

Domestic Trade and Foreign Economy of Major Cities(2016)

城市 City		社会消费品零售总额(亿元) Total Retail Sales of Consumer Goods (100 million yuan)	进出口总额(亿美元) Total Imports and Exports (USD 100 million)	出口 Exports	进口 Imports	实际使用外资(亿美元) Actual Use of Foreign Capital (USD 100 million)	星级饭店数(个) Star Class Hotel (unit)
南京市区	Nanjing	5088.20	502.14	295.94	206.20	34.79	79
无锡市区	Wuxi	1787.14	462.28	279.70	182.58	21.99	22
徐州市区	Xuzhou	1655.21	35.45	29.78	5.66	9.31	59
常州市区	Changzhou	1899.81	267.54	201.14	66.40	21.64	31
苏州市区	Suzhou	2558.50	1432.59	846.31	586.28	33.12	62
南通市区	Nantong	1029.13	172.29	119.11	53.18	9.96	28
连云港市区	Lianyungang	544.44	61.23	29.43	31.81	4.29	34
淮安市区	Huaian	739.14	25.98	18.92	7.06	7.80	32
盐城市区	Yancheng	730.21	54.87	25.45	29.41	4.51	11
扬州市区	Yangzhou	928.61	70.09	55.20	14.89	9.75	37
镇江市区	Zhenjiang	638.23	66.07	38.87	27.20	6.90	9
泰州市区	Taizhou	556.91	45.64	30.16	15.48	7.86	12
宿迁市区	Suqian	301.98	12.65	8.82	3.84	1.21	13

18-16 主要城市邮电、电力(2016年)
Post and Telecommunication Service and Power Consumption of Major Cities(2016)

城市 City		邮电业务收入(亿元) Revenue from Posts and Telecommunication Services (100 million yuan)	固定电话用户(万户) Telephones (10000 Subscribers)	年末移动电话用户(万户) Mobile Telephones (10000 Subscribers)	互联网宽带接入用户(万户) Internet Service (10000 Subscribers)	全年用电量(亿千瓦时) Power Consumption (100 million kW·h)	#城乡居民生活用电 Urban and Rural Residents Power Consumption
南京市区	Nanjing	203.16	243.50	1114.72	373.66	524.79	76.45
无锡市区	Wuxi	106.51	95.45	528.57	178.33	301.50	35.34
徐州市区	Xuzhou	41.86	61.30	403.30	105.26	204.08	23.20
常州市区	Changzhou	56.43	104.64	452.62	186.67	357.18	36.12
苏州市区	Suzhou	188.75	139.25	916.79	240.70	607.00	58.10
南通市区	Nantong	67.53	63.83	331.38	43.11	151.50	19.73
连云港市区	Lianyungang	26.32	42.18	231.40	68.22	63.68	8.89
淮安市区	Huaian	12.10	54.19	172.80	29.03	118.22	29.98
盐城市区	Yancheng	28.84	37.81	253.29	70.11	107.02	16.29
扬州市区	Yangzhou	76.60	74.81	164.61	57.83	132.73	20.99
镇江市区	Zhenjiang	18.10	33.53	132.19	46.99	116.56	10.82
泰州市区	Taizhou	21.71	37.79	192.16	57.19	84.13	12.83
宿迁市区	Suqian	15.45	15.67	153.55	42.50	78.36	8.92

18-17 主要城市文教、科技、卫生(2016年)
Culture, Education, Science and Technology and Public Health of Major Cities(2016)

城市 City		高等学校在校学生数(万人) Number of Students Enrollement in Regular Institutions of High Education (10000 persons)	专利申请受理量(件) Applications Accepted (unit)	公共图书馆图书藏量(千册) Total Volume of Collections of Public Libraries (1000 volumes)	卫生机构数(个) Number of Health Care Institutions (unit)	卫生机构床位数(万张) Number of Beds in Health Care Institutions (10000 units)	执业(助理)医师(万人) Practitioner Doctors (Assistant) (10000 persons)
南京市区	Nanjing	82.78	65198	19886	2383	4.99	2.53
无锡市区	Wuxi	10.23	45782	3755	1281	2.63	1.14
徐州市区	Xuzhou	14.08	14639	1628	1571	2.96	1.05
常州市区	Changzhou	12.34	42425	4102	1015	2.24	1.06
苏州市区	Suzhou	16.12	64855	10940	1514	3.48	1.39
南通市区	Nantong	9.48	18101	2085	991	1.68	0.76
连云港市区	Lianyungang	3.86	6041	1472	1395	1.26	0.61
淮安市区	Huaian	6.95	11817	2173	1261	1.83	0.83
盐城市区	Yancheng	6.87	13611	1945	1044	1.42	0.67
扬州市区	Yangzhou	7.44	15802	2717	1045	1.33	0.64
镇江市区	Zhenjiang	8.75	15994	1935	420	0.85	0.41
泰州市区	Taizhou	5.92	16893	1523	640	0.99	0.44
宿迁市区	Suqian	1.99	3608	580	671	0.88	0.33

18－18　主要城市居民收支情况（2016 年）

Household Income and Expenditure of Major Cities(2016)

单位:元 (yuan)

城市 City		城市常住居民人均可支配收入 Per Capita Disposable Income of Urban Residents	城市常住居民人均消费性支出 Per Capita Living Expenditure of Urban Residents	食品烟酒 Food, Tobacco and Wine	衣着 Clothing Articles	居住 Residence	生活用品及服务 Articles for Daily Use and Services
南京市区	Nanjing	49997	29772	7642	2192	6514	1792
无锡市区	Wuxi	46979	29332	8259	2432	6180	1593
徐州市区	Xuzhou	31763	20963	6068	1545	3585	1626
常州市区	Changzhou	46611	27159	7395	2043	5603	1673
苏州市区	Suzhou	54200	33497	9077	2036	8317	1669
南通市区	Nantong	41628	24382	7064	1761	5728	1446
连云港市区	Lianyungang	30120	18700	5416	1655	3977	1420
淮安市区	Huaian	31221	16474	4941	1538	3057	1195
盐城市区	Yancheng	34005	19727	5808	1661	3512	1296
扬州市区	Yangzhou	38475	25918	8003	2059	5015	1412
镇江市区	Zhenjiang	41324	25717	7300	2026	5302	1507
泰州市区	Taizhou	37459	22680	6700	1913	5259	1189
宿迁市区	Suqian	25095	15578	5253	1204	2776	1012

18－18　续表　Continued

单位:元 (yuan)

城市 City		交通通信 Transport and Communication	教育文化娱乐 Education, Culture and Recreation	医疗保健 Healthcare and Medical Services	其他用品和服务 Other Goods and Services	人均住房建筑面积(平方米) Per Capita Construction Floor Space of Residential Building (sq. m)	居民消费价格指数(上年=100) Consumer Price Index (preceding year=100)
南京市区	Nanjing	3710	5311	1734	877	36.7	102.7
无锡市区	Wuxi	4305	3787	1800	976	42.5	102.3
徐州市区	Xuzhou	3002	2234	2280	623	33.8	102.3
常州市区	Changzhou	4204	3832	1718	691	45.4	102.5
苏州市区	Suzhou	5952	4244	1285	917	38.6	102.7
南通市区	Nantong	3542	2529	1580	732	43.0	102.3
连云港市区	Lianyungang	1968	2366	1359	539	46.6	102.1
淮安市区	Huaian	1636	2544	1142	421	43.0	102.2
盐城市区	Yancheng	3514	2068	1115	753	41.6	102.1
扬州市区	Yangzhou	2971	4135	1484	839	43.2	102.4
镇江市区	Zhenjiang	3746	3824	1104	908	40.8	102.2
泰州市区	Taizhou	2877	2684	1368	690	50.0	102.1
宿迁市区	Suqian	1484	2659	971	219	45.6	102.0

18－19 市辖区主要指标（2016 年）

市辖区	Municipal District	年末户籍人口（万人）Registered Population at Year-end (10000 persons)	土地面积（平方公里）Land Area (sq. m)	地区生产总值（亿元）Gross Domestic Product (100 million yuan)	#第二产业 Secondary Industry	#第三产业 Tertiary Industry
南京市	**Nanjing City**					
玄武区	Xuanwu District	47.87	75	590.20	18.83	571.37
秦淮区	Qinhuai District	69.46	49	690.22	54.81	635.41
建邺区	Jianye District	31.59	83	325.47	51.07	274.40
鼓楼区	Gulou District	92.49	53	1123.03	84.93	1038.10
浦口区	Pukou District	66.69	910	820.34	394.12	384.90
栖霞区	Qixia District	46.70	395	927.23	565.87	353.76
雨花台区	Yuhuatai District	26.92	132	444.69	74.70	369.14
江宁区	Jiangning District	102.52	1563	1680.52	892.56	727.08
六合区	Luhe District	90.89	1471	804.54	421.44	321.35
溧水区	Lishui District	43.37	1064	624.96	328.53	256.38
高淳区	Gaochun District	44.29	790	573.73	285.61	247.99
无锡市	**Wuxi City**					
锡山区	Xishan District	44.33	399	708.25	368.54	322.26
惠山区	Huishan District	46.83	325	722.40	427.18	278.45
滨湖区	Binhu District	49.26	628	829.07	364.37	460.49
梁溪区	Liangxi District	77.23	71	1071.30	170.30	901.00
新吴区	Xinwu District	35.41	220	1408.01	883.88	521.40
徐州市	**Xuzhou City**					
鼓楼区	Gulou District	31.84	66	232.40	49.50	182.75
云龙区	Yunlong District	34.95	120	279.27	31.59	246.92
贾汪区	Jiawang District	52.56	620	284.25	142.30	119.72
泉山区	Quanshan District	57.03	100	519.60	77.16	442.03
铜山区	Tongshan District	131.71	1871	974.81	505.35	391.47
常州市	**Changzhou City**					
天宁区	Tianning District	46.71	155	694.51	196.42	488.93
钟楼区	Zhonglou District	42.57	133	649.73	217.76	428.90
新北区	Xinbei District	56.30	509	1155.03	606.44	530.51
武进区	Wujin District	94.32	1065	1968.99	1074.23	854.54
金坛区	Jintan District	55.04	976	600.02	302.26	263.93
苏州市	**Suzhou City**					
虎丘区	Huqiu District	37.53	332	1066.41	673.28	390.84
吴中区	Wuzhong District	64.73	2231	1010.72	469.99	517.60

Major Indicators of Municipal Districts(2016)

一般公共预算收入(亿元) General Public Budget Revenue (100 million yuan)	固定资产投资(亿元) Investment in Fixed Assets (100 million yuan)	#房地产开发 Real Estate Development	社会消费品零售总额(亿元) Total Retail Sales of Consumer Goods (100 million yuan)	进出口总额(亿美元) Total Imports and Exports (USD 100 million)	#出口 Exports	实际使用外资(万美元) Actual Use of Foreign Capital (USD 10000)
48.91	133.93	90.66	475.17	64.00	28.78	22585
70.14	226.19	104.62	925.67	80.95	57.03	9022
90.84	323.86	225.82	198.58	10.11	7.29	27028
94.12	251.44	132.59	884.84	45.10	29.54	28042
109.62	1070.04	312.59	302.25	13.39	11.37	49203
112.51	603.66	318.62	239.16	104.12	42.60	52657
69.72	242.01	179.27	366.62	31.07	21.71	27873
210.25	874.59	253.22	469.43	113.84	74.51	78755
98.57	485.86	135.24	381.48	18.59	10.96	37378
51.28	552.33	47.49	193.53	6.31	5.51	19219
25.45	463.75	24.62	187.70	6.19	4.62	10476
72.24	713.88	67.89	164.65	42.63	33.46	35052
81.41	656.53	79.34	176.32	26.98	23.30	30266
92.78	600.39	343.01	259.78	23.77	17.80	25157
42.43	197.59	98.72	903.55	22.53	20.28	3106
160.54	128.46	74.87	282.83	346.36	184.87	126366
15.72	285.13	84.92	396.79	0.31	0.29	4079
21.54	294.90	76.73	403.11	2.47	2.28	11602
21.74	250.62	9.27	69.99	3.06	3.00	7263
27.79	274.54	97.85	527.99	2.85	2.79	10373
68.36	783.45	35.90	242.12	3.69	2.99	14924
46.82	381.44	67.00	476.28	28.35	24.62	26040
37.21	350.90	88.94	348.31	25.14	23.40	18912
102.58	807.46	83.51	292.33	100.74	70.29	85005
147.52	1029.46	120.18	530.51	94.77	68.36	85037
43.38	403.68	43.01	252.38	16.72	13.20	32003
129.80	530.06	219.81	251.50	340.18	227.66	60846
134.43	561.67	297.73	373.28	76.60	51.76	36055

市　辖　区 Municipal District		年末户籍人口（万人）Registered Population at Year-end (10000 persons)	土地面积（平方公里）Land Area (sq. m)	地区生产总值（亿元）Gross Domestic Product (100 million yuan)	#第二产业 Secondary Industry	#第三产业 Tertiary Industry
相城区	Xiangcheng District	41.33	490	633.75	308.66	313.71
姑苏区	Gushu District	73.21	83	622.30	66.32	555.98
吴江区	Wujiang District	82.45	1237	1628.33	834.85	750.67
南通市	**Nantong City**					
崇川区	Chongchuan District	52.61	160	682.69	170.45	512.11
港闸区	Gangzha District	19.40	152	337.27	190.60	144.80
通州区	Tongzhou District	126.42	267	1026.66	507.36	462.89
连云港市	**Lianyungang City**					
连云区	Lianyun District	17.74	797	126.81	47.39	73.89
海州区	Haizhou Distric	76.64	701	310.73	87.38	205.92
赣榆区	Ganyu Distric	120.30	1514	519.21	245.56	197.10
淮安市	**Huaian City**					
淮安区	Huaian District	118.45	1452	448.61	172.62	211.56
淮阴区	Huaiyin District	93.36	1307	435.72	182.39	184.28
清江浦区	Qingjiangpu District	55.99	310	400.30	94.27	295.78
洪泽区	Hongze District	37.88	1273	255.31	103.71	117.97
盐城市	**Yancheng City**					
亭湖区	Tinghu District	70.66	800	392.71	141.40	218.07
盐都区	Yandu District	71.49	1015	443.62	214.13	185.84
大丰区	Dafeng District	71.65	3008	579.07	223.77	277.61
扬州市	**Yangzhou City**					
广陵区	Guangling District	49.46	335	657.27	301.26	346.64
邗江区	Hanjiang District	60.06	553	743.01	295.44	426.54
江都区	Jiangdu District	105.94	1330	939.63	453.94	426.03
镇江市	**Zhenjiang City**					
京口区	Jingkou District	31.40	125	449.24	121.70	326.19
润州区	Runzhou District	24.41	124	369.00	131.76	235.68
丹徒区	Dantu District	29.11	617	371.22	194.42	158.27
泰州市	**Taizhou City**					
海陵区	Hailing District	42.91	237	516.80	240.25	268.96
高港区	Gaogang District	26.29	287	423.06	245.74	165.32
姜堰区	Jiangyan District	78.66	928	583.19	264.44	278.65
宿迁市	**Suqian City**					
宿城区	Sucheng District	94.81	917	286.20	109.98	154.26
宿豫区	Suyu District	66.54	1237	252.13	146.23	79.17

一般公共预算收入(亿元) General Public Budget Revenues (100 million yuan)	固定资产投资(亿元) Investment in Fixed Assets (100 million yuan)	#房地产开发 Real Estate Development	社会消费品零售总额(亿元) Total Retail Sales of Consumer Goods (100 million yuan)	进出口总额(亿美元) Total Imports and Exports (USD 100 million)	#出口 Exports	实际使用外资(万美元) Actual Use of Foreign Capital (USD 10000)
80.11	476.21	227.66	223.09	41.56	30.78	19107
50.00	230.32	118.29	836.13	20.08	17.85	530
165.25	681.02	289.51	467.66	211.35	140.20	61640
67.62	331.74	105.16	398.30	54.78	34.11	11476
36.50	309.30	153.70	134.36	27.09	20.63	11569
72.22	681.49	30.50	341.12	37.33	33.69	24384
9.43	303.88	16.30	72.34	11.66	4.26	3664
31.43	329.82	75.39	270.86	10.27	8.74	6937
25.02	372.00	25.46	172.46	5.13	4.04	9605
33.44	354.20	49.07	172.23	2.43	2.31	14483
40.58	339.56	35.01	119.08	2.20	1.60	15777
50.08	376.05	89.30	285.87	3.60	3.11	6870
23.24	202.65	12.50	94.03	1.24	1.13	15063
35.31	392.50	49.01	251.14	5.60	5.11	3404
38.13	354.81	25.58	208.79	6.29	3.32	6835
59.26	453.80	38.98	172.77	16.21	8.74	14456
40.03	443.71	94.14	288.35	13.12	12.18	10060
63.97	592.53	148.92	287.09	19.57	16.81	20784
55.15	709.43	51.86	252.44	13.95	10.55	11024
18.06	434.74	58.52	288.83	13.33	10.13	6937
20.66	427.57	122.43	177.85	5.29	4.41	6180
25.70	354.53	15.52	68.42	5.64	5.18	10728
39.05	273.61	51.34	243.08	12.99	10.73	10470
40.44	380.16	12.30	49.33	14.56	6.79	26651
35.60	494.82	30.72	172.41	9.55	8.26	13702
23.02	228.49	52.52	178.64	4.03	2.66	5237
23.82	252.94	19.66	53.69	3.50	3.26	4294

18－20 市辖区法人单位数（2016 年）
Number of Corporations of Municipal District(2016)

单位:个 (unit)

市辖区 Municipal District	合计 Total	企业 Enterprises	事业单位 Institutions	机关 Agencies& Organizations	社会团体 Social Organizations	民办非企业单位 Non-enterprise Units Run by NGO	其他组织机构 Others
南京市 Nanjing City							
玄武区 Xuanwu District	19012	17686	318	122	399	326	161
秦淮区 Qinhuai District	31050	29434	364	105	275	558	314
建邺区 Jianye District	15165	14139	223	111	208	241	243
鼓楼区 Gulou District	34116	31817	658	240	697	359	345
浦口区 Pukou District	18864	17416	272	87	107	297	685
栖霞区 Qixia District	20349	18970	201	92	122	635	329
雨花台区 Yuhuatai District	9992	9408	141	66	82	193	102
江宁区 Jiangning District	32726	30289	374	86	108	675	1194
六合区 Luhe District	16766	15272	341	97	83	93	880
溧水区 Lishui District	11206	9762	305	75	75	57	932
高淳区 Gaochun District	8435	7217	252	102	129	76	659
无锡市 Wuxi City							
锡山区 Xishan District	18757	17917	199	76	125	88	352
惠山区 Huishan District	23975	22807	312	73	172	153	458
滨湖区 Binhu District	26369	24892	488	150	195	258	386
梁溪区 Liangxi District	42037	40103	587	172	405	477	293
新吴区 Xinwu District	22233	21753	151	16	33	70	210
徐州市 Xuzhou City							
鼓楼区 Gulou District	12321	11742	142	55	45	223	114
云龙区 Yunlong District	17059	15683	330	160	249	326	311
贾汪区 Jiawang District	5743	4598	218	60	123	123	621
泉山区 Quanshan District	17886	16630	306	95	290	324	241
铜山区 Tongshan District	13641	11022	412	105	250	242	1610
常州市 Changzhou City							
天宁区 Tianning District	22051	20390	269	52	741	196	403
钟楼区 Zhonglou District	19528	18011	312	67	639	260	239
新北区 Xinbei District	34672	32717	277	124	730	167	657
武进区 Wujin District	44623	40885	574	163	1440	221	1340
金坛区 Jintan District	11370	9645	351	74	195	161	944
苏州市 Suzhou City							
虎丘区 Huqiu District	27021	26066	250	54	100	256	295

单位:个 (unit)

市辖区 Municipal District	合计 Total	企业 Enterprises	事业单位 Institutions	机关 Agencies& Organizations	社会团体 Social Organizations	民办非企业单位 Non-enterprise Units Run by NGO	其他组织机构 Others
吴中区 Wuzhong District	47380	45860	370	108	198	96	748
相城区 Xiangcheng District	25708	24820	197	66	92	56	477
姑苏区 Gushu District	53058	50842	475	141	577	497	526
吴江区 Wujiang District	50539	48613	488	101	312	120	905
南通市 Nantong City							
崇川区 Chongchuan District	27678	25821	407	152	535	516	247
港闸区 Gangzha District	6990	6305	153	54	59	284	135
通州区 Tongzhou District	18852	16729	483	107	227	149	1157
连云港市 Lianyungang City							
连云区 Lianyun District	3778	3368	144	63	35	70	98
海州区 Haizhou Distric	21244	19778	366	122	190	180	608
赣榆区 Ganyu Distric	9791	7922	352	66	187	85	1179
淮安市 Huaian City							
淮安区 Huaian District	10658	8248	527	134	188	167	1394
淮阴区 Huaiyin District	10243	8155	495	117	222	142	1112
清江浦区 Qingjiangpu District	19635	17177	693	289	599	238	639
洪泽区 Hongze District	7234	5477	347	103	141	107	1059
盐城市 Yancheng City							
亭湖区 Tinghu District	18158	16886	453	117	124	204	374
盐都区 Yandu District	13840	12478	386	155	60	66	695
大丰区 Dafeng District	12480	10757	404	82	255	349	633
扬州市 Yangzhou City							
广陵区 Guangling District	17282	15664	364	156	280	314	504
邗江区 Hanjiang District	18456	16555	534	187	301	254	625
江都区 Jiangdu District	17252	14513	666	91	273	215	1494
镇江市 Zhenjiang City							
京口区 Jingkou District	11238	9990	330	63	504	196	155
润州区 Runzhou District	9705	8460	318	125	391	194	217
丹徒区 Dantu District	7955	6651	273	72	252	110	597
泰州市 Taizhou City							
海陵区 Hailing District	13800	11725	604	148	502	311	510
高港区 Gaogang District	7711	6693	228	64	156	127	443
姜堰区 Jiangyan District	12557	10094	418	75	190	340	1440
宿迁市 Suqian City							
宿城区 Sucheng District	12447	10191	495	181	603	253	724
宿豫区 Suyu District	7070	5464	329	113	167	119	878

18－21 市辖区人口、面积(2016年)

Population and Land Area of Municipal District(2016)

市辖区	Municipal District	年末户籍人口(万人) Registered Population at Year-end (10000 persons)	出生人口(人) Births (person)	死亡人口(人) Deaths (person)	年末总户数(万户) Total Households at Year-end (10000 household)	土地面积(平方公里) Land Area (sq. m)	人口密度(人/平方公里) Population Density (person/sq. m)
南京市浦口区	Nanjing Pukou District	66.69	10797	3166	22.73	910	846
南京市栖霞区	Nanjing Qixia District	46.70	5802	2435	16.25	395	1755
南京市雨花台区	Nanjing Yuhuatai District	26.92	3611	1295	9.82	132	3305
南京市江宁区	Nanjing Jiangning District	102.52	15157	5019	37.01	1563	778
南京市六合区	Nanjing Luhe District	90.89	9762	5854	29.96	1471	642
南京市溧水区	Nanjing Lishui District	43.37	6249	2870	15.32	1064	406
南京市高淳区	Nanjing Gaochun District	44.29	6619	3067	15.48	790	545
无锡市锡山区	Wuxi Xishan District	44.33	3960	3006	13.30	399	1765
无锡市惠山区	Wuxi Huishan District	46.83	4575	2481	14.64	325	2183
无锡市滨湖区	Wuxi Binhu District	49.26	5008	2738	18.90	628	1117
徐州市贾汪区	Xuzhou Jiawang District	52.56	3204	971	13.90	620	691
徐州市铜山区	Xuzhou Tongshan District	131.71	12765	3726	35.50	1871	561
常州市新北区	Changzhou Xinbei District	56.30	6721	3347	18.29	509	1355
常州市武进区	Changzhou Wujin District	94.32	9121	6190	33.28	1065	1352
常州市金坛区	Changzhou Jintan District	55.04	5092	3937	20.17	976	574
苏州市吴中区	Suzhou Wuzhong District	64.73	8656	3724	19.42	2231	504
苏州市相城区	Suzhou Xiangcheng District	41.33	5544	2573	12.90	490	1493
苏州市吴江区	Suzhou Wujiang District	82.45	8734	5759	25.89	1237	1051
南通市崇川区	Nantong Chongchuan District	52.61	4729	2778	19.20	160	4444
南通市港闸区	Nantong Gangzha District	19.40	1794	1636	7.52	152	1870
南通市通州区	Nantong Tongzhou District	126.42	9289	10922	50.16	1562	731
连云港市连云区	Lianyungang Lianyun District	17.74	1982	605	5.78	797	243
连云港市赣榆区	Lianyungang Ganyu District	120.30	13625	3025	34.23	1514	638
淮安市淮安区	Huaian Huaian District	118.45	11875	4523	32.87	1452	681
淮安市淮阴区	Huaian Huaiyin District	93.36	10916	2777	28.28	1307	598
淮安市洪泽区	Huaian Hongze District	37.88	3749	1608	11.80	1273	266
盐城市盐都区	Yancheng Yandu District	71.49	7813	5364	23.93	1015	628
盐城市大丰区	Yancheng Dafeng District	71.65	6493	5430	27.25	3008	233
扬州市邗江区	Yangzhou Hanjiang District	60.06	6501	3607	18.84	553	1248
扬州市江都区	Yangzhou Jiangdu District	105.94	7864	8912	35.16	1330	758
镇江市丹徒区	Zhenjiang Dantu District	29.11	2419	1916	10.35	617	500
泰州市海陵区	Taizhou Hailing District	42.91	3995	2678	15.73	237	2022
泰州市高港区	Taizhou Gaogang District	26.29	2480	2317	8.05	287	882
泰州市姜堰区	Taizhou Jiangyan District	78.66	7128	6894	26.82	928	787
宿迁市宿豫区	Suqian Suyu District	66.54	10559	2551	16.55	1237	505

18－22　市辖区就业人员(2016年)
Employment of Municipal District(2016)

单位:万人　　(10000 persons)

市辖区	Municipal District	就业人员 Employment	第一产业 Primary Industry	第二产业 Secondary Industry	第三产业 Tertiary Industry	私营企业就业人员 Employment in Private Enterprises	个体就业人员 Employment in Self-employed Individuals
南京市浦口区	Nanjing Pukou District	41.30	2.30	17.87	21.13	16.23	11.28
南京市栖霞区	Nanjing Qixia District	36.50	1.39	14.25	20.86	19.83	7.29
南京市雨花台区	Nanjing Yuhuatai District	21.70	0.46	3.83	17.41	11.17	6.89
南京市江宁区	Nanjing Jiangning District	74.50	6.58	34.65	33.27	36.01	19.06
南京市六合区	Nanjing Luhe District	49.10	6.12	23.59	19.39	22.47	9.16
南京市溧水区	Nanjing Lishui District	31.26	3.90	16.30	11.06	14.26	4.71
南京市高淳区	Nanjing Gaochun District	31.28	5.95	16.35	8.98	17.42	3.50
无锡市锡山区	Wuxi Xishan District	45.28	1.70	30.03	13.55	22.20	6.66
无锡市惠山区	Wuxi Huishan District	45.36	1.42	28.75	15.19	29.23	6.64
无锡市滨湖区	Wuxi Binhu District	34.83	0.47	14.96	19.40	25.65	5.34
徐州市贾汪区	Xuzhou Jiawang District	22.82	8.40	6.91	7.51	7.08	2.21
徐州市铜山区	Xuzhou Tongshan District	56.27	21.10	17.39	17.78	13.09	5.64
常州市新北区	Changzhou Xinbei District	43.65	2.39	24.25	17.01	30.73	9.83
常州市武进区	Changzhou Wujin District	88.96	7.92	52.15	28.89	61.12	15.48
常州市金坛区	Changzhou Jintan District	37.07	5.76	18.69	12.62	18.08	5.97
苏州市吴中区	Suzhou Wuzhong District	74.39	5.14	43.08	26.17	52.81	18.17
苏州市相城区	Suzhou Xiangcheng District	49.20	1.01	30.88	17.31	31.84	11.75
苏州市吴江区	Suzhou Wujiang District	86.18	3.74	53.57	28.87	44.75	12.53
南通市崇川区	Nantong Chongchuan District	37.00	0.00	7.30	29.70	16.26	14.23
南通市港闸区	Nantong Gangzha District	16.75	0.45	9.80	6.50	7.93	3.32
南通市通州区	Nantong Tongzhou District	69.80	16.40	33.40	20.00	21.80	12.32
连云港市连云区	Lianyungang Lianyun District	7.81	0.37	2.17	5.27	4.90	2.34
连云港市赣榆区	Lianyungang Ganyu District	57.46	18.54	22.10	16.82	8.62	4.60
淮安市淮安区	Huaian Huaian District	57.14	18.98	17.99	20.17	11.36	5.19
淮安市淮阴区	Huaian Huaiyin District	45.86	15.11	14.55	16.20	8.88	6.22
淮安市洪泽区	Huaian Hongze District	20.25	5.86	7.01	7.38	8.45	4.19
盐城市盐都区	Yancheng Yandu District	39.96	8.00	15.75	16.21	11.17	5.72
盐城市大丰区	Yancheng Dafeng District	46.01	11.72	15.70	18.59	17.20	6.35
扬州市邗江区	Yangzhou Hanjiang District	37.38	0.75	15.78	20.85	21.02	9.76
扬州市江都区	Yangzhou Jiangdu District	61.08	10.93	27.33	22.82	33.52	7.95
镇江市丹徒区	Zhenjiang Dantu District	19.87	3.72	8.25	7.90	9.22	5.16
泰州市海陵区	Taizhou Hailing District	28.90	0.90	11.10	16.90	12.96	6.77
泰州市高港区	Taizhou Gaogang District	15.10	2.50	7.00	5.60	8.76	4.58
泰州市姜堰区	Taizhou Jiangyan District	43.70	10.50	17.10	16.10	20.92	5.51
宿迁市宿豫区	Suqian Suyu District	36.14	10.33	13.21	12.60	7.84	4.82

18-23 市辖区地区生产总值(2016 年)

Gross Domestic Product of Municipal District(2016)

市辖区	Municipal District	地区生产总值(亿元) Gross Domestic Product (100 million yuan)	第一产业 Primary Industry	第二产业 Secondary Industry	第三产业 Tertiary Industry	#工业 Industry	地区生产总值指数(上年=100) GDP Index (preceding year =100)
南京市浦口区	Nanjing Pukou District	885.06	41.32	424.47	419.27	377.63	110.6
南京市栖霞区	Nanjing Qixia District	1302.54	7.60	866.07	428.87	810.71	109.0
南京市雨花台区	Nanjing Yuhuatai District	498.96	0.85	103.53	394.58	74.90	108.6
南京市江宁区	Nanjing Jiangning District	1747.79	60.88	892.67	794.24	765.18	109.5
南京市六合区	Nanjing Luhe District	1079.64	61.75	669.47	348.42	611.15	108.0
南京市溧水区	Nanjing Lishui District	642.43	40.05	328.58	273.80	279.61	109.3
南京市高淳区	Nanjing Gaochun District	587.05	40.13	285.68	261.24	225.05	108.0
无锡市锡山区	Wuxi Xishan District	708.25	17.45	368.54	322.26	316.05	107.7
无锡市惠山区	Wuxi Huishan District	722.40	16.77	427.18	278.45	392.29	107.7
无锡市滨湖区	Wuxi Binhu District	829.07	4.21	364.37	460.49	318.39	108.4
徐州市贾汪区	Xuzhou Jiawang District	284.25	22.23	142.30	119.72	137.01	108.5
徐州市铜山区	Xuzhou Tongshan District	974.81	77.99	505.35	391.47	448.92	108.0
常州市新北区	Changzhou Xinbei District	1155.03	18.08	606.44	530.51	580.33	109.5
常州市武进区	Changzhou Wujin District	1968.99	40.22	1074.23	854.54	1025.22	108.0
常州市金坛区	Changzhou Jintan District	600.02	33.83	302.26	263.93	253.35	112.8
苏州市吴中区	Suzhou Wuzhong District	1010.72	23.13	469.99	517.60	426.99	107.6
苏州市相城区	Suzhou Xiangcheng District	633.75	11.38	308.66	313.71	243.92	107.1
苏州市吴江区	Suzhou Wujiang District	1628.33	42.81	834.85	750.67	783.74	107.5
南通市崇川区	Nantong Chongchuan District	682.69	0.13	170.45	512.11	115.82	109.0
南通市港闸区	Nantong Gangzha District	337.27	1.87	190.60	144.80	160.83	109.0
南通市通州区	Nantong Tongzhou District	1026.66	56.41	507.36	462.89	424.85	109.3
连云港市连云区	Lianyungang Lianyun District	126.81	5.53	47.39	73.89	40.05	107.5
连云港市赣榆区	Lianyungang Ganyu District	519.21	76.55	245.56	197.10	192.63	108.2
淮安市淮安区	Huaian Huaian District	448.61	64.43	172.62	211.56	118.53	109.9
淮安市淮阴区	Huaian Huaiyin District	435.72	69.05	182.39	184.28	156.51	109.8
淮安市洪泽区	Huaian Hongze District	255.31	33.63	103.71	117.97	89.26	108.9
盐城市盐都区	Yancheng Yandu District	443.62	43.65	214.13	185.84	182.38	109.3
盐城市大丰区	Yancheng Dafeng District	579.07	77.69	223.77	277.61	192.89	109.5
扬州市邗江区	Yangzhou Hanjiang District	743.01	21.03	295.44	426.54	242.04	109.6
扬州市江都区	Yangzhou Jiangdu District	939.63	59.65	453.94	426.03	384.55	109.2
镇江市丹徒区	Zhenjiang Dantu District	371.22	18.53	194.42	158.27	183.82	109.3
泰州市海陵区	Taizhou Hailing District	516.80	7.59	240.25	268.96	202.76	110.0
泰州市高港区	Taizhou Gaogang District	423.06	12.00	245.74	165.32	225.26	111.2
泰州市姜堰区	Taizhou Jiangyan District	583.19	40.10	264.44	278.65	216.02	110.0
宿迁市宿豫区	Suqian Suyu District	252.13	26.73	146.23	79.17	129.82	109.2

18－24 市辖区投资、财政收支(2016年)

Investment, Government Revenue and Expenditure of Municipal District (2016)

单位:亿元 (100 million yuan)

市辖区	Municipal District	固定资产投资 Investment in Fixed Assets	房地产开发投资 Investment in Real Estate Development	#住宅 Resdential Building	一般公共预算收入 General Public Budget Revenue	#税收收入 Taxes	一般公共预算支出 General Public Budget Expenditure
南京市浦口区	Nanjing Pukou District	1070.04	312.59	240.61	109.62	100.19	98.47
南京市栖霞区	Nanjing Qixia District	603.66	318.62	279.03	112.51	102.68	65.59
南京市雨花台区	Nanjing Yuhuatai District	242.01	179.27	118.04	69.72	63.83	55.32
南京市江宁区	Nanjing Jiangning District	874.59	253.22	192.69	210.25	188.00	180.62
南京市六合区	Nanjing Luhe District	485.86	135.24	115.94	98.57	86.29	86.49
南京市溧水区	Nanjing Lishui District	552.33	47.49	33.61	51.28	41.04	67.87
南京市高淳区	Nanjing Gaochun District	463.75	24.62	17.93	25.45	21.51	46.84
无锡市锡山区	Wuxi Xishan District	713.88	67.89	52.79	72.24	64.03	73.13
无锡市惠山区	Wuxi Huishan District	656.53	79.34	61.06	81.41	66.79	77.13
无锡市滨湖区	Wuxi Binhu District	600.39	343.01	199.38	92.78	73.77	66.89
徐州市贾汪区	Xuzhou Jiawang District	250.62	9.27	7.53	21.74	16.93	32.95
徐州市铜山区	Xuzhou Tongshan District	783.45	35.90	23.76	68.36	53.63	108.00
常州市新北区	Changzhou Xinbei District	807.46	83.51	68.16	102.58	87.68	58.22
常州市武进区	Changzhou Wujin District	1029.46	120.18	92.75	147.52	122.36	145.44
常州市金坛区	Changzhou Jintan District	403.68	43.01	28.82	43.38	38.23	52.98
苏州市吴中区	Suzhou Wuzhong District	561.67	297.73	242.10	134.43	122.19	108.04
苏州市相城区	Suzhou Xiangcheng District	476.21	227.66	173.33	80.11	72.14	56.42
苏州市吴江区	Suzhou Wujiang District	681.02	289.51	222.79	165.25	144.99	159.29
南通市崇川区	Nantong Chongchuan District	331.74	105.16	68.94	67.62	57.62	44.06
南通市港闸区	Nantong Gangzha District	309.30	153.70	105.63	36.50	32.43	22.65
南通市通州区	Nantong Tongzhou District	681.49	30.50	20.13	72.22	54.15	85.75
连云港市连云区	Lianyungang Lianyun District	303.88	16.30	3.65	9.43	8.05	9.71
连云港市赣榆区	Lianyungang Ganyu District	372.00	25.46	20.27	25.02	21.27	60.22
淮安市淮安区	Huaian Huaian District	354.20	49.07	39.74	33.44	26.04	67.94
淮安市淮阴区	Huaian Huaiyin District	339.56	35.01	26.23	40.58	30.12	62.71
淮安市洪泽区	Huaian Hongze District	202.65	12.50	8.58	23.24	18.42	41.48
盐城市盐都区	Yancheng Yandu District	354.81	25.58	25.51	38.13	31.15	57.93
盐城市大丰区	Yancheng Dafeng District	453.80	38.98	23.68	59.26	47.55	89.38
扬州市邗江区	Yangzhou Hanjiang District	592.53	148.92	96.34	63.97	49.82	61.72
扬州市江都区	Yangzhou Jiangdu District	709.43	51.86	44.97	55.15	42.39	85.24
镇江市丹徒区	Zhenjiang Dantu District	354.53	15.52	11.81	25.70	22.07	29.24
泰州市海陵区	Taizhou Hailing District	273.61	51.34	39.00	39.05	31.89	28.82
泰州市高港区	Taizhou Gaogang District	380.16	12.30	9.24	40.44	33.25	35.50
泰州市姜堰区	Taizhou Jiangyan District	494.82	30.72	21.70	35.60	27.45	66.96
宿迁市宿豫区	Suqian Suyu District	252.94	19.66	15.87	23.82	17.99	41.08

18-25 市辖区规模以上工业产值(2016 年)

Gross Output Value of above Designated Size Industry of Municipal District (2016)

市辖区	Municipal District	规模以上工业企业个数(个) Number of Industrial Enterprises (unit)	工业总产值(亿元) Tatal Output Value of Industry (100 million yuan)	内资企业 Inner Funded Enterprises	港澳台商投资企业 Hong Kong, Macao and Taiwan Funded Enterprises	外商投资企业 Foreign Funded Enterprises
南京市浦口区	Nanjing Pukou District	349	1690.99	1215.40	303.04	172.55
南京市栖霞区	Nanjing Qixia District	207	3037.83	1139.59	224.21	1674.03
南京市雨花台区	Nanjing Yuhuatai District	55	259.58	253.98	3.44	2.17
南京市江宁区	Nanjing Jiangning District	658	2918.90	983.86	135.77	1799.28
南京市六合区	Nanjing Luhe District	487	2339.90	1671.16	162.00	506.74
南京市溧水区	Nanjing Lishui District	499	1087.89	898.74	112.32	76.83
南京市高淳区	Nanjing Gaochun District	331	939.19	831.48	58.58	49.13
无锡市锡山区	Wuxi Xishan District	637	1130.91	736.98	158.44	235.50
无锡市惠山区	Wuxi Huishan District	808	1225.78	858.88	238.93	127.97
无锡市滨湖区	Wuxi Binhu District	404	492.87	335.33	48.98	108.56
徐州市贾汪区	Xuzhou Jiawang District	171	728.33	637.66	72.13	18.54
徐州市铜山区	Xuzhou Tongshan District	416	3552.96	3329.60	95.81	127.55
常州市新北区	Changzhou Xinbei District	988	2837.18	1127.49	596.09	1113.59
常州市武进区	Changzhou Wujin District	1598	4676.51	3754.93	558.42	363.16
常州市金坛区	Changzhou Wujin District	448	1210.26	936.98	146.64	126.63
苏州市吴中区	Suzhou Wuzhong District	835	1226.49	559.55	191.66	475.27
苏州市相城区	Suzhou Xiangcheng District	742	1104.01	759.62	101.31	243.09
苏州市吴江区	Suzhou Wujiang District	1304	3116.81	1465.10	723.37	928.34
南通市崇川区	Nantong Chongchuan District	75	307.61	149.36	30.02	128.23
南通市港闸区	Nantong Gangzha District	232	541.85	319.20	83.57	139.08
南通市通州区	Nantong Tongzhou District	736	2142.58	1458.75	257.16	426.67
连云港市连云区	Lianyungang Lianyun District	49	113.09	75.68	11.19	26.21
连云港市赣榆区	Lianyungang Ganyu District	507	1636.15	1528.80	28.02	79.32
淮安市淮安区	Huaian Huaian District	368	840.48	777.03	43.28	20.18
淮安市淮阴区	Huaian Huaiyin District	453	1457.21	1351.27	27.94	78.00
淮安市洪泽区	Huaian Hongze District	329	727.03	653.49	58.09	15.44
盐城市盐都区	Yancheng Yandu District	370	1001.83	846.54	50.66	104.63
盐城市大丰区	Yancheng Dafeng District	435	944.76	802.09	39.53	103.15
扬州市邗江区	Yangzhou Hanjiang District	375	1325.14	1017.84	171.51	135.79
扬州市江都区	Yangzhou Jiangdu District	583	2239.45	1990.14	91.34	157.97
镇江市丹徒区	Zhenjiang Dantu District	356	1115.01	835.27	163.71	116.03
泰州市海陵区	Taizhou Hailing District	271	1349.91	1018.43	28.81	302.67
泰州市高港区	Taizhou Gaogang District	247	1994.38	1706.35	19.68	268.35
泰州市姜堰区	Taizhou Jiangyan District	521	1447.63	1279.05	49.88	118.71
宿迁市宿豫区	Suqian Suyu District	247	416.64	370.78	28.62	17.24

18－26 市辖区规模以上工业效益(2016年)

Economic Benefit of above Designated Size Industry of Municipal District (2016)

市辖区 Municipal District		资产合计(亿元) Total Assets (100 million yuan)	负债合计(亿元) Total Liabilities (100 million yuan)	主营业务收入(亿元) Revenue from principal Business (100 million yuan)	利润总额(亿元) Total Profits (100 million yuan)	从业人员年平均人数(万人) Annual Average Persons Employed (10000 persons)
南京市浦口区	Nanjing Pukou District	1435.85	787.58	1668.07	120.69	8.86
南京市栖霞区	Nanjing Qixia District	2618.18	1376.64	3043.67	136.95	11.88
南京市雨花台区	Nanjing Yuhuatai District	438.90	276.65	255.33	7.69	1.56
南京市江宁区	Nanjing Jiangning District	2523.54	1395.47	2355.38	271.72	18.32
南京市六合区	Nanjing Luhe District	2097.09	1061.73	2347.91	175.66	13.27
南京市溧水区	Nanjing Lishui District	709.34	421.12	1081.37	117.87	7.97
南京市高淳区	Nanjing Gaochun District	490.24	271.71	930.87	67.13	8.27
无锡市锡山区	Wuxi Xishan District	1247.88	613.34	1101.48	72.75	12.90
无锡市惠山区	Wuxi Huishan District	1109.93	662.62	1195.26	87.48	11.04
无锡市滨湖区	Wuxi Binhu District	664.28	293.78	476.48	43.61	6.24
徐州市贾汪区	Xuzhou Jiawang District	407.35	210.74	745.16	51.98	3.50
徐州市铜山区	Xuzhou Tongshan District	1438.77	523.13	3661.18	341.43	16.01
常州市新北区	Changzhou Xinbei District	2173.85	1177.69	2811.35	141.33	18.70
常州市武进区	Changzhou Wujin District	3565.80	1820.36	4945.20	280.02	37.12
常州市金坛区	Changzhou Jintan District	1024.77	678.93	1250.88	97.26	9.45
苏州市吴中区	Suzhou Wuzhong District	1365.02	717.37	1214.98	70.50	18.95
苏州市相城区	Suzhou Xiangcheng District	1109.15	601.85	1065.33	52.01	15.71
苏州市吴江区	Suzhou Wujiang District	3303.50	1837.93	3016.07	164.94	39.26
南通市崇川区	Nantong Chongchuan District	454.39	223.39	310.78	27.96	2.80
南通市港闸区	Nantong Gangzha District	478.32	229.15	514.70	37.80	4.06
南通市通州区	Nantong Tongzhou District	1059.38	506.09	2113.40	150.13	16.80
连云港市连云区	Lianyungang Lianyun District	105.41	57.88	110.07	3.11	3.11
连云港市赣榆区	Lianyungang Ganyu District	589.17	207.87	1648.51	110.88	110.88
淮安市淮安区	Huaian Huaian District	218.95	112.03	842.44	30.53	4.46
淮安市淮阴区	Huaian Huaiyin District	525.47	178.20	1438.61	102.49	6.34
淮安市洪泽区	Huaian Hongze District	388.80	195.36	717.64	43.64	4.40
盐城市盐都区	Yancheng Yandu District	454.43	165.04	985.65	51.58	7.11
盐城市大丰区	Yancheng Dafeng District	740.51	448.81	920.18	56.24	7.27
扬州市邗江区	Yangzhou Hanjiang District	755.34	398.17	1269.26	75.87	12.60
扬州市江都区	Yangzhou Jiangdu District	810.91	479.04	2199.79	165.70	12.84
镇江市丹徒区	Zhenjiang Dantu District	862.45	481.10	1116.35	78.69	7.01
泰州市海陵区	Taizhou Hailing District	642.39	324.60	1356.44	83.92	5.55
泰州市高港区	Taizhou Gaogang District	989.16	447.30	1971.96	169.39	9.09
泰州市姜堰区	Taizhou Jiangyan District	638.12	340.29	1349.74	100.38	6.41
宿迁市宿豫区	Suqian Suyu District	286.88	151.07	381.24	18.23	4.98

18－27 市辖区贸易、外资(2016年)

Trade and Foreign Economy of Municipal District(2016)

市辖区	Municipal District	社会消费品零售总额(亿元) Total Retail Sales of Consumer Goods (100 million yuan)	进出口总额(亿美元) Total Imports and Exports (USD 100 million)	出口总额(亿美元) Total Exports (USD 100 million)	协议注册外资(亿美元) Agreement Registered Foreign(USD 100 million)	实际使用外资(亿美元) Actual Use of Foreign Capital (USD 100 million)
南京市浦口区	Nanjing Pukou District	302.25	13.39	11.37	3.12	4.92
南京市栖霞区	Nanjing Qixia District	239.16	104.12	42.60	0.78	5.27
南京市雨花台区	Nanjing Yuhuatai District	366.62	31.07	21.71	3.24	2.79
南京市江宁区	Nanjing Jiangning District	469.43	113.84	74.51	3.17	7.88
南京市六合区	Nanjing Luhe District	381.48	18.59	10.96	1.54	3.74
南京市溧水区	Nanjing Lishui District	193.53	6.31	5.51	0.05	1.92
南京市高淳区	Nanjing Gaochun District	187.70	6.19	4.62	0.49	1.05
无锡市锡山区	Wuxi Xishan District	164.65	42.63	33.46	4.71	3.51
无锡市惠山区	Wuxi Huishan District	176.32	26.98	23.30	4.90	3.03
无锡市滨湖区	Wuxi Binhu District	259.78	23.77	17.80	4.16	2.52
徐州市贾汪区	Xuzhou Jiawang District	69.99	3.06	3.00	2.21	0.73
徐州市铜山区	Xuzhou Tongshan District	242.12	3.69	2.99	4.17	1.49
常州市新北区	Changzhou Xinbei District	292.33	100.74	70.29	11.01	8.50
常州市武进区	Changzhou Wujin District	530.51	94.77	68.36	14.08	8.50
常州市金坛区	Changzhou Jintan District	252.38	16.72	13.20	4.67	3.20
苏州市吴中区	Suzhou Wuzhong District	373.28	76.60	51.76	2.15	3.61
苏州市相城区	Suzhou Xiangcheng District	223.09	41.56	30.78	1.92	1.91
苏州市吴江区	Suzhou Wujiang District	467.66	211.35	140.20	11.11	6.16
南通市崇川区	Nantong Chongchuan District	398.30	54.78	34.11	1.33	1.15
南通市港闸区	Nantong Gangzha District	134.36	27.09	20.63	2.11	1.16
南通市通州区	Nantong Tongzhou District	341.12	37.33	33.69	8.16	2.44
连云港市连云区	Lianyungang Lianyun District	72.34	11.66	4.26	1.03	0.37
连云港市赣榆区	Lianyungang Ganyu District	172.46	5.13	4.04	0.80	0.96
淮安市淮安区	Huaian Huaian District	172.23	2.43	2.31	4.75	1.45
淮安市淮阴区	Huaian Huaiyin District	119.08	2.20	1.60	4.75	1.58
淮安市洪泽区	Huaian Hongze District	94.03	1.24	1.13	3.22	1.51
盐城市盐都区	Yancheng Yandu District	208.79	6.29	3.32	1.55	0.68
盐城市大丰区	Yancheng Dafeng District	172.77	16.21	8.74	4.74	1.45
扬州市邗江区	Yangzhou Hanjiang District	287.09	19.57	16.81	2.04	2.08
扬州市江都区	Yangzhou Jiangdu District	252.44	13.95	10.55	1.26	1.10
镇江市丹徒区	Zhenjiang Dantu District	68.42	5.64	5.18	2.79	1.07
泰州市海陵区	Taizhou Hailing District	243.08	12.99	10.73	4.40	1.05
泰州市高港区	Taizhou Gaogang District	49.33	14.56	6.79	4.94	2.67
泰州市姜堰区	Taizhou Jiangyan District	172.41	9.55	8.26	1.84	1.37
宿迁市宿豫区	Suqian Suyu District	53.69	3.50	3.26	0.55	0.43

18－28 市辖区教育、卫生、收入(2016年)

Education, Public Health and Income of Municipal District(2016)

市辖区	Municipal District	普通中学在校学生(万人) Regular Secondary School Students Enrollment (10000 persons)	小学在校学生(万人) Primary School Student Enrollment (10000 persons)	医院个数(个) Number of Hospitals (unit)	医院床位数(张) Number of Beds in Hospitals (unit)	执业(助理)医师(人) Practitioner (Assistant) Doctors (person)	城镇常住居民人均可支配收入(元) Per Capita Annual Disposable Income of Urban Residents (yuan)
南京市浦口区	Nanjing Pukou District	1.86	3.87	17	2315	1372	47374
南京市栖霞区	Nanjing Qixia District	1.41	2.59	16	2344	1508	48379
南京市雨花台区	Nanjing Yuhuatai District	1.30	1.82	10	1315	706	48289
南京市江宁区	Nanjing Jiangning District	3.64	6.47	28	6639	2897	48526
南京市六合区	Nanjing Luhe District	2.79	4.04	12	3465	2022	46147
南京市溧水区	Nanjing Lishui District	1.43	2.26	6	1633	778	44082
南京市高淳区	Nanjing Gaochun District	1.38	1.91	15	1715	886	45054
无锡市锡山区	Wuxi Xishan District	2.26	4.02	8	2133	1181	46295
无锡市惠山区	Wuxi Huishan District	2.63	4.57	5	2394	1278	47190
无锡市滨湖区	Wuxi Binhu District	1.61	3.34	29	9904	3034	48503
徐州市贾汪区	Xuzhou Jiawang District	1.53	4.24	5	2397	885	27943
徐州市铜山区	Xuzhou Tongshan District	4.37	12.70	11	3426	1812	31960
常州市新北区	Changzhou Xinbei District	2.33	4.63	5	2149	1497	48239
常州市武进区	Changzhou Wujin District	5.08	9.98	12	5153	2662	48203
常州市金坛区	Changzhou Jintan District	1.83	2.59	10	2564	1289	43246
苏州市吴中区	Suzhou Wuzhong District	2.41	7.04	25	5868	2099	56013
苏州市相城区	Suzhou Xiangcheng District	1.66	4.28	11	3451	1172	49749
苏州市吴江区	Suzhou Wujiang District	3.89	8.69	13	5723	2547	54321
南通市崇川区	Nantong Chongchuan District	0.67	4.10	24	8299	3927	41870
南通市港闸区	Nantong Gangzha District	0.47	1.38	10	2016	800	41639
南通市通州区	Nantong Tongzhou District	3.27	4.92	7	5741	2376	40741
连云港市连云区	Lianyungang Lianyun District	1.14	1.88	8	1523	885	34473
连云港市赣榆区	Lianyungang Ganyu District	5.59	10.13	13	4077	2025	27199
淮安市淮安区	Huaian Huaian District	4.17	5.85	7	4592	2198	26144
淮安市淮阴区	Huaian Huaiyin District	3.08	6.05	6	6624	2769	28393
淮安市洪泽区	Huaian Hongze District	1.29	1.82	2	1560	716	30291
盐城市盐都区	Yancheng Yandu District	2.43	3.60	3	2992	1743	32796
盐城市大丰区	Yancheng Dafeng District	2.25	2.71	21	3514	1830	31140
扬州市邗江区	Yangzhou Hanjiang District	2.03	3.35	19	2721	1773	40260
扬州市江都区	Yangzhou Jiangdu District	3.71	4.22	13	4313	1973	36558
镇江市丹徒区	Zhenjiang Dantu District	0.89	1.41	2	850	510	40891
泰州市海陵区	Taizhou Hailing District	1.27	2.41	19	4565	2405	38074
泰州市高港区	Taizhou Gaogang District	0.55	1.18	4	568	422	37224
泰州市姜堰区	Taizhou Jiangyan District	3.18	3.16	12	2688	1610	36898
宿迁市宿豫区	Suqian Suyu District	1.08	3.28	28	2677	1021	21741

主要统计指标解释

供水综合生产能力 指按供水设施取水、净化、送水、出厂输水干管等环节实际测定计算的综合生产能力。

供水管道长度 指从送水泵到用户水表之间所有管道的长度。在同一条街道埋设两条或两条以上管道时,应按每条管道的长度计算。

供水总量 指报告期供水企业(单位)供出的全部水量。包括有效供水量及损失水量。

生活用水量 指居民日常生活与公共福利设施的用水量,包括居民、饮食店、旅馆、医院、理发店、浴池、洗衣店、游泳池、商店、学校、机关、部队等单位的用水量。

城市人口用水普及率 指城市用水人口数与城市人口总数之比。计算公式为:

用水普及率 = 城市用水人口数/城市人口总数 × 100%

燃气综合生产能力 指报告期末燃气生产厂制气、净化、输送等环节的综合生产能力,不包括备用设备能力。一般按设计能力计算,如果实际生产能力大于设计能力时,应按实际测定的生产能力计算。测定时应以制气、净化、输送三个环节中最薄弱的环节为主。

燃气供气管道长度 指报告期末从气源厂压缩机的出口或门站出口到各类用户引入管之间的全部已经通气投入使用的管道长度。不包括煤气生产厂、输配站、液化气储存站、灌瓶站、储配站、气化站、混气站、供应站等厂(站)内的管道。按不同的材质、压力级别、管径分别统计。

燃气供应总量 指报告期燃气企业(单位)向用户供应的燃气数量。包括销售量及损失量。

燃气普及率 指报告期末使用燃气的城市人口数与城市人口总数的比率。计算公式为:

燃气普及率 = 用气人口数/城市人口总数 × 100%

道路长度 指道路长度和与道路相通的桥梁、隧道的长度,按车行道中心线计算。

排水管道长度 指所有排水总管、干管、支管、检查井及连接井进出口等长度之和。

计算时应按单管计算,即在同一条街道上如有两条或两条以上并排的排水管道时,应按每条排水管道的长度相加计算。

城市污水处理能力 指污水处理厂(或处理装置)每昼夜处理污水量的设计能力。

营运车数 指报告期末公交企业(单位)用于运营业务的全部车辆数。以企业(单位)固定资产台帐中已投入运营的车辆数为准;新购、新制和调入的运营车辆,自投入之日起开始计算;调出、报废和调作他用的运营车辆,自上级主管机关批准之日起不再计入。

园林绿地面积 指报告期末用于园林和绿化的各种绿地面积。包括公共绿地、居住区绿地、单位附属绿地、防护绿地、生产绿地、道路绿地和风景林地面积。不包括:

1. 屋顶绿化、垂直绿化、阳台绿化和室内绿化。
2. 以物质生产为主的林地、耕地、牧草地、果园和竹园等。
3. 城市总体规划中不列入绿地的水域。

公园绿地 指城市中向公众开放的以游憩为主要功能,有一定的游憩设施和服务设施,同时兼有健全生态、美化景观,防灾减灾等综合作用的绿化用地。包括综合公园、社区公园、专类公园、带状公园和街旁绿地。其中综合公园、专类公园和带状公园面积之和为公园面积。

Explanatory Notes on Main Statistical Indicators

Comprehensive Production Capacity of Tap Water refers to the actual comprehensive production capacity of the waterworks, taking the capacity of the main links such as waterflow, purification, conveyance and outflow of the trunk pilelines into account.

Length of Water Pipelines refers to the total length of all the pipelines between the water pumps and the user's water meters. If there are two or more than two pipelies buried in a same street, the length of every pipeline should be taken into account.

Volume of Water Supply refers to the total volume of water supply by the water supply enterprises (units) during the reference period, including both the effective water supply and loss.

Consumption of Water for Residential Use refers to the water consumption of households for daily life and the water consumption of public welfare facilities, including the consumption of restaurants, hotels, hospitals, barber shops, public bathhouses, laundries, swimming pools, shops, schools, institutions, army units and other units.

Percentage of Urban Population with Access to Tap Water refers to the ratio of the urban population with access to tap water to the total urban population. The formula is:

Percentage of Population with Access to Tap Water = (Urban Population with Access to Tap Water)/(Urban Population) × 100%

Comprehensive Production Capacity of Burning Gas refers to the comprehensive production capacity of the burning gas—works in burning gas generation, purification and delivering, excluding the reserve capacity of the equipment. In general, the capacity is counted in accordance with the designed requirement. If the actual production capacity is larger than designed requirement, it should be counted according to the actual capacity through determination. In determination, the most weak link should be determined as the main one among the three links of burning gas generation, purification and delivering.

Length of Burning Gas Pipelines refers to the total length of pipelines between the outlet of the compressor, blower or burning gas tank of the source factory and the burning gas meters of users, which are all put in use, excluding the pipelines in burning gas—works (stations) and the pipelines of transportation and distribution station, liquefied petroluem gas storage station, pipeline and bottle station, storage and distribution station, gasification station, gas mixed station, supply station. They are counted respectively according to the different quality of materials, level of preasure and the size of bores.

Volume of Burning Gas Supply refers to the volume of burning gas supplied by the burning gas enterprises, including both the sales volume and loss.

Percentage of Urban Population with Access to Burning Gas refers to the ratio of the urban population with access to burning gas to the urban population at the reference period. The formula is:

Percentage of Urban Population with Access to Burning Gas = (Urban Population with Access to Burning Gas)/Urban Population) ×100%

Length of Roads refers to the length of roads, as well as the length of bridges and tunnels, the same as the roads, and taking the middle line of traffic lane into account.

Length of Sewage Pipes refers to the total length of general drainage, trunks, branch and blind drainages, inspection wells, connection wells, inlets and outlets, ete., taking the single pipe into account. Namely if there are two or more than two pipes standing side by side in a street, the length of every pipe should put into account.

Daily Disposal Capacity of Urban Sewage refers to the designed 24 hour capacity of sewage disposal at the sewage treatment works.

Number of Vehicles (Public Transit) in Working refers to the total of operatoinal vehicles (buses and trolley buses) available at the end of the reference period, taking them as the fixed assets registered in account book of the enterprises and put in operation as the accounting standard. Vehicles, newly bought, newly manufactured and transfered in from other units, should be put into account since the day of putting into operation, while the vehicles, transfered to other units, being scrapped and turned to other use, should not be put into account since the day of permission made by higher responsible department.

Area of Gardens and Green Areas refers to the various green land used for gardening and afforestation at the end of reference period, including public green land, residential area green land, subsidiary green land of the units, protection green land, production green land, roadside green land and scenic forest land, excluding:

1. Roof, perpendicular, balcony and indoor green area.
2. Areas taking the material production as the main aim, such as forest land, cultivated land, pasture, orchard and bamboo forest.
3. Water areas which are not listed in the urban general plan.

Park Green Area refers to green areas open to the public for amusement and rest with the facilities of amusement, rest and services. Its function includes perfecting ecology, beautifying landscape, and preventing and reducing disaster. Park green areas include comprehensive park, community park, topic park, belt-shaped park and green area nearby street. Total areas of comprehensive park, topic park and belt-shaped is the area of park.

19

区域经济

Regional Economy

简要说明

一、本篇资料的主要内容

本篇资料反映苏南苏中苏北、沿江、沿海、沿东陇海线及长江三角洲地区经济社会发展情况。

二、资料来源

本篇资料主要根据市县社会经济基本情况统计年报加工整理。

Brief Introduction

I. Main Contents

Data in this chapter reflect economic and social development of the Southern, Mid and Northern Jiangsu; zone along the Yangtze rive; Coastal region; region along the Long – hai rarlway; Yangtze River Delta.

Ⅱ. Date Source

Data in this chapter mainly based on the basic socio – economic situation annual report.

19－1 三大区域主要经济指标（2016 年）
Major Economic Indicators of Three Regions（2016）

指标	Item	苏南 Southern Jiangsu	苏中 Mid Jiangsu	苏北 Northern Jiangsu
年末常住人口（万人）	Permanent Resident Population at Year-end（10000 persons）	3333.60	1643.92	3021.08
土地面积（平方公里）	Land Area（sq. km）	28084	22927	54865
地区生产总值（亿元）	Gross Domestic Product（100 million yuan）	44795.83	15319.36	18160.20
第一产业	Primary Industry	899.99	858.05	1978.19
第二产业	Secondary Industry	20294.42	7301.82	8021.89
第三产业	Tertiary Industry	23601.42	7159.49	8160.12
#工业	Industry	18425.16	6238.81	6794.96
人均地区生产总值（元）	Per Capita GDP（yuan）	134569	93228	60225
地区生产总值指数（上年＝100）	Indices of GDP（preceding year＝100）	107.9	109.4	109.9
粮食产量（万吨）	Grain（10000 tons）	477.37	938.52	2360.35
油料产量（万吨）	Oil-bearing Crops（10000 tons）	18.83	54.88	62.60
棉花产量（万吨）	Cotton（10000 tons）	0.49	2.67	3.32
规模以上工业利润总额（亿元）	Profits and Taxes of above Designated Size Industrial Enterprises（100 million yuan）	5007.55	2651.66	2871.03
固定资产投资额（亿元）	Urban Completed Investment in Fixed Assets（100 million yuan）	22454.26	11256.51	15660.09
社会消费品零售总额（亿元）	Total Retail Sale of Consumer Goods（100 million yuan）	16584.16	5110.01	7012.94
进出口总额（亿美元）	Total Imports and Exports（USD 100 million）	4316.78	508.65	271.58
#出口	Exports	2642.56	369.45	182.39
实际使用外资（亿美元）	Actual Use of Foreign Capital（USD 100 million）	167.46	49.36	43.74
一般公共预算收入（亿元）	General Public Budget Revenue（100 million yuan）	4520.94	1256.66	1696.30
一般公共预算支出（亿元）	General Public Budget Expenditure（100 million yuan）	4529.36	1677.12	2809.48
金融机构存款余额（亿元）	Deposits Balance of Banking Institution（100 million yuan）	80846.02	21734.91	18525.64
#住户存款	Household Deposits	23921.70	10590.58	9388.22
金融机构贷款余额（亿元）	Loans Balance of Banking Institution（100 million yuan）	63476.16	14000.39	13631.05
居民人均可支配收入（元）	Per Capita Disposable Income of Residents（100 million yuan）	42795	29138	22174
城镇常住居民人均可支配收入（元）	Per Capita Annual Disposable Income of Urban Permanent Residents（yuan）	49920	37585	28515
农村常住居民人均可支配收入（元）	Per Capita Annual Disposable Income of Rural Permanent Residents（yuan）	24638	18320	15102

19－2 三大区域经济社会基本情况（2016年）

指标	Item	苏南合计 Southern Jiangsu	南京 Nanjing	无锡 Wuxi	常州 Changzhou	苏州 Suzhou
人口、就业	**Population and Employment**					
土地面积 （平方公里）	Land Area (sq. km)	28084	6587	4627	4373	8657
年末户籍人口 （万人）	Population (Registered) (year-end) (10000 persons)	2474.07	662.79	486.20	374.90	678.20
男	Male	1223.15	330.86	240.02	185.22	332.53
女	Female	1250.92	331.93	246.18	189.68	345.67
年均户籍人口 （万人）	Yearly Average Population(Registered) (10000 persons)	2458.95	658.10	483.55	372.88	672.61
年末常住人口 （万人）	Population(Permanent) (10000 persons)	3333.60	827.00	652.90	470.83	1064.74
城镇化率 （%）	Rate of Urbanization (%)	75.9	82.0	75.8	71.0	75.5
年末总户数 （万户）	Households(year-end) (10000 subs)	848.95	229.95	163.87	131.45	222.44
#乡村户数	Rural Households	340.91	63.25	59.91	72.68	87.50
出生人口 （万人）	Births (10000 persons)	25.91	8.03	4.48	3.70	7.53
死亡人口 （万人）	Deaths (10000 persons)	15.05	3.72	3.13	2.26	4.27
人口密度 （人/平方公里）	Density of Population (person/sq. km)	1187	1256	1411	1077	1230
就业人员 （万人）	Employed Persons (10000 persons)	2010.0	456.0	387.0	281.4	691.3
第一产业	Primary Industry	138.8	46.0	17.1	30.0	23.5
第二产业	Secondary Industry	1006.2	148.9	214.9	142.2	412.1
第三产业	Tertiary Industry	865.0	261.1	155.0	109.2	255.7
私营企业就业人员 （万人）	Number of Employed Persons in Private Enterprises (10000 persons)	1315.17	371.68	262.45	168.48	440.87
个体就业人员 （万人）	Number of Self-employed Individuals (10000 persons)	376.61	94.60	60.24	56.75	126.95
年末城镇登记失业人员 （万人）	Registered Unemployed Persons in Urban Areas at Year-end (10000 persons)	19.19	6.54	3.98	3.29	3.96
年末城镇登记失业率 （%）	Registered Unemployed Rate in Urban Areas at Year-end (%)	1.87	1.88	1.85	1.85	1.89
国民核算	**National Accounting**					
地区生产总值 （亿元）	Gross Domestic Product (100 million yuan)	44795.83	10503.02	9210.02	5773.86	15475.09
第一产业	Primary Industry	899.99	252.54	135.19	152.67	221.81
第二产业	Secondary Industry	20294.42	4117.32	4346.78	2682.46	7277.46

Basic Statistics on Economy and Society of Three Regions (2016)

镇 江 Zhenjiang	苏中合计 Mid Jiangsu	南 通 Nantong	扬 州 Yangzhou	泰 州 Taizhou	苏北合计 Northern Jiangsu	徐 州 Xuzhou	连云港 Lianyungang	淮 安 Huaian	盐 城 Yancheng	宿 迁 Suqian
3840	22927	10549	6591	5787	54865	11765	7615	10030	16931	8524
271.98	1736.54	766.66	461.67	508.21	3566.08	1042.40	533.99	567.56	830.53	591.60
134.52	866.80	377.29	230.55	258.96	1845.46	540.01	278.75	291.25	428.50	306.95
137.46	869.74	389.37	231.12	249.25	1720.62	502.39	255.24	276.31	402.03	284.65
271.83	1736.14	766.72	461.40	508.03	3552.05	1035.55	532.28	566.00	829.28	588.94
318.13	1643.92	730.20	449.14	464.58	3021.08	871.00	449.64	489.00	723.50	487.94
69.2	64.0	64.4	64.4	63.2	60.7	62.4	60.2	59.7	61.6	57.5
101.24	598.17	281.88	148.63	167.66	1006.78	278.54	142.10	164.82	271.20	150.12
57.57	418.71	198.67	100.85	119.19	659.82	175.79	93.07	99.50	183.00	108.46
2.17	14.37	5.71	4.00	4.66	40.04	9.42	6.19	6.41	9.15	8.88
1.69	12.73	5.94	3.11	3.67	14.01	2.77	1.51	2.31	5.00	2.42
828	717	692	681	803	551	740	590	488	427	572
194.3	999.5	458.0	263.4	278.1	1746.7	483.4	250.5	283.6	446.0	283.2
22.2	202.3	96.0	46.2	60.1	500.7	144.3	78.6	78.3	110.2	89.3
88.1	442.2	213.0	116.4	112.8	596.8	159.9	80.7	89.6	159.8	106.8
84.0	355.0	149.0	100.8	105.2	649.2	179.2	91.2	115.7	176.0	87.1
98.25	460.72	211.26	133.53	115.93	510.69	136.89	50.19	79.26	145.28	98.18
39.79	175.56	76.03	49.71	50.42	247.41	68.54	28.63	45.33	55.53	49.38
1.42	7.56	3.52	2.44	1.60	9.19	3.10	1.18	2.03	1.82	1.07
1.85	1.86	1.85	1.88	1.87	1.86	1.85	1.88	1.87	1.85	1.88
3833.84	15319.36	6768.20	4449.38	4101.78	18160.20	5808.52	2376.48	3048.00	4576.08	2351.12
137.78	858.05	366.66	251.39	240.00	1978.19	542.88	301.56	324.61	533.91	275.23
1870.40	7301.82	3170.30	2197.63	1933.89	8021.89	2513.85	1049.90	1268.15	2050.02	1139.97

指 标	Item	苏南合计 Southern Jiangsu	南京 Nanjing	无锡 Wuxi	常州 Changzhou	苏州 Suzhou
第三产业	Tertiary Industry	23601.42	6133.16	4728.05	2938.73	7975.82
#工业	Industry	18425.16	3581.72	3977.58	2428.84	6709.02
人均地区生产总值（按常住人口计算，元）	Per Capita GDP(Permanent) (yuan)	134569	127264	141258	122721	145556
人均地区生产总值（按户籍人口计算，元）	Per Capita GDP(Registered) (yuan)	182174	159597	190467	154847	230077
地区生产总值指数（上年＝100）	Indices of GDP (preceding year＝100)	107.9	108.0	107.5	108.5	107.5
第一产业	Primary Industry	99.5	101.1	97.6	99.1	99.0
第二产业	Secondary Industry	106.2	105.3	106.8	107.4	105.4
第三产业	Tertiary Industry	109.7	110.3	108.6	110.1	109.7
#工业	Industry	106.3	104.8	107.0	107.7	105.5
地区生产总值构成（%）	Composition of GDP (%)					
第一产业	Primary Industry	2.0	2.4	1.5	2.6	1.5
第二产业	Secondary Industry	45.3	39.2	47.2	46.5	47.0
第三产业	Tertiary Industry	52.7	58.4	51.3	50.9	51.5
#工业	Industry	41.1	34.1	43.2	42.1	43.4
固定资产投资	**Investment in Fixed Assets**					
固定资产投资额（亿元）	Urban Investment in Fixed Assets (100 million yuan)	22454.26	5533.56	4793.69	3605.08	5648.49
#房地产投资	Investment in Real Estate Development	5937.81	1845.60	1033.62	446.70	2163.24
#住宅	Residence	4390.35	1392.76	684.42	316.48	1655.24
固定资产投资本年资金来源构成（%）	Grouped by Source of Finance (%)					
国家预算内资金	State Appropriation	1.5	1.2	1.1	2.6	1.7
国内贷款	Domestic Loans	13.3	14.0	7.2	16.4	14.1
利用外资	Foreign Inventment	1.8	0.1	5.5	1.3	2.0
自筹资金	Fund Raising	54.0	49.0	67.9	64.0	41.4
其他资金	Others	29.4	35.6	18.4	15.7	40.9
新增固定资产（亿元）	Newly Increased Investment in Fixed Assets (100 million yuan)	14872.11	3019.53	3730.42	2645.73	3682.31
商品房销售建筑面积（万平方米）	Floor Space of Selling Commercial Houses (10000 sq. m)	7258.34	1558.18	1276.41	933.20	2494.05
#住宅	Residencial Buildings	6592.05	1406.29	1168.43	810.80	2258.60
财政、金融、保险	**Finance, Banking and Insurance**					
财政总收入（新口径）（亿元）	Total Financial Budgetary Revenue (New Statistical Scale) (100 million yuan)	7968.57	2198.54	1470.13	786.29	3076.90

19－2　Continued 1

镇 江 Zhenjiang	苏中合计 Mid Jiangsu	南 通 Nantong	扬 州 Yangzhou	泰 州 Taizhou	苏北合计 Northern Jiangsu	徐 州 Xuzhou	连云港 Lianyungang	淮 安 Huaian	盐 城 Yancheng	宿 迁 Suqian
1825.66	7159.49	3231.24	2000.36	1927.89	8160.12	2751.79	1025.02	1455.24	1992.15	935.92
1728.00	6238.81	2633.06	1925.92	1679.83	6794.96	2122.58	851.82	1071.99	1771.68	976.89
120603	93228	92702	99151	88330	60225	66845	52987	62446	63278	48311
141040	88238	88275	96433	80739	51126	56091	44648	53851	55181	39921
109.3	109.4	109.3	109.4	109.5	109.9	108.2	107.8	109.0	108.9	109.1
100.2	100.7	100.7	100.0	101.4	101.6	102.0	101.6	101.7	100.9	102.0
108.6	108.7	109.0	108.3	108.8	107.7	108.7	107.8	109.1	109.2	110.1
110.7	111.2	110.6	112.0	111.4	110.1	109.1	109.8	110.6	110.8	110.2
108.9	109.3	109.6	108.7	109.4	108.0	109.4	108.6	109.7	109.9	110.6
3.6	5.6	5.4	5.7	5.9	10.9	9.3	12.7	10.6	11.7	11.7
48.8	47.7	46.8	49.4	47.1	44.2	43.3	44.2	41.6	44.8	48.5
47.6	46.7	47.7	45.0	47.0	44.9	47.4	43.1	47.7	43.5	39.8
45.1	40.7	38.9	43.3	41.0	37.4	36.5	35.8	35.2	38.7	41.5
2873.43	11256.51	4811.95	3288.68	3155.87	15660.09	4797.33	2385.16	2535.19	3882.83	2059.58
448.64	1244.27	584.14	410.18	249.96	1774.28	549.13	235.41	321.41	358.57	309.76
341.45	910.06	425.88	289.28	194.91	1329.06	415.04	192.92	222.99	273.02	225.10
1.2	2.2	3.8	1.1	0.5	2.2	2.9	1.2	1.2	1.4	4.0
15.2	4.1	5.4	5.1	5.0	10.1	13.4	11.7	4.7	11.5	4.8
0.1	0.3	0.5	0.0	0.2	0.5	0.2	0.6	0.3	0.6	1.2
65.5	86.2	79.2	82.2	83.0	78.5	72.3	77.3	82.0	78.4	78.7
18.0	7.2	11.0	11.6	11.3	8.7	11.3	9.3	11.7	8.2	11.3
1794.13	8184.52	3240.33	2263.68	2680.51	10907.08	3321.67	1541.93	1612.42	2960.76	1470.29
996.50	2630.43	1200.80	734.76	694.87	4073.32	1071.43	524.44	869.80	842.55	765.10
947.93	2443.29	1115.64	682.21	645.44	3626.01	917.89	503.30	749.08	751.32	704.42
436.70	1923.21	879.28	529.45	514.48	2641.48	802.02	315.10	483.13	597.24	444.00

指 标	Item	苏南合计 Southern Jiangsu	南京 Nanjing	无锡 Wuxi	常州 Changzhou	苏州 Suzhou
上划中央收入	Turn Over Revenue to the Central Government	3447.63	1055.94	595.13	306.01	1346.86
一般公共预算收入	General Public Budget Revenue	4520.94	1142.60	875.00	480.29	1730.04
#税收收入	Taxes	3783.07	956.62	706.04	383.19	1505.82
一般公共预算支出（亿元）	General Public Budget Expenditure (100 million yuan)	4529.36	1173.84	867.36	508.11	1617.11
人均一般公共预算收入（元）	Per Capita General Public Budget Revenue (yuan)	13581	13845	13420	10208	16272
一般公共预算收入占GDP比重（%）	Percentage of General Public Budget Revenue to GDP (%)	10.1	10.9	9.5	8.3	11.2
金融机构存款余额（亿元）	Deposits Balance of Banking Institutions (100 million yuan)	80846.02	27633.55	14101.40	8540.82	25864.26
#住户存款	Household Deposits	23921.70	5894.47	4867.43	3366.85	7913.85
金融机构贷款余额（亿元）	Loans Balance of Banking Institutions (100 million yuan)	63476.16	21681.28	10382.93	6043.16	21924.44
农业	**Agriculture**					
乡村从业人员（万人）	Rural Employees (10000 persons)	627.99	116.97	109.81	128.05	171.89
#农林牧渔业	Farming, Forestry, Animal Husbandry and Fishery	106.24	23.21	16.30	23.22	21.83
工业	Industry	317.02	36.65	67.21	59.45	103.57
建筑业	Construction	68.86	23.81	6.39	17.36	9.66
农林牧渔业总产值（亿元）	Gross Output Value of Farming, Forestry, Animal Husbandry and Fishery (100 million yuan)	1650.49	451.16	249.98	283.97	424.67
农业	Farming	864.42	258.75	140.30	152.43	178.81
林业	Forestry	78.61	24.26	18.53	1.97	24.76
牧业	Animal Husbandry	182.63	46.83	27.46	39.43	37.39
渔业	Fishery	378.68	99.36	35.36	72.98	136.08
农林牧渔服务业	Service Industry of FFAF	146.15	21.97	28.32	17.18	47.62

19－2 Continued 2

镇 江 Zhenjiang	苏中合计 Mid Jiangsu	南 通 Nantong	扬 州 Yangzhou	泰 州 Taizhou	苏北合计 Northern Jiangsu	徐 州 Xuzhou	连云港 Lianyungang	淮 安 Huaian	盐 城 Yancheng	宿 迁 Suqian
143.69	653.80	289.10	184.15	180.55	849.99	285.95	103.63	167.62	182.06	110.73
293.01	1256.66	590.18	345.30	321.18	1696.30	516.06	211.47	315.51	415.18	238.08
231.40	981.55	456.77	267.16	257.62	1307.19	390.30	170.80	235.15	324.67	186.27
362.94	1677.12	749.22	478.97	448.93	2809.48	797.99	373.12	483.47	730.33	424.57
9217	7687	8084	7695	6916	5625	5939	4715	6464	5741	4892
7.6	8.2	8.7	7.8	7.8	9.3	8.9	8.9	10.4	9.1	10.1
4705.99	21734.91	11097.74	5361.55	5275.62	18525.64	5495.31	2501.84	3066.00	5255.06	2207.43
1879.10	10590.58	5554.89	2560.98	2474.71	9388.22	3090.21	1168.71	1360.51	2682.46	1086.33
3444.36	14000.39	6835.46	3508.13	3656.79	13631.05	3620.21	2046.93	2304.22	3699.32	1960.37
101.27	693.31	299.48	181.49	212.34	1273.48	358.55	177.97	211.79	299.92	225.25
21.68	139.70	63.55	33.22	42.93	490.18	130.56	80.84	86.13	107.93	84.72
50.14	213.71	86.19	64.44	63.08	301.54	104.30	31.00	42.36	60.76	63.12
11.64	133.61	62.50	34.69	36.42	180.63	51.80	31.30	31.91	36.68	28.94
240.71	1585.47	691.55	477.95	415.96	3861.08	1046.76	589.42	602.72	1104.93	517.24
134.13	744.64	294.61	221.18	228.85	2079.23	650.95	275.56	373.23	480.98	298.51
9.08	20.23	4.60	12.02	3.60	94.65	18.47	16.54	13.59	27.95	18.09
31.52	316.05	159.06	78.05	78.94	966.63	301.90	119.01	139.93	303.65	102.14
34.91	388.26	163.99	140.97	83.30	550.70	43.22	143.24	64.63	214.72	84.90
31.07	116.28	69.29	25.73	21.27	169.87	32.21	35.07	11.34	77.64	13.61

指标	Item	苏南合计 Southern Jiangsu	南京 Nanjing	无锡 Wuxi	常州 Changzhou	苏州 Suzhou
农业机械总动力 （万千瓦）	Total Power of Agricultural Machinery (10000 kw)	782.69	227.61	99.22	146.25	163.89
化肥施用量 （万吨）	Consumption of Chemical Fertilizer (10000 tons)	31.10	7.39	5.18	6.04	7.11
农村用电量 （亿千瓦小时）	Electricity Consumed in Rural Areas (100 million kw·h)	1270.27	32.08	394.38	156.59	609.78
农作物总播种面积 （千公顷）	Total Sown Area (1000 hectares)	1133.91	289.25	160.31	209.20	241.40
#粮食	Grain	698.93	153.05	94.06	132.79	145.01
主要产品产量 （万吨）	Total Output of Major Products (10000 tons)					
粮食	Grain	477.37	108.04	59.16	93.74	97.68
油料	Oil-bearing Crops	18.83	7.43	0.81	3.41	1.34
棉花 （吨）	Cotton (ton)	4852	3071		371	500
肉类	Meat	48.39	9.81	7.35	13.52	9.76
#猪肉	Pork	28.21	5.32	5.17	6.70	6.18
牛肉	Beef	0.18	0.08		0.03	
羊肉	Mutton	0.77	0.26	0.03	0.15	0.20
水产品	Aquatic Products	86.96	22.31	12.67	16.64	25.49
工业（规模以上）	**Industry (above Designated Size)**					
工业企业单位数 （个）	Number of Industrial Enterprises (unit)	23939	2661	4888	4139	9616
工业总产值 （亿元）	Gross Output Value of Industry (100 million yuan)	78831.63	12945.02	14352.96	12096.82	30713.99
#内资企业	Domestic Funded Enterprises	41483.42	7554.24	9108.05	8050.37	10845.61
外商港澳台商投资企业	Enterprises Funded by Foreign, Hong Kong, Macao and Taiwan Enterprises	37348.21	5390.78	5244.91	4046.45	19868.37
#国有控股企业	State-owned Share Holding Enterprises	7442.65	4920.80	784.92	444.07	783.36
#大中型企业	Large and Medium-sized Enterprises	55400.55	8824.62	9734.20	7703.92	22961.02
#轻工业	Light Industry	18602.51	2958.57	3642.34	2769.91	7695.83
#制造业	Manufacturing	77449.31	12654.34	14096.56	11957.05	30193.41
电力、热力、燃气及水的生产和供应业	Production and Supply of Electric Power, Heat Power, Gas and Water	1293.28	238.34	256.40	131.83	518.70
资产总计 （亿元）	Total Industrial Assets (100 million yuan)	69701.23	11448.85	15095.63	8942.07	28356.50
负债合计 （亿元）	Total Liabilities (100 million yuan)	37206.78	6166.10	8085.84	4945.73	14838.02
主营业务收入 （亿元）	Major Business Revenue (100 million yuan)	78119.21	12442.36	14120.24	12435.86	30380.18

镇 江 Zhenjiang	苏中合计 Mid Jiangsu	南 通 Nantong	扬 州 Yangzhou	泰 州 Taizhou	苏北合计 Northern Jiangsu	徐 州 Xuzhou	连云港 Lianyungang	淮 安 Huaian	盐 城 Yancheng	宿 迁 Suqian
145.72	943.98	398.28	270.19	275.52	3179.88	712.33	588.06	622.60	679.12	577.77
5.36	58.40	22.24	20.03	16.12	223.02	60.46	34.57	38.85	50.56	38.59
77.44	355.89	170.31	61.14	124.44	243.11	66.11	34.28	16.00	80.30	46.42
233.75	1906.44	824.10	507.16	575.18	4701.51	1154.55	631.90	797.17	1399.86	718.03
174.02	1372.77	518.87	418.85	435.05	3460.27	737.77	501.53	659.99	981.57	579.41
118.74	938.52	325.20	300.30	313.03	2360.35	469.16	360.80	458.55	687.31	384.54
5.83	54.88	35.82	6.87	12.20	62.60	13.45	11.40	8.80	24.30	4.65
910	26711	23797	1144	1770	33185	20653	549	84	11262	637
7.95	90.39	45.73	18.01	26.65	264.92	90.77	29.50	30.39	81.40	32.86
4.85	56.64	25.64	9.87	21.13	148.96	39.89	21.13	18.45	51.71	17.79
0.06	0.14	0.03	0.06	0.05	5.18	1.20	2.01	0.37	0.37	1.24
0.13	3.23	2.65	0.19	0.39	8.15	3.82	0.62	0.63	2.52	0.56
9.85	168.79	89.03	40.12	39.64	266.82	18.88	75.30	26.10	119.43	27.11
2635	10775	5071	2686	3018	13200	2992	1815	2609	3185	2599
8722.84	36740.87	14525.72	9661.65	12170.80	40094.53	13644.36	5974.81	6951.32	9180.84	4096.70
5925.14	26986.65	10167.43	7043.23	9775.98	33839.92	12442.52	4855.40	5758.55	7104.34	3679.11
2797.70	9754.22	4573.17	2786.24	2394.82	6254.62	1201.85	1366.39	1192.77	2076.03	417.58
509.50	2947.65	632.12	1634.89	680.64	2120.41	917.50	356.03	375.56	365.87	105.45
6176.79	20036.01	7692.30	6205.37	6138.34	19648.00	7983.71	3502.70	2536.24	4282.24	1343.12
1535.87	10533.54	4585.27	2540.76	3407.52	14907.52	4610.40	2042.27	2964.07	3143.41	2147.38
8547.95	36224.47	14519.62	9688.01	12016.85	39088.41	13172.19	6041.34	6777.91	9015.88	4081.09
148.02	468.02	220.98	93.32	153.72	571.98	169.69	117.83	82.42	162.14	39.90
5858.18	20134.47	8801.91	4678.72	6653.84	22282.65	6952.73	3650.60	3071.44	5261.76	3346.13
3171.09	10259.69	4423.65	2430.70	3405.33	10491.70	3159.11	1856.14	1370.93	2768.09	1337.44
8632.13	36383.51	14650.80	9502.36	12139.45	39846.19	13947.04	5946.41	7014.24	8870.47	3896.33

指 标	Item	苏南合计 Southern Jiangsu	南京 Nanjing	无锡 Wuxi	常州 Changzhou	苏州 Suzhou
主营业务成本 （亿元）	Cost of Principle Business (100 million yuan)	66749.46	10182.08	12097.75	10880.58	26169.61
利润总额 （亿元）	Total Profits (100 million yuan)	5007.55	959.35	968.02	725.27	1772.74
从业人员年平均人数 （万人）	Annual Average Employed Persons (10000 persons)	619.04	74.44	116.78	85.68	286.58
建筑业	**Construction**					
建筑企业单位数 （个）	Number of Construction Enterprise (unit)	4383	1458	550	612	1396
建筑业总产值 （亿元）	Gross Output Value of Construction (100 million yuan)	7388.10	3094.65	633.52	1273.35	1855.90
房屋建筑施工面积 （万平方米）	Floor Space of Building under Construction (10000 sq. m)	43687.10	19228.82	3133.48	9236.17	9681.78
房屋建筑竣工面积 （万平方米）	Floor Space of Buildings Completed (10000 sq. m)	14344.48	5012.89	1308.62	3575.17	3569.78
公路里程 （公里）	Total Length of Highways (km)	47972	11211	7695	9031	12681
#等级公路	Expressway and Class Ⅰ to Ⅳ Highways	47752	10991	7695	9031	12681
#高速公路	Expressway	1915	555	274	306	598
公路客运量 （万人）	Passenger Traffic of Highways (10000 persons)	54861	8490	5785	5423	31589
公路货运量 （万吨）	Freight Traffic of Highways (10000 tons)	56020	12463	13225	11095	12287
民用汽车拥有量（万辆）	Number of Civil Motor Vehicles Owned (10000 units)	853.29	221.68	160.01	109.80	312.60
#私人汽车拥有量	Number of Private-owned Vehicles	731.44	192.71	134.08	93.93	267.03
邮政业务总量 （亿元）	Total Post Services (100 million yuan)	437.70	102.89	84.02	40.57	193.61
电信业务总量 （亿元）	Total Telecommunication Revenue (100 million yuan)	1587.46	422.38	284.84	191.38	595.60
固定电话用户 （万户）	Number of Fixed Telephone Subscribers (10000 subscribers)	925.07	243.50	168.09	123.49	314.20
移动电话用户 （万户）	Number of Mobile Telephone Subscribers (10000 subscribers)	4208.01	1114.72	799.86	539.94	1447.59
互联网宽带接入用户 （万户）	Number of Subscribers of Internet Service (10000 subscriber)	1418.24	373.66	269.95	195.15	471.80
全年用电量 （亿千瓦小时）	Total Consumption of Electricity (100 million kw·h)	3208.38	524.79	638.67	429.93	1382.58
#工业用电	Consumption of Electricity for Industrial Use	2429.39	310.81	493.73	334.78	1116.30
居民生活用电	Consumption of Electricity for Living Use by Residents	313.00	76.45	60.40	41.84	108.26

镇 江 Zhenjiang	苏中合计 Mid Jiangsu	南 通 Nantong	扬 州 Yangzhou	泰 州 Taizhou	苏北合计 Northern Jiangsu	徐 州 Xuzhou	连云港 Lianyungang	淮 安 Huaian	盐 城 Yancheng	宿 迁 Suqian
7419.44	31231.25	12761.31	8336.30	10133.65	33825.32	11725.51	5040.36	6079.35	7701.31	3278.80
582.17	2651.66	1118.27	593.15	938.67	2871.03	1108.89	496.53	404.81	475.83	391.93
55.56	231.81	101.55	70.59	59.68	713.19	81.07	489.63	46.75	54.90	40.85
367	2219	900	686	633	2421	436	288	547	776	374
530.67	12890.31	6619.39	3346.48	2924.44	5513.35	1387.79	648.73	1337.29	1422.73	716.82
2406.84	128668.51	71731.81	26807.86	30128.84	49137.96	11880.35	5309.08	12889.05	12769.72	6289.76
878.01	42100.55	19160.04	10094.65	12845.86	18545.26	4613.18	2306.10	3676.99	4954.27	2994.74
7354	37608	18427	9546	9635	71723	16277	12027	13351	19568	10500
7354	37221	18427	9166	9628	69434	15405	12027	12589	19303	10110
182	889	334	271	284	1855	459	354	401	396	245
3574	19344	8204	3840	7300	39289	13217	4654	7226	8283	5909
6950	20658	11535	6546	2577	40488	17586	8378	5663	5076	3785
49.20	260.39	134.95	63.53	61.91	318.97	101.61	47.85	45.27	75.57	48.67
43.68	232.23	120.41	56.27	55.54	288.54	92.64	43.16	40.31	67.55	44.88
16.62	101.00	56.14	26.61	18.25	124.99	39.30	17.38	21.04	22.65	24.63
93.25	448.00	205.78	129.27	112.95	671.10	207.39	102.58	105.02	150.52	105.58
75.79	393.42	179.98	108.59	104.85	389.84	115.78	71.20	57.06	98.80	47.00
305.89	1520.81	678.69	437.36	404.76	2469.94	762.01	368.05	383.34	584.97	371.56
107.69	507.05	225.34	146.95	134.75	729.85	223.61	114.94	111.15	174.43	105.72
232.41	839.70	374.79	225.37	239.55	1141.38	353.91	166.15	163.20	289.29	168.83
173.77	598.45	265.65	156.60	176.20	784.10	250.22	110.00	106.70	201.37	115.81
26.05	333.51	265.65	34.41	33.44	174.22	52.92	17.17	29.98	46.39	27.76

指 标	Item	苏南合计 Southern Jiangsu	南京 Nanjing	无锡 Wuxi	常州 Changzhou	苏州 Suzhou
批发零售贸易、餐饮业	**Wholesale and Retail Trade and Catering Services**					
社会消费品零售总额（亿元）	Total Retail Sale of Consumer Goods (100 million yuan)	16584.16	5088.20	3119.56	2202.83	4936.79
#批发和零售业	Wholesale and Retail Trade	14965.42	4638.45	2880.94	2016.06	4343.02
住宿和餐饮业	Catering Services	1618.74	449.74	238.62	186.77	593.77
对外经济贸易、旅游	**Foreign Economy, Trade and Tourism**					
进出口总额（亿美元）	Total Imports and Exports (USD 100 million)	4316.78	502.14	698.05	275.84	2737.58
出口	Exports	2642.56	295.94	429.10	208.60	1639.41
进口	Imports	1674.22	206.20	268.95	67.25	1098.18
外贸依存度（%）	Interdependent Level to Foreign Trade (%)	63.6	31.6	50.1	31.5	116.7
实际使用外资（亿美元）	Actual Use of Foreign Capital (USD 100 million)	167.46	34.79	34.13	25.00	60.03
接待境外旅游者人数（万人次）	Number of Overseas Recieved Tourists (10000 person-times)	289.07	63.78	43.92	14.59	161.28
星级饭店数（个）	Star Class Hotels (unit)	310	91	42	42	116
旅游外汇收入（亿美元）	Foreign Exchange Earnings from Tourism (USD 100 million)	34.29	6.76	3.90	1.31	21.67
教育	**Education**					
学校数（所）	Total Number of School (unit)					
#普通高校	Institutions of Regular Higher Education	94	44	12	10	22
普通中等专业学校	Regular Specialized Secondary Schools	84	22	20	11	21
普通中学	Regular Secondary Schools	972	227	183	160	292
小学	Primary Schools	1246	346	197	201	391
在校学生数（万人）	Total Number of Students Enrollment (10000 persons)					
#普通高校	Institutions of Regular Higher Education	135.24	82.78	11.37	10.41	21.93
普通中等专业学校	Regular Specialized Secondary Schools	21.24	5.50	4.43	3.50	5.91
普通中学	Regular Secondary Schools	101.03	22.45	21.54	16.53	30.98

镇 江 Zhenjiang	苏中合计 Mid Jiangsu	南 通 Nantong	扬 州 Yangzhou	泰 州 Taizhou	苏北合计 Northern Jiangsu	徐 州 Xuzhou	连云港 Lianyungang	淮 安 Huaian	盐 城 Yancheng	宿 迁 Suqian
1236.78	5110.01	2632.87	1358.80	1118.34	7012.94	2659.39	933.31	1083.83	1630.88	705.54
1086.95	4573.11	2406.78	1201.39	964.94	6321.27	2433.52	829.64	978.30	1465.26	614.55
149.83	536.90	226.09	157.41	153.40	691.67	225.87	103.67	105.53	165.62	90.99
103.17	508.65	308.59	96.25	103.81	271.58	62.42	70.40	35.04	79.51	24.22
69.52	369.45	230.11	72.59	66.74	182.39	52.48	36.84	26.98	47.38	18.71
33.65	139.21	78.48	23.66	37.07	89.19	9.94	33.56	8.06	32.12	5.51
17.7	21.9	30.1	14.2	16.7	9.9	7.1	19.5	7.6	11.5	7.1
13.51	49.36	23.87	12.04	13.44	43.74	15.06	5.50	11.61	7.07	4.50
5.49	27.48	18.02	5.86	3.61	13.22	3.41	2.26	1.82	5.31	0.42
34	160	80	48	28	237	73	34	48	36	24
0.65	2.24	1.25	0.63	0.36	1.53	0.39	0.23	0.17	0.64	0.07
6	17	8	6	3	30	10	4	7	6	3
10	24	5	10	9	57	11	9	16	5	16
110	558	206	166	186	1162	337	174	188	277	186
111	674	322	203	149	2116	928	451	252	329	156
8.75	22.71	8.75	8.05	5.92	32.78	14.08	3.86	6.97	6.12	1.76
1.90	11.31	5.00	4.18	2.13	18.58	3.63	3.75	4.34	2.08	4.78
9.52	58.23	23.59	17.56	17.08	130.83	36.10	23.01	21.52	27.00	23.20

指 标 Item		苏南合计 Southern Jiangsu	南京 Nanjing	无锡 Wuxi	常州 Changzhou	苏州 Suzhou
小学	Primary Schools	185.53	37.54	36.13	28.11	69.37
专任教师数 （万人）	Total Number of Full-time Teachers (10000 persons)					
#普通高校	Institutions of Regular Higher Education	7.84	4.89	0.61	0.56	1.21
普通中等专业学校	Regular Specialized Secondary Schools	1.60	0.37	0.40	0.25	0.43
普通中学	Regular Secondary Schools	9.48	2.30	2.00	1.41	2.77
小学	Primary Schools	10.33	2.36	2.01	1.42	3.58
成人高等学校在校学生数 （万人）	Total Number of Adult Students in Institutions of Higher Education (10000 persons)	31.83	17.94	2.18	4.75	3.96
科技、文化、卫生	**Science, Culture and Public Health**					
专利申请受理量 （件）	Applications Accepted (unit)	321691	65198	71673	43860	106700
#发 明	Inventions	140458	31556	32610	15349	47429
专利申请授权量 （件）	Patents Granted (unit)	143801	28782	29865	17790	53528
#发 明	Inventions	33354	8697	5583	2865	13267
公共图书馆 （个）	Public Libraries (unit)	47	14	8	5	11
公共图书馆藏书量 （千册、件）	Total Collections of Public Libraries (1000 volumes)	39790	6240	7100	4520	18780
卫生机构数 （个）	Number of Health Institutions (unit)	10109	2383	2308	1267	3175
#医院	Hospitals	677	209	159	56	206
卫生院	Commune Hospitals	233	16	32	58	77
卫生机构床位数 （万张）	Number of Beds in Health Institutions (10000 units)	19.28	4.99	3.97	2.54	6.32
#医院	Hospital	16.74	4.48	3.54	1.97	5.67
卫生院	Commune Hospitals	1.09	0.04	0.08	0.37	0.42
卫生技术人员 （万人）	Number of Medical and Technical Personnel (10000 persons)	24.10	7.07	4.75	3.12	7.22

镇 江 Zhenjiang	苏中合计 Mid Jiangsu	南 通 Nantong	扬 州 Yangzhou	泰 州 Taizhou	苏北合计 Northern Jiangsu	徐 州 Xuzhou	连云港 Lianyungang	淮 安 Huaian	盐 城 Yancheng	宿 迁 Suqian
14.38	75.96	32.71	21.26	22.00	260.71	90.54	43.20	35.05	45.02	46.90
0.57	1.29	0.49	0.48	0.31	1.86	0.82	0.21	0.38	0.35	0.09
0.16	0.40	0.06	0.17	0.17	0.98	0.18	0.15	0.29	0.08	0.27
1.01	6.00	2.45	1.65	1.90	11.68	3.37	2.00	1.95	2.66	1.71
0.96	4.73	1.96	1.36	1.41	13.85	4.27	2.36	2.11	2.65	2.46
3.01	5.99	2.43	2.50	1.06	6.08	3.83	0.94	1.32		
34260	104198	45557	27043	31598	86615	21511	8780	17293	28509	10522
13514	25799	9303	6124	10372	18411	5414	1760	4061	5624	1552
13836	50079	24337	13253	12489	37124	11458	4599	8081	8076	4910
2942	4402	2725	738	939	3193	1330	453	406	842	162
9	24	10	7	7	42	8	8	9	11	6
3150	11250	5000	3540	2710	13600	3300	2650	2860	3350	1440
976	6881	3131	1787	1963	15145	4584	2726	2237	3233	2365
47	352	216	69	67	650	131	80	57	151	231
50	294	105	73	116	514	160	91	128	135	
1.46	8.32	3.91	2.07	2.33	16.72	5.22	2.33	2.75	3.87	2.54
1.08	6.25	3.06	1.53	1.67	12.64	3.82	1.66	1.76	2.87	2.53
0.19	1.60	0.76	0.32	0.52	3.19	1.07	0.48	0.79	0.84	
1.94	9.49	4.36	2.53	2.61	18.11	5.55	2.62	3.15	3.95	2.84

指 标	Item	苏南合计 Southern Jiangsu	南京 Nanjing	无锡 Wuxi	常州 Changzhou	苏州 Suzhou
#执业(助理)医师	Practitioner (Assistant) Doctors	9.14	2.53	1.81	1.24	2.77
注册护士	Registered Nurses	10.51	3.21	2.05	1.35	3.07
人民生活	**People's Livelihood**					
居民人均可支配收入	Per Capita Disposable Income of Residents	42795	44009	42757	38435	46595
城镇常住居民人均可支配收入 (元)	Per Capita Disposable Income of Urban Permanent Residents (yuan)	49920	49997	48628	46058	54341
城镇常住居民人均生活消费支出 (元)	Per Capita Consumption Expanditure of Urban Permanent Residents (yuan)	30444	29772	31438	27080	33305
#食品烟酒	Food, Tobacco and Wine	8184	7642	8818	7357	8882
恩格尔系数(城镇)(%)	Engle Coefficient(Urban) (%)	26.9	25.7	28.0	27.2	26.7
农村常住居民人均可支配收入 (元)	Per Capita Disposable Income of Rural Permanent Residents (yuan)	24638	21156	26158	23780	27691
农村常住居民人均生活消费支出 (元)	Per Capita Consumption Expanditure of Rural Permanent Residents (yuan)	17423	15773	18463	16567	18820
#食品烟酒	Food, Tobacco and Wine	4956	4745	5502	5102	4832
恩格尔系数(农村)(%)	Engle Coefficient(Rural) (%)	28.4	30.1	29.8	30.8	25.7
城镇人均住房建筑面积 (平方米)	Per Capita Existing Residential Building Space in Urban Areas (sq. m)	42.6	36.7	46.7	44.3	43.3
农村人均住房建筑面积 (平方米)	Per Capita Existing Residential Building Space in Rural Areas (sq. m)	60.7	56.6	56.4	64.7	65.6
居民消费价格指数 (上年=100)	Consumer Price Indices (preceding year=100)	—	102.7	102.3	102.5	102.7

镇 江 Zhenjiang	苏中合计 Mid Jiangsu	南 通 Nantong	扬 州 Yangzhou	泰 州 Taizhou	苏北合计 Northern Jiangsu	徐 州 Xuzhou	连云港 Lianyungang	淮 安 Huaian	盐 城 Yancheng	宿 迁 Suqian
0.79	3.97	1.80	1.04	1.13	7.37	2.18	1.10	1.24	1.81	1.03
0.83	3.88	1.82	1.04	1.02	7.73	2.43	1.09	1.43	1.48	1.28
34064	29138	30084	28633	28259	22174	22348	21230	22762	24463	18957
41794	37585	39247	35659	36828	28515	28421	27853	30335	30496	24086
24388	23311	25217	21064	22480	17163	17255	18344	16912	17546	15521
6939	6826	7227	6551	6470	5384	5182	5924	5054	5532	5390
28.5	29.3	28.7	31.1	28.8	31.4	30.0	32.3	29.9	31.5	34.7
20922	18320	18741	18057	17861	15102	15274	13932	14319	17172	13929
15925	13460	13440	13722	13250	10929	11059	10113	9633	13145	9395
4547	4022	3923	4185	4025	3525	3475	3298	3055	4159	3358
28.6	29.9	29.2	30.5	30.4	32.3	31.4	32.6	31.7	31.6	35.7
44.7	47.8	47.8	46.4	49.0	43.8	41.4	46.1	44.2	43.1	46.7
57.7	60.3	61.5	54.2	64.0	50.9	53.3	48.7	51.2	50.9	47.8
102.2	—	102.3	102.4	102.1	—	102.3	102.1	102.2	102.1	102.0

19-3 江苏主要指标占长江三角洲比重（2016年）
Proportion of Main Indicators of Jiangsu in Yangtze River Delta (2016)

指标	Item	长江三角洲三省市合计 Yangtze River Delta	长江三角洲占全国比重(%) Proportion of Yangtze River Delta in the Country(%)	江苏占长江三角洲比重(%) Proportion of Jiangsu in Yangtze River Delta(%)
土地面积（万平方公里）	Land Area (10000 sq. km)	21.5	2.2	49.8
年末总人口（万人）	Year-end Total Population (10000 persons)	16008.3	11.6	50.0
地区生产总值（亿元）	Gross Domestic Product (100 million yuan)	150037.3	20.2	50.7
第一产业	Primary Industry	6153.2	9.7	66.3
第二产业	Secondary Industry	62062.7	21.0	54.1
第三产业	Tertiary Industry	81821.4	21.3	47.0
#工业	Industry	54808.9	22.1	46.8
固定资产投资（亿元）	Total Investment in Fixed Assets (100 million yuan)	85693.5	14.4	57.6
#房地产开发	Investment in Real Estate Development	20134.8	19.6	44.5
一般公共预算收入（亿元）	General Public Budget Revenue (100 million yuan)	19829.2	22.7	41.0
金融机构本外币存款余额（亿元）	Deposits Balance of Banking Institutions (100 million yuan)	335618.2	21.6	37.4
金融机构本外币贷款余额（亿元）	Loans Balance of Banking Institutions (100 million yuan)	234743.8	20.9	39.6
社会消费品零售总额（亿元）	Total Rtail Sales of Consumer Goods (100 million yuan)	61624.5	18.5	46.6
进出口总额（亿美元）	Total Imports and Exports (USD 100 million)	12798.7	34.7	39.8
出口	Exports	7706.1	36.7	41.4
进口	Imports	5092.6	32.1	37.4
实际使用外资（亿美元）	Actual Use of Foreign Capital (USD 100 million)	533.6	42.3	46.0
旅游外汇收入（亿美元）	Foreign Exchange Earnings from Tourism (USD 100 million)	177.6	14.8	21.4
在读研究生（万人）	Postgraduates (10000 persons)	37.4	18.9	43.2
普通高等学校本专科在校学生（万人）	University and College Students (10000 persons)	311.2	11.5	56.1
专利申请受理量（万件）	Applications Accepted (10000 units)	102.5	29.6	50.0
专利申请授权量（万件）	Patents Granted (10000 units)	51.6	29.4	44.8
图书出版量（亿册）	Books Pubished (100 million copies)	14.4	16.8	43.3
执业医师数（万人）	Doctors (10000 persons)	43.8	13.7	46.7

19－4　沿江开发区域主要指标占全省比重（2016 年）
Proportion of Main Indicators of Development Zones along the Yangtze River in Jiangsu Province (2016)

指标	Item	全省 Province	沿江开发区域 Development Zones along the Yangtze River	沿江开发区域占全省比重（%） Proportion of Development Zones along the Yangtze River in Jiangsu Province (%)
年末户籍人口　（万人）	Registered Population at Year-end (10000 persons)	7775.66	2810.55	36.1
土地面积　（万平方公里）	Land Area (10000 sq. km)	10.72	3.05	28.4
地区生产总值　（亿元）	Gross Domestic Product (100 million yuan)	76086.17	40078.50	52.7
第一产业	Primary Industry	4078.48	1145.28	28.1
第二产业	Secondary Industry	33855.73	18695.56	55.2
第三产业	Tertiary Industry	38151.96	20237.79	53.0
#工业	Industry	29689.92	16768.6	56.5
规模以上工业总产值　（亿元）	Gross Industrial Output Value of Over Scale Enterprises (100 million yuan)	157640.23	76616.63	48.6
#制造业	Manufacturing	151934.14	75153.06	49.5
固定资产投资额　（亿元）	Urban Investment in Fixed Assets (100 million yuan)	49370.85	23280.10	47.2
#房地产开发投资	Real Estate Dvelopment	8956.37	4455.85	49.8
社会消费品零售总额　（亿元）	Total Retail Sales of Consumer Goods (100 million yuan)	28707.12	14590.06	50.8
进出口总额　（亿美元）	Total Imports and Exports (USD 100 million)	5096.12	2100.39	41.2
#出口	Exports	3193.44	1338.94	41.9
实际使用外资　（亿美元）	Actual Use of Foreign Cpaital (USD 100 million)	245.43	139.06	56.7
一般公共预算收入　（亿元）	General Public Budget Revenue (100 million yuan)	8121.23	3627.22	44.7
一般公共预算支出　（亿元）	General Public Budget Expenditure (100 million yuan)	8754.50	3948.39	45.1
金融机构存款余额　（亿元）	Deposits Balance of Banking Institutions (100 million yuan)	121106.58	67717.28	55.9
#住户存款	Household Deposits	43900.50	22651.58	51.6
金融机构贷款余额　（亿元）	Loans Balance of Banking Institutions (100 million yuan)	91107.60	50100.54	55.0

19－5 沿江地区主要指标（2016年）
Main Indicators of the Region along the Yangtze River（2016）

地　区	Region	年末户籍人口（万人）Registered Population at Year-end（10000 persons）	土地面积（平方公里）Land Area（sq. km）	人口密度（人/平方公里）Density of Population（person/sq. km）	就业人员（万人）Employed Persons（10000 persons）	#第二产业 Secondary Industry	#第三产业 Tertiary Industry
沿江八市	**Eight Cities**	**4210.61**	**51011**	**976**	**3009.50**	**1448.40**	**1220.00**
沿江开发区域	**Development Regions**	**2810.55**	**30499**	**1061**	**1966.82**	**896.52**	**856.67**
南京市区	Nanjing	662.79	6587	1256	493.20	172.70	293.80
江阴市	Jiangyin	124.80	987	1663	98.99	61.03	33.10
常州市区	Changzhou	294.95	2838	1391	231.56	116.73	96.39
常熟市	Changshu	106.87	1276	1185	104.55	64.17	36.43
张家港市	Zhangjiagang	92.66	987	1272	77.27	46.51	26.35
太仓市	Taicang	48.30	810	879	45.80	26.81	16.39
南通市区	Nantong	213.57	2140	1097	135.80	58.75	59.80
启东市	Qidong	111.95	1715	555	67.00	29.20	19.50
如皋市	Rugao	143.68	1575	794	74.30	34.60	20.40
海门市	Haimen	100.10	1144	791	64.70	31.20	17.00
扬州市区	Yangzhou	232.47	2306	1053	137.15	62.04	61.94
仪征市	Yizheng	56.47	902	627	39.18	18.02	12.54
镇江市区	Zhenjiang	103.42	1088	1132	69.74	26.97	37.25
丹阳市	Danyang	81.15	1047	938	63.56	33.76	24.00
扬中市	Yangzhong	28.20	327	1048	21.72	11.73	8.66
句容市	Jurong	59.21	1378	454	39.30	15.60	14.12
泰州市区	Taizhou	163.98	1567	1038	97.50	39.70	43.50
靖江市	Jingjiang	66.67	655	1049	41.10	20.60	13.60
泰兴市	Taixing	119.31	1170	921	64.40	26.40	21.90

地 区	Region	地区生产总值（亿元） Gross Domectic Product (100 million yuan)	第一产业 Primary Industry	第二产业 Seconary Industry	第三产业 Tertiary Industry	#工 业 Industry	人均地区生产总值（元） Per Capita GDP (yuan)
沿江八市	**Eight Cities**	**60115.19**	**1758.04**	**27596.24**	**30760.91**	**24663.97**	**120906**
沿江开发区域	**Development Regions**	**40078.76**	**1145.62**	**18695.55**	**20238.60**	**16768.30**	**123994**
南京市区	Nanjing	10503.02	252.54	4117.32	6133.16	3581.72	127264
江 阴 市	Jiangyin	3083.26	44.34	1681.99	1357.93	1612.25	188101
常州市区	Changzhou	4985.66	104.37	2291.09	2590.20	2094.66	126424
常 熟 市	Changshu	2112.39	42.76	1082.43	987.20	1026.16	139768
张家港市	Zhangjiagang	2317.24	31.34	1214.70	1071.21	1155.30	184747
太 仓 市	Taicang	1155.13	36.76	583.87	534.50	547.67	162526
南通市区	Nantong	2475.03	59.97	1113.84	1301.22	933.36	105599
启 东 市	Qidong	881.85	66.58	422.85	392.42	336.94	92534
如 皋 市	Rugao	904.27	62.99	434.36	406.92	364.30	72255
海 门 市	Haimen	1005.06	53.28	504.53	447.25	420.99	111099
扬州市区	Yangzhou	2900.30	92.21	1420.61	1388.48	1262.32	119578
仪 征 市	Yizheng	557.05	23.36	294.27	239.42	262.33	98558
镇江市区	Zhenjiang	1711.60	29.33	829.74	852.53	739.42	139126
丹 阳 市	Danyang	1136.04	52.31	567.57	516.16	544.57	115816
扬 中 市	Yangzhong	504.73	12.96	261.44	230.33	250.74	147431
句 容 市	Jurong	493.20	43.11	231.90	218.19	206.81	78862
泰州市区	Taizhou	1718.27	60.95	863.57	793.75	737.30	105789
靖 江 市	Jingjiang	801.75	22.51	391.95	387.29	351.39	116703
泰 兴 市	Taixing	832.91	53.95	388.52	390.44	340.07	77315

单位:% (%)

地区	Region	三次产业占GDP比重 Percentage of Three Industries to GDP 第一产业 Primary Industry	第二产业 Seconary Industry	第三产业 Tertiary Industry	#工业 Industry	一般公共预算收入占GDP比重 Percentage of General Public Budget Revenue to GDP	外贸依存度 Interdependent Level to Foreign Trade
沿江八市	**Eight Cities**	**2.9**	**45.9**	**51.2**	**41.0**	**9.6**	**53.0**
沿江开发区域	**Development Regions**	**2.9**	**46.6**	**50.5**	**41.8**	**9.1**	**30.2**
南京市区	Nanjing	2.4	39.2	58.4	34.1	10.9	31.6
江阴市	Jiangyin	1.4	54.5	44.0	52.3	7.5	42.5
常州市区	Changzhou	2.1	46.0	52.0	42.0	8.4	35.6
常熟市	Changshu	2.0	51.2	46.7	48.6	8.2	62.1
张家港市	Zhangjiagang	1.4	52.4	46.2	49.9	8.2	78.1
太仓市	Taicang	3.2	50.5	46.3	47.4	11.1	62.6
南通市区	Nantong	2.4	45.0	52.6	37.7	10.6	45.9
启东市	Qidong	7.6	48.0	44.5	38.2	8.1	22.5
如皋市	Rugao	7.0	48.0	45.0	40.3	7.9	18.4
海门市	Haimen	5.3	50.2	44.5	41.9	7.2	25.6
扬州市区	Yangzhou	3.2	49.0	47.8	43.5	8.1	15.8
仪征市	Yizheng	4.2	52.8	43.0	47.1	8.0	12.7
镇江市区	Zhenjiang	1.7	48.5	49.8	43.2	9.0	25.5
丹阳市	Danyang	4.6	50.0	45.4	47.9	5.8	14.8
扬中市	Yangzhong	2.6	51.8	45.6	49.7	6.4	7.5
句容市	Jurong	8.7	47.0	44.2	41.9	8.2	7.9
泰州市区	Taizhou	3.5	50.3	46.2	42.9	10.2	17.6
靖江市	Jingjiang	2.8	48.9	48.3	43.8	7.4	22.2
泰兴市	Taixing	6.5	46.6	46.9	40.8	6.9	20.4

地　区	Region	规模以上工业企业个数（个）Number of Over Scale Industrial Enterprises (unit)	工业总产值（亿元）Total Output Value of Industry (100 million yuan)	#制造业 Manufacturing	资产合计（亿元）Total Assets (100 million yuan)	主营业务收入（亿元）Revenue from Principal Business (100 million yuan)	利润总额（亿元）Total Profits (100 million yuan)
沿江八市	**Eight Cities**	**34714**	**115572.49**	**113673.78**	**89835.70**	**114502.72**	**7659.21**
沿江开发区域	**Development Regions**	**21436**	**76616.63**	**75153.06**	**58351.93**	**76241.33**	**5210.00**
南京市区	Nanjing	2661	12945.02	12654.34	11448.85	12442.36	959.35
江 阴 市	Jiangyin	1356	5376.01	5245.73	6163.53	5393.26	337.84
常州市区	Changzhou	3746	10733.40	10607.49	7997.81	11086.35	646.19
常 熟 市	Changshu	1309	3684.89	3572.97	3939.37	3633.14	235.76
张家港市	Zhangjiagang	1078	4571.66	4479.70	4746.81	4683.67	177.08
太 仓 市	Taicang	1020	2027.67	1929.30	2108.82	1968.23	154.73
南通市区	Nantong	1515	4771.88	4679.92	3367.16	4688.23	332.71
启 东 市	Qidong	503	1829.18	1777.07	1200.83	1839.18	130.52
如 皋 市	Rugao	819	1985.12	1980.11	955.73	2009.77	128.77
海 门 市	Haimen	650	2053.24	2047.58	1017.11	2072.14	220.61
扬州市区	Yangzhou	1385	5918.50	5803.45	2891.00	5775.55	334.19
仪 征 市	Yizheng	363	1616.84	1598.00	746.22	1558.76	137.14
镇江市区	Zhenjiang	906	3421.62	3297.97	2465.13	3464.56	256.80
丹 阳 市	Danyang	724	2529.31	2522.03	1494.37	2521.56	159.66
扬 中 市	Yangzhong	460	1372.66	1370.88	1050.04	1365.95	94.16
句 容 市	Jurong	545	1399.25	1357.07	848.64	1388.50	71.56
泰州市区	Taizhou	1210	5489.57	5403.02	2711.41	5394.22	407.02
靖 江 市	Jingjiang	488	1888.79	1840.70	1550.00	1865.42	147.87
泰 兴 市	Taixing	698	3002.02	2985.75	1649.12	3090.49	278.07

地 区	Region	固定资产投资（亿元）Investment in Fixed Assets (100 million yuan)	#房地产开发 Real Estate Development	社会消费品零售总额（亿元）Total Retail Sales of Consumer Goods (100 million yuan)	进出口总额（亿美元）Total Imports and Exports (USD 100 million)	#出 口 Exports	实际使用外资（亿美元）Actual Use of Foreign Capital (USD 100 million)
沿江八市	**Eight Cities**	**33720.56**	**7182.83**	**21694.17**	**4825.44**	**3012.01**	**216.82**
沿江开发区域	**Development Regions**	**23280.10**	**4455.85**	**14590.06**	**2100.39**	**1338.94**	**139.06**
南京市区	Nanjing	5533.56	1845.60	5088.20	502.14	295.94	34.79
江 阴 市	Jiangyin	1133.03	281.10	776.05	198.77	119.22	10.55
常州市区	Changzhou	3118.52	402.64	1899.81	267.54	201.14	21.64
常 熟 市	Changshu	544.91	143.71	740.78	198.53	133.56	6.30
张家港市	Zhangjiagang	724.77	163.81	535.16	274.17	142.02	6.04
太 仓 市	Taicang	465.00	94.73	287.31	109.64	54.30	5.61
南通市区	Nantong	1878.80	351.37	1029.13	172.29	119.11	9.96
启 东 市	Qidong	614.84	55.63	324.57	30.22	26.51	2.84
如 皋 市	Rugao	575.25	52.68	342.21	25.29	20.15	2.77
海 门 市	Haimen	613.19	49.77	344.60	39.14	35.79	2.40
扬州市区	Yangzhou	1989.33	315.84	928.61	70.09	55.20	9.75
仪 征 市	Yizheng	471.00	22.11	109.75	10.83	4.64	1.29
镇江市区	Zhenjiang	1693.52	239.59	638.23	66.07	38.87	6.90
丹 阳 市	Danyang	514.01	71.73	315.61	25.44	21.40	3.22
扬 中 市	Yangzhong	305.10	24.86	140.92	5.73	4.54	1.18
句 容 市	Jurong	360.81	112.46	142.02	5.93	4.71	2.21
泰州市区	Taizhou	1557.00	125.45	556.91	45.64	30.16	7.86
靖 江 市	Jingjiang	500.00	35.08	176.24	27.18	19.36	0.23
泰 兴 市	Taixing	687.46	67.69	213.95	25.75	12.33	3.53

19－5　续　表5　Continued 5

单位:亿元　　(100 million yuan)

地　　区	Region	一般公共预算收入 General Public Budget Revenue	#税收收入 Taxes	一般公共预算支出 General Public Budget Expenditure	年末金融机构存款余　额 Deposits Balance of Banking Institutions (year-end)	#住户存款 Household Deposits	年末金融机构贷款余　额 Loans Balance of Banking Institutions (year-end)
沿江八市	**Eight Cities**	**5784.02**	**4770.74**	**6208.42**	**102581.36**	**34512.28**	**77476.55**
沿江开发区域	**Development Regions**	**3627.22**	**2941.70**	**3948.39**	**67717.28**	**22651.58**	**50100.54**
南京市区	Nanjing	1142.60	956.62	1173.79	27633.55	5894.47	21681.28
江 阴 市	Jiangyin	229.91	191.20	226.26	3509.40	1079.72	2689.91
常州市区	Changzhou	421.29	336.45	438.67	7546.00	2888.34	5244.21
常 熟 市	Changshu	173.58	145.54	158.74	2692.88	1192.75	2139.49
张家港市	Zhangjiagang	190.00	160.11	184.86	2508.27	1018.23	1994.40
太 仓 市	Taicang	127.71	110.52	115.84	1395.41	522.74	1245.07
南通市区	Nantong	263.54	201.73	294.55	5064.90	2005.85	3302.70
启 东 市	Qidong	71.03	54.95	89.03	1232.03	767.24	705.13
如 皋 市	Rugao	71.21	54.26	96.38	1135.62	716.86	709.99
海 门 市	Haimen	72.41	53.23	85.75	1368.55	766.55	824.32
扬州市区	Yangzhou	235.63	173.45	306.71	3724.09	1632.92	2548.23
仪 征 市	Yizheng	44.74	38.57	50.95	606.06	295.73	343.07
镇江市区	Zhenjiang	154.48	114.07	191.74	2457.48	748.20	1487.41
丹 阳 市	Danyang	65.55	54.23	79.01	1040.33	566.31	964.49
扬 中 市	Yangzhong	32.50	26.72	38.66	578.31	276.78	431.43
句 容 市	Jurong	40.48	36.38	53.54	629.87	287.82	561.03
泰州市区	Taizhou	174.41	138.43	223.39	2742.07	1053.58	1952.97
靖 江 市	Jingjiang	58.93	48.08	64.15	940.16	472.16	694.02
泰 兴 市	Taixing	57.20	47.16	76.38	912.30	465.34	581.39

19－5 续 表6 Continued 6

地 区	Region	公路里程（公里）Total Length of Highways (km)	民用汽车拥有量（万辆）Number of Civil Motor Vehicles Owned (10000 units)	公路客运量（万人）Passenger Traffic (10000 persons)	公路货运量（万吨）Freight Traffic (10000 tons)	全社会用电量（亿千瓦时）Total Consumption of Electricity (100 million kW·h)	#工业用电 Consumption of Electricity for Industrial Use
沿江八市	**Eight Cities**	**86359**	**1053.25**	**76410**	**77556**	**4048.08**	**3027.84**
沿江开发区域	**Development Regions**	**59394**	**693.81**	**43696**	**52195**	**2538.80**	**1753.93**
南京市区	Nanjing	11211	221.68	10694	13341	524.79	310.81
江 阴 市	Jiangyin	2373	40.40	420	2947	244.93	214.41
常州市区	Changzhou	6474	96.34	4477	9066	357.18	274.42
常 熟 市	Changshu	3120	39.14	3528	1275	172.33	144.18
张家港市	Zhangjiagang	1617	33.65	3129	1599	288.81	264.91
太 仓 市	Taicang	1304	19.66	2796	1302	96.93	81.30
南通市区	Nantong	3976	53.11	4754	4941	151.50	19.73
启 东 市	Qidong	3595	16.03	1198	548	31.02	6.79
如 皋 市	Rugao	3270	20.78	548	2137	50.31	8.86
海 门 市	Haimen	2521	16.39	482	780	38.60	6.48
扬州市区	Yangzhou	4186	28.62	1968	4260	132.73	88.12
仪 征 市	Yizheng	1510	7.80	451	914	41.10	34.40
镇江市区	Zhenjiang	1637	22.93	1816	3901	116.56	89.22
丹 阳 市	Danyang	2189	16.05	761	1583	71.50	55.67
扬 中 市	Yangzhong	1031	5.70	360	423	18.26	12.96
句 容 市	Jurong	2498	4.51	637	1043	26.09	15.93
泰州市区	Taizhou	3364	26.52	2915	1298	84.13	56.85
靖 江 市	Jingjiang	1327	12.00	1046	342	37.47	26.43
泰 兴 市	Taixing	2191	12.48	1716	496	54.57	42.46

19－6　沿海地区主要指标（2016 年）
Main Indicators of the Coastal Regions(2016)

地　区	Region	年末户籍人口(万人) Registered Population at Year-end (10000 persons)	土地面积(平方公里) Land Area (sq. km)	人口密度(人/平方公里) Density of Population (person/sq. km)	就业人员(万人) Employed Persons (10000 persons)	#第二产业 Secondary Industry	#第三产业 Tertiary Industry
沿海三市合计	**Three Cities**	**2131.18**	**35095**	**542**	**1154.50**	**453.5**	**416.2**
沿海地带合计	**Coastal Regions**	**1671.04**	**28887**	**528**	**928.01**	**366.72**	**340.74**
南通市区	Nantong	213.57	2140	1097	135.80	58.75	59.80
海 安 县	Haian	93.83	1184	731	54.20	28.55	14.35
如 东 县	Rudong	103.53	2791	352	62.00	30.70	17.95
启 东 市	Qidong	111.95	1715	555	67.00	29.20	19.50
海 门 市	Haimen	100.10	1144	791	64.70	31.20	17.00
连云港市区	Lianyungang	222.69	3012	693	109.60	39.01	44.20
灌 云 县	Guanyun	105.21	1538	523	47.87	12.92	16.46
灌 南 县	Guannan	82.64	1028	618	36.44	10.96	10.39
盐城市区	Yancheng	243.34	5129	463	143.08	54.01	62.61
响 水 县	Xiangshui	62.49	1474	340	28.74	9.97	10.56
滨 海 县	Binhai	123.00	1950	479	56.40	18.77	20.78
射 阳 县	Sheyang	96.23	2606	339	57.01	19.55	21.42
东 台 市	Dongtai	112.46	3176	309	65.17	23.13	25.72

地　区	Region	地区生产总值（亿元）Gross Domectic Product (100 million yuan)	第一产业 Primary Industry	第二产业 Seconary Industry	第三产业 Tertiary Industry	#工　业 Industry	人均地区生产总值（元）Per Capita GDP (yuan)
沿海三市合计	**Three Cities**	**13720.76**	**1202.13**	**6270.22**	**6248.41**	**5256.56**	**72147**
沿海地带合计	**Coastal Regions**	**11522.52**	**970.53**	**5282.55**	**5269.44**	**4433.40**	**75649**
南通市区	Nantong	2475.03	59.97	1113.84	1301.22	933.36	105599
海 安 县	Haian	755.29	55.97	354.15	345.17	290.67	87201
如 东 县	Rudong	746.69	67.87	340.57	338.25	286.80	76045
启 东 市	Qidong	881.85	66.58	422.85	392.42	336.94	92534
海 门 市	Haimen	1005.06	53.28	504.53	447.25	420.99	111099
连云港市区	Lianyungang	1307.59	118.67	575.43	613.49	453.52	62788
灌 云 县	Guanyun	328.66	64.10	143.12	121.44	109.30	40926
灌 南 县	Guannan	306.80	51.51	144.78	110.51	125.92	48429
盐城市区	Yancheng	1884.64	160.69	951.98	771.97	831.76	80122
响 水 县	Xiangshui	270.64	41.42	126.77	102.45	113.66	53971
滨 海 县	Binhai	391.61	57.99	156.72	176.90	132.74	41761
射 阳 县	Sheyang	441.65	81.01	155.78	204.86	142.01	49749
东 台 市	Dongtai	727.01	91.47	292.03	343.51	255.73	73902

单位:%　　(%)

地　区	Region	三次产业占GDP比重 Percentage of Three Industries to GDP 第一产业 Primary Industry	第二产业 Seconary Industry	第三产业 Tertiary Industry	#工　业 Industry	一般公共预算收入占GDP比重 Percentage of General Public Budget Revenue to GDP	外贸依存度 Interdependent Level to Foreign Trade
沿海三市合计	**Three Cities**	**8.8**	**45.7**	**45.5**	**38.3**	**8.9**	**22.2**
沿海地带合计	**Coastal Regions**	**8.4**	**45.8**	**45.7**	**38.5**	**9.1**	**24.4**
南通市区	Nantong	2.4	45.0	52.6	37.7	10.6	46.2
海安县	Haian	7.4	46.9	45.7	38.5	7.6	14.6
如东县	Rudong	9.1	45.6	45.3	38.4	7.3	22.3
启东市	Qidong	7.6	48.0	44.5	38.2	8.1	22.8
海门市	Haimen	5.3	50.2	44.5	41.9	7.2	25.9
连云港市区	Lianyungang	9.1	44.0	46.9	34.7	11.1	31.1
灌云县	Guanyun	19.5	43.5	37.0	33.3	6.5	4.7
灌南县	Guannan	16.8	47.2	36.0	41.0	7.3	4.9
盐城市区	Yancheng	8.5	50.5	41.0	44.1	10.5	19.3
响水县	Xiangshui	15.3	46.8	37.9	42.0	10.9	11.9
滨海县	Binhai	14.8	40.0	45.2	33.9	8.7	6.4
射阳县	Sheyang	18.3	35.3	46.4	32.2	4.9	4.3
东台市	Dongtai	12.6	40.2	47.2	35.2	8.3	6.7

地　　区	Region	规模以上工业企业个数（个）Number of Over Scale Industrial Enterprises (unit)	工业总产值（亿元）Total Output Value of Industry (100 million yuan)	#制造业 Manufacturing	资产合计（亿元）Total Assets (100 million yuan)	主营业务收入（亿元）Revenue from Principal Business (100 million yuan)	利润总额（亿元）Total Profits (100 million yuan)
沿海三市合计	**Three Cities**	**10071**	**29681.37**	**29576.84**	**17714.26**	**29467.68**	**2090.63**
沿海地带合计	**Coastal Regions**	**7991**	**25352.43**	**24842.03**	**15642.76**	**24982.76**	**1796.04**
南通市区	Nantong	1515	4771.88	4679.92	3367.16	4688.23	332.71
海 安 县	Haian	895	2204.77	2194.69	1060.75	2213.06	159.99
如 东 县	Rudong	689	1896.41	1840.26	1200.34	1883.91	147.18
启 东 市	Qidong	503	1829.18	1777.07	1200.83	1839.18	130.52
海 门 市	Haimen	650	2053.24	2047.58	1017.11	2072.14	220.61
连云港市区	Lianyungang	798	3663.54	3547.13	2708.96	3627.12	323.48
灌 云 县	Guanyun	279	762.14	742.69	192.73	715.77	44.99
灌 南 县	Guannan	192	671.18	670.38	315.35	666.61	46.83
盐城市区	Yancheng	1204	3932.36	3878.79	2298.20	3791.86	202.25
响 水 县	Xiangshui	166	924.82	888.47	767.14	922.06	53.93
滨 海 县	Binhai	228	705.15	689.86	418.51	685.29	35.01
射 阳 县	Sheyang	312	751.19	711.71	383.45	731.74	32.58
东 台 市	Dongtai	560	1186.59	1173.50	712.24	1145.78	65.96

地　　区	Region	固定资产投资（亿元）Investment in Fixed Assets（100 million yuan）	#房地产开发 Real Estate Development	社会消费品零售总额（亿元）Total Retail Sales of Consumer Goods（100 million yuan）	进出口总额（亿美元）Total Imports and Exports（USD 100 million）	#出　口 Exports	实际使用外　资（亿美元）Actual Use of Foreign Capital（USD 100 million）
沿海三市合计	**Three Cities**	**11079.94**	**1178.12**	**5197.06**	**458.50**	**314.34**	**36.44**
沿海地带合计	**Coastal Regions**	**9495.89**	**1063.76**	**4376.69**	**422.83**	**285.37**	**32.06**
南通市区	Nantong	1878.80	351.37	1029.13	172.29	119.11	9.96
海安县	Haian	584.46	52.44	273.74	16.55	14.05	2.96
如东县	Rudong	545.42	22.24	318.62	25.10	14.51	2.94
启东市	Qidong	614.84	55.63	324.57	30.22	26.51	2.84
海门市	Haimen	613.19	49.77	344.60	39.14	35.79	2.40
连云港市区	Lianyungang	1564.32	165.86	544.44	61.23	29.43	4.29
灌云县	Guanyun	272.19	27.26	119.45	2.33	2.03	0.24
灌南县	Guannan	218.06	22.51	93.52	2.25	1.70	0.03
盐城市区	Yancheng	1658.29	209.37	730.21	54.87	25.45	4.51
响水县	Xiangshui	287.25	11.07	66.52	4.86	4.70	0.29
滨海县	Binhai	377.87	21.34	110.46	3.77	3.08	0.53
射阳县	Sheyang	300.16	26.21	167.90	2.84	1.95	0.45
东台市	Dongtai	581.03	48.68	253.53	7.37	7.07	0.62

19－6 续 表5 Continued 5

单位:亿元 (100 million yuan)

地 区	Region	一般公共预算收入 General Public Budget Revenue	#税收收入 Taxes	一般公共预算支出 General Public Budget Expenditure	年末金融机构存款余额 Deposits Balance of Banking Institutions (year-end)	#住户存款 Household Deposits	年末金融机构贷款余额 Loans Balance of Banking Institutions (year-end)
沿海三市合计	**Three Cities**	**1216.83**	**952.24**	**1852.67**	**18854.65**	**9406.06**	**12581.71**
沿海地带合计	**Coastal Regions**	**1051.76**	**825.22**	**1548.44**	**16598.95**	**7600.31**	**11080.74**
南通市区	Nantong	263.54	201.73	294.55	5064.90	2005.85	3302.70
海 安 县	Haian	57.58	48.16	81.35	1286.53	696.77	798.77
如 东 县	Rudong	54.41	44.44	102.16	1010.55	601.62	494.56
启 东 市	Qidong	71.03	54.95	89.03	1232.03	767.24	705.13
海 门 市	Haimen	72.41	53.23	85.75	1368.55	766.55	824.32
连云港市区	Lianyungang	144.91	115.24	217.35	1743.70	470.61	1480.37
灌 云 县	Guanyun	21.52	17.64	49.64	260.88	82.62	183.80
灌 南 县	Guannan	22.43	19.33	48.04	179.88	77.90	134.05
盐城市区	Yancheng	198.42	156.94	299.37	2835.08	1072.21	2108.63
响 水 县	Xiangshui	29.60	20.39	50.13	178.13	93.58	139.77
滨 海 县	Binhai	34.07	25.08	70.89	308.75	176.66	249.46
射 阳 县	Sheyang	21.58	17.40	64.60	413.98	277.99	264.42
东 台 市	Dongtai	60.26	50.70	95.58	715.99	510.70	394.75

19－6　续　表6　Continued 6

地　　区	Region	公路里程（公里） Total Length of Highways (km)	民用汽车拥有量（万辆） Number of Civil Motor Vehicles Owned (10000 units)	公路客运量（万人） Passenger Traffic (10000 persons)	公路货运量（万吨） Freight Traffic (10000 tons)	全社会用电量（亿千瓦时） Total Consumption of Electricity (100 million kW·h)	#工业用电 Consumption of Electricity for Industrial Use
沿海三市合计	**Three Cities**	**50022**	**258.38**	**21141**	**24989**	**830.23**	**577.02**
沿海地带合计	**Coastal Regions**	**40047**	**214.79**	**18650**	**20572**	**663.05**	**283.22**
南通市区	Nantong	3976	53.11	4754	4941	151.50	19.73
海安县	Haian	2374	12.89	544	1794	46.72	5.30
如东县	Rudong	2691	15.03	679	1335	49.12	6.29
启东市	Qidong	3595	16.03	1198	548	31.02	6.79
海门市	Haimen	2521	16.39	482	780	38.60	6.48
连云港市区	Lianyungang	4489	27.04	3359	5006	63.68	41.30
灌云县	Guanyun	2649	7.29	439	873	12.83	6.05
灌南县	Guannan	1921	4.97	359	694	31.48	24.87
盐城市区	Yancheng	6105	32.59	3824	1650	107.02	70.56
响水县	Xiangshui	1806	4.08	426	359	42.08	36.08
滨海县	Binhai	2158	7.67	900	1052	26.26	17.22
射阳县	Sheyang	2498	8.06	796	672	21.64	12.42
东台市	Dongtai	3264	9.64	890	868	41.10	30.12

19-7 沿东陇海线地区主要指标（2016年）
Main Indicators of the East Region along the Long-hai Railway(2016)

地 区	Region	年末户籍人口（万人）Registered Population at Year-end (10000 persons)	土地面积（平方公里）Land Area (sq. km)	人口密度（人/平方公里）Density of Population (person/sq. km)	就业人员（万人）Employed Persons (10000 persons)	#第二产业 Secondary Industry	#第三产业 Tertiary Industry
东陇海合计	**Total**	**992.02**	**11789**	**736**	**466.15**	**154.35**	**186.46**
徐州市区	Xuzhou	338.09	3063	1067	156.82	48.89	74.58
新 沂 市	Xinyi	113.69	1592	572	55.35	18.87	18.65
邳 州 市	Pizhou	194.10	2085	690	87.79	29.77	28.88
连云港市区	Lianyungang	222.69	3012	693	109.60	39.01	44.20
东 海 县	Donghai	123.45	2037	475	56.59	17.81	20.15

19-7 续表1 Continued 1

地 区	Region	地区生产总 值（亿元）Gross Domectic Product (100 million yuan)	第一产业 Primary Industry	第二产业 Seconary Industry	第三产业 Tertiary Industry	#工 业 Industry	人均地区生产总值（元）Per Capita GDP (yuan)
东陇海合计	**Total**	**6179.40**	**462.33**	**2762.71**	**2916.10**	**2386.95**	**71439**
徐州市区	Xuzhou	3072.18	109.01	1442.79	1520.39	1268.39	94402
新 沂 市	Xinyi	562.06	64.91	232.17	264.98	198.89	61765
邳 州 市	Pizhou	804.14	111.92	347.27	344.95	303.07	55960
连云港市区	Lianyungang	1307.59	113.91	550.35	612.33	453.52	62788
东 海 县	Donghai	433.43	62.58	190.13	173.45	163.08	44871

19－7 续 表2 Continued 2

地 区	Region	规模以上工业企业个数(个) Number of over Scale Industrial Enterprises (unit)	工业总产值(亿元) Total Output Value (100 million yuan)	#制造业 Manufacturing	资产合计(亿元) Total Assets (100 million yuan)	主营业务收入(亿元) Revenue from Principal Business (100 million yuan)	利润总额(亿元) Total Profits (100 million yuan)
东陇海合计	**Total**	**3151**	**14894.75**	**12571.20**	**9137.26**	**15163.22**	**1230.27**
徐州市区	Xuzhou	779	5701.27	4999.47	4615.69	5888.95	488.16
新沂市	Xinyi	504	1812.43	1709.27	539.15	1861.13	138.29
邳州市	Pizhou	524	2592.57	2400.59	839.90	2676.86	206.01
连云港市区	Lianyungang	798	3663.54	2453.97	2708.96	3627.12	323.48
东海县	Donghai	546	1124.94	1007.90	433.55	1109.15	74.33

19－7 续表3 Continued 3

地 区	Region	固定资产投资(亿元) Urban Investment in Fixed Assets (100 million yuan)	#房地产开发 Real Estate Development	社会消费品零售总额(亿元) Total Retail Sales of Consumer Goods (100 million yuan)	进出口总额(亿美元) Total Imports and Exports (USD 100 million)	#出 口 Export	实际使用外资(亿美元) Actual Use of Foreign Capital (USD 100 million)
东陇海合计	**Total**	**5560.31**	**633.94**	**2803.51**	**116.16**	**75.04**	**17.38**
徐州市区	Xuzhou	2352.23	326.39	1655.21	35.45	29.78	9.31
新沂市	Xinyi	550.05	49.08	174.56	4.58	2.98	1.00
邳州市	Pizhou	763.12	72.83	253.41	10.32	9.16	1.83
连云港市区	Lianyungang	1564.32	165.86	544.44	61.23	29.43	4.29
东海县	Donghai	330.59	19.77	175.89	4.58	3.68	0.94

19－7 续 表4 Continued 4

单位:亿元 (100 million yuan)

地 区	Region	一般公共预算收入 General Public Budget Revenue	#税收收入 Taxes	一般公共预算支出 General Public Budget Expenditure	年末金融机构存款余 额 Deposits Balance of Banking Institutions (year-end)	#住户存款 Household Deposits	年末金融机构贷款余 额 Loans Balance of Banking Institutions (year-end)
东陇海合计	**Total**	**548.38**	**421.05**	**827.46**	**6346.25**	**2860.83**	**4725.00**
徐州市区	Xuzhou	268.56	201.42	350.13	3372.86	1649.21	2383.41
新 沂 市	Xinyi	49.91	37.71	91.82	386.97	217.87	246.38
邳 州 市	Pizhou	62.40	48.10	110.08	525.34	361.35	366.13
连云港市区	Lianyungang	144.91	115.24	217.35	1743.70	470.61	1480.37
东 海 县	Donghai	22.61	18.59	58.09	317.38	161.78	248.71

19－7 续 表5 Continued 5

地 区	Region	公路里程(公里) Total Length of Highways (km)	民用汽车拥用量(万辆) Number of Civil Motor Vehicles Owned (10000 units)	公路客运量(万人) Passenger Traffic (10000 persons)	公路货运量(万吨) Freight Traffic (10000 tons)	全社会用电量(亿千瓦时) Total Consumption of Electricity (100 million kW·h)	#工业用电 Consumption of Electricity for Industrial Use
东陇海合计	**Total**	**17207**	**111.84**	**14582**	**19698**	**358.65**	**252.44**
徐州市区	Xuzhou	3882	54.79	9093	9423	204.08	150.60
新 沂 市	Xinyi	2719	7.32	889	1510	39.27	30.97
邳 州 市	Pizhou	3118	11.71	744	1954	28.40	15.88
连云港市区	Lianyungang	4489	27.04	3359	5006	63.68	41.30
东 海 县	Donghai	2999	10.98	497	1805	23.22	13.69

20

市县社会经济

Social Economy of Cities and Counties

简 要 说 明

一、本篇资料的主要内容

本篇资料反映市县经济社会发展情况。

二、资料来源

本篇资料主要根据市县社会经济基本情况统计年报加工整理。

Brief Introduction

I. Main Contents

Data in this chapter reflect the economic and social development of cities and counties.

Ⅱ. Date Source

Data in this chapter mainly based on the basic socio-economic situation annual report.

20-1 人　　口（2016年）
Population (2016)

市　县 City and County		年末户籍人口（万人） Registered Population at Year-end (10000 persons)	#女 Female	年末常住人口（万人） Permanent Population at Year-end (10000 persons)	出生人数（人） Birth (person)	死亡人数（人） Death (person)	人口密度（人/平方公里） Density of Population (person/sq. km)
南京市	**Nanjing City**	**662.79**	**331.93**	**827.00**	**80332**	**37156**	**1256**
无锡市	**Wuxi City**	**486.20**	**246.18**	**652.90**	**44836**	**31253**	**1411**
江阴市	Jiangyin City	124.80	62.85	164.15	11617	8079	1663
宜兴市	Yixing City	108.34	54.93	125.44	9218	8108	628
徐州市	**Xuzhou City**	**1042.40**	**502.39**	**871.00**	**94163**	**27713**	**740**
丰　县	Fengxian County	121.43	57.99	94.89	11506	4734	654
沛　县	Peixian County	124.93	62.73	111.68	11055	6129	618
睢宁县	Suining County	144.16	69.05	102.59	8827	6363	580
新沂市	Xinyi City	113.56	54.79	91.09	7363	1303	572
邳州市	Pizhou City	193.87	93.11	143.86	22632	2541	690
常州市	**Changzhou City**	**374.90**	**189.68**	**470.83**	**36984**	**22573**	**1077**
溧阳市	Liyang City	79.95	39.65	76.16	7999	3509	496
苏州市	**Suzhou City**	**678.20**	**345.67**	**1064.74**	**75303**	**42685**	**1230**
常熟市	Changshu City	106.87	55.04	151.26	8025	8167	1185
张家港市	Zhangjiagang City	92.66	47.26	125.55	8895	6077	1272
昆山市	Kunshan City	82.35	41.63	165.70	11313	4097	1778
太仓市	Taicang City	48.30	24.94	71.20	3813	3590	879
南通市	**Nantong City**	**766.66**	**389.37**	**730.20**	**57103**	**59429**	**692**
海安县	Haian County	93.83	47.42	86.60	6985	7865	731
如东县	Rudong County	103.54	52.60	98.18	6125	9544	352
启东市	Qidong City	111.95	57.13	95.20	7427	8088	555
如皋市	Rugao City	143.68	72.10	125.00	12209	10750	794
海门市	Haimen City	100.10	50.89	90.50	6870	6915	791
连云港市	**Lianyungang City**	**533.99**	**255.24**	**449.64**	**61852**	**15114**	**590**
东海县	Donghai County	123.45	59.12	96.84	15623	6315	475
灌云县	Guanyun County	105.21	49.88	80.51	11233	1504	523
灌南县	Guannan County	82.64	38.93	63.51	9539	1475	618

市 县 City and County		年末户籍人口（万人）Registered Population at Year-end (10000 persons)	#女 Female	年末常住人口（万人）Permanent Population at Year-end (10000 persons)	出生人数（人）Birth (person)	死亡人数（人）Death (person)	人口密度（人/平方公里）Density of Population (person/sq. km)
淮安市	**Huaian City**	**567.56**	**276.31**	**489.00**	**64090**	**23097**	**488**
涟水县	Lianshui County	115.38	55.46	84.80	14114	5269	505
盱眙县	Xuyi County	80.47	39.38	65.35	9084	3323	262
金湖县	Jinhu County	35.96	17.95	33.18	3594	2370	241
盐城市	**Yancheng City**	**830.53**	**402.03**	**723.50**	**91500**	**50039**	**427**
响水县	Xiangshui County	62.49	29.55	50.10	7451	4037	340
滨海县	Binhai County	123.00	58.28	93.45	16920	8604	479
阜宁县	Funing County	112.95	53.80	83.17	15450	4241	578
射阳县	Sheyang County	96.23	46.86	88.45	9554	5646	339
建湖县	Jianhu County	80.06	38.72	73.07	7485	4789	632
东台市	Dongtai City	112.46	55.74	98.04	8723	7289	309
扬州市	**Yangzhou City**	**461.67**	**231.12**	**449.14**	**40003**	**31112**	**681**
宝应县	Baoying County	91.25	44.99	75.68	7954	3945	518
仪征市	Yizheng City	59.62	28.07	56.57	5294	3842	627
高邮市	Gaoyou City	81.48	40.92	74.14	6714	6210	386
镇江市	**Zhenjiang City**	**271.98**	**137.46**	**318.13**	**21686**	**16869**	**828**
丹阳市	Danyang City	81.15	41.06	98.16	5948	5756	938
扬中市	Yangzhong City	28.20	14.40	34.26	2341	2142	1048
句容市	Jurong City	59.21	29.87	62.58	5071	3244	454
泰州市	**Taizhou City**	**508.21**	**249.25**	**464.58**	**46618**	**36734**	**803**
兴化市	Xinghua City	158.25	75.15	125.53	15847	9777	524
靖江市	Jingjiang City	66.67	33.71	68.71	5114	4273	1049
泰兴市	Taixing City	119.31	58.56	107.74	9810	9624	921
宿迁市	**Suqian City**	**591.60**	**284.65**	**487.94**	**88802**	**24165**	**572**
沭阳县	Shuyang County	197.05	94.16	154.88	31344	9755	674
泗阳县	Siyang County	107.34	51.24	84.09	14085	5447	610
泗洪县	Sihong County	111.06	53.75	89.23	15706	2619	331

20－2　户数及土地面积（2016 年）
Number of Households and Land Area (2016)

市　县 City and County		年末总户数（万户） Number of Households at Year-end (10000 households)	#乡村户数 Rural Household	土地面积（平方公里） Land Area (sq. km)	建成区面积（平方公里） Developed Areas (sq. km)	建成区绿化覆盖面积（公顷） Coverage Space of Green Areas Developed (hectare)
南 京 市	**Nanjing City**	**229.95**	**63.25**	**6587**	**774**	**34625**
无 锡 市	**Wuxi City**	**163.87**	**59.91**	**4627**	**538**	**23115**
江 阴 市	Jiangyin City	37.32	18.43	987	125	5358
宜 兴 市	Yixing City	37.60	20.66	1997	81	3487
徐 州 市	**Xuzhou City**	**278.54**	**175.79**	**11765**	**455**	**19453**
丰　县	Fengxian County	32.62	23.48	1450	31	1248
沛　县	Peixian County	36.92	23.84	1806	47	1923
睢 宁 县	Suining County	33.41	25.18	1769	34	1357
新 沂 市	Xinyi City	31.71	21.37	1592	36	1515
邳 州 市	Pizhou City	45.92	33.65	2085	46	1975
常 州 市	**Changzhou City**	**131.45**	**72.68**	**4373**	**290**	**12502**
溧 阳 市	Liyang City	26.26	19.99	1535	29	1246
苏 州 市	**Suzhou City**	**222.44**	**87.50**	**8657**	**733**	**31289**
常 熟 市	Changshu City	32.63	17.75	1276	98	4487
张家港市	Zhangjiagang City	32.95	18.47	987	51	2068
昆 山 市	Kunshan City	27.85	10.29	932	72	3160
太 仓 市	Taicang City	15.09	6.70	810	51	2190
南 通 市	**Nantong City**	**281.88**	**198.67**	**10549**	**370**	**15662**
海 安 县	Haian County	33.98	24.88	1184	32	1314
如 东 县	Rudong County	36.78	30.50	2791	25	1046
启 东 市	Qidong City	45.37	38.55	1715	30	1245
如 皋 市	Rugao City	44.99	35.40	1575	39	1629
海 门 市	Haimen City	37.74	29.85	1144	28	1096
连云港市	**Lianyungang City**	**142.10**	**93.07**	**7615**	**297**	**11979**
东 海 县	Donghai County	29.02	22.23	2037	29	1180
灌 云 县	Guanyun County	26.39	19.57	1538	28	1114
灌 南 县	Guannan County	20.88	14.42	1028	27	1076

市 县 City and County		年末总户数（万户）Number of Households at Year-end (10000 households)	#乡村户数 Rural Household	土地面积（平方公里）Land Area (sq. km)	建成区面积（平方公里）Developed Areas (sq. km)	建成区绿化覆盖面积（公顷）Coverage Space of Green Areas Developed (hectare)
淮安市	**Huaian City**	**164.82**	**99.50**	**10030**	**275**	**11494**
涟水县	Lianshui County	29.92	22.21	1679	36	1458
盱眙县	Xuyi County	21.65	15.30	2497	37	1531
金湖县	Jinhu County	12.73	8.17	1378	24	999
盐城市	**Yancheng City**	**271.20**	**183.00**	**16931**	**336**	**13898**
响水县	Xiangshui County	16.86	11.71	1474	22	912
滨海县	Binhai County	34.14	24.82	1950	34	1390
阜宁县	Funing County	35.77	21.79	1439	45	1842
射阳县	Sheyang County	31.47	21.08	2606	25	1005
建湖县	Jianhu County	29.45	18.96	1157	27	1100
东台市	Dongtai City	39.11	32.16	3176	36	1508
扬州市	**Yangzhou City**	**148.63**	**100.85**	**6591**	**248**	**10641**
宝应县	Baoying County	27.72	20.86	1462	33	1358
仪征市	Yizheng City	18.64	11.90	902	39	1642
高邮市	Gaoyou City	25.51	19.19	1922	27	1113
镇江市	**Zhenjiang City**	**101.24**	**57.57**	**3840**	**214**	**9046**
丹阳市	Danyang City	27.80	19.48	1047	34	1381
扬中市	Yangzhong City	10.54	7.81	327	14	575
句容市	Jurong City	22.70	15.65	1378	27	1115
泰州市	**Taizhou City**	**167.66**	**119.19**	**5787**	**216**	**9048**
兴化市	Xinghua City	51.84	37.21	2395	38	1635
靖江市	Jingjiang City	21.19	14.43	655	34	1422
泰兴市	Taixing City	39.16	30.96	1170	29	1182
宿迁市	**Suqian City**	**150.12**	**108.46**	**8524**	**224**	**9546**
沭阳县	Shuyang County	49.44	37.57	2299	65	2709
泗阳县	Siyang County	26.91	20.16	1378	37	1547
泗洪县	Sihong County	29.55	19.15	2694	36	1504

20－3 法人单位数(2016 年)
Number of Corporations (2016)

单位:个 (unit)

地区	City and County	合计 Total	企业 Enterprises	事业单位 Institutions	机关 Agencies & Organizations	社会团体 Social Organizations	民办非企业单位 Non-enterprise Units Run by NGO	其他组织机构 Others
南京市	**Nanjing City**	**217681**	**201410**	**3449**	**1183**	**2285**	**3510**	**5844**
无锡市	**Wuxi City**	**216409**	**204239**	**3049**	**762**	**1566**	**1579**	**5214**
江阴市	Jiangyin City	46372	43503	642	139	347	231	1510
宜兴市	Yixing City	36666	33264	670	136	289	302	2005
徐州市	**Xuzhou City**	**137809**	**117453**	**3661**	**1005**	**1695**	**1913**	**12082**
丰县	Fengxian County	10562	8313	507	112	212	141	1277
沛县	Peixian County	10307	7838	423	100	132	103	1711
睢宁县	Suining County	11865	9668	379	80	121	171	1446
新沂市	Xinyi City	13825	11600	342	90	119	85	1589
邳州市	Pizhou City	17981	14289	508	138	140	94	2812
常州市	**Changzhou City**	**145469**	**132065**	**2226**	**581**	**4374**	**1124**	**5099**
溧阳市	Liyang City	13225	10417	443	101	629	119	1516
苏州市	**Suzhou City**	**456803**	**439290**	**3972**	**941**	**3093**	**2384**	**7123**
常熟市	Changshu City	39307	36964	533	99	407	251	1053
张家港市	Zhangjiagang City	38359	36021	491	137	446	288	976
昆山市	Kunshan City	94599	92074	612	113	436	438	926
太仓市	Taicang City	23117	21394	383	86	286	127	841
南通市	**Nantong City**	**143824**	**126582**	**3677**	**898**	**2316**	**2945**	**7406**
海安县	Haian County	18571	16203	602	108	264	534	860
如东县	Rudong County	13868	11860	586	105	283	307	727
启东市	Qidong City	14864	12258	395	125	306	403	1377
如皋市	Rugao City	19665	16972	531	118	191	242	1611
海门市	Haimen City	13703	11172	472	116	239	487	1217
连云港市	**Lianyungang City**	**63057**	**51938**	**2295**	**614**	**1074**	**1003**	**6133**
东海县	Donghai County	10452	8279	470	111	114	155	1323
灌云县	Guanyun County	7916	5606	417	89	141	139	1524
灌南县	Guannan County	6475	3934	442	97	358	344	1300

单位:个 (unit)

地区 City and County		合计 Total	企业 Enterprises	事业单位 Institutions	机关 Agencies & Organizations	社会团体 Social Organizations	民办非企业单位 Non-enterprise Units Run by NGO	其他组织机构 Others
淮安市	**Huaian City**	**83325**	**66766**	**3697**	**1124**	**1802**	**1055**	**8881**
涟水县	Lianshui County	10551	7409	652	141	176	234	1939
盱眙县	Xuyi County	8755	6429	493	195	298	92	1248
金湖县	Jinhu County	7772	5881	356	98	155	42	1240
盐城市	**Yancheng City**	**114796**	**99620**	**3426**	**899**	**1810**	**1701**	**7340**
响水县	Xiangshui County	7625	5975	301	75	420	152	702
滨海县	Binhai County	8298	6609	372	71	289	92	865
阜宁县	Funing County	12784	11274	230	81	66	143	990
射阳县	Sheyang County	12802	11203	377	110	69	241	802
建湖县	Jianhu County	12453	10931	399	107	174	91	751
东台市	Dongtai City	14350	11651	459	81	344	342	1473
扬州市	**Yangzhou City**	**90993**	**77781**	**3164**	**810**	**1472**	**1140**	**6626**
宝应县	Baoying County	10387	7890	519	85	149	112	1632
仪征市	Yizheng City	11059	9097	530	147	276	91	918
高邮市	Gaoyou City	11646	9403	472	132	160	121	1358
镇江市	**Zhenjiang City**	**80882**	**70868**	**2237**	**541**	**2096**	**1024**	**4116**
丹阳市	Danyang City	21128	18753	477	104	329	197	1268
扬中市	Yangzhong City	11780	10653	321	74	160	131	441
句容市	Jurong City	11610	9437	393	84	321	139	1236
泰州市	**Taizhou City**	**84747**	**70662**	**2925**	**579**	**1504**	**1565**	**7512**
兴化市	Xinghua City	13160	9232	568	103	264	421	2572
靖江市	Jingjiang City	15042	13045	441	80	187	176	1113
泰兴市	Taixing City	15433	13219	526	84	170	115	1319
宿迁市	**Suqian City**	**71928**	**58461**	**2045**	**681**	**1634**	**2126**	**6981**
沭阳县	Shuyang County	23984	21058	483	132	105	444	1762
泗阳县	Siyang County	11370	8329	270	104	508	460	1699
泗洪县	Sihong County	11366	7968	423	142	233	802	1798

20－4 年末就业人员（2016年）
Number of Employed Persons (Year-end) (2016)

单位：万人 (10000 persons)

市县 City and County		就业人员 Total Employed Persons	第一产业 Primary Industry	第二产业 Secondary Industry	第三产业 Tertiary Industry	私营企业就业人员 Employed Persons in Private Enterprises	个体就业人员 Self-employed Individuals
南京市	**Nanjing City**	**456.00**	**46.00**	**148.90**	**261.10**	**371.68**	**94.60**
无锡市	**Wuxi City**	**387.00**	**17.10**	**214.90**	**155.00**	**262.45**	**60.24**
江阴市	Jiangyin City	98.99	4.86	61.03	33.10	67.13	16.22
宜兴市	Yixing City	73.92	8.62	40.36	24.94	57.59	7.82
徐州市	**Xuzhou City**	**483.40**	**144.30**	**159.90**	**179.20**	**136.89**	**68.54**
丰县	Fengxian County	55.78	19.58	5.87	17.18	11.16	5.99
沛县	Peixian County	64.77	22.09	19.02	20.60	14.76	4.62
睢宁县	Suining County	62.89	22.33	22.09	19.31	16.82	6.97
新沂市	Xinyi City	55.35	17.82	21.26	18.65	18.28	6.67
邳州市	Pizhou City	87.79	29.14	18.87	28.88	17.30	13.23
常州市	**Changzhou City**	**281.40**	**30.00**	**142.20**	**109.20**	**168.48**	**56.75**
溧阳市	Liyang City	49.84	11.56	25.47	12.81	22.25	7.74
苏州市	**Suzhou City**	**691.30**	**23.50**	**412.10**	**255.70**	**440.87**	**126.95**
常熟市	Changshu City	104.55	3.95	64.17	36.43	50.25	17.14
张家港市	Zhangjiagang City	77.27	4.41	46.51	26.35	57.81	14.31
昆山市	Kunshan City	116.27	1.73	74.40	40.14	67.68	22.97
太仓市	Taicang City	45.80	2.60	26.81	16.39	25.15	6.28
南通市	**Nantong City**	**458.00**	**96.00**	**213.00**	**149.00**	**211.26**	**76.03**
海安县	Haian County	54.20	11.30	28.55	14.35	32.40	8.76
如东县	Rudong County	62.00	13.35	30.70	17.95	26.38	7.24
启东市	Qidong City	67.00	18.30	29.20	19.50	20.80	5.99
如皋市	Rugao City	74.30	19.30	34.60	20.40	32.58	10.60
海门市	Haimen City	64.70	16.50	31.20	17.00	23.56	9.03
连云港市	**Lianyungang City**	**250.50**	**78.60**	**80.70**	**91.20**	**50.19**	**28.63**
东海县	Donghai County	56.59	18.63	17.81	20.15	7.97	6.50
灌云县	Guanyun County	47.87	18.49	12.92	16.46	5.22	4.59
灌南县	Guannan County	36.44	15.09	10.96	10.39	4.51	3.48

单位:万人 (10000 persons)

市 县	City and County	就业人员 Total Employed Persons	第一产业 Primary Industry	第二产业 Secondary Industry	第三产业 Tertiary Industry	私营企业就业人员 Employed Persons in Private Enterprises	个 体 就业人员 Self-employed Individuals
淮 安 市	**Huaian City**	**283.60**	**78.30**	**89.60**	**115.70**	**79.26**	**45.33**
涟 水 县	Lianshui County	48.92	17.17	11.86	19.89	10.41	5.89
盱 眙 县	Xuyi County	38.48	11.72	12.86	13.90	9.21	5.46
金 湖 县	Jinhu County	19.27	5.53	6.65	7.09	7.19	3.25
盐 城 市	**Yancheng City**	**446.00**	**110.20**	**159.80**	**176.00**	**145.28**	**55.53**
响 水 县	Xiangshui County	28.74	8.21	9.97	10.56	5.78	3.58
滨 海 县	Binhai County	56.40	16.85	18.77	20.78	12.43	5.20
阜 宁 县	Funing County	51.42	15.46	17.33	18.63	20.21	6.58
射 阳 县	Sheyang County	57.01	16.04	19.55	21.42	11.21	5.98
建 湖 县	Jianhu County	44.18	10.86	17.04	16.28	14.24	5.40
东 台 市	Dongtai City	65.17	16.32	23.13	25.72	25.91	6.76
扬 州 市	**Yangzhou City**	**263.40**	**46.20**	**116.40**	**100.80**	**133.53**	**49.71**
宝 应 县	Baoying County	41.56	12.12	17.24	12.20	15.81	6.40
仪 征 市	Yizheng City	39.18	8.62	18.02	12.54	13.43	6.08
高 邮 市	Gaoyou City	45.52	12.29	19.11	14.12	22.56	7.24
镇 江 市	**Zhenjiang City**	**194.30**	**22.20**	**88.10**	**84.00**	**98.25**	**39.79**
丹 阳 市	Danyang City	63.56	5.80	33.76	24.00	34.55	12.10
扬 中 市	Yangzhong City	21.72	1.33	11.73	8.66	16.80	2.82
句 容 市	Jurong City	39.30	9.58	15.60	14.12	11.54	7.06
泰 州 市	**Taizhou City**	**278.10**	**60.10**	**112.80**	**105.20**	**115.93**	**50.42**
兴 化 市	Xinghua City	75.10	22.80	26.10	26.20	18.42	11.98
靖 江 市	Jingjiang City	41.10	6.90	20.60	13.60	19.88	6.74
泰 兴 市	Taixing City	64.40	16.10	26.40	21.90	23.10	12.69
宿 迁 市	**Suqian City**	**283.20**	**89.30**	**106.80**	**87.10**	**98.18**	**49.38**
沭 阳 县	Shuyang County	93.80	28.44	37.73	27.63	48.78	10.80
泗 阳 县	Siyang County	49.49	18.90	16.91	13.68	12.73	9.07
泗 洪 县	Sihong County	48.46	17.34	16.72	14.40	10.69	8.62

20－5 乡村就业人员(2016年)
Rural Employment (2016)

单位:万人　　(10000 persons)

市县	City and County	乡村就业人员 Total Employment	#农林牧渔业 Farming, Forestry, Animal Husbandry and Fishery	#工业 Industry	#建筑业 Construction	#交通运输、仓储及邮政业 Transportation, Storage, and Postal Services	#批发和零售业 Wholesale and Retail Trade
南京市	**Nanjing City**	**116.97**	**23.21**	**36.65**	**23.81**	**7.14**	**7.99**
无锡市	**Wuxi City**	**109.81**	**16.30**	**67.21**	**6.39**	**3.34**	**5.85**
江阴市	Jiangyin City	35.20	4.93	21.75	1.76	1.30	2.23
宜兴市	Yixing City	35.15	7.97	18.66	3.21	1.03	1.55
徐州市	**Xuzhou City**	**358.55**	**130.56**	**104.30**	**51.80**	**15.63**	**22.39**
丰县	Fengxian County	53.11	22.98	15.30	7.32	1.64	2.67
沛县	Peixian County	49.57	16.91	14.16	9.70	1.80	2.40
睢宁县	Suining County	59.72	23.00	17.43	8.65	1.44	2.90
新沂市	Xinyi City	44.42	17.89	10.01	8.57	1.24	2.54
邳州市	Pizhou City	65.49	20.61	21.25	6.51	4.18	5.65
常州市	**Changzhou City**	**128.05**	**23.22**	**59.45**	**17.36**	**5.18**	**6.65**
溧阳市	Liyang City	31.73	7.82	8.82	9.08	1.78	1.82
苏州市	**Suzhou City**	**171.89**	**21.83**	**103.57**	**9.66**	**5.48**	**10.24**
常熟市	Changshu City	38.42	3.58	23.87	1.98	1.17	2.30
张家港市	Zhangjiagang City	30.42	3.05	19.81	1.45	1.29	1.69
昆山市	Kunshan City	20.78	1.67	12.89	1.09	0.62	1.36
太仓市	Taicang City	15.52	2.87	9.92	0.59	0.37	0.35
南通市	**Nantong City**	**299.48**	**63.55**	**86.19**	**62.50**	**15.58**	**27.65**
海安县	Haian County	37.32	6.87	11.33	8.55	2.88	3.13
如东县	Rudong County	47.59	8.11	17.79	9.82	2.50	2.78
启东市	Qidong City	49.22	12.05	12.22	10.32	2.24	4.93
如皋市	Rugao City	60.00	13.20	18.10	10.50	2.10	3.50
海门市	Haimen City	48.88	11.57	11.40	11.36	2.30	6.70
连云港市	**Lianyungang City**	**177.97**	**80.84**	**31.00**	**31.30**	**8.08**	**8.50**
东海县	Donghai County	43.84	19.05	7.80	8.62	2.26	2.00
灌云县	Guanyun County	38.91	20.17	5.53	4.19	1.13	1.40
灌南县	Guannan County	29.88	15.18	4.39	4.34	1.96	1.59

单位:万人 (10000 persons)

市 县	City and County	乡 村 就业人员 Total Employment	#农林牧渔业 Farming, Forestry, Animal Husbandry and Fishery	#工 业 Industry	#建筑业 Construction	#交通运输、仓储及邮政业 Transportation, Storage, and Postal Services	#批发和零售业 Wholesale and Retail Trade
淮安市	**Huaian City**	**211.79**	**86.13**	**42.36**	**31.91**	**6.79**	**9.03**
涟水县	Lianshui County	49.48	20.38	5.93	5.56	1.19	1.56
盱眙县	Xuyi County	33.90	13.34	7.10	4.13	1.11	1.26
金湖县	Jinhu County	13.45	4.60	3.90	2.67	0.44	0.58
盐城市	**Yancheng City**	**299.92**	**107.93**	**60.76**	**36.68**	**13.71**	**14.00**
响水县	Xiangshui County	21.57	8.88	5.60	1.37	0.74	0.85
滨海县	Binhai County	44.09	16.12	5.89	4.81	2.49	1.87
阜宁县	Funing County	36.76	14.75	4.88	5.43	1.49	1.48
射阳县	Sheyang County	34.64	12.50	5.36	3.79	1.69	1.94
建湖县	Jianhu County	30.31	9.21	9.32	3.59	1.35	1.68
东台市	Dongtai City	48.23	19.01	10.22	6.64	2.04	2.24
扬州市	**Yangzhou City**	**181.49**	**33.22**	**64.44**	**34.69**	**7.61**	**12.13**
宝应县	Baoying County	41.78	10.30	11.65	10.10	1.94	3.01
仪征市	Yizheng City	23.02	3.18	7.76	5.22	0.93	1.25
高邮市	Gaoyou City	36.52	8.98	13.92	6.79	1.32	1.96
镇江市	**Zhenjiang City**	**101.27**	**21.68**	**50.14**	**11.64**	**3.65**	**3.54**
丹阳市	Danyang City	36.48	7.12	21.28	3.06	1.09	1.17
扬中市	Yangzhong City	13.66	2.01	8.71	0.69	0.38	0.53
句容市	Jurong City	25.97	7.58	7.91	5.70	1.10	0.84
泰州市	**Taizhou City**	**212.34**	**42.93**	**63.08**	**36.42**	**13.34**	**17.24**
兴化市	Xinghua City	60.97	19.85	10.37	5.99	4.31	5.64
靖江市	Jingjiang City	26.96	5.19	13.19	2.50	1.59	1.58
泰兴市	Taixing City	56.73	8.53	16.56	11.62	3.50	5.82
宿迁市	**Suqian City**	**225.25**	**84.72**	**63.12**	**28.94**	**8.41**	**13.31**
沭阳县	Shuyang County	82.01	28.30	27.60	8.50	3.29	4.42
泗阳县	Siyang County	40.81	14.95	11.86	4.82	1.24	2.20
泗洪县	Sihong County	38.32	20.36	6.30	4.61	1.12	2.10

20-6 地区生产总值(2016年)

Gross Domestic Product (2016)

单位:亿元 (100 million yuan)

市县 City and County		地区生产总值 Gross Domestic Product	第一产业 Primary Industry	第二产业 Secondary Industry	第三产业 Tertiary Industry	#工业 Industry	人均地区生产总值(元) Per Capita GDP(yuan)
南京市	**Nanjing City**	**10503.02**	**252.54**	**4117.32**	**6133.16**	**3581.72**	**127264**
无锡市	**Wuxi City**	**9210.02**	**135.19**	**4346.78**	**4728.05**	**3977.58**	**141258**
江阴市	Jiangyin City	3083.26	44.34	1680.99	1357.93	1612.25	188101
宜兴市	Yixing City	1377.74	48.74	709.51	619.49	608.05	109881
徐州市	**Xuzhou City**	**5808.52**	**542.88**	**2513.85**	**2751.79**	**2122.58**	**66845**
丰县	Fengxian County	405.19	74.81	171.60	158.78	132.52	42739
沛县	Peixian County	665.03	91.29	305.05	268.69	234.93	59604
睢宁县	Suining County	497.38	84.09	207.65	205.64	163.98	48556
新沂市	Xinyi City	562.06	64.91	232.17	264.98	198.89	61765
邳州市	Pizhou City	804.14	111.92	347.27	344.95	303.07	55960
常州市	**Changzhou City**	**5773.86**	**152.67**	**2682.46**	**2938.73**	**2428.84**	**122721**
溧阳市	Liyang City	801.26	48.29	392.29	360.68	334.26	105256
苏州市	**Suzhou City**	**15475.09**	**221.81**	**7277.46**	**7975.82**	**6709.02**	**145556**
常熟市	Changshu City	2112.39	42.76	1082.43	987.20	1026.16	139768
张家港市	Zhangjiagang City	2317.24	31.34	1214.70	1071.21	1155.30	184744
昆山市	Kunshan City	3160.29	30.07	1708.82	1421.40	1608.39	191058
太仓市	Taicang City	1155.13	36.76	583.87	534.50	547.67	162523
南通市	**Nantong City**	**6768.20**	**366.66**	**3170.30**	**3231.24**	**2633.06**	**92702**
海安县	Haian County	755.29	55.97	354.15	345.17	290.67	87201
如东县	Rudong County	746.69	67.87	340.57	338.25	286.80	76045
启东市	Qidong City	881.85	66.58	422.85	392.42	336.94	92534
如皋市	Rugao City	904.27	62.99	434.36	406.92	364.30	72255
海门市	Haimen City	1005.06	53.28	504.53	447.25	420.99	111099
连云港市	**Lianyungang City**	**2376.48**	**301.56**	**1049.90**	**1025.02**	**851.82**	**52987**
东海县	Donghai County	433.43	67.28	186.57	179.58	163.08	44871
灌云县	Guanyun County	328.66	64.10	143.12	121.44	109.30	40926
灌南县	Guannan County	306.80	51.51	144.78	110.51	125.92	48429

单位:亿元 (100 million yuan)

市 县	City and County	地区生产总值 Gross Domestic Product	第一产业 Primary Industry	第二产业 Secondary Industry	第三产业 Tertiary Industry	#工 业 Industry	人均地区生产总值(元) Per Capita GDP(yuan)
淮安市	**Huaian City**	**3048.00**	**324.61**	**1268.15**	**1455.24**	**1071.99**	**62446**
涟水县	Lianshui County	387.09	56.64	147.51	182.94	121.88	45680
盱眙县	Xuyi County	356.70	54.20	140.30	162.20	113.46	54625
金湖县	Jinhu County	241.88	33.11	90.31	118.46	79.90	72987
盐城市	**Yancheng City**	**4576.08**	**533.91**	**2050.02**	**1992.15**	**1771.68**	**63278**
响水县	Xiangshui County	270.64	41.42	126.77	102.45	113.66	53971
滨海县	Binhai County	391.61	57.99	156.72	176.90	132.74	41761
阜宁县	Funing County	394.40	54.60	169.15	170.65	126.96	47236
射阳县	Sheyang County	441.65	81.01	155.78	204.86	142.01	49749
建湖县	Jianhu County	466.13	46.73	197.59	221.81	168.82	63514
东台市	Dongtai City	727.01	91.47	292.03	343.51	255.73	73902
扬州市	**Yangzhou City**	**4449.38**	**251.39**	**2197.63**	**2000.36**	**1925.92**	**99151**
宝应县	Baoying County	506.30	66.44	226.31	213.55	187.64	66962
仪征市	Yizheng City	557.05	23.36	294.27	239.42	262.33	98558
高邮市	Gaoyou City	537.50	69.59	237.86	230.05	194.85	72562
镇江市	**Zhenjiang City**	**3833.84**	**137.78**	**1870.40**	**1825.66**	**1728.00**	**120603**
丹阳市	Danyang City	1136.04	52.31	567.57	516.16	544.57	115816
扬中市	Yangzhong City	504.73	12.96	261.44	230.33	250.74	147431
句容市	Jurong City	493.20	43.11	231.90	218.19	206.81	78862
泰州市	**Taizhou City**	**4101.78**	**240.00**	**1933.89**	**1927.89**	**1679.83**	**88330**
兴化市	Xinghua City	748.85	102.59	289.85	356.41	251.07	59662
靖江市	Jingjiang City	801.75	22.51	391.95	387.29	351.39	116703
泰兴市	Taixing City	832.91	53.95	388.52	390.44	340.07	77315
宿迁市	**Suqian City**	**2351.12**	**275.23**	**1139.97**	**935.92**	**976.89**	**48311**
沭阳县	Shuyang County	697.31	91.27	317.95	288.09	284.04	45107
泗阳县	Siyang County	402.75	57.85	199.21	145.69	166.95	48006
泗洪县	Sihong County	401.14	61.13	168.93	171.08	142.09	45039

20－7 地区生产总值构成(2016 年)

Composition and Indices of Gross Domestic Product (2016)

市 县 City and County		地区生产总值指数(上年＝100) GDP Index (preceding year＝100)	三次产业占 GDP 比重(%) Percentage of Three Industries to GDP			一般公共预算收入占 GDP 比重(%) General Public Budget Revenue to GDP	外贸依存度(%) Interdependent Level to Foreign Trade(%)
			第一产业 Primary Industry	第二产业 Secondary Industry	第三产业 Tertiary Industry		
南 京 市	**Nanjing City**	**108.0**	**2.4**	**39.2**	**58.4**	**10.9**	**31.8**
无 锡 市	**Wuxi City**	**107.5**	**1.5**	**47.2**	**51.3**	**9.5**	**50.3**
江 阴 市	Jiangyin City	107.4	1.4	54.5	44.0	7.5	42.8
宜 兴 市	Yixing City	106.7	3.5	51.5	45.0	7.9	17.8
徐 州 市	**Xuzhou City**	**108.2**	**9.3**	**43.3**	**47.4**	**8.9**	**7.1**
丰 县	Fengxian County	107.9	18.5	42.4	39.2	8.6	2.4
沛 县	Peixian County	109.1	13.7	45.9	40.4	8.7	3.1
睢 宁 县	Suining County	108.5	16.9	41.7	41.3	8.5	10.0
新 沂 市	Xinyi City	109.4	11.5	41.3	47.1	8.9	5.4
邳 州 市	Pizhou City	108.7	13.9	43.2	42.9	7.8	8.5
常 州 市	**Changzhou City**	**108.5**	**2.6**	**46.5**	**50.9**	**8.3**	**31.7**
溧 阳 市	Liyang City	108.6	6.0	49.0	45.0	7.4	6.9
苏 州 市	**Suzhou City**	**107.5**	**1.5**	**47.0**	**51.5**	**11.2**	**117.5**
常 熟 市	Changshu City	107.5	2.0	51.2	46.7	8.2	62.4
张家港市	Zhangjiagang City	107.0	1.4	52.4	46.2	8.2	78.6
昆 山 市	Kunshan City	107.4	0.9	54.1	45.0	10.1	151.9
太 仓 市	Taicang City	107.3	3.2	50.5	46.3	11.1	63.0
南 通 市	**Nantong City**	**109.3**	**5.4**	**46.8**	**47.7**	**8.7**	**30.3**
海 安 县	Haian County	109.6	7.4	46.9	45.7	7.6	14.6
如 东 县	Rudong County	109.2	9.1	45.6	45.3	7.3	22.3
启 东 市	Qidong City	109.5	7.6	48.0	44.5	8.1	22.8
如 皋 市	Rugao City	109.6	7.0	48.0	45.0	7.9	18.6
海 门 市	Haimen City	109.4	5.3	50.2	44.5	7.2	25.9
连云港市	**Lianyungang City**	**107.8**	**12.7**	**44.2**	**43.1**	**8.9**	**19.7**
东 海 县	Donghai County	108.3	15.5	43.0	41.4	5.2	7.0
灌 云 县	Guanyun County	108.2	19.5	43.5	37.0	6.5	4.7
灌 南 县	Guannan County	107.5	16.8	47.2	36.0	7.3	4.9

市 县 City and County		地区生产总值指数（上年=100）GDP Index (preceding year=100)	三次产业占GDP比重(%) Percentage of Three Industries to GDP			一般公共预算收入占GDP比重(%) General Public Budget Revenue to GDP	外贸依存度(%) Interdependent Level to Foreign Trade(%)
			第一产业 Primary Industry	第二产业 Secondary Industry	第三产业 Tertiary Industry		
淮 安 市	**Huaian City**	**109.0**	**10.6**	**41.6**	**47.7**	**10.4**	**7.6**
涟 水 县	Lianshui County	109.4	14.6	38.1	47.3	7.5	6.4
盱 眙 县	Xuyi County	108.9	15.2	39.3	45.5	8.6	3.5
金 湖 县	Jinhu County	109.7	13.7	37.3	49.0	9.1	9.5
盐 城 市	**Yancheng City**	**108.9**	**11.7**	**44.8**	**43.5**	**9.1**	**11.5**
响 水 县	Xiangshui County	109.8	15.3	46.8	37.9	10.9	11.9
滨 海 县	Binhai County	108.9	14.8	40.0	45.2	8.7	6.4
阜 宁 县	Funing County	108.9	13.8	42.9	43.3	9.2	4.7
射 阳 县	Sheyang County	108.9	18.3	35.3	46.4	4.9	4.3
建 湖 县	Jianhu County	108.7	10.0	42.4	47.6	7.5	4.3
东 台 市	Dongtai City	108.9	12.6	40.2	47.2	8.3	6.7
扬 州 市	**Yangzhou City**	**109.4**	**5.7**	**49.4**	**45.0**	**7.8**	**14.4**
宝 应 县	Baoying County	109.4	13.1	44.7	42.2	6.1	13.9
仪 征 市	Yizheng City	109.4	4.2	52.8	43.0	8.0	12.9
高 邮 市	Gaoyou City	109.5	12.9	44.3	42.8	6.3	5.9
镇 江 市	**Zhenjiang City**	**109.3**	**3.6**	**48.8**	**47.6**	**7.6**	**17.9**
丹 阳 市	Danyang City	109.1	4.6	50.0	45.4	5.8	14.9
扬 中 市	Yangzhong City	109.5	2.6	51.8	45.6	6.4	7.5
句 容 市	Jurong City	109.3	8.7	47.0	44.2	8.2	8.0
泰 州 市	**Taizhou City**	**109.5**	**5.9**	**47.1**	**47.0**	**7.8**	**16.8**
兴 化 市	Xinghua City	110.6	13.7	38.7	47.6	4.9	4.6
靖 江 市	Jingjiang City	105.7	2.8	48.9	48.3	7.4	22.5
泰 兴 市	Taixing City	110.8	6.5	46.6	46.9	6.9	20.5
宿 迁 市	**Suqian City**	**109.1**	**11.7**	**48.5**	**39.8**	**10.1**	**6.8**
沭 阳 县	Shuyang County	109.0	13.1	45.6	41.3	10.3	6.1
泗 阳 县	Siyang County	109.3	14.4	49.5	36.2	8.3	5.8
泗 洪 县	Sihong County	109.0	15.2	42.1	42.6	7.9	2.7

20－8 农林牧渔业总产值(2016年)
Gross Output Value of Agriculture, Forestry, Animal Husbandry and Fishery (2016)

单位:亿元 (100 million yuan)

市县	City and County	农林牧渔业总产值 Total Output Value of Agriculture, Forestry, Animal Husbandry and Fishery	农业 Farming	林业 Forestry	畜牧业 Animal Husbandry	渔业 Fishery	农林牧渔服务业 Service in Support of Agriculture
南京市	**Nanjing City**	**451.16**	**258.75**	**24.26**	**46.83**	**99.36**	**21.97**
无锡市	**Wuxi City**	**249.98**	**140.30**	**18.53**	**27.46**	**35.36**	**28.32**
江阴市	Jiangyin City	87.83	41.06	8.18	16.56	9.77	12.26
宜兴市	Yixing City	86.58	50.68	3.50	7.16	17.86	7.37
徐州市	**Xuzhou City**	**1046.76**	**650.95**	**18.47**	**301.90**	**43.22**	**32.21**
丰县	Fengxian County	147.91	105.49	1.16	35.30	1.19	4.78
沛县	Peixian County	173.84	107.50	0.98	49.99	6.75	8.62
睢宁县	Suining County	158.62	93.82	2.67	52.00	5.22	4.91
新沂市	Xinyi City	136.09	67.18	4.65	41.49	17.71	5.06
邳州市	Pizhou City	223.30	143.75	3.90	57.52	8.63	9.50
常州市	**Changzhou City**	**283.97**	**152.43**	**1.97**	**39.43**	**72.98**	**17.18**
溧阳市	Liyang City	89.72	49.07	1.14	6.55	29.09	3.88
苏州市	**Suzhou City**	**424.67**	**178.81**	**24.76**	**37.39**	**136.08**	**47.62**
常熟市	Changshu City	79.80	47.53	3.14	5.32	14.39	9.43
张家港市	Zhangjiagang City	61.14	34.49	7.29	5.17	6.09	8.10
昆山市	Kunshan City	54.51	15.32	4.80	2.77	28.42	3.20
太仓市	Taicang City	69.48	29.95	3.47	13.43	15.56	7.08
南通市	**Nantong City**	**691.55**	**294.61**	**4.60**	**159.06**	**163.99**	**69.29**
海安县	Haian County	113.29	44.34	0.33	48.60	9.74	10.28
如东县	Rudong County	139.88	46.52	1.03	33.35	50.08	8.91
启东市	Qidong City	131.73	43.07	0.76	13.73	59.96	14.21
如皋市	Rugao City	108.88	59.63	0.25	35.45	6.25	7.30
海门市	Haimen City	94.12	46.93	1.05	12.57	21.80	11.77
连云港市	**Lianyungang City**	**589.42**	**275.56**	**16.54**	**119.01**	**143.24**	**35.07**
东海县	Donghai County	130.31	74.42	4.55	26.52	12.27	12.57
灌云县	Guanyun County	128.00	62.47	2.84	35.46	16.43	10.79
灌南县	Guannan County	97.07	60.11	2.11	23.11	7.54	4.21

单位:亿元 (100 million yuan)

市 县 City and County		农林牧渔业总产值 Total Output Value of Agriculture, Forestry, Animal Husbandry and Fishery	农 业 Farming	林 业 Forestry	畜牧业 Animal Husbandry	渔 业 Fishery	农林牧渔服务业 Service in Support of Agriculture
淮 安 市	**Huaian City**	**602.72**	**373.23**	**13.59**	**139.93**	**64.63**	**11.34**
涟 水 县	Lianshui County	109.49	75.67	3.12	25.30	3.00	2.40
盱 眙 县	Xuyi County	100.75	60.03	1.67	19.01	18.30	1.73
金 湖 县	Jinhu County	62.56	35.89	1.88	7.36	15.64	1.80
盐 城 市	**Yancheng City**	**1104.93**	**480.98**	**27.95**	**303.65**	**214.72**	**77.64**
响 水 县	Xiangshui County	75.13	35.16	1.41	23.35	8.54	6.68
滨 海 县	Binhai County	110.69	56.14	4.59	24.60	22.00	3.35
阜 宁 县	Funing County	110.41	41.61	3.86	37.32	18.17	9.44
射 阳 县	Sheyang County	181.07	70.42	4.75	42.42	48.71	14.77
建 湖 县	Jianhu County	92.99	34.77	1.59	26.21	22.24	8.18
东 台 市	Dongtai City	203.11	93.90	4.40	59.08	30.56	15.17
扬 州 市	**Yangzhou City**	**477.95**	**221.18**	**12.02**	**78.05**	**140.97**	**25.73**
宝 应 县	Baoying County	124.99	47.50	2.22	18.68	50.78	5.82
仪 征 市	Yizheng City	45.84	27.46	2.30	10.16	1.98	3.94
高 邮 市	Gaoyou City	135.64	50.24	2.08	21.97	54.08	7.27
镇 江 市	**Zhenjiang City**	**240.71**	**134.13**	**9.08**	**31.52**	**34.91**	**31.07**
丹 阳 市	Danyang City	86.64	50.31	2.02	10.71	12.20	11.41
扬 中 市	Yangzhong City	25.53	12.46	0.97	3.37	4.08	4.65
句 容 市	Jurong City	73.32	43.08	5.01	8.08	8.04	9.10
泰 州 市	**Taizhou City**	**415.96**	**228.85**	**3.60**	**78.94**	**83.30**	**21.27**
兴 化 市	Xinghua City	179.94	85.10	1.56	18.70	64.68	9.89
靖 江 市	Jingjiang City	39.81	22.53	0.50	9.77	3.33	3.68
泰 兴 市	Taixing City	91.76	56.05	1.01	26.91	4.91	2.88
宿 迁 市	**Suqian City**	**517.24**	**298.51**	**18.09**	**102.14**	**84.90**	**13.61**
沭 阳 县	Shuyang County	172.56	129.89	5.27	31.65	3.10	2.65
泗 阳 县	Siyang County	106.53	54.72	7.43	18.72	21.69	3.96
泗 洪 县	Sihong County	121.89	51.02	1.54	22.13	44.52	2.67

20－9 农业生产情况(2016年)
Basic Conditions of Agricultural Production (2016)

市 县	City and County	农作物总播种面积(千公顷) Total Sown Area (1000 hectares)	#粮食作物 Grain Grops	农业机械总动力(万千瓦) Total Power of Agricultural Machinery (10000 kW)	农用化肥施用量(万吨) Consumption of Chemical Fertilizer (10000 tons)	农村用电量(亿千瓦小时) Electricity Consumed in Rural Area (100 million kW·h)
南京市	**Nanjing City**	**289.25**	**153.05**	**227.61**	**7.39**	**32.08**
无锡市	**Wuxi City**	**160.31**	**94.06**	**99.22**	**5.18**	**394.38**
江阴市	Jiangyin City	40.15	22.72	25.63	1.31	170.16
宜兴市	Yixing City	87.17	59.54	52.15	2.42	84.26
徐州市	**Xuzhou City**	**1154.55**	**737.77**	**712.33**	**60.46**	**66.11**
丰县	Fengxian County	143.77	87.26	82.84	8.36	4.95
沛县	Peixian County	150.88	90.98	102.08	7.23	7.01
睢宁县	Suining County	189.57	148.77	122.05	12.16	8.22
新沂市	Xinyi City	188.92	101.30	115.86	7.69	3.99
邳州市	Pizhou City	230.21	124.86	118.52	11.85	15.70
常州市	**Changzhou City**	**209.20**	**132.79**	**146.25**	**6.04**	**156.59**
溧阳市	Liyang City	90.98	66.54	55.86	2.17	50.66
苏州市	**Suzhou City**	**241.40**	**145.01**	**163.89**	**7.11**	**609.78**
常熟市	Changshu City	68.40	41.24	32.03	2.44	78.52
张家港市	Zhangjiagang City	51.67	33.87	29.99	1.11	150.53
昆山市	Kunshan City	21.46	15.37	18.00	0.75	104.55
太仓市	Taicang City	44.21	24.26	20.85	0.96	54.70
南通市	**Nantong City**	**824.10**	**518.87**	**398.28**	**22.24**	**170.31**
海安县	Haian County	102.30	78.69	65.55	4.37	24.30
如东县	Rudong County	166.65	133.00	92.43	4.09	22.61
启东市	Qidong City	138.71	70.98	59.28	3.23	11.21
如皋市	Rugao City	152.26	107.17	81.12	3.13	38.12
海门市	Haimen City	112.57	39.94	38.19	4.40	26.94
连云港市	**Lianyungang City**	**631.90**	**501.53**	**588.06**	**34.57**	**34.28**
东海县	Donghai County	205.49	159.80	151.66	6.84	10.20
灌云县	Guanyun County	135.95	112.67	126.49	10.28	6.37
灌南县	Guannan County	109.87	87.03	124.14	4.51	2.35

市 县 City and County		农作物总播种面积(千公顷) Total Sown Area (1000 hectares)	#粮食作物 Grain Grops	农业机械总动力(万千瓦) Total Power of Agricultural Machinery (10000 kW)	农用化肥施用量(万吨) Consumption of Chemical Fertilizer (10000 tons)	农村用电量(亿千瓦小时) Electricity Consumed in Rural Area (100 million kW·h)
淮 安 市	**Huaian City**	**797.17**	**659.99**	**622.60**	**38.85**	**16.00**
涟 水 县	Lianshui County	167.88	132.93	119.12	6.29	2.01
盱 眙 县	Xuyi County	162.74	143.58	123.57	5.31	2.76
金 湖 县	Jinhu County	82.43	74.35	87.07	2.59	2.50
盐 城 市	**Yancheng City**	**1399.86**	**981.57**	**679.12**	**50.56**	**80.30**
响 水 县	Xiangshui County	113.44	78.97	75.48	4.70	2.94
滨 海 县	Binhai County	170.63	130.08	84.52	6.89	9.55
阜 宁 县	Funing County	168.24	125.54	84.02	3.91	6.80
射 阳 县	Sheyang County	200.27	158.47	102.03	9.32	9.90
建 湖 县	Jianhu County	115.77	99.71	61.84	3.32	9.53
东 台 市	Dongtai City	243.88	146.57	94.00	5.09	16.11
扬 州 市	**Yangzhou City**	**507.16**	**418.85**	**270.19**	**20.03**	**61.14**
宝 应 县	Baoying County	138.48	120.25	58.36	3.62	11.77
仪 征 市	Yizheng City	58.11	46.12	40.22	1.21	6.28
高 邮 市	Gaoyou City	139.94	117.76	71.36	4.93	11.52
镇 江 市	**Zhenjiang City**	**233.75**	**174.02**	**145.72**	**5.36**	**77.44**
丹 阳 市	Danyang City	84.59	71.39	37.35	1.50	50.32
扬 中 市	Yangzhong City	17.85	12.70	13.65	0.35	10.52
句 容 市	Jurong City	77.01	49.68	56.26	2.11	6.67
泰 州 市	**Taizhou City**	**575.18**	**435.05**	**275.52**	**16.12**	**124.44**
兴 化 市	Xinghua City	223.43	185.52	119.76	6.32	39.08
靖 江 市	Jingjiang City	53.88	44.60	28.39	1.98	15.97
泰 兴 市	Taixing City	139.55	95.90	62.57	2.84	37.53
宿 迁 市	**Suqian City**	**718.03**	**579.41**	**577.77**	**38.59**	**46.42**
沭 阳 县	Shuyang County	251.39	185.40	207.95	14.97	24.62
泗 阳 县	Siyang County	115.38	92.93	99.08	3.66	5.60
泗 洪 县	Sihong County	189.06	166.91	148.45	10.16	3.97

20－10 农产品产量(2016年)
Output of Agricultural Products (2016)

单位:万吨 (10000 tons)

市 县	City and County	粮食产量 Grain	油料产量 Oil-bearing Crops	棉花产量(吨) Cotton (ton)	肉类总产量 Meat	#猪牛羊肉 Pork, Beef and Mutton	水产品产量 Aquatic Products
南京市	**Nanjing City**	**108.04**	**7.43**	**3071**	**9.81**	**5.66**	**22.31**
无锡市	**Wuxi City**	**59.16**	**0.81**		**7.35**	**5.20**	**12.67**
江阴市	Jiangyin City	14.49	0.27		3.96	2.77	2.70
宜兴市	Yixing City	37.05	0.51		2.46	1.71	8.19
徐州市	**Xuzhou City**	**469.16**	**13.45**	**20653**	**90.77**	**44.91**	**18.88**
丰县	Fengxian County	52.54	0.44	10157	13.86	6.68	0.30
沛县	Peixian County	60.27	0.24	3976	17.55	5.90	1.72
睢宁县	Suining County	92.78	3.07	850	12.15	7.21	2.25
新沂市	Xinyi City	66.06	7.54		11.68	7.39	5.90
邳州市	Pizhou City	80.75	1.40	703	19.94	7.48	3.08
常州市	**Changzhou City**	**93.74**	**3.41**	**371**	**13.52**	**6.88**	**16.64**
溧阳市	Liyang City	48.66	2.55	359	2.25	1.29	5.46
苏州市	**Suzhou City**	**97.68**	**1.34**	**500**	**9.76**	**6.38**	**25.49**
常熟市	Changshu City	27.76	0.35	288	1.06	0.96	3.68
张家港市	Zhangjiagang City	22.17	0.38	27	0.76	0.58	1.61
昆山市	Kunshan City	10.13	0.16	22	0.63	0.58	4.10
太仓市	Taicang City	16.53	0.36	163	4.24	1.56	2.16
南通市	**Nantong City**	**325.20**	**35.82**	**23797**	**45.73**	**28.32**	**89.03**
海安县	Haian County	60.12	1.51		8.03	5.79	4.86
如东县	Rudong County	90.90	4.02	4505	9.99	6.17	30.49
启东市	Qidong City	26.14	8.37	6310	5.67	2.68	36.55
如皋市	Rugao City	70.95	3.78	82	11.13	7.37	2.76
海门市	Haimen City	19.16	8.58	10593	4.09	1.59	7.22
连云港市	**Lianyungang City**	**360.80**	**11.40**	**549**	**29.50**	**23.75**	**75.30**
东海县	Donghai County	114.53	4.80		7.39	6.11	6.81
灌云县	Guanyun County	81.88	0.09		5.24	4.68	5.77
灌南县	Guannan County	63.34	0.16		5.33	4.91	3.73

单位:万吨 (10000 tons)

市 县	City and County	粮食产量 Grain	油料产量 Oil-bearing Crops	棉花产量(吨) Cotton (ton)	肉类总产量 Meat	#猪牛羊肉 Pork, Beef and Mutton	水产品产量 Aquatic Products
淮安市	**Huaian City**	**458.55**	**8.80**	**84**	**30.39**	**19.45**	**26.10**
涟水县	Lianshui County	88.44	3.73		6.34	4.74	1.86
盱眙县	Xuyi County	97.86	1.20	84	7.30	3.12	5.87
金湖县	Jinhu County	53.56	0.84		1.39	0.79	4.71
盐城市	**Yancheng City**	**687.31**	**24.30**	**11262**	**81.40**	**54.60**	**119.43**
响水县	Xiangshui County	53.51	2.06		5.86	4.29	6.81
滨海县	Binhai County	95.62	3.14	252	9.92	6.74	10.10
阜宁县	Funing County	91.50	1.70	74	16.20	11.37	7.57
射阳县	Sheyang County	111.90	1.33	2244	8.26	5.37	21.28
建湖县	Jianhu County	72.86	1.88	87	6.49	4.24	10.22
东台市	Dongtai City	97.28	6.12	636	13.73	8.63	18.50
扬州市	**Yangzhou City**	**300.30**	**6.87**	**1144**	**18.01**	**10.12**	**40.12**
宝应县	Baoying County	90.04	1.61		4.72	3.13	15.06
仪征市	Yizheng City	31.14	0.93	26	2.13	1.24	0.77
高邮市	Gaoyou City	85.98	2.00	51	4.93	2.66	16.23
镇江市	**Zhenjiang City**	**118.74**	**5.83**	**910**	**7.95**	**5.04**	**9.85**
丹阳市	Danyang City	49.33	0.85		2.45	1.82	4.09
扬中市	Yangzhong City	9.19	0.16		0.88	0.66	0.78
句容市	Jurong City	33.18	3.71	898	1.66	1.13	2.70
泰州市	**Taizhou City**	**313.03**	**12.20**	**1770**	**26.65**	**21.57**	**39.64**
兴化市	Xinghua City	137.91	3.45	1496	5.99	4.35	30.33
靖江市	Jingjiang City	30.98	0.56		3.13	2.74	1.02
泰兴市	Taixing City	68.47	4.17		8.56	7.69	2.50
宿迁市	**Suqian City**	**384.54**	**4.65**	**637**	**32.86**	**19.58**	**27.11**
沭阳县	Shuyang County	127.49	1.51		9.02	6.82	1.83
泗阳县	Siyang County	60.37	0.88	12	4.93	3.47	8.77
泗洪县	Sihong County	105.55	1.82	558	7.18	4.71	10.17

20-11 工业总产值(2016年)
Gross Output Value of Industry (2016)

单位:亿元 (100 million yuan)

市　　县	City and County	工业总产值 Gross Output Value of Industry	内资企业 Domestic Funded Enterprises	外商港澳台商投资企业 Foreign, Hong Kong Macao and Taiwan Invested Enterprises	#国有控股企业 State-owned Share Holding Enterprises	#大中型企业 Large and Medium Scale Enterprises	#轻工业 Light Industry
南京市	**Nanjing City**	**12945.02**	**7554.24**	**5390.78**	**4920.80**	**8824.62**	**2958.57**
无锡市	**Wuxi City**	**14352.96**	**9108.05**	**5244.91**	**784.92**	**9734.20**	**3642.34**
江阴市	Jiangyin City	5376.01	4169.01	1207.00	128.51	4080.44	1655.16
宜兴市	Yixing City	2588.86	2133.81	455.05	118.46	1384.28	306.24
徐州市	**Xuzhou City**	**13644.36**	**12442.52**	**1201.85**	**917.50**	**7983.71**	**4610.40**
丰　县	Fengxian County	715.31	664.90	50.41	35.66	117.83	336.06
沛　县	Peixian County	1738.40	1715.17	23.23	1.37	1237.84	697.21
睢宁县	Suining County	1084.38	953.12	131.26		418.92	576.46
新沂市	Xinyi City	1812.43	1709.27	103.16	0.23	583.40	581.97
邳州市	Pizhou City	2592.57	2400.59	191.98	19.81	1339.24	726.92
常州市	**Changzhou City**	**12096.82**	**8050.37**	**4046.45**	**444.07**	**7703.92**	**2769.91**
溧阳市	Liyang City	1363.42	923.08	440.34	43.46	1004.09	130.26
苏州市	**Suzhou City**	**30713.99**	**10845.61**	**19868.37**	**783.36**	**22961.02**	**7695.83**
常熟市	Changshu City	3684.89	1893.21	1791.69	38.86	2634.37	1499.50
张家港市	Zhangjiagang City	4571.66	3046.22	1525.44	188.33	3618.93	1067.57
昆山市	Kunshan City	8383.24	1294.31	7088.93	119.96	6828.77	1057.15
太仓市	Taicang City	2027.67	968.31	1059.36	131.68	1092.95	702.61
南通市	**Nantong City**	**14525.72**	**10167.43**	**4573.17**	**632.12**	**7692.30**	**4585.27**
海安县	Haian County	2204.77	1827.10	377.67	1.06	1098.72	786.84
如东县	Rudong County	1896.41	1348.16	548.25	65.34	791.59	839.75
启东市	Qidong City	1829.18	1300.61	528.57	63.23	702.30	324.37
如皋市	Rugao City	1985.12	1680.32	304.80	29.96	1251.12	570.43
海门市	Haimen City	2053.24	1291.91	761.32	35.41	1082.19	492.09
连云港市	**Lianyungang City**	**5974.81**	**4855.40**	**1366.39**	**356.03**	**3502.70**	**2042.27**
东海县	Donghai County	1124.94	1007.90	117.04	4.71	143.65	424.24
灌云县	Guanyun County	762.14	741.68	20.46	10.37	228.42	283.71
灌南县	Guannan County	671.18	651.86	19.32	0.80	536.22	49.59

20－11 续 表 Continued

单位:亿元 (100 million yuan)

市 县	City and County	工业总产值 Gross Output Value of Industry	内资企业 Domestic Funded Enterprises	外商港澳台商投资企业 Foreign, Hong Kong Macao and Taiwan Invested Enterprises	#国有控股企业 State-owned Share Holding Enterprises	#大中型企业 Large and Medium Scale Enterprises	#轻工业 Light Industry
淮安市	**Huaian City**	**6951.32**	**5758.55**	**1192.77**	**375.56**	**2536.24**	**2964.07**
涟水县	Lianshui County	808.17	733.53	74.64	35.94	336.34	479.49
盱眙县	Xuyi County	1038.08	986.35	51.74	7.54	248.97	403.16
金湖县	Jinhu County	547.97	516.53	31.44	0.90	143.02	243.21
盐城市	**Yancheng City**	**9180.84**	**7104.34**	**2076.03**	**365.87**	**4282.24**	**3143.41**
响水县	Xiangshui County	924.82	830.30	94.51	35.09	540.30	278.71
滨海县	Binhai County	705.15	675.32	29.84	5.68	287.89	389.66
阜宁县	Funing County	804.18	741.63	62.55	14.79	157.40	271.65
射阳县	Sheyang County	751.19	664.46	86.73	47.95	137.69	506.57
建湖县	Jianhu County	876.09	733.13	142.96		358.28	322.73
东台市	Dongtai City	1186.59	1008.90	177.69	84.19	330.71	461.65
扬州市	**Yangzhou City**	**9661.65**	**7043.23**	**2786.24**	**1634.89**	**6205.37**	**2540.76**
宝应县	Baoying County	1075.78	979.50	96.27	253.55	732.32	219.11
仪征市	Yizheng City	1616.84	802.59	814.25	824.21	1041.10	346.93
高邮市	Gaoyou City	1218.35	1067.15	151.21	5.17	495.73	445.16
镇江市	**Zhenjiang City**	**8722.84**	**5925.14**	**2797.70**	**509.50**	**6176.79**	**1535.87**
丹阳市	Danyang City	2529.31	1845.89	683.42	7.53	1901.26	492.59
扬中市	Yangzhong City	1372.66	1222.70	149.96	0.75	1064.72	61.22
句容市	Jurong City	1399.25	986.99	412.25	39.76	703.81	435.91
泰州市	**Taizhou City**	**12170.80**	**9775.98**	**2394.82**	**680.64**	**6138.34**	**3407.52**
兴化市	Xinghua City	1790.42	1669.90	120.52	6.76	237.65	438.80
靖江市	Jingjiang City	1888.79	1365.00	523.79	173.42	1375.97	249.36
泰兴市	Taixing City	3002.02	2419.32	582.70	55.20	1508.49	733.46
宿迁市	**Suqian City**	**4096.70**	**3679.11**	**417.58**	**105.45**	**1343.12**	**2147.38**
沭阳县	Shuyang County	1375.83	1259.77	116.06	1.93	293.30	638.53
泗阳县	Siyang County	708.99	682.46	26.53	2.16	168.34	347.33
泗洪县	Sihong County	744.10	705.49	38.61	36.32	145.31	426.05

注：统计范围为年主营业务收入2000万元以上工业企业(下同)。

a) The statistical scope of industry covers industrial enterprises with major business revenue of over 20 million yuan. (Similarly in following tables.)

20-12 工业企业主要经济指标(2016年)
Major Economic Indicators on Industrial Enterprises (2016)

单位:亿元 (100 million yuan)

市县	City and County	资产合计 Total Assets	负债合计 Total Liabilities	主营业务收入 Major Business Revenue	主营业务成本 Cost of Principle Business	利润总额 Total Profits	从业人员年平均人数(万人) Annual Average Employed Person (10000 persons)
南京市	**Nanjing City**	**11448.85**	**6166.10**	**12442.36**	**10182.08**	**959.35**	**74.44**
无锡市	**Wuxi City**	**15095.63**	**8085.84**	**14120.24**	**12097.75**	**968.02**	**116.78**
江阴市	Jiangyin City	6163.53	3481.17	5393.26	4751.64	337.84	41.42
宜兴市	Yixing City	2384.60	1422.59	2446.33	2113.14	137.10	15.13
徐州市	**Xuzhou City**	**6952.73**	**3159.11**	**13947.04**	**11725.51**	**1108.89**	**81.07**
丰县	Fengxian County	275.09	103.11	713.22	622.91	57.40	4.82
沛县	Peixian County	354.86	192.02	1734.65	1508.55	104.09	12.99
睢宁县	Suining County	328.04	132.70	1072.23	924.94	114.94	6.69
新沂市	Xinyi City	539.15	219.59	1861.13	1605.02	138.29	9.33
邳州市	Pizhou City	839.90	195.88	2676.86	2356.44	206.01	13.29
常州市	**Changzhou City**	**8942.07**	**4945.73**	**12435.86**	**10880.58**	**725.27**	**85.68**
溧阳市	Liyang City	944.26	641.12	1349.51	1166.94	79.08	7.14
苏州市	**Suzhou City**	**28356.50**	**14838.02**	**30380.18**	**26169.61**	**1772.74**	**286.58**
常熟市	Changshu City	3939.37	2189.04	3633.14	3052.59	235.76	32.97
张家港市	Zhangjiagang City	4746.81	2777.48	4683.67	4195.29	177.08	27.33
昆山市	Kunshan City	5573.49	2779.55	8369.39	7446.02	446.81	75.68
太仓市	Taicang City	2108.82	1093.69	1968.23	1633.32	154.73	18.48
南通市	**Nantong City**	**8801.91**	**4423.65**	**14650.80**	**12761.31**	**1118.27**	**101.55**
海安县	Haian County	1060.75	540.03	2213.06	1926.25	159.99	12.47
如东县	Rudong County	1200.34	556.42	1883.91	1650.52	147.18	11.55
启东市	Qidong City	1200.83	637.96	1839.18	1590.55	130.52	11.47
如皋市	Rugao City	955.73	496.88	2009.77	1783.00	128.77	20.89
海门市	Haimen City	1017.11	506.67	2072.14	1769.24	220.61	12.21
连云港市	**Lianyungang City**	**3650.60**	**1856.14**	**5946.41**	**5040.36**	**496.53**	**489.63**
东海县	Donghai County	433.55	158.38	1109.15	981.91	74.33	74.33
灌云县	Guanyun County	192.73	80.24	715.77	603.33	44.99	44.99
灌南县	Guannan County	315.35	181.05	666.61	591.29	46.83	46.83

单位:亿元 (100 million yuan)

市 县 City and County		资产合计 Total Assets	负债合计 Total Liabilities	主营业务收入 Major Business Revenue	主营业务成本 Cost of Principle Business	利润总额 Total Profits	从业人员年平均人数(万人) Annual Average Employed Person (10000 persons)
淮安市	**Huaian City**	**3071.44**	**1370.93**	**7014.24**	**6079.35**	**404.81**	**46.75**
涟水县	Lianshui County	259.30	112.63	762.17	685.19	37.32	8.10
盱眙县	Xuyi County	444.04	217.43	1085.70	953.09	42.86	7.52
金湖县	Jinhu County	229.66	127.44	542.75	492.89	22.96	3.12
盐城市	**Yancheng City**	**5261.76**	**2768.09**	**8870.47**	**7701.31**	**475.83**	**54.90**
响水县	Xiangshui County	767.14	390.31	922.06	843.21	53.93	3.27
滨海县	Binhai County	418.51	194.16	685.29	580.79	35.01	4.14
阜宁县	Funing County	347.53	186.50	757.17	671.45	31.82	4.54
射阳县	Sheyang County	383.45	207.09	731.74	605.96	32.58	4.37
建湖县	Jianhu County	334.68	132.52	836.04	679.90	54.23	6.25
东台市	Dongtai City	712.24	408.24	1145.78	1037.57	65.96	8.71
扬州市	**Yangzhou City**	**4678.72**	**2430.70**	**9502.36**	**8336.30**	**593.15**	**70.59**
宝应县	Baoying County	550.34	284.42	1022.58	888.70	59.59	9.19
仪征市	Yizheng City	746.22	404.14	1558.76	1332.43	137.14	6.66
高邮市	Gaoyou City	491.17	228.06	1180.87	1041.42	62.28	9.69
镇江市	**Zhenjiang City**	**5858.18**	**3171.09**	**8632.13**	**7419.44**	**582.17**	**55.56**
丹阳市	Danyang City	1494.37	812.11	2521.56	2076.24	159.66	18.29
扬中市	Yangzhong City	1050.04	595.62	1365.95	1102.28	94.16	7.90
句容市	Jurong City	848.64	497.54	1388.50	1232.70	71.56	13.14
泰州市	**Taizhou City**	**6653.84**	**3405.33**	**12139.45**	**10133.65**	**938.67**	**59.68**
兴化市	Xinghua City	743.31	309.77	1789.33	1567.08	105.72	6.99
靖江市	Jingjiang City	1550.00	816.15	1865.42	1639.61	147.87	12.13
泰兴市	Taixing City	1649.12	873.83	3090.49	2546.80	278.07	15.87
宿迁市	**Suqian City**	**3346.13**	**1337.44**	**3896.33**	**3278.80**	**391.93**	**40.85**
沭阳县	Shuyang County	744.27	262.57	1356.37	1185.78	119.92	10.48
泗阳县	Siyang County	729.21	273.30	693.26	586.11	51.22	8.94
泗洪县	Sihong County	534.50	205.73	660.92	561.43	64.41	6.00

20-13 交 通 运 输 (2016年)

Transportation (2016)

市 县 City and County		公路里程(公里) Total Length of Highway (km)	#等级公路 Grade Highway	公路客运量(万人) Passenger Traffic of Highways (10000 persons)	公路货运量(万吨) Freight Traffic of Highways (10000 tons)	民用汽车拥有量(万辆) Civil Vehicles Owned (10000 units)	#私人汽车 Private Vehicles
南京市	**Nanjing City**	**11211**	**10991**	**8490**	**12463**	**221.68**	**192.71**
无锡市	**Wuxi City**	**7695**	**7695**	**5785**	**13225**	**160.01**	**134.08**
江阴市	Jiangyin City	2373	2373	420	2947	40.40	35.49
宜兴市	Yixing City	2388	2388	564	1683	24.96	21.84
徐州市	**Xuzhou City**	**16277**	**15405**	**13217**	**17586**	**101.61**	**92.64**
丰县	Fengxian County	1834	1834	554	1408	8.92	8.46
沛县	Peixian County	2328	2328	862	1527	8.96	8.24
睢宁县	Suining County	2396	2281	1074	1763	9.92	9.24
新沂市	Xinyi City	2719	2358	889	1510	7.32	6.70
邳州市	Pizhou City	3118	2806	744	1954	11.71	11.07
常州市	**Changzhou City**	**9031**	**9031**	**5423**	**11095**	**109.80**	**93.93**
溧阳市	Liyang City	2557	2557	946	2029	13.24	11.89
苏州市	**Suzhou City**	**12681**	**12681**	**31589**	**12287**	**312.60**	**267.03**
常熟市	Changshu City	3120	3120	3528	1275	39.14	34.52
张家港市	Zhangjiagang City	1617	1617	3129	1599	33.65	29.20
昆山市	Kunshan City	1893	1893	4048	1339	49.88	41.60
太仓市	Taicang City	1304	1304	2796	1302	19.66	16.73
南通市	**Nantong City**	**18427**	**18427**	**8204**	**11535**	**134.95**	**120.41**
海安县	Haian County	2374	2374	544	1794	12.89	11.75
如东县	Rudong County	2691	2691	679	1335	15.03	14.07
启东市	Qidong City	3595	3595	1198	548	16.03	15.01
如皋市	Rugao City	3270	3270	548	2137	20.78	19.41
海门市	Haimen City	2521	2521	482	780	16.39	15.21
连云港市	**Lianyungang City**	**12027**	**12027**	**4654**	**8378**	**47.85**	**43.16**
东海县	Donghai County	2999	2999	497	1805	10.98	10.37
灌云县	Guanyun County	2649	2649	439	873	7.29	6.85
灌南县	Guannan County	1921	1921	359	694	4.97	4.66

市 县 City and County		公路里程（公里）Total Length of Highway（km）	#等级公路 Grade Highway	公路客运量（万人）Passenger Traffic of Highways（10000 persons）	公路货运量（万吨）Freight Traffic of Highways（10000 tons）	民用汽车拥有量（万辆）Civil Vehicles Owned（10000 units）	#私人汽车 Private Vehicles
淮安市	**Huaian City**	**13351**	**12589**	**7226**	**5663**	**45.27**	**40.31**
涟水县	Lianshui County	2554	2307	1510	1531	6.61	6.51
盱眙县	Xuyi County	2724	2724	1157	1438	3.85	3.80
金湖县	Jinhu County	1499	1334	686	228	2.31	2.29
盐城市	**Yancheng City**	**19568**	**19303**	**8283**	**5076**	**75.57**	**67.55**
响水县	Xiangshui County	1806	1806	426	359	4.08	3.68
滨海县	Binhai County	2158	2145	900	1052	7.67	6.88
阜宁县	Funing County	1932	1925	636	225	6.53	6.06
射阳县	Sheyang County	2498	2298	796	672	8.06	7.54
建湖县	Jianhu County	1805	1791	811	250	5.55	4.97
东台市	Dongtai City	3264	3264	890	868	9.64	8.91
扬州市	**Yangzhou City**	**9546**	**9166**	**3840**	**6546**	**63.53**	**56.27**
宝应县	Baoying County	1932	1819	601	542	4.90	4.20
仪征市	Yizheng City	1510	1510	451	914	7.80	7.14
高邮市	Gaoyou City	2134	2092	820	830	7.68	6.80
镇江市	**Zhenjiang City**	**7354**	**7354**	**3574**	**6950**	**49.20**	**43.68**
丹阳市	Danyang City	2189	2189	761	1583	16.05	14.49
扬中市	Yangzhong City	1031	1031	360	423	5.70	5.14
句容市	Jurong City	2498	2498	637	1043	4.51	3.96
泰州市	**Taizhou City**	**9635**	**9628**	**7300**	**2577**	**61.91**	**55.54**
兴化市	Xinghua City	2753	2747	1623	441	10.92	10.20
靖江市	Jingjiang City	1327	1327	1046	342	12.00	10.76
泰兴市	Taixing City	2191	2191	1716	496	12.48	11.37
宿迁市	**Suqian City**	**10500**	**10110**	**5909**	**3785**	**48.67**	**44.88**
沭阳县	Shuyang County	3299	219	1649	1981	14.53	13.29
泗阳县	Siyang County	1647	136	1085	472	7.54	7.06
泗洪县	Sihong County	2300	194	2007	459	6.63	6.12

20－14 邮电、电力（2016年）

Postal and Telecommunications, Power Services (2016)

市县 City and County		邮电业务总量（亿元） Post & Telecommunication Services (100 million yuan)	固定电话用户（万户） Telephone Subscribers (10000 subscribers)	移动电话用户（万户） Number of Mobile Telephones Subscribers at Year-end (10000 subscribers)	互联网宽带接入用户（万户） International Exchange Network Users (10000 subscribers)	全年用电量（亿千瓦时） Total Consumption of Electricity of the Year (100 million kW·h)	#工业用电 Consumption of Electricity for Industrial Use
南京市	**Nanjing City**	**525.27**	**243.50**	**1114.72**	**373.66**	**524.79**	**310.81**
无锡市	**Wuxi City**	**368.86**	**168.09**	**799.86**	**269.95**	**638.67**	**493.73**
江阴市	Jiangyin City	35.26	33.53	201.45	65.05	244.93	214.41
宜兴市	Yixing City	22.11	26.17	144.97	49.15	92.25	70.35
徐州市	**Xuzhou City**	**246.69**	**115.78**	**762.01**	**223.61**	**353.91**	**250.22**
丰县	Fengxian County	19.39	7.90	83.24	17.93	21.27	12.31
沛县	Peixian County	22.26	9.96	98.12	21.63	35.85	25.85
睢宁县	Suining County	26.96	11.51	82.43	22.13	25.04	14.61
新沂市	Xinyi City	24.94	9.17	75.11	21.32	39.27	30.97
邳州市	Pizhou City	29.92	11.35	121.87	26.48	28.40	15.88
常州市	**Changzhou City**	**231.95**	**123.49**	**539.94**	**195.15**	**429.93**	**334.78**
溧阳市	Liyang City	8.34	18.80	73.62	29.47	72.75	60.36
苏州市	**Suzhou City**	**789.21**	**314.20**	**1447.59**	**471.80**	**1382.58**	**1116.30**
常熟市	Changshu City	67.71	33.05	202.59	63.03	172.33	144.18
张家港市	Zhangjiagang City	26.71	24.32	171.70	50.99	288.81	264.91
昆山市	Kunshan City	63.96	40.08	299.55	87.66	217.51	171.12
太仓市	Taicang City	17.26	15.30	99.99	31.15	96.93	81.30
南通市	**Nantong City**	**261.92**	**179.98**	**678.69**	**225.34**	**374.79**	**265.65**
海安县	Haian County	24.60	22.86	82.59	92.00	46.72	5.30
如东县	Rudong County	21.27	19.40	86.48	91.45	49.12	6.29
启东市	Qidong City	26.32	24.59	97.19	105.29	31.02	6.79
如皋市	Rugao City	27.93	25.46	127.15	130.76	50.31	8.86
海门市	Haimen City	27.05	23.59	94.18	108.28	38.60	6.48
连云港市	**Lianyungang City**	**119.96**	**71.20**	**368.05**	**114.94**	**166.15**	**110.00**
东海县	Donghai County	10.01	10.81	82.21	24.37	23.22	13.69
灌云县	Guanyun County	7.00	8.88	62.84	15.87	12.83	6.05
灌南县	Guannan County	4.37	6.80	49.85	12.44	31.48	24.87

市 县 City and County		邮电业务总量（亿元）Post & Telecommunication Services (100 million yuan)	固定电话用户（万户）Telephone Subscribers (10000 subscribers)	移动电话年末用户（万户）Number of Mobile Telephones Subscribers at Year-end (10000 subscribers)	国际互联网用户（万户）International Exchange Network Users (10000 subscribers)	全年用电量（亿千瓦时）Total Consumption of Electricity of the Year (100 million kW·h)	#工业用电 Consumption of Electricity for Industrial Use
淮安市	**Huaian City**	**126.06**	**57.06**	**383.34**	**111.15**	**163.20**	**106.70**
涟水县	Lianshui County	5.17	10.48	169.00	27.88	16.69	8.94
盱眙县	Xuyi County	4.35	9.82	56.50	13.64	17.51	10.26
金湖县	Jinhu County	2.83	3.51	23.70	7.55	10.78	6.86
盐城市	**Yancheng City**	**173.17**	**98.80**	**584.97**	**174.43**	**289.29**	**201.37**
响水县	Xiangshui County	3.43	4.84	41.39	10.19	42.08	36.08
滨海县	Binhai County	6.66	10.40	66.19	15.87	26.26	17.22
阜宁县	Funing County	6.18	8.21	68.66	15.98	29.06	20.65
射阳县	Sheyang County	6.54	9.35	79.99	17.37	21.64	12.42
建湖县	Jianhu County	6.24	7.63	65.59	15.67	22.13	14.32
东台市	Dongtai City	8.55	15.92	88.33	22.02	41.10	30.12
扬州市	**Yangzhou City**	**155.88**	**108.59**	**437.36**	**146.95**	**225.37**	**156.60**
宝应县	Baoying County	29.43	12.18	22.92	9.07	19.76	11.70
仪征市	Yizheng City	27.03	13.50	23.26	9.87	41.10	34.40
高邮市	Gaoyou City	31.52	15.18	28.54	11.73	31.78	22.38
镇江市	**Zhenjiang City**	**109.87**	**75.79**	**305.89**	**107.69**	**232.41**	**173.77**
丹阳市	Danyang City	27.76	21.00	89.32	29.81	71.50	55.67
扬中市	Yangzhong City	10.31	9.15	34.16	12.70	18.26	12.96
句容市	Jurong City	14.36	12.11	50.22	18.21	26.09	15.93
泰州市	**Taizhou City**	**131.20**	**104.85**	**404.76**	**134.75**	**239.55**	**176.20**
兴化市	Xinghua City	20.27	20.09	98.12	26.78	63.38	50.46
靖江市	Jingjiang City	20.14	18.00	73.87	21.80	37.47	26.43
泰兴市	Taixing City	25.53	24.58	96.95	28.62	54.57	42.46
宿迁市	**Suqian City**	**130.21**	**47.00**	**371.56**	**105.72**	**168.83**	**115.81**
沭阳县	Shuyang County	26.89	15.35	130.09	33.71	47.97	32.62
泗阳县	Siyang County	8.47	8.40	71.16	18.22	24.53	15.30
泗洪县	Sihong County	7.76	6.06	77.91	19.12	17.97	8.82

20-15 固定资产投资完成额(2016年)

Completed Investment in Fixed Assets (2016)

单位:亿元 (100 million yuan)

市县	City and County	固定资产投资 Investment in Fixed Assets	房地产开发投资 Investment in Real Estate Development	#住宅 Residential Buildings	新增固定资产 Newly Added Fixed Assets	商品房屋销售建筑面积(万平方米) Constraction Floor Space of the Commercial Houses Sold (10000 sq. m)	#住宅 Residential Buildings
南京市	**Nanjing City**	**5533.56**	**1845.60**	**1392.76**	**3019.53**	**1558.18**	**1406.29**
无锡市	**Wuxi City**	**4793.69**	**1033.62**	**684.42**	**3730.42**	**1276.41**	**1168.43**
江阴市	Jiangyin City	1133.03	281.10	202.75	655.31	233.05	214.81
宜兴市	Yixing City	537.31	88.70	62.38	522.59	135.13	117.16
徐州市	**Xuzhou City**	**4797.33**	**549.13**	**415.04**	**3321.67**	**1071.43**	**917.89**
丰县	Fengxian County	251.10	32.62	27.44	174.92	98.33	93.05
沛县	Peixian County	560.35	24.68	19.12	510.16	92.78	83.51
睢宁县	Suining County	320.49	43.53	31.32	203.09	119.52	103.80
新沂市	Xinyi City	550.05	49.08	41.07	298.07	134.35	101.69
邳州市	Pizhou City	763.12	72.83	63.42	562.24	142.49	130.32
常州市	**Changzhou City**	**3605.08**	**446.70**	**316.48**	**2645.73**	**933.20**	**810.80**
溧阳市	Liyang City	486.55	44.06	35.51	335.53	75.55	71.49
苏州市	**Suzhou City**	**5648.49**	**2163.24**	**1655.24**	**3682.31**	**2494.05**	**2258.60**
常熟市	Changshu City	544.91	143.71	109.33	365.22	213.15	192.80
张家港市	Zhangjiagang City	724.77	163.81	130.62	488.41	196.62	171.75
昆山市	Kunshan City	757.42	379.80	285.38	686.93	633.43	575.97
太仓市	Taicang City	465.00	94.73	69.70	357.52	178.09	170.42
南通市	**Nantong City**	**4811.95**	**584.14**	**425.88**	**3240.33**	**1200.80**	**1115.64**
海安县	Haian County	584.46	52.44	40.01	147.71	101.25	97.00
如东县	Rudong County	545.42	22.24	15.55	411.67	39.78	36.63
启东市	Qidong City	614.84	55.63	48.01	416.77	155.93	151.87
如皋市	Rugao City	575.25	52.68	36.34	326.78	120.26	109.97
海门市	Haimen City	613.19	49.77	42.56	375.69	107.02	98.22
连云港市	**Lianyungang City**	**2385.16**	**235.41**	**192.92**	**1541.93**	**524.44**	**503.30**
东海县	Donghai County	330.59	19.77	17.64	245.76	88.42	83.22
灌云县	Guanyun County	272.19	27.26	24.25	233.37	47.78	46.59
灌南县	Guannan County	218.06	22.51	21.11	155.37	43.61	41.50

单位：亿元 (100 million yuan)

市 县	City and County	固定资产投资 Investment in Fixed Assets	房地产开发投资 Investment in Real Estate Development	#住宅 Residential Buildings	新增固定资产 Newly Added Fixed Assets	商品房屋销售建筑面积（万平方米） Constraction Floor Space of the Commercial Houses Sold (10000 sq. m)	#住宅 Residential Buildings
淮 安 市	**Huaian City**	**2535.19**	**321.41**	**222.99**	**1612.42**	**869.80**	**749.08**
涟 水 县	Lianshui County	335.29	23.83	20.22	214.30	118.43	96.32
盱 眙 县	Xuyi County	350.65	45.66	20.11	190.51	108.17	77.08
金 湖 县	Jinhu County	195.54	11.88	9.43	146.84	39.98	31.90
盐 城 市	**Yancheng City**	**3882.83**	**358.57**	**273.02**	**2960.76**	**842.55**	**751.32**
响 水 县	Xiangshui County	287.25	11.07	9.00	198.37	42.83	36.95
滨 海 县	Binhai County	377.87	21.34	16.62	246.26	67.76	60.33
阜 宁 县	Funing County	320.52	28.29	20.91	265.85	72.21	65.83
射 阳 县	Sheyang County	300.16	26.21	23.44	212.45	56.55	54.24
建 湖 县	Jianhu County	357.70	13.61	10.45	275.84	52.41	43.81
东 台 市	Dongtai City	581.03	48.68	35.34	540.90	114.96	103.43
扬 州 市	**Yangzhou City**	**3288.68**	**410.18**	**289.28**	**2263.68**	**734.76**	**682.21**
宝 应 县	Baoying County	372.72	40.58	38.35	288.67	98.67	96.18
仪 征 市	Yizheng City	471.00	22.11	18.83	380.87	87.52	85.20
高 邮 市	Gaoyou City	455.62	31.64	23.94	346.10	99.50	90.88
镇 江 市	**Zhenjiang City**	**2873.43**	**448.64**	**341.45**	**1794.13**	**996.50**	**947.93**
丹 阳 市	Danyang City	514.01	71.73	60.88	380.04	150.23	134.33
扬 中 市	Yangzhong City	305.10	24.86	21.43	122.08	54.94	50.45
句 容 市	Jurong City	360.81	112.46	89.47	139.13	461.40	450.77
泰 州 市	**Taizhou City**	**3155.87**	**249.96**	**194.91**	**2680.51**	**694.87**	**645.44**
兴 化 市	Xinghua City	419.66	22.49	15.25	383.18	93.01	81.76
靖 江 市	Jingjiang City	500.00	35.08	29.91	453.64	80.99	73.94
泰 兴 市	Taixing City	687.46	67.69	51.36	577.07	146.47	134.22
宿 迁 市	**Suqian City**	**2059.58**	**309.76**	**225.10**	**1470.29**	**765.10**	**704.42**
沭 阳 县	Shuyang County	515.03	74.81	43.87	352.34	182.22	164.71
泗 阳 县	Siyang County	379.23	64.29	55.63	289.13	138.20	130.42
泗 洪 县	Sihong County	380.41	49.86	39.64	307.81	158.00	148.00

20-16 国内贸易、对外经济(2016 年)

Domestic and Foreign Trade, Foreign Economy (2016)

市 县	City and County	社会消费品零售总额(亿元) Total Retail of Consumer Goods (100 million Yuan)	#批发和零售业 Wholesale and Retail Trade	进出口总额(亿美元) Total Imports and Exports (USD 100 million)	出口 Exports	进口 Imports	实际使用外资(亿美元) Actual Use of Foreign Capital (USD 100 million)
南京市	**Nanjing City**	**5088.20**	**4638.45**	**502.14**	**295.94**	**206.20**	**34.79**
无锡市	**Wuxi City**	**3119.56**	**2880.94**	**698.05**	**429.10**	**268.95**	**34.13**
江阴市	Jiangyin City	776.05	730.46	198.77	119.22	79.55	10.55
宜兴市	Yixing City	556.37	530.87	37.00	30.17	6.82	1.58
徐州市	**Xuzhou City**	**2659.39**	**2433.52**	**62.42**	**52.48**	**9.94**	**15.06**
丰县	Fengxian County	151.04	139.32	1.46	1.26	0.20	0.41
沛县	Peixian County	245.59	220.70	3.09	2.94	0.15	1.30
睢宁县	Suining County	179.58	166.04	7.52	6.35	1.17	1.11
新沂市	Xinyi City	174.56	157.84	4.58	2.98	1.60	1.00
邳州市	Pizhou City	253.41	231.56	10.32	9.16	1.16	1.83
常州市	**Changzhou City**	**2202.83**	**2016.06**	**275.84**	**208.60**	**67.25**	**25.00**
溧阳市	Liyang City	303.03	276.51	8.30	7.46	0.85	3.36
苏州市	**Suzhou City**	**4936.79**	**4343.02**	**2737.58**	**1639.41**	**1098.18**	**60.03**
常熟市	Changshu City	740.78	678.32	198.53	133.56	64.97	6.30
张家港市	Zhangjiagang City	535.16	457.54	274.17	142.02	132.14	6.04
昆山市	Kunshan City	815.04	663.93	722.66	463.21	259.44	8.96
太仓市	Taicang City	287.31	247.05	109.64	54.30	55.34	5.61
南通市	**Nantong City**	**2632.87**	**2406.78**	**308.59**	**230.11**	**78.48**	**23.87**
海安县	Haian County	273.74	236.65	16.55	14.05	2.50	2.96
如东县	Rudong County	318.62	301.31	25.10	14.51	10.59	2.94
启东市	Qidong City	324.57	295.57	30.22	26.51	3.71	2.84
如皋市	Rugao City	342.21	304.74	25.29	20.15	5.13	2.77
海门市	Haimen City	344.60	317.46	39.14	35.79	3.36	2.40
连云港市	**Lianyungang City**	**933.31**	**829.64**	**70.40**	**36.84**	**33.56**	**5.50**
东海县	Donghai County	175.89	154.06	4.58	3.68	0.90	0.94
灌云县	Guanyun County	119.45	103.80	2.33	2.03	0.30	0.24
灌南县	Guannan County	93.52	85.23	2.25	1.70	0.55	0.03

市 县	City and County	社会消费品零售总额（亿元）Total Retail of Consumer Goods (100 million Yuan)	#批发和零售业 Wholesale and Retail Trade	进出口总额（亿美元）Total Imports and Exports (USD 100 million)	出口 Exports	进口 Imports	实际使用外资（亿美元）Actual Use of Foreign Capital (USD 100 million)
淮安市	**Huaian City**	**1083.83**	**978.30**	**35.04**	**26.98**	**8.06**	**11.61**
涟水县	Lianshui County	130.03	119.90	3.71	3.30	0.41	1.41
盱眙县	Xuyi County	123.89	109.89	1.88	1.34	0.54	1.20
金湖县	Jinhu County	90.76	81.35	3.47	3.42	0.06	1.20
盐城市	**Yancheng City**	**1630.88**	**1465.26**	**79.51**	**47.38**	**32.12**	**7.07**
响水县	Xiangshui County	66.52	60.92	4.86	4.70	0.17	0.29
滨海县	Binhai County	110.46	99.56	3.77	3.08	0.70	0.53
阜宁县	Funing County	130.29	122.73	2.77	2.22	0.55	0.12
射阳县	Sheyang County	167.90	149.09	2.84	1.95	0.89	0.45
建湖县	Jianhu County	171.98	144.77	3.03	2.92	0.11	0.55
东台市	Dongtai City	253.53	227.36	7.37	7.07	0.30	0.62
扬州市	**Yangzhou City**	**1358.80**	**1201.39**	**96.25**	**72.59**	**23.66**	**12.04**
宝应县	Baoying County	150.34	135.96	10.59	8.43	2.16	0.50
仪征市	Yizheng City	109.75	97.09	10.83	4.64	6.19	1.29
高邮市	Gaoyou City	170.10	145.60	4.75	4.33	0.42	0.50
镇江市	**Zhenjiang City**	**1236.78**	**1086.95**	**103.17**	**69.52**	**33.65**	**13.51**
丹阳市	Danyang City	315.61	279.39	25.44	21.40	4.04	3.22
扬中市	Yangzhong City	140.92	114.88	5.73	4.54	1.19	1.18
句容市	Jurong City	142.02	126.33	5.93	4.71	1.22	2.21
泰州市	**Taizhou City**	**1118.34**	**964.94**	**103.81**	**66.74**	**37.07**	**13.44**
兴化市	Xinghua City	171.24	145.74	5.24	4.90	0.34	1.83
靖江市	Jingjiang City	176.24	148.23	27.18	19.36	7.82	0.23
泰兴市	Taixing City	213.95	173.32	25.75	12.33	13.42	3.53
宿迁市	**Suqian City**	**705.54**	**614.55**	**24.22**	**18.71**	**5.51**	**4.50**
沭阳县	Shuyang County	197.68	161.96	6.39	5.12	1.26	0.80
泗阳县	Siyang County	100.47	86.93	3.53	3.43	0.10	0.51
泗洪县	Sihong County	105.40	98.28	1.66	1.34	0.32	0.33

20-17 财政、金融(2016年)
Government Finance, Financial Intermediation (2016)

单位:亿元 (100 million yuan)

市县	City and County	一般公共预算收入 General Public Budget Revenue	#税收收入 Taxes	一般公共预算支出 General Public Budget Expenditure	年末金融机构存款余额 Deposits Balance of Banking Institutions (Year-end)	#住户存款 Household Deposits	年末金融机构贷款余额 Loans Balance of Banking Institutions (Year-end)
南京市	**Nanjing City**	**1142.60**	**956.62**	**1173.84**	**27633.55**	**5894.47**	**21681.28**
无锡市	**Wuxi City**	**875.00**	**706.04**	**867.36**	**14101.40**	**4867.43**	**10382.93**
江阴市	Jiangyin City	229.91	191.20	226.26	3509.40	1079.72	2689.91
宜兴市	Yixing City	108.65	91.21	117.42	1903.25	958.60	1392.03
徐州市	**Xuzhou City**	**516.06**	**390.30**	**797.99**	**5495.31**	**3090.21**	**3620.21**
丰县	Fengxian County	35.00	25.03	70.90	354.14	251.75	177.31
沛县	Peixian County	57.68	45.08	94.86	454.10	324.35	222.60
睢宁县	Suining County	42.52	32.97	80.21	401.90	285.67	224.39
新沂市	Xinyi City	49.91	37.71	91.82	386.97	217.87	246.38
邳州市	Pizhou City	62.40	48.10	110.08	525.34	361.35	366.13
常州市	**Changzhou City**	**480.29**	**383.19**	**508.11**	**8540.82**	**3366.85**	**6043.16**
溧阳市	Liyang City	59.00	46.74	69.44	994.82	478.51	798.94
苏州市	**Suzhou City**	**1730.04**	**1505.82**	**1617.11**	**25864.26**	**7913.85**	**21924.44**
常熟市	Changshu City	173.58	145.54	158.74	2692.88	1192.75	2139.49
张家港市	Zhangjiagang City	190.00	160.11	184.81	2508.27	1018.23	1994.40
昆山市	Kunshan City	318.92	284.07	269.00	3562.27	1155.13	2552.22
太仓市	Taicang City	127.71	110.52	115.84	1395.41	522.74	1245.07
南通市	**Nantong City**	**590.18**	**456.77**	**749.22**	**11097.74**	**5554.89**	**6835.46**
海安县	Haian County	57.58	48.16	81.35	1286.53	696.77	798.77
如东县	Rudong County	54.41	44.44	102.16	1010.55	601.62	494.56
启东市	Qidong City	71.03	54.95	89.03	1232.03	767.24	705.13
如皋市	Rugao City	71.21	54.26	96.38	1135.62	716.86	709.99
海门市	Haimen City	72.41	53.23	85.75	1368.55	766.55	824.32
连云港市	**Lianyungang City**	**211.47**	**170.80**	**373.12**	**2501.84**	**1168.71**	**2046.93**
东海县	Donghai County	22.61	18.59	58.09	317.38	161.78	248.71
灌云县	Guanyun County	21.52	17.64	49.64	260.88	82.62	183.80
灌南县	Guannan County	22.43	19.33	48.04	179.88	77.90	134.05

单位:亿元 (100 million yuan)

市 县 City and County		一般公共预算收入 General Public Budget Revenue	#税收收入 Taxes	一般公共预算支出 General Public Budget Expenditure	年末金融机构存款余额 Deposits Balance of Banking Institutions (Year-end)	#住户存款 Household Deposits	年末金融机构贷款余额 Loans Balance of Banking Institutions (Year-end)
淮安市	**Huaian City**	**315.51**	**235.15**	**483.47**	**3066.00**	**1360.51**	**2304.22**
涟水县	Lianshui County	28.98	23.49	64.11	330.06	187.51	197.10
盱眙县	Xuyi County	30.78	23.02	54.65	278.07	161.88	222.34
金湖县	Jinhu County	22.00	19.19	41.84	221.07	129.57	171.67
盐城市	**Yancheng City**	**415.18**	**324.67**	**730.33**	**5255.06**	**2682.46**	**3699.32**
响水县	Xiangshui County	29.60	20.39	50.13	178.13	93.58	139.77
滨海县	Binhai County	34.07	25.08	70.89	308.75	176.66	249.46
阜宁县	Funing County	36.24	26.87	76.55	392.18	266.81	240.78
射阳县	Sheyang County	21.58	17.40	64.60	413.98	277.99	264.42
建湖县	Jianhu County	35.01	27.30	73.22	409.79	284.50	301.49
东台市	Dongtai City	60.26	50.70	95.58	715.99	510.70	394.75
扬州市	**Yangzhou City**	**345.30**	**267.16**	**478.97**	**5361.55**	**2560.98**	**3508.13**
宝应县	Baoying County	30.81	26.60	64.38	478.68	286.71	294.60
仪征市	Yizheng City	44.74	38.57	50.95	606.06	295.73	343.07
高邮市	Gaoyou City	34.12	28.54	56.93	552.73	345.62	322.23
镇江市	**Zhenjiang City**	**293.01**	**231.40**	**362.94**	**4705.99**	**1879.10**	**3444.36**
丹阳市	Danyang City	65.55	54.23	79.01	1040.33	566.31	964.49
扬中市	Yangzhong City	32.50	26.72	38.66	578.31	276.78	431.43
句容市	Jurong City	40.48	36.38	53.54	629.87	287.82	561.03
泰州市	**Taizhou City**	**321.18**	**257.62**	**448.93**	**5275.62**	**2474.71**	**3656.79**
兴化市	Xinghua City	37.06	30.07	85.00	681.08	483.63	428.41
靖江市	Jingjiang City	58.93	48.08	64.15	940.16	472.16	694.02
泰兴市	Taixing City	57.20	47.16	76.38	912.30	465.34	581.39
宿迁市	**Suqian City**	**238.08**	**186.27**	**424.57**	**2207.43**	**1086.33**	**1960.37**
沭阳县	Shuyang County	71.75	54.48	117.29	461.62	323.19	403.49
泗阳县	Siyang County	33.34	25.46	70.29	320.87	194.68	314.93
泗洪县	Sihong County	31.75	25.43	66.59	299.28	192.89	288.55

20－18 科技、教育(2016年)
Science, Technology and Education (2016)

市县 City and County		专利申请受理量(件) Applications Accepted (unit)	专利申请受权量(件) Patents Granted (unit)	普通中学在校学生(万人) Regular Secondary Schools Student Enrollment (10000 persons)	小学在校学生(万人) Primary Schools Student Enrollment (10000 persons)	普通中学专任教师(人) Full-time Teachers in Regular Secondary Schools (person)	小学专任教师(人) Full-time Teachers in Primary Schools (person)
南京市	**Nanjing City**	**65198**	**28782**	**22.45**	**37.54**	**22982**	**23644**
无锡市	**Wuxi City**	**71673**	**29865**	**21.54**	**36.13**	**19991**	**20119**
江阴市	Jiangyin City	18537	4912	5.63	9.33	5545	4670
宜兴市	Yixing City	7354	3305	4.13	6.04	4181	3647
徐州市	**Xuzhou City**	**21511**	**11458**	**36.10**	**90.54**	**33695**	**42716**
丰县	Fengxian County	1053	687	4.27	8.93	4760	4470
沛县	Peixian County	1520	982	3.74	10.76	3689	5138
睢宁县	Suining County	1715	843	4.72	10.26	4849	5951
新沂市	Xinyi City	1321	704	3.58	12.21	3175	4347
邳州市	Pizhou City	1263	728	7.49	19.18	5707	9551
常州市	**Changzhou City**	**43860**	**17790**	**16.53**	**28.11**	**14060**	**14173**
溧阳市	Liyang City	1435	764	2.62	3.86	2733	2471
苏州市	**Suzhou City**	**106700**	**53528**	**30.98**	**69.37**	**27726**	**35770**
常熟市	Changshu City	6571	3078	4.45	8.15	3697	4611
张家港市	Zhangjiagang City	8889	4162	4.23	8.01	3525	4083
昆山市	Kunshan City	18159	9833	4.76	13.02	3589	6094
太仓市	Taicang City	8226	3632	2.11	4.42	1813	2256
南通市	**Nantong City**	**45557**	**24337**	**23.59**	**32.71**	**24493**	**19636**
海安县	Haian County	6125	3413	2.68	3.21	3356	2262
如东县	Rudong County	3399	1424	2.52	2.92	2839	2195
启东市	Qidong City	6127	2598	2.82	3.72	3250	2599
如皋市	Rugao City	5132	2422	4.78	6.14	4489	3430
海门市	Haimen City	6673	3019	3.30	4.74	3644	2683
连云港市	**Lianyungang City**	**8780**	**4599**	**23.01**	**43.20**	**19959**	**23614**
东海县	Donghai County	954	504	5.25	11.82	4512	6086
灌云县	Guanyun County	1100	95	4.14	7.01	3086	3333
灌南县	Guannan County	685	680	3.33	6.25	2753	3806

市 县 City and County		专利申请受理量(件) Applications Accepted (unit)	专利申请受权量(件) Patents Granted (unit)	普通中学在校学生(万人) Regular Secondary Schools Student Enrollment (10000 persons)	小学在校学生(万人) Primary Schools Student Enrollment (10000 persons)	普通中学专任教师(人) Full-time Teachers in Regular Secondary Schools (person)	小学专任教师(人) Full-time Teachers in Primary Schools (person)
淮安市	**Huaian City**	**17293**	**8081**	**21.52**	**35.05**	**19454**	**21067**
涟水县	Lianshui County	2299	901	4.45	8.10	3982	4841
盱眙县	Xuyi County	1555	627	3.03	5.63	2924	3155
金湖县	Jinhu County	1622	921	0.94	1.29	937	926
盐城市	**Yancheng City**	**28509**	**8076**	**27.00**	**45.02**	**26634**	**26548**
响水县	Xiangshui County	1161	432	2.24	4.87	1915	2791
滨海县	Binhai County	2018	257	3.49	8.47	3279	4631
阜宁县	Funing County	3061	392	3.47	6.49	3262	3828
射阳县	Sheyang County	1976	672	3.13	4.85	3072	3046
建湖县	Jianhu County	3044	942	2.71	4.01	2790	2547
东台市	Dongtai City	3638	1032	3.01	3.45	3645	2370
扬州市	**Yangzhou City**	**27043**	**13253**	**17.56**	**21.26**	**16467**	**13593**
宝应县	Baoying County	3807	1156	3.21	3.63	2951	2319
仪征市	Yizheng City	3472	1190	1.90	2.35	1825	1600
高邮市	Gaoyou City	3962	2750	2.65	2.68	2801	1938
镇江市	**Zhenjiang City**	**34260**	**13836**	**9.52**	**14.38**	**10088**	**9632**
丹阳市	Danyang City	8415	3006	3.25	4.91	3452	3381
扬中市	Yangzhong City	4510	1208	0.97	1.43	1041	962
句容市	Jurong City	5341	3061	1.67	2.47	1992	1733
泰州市	**Taizhou City**	**31598**	**12489**	**17.08**	**22.00**	**19014**	**14108**
兴化市	Xinghua City	4524	2751	3.99	6.41	4251	4116
靖江市	Jingjiang City	5391	2453	2.38	2.83	2934	2012
泰兴市	Taixing City	5117	1041	4.24	4.89	5102	3067
宿迁市	**Suqian City**	**10522**	**4910**	**23.20**	**46.90**	**17104**	**24582**
沭阳县	Shuyang County	3706	1862	7.58	16.34	5533	8684
泗阳县	Siyang County	2004	1064	5.04	9.02	3168	4469
泗洪县	Sihong County	816	229	4.41	9.02	3263	4686

20－19 文化、卫生（2016年）

Culture and Public Health (2016)

市县	City and County	公共图书馆（个） Public Libraries (unit)	公共图书馆图书藏量（千册） Total Collections of Public Libraries (1000 volumes)	卫生机构数（个） Number of Health Institutions (unit)	卫生机构床位数（张） Number of Hospital Beds (unit)	卫生技术人员（人） Medical Technical Personnel (person)	#执业（助理）医师 Practitioner (Assistant) Doctors
南京市	**Nanjing City**	**14**	**6240**	**2383**	**49857**	**70687**	**25272**
无锡市	**Wuxi City**	**8**	**7100**	**2308**	**39732**	**47549**	**18107**
江阴市	Jiangyin City	1	2528	584	8080	9405	3702
宜兴市	Yixing City	1	815	443	5320	7887	2996
徐州市	**Xuzhou City**	**8**	**3300**	**4584**	**52247**	**55523**	**21836**
丰县	Fengxian County	1	220	554	4053	4635	2076
沛县	Peixian County	1	353	612	4876	5398	2481
睢宁县	Suining County	1	412	596	4540	4900	2050
新沂市	Xinyi City	1	190	483	3549	4848	2192
邳州市	Pizhou City	1	493	768	5678	7203	2560
常州市	**Changzhou City**	**5**	**4520**	**1267**	**25370**	**31194**	**12447**
溧阳市	Liyang City	1	415	252	2956	4189	1879
苏州市	**Suzhou City**	**11**	**18780**	**3175**	**63241**	**72166**	**27667**
常熟市	Changshu City	1	2533	481	7882	9114	3834
张家港市	Zhangjiagang City	1	2170	429	9601	9288	3814
昆山市	Kunshan City	1	2433	504	7148	11070	4312
太仓市	Taicang City	1	1150	247	3853	4520	1778

市 县 City and County		公共图书馆（个）Public Libraries (unit)	公共图书馆图书藏量（千册）Total Collections of Public Libraries (1000 volumes)	卫生机构数（个）Number of Health Institutions (unit)	卫生机构床位数（张）Number of Hospital Beds (unit)	卫生技术人员（人）Medical Technical Personnel (person)	#执业(助理)医师 Practitioner (Assistant) Doctors
南通市	**Nantong City**	**10**	**5000**	**3131**	**39147**	**43570**	**17967**
海安县	Haian County	1	467	395	4974	4815	2183
如东县	Rudong County	1	431	461	3599	4311	1981
启东市	Qidong City	1	493	385	4094	4185	1667
如皋市	Rugao City	2	960	522	5988	6181	2820
海门市	Haimen City	1	564	377	3694	4154	1712
连云港市	**Lianyungang City**	**8**	**2650**	**2726**	**23281**	**26152**	**10979**
东海县	Donghai County	1	748	549	3902	4054	1883
灌云县	Guanyun County	1	249	415	3368	3350	1471
灌南县	Guannan County	1	183	367	3400	3562	1535
淮安市	**Huaian City**	**9**	**2860**	**2237**	**27529**	**31524**	**12385**
涟水县	Lianshui County	1	133	477	4110	4539	1926
盱眙县	Xuyi County	1	316	355	3607	3600	1455
金湖县	Jinhu County	1	238	144	1557	1855	739
盐城市	**Yancheng City**	**11**	**3350**	**3233**	**38663**	**39472**	**18124**
响水县	Xiangshui County	1	89	226	2616	2871	1339
滨海县	Binhai County	1	208	413	4940	4293	1904
阜宁县	Funing County	2	304	382	4203	3828	1990

市 县 City and County		公共图书馆(个) Public Libraries (unit)	公共图书馆图书藏量(千册) Total Collections of Public Libraries (1000 volumes)	卫生机构数(个) Number of Health Institutions (unit)	卫生机构床位数(张) Number of Hospital Beds (unit)	卫生技术人员(人) Medical Technical Personnel (person)	#执业(助理)医师 Practitioner (Assistant) Doctors
射阳县	Sheyang County	1	256	340	3941	4314	2208
建湖县	Jianhu County	1	263	358	3638	3503	1751
东台市	Dongtai City	1	284	470	5109	4649	2211
扬州市	**Yangzhou City**	**7**	**3540**	**1787**	**20683**	**25273**	**10405**
宝应县	Baoying County	1	182	342	2313	3125	1386
仪征市	Yizheng City	1	389	154	2376	2840	1158
高邮市	Gaoyou City	1	254	246	2646	3292	1488
镇江市	**Zhenjiang City**	**9**	**3150**	**976**	**14585**	**19449**	**7884**
丹阳市	Danyang City	2	629	255	3232	4622	1938
扬中市	Yangzhong City	1	337	94	1100	1733	756
句容市	Jurong City	1	254	207	1759	2698	1140
泰州市	**Taizhou City**	**7**	**2710**	**1963**	**23324**	**26094**	**11287**
兴化市	Xinghua City	1	251	669	4783	5730	2850
靖江市	Jingjiang City	1	606	289	4275	4484	1934
泰兴市	Taixing City	1	325	365	4371	4628	2066
宿迁市	**Suqian City**	**6**	**1440**	**2365**	**25441**	**28412**	**10327**
沭阳县	Shuyang County	1	167	753	7318	10276	3279
泗阳县	Siyang County	1	313	438	4770	6898	1658
泗洪县	Sihong County	1	100	503	4591	7140	2076

20-20 人民生活(2016年)

市　县 City and County		居民人均可支配收入(元) Per Capita Disposable Income of Residents (yuan)	居民人均生活消费支出(元) Per Capita Consumption Expanditure of Residents (yuan)	#食品烟酒 Food, Tobacco and Wine	居民恩格尔系数(%) Engle Coefficient of Residents (%)	居民人均住房建筑面积(平方米) Per Capital Construction Floor Space of Residential Building (sq. m)	城镇常住居民人均可支配收入(元) Per Capita Annual Disposable Income of Urban Residents (yuan)	城镇常住居民人均生活消费支出(元) Per Capita Annual Consumption Expanditure of Urban Residents (yuan)
南京市	**Nanjing City**	**44009**	**26802**	**7027**	**26.2**	**40.8**	**49997**	**29772**
无锡市	**Wuxi City**	**42757**	**27932**	**7922**	**28.4**	**49.7**	**48628**	**31438**
江阴市	Jiangyin City	46337	25562	7516	29.4	51.6	54631	28775
宜兴市	Yixing City	37326	23968	7067	29.5	56.9	46092	28767
徐州市	**Xuzhou City**	**22348**	**14321**	**4374**	**30.5**	**46.4**	**28421**	**17255**
丰县	Fengxian County	18056	12551	3925	31.3	45.0	22971	16711
沛县	Peixian County	21221	13552	3836	28.3	45.5	27277	17050
睢宁县	Suining County	18127	10867	3557	32.7	50.4	23403	13185
新沂市	Xinyi City	18786	12594	4166	33.1	47.7	24928	16382
邳州市	Pizhou City	20675	12072	3684	30.5	66.1	28546	15765
常州市	**Changzhou City**	**38435**	**23980**	**6751**	**28.2**	**50.6**	**46058**	**27080**
溧阳市	Liyang City	31833	19116	6540	34.2	47.3	42063	21550
苏州市	**Suzhou City**	**46595**	**28983**	**7674**	**26.5**	**51.1**	**54341**	**33305**
常熟市	Changshu City	45061	27337	7807	28.6	58.4	54411	31520
张家港市	Zhangjiagang City	44977	26837	7648	28.5	62.6	54602	31590
昆山市	Kunshan City	46339	28161	8006	28.4	40.2	54728	32578
太仓市	Taicang City	43867	28120	8502	30.2	68.8	54099	33721
南通市	**Nantong City**	**30084**	**19827**	**5715**	**28.8**	**53.1**	**39247**	**25217**
海安县	Haian County	27230	18780	5599	29.8	56.1	37297	22949
如东县	Rudong County	26683	17119	5578	32.6	57.2	37133	21470
启东市	Qidong City	28446	21794	6889	31.6	52.2	37390	29629
如皋市	Rugao City	26695	17043	5075	29.8	57.9	36590	21810
海门市	Haimen City	30092	19853	5817	29.3	54.0	40509	25928
连云港市	**Lianyungang City**	**21230**	**14333**	**4645**	**32.4**	**47.2**	**27853**	**18344**
东海县	Donghai County	20128	13779	4782	34.7	51.0	27391	18633
灌云县	Guanyun County	17565	11301	3925	35.0	42.1	22979	13980
灌南县	Guannan County	17446	11701	4198	35.9	53.1	24494	15734

#食品烟酒 Food, Tobacco and Wine	城镇常住居民恩格尔系数(%) Engle Coefficient of Urban Residents (%)	城镇常住居民人均住房建筑面积(平方米) Per Capital Construction Floor Space of Urban Residential Building (sq. m)	农村常住居民人均可支配收入(元) Per Capita Annual Disposable Income of Rural Residents (yuan)	农村常住居民人均生活消费支出(元) Per Capita Annual Consumption Expanditure of Rural Residents (yuan)	#食品烟酒 Food, Tobacco and Wine	农村常住居民恩格尔系数(%) Engle Coefficient of Rural Residents (%)	农村常住居民人均住房建筑面积(平方米) Per Capital Construction Floor Space of Rural Residential Building (sq. m)
7642	**25.7**	**36.7**	**21156**	**15773**	**4745**	**30.1**	**56.6**
8818	**28.0**	**46.7**	**26158**	**18463**	**5502**	**29.8**	**56.4**
8402	29.2	54.0	28181	18791	5648	30.1	47.8
8409	29.2	47.5	23709	16771	5055	30.1	71.5
5182	**30.0**	**41.4**	**15274**	**11059**	**3475**	**31.4**	**53.3**
5080	30.4	40.9	14026	9277	2966	32.0	48.5
4756	27.9	42.8	15791	10573	3051	28.9	47.9
4195	31.8	46.5	13822	9064	2923	32.2	54.4
5351	32.7	46.0	14526	10101	3386	33.5	49.1
4812	30.5	64.3	15321	9699	2960	30.5	67.3
7357	**27.2**	**44.3**	**23780**	**16567**	**5102**	**30.8**	**64.7**
7180	33.3	39.0	21899	16895	5840	34.6	58.3
8882	**26.7**	**43.3**	**27691**	**18820**	**4832**	**25.7**	**65.6**
9087	28.8	50.0	27956	21024	5876	28.0	72.6
9025	28.6	60.1	27849	18687	5286	28.3	66.4
9194	28.2	36.2	28178	18890	5511	29.2	44.8
10148	30.1	57.7	27766	19589	5994	30.6	77.5
7227	**28.7**	**47.8**	**18741**	**13440**	**3923**	**29.2**	**61.5**
6593	28.7	51.6	17978	15120	4728	31.3	60.7
7386	34.4	54.0	17119	13314	3994	30.0	60.5
9161	30.9	45.4	19875	14615	4712	32.2	64.1
6347	29.1	55.4	16883	12526	3871	30.9	62.1
7597	29.3	47.5	20608	14570	4269	29.3	63.0
5924	**32.3**	**46.1**	**13932**	**10113**	**3299**	**32.6**	**48.7**
6423	34.5	45.5	14487	10194	3571	35.0	56.9
4865	34.8	42.5	12969	9140	3127	34.2	41.9
5475	34.8	51.8	12430	8978	3335	37.1	54.3

市 县	City and County	居民人均可支配收入(元) Per Capita Disposable Income of Residents (yuan)	居民人均生活消费支出(元) Per Capita Consumption Expanditure of Residents (yuan)	#食品烟酒 Food, Tobacco and Wine	居民恩格尔系数(%) Engle Coefficient of Residents (%)	居民人均住房建筑面积(平方米) Per Capital Construction Floor Space of Residential Building (sq. m)	城镇常住居民人均可支配收入(元) Per Capita Annual Disposable Income of Urban Residents (yuan)	城镇常住居民人均生活消费支出(元) Per Capita Annual Consumption Expanditure of Urban Residents (yuan)
淮 安 市	**Huaian City**	**22762**	**13381**	**4044**	**30.2**	**46.3**	**30335**	**16912**
涟 水 县	Lianshui County	18302	11310	3620	32.0	58.0	25230	15768
盱 眙 县	Xuyi County	21923	11635	3680	31.6	51.0	30684	16234
金 湖 县	Jinhu County	22542	16225	5079	31.3	51.0	30799	19833
盐 城 市	**Yancheng City**	**24463**	**15503**	**4913**	**31.7**	**46.4**	**30496**	**17546**
响 水 县	Xiangshui County	19629	10360	3240	31.3	40.2	25564	11190
滨 海 县	Binhai County	20257	13319	4254	31.9	37.8	26543	15922
阜 宁 县	Funing County	20262	14005	4826	34.5	39.1	25543	20603
射 阳 县	Sheyang County	21710	15119	5018	33.2	39.2	26509	21882
建 湖 县	Jianhu County	22993	13300	4306	32.4	44.6	29637	16084
东 台 市	Dongtai City	26565	15269	4940	32.4	57.8	32686	17641
扬 州 市	**Yangzhou City**	**28633**	**18054**	**5581**	**30.9**	**49.5**	**35659**	**21064**
宝 应 县	Baoying County	21396	13975	4642	33.2	46.0	26842	16263
仪 征 市	Yizheng City	26952	18493	5816	31.4	56.6	36523	20710
高 邮 市	Gaoyou City	23854	16708	5241	31.4	45.5	31430	20610
镇 江 市	**Zhenjiang City**	**34064**	**21167**	**6029**	**28.5**	**50.5**	**41794**	**24388**
丹 阳 市	Danyang City	33089	20843	6831	32.8	50.4	41653	22452
扬 中 市	Yangzhong City	35729	20552	6071	29.5	58.0	45842	24103
句 容 市	Jurong City	28994	18564	5591	30.3	46.9	40582	22893
泰 州 市	**Taizhou City**	**28259**	**18218**	**5340**	**29.3**	**54.0**	**36828**	**22480**
兴 化 市	Xinghua City	24602	14989	4670	31.3	42.9	33614	19029
靖 江 市	Jingjiang City	29544	21600	6537	30.3	61.9	39713	26570
泰 兴 市	Taixing City	27806	17672	4597	26.0	59.0	36521	22891
宿 迁 市	**Suqian City**	**18957**	**12315**	**4327**	**35.1**	**47.2**	**24086**	**15521**
沭 阳 县	Shuyang County	19132	12743	4819	37.8	47.9	23933	15802
泗 阳 县	Siyang County	18510	12728	4430	34.8	48.5	23535	15028
泗 洪 县	Sihong County	17726	11522	4169	36.2	45.9	22953	15146

#食品烟酒 Food, Tobacco and Wine	城镇常住居民恩格尔系数(%) Engle Coefficient of Urban Residents (%)	城镇常住居民人均住房建筑面积(平方米) Per Capital Construction Floor Space of Urban Residential Building (sq. m)	农村常住居民人均可支配收入(元) Per Capita Annual Disposable Income of Rural Residents (yuan)	农村常住居民人均生活消费支出(元) Per Capita Annual Consumption Expanditure of Rural Residents (yuan)	#食品烟酒 Food, Tobacco and Wine	农村常住居民恩格尔系数(%) Engle Coefficient of Rural Residents (%)	农村常住居民人均住房建筑面积(平方米) Per Capital Construction Floor Space of Rural Residential Building (sq. m)
5054	**29.9**	**44.2**	**14319**	**9633**	**3055**	**31.7**	**51.2**
5109	32.4	52.1	13372	8324	2622	31.5	62.0
5099	31.4	49.2	14495	7938	2540	32.0	53.2
6047	30.5	41.9	15683	13385	4210	31.5	60.6
5532	**31.5**	**43.1**	**17172**	**13145**	**4159**	**31.6**	**50.9**
3499	31.3	36.2	14299	9651	2987	30.9	48.1
5160	32.4	31.8	14931	11225	3525	31.4	43.7
7268	35.3	34.8	15439	8275	2786	33.7	43.8
7077	32.3	41.4	16536	8161	2897	35.5	36.9
4976	30.9	43.7	17083	10989	3750	34.1	45.8
5684	32.2	57.6	19727	12771	4157	32.6	58.0
6551	**31.1**	**46.4**	**18057**	**13722**	**4185**	**30.5**	**54.2**
5501	33.8	40.3	16856	12145	3955	32.6	50.7
6723	32.5	46.3	17516	16390	5002	30.5	66.7
6455	31.3	45.3	16952	13280	4175	31.4	45.8
6939	**28.5**	**44.7**	**20922**	**15925**	**4547**	**28.6**	**57.7**
7642	34.0	44.8	21706	18791	5795	30.8	55.6
7111	29.5	54.7	23855	16574	4906	29.6	61.2
6970	30.4	42.3	18893	14484	4604	31.8	49.3
6470	**28.8**	**49.0**	**17861**	**13250**	**4025**	**30.4**	**64.0**
5675	29.8	37.4	16915	11691	3849	32.9	51.9
7955	29.9	56.7	19605	16958	5213	30.7	74.1
6539	28.6	50.0	17842	11935	2485	20.8	69.0
5390	**34.7**	**46.7**	**13929**	**9395**	**3358**	**35.7**	**47.8**
6035	38.2	45.8	14107	10044	3769	37.5	49.9
5176	34.4	50.7	13952	10599	3705	35.0	46.2
5427	35.8	46.1	13625	7777	2875	37.0	45.7

21

县(市)社会经济发展序列

Social Economy Development Alignment of Counties (Cities)

简 要 说 明

一、本篇资料的主要内容

本篇资料反映县(市)经济社会发展水平序列情况。

二、资料来源

本篇资料主要根据市县社会经济基本情况统计年报加工整理。

Brief Introduction

I. Main Contents

Data in this chapter reflects the counties (cities) rankings of economic and social development

Ⅱ. Date Source

Data in this chapter mainly based on the basic socio – economic situation annual report.

21－1 年末户籍人口（2016年）
Total Registered Population at Year-end (2016)

位次 No.	县（市）名称 County (City)		绝对数（万人） Absolute Figure (10000 persons)
1	沭阳县	Shuyang County	197.05
2	邳州市	Pizhou City	193.87
3	兴化市	Xinghua City	158.25
4	睢宁县	Suining County	144.16
5	如皋市	Rugao City	143.68
6	沛县	Peixian County	124.93
7	江阴市	Jiangyin City	124.80
8	东海县	Donghai County	123.45
9	滨海县	Binhai County	123.00
10	丰县	Fengxian County	121.43
11	泰兴市	Taixing City	119.31
12	涟水县	Lianshui County	115.38
13	新沂市	Xinyi City	113.56
14	阜宁县	Funing County	112.95
15	东台市	Dongtai City	112.46
16	启东市	Qidong City	111.95
17	泗洪县	Sihong County	111.06
18	宜兴市	Yixing City	108.34
19	泗阳县	Siyang County	107.34
20	常熟市	Changshu City	106.87
21	灌云县	Guanyun County	105.21
22	如东县	Rugao City	103.53
23	海门市	Haimen City	100.10
24	射阳县	Sheyang County	96.23
25	海安县	Haian County	93.83
26	张家港市	Zhangjiagang City	92.66
27	宝应县	Baoying County	91.25
28	灌南县	Guannan County	82.64
29	昆山市	Kunshan City	82.35
30	高邮市	Gaoyou City	81.48
31	丹阳市	Danyang City	81.15
32	盱眙县	Xuyi County	80.47
33	建湖县	Jianhu County	80.06
34	溧阳市	Liyang City	79.95
35	靖江市	Jingjiang City	66.67
36	响水县	Xiangshui County	62.49
37	仪征市	Yizheng City	59.62
38	句容市	Jurong City	59.21
39	太仓市	Taicang City	48.30
40	金湖县	Jinhu County	35.96
41	扬中市	Yangzhong City	28.20

21-2 地区生产总值（2016年）
Gross Domestic Product (2016)

位次 No.	县（市）名称 County (City)		绝对数（亿元）Absolute Figure (100 million yuan)	位次 No.	县（市）名称 County (City)		绝对数（亿元）Absolute Figure (100 million yuan)
1	昆 山 市	Kunshan City	3160.29	22	仪 征 市	Yizheng City	557.05
2	江 阴 市	Jiangyin City	3083.26	23	高 邮 市	Gaoyou City	537.50
3	张家港市	Zhangjiagang City	2317.24	24	宝 应 县	Baoying County	506.30
4	常 熟 市	Changshu City	2112.39	25	扬 中 市	Yangzhong City	504.73
5	宜 兴 市	Yixing City	1377.74	26	睢 宁 县	Suining County	497.38
6	太 仓 市	Taicang City	1155.13	27	句 容 市	Jurong City	493.20
7	丹 阳 市	Danyang City	1136.04	28	建 湖 县	Jianhu County	466.13
8	海 门 市	Haimen City	1005.06	29	射 阳 县	Sheyang County	441.65
9	如 皋 市	Rugao City	904.27	30	东 海 县	Donghai County	433.43
10	启 东 市	Qidong City	881.85	31	丰 县	Fengxian County	405.19
11	泰 兴 市	Taixing City	832.91	32	泗 阳 县	Siyang County	402.75
12	邳 州 市	Pizhou City	804.14	33	泗 洪 县	Sihong County	401.14
13	靖 江 市	Jingjiang City	801.75	34	阜 宁 县	Funing County	394.40
14	溧 阳 市	Liyang City	801.26	35	滨 海 县	Binhai County	391.61
15	海 安 县	Haian County	755.29	36	涟 水 县	Lianshui County	387.09
16	兴 化 市	Xinghua City	748.85	37	盱 眙 县	Xuyi County	356.70
17	如 东 县	Rugao City	746.69	38	灌 云 县	Guanyun County	328.66
18	东 台 市	Dongtai City	727.01	39	灌 南 县	Guannan County	306.80
19	沭 阳 县	Shuyang County	697.31	40	响 水 县	Xiangshui County	270.64
20	沛 县	Peixian County	665.03	41	金 湖 县	Jinhu County	241.88
21	新 沂 市	Xinyi City	562.06				

21－3 第一产业增加值（2016年）
Value-added of the Primary Industry (2016)

位次 No.	县（市）名称 County (City)		绝对数（亿元）Absolute Figure (100 million yuan)	位次 No.	县（市）名称 County (City)		绝对数（亿元）Absolute Figure (100 million yuan)
1	邳州市	Pizhou City	111.92	22	阜宁县	Funing County	54.60
2	兴化市	Xinghua City	102.59	23	盱眙县	Xuyi County	54.20
3	东台市	Dongtai City	91.47	24	泰兴市	Taixing City	53.95
4	沛县	Peixian County	91.29	25	海门市	Haimen City	53.28
5	沭阳县	Shuyang County	91.27	26	丹阳市	Danyang City	52.31
6	睢宁县	Suining County	84.09	27	灌南县	Guannan County	51.51
7	射阳县	Sheyang County	81.01	28	宜兴市	Yixing City	48.74
8	丰县	Fengxian County	74.81	29	溧阳市	Liyang City	48.29
9	高邮市	Gaoyou City	69.59	30	建湖县	Jianhu County	46.73
10	如东县	Rugao City	67.87	31	江阴市	Jiangyin City	44.31
11	东海县	Donghai County	67.28	32	句容市	Jurong City	43.11
12	启东市	Qidong City	66.58	33	常熟市	Changshu City	42.76
13	宝应县	Baoying County	66.44	34	响水县	Xiangshui County	41.42
14	新沂市	Xinyi City	64.91	35	太仓市	Taicang City	36.76
15	灌云县	Guanyun County	64.10	36	金湖县	Jinhu County	33.11
16	如皋市	Rugao City	62.99	37	张家港市	Zhangjiagang City	31.34
17	泗洪县	Sihong County	61.13	38	昆山市	Kunshan City	30.07
18	滨海县	Binhai County	57.99	39	仪征市	Yizheng City	23.36
19	泗阳县	Siyang County	57.85	40	靖江市	Jingjiang City	22.51
20	涟水县	Lianshui County	56.64	41	扬中市	Yangzhong City	12.96
21	海安县	Haian County	55.97				

21－4 第二产业增加值（2016年）
Value-added of the Secondary Industry（2016）

位次 No.	县（市）名称 County（City）		绝对数（亿元） Absolute Figure（100 million yuan）	位次 No.	县（市）名称 County（City）		绝对数（亿元） Absolute Figure（100 million yuan）
1	昆 山 市	Kunshan City	1708.82	22	扬 中 市	Yangzhong City	261.44
2	江 阴 市	Jiangyin City	1680.99	23	高 邮 市	Gaoyou City	237.86
3	张家港市	Zhangjiagang City	1214.70	24	新 沂 市	Xinyi City	232.17
4	常 熟 市	Changshu City	1082.43	25	句 容 市	Jurong City	231.90
5	宜 兴 市	Yixing City	709.51	26	宝 应 县	Baoying County	226.31
6	太 仓 市	Taicang City	583.87	27	睢 宁 县	Suining County	207.65
7	丹 阳 市	Danyang City	567.57	28	泗 阳 县	Siyang County	199.21
8	海 门 市	Haimen City	504.53	29	建 湖 县	Jianhu County	197.59
9	如 皋 市	Rugao City	434.36	30	东 海 县	Donghai County	186.57
10	启 东 市	Qidong City	422.85	31	丰 县	Fengxian County	171.60
11	溧 阳 市	Liyang City	392.29	32	阜 宁 县	Funing County	169.15
12	靖 江 市	Jingjiang City	391.95	33	泗 洪 县	Sihong County	168.93
13	泰 兴 市	Taixing City	388.52	34	滨 海 县	Binhai County	156.72
14	海 安 县	Haian County	354.15	35	射 阳 县	Sheyang County	155.78
15	邳 州 市	Pizhou City	347.27	36	涟 水 县	Lianshui County	147.51
16	如 东 县	Rugao City	340.57	37	灌 南 县	Guannan County	144.78
17	沭 阳 县	Shuyang County	317.95	38	灌 云 县	Guanyun County	143.12
18	沛 县	Peixian County	305.05	39	盱 眙 县	Xuyi County	140.30
19	仪 征 市	Yizheng City	294.27	40	响 水 县	Xiangshui County	126.77
20	东 台 市	Dongtai City	292.03	41	金 湖 县	Jinhu County	90.31
21	兴 化 市	Xinghua City	289.85				

21－5 第三产业增加值（2016年）
Value-added of the Tertiary Industry（2016）

位次 No.	县（市）名称 County（City）		绝对数（亿元）Absolute Figure（100 million yuan）	位次 No.	县（市）名称 County（City）		绝对数（亿元）Absolute Figure（100 million yuan）
1	昆山市	Kunshan City	1421.40	22	仪征市	Yizheng City	239.42
2	江阴市	Jiangyin City	1357.93	23	扬中市	Yangzhong City	230.33
3	张家港市	Zhangjiagang City	1071.21	24	高邮市	Gaoyou City	230.05
4	常熟市	Changshu City	987.20	25	建湖县	Jianhu County	221.81
5	宜兴市	Yixing City	619.49	26	句容市	Jurong City	218.19
6	太仓市	Taicang City	534.50	27	宝应县	Baoying County	213.55
7	丹阳市	Danyang City	516.16	28	睢宁县	Suining County	205.64
8	海门市	Haimen City	447.25	29	射阳县	Sheyang County	204.86
9	如皋市	Rugao City	406.92	30	涟水县	Lianshui County	182.94
10	启东市	Qidong City	392.42	31	东海县	Donghai County	179.58
11	泰兴市	Taixing City	390.44	32	滨海县	Binhai County	176.90
12	靖江市	Jingjiang City	387.29	33	泗洪县	Sihong County	171.08
13	溧阳市	Liyang City	360.68	34	阜宁县	Funing County	170.65
14	兴化市	Xinghua City	356.41	35	盱眙县	Xuyi County	162.20
15	海安县	Haian County	345.17	36	丰县	Fengxian County	158.78
16	邳州市	Pizhou City	344.95	37	泗阳县	Siyang County	145.69
17	东台市	Dongtai City	343.51	38	灌云县	Guanyun County	121.44
18	如东县	Rugao City	338.25	39	金湖县	Jinhu County	118.46
19	沭阳县	Shuyang County	288.09	40	灌南县	Guannan County	110.51
20	沛县	Peixian County	268.69	41	响水县	Xiangshui County	102.45
21	新沂市	Xinyi City	264.98				

21－6 全部工业增加值(2016 年)

Value-added of All Industries (2016)

位 次 No.	县(市)名称 County (City)		绝对数(亿元) Absolute Figure (100 million yuan)	位 次 No.	县(市)名称 County (City)		绝对数(亿元) Absolute Figure (100 million yuan)
1	江 阴 市	Jiangyin City	1612.25	22	沛 县	Peixian County	234.93
2	昆 山 市	Kunshan City	1608.39	23	句 容 市	Jurong City	206.81
3	张家港市	Zhangjiagang City	1155.30	24	新 沂 市	Xinyi City	198.89
4	常 熟 市	Changshu City	1026.16	25	高 邮 市	Gaoyou City	194.85
5	宜 兴 市	Yixing City	608.05	26	宝 应 县	Baoying County	187.64
6	太 仓 市	Taicang City	547.67	27	建 湖 县	Jianhu County	168.82
7	丹 阳 市	Danyang City	544.57	28	泗 阳 县	Siyang County	166.95
8	海 门 市	Haimen City	420.99	29	睢 宁 县	Suining County	163.98
9	如 皋 市	Rugao City	364.30	30	东 海 县	Donghai County	163.08
10	靖 江 市	Jingjiang City	351.39	31	泗 洪 县	Sihong County	142.09
11	泰 兴 市	Taixing City	340.07	32	射 阳 县	Sheyang County	142.01
12	启 东 市	Qidong City	336.94	33	滨 海 县	Binhai County	132.74
13	溧 阳 市	Liyang City	334.26	34	丰 县	Fengxian County	132.52
14	邳 州 市	Pizhou City	303.07	35	阜 宁 县	Funing County	126.96
15	海 安 县	Haian County	290.67	36	灌 南 县	Guannan County	125.92
16	如 东 县	Rugao City	286.80	37	涟 水 县	Lianshui County	121.88
17	沭 阳 县	Shuyang County	284.04	38	响 水 县	Xiangshui County	113.66
18	仪 征 市	Yizheng City	262.33	39	盱 眙 县	Xuyi County	113.46
19	东 台 市	Dongtai City	255.73	40	灌 云 县	Guanyun County	109.30
20	兴 化 市	Xinghua City	251.07	41	金 湖 县	Jinhu County	79.90
21	扬 中 市	Yangzhong City	250.74				

21-7 人均地区生产总值（2016年）
Per Capita Gross Domestic Product（2016）

位次 No.	县（市）名称 County（City）		绝对数（元） Absolute Figure（yuan）	位次 No.	县（市）名称 County（City）		绝对数（元） Absolute Figure（yuan）
1	昆山市	Kunshan City	191056	22	宝应县	Baoying County	66962
2	江阴市	Jiangyin City	188101	23	建湖县	Jianhu County	63514
3	张家港市	Zhangjiagang City	184747	24	新沂市	Xinyi City	61765
4	太仓市	Taicang City	162526	25	兴化市	Xinghua City	59662
5	扬中市	Yangzhong City	147431	26	沛县	Peixian County	59604
6	常熟市	Changshu City	139768	27	邳州市	Pizhou City	55960
7	靖江市	Jingjiang City	116703	28	盱眙县	Xuyi County	54625
8	丹阳市	Danyang City	115816	29	响水县	Xiangshui County	53971
9	海门市	Haimen City	111099	30	射阳县	Sheyang County	49749
10	宜兴市	Yixing City	109881	31	睢宁县	Suining County	48556
11	溧阳市	Liyang City	105256	32	灌南县	Guannan County	48429
12	仪征市	Yizheng City	98558	33	泗阳县	Siyang County	48006
13	启东市	Qidong City	92534	34	阜宁县	Funing County	47236
14	海安县	Haian County	87201	35	涟水县	Lianshui County	45680
15	句容市	Jurong City	78862	36	沭阳县	Shuyang County	45107
16	泰兴市	Taixing City	77315	37	泗洪县	Sihong County	45039
17	如东县	Rugao City	76045	38	东海县	Donghai County	44871
18	东台市	Dongtai City	73902	39	丰县	Fengxian County	42739
19	金湖县	Jinhu County	72987	40	滨海县	Binhai County	41761
20	高邮市	Gaoyou City	72562	41	灌云县	Guanyun County	40926
21	如皋市	Rugao City	72255				

21－8 固定资产投资（2016年）

Completed Investment in Fixed Assetes (2016)

位次 No.	县（市）名称 County (City)		绝对数（亿元） Absolute Figure (100 million yuan)	位次 No.	县（市）名称 County (City)		绝对数（亿元） Absolute Figure (100 million yuan)
1	江阴市	Jiangyin City	1133.03	22	高邮市	Gaoyou City	455.62
2	邳州市	Pizhou City	763.12	23	兴化市	Xinghua City	419.66
3	昆山市	Kunshan City	757.42	24	泗洪县	Sihong County	380.41
4	张家港市	Zhangjiagang City	724.77	25	泗阳县	Siyang County	379.23
5	泰兴市	Taixing City	687.46	26	滨海县	Binhai County	377.87
6	启东市	Qidong City	614.84	27	宝应县	Baoying County	372.72
7	海门市	Haimen City	613.19	28	句容市	Jurong City	360.81
8	海安县	Haian County	584.46	29	建湖县	Jianhu County	357.70
9	东台市	Dongtai City	581.03	30	盱眙县	Xuyi County	350.65
10	如皋市	Rugao City	575.25	31	涟水县	Lianshui County	335.29
11	沛县	Peixian County	560.35	32	东海县	Donghai County	330.59
12	新沂市	Xinyi City	550.05	33	阜宁县	Funing County	320.52
13	如东县	Rugao City	545.42	34	睢宁县	Suining County	320.49
14	常熟市	Changshu City	544.91	35	扬中市	Yangzhong City	305.10
15	宜兴市	Yixing City	537.31	36	射阳县	Sheyang County	300.16
16	沭阳县	Shuyang County	515.03	37	响水县	Xiangshui County	287.25
17	丹阳市	Danyang City	514.01	38	灌云县	Guanyun County	272.19
18	靖江市	Jingjiang City	500.00	39	丰县	Fengxian County	251.10
19	溧阳市	Liyang City	486.55	40	灌南县	Guannan County	218.06
20	仪征市	Yizheng City	471.00	41	金湖县	Jinhu County	195.54
21	太仓市	Taicang City	465.00				

21－9　一般公共预算收入（2016年）
General Public Budget Revenue(2016)

位次 No.	县（市）名称 County (City)		绝对数（亿元）Absolute Figure (100 million yuan)	位次 No.	县（市）名称 County (City)		绝对数（亿元）Absolute Figure (100 million yuan)
1	昆　山　市	Kunshan City	318.92	22	睢　宁　县	Suining County	42.52
2	江　阴　市	Jiangyin City	229.91	23	句　容　市	Jurong City	40.48
3	张家港市	Zhangjiagang City	190.00	24	兴　化　市	Xinghua City	37.06
4	常　熟　市	Changshu City	173.58	25	阜　宁　县	Funing County	36.24
5	太　仓　市	Taicang City	127.71	26	建　湖　县	Jianhu County	35.01
6	宜　兴　市	Yixing City	108.65	27	丰　　　县	Fengxian County	35.00
7	海　门　市	Haimen City	72.41	28	高　邮　市	Gaoyou City	34.12
8	沭　阳　县	Shuyang County	71.75	29	滨　海　县	Binhai County	34.07
9	如　皋　市	Rugao City	71.21	30	泗　阳　县	Siyang County	33.34
10	启　东　市	Qidong City	71.03	31	扬　中　市	Yangzhong City	32.50
11	丹　阳　市	Danyang City	65.55	32	泗　洪　县	Sihong County	31.75
12	邳　州　市	Pizhou City	62.40	33	宝　应　县	Baoying County	30.81
13	东　台　市	Dongtai City	60.26	34	盱　眙　县	Xuyi County	30.78
14	溧　阳　市	Liyang City	59.00	35	响　水　县	Xiangshui County	29.60
15	靖　江　市	Jingjiang City	58.93	36	涟　水　县	Lianshui County	28.98
16	沛　　　县	Peixian County	57.68	37	东　海　县	Donghai County	22.61
17	海　安　县	Haian County	57.58	38	灌　南　县	Guannan County	22.43
18	泰　兴　市	Taixing City	57.20	39	金　湖　县	Jinhu County	22.00
19	如　东　县	Rugao City	54.41	40	射　阳　县	Sheyang County	21.58
20	新　沂　市	Xinyi City	49.91	41	灌　云　县	Guanyun County	21.52
21	仪　征　市	Yizheng City	44.74				

注：靖江包含江阴—靖江工业园区（下表同）。

a) Data of Jingjiang included jiangyin & Jingjiang Industrial Park. (The same as in the following table.)

21－10 人均一般公共预算收入（2016年）

Per Capita General Public Budget Revenue(2016)

位次 No.	县（市）名称 County (City)		绝对数（元）Absolute Figure (yuan)	位次 No.	县（市）名称 County (City)		绝对数（元）Absolute Figure (yuan)
1	昆山市	Kunshan City	19280	22	泰兴市	Taixing City	5310
2	太仓市	Taicang City	17969	23	沛县	Peixian County	5170
3	张家港市	Zhangjiagang City	15148	24	建湖县	Jianhu County	4770
4	江阴市	Jiangyin City	14026	25	盱眙县	Xuyi County	4714
5	常熟市	Changshu City	11485	26	沭阳县	Shuyang County	4641
6	扬中市	Yangzhong City	9494	27	高邮市	Gaoyou City	4606
7	宜兴市	Yixing City	8665	28	邳州市	Pizhou City	4342
8	靖江市	Jingjiang City	8578	29	阜宁县	Funing County	4341
9	海门市	Haimen City	8004	30	睢宁县	Suining County	4150
10	仪征市	Yizheng City	7917	31	宝应县	Baoying County	4075
11	溧阳市	Liyang City	7750	32	泗阳县	Siyang County	3974
12	启东市	Qidong City	7453	33	丰县	Fengxian County	3692
13	丹阳市	Danyang City	6682	34	滨海县	Binhai County	3633
14	海安县	Haian County	6647	35	泗洪县	Sihong County	3565
15	金湖县	Jinhu County	6639	36	灌南县	Guannan County	3541
16	句容市	Jurong City	6473	37	涟水县	Lianshui County	3420
17	东台市	Dongtai City	6125	38	兴化市	Xinghua City	2952
18	响水县	Xiangshui County	5903	39	灌云县	Guanyun County	2680
19	如皋市	Rugao City	5690	40	射阳县	Sheyang County	2431
20	如东县	Rugao City	5541	41	东海县	Donghai County	2340
21	新沂市	Xinyi City	5485				

21-11 粮食产量（2016年）
Output of Grain (2016)

位次 No.	县（市）名称 County (City)		绝对数（万吨）Absolute Figure (10000 tons)	位次 No.	县（市）名称 County (City)		绝对数（万吨）Absolute Figure (10000 tons)
1	兴化市	Xinghua City	137.91	22	泗阳县	Siyang County	60.37
2	沭阳县	Shuyang County	127.49	23	沛县	Peixian County	60.27
3	东海县	Donghai County	114.53	24	海安县	Haian County	60.12
4	射阳县	Sheyang County	111.90	25	金湖县	Jinhu County	53.56
5	泗洪县	Sihong County	105.55	26	响水县	Xiangshui County	53.51
6	盱眙县	Xuyi County	97.86	27	丰县	Fengxian County	52.54
7	东台市	Dongtai City	97.28	28	丹阳市	Danyang City	49.33
8	滨海县	Binhai County	95.62	29	溧阳市	Liyang City	48.66
9	睢宁县	Suining County	92.78	30	宜兴市	Yixing City	37.05
10	阜宁县	Funing County	91.50	31	句容市	Jurong City	33.18
11	如东县	Rugao City	90.90	32	仪征市	Yizheng City	31.14
12	宝应县	Baoying County	90.04	33	靖江市	Jingjiang City	30.98
13	涟水县	Lianshui County	88.44	34	常熟市	Changshu City	27.76
14	高邮市	Gaoyou City	85.98	35	启东市	Qidong City	26.14
15	灌云县	Guanyun County	81.88	36	张家港市	Zhangjiagang City	22.17
16	邳州市	Pizhou City	80.75	37	海门市	Haimen City	19.16
17	建湖县	Jianhu County	72.86	38	太仓市	Taicang City	16.53
18	如皋市	Rugao City	70.95	39	江阴市	Jiangyin City	14.49
19	泰兴市	Taixing City	68.47	40	昆山市	Kunshan City	10.13
20	新沂市	Xinyi City	66.06	41	扬中市	Yangzhong City	9.19
21	灌南县	Guannan County	63.34				

21－12　油料产量（2016年）
Output of Oil-bearing Crops（2016）

位次 No.	县（市）名称 County（City）	绝对数（万吨） Absolute Figure （10000 tons）	位次 No.	县（市）名称 County（City）	绝对数（万吨） Absolute Figure （10000 tons）
1	海　门　市　Haimen City	8.58	22	海　安　县　Haian County	1.51
2	启　东　市　Qidong City	8.37	23	邳　州　市　Pizhou City	1.40
3	新　沂　市　Xinyi City	7.54	24	射　阳　县　Sheyang County	1.33
4	东　台　市　Dongtai City	6.12	25	盱　眙　县　Xuyi County	1.20
5	东　海　县　Donghai County	4.80	26	仪　征　市　Yizheng City	0.93
6	泰　兴　市　Taixing City	4.17	27	泗　阳　县　Siyang County	0.88
7	如　东　县　Rugao City	4.02	28	丹　阳　市　Danyang City	0.85
8	如　皋　市　Rugao City	3.78	29	金　湖　县　Jinhu County	0.84
9	涟　水　县　Lianshui County	3.73	30	靖　江　市　Jingjiang City	0.56
10	句　容　市　Jurong City	3.71	31	宜　兴　市　Yixing City	0.51
11	兴　化　市　Xinghua City	3.45	32	丰　　　县　Fengxian County	0.44
12	滨　海　县　Binhai County	3.14	33	张家港市　Zhangjiagang City	0.38
13	睢　宁　县　Suining County	3.07	34	太　仓　市　Taicang City	0.36
14	溧　阳　市　Liyang City	2.55	35	常　熟　市　Changshu City	0.35
15	响　水　县　Xiangshui County	2.06	36	江　阴　市　Jiangyin City	0.27
16	高　邮　市　Gaoyou City	2.00	37	沛　　　县　Peixian County	0.24
17	建　湖　县　Jianhu County	1.88	38	灌　南　县　Guannan County	0.16
18	泗　洪　县　Sihong County	1.82	39	扬　中　市　Yangzhong City	0.16
19	阜　宁　县　Funing County	1.70	40	昆　山　市　Kunshan City	0.16
20	宝　应　县　Baoying County	1.61	41	灌　云　县　Guanyun County	0.09
21	沭　阳　县　Shuyang County	1.51			

21-13 规模以上工业企业利润总额（2016年）

Profits of above Designated Size Industrial Enterprises (2016)

位次 No.	县（市）名称 County (City)		绝对数（亿元）Absolute Figure (100 million yuan)	位次 No.	县（市）名称 County (City)		绝对数（亿元）Absolute Figure (100 million yuan)
1	昆 山 市	Kunshan City	446.81	22	扬 中 市	Yangzhong City	94.16
2	江 阴 市	Jiangyin City	337.84	23	溧 阳 市	Liyang City	79.08
3	泰 兴 市	Taixing City	278.07	24	东 海 县	Donghai County	74.33
4	常 熟 市	Changshu City	235.76	25	句 容 市	Jurong City	71.56
5	海 门 市	Haimen City	220.61	26	东 台 市	Dongtai City	65.96
6	邳 州 市	Pizhou City	206.01	27	泗 洪 县	Sihong County	64.41
7	张家港市	Zhangjiagang City	177.08	28	高 邮 市	Gaoyou City	62.28
8	海 安 县	Haian County	159.99	29	宝 应 县	Baoying County	59.59
9	丹 阳 市	Danyang City	159.66	30	丰 县	Fengxian County	57.40
10	太 仓 市	Taicang City	154.73	31	建 湖 县	Jianhu County	54.23
11	靖 江 市	Jingjiang City	147.87	32	响 水 县	Xiangshui County	53.93
12	如 东 县	Rugao City	147.18	33	泗 阳 县	Siyang County	51.22
13	新 沂 市	Xinyi City	138.29	34	灌 南 县	Guannan County	46.83
14	仪 征 市	Yizheng City	137.14	35	灌 云 县	Guanyun County	44.99
15	宜 兴 市	Yixing City	137.10	36	盱 眙 县	Xuyi County	42.86
16	启 东 市	Qidong City	130.52	37	涟 水 县	Lianshui County	37.32
17	如 皋 市	Rugao City	128.77	38	滨 海 县	Binhai County	35.01
18	沭 阳 县	Shuyang County	119.92	39	射 阳 县	Sheyang County	32.58
19	睢 宁 县	Suining County	114.94	40	阜 宁 县	Funing County	31.82
20	兴 化 市	Xinghua City	105.72	41	金 湖 县	Jinhu County	22.96
21	沛 县	Peixian County	104.09				

21－14 社会消费品零售总额（2016 年）
Total Retail Sale of Consumer Goods（2016）

位次 No.	县（市）名称 County（City）		绝对数（亿元） Absolute Figure（100 million yuan）	位次 No.	县（市）名称 County（City）		绝对数（亿元） Absolute Figure（100 million yuan）
1	昆山市	Kunshan City	815.04	22	新沂市	Xinyi City	174.56
2	江阴市	Jiangyin City	776.05	23	建湖县	Jianhu County	171.98
3	常熟市	Changshu City	740.78	24	兴化市	Xinghua City	171.24
4	宜兴市	Yixing City	556.37	25	高邮市	Gaoyou City	170.10
5	张家港市	Zhangjiagang City	535.16	26	射阳县	Sheyang County	167.90
6	海门市	Haimen City	344.60	27	丰县	Fengxian County	151.04
7	如皋市	Rugao City	342.21	28	宝应县	Baoying County	150.34
8	启东市	Qidong City	324.57	29	句容市	Jurong City	142.02
9	如东县	Rugao City	318.62	30	扬中市	Yangzhong City	140.92
10	丹阳市	Danyang City	315.61	31	阜宁县	Funing County	130.29
11	溧阳市	Liyang City	303.03	32	涟水县	Lianshui County	130.03
12	太仓市	Taicang City	287.31	33	盱眙县	Xuyi County	123.89
13	海安县	Haian County	273.74	34	灌云县	Guanyun County	119.45
14	东台市	Dongtai City	253.53	35	滨海县	Binhai County	110.46
15	邳州市	Pizhou City	253.41	36	仪征市	Yizheng City	109.75
16	沛县	Peixian County	245.59	37	泗洪县	Sihong County	105.40
17	泰兴市	Taixing City	213.95	38	泗阳县	Siyang County	100.47
18	沭阳县	Shuyang County	197.68	39	灌南县	Guannan County	93.52
19	睢宁县	Suining County	179.58	40	金湖县	Jinhu County	90.76
20	靖江市	Jingjiang City	176.24	41	响水县	Xiangshui County	66.52
21	东海县	Donghai County	175.89				

21－15 出口总额（2016年）
Total Exports（2016）

位次 No.	县（市）名称	County（City）	绝对数（亿美元）Absolute Figure（100 million USD）	位次 No.	县（市）名称	County（City）	绝对数（亿美元）Absolute Figure（100 million USD）
1	昆山市	Kunshan City	463.21	22	句容市	Jurong City	4.71
2	张家港市	Zhangjiagang City	142.02	23	响水县	Xiangshui County	4.70
3	常熟市	Changshu City	133.56	24	仪征市	Yizheng City	4.64
4	江阴市	Jiangyin City	119.22	25	扬中市	Yangzhong City	4.54
5	太仓市	Taicang City	54.30	26	高邮市	Gaoyou City	4.33
6	海门市	Haimen City	35.79	27	东海县	Donghai County	3.68
7	宜兴市	Yixing City	30.17	28	泗阳县	Siyang County	3.43
8	启东市	Qidong City	26.51	29	金湖县	Jinhu County	3.42
9	丹阳市	Danyang City	21.40	30	涟水县	Lianshui County	3.30
10	如皋市	Rugao City	20.15	31	滨海县	Binhai County	3.08
11	靖江市	Jingjiang City	19.36	32	新沂市	Xinyi City	2.98
12	如东县	Rugao City	14.51	33	沛县	Peixian County	2.94
13	海安县	Haian County	14.05	34	建湖县	Jianhu County	2.92
14	泰兴市	Taixing City	12.33	35	阜宁县	Funing County	2.22
15	邳州市	Pizhou City	9.16	36	灌云县	Guanyun County	2.03
16	宝应县	Baoying County	8.43	37	射阳县	Sheyang County	1.95
17	溧阳市	Liyang City	7.46	38	灌南县	Guannan County	1.70
18	东台市	Dongtai City	7.07	39	泗洪县	Sihong County	1.34
19	睢宁县	Suining County	6.35	40	盱眙县	Xuyi County	1.34
20	沭阳县	Shuyang County	5.12	41	丰县	Fengxian County	1.26
21	兴化市	Xinghua City	4.90				

21－16　实际使用外资（2016 年）
Actual Use of Foreign Capital(2016)

位次 No.	县（市）名称 County (City)		绝对数（亿美元）Absolute Figure (100 million USD)	位次 No.	县（市）名称 County (City)		绝对数（亿美元）Absolute Figure (100 million USD)
1	江阴市	Jiangyin City	10.55	22	盱眙县	Xuyi County	1.20
2	昆山市	Kunshan City	8.96	23	扬中市	Yangzhong City	1.18
3	常熟市	Changshu City	6.30	24	睢宁县	Suining County	1.11
4	张家港市	Zhangjiagang City	6.04	25	新沂市	Xinyi City	1.00
5	太仓市	Taicang City	5.61	26	东海县	Donghai County	0.94
6	泰兴市	Taixing City	3.53	27	沭阳县	Shuyang County	0.80
7	溧阳市	Liyang City	3.36	28	东台市	Dongtai City	0.62
8	丹阳市	Danyang City	3.22	29	建湖县	Jianhu County	0.55
9	海安县	Haian County	2.96	30	滨海县	Binhai County	0.53
10	如东县	Rugao City	2.94	31	泗阳县	Siyang County	0.51
11	启东市	Qidong City	2.84	32	高邮市	Gaoyou City	0.50
12	如皋市	Rugao City	2.77	33	宝应县	Baoying County	0.50
13	海门市	Haimen City	2.40	34	射阳县	Sheyang County	0.45
14	句容市	Jurong City	2.21	35	丰县	Fengxian County	0.41
15	邳州市	Pizhou City	1.83	36	泗洪县	Sihong County	0.33
16	兴化市	Xinghua City	1.83	37	响水县	Xiangshui County	0.29
17	宜兴市	Yixing City	1.58	38	灌云县	Guanyun County	0.24
18	涟水县	Lianshui County	1.41	39	靖江市	Jingjiang City	0.23
19	沛县	Peixian County	1.30	40	阜宁县	Funing County	0.12
20	仪征市	Yizheng City	1.29	41	灌南县	Guannan County	0.03
21	金湖县	Jinhu County	1.20				

21－17 金融机构各项存款余额(2016年)

The Balance of Deposits of Financial Institutions (2016)

位次 No.	县(市)名称 County (City)	绝对数(亿元) Absolute Figure (100 million yuan)	位次 No.	县(市)名称 County (City)	绝对数(亿元) Absolute Figure (100 million yuan)
1	昆山市 Kunshan City	3562.27	22	邳州市 Pizhou City	525.34
2	江阴市 Jiangyin City	3509.40	23	宝应县 Baoying County	478.68
3	常熟市 Changshu City	2692.88	24	沭阳县 Shuyang County	461.62
4	张家港市 Zhangjiagang City	2508.27	25	沛县 Peixian County	454.10
5	宜兴市 Yixing City	1903.25	26	射阳县 Sheyang County	413.98
6	太仓市 Taicang City	1395.41	27	建湖县 Jianhu County	409.79
7	海门市 Haimen City	1368.55	28	睢宁县 Suining County	401.90
8	海安县 Haian County	1286.53	29	阜宁县 Funing County	392.18
9	启东市 Qidong City	1232.03	30	新沂市 Xinyi City	386.97
10	如皋市 Rugao City	1135.62	31	丰县 Fengxian County	354.14
11	丹阳市 Danyang City	1040.33	32	涟水县 Lianshui County	325.80
12	如东县 Rugao City	1010.55	33	泗阳县 Siyang County	320.87
13	溧阳市 Liyang City	994.82	34	东海县 Donghai County	317.38
14	靖江市 Jingjiang City	940.16	35	滨海县 Binhai County	308.75
15	泰兴市 Taixing City	912.30	36	泗洪县 Sihong County	299.28
16	东台市 Dongtai City	715.99	37	盱眙县 Xuyi County	277.13
17	兴化市 Xinghua City	681.08	38	灌云县 Guanyun County	260.88
18	句容市 Jurong City	629.87	39	金湖县 Jinhu County	220.07
19	仪征市 Yizheng City	606.06	40	灌南县 Guannan County	179.88
20	扬中市 Yangzhong City	578.31	41	响水县 Xiangshui County	178.13
21	高邮市 Gaoyou City	552.73			

21-18 金融机构各项贷款余额(2016年)
The Balance of Loans of Financial Institutions (2016)

位次 No.	县(市)名称 County (City)		绝对数(亿元) Absolute Figure (100 million yuan)	位次 No.	县(市)名称 County (City)		绝对数(亿元) Absolute Figure (100 million yuan)
1	江阴市	Jiangyin City	2689.91	22	仪征市	Yizheng City	343.07
2	昆山市	Kunshan City	2552.22	23	高邮市	Gaoyou City	322.23
3	常熟市	Changshu City	2139.49	24	泗阳县	Siyang County	314.93
4	张家港市	Zhangjiagang City	1994.40	25	建湖县	Jianhu County	301.49
5	宜兴市	Yixing City	1392.03	26	宝应县	Baoying County	294.60
6	太仓市	Taicang City	1245.07	27	泗洪县	Sihong County	288.55
7	丹阳市	Danyang City	964.49	28	射阳县	Sheyang County	264.42
8	海门市	Haimen City	824.32	29	滨海县	Binhai County	249.46
9	溧阳市	Liyang City	798.94	30	东海县	Donghai County	248.71
10	海安县	Haian County	798.77	31	新沂市	Xinyi City	246.38
11	如皋市	Rugao City	709.99	32	阜宁县	Funing County	240.78
12	启东市	Qidong City	705.13	33	睢宁县	Suining County	224.39
13	靖江市	Jingjiang City	694.02	34	沛县	Peixian County	222.60
14	泰兴市	Taixing City	581.39	35	盱眙县	Xuyi County	222.34
15	句容市	Jurong City	561.03	36	涟水县	Lianshui County	197.02
16	如东县	Rugao City	494.56	37	灌云县	Guanyun County	183.80
17	扬中市	Yangzhong City	431.43	38	丰县	Fengxian County	177.31
18	兴化市	Xinghua City	428.41	39	金湖县	Jinhu County	171.54
19	沭阳县	Shuyang County	403.49	40	响水县	Xiangshui County	139.77
20	东台市	Dongtai City	394.75	41	灌南县	Guannan County	134.05
21	邳州市	Pizhou City	366.13				

21－19 居民人均可支配收入（2016年）
Per Capita Disposable Income of Residents(2016)

位次 No.	县（市）名称 County (City)	绝对数（元）Absolute Figure (yuan)	位次 No.	县（市）名称 County (City)	绝对数（元）Absolute Figure (yuan)
1	昆 山 市 Kunshan City	46339	22	建 湖 县 Jianhu County	22993
2	江 阴 市 Jiangyin City	46337	23	金 湖 县 Jinhu County	22541
3	常 熟 市 Changshu City	45061	24	盱 眙 县 Xuyi County	21923
4	张家港市 Zhangjiagang City	44977	25	射 阳 县 Sheyang County	21710
5	太 仓 市 Taicang City	43867	26	宝 应 县 Baoying County	21396
6	宜 兴 市 Yixing City	37326	27	沛 县 Peixian County	21221
7	扬 中 市 Yangzhong City	35729	28	邳 州 市 Pizhou City	20675
8	丹 阳 市 Danyang City	33089	29	阜 宁 县 Funing County	20262
9	溧 阳 市 Liyang City	31833	30	滨 海 县 Binhai County	20257
10	海 门 市 Haimen City	30092	31	东 海 县 Donghai County	20128
11	靖 江 市 Jingjiang City	29544	32	响 水 县 Xiangshui County	19629
12	句 容 市 Jurong City	28994	33	沭 阳 县 Shuyang County	19132
13	启 东 市 Qidong City	28446	34	新 沂 市 Xinyi City	18786
14	泰 兴 市 Taixing City	27806	35	泗 阳 县 Siyang County	18510
15	海 安 县 Haian County	27230	36	涟 水 县 Lianshui County	18302
16	仪 征 市 Yizheng City	26952	37	睢 宁 县 Suining County	18127
17	如 皋 市 Rugao City	26695	38	丰 县 Fengxian County	18056
18	如 东 县 Rugao City	26683	39	泗 洪 县 Sihong County	17726
19	东 台 市 Dongtai City	26565	40	灌 云 县 Guanyun County	17565
20	兴 化 市 Xinghua City	24602	41	灌 南 县 Guannan County	17446
21	高 邮 市 Gaoyou City	23854			

21-20 城镇常住居民人均可支配收入（2016年）
Per Capita Disposable Income of Urban Permanent Residents(2016)

位次 No.	县（市）名称 County (City)		绝对数（元）Absolute Figure (yuan)	位次 No.	县（市）名称 County (City)		绝对数（元）Absolute Figure (yuan)
1	昆山市	Kunshan City	54728	22	金湖县	Jinhu County	30799
2	江阴市	Jiangyin City	54631	23	盱眙县	Xuyi County	30684
3	张家港市	Zhangjiagang City	54602	24	建湖县	Jianhu County	29637
4	常熟市	Changshu City	54411	25	邳州市	Pizhou City	28546
5	太仓市	Taicang City	54099	26	东海县	Donghai County	27391
6	宜兴市	Yixing City	46092	27	沛县	Peixian County	27277
7	扬中市	Yangzhong City	45842	28	宝应县	Baoying County	26842
8	溧阳市	Liyang City	42062	29	滨海县	Binhai County	26543
9	丹阳市	Danyang City	41652	30	射阳县	Sheyang County	26509
10	句容市	Jurong City	40582	31	响水县	Xiangshui County	25564
11	海门市	Haimen City	40509	32	阜宁县	Funing County	25543
12	靖江市	Jingjiang City	39713	33	涟水县	Lianshui County	25230
13	启东市	Qidong City	37390	34	新沂市	Xinyi City	24928
14	海安县	Haian County	37297	35	灌南县	Guannan County	24494
15	如东县	Rugao City	37133	36	沭阳县	Shuyang County	23933
16	如皋市	Rugao City	36590	37	泗阳县	Siyang County	23535
17	仪征市	Yizheng City	36523	38	睢宁县	Suining County	23403
18	泰兴市	Taixing City	36521	39	灌云县	Guanyun County	22979
19	兴化市	Xinghua City	33614	40	丰县	Fengxian County	22971
20	东台市	Dongtai City	32686	41	泗洪县	Sihong County	22953
21	高邮市	Gaoyou City	31430				

21－21 农村常住居民人均可支配收入(2016年)
Per Capita Disposable Income of Rural Permanent Residents(2016)

位次 No.	县(市)名称 County (City)		绝对数(元) Absolute Figure (yuan)	位次 No.	县(市)名称 County (City)		绝对数(元) Absolute Figure (yuan)
1	江阴市	Jiangyin City	28181	22	如皋市	Rugao City	16883
2	昆山市	Kunshan City	28178	23	宝应县	Baoying County	16856
3	常熟市	Changshu City	27956	24	射阳县	Sheyang County	16536
4	张家港市	Zhangjiagang City	27849	25	沛县	Peixian County	15791
5	太仓市	Taicang City	27766	26	金湖县	Jinhu County	15683
6	扬中市	Yangzhong City	23855	27	阜宁县	Funing County	15439
7	宜兴市	Yixing City	23709	28	邳州市	Pizhou City	15321
8	溧阳市	Liyang City	21899	29	滨海县	Binhai County	14931
9	丹阳市	Danyang City	21706	30	新沂市	Xinyi City	14526
10	海门市	Haimen City	20608	31	盱眙县	Xuyi County	14495
11	启东市	Qidong City	19875	32	东海县	Donghai County	14487
12	东台市	Dongtai City	19727	33	响水县	Xiangshui County	14299
13	靖江市	Jingjiang City	19605	34	沭阳县	Shuyang County	14107
14	句容市	Jurong City	18893	35	丰县	Fengxian County	14026
15	海安县	Haian County	17978	36	泗阳县	Siyang County	13952
16	泰兴市	Taixing City	17842	37	睢宁县	Suining County	13822
17	仪征市	Yizheng City	17516	38	泗洪县	Sihong County	13625
18	如东县	Rugao City	17119	39	涟水县	Lianshui County	13372
19	建湖县	Jianhu County	17083	40	灌云县	Guanyun County	12969
20	高邮市	Gaoyou City	16952	41	灌南县	Guannan County	12430
21	兴化市	Xinghua City	16915				

附录

全国分省主要指标

Appendix. Major Indicators by Region

简 要 说 明

一、主要内容

包括全国各省、自治区、直辖市经济社会主要指标。

二、资料来源

资料均来自中国统计出版社出版的《中国统计摘要 2017》，部分数据为初步统计数。其中江苏的数据与相应篇章内容保持一致。

Brief Introduction

I. Main Content

Data in this charter include social and economic indicators of provinces, autonomous regions and municipalities.

II. Source of Data

Data in this charter come from *china statistics abstract 2017* published by china statistics press, and part of the data are preliminary statistics. Data of Jiangsu province are consistent with corresponding chapter.

附录1－1　人口及地区生产总值（2016年）
Population and Gross Domestic Product (2016)

地　区 Region		年末常住人口（万人）Permanent Population at Year-end (10000 persons)	年末城镇人口比重（%）Proportion of Urban Population at Year-end (%)	地区生产总值（亿元）Gross Domestic Products (100 million yuan)				人均地区生产总值（元）Per Capita GDP (yuan)
					第一产业 Primary Industry	第二产业 Secondary Industry	第三产业 Tertiary Industry	
全　国	**National Total**	**138271**	**57.4**	**744127**	**63671**	**296236**	**384221**	**53980**
北　京	Beijing	2172.9	86.5	24899.26	122.58	4774.38	19995.30	114653
天　津	Tianjin	1562.12	82.9	17885.39	220.22	8003.87	9661.30	115053
河　北	Hebei	7470.05	53.3	31827.86	3492.81	15058.51	13276.54	42736
山　西	Shanxi	3682.00	56.2	12928.34	784.57	4926.40	7217.37	35198
内蒙古	Inner Mongolia	2520.13	61.2	18632.57	1628.65	9078.87	7925.05	74069
辽　宁	Liaoning	4377.80	67.4	22037.88	2173.04	8504.84	11360.00	50314
吉　林	Jilin	2733.03	56.0	14886.23	1498.52	7147.18	6240.53	54266
黑龙江	Heilongjiang	3799.23	59.2	15386.09	2670.46	4441.38	8274.25	40432
上　海	Shanghai	2419.70	87.9	27466.15	109.47	7994.34	19362.34	113615
江　苏	**Jiangsu**	**7998.60**	**67.7**	**76086.17**	**4077.18**	**33550.54**	**38458.45**	**95257**
浙　江	Zhejiang	5590.00	67.0	46484.98	1966.54	20517.83	24000.61	83538
安　徽	Anhui	6195.50	52.0	24117.87	2567.72	11666.58	9883.57	39092
福　建	Fujian	3874.00	63.6	28519.15	2364.14	13912.73	12242.28	73951
江　西	Jiangxi	4592.27	53.1	18364.41	1904.53	9032.05	7427.83	40106
山　东	Shandong	9946.64	59.0	67008.19	4929.13	30410.03	31669.03	67706
河　南	Henan	9532.00	48.5	40160.01	4286.30	19055.44	16818.27	42247
湖　北	Hubei	5885.00	58.1	32297.91	3499.30	14375.13	14423.48	55038
湖　南	Hunan	6822.02	52.8	31244.68	3578.37	13180.97	14485.34	45931
广　东	Guangdong	10999.00	69.2	79512.05	3693.58	34372.46	41446.01	72787
广　西	Guangxi	4838.00	48.1	18245.07	2798.61	8219.86	7226.60	37876
海　南	Hainan	917.13	56.8	4044.51	970.93	901.68	2171.90	44252
重　庆	Chongqing	3048.43	62.6	17558.76	1303.24	7755.16	8500.36	57902
四　川	Sichuan	8262.00	49.2	32680.50	3924.08	13924.73	14831.69	39695
贵　州	Guizhou	3555.00	44.2	11734.43	1846.54	4636.74	5251.15	33127
云　南	Yunnan	4770.50	45.0	14869.95	2195.04	5799.34	6875.57	31265
西　藏	Tibet	330.54	29.6	1150.07	104.98	429.92	615.17	35143
陕　西	Shaanxi	3812.62	55.3	19165.39	1693.84	9390.88	8080.67	50398
甘　肃	Gansu	2609.95	44.7	7152.04	973.47	2491.53	3687.04	27458
青　海	Qinghai	593.46	51.6	2572.49	221.19	1249.98	1101.32	43531
宁　夏	Ningxia	674.90	56.3	3150.06	239.96	1475.51	1434.59	46918
新　疆	Xinjiang	2398.08	48.4	9617.23	1648.97	3585.22	4383.04	40427

注：地区生产总值为初步核算数。

a) Data of gross domestic products are preliminary verification data.

附录 1-2　地区生产总值构成及增速（2016 年）
Structure and Growth Rate of Gross Domestic Product (2016)

地区 Region		地区生产总值构成（%）Structure of GDP(%)	第一产业 Primary Industry	第二产业 Secondary Industry	第三产业 Tertiary Industry	地区生产总值比上年增长（%）Growth Rate of GDP Over Preceding Year (%)
全　国	**National Total**	**100.0**	**8.6**	**39.8**	**51.6**	**6.7**
北　京	Beijing	100.0	0.5	19.2	80.3	6.7
天　津	Tianjin	100.0	1.2	44.8	54.0	9.0
河　北	Hebei	100.0	11.0	47.3	41.7	6.8
山　西	Shanxi	100.0	6.1	38.1	55.8	4.5
内蒙古	Inner Mongolia	100.0	8.7	48.7	42.5	7.2
辽　宁	Liaoning	100.0	9.9	38.6	51.5	-2.5
吉　林	Jilin	100.0	10.1	48.0	41.9	6.9
黑龙江	Heilongjiang	100.0	17.4	28.9	53.8	6.1
上　海	Shanghai	100.0	0.4	29.1	70.5	6.8
江　苏	**Jiangsu**	**100.0**	**5.4**	**44.1**	**50.5**	**7.8**
浙　江	Zhejiang	100.0	4.2	44.1	51.6	7.5
安　徽	Anhui	100.0	10.6	48.4	41.0	8.7
福　建	Fujian	100.0	8.3	48.8	42.9	8.4
江　西	Jiangxi	100.0	10.4	49.2	40.4	9.0
山　东	Shandong	100.0	7.4	45.4	47.3	7.6
河　南	Henan	100.0	10.7	47.4	41.9	8.1
湖　北	Hubei	100.0	10.8	44.5	44.7	8.1
湖　南	Hunan	100.0	11.5	42.2	46.4	7.9
广　东	Guangdong	100.0	4.6	43.2	52.1	7.5
广　西	Guangxi	100.0	15.3	45.1	39.6	7.3
海　南	Hainan	100.0	24.0	22.3	53.7	7.5
重　庆	Chongqing	100.0	7.4	44.2	48.4	10.7
四　川	Sichuan	100.0	12.0	42.6	45.4	7.7
贵　州	Guizhou	100.0	15.7	39.5	44.7	10.5
云　南	Yunnan	100.0	14.8	39.0	46.2	8.7
西　藏	Tibet	100.0	9.1	37.4	53.5	10.0
陕　西	Shaanxi	100.0	8.8	49.0	42.2	7.6
甘　肃	Gansu	100.0	13.6	34.8	51.6	7.6
青　海	Qinghai	100.0	8.6	48.6	42.8	8.0
宁　夏	Ningxia	100.0	7.6	46.8	45.5	8.1
新　疆	Xinjiang	100.0	17.1	37.3	45.6	7.6

附录1-3 固定资产投资完成额（2016年）
Completed Investment in Fixed Assets（2016）

地区 Region		固定资产投资（含农户）（亿元）Investment in Fixed Assets (Including Farm Households)（100 million yuan）	固定资产投资（不含农户）（亿元）Investment in Fixed Assets (Excluding Farm Households)（100 million yuan）	#房地产开发 Real Estate Development	商品房销售额（亿元）Sales Value of Commercial Housing（100 million yuan）	#住宅 Residence	商品房竣工面积（万平方米）Floor Space of Commercial Housing Completed（10000 sq. m）	商品房销售面积（万平方米）Sales Floor Space of Commercial Residence（10000 sq. m）
全　国	**National Total**	**606466**	**596501**	**102581**	**117627**	**99064**	**106128**	**157349**
北　京	Beijing	7943.89	7888.69	4000.57	4561.60	2795.81	2369.95	1658.93
天　津	Tianjin	12779.39	12756.36	2300.01	3478.22	3245.60	2914.25	2711.08
河　北	Hebei	31750.02	31340.07	4695.63	4301.83	3710.88	4287.78	6682.29
山　西	Shanxi	14197.98	13859.35	1597.35	1027.14	900.79	2683.59	2061.06
内蒙古	Inner Mongolia	15080.01	14893.96	1133.48	1149.08	838.08	1664.02	2527.85
辽　宁	Liaoning	6692.25	6436.33	2094.85	2256.91	1988.03	2709.29	3711.90
吉　林	Jilin	13923.20	13773.17	1016.76	1029.58	806.49	1351.65	1919.30
黑龙江	Heilongjiang	10648.35	10432.55	864.84	1121.04	903.66	2375.61	2117.29
上　海	Shanghai	6755.88	6751.68	3709.03	6695.85	5233.29	2550.64	2705.69
江　苏	**Jiangsu**	**49663.21**	**49370.85**	**8956.37**	**12293.02**	**11055.36**	**10073.96**	**13962.09**
浙　江	Zhejiang	30276.07	29571.00	7469.37	9605.10	8280.85	7925.40	8636.79
安　徽	Anhui	27033.38	26577.37	4603.56	5035.55	4231.59	5382.95	8499.65
福　建	Fujian	23237.35	22927.99	4588.83	4530.79	3793.41	3665.25	4915.35
江　西	Jiangxi	19694.21	19378.69	1770.94	2678.37	2207.17	1635.61	4691.84
山　东	Shandong	53322.94	52364.49	6323.38	6902.90	6070.54	8253.50	11789.88
河　南	Henan	40415.09	39753.93	6179.13	5612.90	4839.03	6299.44	11306.27
湖　北	Hubei	30011.65	29503.88	4296.38	4994.05	4383.81	3127.49	7427.16
湖　南	Hunan	28353.33	27688.45	2957.04	3751.86	3113.62	4533.74	8085.36
广　东	Guangdong	33303.64	32947.30	10307.80	16214.61	14240.33	6593.75	14611.60
广　西	Guangxi	18236.78	17652.95	2397.99	2207.47	1948.23	1735.05	4215.39
海　南	Hainan	3890.45	3747.03	1787.60	1490.20	1385.26	1674.61	1508.53
重　庆	Chongqing	16048.10	15931.78	3725.95	3432.00	2635.64	4421.30	6257.15
四　川	Sichuan	28811.95	28229.79	5282.64	5358.91	4296.27	7050.24	9300.47
贵　州	Guizhou	13204.00	12929.17	2148.96	1790.53	1269.43	1901.45	4156.93
云　南	Yunnan	16119.40	15662.49	2688.34	1917.76	1411.38	2115.08	3639.75
西　藏	Tibet	1596.05	1596.05	48.54	38.14	34.70	31.53	74.61
陕　西	Shaanxi	20825.25	20474.85	2736.75	1785.17	1585.71	2431.70	3262.70
甘　肃	Gansu	9663.99	9534.10	850.03	873.46	712.35	991.73	1679.49
青　海	Qinghai	3528.05	3455.51	396.92	236.44	172.06	386.67	437.85
宁　夏	Ningxia	3794.25	3709.04	728.16	409.71	325.89	1294.55	966.07
新　疆	Xinjiang	10287.53	9983.86	923.40	846.84	648.94	1695.91	1828.22

附录1－4 居民人均收入与支出(2016年)

Per Capita Disposable Income and Comsumption Expenditure of Residents(2016)

单位:元 (yuan)

地区 Region	全体居民 All Residents		城镇常住居民 Urban Residents		农村常住居民 Rural Resident	
	人均可支配收入 Per Capita Disposable Income	人均消费支出 Per Capita Consumption Expenditure	人均可支配收入 Per Capita Disposable Income	人均消费支出 Per Capita Consumption Expenditure	人均可支配收入 Per Capita Disposable Income	人均消费支出 Per Capita Consumption Expenditure
全国 National Total	**23821**	**17111**	**33616**	**23079**	**12363**	**10130**
北京 Beijing	52530	35416	57275	38256	22310	17329
天津 Tianjin	34074	26129	37110	28345	20076	15912
河北 Hebei	19725	14247	28249	19106	11919	9798
山西 Shanxi	19049	12683	27352	16993	10082	8029
内蒙古 Inner Mongolia	24127	18072	32975	22744	11609	11463
辽宁 Liaoning	26040	19853	32876	24996	12881	9953
吉林 Jilin	19967	14773	26530	19166	12123	9521
黑龙江 Heilongjiang	19838	14446	25736	18145	11832	9424
上海 Shanghai	54032	37265	57692	39857	25520	17071
江苏 Jiangsu	**32070**	**22130**	**40152**	**26433**	**17606**	**14428**
浙江 Zhejiang	38529	25527	47237	30068	22866	17359
安徽 Anhui	19998	14712	29156	19606	11720	10287
福建 Fujian	27608	20167	36014	25006	14999	12911
江西 Jiangxi	20110	13259	28673	17696	12138	9128
山东 Shandong	24685	15926	34012	21495	13954	9519
河南 Henan	18443	12712	27233	18088	11697	8587
湖北 Hubei	21787	15889	29386	20040	12725	10938
湖南 Hunan	21115	15750	31284	21420	11930	10630
广东 Guangdong	30296	23448	37684	28613	14512	12415
广西 Guangxi	18305	12295	28324	17268	10359	8351
海南 Hainan	20653	14275	28453	19015	11843	8921
重庆 Chongqing	22034	16385	29610	21031	11549	9954
四川 Sichuan	18808	14839	28335	20660	11203	10192
贵州 Guizhou	15121	11932	26743	19202	8090	7533
云南 Yunnan	16720	11769	28611	18622	9020	7331
西藏 Tibet	13639	9319	27802	19440	9094	6070
陕西 Shaanxi	18874	13943	28440	19369	9396	8568
甘肃 Gansu	14670	12254	25693	19539	7457	7487
青海 Qinghai	17302	14775	26757	20853	8664	9222
宁夏 Ningxia	18832	14965	27153	20364	9852	9138
新疆 Xinjiang	18355	14066	28463	21229	10183	8277

附录1－5　居民消费价格指数（2016年）
Consumer Price Index(2016)

上年＝100

地　区 Region	居民消费价格指数 Consumer Price Index	食品烟酒 Food or somke wine	衣着 Clothing	居住 Residence	生活用品及服务 Daily Necessities and services	交通和通信 Transportation and Communication	教育文化和娱乐 Education and Culture Artides	医疗保健 Health Care	其他用品和服务 Other Supplies and Services
全　国 National Total	**102.0**	**103.8**	**101.4**	**101.6**	**100.5**	**98.7**	**101.6**	**103.8**	**102.8**
北　京 Beijing	101.4	103.0	100.2	103.7	99.2	96.6	98.3	102.6	104.3
天　津 Tianjin	102.1	102.1	100.1	103.6	99.4	98.3	100.6	108.8	103.8
河　北 Hebei	101.5	102.6	101.8	100.7	100.5	98.3	101.3	104.4	103.3
山　西 Shanxi	101.1	102.8	101.0	99.9	100.0	98.3	101.3	102.4	101.2
内蒙古 Inner Mongolia	101.2	102.2	101.4	100.0	100.1	98.9	100.7	104.4	101.8
辽　宁 Liaoning	101.6	102.5	101.4	100.5	100.7	99.8	102.8	102.5	101.6
吉　林 Jilin	101.6	103.2	101.8	99.7	100.5	98.7	100.6	106.1	102.2
黑龙江 Heilongjiang	101.5	102.6	101.0	100.0	100.4	100.0	101.7	103.7	102.1
上　海 Shanghai	103.2	103.7	100.8	105.1	101.2	97.0	102.7	109.0	103.3
江　苏 Jiangsu	**102.3**	**103.8**	**101.8**	**101.2**	**101.6**	**98.8**	**100.9**	**109.1**	**102.7**
浙　江 Zhejiang	101.9	104.4	101.5	101.0	100.2	98.7	102.7	101.3	102.5
安　徽 Anhui	101.8	103.7	100.8	101.1	100.2	97.6	102.3	103.6	102.3
福　建 Fujian	101.7	103.9	100.3	100.7	99.8	99.4	101.2	102.9	102.5
江　西 Jiangxi	102.0	104.4	100.9	101.0	100.1	98.8	101.5	102.7	102.6
山　东 Shandong	102.1	103.6	101.7	100.9	100.8	99.6	101.9	104.9	102.9
河　南 Henan	101.9	103.2	100.7	102.2	100.2	98.3	102.4	102.8	103.9
湖　北 Hubei	102.2	104.0	102.3	102.8	100.4	97.2	102.2	101.9	102.8
湖　南 Hunan	101.9	104.3	101.5	101.2	100.0	98.4	100.8	103.1	101.6
广　东 Guangdong	102.3	104.8	102.7	101.7	100.2	98.5	101.4	102.8	102.8
广　西 Guangxi	101.6	103.4	101.3	100.3	99.9	98.8	101.6	103.7	101.9
海　南 Hainan	102.8	105.1	97.9	102.6	100.8	98.5	103.0	104.4	103.6
重　庆 Chongqing	101.8	103.6	102.4	101.1	100.6	100.6	99.5	101.8	102.6
四　川 Sichuan	101.9	104.1	100.6	101.2	100.3	98.6	102.5	101.6	102.9
贵　州 Guizhou	101.4	103.6	99.6	100.8	99.9	98.7	101.3	101.5	101.0
云　南 Yunnan	101.5	103.5	100.2	101.2	100.0	99.3	100.7	102.4	101.3
西　藏 Tibet	102.5	104.9	103.2	100.8	101.5	99.5	101.1	102.1	103.1
陕　西 Shaanxi	101.3	103.1	101.1	100.9	99.5	98.3	100.0	102.4	102.2
甘　肃 Gansu	101.3	103.2	101.4	100.8	100.4	99.0	100.0	100.8	101.5
青　海 Qinghai	101.8	102.3	101.2	105.2	100.4	97.3	100.6	102.6	102.4
宁　夏 Ningxia	101.5	102.4	101.7	100.4	100.3	98.6	102.2	102.9	103.2
新　疆 Xinjiang	101.4	101.9	101.3	101.2	100.6	99.3	101.6	102.7	103.1

附录 1－6 农林牧渔业总产值和增速(2016 年)

Gross Output Value and Growth Rate of Agriculture, Forestry, Animal Husbandry and Fishery (2016)

地区 Region		农林牧渔业总产值(亿元)	Gross Output Value of Agriculture, Forestry, Animal Husbandry and Fishery (100 million yuan)				农林牧渔业总产值比上年增长(%) Grouth Rate of Gross Output Value of Agriculture, Forestry, Animal Husbandry and Fishery Over Preceding Year(%)
			#农业 Farming	#林业 Forestry	#畜牧业 Animal Husbandry	#渔业 Fishery	
全国	National Total	112091	59288	4632	31703	11603	3.5
北京	Beijing	338.06	145.20	52.21	122.69	9.23	-9.9
天津	Tianjin	494.44	244.31	8.35	140.86	88.97	3.3
河北	Hebei	6083.86	3459.39	132.31	1939.22	210.95	3.5
山西	Shanxi	1534.03	958.11	100.31	376.17	9.91	3.2
内蒙古	Inner Mongolia	2794.22	1415.07	98.64	1202.90	33.03	3.1
辽宁	Liaoning	4421.78	1859.55	143.73	1575.75	639.64	-2.6
吉林	Jilin	2724.88	1231.98	107.21	1252.85	42.99	3.2
黑龙江	Heilongjiang	5197.75	2873.86	219.87	1854.75	129.19	5.5
上海	Shanghai	285.09	148.53	13.20	62.62	50.16	-9.2
江苏	**Jiangsu**	**7235.06**	**3714.64**	**129.33**	**1331.55**	**1621.88**	**0.8**
浙江	Zhejiang	3146.06	1521.19	158.15	434.32	962.01	2.5
安徽	Anhui	4655.53	2234.14	291.08	1375.68	513.15	3.4
福建	Fujian	4155.68	1782.01	315.14	681.68	1235.48	3.7
江西	Jiangxi	3130.29	1446.89	324.61	788.61	458.86	4.1
山东	Shandong	9325.89	4641.35	147.48	2540.82	1485.58	4.4
河南	Henan	7799.67	4577.16	121.28	2611.33	128.32	4.5
湖北	Hubei	6278.35	2921.27	203.43	1715.18	1030.01	4.9
湖南	Hunan	6081.92	3255.11	321.60	1762.65	396.66	3.6
广东	Guangdong	6078.43	3134.44	314.74	1221.75	1195.63	2.9
广西	Guangxi	4591.37	2347.90	323.53	1266.37	464.25	3.3
海南	Hainan	1470.41	695.64	100.02	267.10	353.77	4.3
重庆	Chongqing	1968.28	1151.77	73.43	627.45	85.30	4.5
四川	Sichuan	6831.08	3710.97	219.09	2551.71	223.90	4.0
贵州	Guizhou	3097.19	1888.64	195.00	797.21	68.74	6.2
云南	Yunnan	3633.12	1943.65	330.37	1141.82	94.24	5.8
西藏	Tibet	172.97	52.23	2.39	113.84	0.24	12.6
陕西	Shaanxi	2985.76	2027.56	85.54	695.93	26.25	4.1
甘肃	Gansu	1778.00	1274.71	30.83	299.75	2.17	4.2
青海	Qinghai	338.80	155.52	8.28	165.72	3.25	5.4
宁夏	Ningxia	493.60	311.89	10.11	131.71	16.97	4.4
新疆	Xinjiang	2969.70	2163.11	50.28	653.15	22.18	6.0

注：本表绝对数按当年价格计算，增速按可比价格计算。

a) In this table the absolute value is counted with current price, while the growth rate is counted with comparable price.

附录1-7　主要农产品产量（2016年）
Output of Major Agricultural Products (2016)

单位：万吨　　(10000 tons)

地区 Region		粮食 Grain	油料 Oil-bearing Crops	棉花 Cotton	肉类 Meat	奶类 Milk	水果 Fruit
全国	**National Total**	**61625**	**3629**	**530**	**8538**	**3712**	**28351**
北京	Beijing	53.69	0.56	0.01	30.37	45.70	78.97
天津	Tianjin	196.37	1.60	2.33	45.52	68.02	61.50
河北	Hebei	3460.24	156.50	29.95	457.67	448.04	2138.51
山西	Shanxi	1318.51	15.43	1.03	84.43	95.88	840.77
内蒙古	Inner Mongolia	2780.25	220.02	0.02	258.89	741.34	316.28
辽宁	Liaoning	2100.63	81.33	0.11	430.92	144.24	802.26
吉林	Jilin	3717.21	82.54		260.41	53.38	241.10
黑龙江	Heilongjiang	6058.50	21.75		231.16	548.59	259.88
上海	Shanghai	99.16	0.90	0.03	17.41	26.04	50.64
江苏	**Jiangsu**	**3466.01**	**131.93**	**7.38**	**355.63**	**59.01**	**893.00**
浙江	Zhejiang	752.20	29.09	1.65	118.09	15.33	724.32
安徽	Anhui	3417.40	214.83	18.46	411.39	32.68	1043.49
福建	Fujian	650.87	31.03	0.01	225.64	15.86	853.81
江西	Jiangxi	2138.11	122.02	7.33	330.90	13.45	617.40
山东	Shandong	4700.71	326.78	54.83	777.51	276.80	3255.43
河南	Henan	5946.60	619.09	9.75	697.02	336.59	2871.26
湖北	Hubei	2554.12	329.75	18.85	425.24	16.86	1010.40
湖南	Hunan	2953.20	242.87	12.27	529.82	10.10	1048.18
广东	Guangdong	1360.22	113.29		415.49	12.98	1717.01
广西	Guangxi	1521.30	68.95	0.25	411.19	9.66	1882.50
海南	Hainan	177.86	11.18		76.33	0.22	395.39
重庆	Chongqing	1166.00	62.72		210.85	5.45	408.69
四川	Sichuan	3483.50	311.29	0.88	696.29	62.77	979.32
贵州	Guizhou	1192.38	103.43	0.12	199.28	6.39	243.88
云南	Yunnan	1902.89	68.50	0.00	375.63	64.11	759.11
西藏	Tibet	101.91	6.21		27.72	34.70	1.53
陕西	Shaanxi	1228.29	63.80	3.38	111.72	189.14	2017.84
甘肃	Gansu	1140.59	76.02	1.99	97.32	40.68	737.96
青海	Qinghai	103.45	30.04		36.04	34.22	4.02
宁夏	Ningxia	370.60	14.65		30.89	139.47	305.77
新疆	Xinjiang	1512.28	71.39	359.38	160.97	164.39	1790.88

附录1－8 规模以上工业企业主要经济指标(2016年)

Main Economic Indicators of above Designated Size Industrial Enterprises (2016)

单位:亿元 (100 million yuan)

地区		Region	主营业务收入 Revenue from Principal Business	主营业务成本 Cost of Principal Business	利润总额 Total Profits	应收账款 Accounts Receivable	产成品 Finished Goods	资产总计 Total Assets
全	**国**	**National Total**	**1151618**	**984903**	**68803**	**125800**	**39752**	**1068297**
北	京	Beijing	19413.60	16167.30	1549.30	4298.30	802.40	42848.60
天	津	Tianjin	27835.80	23812.40	1984.90	3785.20	1020.80	24646.80
河	北	Hebei	46729.40	40926.60	2610.00	3553.90	1496.40	43754.20
山	西	Shanxi	13957.00	11813.20	208.70	2320.60	743.60	33194.10
内蒙古		Inner Mongolia	19797.90	16537.60	1242.10	1840.80	585.40	29677.60
辽	宁	Liaoning	23802.00	20203.80	657.60	3646.90	1333.20	35829.10
吉	林	Jilin	23268.30	19524.10	1241.80	1470.60	736.30	18785.40
黑龙江		Heilongjiang	11166.50	9595.00	244.00	1325.10	449.50	14744.80
上	海	Shanghai	33844.30	27001.50	2906.20	6977.90	1492.00	39258.20
江	**苏**	**Jiangsu**	**156591.04**	**134083.08**	**10574.40**	**19022.03**	**4787.06**	**114536.32**
浙	江	Zhejiang	65307.60	54908.20	4322.70	11173.70	3312.20	69755.30
安	徽	Anhui	41645.90	36471.00	2078.90	4476.30	1338.40	32845.40
福	建	Fujian	42124.10	36310.50	2643.30	4200.20	1443.70	31317.50
江	西	Jiangxi	35518.70	31181.80	2399.40	2094.60	863.40	21432.70
山	东	Shandong	150034.90	131911.30	8643.10	8957.00	4547.20	104715.50
河	南	Henan	79195.70	69430.10	5174.10	5745.30	1678.40	59165.50
湖	北	Hubei	45169.90	38784.30	2441.40	4234.60	1594.30	36640.10
湖	南	Hunan	37686.50	31823.10	1620.50	3172.70	900.70	24743.20
广	东	Guangdong	127363.10	107569.00	8025.40	18500.60	4701.40	104720.00
广	西	Guangxi	21978.40	18819.20	1287.70	1495.90	786.50	15838.80
海	南	Hainan	1660.30	1296.50	103.50	190.70	79.50	2740.50
重	庆	Chongqing	22947.60	19510.50	1584.20	2485.20	716.00	19313.40
四	川	Sichuan	40639.30	34491.70	2176.10	3968.00	1322.30	40163.60
贵	州	Guizhou	10654.90	8668.30	658.70	921.10	333.40	13468.90
云	南	Yunnan	10342.00	8166.60	309.10	1100.90	527.20	19427.40
西	藏	Tibet	170.70	129.40	16.50	21.10	10.20	1076.40
陕	西	Shaanxi	19776.80	16118.60	1472.40	2060.40	829.20	28153.30
甘	肃	Gansu	7711.50	6733.90	116.10	830.80	513.90	11883.10
青	海	Qinghai	2227.10	1871.40	76.90	309.50	116.80	6107.00
宁	夏	Ningxia	3636.10	3066.90	137.70	581.60	275.10	8477.10
新	疆	Xinjiang	8222.30	6634.40	345.10	1041.90	447.10	19265.60

附录1-9 主要工业产品产量(2016年)
Output of Major Industrial Products (2016)

地区	Region	发电量(亿千瓦小时) Electricity (100 million kW·h)	生铁(万吨) Pig Irom (10000 tons)	粗钢(万吨) Rough Steel (10000 tons)	钢材(万吨) Steel Products (10000 tons)	水泥(万吨) Cement (10000 tons)	农用化肥(万吨) Chemical Fertilizers (10000 tons)	汽车(万辆) Truck (10000 units)	布(亿米) Cloth (100 million meter)
全　国	**National Total**	**61425**	**70074**	**80837**	**113801**	**241353**	**7129**	**2812**	**907**
北　京	Beijing	434.40			162.80	510.30		238.00	0.00
天　津	Tianjin0	617.50	1660.80	1798.90	8667.10	788.60	13.40	52.90	2.40
河　北	Hebei0	2630.60	18398.40	19260.00	26150.40	9898.60	226.20	128.60	73.90
山　西	Shanxi	2535.10	3641.10	3936.10	4279.00	3851.50	438.70	0.70	0.70
内蒙古	Inner Mongolia	3949.80	1469.40	1813.20	2016.80	6298.40	250.20	2.10	
辽　宁	Liaoning	1778.80	6033.90	6029.00	5906.30	4011.00	58.80	107.90	1.60
吉　林	Jilin	760.30	847.60	832.00	961.40	3086.80	15.90	254.00	0.30
黑龙江	Heilongjiang	900.40	354.00	372.30	332.80	3381.00	63.50	7.60	0.10
上　海	Shanghai	807.30	1587.20	1709.10	2080.10	418.40	1.80	260.80	1.10
江　苏	**Jiangsu**	**4667.73**	**7174.10**	**11080.50**	**13469.70**	**17989.78**	**207.17**	**144.89**	**91.46**
浙　江	Zhejiang0	3197.70	848.00	1299.60	3760.90	10848.00	32.30	58.10	256.90
安　徽	Anhui	2252.70	2242.70	2731.30	3225.80	13584.10	291.70	139.10	16.50
福　建	Fujian	2007.40	980.40	1516.80	2859.60	8106.00	52.00	21.80	87.10
江　西	Jiangxi	1085.40	2082.00	2241.50	2585.00	9553.30	149.40	53.60	13.60
山　东	Shandong	5329.30	6769.20	7167.10	9788.20	16156.10	531.40	86.90	127.50
河　南	Henan	2652.70	2862.90	2849.50	4667.90	15672.10	542.10	58.50	28.70
湖　北	Hubei	2479.00	2323.30	2948.50	3563.80	11600.50	1164.90	243.50	82.20
湖　南	Hunan	1385.10	1791.40	1827.80	1998.70	12239.70	109.50	47.70	4.40
广　东	Guangdong	4263.70	1670.20	2283.20	4113.30	15080.60	69.50	280.10	31.90
广　西	Guangxi	1346.50	1216.40	2109.60	3644.70	12034.90	94.30	245.30	0.50
海　南	Hainan	287.70		27.60	36.30	2227.90	51.70	6.70	
重　庆	Chongqing	701.20	287.80	366.50	1234.20	6790.20	182.00	266.30	5.40
四　川	Sichuan	3273.90	1733.20	2007.70	2837.20	14615.50	531.00	53.00	20.00
贵　州	Guizhou	1904.00	371.40	515.90	526.20	10798.50	639.70	1.60	0.30
云　南	Yunnan	2692.50	1277.20	1417.30	1654.70	11104.40	279.50	13.30	0.00
西　藏	Tibet	54.50			1.80	623.30			
陕　西	Shaanxi	1757.40	856.00	924.70	1233.80	7264.00	153.40	42.00	8.80
甘　肃	Gansu	1214.30	494.30	628.40	665.90	4640.40	32.10	1.20	
青　海	Qinghai	553.00	96.60	114.90	125.10	1895.40	552.40		
宁　夏	Ningxia	1144.40	154.30	159.20	164.10	1984.70	55.00		0.10
新　疆	Xinjiang	2719.10	849.90	868.40	1087.60	4250.20	336.30	2.10	1.80

附录1－10　建筑业主要指标(2016年)

Main Indicators on Construction (2016)

地区	Region	企业个数(个) Number of Construction Enterprises (unit)	从事建筑业活动的从业人员平均人数(万人) the Average Number of Employees Engaged in Principal Business (10000 persons)	建筑业总产值(亿元) Gross Output Value of Construction (100 million yuan)	房屋建筑面积施工面积(万平方米) Floor Space of Building under Construction (10000 sq. m)	房屋建筑面积竣工面积(万平方米) Floor Space of Building Completed (10000 sq. m)	按建筑业总产值计算的劳动生产率(元/人) Calculated by the Gross Output Value of Construction Labor Productivity (yuan/person)
全　国	**National Total**	**83017**	**5757**	**193567**	**1264220**	**422376**	**336227**
北　京	Beijing	2858	165.60	8841.19	61097.53	10703.46	533880
天　津	Tianjin	1500	99.25	4891.81	17036.16	3428.73	492879
河　北	Hebei	2467	145.27	5517.69	34616.12	11145.14	379815
山　西	Shanxi	2532	112.27	3318.47	14620.58	3353.26	295590
内蒙古	Inner Mongolia	870	41.30	1220.81	6296.04	2538.64	295574
辽　宁	Liaoning	5238	130.49	3926.71	20390.69	6852.47	300927
吉　林	Jilin	2191	80.07	2283.56	10634.39	5211.38	285207
黑龙江	Heilongjiang	1566	67.04	1716.61	5404.13	2746.95	256076
上　海	Shanghai	2662	126.49	6046.19	36019.72	7481.15	477994
江　苏	**Jiangsu**	**9023**	**845.84**	**25791.76**	**221493.57**	**74990.29**	**304925**
浙　江	Zhejiang	6174	777.33	24989.37	198401.24	68818.52	321476
安　徽	Anhui	2929	169.81	6047.29	40130.03	14588.44	356129
福　建	Fujian	3608	321.89	8531.45	62920.69	18121.20	265043
江　西	Jiangxi	1873	168.42	5179.03	28446.16	14835.79	307509
山　东	Shandong	6013	322.58	10087.43	72090.61	23721.32	312707
河　南	Henan	5123	272.61	8807.99	55784.03	19425.80	323100
湖　北	Hubei	3368	270.56	11862.40	72835.05	28613.46	438438
湖　南	Hunan	2067	229.17	7304.22	50329.04	18629.18	318730
广　东	Guangdong	4437	230.46	9652.31	54358.29	15661.71	418829
广　西	Guangxi	1139	114.08	3449.19	26531.93	7998.04	302337
海　南	Hainan	155	8.11	307.76	2085.41	652.44	379671
重　庆	Chongqing	2577	217.41	7035.81	32077.14	13751.59	323617
四　川	Sichuan	3809	324.28	9959.68	54048.32	21084.85	307129
贵　州	Guizhou	891	71.44	2362.95	19354.57	4112.08	330753
云　南	Yunnan	2544	132.24	3867.22	17052.86	7102.03	292428
西　藏	Tibet	173	3.32	111.28	244.20	143.99	335094
陕　西	Shaanxi	2114	136.73	5329.23	24528.29	6758.89	389771
甘　肃	Gansu	1323	62.92	1947.24	10422.41	3915.21	309498
青　海	Qinghai	371	14.49	410.62	886.79	301.94	283457
宁　夏	Ningxia	531	19.11	511.25	2771.34	1017.77	267566
新　疆	Xinjiang	1144	76.46	2258.24	11312.61	4669.94	295359

附录1－11　客运量和旅客周转量（2016年）

Passenger Traffic and Turnover Volume of Passenger Traffic（2016）

地区 Region	客运量（万人）Passenger Traffic（10000 persons）	铁路 Railway	公路 Highway	水运 Waterway	旅客周转量（亿人公里）Turnover Volume of Passenger Traffic（100 million person-km）	铁路 Railway	公路 Highway	水运 Waterway
全国 National Total	**1900194**	**281405**	**1542759**	**27234**	**31258**	**12579**	**10229**	**72**
北京 Beijing	61519	13479	48040		268.50	150.80	117.70	
天津 Tianjin	18377	4543	13741	93	262.00	183.50	78.40	0.10
河北 Hebei	50701	10771	39925	5	1238.10	993.60	244.20	0.40
山西 Shanxi	26374	7530	18702	142	360.60	219.30	141.10	0.10
内蒙古 Inner Mongolia	15735	5388	10347		375.00	222.20	152.70	
辽宁 Liaoning	73632	14040	59054	538	936.10	623.40	306.70	6.00
吉林 Jilin	34910	7567	27186	156	431.30	262.30	168.70	0.20
黑龙江 Heilongjiang	39386	10480	28550	355	471.10	270.60	200.10	0.40
上海 Shanghai	14416	10609	3402	404	214.40	98.70	115.00	0.70
江苏 Jiangsu	**134605**	**17814**	**113493**	**2272**	**1591.93**	**672.65**	**779.98**	**2.39**
浙江 Zhejiang	105018	18035	83033	3950	1075.00	604.00	465.10	5.80
安徽 Anhui	81106	10370	70523	213	1187.40	695.70	491.30	0.40
福建 Fujian	51649	10496	39137	2016	593.30	338.60	251.90	2.70
江西 Jiangxi	62876	9249	53366	261	970.70	688.00	282.30	0.30
山东 Shandong	63463	12639	48823	2000	1188.90	704.50	472.40	12.00
河南 Henan	120528	13825	106415	289	1684.30	923.10	760.60	0.60
湖北 Hubei	102990	14197	88221	572	1232.30	741.60	487.30	3.40
湖南 Hunan	121760	11518	108627	1615	1500.80	920.60	577.00	3.20
广东 Guangdong	130345	25603	102094	2648	1887.40	797.30	1079.80	10.30
广西 Guangxi	48699	8388	39750	561	743.80	351.10	390.10	2.70
海南 Hainan	13912	2292	9920	1699	120.40	41.50	75.40	3.50
重庆 Chongqing	61255	4911	55594	750	506.30	164.40	336.70	5.10
四川 Sichuan	123746	11456	109716	2573	941.60	341.30	597.80	2.40
贵州 Guizhou	89464	5169	82199	2096	674.90	226.00	443.10	5.80
云南 Yunnan	46519	4056	41208	1255	446.10	123.40	320.00	2.70
西藏 Tibet	1155	265	889		39.80	16.00	23.70	
陕西 Shaanxi	69820	8302	61093	425	755.70	464.20	290.80	0.70
甘肃 Gansu	41626	3604	37932	90	613.40	360.00	253.30	0.20
青海 Qinghai	5934	994	4873	66	125.10	77.50	47.50	0.10
宁夏 Ningxia	8757	659	7910	188	109.70	45.20	64.40	0.10
新疆 Xinjiang	32148	3155	28993		458.10	244.60	213.50	

附录1-12 货运量和货物周转量（2016年）
Freight Traffic and Turnover Volume of Freight Traffic（2016）

地区	Region	货运量（万吨）Freight Traffic（10000 tons）	铁路 Railway	公路 Highway	水运 Waterway	货物周转量（亿吨公里）Turnover Volume of Freight Traffic（100 million ton-km）	铁路 Railway	公路 Highway	水运 Waterway
全国	**National Total**	**4386762**	**333186**	**3341259**	**638238**	**186629**	**23792**	**61080**	**97339**
北京	Beijing	20734	762	19972		825.40	664.10	161.30	
天津	Tianjin	50506	8150	32841	9515	2302.30	399.80	372.50	1530.00
河北	Hebei	210586	16313	189822	4451	12332.70	3704.50	7294.60	1333.60
山西	Shanxi	167076	64861	102200	16	3565.50	2113.30	1452.10	0.10
内蒙古	Inner Mongolia	186726	56113	130613		4341.70	1918.10	2423.60	
辽宁	Liaoning	207064	16230	177371	13464	12113.50	900.90	2936.80	8275.80
吉林	Jilin	45060	3944	40777	339	1478.50	393.10	1084.80	0.60
黑龙江	Heilongjiang	53569	9542	42897	1130	1532.50	620.50	904.80	7.30
上海	Shanghai	88324	482	39055	48787	19317.80	10.20	282.00	19025.60
江苏	**Jiangsu**	**215651**	**5335**	**117166**	**79314**	**8290.69**	**282.46**	**2140.33**	**5224.60**
浙江	Zhejiang	215558	3913	133999	77646	9789.30	212.00	1626.80	7950.60
安徽	Anhui	364567	9265	244526	110776	10896.40	719.70	4915.70	5261.00
福建	Fujian	120352	2918	85770	31664	6070.60	129.40	1094.70	4846.40
江西	Jiangxi	138118	4357	122872	10889	3897.80	515.00	3147.50	235.30
山东	Shandong	285386	20574	249752	15060	8884.30	1225.50	6071.40	1587.40
河南	Henan	206087	10287	184255	11544	7383.50	1736.40	4838.50	808.60
湖北	Hubei	162460	4088	122656	35716	5922.90	735.70	2506.90	2680.30
湖南	Hunan	206527	4114	178968	23445	4056.90	750.80	2686.60	619.50
广东	Guangdong	366839	8380	272826	85633	21801.60	259.40	3381.90	18160.30
广西	Guangxi	160761	5898	128247	26615	4260.40	679.00	2248.50	1332.90
海南	Hainan	21786	793	10879	10114	1060.80	12.10	76.10	972.50
重庆	Chongqing	107966	1928	89390	16648	2968.30	156.70	935.40	1876.10
四川	Sichuan	160970	6794	146046	8131	2504.10	716.10	1565.30	222.70
贵州	Guizhou	89526	5635	82237	1654	1482.30	566.70	873.20	42.40
云南	Yunnan	115505	5372	109487	646	1600.10	411.80	1173.10	15.20
西藏	Tibet	1971	65	1906		124.60	30.10	94.50	
陕西	Shaanxi	149046	35459	113363	224	3444.90	1518.30	1925.80	0.80
甘肃	Gansu	60661	5866	54761	34	2170.00	1220.30	949.60	0.10
青海	Qinghai	16881	2834	14047		475.80	239.80	236.00	
宁夏	Ningxia	43260	5839	37421		819.90	242.40	577.60	
新疆	Xinjiang	71961	6822	65139		1803.90	701.70	1102.20	

附录1－13　国内外贸易（2016年）
Domestic and Foreign Trade (2016)

地区	Region	社会消费品零售总额（亿元）Total Ratail Sales of Consumer Goods (100 million yuan)	进出口总额（亿美元）Total Value of Imports and Exports Through Customs (USD 100 million)	出口 Exports	进口 Imports
全　国	**National Total**	**332316**	**36856**	**20982**	**15874**
北　京	Beijing	11005.10	2820.32	518.45	2301.88
天　津	Tianjin	5635.80	1026.52	442.86	583.66
河　北	Hebei	14364.70	466.23	305.77	160.46
山　西	Shanxi	6480.50	166.44	99.32	67.12
内蒙古	Inner Mongolia	6700.80	116.15	43.74	72.41
辽　宁	Liaoning	13414.10	865.21	430.65	434.56
吉　林	Jilin	7310.40	184.42	42.06	142.37
黑龙江	Heilongjiang	8402.50	165.38	50.44	114.94
上　海	Shanghai	10946.60	4338.44	1834.73	2503.71
江　苏	**Jiangsu**	**28707.12**	**5096.12**	**3193.44**	**1902.68**
浙　江	Zhejiang	21970.80	3365.00	2678.64	686.36
安　徽	Anhui	10000.20	443.34	284.45	158.90
福　建	Fujian	11674.50	1568.47	1036.76	531.71
江　西	Jiangxi	6634.60	400.76	298.14	102.62
山　东	Shandong	30645.80	2342.10	1371.56	970.54
河　南	Henan	17618.40	711.89	427.93	283.95
湖　北	Hubei	15649.20	393.50	260.25	133.25
湖　南	Hunan	13436.50	262.49	176.69	85.80
广　东	Guangdong	34739.10	9555.12	5988.62	3566.49
广　西	Guangxi	7027.30	478.28	229.57	248.71
海　南	Hainan	1453.70	113.28	21.23	92.05
重　庆	Chongqing	7271.40	627.71	406.94	220.77
四　川	Sichuan	15601.90	493.19	279.33	213.86
贵　州	Guizhou	3709.00	56.93	47.36	9.57
云　南	Yunnan	5722.90	198.90	114.83	84.08
西　藏	Tibet	459.40	7.82	4.72	3.10
陕　西	Shaanxi	7367.60	299.19	158.25	140.94
甘　肃	Gansu	3184.40	68.75	40.88	27.88
青　海	Qinghai	767.30	15.25	13.66	1.59
宁　夏	Ningxia	850.10	32.73	24.97	7.76
新　疆	Xinjiang	2825.90	176.58	156.07	20.51

溧阳市

溧阳位于苏浙皖三省交界，是宁杭经济带的区域中心城市，现辖10个镇、1个街道、1个国家级旅游度假区、1个省级经济开发区，获批筹建1个省级高新技术开发区，面积1535平方公里，人口约80万。5条高速公路覆盖全境，宁杭高铁在溧阳设有2个站台，溧阳已全面融入长三角“1小时经济圈”。溧阳秦代建县，是人类祖先“中华曙猿”发源地，被誉为焦尾琴故里，历代文人李白、陆游、孟郊等都曾留下过足迹和名篇。溧阳生态环境优美，拥有天目湖国家森林公园、国家湿地公园以及长荡湖国家湿地公园，是全国唯一拥有两个国家级湿地公园的县级市，天目湖旅游度假区集国家级旅游度假区、国家5A级旅游景区、国家级生态旅游示范区于一体，是华东唯一、全国两家之一的“三区一体”旅游度假区，溧阳先后被评为国家卫生城市、国家生态市、中国长寿之乡和世界长寿之乡。溧阳产业基础扎实，拥有江苏中关村科技产业园，已形成智能电网装备、农机和工程机械制造、汽车及零部件制造等主导产业，百亿级动力电池产业基地正加快培育。智能电网、汽车零部件产业集群双双入选江苏省特色产业集群。2016年，全市实现地区生产总值801.3亿元、规模以上工业总产值1363.4亿元、一般公共预算收入59亿元，位居全国“百强县”第36位。

燕山新区夜景

天目湖国家湿地公园

天目湖国家森林公园

江苏省江阴市

江阴，简称“澄”，古称暨阳，北临长江，南接太湖，是历史上著名的军事重镇和重要商港，素有“江海门户”、“锁航要塞”之称。现辖10个镇、5个街道办事处、1个国家级高新区、2个省级开发区，总面积986.97平方公里，户籍人口124.80万，境内35公里长江深水岸线，被专家称为黄金水道的黄金地段。江阴交通便利发达，距上海、南京各150公里，以江阴为圆心，半径160公里范围内有6个机场，江阴大桥连接长江南北，京沪高速、沿江高速、新长铁路、锡澄运河穿境而过，是长江下游新兴的滨江港口城市和交通枢纽城市。

江阴地处温带，四季分明，气候宜人。辖内水网密布，土地肥沃，物产丰富。特产“长江三鲜”（长江鲥鱼、刀鱼、河豚），是江南著名的“鱼米之乡”。这里自古钟灵毓秀，人文荟萃，拥有7000年人文史、5000年文明史和2500年文字记载的历史，是良渚文化重要的发祥地之一。明清以来，江阴涌现了地理学家徐霞客、“中国近代图书馆之父”缪荃孙、现代文学家刘半农、民族音乐家刘天华、佛学家巨赞等一大批杰出人物，拥有近百名大学校长、近20名院士和40多位共和国将军。

改革开放以来，“人心齐、民性刚、敢攀登、创一流”的江阴人坚持科学发展、创新发展、率先发展，乡镇企业异军突起，成为“苏南模式”的重要发源地。江阴先后荣获全国双拥模范城、国家卫生城市、国家环保模范城市、全国科技进步示范市、国家生态市、中国优秀旅游城市、中国最佳经济活力魅力城市、首批国家可持续发展先进示范区等100多项全国性荣誉称号，被中央确定为改革开放30年全国18个典型地区之一，被誉为“科学发展的先行者”。2016年江阴连续14年蝉联全国县域经济和县域基本竞争力百强县排名第一名，连续9年蝉联中国全面小康十大示范县市（第一名）。全年实现地区生产总值3083.26亿元，一般公共预算收入达到229.91亿元，拥有42家上市公司，成为证券界独特的“江阴板块”。

江阴将全面贯彻党的十八大和十八届三中、四中、五中、六中全会精神，深入贯彻习近平总书记系列重要讲话特别是视察江苏重要讲话精神，紧紧围绕高水平全面建成小康社会、建设“强富美高”新江阴的总目标，积极弘扬江阴精神，开拓进取、埋头实干，铸牢创新之魂，借好资本之力，用足人才之长，塑优环境之本，推动江阴实体经济枝繁叶茂、开花结果。

昆山市

中环夜景

2016年，在苏州市委、市政府的坚强领导下，昆山深入贯彻落实党的十八大和十八届三中、四中、五中、六中全会精神，深入贯彻落实习近平总书记系列重要讲话特别是视察江苏重要讲话精神，认真贯彻落实省第十三次党代会和苏州市第十二次党代会精神，积极践行“五大发展理念”，全力做好稳增长、促改革、调结构、惠民生、防风险各项工作。围绕“两聚一高”总要求，结合昆山实际，提出“聚力创新求突破，聚焦富民补短板”，争当“强富美高”新江苏建设排头兵。2016年，全市完成地区生产总值3160.3亿元，一般公共预算收入318.9亿元，成为全国首个GDP突破3000亿、财政收入突破300亿的县级市。规上工业总产值8383.2亿元；固定资产投资757.4亿元；社会消费品零售总额815亿元；进出口总额722.7亿美元，其中出口463.2亿美元；居民人均可支配收入46339元。

在“聚力创新求突破”方面，紧紧围绕“创新四问”要求，重点做好五项工作：

一是坚持稳中求进工作总基调，为聚力创新夯实基础。坚持把稳增长作为首要前提，一着不让抓好经济组织运行，确保经济增长保持在合理区间。

二是精心打造三大高端产业。重点抓好电子信息产业、小核酸生物医药产业和人工智能产业。

三是加快聚升区域创新浓度。积极抢抓苏南国家自主创新示范区建设机遇，下大力气整合资源，全力建设15平方公里阳澄湖科技园核心区，推动创新资源、科技人才、科技金融融合互动，营造良好创新生态。

中国（昆山）品牌产品进口交易会

昆山杜克大学

汤 尤 杯

四是提升企业创新能力，尤其要让民营企业成为创新发展的主力军、生力军。目前，昆山有940家国家高新技术企业、1229家省民营科技企业。2016年，新兴产业、高新技术产业产值占规模以上工业比重分别为45.3%、51%。全社会研发投入占比达3.1%，科技进步贡献率达62.6%。

五是充分发挥沿沪对台优势，争取重大政策突破。昆山深化两岸产业合作试验区获国务院批准设立，并写入国家“十三五”发展规划。同时，积极复制上海自贸区成功经验，加强与苏州工业园区的对接，增创开放型经济发展新优势。

在“聚焦富民补短板”方面，坚持问题导向，强化靶向思维，围绕教育、医疗、养老“三个焦点问题”，生态环境和公共安全“两大公共产品”，突出工作重点，补齐发展短板，全力解决好群众最关心最直接最现实的利益问题。

一是把提高居民收入作为首要任务。2016年城乡居民收入水平进一步提升，分别达54728元、28178元，分别比上年增长7.8%、8.5%。

二是把改善生态环境作为当务之急。我们通过开展环境保护、安全生产、城市管理“三大百日行动”，解决了一批群众反映强烈的突出问题，形成了一批长效化、常态化制度，排出了一批基础性、工程性项目。

三是把优化公共服务作为重中之重。教育上，“十三五”期间完成94所学校项目建设。医疗上，投资45亿元，加快建设东西部医疗中心和公共卫生中心，优化医疗布局。交通上，全国第一条跨省际地铁——上海轨道交通11号线延伸到昆山，建成全长44.2公里的全国县级市首条环城快速路。

四是把开展创建工作作为有效抓手。深入开展文明城市创建活动，不断提高市民文明素养，实现城市干净、有序、诚信、文明。依托大数据、云计算、移动互联网，在城市管理、综合治理、治安防控、安全生产、环境保护、公共服务等领域推进信息化、智能化建设。

上海轨道交通11号线通往花桥

智能数控机床与机械手完美结合

海纳百川 安居乐业

HAINABAICHUANANJULEYE

南通市人民政府副市长
中共海安县委书记 陆卫东

海安县人民政府县长 顾国标

海安是苏中水陆交通要冲，气候宜人，雨水充沛，河道成网，物产丰富。全县总面积1184平方公里，总人口93.8万，下辖10个区镇，含一个国家级开发区，一个省级高新区，一个省级商贸物流园，一个老坝港滨海新区。

综合实力持续攀升。实现地区生产总值755.3亿元；一般公共预算收入57.6亿元；完成固定资产投资584.5亿元；工业开票销售总量1134.4亿元。

转型升级成效明显。新兴工业产值占规模工业产值的比重比上年提升1.1个百分点。三次产业结构由上年的7.9:47.5:44.6调整为7.4:46.9:45.7，服务业增加值占GDP的比重较上年提升1.1个百分点。财政收入占地区生产总值比重为7.6%。

开放开发势头强劲。全年实际利用外资3.0亿美元，获批全省首家苏台产业合作园。全年新开工亿元产业类项目126个，22个入选省市重大项目库。商贸物流园区获评省级示范物流园区、全国优秀物流园区。

创新活力竞相迸发。高新技术产业产值占规模工业比重48.6%。全年支付各类合作经费1.2亿元，获中国专利优秀奖3个。产学研合作项目销售占全县净增工业开票销售41.6%。依靠创新驱动稳增长的做法和成效得到了国务院督查组的充分肯定。

城乡统筹步伐加快。城市防洪工程经受住50年一遇的强降雨考验。铁路综合枢纽汽车客运站建设进展顺利。新增绿化1.6万亩，获评全省园林城市。城市环境综合整治工作全省放样，获评省优秀管理城市。“清水工程”三年行动计划圆满收官。

社会事业均衡发展。民生财政支出增长20%，15件民生实事扎实推进。南通理工学院海安校区顺利开学。公共服务水平日渐提高，社会保障体系日趋完善，人民群众福祉切实增进。全国普法先进县实现“五连冠”。

海安将紧紧围绕**“枢纽海安、物流天下”**战略取向，充分发挥**“动车时代、节点城市”**新优势，立足**“区域性枢纽城市”**的战略追求，坚持创新争先，聚焦发展富民，为高水平全面建成小康社会、实现经济社会发展全面领先打下坚实基础。

第三届创新创业在海安

春到东洲

田升光电检验车间

圣德曼生产车间

美丽富饶的南黄海滩涂

银装素裹的七星广场

"世界水晶之都"

东海县

滨湖小城

2016年是“十三五”开局之年，东海县全面贯彻党的十八大和十八届三中四中五中六中全会精神，深入贯彻习近平总书记系列重要讲话特别是视察江苏重要讲话精神，以“五位一体”总体布局和“四个全面”战略布局为统领，践行创新、协调、绿色、开放、共享发展理念，抓住用好战略机遇，突出“全面建成小康社会、建设幸福东海”奋斗目标，统筹实施创新驱动、产业强县、双向开放、新型城镇化、绿色发展、民生共享六大战略，围绕“两聚一高”，努力谱写经济强、百姓富、环境美、社会文明程度高的新东海篇章。

多措并举稳定增长。实施“大产业、大园区、大企业”培育工程和“特色型、科技型、成长型”企业培育计划，设立3000万元企业奖补资金和2亿元产业发展基金，树立重抓“工业立县、产业强县”的政策导向。常态化开展企业座谈和银企对接，新增中小企业贷款14.5亿元，使用应急转贷资金4.5亿元，切实解决了一批企业发展难题。

工业经济扩量提质。规模以上工业总产值突破1100亿元，规模以上工业增加值增长11.3%。主导产业持续壮大，硅工业、食品工业、新型建材、机械汽配“四大板块”规模工业产值增长17.8%，其中硅工业产值540亿元，增长18.7%。质量效益稳步向好，工业应税销售收入、工业增值税、企业所得税等提质增效指标分别增长9%、23.7%和17%。企业培育成效明显，净增规模企业33家，17家企业省股权交易中心挂牌，晶海洋列入市培优培强计划。

现代农业稳步发展。粮食总产增加1.6万吨，新增高效农业8.1万亩，其中设施农业4.2万亩。“黄川草莓”获评中国驰名商标，“东海西红柿”荣获国家地理标志保护产品，“东海大米”品牌提升成效明显，新增“三品”品牌37个。举办东海名特优新农产品（南京）博览会，一批优质农产品亮相第18届省农洽会。基础保障更加扎实，新增粮食烘干中心27个，秸

多晶硅生产车间

石英管精检

秆机械化还田率86%，完成小型农田水利重点县工程。

现代服务业特色明显。服务业增加值180亿元，增长9.8%。正式荣膺“世界水晶之都”，在北京举办东海水晶精品展暨“晶韵华章”新书发布会，在南京举办“岁月鎏晶·东海水晶”专场拍卖会。中国东海水晶城投入运营，入驻商户3000余家，餐饮、物流、电子商务、检测鉴定等配套功能逐步完善，获评国家知识产权保护培育基地。水晶文化创意产业园新增入园企业8家，获评省首批众创集聚区。旅游业活力彰显，获批建设国家全域旅游示范区，荣获长三角十大最美骑行城市，举办第六届花卉博览会、西双湖梦幻音乐节，温泉旅游度假区入围最美中国榜百强，西双湖通过国家级湿地公园评审，李埝林场千亩薰衣草园、御园欢乐谷等一批特色景点建成开放，游客接待量和旅游总收入分别增长9.2%和11%。电子商务增势明显，实现电商交易额54亿元，位列中国电商百佳县81位，荣获省农村电子商务十强县。

党员爱心水站

百合花开

西双湖的晨辉

盐城市盐都区

江苏省盐城市盐都区，地处苏北平原中部，位于国家沿海大开发的腹部黄金地段，东濒黄海，西临淮扬，北通陇海线，南跨苏通大桥而联袂苏锡常、接轨大上海，是长江三角洲城市群中的重要区域中心城市盐城的核心区。现辖8个镇、4个街道、1个国家级高新区和1个省级度假区。拥有250个村（居），面积1015平方公里，户籍人口71.5万人。

今日的盐都，是一个交通越来越发达、环境越来越优越的投资兴业的热土乐园。区政府所在地西面4公里有宁靖盐高速、90公里有京沪高速；南面4公里有盐淮高速；东面2公里有204国道、6公里有新长铁路、10公里有沿海高速大通道、13公里有盐城机场、50公里有大丰港、70公里有射阳港；东侧还有国家三级航道通榆河。行驶高速到达南京仅需2.5小时、上海3.5小时、北京10小时。铁路南接京沪线和宣杭线，北接陇海线。盐城机场直通北京、广州、温州和韩国首尔，其黄金航线开辟了世界各地客商来盐都投资、旅游的通途。

今日的盐都，是黄海之滨自然生态风景怡人、人文景观异彩纷呈的旅游胜地。碧波荡漾的大纵湖，不仅以盛产河蟹、河鳗著称，也以风光旖旎驰名遐迩，省政府批准设立的大纵湖旅游度假区正吸引着越来越多的游客来这里观光旅游。陈琳墓、宋曹故居、胡乔木故居、郑板桥教书馆、郝氏宗祠、华都森林公园、新区世纪广场等遍布境内的景点，处处射显出丰富的历史文化底蕴的魅力光辉，也时时闪耀着新时代的盐都与时俱进的活力光华。

江苏盐芯微电子科技有限公司

今日的盐都，是一个渐成规模后势强劲的新兴工业发展高地。通过建国以后几十年的发展，特别是改革开放后的快速推进，奠定并提升了工业主体地位，纺织、服装、机械、化工、建材、食品等传统的支柱产业经过市场经济的洗礼老树开新花，焕发出无限的生机；随着盐城高新区和各镇（区、街道）特色工业园区的开发建设，一批又一批的大型、特大型高科技项目被陆续引进和建成投产，智能终端、高端装备、新能源、电商物流等行业崛起后迅速形成先进生产力，支撑区域经济一路攀升。盐都区将用创新驱动，生态富民的理念，建设成为强富美高的新盐都。

“我见青山多妩媚，料青山见我应如是”。盐都，是世界的盐都；盐都，是发展的盐都；盐都，是青春年少意气风发的盐都。今日的盐都已美好，明天的盐都更辉煌。

高新区科技广场

智创园

永宁国际汽车城

研创大厦

4A级风景区大纵湖芦荡迷宫

4A级风景区大纵湖风光

盐城万达广场

江苏最美乡村杨侍欢迎你

DAFENG 盐城市 大丰区

大丰位于江苏沿海中部，是国务院批复的长三角城市群规划中苏北唯一城市盐城的临海新城区，也是江苏省面积最大的城市区。大丰总人口72万，总面积3008平方公里，下辖12个镇、两个省级开发区，境内有江苏省属农场3家、上海市属农场1家。大丰是麋鹿故乡、黄海港城、上海“飞地”、革命老区、长寿之乡，历史悠久，人文荟萃，开放包容，建成国家首批可持续发展先进示范区、国家首批生态示范区、国家卫生城市、国家园林城市和中国优秀旅游城市。

2016年，全区实现GDP579.07亿元，一般公共预算收入59.26亿元，城镇居民人均可支配收入31104元、农村居民人均可支配收入19480元。全社会用电量、工业用电量、全口径工业开票销售收入、出口总额、金融机构贷款余额等指标盐城第一。

· 实干为先

· 项目为王

· 民生为本

· 盐城领先

· 沿海当先

· 全省争先

张家港的发展

虞姬故里 花乡沭阳

沭阳县地处江苏省北部，公元578年设县沭阳县，因位于沭水之阳而得名。京沪高速公路在沭阳有四个出口，新长铁路在沭阳设站;新G205、S245、S326、S344等国省干道的通达使得沭阳交通便捷。全县水路畅通，新沂河横贯东西，淮沭新河纵穿南北。

沭阳陆域面积2299平方千米，全县辖1个国家级经济技术开发区、40个乡镇场（街道），2016年末总人口197.06万。在第十六届（2016年）全国县域经济与县域基本竞争力评价中，沭阳列第41位，沭阳连续五年跻身全国“县域经济与县域基本竞争力”前100名行列。连续两届入选“全国工业百强县”，名列第79位。沭阳经济技术开发区是苏北唯一一家落户县级城市的国家级经济技术开发区。

2016年沭阳县实现地区生产总值697.31亿元，增长9.0%；完成一般公共预算收入71.75亿元，同口径增长9.9%，总量稳居苏北21县（市）首位。全县规模以上工业企业881家，规模以上工业实现总产值1375.83亿元，增长14.0%；纺织服装业实现产值220.39亿元，增长23.9%，纺织服装产业总量稳居苏北21县（市）前列，成为省内发展最快的纺织服装产业集群。

2016年全县网上交易额突破130亿元，快递发货量达8500万件。成功创建国家级电子商务进农村综合示范县，全县共有32个“中国淘宝村”、3个“中国淘宝镇”，第四届（2016）“中国淘宝村高峰论坛”落户沭阳县，央视《新闻联播》等多家媒体连续聚焦沭阳县电子商务和网络创业情况，“全省领先、全国知名”的沭阳电商品牌逐步形成。